10e

Social Psychology

David G. Myers

Hope College
Holland, Michigan

Mc
Graw
Hill

*Connect
Learn
Succeed*™

About the Author

Since receiving his Ph.D. from the University of Iowa, David Myers has spent his career at Michigan's Hope College and has taught dozens of social psychology sections. Hope College students have invited him to be their commencement speaker and voted him "outstanding professor."

Myers' scientific articles have appeared in some three dozen scientific books and periodicals, including *Science*, the *American Scientist*, *Psychological Science*, and the *American Psychologist*.

In addition to his scholarly writing and his textbooks, he communicates psychological science to the general public. His writings have appeared in three dozen magazines, from *Today's Education* to *Scientific American*. He also has published general audience books, including *The Pursuit of Happiness* and *Intuition: Its Powers and Perils*.

David Myers has chaired his city's Human Relations Commission, helped found a thriving assistance center for families in poverty, and spoken to hundreds of college and community groups. Drawing on his own experience, he also has written articles and a book (*A Quiet World*) about hearing loss, and he is advocating a revolution in American hearing-assistance technology (hearingloop.org).

He bikes to work year-round and still plays daily pick-up basketball. David and Carol Myers are parents of two sons and a daughter.

Brief Contents

Table of Contents

Part Two: Social Influence

Preface

Regardless of background or major, students will see their world reflected in *Social Psychology*

Social psychology is a young science, barely a century old. Yet already its scientific explorations have shed light on love and hate, conformity and independence—social behaviors that we encounter each day. In the findings and concepts of social psychology, students will see themselves and the world in which they live and love, work and play.

SOCIAL PSYCHOLOGY

TENTH EDITION

David G. Myers

When first invited to write this book, and even now when preparing this tenth edition, I envisioned a text that would be at once solidly scientific and warmly human, factually rigorous and intellectually provocative. It would reveal important social phenomena, as well as how scientists discover and explain such phenomena. It would also *stimulate students' thinking*—their motivation to inquire, to analyze, to relate principles to everyday happenings. Social phenomena that are important and relevant to today's students would be revealed both in the narrative and in enriching margin notes and chapter-ending personal postscripts.

Understanding that students majoring in psychology, business, law, teaching, or many other areas may be drawn to the study of social psychology, *this text is written in the intellectual tradition of the liberal arts.* As with great literature, philosophy, and science, liberal arts education seeks to expand our thinking and awareness beyond the confines of the present. By focusing on humanly significant issues I offer the core content in ways that appeal to, and draw on applications from, a wide array of behaviors and experiences.

Much about human behavior remains a mystery, yet social psychology can now offer partial answers to many intriguing questions:

- How does our thinking—both conscious and unconscious—drive our behavior?

- What leads people sometimes to hurt and sometimes to help one another?

- What kindles social conflict, and how can we transform closed fists into helping hands?

Answering these and many other questions—my mission in the pages that lie ahead—expands our self-understanding and sensitizes us to the social forces that work upon us.

Engaging research reflects students' interests and their environment

In addition to part openers, chapter outlines, and summaries, each chapter includes the following features:

The Inside Story essays capture compelling stories of famous researchers *in their own words*, highlighting the interests and questions that guided—and sometimes misguided—their findings. For example, Chapter 4 offers an essay by Mahzarin R. Banaji on her journey from being a secretarial assistant in India to being a Harvard professor.

Focus On features give students an in-depth exploration of a topic presented in the text. The "Focus On" in Chapter 11, for example, describes what Brett Pelham and colleagues call implicit egotism, which is the predisposition that we like what we associate with ourselves.

research
CLOSE-UP   Ingroup Similarity and Helping

Likeness breeds liking, and liking elicits helping. So, do people offer more help to others who display similarities to themselves? To explore the similarity-helping relationship, Mark Levine, Amy Prosser, and David Evans at Lancaster University joined with Stephen Reicher at St. Andrews University (2005) to study the behavior of some Lancaster students who earlier had identified themselves as fans of the nearby Manchester United soccer football team. Taking their cue from John Darley and Daniel Batson's (1973) famous Good Samaritan experiment, they directed each newly arrived participant to the laboratory in an adjacent building. En route, a confederate jogger—wearing a shirt from either Manchester United or rival Liverpool—seemingly slipped on a grass bank just in front of them, grasped his ankle, and groaned in apparent pain. As Figure 12.8 shows, the Manchester fans routinely paused to offer help to their fellow Manchester supporter but usually did not offer such help to a supposed Liverpool supporter.

But, the researchers wondered, what if we remind Manchester fans of the identity they share with Liverpool supporters—as football fans rather than as detractors

who scorn football fans as violent hooligans? So they repeated the experiment, but with one difference. Before participants witnessed the jogger's fall, the researcher explained that the study concerned the positive aspects of being a football fan. Given that only a small minority of fans are troublemakers, this research aimed to explore what fans get out of their love for "the beautiful game." Now a jogger wearing a football club shirt, whether for Manchester or Liverpool, became one of "us fans." And as Figure 12.9 shows, the grimacing jogger was helped regardless of which team he supported—and more so than if wearing a plain shirt.

The principle in the two cases is the same, notes the Lancaster research team: People are predisposed to help their fellow group members, whether those are defined more narrowly (as "us Manchester fans") or more inclusively (as "us football fans"). If even rival fans can be persuaded to help one another if they think about what unites them, then surely other antagonists can as well. One way to increase people's willingness to help others is to promote social identities that are inclusive rather than exclusive.

FIGURE :: 12.8
Percent of Manchester United Fans Who Helped Victim Wearing Manchester or Liverpool Shirt

FIGURE :: 12.9
Common Fan Identity Condition: Percent of Manchester United Fans Who Helped Victim Wearing Manchester or Liverpool Shirt

- Some studies found a same-race bias (Benson & others, 1976; Clark, 1974; Franklin, 1974; Gaertner, 1973; Gaertner & Bickman, 1971; Sissons, 1981).
- Others found no bias (Gaertner, 1975; Lerner & Frank, 1974; Wilson & Donnerstein, 1979; Wispe & Freshley, 1971).
- Still others—especially those involving face-to-face situations—found a bias toward helping those of a different race (Dutton, 1971, 1973; Dutton & Lake, 1973; Katz & others, 1975).

Research Close-Up boxes offer in-depth looks at scientific exploration of a fascinating variety of topics, ranging from when people yawn to how pedestrians in different cultures interact. "Research Close-Ups" provide students with a detailed, yet accessible understanding of how social psychologists use various research methods, from laboratory studies, Internet experiments, and creating virtual realities to naturalistic observation and harvesting archival data.

When an apt combination of intelligence, skill, determination, self-confidence, and social charisma meets a rare opportunity, the result is sometimes a championship, a Nobel Prize, or a social revolution.

Summing Up: The Influence of the Minority: How Do Individuals Influence the Group?

- Although a majority opinion often prevails, sometimes a minority can influence and even overturn a majority position. Even if the majority does not adopt the minority's views, the minority's speaking up can increase the majority's self-doubts and prompt it to consider other alternatives, often leading to better, more creative decisions.
- In experiments, a minority is most influential when it is consistent and persistent in its views, when its

actions convey self-confidence, and after it begins to elicit some defections from the majority.

- Through their task and social leadership, formal and informal group leaders exert disproportionate influence. Those who consistently press toward their goals and exude a self-confident charisma often engender trust and inspire others to follow.

 POSTSCRIPT: Are Groups Bad for Us?

A selective reading of this chapter could, I must admit, leave readers with the impression that, on balance, groups are bad. In groups we become more aroused, more stressed, more tense, more error-prone on complex tasks. Submerged in a group that gives us anonymity, we have a tendency to loaf or leave our worst impulses unleashed by deindividuation. Police brutality, lynchings, gang destruction, and terrorism are all group phenomena. Discussion in groups often polarizes our views, enhancing mutual racism or hostility. It may also suppress dissent, creating a homogenized groupthink that produces disastrous decisions. No wonder we celebrate those individuals—minorities of one—who, alone against a group, have stood up for truth and justice. Groups, it seems, are ba-a-a-d.

All that is true, but it's only half the truth. The other half is that, as social animals, we are group-dwelling creatures. Like our distant ancestors, we depend on one another for sustenance, support, and security. Moreover, when our individual tendencies are positive, group interaction accentuates our best. In groups, runners run faster, audiences laugh louder, and givers become more generous. In self-help groups, people strengthen their resolve to stop drinking, lose weight, and study harder. In kindred-spirited groups, people expand their spiritual consciousness. "A devout communing on spiritual things sometimes greatly helps the health of the soul," observed fifteenth-century cleric Thomas à Kempis, especially when people of faith "meet and speak and commune together."

Depending on which tendency a group is magnifying or disinhibiting, groups can be very, very bad or very, very good. So we had best choose our groups wisely and intentionally.

Making the Social Connection

In this chapter we discussed group polarization and whether groups intensify opinions. This phenomenon will also be covered in Chapter 15 when we look at juries and how they make decisions. Can you think of other situations where group polarization might be in effect? Go to the Online Learning Center for this book to view a clip about cliques and the influence of the group.

Postscripts are chapter-ending vignettes that engage students with thought-provoking questions and insights from the chapter. For example, Chapter 8 ("Group Influence") explores the question, "Are Groups Bad for Us?"

Updated material in the tenth edition

With some 650 new bibliographic citations, David Myers, who subscribes to nearly all English-language social psychology periodicals (including those from Europe), has comprehensively updated *Social Psychology*. In addition to new margin quotes, photos, and cartoons, new content includes:

Chapter 1   Introducing Social Psychology

- Hindsight bias and the world financial crisis
- 2008 U.S. presidential election examples
- Framing and nudging organ donation and retirement savings

Chapter 2   The Self in a Social World

- Chapter opening example
- Section on narcissism
- Research on self-esteem and self-serving bias

Chapter 3   Social Beliefs and Judgments

- Constructed memories and biased perceptions in politics
- Research on unconscious information processing
- Data on "probability neglect" in judgments of risk

Chapter 4   Behavior and Attitudes

- Enhanced coverage of implicit attitudes and Implicit Association Test
- Recent studies and examples of behavior feeding attitudes
- Updated coverage of dissonance research

Chapter 5   Genes, Culture, and Gender

- Research on social norms and rule-breaking
- Group conflict and preference for male leader
- International data on gender and sexuality, and gender and social roles

Chapter 6   Conformity and Obedience

- Examples of suggestibility, conformity, and obedience
- Replication of Milgram obedience experiment
- Research on cohesion, conformity, and genocide

Chapter 7   Persuasion

- Research on effective anti-smoking ads
- Examples of political persuasion
- Two-step flow of medical information

Chapter 8   Group Influence

- Deindividuation effects on the Internet
- Group polarization in liberal and conservative communities
- The wisdom of crowds, prediction markets, and "the crowd within"

Chapter 9 Prejudice: Disliking Others

- Contemporary examples and data regarding various forms of prejudice
- Recent studies of implicit prejudice
- Research on prejudice phenomena, including infrahumanization, own-age bias, just-world thinking

Chapter 10 Aggression: Hurting Others

- Updated information on human aggression, including the Congo and Iraq
- Studies of testosterone and aggression
- Recent research on media influences

Chapter 11 Attraction and Intimacy: Liking and Loving Others

- Studies of social exclusion and social pain
- Speed dating experiments
- Recent evolutionary psychology-based studies of fertility and attraction

Chapter 12 Helping

- Examples of heroic altruism
- Research on generosity and happiness
- Experiments on priming on materialistic versus spiritual concepts

Chapter 13 Conflict and Peacemaking

- Experiments on counterproductive effects of punishment
- "The Inside Story" (Nicole Shelton and Jennifer Richeson) on cross-racial friendships
- Cross-cultural and political examples of common enemies and superordinate goals

Chapter 14 Social Psychology in the Clinic

- The social construction of mental illness
- Trends in close relationships, and implications for health
- Neuroscience of supportive friends and partners

Chapter 15 Social Psychology in Court

- Fresh examples of eyewitness misidentification
- The post-identification feedback effect
- Juror expectations of forensic evidence in the *CSI* generation

Chapter 16 Social Psychology and the Sustainable Future

- IPCC consensus on global climate change
- Data on public opinion about effects of climate change
- Prospects for a "new consciousness" that fosters sustainability

For a more detailed list of chapter-by-chapter changes, please contact your local McGraw-Hill sales representative.

Supplements

For the Student

SocialSense Videos

Now available at the Online Learning Center, the *SocialSense* videos are organized according to the text chapters. There is also a video library available containing all of the videos alphabetically. Taking advantage of McGraw-Hill's exclusive Discovery Channel® licensing arrangement, the video segments chosen illustrate core concepts of social psychology and contemporary applications. Each video includes a pre-test, a post-test, and Web resources.

Online Learning Center for Students

The official website for the text (www.mhhe.com/myers10e) contains chapter outlines, practice quizzes, a practice midterm and final, and Internet Connections and Internet Exercises updated by Jill Cohen of Los Angeles Community College. Also available are Scenarios, Interactivities, and "What Do You Think?" exercises for each chapter.

For the Instructor

Online Learning Center for Instructors

The password-protected instructor side of the Online Learning Center www.mhhe .com/myers10e contains the Instructor's Manual, PowerPoint presentations, Web links, image gallery, and other teaching resources. Ask your McGraw-Hill representative for your password.

Instructor's Manual
Jonathan Mueller, North Central College

This manual provides many useful tools to enhance your teaching. For each chapter you will find lecture ideas, assignment ideas, suggested class discussion topics, classroom demonstrations and demonstration materials, suggested films, and more.

Test Bank
Donna Walsh, Beaufort Community College

The test bank includes over 100 questions per chapter, including factual, conceptual, and applied questions. The test bank can be used with McGraw-Hill's EZ Test, a flexible and easy-to-use electronic testing program allowing instructors to create tests from the test bank as well as their own questions.

PowerPoint Presentations
Kim Foreman

Available on the instructor side of the Online Learning Center, these presentations cover the key points of each chapter and include charts and graphs from the text. They can be used as is or modified to meet your needs.

Classroom Performance System (CPS) by eInstruction
Alisha Janowsky, University of Central Florida

CPS, or "clickers," is a superb way to give interactive quizzes, maximize student participation in class discussions, and take attendance. The CPS content may be used as is or modified to suit your needs.

Image Gallery

These files include all the figures from the Myers textbook for which McGraw-Hill holds copyright.

Annual Editions: Social Psychology
Karen Duffy of SUNY–Geneseo

This annually updated reader is a compilation of current, carefully selected articles from respected journals, magazines, and newspapers. Additional support for the readings can be found on our student website, www.mhcls.com/online. An Instructor's Manual and the guide *Using Annual Editions in the Classroom* are available as support materials for instructors.

Taking Sides: Clashing Views in Social Psychology
Jason A. Nier, Connecticut College

This debate-style reader is designed to introduce students to controversial viewpoints on the field's most crucial issues. Each issue is carefully framed for the student, and the pro and con essays represent the arguments of leading scholars and commentators in their fields.

Film Clips from Films for the Humanities and Social Sciences

Depending on adoption size, you may qualify for FREE videos from this resource. View more than 700 psychology-related videos at www.films.com.

As a full-service publisher of quality educational products, McGraw-Hill does much more than just sell textbooks to your students. We create and publish an extensive array of print, video, and digital supplements to support instruction on your campus. Orders of new (rather than used) textbooks help us to defray the cost of developing such supplements, which is substantial. We have a broad range of other supplements in psychology that you may wish to tap for your introductory psychology course. Ask your local McGraw-Hill representative about the availability of these and other supplements that may help you with your course design.

In Appreciation

Although only one person's name appears on this book's cover, the truth is that a whole community of scholars has invested itself in it. Although none of these people should be held responsible for what I have written—nor do any of them fully agree with everything said—their suggestions made this a better book than it could otherwise have been.

A special "thank you" goes to Jean Twenge, San Diego State University, for her contribution to Chapter 2, "The Self in a Social World." Drawing on her extensive knowledge of and research on the self and cultural changes, Professor Twenge updated and revised this chapter.

This new edition retains many of the improvements contributed by consultants and reviewers on the first nine editions. To these esteemed colleagues I therefore remain indebted. I have also benefited from the input of instructors who reviewed the ninth edition in preparation for this revision, rescuing me from occasional mistakes and offering constructive suggestions (and encouragement). I am indebted to each of these many colleagues:

Mike Aamodt, Radford University

Robert Arkin, Ohio State University

Robert Armenta, University of Nebraska–Lincoln

Jahna Ashlyn, San Diego State University

Nancy L. Ashton, Richard Stockton College of New Jersey

Steven H. Baron, Montgomery County Community College

Charles Daniel Batson, University of Kansas

Steve Baumgardner, University of Wisconsin—Eau Claire

Susan Beers, Sweet Briar College

George Bishop, National University of Singapore

Galen V. Bodenhausen, Northwestern University

Martin Bolt, Calvin College

Kurt Boniecki, University of Central Arkansas

Amy Bradfield, Iowa State University

Dorothea Braginsky, Fairfield University

Timothy C. Brock, Ohio State University

Jonathon D. Brown, University of Washington

Fred B. Bryant, Loyola University Chicago

Jeff Bryson, San Diego State University

Shawn Meghan Burn, California Polytechnic State University

David Buss, University of Texas

Thomas Cafferty, University of South Carolina

Jerome M. Chertkoff, Indiana University

Nicholas Christenfeld, University of California at San Diego

Russell Clark, University of North Texas

Diana I. Cordova, Yale University

Karen A. Couture, New Hampshire College

Traci Craig, University of Idaho

Cynthia Crown, Xavier University

Jack Croxton, State University of New York at Fredonia

Jennifer Daniels, University of Connecticut

Anthony Doob, University of Toronto

David Dunning, Cornell University

Alice H. Eagly, Northwestern University

Jason Eggerman, Palomar College

Leandre Fabrigar, Queen's University

Philip Finney, Southeast Missouri State University

Carie Forden, Clarion University

Kenneth Foster, City University of New York

Dennis Fox, University of Illinois at Springfield

Robin Franck, Southwestern College

Carrie B. Fried, Winona State University

William Froming, Pacific Graduate School of Psychology

Madeleine Fugere, Eastern Connecticut State University

Stephen Fugita, Santa Clara University

David A. Gershaw, Arizona Western College

Tom Gilovich, Cornell University

Mary Alice Gordon, Southern Methodist University

Tresmaine Grimes, Iona College

Rosanna Guadagno, University of Alabama

Ranald Hansen, Oakland University

Allen Hart, Amherst College

Elaine Hatfield, University of Hawaii

James L. Hilton, University of Michigan

Bert Hodges, Gordon College

William Ickes, University of Texas at Arlington

Marita Inglehart, University of Michigan

Chester Insko, University of North Carolina

Jonathan Iuzzini, Texas A&M University

Miles Jackson, Portland State University

Bethany Johnsin, University of Nebraska–Lincoln

Meighan Johnson, Shorter College

Edward Jones, Princeton University [deceased]

Judi Jones, Georgia Southern College

Deana Julka, University of Portland

Martin Kaplan, Northern Illinois University

Timothy J. Kasser, Knox College

Janice Kelly, Purdue University

Douglas Kenrick, Arizona State University

Jared Kenworthy, University of Texas at Arlington

Norbert Kerr, Michigan State University

Suzanne Kieffer, University of Houston

Charles Kiesler, University of Missouri

Steve Kilianski, Rutgers University–New Brunswick

Robin Kowalski, Clemson University

Marjorie Krebs, Gannon University

Joachim Krueger, Brown University

Travis Langley, Henderson State University

Dianne Leader, Georgia Institute of Technology

Juliana Leding, University of North Florida

Maurice J. Levesque, Elon University

Helen E. Linkey, Marshall University

Deborah Long, East Carolina University

Karsten Look, Columbus State Community College

Amy Lyndon, East Carolina University

Kim MacLin, University of Northern Iowa

Diane Martichuski, University of Colorado

John W. McHoskey, Eastern Michigan University

Daniel N. McIntosh, University of Denver

Rusty McIntyre, Amherst College

Annie McManus, Parkland College

David McMillen, Mississippi State University

Robert Millard, Vassar College

Arthur Miller, Miami University

Daniel Molden, Northwestern University

Teru Morton, Vanderbilt University

Todd D. Nelson, California State University

K. Paul Nesselroade, Jr., Simpson College

Darren Newtson, University of Virginia

Cindy Nordstrom, Southern Illinois University, Edwardsville

Michael Olson, University of Tennessee at Knoxville

Stuart Oskamp, Claremont Graduate University

Chris O'Sullivan, Bucknell University

Ellen E. Pastorino, Valencia Community College

Sandra Sims Patterson, Spelman College

Paul Paulus, University of Texas at Arlington

Terry F. Pettijohn, Mercyhurst College

Scott Plous, Wesleyan University

Greg Pool, St. Mary's University

Jennifer Pratt-Hyatt, Michigan State University

Michelle R. Rainey, Indiana University–Purdue University at Indianapolis

Cynthia Reed, Tarrant County College

Nicholas Reuterman, Southern Illinois University of Edwardsville

Robert D. Ridge, Brigham Young University

Judith Rogers, American River College

Hilliard Rogers, American River College

Paul Rose, Southern Illinois University, Edwardsville

Gretchen Sechrist, University at Buffalo, the State University of New York

Nicole Schnopp-Wyatt, Pikeville College

Wesley Schultz, California State University, San Marcos

Vann Scott, Armstrong Atlantic State University

John Seta, University of North Carolina at Greensboro

Robert Short, Arizona State University

Linda Silka, University of Massachusetts–Lowell

Royce Singleton, Jr., College of the Holy Cross

Stephen Slane, Cleveland State University

Christopher Sletten, University of North Florida

Christine M. Smith, Grand Valley State University

Richard A. Smith, University of Kentucky

C. R. Snyder, University of Kansas

Mark Snyder, University of Minnesota

Sheldon Solomon, Skidmore College

Matthew Spackman, Brigham Young University

Charles Stangor, University of Maryland at College Park

Garold Stasser, Miami University

Homer Stavely, Keene State College

Mark Stewart, American River College

JoNell Strough, West Virginia University

Eric Sykes, Indiana University Kokomo

Elizabeth Tanke, University of Santa Clara

Cheryl Terrance, University of North Dakota

William Titus, Arkansas Tech University

Christopher Trego, Florida Community College at Jacksonville

Tom Tyler, New York University

Rhoda Unger, Montclair State University

Billy Van Jones, Abilene Christian College

Mary Stewart Van Leeuwen, Eastern College

Ann L. Weber, University of North Carolina at Asheville

David Wilder, Rutgers University–New Brunswick

Daniel M. Wegner, Harvard University

Kipling Williams, Purdue University

Gary Wells, Iowa State University

Midge Wilson, DePaul University

Mike Wessells, Randolph-Macon College

Doug Woody, University of Northern Colorado

Bernard Whitley, Ball State University

Elissa Wurf, Muhlenberg College.

Carolyn Whitney, Saint Michael's University

Hope College, Michigan, has been wonderfully supportive of these successive editions. Both the people and the environment have helped make the gestation of ten editions of Social Psychology a pleasure. At Hope College, poet Jack Ridl helped shape the voice you will hear in these pages. Kathy Adamski has again contributed her good cheer and secretarial support. And Kathryn Brownson did library research, edited and prepared the manuscript, managed the paper flow, and proofed the pages and art. All in all, she midwifed this book.

Were it not for the inspiration of Nelson Black of McGraw-Hill, writing a textbook never would have occurred to me. Alison Meersschaert guided and encouraged the formative first edition. Publisher Mike Sugarman helped envision the execution of the ninth and tenth editions and their teaching supplements. Augustine Laferrrera ably served as editorial coordinator. Sarah Colwell managed the supplements, and production editor Holly Paulsen patiently guided the process of converting the manuscript into the finished book, assisted by copyeditor Janet Tilden's fine-tuning.

After hearing countless dozens of people say that this book's supplements have taken their teaching to a new level, I also pay tribute to Martin Bolt (Calvin College), for his pioneering the extensive instructor's resources, with their countless ready-to-use demonstration activities. How fortunate we are to have as part of our team Jonathan Mueller (North Central College) as author of the instructor's resources for the eighth, ninth, and tenth editions. Jon is able to draw on his acclaimed online resources for the teaching of social psychology and his monthly listserv offering resources to social psychology instructors (see jonathan.mueller.faculty.noctrl.edu/crow).

Kudos also go to Donna Walsh for her gift to the teaching of Social Psychology by authoring the testing resources. Thanks also to Kim Foreman for creating the PowerPoint presentations and Alisha Janowsky for preparing the classroom clicker materials.

To all in this supporting cast, I am indebted. Working with all these people has made the creation of this book a stimulating, gratifying experience.

David G. Myers
www.davidmyers.org

Social
Psychology

Introducing Social Psychology

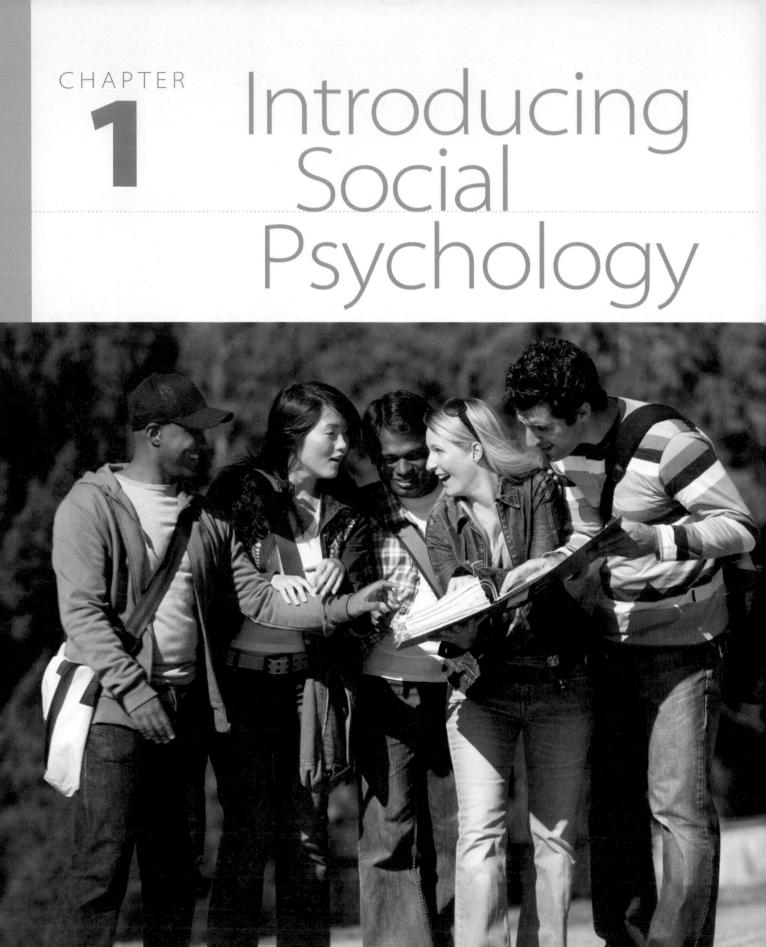

There once was a man whose second wife was a vain and selfish woman. This woman's two daughters were similarly vain and selfish. The man's own daughter, however, was meek and unselfish. This sweet, kind daughter, whom we all know as Cinderella, learned early on that she should do as she was told, accept ill treatment and insults, and avoid doing anything to upstage her stepsisters and their mother.

But then, thanks to her fairy godmother, Cinderella was able to escape her situation for an evening and attend a grand ball, where she attracted the attention of a handsome prince. When the love-struck prince later encountered Cinderella back in her degrading home, he failed to recognize her.

Implausible? The folktale demands that we accept the power of the situation. In the presence of her oppressive stepmother, Cinderella was humble and unattractive. At the ball, Cinderella felt more beautiful—and walked and talked and smiled as if she were. In one situation, she cowered. In the other, she charmed.

The French philosopher-novelist Jean-Paul Sartre (1946) would have had no problem accepting the Cinderella premise. We humans are "first of all beings in a situation," he wrote. "We cannot be distinguished from our situations, for they form us and decide our possibilities" (pp. 59–60, paraphrased).

What Is Social Psychology?

social psychology
The scientific study of how people think about, influence, and relate to one another.

Social psychology is a science that studies the influences of our situations, with special attention to how we view and affect one another. More precisely, it is *the scientific study of how people think about, influence, and relate to one another* (Figure 1.1).

Social psychology lies at psychology's boundary with sociology. Compared with sociology (the study of people in groups and societies), social psychology focuses more on individuals and uses more experimentation. Compared with personality psychology, social psychology focuses less on individuals' differences and more on how individuals, in general, view and affect one another.

Social psychology is still a young science. The first social psychology experiments were reported barely more than a century ago (1898), and the first social psychology texts did not appear until just before and after 1900 (Smith, 2005). Not until the 1930s did social psychology assume its current form. And not until World War II did it begin to emerge as the vibrant field it is today.

Social psychology studies our thinking, influence, and relationships by asking questions that have intrigued us all. Here are some examples:

How Much of Our Social World Is Just in Our Heads? As we will see in later chapters, our social behavior varies not just with the objective situation but also with how we construe it. Social beliefs can be self-fulfilling. For example, happily married people will attribute their spouse's acid remark ("Can't you ever put that where it belongs?") to something external ("He must have had a frustrating day"). Unhappily married people will attribute the same remark to a mean disposition ("Is he ever hostile!") and may respond with a counterattack. Moreover, expecting hostility from their spouse, they may behave resentfully, thereby eliciting the hostility they expect.

Would People Be Cruel If Ordered? How did Nazi Germany conceive and implement the unconscionable slaughter of 6 million Jews? Those evil acts occurred partly because thousands of people followed orders. They put the prisoners on trains, herded them into crowded "showers," and poisoned them with gas. How could people engage in such horrific actions? Were those individuals normal human beings? Stanley Milgram (1974) wondered. So he set up a situation where people were ordered to administer increasing

Throughout this book, sources for information are cited parenthetically. The complete source is provided in the reference section that begins on page R-1.

FIGURE :: 1.1

Social Psychology Is . . .

Social psychology is the scientific study of . . .

Social thinking	**Social influence**	**Social relations**
• How we perceive ourselves and others	• Culture	• Prejudice
• What we believe	• Pressures to conform	• Aggression
• Judgments we make	• Persuasion	• Attraction and intimacy
• Our attitudes	• Groups of people	• Helping

levels of electric shock to someone who was having difficulty learning a series of words. As we will see in Chapter 6, nearly two-thirds of the participants fully complied.

To Help? Or to Help Oneself? As bags of cash tumbled from an armored truck one fall day, $2 million was scattered along a Columbus, Ohio, street. Some motorists stopped to help, returning $100,000. Judging from the $1,900,000 that disappeared, many more stopped to help themselves. (What would you have done?) When similar incidents occurred several months later in San Francisco and Toronto, the results were the same: Passersby grabbed most of the money (Bowen, 1988). What situations trigger people to be helpful or greedy? Do some cultural contexts—perhaps villages and small towns— breed greater helpfulness?

A common thread runs through these questions: They all deal with how people view and affect one another. And that is what social psychology is all about. Social psychologists study attitudes and beliefs, conformity and independence, love and hate.

Tired of looking at the stars, Professor Mueller takes up social psychology.

Reprinted with permission of Jason Love at www.jasonlove.com.

Social Psychology's Big Ideas

What are social psychology's big lessons—its overarching themes? In many academic fields, the results of tens of thousands of studies, the conclusions of thousands of investigators, and the insights of hundreds of theorists can be boiled down to a few central ideas. Biology offers us principles such as natural selection and adaptation. Sociology builds on concepts such as social structure and organization. Music harnesses our ideas of rhythm, melody, and harmony.

What concepts are on social psychology's short list of big ideas? What themes, or fundamental principles, will be worth remembering long after you have forgotten most of the details? My short list of "great ideas we ought never to forget" includes these, each of which we will explore further in chapters to come (Figure 1.2).

We Construct Our Social Reality

We humans have an irresistible urge to explain behavior, to attribute it to some cause, and therefore to make it seem orderly, predictable, and controllable. You and I may react differently to similar situations because we *think* differently. How we react to a friend's insult depends on whether we attribute it to hostility or to a bad day.

A 1951 Princeton-Dartmouth football game provided a classic demonstration of how we construct reality (Hastorf & Cantril, 1954; see also Loy & Andrews, 1981). The game lived up to its billing as a grudge match; it turned out to be one of the roughest and dirtiest games in the history of either school. A Princeton All-American was gang-tackled, piled on, and finally forced out of the game with a broken nose. Fistfights erupted, and there were further injuries on both sides. The whole performance hardly fit the Ivy League image of upper-class gentility.

Not long afterward, two psychologists, one from each school, showed films of the game to students on each campus. The students played the role of scientist-observer, noting each infraction as they watched and who was responsible for it. But they could not set aside their loyalties. The Princeton students, for example, saw twice as many Dartmouth violations as the Dartmouth students saw. The conclusion: There *is* an objective reality out there, but we always view it through the lens of our beliefs and values.

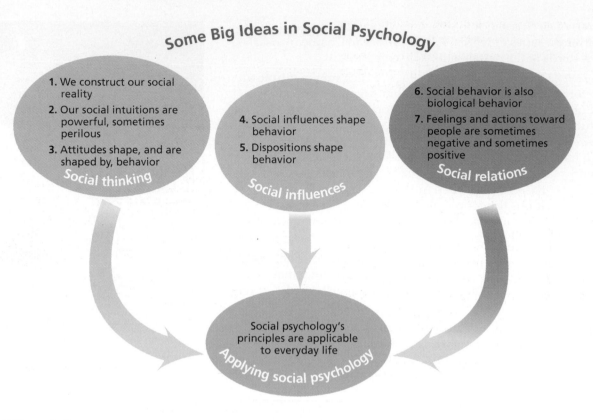

FIGURE :: 1.2

Some Big Ideas in Social Psychology

We are all intuitive scientists. We explain people's behavior, usually with enough speed and accuracy to suit our daily needs. When someone's behavior is consistent and distinctive, we attribute that behavior to his or her personality. For example, if you observe someone who makes repeated snide comments, you may infer that this person has a nasty disposition, and then you might try to avoid the person.

Our beliefs about ourselves also matter. Do we have an optimistic outlook? Do we see ourselves as in control of things? Do we view ourselves as relatively superior or inferior? Our answers influence our emotions and actions. *How we construe the world, and ourselves, matters.*

Our Social Intuitions Are Often Powerful but Sometimes Perilous

Our instant intuitions shape our fears (is flying dangerous?), impressions (can I trust him?), and relationships (does she like me?). Intuitions influence presidents in times of crisis, gamblers at the table, jurors assessing guilt, and personnel directors screening applicants. Such intuitions are commonplace.

Indeed, psychological science reveals a fascinating unconscious mind—an intuitive backstage mind—that Freud never told us about. More than psychologists realized until recently, thinking occurs offstage, out of sight. Our intuitive capacities are revealed by studies of what later chapters will explain: "automatic processing," "implicit memory," "heuristics," "spontaneous trait inference," instant emotions, and nonverbal communication. Thinking, memory, and attitudes all operate on two levels—one conscious and deliberate, the other unconscious and automatic. "Dual processing," today's researchers call it. We know more than we know we know.

Intuition is huge, but intuition is also perilous. An example: As we cruise through life, mostly on automatic pilot, we intuitively judge the likelihood of things by how easily various instances come to mind. Especially since September 11, 2001, we carry readily available mental images of plane crashes. Thus, most people fear flying more than driving, and many will drive great distances to avoid risking the skies. Actually, we're many times safer (per mile traveled) in a commercial plane than in a motor vehicle (in the United States, air travel was 230 times safer between 2002 and 2005, reports the National Safety Council [2008]).

Even our intuitions about ourselves often err. We intuitively trust our memories more than we should. We misread our own minds; in experiments, we deny being affected by things that do influence us. We mispredict our own feelings—how bad we'll feel a year from now if we lose our job or our romance breaks up, and how good we'll feel a year from now, or even a week from now, if we win our state's lottery. And we often mispredict our own future. For example, when selecting clothes, people approaching middle age will still buy snug ("I anticipate shedding a few pounds"); rarely does anyone say, more realistically, "I'd better buy a relatively loose fit; people my age tend to put on pounds."

Our social intuitions, then, are noteworthy for both their powers and their perils. By reminding us of intuition's gifts and alerting us to its pitfalls, social psychologists aim to fortify our thinking. In most situations, "fast and frugal" snap judgments serve us well enough. But in others, where accuracy matters—as when needing to fear the right things and spend our resources accordingly—we had best restrain our impulsive intuitions with critical thinking. *Our intuitions and unconscious information processing are routinely powerful and sometimes perilous.*

"He didn't actually threaten me, but I perceived him as a threat."

Social cognition matters. Our behavior is influenced not just by the objective situation, but also by how we construe it.

Social Influences Shape Our Behavior

We are, as Aristotle long ago observed, social animals. We speak and think in words we learned from others. We long to connect, to belong, and to be well thought of. Matthias Mehl and James Pennebaker (2003) quantified their University of Texas students' social behavior by inviting them to wear microcassette recorders and microphones. Once every 12 minutes during their waking hours, the computer-operated recorder would imperceptibly record for 30 seconds. Although the observation period covered only weekdays (including class time), almost 30 percent of the students' time was spent in conversation. Relationships are a large part of being human.

As social creatures, we respond to our immediate contexts. Sometimes the power of a social situation leads us to act contrary to our expressed attitudes. Indeed, powerfully evil situations sometimes overwhelm good intentions, inducing people to agree with falsehoods or comply with cruelty. Under Nazi influence, many decent-seeming people became instruments of the Holocaust. Other situations may elicit great generosity and compassion. After the 9/11 catastrophe, New York City was overwhelmed with donations of food, clothing, and help from eager volunteers.

The power of the situation was also dramatically evident in varying attitudes toward the 2003 invasion of Iraq. Opinion polls revealed that Americans and Israelis overwhelmingly favored the war. Their distant cousins elsewhere in the world overwhelmingly opposed it. Tell me where you live and I'll make a reasonable guess as to what your attitudes were as the war began. Tell me your educational level and what media you watch and read, and I'll make an even more confident guess. Our situations matter.

Our cultures help define our situations. For example, our standards regarding promptness, frankness, and clothing vary with our culture.

- Whether you prefer a slim or voluptuous body depends on when and where in the world you live.
- Whether you define social justice as equality (all receive the same) or as equity (those who earn more receive more) depends on whether your ideology has been shaped more by socialism or by capitalism.
- Whether you tend to be expressive or reserved, casual or formal, hinges partly on your culture and your ethnicity.
- Whether you focus primarily on yourself—your personal needs, desires, and morality—or on your family, clan, and communal groups depends on how much you are a product of modern Western individualism.

Social psychologist Hazel Markus (2005) sums it up: "People are, above all, malleable." Said differently, we adapt to our social context. *Our attitudes and behavior are shaped by external social forces.*

Personal Attitudes and Dispositions Also Shape Behavior

Internal forces also matter. We are not passive tumbleweeds, merely blown this way and that by the social winds. Our inner attitudes affect our behavior. Our political attitudes influence our voting behavior. Our smoking attitudes influence our susceptibility to peer pressures to smoke. Our attitudes toward the poor influence our willingness to help them. (As we will see, our attitudes also follow our behavior, which leads us to believe strongly in those things we have committed ourselves to or suffered for.)

Personality dispositions also affect behavior. Facing the same situation, different people may react differently. Emerging from years of political imprisonment, one person exudes bitterness and seeks revenge. Another, such as South Africa's Nelson Mandela, seeks reconciliation and unity with his former enemies. *Attitudes and personality influence behavior.*

Social Behavior Is Biologically Rooted

Twenty-first-century social psychology is providing us with ever-growing insights into our behavior's biological foundations. Many of our social behaviors reflect a deep biological wisdom.

Everyone who has taken introductory psychology has learned that nature and nurture together form who we are. As the area of a rectangle is determined by both its length and its width, so do biology and experience together create us. As *evolutionary psychologists* remind us (see Chapter 5), our inherited human nature predisposes us to behave in ways that helped our ancestors survive and reproduce. We carry the genes of those whose traits enabled them and their children to survive and reproduce. Thus, evolutionary psychologists ask how natural selection might predispose our actions and reactions when dating and mating, hating and hurting, caring and sharing. Nature also endows us with an enormous capacity to learn and to adapt to varied environments. We are sensitive and responsive to our social context.

If every psychological event (every thought, every emotion, every behavior) is simultaneously a biological event, then we can also examine the neurobiology that underlies social behavior. What brain areas enable our experiences of love and contempt, helping and aggression, perception and belief? How do brain, mind, and behavior function together as one coordinated system? What does the timing of brain events reveal about how we process information? Such questions are asked by those in **social neuroscience** (Cacioppo & others, 2007).

Social neuroscientists do not reduce complex social behaviors, such as helping and hurting, to simple neural or molecular mechanisms. Their point is this: To understand social behavior, we must consider both under-the-skin (biological) and between-skins (social) influences. Mind and body are one grand system. Stress hormones affect how we feel and act. Social ostracism elevates blood pressure. Social support strengthens the disease-fighting immune system. *We are bio-psycho-social organisms.* We reflect the interplay of our biological, psychological, and social influences. And that is why today's psychologists study behavior from these different levels of analysis.

social neuroscience
An integration of biological and social perspectives that explores the neural and psychological bases of social and emotional behaviors.

Social Psychology's Principles Are Applicable in Everyday Life

Social psychology has the potential to illuminate your life, to make visible the subtle influences that guide your thinking and acting. And, as we will see, it offers many ideas about how to know ourselves better, how to win friends and influence people, how to transform closed fists into open arms.

Scholars are also applying social psychological insights. Principles of social thinking, social influence, and social relations have implications for human health and well-being, for judicial procedures and juror decisions in courtrooms, and for influencing behaviors that will enable an environmentally sustainable human future.

As but one perspective on human existence, psychological science does not seek to engage life's ultimate questions: What is the meaning of human life? What should be our purpose? What is our ultimate destiny? But social psychology does give us a method for asking and answering some exceedingly interesting and important questions. *Social psychology is all about life—your life: your beliefs, your attitudes, your relationships.*

The rest of this chapter takes us inside social psychology. Let's first consider how social psychologists' own values influence their work in obvious and subtle ways. And then let's focus on this chapter's biggest task: glimpsing how we *do* social psychology. How do social psychologists search for explanations of social thinking, social influence, and social relations? And how might you and I use these analytical tools to think smarter?

Throughout this book, a brief summary will conclude each major section. I hope these summaries will help you assess how well you have learned the material in each section.

Summing Up: Social Psychology's Big Ideas

Social psychology is the scientific study of how people think about, influence, and relate to one another. Its central themes include the following:

- How we construe our social worlds
- How our social intuitions guide and sometimes deceive us

- How our social behavior is shaped by other people, by our attitudes and personalities, and by our biology
- How social psychology's principles apply to our everyday lives and to various other fields of study

Social Psychology and Human Values

Social psychologists' values penetrate their work in ways both obvious and subtle. What are such ways?

Social psychology is less a collection of findings than a set of strategies for answering questions. In science, as in courts of law, personal opinions are inadmissible. When ideas are put on trial, evidence determines the verdict.

But are social psychologists really that objective? Because they are human beings, don't their *values*—their personal convictions about what is desirable and how people ought to behave—seep into their work? If so, can social psychology really be scientific?

Obvious Ways Values Enter Psychology

Values enter the picture when social psychologists *choose research topics*. It was no accident that the study of prejudice flourished during the 1940s as fascism raged in Europe; that the 1950s, a time of look-alike fashions and intolerance of differing views, gave us studies of conformity; that the 1960s saw interest in aggression increase with riots and rising crime rates; that the feminist movement of the 1970s helped stimulate a wave of research on gender and sexism; that the 1980s offered a resurgence of attention to psychological aspects of the arms race; and that the 1990s and the early twenty-first century were marked by heightened interest in how people respond to diversity in culture, race, and sexual orientation. Social psychology reflects social history (Kagan, 2009).

Values differ not only across time but also across cultures. In Europe, people take pride in their nationalities. The Scots are more self-consciously distinct from the English, and the Austrians from the Germans, than are similarly adjacent Michiganders from Ohioans. Consequently, Europe has given us a major theory of "social identity," whereas American social psychologists have focused more on individuals—how one person thinks about others, is influenced by them, and relates to them (Fiske, 2004; Tajfel, 1981; Turner, 1984). Australian social psychologists have drawn theories and methods from both Europe and North America (Feather, 2005).

Values also influence the *types of people* who are attracted to various disciplines (Campbell, 1975a; Moynihan, 1979). At your school, do the students majoring in the humanities, the arts, the natural sciences, and the social sciences differ noticeably from one another? Do social psychology and sociology attract people who are—for example—relatively eager to challenge tradition, people more inclined to shape the future than preserve the past?

Finally, values obviously enter the picture as the *object* of social-psychological analysis. Social psychologists investigate how values form, why they change, and how they influence attitudes and actions. None of that, however, tells us which values are "right."

Different sciences offer different perspectives.
ScienceCartoonsPlus.com

Not-So-Obvious Ways Values Enter Psychology

We less often recognize the subtler ways in which value commitments masquerade as objective truth. Consider three not-so-obvious ways values enter psychology.

THE SUBJECTIVE ASPECTS OF SCIENCE

Scientists and philosophers now agree: Science is not purely objective. Scientists do not simply read the book of nature. Rather, they interpret nature, using their own mental categories. In our daily lives, too, we view the world through the lens of our preconceptions. Pause a moment: What do you see in Figure 1.3? Can you see a Dalmatian sniffing the ground at the picture's center? Without that preconception, most people are blind to the Dalmatian. Once your mind grasps the concept, it informs your interpretation of the picture—so much so that it becomes difficult *not* to see the dog.

This is the way our minds work. While reading these words, you have been unaware that you are also looking at your nose. Your mind blocks from awareness something that is there, if only you were predisposed to perceive it. This tendency to prejudge reality based on our expectations is a basic fact about the human mind.

Because scholars at work in any given area often share a common viewpoint or come from the same **culture,** their assumptions may go unchallenged. What we take for granted—the shared beliefs that some European social psychologists call our **social representations** (Augoustinos & Innes, 1990; Moscovici, 1988, 2001)—are often our most important yet most unexamined convictions. Sometimes, however, someone from outside the camp will call attention to those assumptions. During the 1980s feminists and Marxists exposed some of social psychology's unexamined assumptions. Feminist critics called attention to subtle biases—for example, the political conservatism of some scientists who favored a biological interpretation of gender differences in social behavior (Unger, 1985). Marxist critics called attention to competitive, individualist biases—for example, the assumption that conformity is bad and that individual rewards are good. Marxists and feminists, of course, make their own assumptions, as critics of academic "political correctness" are fond of noting. Social psychologist Lee Jussim (2005), for example, argues that progressive social psychologists sometimes feel compelled to deny group differences and to assume that stereotypes of group difference are never rooted in reality but always in racism.

> "Science does not simply describe and explain nature; it is part of the interplay between nature and ourselves; it describes nature as exposed to our method of questioning."
> —*WERNER HEISENBERG, PHYSICS AND PHILOSOPHY, 1958*

culture
The enduring behaviors, ideas, attitudes, and traditions shared by a large group of people and transmitted from one generation to the next.

social representations
Socially shared beliefs—widely held ideas and values, including our assumptions and cultural ideologies. Our social representations help us make sense of our world.

FIGURE :: 1.3
What Do You See?

In Chapter 3 we will see more ways in which our preconceptions guide our interpretations. As those Princeton and Dartmouth football fans remind us, what guides our behavior is less the situation-as-it-is than the situation-as-we-construe-it.

PSYCHOLOGICAL CONCEPTS CONTAIN HIDDEN VALUES

Implicit in our understanding that psychology is not objective is the realization that psychologists' own values may play an important part in the theories and judgments they support. Psychologists may refer to people as mature or immature, as well adjusted or poorly adjusted, as mentally healthy or mentally ill. They may talk as if they were stating facts, when they are really making *value judgments*. Here are some examples:

Defining the Good Life. Values influence our idea of the best way to live our lives. The personality psychologist Abraham Maslow, for example, was known for his sensitive descriptions of "self-actualized" people—people who, with their needs for survival, safety, belonging, and self-esteem satisfied, go on to fulfill their human potential. Few readers noticed that Maslow himself, guided by his own values, selected the sample of self-actualized people he described. The resulting description of self-actualized personalities—as spontaneous, autonomous, mystical, and so forth—reflected Maslow's personal values. Had he begun with someone else's heroes—say, Napoleon, Alexander the Great, and John D. Rockefeller—his resulting description of self-actualization would have differed (Smith, 1978).

Professional Advice. Psychological advice also reflects the advice giver's personal values. When mental health professionals advise us how to get along with our spouse or our co-workers, when child-rearing experts tell us how to handle our children, and when some psychologists advocate living free of concern for others' expectations, they are expressing their personal values. (In Western cultures, those values usually will be individualistic—encouraging what feels best for "me." Non-Western cultures more often encourage what's best for "we.") Many people, unaware of those hidden values, defer to the "professional." But professional psychologists cannot answer questions of ultimate moral obligation, of purpose and direction, and of life's meaning.

Forming Concepts. Hidden values even seep into psychology's research-based *concepts*. Pretend you have taken a personality test and the psychologist, after scoring your answers, announces: "You scored high in self-esteem. You are low in anxiety. And you have exceptional ego-strength." "Ah," you think, "I suspected as much, but it feels good to know that." Now another psychologist gives you a similar test. For some peculiar reason, this test asks some of the same questions. Afterward, the psychologist informs you that you seem defensive, for you scored high in "repressiveness." "How could this be?" you wonder. "The other psychologist said such nice things about me." It could be because all these labels describe the same set of responses (a tendency to say nice things about oneself and not to acknowledge problems). Shall we call it high self-esteem or defensiveness? The label reflects the judgment.

Hidden (and not-so-hidden) values seep into psychological advice. They permeate popular psychology books that offer guidance on living and loving.

Labeling. Value judgments, then, are often hidden within our social-psychological language—but that is also true of everyday language:

• Whether we label a quiet child as "bashful" on "cautious," as "holding back" or as "an observer," conveys a judgment.

- Whether we label someone engaged in guerrilla warfare a "terrorist" or a "freedom fighter" depends on our view of the cause.
- Whether we view wartime civilian deaths as "the loss of innocent lives" or as "collateral damage" affects our acceptance of such.
- Whether we call public assistance "welfare" or "aid to the needy" reflects our political views.
- When "they" exalt their country and people, it's nationalism; when "we" do it, it's patriotism.
- Whether someone involved in an extramarital affair is practicing "open marriage" or "adultery" depends on one's personal values.
- "Brainwashing" is social influence we do not approve of.
- "Perversions" are sex acts we do not practice.
- Remarks about "ambitious" men and "aggressive" women convey a hidden message.

As these examples indicate, values lie hidden within our cultural definitions of mental health, our psychological advice for living, our concepts, and our psychological labels. Throughout this book I will call your attention to additional examples of hidden values. The point is never that the implicit values are necessarily bad. The point is that scientific interpretation, even at the level of labeling phenomena, is a human activity. It is therefore natural and inevitable that prior beliefs and values will influence what social psychologists think and write.

Should we dismiss science because it has its subjective side? Quite the contrary: The realization that human thinking always involves interpretation is precisely why we need researchers with varying biases to undertake scientific analysis. By constantly checking our beliefs against the facts, as best we know them, we check and restrain our biases. Systematic observation and experimentation help us clean the lens through which we see reality.

Summing Up: Social Psychology and Human Values

- Social psychologists' values penetrate their work in obvious ways, such as their choice of research topics and the types of people who are attracted to various fields of study.
- They also do this in subtler ways, such as their hidden assumptions when forming concepts, choosing labels, and giving advice.

- This penetration of values into science is not a reason to fault social psychology or any other science. That human thinking is seldom dispassionate is precisely why we need systematic observation and experimentation if we are to check our cherished ideas against reality.

I Knew It All Along: Is Social Psychology Simply Common Sense?

Do social psychology's theories provide new insight into the human condition? Or do they only describe the obvious?

Many of the conclusions presented in this book may have already occurred to you, for social psychological phenomena are all around you. We constantly observe people thinking about, influencing, and relating to one another. It pays to discern what a facial expression predicts, how to get someone to do something, or whether to regard another as friend or foe. For centuries, philosophers, novelists, and poets have observed and commented on social behavior.

Does this mean that social psychology is just common sense in fancy words? Social psychology faces two contradictory criticisms: first, that it is trivial because it documents the obvious; second, that it is dangerous because its findings could be used to manipulate people.

We will explore the second criticism in Chapter 7. For the moment, let's examine the first objection.

Do social psychology and the other social sciences simply formalize what any amateur already knows intuitively? Writer Cullen Murphy (1990) took that view: "Day after day social scientists go out into the world. Day after day they discover that people's behavior is pretty much what you'd expect." Nearly a half-century earlier, historian Arthur Schlesinger, Jr. (1949), reacted with similar scorn to social scientists' studies of American World War II soldiers. Sociologist Paul Lazarsfeld (1949) reviewed those studies and offered a sample with interpretive comments, a few of which I paraphrase:

1. Better-educated soldiers suffered more adjustment problems than did less-educated soldiers. (Intellectuals were less prepared for battle stresses than street-smart people.)
2. Southern soldiers coped better with the hot South Sea Island climate than did Northern soldiers. (Southerners are more accustomed to hot weather.)
3. White privates were more eager for promotion than were Black privates. (Years of oppression take a toll on achievement motivation.)
4. Southern Blacks preferred Southern to Northern White officers. (Southern officers were more experienced and skilled in interacting with Blacks.)

As you read those findings, did you agree that they were basically common sense? If so, you may be surprised to learn that Lazarsfeld went on to say, *"Every one of these statements is the direct opposite of what was actually found."* In reality, the studies found that less-educated soldiers adapted more poorly. Southerners were not more likely than northerners to adjust to a tropical climate. Blacks were more eager than Whites for promotion, and so forth. "If we had mentioned the actual results of the investigation first [as Schlesinger experienced], the reader would have labeled these 'obvious' also."

One problem with common sense is that we invoke it after we know the facts. Events are far more "obvious" and predictable in hindsight than beforehand. Experiments reveal that when people learn the outcome of an experiment, that outcome suddenly seems unsurprising—certainly less surprising than it is to people who are simply told about the experimental procedure and the possible outcomes (Slovic & Fischhoff, 1977).

Likewise, in everyday life we often do not expect something to happen until it does. *Then* we suddenly see clearly the forces that brought the event about and feel unsurprised. Moreover, we may also misremember our earlier view (Blank & others, 2008). Errors in judging the future's foreseeability and in remembering our past combine to create **hindsight bias** (also called the *I-knew-it-all-along phenomenon*).

hindsight bias
The tendency to exaggerate, after learning an outcome, one's ability to have foreseen how something turned out. Also known as the *I-knew-it-all-along phenomenon*.

Thus, after elections or stock market shifts, most commentators find the turn of events unsurprising: "The market was due for a correction." After the widespread flooding in New Orleans as a result of Hurricane Katrina in 2005, it seemed obvious that public officials should have anticipated the situation: Studies of the levees' vulnerability had been done. Many residents did not own cars and were too poor to afford transportation and lodging out of town. Meteorologic assessment of the storm's severity clearly predicted an urgent need to put security and relief supplies in place. As the Danish philosopher-theologian Søren Kierkegaard put it, "Life is lived forwards, but understood backwards."

If hindsight bias is pervasive, you may now be feeling that you already knew about this phenomenon. Indeed, almost any conceivable result of a psychological experiment can seem like common sense—*after* you know the result.

You can demonstrate the phenomenon yourself. Take a group of people and tell half of them one psychological finding and the other half the opposite result. For example, tell half as follows:

> Social psychologists have found that, whether choosing friends or falling in love, we are most attracted to people whose traits are different from our own. There seems to be wisdom in the old saying "Opposites attract."

Tell the other half:

> Social psychologists have found that, whether choosing friends or falling in love, we are most attracted to people whose traits are similar to our own. There seems to be wisdom in the old saying "Birds of a feather flock together."

In hindsight, events seem obvious and predictable.
ScienceCartoonsPlus.com

Ask the people first to explain the result. Then ask them to say whether it is "surprising" or "not surprising." Virtually all will find a good explanation for whichever result they were given and will say it is "not surprising."

Indeed, we can draw on our stockpile of proverbs to make almost any result seem to make sense. If a social psychologist reports that separation intensifies romantic attraction, John Q. Public responds, "You get paid for this? Everybody knows that 'absence makes the heart grow fonder.'" Should it turn out that separation *weakens* attraction, John will say, "My grandmother could have told you, 'Out of sight, out of mind.'"

Karl Teigen (1986) must have had a few chuckles when he asked University of Leicester (England) students to evaluate actual proverbs and their opposites. When given the proverb "Fear is stronger than love," most rated it as true. But so did students who were given its reversed form, "Love is stronger than fear." Likewise, the genuine proverb "He that is fallen cannot help him who is down" was rated highly; but so too was "He that is fallen can help him who is down." My favorites, however, were two highly rated proverbs: "Wise men make proverbs and fools repeat them" (authentic) and its made-up counterpart, "Fools make proverbs and wise men repeat them." For more dueling proverbs, see "Focus On: I Knew It All Along."

The hindsight bias creates a problem for many psychology students. Sometimes results are genuinely surprising (for example, that Olympic *bronze* medalists take more joy in their achievement than do silver medalists). More often, when you read the results of experiments in your textbooks, the material seems easy, even obvious. When you later take a multiple-choice test on which you must choose among several plausible conclusions, the task may become surprisingly difficult. "I don't know what happened," the befuddled student later moans. "I thought I knew the material."

focus
ON   I Knew It All Along

Cullen Murphy (1990), managing editor of the *Atlantic*, faulted "sociology, psychology, and other social sciences for too often merely discerning the obvious or confirming the commonplace." His own casual survey of social science findings "turned up no ideas or conclusions that can't be found in *Bartlett's* or any other encyclopedia of quotations." Nevertheless, to sift through competing sayings, we need research. Consider some dueling proverbs:

Is it more true that . . .
- Too many cooks spoil the broth.
- The pen is mightier than the sword.
- You can't teach an old dog new tricks.
- Blood is thicker than water.
- He who hesitates is lost.
- Forewarned is forearmed.

Or that . . .
- Two heads are better than one.
- Actions speak louder than words.
- You're never too old to learn.

- Many kinfolk, few friends.
- Look before you leap.
- Don't cross the bridge until you come to it.

The I-knew-it-all-along phenomenon can have unfortunate consequences. It is conducive to arrogance—an overestimation of our own intellectual powers. Moreover, because outcomes seem as if they should have been foreseeable, we are more likely to blame decision makers for what are in retrospect "obvious" bad choices than to praise them for good choices, which also seem "obvious."

Starting *after* the morning of 9/11 and working backward, signals pointing to the impending disaster seemed obvious. A U.S. Senate investigative report listed the missed or misinterpreted clues (Gladwell, 2003), which included the following. The CIA knew that al Qaeda operatives had entered the country. An FBI agent sent a memo to headquarters that began by warning "the Bureau and New York of the possibility of a coordinated effort by Osama bin Laden to send students to the United States to attend civilian aviation universities and colleges." The FBI ignored that accurate warning and failed to relate it to other reports that terrorists were planning to use planes as weapons. The president received a daily briefing titled "Bin Laden Determined to Strike Inside the United States" and stayed on holiday. "The dumb fools!" it seemed to hindsight critics. "Why couldn't they connect the dots?"

But what seems clear in hindsight is seldom clear on the front side of history. The intelligence community is overwhelmed with "noise"—piles of useless information surrounding the rare shreds of useful information. Analysts must therefore be selective in deciding which to pursue, and only when a lead is pursued does it stand a chance of being connected to another lead. In the six years before 9/11, the FBI's counterterrorism unit could never have pursued all 68,000 uninvestigated leads. In hindsight, the few useful ones are now obvious.

In the aftermath of the 2008 world financial crisis, it seemed obvious that government regulators should have placed safeguards against the ill-fated bank lending practices. But what was obvious in hindsight was unforeseen by the chief American regulator, Alan Greenspan, who found himself "in a state of shocked disbelief" at the economic collapse.

We sometimes blame ourselves for "stupid mistakes"—perhaps for not having handled a person or a situation better. Looking back, we see how we should have handled it. "I should have known how busy I would be at the semester's end and started that paper earlier." But sometimes we are too hard on ourselves. We forget that what is obvious to us *now* was not nearly so obvious at the time.

Physicians who are told both a patient's symptoms and the cause of death (as determined by autopsy) sometimes wonder how an incorrect diagnosis could have been made. Other physicians, given only the symptoms, don't find the diagnosis nearly so obvious (Dawson & others, 1988). Would juries be slower to assume malpractice if they were forced to take a foresight rather than a hindsight perspective?

What do we conclude—that common sense is usually wrong? Sometimes it is. At other times, conventional wisdom is right—or it falls on both sides of an issue: Does happiness come from knowing the truth, or from preserving illusions? From being with others, or from living in peaceful solitude? Opinions are a dime a dozen. No matter what we find, there will be someone who foresaw it. (Mark Twain jested that Adam was the only person who, when saying a good thing, knew that nobody had said it before.) But which of the many competing ideas best fit reality? Research can specify the circumstances under which a common-sense truism is valid.

The point is not that common sense is predictably wrong. Rather, common sense usually is right—*after the fact*. We therefore easily deceive ourselves into thinking that we know and knew more than we do and did. And that is precisely why we need science to help us sift reality from illusion and genuine predictions from easy hindsight.

"It is easy to be wise after the event."

—SHERLOCK HOLMES, IN ARTHUR CONAN DOYLE'S STORY "THE PROBLEM OF THOR BRIDGE"

"Everything important has been said before."

—PHILOSOPHER ALFRED NORTH WHITEHEAD (1861–1947)

Summing Up: I Knew It All Along: Is Social Psychology Simply Common Sense?

- Social psychology is criticized for being trivial because it documents things that seem obvious.

- Experiments, however, reveal that outcomes are more "obvious" *after* the facts are known.

- This hindsight bias (the *I-knew-it-all-along phenomenon*) often makes people overconfident about the validity of their judgments and predictions.

Research Methods: How We Do Social Psychology

We have considered some of the intriguing questions social psychology seeks to answer. We have also seen how subjective, often unconscious, processes influence social psychologists' work. Now let's consider the scientific methods that make social psychology a science.

In their quest for insight, social psychologists propose *theories* that organize their observations and imply testable *hypotheses* and practical predictions. To test a hypothesis, social psychologists may do research that predicts behavior using *correlational* studies, often conducted in natural settings. Or they may seek to explain behavior by conducting *experiments* that manipulate one or more factors under controlled conditions. Once they have conducted a research study, they explore ways to apply their findings to improve people's everyday lives.

We are all amateur social psychologists. People-watching is a universal hobby. As we observe people, we form ideas about how human beings think about, influence, and relate to one another. Professional social psychologists do the same, only more systematically (by forming theories) and painstakingly (often with experiments that create miniature social dramas that pin down cause and effect). And they have done it extensively, in 25,000 studies of 8 million people by one count (Richard & others, 2003).

> "Nothing has such power to broaden the mind as the ability to investigate systematically and truly all that comes under thy observation in life."
> —*MARCUS AURELIUS,* MEDITATIONS

Forming and Testing Hypotheses

We social psychologists have a hard time thinking of anything more fascinating than human existence. As we wrestle with human nature to pin down its secrets, we organize our ideas and findings into theories. A **theory** is *an integrated set of principles that explain and predict* observed events. Theories are a scientific shorthand.

In everyday conversation, "theory" often means "less than fact"—a middle rung on a confidence ladder from guess to theory to fact. Thus, people may, for example, dismiss Charles Darwin's theory of evolution as "just a theory." Indeed, notes Alan Leshner (2005), chief officer of the American Association for the Advancement of Science, "Evolution *is* only a theory, but so is gravity." People often respond that gravity is a fact—but the *fact* is that your keys fall to the ground when dropped. Gravity is the *theoretical explanation* that accounts for such observed facts.

To a scientist, facts and theories are apples and oranges. Facts are agreed-upon statements about what we observe. Theories are *ideas* that summarize and explain facts. "Science is built up with facts, as a house is with stones," wrote the French scientist Jules Henri Poincaré, "but a collection of facts is no more a science than a heap of stones is a house."

theory
An integrated set of principles that explain and predict observed events.

hypothesis
A testable proposition that describes a relationship that may exist between events.

For humans, the most fascinating subject is people.
© The New Yorker Collection, 1987, Warren Miller, from cartoonbank.com. All Rights Reserved.

Theories not only summarize but also imply testable predictions, called **hypotheses.** Hypotheses serve several purposes. First, they allow us to *test* a theory by suggesting how we might try to falsify it. Second, predictions give *direction* to research and sometimes send investigators looking for things they might never have thought of. Third, the predictive feature of good theories can also make them *practical.* A complete theory of aggression, for example, would predict when to expect aggression and how to control it. As the pioneering social psychologist Kurt Lewin declared, "There is nothing so practical as a good theory."

Consider how this works. Say we observe that people who loot, taunt, or attack often do so in groups or crowds. We might therefore theorize that being part of a crowd, or group, makes individuals feel anonymous and lowers their inhibitions. How could we test this theory? Perhaps (I'm playing with this theory) we could devise a laboratory experiment simulating aspects of execution by electric chair. What if we asked individuals in groups to administer punishing shocks to a hapless victim without knowing which member of the group was actually shocking the victim? Would these individuals administer stronger shocks than individuals acting alone, as our theory predicts?

We might also manipulate anonymity: Would people deliver stronger shocks if they were wearing masks? If the results confirm our hypothesis, they might suggest some practical applications. Perhaps police brutality could be reduced by having officers wear large name tags and drive cars identified with large numbers, or by videotaping their arrests—all of which have, in fact, become common practice in many cities.

But how do we conclude that one theory is better than another? A good theory

- effectively *summarizes many observations,* and
- *makes clear predictions* that we can use to
  - confirm or modify the theory,
  - generate new exploration, and
  - suggest practical applications.

When we discard theories, usually it's not because they have been proved false. Rather, like old cars, they are replaced by newer, better models.

Correlational Research: Detecting Natural Associations

Most of what you will learn about social-psychological research methods you will absorb as you read later chapters. But let's now go backstage and see how social psychology is done. This glimpse behind the scenes should be just enough for you to appreciate findings discussed later. Understanding the logic of research can also help you think critically about everyday social events.

Social-psychological research varies by location. It can take place in the *laboratory* (a controlled situation) or in the **field** (everyday situations). And it varies by

field research
Research done in natural, real-life settings outside the laboratory.

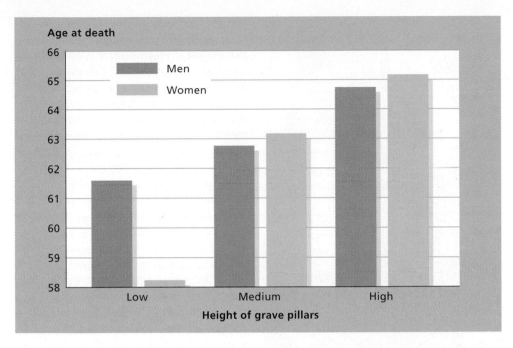

Correlating Status
and Longevity

Tall grave pillars commemorated
people who also tended to live
longer.

method—whether **correlational** (asking whether two or more factors are naturally associated) or **experimental** (manipulating some factor to see its effect on another). If you want to be a critical reader of psychological research reported in newspapers and magazines, it will pay you to understand the difference between correlational and experimental research.

Using some real examples, let's first consider the advantages of correlational research (often involving important variables in natural settings) and its major disadvantage (ambiguous interpretation of cause and effect). As we will see in Chapter 14, today's psychologists relate personal and social factors to human health. Among the researchers have been Douglas Carroll at Glasgow Caledonian University and his colleagues, George Davey Smith and Paul Bennett (1994). In search of possible links between socioeconomic status and health, the researchers ventured into Glasgow's old graveyards. As a measure of health, they noted from grave markers the life spans of 843 individuals. As an indication of status, they measured the height of the pillars over the graves, reasoning that height reflected cost and therefore affluence. As Figure 1.4 shows, taller grave markers were related to longer lives, for both men and women.

Carroll and his colleagues report that other researchers, using contemporary data, have confirmed the status-longevity correlation. Scottish postal-code regions having the least overcrowding and unemployment also have the greatest longevity. In the United States, income correlates with longevity (poor and lower-status people are more at risk for premature death). In today's Britain, occupational status correlates with longevity. One study followed 17,350 British civil service workers over 10 years. Compared with top-grade administrators, those at the professional-executive grade were 1.6 times more likely to have died. Clerical workers were 2.2 times and laborers 2.7 times more likely to have died (Adler & others, 1993, 1994). Across times and places, the status-health correlation seems reliable.

correlational research
The study of the naturally occurring relationships among variables.

experimental research
Studies that seek clues to cause-effect relationships by manipulating one or more factors (independent variables) while controlling others (holding them constant).

CORRELATION AND CAUSATION

The status-longevity question illustrates the most irresistible thinking error made by both amateur and professional social psychologists: When two factors such as status and health go together, it is terribly tempting to conclude that one is causing the

Commemorative markers in Glasgow Cathedral graveyard.

other. Status, we might presume, somehow protects a person from health risks. But might it be the other way around? Could it be that health promotes vigor and success? Perhaps people who live longer simply have more time to accumulate wealth (enabling them to have more expensive grave markers). Or might a third variable, such as diet, be involved (did wealthy and working-class people tend to eat differently)? Correlations indicate a relationship, but that relationship is not necessarily one of cause and effect. Correlational research allows us to *predict*, but it cannot tell us whether changing one variable (such as social status) will *cause* changes in another (such as health).

An amusing correlation-causation confusion surfaced during the 2008 presidential campaign when the Associated Press reported a survey showing that most dog owners favored John McCain (who had two dogs) over Barack Obama (who didn't own a pet), while those without a dog favored Obama. "The pet owning public seems to have noticed," noted the writer, inferring that McCain's dog ownership drew support from fellow dog owners (Schmid, 2008). But had the public noticed and cared who had pets? Or was the pet-preference correlation merely a reflection of some "confounded" third factors? For example, the survey also found dog ownership rates much higher among White and married people (who are more often Republicans and therefore McCain's natural constituency) than among Black and single people.

The correlation-causation confusion is behind much muddled thinking in popular psychology. Consider another very real correlation—between self-esteem and academic achievement. Children with high self-esteem tend also to have high academic achievement. (As with any correlation, we can also state this the other way around: High achievers tend to have high self-esteem.) Why do you suppose that is true (Figure 1.5)?

FIGURE :: 1.5

Correlation and Causations

When two variables correlate, any combination of three explanations is possible. Either one may cause the other, or both may be affected by an underlying "third factor."

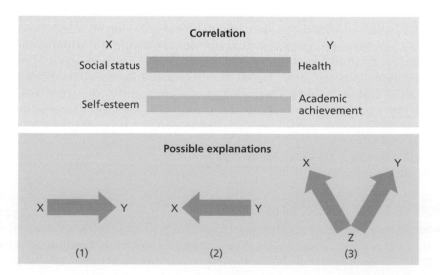

Some people believe a "healthy self-concept" contributes to achievement. Thus, boosting a child's self-image may also boost school achievement. Believing so, 30 U.S. states have enacted more than 170 self-esteem-promoting statutes.

But other people, including psychologists William Damon (1995), Robyn Dawes (1994), Mark Leary (1999), Martin Seligman (1994, 2002), and Roy Baumeister and colleagues (2003, 2005), doubt that self-esteem is really "the armor that protects kids" from underachievement (or drug abuse and delinquency). Perhaps it's the other way around: Perhaps problems and failures cause low self-esteem. Perhaps self-esteem often reflects the reality of how things are going for us. Perhaps self-esteem grows from hard-won achievements. Do well and you will feel good about yourself; goof off and fail and you will feel like a dolt. A study of 635 Norwegian schoolchildren showed that a (legitimately earned) string of gold stars by one's name on the spelling chart and accompanying praise from the admiring teacher can boost a child's self-esteem (Skaalvik & Hagtvet, 1990). Or perhaps, as in a study of nearly 6,000 German seventh-graders, the traffic between self-esteem and academic achievements runs both ways (Trautwein & Lüdtke, 2006).

It's also possible that self-esteem and achievement correlate because both are linked to underlying intelligence and family social status. That possibility was raised in two studies—one a nationwide sample of 1,600 young American men, another of 715 Minnesota youngsters (Bachman & O'Malley, 1977; Maruyama & others, 1981). When the researchers mathematically removed the predictive power of intelligence and family status, the relationship between self-esteem and achievement evaporated.

Correlations quantify, with a coefficient known as r, the degree of relationship between two factors—from 1.0 (as one factor score goes up, the other goes down) through 0 to +1.0 (the two factors' scores rise and fall together). Scores on self-esteem and depression tests correlate negatively (about −.6). Identical twins' intelligence scores correlate positively (above +.8). The great strength of correlational research is that it tends to occur in real-world settings where we can examine factors such as race, gender, and social status (factors that we cannot manipulate in the laboratory). Its great disadvantage lies in the ambiguity of the results. This point is so important that even if it fails to impress people the first 25 times they hear it, it is worth repeating a twenty-sixth time: *Knowing that two variables change together (correlate) enables us to predict one when we know the other, but correlation does not specify cause and effect.*

Advanced correlational techniques can, however, suggest cause-effect relationships. *Time-lagged* correlations reveal the *sequence* of events (for example, by indicating whether changed achievement more often precedes or follows changed self-esteem). Researchers can also use statistical techniques that extract the influence of "confounded" variables, as when the correlation between self-esteem *and* achievement evaporated after extracting intelligence and family status. Recall our earlier mention of a *third variable*, such as diet. Thus, the Scottish research team wondered whether the status-longevity relationship would survive their removing the effect of cigarette smoking, which is now much less common among those of higher status. It did, which suggested that some other factors, such as increased stress and decreased feelings of control, may also account for poorer people's earlier mortality.

SURVEY RESEARCH

How do we measure variables such as status and health? One way is by surveying representative samples of people. If survey researchers want to describe a whole population (which for many psychology surveys is not the aim), then they will obtain a *representative* group by taking a **random sample**—*one in which every person in the population being studied has an equal chance of inclusion.* With

random sample
Survey procedure in which every person in the population being studied has an equal chance of inclusion.

Even exit polls require a random (and therefore representative) sample of voters.

this procedure any subgroup of people—blondes, joggers, liberals—will tend to be represented in the survey to the extent that they are represented in the total population.

It is an amazing fact that whether we survey people in a city or in a whole country, 1,200 randomly selected participants will enable us to be 95 percent confident of describing the entire population with an error margin of 3 percentage points or less. Imagine a huge jar filled with beans, 50 percent red and 50 percent white. Randomly sample 1,200 of these, and you will be 95 percent certain to draw out between 47 percent and 53 percent red beans—regardless of whether the jar contains 10,000 beans or 100 million beans. If we think of the red beans as supporters of one presidential candidate and the white beans as supporters of the other candidate, we can understand why, since 1950, the Gallup polls taken just before U.S. national elections have diverged from election results by an average of less than 2 percent. As a few drops of blood can speak for the whole body, so can a random sample speak for a population.

Bear in mind that polls do not literally *predict* voting; they only *describe* public opinion at the moment they are taken. Public opinion can shift. To evaluate surveys, we must also bear in mind four potentially biasing influences: unrepresentative samples, question order, response options, and question wording.

UNREPRESENTATIVE SAMPLES   How closely the sample represents the population under study greatly matters. In 1984 columnist Ann Landers accepted a letter writer's challenge to poll her readers on the question of whether women find affection more important than sex. Her question: "Would you be content to be held close and treated tenderly and forget about 'the act'?" Of the more than 100,000 women who replied, 72 percent said yes. An avalanche of worldwide publicity followed. In response to critics, Landers (1985, p. 45) granted that "the sampling may not be representative of all American women. But it does provide honest—valuable—insights from a cross section of the public. This is because my column is read by people from every walk of life, approximately 70 million of them." Still, one wonders, are the 70 million readers representative of the entire population? And are the 1 in 700 readers who took the trouble to reply to the survey representative of the 699 in 700 who did not?

The importance of representativeness was effectively demonstrated in 1936, when a weekly newsmagazine, *Literary Digest,* mailed a postcard presidential election poll to 10 million Americans. Among the more than 2 million returns, Alf

SRC's Survey Services Laboratory at the University of Michigan's Institute for Social Research has interviewing carrels with monitoring stations. Staff and visitors must sign a pledge to honor the strict confidentiality of all interviews.

Landon won by a landslide over Franklin D. Roosevelt. When the actual votes were counted a few days later, Landon carried only two states. The magazine had sent the poll only to people whose names it had obtained from telephone books and automobile registrations—thus ignoring the millions of voters who could afford neither a telephone nor a car (Cleghorn, 1980).

ORDER OF QUESTIONS   Given a representative sample, we must also contend with other sources of bias, such as the order of questions in a survey. Americans' support for civil unions of gays and lesbians rises if they are first asked their opinion of gay marriage, compared with which civil unions seem a more acceptable alternative (Moore, 2004a, 2004b).

RESPONSE OPTIONS   Consider, too, the dramatic effects of the response options. When Joop van der Plight and his co-workers (1987) asked English voters what percentage of Britain's energy they wished came from nuclear power, the average preference was 41 percent. They asked other voters what percentage they wished came from (1) nuclear, (2) coal, and (3) other sources. The average preference for nuclear power among these respondents was 21 percent.

WORDING OF QUESTIONS   The precise wording of questions may also influence answers. One poll found that only 23 percent of Americans thought their government was spending too much "on assistance to the poor." Yet 53 percent thought the government was spending too much "on welfare" (*Time,* 1994). Likewise, most people favor cutting "foreign aid" and *increasing* spending "to help hungry people in other nations" (Simon, 1996).

Survey questioning is a very delicate matter. Even subtle changes in the tone of a question can have marked effects (Krosnick & Schuman, 1988; Schuman & Kalton, 1985). "Forbidding" something may be the same as "not allowing" it. But in 1940, 54 percent of Americans said the United States should "forbid" speeches against democracy, and 75 percent said the United States should "not allow" them. Even when people say they feel strongly about an issue, a question's form and wording may affect their answer.

Order, response, and wording effects enable political manipulators to use surveys to show public support for their views. Consultants, advertisers, and physicians can have similar disconcerting influences upon our decisions by how they **frame** our choices. No wonder the meat lobby in 1994 objected to a new U.S. food labeling law that required declaring ground beef, for example, as "30 percent fat," rather than "70 percent lean, 30 percent fat." To 9 in 10 college students, a condom

framing
The way a question or an issue is posed; framing can influence people's decisions and expressed opinions.

Survey researchers must be sensitive to subtle and not-so-subtle biases.

seems effective if its protection against the AIDS virus has a "95 percent success rate." Told that it has a "5 percent failure rate," only 4 in 10 students say they find it effective (Linville & others, 1992).

Framing research also has applications in the definition of everyday default options:

- *Opting in or opting out of organ donation.* In many countries, people decide, when renewing their drivers' license, whether they want to make their body available for organ donation. In countries where the default option is *yes*, but one can "opt out," nearly 100 percent of people choose to be donors. In the United States, Britain, and Germany, where the default option is *no* but one can "opt in," about 1 in 4 choose to be donors (Johnson & Goldstein, 2003).

- *Opting in or opting out of retirement savings.* For many years, American employees who wanted to defer part of their compensation to a 401(k) retirement plan had to elect to lower their take-home pay. Most chose not to do so. A 2006 pension law, influenced by framing research, reframed the choice. Now companies are given an incentive to enroll their employees automatically in the plan, and to allow them to opt out (and to raise their take-home pay). The choice was preserved. But one study found that with the "opt out" framing, enrollments soared from 49 to 86 percent (Madrian & Shea, 2001).

The lesson of framing research is told in the story of a sultan who dreamed he had lost all his teeth. Summoned to interpret the dream, the first interpreter said, "Alas! The lost teeth mean you will see your family members die." Enraged, the sultan ordered 50 lashes for this bearer of bad news. When a second dream interpreter heard the dream, he explained the sultan's good fortune: "You will outlive your whole clan!" Reassured, the sultan ordered his treasurer to go and fetch 50 pieces of gold for this bearer of good news. On the way, the bewildered treasurer observed to the second interpreter, "Your interpretation was no different from that of the first interpreter." "Ah yes," the wise interpreter replied, "but remember: What matters is not only what you say, but how you say it."

A young monk was once rebuffed when asking if he could smoke while he prayed. Ask a different question, advised a friend: Ask if you can pray while you smoke (Crossen, 1993).

Experimental Research: Searching for Cause and Effect

The difficulty of discerning cause and effect among naturally correlated events prompts most social psychologists to create laboratory simulations of everyday processes whenever this is feasible and ethical. These simulations are akin to aeronautical wind tunnels. Aeronautical engineers don't begin by observing how flying objects perform in various natural environments. The variations in both atmospheric conditions and flying objects are too complex. Instead, they construct a simulated reality in which they can manipulate wind conditions and wing structures.

CONTROL: MANIPULATING VARIABLES

Like aeronautical engineers, social psychologists experiment by constructing social situations that simulate important features of our daily lives. By varying just one or two factors at a time—called **independent variables**—the experimenter pinpoints their influence. As the wind tunnel helps the aeronautical engineer discover principles of aerodynamics, so the experiment enables the social psychologist to discover principles of social thinking, social influence, and social relations.

Historically, social psychologists have used the experimental method in about three-fourths of their research studies (Higbee & others, 1982), and in two out of three studies the setting has been a research laboratory (Adair & others, 1985). To illustrate the laboratory experiment, consider two experiments that typify research from upcoming chapters on prejudice and aggression. Each suggests possible cause-effect explanations of correlational findings.

CORRELATIONAL AND EXPERIMENTAL STUDIES OF PREJUDICE AGAINST THE OBESE The first experiment concerns prejudice against people who are obese. People often perceive the obese as slow, lazy, and sloppy (Roehling & others, 2007; Ryckman & others, 1989). Do such attitudes spawn discrimination? In hopes of finding out, Steven Gortmaker and his colleagues (1993) studied 370 obese 16- to 24-year-old women. When they restudied them seven years later, two-thirds of the women were still obese and were less likely to be married and earning high salaries than a comparison group of some 5,000 other women. Even after correcting for any differences in aptitude test scores, race, and parental income, the obese women's incomes were $7,000 a year below average.

Correcting for certain other factors makes it look as though discrimination might explain the correlation between obesity and lower status. But we can't be sure. (Can you think of other possibilities?) Enter social psychologists Mark Snyder and Julie Haugen (1994, 1995). They asked 76 University of Minnesota male students to have a get-acquainted phone conversation with 1 of 76 female students. Unknown to the women, each man was shown a photo *said* to picture his conversational partner. Half were shown an obese woman (not the actual partner); the other half a normal-weight woman. Later analysis of just the women's side of the conversation revealed that *they spoke less warmly and happily if they were presumed obese.* Clearly, something in the men's tone of voice and conversational content induced the supposedly obese women to speak in a way that confirmed the idea that obese women are undesirable. Prejudice and discrimination were having an effect. Recalling the effect of the stepmother's behavior, perhaps we should call this the "Cinderella effect."

CORRELATIONAL AND EXPERIMENTAL STUDIES OF TV VIOLENCE VIEWING As a second example of how experiments clarify causation, consider the correlation between television viewing and children's behavior. *The more violent television children watch, the more aggressive they tend to be.* Are children learning and reenacting what they see on the screen? As I hope you now recognize, this is a correlational finding. Figure 1.5 reminds us that there are two other cause-effect interpretations. (What are they?)

Social psychologists have therefore brought television viewing into the laboratory, where they control the amount of violence the children see. By exposing children to violent and nonviolent programs, researchers can observe how the amount of violence affects behavior. Chris Boyatzis and his colleagues (1995) showed some elementary school children, but not others, an episode of the most popular—and violent—children's television program of the 1990s, *Power Rangers.* Immediately

independent variable
The experimental factor that a researcher manipulates.

Future chapters will offer many research-based insights, a few of which will be highlighted in "Research Close-Up" boxes that describe a sample study in depth.

Note: Obesity correlated with marital status and income.

Whom the men were shown—a normal or an overweight woman—was the independent variable.

Does viewing violence on TV or in other media lead to imitation, especially among children? Experiments suggest that it does.

dependent variable
The variable being measured, so called because it may depend on manipulations of the independent variable.

after viewing the episode, the viewers committed seven times as many aggressive acts per two-minute interval as the nonviewers. The observed aggressive acts we call the **dependent variable.** Such experiments indicate that television can be one cause of children's aggressive behavior.

So far we have seen that the logic of experimentation is simple: By creating and controlling a miniature reality, we can vary one factor and then another and discover how those factors, separately or in combination, affect people. Now let's go a little deeper and see how an experiment is done.

Every social-psychological experiment has two essential ingredients. We have just considered one—*control.* We manipulate one or more independent variables while trying to hold everything else constant. The other ingredient is *random assignment.*

RANDOM ASSIGNMENT: THE GREAT EQUALIZER

Recall that we were reluctant, on the basis of a correlation, to assume that obesity *caused* lower status (via discrimination) or that violence viewing *caused* aggressiveness (see Table 1.1 for more examples). A survey researcher might measure and

TABLE :: 1.1   Recognizing Correlational and Experimental Research

	Can Participants Be Randomly Assigned to Condition?	Independent Variable	Dependent Variable
Are early-maturing children more confident?	No → Correlational		
Do students learn more in online or classroom courses?	Yes → Experimental	Take class online or in classroom	Learning
Do school grades predict vocational success?	No → Correlational		
Does playing violent video games increase aggressiveness?	Yes → Experimental	Play violent or nonviolent game	Aggressiveness
Do people find comedy funnier when alone or with others?	(you answer)		
Do higher-income people have higher self-esteem?	(you answer)		

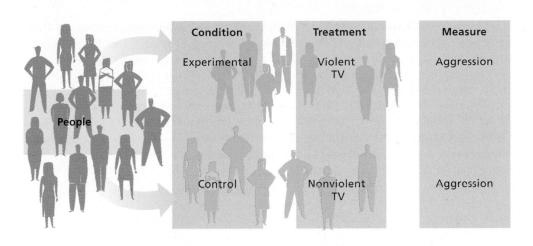

FIGURE :: 1.6

Random Assignment

Experiments randomly assign
people either to a condition
that receives the experimental
treatment or to a control condition that does not. This gives
the researcher confidence that
any later difference is somehow
caused by the treatment.

statistically extract other possibly pertinent factors and see if the correlations survive. But one can never control for all the factors that might distinguish obese from
nonobese, and viewers of violence from nonviewers. Maybe viewers of violence
differ in education, culture, intelligence—or in dozens of ways the researcher hasn't
considered.

In one fell swoop, **random assignment** eliminates all such extraneous factors.
With random assignment, each person has an equal chance of viewing the violence
or the nonviolence. Thus, the people in both groups would, in every conceivable
way—family status, intelligence, education, initial aggressiveness—average about
the same. Highly intelligent people, for example, are equally likely to appear in both
groups. Because random assignment creates equivalent groups, any later aggression difference between the two groups will almost surely have something to do
with the only way they differ—whether or not they viewed violence (Figure 1.6).

THE ETHICS OF EXPERIMENTATION

Our television example illustrates why some conceivable experiments raise ethical
issues. Social psychologists would not, over long time periods, expose one group
of children to brutal violence. Rather, they briefly alter people's social experience
and note the effects. Sometimes the experimental treatment is a harmless, perhaps
even enjoyable, experience to which people give their knowing consent. Sometimes,
however, researchers find themselves operating in a gray area between the harmless and the risky.

Social psychologists often venture into that ethical gray area when they design
experiments that engage intense thoughts and emotions. Experiments need not
have what Elliot Aronson, Marilynn Brewer, and Merrill Carlsmith (1985) call
mundane realism. That is, laboratory behavior (for example, delivering electric
shocks as part of an experiment on aggression) need not be literally the same as
everyday behavior. For many researchers, that sort of realism is indeed mundane—
not important. But the experiment *should* have **experimental realism**—it should
engage the participants. Experimenters do not want their people consciously playacting or ho-humming it; they want to engage real psychological processes. Forcing people to choose whether to give intense or mild electric shock to someone else
can, for example, be a realistic measure of aggression. It functionally simulates
real aggression.

Achieving experimental realism sometimes requires deceiving people with a
plausible cover story. If the person in the next room actually is not receiving the
shocks, the experimenter does not want the participants to know that. That would
destroy the experimental realism. Thus, about one-third of social-psychological
studies (though a decreasing number) have used **deception** in their search for truth
(Korn & Nicks, 1993; Vitelli, 1988).

random assignment
The process of assigning
participants to the conditions
of an experiment such that
all persons have the same
chance of being in a given
condition. (Note the dis-
tinction between random
assignment in experiments
and random *sampling* in
surveys. Random assignment
helps us infer cause and
effect. Random sampling
helps us generalize to a
population.)

mundane realism
Degree to which an
experiment is superficially
similar to everyday situations.

experimental realism
Degree to which an
experiment absorbs and
involves its participants.

deception
In research, an effect by
which participants are
misinformed or misled about
the study's methods and
purposes.

Experimenters also seek to hide their predictions lest the participants, in their eagerness to be "good subjects," merely do what's expected or, in an ornery mood, do the opposite. Small wonder, says Ukrainian professor Anatoly Koladny, that only 15 percent of Ukrainian survey respondents declared themselves "religious" while under Soviet communism in 1990 when religion was oppressed by the government— and that 70 percent declared themselves "religious" in postcommunist 1997 (Nielsen, 1998). In subtle ways, too, the experimenter's words, tone of voice, and gestures may call forth desired responses. To minimize such **demand characteristics**—cues that seem to "demand" certain behavior—experimenters typically standardize their instructions or even use a computer to present them.

Researchers often walk a tightrope in designing experiments that will be involving yet ethical. To believe that you are hurting someone, or to be subjected to strong social pressure, may be temporarily uncomfortable. Such experiments raise the age-old question of whether ends justify means. The social psychologists' deceptions are usually brief and mild compared with many misrepresentations in real life, and in some of television's *Candid Camera* and reality shows. (One network reality TV series deceived women into competing for the hand of a handsome supposed millionaire, who turned out to be an ordinary laborer.)

University ethics committees review social-psychological research to ensure that it will treat people humanely and that the scientific merit justifies any temporary deception or distress. Ethical principles developed by the American Psychological Association (2002), the Canadian Psychological Association (2000), and the British Psychological Society (2000) mandate investigators to do the following:

- Tell potential participants enough about the experiment to enable their **informed consent.**
- Be truthful. Use deception only if essential and justified by a significant purpose and not "about aspects that would affect their willingness to participate."
- Protect participants (and bystanders, if any) from harm and significant discomfort.
- Treat information about the individual participants confidentially.
- **Debrief** participants. Fully explain the experiment afterward, including any deception. The only exception to this rule is when the feedback would be distressing, such as by making participants realize they have been stupid or cruel.

The experimenter should be sufficiently informative *and* considerate that people leave feeling at least as good about themselves as when they came in. Better yet, the participants should be compensated by having learned something. When treated respectfully, few participants mind being deceived (Epley & Huff, 1998; Kimmel, 1998). Indeed, say social psychology's advocates, professors provoke far greater anxiety and distress by giving and returning course exams than researchers provoke in their experiments.

Generalizing from Laboratory to Life

As the research on children, television, and violence illustrates, social psychology mixes everyday experience and laboratory analysis. Throughout this book we will do the same by drawing our data mostly from the laboratory and our illustrations mostly from life. Social psychology displays a healthy interplay between laboratory research and everyday life. Hunches gained from everyday experience often inspire laboratory research, which deepens our understanding of our experience.

This interplay appears in the children's television experiment. What people saw in everyday life suggested correlational research, which led to experimental research. Network and government policymakers, those with the power to make changes, are

---

demand characteristics
Cues in an experiment that tell the participant what behavior is expected.

informed consent
An ethical principle requiring that research participants be told enough to enable them to choose whether they wish to participate.

debriefing
In social psychology, the postexperimental explanation of a study to its participants. Debriefing usually discloses any deception and often queries participants regarding their understandings and feelings.

now aware of the results. The consistency of findings on television's effects—in the lab and in the field—is true of research in many other areas, including studies of helping, leadership style, depression, and self-efficacy. The effects one finds in the lab have been mirrored by effects in the field. "The psychology laboratory has generally produced psychological truths rather than trivialities," note Craig Anderson and his colleagues (1999).

We need to be cautious, however, in generalizing from laboratory to life. Although the laboratory uncovers basic dynamics of human existence, it is still a simplified, controlled reality. It tells us what effect to expect of variable X, all other things being equal—which in real life they never are! Moreover, as you will see, the participants in many experiments are college students. Although that may help you identify with them, college students are hardly a random sample of all humanity. Would we get similar results with people of different ages, educational levels, and cultures? That is always an open question.

Nevertheless, we can distinguish between the *content* of people's thinking and acting (their attitudes, for example) and the *process* by which they think and act (for example, *how* attitudes affect actions and vice versa). The content varies more from culture to culture than does the process. People from various cultures may hold different opinions yet form them in similar ways. Consider:

- College students in Puerto Rico have reported greater loneliness than do collegians on the U.S. mainland. Yet in the two cultures the ingredients of loneliness have been much the same—shyness, uncertain purpose in life, low self-esteem (Jones & others, 1985).

- Ethnic groups differ in school achievement and delinquency, but the differences are "no more than skin deep," report David Rowe and his colleagues (1994). To the extent that family structure, peer influences, and parental education predict achievement or delinquency for one ethnic group, they do so for other groups.

Although our behaviors may differ, we are influenced by the same social forces. Beneath our surface diversity, we are more alike than different.

Summing Up: Research Methods: How We Do Social Psychology

- Social psychologists organize their ideas and findings into theories. A good theory will distill an array of facts into a much shorter list of predictive principles. We can use those predictions to confirm or modify the theory, to generate new research, and to suggest practical application.

- Most social-psychological research is either correlational or experimental. Correlational studies, sometimes conducted with systematic survey methods, discern the relationship between variables, such as between amount of education and amount of income. Knowing two things are naturally related is valuable information, but it is not a reliable indicator of what is causing what—or whether a third variable is involved.

- When possible, social psychologists prefer to conduct experiments that explore cause and effect. By constructing a miniature reality that is under their control, experimenters can vary one thing and then another and discover how those things, separately or in combination, affect behavior. We randomly assign participants to an experimental condition, which receives the experimental treatment, or to a control condition, which does not. We can then attribute any resulting difference between the two conditions to the independent variable (Figure 1.7).

- In creating experiments, social psychologists sometimes stage situations that engage people's emotions. In doing so, they are obliged to follow professional ethical guidelines, such as obtaining people's informed consent, protecting them from harm, and fully disclosing afterward any temporary deceptions. Laboratory experiments enable social psychologists to test ideas gleaned from life experience and then to apply the principles and findings to the real world.

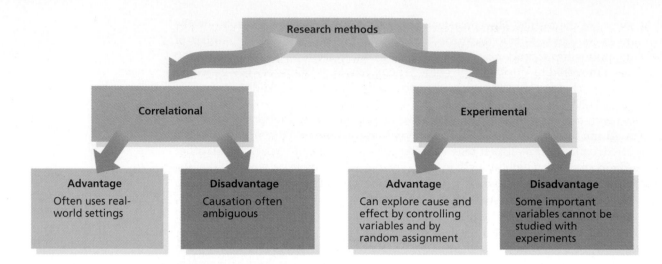

FIGURE :: 1.7

Two Methods of Doing Research: Correlational and Experimental

---

POSTSCRIPT: Why I Wrote This Book

I conclude each chapter with a brief reflection on social psychology's human significance.

I write this text to offer social psychology's powerful, hard-wrought principles. They have, I believe, the power to expand your mind and enrich your life. If you finish this book with sharpened critical thinking skills and with a deeper understanding of how we view and affect one another—and why we sometimes like, love, and help one another and sometimes dislike, hate, and harm one another—then I will be a satisfied author and you, I trust, will be a rewarded reader.

I write knowing that many readers are in the process of defining their life goals, identities, values, and attitudes. The novelist Chaim Potok recalls being urged by his mother to forgo writing: "Be a brain surgeon. You'll keep a lot of people from dying; you'll make a lot more money." Potok's response: "Mama, I don't want to keep people from dying; I want to show them how to live" (quoted by Peterson, 1992, p. 47).

Many of us who teach and write psychology are driven not only by a love for giving psychology away but also by wanting to help students live better lives—wiser, more fulfilling, more compassionate lives. In this we are like teachers and writers in other fields. "Why do we write?" asks theologian Robert McAfee Brown. "I submit that beyond all rewards . . . *we write because we want to change things. We write because we have this* [conviction that we] *can make a difference.* The 'difference' may be a new perception of beauty, a new insight into self-understanding, a new experience of joy, or a decision to join the revolution" (quoted by Marty, 1988). Indeed, I write hoping to do my part to restrain intuition with critical thinking, refine judgmentalism with compassion, and replace illusion with understanding.

Making the Social Connection

As you read this book, you'll find many interesting connections: connections between one researcher's work and other social psychology topics; connections between a concept discussed in one chapter and in other chapters.

Also, you will notice that many concepts introduced in early chapters connect to our everyday lives. Some of these social-psychological concepts are also applicable in clinical psychology, the courtroom, and care for our environment. These applications appear throughout the book and particularly in Part Four: Applying Social Psychology.

So, keep an eye out for each of these connections—to the work of researchers, to other topics in social psychology, and to applications to everyday life.

We make some of these connections for you, right here in Making the Social Connection. As a way to broaden your understanding of these connections, you are invited to view a video clip of either an important concept discussed in the chapter or a famous social psychologist discussing what sparked his or her research interests. These short videos offer examples of how social psychology's topics relate to one another and to everyday experiences.

Go to the Online Learning Center for this text at www.mhhe.com/myers10e to view the video clip "How Dave Myers became a social psychologist."

Social
partone Thinking

This book unfolds around its definition of social psychology: the scientific study of how we *think about* (Part One), *influence* (Part Two), and *relate to* (Part Three) one another. Part Four offers additional, focused examples of how the research and the theories of social psychology are applied to real life.

Part One examines the scientific study of how we think about one another (also called *social cognition*). Each chapter confronts some overriding questions: How reasonable are our social attitudes, explanations, and beliefs? Are our impressions of ourselves and others generally accurate? How does our social thinking form? How is it prone to bias and error, and how might we bring it closer to reality?

Chapter 2 explores the interplay between our sense of self and our social worlds. How do our social surroundings shape our self-identities? How does self-interest color our social judgments and motivate our social behavior?

Chapter 3 looks at the amazing and sometimes rather amusing ways we form beliefs about our social worlds. It also alerts us to some pitfalls of social thinking and suggests how to avoid them and think smarter.

Chapter 4 explores the links between our thinking and our actions, between our attitudes and our behaviors: Do our attitudes determine our behaviors, or vice versa? Or does it work both ways?

The Self in a Social World*

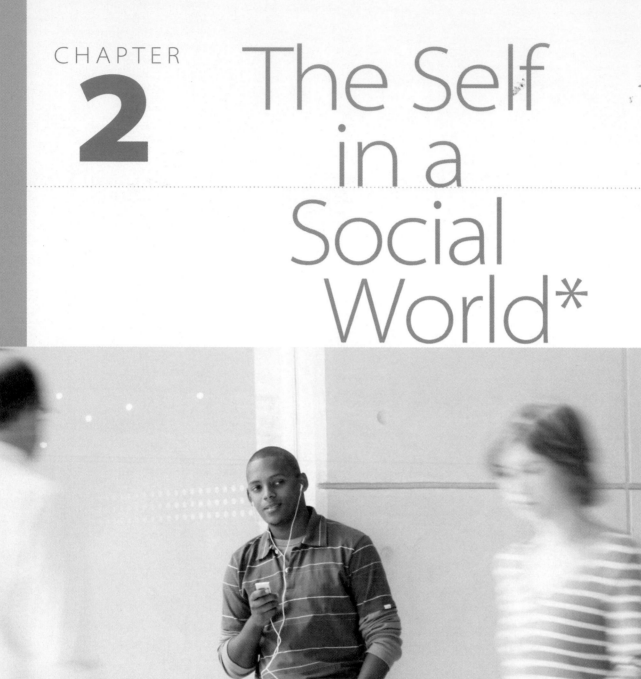

> "There are three things extremely hard, Steel, a Diamond, and to know one's self."

—Benjamin Franklin

At the center of our worlds, more pivotal for us than anything else, is ourselves. As we navigate our daily lives, our sense of self continually engages the world.

Consider this example: One morning, you wake up to find your hair sticking up at weird angles on your head. It's too late to jump in the shower and you can't find a hat, so you smooth down the random spikes of your hair and dash out the door to class. All morning, you're acutely self-conscious about your very bad hair day. To your surprise, your friends in class don't say anything. Are they secretly laughing to themselves about how ridiculous you look, or are they too preoccupied with themselves to notice your spiky hair?

*This 10th edition chapter is co-authored by Jean Twenge, professor of psychology at San Diego State University. Professor Twenge's research on social rejection and on generational changes in personality and the self has been published in many articles and books, including *Generation Me: Why Today's Young Americans Are More Confident, Assertive, Entitled—and More Miserable Than Ever Before* (2006) and *The Narcissism Epidemic: Living in the Age of Entitlement* (with W. Keith Campbell, 2009).

spotlight effect
The belief that others are paying more attention to one's appearance and behavior than they really are.

illusion of transparency
The illusion that our concealed emotions leak out and can be easily read by others.

Spotlights and Illusions

From our self-focused perspective, we overestimate our conspicuousness. This **spotlight effect** means that we tend to see ourselves at center stage, so we intuitively overestimate the extent to which others' attention is aimed at us.

Thomas Gilovich, Victoria Medvec, and Kenneth Savitsky (2000) explored the spotlight effect by having individual Cornell University students don embarrassing Barry Manilow T-shirts before entering a room with other students. The self-conscious T-shirt wearers guessed that nearly half their peers would notice the shirt. Actually, only 23 percent did.

What's true of our dorky clothes and bad hair is also true of our emotions: our anxiety, irritation, disgust, deceit, or attraction (Gilovich & others, 1998). Fewer people notice than we presume. Keenly aware of our own emotions, we often suffer an **illusion of transparency.** If we're happy and we know it, then our face will surely show it. And others, we presume, will notice. Actually, we can be more opaque than we realize. (See "Research Close-Up: On Being Nervous about Looking Nervous.")

research CLOSE-UP   On Being Nervous about Looking Nervous

Have you ever felt self-conscious when approaching someone you felt attracted to, concerned that your nervousness was obvious? Or have you felt yourself trembling while speaking before an audience and presumed that everyone was noticing?

Kenneth Savitsky and Thomas Gilovich (2003) knew from their own and others' studies that people overestimate the extent to which their internal states "leak out." People who are asked to tell lies presume that others will detect their deceit, which feels so obvious. People who are asked to sample horrid-tasting drinks presume that others notice their disgust, which they can barely suppress.

Many people who find themselves having to make a presentation report being not only nervous but also anxious that they will seem so. And if they feel their knees shaking and hands trembling during their presentation, their presumption that others are noticing may compound and perpetuate their anxiety. This is similar to fretting about not falling asleep, which further impedes one's falling asleep, or feeling anxious about stuttering, which worsens the stuttering. (As a former stutterer and speech therapy patient, I know this is true.)

Savitsky and Gilovich wondered whether an "illusion of transparency" might surface among inexperienced public speakers—and whether it might disrupt their performance. To find out, they invited 40 Cornell University students to their laboratory in pairs. As one person stood at a podium with the other seated, Savitsky assigned a topic, such as "The Best and Worst Things About Life Today," and asked the person to speak for three minutes. Then the two switched positions and the other person gave a three-minute impromptu talk on a different topic. Afterward, each rated how nervous they thought they appeared while speaking (from 0, *not at all,* to 10, *very*) and how nervous the other person seemed.

The results? People rated themselves as appearing relatively nervous (6.65, on average). But to their partner they appeared not so nervous (5.25), a difference great enough to be statistically significant (meaning that a difference this great, for this sample of people, is very unlikely to have been due to chance variation). Twenty-seven of the 40 participants (68 percent) believed that they appeared more nervous than did their partner.

To check on the reliability of their finding, Savitsky and Gilovich *replicated* (repeated) the experiment by having people speak before passive audiences that weren't distracted by their own speech-giving. Once again, speakers overestimated the transparency of their nervousness.

Savitsky and Gilovich next wondered whether informing speakers that their nervousness isn't so obvious might help them relax and perform better. They invited 77 more Cornell students to come to the lab and, after five minutes' preparation, give a three-minute videotaped speech on race relations at their university. Those in one group—the *control condition*—were given no further instructions. Those in the *reassured condition* were told that it was natural to feel anxious but that "You shouldn't worry much about what other people think. . . . With this in mind you should just relax and try to do your best. Know that if you become nervous, you probably shouldn't worry about it." To those in the *informed condition* he explained the illusion of transparency. After telling them it was natural to feel anxious, the experimenter added that "Research has found that audiences can't pick up on your anxiety as well as you might expect. . . . Those speaking feel that their nervousness is transparent, but in reality their feelings are not so apparent. . . . With this in mind, you should just relax and try to do your best. Know that if you become nervous, you'll probably be the only one to know."

After the speeches, the speakers rated their speech quality and their perceived nervousness (this time using a 7-point scale), and were also rated by the observers. As Table 2.1 shows, those informed about the illusion-of-transparency phenomenon felt better about their speech and their appearance than did those in the control and reassurance conditions. What's more, the observers confirmed the speakers' self-assessments.

So, the next time you feel nervous about looking nervous, pause to remember the lesson of these experiments: Other people are noticing less than you might suppose.

TABLE :: 2.1 Average Ratings of Speeches by Speakers and Observers on a 1 to 7 Scale

Type of Rating	Control Condition	Reassured Condition	Informed Condition
Speakers' self-ratings			
Speech quality	3.04	2.83	3.50*
Relaxed appearance	3.35	2.69	4.20*
Observers' ratings			
Speech quality	3.50	3.62	4.23*
Composed appearance	3.90	3.94	4.65*

*Each of these results differs by a statistically significant margin from those of the control and reassured condition.

We also overestimate the visibility of our social blunders and public mental slips. When we trigger the library alarm or accidentally insult someone, we may be mortified ("Everyone thinks I'm a jerk"). But research shows that what we agonize over, others may hardly notice and soon forget (Savitsky & others, 2001).

The spotlight effect and the related illusion of transparency are but two of many examples of the interplay between our sense of self and our social worlds. Here are more examples:

- *Social surroundings affect our self-awareness.* When we are the only member of our race, gender, or nationality in a group, we notice how we differ and how others are reacting to our difference. A White American friend once told me how self-consciously White he felt while living in a rural village in Nepal; an hour later, an African American friend told me how self-consciously American she felt while in Africa.
- *Self-interest colors our social judgment.* When problems arise in a close relationship such as marriage, we usually attribute more responsibility to our partners than to ourselves. When things go *well* at home or work or play, we see ourselves as more responsible.
- *Self-concern motivates our social behavior.* In hopes of making a positive impression, we agonize about our appearance. Like savvy politicians, we also monitor others' behavior and expectations and adjust our behavior accordingly.
- *Social relationships help define our self.* In our varied relationships, we have varying selves, note Susan Andersen and Serena Chen (2002). We may be one self with Mom, another with friends, another with teachers. How we think of ourselves is linked to the person we're with at the moment.

As these examples suggest, the traffic between ourselves and others runs both ways. Our ideas and feelings about ourselves affect how we respond to others. And others help shape our sense of self.

No topic in psychology today is more heavily researched than the self. In 2009 the word "self" appeared in 6,935 book and article summaries in *PsycINFO* (the online archive of psychological research)—more than four times the number that appeared in 1970. Our sense of self organizes our thoughts, feelings, and actions. Our sense of self enables us to remember our past, assess our present, and project our future—and thus to behave adaptively.

In later chapters we will see that much of our behavior is not consciously controlled, but rather, automatic and unself-conscious. However, the self does enable long-term planning, goal-setting, and restraint. It imagines alternatives, compares itself with others, and manages its reputation and relationships. Moreover, as Mark Leary (2004a) has noted, the self can sometimes be an impediment to a satisfying life. Its egocentric preoccupations are what religious meditation practices seek to prune, by quieting the self, reducing its attachments to material pleasures, and redirecting it. "Mysticism," adds fellow psychologist Jonathan Haidt (2006), "everywhere and always, is about losing the self, transcending the self, and merging with something larger than the self."

In the remainder of this chapter, we will take a look at self-concept (how we come to know ourselves) and at the self in action (how our sense of self drives our attitudes and actions).

"No topic is more interesting to people than people. For most people, moreover, the most interesting person is the self."

—ROY F. BAUMEISTER,
THE SELF IN SOCIAL
PSYCHOLOGY, 1999

Summing Up: Spotlights and Illusions

- Concerned with the impression we make on others, we tend to believe that others are paying more attention to us than they are (the spotlight effect).
- We also tend to believe that our emotions are more obvious than they are (the illusion of transparency).

Self-Concept: Who Am I?

How, and how accurately, do we know ourselves? What determines our self-concept?

You have many ways to complete the sentence "I am _____." (What five answers might you give?) Taken together, your answers define your **self-concept.**

self-concept
A person's answers to the question, "Who am I?"

At the Center of Our Worlds: Our Sense of Self

The most important aspect of yourself is your self. You know who you are, your gender, whose feelings and memories you experience.

To discover where this sense of self arises, neuroscientists are exploring the brain activity that underlies our constant sense of being oneself. Some studies suggest an important role for the right hemisphere. Put yours to sleep (with an anesthetic to your right carotid artery) and you likely will have trouble recognizing your own face. One patient with right hemisphere damage failed to recognize that he owned and was controlling his left hand (Decety & Sommerville, 2003). The "medial prefrontal cortex," a neuron path located in the cleft between your brain hemispheres just behind your eyes, seemingly helps stitch together your sense of self. It becomes more active when you think about yourself (Zimmer, 2005). The elements of your self-concept, the specific beliefs by which you define yourself, are your **self-schemas** (Markus & Wurf, 1987). *Schemas* are mental templates by which we organize our worlds. Our *self*-schemas—our perceiving ourselves as athletic, overweight, smart, or whatever—powerfully affect how we perceive, remember, and evaluate other people and ourselves. If athletics is central to your self-concept (if being an athlete is one of your self-schemas), then you

self-schema
Beliefs about self that organize and guide the processing of self-relevant information.

will tend to notice others' bodies and skills. You will quickly recall sports-related experiences. And you will welcome information that is consistent with your self-schema (Kihlstrom & Cantor, 1984). The self-schemas that make up our self-concepts help us organize and retrieve our experiences.

POSSIBLE SELVES

Our self-concepts include not only our self-schemas about who we currently are but also who we might become—our **possible selves.** Hazel Markus and her colleagues (Inglehart & others, 1989; Markus & Nurius, 1986) note that our possible selves include our visions of the self we dream of becoming—the rich self, the thin self, the passionately loved and loving self. They also include the self we fear

possible selves
Images of what we dream of or dread becoming in the future.

Oprah Winfrey's imagined possible selves, including the dreaded overweight self, the rich self, and the helpful self, motivated her to work to achieve the life she wanted.

FIGURE :: 2.1
The Self

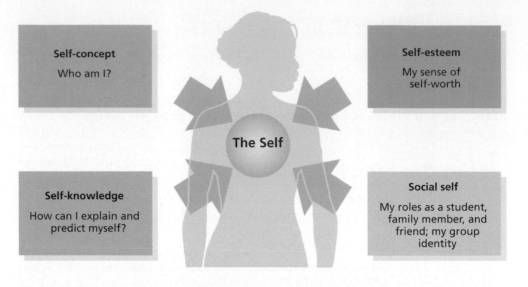

becoming—the underemployed self, the unloved self, the academically failed self. Such possible selves motivate us with a vision of the life we long for.

Development of the Social Self

The self-concept has become a major social-psychological focus because it helps organize our thinking and guide our social behavior (Figure 2.1). But what determines our self-concepts? Studies of twins point to genetic influences on personality and self-concept, but social experience also plays a part. Among these influences are the following:

- the roles we play
- the social identities we form
- the comparisons we make with others
- our successes and failures
- how other people judge us
- the surrounding culture

THE ROLES WE PLAY

As we enact a new role—college student, parent, salesperson—we initially feel self-conscious. Gradually, however, what begins as playacting in the theater of life is absorbed into our sense of self. For example, while playing our roles we may support something we haven't really thought much about. Having made a pitch on behalf of our organization, we then justify our words by believing more strongly in it. Role playing becomes reality (see Chapter 4).

SOCIAL COMPARISONS

social comparison
Evaluating one's abilities and opinions by comparing oneself with others.

How do we decide if we are rich, smart, or short? One way is through **social comparisons** (Festinger, 1954). Others around us help to define the standard by which we define ourselves as rich or poor, smart or dumb, tall or short: We compare ourselves with them and consider how we differ. Social comparison explains why students tend to have a higher academic self-concept if they attend a high school with mostly average students (Marsh & others, 2000), and how that self-concept can be threatened after graduation when a student who excelled in an average high school goes on to an academically selective university. The "big fish" is no longer in a small pond.

Much of life revolves around social comparisons. We feel handsome when others seem homely, smart when others seem dull, caring when others seem callous. When we witness a peer's performance, we cannot resist implicitly comparing ourselves (Gilbert & others, 1995; Stapel & Suls, 2004). We may, therefore, privately take some pleasure in a peer's failure, especially when it happens to someone we envy and when we don't feel vulnerable to such misfortune ourselves (Lockwood, 2002; Smith & others, 1996).

Social comparisons can also diminish our satisfaction. When we experience an increase in affluence, status, or achievement, we "compare upward"—we raise the standards by which we evaluate our attainments. When climbing the ladder of success, we tend to look up, not down; we compare ourselves with others doing even better (Gruder, 1977; Suls & Tesch, 1978; Wheeler & others, 1982). When facing competition, we often protect our shaky self-concept by perceiving the competitor as advantaged. For example, college swimmers believed that their competitors had better coaching and more practice time (Shepperd & Taylor, 1999).

"Make no comparisons!"
—*KING CHARLES I, 1600–1649*

SUCCESS AND FAILURE

Self-concept is fed not only by our roles, our social identity, and our comparisons but also by our daily experiences. To undertake challenging yet realistic tasks and to succeed is to feel more competent. After mastering the physical skills needed to repel a sexual assault, women feel less vulnerable, less anxious, and more in control (Ozer & Bandura, 1990). After experiencing academic success, students believe they are better at school, which often stimulates them to work harder and achieve more (Felson, 1984; Marsh & Young, 1997). To do one's best and achieve is to feel more confident and empowered.

As noted in Chapter 1, the success-feeds-self-esteem principle has led several research psychologists to question efforts to boost achievement by raising self-esteem with positive messages ("You are somebody! You're special!"). Self-esteem comes not only from telling children how wonderful they are but also from hard-earned achievements. Feelings follow reality.

Low self-esteem does sometimes cause problems. Compared with those with low self-esteem, people with a sense of self-worth are happier, less neurotic, less troubled by insomnia, less prone to drug and alcohol addictions, and more persistent after failure (Brockner & Hulton, 1978; Brown, 1991; Tafarodi & Vu, 1997). But as we will see, critics argue that it's at least as true the other way around: Problems and failures can cause low self-esteem.

OTHER PEOPLE'S JUDGMENTS

When people think well of us, it helps us think well of ourselves. Children whom others label as gifted, hardworking, or helpful tend to incorporate such ideas into their self-concepts and behavior (see Chapter 3). If minority students feel threatened by negative stereotypes of their academic ability, or if women feel threatened by low expectations for their math and science performance, they may "disidentify" with those realms. Rather than fight such prejudgments, they may identify their interests elsewhere (Steele, 1997, and see Chapter 9).

The looking-glass self was how sociologist Charles H. Cooley (1902) described our use of how we think others perceive us as a mirror for perceiving ourselves. Fellow sociologist George Herbert Mead (1934) refined this concept, noting that what matters for our self-concepts is not how others actually see us but the way we *imagine* they see us. People generally feel freer to praise than to criticize; they voice their compliments and restrain their gibes. We may, therefore, overestimate others' appraisal, inflating our self-images (Shrauger & Schoeneman, 1979).

Self-inflation, as we will see, is found most strikingly in Western countries. Shinobu Kitayama (1996) reports that Japanese visitors to North America are routinely struck by the many words of praise that friends offer one another. When he and his colleagues asked people how many days ago they last complimented someone, the most common American response was one day. In Japan, where people are socialized less to feel pride in personal achievement and more to feel shame in failing others, the most common response was four days.

Our ancestors' fate depended on what others thought of them. Their survival was enhanced when protected by their group. When perceiving their group's disapproval, there was biological wisdom to their feeling shame and low self-esteem. As their heirs, having a similar deep-seated need to belong, we feel the pain of low self-esteem when we face social exclusion, notes Mark Leary (1998, 2004b). Self-esteem, he argues, is a psychological gauge by which we monitor and react to how others appraise us.

Self and Culture

How did you complete the "I am _____" statement on page 39? Did you give information about your personal traits, such as "I am honest," "I am tall," or "I am outgoing"? Or did you also describe your social identity, such as "I am a Pisces," "I am a MacDonald," or "I am a Muslim"?

individualism
The concept of giving priority to one's own goals over group goals and defining one's identity in terms of personal attributes rather than group identifications.

For some people, especially those in industrialized Western cultures, **individualism** prevails. Identity is self-contained. Adolescence is a time of separating from parents, becoming self-reliant, and defining one's personal, *independent self*. One's identity—as a unique individual with particular abilities, traits, values, and dreams—remains fairly constant.

The psychology of Western cultures assumes that your life will be enriched by believing in your power of personal control. Western literature, from *The Iliad* to *The Adventures of Huckleberry Finn*, celebrates the self-reliant individual. Movie plots feature rugged heroes who buck the establishment. Songs proclaim "I Gotta Be Me," declare that "The Greatest Love of All" is loving oneself (Schoeneman, 1994) and state without irony that "I Believe the World Should Revolve Around Me." Individualism flourishes when people experience affluence, mobility, urbanism, and mass media (Freeman, 1997; Marshall, 1997; Triandis, 1994).

collectivism
Giving priority to the goals of one's groups (often one's extended family or work group) and defining one's identity accordingly.

interdependent self
Construing one's identity in relation to others.

Most cultures native to Asia, Africa, and Central and South America place a greater value on **collectivism.** They nurture what Shinobu Kitayama and Hazel Markus (1995) call the **interdependent self.** In these cultures, people are more self-critical and have less need for positive self-regard (Heine & others, 1999). Malaysians, Indians, Japanese, and traditional Kenyans such as the Maasai, for example, are much more likely than Australians, Americans, and the British to complete the "I am" statement with their group identities (Kanagawa & others, 2001; Ma & Schoeneman, 1997). When speaking, people using the languages of collectivist countries say "I" less often (Kashima & Kashima, 1998, 2003). A person might say "Went to the movie" rather than "I went to the movie."

Pigeonholing cultures as solely individualist or collectivist oversimplifies, because within any culture individualism varies from person to person (Oyserman & others, 2002a, 2002b). There are individualist Chinese and collectivist Americans, and most of us sometimes behave communally, sometimes individualistically (Bandura, 2004). Individualism-collectivism also varies across a country's regions and political views. In the United States, Hawaiians and those living in the deep South exhibit greater collectivism than do those in Mountain West states such as Oregon and Montana (Vandello & Cohen, 1999). Conservatives tend to be economic individualists ("don't tax or regulate me") and moral collectivists ("legislate against immorality"). Liberals, on the other hand, tend to be economic collectivists (supporting national health care) and moral individualists ("keep your laws off my body"). Despite individual and subcultural variations, researchers continue to regard individualism and collectivism as genuine cultural variables (Schimmack & others, 2005).

GROWING INDIVIDUALISM

Cultures can also change over time, and many seem to be growing more individualistic. China's young people have acquired the label "The Me Generation," and new economic opportunities have challenged traditional collectivistic ways in India. Chinese citizens under 25 are more likely than those over 25 to agree with individualistic statements such as "make a name for yourself" and "live a life that suits your tastes" (Arora, 2005). In the United States, younger generations report significantly more positive self-feelings than young people did in the 1960s and 1970s (Gentile & others, 2009; Twenge & Campbell, 2001).

Even your name might show the shift toward individualism: American parents are now less likely to give their children common names and more likely to help them stand out with an unusual name. While nearly 20 percent of boys born in 1990 received one of the 10 most common names, only 9 percent received such a common name by 2007 (Twenge & others, 2009). Today, you don't have to be the child of a celebrity to get a name as unique as Shiloh, Suri, Knox, or Apple.

These changes demonstrate something that goes deeper than a name: The interaction between individuals and society. Did the culture focus on uniqueness first and cause the parents' name choices, or did individual parents decide they wanted their children to be unique, thus creating the culture? The answer, though not yet fully understood, is probably both.

CULTURE AND COGNITION

In his book *The Geography of Thought* (2003), social psychologist Richard Nisbett contends that collectivism also results in different ways of thinking. Consider: Which two—of a panda, a monkey, and a banana—go together? Perhaps a monkey and a panda, because they both fit the category "animal"? Asians more often than Americans see relationships: monkey eats banana. When shown an animated underwater scene (Figure 2.2), Japanese spontaneously recalled 60 percent more background features than did Americans, and they spoke of more relationships (the frog beside the plant). Americans look more at the focal object, such as a single big fish, and less at the surroundings (Chua & others, 2005; Nisbett, 2003), a result duplicated in studies examining activation in different areas of the brain (Goh & others, 2007; Lewis & others, 2008). When shown drawings of groups of children, Japanese students took the facial expressions of all of the children into account when rating the happiness or anger of an individual

FIGURE :: 2.2

Asian and Western Thinking

When shown an underwater scene, Asians often describe the environment and the relationships among the fish. Americans attend more to a single big fish (Nisbett, 2003).

FIGURE :: 2.3

Which Pen Would You Choose?

When Heejun Kim and Hazel Markus (1999) invited people to choose one of these pens, 77 percent of Americans but only 31 percent of Asians chose the uncommon color (regardless of whether it was orange, as here, or green). This result illustrates differing cultural preferences for uniqueness and conformity, note Kim and Markus.

child, whereas Americans focused on only the child they were asked to rate (Masuda & others, 2008). Nisbett and Takahido Masuda (2003) conclude from such studies that East Asians think more holistically—perceiving and thinking about objects and people in relationship to one another and to their environment.

If you grew up in a Western culture, you were probably told to "express yourself"—through writing, the choices you make, and the products you buy, and perhaps through your tattoos or piercings. When asked about the purpose of language, American students were more likely to explain that it allows self-expression, whereas Korean students focused on how language allows communication with others. American students were also more likely to see their choices as expressions of themselves and to evaluate their choices more favorably (Kim & Sherman, 2007). The individualized latté—"decaf, single shot, skinny, extra hot"—that seems just right at a North American espresso shop would seem strange in Seoul, note Heejung Kim and Hazel Markus (1999). In Korea, people place less value on expressing their uniqueness and more on tradition and shared practices (Choi & Choi, 2002, and Figure 2.3). Korean advertisements tend to feature people together; they seldom highlight personal choice or freedom (Markus, 2001; Morling & Lamoreaux, 2008).

With an interdependent self, one has a greater sense of belonging. If they were uprooted and cut off from family, colleagues, and loyal friends, interdependent people would lose the social connections that define who they are. They have not one self but many selves: self-with-parents, self-at-work, self-with-friends (Cross & others, 1992). As Figure 2.4 and Table 2.2 suggest, the interdependent self is embedded in social memberships. Conversation is less direct and more polite (Holtgraves, 1997), and people focus more on gaining social approval (Lalwani & others, 2006). The goal of social life is to harmonize with and support one's communities, not—as it is in more individualistic societies—to enhance one's individual self.

Even within one culture, personal history can influence self-views. People who have moved from place to place are happier when people understand their constant, personal selves; people who have always lived in the same town are more pleased when someone recognizes their collective identity (Oishi & others, 2007). Our self-concepts seem to adjust to our situation: If you interact with the same people all your life, they are more important to your identity than if you are uprooted every few years and must make new friends. Your self becomes your constant companion (echoing the nonsensical but correct statement "Wherever you go, there you are").

FIGURE :: 2.4

Self-Construal as Independent or Interdependent

The independent self acknowledges relationships with others. But the interdependent self is more deeply embedded in others (Markus & Kitayama, 1991).

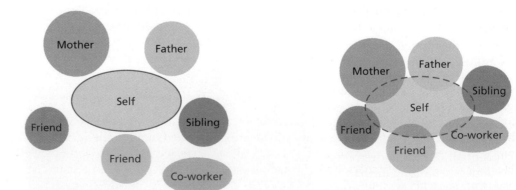

Independent view of self   Interdependent view of self

TABLE :: 2.2 Self-Concept: Independent or Interdependent

	Independent	Interdependent
Identity is	Personal, defined by individual traits and goals	Social, defined by connections with others
What matters	Me—personal achievement and fulfilment; my rights and liberties	We—group goals and solidarity; our social responsibilities and relationships
Disapproves of	Conformity	Egotism
Illustrative motto	"To thine own self be true"	"No one is an island"
Cultures that support	Individualistic Western	Collectivistic Asian and Third World

CULTURE AND SELF-ESTEEM

Self-esteem in collectivist cultures correlates closely with "what others think of me and my group." Self-concept is malleable (context-specific) rather than stable (enduring across situations). In one study, four in five Canadian students but only one in three Chinese and Japanese students agreed that "the beliefs that you hold about who you are (your inner self) remain the same across different activity domains" (Tafarodi & others, 2004).

For those in individualistic cultures, self-esteem is more personal and less relational. Threaten our *personal* identity and we'll feel angrier and gloomier than when someone threatens our collective identity (Gaertner & others, 1999). Unlike Japanese, who persist more on tasks when they are failing (wanting not to fall short of others' expectations), people in individualistic countries persist more when succeeding, because success elevates self-esteem (Heine & others, 2001). Western individualists like to make comparisons with others that boost their self-esteem. Asian collectivists make comparisons (often upward, with those doing better) in ways that facilitate self-improvement (White & Lehman, 2005).

So when, do you suppose, are university students in collectivist Japan and individualist United States most likely to report positive emotions such as happiness and elation? For Japanese students, happiness comes with positive social engagement—with feeling close, friendly, and respectful. For American students, it more often comes with disengaged emotions—with feeling effective, superior, and proud (Kitayama & Markus, 2000). Conflict in collectivist cultures often takes place between groups; individualist cultures breed more conflict (and crime and divorce) between individuals (Triandis, 2000).

When Kitayama (1999), after ten years of teaching and researching in America, visited his Japanese alma mater, Kyoto University, graduate students were "astounded" when he explained the Western idea of the independent self. "I persisted in explaining this Western notion of self-concept—one that my American students understood intuitively—and finally began to persuade them that, indeed, many Americans do have such a disconnected notion of self. Still, one of them, sighing deeply, said at the end, 'Could this *really* be true?'"

When East meets West—as happens, for example, thanks to Western influences in urban Japan and to Japanese exchange students visiting Western countries—does the self-concept become more individualized? Are the Japanese influenced when exposed to Western promotions based on individual achievement, with admonitions to "believe in one's own possibilities," and with movies in which the heroic individual police officer catches the crook *despite* others' interference? They seem to be, report Steven Heine and his co-researchers (1999). Personal self-esteem increased among Japanese exchange students after spending seven months at the University of British Columbia. In Canada individual self-esteem is also higher among long-term Asian immigrants than among more recent immigrants (and than it is among those living in Asia).

"One needs to cultivate the spirits of sacrificing the *little me* to achieve the benefits of the *big me.*"
—*CHINESE SAYING*

THE inside STORY

We began our collaboration by wondering out loud. Shinobu wondered why American life was so weird. Hazel countered with anecdotes about the strangeness of Japan. Cultural psychology is about making the strange familiar and the familiar strange. Our shared cultural encounters astonished us and convinced us that when it comes to psychological functioning, place matters.

After weeks of lecturing in Japan to students with a good command of English, Hazel wondered why the students did not say anything—no questions, no comments. She assured students she was interested in ideas that were different from hers, so why was there no response? Where were the arguments, debates, and signs of critical thinking? Even if she asked a straightforward question, "Where is the best noodle shop?" the answer was invariably an audible intake of air followed by, "It depends." Didn't Japanese students have preferences, ideas, opinions, and attitudes? What is inside a head if it isn't these things? How could you know someone if she didn't tell you what she was thinking?

Shinobu was curious about why students shouldn't just listen to a lecture and why American students felt the need to be constantly interrupting each other and talking over each other and the professor. Why did the comments and questions reveal strong emotions and have a competitive edge? What was the point of this arguing? Why did intelligence seem to be associated with getting the best of another person, even within a class where people knew each other well?

Shinobu expressed his amazement at American hosts who bombard their guests with choices. Do you want wine or beer, or soft drinks or juice, or coffee or tea? Why burden the guest with trivial decisions? Surely the host knew what would be good refreshment on this occasion and could simply provide something appropriate.

Choice as a burden? Hazel wondered if this could be the key to one particularly humiliating experience in Japan. A group of eight was in a French restaurant, and everyone was following the universal restaurant script and was studying the menu. The waiter approached and stood nearby. Hazel announced her choice of appetizer and entrée. Next was a tense conversation among the Japanese host and the Japanese guests. When the meal was served, it was not what she had ordered. Everyone at the table was served the same meal. This was deeply disturbing. If you can't choose your own dinner, how could it be enjoyable? What was the point of the menu if everybody is served the same meal?

Could a sense of sameness be a good or a desirable feeling in Japan? When Hazel walked around the grounds of a temple in Kyoto, there was a fork in the path and a sign that read: "ordinary path." Who would want to take the ordinary path? Where was the special, less traveled path? Choosing the non-ordinary path may be an obvious course for Americans, but in this case it led to the temple dump outside the temple grounds. The ordinary path did not denote the dull and unchallenging way, but meant the appropriate and the good way.

These exchanges inspired our experimental studies and remind us that there are ways of life beyond the ones that each of us knows best. So far, most of psychology has been produced by psychologists in middle-class White American settings studying middle-class White American respondents. In other sociocultural contexts, there can be different ideas and practices about how to be a person and how to live a meaningful life, and these differences have an influence on psychological functioning. It is this realization that fuels our continuing interest in collaboration and in cultural psychology.

Hazel Rose Markus,
Stanford University

Shinobu Kitayama,
University of Michigan

Collectivism in action: Following the 2004 tsunami, people acted together to help one another.

Self-Knowledge

"Know thyself," admonished an ancient Greek oracle. We certainly try. We readily form beliefs about ourselves, and we in Western cultures don't hesitate to explain why we feel and act as we do. But how well do we actually know ourselves?

"There is one thing, and only one in the whole universe which we know more about than we could learn from external observation," noted C. S. Lewis (1952, pp. 18–19). "That one thing is [ourselves]. We have, so to speak, inside information; we are in the know." Indeed. Yet sometimes we *think* we know, but our inside information is wrong. That is the unavoidable conclusion of some fascinating research.

EXPLAINING OUR BEHAVIOR

Why did you choose where to go to college? Why did you lash out at your roommate? Why did you fall in love with that special person? Sometimes we know. Sometimes we don't. Asked why we have felt or acted as we have, we produce plausible answers. Yet, when causes are subtle, our self-explanations are often wrong. We may dismiss factors that matter and inflate others that don't. People may misattribute their rainy-day gloom to life's emptiness (Schwarz & Clore, 1983). And people routinely deny being influenced by the media, which, they readily acknowledge, affects *others*.

Also thought provoking are studies in which people recorded their moods every day for two or three months (Stone & others, 1985; Weiss & Brown, 1976; Wilson & others, 1982). They also recorded factors that might affect their moods: the day of the week, the weather, the amount they slept, and so forth. At the end of each study, the people judged how much each factor had affected their moods. Even with their attention on their daily moods, there was little relationship between their perceptions of how well a factor predicted their mood and how well it really did. For example, people thought they would experience more negative moods on Mondays, but in fact their moods were no more negative on Mondays than other weekdays. This raises a disconcerting question: How much insight do we really have into what makes us happy or unhappy? As Daniel Gilbert notes in *Stumbling on Happiness* (2007), not much: We are remarkably bad predictors of what will make us happy.

"In sooth, I know not why I am so sad."
—*WILLIAM SHAKESPEARE*, THE MERCHANT OF VENICE, *1596*

PREDICTING OUR BEHAVIOR

People also err when predicting their behavior. Dating couples tend to predict the longevity of their relationships through rose-colored glasses. Their friends and family often know better, report Tara MacDonald and Michael Ross (1997). Among University of Waterloo students, their roommates were better predictors of whether their romances would survive than they were. Medical residents weren't very good at predicting whether they would do well on a surgical skills exam, but their peers in the program predicted each others' performance with startling accuracy (Lutsky & others, 1993). So if you're in love and want to know whether it will last, don't listen to your heart—ask your roommate. And if you want to predict your routine daily behaviors—how much time you will spend laughing, on the phone, or watching TV, for example—your close friends' estimates will likely prove at least as accurate as your own (Vazire & Mehl, 2008).

planning fallacy
The tendency to underestimate how long it will take to complete a task.

One of the most common errors in behavior prediction is underestimating how long it will take to complete a task (called the **planning fallacy**.) The Big Dig freeway construction project in Boston was supposed to take 10 years and actually took 20 years. The Sydney Opera House was supposed to be completed in 6 years; it took 16. In one study, college students writing a senior thesis paper were asked to predict when they would complete the project. On average, students finished three weeks later than their "most realistic" estimate—and a week later than their "worst-case scenario" estimate (Buehler & others, 2002)! However, friends and teachers were able to predict just how late these papers would be. Just as you should ask your friends how long your relationship is likely to survive, if you want to know when you will finish your term paper, ask your roommate or your mom. You could also do what Microsoft does: Managers automatically add 30 percent onto a software developer's estimate of completion—and 50 percent if the project involves a new operating system (Dunning, 2006).

So, how can you improve your self-predictions? The best way is to be more realistic about how long tasks took in the past. Apparently people underestimate how long something will take because they misremember previous tasks as taking less time (Roy & others, 2005).

Or you can try predicting someone else's actions. A month before a presidential election, Nicholas Epley and David Dunning (2006) asked students to predict whether they would vote. Almost all (90 percent) predicted they would vote, but only 69 percent did—virtually identical to the 70 percent who predicted that a peer would vote. So if the students had only considered what their peers were likely to do, they would have predicted their own behavior very accurately. If Lao-tzu was right that "he who knows others is learned. He who knows himself is enlightened," then most people, it would seem, are more learned than enlightened.

PREDICTING OUR FEELINGS

Many of life's big decisions involve predicting our future feelings. Would marrying this person lead to lifelong contentment? Would entering this profession make for satisfying work? Would going on this vacation produce a happy experience? Or would the likelier results be divorce, job burnout, and holiday disappointment?

Sometimes we know how we will feel—if we fail that exam, win that big game, or soothe our tensions with a half-hour jog. We know what exhilarates us and what makes us anxious or bored. Other times we may mispredict our responses. Asked how they would feel if asked sexually harassing questions on a job interview, most women studied by Julie Woodzicka and Marianne LaFrance (2001) said they would feel angry. When actually asked such questions, however, women more often experienced fear.

Studies of "affective forecasting" reveal that people have greatest difficulty predicting the *intensity* and the *duration* of their future emotions (Wilson & Gilbert,

2003). People have mispredicted how they would feel some time after a romantic breakup, receiving a gift, losing an election, winning a game, and being insulted (Gilbert & Ebert, 2002; Loewenstein & Schkade, 1999). Some examples:

- When male youths are sexually aroused by erotic photographs, then exposed to a passionate date scenario in which their date asks them to "stop," they admit that they might not stop. If not shown sexually arousing pictures first, they more often deny the possibility of being sexually aggressive. When not aroused, one easily mispredicts how one will feel and act when aroused—a phenomenon that leads to unexpected professions of love during lust, to unintended pregnancies, and to repeat offenses among sex abusers who have sincerely vowed "never again."

- Hungry shoppers do more impulse buying ("Those doughnuts would be delicious!") than do shoppers who have just enjoyed a quarter-pound blue-berry muffin (Gilbert & Wilson, 2000). When we are hungry, we mispredict how gross those deep-fried doughnuts will seem when we are sated. When stuffed, we may underestimate how yummy a doughnut might be with a late-night glass of milk—a purchase whose appeal quickly fades when we have eaten one or two.

- Undergraduates who experienced a romantic breakup were less upset afterward than they predicted they would be (Eastwick & others, 2007). Their distress lasted just about as long as they thought it would, but the heartbroken students were not as hard-hit as they imagined they would be. European track athletes similarly overestimated how badly they would feel if they failed to reach their goal in an upcoming meet (van Dijk & others, 2008).

- When natural disasters like hurricanes occur, people predict that their sad-ness will be greater if more people are killed. But after Hurricane Katrina struck in 2005, students' sadness was similar when it was believed that 50 people had been killed or 1,000 had been killed (Dunn & Ashton-James, 2008). What *did* influence how sad people felt? Seeing pictures of victims. No wonder poignant images on TV have so much influence on us after disasters.

- People overestimate how much their well-being would be affected by warmer winters, weight loss, more television channels, or more free time. Even extreme events, such as winning a state lottery or suffering a paralyz-ing accident, affect long-term happiness less than most people suppose.

Our intuitive theory seems to be: We want. We get. We are happy. If that were true, this chapter would have fewer words. In reality, note Daniel Gilbert and Timothy Wilson (2000), we often "miswant." People who imagine an idyl-lic desert island holiday with sun, surf, and sand may be disappointed when they discover "how much they require daily structure, intellectual stimulation, or regular infusions of Pop Tarts." We think that if our candidate or team wins we will be delighted for a long while. But study after study reveals our vulnerability to **impact bias**—overestimating the enduring impact of emotion-causing events. Faster than we expect, the emotional traces of such good tidings evaporate.

Moreover, we are especially prone to impact bias after *negative* events. When Gilbert and his colleagues (1998) asked assistant professors to predict their happiness a few years after achieving tenure or not, most believed

"When a feeling was there, they felt as if it would never go; when it was gone, they felt as if it had never been; when it returned, they felt as if it had never gone."
—*GEORGE MACDONALD,*
WHAT'S MINE'S MINE, *1886*

impact bias
Overestimating the enduring impact of emotion-causing events.

Predicting behavior, even one's own, is no easy matter, which may be why some people go to tarot card readers in hope of help.

a favorable outcome was important for their future happiness: "Losing my job would crush my life's ambitions. It would be terrible." Yet when surveyed several years after the event, those denied tenure were about as happy as those who received it. Impact bias is important, say Wilson and Gilbert (2005), because people's "affective forecasts"—their predictions of their future emotions—influence their decisions. If people overestimate the intensity and the duration of the pleasure they will gain from purchasing a new car or undergoing cosmetic surgery, then they may make ill-advised investments in that new Mercedes or extreme makeover.

Let's make this personal. Gilbert and Wilson invite us to imagine how we might feel a year after losing our nondominant hands. Compared with today, how happy would you be?

Thinking about that, you perhaps focused on what the calamity would mean: no clapping, no shoe tying, no competitive basketball, no speedy keyboarding. Although you likely would forever regret the loss, your general happiness some time after the event would be influenced by "two things: (a) the event, and (b) everything else" (Gilbert & Wilson, 2000). In focusing on the negative event, we discount the importance of everything else that contributes to happiness and so overpredict our enduring misery. "Nothing that you focus on will make as much difference as you think," write researchers David Schkade and Daniel Kahneman (1998).

Moreover, say Wilson and Gilbert (2003), people neglect the speed and the power of their *psychological immune system,* which includes their strategies for rationalizing, discounting, forgiving, and limiting emotional trauma. Being largely ignorant of our psychological immune system (a phenomenon Gilbert and Wilson call **immune neglect**), we adapt to disabilities, romantic breakups, exam failures, tenure denials, and personal and team defeats more readily than we would expect. Ironically, as Gilbert and his colleagues report (2004), major negative events (which activate our psychological defenses) can be less enduringly distressing than minor irritations (which don't activate our defenses). We are, under most circumstances, amazingly resilient.

immune neglect
The human tendency to underestimate the speed and the strength of the "psychological immune system," which enables emotional recovery and resilience after bad things happen.

THE WISDOM AND ILLUSIONS OF SELF-ANALYSIS

To a striking extent, then, our intuitions are often dead wrong about what has influenced us and what we will feel and do. But let's not overstate the case. When the causes of our behavior are conspicuous and the correct explanation fits our intuition, our self-perceptions will be accurate (Gavanski & Hoffman, 1987). When the causes of behavior are obvious to an observer, they are usually obvious to us as well.

As Chapter 3 will explore further, we are unaware of much that goes on in our minds. Perception and memory studies show that we are more aware of the *results* of our thinking than of its process. For example, we experience the results of our mind's unconscious workings when we set a mental clock to record the passage of time or to awaken us at an appointed hour, or when we somehow achieve a spontaneous creative insight after a problem has unconsciously "incubated." Similarly, creative scientists and artists often cannot report the thought processes that produced their insights, although they have superb knowledge of the results.

Timothy Wilson (1985, 2002) offers a bold idea: The mental processes that *control* our social behavior are distinct from the mental processes through which we *explain* our behavior. Our rational explanations may therefore omit the unconscious attitudes that actually guide our behavior. In nine experiments, Wilson and his colleagues (1989, 2008) found that the attitudes people consciously expressed toward things or people usually predicted their subsequent behavior reasonably well. Their attitude reports became useless, however, if the participants were first asked to *analyze* their feelings. For example, dating couples' level of happiness with their relationship accurately predicted whether they would still be dating several months later. But participants who first listed all the *reasons* they could think of why their relationship was good or bad before rating their happiness were misled—their happiness ratings were useless in predicting the future of the relationship! Apparently, the process of dissecting the relationship drew attention to easily verbalized factors that were actually not as important as harder-to-verbalize happiness. We are often "strangers to ourselves," Wilson concluded (2002).

Such findings illustrate that we have a **dual attitude** system, say Wilson and his colleagues (2000). Our automatic *implicit* attitudes regarding someone or something often differ from our consciously controlled, *explicit* attitudes (Gawronski & Bodenhausen, 2006; Nosek, 2007). From childhood, for example, we may retain a habitual, automatic fear or dislike of people for whom we now consciously verbalize respect and appreciation. Although explicit attitudes may change with relative ease, notes Wilson, "implicit attitudes, like old habits, change more slowly." With repeated practice, however, new habitual attitudes can replace old ones.

Murray Millar and Abraham Tesser (1992) have argued that Wilson overstates our ignorance of self. Their research suggests that, yes, drawing people's attention to *reasons* diminishes the usefulness of attitude reports in predicting behaviors that are driven by *feelings*. They argue that if, instead of having people analyze their romantic relationships, Wilson had first asked them to get more in touch with their feelings ("How do you feel when you are with and apart from your partner?"), the attitude reports might have been more insightful. Other decisions people make—say, choosing which school to attend based on considerations of cost, career advancement, and so forth—seem more cognitively driven. For these, an analysis of reasons rather than feelings may be most useful. Although the heart has its reasons, sometimes the mind's own reasons are decisive.

This research on the limits of our self-knowledge has two practical implications. The first is for psychological inquiry. *Self-reports are often untrustworthy.* Errors in self-understanding limit the scientific usefulness of subjective personal reports.

The second implication is for our everyday lives. The sincerity with which people report and interpret their experiences is no guarantee of the validity of those reports. Personal testimonies are powerfully persuasive (as we will see in Chapter 15, Social Psychology in Court). But they may also be wrong. Keeping this potential for error in mind can help us feel less intimidated by others and be less gullible.

dual attitudes
Differing implicit (automatic) and explicit (consciously controlled) attitudes toward the same object. Verbalized explicit attitudes may change with education and persuasion; implicit attitudes change slowly, with practice that forms new habits.

Summing Up: Self-Concept: Who Am I?

- Our sense of self helps organize our thoughts and actions. When we process information with reference to ourselves, we remember it well (the self-reference effect). Self-concept consists of two elements: the self-schemas that guide our processing of self-relevant information, and the possible selves that we dream of or dread.

- Cultures shape the self, too. Many people in individualistic Western cultures assume an independent self. Others, often in collectivistic cultures, assume a more interdependent self. As Chapter 5 will further explain, these contrasting ideas contribute to cultural differences in social behavior.

- Our self-knowledge is curiously flawed. We often do not know why we behave the way we do. When influences upon our behavior are not conspicuous enough for any observer to see, we, too, can miss them. The unconscious, implicit processes that control our behavior may differ from our conscious, explicit explanations of it. We also tend to mispredict our emotions. We underestimate the power of our psychological immune systems and thus tend to overestimate the durability of our emotional reactions to significant events.

Self-Esteem

People desire self-esteem, which they are motivated to enhance. But inflated self-esteem also has a dark side.

self-esteem
A person's overall self-evaluation or sense of self-worth.

Is **self-esteem**—our overall self-evaluation—the sum of all our self-schemas and possible selves? If we see ourselves as attractive, athletic, smart, and destined to be rich and loved, will we have high self-esteem? Yes, say Jennifer Crocker and Connie Wolfe (2001)—when we feel good about the domains (looks, smarts, or whatever) important to our self-esteem. "One person may have self-esteem that is highly contingent on doing well in school and being physically attractive, whereas another may have self-esteem that is contingent on being loved by God and adhering to moral standards." Thus, the first person will feel high self-esteem when made to feel smart and good looking, the second person when made to feel moral.

But Jonathon Brown and Keith Dutton (1994) argue that this "bottom-up" view of self-esteem is not the whole story. The causal arrow, they believe, also goes the other way. People who value themselves in a general way—those with high self-esteem—are more likely to value their looks, abilities, and so forth. They are like new parents who, loving their infant, delight in the baby's fingers, toes, and hair: The parents do not first evaluate their infant's fingers or toes and then decide how much to value the whole baby.

Specific self-perceptions do have some influence, however. If you think you're good at math, you will be more likely to do well at math. Although general self-esteem does not predict academic performance very well, academic self-concept—whether you think you are good in school—does predict performance (Marsh & O'Mara, 2008). Of course, each causes the other: Doing well at math makes you think you are good at math, which then motivates you to do even better. So if you want to encourage someone (or yourself!), it's better if your praise is specific ("you're good at math") instead of general ("you're great") and if your kind words reflect true ability and performance ("you really improved on your last test") rather than unrealistic optimism ("You can do anything"). Feedback is best when it is true and specific (Swann & others, 2007).

Imagine you're getting your grade back for the first test in a psychology class. When you see your grade, you groan—you're hovering somewhere between a D and an F. But then you get an encouraging e-mail with some review questions for the class and this message: "Students who have high self-esteem not only get better grades, but they remain self-confident and assured. . . . Bottom line: Hold your head—and your self-esteem—high." Another group of students instead get a message about taking personal control of their performance, or receive review questions only. So how would each group do on the final exam? To the surprise of the researchers in one study, the students whose self-esteem was boosted did by far the worst on the final—in fact, they flunked it (Forsyth & others, 2007). Poor students told to feel good about themselves, the researchers muse, may have thought, "I'm already great—why study?"

Self-Esteem Motivation

Abraham Tesser (1988) reported that a "self-esteem maintenance" motive predicts a variety of interesting findings, even friction among brothers and sisters. Do you have a sibling of the same gender who is close to you in age? If so, people probably compared the two of you as you grew up. Tesser presumes that people's perceiving one of you as more capable than the other will motivate the less able one to act in ways that maintain self-esteem. (Tesser thinks the threat to self-esteem is greatest for an older child with a highly capable younger sibling.) Men with a brother with markedly different ability levels typically recall not getting along well with him; men with a similarly able brother are more likely to recall very little friction.

Among sibling relationships, the threat to self-esteem is greatest for an older child with a highly capable younger brother or sister.

Self-esteem threats occur among friends, whose success can be more threatening than that of strangers (Zuckerman & Jost, 2001). And they can occur among married partners, too. Although shared interests are healthy, *identical* career goals may produce tension or jealousy (Clark & Bennett, 1992). When a partner outperforms us in a domain important to both our identities, we may reduce the threat by affirming our relationship, saying, "My capable partner, with whom I'm very close, is part of who I am" (Lockwood & others, 2004).

What underlies the motive to maintain or enhance self-esteem? Mark Leary (1998, 2004b, 2007) believes that our self-esteem feelings are like a fuel gauge. Relationships enable surviving and thriving. Thus, the self-esteem gauge alerts us to threatened social rejection, motivating us to act with greater sensitivity to others' expectations. Studies confirm that social rejection lowers our self-esteem and makes us more eager for approval. Spurned or jilted, we feel unattractive or inadequate. Like a blinking dashboard light, this pain can motivate action—self-improvement and a search for acceptance and inclusion elsewhere.

Jeff Greenberg (2008) offers another perspective. If self-esteem were only about acceptance, he counters, why do "people strive to be great rather than to just be accepted"? The reality of our own death, he argues, motivates us to gain recognition from our work and values. There's a worm in the apple, however: Not everyone can achieve such recognition, which is exactly why it is valuable, and why self-esteem can never be wholly unconditional ("You're special just for being you" is an example of self-esteem being granted unconditionally). To feel our lives are not in vain, Greenberg maintains, we must continually pursue self-esteem by meeting the standards of our societies.

The "Dark Side" of Self-Esteem

People with low self-esteem often have problems in life—they make less money, abuse drugs, and are more likely to be depressed (Salmela-Aro & Nurmi, 2007; Trzesniewski & others, 2006). As you learned in Chapter 1, though, a correlation between two variables is sometimes caused by a third factor. Maybe people low in self-esteem also faced poverty as children, experienced sexual abuse, or had parents who used drugs, all possible causes of later struggling. Sure enough, a study that controlled for these factors found that the link between self-esteem and negative outcomes disappeared (Boden & others, 2008). In other words, low self-esteem was not the cause of these young adults' problems—the seeming cause, instead, was that many could not escape their tough childhoods.

High self-esteem does have some benefits—it fosters initiative, resilience, and pleasant feelings (Baumeister & others, 2003). Yet teen males who engage in sexual activity at an "inappropriately young age" tend to have *higher* than average self-esteem. So do teen gang leaders, extreme ethnocentrists, terrorists, and men in prison for committing violent crimes (Bushman & Baumeister, 2002; Dawes, 1994, 1998). "Hitler had very high self-esteem," note Baumeister and his co-authors (2003).

NARCISSISM: SELF-ESTEEM'S CONCEITED SISTER

High self-esteem becomes especially problematic if it crosses over into narcissism, or having an inflated sense of self. Most people with high self-esteem value both individual achievement and relationships with others. Narcissists usually have high self-esteem, but they are missing the piece about caring for others (Campbell & others, 2002). Although narcissists are often outgoing and charming early on, their self-centeredness often leads to relationship problems in the long run (Campbell, 2005). The link between narcissism and problematic social relations led Delroy Paulhus and Kevin Williams (2002) to include narcissism in "The Dark Triad" of negative traits. The other two are Machiavellianism (manipulativeness) and antisocial psychopathy.

In a series of experiments conducted by Brad Bushman and Roy Baumeister (1998), undergraduate volunteers wrote essays and received rigged feedback that said, "This is one of the worst essays I've read!" Those who scored high on narcissism were much more likely to retaliate, blasting painful noise into the headphones of the student they believed had criticized them. Narcissists weren't aggressive toward someone who praised them ("great essay!"). It was the insult that set them off. But what about self-esteem? Maybe only the "insecure" narcissists—those low in self-esteem—would lash out. But that's not how it turned out—instead, the students high in both self-esteem and narcissism were the most aggressive. The same was true in a classroom setting—those who were high in both self-esteem and narcissism were the most likely to retaliate against a classmate's criticism by giving him or her a bad grade (Bushman & others, 2009; Figure 2.5). Narcissists can be charming and entertaining. But as one wit has said, "God help you if you cross them."

> "After all these years, I'm sorry to say, my recommendation is this: Forget about self-esteem and concentrate more on self-control and self-discipline. Recent work suggests this would be good for the individual and good for society."
>
> —ROY BAUMEISTER, 2005

FIGURE :: 2.5

Narcissism, Self-Esteem, and Aggression

Narcissism and self-esteem interact to influence aggression. In an experiment by Brad Bushman and colleagues (2009), the recipe for retaliation against a critical classmate required both narcissism and high self-esteem.

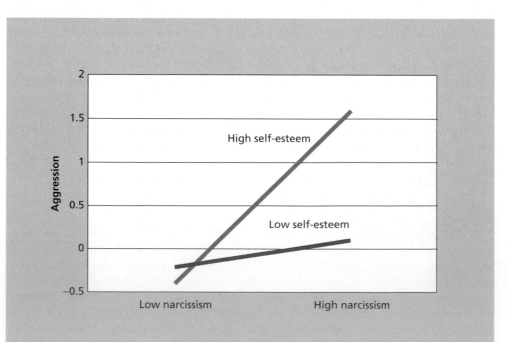

Some studies have found small correlations between low self-esteem and antisocial behavior, even when IQ and family income were taken into account (Donnellan & others, 2005; Trzesniewski & others, 2006). However, another study found that the link between low self-esteem and antisocial behavior disappeared when things like sexual abuse and earlier behavioral problems were considered (Boden & others, 2007). So kids aren't acting aggressively because they have low self-esteem, but because they were hurt in the past. "The enthusiastic claims of the self-esteem movement mostly range from fantasy to hogwash," says Baumeister (1996), who suspects he has "probably published more studies on self-esteem than anybody else. . . . The effects of self-esteem are small, limited, and not all good." Folks with high self-esteem, he reports, are more likely to be obnoxious, to interrupt, and to talk at people rather than with them (in contrast to the more shy, modest, self-effacing folks with low self-esteem). "My conclusion is that self-control is worth 10 times as much as self-esteem."

What about the idea that an overinflated ego is just a cover for deep-seated insecurity? Do narcissistic people actually hate themselves "deep down inside?" Recent studies show that the answer is *no*. People who score high on measures of narcissistic personality traits also score high on measures of self-esteem. In case narcissists were claiming high self-esteem just for show, researchers also asked undergraduates to play a computer game where they had to press a key as quickly as possible to match the word "me" with words like good, wonderful, great, and right, and words like bad, awful, terrible, and wrong. High scorers on the narcissism scale were faster than others to associate themselves with good words, and slower than others to pair themselves with bad words (Campbell & others, 2007). And narcissists were even faster to identify with words like outspoken, dominant, and assertive. Although it might be comforting to think that an arrogant classmate is just covering for his insecurity, chances are that deep down inside he thinks he's *awesome*.

NARCISSISM ON THE RISE

There was one area where narcissists were only average—though still not insecure. Narcissism had no effect on pairing words like kind, friendly, and affectionate with self words. This is consistent with the idea that narcissists love being winners, but aren't as concerned with being emotionally close to others. There also seem to be more narcissists. After tracking self-importance across the last several decades, psychologist Jean Twenge (2006; Twenge & others, 2008) reports that today's young generation—*Generation Me*, she calls it—express more narcissism (by agreeing with statements such as "If I ruled the world, it would be a better place" or "I think I am a special person"). Agreement with narcissistic items correlates with materialism, desire to be famous, inflated expectations, fewer committed relationships and more "hooking up," more gambling, and more cheating, all of which have also risen as narcissism has increased.

Another data set on narcissism over time showed the influence of both time and ethnicity. Narcissism did not change among samples of University of California students over time (Trzesniewski & others, 2008), possibly because more Asian American students—from a culture that discourages self-importance—enrolled over the years. When analyzed separately by ethnicity and campus, these data showed increases in narcissism across all ethnic groups (Twenge & Foster, 2008). Although Asian American students scored lower on narcissism, on average, than White students, both groups increased in narcissism over time as American culture presumably became more accepting of self-importance.

LOW VERSUS SECURE SELF-ESTEEM

The findings linking a highly positive self-concept with negative behavior exist in tension with the findings that people expressing low self-esteem are more vulnerable to assorted clinical problems, including anxiety, loneliness, and eating disorders.

When feeling bad or threatened, low-self-esteem people often take a negative view of everything. They notice and remember others' worst behaviors and think their partners don't love them (Murray & others, 1998, 2002; Ybarra, 1999). Although there is no evidence that low-self-esteem people choose less desirable partners, they are quick to believe that their partners are criticizing or rejecting them. Perhaps as a result, low-self-esteem people are less satisfied with their relationships (Fincham & Bradbury, 1993). They may also be more likely to leave those relationships. Low-self-esteem undergraduates decided not to stay with roommates who saw them in a positive light (Swann & Pelham, 2002).

Secure self-esteem—one rooted more in feeling good about who one is than in grades, looks, money, or others' approval—is conducive to long-term well-being (Kernis, 2003; Schimel & others, 2001). Jennifer Crocker and her colleagues (2002, 2003, 2004, 2005) confirmed this in studies with University of Michigan students. Those whose self-worth was most fragile—most contingent on external sources— experienced more stress, anger, relationship problems, drug and alcohol use, and eating disorders than did those whose sense of self-worth was rooted more in internal sources, such as personal virtues.

Ironically, note Crocker and Lora Park (2004), those who pursue self-esteem, perhaps by seeking to become beautiful, rich, or popular, may lose sight of what really makes for quality of life. Moreover, if feeling good about ourselves is our goal, then we may become less open to criticism, more likely to blame than empathize with others, and more pressured to succeed at activities rather than enjoy them. Over time, such pursuit of self-esteem can fail to satisfy our deep needs for competence, relationship, and autonomy, note Crocker and Park. To focus less on one's self-image, and more on developing one's talents and relationships, eventually leads to greater well-being.

Summing Up: Self-Esteem

- Self-esteem is the overall sense of self-worth we use to appraise our traits and abilities. Our self-concepts are determined by multiple influences, including the roles we play, the comparisons we make, our social identities, how we perceive others appraising us, and our experiences of success and failure.

- Self-esteem motivation influences our cognitive processes: Facing failure, high-self-esteem people sustain their self-worth by perceiving other people as failing, too, and by exaggerating their superiority over others.

- Although high self-esteem is generally more beneficial than low, researchers have found that people high in both self-esteem and narcissism are the most aggressive. Someone with a big ego who is threatened or deflated by social rejection is potentially aggressive.

Perceived Self-Control

Several lines of research point to the significance of our perceived self-control. What concepts emerge from this research?

So far we have considered what a self-concept is, how it develops, and how well (or poorly) we know ourselves. Now let's see why our self-concepts matter, by viewing the self in action.

The self's capacity for action has limits, note Roy Baumeister and his colleagues (1998, 2000; Muraven & others, 1998). Consider:

- People who exert self-control—by forcing themselves to eat radishes rather than chocolates, or by suppressing forbidden thoughts—subsequently quit faster when given unsolvable puzzles.

- People who have tried to control their emotional responses to an upsetting movie exhibit decreased physical stamina.

- People who have spent their willpower on tasks such as controlling their emotions during an upsetting film later become more aggressive and more likely to fight with their partners (de Wall & others, 2007; Finkel & Campbell, 2001). They also become less restrained in their sexual thoughts and behaviors. In one study, students who depleted their willpower by focusing their attention on a difficult task were later, when asked to express a comfortable level of intimacy with their partner, more likely to make out and even remove some clothing (Gailliot & Baumeister, 2007).

Effortful self-control depletes our limited willpower reserves. Our brain's "central executive" consumes available blood sugar when engaged in self-control (Gailliot, 2008). Self-control therefore operates similarly to muscular strength, conclude Baumeister and Julia Exline (2000): Both are weaker after exertion, replenished with rest, and strengthened by exercise.

Although the self's energy can be temporarily depleted, our self-concepts do influence our behavior (Graziano & others, 1997). Given challenging tasks, people who imagine themselves as hardworking and successful outperform those who imagine themselves as failures (Ruvolo & Markus, 1992). Envision your positive possibilities and you become more likely to plan and enact a successful strategy.

Self-Efficacy

Stanford psychologist Albert Bandura (1997, 2000, 2008) captured the power of positive thinking in his research and theorizing about **self-efficacy** (how competent we feel on a task). Believing in our own competence and effectiveness pays dividends (Bandura & others, 1999; Maddux and Gosselin, 2003). Children and adults with strong feelings of self-efficacy are more persistent, less anxious, and less depressed. They also live healthier lives and are more academically successful.

In everyday life, self-efficacy leads us to set challenging goals and to persist. More than a hundred studies show that self-efficacy predicts worker productivity (Stajkovic & Luthans, 1998). When problems arise, a strong sense of self-efficacy leads workers to stay calm and seek solutions rather than ruminate on their inadequacy. Competence plus persistence equals accomplishment. And with accomplishment, self-confidence grows. Self-efficacy, like self-esteem, grows with hard-won achievements.

Even subtle manipulations of self-efficacy can affect behavior. Becca Levy (1996) discovered this when she subliminally exposed 90 older adults to words that evoked (primed) either a negative or a positive stereotype of aging. Some subjects viewed .066-second presentations of negative words such as "decline," "forgets," and "senile," or of positive words such as "sage," "wise," and "learned." At the conscious level, the participants perceived only a flash of light. Yet being given the positive words led to heightened "memory self-efficacy" (confidence in one's memory) and better memory performance. Viewing the negative words had the opposite effect. We can observe a similar phenomenon outside the laboratory: Older adults in China, where positive images of aging prevail and memory self-efficacy may be greater, seem to suffer less memory decline than is commonly observed in Western countries (Schacter & others, 1991).

If you believe you can do something, will that belief necessarily make a difference? That depends on a second factor: Do you have *control* over your outcomes? You may, for example, feel like an effective driver (high self-efficacy), yet feel endangered by drunken drivers (low control). You may feel like a competent student or worker but, fearing discrimination based on your age, gender, or appearance, you may think your prospects for success are dim.

Many people confuse self-efficacy with self-esteem. If you believe you can do something, that's self-efficacy. If you like yourself overall, that's self-esteem. When you were a child, your parents may have encouraged you by saying things like, "You're special!" (intended to build self-esteem) instead of "I know you can do it!"

self-efficacy
A sense that one is competent and effective, distinguished from self-esteem, which is one's sense of self-worth. A bombardier might feel high self-efficacy and low self-esteem.

(intended to build self-efficacy). One study showed that self-efficacy feedback ("You tried really hard") led to better performance than self-esteem feedback ("You're really smart"). Children told they were smart were afraid to try again—maybe they wouldn't look so smart next time. Those praised for working hard, however, knew they could exert more effort again (Mueller & Dweck, 1998). If you want to encourage someone, focus on their self-efficacy, not their self-esteem.

Locus of Control

"I have no social life," complained a 40-something single man to student therapist Jerry Phares. At Phares's urging, the patient went to a dance, where several women danced with him. "I was just lucky," he later reported. "It would never happen again." When Phares reported this to his mentor, Julian Rotter, it crystallized an idea he had been forming. In Rotter's experiments and in his clinical practice, some people seemed to persistently "feel that what happens to them is governed by external forces of one kind or another, while others feel that what happens to them is governed largely by their own efforts and skills" (quoted by Hunt, 1993, p. 334).

What do you think about your own life? Are you more often in charge of your destiny, or a victim of circumstance? Rotter called this dimension **locus of control.** With Phares, he developed 29 paired statements to measure a person's locus of control. Imagine taking this test. Which statements do you more strongly believe?

a. In the long run, people get the respect they deserve in this world.

or

b. Unfortunately, people's worth passes unrecognized no matter how hard they try.

a. What happens to me is my own doing.

or

b. Sometimes I feel that I don't have enough control over the direction my life is taking.

a. The average person can have an influence in government decisions.

or

b. This world is run by the few people in power, and there is not much the little guy can do about it.

If your answers to these questions (from Rotter, 1973) were mostly "a," you probably believe you control your own destiny (*internal* locus of control). If your answers were mostly "b," you probably feel chance or outside forces determine your fate (*external* locus of control, as in Figure 2.6). Those who see themselves as *internally* controlled are more likely to do well in school, successfully stop smoking, wear seat belts, deal with marital problems directly, earn a substantial income, and delay instant gratification to achieve long-term goals (Findley & Cooper, 1983; Lefcourt, 1982; Miller & others, 1986).

How much control we feel is related to how we explain setbacks. Perhaps you have known students who view themselves as victims—who blame poor grades on things beyond their control, such as their feelings of stupidity or their "poor" teachers, texts, or tests. If such students are coached to adopt a more hopeful attitude—to believe that effort, good study habits, and self-discipline can make a difference—their academic performance tends to go up (Noel & others, 1987; Peterson & Barrett, 1987). In general, students who feel in control—who, for example, agree that "I am good at resisting temptation"—get better grades, enjoy better relationships, and exhibit better mental health (Tangney & others, 2004). They are also less likely to cheat: Students who were told that free will is an illusion—that what happened to them is outside their control—peeked at answers and paid themselves more money for mediocre work (Vohs & Schooler, 2008).

When faced with a setback, successful people are likely to see it as a fluke or to think, "I need a new approach." New life insurance sales representatives who view failures as controllable ("It's difficult, but with persistence I'll get better") sell more policies. They are only half as likely as their more pessimistic colleagues to quit

---

locus of control

The extent to which people perceive outcomes as internally controllable by their own efforts or as externally controlled by chance or outside forces.

"If my mind can conceive it and my heart can believe it, I know I can achieve it. Down with dope! Up with hope! I am somebody!"

—*JESSE JACKSON, THE MARCH ON WASHINGTON, 1983*

during their first year (Seligman & Schulman, 1986). Among college swim team members, those with an optimistic "explanatory style" are more likely than pessimists to perform beyond expectations (Seligman & others, 1990). As the Roman poet Virgil said in the *Aeneid*, "They can because they think they can."

Some people, however, have taken these ideas a little too far. The popular book *The Secret*, for example, claims that thinking positive thoughts causes positive things to happen to you ("The only reason any person does not have enough money is because they are blocking money from coming to them with their thoughts"). So let's not help those poor Zimbabweans—all they need to do is think happy thoughts. And if you are sick, your thoughts just aren't positive enough—despite the thousands of cancer patients who desperately want to get well. Obviously, there are limits to the power of positive thinking. Being optimistic and feeling in control can reap great benefits, but poverty and sickness can happen to anyone.

Learned Helplessness versus Self-Determination

The benefits of feelings of control also appear in animal research. Dogs confined in a cage and taught that they cannot escape shocks will learn a sense of helplessness. Later, these dogs cower passively in other situations when they *could* escape punishment. Dogs that learn personal control (by successfully escaping their first shocks) adapt easily to a new situation. Researcher Martin Seligman (1975, 1991) noted similarities to this **learned helplessness** in human situations. Depressed or oppressed people, for example, become passive because they believe their efforts have no effect. Helpless dogs and depressed people both suffer paralysis of the will, passive resignation, even motionless apathy (Figure 2.7).

On the other hand, people benefit by training their self-control "muscles." That's the conclusion of studies by Megan Oaten and Ken Cheng (2006) at Sydney's Macquarie University. For example, students who were engaged in practicing self-control by daily exercise, regular study, and time management became more capable of self-control in other settings, both in the laboratory and when taking exams. If you develop your self-discipline in one area of your life, it may spill over into other areas as well.

Ellen Langer and Judith Rodin (1976) tested the importance of personal control by treating elderly patients in a highly rated Connecticut nursing home in

"Argue for your limitations, and sure enough they're yours."
—*RICHARD BACH*, ILLUSIONS: ADVENTURES OF A RELUCTANT MESSIAH, *1977*

learned helplessness
The sense of hopelessness and resignation learned when a human or animal perceives no control over repeated bad events.

FIGURE :: 2.7

Learned Helplessness

When animals and people experience uncontrollable bad events, they learn to feel helpless and resigned.

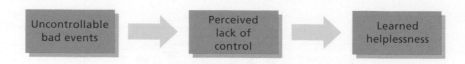

| Uncontrollable bad events | ⇒ | Perceived lack of control | ⇒ | Learned helplessness |

"Yes, we can."

—*BARACK OBAMA, NOVEMBER 4, 2008*

one of two ways. With one group, the benevolent caregivers emphasized "our responsibility to make this a home you can be proud of and happy in." They gave the patients their normal well-intentioned, sympathetic care and allowed them to assume a passive care-receiving role. Three weeks later, most of these patients were rated by themselves, by interviewers, and by nurses as further debilitated. Langer and Rodin's other treatment promoted personal control. It emphasized opportunities for choice, the possibilities for influencing nursing-home policy, and the person's responsibility "to make of your life whatever you want." These patients were given small decisions to make and responsibilities to fulfill. Over the ensuing three weeks, 93 percent of this group showed improved alertness, activity, and happiness.

Studies confirm that systems of governing or managing people that promote personal control will indeed promote health and happiness (Deci & Ryan, 1987). Here are some additional examples:

- Prisoners given some control over their environments—by being able to move chairs, control TV sets, and operate the lights—experience less stress, exhibit fewer health problems, and commit less vandalism (Ruback & others, 1986; Wener & others, 1987).

- Workers given leeway in carrying out tasks and making decisions experience improved morale (Miller & Monge, 1986). So do telecommuting workers who have more flexibility in balancing their work and personal life (Valcour, 2007).

- Institutionalized residents allowed choice in matters such as what to eat for breakfast, when to go to a movie, whether to sleep late or get up early, may live longer and certainly are happier (Timko & Moos, 1989).

- Homeless shelter residents who perceive little choice in when to eat and sleep, and little control over their privacy, are more likely to have a passive, helpless attitude regarding finding housing and work (Burn, 1992).

- In all countries studied, people who perceive themselves as having free choice experience greater satisfaction with their lives (Figure 2.8). And countries where people experience more freedom have more satisfied citizens (Inglehart & others, 2008).

Personal control: Inmates of Spain's modern Valencia prison have, with work and appropriate behavior, gained access to classes, sports facilities, cultural opportunities, and money in an account that can be charged for snacks.

THE COSTS OF EXCESS CHOICE

Can there ever be too much of a good thing such as freedom and self-determination? Barry Schwartz (2000, 2004) contends that individualistic modern cultures indeed have "an excess of freedom," causing decreased life satisfaction and increased rates of clinical depression. Too many choices can lead to paralysis, or what Schwartz calls "the tyranny of freedom." After choosing from among 30 kinds of jams or chocolates, people express less satisfaction with their choices than those choosing from among 6 options (Iyengar & Lepper, 2000). Making choices is also tiring. Students who chose which classes they would take during the upcoming semester— versus those who simply read over the course catalog—were later less likely to study for an important test and more likely to procrastinate by playing

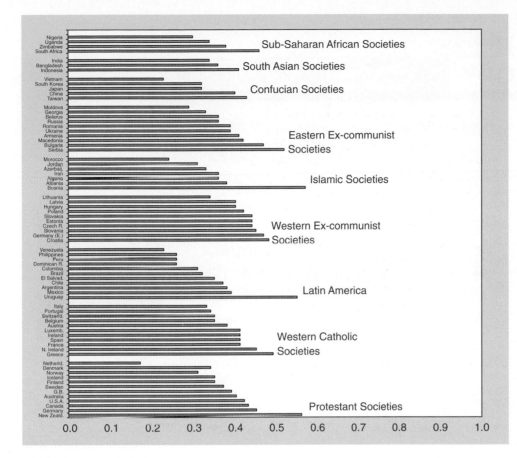

FIGURE :: 2.8

Correlations between individuals' perceived free choice and their self-reported life satisfaction, for each of 73 countries (Inglehart & Welzel, 2005).

video games and reading magazines. In another study, students who chose among an array of consumer products were later less able to consume an unsavory but healthy drink (Vohs & others, 2008). So after choosing among the 19,000 possible beverage combinations at Starbucks or the 40,000 items at the average supermarket, you might be less satisfied with your choices and more likely to go home and eat the ice cream straight from the container.

Christopher Hsee and Reid Hastie (2006) illustrate how choice may enhance regret. Give employees a free trip to either Paris or Hawaii and they will be happy. But give them a choice between the two and they may be less happy. People who choose Paris may regret that it lacks the warmth and the ocean. Those who choose Hawaii may regret the lack of great museums. Something like that may explain why the seniors from 11 colleges in one recent study who spent the most time seeking and assessing various job possibilities ended up with higher starting salaries but lower satisfaction (Iyengar & others, 2006).

In other experiments, people have expressed greater satisfaction with irrevocable choices (such as those made in an "all purchases final" sale) than with reversible choices (as when allowing refunds or exchanges). Ironically, people like and will pay for the freedom to reverse their choices. Yet, note Daniel Gilbert and Jane Ebert (2002), that same freedom "can inhibit the psychological processes that manufacture satisfaction."

That principle may help explain a curious social phenomenon (Myers, 2000a): National surveys show that people expressed more satisfaction with their marriages several decades ago when marriage was more irrevocable ("all purchases final"). Today, despite greater freedom to escape bad marriages and try new ones, people tend to express somewhat less satisfaction with the marriage that they have.

Research on self-control gives us greater confidence in traditional virtues such as perseverance and hope. Bandura (2004) acknowledges that self-efficacy is fed by social

THE inside STORY

In 2002 I changed my mind about the benefit of being able to change my mind.

Jane Ebert and I discovered that people are generally happier with decisions when they can't undo them. When participants in our experiments were able to undo their decisions they tended to consider both the positive and negative features of the decisions they had made. When they couldn't undo their decisions they tended to concentrate on the good features and ignore the bad. As such, they were more satisfied when they made irrevocable than revocable decisions. Ironically, subjects did not realize this would happen and strongly preferred to have the opportunity to change their minds.

Now, up until this point I had always believed that love causes marriage. But these experiments suggested to me that marriage would also cause love. If you take data seriously you act on it, so when these results came in I went home and proposed to the woman I was living with. She said yes, and it turned out that the right were right: I love my wife more than I loved my girlfriend. (Excerpted with permission from edge.org)

Daniel Gilbert,
Harvard University

"*This gives my confidence a real boost.*"

Confidence and feelings of self-efficacy grow from successes.

persuasion ("you have what it takes to succeed") and by self-persuasion ("I think I can, I think I can"). Modeling—seeing similar others succeed with effort—helps, too. But the biggest source of self-efficacy, he says, is *mastery experiences*. "Successes build a robust belief in one's efficacy." If your initial efforts to lose weight, stop smoking, or improve your grades succeed, your self-efficacy increases.

A team of researchers led by Roy Baumeister (2003) concurs. "Praising all the children just for being themselves," they contend, "simply devalues praise." Better to praise and bolster self-esteem "in recognition of good performance. . . . As the person performs or behaves better, self-esteem is encouraged to rise, and the net effect will be to reinforce both good behavior and improvement. Those outcomes are conducive to both the happiness of the individual and the betterment of society."

Summing Up: Perceived Self-Control

- Several lines of research show the benefits of a sense of self-efficacy and feelings of control. People who believe in their own competence and effectiveness, and who have an internal locus of control, cope better and achieve more than others.

- Learned helplessness often occurs when attempts to improve a situation have proven fruitless; self-determination, in contrast, is bolstered by experiences of successfully exercising control and improving one's situation.

- When people are given too many choices, they may be less satisfied with what they have than when offered a smaller range of choices.

Self-Serving Bias

As we process self-relevant information, a potent bias intrudes. We readily excuse our failures, accept credit for our successes, and in many ways see ourselves as better than average. Such self-enhancing perceptions enable most people to enjoy the bright side of high self-esteem, while occasionally suffering the dark side.

Most of us have a good reputation with ourselves. In studies of self-esteem, even low-scoring people respond in the midrange of possible scores. (A low-self-esteem person responds to statements such as "I have good ideas" with a qualifying adjective, such as "somewhat" or "sometimes.") In a study of self-esteem across 53 nations, the average self-esteem score was above the midpoint in every single country (Schmitt & Allik, 2005). One of social psychology's most provocative yet firmly established conclusions concerns the potency of **self-serving bias.**

self-serving bias
The tendency to perceive oneself favorably.

Explaining Positive and Negative Events

Many dozens of experiments have found that people accept credit when told they have succeeded. They attribute the success to their ability and effort, but they attribute failure to external factors such as bad luck or the problem's inherent "impossibility" (Campbell & Sedikides, 1999). Similarly, in explaining their victories, athletes commonly credit themselves, but they attribute losses to something else: bad breaks, bad referee calls, or the other team's super effort or dirty play (Grove & others, 1991; Lalonde, 1992; Mullen & Riordan, 1988). And how much responsibility do you suppose car drivers tend to accept for their accidents? On insurance forms, drivers have described their accidents in words such as these: "An invisible car came out of nowhere, struck my car, and vanished"; "As I reached an intersection, a hedge sprang up, obscuring my vision, and I did not see the other car"; "A pedestrian hit me and went under my car" (*Toronto News,* 1977).

Situations that combine skill and chance (games, exams, job applications) are especially prone to the phenomenon. When I win at Scrabble, it's because of my verbal dexterity; when I lose, it's because "Who could get anywhere with a *Q* but no *U?*" Politicians similarly tend to attribute their wins to themselves (hard work, constituent service, reputation, and strategy) and their losses to factors beyond their control (their district's party makeup, their opponent's name, political trends) (Kingdon, 1967). When corporate profits are up, the CEOs welcome big bonuses for their managerial skill. When profits turn to losses, well, what could you expect in a down economy? This phenomenon of **self-serving attributions** (attributing positive outcomes to oneself and negative outcomes to something else) is one of the most potent of human biases (Mezulis & others, 2004).

self-serving attributions
A form of self-serving bias; the tendency to attribute positive outcomes to oneself and negative outcomes to other factors.

Self-serving attributions contribute to marital discord, worker dissatisfaction, and bargaining impasses (Kruger & Gilovich, 1999). Small wonder that divorced people usually blame their partner for the breakup (Gray & Silver, 1990), or that managers often blame poor performance on workers' lack of ability or effort (Imai, 1994; Rice, 1985). (Workers are more likely to blame something external—inadequate supplies, excessive workload, difficult co-workers, ambiguous assignments.) Small wonder, too, that people evaluate pay raises as fairer when they receive a bigger raise than most of their co-workers (Diekmann & others, 1997).

We help maintain our positive self-images by associating ourselves with success and distancing ourselves from failure. For example, "I got an A on my econ test" versus "The prof gave me a C on my history exam." Blaming failure or rejection on something external, even another's prejudice, is less depressing than seeing oneself as undeserving (Major & others, 2003). We will, however, acknowledge our distant past failings—those by our "former" self, note Anne Wilson and Michael Ross (2001). Describing their old precollege selves, their University of Waterloo students offered

nearly as many negative as positive statements. When describing their present selves, they offered three times more positive statements. "I've learned and grown, and I'm a better person today," most people surmise. Chumps yesterday, champs today.

Ironically, we are even biased against seeing our own bias. People claim they avoid self-serving bias themselves, but readily acknowledge that others commit this bias (Pronin & others, 2002). This "bias blind spot" can have serious consequences during conflicts. If you're negotiating with your roommate over who does household chores and you believe your roommate has a biased view of the situation, you're much more likely to become angry (Pronin & Ross, 2006). Apparently we see ourselves as objective and everyone else as biased. No wonder we fight, because we're each convinced we're "right" and free from bias. As the T-shirt slogan says, "Everyone is entitled to my opinion."

Is the self-serving bias universal, or are people in collectivistic cultures immune? People in collectivistic cultures associate themselves with positive words and valued traits (Gaertner & others, 2008; Yamaguchi & others, 2007). However, in some studies, collectivists are less likely to self-enhance by believing they are better than others (Heine & Hamamura, 2007), particularly in individualistic domains (Sedikides & others, 2003).

Can We All Be Better than Average?

Self-serving bias also appears when people compare themselves with others. If the sixth-century B.C. Chinese philosopher Lao-tzu was right that "at no time in the world will a man who is sane over-reach himself, over-spend himself, over-rate himself," then most of us are a little insane. For on *subjective, socially desirable,* and *common* dimensions, most people see themselves as better than the average person. Compared with people in general, most people see themselves as more ethical, more competent at their job, friendlier, more intelligent, better looking, less prejudiced, healthier, and even more insightful and less biased in their self-assessments. (See "Focus On: Self-Serving Bias—How Do I Love Me? Let Me Count the Ways.")

Every community, it seems, is like Garrison Keillor's fictional Lake Wobegon, where "all the women are strong, all the men are good-looking, and all the children are above average." Many people believe that they will become even more above average in the future—if I'm good now, I will be even better soon, they seem to think (Kanten & Teigen, 2008). One of Freud's favorite jokes was the husband who told his wife, "If one of us should die, I think I would go live in Paris."

Michael Ross and Fiore Sicoly (1979) observed a marital version of self-serving bias. They found that young married Canadians usually believed they took more responsibility for such activities as cleaning the house and caring for the children than their spouses credited them for. In a more recent study of 265 U.S. married couples with children, husbands estimated they did 42 percent of the housework. The wives estimated their husbands did 33 percent. When researchers tracked actual housework (by sampling participants' activity at random times using beepers),

focus
ON
Self-Serving Bias—How Do I Love Me? Let Me Count the Ways

"The one thing that unites all human beings, regardless of age, gender, religion, economic status or ethnic background," notes columnist Dave Barry (1998), "is that deep down inside, we all believe that we are above average drivers." We also believe we are above average on most any other subjective and desirable trait. Among the many faces of self-serving bias are these:

- *Ethics.* Most business people see themselves as more ethical than the average business person (Baumhart, 1968; Brenner & Molander, 1977). One national survey asked, "How would you rate your own morals and values on a scale from 1 to 100 (100 being perfect)?" Fifty percent of people rated themselves 90 or above; only 11 percent said 74 or less (Lovett, 1997).

- *Professional competence.* In one survey, 90 percent of business managers rated their performance as superior to their average peer (French, 1968). In Australia, 86 percent of people rated their job performance as above average, 1 percent as below average (Headey & Wearing, 1987). Most surgeons believe *their* patients' mortality rate to be lower than average (Gawande, 2002).

- *Virtues.* In the Netherlands, most high school students rate themselves as more honest, persistent, original, friendly, and reliable than the average high school student (Hoorens, 1993, 1995).

- *Intelligence.* Most people perceive themselves as more intelligent, better looking, and much less prejudiced than their average peer (*Public Opinion*, 1984; Wylie, 1979). When someone outperforms them, people tend to think of the other as a genius (Lassiter & Munhall, 2001).

- *Tolerance.* In a 1997 Gallup Poll, only 14 percent of White Americans rated their prejudice against Blacks as 5 or higher on a 0 to 10 scale. Yet Whites perceived high prejudice (5 or above) among 44 percent of *other* Whites.

- *Parental support.* Most adults believe they support their aging parents more than do their siblings (Lerner & others, 1991).

- *Health.* Los Angeles residents view themselves as healthier than most of their neighbors, and most college students believe they will outlive their actuarially predicted age of death by about 10 years (Larwood, 1978; C. R. Snyder, 1978).

- *Insight.* Others' public words and deeds reveal their natures, we presume. Our *private* thoughts do the same. Thus, most of us believe we know and understand others better than they know and understand us. We also believe we know ourselves better than others know themselves (Pronin & others, 2001).

- *Attractiveness.* Is it your experience, as it is mine, that most photos of you seem not to do you justice? One experiment showed people a lineup of faces—one their own, the others being their face morphed into those of less and more attractive faces (Epley & Whitchurch, 2008). When asked which was their actual face, people tended to identify an attractively enhanced version of their face.

- *Driving.* Most drivers—even most drivers who have been hospitalized for accidents—believe themselves to be safer and more skilled than the average driver (Guerin, 1994; McKenna & Myers, 1997; Svenson, 1981). Dave Barry was right.

they found husbands actually carrying 39 percent of the domestic workload (Lee & Waite, 2005). The general rule: Group members' estimates of how much they contribute to a joint task typically sum to more than 100 percent (Savitsky & others, 2005).

My wife and I used to pitch our laundry at the foot of our bedroom clothes hamper. In the morning, one of us would put it in. When she suggested that I take more responsibility for this, I thought, "Huh? I already do it 75 percent of the time." So I asked her how often she thought she picked up the clothes. "Oh," she replied, "about 75 percent of the time."

But what if you had to estimate how often you performed rare household chores, like cleaning the oven? Here, you're likely to say that you do this less than 50 percent of the time (Kruger & Savitsky, 2009). Apparently this occurs because

I DO EVERYTHING AROUND HERE

© Jean Sorensen.

we have more knowledge about our behavior than about someone else's, and we assume that other people's behavior will be less extreme than ours (Kruger & others, 2008; Moore & Small, 2007). If you can remember cleaning an oven only a few times, you might assume you are unusual and that your partner must do this more often. Same for a trivia contest: Students say they have only a small chance of winning if the questions are about the history of Mesopotamia, apparently not recognizing that their fellow students are probably equally clueless about this subject area (Windschitl & others, 2003). When people receive more information about others' actions, the discrepancy disappears.

Within commonly considered domains, subjective behavioral dimensions (such as "disciplined") trigger even greater self-serving bias than observable behavioral dimensions (such as "punctual"). Subjective qualities give us leeway in constructing our own definitions of success (Dunning & others, 1989, 1991). Rating my "athletic ability," I ponder my basketball play, not the agonizing weeks I spent as a Little League baseball player hiding in right field. Assessing my "leadership ability," I conjure up an image of a great leader whose style is similar to mine. By defining ambiguous criteria in our own terms, each of us can see ourselves as relatively successful. In one College Entrance Examination Board survey of 829,000 high school seniors, *none* rated themselves below average in "ability to get along with others" (a subjective, desirable trait), 60 percent rated themselves in the top 10 percent, and 25 percent saw themselves among the top 1 percent!

Researchers have wondered: Do people really believe their above-average self-estimates? Is their self-serving bias partly a function of how the questions are phrased (Krizan & Suls, 2008)? When Elanor Williams and Thomas Gilovich (2008) had people bet real money when estimating their relative performance on tests, they found that, yes, "people truly believe their self-enhancing self-assessments."

Unrealistic Optimism

Optimism predisposes a positive approach to life. "The optimist," notes H. Jackson Brown (1990, p. 79), "goes to the window every morning and says, 'Good morning, God.' The pessimist goes to the window and says, 'good God, morning.'" Studies of more than 90,000 people across 22 cultures reveal that most humans are more disposed to optimism than pessimism (Fischer & Chalmers, 2008). Indeed, many of us have what researcher Neil Weinstein (1980, 1982) terms "an unrealistic optimism about future life events." Partly because of their relative pessimism about others' fates (Hoorens & others, 2008; Shepperd, 2003), students perceive themselves as far more likely than their classmates to get a good job, draw a good salary, and own a home. They also see themselves as far *less* likely to experience negative events, such as developing a drinking problem, having a heart attack before age 40, or being fired.

"Views of the future are so rosy that they would make Pollyanna blush."

—*SHELLEY E. TAYLOR,*
POSITIVE ILLUSIONS, 1989

Parents extend their unrealistic optimism to their children, assuming their child is less likely to drop out of college, become depressed, or get lung cancer than the average child, but more likely to complete college, remain healthy, and stay happy (Lench & others, 2006).

Illusory optimism increases our vulnerability. Believing ourselves immune to misfortune, we do not take sensible precautions. Sexually active undergraduate women who don't consistently use contraceptives perceive themselves, compared with other women at their university, as much *less* vulnerable to unwanted pregnancy (Burger & Burns, 1988). Elderly drivers who rated themselves as "above average" were four times more likely than more modest drivers to flunk a driving test and be rated "unsafe" (Freund & others, 2005). Students who enter university with inflated assessments of their academic ability often suffer deflating self-esteem and well-being and are more likely to drop out (Robins & Beer, 2001).

Unrealistically optimistic people are also more likely to select credit card offers with low annual fees but high interest rates—a poor choice for the average borrower whose interest charges far exceed the difference of a few dollars in the annual fee (Yang & others, 2007). Because the main source of profit for credit card issuers is interest charges, unrealistic optimism means more profit for them—and more money out of the pockets of those surrounded by a rosy glow.

Those who cheerfully run up credit card debt, deny the effects of smoking, and stumble into ill-fated relationships remind us that blind optimism, like pride, may go before a fall. When gambling, optimists persist longer than pessimists, even when piling up losses (Gibson & Sanbonmatsu, 2004). If those who deal in the stock market or in real estate perceive their business intuition as superior to that of their competitors, they, too, may be in for disappointment. Even the seventeenth-century economist Adam Smith, a defender of human economic rationality, foresaw that people would overestimate their chances of gain. This "absurd presumption in their own good fortune," he said, arises from "the overweening conceit which the greater part of men have of their own abilities" (Spiegel, 1971, p. 243).

Unrealistic optimism appears to be on the rise. In the 1970s, half of American high school seniors predicted that they would be "very good" workers as adults—the highest rating available, and thus the equivalent of giving themselves five stars out of five. By 2006, two-thirds of teens believed they would achieve this stellar outcome—placing themselves in the top 20 percent (Twenge & Campbell, 2008)! Even more striking, half of high school seniors in 2000 believed that they would earn a graduate degree—even though only 9 percent were likely to actually do so (Reynolds & others, 2006). Although aiming high has benefits for success, those who aim too high may struggle with depression as they learn to adjust their goals to more realistic heights (Wrosch & Miller, 2009).

Optimism definitely beats pessimism in promoting self-efficacy, health, and well-being (Armor & Taylor, 1996; Segerstrom, 2001). Being natural optimists, most people believe they will be happier with their lives in the future—a belief that surely helps create happiness in the present (Robinson & Ryff, 1999). If our

"O God, give us grace to accept with serenity the things that cannot be changed, courage to change the things which should be changed, and the wisdom to distinguish the one from the other."

—*REINHOLD NIEBUHR*, THE SERENITY PRAYER, *1943*

Illusory optimism: Most couples marry feeling confident of long-term love. Actually, in individualistic cultures, half of marriages fail.

defensive pessimism
The adaptive value of anticipating problems and harnessing one's anxiety to motivate effective action.

optimistic ancestors were more likely than their pessimistic neighbors to surmount challenges and survive, then small wonder that we are disposed to optimism (Haselton & Nettle, 2006).

Yet a dash of realism—or what Julie Norem (2000) calls **defensive pessimism**—can save us from the perils of unrealistic optimism. Defensive pessimism anticipates problems and motivates effective coping. As a Chinese proverb says, "Be prepared for danger while staying in peace." Students who exhibit excess optimism (as many students destined for low grades do) can benefit from having some self-doubt, which motivates study (Prohaska, 1994; Sparrell & Shrauger, 1984). Students who are overconfident tend to underprepare, whereas their equally able but less confident peers study harder and get higher grades (Goodhart, 1986; Norem & Cantor, 1986; Showers & Ruben, 1987). Viewing things in a more immediate, realistic way often helps. Students in one experiment were wildly optimistic in predicting their test performance when the test was hypothetical, but surprisingly accurate when the test was imminent (Armor & Sackett, 2006). Believing you're great when nothing can prove you wrong is one thing, but with an evaluation fast approaching, best not to look like a bragging fool.

It's also important to be able to listen to criticism. "One gentle rule I often tell my students," writes David Dunning (2006), "is that if two people independently give them the same piece of negative feedback, they should at least consider the possibility that it might be true." In other words, don't audition for *American Idol* if you can't sing. Simple advice, but the laughably bad singers who populate the opening episodes every season prove that unrealistic optimism is alive and well.

There is a power to negative as well as positive thinking. The moral: Success in school and beyond requires enough optimism to sustain hope and enough pessimism to motivate concern.

False Consensus and Uniqueness

We have a curious tendency to enhance our self-images by overestimating or underestimating the extent to which others think and act as we do. On matters of *opinion*, we find support for our positions by overestimating the extent to which others agree—a phenomenon called the **false consensus effect** (Krueger & Clement, 1994; Marks & Miller, 1987; Mullen & Goethals, 1990). Those who have favored a Canadian referendum or supported New Zealand's National Party wishfully overestimated the extent to which others would agree (Babad & others, 1992; Koestner, 1993). The sense we make of the world seems like common sense.

false consensus effect
The tendency to overestimate the commonality of one's opinions and one's undesirable or unsuccessful behaviors.

When we behave badly or fail in a task, we reassure ourselves by thinking that such lapses also are common. After one person lies to another, the liar begins to perceive the *other* person as dishonest (Sagarin & others, 1998). They guess that others think and act as they do: "I lie, but doesn't everyone?" If we cheat on our income taxes or smoke, we are likely to overestimate the number of other people who do likewise. If we feel sexual desire toward another, we may overestimate the other's reciprocal desire. As former *Baywatch* actor David Hasselhoff admitted, "I have had Botox. Everyone has!" Four recent studies illustrate:

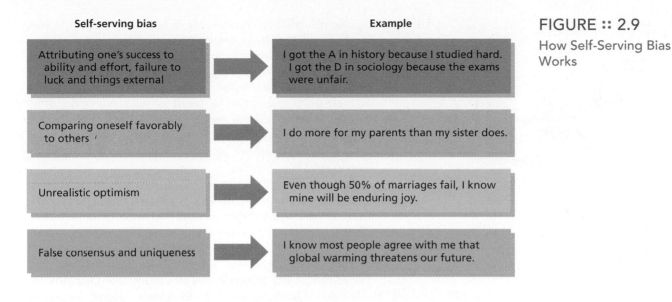

FIGURE :: 2.9

How Self-Serving Bias Works

- People who sneak a shower during a shower ban believe (more than non-bathers) that lots of others are doing the same (Monin & Norton, 2003).
- Those thirsty after hard exercise imagine that lost hikers would become more bothered by thirst than by hunger. That's what 88 percent of thirsty postexercisers guessed in a study by Leaf Van Boven and George Lowenstein (2003), compared with 57 percent of people who were about to exercise.
- As people's own lives change, they see the world changing. Protective new parents come to see the world as a more dangerous place. People who go on a diet judge food ads to be more prevalent (Eibach & others, 2003).
- People who harbor negative ideas about another racial group presume that many others also have negative stereotypes (Krueger, 1996, 2007). Thus, our perceptions of others' stereotypes may reveal something of our own.

"We don't see things as they are," says a proverb. "We see things as we are."

Dawes (1990) proposes that this false consensus may occur because we generalize from a limited sample, which prominently includes ourselves. Lacking other information, why not "project" ourselves; why not impute our own knowledge to others and use our responses as a clue to their likely responses? Most people are in the majority; so when people assume they are in the majority they are usually right. Also, we're more likely to spend time with people who share our attitudes and behaviors and, consequently, to judge the world from the people we know.

On matters of *ability* or when we behave well or successfully, however, a **false uniqueness effect** more often occurs (Goethals & others, 1991). We serve our self-image by seeing our talents and moral behaviors as relatively unusual. For example, those who use marijuana but use seat belts will *overestimate* (false consensus) the number of other marijuana users and *underestimate* (false uniqueness) the number of other seat belt users (Suls & others, 1988). Thus, we may see our failings as relatively normal and our virtues as relatively exceptional.

To sum up, self-serving bias appears as self-serving attributions, self-congratulatory comparisons, illusory optimism, and false consensus for one's failings (Figure 2.9).

Explaining Self-Serving Bias

Why do people perceive themselves in self-enhancing ways? One explanation sees the self-serving bias as a by-product of how we process and remember information about ourselves. Comparing ourselves with others requires us to notice, assess, and recall their behavior and ours. Thus, there are multiple opportunities for flaws

"Everybody says I'm plastic from head to toe. Can't stand next to a radiator or I'll melt. I had (breast) implants, but so has every single person in L.A."

—*ACTRESS PAMELA LEE ANDERSON (QUOTED BY TALBERT, 1997)*

false uniqueness effect
The tendency to underestimate the commonality of one's abilities and one's desirable or successful behaviors.

"I admit it does look very impressive. But you see nowadays everyone graduates in the top ten percent of his class".

Can we all be better than average?

in our information processing (Chambers & Windschitl, 2004). Recall the study in which married people gave themselves credit for doing more housework than their spouses did. Might that not be due, as Michael Ross and Fiore Sicoly (1979) believed, to our greater recall for what we've actively done and our lesser recall for what we've not done or merely observed our partner doing? I could easily picture myself picking up the laundry off the bedroom floor, but I was less aware of the times when I absentmindedly overlooked it.

Are the biased perceptions, then, simply a perceptual error, an emotion-free glitch in how we process information? Or are self-serving *motives* also involved? It's now clear from research that we have multiple motives. Questing for self-knowledge, we're motivated to *assess our competence* (Dunning, 1995). Questing for self-confirmation, we're motivated to *verify our self-conceptions* (Sanitioso & others, 1990; Swann, 1996, 1997). Questing for self-affirmation, we're especially motivated to *enhance our self-image* (Sedikides, 1993). Self-esteem motivation, then, helps power our self-serving bias. As social psychologist Daniel Batson (2006) surmises, "The head is an extension of the heart."

Reflections on Self-Esteem and Self-Serving Bias

If you are like some readers, by now you are finding the self-serving bias either depressing or contrary to your own occasional feelings of inadequacy. Even the people who exhibit the self-serving bias may feel inferior—to specific individuals, especially those who are a step or two higher on the ladder of success, attractiveness, or skill. Moreover, not everyone operates with a self-serving bias. Some people *do* suffer from low self-esteem. Positive self-esteem does have some benefits.

THE SELF-SERVING BIAS AS ADAPTIVE

Self-esteem has its dark side, but also its bright side. When good things happen, people with high self-esteem are more likely to savor and sustain the good feelings (Wood & others, 2003). "Believing one has more talents and positive qualities than one's peers allows one to feel good about oneself and to enter the stressful circumstances of daily life with the resources conferred by a positive sense of self," note Shelley Taylor and her co-researchers (2003).

Self-serving bias and its accompanying excuses also help protect people from depression (Snyder & Higgins, 1988; Taylor & others, 2003). Nondepressed people usually exhibit self-serving bias. They excuse their failures on laboratory tasks or perceive themselves as being more in control than they are. Depressed people's self-appraisals and their appraisals of how others really view them are not inflated (more on this in Chapter 14).

Self-serving bias additionally helps buffer stress. George Bonanno and colleagues (2005) assessed the emotional resiliency of workers who escaped from the World Trade Center or its environs on September 11, 2001. They found that those who displayed self-enhancing tendencies were the most resilient.

In their "terror management theory," Jeff Greenberg, Sheldon Solomon, and Tom Pyszczynski (1997; Greenberg, 2008) propose another reason why positive self-esteem is adaptive: It buffers anxiety, including anxiety related to our certain death. In childhood we learn that when we meet the standards taught us by our parents, we are loved and protected; when we don't, love and protection may be withdrawn. We therefore come to associate viewing ourselves as good with feeling secure. Greenberg and colleagues argue that positive self-esteem—viewing oneself as good and secure—even protects us from feeling terror over our eventual death. Their research shows that reminding people of their mortality (say, by writing a short essay on dying) motivates them to affirm their self-worth. When facing such threats, self-esteem buffers anxiety. In 2004, a year after the U.S. invasion, Iraqi teens who felt their country was under threat reported the highest self-esteem (Carlton-Ford & others, 2008).

As research on depression and anxiety suggests, there is practical wisdom in self-serving perceptions. It may be strategic to believe we are smarter, stronger, and more socially successful than we are. Cheaters may give a more convincing display of honesty if they believe themselves honorable. Belief in our superiority can also motivate us to achieve—creating a self-fulfilling prophecy—and can sustain our hope through difficult times (Willard & Gramzow, 2009).

THE SELF-SERVING BIAS AS MALADAPTIVE

Although self-serving pride may help protect us from depression, it can also be maladaptive. People who blame others for their social difficulties are often unhappier than people who can acknowledge their mistakes (C. A. Anderson & others, 1983; Newman & Langer, 1981; Peterson & others, 1981).

Research by Barry Schlenker (1976; Schlenker & Miller, 1977a, 1977b) has also shown how self-serving perceptions can poison a group. As a rock band guitarist during his college days, Schlenker noted that "rock band members typically overestimated their contributions to a group's success and underestimated their contributions to failure. I saw many good bands disintegrate from the problems caused by these self-glorifying tendencies." In his later life as a University of Florida social psychologist, Schlenker explored group members' self-serving perceptions. In nine experiments, he had people work together on some task. He then falsely informed them that their group had done either well or poorly. In every one of those studies, the members of successful groups claimed more responsibility for their group's performance than did members of groups that supposedly failed at the task.

If most group members believe they are underpaid and underappreciated relative to their better-than-average contributions, disharmony and envy are likely. College presidents and academic deans will readily recognize the phenomenon. Ninety percent or more of college faculty members have rated themselves as superior to their average colleague (Blackburn & others, 1980; Cross, 1977). It is therefore inevitable that when merit salary raises are announced and half receive an average raise or less, many will feel themselves victims of injustice.

Self-serving biases also inflate people's judgments of their *groups,* a phenomenon called **group-serving bias.** When groups are comparable, most people consider their own group superior (Codol, 1976; Jourden & Heath, 1996; Taylor & Doria, 1981).

- Most university sorority members perceive those in their sorority as far less likely to be conceited and snobbish than those in other sororities (Biernat & others, 1996).
- Fifty-three percent of Dutch adults rate their marriage or partnership as better than that of most others; only 1 percent rate it as worse than most (Buunk & van der Eijnden, 1997).

"Victory finds a hundred fathers but defeat is an orphan."
—*COUNT GALEAZZO CIANO,* THE CIANO DIARIES, *1938*

"Other men's sins are before our eyes; our own are behind our back."
—*SENECA,* DE IRA, A.D. *43*

group-serving bias
Explaining away outgroup members' positive behaviors; also attributing negative behaviors to their dispositions (while excusing such behavior by one's own group).

Self-serving pride in group settings can become especially dangerous.

"Then we're in agreement. There's nothing rotten in Denmark. Something is rotten everywhere else."

- Sixty-six percent of Americans give their oldest child's public school a grade of A or B. But nearly as many—64 percent—give the nation's public schools a grade of C or D (Whitman, 1996).
- Most entrepreneurs overpredict their own firms' productivity and growth (Kidd & Morgan, 1969; Larwood & Whittaker, 1977).

That people see themselves and their groups with a favorable bias is hardly new. The tragic flaw portrayed in ancient Greek drama was *hubris*, or pride. Like the subjects of our experiments, the Greek tragic figures were not self-consciously evil; they merely thought too highly of themselves. In literature, the pitfalls of pride are portrayed again and again. In theology, pride has long been first among the "seven deadly sins."

"False humility is the pretence that one is small. True humility is the consciousness of standing in the presence of greatness."

—JONATHAN SACKS, BRITAIN'S CHIEF RABBI, 2000

If pride is akin to the self-serving bias, then what is humility? Is it self-contempt? Humility is not handsome people believing they are ugly and smart people trying to believe they are slow-witted. False modesty can actually be a cover for pride in one's better-than-average humility. (James Friedrich [1996] reports that most students congratulate themselves on being better than average at not thinking themselves better than average!) True humility is more like self-forgetfulness than false modesty. It leaves us free to rejoice in our special talents and, with the same honesty, to recognize the talents of others.

Summing Up: Self-Serving Bias

- Contrary to the presumption that most people suffer from low self-esteem or feelings of inferiority, researchers consistently find that most people exhibit a self-serving bias. In experiments and everyday life, we often take credit for our successes while blaming failures on the situation.
- Most people rate themselves as better than average on subjective, desirable traits and abilities.
- We exhibit unrealistic optimism about our futures.
- We overestimate the commonality of our opinions and foibles (false consensus) while underestimating the commonality of our abilities and virtues (false uniqueness).
- Such perceptions arise partly from a motive to maintain and enhance self-esteem, a motive that protects people from depression but contributes to misjudgment and group conflict.
- Self-serving bias can be adaptive in that it allows us to savor the good things that happen in our lives. When bad things happen, however, self-serving bias can have the maladaptive effect of causing us to blame others or feel cheated out of something we "deserved."

Self-Presentation

Humans seem motivated not only to perceive themselves in self-enhancing ways but also to present themselves favorably to others. How might people's tactics of "impression management" lead to false modesty or to self-defeating behavior?

So far we have seen that the self is at the center of our social worlds, that self-esteem and self-efficacy pay some dividends, and that self-serving bias influences self-evaluations. Perhaps you have wondered: Are self-enhancing expressions always sincere? Do people have the same feelings privately as they express publicly? Or are they just putting on a positive face even while living with self-doubt?

Self-Handicapping

Sometimes people sabotage their chances for success by creating impediments that make success less likely. Far from being deliberately self-destructive, such behaviors typically have a self-protective aim (Arkin & others, 1986; Baumeister & Scher, 1988; Rhodewalt, 1987): "I'm really not a failure—I would have done well except for this problem."

Why would people handicap themselves with self-defeating behavior? Recall that we eagerly protect our self-images by attributing failures to external factors. Can you see why, *fearing failure*, people might handicap themselves by partying half the night before a job interview or playing video games instead of studying before a big exam? When self-image is tied up with performance, it can be more self-deflating to try hard and fail than to procrastinate and have a ready excuse. If we fail while handicapped in some way, we can cling to a sense of competence; if we succeed under such conditions, it can only boost our self-image. Handicaps protect both self-esteem and public image by allowing us to attribute failures to something temporary or external ("I was feeling sick"; "I was out too late the night before") rather than to lack of talent or ability.

Steven Berglas and Edward Jones (1978) confirmed this analysis of **self-handicapping.** One experiment was announced as concerning "drugs and intellectual performance." Imagine yourself in the position of their Duke University participants. You guess answers to some difficult aptitude questions and then are told, "Yours was one of the best scores seen to date!" Feeling incredibly lucky, you are then offered a choice between two drugs before answering more of these items. One drug will aid intellectual performance and the other will inhibit it. Which drug do you want? Most students wanted the drug that would supposedly disrupt their thinking, thus providing a handy excuse for anticipated poorer performance.

Researchers have documented other ways people self-handicap. Fearing failure, people will

- reduce their preparation for important individual athletic events (Rhodewalt & others, 1984).
- give their opponent an advantage (Shepperd & Arkin, 1991).
- perform poorly at the beginning of a task in order not to create unreachable expectations (Baumgardner & Brownlee, 1987).
- not try as hard as they could during a tough, ego-involving task (Hormuth, 1986; Pyszczynski & Greenberg, 1987; Riggs, 1992; Turner & Pratkanis, 1993).

Impression Management

Self-serving bias, false modesty, and self-handicapping reveal the depth of our concern for self-image. To varying degrees, we are continually managing the impressions we create. Whether we wish to impress, intimidate, or seem helpless, we are social animals, playing to an audience.

Self-presentation refers to our wanting to present a desired image both to an external audience (other people) and to an internal audience (ourselves). We work at managing the impressions we create. We excuse, justify, or apologize as necessary to shore up our self-esteem and verify our self-images (Schlenker & Weigold, 1992). Just as we preserve our self-esteem, we also must make sure not to brag too much and risk the disapproval of others (Anderson & others, 2006). Social interaction is a careful balance of looking good while not looking *too* good.

"With no attempt there can be no failure; with no failure no humiliation."
—*WILLIAM JAMES*, PRINCIPLES OF PSYCHOLOGY, *1890*

self-handicapping
Protecting one's self-image with behaviors that create a handy excuse for later failure.

"If you try to fail, and succeed, what have you done?"
—*ANONYMOUS*

After losing to some younger rivals, tennis great Martina Navratilova confessed that she was "afraid to play my best. . . . I was scared to find out if they could beat me when I'm playing my best because if they can, then I am finished" (Frankel & Snyder, 1987).

self-presentation
The act of expressing oneself and behaving in ways designed to create a favorable impression or an impression that corresponds to one's ideals.

© 2008 by P. S. Mueller

MUELLER

In familiar situations, self-presentation happens without conscious effort. In unfamiliar situations, perhaps at a party with people we would like to impress or in conversation with someone we have romantic interest in, we are acutely self-conscious of the impressions we are creating and we are therefore less modest than when among friends who know us well (Leary & others, 1994; Tice & others, 1995). Preparing to have our photographs taken, we may even try out different faces in a mirror. We do this even though active self-presentation depletes energy, which often leads to diminished effectiveness—for example, to less persistence on a tedious experimental task or more difficulty stifling emotional expressions (Vohs & others, 2005). The upside is that self-presentation can unexpectedly improve mood. People felt significantly better than they thought they would after doing their best to "put their best face forward" and concentrate on making a positive impression on their boyfriend or girlfriend. Elizabeth Dunn and her colleagues conclude that "date nights" for long-term couples work because they encourage active self-presentation, which improves mood (Dunn & others, 2008).

Social networking sites such as Facebook provide a new and sometimes intense venue for self-presentation. They are, says communications professor Joseph Walther, "like impression management on steroids" (Rosenbloom, 2008). Users make careful decisions about which pictures, activities, and interests to highlight in their profiles. Some even think about how their friends will affect the impression they make on others; one study found that those with more attractive friends were perceived as more attractive themselves (Walther & others, 2008). Given the concern with status and attractiveness on social networking sites, it is not surprising that people high in narcissistic traits thrive on Facebook, tallying up more friends and choosing more attractive pictures of themselves (Buffardi & Campbell, 2008).

Given our concern for self-presentation, it's no wonder that people will self-handicap when failure might make them look bad. It's no wonder that people take health risks—tanning their skin with wrinkle- and cancer-causing radiation; having piercings or tattoos done without proper hygiene; becoming anorexic; yielding to peer pressures to smoke, get drunk, and do drugs (Leary & others, 1994). It's no wonder that people express more modesty when their self-flattery is vulnerable to being debunked, perhaps by experts who will be scrutinizing their self-evaluations (Arkin & others, 1980; Riess & others, 1981; Weary & others, 1982). Professor Smith will likely express more modesty about the significance of her work when presenting it to professional colleagues than when presenting it to students.

For some people, conscious self-presentation is a way of life. They continually monitor their own behavior and note how others react, then adjust their social performance to gain a desired effect. Those who score high on a scale of **self-monitoring** tendency (who, for example, agree that "I tend to be what people expect me to be") act like social chameleons—they adjust their behavior in

self-monitoring
Being attuned to the way one presents oneself in social situations and adjusting one's performance to create the desired impression.

Group identity. In Asian countries, self-presentation is restrained. Children learn to identify themselves with their groups.

response to external situations (Gangestad & Snyder, 2000; Snyder, 1987). Having attuned their behavior to the situation, they are more likely to espouse attitudes they don't really hold (Zanna & Olson, 1982). Being conscious of others, they are less likely to act on their own attitudes. As Mark Leary (2004b) observed, the self they know often differs from the self they show. As social chameleons, those who score high in self-monitoring are also less committed to their relationships and more likely to be dissatisfied in their marriages (Leone & Hawkins, 2006).

Those who score low in self-monitoring care less about what others think. They are more internally guided and thus more likely to talk and act as they feel and believe (McCann & Hancock, 1983). For example, if asked to list their thoughts about gay couples, they simply express what they think, regardless of the attitudes of their anticipated audience (Klein & others, 2004). As you might imagine, someone who is extremely low in self-monitoring could come across as an insensitive boor, whereas extremely high self-monitoring could result in dishonest behavior worthy of a con artist. Most of us fall somewhere between those two extremes.

Presenting oneself in ways that create a desired impression is a delicate balancing act. People want to be seen as able but also as modest and honest (Carlston & Shovar, 1983). In most social situations, modesty creates a good impression, unsolicited boasting a bad one. Hence the false modesty phenomenon: We often display lower self-esteem than we privately feel (Miller & Schlenker, 1985). But when we have obviously done extremely well, the insincerity of a disclaimer ("I did well, but it's no big deal") may be evident. To make good impressions—to appear modest yet competent—requires social skill.

"Public opinion is always more tyrannical towards those who obviously fear it than towards those who feel indifferent to it."

—*BERTRAND RUSSELL,*
THE CONQUEST
OF HAPPINESS, *1930*

"Hmmm... what shall I wear today...?"

© Mike Marland

Summing Up: Self-Presentation

- As social animals, we adjust our words and actions to suit our audiences. To varying degrees, we note our performance and adjust it to create the impressions we desire.

- Such tactics explain examples of false modesty, in which people put themselves down, extol future competitors, or publicly credit others while privately crediting themselves.

- Sometimes people will even self-handicap with self-defeating behaviors that protect self-esteem by providing excuses for failure.

- Self-presentation refers to our wanting to present a favorable image both to an external audience (other people) and to an internal audience (ourselves). With regard to an external audience, those who score high on a scale of self-monitoring adjust their behavior to each situation, whereas those low in self-monitoring may do so little social adjusting that they seem insensitive.

POSTSCRIPT: Twin Truths—The Perils of Pride, the Powers of Positive Thinking

This chapter offered two memorable truths—the truth of self-efficacy and the truth of self-serving bias. The truth concerning self-efficacy encourages us not to resign ourselves to bad situations. We need to persist despite initial failures and to exert effort without being overly distracted by self-doubts. Secure self-esteem is likewise adaptive. When we believe in our positive possibilities, we are less vulnerable to depression and we feel less insecure.

Thus, it's important to think positively and try hard, but not to be so self-confident that your goals are illusory or you alienate others with your narcissism. Taking self-efficacy too far leads to blaming the victim: If positive thinking can accomplish anything, then we have only ourselves to blame if we are unhappily married, poor, or depressed. For shame! If only we had tried harder, been more disciplined, less stupid. This viewpoint fails to acknowledge that bad things can happen to good people. Life's greatest achievements, but also its greatest disappointments, are born of the highest expectations.

These twin truths—self-efficacy and self-serving bias—remind me of what Pascal taught 300 years ago: No single truth is ever sufficient, because the world is complex. Any truth, separated from its complementary truth, is a half-truth.

 ## Making the Social Connection

This chapter's discussion of self and culture explored the idea of self-concept and suggested that the view of the self can be interdependent and/or independent; we also read Hazel Markus's thoughts on the self and culture. Go to the Online Learning Center at www.mhhe.com/myers10e to watch videos on these topics.

Social Beliefs and Judgments

As U.S. senators, Republican John McCain and Democrat Barack Obama each adopted positions of apparent conscience. In 2001, McCain voted against President Bush's proposed tax cut, saying "I cannot in good conscience support a tax cut in which so many of the benefits go to the most fortunate." In 2008, when McCain was campaigning for the Republican nomination and then for president, he supported and favored extending the cuts that he earlier had opposed.

Barack Obama in 2007 declared himself a "longtime advocate" of public financing of presidential elections and pledged to accept public financing should he win the Democratic nomination for president. But when he won the nomination, supported by unprecedented campaign contributions, he rejected public financing of his own campaign.

For Democrats, McCain's reversal displayed not moral courage and an openness to changing one's mind in the light of new information, but rather expedience and hypocrisy as McCain sought to pick up contributions and votes from wealthy conservatives.

For Republicans, Obama's reversal likewise displayed not a temporary strategy en route to reforming election financing, but rather hypocrisy and the same old do-what-you-can-to-get-elected politics.

As the candidates debated, most McCain partisans were impressed by the reasonableness and power of his straight-talk arguments, while being underwhelmed by the force and cogency of Obama's performance. Most Obama partisans experienced a mirror-image reaction, feeling cheered by what they perceived as their candidate's superior charisma, intelligence, and vision.

These differing reactions, which have been replicated in political perceptions across the world, illustrate the extent to which we construct social perceptions and beliefs as we

- *perceive* and recall events through the filters of our own assumptions;

- *judge* events, informed by our intuition, by implicit rules that guide our snap judgments, and by our moods;

- *explain* events by sometimes attributing them to the situation, sometimes to the person; and

- *expect* certain events, which sometimes helps bring them about.

This chapter therefore explores how we perceive, judge, and explain our social worlds, and how—and to what extent—our expectations matter.

Perceiving Our Social Worlds

Striking research reveals the extent to which our assumptions and prejudgments guide our perceptions, interpretations, and recall.

Chapter 1 noted a significant fact about the human mind: our preconceptions guide how we perceive and interpret information. We construe the world through belief-tinted glasses. "Sure, preconceptions matter," people will agree; yet they fail to realize how great the effect is.

Let's consider some provocative experiments. The first group of experiments examines how predispositions and prejudgments affect how we perceive and interpret information. The second group plants a judgment in people's minds *after* they have been given information to see how after-the-fact ideas bias recall. The overarching point: *We respond not to reality as it is but to reality as we construe it.*

Priming

Unattended stimuli can subtly influence how we interpret and recall events. Imagine yourself, during an experiment, wearing earphones and concentrating on ambiguous spoken sentences such as "We stood by the bank." When a pertinent word (*river* or *money*) is simultaneously sent to your other ear, you don't consciously hear it. Yet the word "primes" your interpretation of the sentence (Baars & McGovern, 1994).

priming
Activating particular
associations in memory.

Our memory system is a web of associations, and **priming** is the awakening or activating of certain associations. Experiments show that priming one thought, even without awareness, can influence another thought, or even an action. John Bargh and his colleagues (1996) asked people to complete a sentence containing words such as "old," "wise," and "retired." Shortly afterward, they observed these people walking more slowly to the elevator than did those not primed with aging-related words. Moreover, the slow walkers had no awareness of their walking speed or of having just viewed words that primed aging.

Often our thinking and acting are subtly primed by unnoticed events. Rob Holland and his colleagues (2005) observed that Dutch students exposed to the scent of an all-purpose cleaner were quicker to identify cleaning-related words. In follow-up experiments, other students exposed to a cleaning scent recalled more cleaning-related activities when describing their day's activities and even kept their desk cleaner while eating a crumbly cookie. Moreover, all these effects occurred without the participants' conscious awareness of the scent and its influence.

Posting the second sign may prime customers to be dissatisfied with the handling of their complaints at the first window.

www.CartoonStock.com

Priming experiments (Bargh, 2006) have their counterparts in everyday life:

- Watching a scary movie alone at home can activate emotions that, without our realizing it, cause us to interpret furnace noises as a possible intruder.
- Depressed moods, as this chapter explains later, prime negative associations. Put people in a *good* mood and suddenly their past seems more wonderful, their future brighter.
- Watching violence primes people to interpret ambiguous actions (a shove) and words ("punch") as aggressive.
- For many psychology students, reading about psychological disorders primes how they interpret their own anxieties and gloomy moods. Reading about disease symptoms similarly primes medical students to worry about their congestion, fever, or headache.

In a host of studies, priming effects surface even when the stimuli are presented subliminally—too briefly to be perceived consciously. What's out of sight may not be completely out of mind. An electric shock that is too slight to be felt may increase the perceived intensity of a later shock. An imperceptibly flashed word, "bread," may prime people to detect a related word such as "butter" more quickly than they detect an unrelated word such as "bottle" or "bubble." A subliminal color name facilitates speedier identification when the color appears on the computer screen, whereas an unseen wrong name delays color identification (Epley & others, 1999; Merikle & others, 2001). In each case, an invisible image or word primes a response to a later task.

Studies of how implanted ideas and images can prime our interpretations and recall illustrate one of this book's take-home lessons from twenty-first-century social psychology: *Much of our social information processing is automatic.* It is unintentional, out of sight, and happens without our conscious awareness.

Perceiving and Interpreting Events

Despite some startling and oft-confirmed biases and logical flaws in how we perceive and understand one another, we're mostly accurate (Jussim, 2005). Our first impressions of one another are more often right than wrong. Moreover, the better we know people, the more accurately we can read their minds and feelings.

FIGURE :: 3.1

Pro-Israeli and pro-Arab students who viewed network news descriptions of the "Beirut massacre" believed the coverage was biased against their point of view.

Source: Data from Vallone, Ross, & Lepper, 1985.

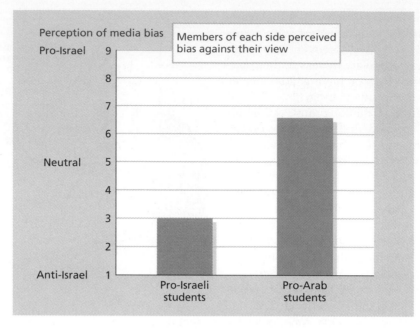

But on occasion our prejudgments err. The effects of prejudgments and expectations are standard fare for psychology's introductory course. Recall the Dalmatian photo in Chapter 1. Or consider this phrase:

A
BIRD
IN THE
THE HAND

Did you notice anything wrong with it? There is more to perception than meets the eye. The same is true of social perception. Because social perceptions are very much in the eye of the beholder, even a simple stimulus may strike two people quite differently. Saying Britain's Gordon Brown is "an okay prime minister" may sound like a put-down to one of his ardent admirers and like praise to someone who regards him with contempt. When social information is subject to multiple interpretations, preconceptions matter (Hilton & von Hippel, 1990).

An experiment by Robert Vallone, Lee Ross, and Mark Lepper (1985) reveals just how powerful preconceptions can be. They showed pro-Israeli and pro-Arab students six network news segments describing the 1982 killing of civilian refugees at two camps in Lebanon. As Figure 3.1 illustrates, each group perceived the networks as hostile to its side.

The phenomenon is commonplace: Sports fans perceive referees as partial to the other side. Political candidates and their supporters nearly always view the news media as unsympathetic to their cause (Richardson & others, 2008). In the 2008 U.S. presidential race, supporters of Hillary Clinton, Barack Obama, and John McCain all noted instances when the media seemed biased against their candidate, sometimes because of seeming prejudice related to gender, race, or age.

But it's not just fans and politicians. People everywhere perceive mediators and media as biased against their position. "There is no subject about which people are less objective than objectivity," noted one media commentator (Poniewozik, 2003). Indeed, people's perceptions of bias can be used to assess their attitudes (Saucier & Miller, 2003). Tell me where you see bias, and you will signal your attitudes.

Our assumptions about the world can even make contradictory evidence seem supportive. For example, Ross and Lepper assisted Charles Lord (1979) in asking two groups of students to evaluate the results of two supposedly new research studies. Half the students favored capital punishment and half opposed it. Of the

"Once you have a belief, it influences how you perceive all other relevant information. Once you see a country as hostile, you are likely to interpret ambiguous actions on their part as signifying their hostility."

—*POLITICAL SCIENTIST ROBERT JERVIS (1985)*

studies they evaluated, one confirmed and the other disconfirmed the students' beliefs about the deterrent effect of the death penalty. The results: Both proponents and opponents of capital punishment readily accepted evidence that confirmed their belief but were sharply critical of disconfirming evidence. Showing the two sides an *identical* body of mixed evidence had not lessened their disagreement but *increased* it.

Is that why, in politics, religion, and science, ambiguous information often fuels conflict? Presidential debates in the United States have mostly reinforced predebate opinions. By nearly a 10-to-1 margin, those who already favored one candidate or the other perceived their candidate as having won (Kinder & Sears, 1985). Thus, report Geoffrey Munro and his colleagues (1997), people on both sides may become even more supportive of their respective candidates after viewing a presidential debate. Moreover, at the end of the Republican presidency of Ronald Reagan (during which inflation fell), only 8 percent of Democrats perceived that inflation had fallen. Republicans—47 percent of whom correctly perceived that it had—were similarly inaccurate and negative in their perceptions at the end of the Democratic Clinton presidency (Brooks, 2004). Partisanship predisposes perceptions.

In addition to these studies of people's preexisting social and political attitudes, researchers have manipulated people's preconceptions—with astonishing effects upon their interpretations and recollections.

Myron Rothbart and Pamela Birrell (1977) had University of Oregon students assess the facial expression of a man (Figure 3.2). Those told he was a Gestapo leader responsible for barbaric medical experiments on concentration camp inmates intuitively judged his expression as cruel. (Can you see that barely suppressed sneer?) Those told he was a leader in the anti-Nazi underground movement whose courage saved thousands of Jewish lives judged his facial expression as warm and kind. (Just look at those caring eyes and that almost smiling mouth.)

Filmmakers control people's perceptions of emotion by manipulating the setting in which they see a face. They call this the "Kulechov effect," after a Russian film director who would skillfully guide viewers' inferences by manipulating their assumptions. Kulechov demonstrated the phenomenon by creating three short films that presented identical footage of the face of an actor with a neutral expression after viewers had first been shown one of three different scenes: a dead woman, a dish of soup, or a girl playing. As a result, in the first film the actor seemed sad, in the second thoughtful, and in the third happy.

Construal processes also color others' perceptions of us. When we say something good or bad about another, people

"I'd like your honest, unbiased and possibly career-ending opinion on something."

Some circumstances make it difficult to be unbiased.

"The error of our eye directs our mind: What error leads must err."
—*SHAKESPEARE*, TROILUS AND CRESSIDA, *1601–1602*

FIGURE :: 3.2

Judge for yourself: Is this person's expression cruel or kind? If told he was a Nazi, would your reading of his face differ?

Supporters of a particular candidate or cause tend to see the media as favoring the other side.

spontaneously tend to associate that trait with us, report Lynda Mae, Donal Carlston, and John Skowronski (1999; Carlston & Skowronski, 2005)—a phenomenon they call *spontaneous trait transference*. If we go around talking about others being gossipy, people may then unconsciously associate "gossip" with us. Call someone a jerk and folks may later construe *you* as one. Describe someone as sensitive, loving, and compassionate, and you may seem more so. There is, it appears, intuitive wisdom in the childhood taunt, "I'm rubber, you're glue; what you say bounces off me and sticks to you."

The bottom line: We view our social worlds through the spectacles of our beliefs, attitudes, and values. That is one reason our beliefs are so important; they shape our interpretation of everything else.

Belief Perseverance

Imagine a grandparent who decides, during an evening with a crying infant, that bottle feeding produces colicky babies: "Come to think of it, cow's milk obviously suits calves better than babies." If the infant turns out to be suffering a high fever, will the sitter nevertheless persist in believing that bottle feeding causes colic (Ross & Anderson, 1982)? To find out, Lee Ross, Craig Anderson, and their colleagues planted a falsehood in people's minds and then tried to discredit it.

Their research reveals that it is surprisingly difficult to demolish a falsehood, once the person conjures up a rationale for it. Each experiment first *implanted a belief*, either by proclaiming it to be true or by showing the participants some anecdotal evidence. Then the participants were asked to *explain why* it is true. Finally, the researchers totally *discredited* the initial information by telling the participants the truth: The information was manufactured for the experiment, and half the participants in the experiment had received opposite information. Nevertheless, the new belief survived about 75 percent intact, presumably because the participants still retained their invented explanations for the belief. This phenomenon, called **belief perseverance,** shows that beliefs can grow their own legs and survive the discrediting of the evidence that inspired them.

An example: Anderson, Lepper, and Ross (1980) asked participants to decide whether individuals who take risks make good or bad firefighters. One group considered a risk-prone person who was a successful firefighter and a cautious person who was unsuccessful. The other group considered cases suggesting the opposite conclusion. After forming their theory that risk-prone people make better or worse firefighters, the participants wrote explanations for it—for example, that risk-prone people are brave or that cautious people have fewer accidents. Once each explanation was formed, it could exist independently of the information that initially created the belief. When that information was discredited, the participants still held their self-generated explanations and therefore continued to believe that risk-prone people really do make better or worse firefighters.

These experiments suggest that the more we examine our theories and explain how they *might* be true, the more closed we become to information that challenges

belief perseverance
Persistence of one's initial conceptions, as when the basis for one's belief is discredited but an explanation of why the belief might be true survives.

our beliefs. Once we consider why an accused person might be guilty, why an offending stranger acts that way, or why a favored stock might rise in value, our explanations may survive challenges (Davies, 1997; Jelalian & Miller, 1984).

The evidence is compelling: Our beliefs and expectations powerfully affect how we mentally construct events. Usually, we benefit from our preconceptions, just as scientists benefit from creating theories that guide them in noticing and interpreting events. But the benefits sometimes entail a cost: We become prisoners of our own thought patterns. Thus, the supposed Martian "canals" that twentieth-century astronomers delighted in spotting turned out to be the product of intelligent life—an intelligence on Earth's side of the telescope. As another example, Germans, who widely believed that the introduction of the Euro currency led to increased prices, overestimated such price increases when comparing actual restaurant menus—the prior menu with German Mark prices and a new one with Euro prices (Traut-Mattausch & others, 2004). As an old Chinese proverb says, "Two-thirds of what we see is behind our eyes."

Belief perseverance may have important consequences, as Stephan Lewandowsky and his international collaborators (2005) discovered when they explored implanted and discredited information about the Iraq war that began in 2003. As the war unfolded, the Western media reported and repeated several claims—for example, that Iraqi forces executed coalition prisoners of war—that later were shown to be false and were retracted. Alas, having accepted the information, which fit their pre-existing assumptions, Americans tended to retain the belief (unlike most Germans and Australians, who had questioned the war's rationale).

Is there a remedy for belief perseverance? There is: *Explain the opposite.* Charles Lord, Mark Lepper, and Elizabeth Preston (1984) repeated the capital punishment study described earlier and added two variations. First, they asked some of their participants, when evaluating the evidence, to be "as *objective* and *unbiased* as possible." That instruction accomplished nothing; whether for or against capital punishment, those who had received the plea made evaluations as biased as those who had not.

The researchers asked a third group to consider the opposite—to ask themselves "whether you would have made the same high or low evaluations had exactly the same study produced results on the *other* side of the issue." After imagining an opposite finding, these people were much less biased in their evaluations of the evidence for and against their views. In his experiments, Craig Anderson (1982; Anderson & Sechler, 1986) consistently found that explaining *why* an opposite theory might be true—why a cautious rather than a risk-taking person might be a better firefighter—reduces or eliminates belief perseverance. Indeed, explaining any alternative outcome, not just the opposite, drives people to ponder various possibilities (Hirt & Markman, 1995).

Constructing Memories of Ourselves and Our Worlds

Do you agree or disagree with this statement?

> Memory can be likened to a storage chest in the brain into which we deposit material and from which we can withdraw it later if needed. Occasionally, something is lost from the "chest," and then we say we have forgotten.

About 85 percent of college students said they agreed (Lamal, 1979). As one magazine ad put it, "Science has proven the accumulated experience of a lifetime is preserved perfectly in your mind."

Actually, psychological research has proved the opposite. Our memories are not exact copies of experiences that remain on deposit in a memory bank. Rather, we construct memories at the time of withdrawal. Like a paleontologist inferring the appearance of a dinosaur from bone fragments, we reconstruct our distant past

"We hear and apprehend only what we already half know."
—*HENRY DAVID THOREAU, 1817–1862*

"No one denies that new evidence can change people's beliefs. Children do eventually renounce their belief in Santa Claus. Our contention is simply that such changes generally occur slowly, and that more compelling evidence is often required to alter a belief than to create it."
—*LEE ROSS & MARK LEPPER (1980)*

"Memory isn't like reading a book: It's more like writing a book from fragmentary notes."
—*JOHN F. KIHLSTROM, 1994*

by using our current feelings and expectations to combine information fragments. Thus, we can easily (though unconsciously) revise our memories to suit our current knowledge. When one of my sons complained, "The June issue of *Cricket* never came," and was then shown where it was, he delightedly responded, "Oh good, I knew I'd gotten it."

When an experimenter or a therapist manipulates people's presumptions about their past, a sizable percentage of people will construct false memories. Asked to imagine vividly a made-up childhood experience in which they ran, tripped, fell, and stuck their hand through a window, or knocked over a punch bowl at a wedding, about one-fourth will later recall the fictitious event as something that actually happened (Loftus & Bernstein, 2005). In its search for truth, the mind sometimes constructs a falsehood.

In experiments involving more than 20,000 people, Elizabeth Loftus (2003, 2007) and her collaborators have explored our mind's tendency to construct memories. In the typical experiment, people witness an event, receive misleading information about it (or not), and then take a memory test. The repeated finding is the **misinformation effect.** People incorporate the misinformation into their memories: They recall a yield sign as a stop sign, hammers as screwdrivers, *Vogue* magazine as *Mademoiselle,* Dr. Henderson as "Dr. Davidson," breakfast cereal as eggs, and a clean-shaven man as a fellow with a mustache. Suggested misinformation may even produce false memories of supposed child sexual abuse, argues Loftus.

This process affects our recall of social as well as physical events. Jack Croxton and his colleagues (1984) had students spend 15 minutes talking with someone. Those who were later informed that this person liked them recalled the person's behavior as relaxed, comfortable, and happy. Those informed that the person disliked them recalled the person as nervous, uncomfortable, and not so happy.

RECONSTRUCTING OUR PAST ATTITUDES

Five years ago, how did you feel about nuclear power? About your country's president or prime minister? About your parents? If your attitudes have changed, what do you think is the extent of the change?

Experimenters have explored such questions, and the results have been unnerving. People whose attitudes have changed often insist that they have always felt much as they now feel. Daryl Bem and Keith McConnell (1970) conducted a survey among Carnegie-Mellon University students. Buried in it was a question concerning student control over the university curriculum. A week later the students agreed to write an essay opposing student control. After doing so, their attitudes shifted toward greater opposition to student control. When asked to recall how they had answered the question before writing the essay, the students "remembered" holding the opinion that they *now* held and denied that the experiment had affected them.

After observing Clark University students similarly denying their former attitudes, researchers D. R. Wixon and James Laird (1976) commented, "The speed, magnitude, and certainty" with which the students revised their own histories "was striking." As George Vaillant (1977) noted after following adults through time, "It is all too common for caterpillars to become butterflies and then to maintain that in their youth they had been little butterflies. Maturation makes liars of us all."

The construction of positive memories brightens our recollections. Terence Mitchell, Leigh Thompson, and their colleagues (1994, 1997) report that people often exhibit *rosy retrospection*—they recall mildly pleasant events more favorably than they experienced them. College students on a three-week bike trip, older adults on a guided tour of Austria, and undergraduates on vacation all reported enjoying their experiences as they were having them. But they later recalled such experiences even more fondly, minimizing the unpleasant or boring aspects and remembering the high points. Thus, the pleasant times during which I have sojourned in Scotland I now (back in my office facing deadlines and interruptions) romanticize

misinformation effect

Incorporating "misinformation" into one's memory of the event, after witnessing an event and receiving misleading information about it.

"A man should never be ashamed to own that he has been in the wrong, which is but saying in other words, that he is wiser today than he was yesterday."

—*JONATHAN SWIFT, THOUGHTS ON VARIOUS SUBJECTS, 1711*

as pure bliss. The mist and the midges are but dim memories. The spectacular scenery and the fresh sea air and the favorite tea rooms are still with me. With any positive experience, some of our pleasure resides in the anticipation, some in the actual experience, and some in the rosy retrospection.

Cathy McFarland and Michael Ross (1985) found that as our relationships change, we also revise our recollections of other people. They had university students rate their steady dating partners. Two months later, they rated them again. Students who were more in love than ever had a tendency to recall love at first sight. Those who had broken up were more likely to recall having recognized the partner as somewhat selfish and bad-tempered.

Diane Holmberg and John Holmes (1994) discovered the phenomenon also operating among 373 newlywed couples, most of whom reported being very happy. When resurveyed two years later, those whose marriages had soured recalled that things had always been bad. The results are "frightening," say Holmberg and Holmes: "Such biases can lead to a dangerous downward spiral. The worse your current view of your partner is, the worse your memories are, which only further confirms your negative attitudes."

It's not that we are totally unaware of how we used to feel, just that when memories are hazy, current feelings guide our recall. When widows and widowers try to recall the grief they felt on their spouse's death five years earlier, their current emotional state colors their memories (Safer & others, 2001). When patients recall their previous day's headache pain, their current feelings sway their recollections (Eich & others, 1985). Parents of every generation bemoan the values of the next generation, partly because they misrecall their youthful values as being closer to their current values. And teens of every generation recall their parents as—depending on their current mood—wonderful or woeful (Bornstein & others, 1991).

RECONSTRUCTING OUR PAST BEHAVIOR

Memory construction enables us to revise our own histories. The hindsight bias, described in Chapter 1, involves memory revision. Hartmut Blank and his colleagues (2003) showed this when inviting University of Leipzig students, after a surprising German election outcome, to recall their voting predictions from two months previous. The students misrecalled their predictions as closer to the actual results.

Our memories reconstruct other sorts of past behaviors as well. Michael Ross, Cathy McFarland, and Garth Fletcher (1981) exposed some University of Waterloo students to a message convincing them of the desirability of toothbrushing. Later, in a supposedly different experiment, these students recalled brushing their teeth more often during the preceding two weeks than did students who had not heard the message. Likewise, people who are surveyed report smoking many fewer cigarettes than are actually sold (Hall, 1985). And they recall casting more votes than were actually recorded (Census Bureau, 1993).

Social psychologist Anthony Greenwald (1980) noted the similarity of such findings to happenings in George Orwell's novel *1984*—in which it was "necessary to remember that events happened in the desired manner." Indeed, argued Greenwald, we all have "totalitarian egos" that revise the past to suit our present views. Thus, we underreport bad behavior and overreport good behavior.

Sometimes our present view is that we've improved—in which case we may misrecall our past as more unlike the present than it actually was. This tendency resolves a puzzling pair of consistent findings: Those who participate in psychotherapy and self-improvement programs for weight control, antismoking, and exercise show only modest improvement on average. Yet they often claim considerable benefit (Myers, 2010). Michael Conway and Michael Ross (1986) explain why: Having expended so much time, effort, and money on self-improvement, people may think, "I may not be perfect now, but I was worse before; this did me a lot of good."

In Chapter 14 we will see that psychiatrists and clinical psychologists are not immune to these human tendencies. We all selectively notice, interpret, and recall events in ways that sustain our ideas. Our social judgments are a mix of observation and expectation, reason and passion.

Summing Up: Perceiving Our Social Worlds

- Our preconceptions strongly influence how we interpret and remember events. In a phenomenon called *priming*, people's prejudgments have striking effects on how they perceive and interpret information.

- Other experiments have planted judgments or false ideas in people's minds *after* they have been given information. These experiments reveal that as *before-the-fact judgments* bias our perceptions and interpretations, so *after-the-fact judgments* bias our recall.

- *Belief perseverance* is the phenomenon in which people cling to their initial beliefs and the reasons why a belief might be true, even when the basis for the belief is discredited.

- Far from being a repository for facts about the past, our memories are actually formed when we retrieve them, and subject to strong influence by the attitudes and feelings we hold at the time of retrieval.

Judging Our Social Worlds

As we have already noted, our cognitive mechanisms are efficient and adaptive, yet occasionally error-prone. Usually they serve us well. But sometimes clinicians misjudge patients, employers misjudge employees, people of one race misjudge people of another, and spouses misjudge their mates. The results can be misdiagnoses, labor strife, prejudices, and divorces. So, how—and how well—do we make intuitive social judgments?

When historians describe social psychology's first century, they will surely record 1980–2010 as the era of social cognition. By drawing on advances in cognitive psychology—in how people perceive, represent, and remember events—social psychologists have shed welcome light on how we form judgments. Let's look at what that research reveals of the marvels and mistakes of our social intuition.

Intuitive Judgments

What are our powers of intuition—of immediately knowing something without reasoning or analysis? Advocates of "intuitive management" believe we should tune into our hunches. When judging others, they say, we should plug into the nonlogical smarts of our "right brain." When hiring, firing, and investing, we should listen to our premonitions. In making judgments, we should follow the example of *Star Wars'* Luke Skywalker by switching off our computer guidance systems and trusting the force within.

Are the intuitionists right that important information is immediately available apart from our conscious analysis? Or are the skeptics correct in saying that intuition is "our knowing we are right, whether we are or not"?

Priming research suggests that the unconscious indeed controls much of our behavior. As John Bargh and Tanya Chartrand (1999) explain, "Most of a person's everyday life is determined not by their conscious intentions and deliberate choices but by mental processes that are put into motion by features of the environment and that operate outside of conscious awareness and guidance." When the light turns red, we react and hit the brake before consciously deciding to do so. Indeed, reflect Neil Macrae and Lucy Johnston (1998), "to be able to do just about anything at all (e.g., driving, dating, dancing), action initiation needs to be decoupled from the inefficient (i.e., slow, serial, resource-consuming) workings of the conscious mind, otherwise inaction inevitably would prevail."

THE POWERS OF INTUITION

"The heart has its reasons which reason does not know," observed seventeenth-century philosopher-mathematician Blaise Pascal. Three centuries later, scientists have proved Pascal correct. We know more than we know we know. Studies of our unconscious information processing confirm our limited access to what's going on in our minds (Bargh & Ferguson, 2000; Greenwald & Banaji, 1995; Strack & Deutsch, 2004). Our thinking is partly **controlled** (reflective, deliberate, and conscious) and—more than psychologists once supposed—partly **automatic** (impulsive, effortless, and without our awareness). Automatic, intuitive thinking occurs not "on-screen" but off-screen, out of sight, where reason does not go. Consider these examples of automatic thinking:

controlled processing
"Explicit" thinking that is deliberate, reflective, and conscious.

automatic processing
"Implicit" thinking that is effortless, habitual, and without awareness, roughly corresponds to "intuition."

- *Schemas* are mental concepts or templates that intuitively guide our perceptions and interpretations. Whether we hear someone speaking of religious *sects* or *sex* depends not only on the word spoken but also on how we automatically interpret the sound.

- *Emotional reactions* are often nearly instantaneous, happening before there is time for deliberate thinking. One neural shortcut takes information from the eye or the ear to the brain's sensory switchboard (the thalamus) and out to its emotional control center (the amygdala) before the thinking cortex has had any chance to intervene (LeDoux, 2002). Our ancestors who intuitively feared a sound in the bushes were usually fearing nothing. But when the sound was made by a dangerous predator they became more likely to survive to pass their genes down to us than their more deliberative cousins.

- Given sufficient *expertise,* people may intuitively know the answer to a problem. Master chess players intuitively recognize meaningful patterns that novices miss and often make their next move with only a glance at the board, as the situation cues information stored in their memory. Similarly, without knowing quite how, we recognize a friend's voice after the first spoken word of a phone conversation.

- Faced with a decision but lacking the expertise to make an informed snap judgment, our *unconscious thinking* may guide us toward a satisfying choice. That's what University of Amsterdam psychologist Ap Dijksterhuis and his co-workers (2006a, 2006b) discovered after showing people, for example, a dozen pieces of information about each of four potential apartments. Compared to people who made instant decisions or were given time to analyze the information, the most satisfying decisions were made by those who were distracted and unable to focus consciously on the problem. Although these findings are controversial (González-Vallejo & others, 2008; Newell & others, 2008), this much seems true: When facing a tough decision it often pays to take our time—even to sleep on it—and to await the intuitive result of our out-of-sight information processing.

Some things—facts, names, and past experiences—we remember explicitly (consciously). But other things—skills and conditioned dispositions—we remember *implicitly,* without consciously knowing or declaring that we know. It's true of us all but most strikingly evident in people with brain damage who cannot form new explicit memories. One such person never could learn to recognize her physician, who would need to reintroduce himself with a handshake each day. One day the physician affixed a tack to his hand, causing the patient to jump with pain. When the physician next returned, he was still unrecognized (explicitly). But the patient, retaining an implicit memory, would not shake his hand.

Equally dramatic are the cases of *blindsight.* Having lost a portion of the visual cortex to surgery or stroke, people may be functionally blind in part of their field of vision. Shown a series of sticks in the blind field, they report seeing nothing. After correctly guessing whether the sticks are vertical or horizontal, the patients are astounded when told, "You got them all right." Like the patient who "remembered" the painful handshake, these people know more than they know they know.

Consider your own taken-for-granted capacity to recognize a face. As you look at it, your brain breaks the visual information into subdimensions such as color, depth, movement, and form and works on each aspect simultaneously before reassembling the components. Finally, using automatic processing, your brain compares the perceived image with previously stored images. Voilà! Instantly and effortlessly, you recognize your grandmother. If intuition is immediately knowing something without reasoned analysis, then perceiving is intuition par excellence.

Subliminal stimuli may, as we have already noted, prime our thinking and reacting. Shown certain geometric figures for less than 0.01 second each, people may deny having seen anything more than a flash of light yet express a preference for the forms they saw.

So, many routine cognitive functions occur automatically, unintentionally, without awareness. We might remember how automatic processing helps us get through life by picturing our minds as functioning like big corporations. Our CEO—our controlled consciousness—attends to many of the most important, complex, and novel issues, while subordinates deal with routine affairs and matters requiring instant action. This delegation of resources enables us to react to many situations quickly and efficiently. The bottom line: Our brain knows much more than it tells us.

THE LIMITS OF INTUITION

We have seen how automatic, intuitive thinking can "make us smart" (Gigerenzer, 2007). Elizabeth Loftus and Mark Klinger (1992) nevertheless speak for other cognitive scientists in having doubts about the brilliance of intuition. They report "a general consensus that the unconscious may not be as smart as previously believed." For example, although subliminal stimuli can trigger a weak, fleeting response—enough to evoke a feeling if not conscious awareness—there is no evidence that commercial subliminal tapes can "reprogram your unconscious mind" for success. In fact, a significant body of evidence indicates that they can't (Greenwald, 1992).

Social psychologists have explored not only our error-prone hindsight judgments but also our capacity for illusion—for perceptual misinterpretations, fantasies, and constructed beliefs. Michael Gazzaniga (1992, 1998, 2008) reports that patients whose brain hemispheres have been surgically separated will instantly fabricate—and believe—explanations of their own puzzling behaviors. If the patient gets up and takes a few steps after the experimenter flashes the instruction "walk" to the patient's nonverbal right hemisphere, the verbal left hemisphere will instantly provide the patient with a plausible explanation ("I felt like getting a drink").

Illusory thinking also appears in the vast new literature on how we take in, store, and retrieve social information. As perception researchers study visual illusions for what they reveal about our normal perceptual mechanisms, social psychologists study illusory thinking for what it reveals about normal information processing. These researchers want to give us a map of everyday social thinking, with the hazards clearly marked.

As we examine some of these efficient thinking patterns, remember this: Demonstrations of how people create counterfeit beliefs do not prove that all beliefs are counterfeit (though, to recognize counterfeiting, it helps to know how it's done).

Overconfidence

So far we have seen that our cognitive systems process a vast amount of information efficiently and automatically. But our efficiency has a trade-off; as we interpret our experiences and construct memories, our automatic intuitions sometimes err. Usually, we are unaware of our flaws. The "intellectual conceit" evident in

DOONESBURY   ## by Garry Trudeau

judgments of past knowledge ("I knew it all along") extends to estimates of current knowledge and predictions of future behavior. We know we've messed up in the past. But we have more positive expectations for our future performance in meeting deadlines, managing relationships, following an exercise routine, and so forth (Ross & Newby-Clark, 1998).

To explore this **overconfidence phenomenon,** Daniel Kahneman and Amos Tversky (1979) gave people factual statements and asked them to fill in the blanks, as in the following sentence: "I feel 98 percent certain that the air distance between New Delhi and Beijing is more than_____ miles but less than_____ miles." Most individuals were overconfident: About 30 percent of the time, the correct answers lay outside the range they felt 98 percent confident about.

To find out whether overconfidence extends to social judgments, David Dunning and his associates (1990) created a little game show. They asked Stanford University students to guess a stranger's answers to a series of questions, such as "Would you prepare for a difficult exam alone or with others?" and "Would you rate your lecture notes as neat or messy?" Knowing the type of question but not the actual questions, the participants first interviewed their target person about background, hobbies, academic interests, aspirations, astrological sign—anything they thought might be helpful. Then, while the targets privately answered 20 of the two-choice questions, the interviewers predicted their target's answers and rated their own confidence in the predictions.

The interviewers guessed right 63 percent of the time, beating chance by 13 percent. But, on average, they *felt* 75 percent sure of their predictions. When guessing their own roommates' responses, they were 68 percent correct and 78 percent confident. Moreover, the most confident people were most likely to be overconfident. People also are markedly overconfident when judging whether someone is telling the truth or when estimating things such as the sexual history of their dating partner or the activity preferences of their roommates (DePaulo & others, 1997; Swann & Gill, 1997).

Ironically, *incompetence feeds overconfidence.* It takes competence to recognize what competence is, note Justin Kruger and David Dunning (1999). Students who score at the bottom on tests of grammar, humor, and logic are most prone to overestimating their gifts at such. Those who don't know what good logic or grammar is are often unaware that they lack it. If you make a list of all the words you can form out of the letters in "psychology," you may feel brilliant—but then stupid when

overconfidence phenomenon
The tendency to be more confident than correct—to overestimate the accuracy of one's beliefs.

The air distance between New Delhi and Beijing is 2,500 miles.

a friend starts naming the ones you missed. Deanna Caputo and Dunning (2005) recreated this phenomenon in experiments, confirming that our ignorance of our ignorance sustains our self-confidence. Follow-up studies indicate that this "ignorance of one's incompetence" occurs mostly on relatively easy-seeming tasks, such as forming words out of "psychology." On really hard tasks, poor performers more often appreciate their lack of skill (Burson & others, 2006).

Ignorance of one's incompetence helps explain David Dunning's (2005) startling conclusion from employee assessment studies that "what others see in us . . . tends to be more highly correlated with objective outcomes than what we see in ourselves." In one study, participants watched someone walk into a room, sit, read a weather report, and walk out (Borkenau & Liebler, 1993). Based on nothing more than that, their estimate of the person's intelligence correlated with the person's intelligence score about as well as did the person's own self-estimate (.30 vs. .32)! If ignorance can beget false confidence, then—yikes!—where, we may ask, are you and I unknowingly deficient?

In Chapter 2 we noted that people overestimate their long-term emotional responses to good and bad happenings. Are people better at predicting their own *behavior*? To find out, Robert Vallone and his colleagues (1990) had college students predict in September whether they would drop a course, declare a major, elect to live off campus next year, and so forth. Although the students felt, on average, 84 percent sure of those self-predictions, they were wrong nearly twice as often as they expected to be. Even when feeling 100 percent sure of their predictions, they erred 15 percent of the time.

In estimating their chances for success on a task, such as a major exam, people's confidence runs highest when the moment of truth is off in the future. By exam day, the possibility of failure looms larger and confidence typically drops (Gilovich & others, 1993; Shepperd & others, 2005). Roger Buehler and his colleagues (1994, 2002, 2003, 2005) report that most students also confidently underestimate how long it will take them to complete papers and other major assignments. They are not alone:

- *The "planning fallacy."* How much free time do you have today? How much free time do you expect you will have a month from today? Most of us overestimate how much we'll be getting done, and therefore how much free time we will have (Zauberman & Lynch, 2005). Professional planners, too, routinely underestimate the time and expense of projects. In 1969, Montreal Mayor Jean Drapeau proudly announced that a $120 million stadium with a retractable roof would be built for the 1976 Olympics. The roof was completed in 1989 and cost $120 million by itself. In 1985, officials estimated that Boston's "Big Dig" highway project would cost $2.6 billion and take until 1998. The cost ballooned to $14.6 billion and the project took until 2006.

- *Stockbroker overconfidence.* Investment experts market their services with the confident presumption that they can beat the stock market average, forgetting that for every stockbroker or buyer saying "Sell!" at a given price, there is another saying "Buy!" A stock's price is the balance point between those mutually confident judgments. Thus, incredible as it may seem, economist Burton Malkiel (2007) reports that mutual fund portfolios selected by investment analysts have not outperformed randomly selected stocks.

- *Political overconfidence.* Overconfident decision makers can wreak havoc. It was a confident Adolf Hitler who from 1939 to 1945 waged war against the rest of Europe. It was a confident Lyndon Johnson who in the 1960s invested U.S. weapons and soldiers in the effort to salvage democracy in South Vietnam. It was a confident Saddam Hussein who in 1990 marched his army into Kuwait and in 2003 promised to defeat invading armies. It was a confident George W. Bush who proclaimed that peaceful democracy would soon prevail in a liberated and thriving Iraq, with its alleged weapons of mass destruction newly destroyed.

"The wise know too well their weakness to assume infallibility; and he who knows most, knows best how little he knows."

—*THOMAS JEFFERSON,*
WRITINGS

Regarding the atomic bomb: "That is the biggest fool thing we have ever done. The bomb will never go off, and I speak as an expert in explosives."

—*ADMIRAL WILLIAM LEAHY TO*
PRESIDENT TRUMAN, 1945

What produces overconfidence? Why doesn't experience lead us to a more realistic self-appraisal? For one thing, people tend to recall their mistaken judgments as times when they were *almost* right. Philip Tetlock (1998, 1999, 2005) observed this after inviting various academic and government experts to project—from their viewpoint in the late 1980s—the future governance of the Soviet Union, South Africa, and Canada. Five years later communism had collapsed, South Africa had become a multiracial democracy, and Canada's French-speaking minority had not seceded. Experts who had felt more than 80 percent confident were right in predicting these turns of events less than 40 percent of the time. Yet, reflecting on their judgments, those who erred believed they were still basically right. I was "almost right," said many. "The hardliners almost succeeded in their coup attempt against Gorbachev." "The Quebecois separatists almost won the secessionist referendum." "But for the coincidence of de Klerk and Mandela, there would have been a much bloodier transition to black majority rule in South Africa." The Iraq war was a good idea, just badly executed, excused many of those who had supported it. Among political experts—and also stock market forecasters, mental health workers, and sports prognosticators—overconfidence is hard to dislodge.

President George W. Bush after the American invasion of Iraq. Overconfidence, as exhibited by presidents and prime ministers who have committed troops to failed wars, underlies many blunders.

CONFIRMATION BIAS

People also tend not to seek information that might disprove what they believe. P. C. Wason (1960) demonstrated this, as you can, by giving participants a sequence of three numbers—2, 4, 6—that conformed to a rule he had in mind. (The rule was simply *any three ascending numbers.*) To enable the participants to discover the rule, Wason invited each person to generate additional sets of three numbers. Each time, Wason told the person whether or not the set conformed to his rule. As soon as participants were sure they had discovered the rule, they were to stop and announce it.

The result? Seldom right but never in doubt: 23 of the 29 participants convinced themselves of a wrong rule. They typically formed some erroneous belief about the rule (for example, counting by twos) and then searched for *confirming* evidence (for example, by testing 8, 10, 12) rather than attempting to *disconfirm* their hunches. We are eager to verify our beliefs but less inclined to seek evidence that might disprove them, a phenomenon called the **confirmation bias.**

Confirmation bias helps explain why our self-images are so remarkably stable. In experiments at the University of Texas at Austin, William Swann and Stephen Read (1981; Swann & others, 1992a, 1992b, 2007) discovered that students seek, elicit, and recall feedback that confirms their beliefs about themselves. People seek as friends and spouses those who bolster their own self views—even if they think poorly of themselves (Swann & others, 1991, 2003).

Swann and Read (1981) liken this *self-verification* to how someone with a domineering self-image might behave at a party. Upon arriving, the person seeks those guests whom she knows will acknowledge her dominance. In conversation she then

"When you know a thing, to hold that you know it; and when you do not know a thing, to allow that you do not know it; this is knowledge."
—*CONFUCIUS,* ANALECTS

confirmation bias
A tendency to search for information that confirms one's preconceptions.

presents her views in ways that elicit the respect she expects. After the party, she has trouble recalling conversations in which her influence was minimal and more easily recalls her persuasiveness in the conversations that she dominated. Thus, her experience at the party confirms her self-image.

REMEDIES FOR OVERCONFIDENCE

What lessons can we draw from research on overconfidence? One lesson is to be wary of other people's dogmatic statements. Even when people are sure they are right, they may be wrong. Confidence and competence need not coincide.

Three techniques have successfully reduced the overconfidence bias. One is *prompt feedback* (Lichtenstein & Fischhoff, 1980). In everyday life, weather forecasters and those who set the odds in horse racing both receive clear, daily feedback. And experts in both groups do quite well at estimating their probable accuracy (Fischhoff, 1982).

To reduce "planning fallacy" overconfidence, people can be asked to *unpack a task*—to break it down into its subcomponents—and estimate the time required for each. Justin Kruger and Matt Evans (2004) report that doing so leads to more realistic estimates of completion time.

When people think about why an idea *might* be true, it begins to seem true (Koehler, 1991). Thus, a third way to reduce overconfidence is to get people to think of one good reason *why* their judgments *might be wrong*; that is, force them to consider disconfirming information (Koriat & others, 1980). Managers might foster more realistic judgments by insisting that all proposals and recommendations include reasons why they might *not* work.

Still, we should be careful not to undermine people's reasonable self-confidence or to destroy their decisiveness. In times when their wisdom is needed, those lacking self-confidence may shrink from speaking up or making tough decisions. Overconfidence can cost us, but realistic self-confidence is adaptive.

Heuristics: Mental Shortcuts

heuristic
A thinking strategy that enables quick, efficient judgments.

With precious little time to process so much information, our cognitive system is fast and frugal. It specializes in mental shortcuts. With remarkable ease, we form impressions, make judgments, and invent explanations. We do so by using **heuristics**—simple, efficient thinking strategies. Heuristics enable us to live and make routine decisions with minimal effort (Shah & Oppenheimer, 2008). In most situations, our snap generalizations—"That's dangerous!"—are adaptive. The speed of these intuitive guides promotes our survival. The biological purpose of thinking is less to make us right than to keep us alive. In some situations, however, haste makes error.

THE REPRESENTATIVENESS HEURISTIC

University of Oregon students were told that a panel of psychologists interviewed a sample of 30 engineers and 70 lawyers and summarized their impressions in thumbnail descriptions. The following description, they were told, was drawn at random from the sample of 30 engineers and 70 lawyers:

> Twice divorced, Frank spends most of his free time hanging around the country club. His clubhouse bar conversations often center around his regrets at having tried to follow his esteemed father's footsteps. The long hours he had spent at academic drudgery would have been better invested in learning how to be less quarrelsome in his relations with other people.
>
> *Question:* What is the probability that Frank is a lawyer rather than an engineer?

Asked to guess Frank's occupation, more than 80 percent of the students surmised he was one of the lawyers (Fischhoff & Bar-Hillel, 1984). Fair enough. But how do you suppose those estimates changed when the sample description was given to another group of students, modified to say that 70 percent were engineers? Not in the slightest. The students took no account of the base rate of engineers and lawyers; in their minds Frank was more *representative* of lawyers, and that was all that seemed to matter.

To judge something by intuitively comparing it to our mental representation of a category is to use the **representativeness heuristic.** Representativeness (typicalness) usually is a reasonable guide to reality. But, as we saw with "Frank" above, it doesn't always work. Consider Linda, who is 31, single, outspoken, and very bright. She majored in philosophy in college. As a student she was deeply concerned with discrimination and other social issues, and she participated in antinuclear demonstrations. Based on that description, would you say it is more likely that

> **a.** Linda is a bank teller.
> **b.** Linda is a bank teller and active in the feminist movement.

Most people think *b* is more likely, partly because Linda better *represents* their image of feminists (Mellers & others, 2001). But ask yourself: Is there a better chance that Linda is *both* a bank teller *and* a feminist than that she's a bank teller (whether feminist or not)? As Amos Tversky and Daniel Kahneman (1983) reminded us, the conjunction of two events cannot be more likely than either one of the events alone.

THE AVAILABILITY HEURISTIC

Consider the following: Do more people live in Iraq or in Tanzania? (See page 96.)

You probably answered according to how readily Iraqis and Tanzanians come to mind. If examples are readily *available* in our memory—as Iraqis tend to be—then we presume that other such examples are commonplace. Usually this is true, so we are often well served by this cognitive rule, called the **availability heuristic** (Table 3.1). Said simply, the more easily we recall something, the more likely it seems.

But sometimes the rule deludes us. If people hear a list of famous people of one sex (Jennifer Lopez, Venus Williams, Hillary Clinton) intermixed with an equal-size list of unfamous people of the other sex (Donald Scarr, William Wood, Mel Jasper), the famous names will later be more cognitively available. Most people will subsequently recall having heard more (in this instance) women's names (McKelvie, 1995, 1997; Tversky & Kahneman, 1973). Vivid, easy-to-imagine events, such as shark attacks or diseases with easy-to-picture symptoms, may likewise seem more likely to occur than harder-to-picture events (MacLeod & Campbell, 1992; Sherman & others, 1985).

representativeness heuristic
The tendency to presume, sometimes despite contrary odds, that someone or something belongs to a particular group if resembling (representing) a typical member.

availability heuristic
A cognitive rule that judges the likelihood of things in terms of their availability in memory. If instances of something come readily to mind, we presume it to be commonplace.

TABLE :: 3.1 Fast and Frugal Heuristics

Heuristic	Definition	Example	But May Lead to
Representativeness	Snap judgments of whether someone or something fits a category	Deciding that Carlos is a librarian rather than a trucker because he better represents one's image of librarians	Discounting other important information
Availability	Quick judgments of likelihood of events (how available in memory)	Estimating teen violence after school shootings	Overweighting vivid instances and thus, for example, fearing the wrong things

Even fictional happenings in novels, television, and movies leave images that later penetrate our judgments (Gerrig & Prentice, 1991; Green & others, 2002; Mar & Oatley, 2008). The more absorbed and "transported" the reader ("I could easily picture the events"), the more the story affects the reader's later beliefs (Diekman & others, 2000). Readers who are captivated by romance novels, for example, may gain readily available sexual scripts that influence their own sexual attitudes and behaviors.

Our use of the availability heuristic highlights a basic principle of social thinking: People are slow to deduce particular instances from a general truth, but they are remarkably quick to infer general truth from a vivid instance. No wonder that after hearing and reading stories of rapes, robberies, and beatings, 9 out of 10 Canadians overestimated—usually by a considerable margin—the percentage of crimes that involved violence (Doob & Roberts, 1988). And no wonder that South Africans, after a series of headline-grabbing gangland robberies and slayings, estimated that violent crime had almost doubled between 1998 and 2004, when actually it had decreased substantially (Wines, 2005).

The availability heuristic explains why powerful anecdotes can nevertheless be more compelling than statistical information and why perceived risk is therefore often badly out of joint with real risks (Allison & others, 1992). We fret over swine flu (H1N1) but don't bother to get vaccinated for common flu, which kills tens of thousands. We fret over extremely rare child abduction, even if we don't buckle our children in the backseat. We fear terrorism, but are indifferent to global climate change—"Armageddon in slow motion." In short, we worry about remote possibilities while ignoring higher probabilities, a phenomenon that Cass Sunstein (2007b) calls our "probability neglect."

Because news footage of airplane crashes is a readily available memory for most of us—especially since September 11, 2001—we often suppose we are more at risk traveling in commercial airplanes than in cars. Actually, from 2003 to 2005, U.S. travelers were 230 times more likely to die in a car crash than on a commercial flight covering the same distance (National Safety Council, 2008). In 2006, reports the Flight Safety Foundation, there was one airliner accident for every 4.2 million flights by Western-built commercial jets (Wald, 2008). For most air travelers, the most dangerous part of the journey is the drive to the airport.

Shortly after 9/11, as many people abandoned air travel and took to the roads, I estimated that if Americans flew 20 percent less and instead drove those unflown miles, we could expect an additional 800 traffic deaths in the ensuing year (Myers, 2001). It took a curious German researcher (why didn't I think of this?) to check that prediction against accident data, which confirmed an excess of some 350 deaths in the last three months of 2001 compared with the three-month average in the preceding five years (Gigerenzer, 2004). The 9/11 terrorists appear to have killed more people unnoticed—on America's roads—than they did with the 266 fatalities on those four planes.

Answer to Question on page 95:
Tanzania's 40 million people greatly outnumber Iraq's 28 million. Most people, having more vivid images of Iraqis, guess wrong.

By now it is clear that our naive statistical intuitions, and our resulting fears, are driven not by calculation and reason but by emotions attuned to the availability heuristic. After this book is published, there likely will be another dramatic natural or terrorist event, which will again propel our fears, vigilance, and resources in a new direction. Terrorists, aided by the media, may again achieve their objective of capturing our attention, draining our resources, and distracting us from the mundane, undramatic, insidious risks that, over time, devastate lives, such as the rotavirus that each day claims the equivalent of four 747s filled with children (Parashar & others, 2006). But then again, dramatic events can also serve to awaken us to real risks. That, say some scientists, is what happened when hurricanes Katrina and Rita in 2005 began to raise concern that global warming, by raising sea levels and spawning extreme weather, is destined to become nature's own weapon of mass destruction.

Vivid, memorable—and therefore cognitively available—events influence our perception of the social world. The resulting "probability neglect" often leads people to fear the wrong things, such as fearing flying or terrorism more than smoking, driving, or climate change. If four jumbo jets filled with children crashed every day—approximating the number of childhood diarrhea deaths resulting from the rotavirus—something would have been done about it.
Illustration by Dave Bohn.

Counterfactual Thinking

Easily imagined (cognitively available) events also influence our experiences of guilt, regret, frustration, and relief. If our team loses (or wins) a big game by one point, we can easily imagine how the game might have gone the other way, and thus we feel regret (or relief). Imagining worse alternatives helps us feel better. Imagining better alternatives, and pondering what we might do differently next time, helps us prepare to do better in the future (Epstude & Roese, 2008).

In Olympic competition, athletes' emotions after an event reflect mostly how they did relative to expectations, but also their **counterfactual thinking**—their *mentally simulating what might have been* (McGraw & others, 2005; Medvec & others, 1995). Bronze medalists (for whom an easily imagined alternative was finishing without a medal) exhibited more joy than silver medalists (who could more easily imagine having won the gold). On the medal stand, it has been said, happiness is as simple as 1-3-2. Similarly, the higher a student's score within a grade category (such as B+), the *worse* they feel (Medvec & Savitsky, 1997). The B+student who misses an A−by a point feels worse than the B+student who actually did worse and just made a B+by a point.

Such counterfactual thinking occurs when we can easily picture an alternative outcome (Kahneman & Miller, 1986; Markman & McMullen, 2003):

- If we barely miss a plane or a bus, we imagine making it *if only* we had left at our usual time, taken our usual route, not paused to talk. If we miss our connection by a half hour or after taking our usual route, it's harder to simulate a different outcome, so we feel less frustration.
- If we change an exam answer, then get it wrong, we will inevitably think "If only . . ." and will vow next time to trust our immediate intuition—although, contrary to student lore, answer changes are more often from incorrect to correct (Kruger & others, 2005).
- The team or the political candidate that barely loses will simulate over and over how they could have won (Sanna & others, 2003).

"Testimonials may be more compelling than mountains of facts and figures (as mountains of facts and figures in social psychology so compellingly demonstrate)."
—*MARK SNYDER (1988)*

counterfactual thinking
Imagining alternative scenarios and outcomes that might have happened, but didn't.

Counterfactual thinking: When *Deal or No Deal* game show contestants deal too late (walking away with a lower amount than they were previously offered) or too early (foregoing their next choice, which would have led to more money) they likely experience counterfactual thinking—imagining what might have been.

People are more often apologetic about actions than inactions (Zeelenberg & others, 1998).

Counterfactual thinking underlies our feelings of luck. When we have barely escaped a bad event—avoiding defeat with a last-minute goal or standing nearest a falling icicle—we easily imagine a negative counterfactual (losing, being hit) and therefore feel "good luck" (Teigen & others, 1999). "*Bad* luck" refers to bad events that did happen but easily might not have.

The more significant the event, the more intense the counterfactual thinking (Roese & Hur, 1997). Bereaved people who have lost a spouse or a child in a vehicle accident, or a child to sudden infant death syndrome, commonly report replaying and undoing the event (Davis & others, 1995, 1996). One friend of mine survived a head-on collision with a drunk driver that killed his wife, daughter, and mother. He recalled, "For months I turned the events of that day over and over in my mind. I kept reliving the day, changing the order of events so that the accident wouldn't occur" (Sittser, 1994).

Across Asian and Western cultures most people, however, live with less regret over things done than over things they failed to do, such as, "I wish I had been more serious in college" or "I should have told my father I loved him before he died" (Gilovich & Medvec, 1994; Rajagopal & others, 2006). In one survey of adults, the most common regret was not taking their education more seriously (Kinnier & Metha, 1989). Would we live with less regret if we dared more often to reach beyond our comfort zone—to venture out, risking failure, but at least having tried?

Illusory Thinking

Another influence on everyday thinking is our search for order in random events, a tendency that can lead us down all sorts of wrong paths.

ILLUSORY CORRELATION

illusory correlation
Perception of a relationship where none exists, or perception of a stronger relationship than actually exists.

It's easy to see a correlation where none exists. When we expect to find significant relationships, we easily associate random events, perceiving an **illusory correlation.** William Ward and Herbert Jenkins (1965) showed people the results of a hypothetical 50-day cloud-seeding experiment. They told participants which of the 50 days the clouds had been seeded and which days it rained. That information was nothing more than a random mix of results: Sometimes it rained after seeding; sometimes it didn't. Participants nevertheless became convinced—in conformity with their ideas about the effects of cloud seeding—that they really had observed a relationship between cloud seeding and rain.

Other experiments confirm that people easily misperceive random events as confirming their beliefs (Crocker, 1981; Jennings & others, 1982; Trolier & Hamilton, 1986). If we believe a correlation exists, we are more likely to notice and recall confirming instances. If we believe that premonitions correlate with events, we notice and remember the joint occurrence of the premonition and the event's later occurrence. If we believe that overweight women are unhappier, we perceive that we have witnessed such a correlation even when we have not (Viken & others, 2005). We seldom notice or remember all the times unusual events do not coincide. If, after we think about a friend, the friend calls us, we notice and remember that coincidence. We don't notice all the times we think of a friend without any ensuing call or receive a call from a friend about whom we've not been thinking.

ILLUSION OF CONTROL

Our tendency to perceive random events as related feeds an **illusion of control**—the idea that *chance events are subject to our influence.* This keeps gamblers going and makes the rest of us do all sorts of unlikely things.

GAMBLING   Ellen Langer (1977) demonstrated the illusion of control with experiments on gambling. Compared with those given an assigned lottery number, people who chose their own number demanded four times as much money when asked if they would sell their ticket. When playing a game of chance against an awkward and nervous person, they bet significantly more than when playing against a dapper, confident opponent. Being the person who throws the dice or spins the wheel increases people's confidence (Wohl & Enzle, 2002). In these and other ways, more than 50 experiments have consistently found people acting as if they can predict or control chance events (Presson & Benassi, 1996; Thompson & others, 1998).

Observations of real-life gamblers confirm these experimental findings. Dice players may throw softly for low numbers and hard for high numbers (Henslin, 1967). The gambling industry thrives on gamblers' illusions. Gamblers attribute wins to their skill and foresight. Losses become "near misses" or "flukes," or for the sports gambler, a bad call by the referee or a freakish bounce of the ball (Gilovich & Douglas, 1986).

Stock traders also like the "feeling of empowerment" that comes from being able to choose and control their own stock trades, as if their being in control can enable them to outperform the market average. One ad declared that online investing "is about control." Alas, the illusion of control breeds overconfidence and frequent losses after stock market trading costs are subtracted (Barber & Odean, 2001).

REGRESSION TOWARD THE AVERAGE   Tversky and Kahneman (1974) noted another way by which an illusion of control may arise: We fail to recognize the statistical phenomenon of **regression toward the average.** Because exam scores fluctuate partly by chance, most students who get extremely high scores on an exam will get lower scores on the next exam. If their first score is at the ceiling, their second score is more likely to fall back ("regress") toward their own average than to push the ceiling even higher. That is why a student who does consistently good work, even if never the best, will sometimes end a course at the top of the class. Conversely, the lowest-scoring students on the first exam are likely to improve. If those who scored lowest go for tutoring after the first exam, the tutors are likely to feel effective when the student improves, even if the tutoring had no effect.

Indeed, when things reach a low point, we will try anything, and whatever we try—going to a psychotherapist, starting a new diet-exercise plan, reading a self-help book—is more likely to be followed by improvement than by further deterioration. Sometimes we recognize that events are not likely to continue at an unusually

THE FAMILY CIRCUS   **By Bil Keane**

8-5
©1998 Bil Keane, Inc.
Dist. by Cowles Synd., Inc.

"I wish they didn't turn on that seatbelt sign so much! Every time they do, it gets bumpy."

illusion of control
Perception of uncontrollable events as subject to one's control or as more controllable than they are.

regression toward the average
The statistical tendency for extreme scores or extreme behavior to return toward one's average.

Regression to the average. When we are at an extremely low point, anything we try will often seem effective. "Maybe a yoga class will improve my life." Events seldom continue at an abnormal low.

good or bad extreme. Experience has taught us that when everything is going great, something will go wrong, and that when life is dealing us terrible blows, we can usually look forward to things getting better. Often, though, we fail to recognize this regression effect. We puzzle at why baseball's rookie of the year often has a more ordinary second year—did he become overconfident? Self-conscious? We forget that exceptional performance tends to regress toward normality.

By simulating the consequences of using praise and punishment, Paul Schaffner (1985) showed how the illusion of control might infiltrate human relations. He invited Bowdoin College students to train an imaginary fourth-grade boy, "Harold," to come to school by 8:30 each morning. For each school day of a three-week period, a computer displayed Harold's arrival time, which was always between 8:20 and 8:40. The students would then select a response to Harold, ranging from strong praise to strong reprimand. As you might expect, they usually praised Harold when he arrived before 8:30 and reprimanded him when he arrived after 8:30. Because Schaffner had programmed the computer to display a random sequence of arrival times, Harold's arrival time tended to improve (to regress toward 8:30) after he was reprimanded. For example, if Harold arrived at 8:39, he was almost sure to be reprimanded, and his randomly selected next-day arrival time was likely to be earlier than 8:39. Thus, *even though their reprimands were having no effect,* most students ended the experiment believing that their reprimands had been effective.

This experiment demonstrates Tversky and Kahneman's provocative conclusion: Nature operates in such a way that we often feel punished for rewarding others and rewarded for punishing them. In actuality, as every student of psychology knows, positive reinforcement for doing things right is usually more effective and has fewer negative side effects.

Moods and Judgments

Social judgment involves efficient, though fallible, information processing. It also involves our feelings: Our moods infuse our judgments. We are not cool computing machines; we are emotional creatures. The extent to which feeling infuses cognition appears in new studies comparing happy and sad individuals (Myers, 1993, 2000b). Unhappy people—especially those bereaved or depressed—tend to be more self-focused and brooding. A depressed mood motivates intense thinking—a search for information that makes one's environment more understandable and controllable (Weary & Edwards, 1994).

Happy people, by contrast, are more trusting, more loving, more responsive. If people are made temporarily happy by receiving a small gift while mall-shopping, they will report, a few moments later on an unrelated survey, that their cars and TV sets are working beautifully—better, if you took their word for it, than those belonging to folks who replied after not receiving gifts.

Moods pervade our thinking. To West Germans enjoying their team's World Cup soccer victory (Schwarz & others, 1987) and to Australians emerging from

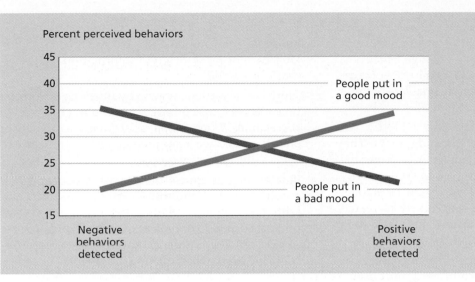

FIGURE :: 3.3

A temporary good or bad mood strongly influenced people's ratings of their videotaped behavior. Those in a bad mood detected far fewer positive behaviors.

Source: Forgas & others, 1984.

a heartwarming movie (Forgas & Moylan, 1987), people seem good-hearted, life seems wonderful. After (but not before) a 1990 football game between rivals Alabama and Auburn, victorious Alabama fans deemed war less likely and potentially devastating than did the gloomier Auburn fans (Schweitzer & others, 1992). When we are in a happy mood, the world seems friendlier, decisions are easier, good news more readily comes to mind (DeSteno & others, 2000; Isen & Means, 1983; Stone & Glass, 1986).

Let a mood turn gloomy, however, and thoughts switch onto a different track. Off come the rose-colored glasses; on come the dark glasses. Now the bad mood primes our recollections of negative events (Bower, 1987; Johnson & Magaro, 1987). Our relationships seem to sour. Our self-images take a dive. Our hopes for the future dim. And other people's behavior seems more sinister (Brown & Taylor, 1986; Mayer & Salovey, 1987).

University of New South Wales social psychologist Joseph Forgas (1999, 2008) had often been struck by how moody people's "memories and judgments change with the color of their mood." To understand this "mood infusion" he began to experiment. Imagine yourself in one such study. Using hypnosis, Forgas and his colleagues (1984) put you in a good or a bad mood and then have you watch a videotape (made the day before) of yourself talking with someone. If made to feel happy, you feel pleased with what you see, and you are able to detect many instances of your poise, interest, and social skill. If you've been put in a bad mood, viewing the same tape seems to reveal a quite different you—one who is stiff, nervous, and inarticulate (Figure 3.3). Given how your mood colors your judgments, you feel relieved at how things brighten when the experimenter switches you to a happy mood before leaving the experiment. Curiously, note Michael Ross and Garth Fletcher (1985), we don't attribute our changing perceptions to our mood shifts. Rather, the world really seems different.

Our moods color how we judge our worlds partly by bringing to mind past experiences associated with the mood. When we are in a bad mood, we have more depressing thoughts. Mood-related thoughts may distract us from complex thinking about something else. Thus, when emotionally aroused—when angry or even in a very good mood—we become more likely to make snap judgments and evaluate others based on stereotypes (Bodenhausen & others, 1994; Paulhus & Lim, 1994).

Summing Up: Judging Our Social World

- We have an enormous capacity for automatic, efficient, intuitive thinking. Our cognitive efficiency, though generally adaptive, comes at the price of occasional error. Since we are generally unaware of those errors entering our thinking, it is useful to identify ways in which we form and sustain false beliefs.

- First, we often overestimate our judgments. This *overconfidence phenomenon* stems partly from the much greater ease with which we can imagine why we might be right than why we might be wrong. Moreover, people are much more likely to search for information that can confirm their beliefs than for information that can disconfirm them.

- Second, when given compelling anecdotes or even useless information, we often ignore useful base-rate information. This is partly due to the later ease of recall of vivid information (the *availability heuristic*).

- Third, we are often swayed by illusions of correlation and personal control. It is tempting to perceive correlations where none exist (*illusory correlation*) and to think we can predict or control chance events (the *illusion of control*).

- Finally, moods infuse judgments. Good and bad moods trigger memories of experiences associated with those moods. Moods color our interpretations of current experiences. And by distracting us, moods can also influence how deeply or superficially we think when making judgments.

Explaining Our Social Worlds

People make it their business to explain other people, and social psychologists make it their business to explain people's explanations. So, how—and how accurately—do people explain others' behavior? Attribution theory suggests some answers.

Our judgments of people depend on how we explain their behavior. Depending on our explanation, we may judge killing as murder, manslaughter, self-defense, or heroism. Depending on our explanation, we may view a homeless person as lacking initiative or as victimized by job and welfare cutbacks. Depending on our explanation, we may interpret someone's friendly behavior as genuine warmth or as ingratiation.

Attributing Causality: To the Person or the Situation

We endlessly analyze and discuss why things happen as they do, especially when we experience something negative or unexpected (Bohner & others, 1988; Weiner, 1985). If worker productivity declines, do we assume the workers are getting lazier? Or has their workplace become less efficient? Does a young boy who hits his classmates have a hostile personality? Or is he responding to relentless teasing? Amy Holtzworth-Munroe and Neil Jacobson (1985, 1988) found that married people often analyze their partners' behaviors, especially their negative behaviors. Cold hostility, more than a warm hug, is likely to leave the partner wondering *why?*

Spouses' answers correlate with marriage satisfaction. Unhappy couples usually offer distress-maintaining explanations for negative acts ("she was late because she doesn't care about me"). Happy couples more often externalize ("she was late because of heavy traffic"). With positive partner behavior, their explanations similarly work either to maintain distress ("he brought me flowers because he wants sex") or to enhance the relationship ("he brought me flowers to show he loves me") (Hewstone & Fincham, 1996; McNulty & others, 2008; Weiner, 1995).

Antonia Abbey (1987, 1991; Abbey & Ross, 1998) and her colleagues have repeatedly found that men are more likely than women to attribute a woman's friendliness to mild sexual interest. That misreading of warmth as a sexual come-on—an example of **misattribution**—can contribute to behavior that women regard as sexual harassment or even rape (Farris & others, 2008; Kolivas & Gross, 2007; Pryor &

misattribution
Mistakenly attributing a behavior to the wrong source.

others, 1997). Many men believe women are flattered by repeated requests for dates, which women more often view as harassment (Rotundo & others, 2001).

Misattribution is particularly likely when men are in positions of power. A manager may misinterpret a subordinate woman's submissive or friendly behavior and, full of himself, see her in sexual terms (Bargh & Raymond, 1995). Men more often than women think about sex (see Chapter 5). Men also are more likely than women to assume that others share their feelings (recall from Chapter 2 the "false consensus effect"). Thus, a man may greatly overestimate the sexual significance of a woman's courtesy smile (Levesque & others, 2006; Nelson & LeBoeuf, 2002).

Such misattributions help explain the greater sexual assertiveness exhibited by men across the world and the greater tendency of men in various cultures, from Boston to Bombay, to justify rape by arguing that the victim consented or implied consent (Kanekar & Nazareth, 1988; Muehlenhard, 1988; Shotland, 1989). Women more often judge forcible sex as meriting conviction and a stiff sentence (Schutte & Hosch, 1997). Misattributions also help explain why the 23 percent of American women who say they have been forced into unwanted sexual behavior is eight times greater than the 3 percent of American men who say they have ever forced a woman into a sexual act (Laumann & others, 1994).

A misattribution? Date rape sometimes results from a man's misreading a woman's warmth as a sexual come-on.

Attribution theory analyzes how we explain people's behavior. The variations of attribution theory share some common assumptions. As Daniel Gilbert and Patrick Malone (1995) explain, each "construes the human skin as a special boundary that separates one set of 'causal forces' from another. On the sunny side of the epidermis are the external or situational forces that press inward upon the person, and on the meaty side are the internal or personal forces that exert pressure outward. Sometimes these forces press in conjunction, sometimes in opposition, and their dynamic interplay manifests itself as observable behavior."

attribution theory
The theory of how people explain others' behavior—for example, by attributing it either to internal dispositions (enduring traits, motives, and attitudes) or to external situations.

To what should we attribute a student's sleepiness? To lack of sleep? To boredom? Whether we make internal or external attributions depends on whether we notice her consistently sleeping in this and other classes, and on whether other students react as she does to this particular class.

Attribution theory pioneer Fritz Heider (1958) and others after him analyzed the "commonsense psychology" by which people explain everyday events. They concluded that when we observe someone acting intentionally, we sometimes attribute that person's behavior to *internal* causes (for example, the person's disposition) and sometimes to *external* causes (for example, something about the person's situation). A teacher may wonder whether a child's underachievement is due to lack of motivation and ability (a **dispositional attribution**) or to physical and social circumstances (a **situational attribution**). Also, some of us are more inclined to attribute behavior to stable personality; others tend more to attribute behavior to situations (Bastian & Haslam, 2006; Robins & others, 2004).

dispositional attribution
Attributing behavior to the person's disposition and traits.

situational attribution
Attributing behavior to the environment.

INFERRING TRAITS

Edward Jones and Keith Davis (1965) noted that we often infer that other people's actions are indicative of their intentions and dispositions. If I observe Rick making a sarcastic comment to Linda, I infer that Rick is a hostile person. Jones and Davis's "theory of correspondent inferences" specified the conditions under which people infer traits. For example, normal or expected behavior tells us less about the person than does unusual behavior. If Samantha is sarcastic in a job interview, where a person would normally be pleasant, that tells us more about Samantha than if she is sarcastic with her siblings.

spontaneous trait inference
An effortless, automatic inference of a trait after exposure to someone's behavior.

The ease with which we infer traits—a phenomenon called **spontaneous trait inference**—is remarkable. In experiments at New York University, James Uleman (1989; Uleman & others, 2008) gave students statements to remember, such as "The librarian carries the old woman's groceries across the street." The students would instantly, unintentionally, and unconsciously infer a trait. When later they were helped to recall the sentence, the most valuable clue word was not "books" (to cue librarian) or "bags" (to cue groceries) but "helpful"—the inferred trait that I suspect you, too, spontaneously attributed to the librarian. Given even just 1/10th of a second exposure to someone's face, people will spontaneously infer some personality traits (Willis & Todorov, 2006).

COMMONSENSE ATTRIBUTIONS

As the theory of correspondent inferences suggests, attributions often are rational. Pioneering attribution theorist Harold Kelley (1973) described how we explain behavior by using information about "consistency," "distinctiveness," and "consensus" (Figure 3.4).

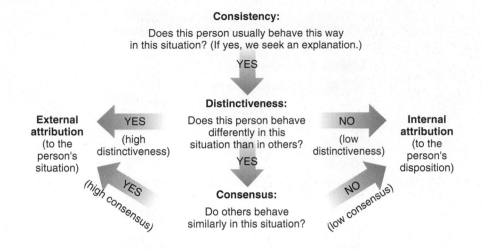

FIGURE :: 3.4

Harold Kelley's Theory
of Attributions

Three factors—consistency,
distinctiveness, and consensus—
influence whether we attribute
someone's behavior to internal
or external causes. Try creating
your own examples, such as: If
Mary and many others criticize
Steve (with consensus), and if
Mary isn't critical of others (high
distinctiveness), then we make
an external attribution (it's something about Steve). If Mary alone
(low consensus) criticizes Steve,
and if she criticizes many other
people, too (low distinctiveness),
then we are drawn to an internal
attribution (it's something about
Mary).

Consistency: How consistent is the person's behavior in this situation?

Distinctiveness: How specific is the person's behavior to this particular situation?

Consensus: To what extent do others in this situation behave similarly?

When explaining why Edgar is having trouble with his computer, most people use information concerning *consistency* (Is Edgar usually unable to get his computer to work?), *distinctiveness* (Does Edgar have trouble with other computers, or only this one?), and *consensus* (Do other people have similar problems with this make of computer?). If we learn that Edgar alone consistently has trouble with this and other computers, we likely will attribute the troubles to Edgar, not to defects in this computer.

So our commonsense psychology often explains behavior logically. But Kelley also found that people often discount a contributing cause of behavior if other plausible causes are already known. If we can specify one or two sufficient reasons a student might have done poorly on an exam, we often ignore or discount alternative possibilities (McClure, 1998). Or consider this: Would you guess that people would overestimate or underestimate the frequency of a very famous name, such as "Bush," in the American population? It surprised me—you, too?—to read Daniel Oppenheimer's (2004) discovery that people *under*estimate the frequency of hyperfamous names such as Bush relative to an equally common name such as Stevenson. They do so because their familiarity with the name can be attributed to President Bush, which leads them to discount other reasons for their familiarity with "Bush."

The Fundamental Attribution Error

Social psychology's most important lesson concerns the influence of our social environment. At any moment, our internal state, and therefore what we say and do, depends on the situation as well as on what we bring to the situation. In experiments, a slight difference between two situations sometimes greatly affects how people respond. As a professor, I have seen this when teaching the same subject at both 8:30 A.M. and 7:00 P.M. Silent stares would greet me at 8:30; at 7:00 I had to break up a party. In each situation some individuals were more talkative than others, but the difference between the two situations exceeded the individual differences.

Attribution researchers have found a common problem with our attributions. When explaining someone's behavior, we often underestimate the impact of the situation and overestimate the extent to which it reflects the individual's traits and attitudes. Thus, even knowing the effect of the time of day on classroom

FIGURE :: 3.5

The Fundamental Attribution Error

When people read a debate speech supporting or attacking Fidel Castro, they attributed corresponding attitudes to the speechwriter, even when the debate coach assigned the writer's position.

Source: Data from Jones & Harris, 1967.

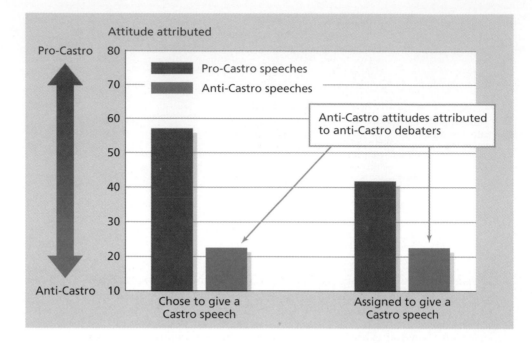

fundamental attribution error

The tendency for observers to underestimate situational influences and overestimate dispositional influences upon others' behavior. (Also called *correspondence bias,* because we so often see behavior as corresponding to a disposition.)

conversation, I found it terribly tempting to assume that the people in the 7:00 P.M. class were more extraverted than the "silent types" who came at 8:30 A.M. Likewise, we may infer that people fall because they're clumsy, rather than because they were tripped; that people smile because they're happy rather than faking friendliness; that people speed past us on the highway because they're aggressive rather than late for an important meeting.

This discounting of the situation, dubbed by Lee Ross (1977) the **fundamental attribution error,** appears in many experiments. In the first such study, Edward Jones and Victor Harris (1967) had Duke University students read debaters' speeches supporting or attacking Cuba's leader, Fidel Castro. When told that the debater chose which position to take, the students logically enough assumed it reflected the person's own attitude. But what happened when the students were told that the debate coach had assigned the position? People who are merely feigning a position write more forceful statements than you'd expect (Allison & others, 1993; Miller & others, 1990). Thus, even knowing that the debater had been told to take a pro- or anti-Castro position did not prevent students from inferring that the debater in fact had the assigned leanings (Figure 3.5). People seemed to think, "Yeah, I know he was assigned that position, but, you know, I think he really believes it."

The error is so irresistible that even when people know they are *causing* someone else's behavior, they still underestimate external influences. If individuals dictate an opinion that someone else must then express, they still tend to see the person as actually holding that opinion (Gilbert & Jones, 1986). If people are asked to be either self-enhancing or self-deprecating during an interview, they are very aware of why they are acting so. But they are *un*aware of their effect on another person. If Juan acts modestly, his naive partner Bob is likely to exhibit modesty as well. Juan will easily understand his own behavior, but he will think that poor Bob suffers from low self-esteem (Baumeister & others, 1988). In short, we tend to presume that others *are* the way they act. Observing Cinderella cowering in her oppressive home, people (ignoring the situation) infer that she is meek; dancing with her at the ball, the prince sees a suave and glamorous person.

The discounting of social constraints was evident in a thought-provoking experiment by Lee Ross and his collaborators (Ross & others, 1977). The experiment re-created Ross's firsthand experience of moving from graduate student to professor. His doctoral oral exam had proved a humbling experience as his apparently brilliant professors quizzed him on topics they specialized in. Six months later,

When viewing a movie actor playing a "good-guy" or a "bad-guy" role, we find it difficult to escape the illusion that the scripted behavior reflects an inner disposition. Perhaps that is why Leonard Nimoy, who played Mr. Spock in the original "Star Trek" series, titled one of his books *I Am Not Spock.*

Dr. Ross was himself an examiner, now able to ask penetrating questions on *his* favorite topics. Ross's hapless student later confessed to feeling exactly as Ross had a half-year before—dissatisfied with his ignorance and impressed with the apparent brilliance of the examiners.

In the experiment, with Teresa Amabile and Julia Steinmetz, Ross set up a simulated quiz game. He randomly assigned some Stanford University students to play the role of questioner, some to play the role of contestant, and others to observe. The researchers invited the questioners to make up difficult questions that would demonstrate their wealth of knowledge. Any one of us can imagine such questions using one's own domain of competence: "Where is Bainbridge Island?" "How did Mary, Queen of Scots, die?" "Which has the longer coastline, Europe or Africa?" If even those few questions have you feeling a little uninformed, then you will appreciate the results of this experiment.*

Everyone had to know that the questioner would have the advantage. Yet both contestants and observers (but not the questioners) came to the erroneous conclusion that the questioners *really were* more knowledgeable than the contestants (Figure 3.6). Follow-up research shows that these misimpressions are hardly a reflection of low social intelligence. If anything, intelligent and socially competent people are *more* likely to make the attribution error (Block & Funder, 1986).

In real life, those with social power usually initiate and control conversations, which often leads underlings to overestimate their knowledge and intelligence. Medical doctors, for example, are often presumed to be experts on all sorts of questions unrelated to medicine. Similarly, students often overestimate the brilliance of their teachers. (As in the experiment, teachers are questioners on subjects of their special expertise.) When some of these students later become teachers, they are usually amazed to discover that teachers are not so brilliant after all.

To illustrate the fundamental attribution error, most of us need look no further than our own experiences. Determined to make some new friends, Bev plasters a smile on her face and anxiously plunges into a party. Everyone else seems quite relaxed and happy as they laugh and talk with one another. Bev wonders to herself, "Why is everyone always so at ease in groups like this while I'm feeling shy and

---

* Bainbridge Island is across Puget Sound from Seattle. Mary was ordered beheaded by her cousin Queen Elizabeth I. Although the African continent is more than double the area of Europe, Europe's coastline is longer. (It is more convoluted, with lots of harbors and inlets, a geographical fact that contributed to its role in the history of maritime trade.)

FIGURE :: 3.6

Both contestants and observers of a simulated quiz game assumed that a person who had been randomly assigned the role of questioner was far more knowledgeable than the contestant. Actually the assigned roles of questioner and contestant simply made the questioner seem more knowledgeable. The failure to appreciate this illustrates the fundamental attribution error.

Source: Data from Ross, Amabile, & Steinmetz, 1977.

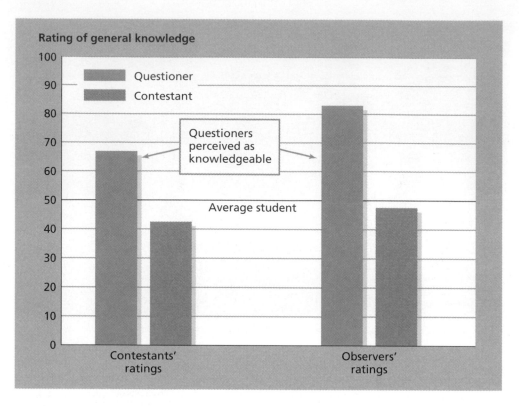

tense?" Actually, everyone else is feeling nervous, too, and making the same attribution error in assuming that Bev and the others *are* as they *appear*—confidently convivial.

WHY DO WE MAKE THE ATTRIBUTION ERROR?

So far we have seen a bias in the way we explain other people's behavior: We often ignore powerful situational determinants. Why do we tend to underestimate the situational determinants of others' behavior but not of our own?

People often attribute keen intelligence to those, such as teachers and quiz show hosts, who test others' knowledge.

PERSPECTIVE AND SITUATIONAL AWARENESS

Actor versus Observer Perspectives? Attribution theorists pointed out that we observe others from a different perspective than we observe ourselves (Jones, 1976; Jones & Nisbett, 1971). When we act, the *environment* commands our attention. When we watch another person act, that *person* occupies the center of our attention and the environment becomes relatively invisible. Auschwitz commandant Rudolph Höss (1959), while acting as a good SS officer "who could not show the slightest trace of emotion," professed inner anguish over his genocidal actions, saying he felt "pity so great that I longed to vanish from the scene." Yet he inferred that his similarly stoic Jewish inmates were uncaring—a "racial characteristic," he presumed—as they led fellow inmates to the gas chambers.

From his analysis of 173 studies, Bertram Malle (2006) concluded that the actor-observer difference is minimal. When our action feels intentional and admirable, we attribute it to our own good reasons, not to the situation. It's only when we behave badly that we're more likely to attribute our behavior to the situation, while someone observing us may spontaneously infer a trait.

The fundamental attribution error: observers underestimating the situation. Driving into a gas station, we may think the person parked at the second pump (blocking access to the first) is inconsiderate. That person, having arrived when the first pump was in use, attributes her behavior to the situation.

The Camera Perspective Bias.   In some experiments, people have viewed a videotape of a suspect confessing during a police interview. If they viewed the confession through a camera focused on the suspect, they perceived the confession as genuine. If they viewed it through a camera focused on the detective, they perceived it as more coerced (Lassiter & others, 1986, 2005, 2007). The camera perspective influenced people's guilt judgments even when the judge instructed them not to allow this to happen (Lassiter & others, 2002).

In courtrooms, most confession videotapes focus on the confessor. As we might expect, noted Daniel Lassiter and Kimberly Dudley (1991), such tapes yield a nearly 100 percent conviction rate when played by prosecutors. Aware of this research, reports Lassiter, New Zealand has made it a national policy that police interrogations be filmed with equal focus on the officer and the suspect, such as by filming them with side profiles of both.

Perspectives Change with Time.   As the once-visible person recedes in their memory, observers often give more and more credit to the situation. As we saw above in the groundbreaking attribution error experiment by Edward Jones and Victor Harris (1967), immediately after hearing someone argue an assigned position, people assume that's how the person really felt. Jerry Burger and M. L. Palmer (1991) found that a week later they are much more ready to credit the situational constraints. The day after a presidential election, Burger and Julie Pavelich (1994) asked voters why the election turned out as it did. Most attributed the outcome to the candidates' personal traits and positions (the winner from the incumbent party was likable). When they asked other voters the same question a year later, only a third attributed the verdict to the candidates. More people now credited circumstances, such as the country's good mood and the robust economy.

Let's make this personal: Are you generally quiet, talkative, or does it depend on the situation? "Depends on the situation" is a common answer. But when asked to describe a friend—or to describe what they were like five years ago—people more often ascribe trait descriptions. When recalling our past, we become like observers of someone else, note researchers Emily Pronin and Lee Ross (2006). For most of us, the "old you" is someone other than today's "real you." We regard our distant past selves (and our distant future selves) almost as if they were other people occupying our body.

"And in imagination he began to recall the best moments of his pleasant life. . . . But the child who had experienced that happiness existed no longer, it was like a reminiscence of somebody else."
—*LEO TOLSTOY,* THE DEATH OF IVAN ILYICH, *1886*

Self-Awareness. Circumstances can also shift our perspective on ourselves. Seeing ourselves on television redirects our attention to ourselves. Seeing ourselves in a mirror, hearing our tape-recorded voices, having our pictures taken, or filling out biographical questionnaires similarly focuses our attention inward, making us *self-*conscious instead of *situation-*conscious. Looking back on ill-fated relationships that once seemed like the unsinkable *Titanic,* people can more easily see the icebergs (Berscheid, 1999).

self-awareness

A self-conscious state in which attention focuses on oneself. It makes people more sensitive to their own attitudes and dispositions.

Robert Wicklund, Shelley Duval, and their collaborators have explored the effects of **self-awareness** (Duval & Wicklund, 1972; Silvia & Duval, 2001). When our attention focuses upon ourselves, we often attribute responsibility to ourselves. Allan Fenigstein and Charles Carver (1978) demonstrated this by having students imagine themselves in hypothetical situations. Some students were made self-aware by thinking they were hearing their own heartbeats while pondering the situation. Compared with those who thought they were just hearing extraneous noises, the self-aware students saw themselves as more responsible for the imagined outcome.

Some people are typically quite self-conscious. In experiments, people who report themselves as privately self-conscious (who agree with statements such as "I'm generally attentive to my inner feelings") behave similarly to people whose attention has been self-focused with a mirror (Carver & Scheier, 1978). Thus, people whose attention focuses on themselves—either briefly during an experiment or because they are self-conscious persons—view themselves more as observers typically do; they attribute their behavior more to internal factors and less to the situation.

All these experiments point to a reason for the attribution error: *We find causes where we look for them.* To see this in your own experience, consider: Would you say your social psychology instructor is a quiet or a talkative person?

My guess is you inferred that he or she is fairly outgoing. But consider: Your attention focuses on your instructor while he or she behaves in a public context that demands speaking. The instructor also observes his or her own behavior in many different situations—in the classroom, in meetings, at home. "Me talkative?" your instructor might say. "Well, it all depends on the situation. When I'm in class or with good friends, I'm rather outgoing. But at conventions and in unfamiliar situations I feel and act rather shy." Because we are acutely aware of how our behavior varies with the situation, we see ourselves as more variable than other people (Baxter & Goldberg, 1987; Kammer, 1982; Sande & others, 1988). "Nigel is uptight, Fiona is relaxed. With me it varies."

Focusing on the person. Would you infer that your professor for this course, or the professor shown here, is naturally outgoing?

CULTURAL DIFFERENCES Cultures also influence attribution error (Ickes, 1980; Watson, 1982). A Western world-view predisposes people to assume that people, not situations, cause events. Internal explanations are more socially approved (Jellison & Green, 1981). "You can do it!" we are assured by the pop psychology of positive-thinking Western culture. You get what you deserve and deserve what you get.

As children grow up in Western culture, they learn to explain behavior in terms of the other's personal characteristics (Rholes & others, 1990; Ross, 1981). As a first-grader, one of my sons brought home an example. He unscrambled the words "gate the sleeve caught Tom on his" into "The gate caught Tom on his sleeve." His teacher, applying the Western cultural assumptions of the curriculum materials, marked that wrong. The "right" answer located the cause within Tom: "Tom caught his sleeve on the gate."

The fundamental attribution error occurs across varied cultures (Krull & others, 1999). Yet people in Eastern Asian cultures are somewhat more sensitive to the importance of situations. Thus, when aware of the social context, they are less inclined to assume that others' behavior corresponds to their traits (Choi & others, 1999; Farwell & Weiner, 2000; Masuda & Kitayama, 2004).

Some languages promote external attributions. Instead of "I was late," Spanish idiom allows one to say, "The clock caused me to be late." In collectivist cultures, people less often perceive others in terms of personal dispositions (Lee & others, 1996; Zebrowitz-McArthur, 1988). They are less likely to spontaneously interpret a behavior as reflecting an inner trait (Newman, 1993). When told of someone's actions, Hindus in India are less likely than Americans to offer dispositional explanations ("She is kind") and more likely to offer situational explanations ("Her friends were with her") (Miller, 1984).

The fundamental attribution error is *fundamental* because it colors our explanations in basic and important ways. Researchers in Britain, India, Australia, and the United States have found that people's attributions predict their attitudes toward the poor and the unemployed (Furnham, 1982; Pandey & others, 1982; Skitka, 1999; Wagstaff, 1983; Zucker & Weiner, 1993). Those who attribute poverty and unemployment to personal dispositions ("They're just lazy and undeserving") tend to adopt political positions unsympathetic to such people (Figure 3.7). This *dispositional attribution* ascribes behavior to the person's disposition and traits. Those who make *situational attributions* ("If you or I were to live with the same overcrowding, poor education, and discrimination, would we be any better off?") tend to adopt political positions that offer more direct support to the poor.

Can we benefit from being aware of the attribution error? I once assisted with some interviews for a faculty position. One candidate was interviewed by six of us at once; each of us had the opportunity to ask two or three questions. I came away thinking, "What a stiff, awkward person he is." The second candidate I met privately over coffee, and we immediately discovered we had a close, mutual friend. As we talked, I became increasingly impressed by what a "warm, engaging, stimulating person she is." Only later did I remember the fundamental attribution error

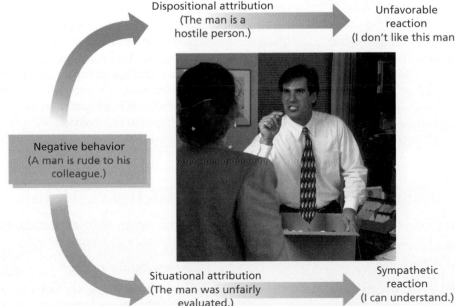

Dispositional attribution
(The man is a hostile person.)

Unfavorable reaction
(I don't like this man.)

Negative behavior
(A man is rude to his colleague.)

Situational attribution
(The man was unfairly evaluated.)

Sympathetic reaction
(I can understand.)

FIGURE :: 3.7

Attributions and Reactions

How we explain someone's negative behavior determines how we feel about it.

and reassess my analysis. I had attributed his stiffness and her warmth to their dispositions; in fact, I later realized, such behavior resulted partly from the difference in their interview situations.

WHY WE STUDY ATTRIBUTION ERRORS

This chapter, like the one before it, explains some foibles and fallacies in our social thinking. Reading about these may make it seem, as one of my students put it, that "social psychologists get their kicks out of playing tricks on people." Actually, the experiments are not designed to demonstrate "what fools these mortals be" (although some of the experiments are rather amusing). Rather, their purpose is to reveal how we think about ourselves and others.

If our capacity for illusion and self-deception is shocking, remember that our modes of thought are generally adaptive. Illusory thinking is often a by-product of our mind's strategies for simplifying complex information. It parallels our perceptual mechanisms, which generally give us useful images of the world but sometimes lead us astray.

A second reason for focusing on thinking biases such as the fundamental attribution error is humanitarian. One of social psychology's "great humanizing messages," note Thomas Gilovich and Richard Eibach (2001), is that people should not always be blamed for their problems. "More often than people are willing to acknowledge," they conclude, "failure, disability, and misfortune are . . . the product of real environmental causes."

A third reason for focusing on biases is that we are mostly unaware of them and can benefit from greater awareness. As with other biases, such as the self-serving bias (Chapter 2), people see themselves as less susceptible than others to attribution errors (Pronin, 2008). My hunch is that you will find more surprises, more challenges, and more benefit in an analysis of errors and biases than you would in a string of testimonies to the human capacity for logic and intellectual achievement. That is also why world literature so often portrays pride and other human failings. Social psychology aims to expose us to fallacies in our thinking in the hope that we will become more rational, more in touch with reality. The hope is not in vain: Psychology students explain behavior less simplistically than similarly intelligent natural science students (Fletcher & others, 1986).

"Most poor people are not lazy. . . . They catch the early bus. They raise other people's children. They clean the streets. No, no, they're not lazy."

—*THE REVEREND JESSE JACKSON, ADDRESS TO THE DEMOCRATIC NATIONAL CONVENTION, JULY 1988*

Summing Up: Explaining Our Social World

- *Attribution theory* involves how we explain people's behavior. Misattribution—attributing a behavior to the wrong source—is a major factor in sexual harassment, as a person in power (typically male) interprets friendliness as a sexual come-on.

- Although we usually make reasonable attributions, we often commit the *fundamental attribution error* (also called *correspondence bias*) when explaining other people's behavior. We attribute their behavior so much to their inner traits and attitudes that we discount situational constraints, even when those are obvious. We make this attribution error partly because when we watch someone act, that *person* is the focus of our attention and the situation is relatively invisible. When *we* act, our attention is usually on what we are reacting to—the situation is more visible.

Expectations of Our Social Worlds

Having considered how we explain and judge others—efficiently, adaptively, but sometimes erroneously—we conclude this chapter by pondering the effects of our social judgments. Do our social beliefs matter? Do they change reality?

Our social beliefs and judgments do matter. They influence how we feel and act, and by so doing may help generate their own reality. When our ideas lead us to act

focus
ON   The Self-Fulfilling Psychology of the Stock Market

On the evening of January 6, 1981, Joseph Granville, a popular Florida investment adviser, wired his clients: "Stock prices will nosedive; sell tomorrow." Word of Granville's advice soon spread, and January 7 became the heaviest day of trading in the previous history of the New York Stock Exchange. All told, stock values lost $40 billion.

Nearly a half-century ago, John Maynard Keynes likened such stock market psychology to the popular beauty contests then conducted by London newspapers. To win, one had to pick the six faces out of a hundred that were, in turn, chosen most frequently by the other newspaper contestants. Thus, as Keynes wrote, "Each competitor has to pick not those faces which he himself finds prettiest, but those which he thinks likeliest to catch the fancy of the other competitors."

Investors likewise try to pick not the stocks that touch their fancy but the stocks that other investors will favor. The name of the game is predicting others' behavior. As one Wall Street fund manager explained, "You may or may not agree with Granville's view—but that's usually beside the point." If you think his advice will cause others to sell, then you want to sell quickly, before prices

drop more. If you expect others to buy, you buy now to beat the rush.

The self-fulfilling psychology of the stock market worked to an extreme on Monday, October 19, 1987, when the Dow Jones Industrial Average lost 20 percent. Part of what happens during such crashes is that the media and the rumor mill focus on whatever bad news is available to explain them. Once reported, the explanatory news stories further diminish people's expectations, causing declining prices to fall still lower. The process also works in reverse by amplifying good news when stock prices are rising.

In April of 2000, the volatile technology market again demonstrated a self-fulfilling psychology, now called "momentum investing." After two years of eagerly buying stocks (because prices were rising), people started frantically selling them (because prices were falling). Such wild market swings—"irrational exuberance" followed by a crash—are mainly self-generated, noted economist Robert Shiller (2000). In 2008 and 2009, the market psychology headed south again as another bubble burst.

in ways that produce their apparent confirmation, they have become what sociologist Robert Merton (1948) termed **self-fulfilling prophecies**—beliefs that lead to their own fulfillment. If, led to believe that their bank is about to crash, its customers race to withdraw their money, then their false perceptions may create reality, noted Merton. If people are led to believe that stocks are about to soar, they will indeed. (See "Focus On: The Self-Fulfilling Psychology of the Stock Market.")

In his well-known studies of *experimenter bias*, Robert Rosenthal (1985, 2006) found that research participants sometimes live up to what they believe experimenters expect of them. In one study, experimenters asked individuals to judge the success of people in various photographs. The experimenters read the same instructions to all their participants and showed them the same photos. Nevertheless, experimenters who expected their participants to see the photographed people as successful obtained higher ratings than did those who expected their participants to see the people as failures. Even more startling—and controversial—are reports that teachers' beliefs about their students similarly serve as self-fulfilling prophecies. If a teacher believes a student is good at math, will the student do well in the class? Let's examine this.

self-fulfilling prophecy
A belief that leads to its own fulfillment.

Rosenthal (2008) recalls submitting a paper describing his early experiments on experimenter bias to a leading journal and to an American Association for the Advancement of Science prize competition. On the same day, some weeks later, he received a letter from the journal rejecting his paper, and from the association naming it the year's best social science research. In science, as in everyday life, some people appreciate what others do not, which is why it often pays to try and, when rebuffed, to try again.

Teacher Expectations and Student Performance

Teachers do have higher expectations for some students than for others. Perhaps you have detected this after having a brother or sister precede you in school, or after receiving a label such as "gifted" or "learning disabled," or after being tracked with "high-ability" or "average-ability" students. Perhaps conversation in the teachers' lounge sent your reputation ahead of you. Or perhaps your new teacher scrutinized your school file or discovered your family's social status. It's clear that teachers' evaluations correlate with student achievement: Teachers think well of students who do well. That's mostly because teachers accurately perceive their students' abilities and achievements (Jussim, 2005).

But are teachers' evaluations ever a *cause* as well as a consequence of student performance? One correlational study of 4,300 British schoolchildren by William Crano and Phyllis Mellon (1978) suggested yes. Not only is high performance followed by higher teacher evaluations, but the reverse is true as well.

Could we test this "teacher-expectations effect" experimentally? Pretend we gave a teacher the impression that Dana, Sally, Todd, and Manuel—four randomly selected students—are unusually capable. Will the teacher give special treatment to these four and elicit superior performance from them? In a now-famous experiment, Rosenthal and Lenore Jacobson (1968) reported precisely that. Randomly selected children in a San Francisco elementary school who were said (on the basis of a fictitious test) to be on the verge of a dramatic intellectual spurt did then spurt ahead in IQ score.

That dramatic result seemed to suggest that the school problems of "disadvantaged" children might reflect their teachers' low expectations. The findings were soon publicized in the national media as well as in many college textbooks. However, further analysis—which was not as highly publicized—revealed the teacher-expectations effect to be not as powerful and reliable as this initial study had led many people to believe (Spitz, 1999). By Rosenthal's own count, in only about 4 in 10 of the nearly 500 published experiments did expectations significantly affect performance (Rosenthal, 1991, 2002). Low expectations do not doom a capable child, nor do high expectations magically transform a slow learner into a valedictorian. Human nature is not so pliable.

High expectations do, however, seem to boost low achievers, for whom a teacher's positive attitude may be a hope-giving breath of fresh air (Madon & others, 1997). How are such expectations transmitted? Rosenthal and other investigators report that teachers look, smile, and nod more at "high-potential students." Teachers also may teach more to their "gifted" students, set higher goals for them, call on them more, and give them more time to answer (Cooper, 1983; Harris & Rosenthal, 1985, 1986; Jussim, 1986).

In one study, Elisha Babad, Frank Bernieri, and Rosenthal (1991) videotaped teachers talking to, or about, unseen students for whom they held high or low expectations. A random 10-second clip of either the teacher's voice or the teacher's face was enough to tell viewers—both children and adults—whether this was a good or a poor student and how much the teacher liked the student. (You read that right: 10 seconds.) Although teachers may think they can conceal their feelings and behave impartially toward the class, students are acutely sensitive to teachers' facial expressions and body movements (Figure 3.8).

Reading the experiments on teacher expectations makes me wonder about the effect of *students'* expectations upon their teachers. You no doubt begin many of your courses having heard "Professor Smith is interesting" and "Professor Jones is a bore." Robert Feldman and Thomas Prohaska (1979; Feldman & Theiss, 1982)

To judge a teacher or professor's overall warmth and enthusiasm also takes but a thin slice of behavior— mere seconds (Ambady & Rosenthal, 1992, 1993).

FIGURE :: 3.8

Self-Fulfilling Prophecies

Teacher expectations can become self-fulfilling prophecies. But for the most part, teachers' expectations accurately reflect reality (Jussim & Harber, 2005).

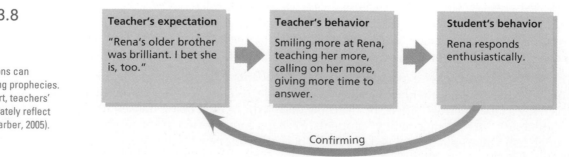

Teacher's expectation	Teacher's behavior	Student's behavior
"Rena's older brother was brilliant. I bet she is, too."	Smiling more at Rena, teaching her more, calling on her more, giving more time to answer.	Rena responds enthusiastically.

Confirming

found that such expectations can affect both student and teacher. Students in a learning experiment who expected to be taught by an excellent teacher perceived their teacher (who was unaware of their expectations) as more competent and interesting than did students with low expectations. Furthermore, the students actually learned more. In a later experiment, women who were led to expect their male instructor to be sexist had a less positive experience with him, performed worse, and rated him as less competent than did women not given the sexist expectation (Adams & others, 2006).

Were these results due entirely to the students' perceptions, or also to a self-fulfilling prophecy that affected the teacher? In a follow-up experiment, Feldman and Prohaska videotaped teachers and had observers rate their performances. Teachers were judged most capable when assigned a student who nonverbally conveyed positive expectations.

To see whether such effects might also occur in actual classrooms, a research team led by David Jamieson (1987) experimented with four Ontario high school classes taught by a newly transferred teacher. During individual interviews, they told students in two of the classes that both other students and the research team rated the teacher very highly. Compared with the control classes, students who were given positive expectations paid better attention during class. At the end of the teaching unit, they also got better grades and rated the teacher as clearer in her teaching. The attitudes that a class has toward its teacher are as important, it seems, as the teacher's attitude toward the students.

Getting from Others What We Expect

So the expectations of experimenters and teachers, though usually reasonably accurate, occasionally act as self-fulfilling prophecies. How widespread are self-fulfilling prophecies? Do we get from others what we expect of them? Studies show that self-fulfilling prophecies also operate in work settings (with managers who have high or low expectations), in courtrooms (as judges instruct juries), and in simulated police contexts (as interrogators with guilty or innocent expectations interrogate and pressure suspects) (Kassin & others, 2003; Rosenthal, 2003, 2006).

Do self-fulfilling prophecies color our personal relationships? There are times when negative expectations of someone lead us to be extra nice to that person, which induces him or her to be nice in return—thus *dis*confirming our expectations. But a more common finding in studies of social interaction is that, yes, we do to some extent get what we expect (Olson & others, 1996).

In laboratory games, hostility nearly always begets hostility: People who perceive their opponents as noncooperative will readily induce them to be noncooperative (Kelley & Stahelski, 1970). Each party's perception of the other as aggressive, resentful, and vindictive induces the other to display those behaviors in self-defense, thus creating a vicious self-perpetuating circle. In another experiment, people anticipated interacting with another person of a different race. When led to expect that the person disliked interacting with someone of their race, they felt more anger and displayed more hostility toward the person (Butz & Plant, 2006). Likewise, whether I expect my wife to be in a bad mood or in a loving mood may affect how I relate to her, thereby inducing her to confirm my belief.

So, do intimate relationships prosper when partners idealize each other? Are positive illusions of the other's virtues self-fulfilling? Or are they more often self-defeating, by creating high expectations that can't be met? Among University of Waterloo dating couples followed by Sandra Murray and her associates (1996a, 1996b, 2000), positive ideals of one's partner were good omens. Idealization helped buffer conflict, bolster satisfaction, and turn self-perceived frogs into princes or princesses. When someone loves and admires us, it helps us become more the person he or she imagines us to be.

When dating couples deal with conflicts, hopeful optimists and their partners tend to perceive each other as engaging constructively. Compared to those with

Behavioral confirmation. When English soccer fans came to France for the 1998 World Cup, they were expected to live up to their reputation as aggressive "hooligans." Local French youth and police, expecting hooligan behavior, reportedly displayed hosility toward the English, who retaliated, thus confirming the expectation (Klein & Snyder, 2003).

behavioral confirmation

A type of self-fulfilling prophecy whereby people's social expectations lead them to behave in ways that cause others to confirm their expectations.

more pessimistic expectations, they then feel more supported and more satisfied with the outcome (Srivastava & others, 2006). Among married couples, too, those who worry that their partner doesn't love and accept them interpret slight hurts as rejections, which motivates them to devalue the partner and distance themselves. Those who presume their partner's love and acceptance respond less defensively, read less into stressful events, and treat the partner better (Murray & others, 2003). Love helps create its presumed reality.

Several experiments conducted by Mark Snyder (1984) at the University of Minnesota show how, once formed, erroneous beliefs about the social world can induce others to confirm those beliefs, a phenomenon called **behavioral confirmation.** In a classic study, Snyder, Elizabeth Tanke, and Ellen Berscheid (1977) had male students talk on the telephone with women they thought (from having been shown a picture) were either attractive or unattractive. Analysis of just the women's comments during the conversations revealed that the supposedly attractive women spoke more warmly than the supposedly unattractive women. The men's erroneous beliefs had become a self-fulfilling prophecy by leading them to act in a way that influenced the women to fulfill the men's stereotype that beautiful people are desirable people.

Behavioral confirmation also occurs as people interact with partners holding mistaken beliefs. People who are believed lonely behave less sociably (Rotenberg & others, 2002). Men who are believed sexist behave less favorably toward women (Pinel, 2002). Job interviewees who are believed to be warm behave more warmly.

Imagine yourself as one of the 60 young men or 60 young women in an experiment by Robert Ridge and Jeffrey Reber (2002). Each man is to interview one of the women to assess her suitability for a teaching assistant position. Before doing so, he is told either that she feels attracted to him (based on his answers to a biographical questionnaire) or not attracted. (Imagine being told that someone you were about to meet reported considerable interest in getting to know you and in dating you, or none whatsoever.) The result was behavioral confirmation: Applicants believed to feel an attraction exhibited more flirtatiousness (and without being aware of doing so). Ridge and Reber believe that this process, like the misattribution phenomenon we discussed earlier, may be one of the roots of sexual harassment. If a woman's behavior seems to confirm a man's beliefs, he may then escalate his overtures until they become sufficiently overt for the woman to recognize and interpret them as inappropriate or harassing.

Expectations influence children's behavior, too. After observing the amount of litter in three classrooms, Richard Miller and his colleagues (1975) had the teacher and others repeatedly tell one class that they should be neat and tidy. This persuasion increased the amount of litter placed in wastebaskets from 15 to 45 percent, but only temporarily. Another class, which also had been placing only 15 percent of its litter in wastebaskets, was repeatedly congratulated for being so neat and tidy. After eight days of hearing this, and still two weeks later, these children were fulfilling the expectation by putting more than 80 percent of their litter in wastebaskets. Tell children they are hardworking and kind (rather than lazy and mean), and they may live up to their labels.

These experiments help us understand how social beliefs, such as stereotypes about people with disabilities or about people of a particular race or sex, may be self-confirming. How others treat us reflects how we and others have treated them.

A note of caution: As with every social phenomenon, the tendency to confirm others' expectations has its limits. Expectations often predict behavior simply because they are accurate (Jussim, 2005).

> "The more he treated her as though she were really very nice, the more Lotty expanded and became really very nice, and the more he, affected in his turn, became really very nice himself; so that they went round and round, not in a vicious but in a highly virtuous circle."
> —*ELIZABETH VON ARNIM*, THE ENCHANTED APRIL, 1922

Summing Up: Expectations of Our Social World

- Our beliefs sometimes take on lives of their own. Usually, our beliefs about others have a basis in reality. But studies of experimenter bias and teacher expectations show that an erroneous belief that certain people are unusually capable (or incapable) can lead teachers and researchers to give those people special treatment. This may elicit superior (or inferior) performance and, therefore, seem to confirm an assumption that is actually false.

- Similarly, in everyday life we often get *behavioral confirmation* of what we expect. Told that someone we are about to meet is intelligent and attractive, we may come away impressed with just how intelligent and attractive he or she is.

Conclusions

Social cognition studies reveal that our information-processing powers are impressive for their efficiency and adaptiveness ("in apprehension how like a god!" exclaimed Shakespeare's Hamlet). Yet we are also vulnerable to predictable errors and misjudgments ("headpiece filled with straw," said T. S. Eliot). What practical lessons, and what insights into human nature, can we take home from this research?

We have reviewed reasons why people sometimes form false beliefs. We cannot easily dismiss these experiments: Most of their participants were intelligent people, often students at leading universities. Moreover, people's intelligence scores are uncorrelated with their vulnerability to many different thinking biases (Stanovich & West, 2008). One can be very smart and exhibit seriously bad judgment.

Trying hard also doesn't eliminate thinking biases. These predictable distortions and biases occurred even when payment for right answers motivated people to think optimally. As one researcher concluded, the illusions "have a persistent quality not unlike that of perceptual illusions" (Slovic, 1972).

Research in cognitive social psychology thus mirrors the mixed review given humanity in literature, philosophy, and religion. Many research psychologists have spent lifetimes exploring the awesome capacities of the human mind. We are smart enough to have cracked our own genetic code, to have invented talking computers, to have sent people to the moon. Three cheers for human reason.

Well, two cheers—because the mind's premium on efficient judgment makes our intuition more vulnerable to misjudgment than we suspect. With remarkable ease, we form and sustain false beliefs. Led by our preconceptions, feeling overconfident, persuaded by vivid anecdotes, perceiving correlations and control even where none may exist, we construct our social beliefs and then influence others to confirm them. "The naked intellect," observed novelist Madeleine L'Engle, "is an extraordinarily inaccurate instrument."

But have these experiments just been intellectual tricks played on hapless participants, thus making them look worse than they are? Richard Nisbett and Lee Ross (1980) contended that, if anything, laboratory procedures overestimate our intuitive powers. The experiments usually present people with clear evidence and warn them that their reasoning ability is being tested. Seldom does real life say to us: "Here is some evidence. Now put on your intellectual Sunday best and answer these questions."

Often our everyday failings are inconsequential, but not always so. False impressions, interpretations, and beliefs can produce serious consequences. Even small biases can have profound social effects when we are making important social judgments: Why are so many people homeless? unhappy? homicidal? Does my friend love me or my money? Cognitive biases even creep into sophisticated scientific thinking. Human nature has hardly changed in the 3,000 years since the Old Testament psalmist noted that "no one can see his own errors."

Is this too cynical? Leonard Martin and Ralph Erber (2005) invite us to imagine that an intelligent being swooped down and begged for information that would help it understand the human species. When you hand it this social psychology text, the alien says "thank you" and zooms back off into space. After (I'd like to presume) resolving your remorse over giving up this book, how would you feel about having offered social psychology's analysis? Joachim Krueger and David Funder (2003a, 2003b) wouldn't feel too good. Social psychology's preoccupation with human foibles needs balancing with "a more positive view of human nature," they argue.

Fellow social psychologist Lee Jussim (2005) agrees, adding, "Despite the oft-demonstrated existence of a slew of logical flaws and systematic biases in lay judgment and social perception, such as the fundamental attribution error, false consensus, over-reliance on imperfect heuristics, self-serving biases, etc., people's perceptions of one another are surprisingly (though rarely perfectly) accurate." The elegant analyses of the imperfections of our thinking are themselves a tribute to human wisdom. Were one to argue that all human thought is illusory, the assertion would be self-refuting, for it, too, would be but an illusion. It would be logically equivalent to contending "All generalizations are false, including this one."

As medical science assumes that any given body organ serves a function, so behavioral scientists find it useful to assume that our modes of thought and behavior are adaptive (Funder, 1987; Kruglanski & Ajzen, 1983; Swann, 1984). The rules of thought that produce false beliefs and striking deficiencies in our statistical intuition usually serve us well. Frequently, the errors are a by-product of our mental shortcuts that simplify the complex information we receive.

Nobel laureate psychologist Herbert Simon (1957) was among the modern researchers who first described the bounds of human reason. Simon contends that to cope with reality, we simplify it. Consider the complexity of a chess game: The number of possible games is greater than the number of particles in the universe. How do we cope? We adopt some simplifying rules—heuristics. These heuristics sometimes lead us to defeat. But they do enable us to make efficient snap judgments.

Illusory thinking can likewise spring from useful heuristics that aid our survival. In many ways, heuristics "make us smart" (Gigerenzer, 2007). The belief in our power to control events helps maintain hope and effort. If things are sometimes subject to control and sometimes not, we maximize our outcomes by positive thinking.

"In creating these problems, we didn't set out to fool people. All our problems fooled us, too."

—AMOS TVERSKY (1985)

"The purposes in the human mind are like deep water, but the intelligent will draw them out."

—PROVERBS 20:5

"Cognitive errors . . . exist in the present because they led to survival and reproductive advantages for humans in the past."

—EVOLUTIONARY PSYCHOLOGISTS MARTIE HASELTON AND DAVID BUSS (2000)

Optimism pays dividends. We might even say that our beliefs are like scientific theories—sometimes in error yet useful as generalizations. As social psychologist Susan Fiske (1992) says, "Thinking is for doing."

As we constantly seek to improve our theories, might we not also work to reduce errors in our social thinking? In school, math teachers teach, teach, teach until the mind is finally trained to process numerical information accurately and automatically. We assume that such ability does not come naturally; otherwise, why bother with the years of training? Research psychologist Robyn Dawes (1980)—who was dismayed that "study after study has shown [that] people have very limited abilities to process information on a conscious level, particularly social information"—suggested that we should also teach, teach, teach how to process social information.

Richard Nisbett and Lee Ross (1980) believe that education could indeed reduce our vulnerability to certain types of error. They offer the following recommendations:

- Train people to recognize likely sources of error in their own social intuition.
- Set up statistics courses geared to everyday problems of logic and social judgment. Given such training, people do in fact reason better about everyday events (Lehman & others, 1988; Nisbett & others, 1987).
- Make such teaching more effective by illustrating it richly with concrete, vivid anecdotes and examples from everyday life.
- Teach memorable and useful slogans, such as "It's an empirical question," "Which hat did you draw that sample out of?" or "You can lie with statistics, but a well-chosen example does the job better."

> "The spirit of liberty is the spirit which is not too sure that it is right; the spirit of liberty is the spirit which seeks to understand the minds of other men and women; the spirit of liberty is the spirit which weighs their interests alongside its own without bias."
> —LEARNED HAND, "THE SPIRIT OF LIBERTY," 1952

Summing Up: Conclusions

Research on social beliefs and judgments reveals how we form and sustain beliefs that usually serve us well but sometimes lead us astray. A balanced social psychology will therefore appreciate both the powers and the perils of social thinking.

POSTSCRIPT: Reflecting on Illusory Thinking

Is research on pride and error too humbling? Surely we can acknowledge the hard truth of our human limits and still sympathize with the deeper message that people are more than machines. Our subjective experiences are the stuff of our humanity—our art and our music, our enjoyment of friendship and love, our mystical and religious experiences.

The cognitive and social psychologists who explore illusory thinking are not out to remake us into unfeeling logical machines. They know that emotions enrich human experience and that intuitions are an important source of creative ideas. They add, however, the humbling reminder that our susceptibility to error also makes clear the need for disciplined training of the mind. The American writer Norman Cousins (1978) called this "the biggest truth of all about learning: that its purpose is to unlock the human mind and to develop it into an organ capable of thought—conceptual thought, analytical thought, sequential thought."

Research on error and illusion in social judgment reminds us to "judge not"—to remember, with a dash of humility, our potential for misjudgment. It also encourages us not to feel intimidated by the arrogance of those who cannot see their own potential for bias and error. We humans are wonderfully intelligent yet fallible creatures. We have dignity but not deity.

> "Rob the average man of his life-illusion, and you rob him also of his happiness."
> —HENRIK IBSEN, THE WILD DUCK, 1884

Such humility and distrust of human authority is at the heart of both religion and science. No wonder many of the founders of modern science were religious people whose convictions predisposed them to be humble before nature and skeptical of human authority (Hooykaas, 1972; Merton, 1938). Science always involves an interplay between intuition and rigorous test, between creative hunch and skepticism. To sift reality from illusion requires both open-minded curiosity and hard-headed rigor. This perspective could prove to be a good attitude for approaching all of life: to be critical but not cynical; curious but not gullible; open but not exploitable.

Making the Social Connection

The Online Learning Center for this book includes a video on each of three important topics from this chapter. First is the manner in which context influenced public perceptions of the televised campaign speech given by presidential candidate Howard Dean after the Iowa Caucus in 2000. In the second video, leading memory researcher Elizabeth Loftus explores the misinformation effect and the way it distorts our memories. Finally, Lee Ross discusses the fundamental attribution error, a concept he formed based on his observations of how people perceive and interpret events. Keep these concepts in mind as you read future chapters, and notice the ways in which you tend to explain others' behavior.

Behavior and Attitudes

> "The ancestor of every action is a thought."
>
> —Ralph Waldo Emerson, *Essays, First Series*, 1841

What is the relationship between what we *are* (on the inside) and what we *do* (on the outside)? Philosophers, theologians, and educators have long speculated about the connections between attitude and action, character and conduct, private word and public deed. Underlying most teaching, counseling, and child rearing is an assumption: Our private beliefs and feelings determine our public behavior, so if we wish to change behavior we must first change hearts and minds.

In the beginning, social psychologists agreed: To know people's attitudes is to predict their actions. As demonstrated by genocidal killers and by suicide bombers, extreme attitudes can produce extreme behavior. But in 1964 Leon Festinger concluded that the evidence showed that *changing* people's attitudes hardly affects their behavior. Festinger believed the attitude-behavior relation works the other way around. As Robert Abelson (1972) put it, we are "very well trained and very good at finding reasons for what we do, but not very good at doing what we find reasons for." This chapter explores the interplay of attitudes and behavior.

When social psychologists talk about someone's attitude, they refer to beliefs and feelings related to a person or an event and the resulting behavior tendency. Taken together, favorable or unfavorable evaluative reactions toward something—often rooted in beliefs and exhibited in feelings and inclinations to act—define a person's **attitude** (Eagly & Chaiken, 2005). Thus, a person may have a negative attitude toward coffee, a neutral attitude toward the French, and a positive attitude toward the next-door neighbor. Attitudes provide an efficient way to size up the world. When we have to respond quickly to something, the way we feel about it can guide how we react. For example, a person who *believes* a particular ethnic group is lazy and aggressive may *feel* dislike for such people and therefore intend to act in a discriminatory manner.

The study of attitudes is close to the heart of social psychology and was one of its first concerns. For much of the last century, researchers wondered how much our attitudes affect our actions. You can remember these three dimensions as the ABCs of attitudes: *affect* (feelings), *behavior* tendency, and *cognition* (thoughts) (Figure 4.1).

attitude
A favorable or unfavorable evaluative reaction toward something or someone (often rooted in one's beliefs, and exhibited in one's feelings and intended behavior).

"All that we are is the result of what we have thought."
—*BUDDHA, 563 B.C.–483 B.C. DHAMMA-PADA*

"Thought is the child of action."
—*BENJAMIN DISRAELI, VIVIAN GRAY, 1926*

How Well Do Our Attitudes Predict Our Behavior?

To what extent, and under what conditions, do the attitudes of the heart drive our outward actions? Why were social psychologists at first surprised by a seemingly small connection between attitudes and actions?

A blow to the supposed power of attitudes came when social psychologist Allan Wicker (1969) reviewed several dozen research studies covering a wide variety of people, attitudes, and behaviors. Wicker offered a shocking conclusion: People's expressed attitudes hardly predicted their varying behaviors.

- Student attitudes toward cheating bore little relation to the likelihood of their actually cheating.
- Attitudes toward the church were only modestly linked with church attendance on any given Sunday.
- Self-described racial attitudes provided little clue to behaviors in actual situations.

An example of the disjuncture between attitudes and actions is what Daniel Batson and his colleagues (1997, 2001, 2002; Valdesolo & DeSteno, 2007, 2008) call "moral hypocrisy" (appearing moral while avoiding the costs of being so). Their studies presented people with an appealing task (where the participant could earn raffle tickets toward a $30 prize) and a dull task with no rewards. The participants had to assign themselves to one of the tasks and a supposed second participant to the other. Only 1 in 20 believed that assigning the

FIGURE :: 4.1
The ABCs of Attitudes

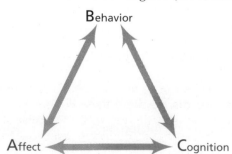

positive task to themselves was the more moral thing to do, yet 80 percent did so. In follow-up experiments on moral hypocrisy, participants were given coins they could flip privately if they wished. Even if they chose to flip, 90 percent assigned themselves to the positive task! (Was that because they could specify the consequences of heads and tails after the coin toss?) In another experiment, Batson put a sticker on each side of the coin, indicating what the flip outcome would signify. Still, 24 of 28 people who made the toss assigned themselves to the positive task. When morality and greed were put on a collision course, greed won.

If people don't walk the same line that they talk, it's little wonder that attempts to change behavior by changing attitudes often fail. Warnings about the dangers of smoking affect only minimally those who already smoke. Increasing public awareness of the desensitizing and brutalizing effects of television violence has stimulated many people to voice a desire for less violent programming—yet they still watch media murder as much as ever. Sex education programs have often influenced *attitudes* toward abstinence and condom use without affecting long-term abstinence and condom use *behaviors*. We are, it seems, a population of hypocrites.

> "It may be desirable to abandon the attitude concept."
> —*ALLAN WICKER (1971)*

All in all, the developing picture of what controls behavior emphasized external social influences, such as others' behavior and expectations, and played down internal factors, such as attitudes and personality. Thus, the original thesis that attitudes determine actions was countered during the 1960s by the antithesis that attitudes determine virtually nothing.

Thesis. Antithesis. Is there a synthesis? The surprising finding that what people *say* often differs from what they *do* sent social psychologists scurrying to find out why. Surely, we reasoned, convictions and feelings must sometimes make a difference.

Indeed. In fact, what I am about to explain now seems so obvious that I wonder why most social psychologists (myself included) were not thinking this way before the early 1970s. I must remind myself, however, that truth never seems obvious until it is known.

When Attitudes Predict Behavior

The reason—now obvious—why our behavior and our expressed attitudes differ is that both are subject to other influences. Many other influences. One social psychologist counted 40 factors that complicate their relationship (Triandis, 1982; see also Kraus, 1995). Our attitudes do predict our behavior when these other influences on what we say and do are minimal, when the attitude is specific to the behavior, and when the attitude is potent.

WHEN SOCIAL INFLUENCES ON WHAT WE SAY ARE MINIMAL

Unlike a physician measuring heart rate, social psychologists never get a direct reading on attitudes. Rather, we measure *expressed* attitudes. Like other behaviors, expressions are subject to outside influences. Sometimes, for example, we say what we think others want to hear. In late 2002, many U.S. legislators, sensing their country's post-9/11 fear, anger, and patriotic fervor, publicly voted support for President Bush's planned war against Iraq while privately having reservations (Nagourney, 2002). On the roll-call vote, strong social influence—fear of criticism—had distorted the true sentiments.

> "I have opinions of my own, strong opinions, but I don't always agree with them."
> —*PRESIDENT GEORGE H. W. BUSH*

Today's social psychologists have some clever means at their disposal for minimizing social influences on people's attitude reports. Some of these complement traditional self-report measures of *explicit* (conscious) attitudes with measures of *implicit* (unconscious) attitudes. One such test measures facial muscle responses to various statements (Cacioppo & Petty, 1981). Those measurements, the researchers

THE inside STORY

Graduating from high school in India at age 15, I had but a single goal—to leave my well-adjusted and secure family to live the patently more daring and exciting life of a secretarial assistant. Proficient at typing scores of words a minute, I looked forward to a life of independence that involved living a block away from my parents. My mother, despite not having attended college, persuaded me to try college—but only for a semester, we agreed, after which I would be free to choose my path.

The end of my first semester at Nizam College came and went. Mother didn't ask about my plans. I didn't have to swallow and tell. Just before one holiday trip home, I bought the five volumes of the 1968 *Handbook of Social Psychology* for the equivalent of a dollar apiece (it seemed like a lot of book for the money). By the end of a 24-hour train ride home, I had polished off one volume and knew with blunt clarity that this science, which studied social processes experimentally, was something I had to do.

Doctoral and postdoctoral fellowships enabled me to work with three remarkable people early in my career: Tony Greenwald at Ohio State, and Claude Steele and Elizabeth Loftus at the University of Washington. At Yale, while still interested in human memory researchers, I discovered that memories come in both explicit (conscious) and implicit (unconscious) forms. Might this also be true of attitudes, beliefs, and values? Hesitantly, I wrote the words "Implicit Attitudes" as the title of a grant proposal, not knowing it would become such a central part of what my students and I would study for the next two decades.

With Tony Greenwald and Brian Nosek, I have enjoyed an extended collaboration on implicit social cognition that few scientists are blessed with. From the hundreds of studies that have used the Implicit Association Test (implicit.harvard.edu) and the millions of tests taken, we now know that people carry knowledge (stereotypes) and feelings (attitudes) of which they are unaware, and which often contrast with their conscious expressions. We know that subcortical brain activity can be an independent marker of implicit attitudes, that people differ in their implicit attitudes, and that such attitudes and stereotypes predict real-life behavior. Most optimistically, we know that implicit attitudes, even old ones, can be modified by experience.

Mahzarin Banaji
Harvard University

---

implicit association test (IAT)

A computer-driven assessment of implicit attitudes. The test uses reaction times to measure people's automatic associations between attitude objects and evaluative words. Easier pairings (and faster responses) are taken to indicate stronger unconscious associations.

hope, can reveal enough of a microsmile or a microfrown to indicate the participant's attitude about a given statement.

A newer and widely used attitude measure, the **implicit association test (IAT),** uses reaction times to measure how quickly people associate concepts (Greenwald & others, 2002, 2003). One can, for example, measure implicit racial attitudes by assessing whether White people take longer to associate positive words with Black than with White faces. Across 126 studies, implicit associations measured by the IAT have correlated, on average, a modest .24 with explicit self-reported attitudes (Hofmann & others, 2005). (See "The Inside Story: Mahzarin R. Banaji on Discovering Experimental Social Psychology.")

A review of more than 100 studies and of more than 2.5 million IATs completed online reveals that explicit (self-report) and implicit attitudes both help predict people's behaviors and judgments (Greenwald & others, 2008; Nosek & others, 2007). Thus, explicit and implicit attitudes may together predict behavior better than either alone (Spence & Townsend, 2007).

For attitudes formed early in life, such as racial and gender attitudes, implicit and explicit attitudes frequently diverge, with implicit attitudes often being the better predictor of behavior. For example, implicit racial attitudes have successfully predicted interracial roommate relationships (Towles-Schwen & Fazio, 2006). For other attitudes, such as those related to consumer behavior and support for political candidates, explicit self-reports are the better predictor.

Recent neuroscience studies have identified brain centers that produce our automatic, implicit reactions (Stanley & others, 2008). One area deep in the brain (the amygdala, a center for threat perception) is active as we automatically evaluate social stimuli. For example, White people who show strong unconscious racial bias on the IAT also exhibit high amygdala activation when viewing unfamiliar Black faces. Other frontal lobe areas are involved in detecting and regulating implicit attitudes.

A word of caution: Despite much excitement over these recent studies of implicit attitudes hiding in the mind's basement, the implicit associations test has detractors (Arkes & Tetlock, 2004; Blanton & others, 2006, 2007). They note that, unlike an aptitude test, the IAT is not reliable enough for use in assessing and comparing individuals. Moreover, a score that suggests some relative bias doesn't distinguish a positive bias for one group (or greater familiarity with one group) from a negative bias against another. The critics also wonder whether compassion and guilt rather than latent hostility might slow one's speed in associating Blacks with positive words. Regardless, the existence of distinct explicit and implicit attitudes confirms one of twenty-first-century psychology's biggest lessons: our "dual processing" capacity for both *controlled* (deliberate, conscious, explicit) and *automatic* (effortless, habitual, implicit) thinking.

WHEN OTHER INFLUENCES ON BEHAVIOR ARE MINIMAL

On any occasion, it's not only our inner attitudes that guide us but also the situation we face. As Chapters 5 to 8 will illustrate again and again, social influences can be enormous—enormous enough to induce people to violate their deepest convictions. So, would *averaging* many occasions enable us to detect more clearly the impact of our attitudes? Predicting people's behavior is like predicting a baseball or cricket player's hitting. The outcome of any particular turn at bat is nearly impossible to predict, because it is affected not only by the batter but also by what the pitcher throws and by a host of chance factors. When we aggregate many times at bat, we neutralize those complicating factors. Knowing the players, we can predict their approximate batting *averages.*

To use a research example, people's general attitude toward religion poorly predicts whether they will go to worship services during the coming week (because attendance is also influenced by the weather, the worship leader, how one is feeling, and so forth). But religious attitudes predict quite well the total quantity of religious behaviors over time (Fishbein & Ajzen, 1974; Kahle & Berman, 1979). The findings define a *principle of aggregation:* The effects of an attitude become more apparent when we look at a person's aggregate or average behavior than when we consider isolated acts.

WHEN ATTITUDES SPECIFIC TO THE BEHAVIOR ARE EXAMINED

Other conditions further improve the predictive accuracy of attitudes. As Icek Ajzen and Martin Fishbein (1977, 2005) point out, when the measured attitude is a general one—say, an attitude toward Asians—and the behavior is very specific—say, a decision whether to help a particular Asian in a particular situation—we should not expect a close correspondence between words and actions. Indeed, report Fishbein and Ajzen, in 26 out of 27 such research studies, attitudes did not predict behavior. But attitudes did predict behavior in all 26 studies they could find in which the measured attitude was directly pertinent to the situation. Thus, attitudes toward the general concept of "health fitness" poorly predict specific exercise and dietary practices, but an individual's attitudes about the costs and benefits of jogging are a fairly strong predictor of whether he or she jogs regularly.

Better yet for predicting behavior, says Ajzen in his and Fishbein's "theory of planned behavior," is knowing people's *intended* behaviors, and their perceived

"There are still barriers out there, often unconscious."
—SENATOR HILLARY RODHAM CLINTON, PRESIDENTIAL CAMPAIGN CONCESSION SPEECH, 2008

"Do I contradict myself? Very well then I contradict myself. (I am large, I contain multitudes.)"
—WALT WHITMAN, SONG OF MYSELF, 1855

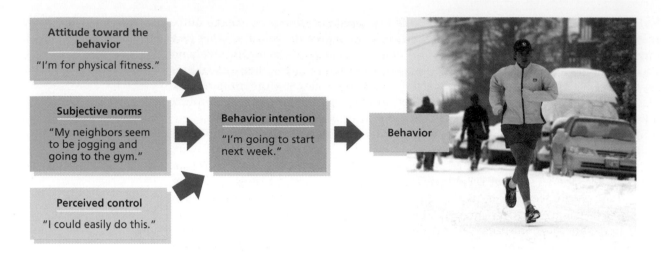

FIGURE :: 4.2

The Theory of Planned Behavior

Icek Ajzen, working with Martin Fishbein, has shown that one's (a) attitudes, (b) perceived social norms, and (c) feelings of control together determine one's intentions, which guide behavior.

Compared with their general attitudes toward a healthy lifestyle, people's specific attitudes regarding jogging predict their jogging behavior much better.

self-efficacy and control (Figure 4.2). Moreover, four dozen experimental tests confirm that inducing new intentions induces new behavior (Webb & Sheeran, 2006). Even simply asking people about their intentions to engage in a behavior increases its likelihood (Levav & Fitzsimons, 2006). Ask people if they intend to floss their teeth in the next two weeks or to vote in an upcoming election, they will become more likely to do so.

Further studies—more than 700 studies with 276,000 participants—confirmed that specific, relevant attitudes do predict intended and actual behavior (Armitage & Conner, 2001; Six & Eckes, 1996; Wallace & others, 2005). For example, attitudes toward condoms strongly predict condom use (Albarracin & others, 2001). And attitudes toward recycling (but not general attitudes toward environmental issues) predict participation in recycling (Oskamp, 1991). To change habits through persuasion, we had best alter people's attitudes toward *specific* practices.

So far we have seen two conditions under which attitudes will predict behavior: (1) when we minimize other influences upon our attitude statements and on our behavior, and (2) when the attitude is specifically relevant to the observed behavior. There is a third condition: An attitude predicts behavior better when the attitude is potent.

WHEN ATTITUDES ARE POTENT

Much of our behavior is automatic. We act out familiar scripts without reflecting on what we're doing. We respond to people we meet in the hall with an automatic "Hi." We answer the restaurant cashier's question "How was your meal?" by saying, "Fine," even if we found it tasteless.

Such mindlessness is adaptive. It frees our minds to work on other things. For habitual behaviors—seat belt use, coffee consumption, class attendance—conscious intentions hardly are activated (Ouellette & Wood, 1998). As the philosopher Alfred North Whitehead argued, "Civilization advances by extending the number of operations which we can perform without thinking about them."

BRINGING ATTITUDES TO MIND. If we were prompted to think about our attitudes before acting, would we be truer to ourselves? Mark Snyder and William Swann (1976) wanted to find out. Two weeks after 120 of their University of Minnesota students indicated their attitudes toward affirmative-action employment policies, Snyder and Swann invited them to act as jurors in a sex-discrimination court case. The participants' attitudes predicted verdicts only for those who were first induced to remember their attitudes—by giving them "a few minutes to organize your thoughts and views on the affirmative-action issue." Our attitudes become potent *if* we think about them.

Self-conscious people usually are in touch with their attitudes (Miller & Grush, 1986). That suggests another way to induce people to focus on their inner convictions: *Make them self-aware*, perhaps by having them act in front of a mirror (Carver & Scheier, 1981). Maybe you, too, can recall suddenly being acutely aware of yourself upon entering a room with a large mirror. Making people self-aware in this way promotes consistency between words and deeds (Froming & others, 1982; Gibbons, 1978).

Edward Diener and Mark Wallbom (1976) noted that nearly all college students say that cheating is morally wrong. But will they follow the advice of Shakespeare's Polonius, "To thine own self be true"? Diener and Wallbom set University of Washington students to work on an anagram-solving task (which, they were told, was to predict IQ) and told them to stop when a bell in the room sounded. Left alone, 71 percent cheated by working past the bell. Among students made self-aware—by working in front of a mirror while hearing their own tape-recorded voices—only 7 percent cheated. It makes one wonder: Would eye-level mirrors in stores make people more self-conscious of their attitudes about stealing?

Remember Batson's studies of moral hypocrisy described on page 124? In a later experiment, Batson and his colleagues (1999) found that mirrors did bring behavior into line with espoused moral attitudes. When people flipped a coin while facing a mirror, the coin flip became scrupulously fair. Exactly half of the self-conscious participants assigned the other person to the positive task.

FORGING STRONG ATTITUDES THROUGH EXPERIENCE. The attitudes that best predict behavior are accessible (easily brought to mind) as well as stable (Glasman & Albarracin, 2006). And when attitudes are forged by experience, not just by hearsay, they are more accessible, more enduring, and more likely to guide actions. In one study, university students all expressed negative attitudes about their school's response to a housing shortage. But given opportunities to act—to sign a petition, solicit signatures, join a committee, or write a letter—only those whose attitudes grew from direct experience acted (Regan & Fazio, 1977).

> "Thinking is easy, acting difficult, and to put one's thoughts into action, the most difficult thing in the world."
> —GERMAN POET GOETHE, 1749–1832

> "Without doubt it is a delightful harmony when doing and saying go together."
> —MONTAIGNE, ESSAYS, 1588

> "It is easier to preach virtue than to practice it."
> —LA ROCHEFOUCAULD, MAXIMS, 1665

Summing Up: How Well Do Our Attitudes Predict Our Behavior?

- How do our inner attitudes (evaluative reactions toward some object or person, often rooted in beliefs) relate to our external behavior? Although popular wisdom stresses the impact of attitudes on behavior, in fact, attitudes are often poor predictors of behaviors. Moreover, changing people's attitudes typically fails to produce much change in their behavior. These findings sent social psychologists scurrying to find out why we so often fail to play the game we talk.

- The answer: Our expressions of attitudes and our behaviors are each subject to many influences. Our attitudes will predict our behavior (1) if these "other influences" are minimized, (2) if the attitude corresponds very closely to the predicted behavior (as in voting studies), and (3) if the attitude is potent (because something reminds us of it, or because we acquired it by direct experience). Under these conditions what we think and feel predicts what we do.

research CLOSE-UP

We have seen that strongly held attitudes predict specific actions, especially when the actions are unconstrained by social pressures. After 9/11, some people formed strongly felt attitudes regarding Arabs. That led University of Michigan social psychologist Brad Bushman and his co-researcher Angelica Bonacci (2004) to wonder how strongly attitudes toward Arab Americans might influence unconstrained *behavior* toward them. They wanted to assess the race-relevant attitudes of university students and then, some time later, to correlate their expressed attitudes with their natural behavior in a situation offering anonymity. (Any ideas as to how you might have done that?)

Their strategy was, first, to embed eleven attitude statements about Arab Americans in a set of questionnaires administered to nearly 1,000 introductory psychology students early in their spring 2002 semester. Using a 1 ("strongly disagree")-to-10 ("strongly agree") scale, the students responded to statements such as these:

- "A major fault of Arab Americans is their conceit, their overbearing pride, and their idea that they are a chosen ethnic group."

- "If there are too many Arab Americans in America, our country will be less safe."

- "If I knew I had been assigned to live in a dorm room with an Arab American, I would ask to change rooms."

Among the many other questions the students answered was one asking if they would be willing to participate later in an "unsolicited e-mail study." With their attitudes now measured, and their informed consent granted, more than 500 of these students (all European American) would, two weeks later, unwittingly participate in a clever experiment. Each person received an e-mail addressed to an individual with an Arabic name (Mohammed Hameed for male participants and Hassan Hameed for female participants) or to a European name (Peter Brice or Julianna Brice). Half the students received an e-mail stating that the intended recipient had received a prestigious scholarship that required acceptance within 48 hours:

> Thank you for applying for a Glassner Foundation Scholarship. These scholarships are highly competitive and are given only to a few select individuals. They cover tuition for four years. . . . Because of the large number of applicants, this year we are late in sending out these notices. . . . We are happy to inform you that you have been selected to receive a Glassner Foundation Scholarship. Congratulations! . . . We ask that you respond to this e-mail within 48 hours to inform us whether you will formally accept our scholarship offer. [If not] we would like to extend offers to other students on our waiting list. . . .

The other half were told the bad news: They did not receive the scholarship (but were welcome to respond if they wanted to be on the waiting list).

Had you received such a misdirected e-mail, without knowing you were actually participating in an experiment, would you have returned the e-mail to the sender, noting the error so that it could be re-sent? Some 26 percent of women but only 16 percent of men did so. And did it matter who the intended recipient was?

As Figure 4.3 shows, it did indeed. The participants (who generally expressed stronger feelings of prejudice toward Arab Americans than toward African Americans, Asian Americans, or Hispanic Americans) were less likely to reconvey the good news of the scholarship award to intended recipients with Arabic names. This discriminatory behavior was most strikingly evident among those students who had earlier expressed higher-than-average prejudice toward Arab Americans. Moreover, as Figure 4.4 shows, the students with highly prejudicial attitudes also were *more* willing than were those low in prejudice to reconvey *bad* news to Arabs. Thus, in the months after 9/11, prejudicial attitudes did indeed predict subtle but relevant discriminatory behavior.

(continued)

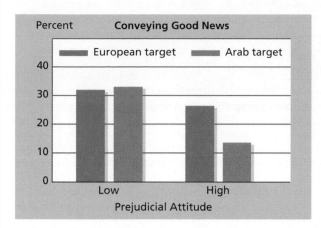

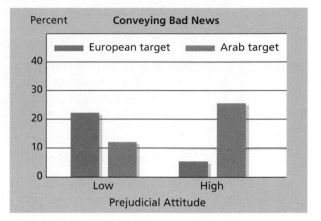

FIGURE :: 4.3

Effect of Prejudicial Attitudes on the Rate of Reconveying Good News to Those with European and Arabic Names

FIGURE :: 4.4

Effect of Prejudicial Attitudes on the Rate of Reconveying Bad News to Those with European and Arabic Names

When Does Our Behavior Affect Our Attitudes?

If social psychology has taught us anything during the last 25 years, it is that we are likely not only to think ourselves into a way of acting but also to act ourselves into a way of thinking. What evidence supports that assertion?

Now we turn to the more startling idea that behavior determines attitudes. It's true that we sometimes stand up for what we believe. But it's also true that we come to believe in what we stand up for. Social-psychological theories inspired much of the research that underlies that conclusion. Instead of beginning with these theories, however, let's first see what there is to explain. As we engage the evidence that behavior affects attitudes, speculate *why* actions affect attitudes and then compare your ideas with social psychologists' explanations.

Consider the following incidents:

- Sarah is hypnotized and told to take off her shoes when a book drops on the floor. Fifteen minutes later a book drops, and Sarah quietly slips out of her loafers. "Sarah," asks the hypnotist, "why did you take off your shoes?" "Well . . . my feet are hot and tired," Sarah replies. "It has been a long day." The act produces the idea.

- George has electrodes temporarily implanted in the brain region that controls his head movements. When neurosurgeon José Delgado (1973) stimulates the electrodes by remote control, George always turns his head. Unaware of the remote stimulation, he offers a reasonable explanation for his head turning: "I'm looking for my slipper." "I heard a noise." "I'm restless." "I was looking under the bed."

- Carol's severe seizures were relieved by surgically separating her two brain hemispheres. Now, in an experiment, psychologist Michael Gazzaniga (1985) flashes a picture of a nude woman to the left half of Carol's field of vision and thus to her nonverbal right brain hemisphere. A sheepish smile spreads over her face, and she begins chuckling. Asked why, she invents—and apparently believes—a plausible explanation: "Oh—that funny machine." Frank, another split-brain patient, has the word "smile" flashed to his non-verbal right hemisphere. He obliges and forces a smile. Asked why, he explains, "This experiment is very funny."

The mental aftereffects of our behavior also appear in many social psychological phenomena. The following examples illustrate such self-persuasion. As we will see over and over, attitudes follow behavior.

Role Playing

role

A set of norms that defines how people in a given social position ought to behave.

"No man, for any considerable period, can wear one face to himself and another to the multitude without finally getting bewildered as to which may be true."

—NATHANIEL HAWTHORNE, 1850

The word **role** is borrowed from the theater and, as in the theater, refers to actions expected of those who occupy a particular social position. When enacting new social roles, we may at first feel phony. But our unease seldom lasts.

Think of a time when you stepped into some new role—perhaps your first days on a job or at college. That first week on campus, for example, you may have been supersensitive to your new social situation and tried valiantly to act mature and to suppress your high school behavior. At such times you may have felt self-conscious. You observed your new speech and actions because they weren't natural to you. Then one day something amazing happened: Your pseudo-intellectual talk no longer felt forced. The role began to fit as comfortably as your old jeans and T-shirt.

In one study, college men volunteered to spend time in a simulated prison constructed in Stanford's psychology department by Philip Zimbardo (1971; Haney & Zimbardo, 1998, 2009). Zimbardo wanted to find out: Is prison brutality a product of evil prisoners and malicious guards? Or do the institutional roles of guard and prisoner embitter and harden even compassionate people? Do the people make the place violent? Or does the place make the people violent?

By a flip of a coin, Zimbardo designated some students as guards. He gave them uniforms, billy clubs, and whistles and instructed them to enforce the rules. The other half, the prisoners, were locked in cells and made to wear humiliating hospital-gown-like outfits. After a jovial first day of "playing" their roles, the guards and the prisoners, and even the experimenters, got caught up in the situation. The guards began to disparage the prisoners, and some devised cruel and degrading routines. The prisoners broke down, rebelled, or became apathetic. There developed, reported Zimbardo (1972), a "growing confusion between reality and illusion, between role-playing and self-identity. . . . This prison which we had created . . . was absorbing us as creatures of its own reality." Observing the emerging social pathology, Zimbardo was forced to call off the planned two-week simulation after only six days.

Guards and prisoners in the Stanford prison simulation quickly absorbed the roles they played.

The point is not that we are powerless to resist imposed roles. In Zimbardo's prison simulation, in Abu Ghraib Prison (where guards degraded Iraq war prisoners), and in other atrocity-producing situations, some people become sadistic and others do not (Haslam & Reicher, 2007; Mastroianni & Reed, 2006; Zimbardo, 2007). In water, salt dissolves and sand does not. So also, notes John Johnson (2007), when placed in a rotten barrel, some people become bad apples and others do not. Behavior is a product of both the individual person and the situation, and the prison study appears to have attracted volunteers who were prone to aggressiveness (McFarland & Carnahan, 2009).

The deeper lesson of the role-playing studies is not that we are powerless machines. Rather, it concerns how what is unreal (an artificial role) can subtly evolve into what is real. In a new career, as teacher, soldier, or businessperson, we enact a role that shapes our attitudes.

Imagine playing the role of slave—not just for six days but for decades. If a few days altered the behavior of those in Zimbardo's "prison," then imagine the corrosive effects of decades of sub-

After the Abu Ghraib degradation of Iraqi prisoners, Philip Zimbardo (2004a, 2004b) noted "direct and sad parallels between similar behavior of the 'guards' in the Stanford Prison Experiment." Such behavior, he contends, is attributable to a toxic situation that can make good people into perpetrators of evil. "It's not that we put bad apples in a good barrel. We put good apples in a bad barrel. The barrel corrupts anything that it touches."

servient behavior. The master may be even more profoundly affected, because the master's role is chosen. Frederick Douglass, a former slave, recalls his new owner's transformation as she absorbed her role:

> My new mistress proved to be all she appeared when I first met her at the door—a woman of the kindest heart and finest feelings. . . . I was utterly astonished at her goodness. I scarcely knew how to behave towards her. She was entirely unlike any other white woman I had ever seen. . . . The meanest slave was put fully at ease in her presence, and none left without feeling better for having seen her. Her face was made of heavenly smiles, and her voice of tranquil music. But, alas! this kind heart had but a short time to remain such. The fatal poison of irresponsible power was already in her hands, and soon commenced its infernal work. That cheerful eye, under the influence of slavery, soon became red with rage; that voice, made all of sweet accord, changed to one of harsh and horrid discord; and that angelic face gave place to that of a demon. (Douglass, 1845, pp. 57–58)

Saying Becomes Believing

People often adapt what they say to please their listeners. They are quicker to tell people good news than bad, and they adjust their message toward their listener's position (Manis & others, 1974; Tesser & others, 1972; Tetlock, 1983). When induced to give spoken or written support to something they doubt, people will often feel bad about their deceit. Nevertheless, they begin to believe what they are saying—*provided* they weren't bribed or coerced into doing so. When there is no compelling external explanation for one's words, saying becomes believing (Klaas, 1978).

Tory Higgins and his colleagues (Higgins & McCann, 1984; Higgins & Rholes, 1978) illustrated how saying becomes believing. They had university students read a personality description of someone and then summarize it for someone else, who was believed either to like or to dislike that person. The students wrote a more positive description when the recipient liked the person. Having said positive things,

focus
ON   Saying Becomes Believing

University of Oregon psychologist Ray Hyman (1981) described how acting the role of a palm reader convinced him that palmistry worked.

> I started reading palms when I was in my teens as a way to supplement my income from doing magic and mental shows. When I started I did not believe in palmistry. But I knew that to "sell" it I had to act as if I did. After a few years I became a firm believer in palmistry. One day the late Stanley Jaks, who was a professional mentalist and a man I respected, tactfully suggested that it would make an interesting experiment if I deliberately gave readings opposite to what the lines indicated. I tried this out with a few clients. To my surprise and horror my readings were just as successful as ever. Ever since then I have been interested in the powerful forces that convince us, [palm] reader and client alike, that something is so when it really isn't. (p. 86)

"Good God! He's giving the white-collar voter's speech to the blue collars."

Impression management: In expressing our thoughts to others, we sometimes tailor our words to what we think the others will want to hear.

© The New Yorker Collection, 1984, Joseph Farris, from cartoonbank.com. All Rights Reserved.

foot-in-the-door phenomenon
The tendency for people who have first agreed to a small request to comply later with a larger request.

they also then liked the person more themselves. Asked to recall what they had read, they remembered the description as more positive than it was. In short, people tend to adjust their messages to their listeners, and, having done so, to believe the altered message.

The Foot-in-the-Door Phenomenon

Most of us can recall times when, after agreeing to help out with a project or an organization, we ended up more involved than we ever intended, vowing that in the future we would say no to such requests. How does this happen? In keeping with the "attitude follows behavior" principle, experiments suggest that if you want people to do a big favor for you, an effective strategy is to get them to do a small favor first. In the best-known demonstration of this **foot-in-the-door phenomenon**, researchers posing as drive-safely volunteers asked Californians to permit the installation of huge, poorly lettered "Drive Carefully" signs in their front yards. Only 17 percent consented. Others were first approached with a small request: Would they display three-inch "Be a safe driver" window signs? Nearly all readily agreed. When approached two weeks later to allow the large, ugly signs in their front yards, 76 percent consented (Freedman & Fraser, 1966). One project helper who went from house to house later recalled that, not knowing who had been previously visited, "I was simply stunned at how easy it was to convince some people and how impossible to convince others" (Ornstein, 1991).

Other researchers have confirmed the foot-in-the-door phenomenon with altruistic behaviors.

- Patricia Pliner and her collaborators (1974) found 46 percent of Toronto suburbanites willing to give to the Canadian Cancer Society when approached directly. Others, asked a day ahead to wear a lapel pin publicizing the drive (which all agreed to do), were nearly twice as likely to donate.
- Angela Lipsitz and others (1989) report that ending blood-drive reminder calls with, "We'll count on seeing you then, OK? [pause for response]," increased the show-up rate from 62 to 81 percent.

The foot-in-the-door phenomenon.
BLONDIE © King Features Syndicate.

- In Internet chat rooms, Paul Markey and his colleagues (2002) requested help ("I can't get my e-mail to work. Is there any way I can get you to send me an e-mail?"). Help increased—from 2 to 16 percent—by including a smaller prior request ("I am new to this whole computer thing. Is there any way you can tell me how to look at someone's profile?").
- Nicolas Guéguen and Céline Jacob (2001) tripled the rate of French Internet users contributing to child land-mine victims organizations (from 1.6 to 4.9 percent) by first inviting them to sign a petition against land mines.

Note that in these experiments, as in many of the 100+ other foot-in-the-door experiments, the initial compliance—wearing a lapel pin, stating one's intention, signing a petition—was voluntary (Burger & Guadagno, 2003). We will see again and again that when people commit themselves to public behaviors *and* perceive those acts to be their own doing, they come to believe more strongly in what they have done.

Social psychologist Robert Cialdini [chal-DEE-nee] is a self-described "patsy." "For as long as I can recall, I've been an easy mark for the pitches of peddlers, fund-raisers, and operators of one sort or another." To better understand why one person says yes to another, he spent three years as a trainee in various sales, fund-raising, and advertising organizations, discovering how they exploit "the weapons of influence." He also put those weapons to the test in simple experiments. In one, Cialdini and his collaborators (1978) explored a variation of the foot-in-the-door phenomenon by experimenting with the **low-ball technique,** a tactic reportedly used by some car dealers. After the customer agrees to buy a new car because of its bargain price and begins completing the sales forms, the salesperson removes the price advantage by charging for options or by checking with a boss who disallows the deal because "we'd be losing money." Folklore has it that more low-balled customers now stick with the higher-priced purchase than would have agreed to it at the outset. Airlines and hotels use the tactic by attracting inquiries with great deals available on only a few seats or rooms, then hoping the customer will agree to a higher-priced option.

Cialdini and his collaborators found that this technique indeed works. When they invited introductory psychology students to participate in an experiment at 7:00 A.M., only 24 percent showed up. But if the students first agreed to participate without knowing the time and only then were asked to participate at 7:00 A.M., 53 percent came.

Marketing researchers and salespeople have found that the principle works even when we are aware of a profit motive (Cialdini, 1988). A harmless initial

"You will easily find folk to do favors if you cultivate those who have done them."
—*PUBLILIUS SYRUS, 42 B.C.*

low-ball technique
A tactic for getting people to agree to something. People who agree to an initial request will often still comply when the requester ups the ante. People who receive only the costly request are less likely to comply with it.

The low-ball technique.

The Born Loser © Newspaper Enterprise Association.

commitment—returning a postcard for more information and a "free gift," agreeing to listen to an investment possibility—often moves us toward a larger commitment. Because salespeople sometimes exploited the power of those small commitments by trying to bind people to purchase agreements, many states now have laws that allow customers a few days to think over their purchases and cancel. To counter the effect of these laws, many companies use what the sales-training program of one company calls "a very important psychological aid in preventing customers from backing out of their contracts" (Cialdini, 1988, p. 78). They simply have the customer, rather than the salesperson, fill out the agreement. Having written it themselves, people usually live up to their commitment.

The foot-in-the-door phenomenon is a lesson worth remembering. Someone trying to seduce us—financially, politically, or sexually—will often use this technique to create a momentum of compliance. The practical lesson: Before agreeing to a small request, think about what may follow.

Cruel acts, such as the 1994 Rwandan genocide, tend to breed even crueler and more hate-filled attitudes.

Evil and Moral Acts

The attitudes-follow-behavior principle works with immoral acts as well. Evil sometimes results from gradually escalating commitments. A trifling evil act can

whittle down one's moral sensitivity, making it easier to perform a worse act. To paraphrase La Rochefoucauld's *Maxims* (1665), it is not as difficult to find a person who has never succumbed to a given temptation as to find a person who has succumbed only once. After telling a "white lie" and thinking, "Well, that wasn't so bad," the person may go on to tell a bigger lie.

Another way in which evil acts influence attitudes is the paradoxical fact that we tend not only to hurt those we dislike but also to dislike those we hurt. Several studies (Berscheid & others, 1968; Davis & Jones, 1960; Glass, 1964) found that harming an innocent victim—by uttering hurtful comments or delivering electric shocks—typically leads aggressors to disparage their victims, thus helping them justify their cruel behavior. This is especially so when we are coaxed into it, not coerced. When we agree to a deed voluntarily, we take more responsibility for it.

The phenomenon appears in wartime. Prisoner-of-war camp guards would sometimes display good manners to captives in their first days on the job, but not for long. Soldiers ordered to kill may initially react with revulsion to the point of sickness over their act. But not for long (Waller, 2002). Often they will denigrate their enemies with dehumanizing nicknames.

Attitudes also follow behavior in peacetime. A group that holds another in slavery will likely come to perceive the slaves as having traits that justify their oppression. Prison staff who participate in executions experience "moral disengagement" by coming to believe (more strongly than do other prison staff) that their victims deserve their fate (Osofsky & others, 2005). Actions and attitudes feed each other, sometimes to the point of moral numbness. The more one harms another and adjusts one's attitudes, the easier harm-doing becomes. Conscience is corroded.

To simulate the "killing begets killing" process, Andy Martens and his collaborators (2007) asked University of Arizona students to kill some bugs. They wondered: Would killing initial bugs in a "practice" trial increase students' willingness to kill more bugs later? To find out, they asked some students to look at one small bug in a container, then to dump it into the coffee grinding machine shown in Figure 4.5, and then to press the "on" button for 3 seconds. (No bugs were actually killed. An unseen stopper at the base of the insert tube prevented the bug from actually entering the opaque killing machine, which had torn bits of paper to simulate the sound of a killing.) Others, who initially killed five bugs (or so they thought), went on to "kill" significantly more bugs during an ensuing 20-second period.

Harmful acts shape the self, but so, thankfully, do moral acts. Our character is reflected in what we do when we think no one is looking. Researchers have tested character by giving children temptations when it seems no one is watching. Consider what happens when children resist the temptation. In a dramatic experiment, Jonathan Freedman (1965) introduced elementary school children to an enticing battery-controlled robot, instructing them not to play with it while he was out of the room. Freedman used a severe threat with half the children and a mild threat with the others. Both were sufficient to deter the children.

Several weeks later a different researcher, with no apparent relation to the earlier events, left each child to play in the same room with the same toys. Of the children who had been given the severe threat, three-fourths now freely played with the robot; but two-thirds of those who had been given the mild deterrent still *resisted* playing with it. Apparently, the deterrent was strong enough to elicit the desired behavior yet mild enough to leave them with a sense of choice. Having earlier chosen consciously *not* to play with the toy, the mildly deterred children apparently internalized their decisions. Moral action, especially when chosen rather than coerced, affects moral thinking.

"Our self-definitions are not constructed in our heads; they are forged by our deeds."
—*ROBERT McAFEE BROWN, CREATIVE DISLOCATION: THE MOVEMENT OF GRACE, 1980*

FIGURE :: 4.5

Killing Begets Killing.

Students who initially perceived themselves as killing several bugs, by dropping them in this apparent killing machine, later killed an increased number of bugs during a self-paced killing period. (In reality, no bugs were harmed.)

"We do not love people so much for the good they have done us, as for the good we have done them."

—*LEO TOLSTOY, WAR AND PEACE, 1867–1869*

Moreover, positive behavior fosters liking for the person. Doing a favor for an experimenter or another participant, or tutoring a student, usually increases liking of the person helped (Blanchard & Cook, 1976). It is a lesson worth remembering: If you wish to love someone more, act as if you do.

In 1793 Benjamin Franklin tested the idea that doing a favor engenders liking. As clerk of the Pennsylvania General Assembly, he was disturbed by opposition from another important legislator. So Franklin set out to win him over:

> I did not . . . aim at gaining his favour by paying any servile respect to him but, after some time, took this other method. Having heard that he had in his library a certain very scarce and curious book I wrote a note to him expressing my desire of perusing that book and requesting he would do me the favour of lending it to me for a few days. He sent it immediately and I return'd it in about a week, expressing strongly my sense of the favour. When we next met in the House he spoke to me (which he had never done before), and with great civility; and he ever after manifested a readiness to serve me on all occasions, so that we became great friends and our friendship continued to his death. (quoted by Rosenzweig, 1972, p. 769)

Interracial Behavior and Racial Attitudes

If moral action feeds moral attitudes, will positive interracial behavior reduce racial prejudice—much as mandatory seat belt use has produced more favorable seat belt attitudes? That was part of social scientists' testimony before the U.S. Supreme Court's 1954 decision to desegregate schools. Their argument ran like this: If we wait for the heart to change—through preaching and teaching—we will wait a long time for racial justice. But if we legislate moral action, we can, under the right conditions, indirectly affect heartfelt attitudes.

That idea runs counter to the presumption that "you can't legislate morality." Yet attitude change has, as some social psychologists predicted, followed desegregation. Consider:

"We become just by the practice of just actions, self-controlled by exercising self-control, and courageous by performing acts of courage."

—*ARISTOTLE*

- Following the Supreme Court decision, the percentage of White Americans favoring integrated schools jumped and now includes nearly everyone. (For other examples of old and current racial attitudes, see Chapter 9.)
- In the 10 years after the Civil Rights Act of 1964, the percentage of White Americans who described their neighborhoods, friends, co-workers, or other students as all-White declined by about 20 percent for each of those measures. Interracial behavior was increasing. During the same period, the percentage of White Americans who said that Blacks should be allowed to live in any neighborhood increased from 65 percent to 87 percent (*ISR Newsletter*, 1975). Attitudes were changing, too.
- More uniform national standards against discrimination were followed by decreasing differences in racial attitudes among people of differing religions, classes, and geographic regions. As Americans came to act more alike, they came to think more alike (Greeley & Sheatsley, 1971; Taylor & others, 1978).

Social Movements

We have now seen that a society's laws and, therefore, its behavior can have a strong influence on its racial attitudes. A danger lies in the possibility of employing the same idea for political socialization on a mass scale. For many Germans during the 1930s, participation in Nazi rallies, displaying the Nazi flag, and especially the public greeting "Heil Hitler" established a profound inconsistency between behavior and belief. Historian Richard Grunberger (1971) reports that for those who had their doubts about Hitler, "the 'German greeting' was a powerful conditioning device. Having once decided to intone it as an outward token of conformity, many experienced . . . discomfort at the contradiction between their words and their feelings. Prevented from saying what they believed, they tried to establish their psychic equilibrium by consciously making themselves believe what they said" (p. 27).

The practice is not limited to totalitarian regimes. Political rituals—the daily flag salute by schoolchildren, singing the national anthem—use public conformity to build a private belief in patriotism. I recall participating in air-raid drills in my elementary school not far from the Boeing Company in Seattle. After we acted repeatedly as if we were the targets of Russian attack, many of us came to fear the Russians.

Many people assume that the most potent social indoctrination comes

Our political rituals—the daily flag salute by schoolchildren, singing the national anthem—use public conformity to build private allegiance.

through *brainwashing,* a term coined to describe what happened to American prisoners of war (POWs) during the 1950s Korean War. Although the "thought-control" program was not as irresistible as this term suggests, the results still were disconcerting. Hundreds of prisoners cooperated with their captors. Twenty-one chose to remain after being granted permission to return to America. And many of those who did return came home believing "although communism won't work in America, I think it's a good thing for Asia" (Segal, 1954).

Edgar Schein (1956) interviewed many of the POWs during their journey home and reported that the captors' methods included a gradual escalation of demands. The captors always started with trivial requests and gradually worked up to more significant ones. "Thus after a prisoner had once been 'trained' to speak or write out trivia, statements on more important issues were demanded." Moreover, they always expected active participation, be it just copying something or participating in group discussions, writing self-criticism, or uttering public confessions. Once a prisoner had spoken or written a statement, he felt an inner need to make his beliefs consistent with his acts. That often drove prisoners to persuade themselves of what they had done wrong. The "start-small-and-build" tactic was an effective application of the foot-in-the-door technique, and it continues to be so today in the socialization of terrorists and torturers (Chapter 6).

Now let me ask you, before reading further, to play theorist. Ask yourself: Why in these studies and real-life examples did attitudes follow behavior? Why might playing a role or making a speech influence your attitude?

"You can use small commitments to manipulate a person's self-image; you can use them to turn citizens into 'public servants,' prospects into 'customers,' prisoners into 'collaborators.'"

—*ROBERT CIALDINI,* INFLUENCE, 1988

Summing Up: When Does Our Behavior Affect Our Attitudes?

- The attitude-action relation also works in the reverse direction: We are likely not only to think ourselves into action but also to act ourselves into a way of thinking. When we act, we amplify the idea underlying what we have done, especially when we feel responsible for it. Many streams of evidence converge on this principle. The actions prescribed by social roles mold the attitudes of the role players.

- Similarly, what we say or write can strongly influence attitudes that we subsequently hold.

- Research on the foot-in-the-door phenomenon reveals that committing a small act makes people more willing to do a larger one later.

- Actions also affect our moral attitudes: That which we have done, even if it is evil, we tend to justify as right.

- Similarly, our racial and political behaviors help shape our social consciousness: We not only stand up for what we believe, we also believe in what we have stood up for.

- Political and social movements may legislate behavior designed to lead to attitude change on a mass scale.

Why Does Our Behavior Affect Our Attitudes?

What theories help explain the attitudes-follow-behavior phenomenon? How does the contest between these competing theories illustrate the process of scientific explanation?

We have seen that several streams of evidence merge to form a river: the effect of actions on attitudes. Do these observations contain any clues to *why* action affects attitude? Social psychology's detectives suspect three possible sources. *Self-presentation theory* assumes that for strategic reasons we express attitudes that make us appear consistent. *Cognitive dissonance theory* assumes that to reduce discomfort, we justify our actions to ourselves. *Self-perception theory* assumes that our actions are self-revealing (when uncertain about our feelings or beliefs, we look to our behavior, much as anyone else would). Let's examine each explanation.

Self-Presentation: Impression Management

The first explanation for why actions affect attitudes began as a simple idea that you may recall from Chapter 2. Who among us does not care what people think? We spend countless dollars on clothes, diets, cosmetics, and now plastic surgery—all because of our fretting over what others think. We see making a good impression as a way to gain social and material rewards, to feel better about ourselves, even to become more secure in our social identities (Leary, 1994, 2001, 2004b, 2007).

No one wants to look foolishly inconsistent. To avoid seeming so, we express

"I see he finally got rid of that idiotic comb-over."

attitudes that match our actions. To appear consistent, we may pretend those attitudes. Even if that means displaying a little insincerity or hypocrisy, it can pay off in managing the impression we are making. Or so self-presentation theory suggests.

Does our feigning consistency explain why expressed attitudes shift toward consistency with behavior? To some extent, yes—people exhibit a much smaller attitude change when a fake lie detector inhibits them from trying to make a good impression (Paulhus, 1982; Tedeschi & others, 1987).

But there is more to attitudes than self-presentation, for people express their changed attitudes even to someone who has no knowledge of their earlier behavior. Two other theories explain why people sometimes internalize their self-presentations as genuine attitude changes.

Self-Justification: Cognitive Dissonance

One theory is that our attitudes change because we are motivated to maintain consistency among our cognitions. That is the implication of Leon Festinger's (1957) famous **cognitive dissonance** theory. The theory is simple, but its range of application is enormous, making "cognitive dissonance" part of the vocabulary of today's educated people. It assumes that we feel tension, or a lack of harmony ("dissonance"), when two simultaneously accessible thoughts or beliefs ("cognitions") are psychologically inconsistent. Festinger argued that to reduce this unpleasant arousal, we often adjust our thinking. This simple idea, and some surprising predictions derived from it, have spawned more than 2,000 studies (Cooper, 1999).

Dissonance theory pertains mostly to discrepancies between behavior and attitudes. We are aware of both. Thus, if we sense some inconsistency, perhaps some hypocrisy, we feel pressure for change. That helps explain why British and U.S. cigarette smokers have been much less likely than nonsmokers to believe that smoking is dangerous (Eiser & others, 1979; Saad, 2002).

After the 2003 Iraq War, noted the director of the Program of International Policy Attitudes, some Americans struggled to reduce their "experience of cognitive dissonance" (Kull, 2003). The war's main premise had been that Saddam Hussein, unlike most other brutal dictators whom the world was tolerating, had weapons of mass destruction that threatened U.S. and British security. As the war began, only 38 percent of Americans said the war was justified even if Iraq did not have weapons of mass destruction (Gallup, 2003). Nearly four in five Americans believed their invading troops would find such, and a similar percentage supported the just-launched war (Duffy, 2003; Newport & others, 2003).

When no such weapons were found, the war-supporting majority experienced dissonance, which was heightened by their awareness of the war's financial and human costs, by scenes of Iraq in chaos, by surging anti-American attitudes in Europe and in Muslim countries, and by inflamed pro-terrorist attitudes. To reduce their dissonance, noted the Program of International Policy Attitudes, some Americans revised their memories of their government's primary rationale for going to war. The reasons now became liberating an oppressed people from tyrannical and genocidal rule, and laying the groundwork for a more peaceful and democratic Middle East. Three months after the war began, the once-minority opinion became, for a time, the majority view: 58 percent of Americans now supported the war even if there were none of the proclaimed weapons of mass destruction (Gallup, 2003). "Whether or not they find weapons of mass destruction doesn't matter," suggested Republican pollster Frank Luntz (2003), "because the rationale for the war changed."

In *Mistakes Were Made (But Not By Me): Why We Justify Foolish Beliefs, Bad Decisions, and Hurtful Acts,* social psychologists Carol Tavris and Elliot Aronson (2007, p. 7) illustrate dissonance reduction by leaders of various political parties when faced with clear evidence that a decision they made or a course of action they chose turned out to be wrong, even disastrous. This human phenomenon is nonpartisan,

cognitive dissonance
Tension that arises when one is simultaneously aware of two inconsistent cognitions. For example, dissonance may occur when we realize that we have, with little justification, acted contrary to our attitudes or made a decision favoring one alternative despite reasons favoring another.

"I made a tough decision. And knowing what I know today, I'd make the decision again."

—GEORGE W. BUSH, DECEMBER 12, 2005

note Tavris and Aronson: "A president who has justified his actions to himself, believing that he has *the truth*, becomes impervious to self-correction." For example, Democratic President Lyndon Johnson's biographer described him as someone who held to his beliefs, even when sinking in the quagmire of Vietnam, regardless "of the facts in the matter." And Republican president George W. Bush, in the years after launching the Iraq war, said that "knowing what I know today, I'd make the decision again" (2005), that "I've never been more convinced that the decisions I made are the right decisions" (2006), and that "this war has . . . come at a high cost in lives and treasure, but those costs are necessary" (2008).

Cognitive dissonance theory offers an explanation for self-persuasion, and it offers several surprising predictions. See if you can anticipate them.

INSUFFICIENT JUSTIFICATION

Imagine you are a participant in a famous experiment staged by the creative Festinger and his student J. Merrill Carlsmith (1959). For an hour, you are required to perform dull tasks, such as turning wooden knobs again and again. After you finish, the experimenter (Carlsmith) explains that the study concerns how expectations affect performance. The next participant, waiting outside, must be led to expect an *interesting* experiment. The seemingly upset experimenter, whom Festinger had spent hours coaching until he became extremely convincing, explains that the assistant who usually creates this expectation couldn't make this session. Wringing his hands, he pleads, "Could you fill in and do this?"

It's for science and you are being paid, so you agree to tell the next participant (who is actually the experimenter's accomplice) what a delightful experience you have just had. "Really?" responds the supposed participant. "A friend of mine was in this experiment a week ago, and she said it was boring." "Oh, no," you respond, "it's really very interesting. You get good exercise while turning some knobs. I'm sure you'll enjoy it." Finally, someone else who is studying how people react to experiments has you complete a questionnaire that asks how much you actually enjoyed your knob-turning experience.

Now for the prediction: Under which condition are you most likely to believe your little lie and say that the experiment was indeed interesting? When paid $1 for fibbing, as some of the participants were? Or when paid a then-lavish $20, as others were? Contrary to the common notion that big rewards produce big effects, Festinger and Carlsmith made an outrageous prediction: Those paid just $1 (hardly sufficient justification for a lie) would be most likely to adjust their attitudes to their actions. Having **insufficient justification** for their actions, they would experience more discomfort (dissonance) and thus be more motivated to believe in what they had done. Those paid $20 had sufficient justification for what they had done and hence should have experienced less dissonance. As Figure 4.6 shows, the results fit this intriguing prediction.*

In dozens of later experiments, this attitudes-follow-behavior effect was strongest when people felt some choice and when their actions had foreseeable consequences. One experiment had people read disparaging lawyer jokes into a recorder (for example, "How can you tell when a lawyer is lying? His lips are moving"). The reading produced more negative attitudes toward lawyers when it was a chosen rather than a coerced activity (Hobden & Olson, 1994). Other experiments have engaged people to write essays for a measly $1.50 or so. When the essay argues something they don't believe in—say, a tuition increase—the underpaid writers begin to feel somewhat greater sympathy with the policy. Pretense becomes reality.

insufficient justification
Reduction of dissonance by internally justifying one's behavior when external justification is "insufficient."

---

* There is a seldom-reported final aspect of this 1950s experiment. Imagine yourself finally back with the experimenter, who is truthfully explaining the whole study. Not only do you learn that you've been duped, but also the experimenter asks for the $20 back. Do you comply? Festinger and Carlsmith note that all their Stanford student participants willingly reached into their pockets and gave back the money. This is a foretaste of some quite amazing observations on compliance and conformity discussed in Chapter 6. As we will see, when the social situation makes clear demands, people usually respond accordingly.

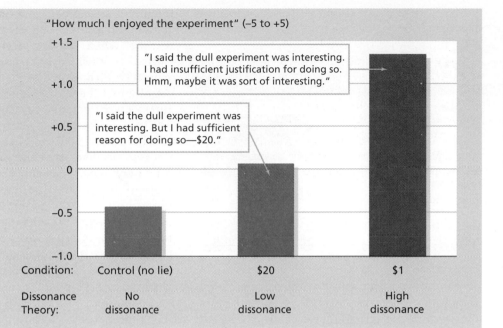

"How much I enjoyed the experiment" (−5 to +5)

"I said the dull experiment was interesting. I had insufficient justification for doing so. Hmm, maybe it was sort of interesting."

"I said the dull experiment was interesting. But I had sufficient reason for doing so—$20."

Condition:	Control (no lie)	$20	$1
Dissonance Theory:	No dissonance	Low dissonance	High dissonance

FIGURE :: 4.6

Insufficient Justification

Dissonance theory predicts that when our actions are not fully explained by external rewards or coercion, we will experience dissonance, which we can reduce by believing in what we have done.

Source: Data from Festinger & Carlsmith, 1959.

Earlier we noted how the insufficient justification principle works with punishments. Children were more likely to internalize a request not to play with an attractive toy if they were given a mild threat that insufficiently justified their compliance. When a parent says, "Clean up your room, Joshua, or else expect a hard spanking," Joshua won't need to internally justify cleaning his room. The severe threat is justification enough.

Note that cognitive dissonance theory focuses not on the relative effectiveness of rewards and punishments administered after the act but, rather, on what induces a desired action. It aims to have Joshua say, "I am cleaning up my room because I want a clean room," rather than, "I am cleaning up my room because my parents will kill me if I don't." Students who perceive their required community service as something they would have chosen to do are more likely to anticipate future volunteering than those who feel coerced (Stukas & others, 1999). The principle: *Attitudes follow behaviors for which we feel some responsibility.*

Authoritarian management will be effective, the theory predicts, only when the authority is present—because people are unlikely to internalize forced behavior. Bree, a formerly enslaved talking horse in C. S. Lewis's *The Horse and His Boy* (1974), observes, "One of the worst results of being a slave and being forced to do things is that when there is no one to force you any more you find you have almost lost the power of forcing yourself" (p. 193). Dissonance theory insists that encouragement and inducement should be enough to elicit the desired action (so that attitudes may follow the behavior). But it suggests that managers, teachers, and parents should use only enough incentive to elicit the desired behavior.

Dissonance theory suggests that parents should aim to elicit desired behavior noncoercively, thus motivating children to internalize the appropriate attitudes.

DISSONANCE AFTER DECISIONS

The emphasis on perceived choice and responsibility implies that decisions produce dissonance. When faced with an important decision—what college to attend, whom to date, which job to accept—we are sometimes torn between two

THE inside STORY

Leon Festinger on Dissonance Reduction

Following a 1934 earthquake in India, there were rumors outside the disaster zone of worse disasters to follow. It occurred to me that these rumors might be "anxiety-justifying"—cognitions that would justify their lingering fears. From that germ of an idea, I developed my theory of dissonance reduction—making your view of the world fit with how you feel or what you've done.

Leon Festinger (1920–1989)

equally attractive alternatives. Perhaps you can recall a time when, having committed yourself, you became painfully aware of dissonant cognitions—the desirable features of what you had rejected and the undesirable features of what you had chosen. If you decided to live on campus, you may have realized you were giving up the spaciousness and freedom of an apartment in favor of cramped, noisy dorm quarters. If you elected to live off campus, you may have realized that your decision meant physical separation from campus and friends, and having to cook and clean for yourself.

After making important decisions, we usually reduce dissonance by upgrading the chosen alternative and downgrading the unchosen option. In the first published dissonance experiment (1956), Jack Brehm brought some of his wedding gifts to his University of Minnesota lab and had women rate eight products, such as a toaster, a radio, and a hair dryer. Brehm then showed the women two objects they had rated closely and told them they could have whichever they chose. Later, when rerating the eight objects, the women increased their evaluations of the item they had chosen and decreased their evaluations of the rejected item. It seems that after we have made our choices, the grass does not then grow greener on the other side of the fence. (Afterwards, Brehm confessed he couldn't afford to let them keep what they chose.)

With simple decisions, this deciding-becomes-believing effect can breed overconfidence (Blanton & others, 2001): "What I've decided must be right." The effect

Big decisions can produce big dissonance when one later ponders the negative aspects of what is chosen and the positive aspects of what was not chosen.

can occur very quickly. Robert Knox and James Inkster (1968) found that racetrack bettors who had just put down their money felt more optimistic about their bets than did those who were about to bet. In the few moments that intervened between standing in line and walking away from the betting window, nothing had changed—except the decisive action and the person's feelings about it. There may sometimes be but a slight difference between two options, as I can recall in helping make faculty tenure decisions. The competence of one faculty member who barely makes it and that of another who barely loses seem not very different—until after you make and announce the decision.

Once made, decisions grow their own self-justifying legs of support. Often, these new legs are strong enough that when one leg is pulled away—perhaps the original one as in the Iraq war case—the decision does not collapse. Rosalia decides to take a trip home if it can be done for an airfare under $400. It can, so she makes her reservation and begins to

I don't like to agonize over my decisions until after I've made them.

Post-decision dissonance.
© David Sipress. Reprinted with permission.

think of additional reasons why she will be glad to see her family. When she goes to buy the tickets, however, she learns there has been a fare increase to $475. No matter; she is now determined to go. As when being low-balled by a car dealer, it never occurs to people, reports Robert Cialdini (1984, p. 103), "that those additional reasons might never have existed had the choice not been made in the first place."

And it's not just grown-ups who do this. A Yale University team led by Louisa Egan (2007), invited 4-year-olds to rate different stickers on a scale of smiley faces. With each child, the researchers then picked three stickers which that child had rated equally, and randomly identified two (let's call them Sticker A and Sticker B) from which the children could choose one to take home. Next they let the child choose one more—either the unchosen sticker or the third one, Sticker C. The result (which put a smiley on my face): The children apparently reduced dissonance by downplaying the appeal of the unchosen first sticker, thus moving them to favor Sticker C 63 percent of the time (rather than half the time, as we might have expected). They repeated the experiment with capuchin monkeys using alternative sweets instead of stickers. As with the children, so with the monkeys: They, too, revised their attitudes after making an initial decision.

Self-Perception

Although dissonance theory has inspired much research, an even simpler theory also explains its phenomena. Consider how we make inferences about other people's attitudes. We see how a person acts in a particular situation, and then we attribute the behavior either to the person's traits and attitudes or to environmental forces. If we see parents coercing 10-year-old Brett into saying, "I'm sorry," we attribute Brett's apology to the situation, not to his personal regret. If we see Brett apologizing with no apparent inducement, we attribute the apology to Brett himself (Figure 4.7).

"Every time you make a choice you are turning the central part of you, the part of you that chooses, into something a little different from what it was before."
—*C. S. LEWIS, MERE CHRISTIANITY, 1942*

Why do actions affect attitudes?

FIGURE :: 4.7

Three Theories Explain Why Attitudes Follow Behavior

self-perception theory
The theory that when we are unsure of our attitudes, we infer them much as would someone observing us, by looking at our behavior and the circumstances under which it occurs.

"Self-knowledge is best learned, not by contemplation, but action."
—GOETHE, 1749–1832

"I can watch myself and my actions, just like an outsider."
—ANNE FRANK, THE DIARY OF A YOUNG GIRL, 1947

Self-perception theory (proposed by Daryl Bem, 1972) assumes that we make similar inferences when we observe our own behavior. When our attitudes are weak or ambiguous, we are in the position of someone observing us from the outside. Hearing myself talk informs me of my attitudes; seeing my actions provides clues to how strong my beliefs are. This is especially so when I can't easily attribute my behavior to external constraints. The acts we freely commit are self-revealing.

The pioneering psychologist William James proposed a similar explanation for emotion a century ago. We infer our emotions, he suggested, by observing our bodies and our behaviors. A stimulus such as a growling bear confronts a woman in the forest. She tenses, her heartbeat increases, adrenaline flows, and she runs away. Observing all this, she then experiences fear. At a college where I am to give a lecture, I awake before dawn and am unable to get back to sleep. Noting my wakefulness, I conclude that I must be anxious.

Do people who observe themselves agreeing to a small request indeed come to perceive themselves as the helpful sort of person who responds positively to requests for help? Is that why, in the foot-in-the-door experiments, people will then later agree to larger requests? Indeed, yes, report Jerry Burger and David Caldwell (2003). Behavior can modify self-concept.

EXPRESSIONS AND ATTITUDE

You may be skeptical of the self-perception effect, as I initially was. Experiments on the effects of facial expressions suggest a way for you to experience it. When James Laird (1974, 1984) induced college students to frown while attaching electrodes to their faces—"contract these muscles," "pull your brows together"—they reported feeling angry. It's more fun to try out Laird's other finding: Those induced to make a smiling face felt happier and found cartoons more humorous. Those induced to repeatedly practice happy (versus sad or angry) expressions may recall more happy memories and find the happy mood lingering (Schnall & Laird, 2003). Viewing one's expressions in a mirror magnifies the self-perception effect (Kleinke & others, 1998).

We have all experienced this phenomenon. We're feeling crabby, but then the phone rings or someone comes to the door and elicits from us warm, polite behavior. "How's everything?" "Just fine, thanks. How are things with you?" "Oh, not bad. . . ." If our feelings are not intense, this warm behavior may change our whole attitude. It's tough to smile and feel grouchy. When Miss Universe parades her smile, she may, after all, be helping herself feel happy. As Rodgers and Hammerstein reminded us, when we are afraid, it may help to "whistle a happy tune." Going through the motions can trigger the emotions. Contrariwise, extending the middle finger makes others' ambiguous expressions seem more hostile (Chandler & Schwarz, 2009).

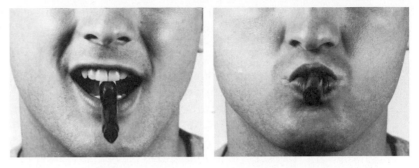

According to German psychologist Fritz Strack and colleagues (1988), people find cartoons funnier while holding a pen with their teeth (using a smiling muscle) than while holding it with their lips (using muscles incompatible with smiling).

Even your gait can affect how you feel. When you get up from reading this chapter, walk for a minute taking short, shuffling steps, with eyes downcast. It's a great way to feel depressed. "Sit all day in a moping posture, sigh, and reply to everything with a dismal voice, and your melancholy lingers," noted William James (1890, p. 463). Want to feel better? Walk for a minute taking long strides with your arms swinging and your eyes straight ahead.

If our expressions influence our feelings, then would imitating others' expressions help us know what they are feeling? An experiment by Katherine Burns Vaughan and John Lanzetta (1981) suggests it would. They asked Dartmouth College students to observe someone receiving electric shock. They told some of the observers to make a pained expression whenever the shock came on. If, as Freud and others supposed, expressing an emotion allows us to discharge it, then the pained expression should be inwardly calming (Cacioppo & others, 1991). Actually, compared with other students who did not act out the expressions, these grimacing students perspired more and had faster heart rates whenever they saw the shock being delivered. Acting out the person's emotion enabled the observers to feel more empathy. The implication: To sense how other people are feeling, let your own face mirror their expressions.

Actually, you hardly need try. Observing others' faces, postures, and voices, we naturally and unconsciously mimic their moment-to-moment reactions (Hatfield & others, 1992). We synchronize our movements, postures, and tones of voice with theirs. Doing so helps us tune in to what they're feeling. It also makes for "emotional contagion," which helps explain why it's fun to be around happy people and depressing to be around depressed people (Chapter 14).

Our facial expressions also influence our attitudes. In a clever experiment, Gary Wells and Richard Petty (1980)

"The free expression by outward signs of emotion intensifies it. On the other hand, the repression, as far as possible, of all outward signs softens our emotions."

—*CHARLES DARWIN,*
THE EXPRESSION OF THE EMOTIONS IN MAN AND ANIMALS, *1897*

All Nippon Airways employees, biting wooden chopsticks, beam during a smile training session.

had University of Alberta students "test headphone sets" by making either vertical or horizontal head movements while listening to a radio editorial. Who most agreed with the editorial? Those who had been nodding their heads up and down. Why? Wells and Petty surmised that positive thoughts are compatible with vertical nodding and incompatible with horizontal motion. Try it yourself when listening to someone: Do you feel more agreeable when nodding rather than shaking your head?

At the University of Cologne, Thomas Mussweiler (2006) likewise discovered that stereotyped actions feed stereotyped thinking. In one clever experiment, he induced some people to move about in the portly manner of an obese person—by having them wear a life vest and by putting weights on their wrists and ankles—and then to give their impressions of someone described on paper. Those whose movements simulated obesity, more than those in a control condition, perceived the target person (described on the paper) as exhibiting traits (friendliness, sluggishness, unhealthiness) that people often perceive in obese people. In follow-up experiments, people induced to move slowly, as an elderly person might, ascribed more elderly stereotypic traits to a target person. Doing influenced thinking.

Postures also affect performance. After noting that people associate an arms-folded posture with determination and persistence, Ron Friedman and Andrew Elliot (2008) had students attempt to solve impossible anagrams. Those instructed to work with their arms folded persevered for an average 55 seconds, nearly double the 30 seconds of those with their hands on their thighs.

OVERJUSTIFICATION AND INTRINSIC MOTIVATIONS

Recall the insufficient justification effect: The smallest incentive that will get people to do something is usually the most effective in getting them to like the activity and keep on doing it. Cognitive dissonance theory offers one explanation for this: When external inducements are insufficient to justify our behavior, we reduce dissonance internally, by justifying the behavior.

Self-perception theory offers a different explanation: People explain their behavior by noting the conditions under which it occurs. Imagine hearing someone proclaim the wisdom of a tuition increase after being paid $20 to do so. Surely the statement would seem less sincere than if you thought the person was expressing those opinions for no pay. Perhaps we make similar inferences when observing ourselves. We observe our uncoerced action and infer our attitude.

Self-perception theory goes a step further. Contrary to the notion that rewards always increase motivation, it suggests that unnecessary rewards can have a hidden cost. Rewarding people for doing what they already enjoy may lead them to attribute their action to the reward. If so, this would undermine their self-perception that they do it because they like it. Experiments by Edward Deci and Richard Ryan (1991, 1997, 2008) at the University of Rochester, by Mark Lepper and David Greene (1979) at Stanford, and by Ann Boggiano and her colleagues (1985, 1987, 1992) at the University of Colorado have confirmed this

Self-perception at work.

"I don't sing because I am happy. I am happy because I sing."

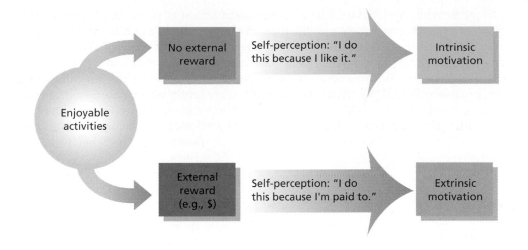

FIGURE :: 4.8

Intrinsic and Extrinsic Motivation

When people do something they enjoy, without reward or coercion, they attribute their behavior to their love of the activity. External rewards undermine intrinsic motivation by leading people to attribute their behavior to the incentive.

overjustification effect. Pay people for playing with puzzles, and they will later play with the puzzles less than will those who play for no pay. Promise children a reward for doing what they intrinsically enjoy (for example, playing with Magic Markers), and you will turn their play into work (Figure 4.8).

A folktale illustrates the overjustification effect. An old man lived alone on a street where boys played noisily every afternoon. The din annoyed him, so one day he called the boys to his door. He told them he loved the cheerful sound of children's voices and promised them each 50 cents if they would return the next day. Next afternoon the youngsters raced back and played more lustily than ever. The old man paid them and promised another reward the next day. Again they returned, whooping it up, and the man again paid them; this time 25 cents. The following day they got only 15 cents, and the man explained that his meager resources were being exhausted. "Please, though, would you come to play for 10 cents tomorrow?" The disappointed boys told the man they would not be back. It wasn't worth the effort, they said, to play all afternoon at his house for only 10 cents.

As self-perception theory implies, an *unanticipated* reward does not diminish intrinsic interest, because people can still attribute their actions to their own motivation (Bradley & Mannell, 1984; Tang & Hall, 1995). (It's like the heroine who, having fallen in love with the woodcutter, now learns that he's really a prince.) And if compliments for a good job make us feel more competent and successful, this can actually increase our intrinsic motivation. When rightly administered, rewards may also boost creativity (Eisenberger & others, 1999, 2001, 2003).

The overjustification effect occurs when someone offers an unnecessary reward beforehand in an obvious effort to control behavior. What matters is what a reward implies: Rewards and praise that inform people of their achievements—that make them feel, "I'm very good at this"—boost intrinsic motivation. Rewards that seek to control people and lead them to believe it was the reward that caused their effort—"I did it for the money"—diminish the intrinsic appeal of an enjoyable task (Rosenfeld & others, 1980; Sansone, 1986).

How then can we cultivate people's enjoyment of initially unappealing tasks? Maria may find her first piano lessons frustrating. Toshi may not have an intrinsic love of ninth-grade science. DeShawn may embark on a career not looking forward to making those first sales calls. In such cases, the parent, the teacher, or the manager should probably use some incentives to coax the desired behavior (Boggiano & Ruble, 1985; Workman & Williams, 1980). After the person complies, suggest an intrinsic reason for doing so: "I'm not surprised that sales call went well, because you are so good at making a first impression."

overjustification effect
The result of bribing people to do what they already like doing; they may then see their actions as externally controlled rather than intrinsically appealing.

If we provide students with just enough justification to perform a learning task and use rewards and labels to help them feel competent, we may enhance their enjoyment and their eagerness to pursue the subject on their own. When there is too much justification—as happens in classrooms where teachers dictate behavior and use rewards to control the children—student-driven learning may diminish (Deci & Ryan, 1985, 1991, 2008). My younger son eagerly consumed 6 or 8 library books a week—until our library started a reading club that promised a party to those who read 10 books in three months. Three weeks later he began checking out only 1 or 2 books during our weekly visits. Why? "Because you only need to read 10 books, you know."

Comparing the Theories

We have seen one explanation of why our actions might only *seem* to affect our attitudes (*self-presentation* theory). And we have seen two explanations of why our actions genuinely affect our attitudes: (1) the *dissonance*-theory assumption that we justify our behavior to reduce our internal discomfort, and (2) the *self-perception*-theory assumption that we observe our behavior and make reasonable inferences about our attitudes, much as we observe other people and infer *their* attitudes.

These two explanations seem to contradict each other. Which is right? It's difficult to find a definitive test. In most instances they make the same predictions, and we can bend each theory to accommodate most of the findings we have considered (Greenwald, 1975). Self-perception theorist Daryl Bem (1972) even suggested it boils down to a matter of personal loyalties and preferences. This illustrates the human element in scientific theorizing. Neither dissonance theory nor self-perception theory has been handed to us by nature. Both are products of human imagination—creative attempts to simplify and explain what we've observed.

It is not unusual in science to find that a principle, such as "attitudes follow behavior," is predictable from more than one theory. Physicist Richard Feynman (1967) marveled that "one of the amazing characteristics of nature" is the "wide range of beautiful ways" in which we can describe it: "I do not understand the reason why it is that the correct laws of physics seem to be expressible in such a tremendous variety of ways" (pp. 53–55). Like different roads leading to the same place, different sets of assumptions can lead to the same principle. If anything, this strengthens our confidence in the principle. It becomes credible not only because of the data supporting it but also because it rests on more than one theoretical pillar.

DISSONANCE AS AROUSAL

Can we say that one of our theories is better? On one key point, strong support has emerged for dissonance theory. Recall that dissonance is, by definition, an aroused state of uncomfortable tension. To reduce that tension, we supposedly change our attitudes. Self-perception theory says nothing about tension being aroused when our actions and attitudes are not in harmony. It assumes merely that when our attitudes are weak to begin with, we will use our behavior and its circumstances as a clue to those attitudes (like the person who said, "How do I tell what I think till I see what I say?" [Forster, 1976]).

Are conditions that supposedly produce dissonance (for example, making decisions or taking actions that are contrary to one's attitudes) indeed uncomfortably arousing? Clearly yes, providing that the behavior has unwanted consequences for which the person feels responsible (Cooper, 1999; Elliot & Devine, 1994). If, in the privacy of your room, you say something you don't believe, dissonance will be minimal. It will be much greater if there are unpleasant results—if someone hears and believes you, if the statement causes harm and the negative effects are irrevocable, and if the person harmed is someone you like. If, moreover, you feel responsible for those consequences—if you can't easily excuse your act because you freely agreed to it and if you were able to foresee its consequences—then uncomfortable dissonance will be aroused. Such dissonance-related arousal is detectable as increased perspiration and heart rate (Cacioppo & Petty, 1986; Croyle & Cooper, 1983; Losch & Cacioppo, 1990).

Why is "volunteering" to say or do undesirable things so arousing? Because, suggests Claude Steele's (1988) **self-affirmation theory,** such acts are embarrassing. They make us feel foolish. They threaten our sense of personal competence and goodness. Justifying our actions and decisions is therefore *self-affirming*; it protects and supports our sense of integrity and self-worth. And when people engage in dissonance-generating actions—uncoerced counterattitudinal actions—their thinking left frontal lobes buzz with extra arousal (Harmon-Jones & others, 2008). This is the grinding gears of belief change at work.

What do you suppose happens, then, if we offer people who have committed self-contradictory acts a way to reaffirm their self-worth, such as doing good deeds? In several experiments Steele found that, with their self-concepts restored, people felt much less need to justify their acts (Steele & others, 1993). People with high and secure self-esteem also engage in less self-justification (Holland & others, 2002).

So, dissonance conditions do indeed arouse tension, especially when they threaten positive feelings of self-worth. But is this arousal necessary for the attitudes-follow-behavior effect? Steele and his colleagues (1981) believe the answer is yes. When drinking alcohol reduces dissonance-produced arousal, the attitudes-follow-behavior effect disappears. In one of their experiments, they induced University of Washington students to write essays favoring a big tuition increase. The students reduced their resulting dissonance by softening their antituition attitudes—*unless* after writing the unpleasant essays they drank alcohol, supposedly as part of a beer- or vodka-tasting experiment.

self-affirmation theory
A theory that (a) people often experience a self-image threat, after engaging in an undesirable behavior; and (b) they can compensate by affirming another aspect of the self. Threaten people's self-concept in one domain, and they will compensate either by refocusing or by doing good deeds in some other domain.

SELF-PERCEIVING WHEN NOT SELF-CONTRADICTING

Dissonance procedures are uncomfortably arousing. That makes for self-persuasion after acting contrary to one's attitudes. But dissonance theory cannot explain attitude changes that occur without dissonance. When people argue a position that is in line with their opinion, although a step or two beyond it, procedures that eliminate arousal do not eliminate attitude change (Fazio & others, 1977, 1979). Dissonance theory also does not explain the overjustification effect, since being paid to do what you like to do should not arouse great tension. And what about situations where the action does not contradict any attitude—when, for example, people are induced to smile or grimace? Here, too, there should be no dissonance. For these cases, self-perception theory has a ready explanation.

In short, it appears that dissonance theory successfully explains what happens when we act contrary to clearly defined attitudes: We feel tension, so we adjust our attitudes to reduce it. Dissonance theory, then, explains attitude *change*. In situations where our attitudes are not well formed, self-perception theory explains attitude *formation*. As we act and reflect, we develop more readily accessible attitudes to guide our future behavior (Fazio, 1987; Roese & Olson, 1994).

"Rather amazingly, 40 years after its publication, the theory of cognitive dissonance looks as strong and as interesting as ever."
—*SOCIAL PSYCHOLOGIST JACK W. BREHM (1999)*

Summing Up: Why Does Our Behavior Affect Our Attitudes?

Three competing theories explain why our actions affect our attitude reports.

- *Self-presentation theory* assumes that people, especially those who self-monitor their behavior hoping to create good impressions, will adapt their attitude reports to appear consistent with their actions. The available evidence confirms that people do adjust their attitude statements out of concern for what other people will think. But it also shows that some genuine attitude change occurs.

Two of these theories propose that our actions trigger genuine attitude change.

- *Dissonance theory* explains this attitude change by assuming that we feel tension after acting contrary to our attitudes or making difficult decisions. To reduce that arousal, we internally justify our behavior. Dissonance theory further proposes that the less external justification we have for our undesirable actions, the more we feel responsible for them, and thus the more dissonance arises and the more attitudes change.

- *Self-perception theory* assumes that when our attitudes are weak, we simply observe our behavior and its circumstances, then infer our attitudes. One interesting implication of self-perception theory is the "overjustification effect": Rewarding people to do what they like doing anyway can turn their pleasure into drudgery (if the reward leads them to attribute their behavior to the reward).

- Evidence supports predictions from both theories, suggesting that each describes what happens under certain conditions.

 POSTSCRIPT: Changing Ourselves through Action

To make anything a habit, do it.
To not make it a habit, do not do it.
To unmake a habit, do something else in place of it.
—*Greek Stoic philosopher Epictetus*

"If we wish to conquer undesirable emotional tendencies in ourselves we must . . . coldbloodedly go through the outward motions of those contrary dispositions we prefer to cultivate."

—*WILLIAM JAMES, "WHAT IS AN EMOTION?" 1884*

This chapter's attitudes-follow-behavior principle offers a powerful lesson for life: If we want to change ourselves in some important way, it's best not to wait for insight or inspiration. Sometimes we need to act—to begin to write that paper, to make those phone calls, to see that person—even if we don't feel like acting. Jacques Barzun (1975) recognized the energizing power of action when he advised aspiring writers to engage in the act of writing even if contemplation had left them feeling uncertain about their ideas:

> If you are too modest about yourself or too plain indifferent about the possible reader and yet are required to write, then you have to pretend. Make believe that you want to bring somebody around to your opinion; in other words, adopt a thesis and start expounding it. . . . With a slight effort of the kind at the start—a challenge to utterance— you will find your pretense disappearing and a real concern creeping in. The subject will have taken hold of you as it does in the work of all habitual writers. (pp. 173–174)

This attitudes-follow-behavior phenomenon is not irrational or magical. That which prompts us to act may also prompt us to think. Writing an essay or role-playing an opposing view forces us to consider arguments we otherwise might have ignored. Also, we remember information best when we have explained it actively in our own terms. As one student wrote me, "It wasn't until I tried to verbalize my beliefs that I really understood them." As a teacher and a writer, I must therefore remind myself not always to lay out finished results. It is better to stimulate students to think through the implications of a theory, to make them active listeners and readers. Even taking notes deepens the impression. William James (1899) made the same point a century ago: "No reception without reaction, no impression without correlative expression—this is the great maxim which the teacher ought never to forget."

Making the Social Connection

In this chapter we discussed self-presentation and the way we manage the impressions we make on others. For an interesting example of self-presentation, go to the Online Learning Center and watch the video on Motivation and Emotional Language of the Face. The OLC also presents a video of Philip Zimbardo describing his famous Stanford Prison Experiment, which we examined as part of this chapter's discussion of attitudes and behavior. In Chapter 8 we will meet Zimbardo again through his study of changes in people's behavior when they believe they are anonymous.

Social
part**two** Influence

So far in this book we have considered mostly "within-the-skin" phenomena—how we think about one another. Now we consider "between-skins" happenings—how we influence and relate to one another. Therefore, in Chapters 5 through 8 we probe social psychology's central concern: the powers of social influence.

What are these unseen social forces that push and pull us? How powerful are they? Research on social influence helps illuminate the invisible strings by which our social worlds move us about. The next four chapters reveal these subtle powers, especially cultural influences (Chapter 5), the forces of social conformity (Chapter 6), the principles of persuasion (Chapter 7), the consequences of participation in groups (Chapter 8), and how all these influences operate together in everyday situations.

Seeing these influences, we may better understand why people feel and act as they do. And we may ourselves become less vulnerable to unwanted manipulation and more adept at pulling our own strings.

Genes, Culture, and Gender

"By birth, the same; by custom, different."

—Confucius, *The Analects*

How are we influenced by human nature and cultural diversity?

How are gender similarities and differences explained?

Evolution and gender: Doing what comes naturally?

Culture and gender: Doing as the culture says?

What can we conclude about genes, culture, and gender?

Postscript: Should we view ourselves as products or architects of our social worlds?

Approaching Earth from light-years away, alien scientists assigned to study the species *Homo sapiens* feel their excitement rising. Their plan: to observe two randomly sampled humans. Their first subject, Jan, is a verbally combative trial lawyer who grew up in Nashville but moved west seeking the "California lifestyle." After an affair and a divorce, Jan is enjoying a second marriage. Friends describe Jan as an independent thinker who is self-confident, competitive, and somewhat domineering.

Their second subject, Tomoko, lives with a spouse and their two children in a rural Japanese village, a walk from the homes of both their parents. Tomoko is proud of being a good child, a loyal spouse, and a protective parent. Friends describe Tomoko as kind, gentle, respectful, sensitive, and supportive of extended family.

From their small sample of two people of different genders and cultures, what might our alien scientists conclude about human nature? Would they wonder whether the two are from different subspecies? Or would they be struck by deeper similarities beneath the surface differences?

The questions faced by our alien scientists are those faced by today's earthbound scientists: How do we humans differ? How are we alike? Those questions are central to a world where social diversity has become, as historian Arthur Schlesinger (1991) said, "the explosive problem of our times." In a world struggling with cultural differences, can we learn to accept our diversity, value our cultural identities, and recognize our human kinship? I believe we can. To see why, let's consider the evolutionary, cultural, and social roots of our humanity. Then let's see how each might help us understand gender similarities and differences.

How Are We Influenced by Human Nature and Cultural Diversity?

Two perspectives dominate current thinking about human similarities and differences: an evolutionary perspective, emphasizing human kinship, and a cultural perspective, emphasizing human diversity. Nearly everyone agrees that we need both: Our genes enable an adaptive human brain—a cerebral hard drive that receives the culture's software.

In many important ways, Jan and Tomoko are more alike than different. As members of one great family with common ancestors, they share not only a common biology but also common behavior tendencies. Each of them sleeps and wakes, feels hunger and thirst, and develops language through identical mechanisms. Jan and Tomoko both prefer sweet tastes to sour, and they divide the visual spectrum into similar colors. They and their kin across the globe all know how to read one another's frowns and smiles.

Jan and Tomoko—and all of us everywhere—are intensely social. We join groups, conform, and recognize distinctions of social status. We return favors, punish offenses, and grieve a child's death. As children, beginning at about 8 months of age, we displayed fear of strangers, and as adults we favor members of our own groups. Confronted by those with dissimilar attitudes or attributes, we react warily or negatively. Anthropologist Donald Brown (1991, 2000) identified several hundred such universal behavior and language patterns. To sample among just those beginning with "v," all human societies have verbs, violence, visiting, and vowels.

Our alien scientists could drop in anywhere and find humans conversing and arguing, laughing and crying, feasting and dancing, singing and worshiping. Everywhere, humans prefer living with others—in families and communal groups—to living alone. Everywhere, the family dramas that entertain us—from Greek tragedies to Chinese fiction to Mexican soap operas—portray similar plots (Dutton, 2006). Ditto adventure stories in which strong and courageous men, supported by wise old people, overcome evil to the delight of beautiful women or threatened children. Such commonalities define our shared human nature. We're all kin beneath the skin.

Genes, Evolution, and Behavior

The universal behaviors that define human nature arise from our biological similarity. We may say "My ancestors came from Ireland" or "My roots are in China" or "I'm Italian," but anthropologists tell us that if we could trace our ancestors back 100,000 or more years, we would see that we are all Africans (Shipman, 2003). In response to climate change and the availability of food, those early hominids migrated across Africa into Asia, Europe, the Australian subcontinent and, eventually, the Americas. As they adapted to their new environments, early humans developed differences that, measured on anthropological scales, are recent and superficial. For example, those who stayed in Africa had darker skin pigment—what Harvard psychologist Steven Pinker (2002) calls "sunscreen for the tropics"—and those who went far north of the equator evolved lighter skins capable of synthesizing vitamin D in less direct sunlight. Still, historically, we all are Africans.

We were Africans recently enough that "there has not been much time to accumulate many new versions of the genes," notes Pinker (2002, p. 143). And, indeed, biologists who study our genes have found that we humans—even humans as seemingly different as Jan and Tomoko—are strikingly similar, like members of one tribe. We may be more numerous than chimpanzees, but chimps are more genetically varied.

To explain the traits of our species, and all species, the British naturalist Charles Darwin (1859) proposed an evolutionary process. Follow the genes, he advised. Darwin's idea, to which philosopher Daniel Dennett (2005) would give "the gold medal for the best idea anybody ever had," was that **natural selection** enables evolution.

The idea, simplified, is this:

- Organisms have many and varied offspring.
- Those offspring compete for survival in their environment.
- Certain biological and behavioral variations increase their chances of reproduction and survival in that environment.
- Those offspring that do survive are more likely to pass their genes to ensuing generations.
- Thus, over time, population characteristics may change.

Natural selection implies that certain genes—those that predisposed traits that increased the odds of surviving long enough to reproduce and nurture descendants—became more abundant. In the snowy Arctic environment, for example, genes programming a thick coat of camouflaging white fur have won the genetic competition in polar bears.

Natural selection, long an organizing principle of biology, has recently become an important principle for psychology as well. **Evolutionary psychology** studies how natural selection predisposes not just physical traits suited to particular contexts—polar bears' coats, bats' sonar, humans' color vision—but also psychological traits and social behaviors that enhance the preservation and spread of one's genes (Buss, 2005, 2007). We humans are the way we are, say evolutionary psychologists, because nature selected those who had our traits—those who, for example, preferred the sweet taste of nutritious, energy-providing foods and who disliked the bitter or sour flavors of foods that are toxic. Those lacking such preferences were less likely to survive to contribute their genes to posterity.

As mobile gene machines, we carry not only the physical legacy but also the psychological legacy of our ancestors' adaptive preferences. We long for whatever helped them survive, reproduce, and nurture their offspring to survive and reproduce. "The purpose of the heart is to pump blood," notes evolutionary psychologist David Barash (2003). "The brain's purpose," he adds, is to direct our organs and our behavior "in a way that maximizes our evolutionary success. That's it."

The evolutionary perspective highlights our universal human nature. We not only share certain food preferences but we also share answers to social questions such as, Whom should I trust, and fear? Whom should I help? When, and with whom, should I mate? Who may dominate me, and whom may I control? Evolutionary psychologists contend that our emotional and behavioral answers to those questions are the same answers that worked for our ancestors.

Because these social tasks are common to people everywhere, humans everywhere tend to agree on the answers. For example, all humans rank others by authority and status. And all have ideas about economic justice (Fiske, 1992). Evolutionary

natural selection
The evolutionary process by which heritable traits that best enable organisms to survive and reproduce in particular environments are passed to ensuing generations.

"The exciting thing about evolution is not that our understanding is perfect or complete but that it is the foundation stone for the rest of biology."
—*DONALD KENNEDY, EDITOR-IN-CHIEF,* SCIENCE, *2005*

evolutionary psychology
The study of the evolution of cognition and behavior using principles of natural selection.

"Psychology will be based on a new foundation."
—*CHARLES DARWIN,* THE ORIGIN OF SPECIES, *1859*

psychologists highlight these universal characteristics that have evolved through natural selection. Cultures, however, provide the specific rules for working out these elements of social life.

Culture and Behavior

Perhaps our most important similarity, the hallmark of our species, is our capacity to learn and adapt. Evolution has prepared us to live creatively in a changing world and to adapt to environments from equatorial jungles to arctic icefields. Compared with bees, birds, and bulldogs, nature has humans on a looser genetic leash. Ironically, it is our shared human biology that enables our cultural diversity. It enables those in one **culture** to value promptness, welcome frankness, or accept premarital sex, whereas those in another culture do not. As social psychologist Roy Baumeister (2005, p. 29) observes, "Evolution made us for culture." (See "Focus On: The Cultural Animal.")

Evolutionary psychology incorporates environmental influences. It recognizes that nature and nurture interact in forming us. Genes are not fixed blueprints; their expression depends on the environment, much as the tea I am now drinking was not expressed until meeting a hot water environment. One study of New Zealand young adults revealed a gene variation that put people at risk for depression, but only if they had also experienced major life stresses such as a marital breakup (Caspi & others, 2003). Neither the stress nor the gene alone produced depression, but the two interacting did.

We humans have been selected not only for big brains and biceps but also for culture. We come prepared to learn language and to bond and cooperate with others in securing food, caring for young, and protecting ourselves. Nature therefore predisposes us to learn whatever culture we are born into (Fiske & others, 1998). The cultural perspective highlights human adaptability. People's "natures are alike," said Confucius; "it is their habits that carry them far apart." And far apart we still are, note world culture researchers Ronald Inglehart and Christian Welzel (2005). Despite increasing education, "we are not moving toward a uniform global culture: cultural convergence is not taking place. A society's cultural heritage is remarkably enduring" (p. 46).

CULTURAL DIVERSITY

The diversity of our languages, customs, and expressive behaviors confirms that much of our behavior is socially programmed, not hardwired. The genetic leash is long. As sociologist Ian Robertson (1987) has noted:

> Americans eat oysters but not snails. The French eat snails but not locusts. The Zulus eat locusts but not fish. The Jews eat fish but not pork. The Hindus eat pork but not beef. The Russians eat beef but not snakes. The Chinese eat snakes but not people. The Jalé of New Guinea find people delicious. (p. 67)

If we all lived as homogeneous ethnic groups in separate regions of the world, as some people still do, cultural diversity would be less relevant to our daily living. In Japan, where there are 127 million people, of whom 125 million are Japanese, internal cultural differences are minimal. In contrast, these differences are encountered many times each day by most residents of New York City, where more than one-third of the 8 million residents are foreign-born and where no ethnic group constitutes more than 37 percent of the population.

Increasingly, cultural diversity surrounds us. More and more we live in a global village, connected to our fellow villagers by e-mail, jumbo jets, and international trade. The mingling of cultures is nothing new. "American" jeans were invented in 1872 by German immigrant Levi Strauss by combining Genes, the trouser style of Genoese sailors, with denim cloth from a French town (Legrain, 2003). From Shakespeare's *Antony and Cleopatra* to Verdi's *Aïda* to Forster's *A Passage to*

"Stand tall, Bipedal Ape. The shark may outswim you, the cheetah outrun you, the swift outfly you, the redwood outlast you. But you have the biggest gifts of all."

—*RICHARD DAWKINS*, THE DEVIL'S CHAPLAIN, *2003*

culture
The enduring behaviors, ideas, attitudes, and traditions shared by a large group of people and transmitted from one generation to the next.

"Somehow the adherents of the 'nurture' side of the arguments have scared themselves silly at the power and inevitability of genes and missed the greatest lesson of all: the genes are on their side."

—*MATT RIDLEY*, NATURE VIA NURTURE, *2003*

focus ON

The Cultural Animal

We are, said Aristotle, the social animal. We humans have at least one thing in common with wolves and bees: We flourish by organizing ourselves into groups and working together.

But more than that, notes Roy Baumeister, we are—as he labels us in the title of his 2005 book—*The Cultural Animal*. Humans more than other animals harness the power of culture to make life better. "Culture is a better way of being social," he writes. We have culture to thank for our communication through language, our driving safely on one side of the road, our eating fruit in winter, and our use of money to pay for our cars and fruit. Culture facilitates our survival and reproduction, and nature has blessed us with a brain that, like no other, enables culture.

Other animals show the rudiments of culture and language. Monkeys have been observed to learn new food-washing techniques, which then are passed across future generations. And chimps exhibit a modest capacity for language. But no species can accumulate progress across generations as smartly as humans. Your nineteenth-century ancestors had no cars, no indoor plumbing, no electricity, no air conditioning, no Internet,

no iPods, and no Post-It notes—all things for which you can thank culture. Intelligence enables innovation, and culture enables dissemination—the transmission of information and innovation across time and place.

The division of labor is "another huge and powerful advantage of culture," notes Baumeister. Few of us grow food or build shelter, yet nearly everyone reading this book enjoys food and shelter. Indeed, books themselves are a tribute to the division of labor enabled by culture. Although only one lucky person gets his name on this book's cover, the product is actually the work of a coordinated team of researchers, reviewers, assistants, and editors. Books and other media disseminate knowledge, providing the engine of progress.

"Culture is what is special about human beings," concludes Baumeister. "Culture helps us to become something much more than the sum of our talents, efforts, and other individual blessings. In that sense, culture is the greatest blessing of all. . . . Alone we would be but cunning brutes, at the mercy of our surroundings. Together, we can sustain a system that enables us to make life progressively better for ourselves, our children, and those who come after."

India, the arts and literature have reflected the fascinating interplay of cultures. In our own day, an unknown pundit has said that nothing typifies globalization like the death of Princess Diana: "An English princess with an Egyptian boyfriend crashes in a French tunnel, riding in a German car with a Dutch engine, driven by a Belgian who was high on Scotch whiskey, followed closely by Italian paparazzi on Japanese motorcycles, and is treated by an American doctor using medicines from Brazil."

Confronting another culture is sometimes a startling experience. American males may feel uncomfortable when Middle Eastern heads of state greet the U.S. president with a kiss on the cheek. A German student, accustomed to speaking to "Herr Professor" only

"Women kiss women good night. Men kiss women good night. But men do not kiss men good night—especially in Armonk."

Although some norms are universal, every culture has its own norms—rules for accepted and expected social behavior.

Cultures mixing. As these London schoolmates illustrate (one of Muslim heritage, the other Anglo Saxon), immigration and globalization are bringing once-distant cultures together.

on rare occasions, considers it strange that at my institution most faculty office doors are open and students stop by freely. An Iranian student on her first visit to an American McDonald's restaurant fumbles around in her paper bag looking for the eating utensils until she sees the other customers eating their french fries with, of all things, their hands. In many areas of the globe, your best manners and mine are serious breaches of etiquette. Foreigners visiting Japan often struggle to master the rules of the social game—when to take off their shoes, how to pour the tea, when to give and open gifts, how to act toward someone higher or lower in the social hierarchy.

Migration and refugee evacuations are mixing cultures more than ever. "East is East and West is West, and never the twain shall meet," wrote the nineteenth-century British author Rudyard Kipling. But today, East and West, and North and South, meet all the time. Italy is home to many Albanians, Germany to Turks, England to Pakistanis, and the result is both friendship and conflict. One in 5 Canadians and 1 in 10 Americans is an immigrant. As we work, play, and live with people from diverse cultural backgrounds, it helps to understand how our cultures influence us and how our cultures differ. In a conflict-laden world, achieving peace requires a genuine appreciation for differences as well as similarities.

NORMS: EXPECTED BEHAVIOR

norms

Standards for accepted and expected behavior. Norms prescribe "proper" behavior. (In a different sense of the word, norms also describe what most others do—what is *normal*.)

As etiquette rules illustrate, all cultures have their accepted ideas about appropriate behavior. We often view these social expectations, or **norms,** as a negative force that imprisons people in a blind effort to perpetuate tradition. Norms do restrain and control us—so successfully and so subtly that we hardly sense their existence. Like fish in the ocean, we are all so immersed in our cultures that we must leap out of them to understand their influence. "When we see other Dutch people behaving in what foreigners would call a Dutch way," note Dutch psychologists Willem Koomen and Anton Dijker (1997), "we often do not realize that the behavior is typically Dutch."

There is no better way to learn the norms of our culture than to visit another culture and see that its members do things *that* way, whereas we do them *this* way. When living in Scotland, I acknowledged to my children that, yes, Europeans eat meat with the fork facing down in the left hand. "But we Americans consider it good manners to cut the meat and then transfer the fork to the right hand. I admit it's inefficient. But it's the way *we* do it."

To those who don't accept them, such norms may seem arbitrary and confining. To most in the Western world, the Muslim woman's veil seems arbitrary and confining, but not to most in Muslim cultures. Just as a stage play moves smoothly when the actors know their lines, so social behavior occurs smoothly when people know what to expect. Norms grease the social machinery. In unfamiliar situations, when the norms may be unclear, we monitor others' behavior and adjust our own accordingly.

Cultures vary in their norms for expressiveness, punctuality, rule-breaking, and personal space. Consider:

EXPRESSIVENESS   To someone from a relatively formal northern European culture, a person whose roots are in an expressive Mediterranean culture may seem "warm, charming, inefficient, and time-wasting." To the Mediterranean person, the northern European may seem "efficient, cold, and overconcerned with time" (Beaulieu, 2004; Triandis, 1981).

PUNCTUALITY   Latin American business executives who arrive late for a dinner engagement may be mystified by how obsessed their North American counterparts are with punctuality. North American tourists in Japan may wonder about the lack of eye contact from passing pedestrians. (See "Research Close-Up: Passing Encounters, East and West.")

RULE-BREAKING   When people see social norms being violated, such as banned graffiti on a wall, they become more likely to follow the rule-breaking norm by violating other rules, such as littering. In six experiments, a Dutch research team led by Kees Keizer (2008) found people more than doubly likely to disobey social rules when it appeared that others were doing so. For example, when useless flyers were put on bike handles, one-third of cyclists tossed the flyer on the ground as litter when there was no graffiti on the adjacent wall. But more than two-thirds did so when the wall was covered with graffiti (Figure 5.1).

PERSONAL SPACE   **Personal space** is a sort of portable bubble or buffer zone that we like to maintain between ourselves and others. As the situation changes, the bubble varies in size. With strangers, most Americans maintain a fairly large personal space, keeping 4 feet or more between us. On uncrowded buses, or in restrooms or libraries, we protect our space and respect others' space. We let friends come closer, often within 2 or 3 feet.

Individuals differ: Some people prefer more personal space than others (Smith, 1981; Sommer, 1969; Stockdale, 1978). Groups differ, too: Adults maintain more distance than children. Men keep more distance from one another than do women. For reasons unknown, cultures near the equator prefer less space and more touching and hugging. Thus, the British and the Scandinavians prefer more distance than the French and the Arabs; North Americans prefer more space than Latin Americans.

To see the effect of encroaching on another's personal space, play space invader. Stand or sit a foot or so from a friend and strike up a conversation. Does the person fidget, look away, back off, show other signs of discomfort? These are the signs of arousal noted by space-invading researchers (Altman & Vinsel, 1978).

FIGURE :: 5.1

Degraded Surroundings Can Degrade Behavior.

In a University of Groningen study, people mostly did not litter the ground with an unwanted flyer when an adjacent wall was clean, but *did* litter when the wall was graffiti-ladon.

personal space
The buffer zone we like to maintain around our bodies. Its size depends on our familiarity with whoever is near us.

"Some 30 inches from my nose, the frontier of my person goes."
—W. H. AUDEN, 1907–1973

research
CLOSE-UP
Passing Encounters, East and West

On my midwestern American campus and in my town, sidewalk passersby routinely glance and smile at one another. In Britain, where I have spent two years, such microinteractions are visibly less common. To a European, our greeting passing strangers might seem a bit silly and disrespectful of privacy; to a midwesterner, avoiding eye contact—what sociologists have called "civil inattention"—might seem aloof.

To quantify the culture difference in pedestrian interactions, an international team led by Miles Patterson and Yuichi Iizuka (2007) conducted a simple field experiment both in the United States and in Japan with the unwitting participation of more than 1,000 American and Japanese pedestrians. Their procedure illustrates how social psychologists sometimes conduct unobtrusive research in natural settings (Patterson, 2008). As Figure 5.2 depicts, a confederate (an accomplice of the experimenter) would initiate one of three behaviors when within about 12 feet of an approaching pedestrian on an uncrowded sidewalk: (1) *avoidance*

(looking straight ahead), (2) *glancing* at the person for less than a second, and (3) *looking* at the person and *smiling*. A trailing observer would then record the pedestrian's reaction. Did the pedestrian glance at the confederate? smile? nod? verbally greet the confederate? (The order of the three conditions was randomized and unknown to the trailing observer, ensuring that the person recording the data was "blind" to the experimental condition.)

As you might expect, the pedestrians, were more likely to look back at someone who looked at them, and to smile at, nod to, or greet someone who also smiled at them, especially when that someone was female rather than male. But as Figure 5.3 shows, the culture differences were nevertheless striking. As the research team expected, in view of Japan's greater respect for privacy and cultural reserve when interacting with outgroups, Americans were much more likely to smile at, nod to, or greet the confederate.

In Japan, they conclude, "there is little pressure to reciprocate the smile of the confederate because there is no relationship with the confederate and no obligation to respond." By contrast, the American norm is to reciprocate a friendly gesture.

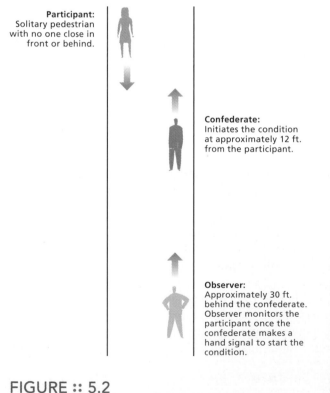

FIGURE :: 5.2
Illustration of Passing Encounter

Source: Patterson & others (2006).

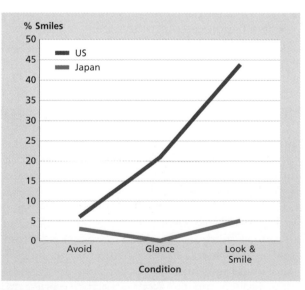

FIGURE :: 5.3
American and Japanese Pedestrian Responses, by Condition

Source: Adapted from Patterson & others (2006).

CULTURAL SIMILARITY

Thanks to human adaptability, cultures differ. Yet beneath the veneer of cultural differences, cross-cultural psychologists see "an essential universality" (Lonner, 1980). As members of one species, we find that the processes that underlie our differing behaviors are much the same everywhere. At ages 4 to 5, for example, children across the world begin to exhibit a "theory of mind" that enables them to infer what others are thinking (Norenzayan & Heine, 2005). If they witness a toy being moved while another child isn't looking, they become able—no matter their culture—to infer that the other child will *think* it still is where it was.

President Bush honored Saudi friendship norms when strolling with Crown Prince Abdullah in 2005. Many heterosexual North American men were, however, startled by the violation of their own norm of distance from other men.

UNIVERSAL FRIENDSHIP NORMS   People everywhere have some common norms for friendship. From studies conducted in Britain, Italy, Hong Kong, and Japan, Michael Argyle and Monika Henderson (1985) noted several cultural variations in the norms that define the role of friend. For example, in Japan it's especially important not to embarrass a friend with public criticism. But there are also some apparently universal norms: Respect the friend's privacy; make eye contact while talking; don't divulge things said in confidence.

UNIVERSAL TRAIT DIMENSIONS   Around the world, people tend to describe others as more or less stable, outgoing, open, agreeable, and conscientious (John & Srivastava, 1999; McCrae & Costa, 1999). If a test specifies where you stand on these "Big Five" personality dimensions, it pretty well describes your personality, no matter where you live. Moreover, a recent 49-country study revealed that nation-to-nation differences in people's scores on Big Five traits such as conscientiousness

"Look, everyone here loves vanilla, right? So let's start there."

Despite enormous cultural variation, we humans do hold some things in common.

FIGURE :: 5.4

Leung and Bond's Universal Social Belief Dimensions

The Big Five Social Beliefs	Sample Questionnaire Item
Cynicism	"Powerful people tend to exploit others."
Social complexity	"One has to deal with matters according to the specific circumstances."
Reward for application	"One will succeed if he/she really tries."
Spirituality	"Religious faith contributes to good mental health."
Fate control	"Fate determines one's success and failures."

and extraversion are smaller than most people suppose (Terracciano & others, 2005). Australians see themselves as unusually outgoing. The German-speaking Swiss see themselves as strikingly conscientious. And Canadians describe themselves as distinctly agreeable. Actually, however, these national stereotypes exaggerate real differences that are quite modest.

UNIVERSAL SOCIAL BELIEF DIMENSIONS   Likewise, say Hong Kong social psychologists Kwok Leung and Michael Harris Bond (2004), there are five universal dimensions of social beliefs. In each of the 38 countries they studied, people vary in the extent to which they endorse and apply these social understandings in their daily lives: cynicism, social complexity, reward for application, spirituality, and fate control (Figure 5.4). People's adherence to these social beliefs appears to guide their living. Those who espouse cynicism express lower life satisfaction and favor assertive influence tactics and right-wing politics. Those who espouse reward for application are inclined to invest themselves in study, planning, and competing.

In The Female Eunuch, *Germaine Greer notes how the language of affection reduces women to foods and baby animals—honey, lamb, sugar, sweetie-pie, kitten, chick.*

UNIVERSAL STATUS NORMS   Roger Brown (1965, 1987; Kroger & Wood, 1992) has studied another universal norm. Wherever people form status hierarchies, they also talk to higher-status people in the respectful way they often talk to strangers. And they talk to lower-status people in the more familiar, first-name way they speak to friends. Patients call their physician "Dr. So and So"; the physician may reply using the patients' first names. Students and professors typically address one another in a similarly nonmutual way.

Most languages have two forms of the English pronoun "you": a respectful form and a familiar form (for example, *Sie* and *du* in German, *vous* and *tu* in French, *usted* and *tu* in Spanish). People typically use the familiar form with intimates and subordinates—with close friends and family members but also in speaking to children and pets. A German adolescent receives a boost when strangers begin addressing him or her as "Sie" instead of "du."

This first aspect of Brown's universal norm—that *forms of address communicate not only social distance but also social status*—correlates with a second aspect: *Advances in intimacy are usually suggested by the higher-status person.* In Europe, where most twosomes begin a relationship with the polite, formal "you" and may eventually progress to the more intimate "you," someone obviously has to initiate the increased intimacy. Who do you suppose does so? On some congenial occasion, the elder or richer or more distinguished of the two is the one to say, "Let's say du to each other."

This norm extends beyond language to every type of advance in intimacy. It is more acceptable to borrow a pen from or put a hand on the shoulder of one's intimates and subordinates than to behave in such a casual way with strangers or superiors. Similarly, the president of my college invites faculty to his home before

Norms—rules for accepted and expected behavior—vary by culture.

they invite him to theirs. In the progression toward intimacy, the higher-status person is typically the pacesetter.

THE INCEST TABOO   The best-known universal norm is the taboo against incest: Parents are not to have sexual relations with their children, nor siblings with one another. Although the taboo apparently is violated more often than psychologists once believed, the norm is still universal. Every society disapproves of incest. Given the biological penalties for inbreeding (through the emergence of disorders linked to recessive genes), evolutionary psychologists can easily understand why people everywhere are predisposed against incest.

NORMS OF WAR   Humans even have cross-cultural norms for conducting war. In the midst of killing one's enemy, there are agreed-upon rules that have been honored for centuries. You are to wear identifiable uniforms, surrender with a gesture of submission, and treat prisoners humanely. (If you can't kill them before they surrender, you should feed them thereafter.) These norms, though cross-cultural, are not universal. When Iraqi forces violated them by showing surrender flags and then attacking, and by dressing soldiers as liberated civilians to set up ambushes, a U.S. military spokesperson complained that "both of these actions are among the most serious violations of the laws of war" (Clarke, 2003).

So, some norms are culture-specific, others are universal. The force of culture appears in varying norms, whereas it is largely our genetic predispositions—our human nature—that account for the universality of some norms. Thus, we might think of nature as universal and nurture as culture-specific.

So far in this chapter, we have affirmed our biological kinship as members of one human family. We have acknowledged our cultural diversity. And we have noted how norms vary within and across cultures. Remember that our quest in social psychology is not just to catalog differences but also to identify universal principles of behavior. Our aim is what cross-cultural psychologist Walter Lonner (1989) has called "a universalistic psychology—a psychology that is as valid and meaningful in Omaha and Osaka as it is in Rome and Botswana."

Attitudes and behaviors will always vary with culture, but the processes by which attitudes influence behavior vary much less. People in Nigeria and Japan define teen roles differently from people in Europe and North America, but in all cultures role expectations guide social relations. G. K. Chesterton had the idea nearly a century ago: When someone "has discovered why men in Bond Street wear black hats he will at the same moment have discovered why men in Timbuctoo wear red feathers."

"I am confident that [if] modern psychology had developed in, let us say, India, the psychologists there would have discovered most of the principles discovered by the Westerners."

—*CROSS-CULTURAL PSYCHOLOGIST JOHN E. WILLIAMS (1993)*

Summing Up: How Are We Influenced by Human Nature and Cultural Diversity?

- How are we humans alike, how do we differ—and why? Evolutionary psychologists study how natural selection favors behavioral traits that promote the perpetuation of one's genes. Although part of evolution's legacy is our human capacity to learn and adapt (and therefore to differ from one another), the *evolutionary perspective* highlights the kinship that results from our shared human nature.

- The *cultural perspective* highlights human diversity—the behaviors and ideas that define a group and that are transmitted across generations. The differences in attitudes and behaviors from one culture to another indicate the extent to which we are the products of cultural norms and roles. Yet cross-cultural psychologists also examine the "essential universality" of all people. For example, despite their differences, cultures have a number of norms in common, such as respecting privacy in friendships and disapproving of incest.

How Are Gender Similarities and Differences Explained?

Both evolutionary psychologists and psychologists working from a cultural perspective have sought to explain gender variations. Before considering their views, let's look at the basic issues: As males and females, how are we alike? How do we differ? And why?

There are many obvious dimensions of human diversity—height, weight, hair color, to name just a few. But for people's self-concepts and social relationships, the two dimensions that matter most, and that people first attune to, are race and, especially, gender (Stangor & others, 1992). When you were born, the first thing people wanted to know about you was, "Is it a boy or a girl?" When an intersex child is born with a combination of male and female sex organs, physicians and family traditionally have felt compelled to assign the child a gender (because they didn't have an approved category of transgendered persons) and to diminish the ambiguity surgically. The simple message: Everyone *must* be assigned a gender. Between day and night there is dusk. But between male and female there has been, socially speaking, essentially nothing.

In Chapter 9, we will consider how race and sex affect the way others regard and treat us. For now, let's consider **gender**—the characteristics people associate with male and female. What behaviors are universally characteristic and expected of males? of females?

"Of the 46 chromosomes in the human genome, 45 are unisex," notes Judith Rich Harris (1998). Females and males are therefore similar in many physical traits and developmental milestones, such as the age of sitting up, teething, and walking. They also are alike in many psychological traits, such as overall vocabulary, creativity, intelligence, self-esteem, and happiness. Women and men feel the same emotions and longings, both dote on their children, and they have similar-appearing brains (although, on average, men have more neurons and women have more neural connections). Indeed, notes Janet Shibley Hyde (2005) from her review of 46 meta-analyses (each a statistical digest of dozens of studies), the common result for most variables studied is *gender similarity*. Your "opposite sex" is actually your nearly identical sex.

So shall we conclude that men and women are essentially the same, except for a few anatomical oddities that hardly matter apart from special occasions? Actually, there are some differences, and it is these differences, not the many similarities, that capture attention and make news. In both science and everyday life, differences excite interest. Compared with males, the average female

gender

In psychology, the characteristics, whether biological or socially influenced, by which people define male and female.

Even in physical traits, individual differences among men and among women far exceed the average differences between the sexes. Don Schollander's world-record-setting 4 minutes, 12 seconds in the 400-meter freestyle swim at the 1964 Olympics trailed the times of all eight women racing in the 2008 Olympic finals for that event.

- has 70 percent more fat, has 40 percent less muscle, is 5 inches shorter, and weighs 40 pounds less.
- is more sensitive to smells and sounds.
- is doubly vulnerable to anxiety disorders and depression.

Compared with females, the average male is

- slower to enter puberty (by about two years) but quicker to die (by four years, worldwide).
- three times more likely to be diagnosed with ADHD (attention deficit/hyperactivity disorder), four times more likely to commit suicide, and five times more likely to be killed by lightning.
- more capable of wiggling the ears.

During the 1970s, many scholars worried that studies of such gender differences might reinforce stereotypes. Would gender differences be construed as women's deficits? Although the findings confirm some stereotypes of women—as less physically aggressive, more nurturant, and more socially sensitive—those traits are not only celebrated by many feminists but also preferred by most people, whether male or female (Prentice & Carranza, 2002; Swim, 1994). Small wonder, then, that most people rate their beliefs and feelings regarding women as more *favorable* than their feelings regarding men (Eagly, 1994; Haddock & Zanna, 1994).

Let's compare men's and women's social connections, dominance, aggressiveness, and sexuality. Once we have described these few differences, we can then consider how the evolutionary and cultural perspectives might explain them. Do gender differences reflect natural selection? Are they culturally constructed—a reflection of the roles that men and women often play and the situations in which they act? Or do genes and culture both bend the genders?

Independence versus Connectedness

Individual men display outlooks and behavior that vary from fierce competitiveness to caring nurturance. So do individual women. Without denying that, psychologists Nancy Chodorow (1978, 1989), Jean Baker Miller (1986), and Carol Gilligan and her colleagues (1982, 1990) have contended that women more than men give priority to close, intimate relationships.

PLAY   Compared with boys, girls talk more intimately and play less aggressively, notes Eleanor Maccoby (2002) from her decades of research on gender development. They also play in smaller groups, often talking with one friend, while boys more often do larger group activities (Rose & Rudolph, 2006). And as they each interact with their own gender, their differences grow.

FRIENDSHIP   As adults, women in individualist cultures describe themselves in more relational terms, welcome more help, experience more relationship-linked emotions, and are more attuned to others' relationships (Addis & Mahalik, 2003; Gabriel & Gardner, 1999; Tamres & others, 2002; Watkins & others, 1998, 2003). In conversation, men more often focus on tasks and on connections with large groups, women on personal relationships (Tannen, 1990). When on the phone, women's conversations with friends last longer (Smoreda & Licoppe, 2000). When on the computer, women spend more time sending e-mails, in which they express more emotion (Crabtree, 2002; Thomson & Murachver, 2001). When in groups, women share more of their lives, and offer more support (Dindia & Allen, 1992; Eagly, 1987). When facing stress, men tend to respond with "fight or flight"; often, their response to a threat is combat. In nearly all studies, notes Shelley Taylor (2002), women who are under stress more often "tend and befriend"; they turn to friends and family for support. Among first-year college students, 5 in 10 males and 7 in 10 females say it is *very* important to "help others who are in difficulty" (Sax & others, 2002).

"There should be no qualms about the forthright study of racial and gender differences; science is in desperate need of good studies that . . . inform us of what we need to do to help underrepresented people to succeed in this society. Unlike the ostrich, we cannot afford to hide our heads for fear of socially uncomfortable discoveries."
—*DEVELOPMENTAL PSYCHOLOGIST SANDRA SCARR (1988)*

"In the different voice of women lies the truth of an ethic of care."
—*CAROL GILLIGAN, IN A DIFFERENT VOICE, 1982*

Girls' play is often in small groups and imitates relationships. Boys' play is more often competitive or aggressive.

"Contrary to what many women believe, it's fairly easy to develop a long-term, stable, intimate, and mutually fulfilling relationship with a guy. Of course this guy has to be a Labrador retriever."
—*DAVE BARRY, DAVE BARRY'S COMPLETE GUIDE TO GUYS, 1995*

empathy
The vicarious experience of another's feelings; putting oneself in another's shoes.

VOCATIONS In general, report Felicia Pratto and her colleagues (1997), men gravitate disproportionately to jobs that enhance inequalities (prosecuting attorney, corporate advertising); women gravitate to jobs that reduce inequalities (public defender, advertising work for a charity). Studies of 640,000 people's job preferences reveal that men more than women value earnings, promotion, challenge, and power; women more than men value good hours, personal relationships, and opportunities to help others (Konrad & others, 2000; Pinker, 2008). Indeed, in most of the North American caregiving professions, such as social worker, teacher, and nurse, women outnumber men. And worldwide, women's vocational interests, compared with men's, usually relate more to people and less to things (Lippa, 2008a).

FAMILY RELATIONS Women's connections as mothers, daughters, sisters, and grandmothers bind families (Rossi & Rossi, 1990). Women spend more time caring for both preschoolers and aging parents (Eagly & Crowley, 1986). Compared with men, they buy three times as many gifts and greeting cards, write two to four times as many personal letters, and make 10 to 20 percent more long-distance calls to friends and family (Putnam, 2000). Asked to provide photos that portray who they are, women include more photos of parents and of themselves with others (Clancy & Dollinger, 1993). For women, especially, a sense of mutual support is crucial to marital satisfaction (Acitelli & Antonucci, 1994).

SMILING Smiling, of course, varies with situations. Yet across more than 400 studies, women's greater connectedness has been expressed in their generally higher rate of smiling (LaFrance & others, 2003). For example, when Marianne LaFrance (1985) analyzed 9,000 college yearbook photos and when Amy Halberstadt and Martha Saitta (1987) studied 1,100 magazine and newspaper photos and 1,300 people in shopping malls, parks, and streets, they consistently found that females were more likely to smile.

EMPATHY When surveyed, women are far more likely to describe themselves as having **empathy,** or being able to feel what another feels—to rejoice with those who rejoice and weep with those who weep. To a lesser extent, the empathy difference extends to laboratory studies. Shown slides or told stories, girls react with more empathy (Hunt, 1990). Given upsetting experiences in the laboratory or in real life, women more than men express empathy for others enduring similar experiences (Batson & others, 1996). Observing another receiving pain after misbehaving, women's empathy-related brain circuits display elevated activity even when men's do not—after the other had misbehaved (Singer & others, 2006). Women are more likely to cry or report feeling distressed at another's distress (Eisenberg & Lennon, 1983). In a 2003 Gallup poll, 12 percent of American men, and 43 percent of women, reported having cried as a result of the war in Iraq.

All of these differences help to explain why, compared with friendships with men, both men and women report friendships with women to be more intimate, enjoyable, and nurturing (Rubin, 1985; Sapadin, 1988). When you want empathy and understanding, someone to whom you can disclose your joys and hurts, to whom do you turn? Most men and women usually turn to women.

One explanation for this male-female empathy difference is that women tend to outperform men at reading others' emotions. In her analysis of 125 studies of men's and women's sensitivity to nonverbal cues, Judith Hall (1984) discerned that women are generally superior at decoding others' emotional messages. For example, shown a 2-second silent film clip of the face of an upset woman, women guess more accurately whether she is criticizing someone or discussing her divorce. Women also are more often strikingly better than men at recalling others' appearance, report Marianne Schmid Mast and Judith Hall (2006).

Finally, women are more skilled at *expressing* emotions nonverbally, says Hall. This is especially so for positive emotion, report Erick Coats and Robert Feldman (1996). They had people talk about times they had been happy, sad, and angry. When shown 5-second silent video clips of those reports, observers could much more accurately discern women's than men's emotions when recalling happiness. Men, however, were slightly more successful in conveying anger.

Social Dominance

Imagine two people: One is "adventurous, autocratic, coarse, dominant, forceful, independent, and strong." The other is "affectionate, dependent, dreamy, emotional, submissive, and weak." If the first person sounds more to you like a man and the second like a woman, you are not alone, report John Williams and Deborah Best (1990, p. 15). From Asia to Africa and Europe to Australia, people rate men as more dominant, driven, and aggressive. Moreover, studies of nearly 80,000 people across 70 countries show that men more than women rate power and achievement as important (Schwartz & Rubel, 2005).

These perceptions and expectations correlate with reality. In essentially every society, men *are* socially dominant. In no known societies do women usually dominate men (Pratto, 1996). As we will see, gender differences vary greatly by culture, and gender differences are shrinking in many industrialized societies as women assume more managerial and leadership positions. Yet consider:

- Women in 2008 were but 18 percent of the world's legislators (IPU, 2008).
- Men more than women are concerned with social dominance and are more likely to favor conservative political candidates and programs that preserve group inequality (Eagly & others, 2004; Sidanius & Pratto, 1999). In 2005, American men, by wide margins, were more supportive of capital punishment and the Iraq war (Gallup, 2005; Newport, 2007a).

What do you think: Should Western women become more self-reliant and more attuned to their culture's individualism? Or might women's relational approach to life help transform power-oriented Western societies (marked by high levels of child neglect, loneliness, and depression) into more caring communities?

Because they are generally empathic and skilled at reading others' emotions, girls are less vulnerable to autism, which to Simon Baron-Cohen (2004, 2005) represents an "extreme male brain."

"That was a fine report, Barbara. But since the sexes speak different languages, I probably didn't understand a word of it."

- Men are half of all jurors but have been 90 percent of elected jury leaders; men are also the leaders of most ad hoc laboratory groups (Colarelli & others, 2006; Davis & Gilbert, 1989; Kerr & others, 1982).

- Women's wages in industrial countries average 77 percent of men's. Only about one-fifth of this wage gap is attributable to gender differences in education, work experience, or job characteristics (World Bank, 2003).

As is typical of those in higher-status positions, men initiate most of the inviting for first dates, do most of the driving, and pick up most of the tabs (Laner & Ventrone, 1998, 2000).

Men's style of communicating undergirds their social power. In situations where roles aren't rigidly scripted, men tend to be more autocratic, women more democratic (Eagly & Carli, 2007). In leadership roles, men tend to excel as directive, task-focused leaders; women excel more often in the "transformational" leadership that is favored by more and more organizations, with inspirational and social skills that build team spirit. Men more than women place priority on winning, getting ahead, and dominating others (Sidanius & others, 1994). This may explain why people's preference for a male leader is greater for competitions between groups, such as when countries are at war, than when conflicts occur within a group (Van Vugt & Spisak, 2008).

Men also take more risks (Byrnes & others, 1999). One study of data from 35,000 stock broker accounts found that "men are more overconfident than women" and therefore made 45 percent more stock trades (Barber & Odean, 2001). Because trading costs money, and because men's trades proved no more successful, their results underperformed the stock market by 2.65 percent, compared with women's 1.72 percent underperformance. The men's trades were riskier—and the men were the poorer for it.

In writing, women tend to use more communal prepositions ("with"), fewer quantitative words, and more present tense. One computer program, which taught itself to recognize gender differences in word usage and sentence structure, successfully identified the author's gender in 80 percent of 920 British fiction and non-fiction works (Koppel & others, 2002).

In conversation, men's style reflects their concern for independence, women's for connectedness. Men are more likely to act as powerful people often do—talking assertively, interrupting intrusively, touching with the hand, staring more, smiling less (Leaper & Ayres, 2007). Stating the results from a female perspective, women's influence style tends to be more indirect—less interruptive, more sensitive, more polite, less cocky.

Some gender differences do not correlate with status and power. For example, women at all status levels tend to smile more (Hall & others, 2005).

So is it right to declare (in the title words of one 1990s best seller), *Men Are from Mars, Women Are from Venus?* Actually, note Kay Deaux and Marianne LaFrance (1998), men's and women's conversational styles vary with the social context. Much of the style we attribute to men is typical of people (men and women) in positions of status and power (Hall & others, 2006). For example, students nod more when speaking with professors than when speaking with peers, and women nod more than men (Helweg-Larsen & others, 2004). Men—and people in high-status roles—tend to talk louder and to interrupt more (Hall & others, 2005). Moreover, individuals vary; some men are characteristically hesitant and deferential, some women direct and assertive. To suggest that women and men are from different emotional planets greatly oversimplifies.

Aggression

By **aggression,** psychologists mean behavior intended to hurt. Throughout the world, hunting, fighting, and warring are primarily male activities (Wood & Eagly, 2007). In surveys, men admit to more aggression than do women. In laboratory experiments, men indeed exhibit more physical aggression, for example, by administering what they believe are hurtful electric shocks (Knight & others, 1996). In Canada, the male-to-female arrest ratio is 9 to 1 for murder (Statistics Canada, 2008). In the United States, where 92 percent of prisoners are male, it is 9 to 1 (FBI, 2008). Almost all suicide terrorists have been young men (Kruglanski & Golec de Zavala, 2005). So also are nearly all battlefield deaths and death row inmates.

But once again the gender difference fluctuates with the context. When there is provocation, the gender gap shrinks (Bettencourt & Kernahan, 1997; Richardson, 2005). And within less assaultive forms of aggression—say, slapping a family member, throwing something, or verbally attacking someone—women are no less aggressive than men (Björkqvist, 1994; White & Kowalski, 1994). Indeed, says John Archer (2000, 2004, 2007) from his statistical digests of dozens of studies, women may be slightly more likely to commit indirect aggressive acts, such as spreading malicious gossip. But all across the world and at all ages, men much more often injure others with physical aggression.

"It's a guy thing."

aggression
Physical or verbal behavior intended to hurt someone. In laboratory experiments, this might mean delivering electric shocks or saying something likely to hurt another's feelings.

Sexuality

There is also a gender gap in sexual attitudes and assertiveness. It's true that in their physiological and subjective responses to sexual stimuli, women and men are "more similar than different" (Griffitt, 1987). Yet consider:

- "I can imagine myself being comfortable and enjoying 'casual' sex with different partners," agreed 48 percent of men and 12 percent of women in an Australian survey (Bailey & others, 2000). One 48-nation study showed country-by-country variation in acceptance of unrestricted sexuality, ranging from relatively promiscuous Finland to relatively monogamous Taiwan (Schmitt, 2005). But in every one of the 48 countries studied, it was the men who expressed more desire for unrestricted sex. Likewise, when the BBC surveyed more than 200,000 people in 53 nations, men everywhere more strongly agreed that "I have a strong sex drive" (Lippa, 2008b).

- The American Council on Education's recent survey of a quarter million first-year college students offers a similar finding. "If two people really like each other, it's all right for them to have sex even if they've known each other for only a very short time," agreed 58 percent of men but only 34 percent of women (Pryor & others, 2005).

• In a survey of 3,400 randomly selected 18- to 59-year-old Americans, half as many men (25 percent) as women (48 percent) cited affection for the partner as a reason for first intercourse. How often do they think about sex? "Every day" or "several times a day," said 19 percent of women and 54 percent of men (Laumann & others, 1994). Ditto Canadians, with 11 percent of women and 46 percent of men saying "several times a day" (Fischstein & others, 2007).

The gender difference in sexual attitudes carries over to behavior. "With few exceptions anywhere in the world," reported cross-cultural psychologist Marshall Segall and his colleagues (1990, p. 244), "males are more likely than females to initiate sexual activity."

Compared with lesbians, gay men also report more interest in uncommitted sex, more frequent sex, more responsiveness to visual stimuli, and more concern with partner attractiveness (Bailey & others, 1994; Peplau & Fingerhut, 2007; Schmitt, 2007). The 47 percent of coupled American lesbians is double the 24 percent of gay men who are coupled (Doyle, 2005). Among those electing civil unions in Vermont and same-sex marriage in Massachusetts, two-thirds have been female couples (Belluck, 2008; Rothblum, 2007). "It's not that gay men are oversexed," observes Steven Pinker (1997). "They are simply men whose male desires bounce off other male desires rather than off female desires."

Indeed, observe Roy Baumeister and Kathleen Vohs (2004; Baumeister & others, 2001), not only do men fantasize more about sex, have more permissive attitudes, and seek more partners, they also are more quickly aroused, desire sex more often, masturbate more frequently, are less successful at celibacy, refuse sex less often, take more risks, expend more resources to gain sex, and prefer more sexual variety. One survey asked 16,288 people from 52 nations how many sexual partners they desired in the next month. Among those unattached, 29 percent of men and 6 percent of women wanted more than one partner (Schmitt, 2003, 2005). These results were identical for straight and gay people (29 percent of gay men and 6 percent of lesbians desired more than one partner).

"Everywhere sex is understood to be something females have that males want," offered anthropologist Donald Symons (1979, p. 253). Small wonder, say Baumeister and Vohs, that cultures everywhere attribute greater value to female than male sexuality, as indicated in gender asymmetries in prostitution and courtship, where men generally offer money, gifts, praise, or commitment in implicit exchange for a woman's sexual engagement. In human sexual economics, they note, women rarely if ever pay for sex. Like labor unions opposing "scab labor" as undermining the value of their own work, most women oppose other women's offering "cheap sex," which reduces the value of their own sexuality. Across 185 countries, the more scarce are available men, the *higher* is the teen pregnancy rate—because when men are scarce "women compete against each other by offering sex at a lower price in terms of commitment" (Barber, 2000; Baumeister & Vohs, 2004). When women are scarce, as is increasingly the case in China and India, the market value of their sexuality rises and they are able to command greater commitment.

Sexual fantasies, too, express the gender difference (Ellis & Symons, 1990). In male-oriented erotica, women are unattached and lust driven. In romance novels, whose primary market is women, a tender male is emotionally consumed by his devoted passion for the heroine. Social scientists aren't the only ones to have noticed. "Women can be fascinated by a four-hour movie with subtitles wherein the entire plot consists of a man and a woman yearning to have, but never actually having a relationship," observes humorist Dave Barry (1995). "Men HATE that. Men can take maybe 45 seconds of yearning, and they want everybody to get naked. Followed by a car chase. A movie called 'Naked People in Car Chases' would do really well among men."

MALE PROSTITUTE

"Oh yeah, baby, I'll listen to you—I'll listen to you all night long."

As detectives are more intrigued by crime than virtue, so psychological detectives are more intrigued by differences than similarities. Let us therefore remind ourselves: *Individual* differences far exceed gender differences. Females and males are hardly opposite (altogether different) sexes. Rather, they differ like two folded hands—similar but not the same, fitting together yet differing as they grasp each other.

Summing Up: How Are Gender Similarities and Differences Explained?

- Boys and girls, and men and women, are in many ways alike. Yet their differences attract more attention than their similarities.

- Social psychologists have explored gender differences in *independence* versus *connectedness*. Women typically do more caring, express more empathy and emotion, and define themselves more in terms of relationships.

- Men and women also tend to exhibit differing social dominance and aggression. In every known culture on earth, men tend to have more social power and are more likely than women to engage in physical aggression.

- Sexuality is another area of marked gender differences. Men more often think about and initiate sex, whereas women's sexuality tends to be inspired by emotional passion.

Evolution and Gender: Doing What Comes Naturally?

In explaining gender differences, inquiry has focused on two influences: evolution and culture.

"What do you think is the main reason men and women have different personalities, interests, and abilities?" asked the Gallup Organization (1990) in a national survey. "Is it mainly because of the way men and women are raised, or are the differences part of their biological makeup?" Among the 99 percent who answered the question (apparently without questioning its assumptions), about the same percentage answered "upbringing" as said "biology."

"I hunt and she gathers—otherwise, we couldn't make ends meet."

There are, of course, certain salient biological sex differences. Men's genes predispose the muscle mass to hunt game; women's the capability to breastfeed infants. Are biological sex differences limited to such obvious distinctions in reproduction and physique? Or do men's and women's genes, hormones, and brains differ in ways that also contribute to behavioral differences?

Gender and Mating Preferences

Noting the worldwide persistence of gender differences in aggressiveness, dominance, and sexuality, evolutionary psychologist Douglas Kenrick (1987) suggested, as have many others since, that "we cannot change the evolutionary history of our species, and some of the differences between us are undoubtedly a function of that history." Evolutionary psychology predicts no sex differences in all those domains in which the sexes faced similar adaptive challenges (Buss, 1995b). Both sexes regulate heat with sweat. The two have similar taste preferences to nourish their bodies. And they both grow calluses where the skin meets friction. But evolutionary psychology does predict sex differences in behaviors relevant to dating, mating, and reproduction.

Consider, for example, the male's greater sexual initiative. The average male produces many trillions of sperm in his lifetime, making sperm cheap compared with eggs. (If you happen to be an average man, you will make more than 1,000 sperm while reading this sentence.) Moreover, whereas a female brings one fetus to term and then nurses it, a male can spread his genes by fertilizing many females. Women's investment in childbearing is, just for starters, nine months; men's investment may be nine seconds.

Thus, say evolutionary psychologists, females invest their reproductive opportunities carefully, by looking for signs of resources and commitment. Males compete with other males for chances to win the genetic sweepstakes by sending their genes into the future, and thus look for healthy, fertile soil in which to plant their seed. Women want to find men who will help them tend the garden—resourceful and monogamous dads rather than wandering cads. Women seek to reproduce wisely, men widely. Or so the theory goes.

Moreover, evolutionary psychology suggests, the physically dominant males were the ones who excelled in gaining access to females, which over generations enhanced male aggression and dominance as the less aggressive males had fewer chances to reproduce. Whatever genes helped Montezuma II to become Aztec king were also given to his offspring, along with those from many of the 4,000 women in his harem (Wright, 1998). If our ancestral mothers benefited from being able to read their infants' and suitors' emotions, then natural selection may have similarly

In species for which males provide more parental investment than females, notes evolutionary psychologist David Schmitt (2006), males have a longer-term mating strategy, are more discriminating among potential mates, and die later.

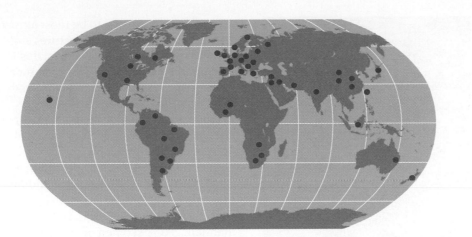

FIGURE :: 5.5

Human Mating Preferences

David Buss and 50 collaborators surveyed more than 10,000 people from all races, religions, and political systems on six continents and five islands. Everywhere, men preferred attractive physical features suggesting youth and health— and reproductive fitness. Everywhere, women preferred men with resources and status.

Source: From Buss (1994b).

favored emotion-detecting ability in females. Underlying all these presumptions is a principle: *Nature selects traits that help send one's genes into the future.*

Little of this process is conscious. Few people in the throes of passion stop to think, "I want to give my genes to posterity." Rather, say evolutionary psychologists, our natural yearnings are our genes' way of making more genes. Emotions execute evolution's dispositions, much as hunger executes the body's need for nutrients.

Medical researcher and author Lewis Thomas (1971) captured the idea of hidden evolutionary predispositions in his fanciful description of a male moth responding to a female's release of bombykol, a single molecule of which will tremble the hairs of any male within miles and send him driving upwind in ardor. But it is doubtful if the moth has an awareness of being caught in an aerosol of chemical attractant. On the contrary, he probably finds suddenly that it has become an excellent day, the weather remarkably bracing, the time appropriate for a bit of exercise of the old wings, a brisk turn upwind.

"Humans are living fossils—collections of mechanisms produced by prior selections pressures," says David Buss (1995a). And that, evolutionary psychologists believe, helps explain not only male aggression but also the differing sexual attitudes and behaviors of females and males. Although a man's interpretation of a woman's smile as sexual interest usually proves wrong, occasionally being right can have reproductive payoff.

Evolutionary psychology also predicts that men will strive to offer what women will desire—external resources and physical protection. Male peacocks strut their feathers; male humans, their abs, Audis, and assets. In one experiment, teen males rated "having lots of money" as more important after they were put alone in a room with a teen female (Roney, 2003). "Male achievement is ultimately a courtship display," says Glenn Wilson (1994). And women may balloon their breasts, Botox their wrinkles, and liposuction their fat to offer men the youthful, healthy appearance (connoting fertility) that men desire—while, in some experiments, demeaning the success and appearance of other attractive women (Agthe & others, 2008; Vukovic & others, 2008). Sure enough, note Buss (1994a) and Alan Feingold (1992a), women's and men's mate preferences extend these observations. Consider:

- Studies in 37 cultures, from Australia to Zambia, reveal that men everywhere feel attracted to women whose physical features, such as youthful faces and forms, suggest fertility. Women everywhere feel attracted to men whose wealth, power, and ambition promise resources for protecting and nurturing offspring (Figure 5.5). Men's greater interest in physical form also makes them the consumers of most of the world's visual pornography. But there are gender similarities, too: Whether residing on an Indonesian island or in urban São Paulo, both women and men desire kindness, love, and mutual attraction.

"A hen is only an egg's way of making another egg."
—*SAMUEL BUTLER, 1835–1901*

Larry King, 25 years older than seventh wife, Shawn Southwick-King.

- Men everywhere tend to be most attracted to women whose age and features suggest peak fertility. For teen boys, this is a woman several years older than themselves. For mid-20s men, it's women their own age. For older men, it's younger women, and the older the man, the greater the age difference he prefers when selecting a mate (Kenrick & others, 2009). One finds this pattern worldwide, in European singles ads, Indian marital ads, and marriage records from the Americas, Africa, and the Philippines (Singh, 1993; Singh & Randall, 2007). Women of all ages prefer men just slightly older than themselves. Once again, say the evolutionary psychologists, we see that natural selection predisposes men to feel attracted to female features associated with fertility.

Reflecting on those findings, Buss (1999) reports feeling somewhat astonished "that men and women across the world differ in their mate preferences in precisely the ways predicted by the evolutionists. Just as our fears of snakes, heights, and spiders provide a window for viewing the survival hazards of our evolutionary ancestors, our mating desires provide a window for viewing the resources our ancestors needed for reproduction. We all carry with us today the desires of our successful forebearers."

Reflections on Evolutionary Psychology

Without disputing natural selection—nature's process of selecting physical and behavioral traits that enhance gene survival—critics see a problem with evolutionary explanations. Evolutionary psychologists sometimes start with an effect (such as the male-female difference in sexual initiative) and then work backward to construct an explanation for it. That approach is reminiscent of functionalism, a dominant theory in psychology during the 1920s, whose logic went like this: "Why does that behavior occur? Because it serves such and such a function." You may recognize both the evolutionary and the functionalist approaches as examples of hindsight reasoning. As biologists Paul Ehrlich and Marcus Feldman (2003) have pointed out, the evolutionary theorist can hardly lose when employing hindsight. Today's evolutionary psychology is like yesterday's Freudian psychology, say such critics: Either theory can be retrofitted to whatever happens.

The way to overcome the hindsight bias is to imagine things turning out otherwise. Let's try it. Imagine that women were stronger and more physically aggressive than men. "But of course!" someone might say, "all the better for protecting their young." And if human males were never known to have extramarital affairs, might we not see the evolutionary wisdom behind their fidelity? Because there is more to bringing offspring to maturity than merely depositing sperm, men and women both gain by investing jointly in their children. Males who are loyal to their mates and offspring are more apt to ensure that their young will survive to perpetuate their genes. Monogamy also increases men's certainty of paternity. (These are, in fact, evolutionary explanations—again based on hindsight—for why humans, and certain other species whose young require a heavy parental investment, tend to pair off and be monogamous).

Outside mainstream science, other critics challenge the teaching of evolution. (See "Focus On: Evolutionary Science and Religion.")

Evolutionary psychologists reply that criticisms of their theories as being hindsight-based are "flat-out wrong." They argue that hindsight plays no less a role in cultural explanations: Why do women and men differ? Because their culture *socializes* their behavior! When people's roles vary across time and place, "culture" *describes* those roles better than it explains them. And far from being mere hindsight conjecture, say

focus
ON
Evolutionary Science and Religion

A century and a half after Charles Darwin wrote *On the Origin of Species,* controversy continues over his big idea: that every earthly creature is descended from another earthly creature. The controversy rages most intensely in the United States, where a Gallup survey reveals that half of adults do not believe that evolution accounts for "how human beings came to exist on Earth" (Newport, 2007b). This skepticism of evolution persists despite evidence, including modern DNA research, which long ago persuaded 95 percent of scientists that "human beings have developed over millions of years" (Gallup, 1996).

For most scientists, mutation and natural selection explain the emergence of life, including its ingenious designs. For example, the human eye, an engineering marvel that encodes and transmits a rich stream of information, has its building blocks "dotted around the animal kingdom," enabling nature to select mutations that over time improved the design (Dennett, 2005). Indeed, many scientists are fond of quoting the famous dictum of geneticist (and Russian Orthodox Church member) Theodosius Dobzhansky, "Nothing makes sense in biology except in the light of evolution."

Alan Leshner (2005), the executive director of the American Association for the Advancement of Science, laments the polarization caused by zealots at both the antiscience and the antireligious extremes. To resolve the growing science-religion tension, he believes "we must take every opportunity to make clear to the general public that science and religion are not adversaries. They can co-exist comfortably, and both have a place and provide important benefits to society."

There are many scientists who concur with Leshner, believing that science offers answers to questions such as "when?" and "how?" and that religion offers answers to "who?" and "why?" In the fifth century, St. Augustine anticipated today's science-affirming people of faith: "The universe was brought into being in a less than fully formed state, but was gifted with the capacity to transform itself from unformed matter into a truly marvelous array of structures and forms" (Wilford, 1999).

And the universe truly is marvelous, say cosmologists. Had gravity been a tiny bit stronger or weaker, or had the carbon proton weighed ever so slightly more or less, our universe—which is so extraordinarily right for producing life—would never have produced us. Although there are questions beyond science (why is there something rather than nothing?), this much appears true, concludes cosmologist Paul Davies (2004, 2007): Nature seems ingeniously devised to produce self-replicating, information-processing systems (us). Although we appear to have been created over eons of time, the end result is our wonderfully complex, meaningful, and hope-filled existence.

---

evolutionary psychologists, their field is an empirical science that tests evolutionary predictions with data from animal behavior, cross-cultural observations, and hormonal and genetic studies. As in many scientific fields, observations inspire a theory that generates new, testable predictions (Figure 5.6). The predictions alert us to unnoticed phenomena and allow us to confirm, refute, or revise the theory.

Critics nevertheless contend that the empirical evidence is not strongly supportive of evolutionary psychology's predictions (Buller, 2005, 2009). They also worry that evolutionary speculation about sex and gender "reinforces male-female stereotypes" (Small, 1999). Might evolutionary explanations for gang violence, homicidal jealousy, and rape reinforce and justify male aggression as natural "boys will be boys" behaviors? But remember, reply the evolutionary psychologists, evolutionary wisdom is wisdom from the past. It tells us what behaviors worked in our early history as a species. Whether such tendencies are still adaptive today is an entirely different question.

Evolutionary psychology's critics acknowledge that evolution helps explain both our commonalities and our differences (a certain amount of diversity aids survival). But they contend that our common evolutionary heritage does not, by itself, predict the enormous cultural variation in human marriage patterns (from one spouse to a succession of spouses to multiple wives to multiple husbands to spouse swapping). Nor does it explain cultural changes in behavior patterns over mere decades of time. The most significant trait that nature has endowed us with, it seems, is the capacity to adapt—to learn and to change. Therein lies what we can all agree is culture's shaping power.

"Sex differences in behavior may have been relevant to our ancestors gathering roots and hunting squirrels on the plains of Northern Africa, but their manifestations in modern society are less clearly 'adaptive.' Modern society is information oriented—big biceps and gushing testosterone have less direct relevance to the president of a computer firm."
—*DOUGLAS KENRICK (1987)*

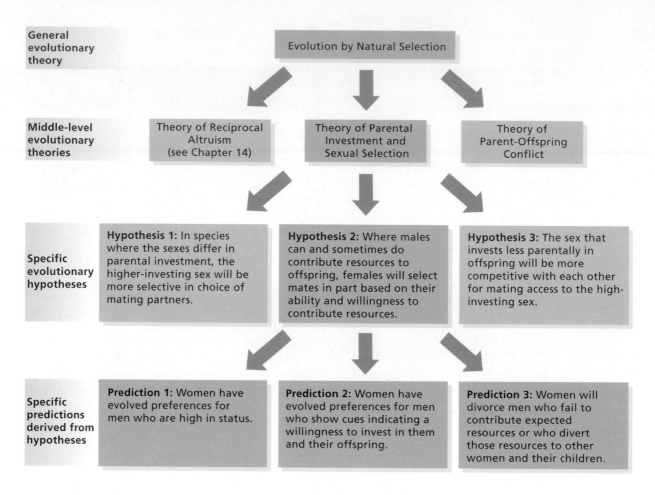

FIGURE :: 5.6

Sample predictions derived from evolutionary psychology by David Buss (1995a).

Gender and Hormones

If genes predispose gender-related traits, they must do so by their effects on our bodies. In male embryos, the genes direct the formation of testes, which begin to secrete testosterone, the male sex hormone that influences masculine appearance. Studies indicate that girls who were exposed to excess testosterone during fetal development tend to exhibit more tomboyish play behavior than other girls (Hines, 2004). Other case studies have followed males who, having been born without penises, are reared as girls (Reiner & Gearhart, 2004). Despite their being put in dresses and treated as girls, most exhibit male-typical play and eventually—in most cases, not without emotional distress—come to have a male identity.

The gender gap in aggression also seems influenced by testosterone. In various animals, administering testosterone heightens aggressiveness. In humans, violent male criminals have higher than normal testosterone levels; so do National Football League players and boisterous fraternity members (Dabbs, 2000). Moreover, for both humans and monkeys, the gender difference in aggression appears early in life (before culture has much effect) and wanes as testosterone levels decline during adulthood. No one of these lines of evidence is conclusive. Taken together, they convince many scholars that sex hormones matter. But so, as we will see, does culture.

As people mature to middle age and beyond, a curious thing happens. Women become more assertive and self-confident, men more empathic and less domineering (Kasen & others, 2006; Lowenthal & others, 1975; Pratt & others, 1990).

"The finest people marry the two sexes in their own person."

—*RALPH WALDO EMERSON*,
JOURNALS, 1843

Hormone changes are one possible explanation for the shrinking gender differences. Role demands are another. Some speculate that during courtship and early parenthood, social expectations lead both sexes to emphasize traits that enhance their roles. While courting, providing, and protecting, men play up their macho sides and forgo their needs for interdependence and nurturance (Gutmann, 1977). While courting and rearing young children, young women restrain their impulses to assert and be independent. As men and women graduate from these early adult roles, they supposedly express more of their restrained tendencies. Each becomes more **androgynous**—capable of both assertiveness and nurturance.

androgynous
From *andro* (man) + *gyn* (woman)—thus mixing both masculine and feminine characteristics.

Summing Up: Evolution and Gender: Doing What Comes Naturally?

• Evolutionary psychologists theorize how evolution might have predisposed gender differences in behaviors such as aggression and sexual initiative. Nature's mating game favors males who take sexual initiative toward females—especially those with physical features suggesting fertility—and who seek aggressive dominance in competing with other males. Females, who have fewer reproductive chances, place a greater priority on selecting mates offering the resources to protect and nurture their young.

• Critics say that evolutionary explanations are sometimes after-the-fact conjectures that fail to account

for the reality of cultural diversity; they also question whether enough empirical evidence exists to support evolutionary psychology's theories, and are concerned that these theories will reinforce troublesome stereotypes.

• Although biology (for example, in the form of male and female hormones) plays an important role in gender differences, social roles are also a major influence. What's agreed is that nature endows us with a remarkable capacity to adapt to differing contexts.

Culture and Gender: Doing as the Culture Says?

Culture's influence is vividly illustrated by differing gender roles across place and time.

Culture, as we noted earlier, is what's shared by a large group and transmitted across generations—ideas, attitudes, behaviors, and traditions. We can see the shaping power of culture in ideas about how men and women should behave. And we can see culture in the disapproval they endure when they violate those expectations (Kite, 2001). In countries everywhere, girls spend more time helping with housework and child care, and boys spend more time in unsupervised play (Edwards, 1991). Even in contemporary, dual-career, North American marriages, men do most of the household repairs and women arrange the child care (Bianchi & others, 2000; Fisher & others, 2007).

Gender socialization, it has been said, gives girls "roots" and boys "wings." Peter Crabb and Dawn Bielawski (1994) surveyed twentieth-century children's books that received the prestigious Caldecott Award and found that the books showed girls four times more often than boys using household objects (such as broom, sewing needle, or pots and pans), and boys five times more often than girls using production objects (such as pitchfork, plow, or gun). For adults, the situation is not much different. "Everywhere," reported the United Nations (1991), "women do most household work." And "everywhere, cooking and dishwashing are the least shared household chores." Analyses of who does what in 185 societies revealed that men hunt big game and harvest lumber, women do about 90 percent of the cooking and the laundry, and the sexes are equally likely to plant and harvest crops and to milk cows. Such behavior expectations for males and females define **gender roles**.

gender role
A set of behavior expectations (norms) for males and females.

Three months after the southeast Asian tsunami on December 26, 2004, Oxfam (2005) counted deaths in eight villages and found that female deaths were at least triple those of men. (The women were more likely to be in or near their homes, near the shore, and less likely to be at sea or away from home on errands or at work.)

"At the United Nations, we have always understood that our work for development depends on building a successful partnership with the African farmer and her husband."

—SECRETARY-GENERAL KOFI ANNAN, 2002

In Western countries, gender roles are becoming more flexible. No longer is preschool teaching necessarily women's work and piloting necessarily men's work.

Does culture construct these gender roles? Or do gender roles merely reflect men's and women's natural behavior tendencies? The variety of gender roles across cultures and over time shows that culture indeed helps construct our gender roles.

Gender Roles Vary with Culture

Despite gender role inequalities, the majority of the world's people would ideally like to see more parallel male and female roles. A Pew Global Attitudes survey asked 38,000 people whether life was more satisfying when both spouses work and share child care, or when women stay home and care for the children while the husband provides. A majority of respondents in 41 of 44 countries chose the first answer (Figure 5.7).

However, there are big country-to-country differences. Egyptians disagreed with the world majority opinion by 2 to 1, whereas Vietnamese concurred by 11 to 1. In its Global Gender Gap Report 2008, the World Economic Forum reported that Norway, Finland, and Sweden have the greatest gender equality, and Saudi Arabia, Chad, and Yemen the least. Even in industrialized societies, roles vary enormously. Women fill 1 in 10 managerial positions in Japan and Germany and nearly 1 in 2 in Australia and the United States (ILO, 1997; Wallace, 2000). In North America most doctors and dentists are men; in Russia most doctors are women, as are most dentists in Denmark.

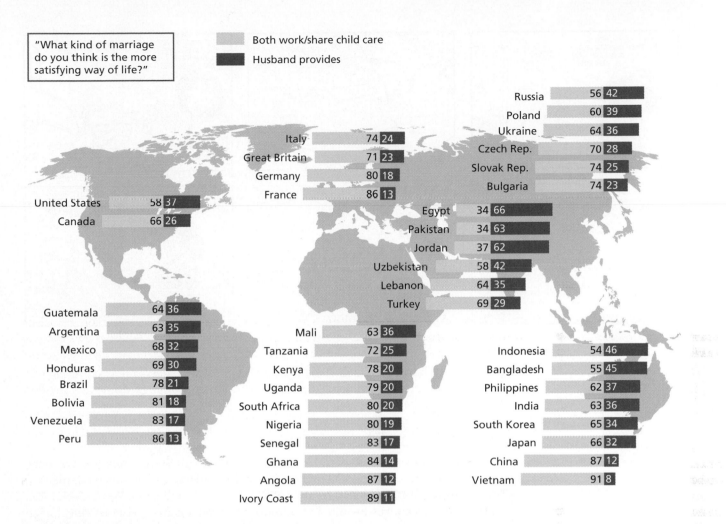

FIGURE :: 5.7

Approved Gender Roles Vary with Culture

Source: Data from the 2003 Pew Global Attitudes survey.

Gender Roles Vary over Time

In the last half-century—a thin slice of our long history—gender roles have changed dramatically. In 1938, just one in five Americans approved "of a married woman earning money in business or industry if she has a husband capable of supporting her." By 1996, four in five approved (Niemi & others, 1989; NORC, 1996). In 1967, 57 percent of first-year American collegians agreed that "the activities of married women are best confined to the home and family." In 2005, only 20 percent agreed (Astin & others, 1987; Pryor & others, 2005). (With the culture approaching a consensus on these matters, the questions are no longer asked in these surveys.)

Behavioral changes have accompanied this attitude shift. In 1965 the Harvard Business School had never granted a degree to a woman. At the turn of the twenty-first century, 30 percent of its graduates were women. From 1960 to 2005, women rose from 6 percent to 50 percent of U.S. medical students and from 3 percent to 50 percent of law students (AMA, 2004; Cynkar, 2007; Hunt, 2000; Richardson, 2005). In the mid-1960s American married women devoted *seven times* as many hours to housework as did their husbands; by the mid-1990s this was down to twice as many hours (Bianchi & others, 2000; Fisher & others, 2007).

The changing male-female roles cross many cultures, as illustrated by women's gradually increasing representation in the parliaments of nations from Morocco to

In Western cultures, gender roles are changing, but not this much.

Sweden (Inglehart & Welzel, 2005; IPU, 2008). Such changes, across cultures and over a remarkably short time, signal that evolution and biology do not fix gender roles: Time also bends the genders.

Peer-Transmitted Culture

Cultures, like ice cream, come in many flavors. On Wall Street, men mostly wear suits and women often wear skirts and dresses; in Scotland, many men wear pleated skirts (kilts) as formal dress; in some equatorial cultures, men and women wear virtually nothing at all. How are such traditions preserved across generations?

The prevailing assumption is what Judith Rich Harris (1998, 2007) calls *The Nurture Assumption:* Parental nurture, the way parents bring their children up, governs who their children become. On that much, Freudians and behaviorists—and your next-door neighbor—agree. Comparing the extremes of loved children and abused children suggests that parenting *does* matter. Moreover, children do acquire many of their values, including their political affiliation and religious faith, at home. But if children's personalities are molded by parental example and nurture, then children who grow up in the same families should be noticeably alike, shouldn't they?

That presumption is refuted by the most astonishing, agreed-upon, and dramatic finding of developmental psychology. In the words of behavior geneticists Robert Plomin and Denise Daniels (1987), "Two children in the same family [are on average] as different from one another as are pairs of children selected randomly from the population."

The evidence from studies of twins and biological and adoptive siblings indicates that genetic influences explain roughly 50 percent of individual variations in personality traits. Shared environmental influences—including the shared home influence—account for only 0 to 10 percent of their personality differences. So what accounts for the other 40 to 50 percent? It's largely *peer influence*, Harris argues. What children and teens care most about is not what their parents think but what peers think. Children and youth learn their culture—their games, their musical tastes, their accents, even their dirty words—mostly from peers. In hindsight, that makes sense. It's their peers with whom they play and eventually will work and mate. Consider:

- Preschoolers will often refuse to try a certain food despite parents' urgings—until they are put at a table with a group of children who like it.

Children learn many of their attitudes from their peers.

- Although children of smokers have an elevated smoking rate, the effect seems largely peer mediated. Such children more often have friends who model smoking, who suggest its pleasures, and who offer cigarettes.
- Young immigrant children whose families are transplanted into foreign cultures usually grow up preferring the language and norms of their new peer culture. They may "code-switch" when they step back into their homes, but their hearts and minds are with their peer groups. Likewise, deaf children of hearing parents who attend schools for the deaf usually leave their parents' culture and assimilate into deaf culture.

Ergo, if we left a group of children with their same schools, neighborhoods, and peers but switched the parents around, says Harris (1996) in taking her argument to its limits, they "would develop into the same sort of adults." Parents have an important influence, but it's substantially indirect; parents help define the schools, neighborhoods, and peers that directly influence whether their children become delinquent, use drugs, or get pregnant. Moreover, children often take their cues from slightly older children, who get their cues from older youth, who take theirs from young adults in the parents' generation.

The links of influence from parental group to child group are loose enough that the cultural transmission is never perfect. And in both human and primate cultures, change comes from the young. When one monkey discovers a better way of washing food or when people develop a new idea about fashion or gender roles, the innovation usually comes from the young and is more readily embraced by younger adults. Thus, cultural traditions continue, yet cultures change.

Summing Up: Culture and Gender: Doing as the Culture Says?

- The most heavily researched of roles, gender roles, reflect biological influence, but also illustrate culture's strong impact. The universal tendency has been for males, more than females, to occupy socially dominant roles.

- Gender roles show significant variation from culture to culture and from time to time.
- Much of culture's influence is transmitted to children by their peers.

FIGURE :: 5.8

A Social-Role Theory of Gender Differences in Social Behavior

Various influences, including childhood experiences and factors, bend males and females toward differing roles. It is the expectations and the skills and beliefs associated with these differing roles that affect men's and women's behavior.

Source: Adapted from Eagly (1987), and Eagly & Wood (1991).

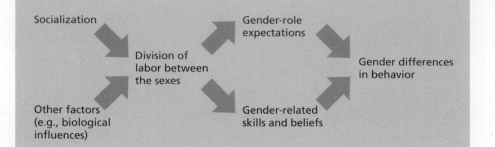

What Can We Conclude about Genes, Culture, and Gender?

Biology and culture play out in the context of each other. How, then, do biology and culture interact? And how do our individual personalities interact with our situations?

Biology *and* Culture

We needn't think of evolution and culture as competitors. Cultural norms subtly yet powerfully affect our attitudes and behavior. But they don't do so independent of biology. Everything social and psychological is ultimately biological. If others' expectations influence us, that is part of our biological programming. Moreover, what our biological heritage initiates, culture may accentuate. If genes and hormones predispose males to be more physically aggressive than females, culture may amplify that difference through norms that expect males to be tough and females to be the kinder, gentler sex.

Biology and culture may also **interact.** Advances in genetic science indicate how experience uses genes to change the brain (Quarts & Sejnowski, 2002). Environmental stimuli can activate genes that produce new brain cell branching receptors. Visual experience activates genes that develop the brain's visual area. Parental touch activates genes that help offspring cope with future stressful events. Genes are not set in stone; they respond adaptively to our experiences.

Biology and experience interact when biological traits influence how the environment reacts. Men, being 8 percent taller and averaging almost double the proportion of muscle mass, are bound to experience life differently from women. Or consider this: A very strong cultural norm dictates that males should be taller than their female mates. In one U.S. study, only 1 in 720 married couples violated that norm (Gillis & Avis, 1980). With hindsight, we can speculate a psychological explanation: Perhaps being taller helps men perpetuate their social power over women. But we can also speculate evolutionary wisdom that might underlie the cultural norm: If people preferred partners of their own height, tall men and short women would often be without partners. As it is, evolution dictates that men tend to be taller than women, and culture dictates the same for couples. So the height norm might well be a result of biology *and* culture.

Alice Eagly and Wendy Wood (1999; Wood & Eagly, 2007) theorize how biology and culture interact (Figure 5.8). They believe that a variety of factors, including biological influences and childhood socialization, predispose a sexual division of labor. In adult life the immediate causes of gender differences in social behavior are the *roles* that reflect this sexual division of labor. Men, because of their biologically endowed strength and speed, tend to be found in roles demanding physical power.

interaction

A relationship in which the effect of one factor (such as biology) depends on another factor (such as environment).

THE inside STORY

I began my work on gender with a project on social influence in the early 1970s. Like many feminist activists of the day, I initially assumed that, despite negative cultural stereotypes about women, the behavior of women and men is substantially equivalent. Over the years, my views have evolved considerably. I have found that some social behaviors of women and men are somewhat different, especially in situations that bring gender roles to mind.

People should not assume that these differences necessarily reflect unfavorably on women. Women's tendencies to be more attuned to other people's concerns and to treat others more democratically are favorably evaluated and can be assets in many situations. In fact, my research on gender stereotypes shows that, if we take both negative and positive qualities into account, the stereotype of women is currently more favorable than the stereotype of men. However, the qualities of niceness and nurturance that are important in expectations about women may decrease their power and effectiveness in situations that call for assertive and competitive behavior.

Alice Eagly,
Northwestern University

Women's capacity for childbearing and breastfeeding inclines them to more nurturant roles. Each sex then tends to exhibit the behaviors expected of those who fill such roles and to have their skills and beliefs shaped accordingly. Nature and nurture are a "tangled web." As role assignments become more equal, Eagly predicts that gender differences "will gradually lessen."

Indeed, note Eagly and Wood, in cultures with greater equality of gender roles the gender difference in mate preferences (men seeking youth and domestic skill, women seeking status and earning potential) is less. Likewise, as women's employment in formerly male occupations has increased, the gender difference in self-reported masculinity/femininity has decreased (Twenge, 1997). As men and women enact more similar roles, some psychological differences shrink.

But not all, report David Schmitt and his international colleagues (2008). Personality tests taken by men and women in 55 nations show that across the world—though (surprise) especially in prosperous, educated, egalitarian countries—women report more extraversion, agreeableness, and conscientiousness. In less fortunate economic and social contexts, suggests Schmitt, "the development of one's inherent personality traits is more restrained."

Although biology predisposes men to strength tasks and women to infant care, Wood and Eagly (2002) conclude that "the behavior of women and men is sufficiently malleable that individuals of both sexes are fully capable of effectively carrying out organizational roles at all levels." For today's high-status and often high-tech work roles, male size and aggressiveness matter less and less. Moreover, lowered birthrates mean that women are less constrained by pregnancy and nursing. The end result, when combined with competitive pressures for employers to hire the best talent regardless of gender, is the inevitable rise in gender equality.

The Power of the Situation *and* the Person

"There are trivial truths and great truths," declared the physicist Niels Bohr. "The opposite of a trivial truth is plainly false. The opposite of a great truth is also true." Each chapter in this unit on social influence teaches a great truth: *the power of the situation.* This great truth about the power of external pressures would explain our behavior if we were passive, like tumbleweeds. But, unlike tumbleweeds, we are not just blown here and there by the situations in which we find ourselves. We act; we react.

Food for thought: If Bohr's statement is a great truth, what is its opposite?

We respond, and we get responses. We can resist the social situation and sometimes even change it. For that reason, I've chosen to conclude each of these "social influence" chapters by calling attention to the opposite of the great truth: *the power of the person.*

Perhaps stressing the power of culture leaves you somewhat uncomfortable. Most of us resent any suggestion that external forces determine our behavior; we see ourselves as free beings, as the originators of our actions (well, at least of our good actions). We worry that assuming cultural reasons for our actions might lead to what philosopher Jean-Paul Sartre called "bad faith"—evading responsibility by blaming something or someone for one's fate.

Actually, social control (the power of the situation) and personal control (the power of the person) no more compete with each other than do biological and cultural explanations. Social and personal explanations of our social behavior are both valid, for at any moment we are both the creatures and the creators of our social worlds. We may well be the products of the interplay of our genes and environment. But it is also true that the future is coming, and it is our job to decide where it is going. Our choices today determine our environment tomorrow.

Social situations do profoundly influence individuals. But individuals also influence social situations. The two *interact.* Asking whether external situations or inner dispositions (or culture or evolution) determine behavior is like asking whether length or width determines a room's area.

The interaction occurs in at least three ways (Snyder & Ickes, 1985).

> "The words of truth are always paradoxical."
> —*LAO-TZU, THE SIMPLE WAY,* 6TH CENTURY B.C.

- *A given social situation often affects different people differently.* Because our minds do not see reality identically or objectively, we respond to a situation as we construe it. And some people (groups as well as individuals) are more sensitive and responsive to social situations than others (Snyder, 1983). The Japanese, for example, are more responsive to social expectations than the British (Argyle & others, 1978).

- *People often choose their situations* (Ickes & others, 1997). Given a choice, sociable people elect situations that evoke social interaction. When you chose your college, you were also choosing to expose yourself to a specific set of social influences. Ardent political liberals are unlikely to choose to live in suburban Dallas and join the Chamber of Commerce. They are more likely to live in San Francisco or Toronto and join Greenpeace—in other words, to choose a social world that reinforces their inclinations.

- *People often create their situations.* Recall again that our preconceptions can be self-fulfilling: If we expect someone to be extraverted, hostile, intelligent, or sexy, our actions toward the person may induce the very behavior we expect. What, after all, makes a social situation but the people in it? A conservative environment is created by conservatives. What takes place in the sorority is created by its members. The social environment is not like the weather— something that just happens to us. It is more like our homes—something we make for ourselves.

Thus, power resides both in persons and in situations. We create and are created by our cultural worlds.

Summing Up: What Can We Conclude about Genes, Culture, and Gender?

- Biological and cultural explanations need not be contradictory. Indeed, they interact. Biological factors operate within a cultural context, and culture builds on a biological foundation.

- The great truth about the power of social influence is but half the truth if separated from its complementary truth: the power of the person. Persons and situations interact in at least three ways. First, individuals vary in how they interpret and react to a given situation. Second, people choose many of the situations that influence them. Third, people help create their social situations.

POSTSCRIPT: Should We View Ourselves as Products or Architects of Our Social Worlds?

The reciprocal causation between situations and persons allows us to see people as either *reacting to* or *acting upon* their environment. Each perspective is correct, for we are both the products and the architects of our social worlds. Is one perspective wiser, however? In one sense, it is wise to see ourselves as the creatures of our environments (lest we become too proud of our achievements and blame ourselves too much for our problems) and to see others as free actors (lest we become paternalistic and manipulative).

Perhaps, however, we would do well more often to assume the reverse—to view ourselves as free agents and to view others as influenced by their environments. We would then assume self-efficacy as we view ourselves, and we would seek understanding and social reform as we relate to others. Most religions, in fact, encourage us to take responsibility for ourselves but to refrain from judging others. Is that because our natural inclination is the opposite: to excuse our own failures while blaming others for theirs?

Making the Social Connection

Gender and culture pervade social psychology. For example, does culture predict how people will conform (Chapter 6, Conformity and Obedience)? How do cultures vary in the way they see love? How do men and women see love differently (Chapter 11, Attraction and Intimacy)? How does the meaning of certain hand gestures vary from one culture to another? Go to the Online Learning Center to see videos on How Biology and Culture Shape Our Social Roles and Cultural Variations in Nonverbal Behavior.

Conformity and Obedience

> "Whatever crushes individuality is despotism, by whatever name it may be called."
>
> —John Stuart Mill, *On Liberty*, 1859

> "The social pressures community brings to bear are a mainstay of our moral values."
>
> —Amitai Etzioni, *The Spirit of Community*, 1993

Y ou have surely experienced the phenomenon: As a controversial speaker or music concert finishes, the adoring fans near the front leap to their feet, applauding. The approving folks just behind them follow their example and join the standing ovation. Now the wave of people standing reaches people who, unprompted, would merely be giving polite applause from their comfortable seats. Seated among them, part of you wants to stay seated ("this speaker doesn't represent my views at all"). But as the wave of standing people sweeps by, will you alone stay seated? It's not easy being a minority of one. Unless you heartily dislike what you've just heard, you will probably rise to your feet, at least briefly.

Such scenes of conformity raise this chapter's questions:

- Why, given our diversity, do we so often behave as social clones?

- Under what circumstances are we most likely to conform?

- Are certain people more likely than others to conform?

- Who resists the pressure to conform?

- Is conformity as bad as my image of a docile "herd" implies? Should I instead be describing their "group solidarity" and "social sensitivity"?

What Is Conformity?

Let us take the last question first. Is conformity good or bad? That question has no scientific answer. Assuming the values most of us share, we can say that conformity is at times bad (when it leads someone to drive drunk or to join in racist behavior), at times good (when it inhibits people from cutting into a theater line), and at times inconsequential (when it disposes tennis players to wear white).

In Western individualistic cultures, where submitting to peer pressure is not admired, the word "conformity" tends to carry a negative value judgment. How would you feel if you overheard someone describing you as a "real conformist"? I suspect you would feel hurt. North American and European social psychologists, reflecting their individualistic cultures, give social influence negative labels (conformity, submission, compliance) rather than positive ones (communal sensitivity, responsiveness, cooperative team play).

In Japan, going along with others is a sign not of weakness but of tolerance, self-control, and maturity (Markus & Kitayama, 1994). "Everywhere in Japan," observed Lance Morrow (1983), "one senses an intricate serenity that comes to a people who know exactly what to expect from each other." Such is also true of self-organized U2 fans whom Marie Helweg-Larsen and Barbara LoMonaco (2008) observed queuing overnight for unreserved concert places at or near the front rail. A U2 fan code of honor mandates first come, first served, with disdain for line cutters.

The moral: We choose labels to suit our values and judgments. Labels both describe and evaluate, and they are inescapable. So let us be clear on the meanings of the following labels: conformity, compliance, obedience, acceptance.

conformity
A change in behavior or belief as the result of real or imagined group pressure.

Conformity is not just acting as other people act; it is also being *affected* by how they act. It is acting or thinking differently from the way you would act and think if you were alone. Thus, **conformity** is a change in behavior or belief to accord with others. When, as part of a crowd, you rise to cheer a game-winning goal, are you conforming? When, along with millions of others, you drink milk or coffee, are you conforming? When you and everyone else agree that women look better with longer hair than with crewcuts, are you conforming? Maybe, maybe not. The key is whether your behavior and beliefs would be the same apart from the group. Would you rise to cheer the goal if you were the only fan in the stands?

compliance
Conformity that involves publicly acting in accord with an implied or explicit request while privately disagreeing.

There are several varieties of conformity (Nail & others, 2000). Consider three: compliance, obedience, and acceptance. Sometimes we conform to an expectation or a request without really believing in what we are doing. We put on the necktie or the dress, though we dislike doing so. This insincere, outward conformity is **compliance.** We comply primarily to reap a reward or avoid a punishment. If our compliance is to an explicit command, we call it **obedience.**

obedience
Acting in accord with a direct order or command.

Sometimes we genuinely believe in what the group has persuaded us to do. We may join millions of others in exercising because we all have been told that exercise is healthy and we accept that as true. This sincere, inward conformity is called **acceptance.** Acceptance sometimes follows compliance; we may come to inwardly believe something we initially questioned. As Chapter 4 emphasized, attitudes follow behavior. Unless we feel no responsibility for our behavior, we usually become sympathetic to what we have stood up for.

acceptance
Conformity that involves both acting and believing in accord with social pressure.

Summing Up: What Is Conformity?

Conformity—changing one's behavior or belief as a result of group pressure—comes in two forms. *Compliance* is outwardly going along with the group while inwardly disagreeing; a subset of compliance is *obedience*, compliance with a direct command. *Acceptance* is believing as well as acting in accord with social pressure.

GREGORY

"Sure, I follow the herd—not out of brainless obedience, mind you, but out of a deep and abiding respect for the concept of community."

What Are the Classic Conformity and Obedience Studies?

How have social psychologists studied conformity in the laboratory? What do their findings reveal about the potency of social forces and the nature of evil?

Researchers who study conformity and obedience construct miniature social worlds—laboratory microcultures that simplify and simulate important features of everyday social influence. Some of these studies revealed such startling findings that they have been widely replicated and widely reported by other researchers, earning them the name of "classic" experiments. We will consider three, each of which provides a method for studying conformity—and plenty of food for thought.

Sherif's Studies of Norm Formation

The first of the three classics bridges Chapter 5's focus on culture's power to create and perpetuate norms and this chapter's focus on conformity. Muzafer Sherif (1935, 1937) wondered whether it was possible to observe the emergence of a social norm in the laboratory. Like biologists seeking to isolate a virus so they can then experiment with it, Sherif wanted to isolate and then experiment with norm formation.

As a participant in one of Sherif's experiments, you might have found yourself seated in a dark room. Fifteen feet in front of you a pinpoint of light appears. At first, nothing happens. Then for a few seconds it moves erratically and finally disappears. Now you must guess how far it moved. The dark room gives you no way to judge distance, so you offer an uncertain "six inches." The experimenter repeats the procedure. This time you say, "Ten inches." With further repetitions, your estimates continue to average about eight inches.

The next day you return to the darkened room, joined by two other participants who had the same experience the day before. When the light goes off for the first time, the other two people offer their best guesses from the day before. "One inch," says one. "Two inches," says the other. A bit taken aback, you nevertheless say, "Six inches." With repetitions of this group experience, both on this day and for the next two days, will your responses change? The Columbia University men whom Sherif tested changed their estimates markedly. As Figure 6.1 illustrates, a group norm typically emerged. (The norm was false. Why? The light never moved! Sherif had taken advantage of an optical illusion called the **autokinetic phenomenon.**)

Sherif and others have used this technique to answer questions about people's suggestibility. When people were retested alone a year later, would their estimates again diverge or would they continue to follow the group norm? Remarkably, they continued to support the group norm (Rohrer & others, 1954). (Does that suggest compliance or acceptance?)

autokinetic phenomenon
Self (*auto*) motion (*kinetic*). The apparent movement of a stationary point of light in the dark.

FIGURE :: 6.1

A Sample Group from Sherif's Study of Norm Formation

Three individuals converge as they give repeated estimates of the apparent movement of a point of light.

Source: Data from Sherif & Sherif (1969), p. 209.

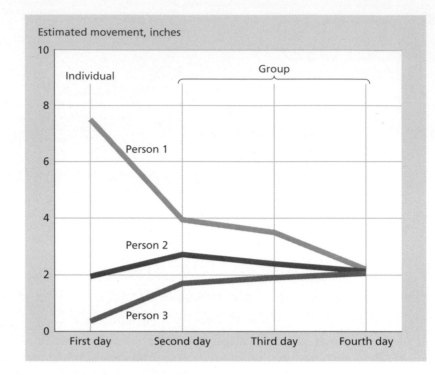

"Why doth one man's yawning make another yawn?"
—*ROBERT BURTON,* ANATOMY OF MELANCHOLY, *1621*

"When people are free to do as they please, they usually imitate each other."
—*ERIC HOFFER,* THE PASSIONATE BELIEVER, *1955*

Struck by culture's seeming power to perpetuate false beliefs, Robert Jacobs and Donald Campbell (1961) studied the transmission of false beliefs in their Northwestern University laboratory. Using the autokinetic phenomenon, they had a confederate give an inflated estimate of how far the light had moved. The confederate then left the experiment and was replaced by another real participant, who was in turn replaced by a still newer member. The inflated illusion persisted (although diminishing) for five generations of participants. These people had become "unwitting conspirators in perpetuating a cultural fraud." The lesson of these experiments: Our views of reality are not ours alone.

In everyday life the results of suggestibility are sometimes amusing. One person coughs, laughs, or yawns, and others are soon doing the same. (See "Research Close-Up: Contagious Yawning.") Comedy-show laugh tracks capitalize on our suggestibility. Laugh tracks work especially well when we presume that the laughing audience is folks like us—"recorded here at La Trobe University" in one study by Michael Platow and colleagues (2004)—rather than a group that's unlike us. Just being around happy people can help us feel happier, a phenomenon that Peter Totterdell and his colleagues (1998) call "mood linkage." In their studies of British nurses and accountants, people within the same work groups tended to share up and down moods.

Another form of social contagion is what Tanya Chartrand and John Bargh (1999) call "the chameleon effect." Picture yourself in one of their experiments, working alongside a confederate who occasionally either rubbed her face or shook her foot. Would you—like their participants—be more likely to rub your face when with a face-rubbing person and shake your foot when with a foot-shaking person? If so, it would quite likely be an automatic behavior, done without any conscious intention to conform. And, because our behavior influences our attitudes and emotions, it would incline you to feel what the other feels (Neumann & Strack, 2000).

An experiment in the Netherlands by Rick van Baaren and his colleagues (2004) indicates that your mimicry would also incline the other to like you and be helpful to you and to others. People become more likely to help pick up dropped pens for someone whose behavior has mimicked their own. Being mimicked seems to enhance social bonds, which even leads to donating more money to a charity. In a follow-up experiment, Chartrand, van Baaren, and their colleagues had an interviewer invite students to try a new sports drink, while sometimes mirroring the

research CLOSE-UP

Contagious Yawning

Yawning is a behavior that you and I share with most vertebrates. Primates do it. So do cats and crocodiles and birds and turtles and even fish. But why, and when?

Sometimes, notes University of Maryland, Baltimore County, psychologist Robert Provine (2005), scientific research neglects commonplace behavior—including the behaviors he loves to study, such as laughing and yawning. To study yawning by the method of naturalistic observation, notes Provine, one needs only a stopwatch, a notepad, and a pencil. Yawning, he reports, is a "fixed action pattern" that lasts about six seconds, with a long inward breath and shorter climactic (and pleasureful) exhalation. It often comes in bouts, with just over a minute between yawns. And it is equally common among men and women. Even patients who are totally paralyzed and unable to move their body voluntarily may yawn normally, indicating that this is automatic behavior.

When do we yawn?

We yawn when we are bored. When Provine asked participants to watch a TV test pattern for 30 minutes, they yawned 70 percent more often than others in a control group who watched less boring music videos. But tension can also elicit yawning, which is commonly observed among paratroopers before their first jump, Olympic athletes before their event, and violinists waiting to go onstage. A friend says she has often been embarrassed when learning something new at work, because her anxiety about getting it right invariably causes her to have a "yawning fit."

We yawn when we are sleepy. No surprise here, except perhaps that people who kept a yawning diary for

Provine recorded even more yawns in the hour after waking than in the yawn-prone hour before sleeping. Often, we awaken and yawn-stretch. And so do our dogs and cats when they rouse from slumber.

We yawn when others yawn. To test whether yawning, like laughter, is contagious, Provine exposed people to a five-minute video of a man yawning repeatedly. Sure enough, 55 percent of viewers yawned, as did only 21 percent of those viewing a video of smiles. A yawning face acts as a stimulus that activates a yawn's fixed action pattern, even if the yawn is presented in black-and-white, upside down, or as a mid-yawn still image. The discovery of brain "mirror neurons"— neurons that rehearse or mimic witnessed actions— suggests a biological mechanism that explains why our yawns so often mirror others' yawns—and why even dogs often yawn after observing a human yawn (Joly-Mascheroni & others, 2008).

To see what parts of the yawning face were most potent, Provine had viewers watch a whole face, a face with the mouth masked, a mouth with the face masked, or (as a control condition) a nonyawning smiling face. As Figure 6.2 shows, the yawning faces triggered yawns even with the mouth masked. Thus, covering your mouth when yawning likely won't suppress yawn contagion.

Just thinking about yawning usually produces yawns, reports Provine—a phenomenon you may have noticed while reading this box. It's a phenomenon I have noticed. While reading Provine's research on contagious yawning, I yawned four times (and felt a little silly).

FIGURE :: 6.2

What Facial Features Trigger Contagious Yawns?

Robert Provine (2005) invited four groups of 30 people each to watch five-minute videotapes of a smiling adult, or a yawning adult, parts of whose face were masked for two of the groups. A yawning mouth triggered some yawns, but yawning eyes and head motion triggered even more.

"I don't know why. I just suddenly felt like calling."

student's postures and movements, with just enough delay to make it not noticeable (Tanner & others, 2008). By the experiment's end the copied students became more likely to consume the new drink and say they would buy it.

Suggestibility can also occur on a large scale. In late March 1954, Seattle newspapers reported damage to car windshields in a city 80 miles to the north. On the morning of April 14, similar windshield damage was reported 65 miles away, and later that day only 45 miles away. By nightfall, whatever was causing this windshield pitting had reached Seattle. Before the end of April 15, the Seattle police department had received complaints of damage to more than 3,000 windshields (Medalia & Larsen, 1958). That evening the mayor of Seattle called on President Eisenhower for help.

I was a Seattle 11-year-old at the time. I recall searching our windshield, frightened by the explanation that a Pacific H-bomb test was raining fallout on Seattle. On April 16, however, the newspapers hinted that the real culprit might be mass suggestibility. After April 17 there were no more complaints. Later analysis of the pitted windshields concluded that the cause was ordinary road damage. Why did local residents notice this only after April 14? Given the suggestion, we had looked carefully *at* our windshields instead of *through* them.

Suggestibility is not always so amusing. Hijackings, UFO sightings, and even suicides tend to come in waves. (See "Focus On: Mass Delusions.") Shortly after the 1774 publication of *The Sorrows of Young Werther,* Johann Wolfgang von Goethe's first novel, young European men started dressing in yellow trousers and blue jackets, as had Goethe's protagonist, a young man named Werther. Although the fashion epidemic triggered by the book was amusing, another apparent effect was less amusing and led to the book's banning in several areas. In the novel, Werther commits suicide with a pistol after being rejected by the woman whose heart he failed to win; after the book's publication, reports began accumulating of young men imitating Werther's desperate act.

Two centuries later, sociologist David Phillips confirmed such imitative suicidal behavior and described it as "the Werther effect." Phillips and his colleagues (1985, 1989) discovered that suicides, as well as fatal auto accidents and private airplane crashes (which sometimes disguise suicides), increase after a highly publicized suicide. For example, following Marilyn Monroe's August 6, 1962, suicide, there were 200 more August suicides in the United States than normal. Moreover, the increase happens only in places where the suicide story is publicized. The more publicity, the greater the increase in later fatalities.

Although not all studies have found the copycat suicide phenomenon, it has surfaced in Germany; in a London psychiatric unit that experienced 14 patient suicides in one year; and in one high school that, within 18 days after one student committed suicide, suffered two suicides, seven suicide attempts, and 23 students reporting suicidal thoughts (Joiner, 1999; Jonas, 1992). In both Germany and the United States, suicide rates rise slightly following fictional suicides on soap operas, and, ironically, even after serious dramas that focus on the suicide problem (Gould & Shaffer, 1986; Hafner & Schmidtke, 1989; Phillips, 1982). Phillips reports that teenagers are most susceptible, a finding that would help explain the occasional clusters of teen copycat suicides. In the days following Saddam Hussein's widely publicized hanging, boys in at least five countries slipped nooses around their own heads and hung themselves, apparently accidentally (AP, 2007b).

focus
ON   Mass Delusions

Suggestibility on a mass scale appears as collective delusions—spontaneous spreading of false beliefs. Occasionally, this appears as "mass hysteria"—the spread of bodily complaints within a school or workplace with no organic basis for the symptoms. One 2,000-student high school was closed for two weeks as 170 students and staff sought emergency treatment for stomach ailments, dizziness, headaches, and drowsiness. After investigators looked high and low for viruses, germs, pesticides, herbicides—anything that would make people ill—they found . . . nothing (Jones & others, 2000).

In the weeks following September 11, 2001, groups of children at schools scattered across the United States started breaking out in itchy red rashes without any apparent cause (Talbot, 2002). Unlike a viral condition, the rash spread by "line of sight." People got the rash as they *saw* others getting it (even if they had no close contact). Also, everyday skin conditions—eczema, acne, dry skin in overheated classrooms—got noticed, and perhaps amplified by anxiety. As with so many mass hysterias, rumors of a problem had caused people to notice their ordinary, everyday symptoms and to attribute them to their school.

Sociologists Robert Bartholomew and Erich Goode (2000) report on other mass delusions from the last millennium. During the Middle Ages, European convents reportedly experienced outbreaks of imitative behaviors. In one large French convent, at a time when it was believed that humans could be possessed by animals, one nun began to meow like a cat. Eventually, "all the nuns meowed together every day at a certain time." In a German convent, a nun reportedly fell to biting her companions, and before long "all the nuns of this convent began biting each other." In time, the biting mania spread to other convents.

On June 24, 1947, Kenneth Arnold was piloting his private plane near Mount Rainier when he spotted nine glittering objects in the sky. Worried that he may have seen foreign guided missiles, he tried reporting what he saw to the FBI. Discovering its office closed, he went to his local newspaper and reported crescent-shaped objects that moved "like a saucer would if you skipped it across the water." When the Associated Press then reported the sighting of "saucers" in more than 150 newspapers, the term "flying saucers" was created by headline writers, triggering a worldwide wave of flying saucer sightings.

Asch's Studies of Group Pressure

Participants in Sherif's darkened-room autokinetic experiments faced an ambiguous reality. Consider a less ambiguous perceptual problem faced by a young boy named Solomon Asch (1907–1996). While attending the traditional Jewish Seder at Passover, Asch recalled,

> I asked my uncle, who was sitting next to me, why the door was being opened. He replied, "The prophet Elijah visits this evening every Jewish home and takes a sip of wine from the cup reserved for him."
>
> I was amazed at this news and repeated, "Does he really come? Does he really take a sip?"
>
> My uncle said, "If you watch very closely, when the door is opened you will see—you watch the cup—you will see that the wine will go down a little."
>
> And that's what happened. My eyes were riveted upon the cup of wine. I was determined to see whether there would be a change. And to me it seemed . . . that indeed something was happening at the rim of the cup, and the wine did go down a little. (Aron & Aron, 1989, p. 27)

Years later, social psychologist Asch recreated his boyhood experience in his laboratory. Imagine yourself as one of Asch's volunteer subjects. You are seated sixth in a row of seven people. The experimenter explains that you will be taking part in a study of perceptual judgments, and then asks you to say which of the three lines in Figure 6.3 matches the standard line. You can easily see that it's line 2. So it's no surprise when the five people responding before you all say, "Line 2."

The next comparison proves as easy, and you settle in for what seems a simple test. But the third trial startles you. Although the correct answer seems just

"He who sees the truth, let him proclaim it, without asking who is for it or who is against it."

—*HENRY GEORGE*, THE IRISH LAND QUESTION, *1881*

FIGURE :: 6.3

Sample Comparison from Solomon Asch's Conformity Procedure

The participants judged which of three comparison lines matched the standard.

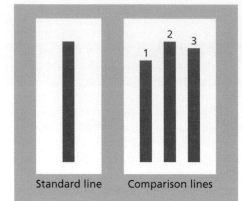

Standard line   Comparison lines

as clear-cut, the first person gives a wrong answer. When the second person gives the same wrong answer, you sit up in your chair and stare at the cards. The third person agrees with the first two. Your jaw drops; you start to perspire. "What is this?" you ask yourself. "Are they blind? Or am I?" The fourth and fifth people agree with the others. Then the experimenter looks at you. Now you are experiencing an epistemological dilemma: "What is true? Is it what my peers tell me or what my eyes tell me?"

Dozens of college students experienced that conflict in Asch's experiments. Those in a control condition who answered alone were correct more than 99 percent of the time. Asch wondered: If several others (confederates coached by the experimenter) gave identical wrong answers, would people declare what they would otherwise have denied? Although some people never conformed, three-quarters did so at least once. All told, 37 percent of the responses were conforming (or should we say *"trusting of others"*). Of course, that means 63 percent of the time people did *not* conform. The experiments show that most people "tell the truth even when others do not," note Bert Hodges and Anne Geyer (2006). Despite the independence shown by many of his participants, Asch's (1955) feelings about the conformity were as clear as the correct answers to his questions: "That reasonably intelligent and well-meaning young people are willing to call white black is a matter of concern. It raises questions about our ways of education and about the values that guide our conduct."

Asch's procedure became the standard for hundreds of later experiments. Those experiments lacked what Chapter 1 called the "mundane realism" of everyday conformity, but they did have "experimental realism." People became emotionally involved in the experience. The Sherif and Asch results are startling because they involved no obvious pressure to conform—there were no rewards for "team play," no punishments for individuality.

Ethical note: Professional ethics usually dictate explaining the experiment afterward (see Chapter 1). Imagine you were an experimenter who had just finished a session with a conforming participant. Could you explain the deception without making the person feel gullible and dumb?

If people are that conforming in response to such minimal pressure, how compliant will they be if they are directly coerced? Could someone force the average North American or European to perform cruel acts? I would have guessed not: Their humane, democratic, individualistic values would make them resist such pressure. Besides, the easy verbal pronouncements of those experiments are a giant step away from actually harming someone; you and I would never yield to coercion to hurt another. Or would we? Social psychologist Stanley Milgram wondered.

In one of Asch's conformity experiments, subject number 6 experienced uneasiness and conflict after hearing five people before him give a wrong answer.

Milgram's Obedience Experiments

Milgram's (1965, 1974) experiments tested what happens when the demands of authority clash with the demands of conscience. These have become social psychology's most famous and controversial experiments. "Perhaps more than any other empirical contributions in the history of social science," notes Lee Ross (1988), "they have become part of our society's shared intellectual legacy—that small body of historical incidents, biblical parables, and classic literature that serious thinkers feel free to draw on when they debate about human nature or contemplate human history."

Although you may therefore recall a mention of this research in a prior course, let's go backstage and examine the studies in depth. Here is the scene staged by Milgram, a creative artist who wrote stories and stage plays: Two men come to Yale University's psychology laboratory to participate in a study of learning and memory. A stern experimenter in a lab coat explains that this is a pioneering study of the effect of punishment on learning. The experiment requires one of them to teach a list of word pairs to the other and to punish errors by delivering shocks of increasing intensity. To assign the roles, they draw slips out of a hat. One of the men (a mild-mannered, 47-year-old accountant who is actually the experimenter's confederate) says that his slip says "learner" and is ushered into an adjacent room. The other man (a volunteer who has come in response to a newspaper ad) is assigned to the role of "teacher." He takes a mild sample shock and then looks on as the experimenter straps the learner into a chair and attaches an electrode to his wrist.

Teacher and experimenter then return to the main room (Figure 6.4), where the teacher takes his place before a "shock generator" with switches ranging from 15 to 450 volts in 15-volt increments. The switches are labeled "Slight Shock," "Very Strong Shock," "Danger: Severe Shock," and so forth. Under the 435- and 450-volt switches appears "XXX." The experimenter tells the teacher to "move one level higher on the shock generator" each time the learner gives a wrong answer. With each flick of a switch, lights flash, relay switches click, and an electric buzzer sounds.

If the participant complies with the experimenter's requests, he hears the learner grunt at 75, 90, and 105 volts. At 120 volts the learner shouts that the shocks are painful. And at 150 volts he cries out, "Experimenter, get me out of here! I won't be in the experiment anymore! I refuse to go on!" By 270 volts his protests have

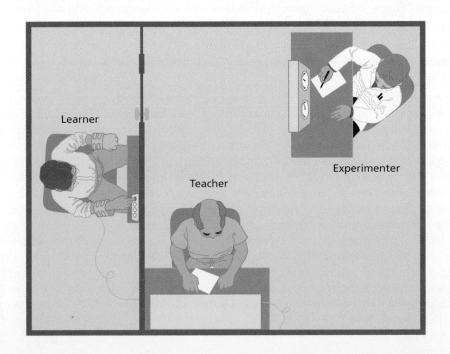

FIGURE :: 6.4

Milgram's Obedience
Experiment

Source: Milgram, 1974.

become screams of agony, and he continues to insist to be let out. At 300 and 315 volts, he screams his refusal to answer. After 330 volts he falls silent. In answer to the teacher's inquiries and pleas to end the experiment, the experimenter states that the nonresponses should be treated as wrong answers. To keep the participant going, he uses four verbal prods:

Prod 1: Please continue (or Please go on).

Prod 2: The experiment requires that you continue.

Prod 3: It is absolutely essential that you continue.

Prod 4: You have no other choice; you must go on.

How far would you go? Milgram described the experiment to 110 psychiatrists, college students, and middle-class adults. People in all three groups guessed that they would disobey by about 135 volts; none expected to go beyond 300 volts. Recognizing that self-estimates may reflect self-serving bias, Milgram asked them how far they thought *other* people would go. Virtually no one expected anyone to proceed to XXX on the shock panel. (The psychiatrists guessed about one in a thousand.)

But when Milgram conducted the experiment with 40 men—a vocational mix of 20- to 50-year-olds—26 of them (65 percent) progressed all the way to 450 volts. Those who stopped often did so at the 150-volt point, when the learner's protestations became more compelling (Packer, 2008).

Wondering if people today would similarly obey, Jerry Burger (2009) replicated Milgram's experiment—though only to the 150-volt point. At that point, 70 percent of participants were still obeying, a slight reduction from Milgram's result. In Milgram's experiment, most who were obedient to this point continued to the end. In fact, all who reached 450 volts complied with a command to *continue* the procedure until, after two further trials, the experimenter called a halt.

Having expected a low rate of obedience, and with plans to replicate the experiment in Germany and assess the culture difference, Milgram was disturbed (A. Milgram, 2000). So instead of going to Germany, Milgram next made the learner's protests even more compelling. As the learner was strapped into the chair, the teacher heard him mention his "slight heart condition" and heard the experimenter's reassurance that "although the shocks may be painful, they cause no permanent tissue damage." The learner's anguished protests were to little avail; of 40 new men in this experiment, 25 (63 percent) fully complied with the experimenter's demands (Figure 6.5). Ten later studies that included women found that women's compliance rates were similar to men's (Blass, 1999).

The Ethics of Milgram's Experiments

The obedience of his subjects disturbed Milgram. The procedures he used disturbed many social psychologists (Miller, 1986). The "learner" in these experiments actually received no shock (he disengaged himself from the electric chair and turned on a tape recorder that delivered the protests). Nevertheless, some critics said that Milgram did to his participants what they presumed they were doing to their victims: He stressed them against their will. Indeed, many of the "teachers" did experience agony. They sweated, trembled, stuttered, bit their lips, groaned, or even broke into uncontrollable nervous laughter. A *New York Times* reviewer complained that the cruelty inflicted by the experiments "upon their unwitting subjects is surpassed only by the cruelty that they elicit from them" (Marcus, 1974).

In a virtual reality recreation of the Milgram experiments, participants responded— when shocking a virtual on-screen woman—much as did Milgram's participants, with perspiration and racing heart (Slater & others, 2006).

Critics also argued that the participants' self-concepts may have been altered. One participant's wife told him, "You can call yourself Eichmann" (referring to Nazi death camp administrator Adolf Eichmann). CBS television depicted the results and the controversy in a two-hour dramatization. "A world of evil so terrifying no one dares penetrate its secret. Until Now!" declared a *TV Guide* ad for the program (Elms, 1995).

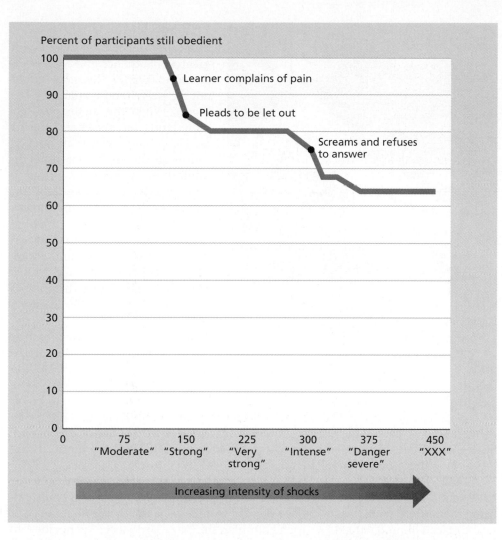

FIGURE :: 6.5

The Milgram
Obedience Experiment

Percentage of participants complying despite the learner's cries of protest and failure to respond.

Source: From Milgram, 1965.

In his own defense, Milgram pointed to the important lessons taught by his nearly two dozen experiments with a diverse sample of more than 1,000 participants. He also reminded critics of the support he received from the participants after the deception was revealed and the experiment explained. When surveyed afterward, 84 percent said they were glad to have participated; only 1 percent regretted volunteering. A year later, a psychiatrist interviewed 40 of those who had suffered most and concluded that, despite the temporary stress, none was harmed.

The ethical controversy was "terribly overblown," Milgram believed:

> There is less consequence to subjects in this experiment from the standpoint of effects on self-esteem, than to university students who take ordinary course examinations, and who do not get the grades they want. . . . It seems that [in giving exams] we are quite prepared to accept stress, tension, and consequences for self-esteem. But in regard to the process of generating new knowledge, how little tolerance we show. (quoted by Blass, 1996)

What Breeds Obedience?

Milgram did more than reveal the extent to which people will obey an authority; he also examined the conditions that breed obedience. When he varied the social conditions, compliance ranged from 0 to 93 percent fully obedient. Four factors that determined obedience were the victim's emotional distance, the authority's closeness and legitimacy, whether or not the authority was part of a respected institution, and the liberating effects of a disobedient fellow participant.

An obedient participant in Milgram's "touch" condition forces the victim's hand onto the shock plate. Usually, however, "teachers" were more merciful to victims who were this close to them.

"Distance negates responsibility."

—*GUY DAVENPORT*

Imagine you had the power to prevent either a tsunami that would kill 25,000 people on the planet's other side, a crash that would kill 250 people at your local airport, or a car accident that would kill a close friend. Which would you prevent?

THE VICTIM'S DISTANCE

Milgram's participants acted with greatest obedience and least compassion when the "learners" could not be seen (and could not see them). When the victim was remote and the "teachers" heard no complaints, nearly all obeyed calmly to the end. That situation minimized the learner's influence relative to the experimenter's. But what if we made the learner's pleas and the experimenter's instructions more equally visible? When the learner was in the same room, "only" 40 percent obeyed to 450 volts. Full compliance dropped to a still-astonishing 30 percent when teachers were required to force the learner's hand into contact with a shock plate.

In everyday life, too, it is easiest to abuse someone who is distant or depersonalized. People who might never be cruel to someone in person may be downright nasty when posting comments aimed at anonymous people on Internet discussion boards. Throughout history, executioners have often depersonalized those being executed by placing hoods over their heads. The ethics of war allow one to bomb a helpless village from 40,000 feet but not to shoot an equally helpless villager. In combat with an enemy they can see, many soldiers either do not fire or do not aim. Such disobedience is rare among those given orders to kill with the more distant artillery or aircraft weapons (Padgett, 1989).

As the Holocaust began, some Germans, under orders, used machine-guns or rifles to kill men, women, and children standing before them. But others could not bring themselves to do so, and some who did were left shaken by the experience of face-to-face killing. That led Heinrich Himmler, the Nazi "architect of genocide," to devise a "more humane" killing, one that would visually separate the killers and their victims. The solution was the construction of concrete gas chambers, where the killers would not see or hear the human consequences of their horror (Russell & Gregory, 2005).

On the positive side, people act most compassionately toward those who are personalized. That is why appeals for the unborn, for the hungry, or for animal rights are nearly always personalized with a compelling photograph or description. Perhaps even more compelling is an ultrasound picture of one's own developing fetus. When queried by researchers John Lydon and Christine Dunkel-Schetter (1994), expectant women expressed more commitment to their pregnancies if they had seen ultrasound pictures of their fetuses that clearly displayed body parts.

CLOSENESS AND LEGITIMACY OF THE AUTHORITY

The physical presence of the experimenter also affected obedience. When Milgram's experimenter gave the commands by telephone, full obedience dropped to 21 percent (although many lied and said they were obeying). Other studies confirm that when the one making the command is physically close, compliance increases. Given a light touch on the arm, people are more likely to lend a dime, sign a petition, or sample a new pizza (Kleinke, 1977; Smith & others, 1982; Willis & Hamm, 1980).

The authority, however, must be perceived as legitimate. In another twist on the basic experiment, the experimenter received a rigged telephone call that required him to leave the laboratory. He said that since the equipment recorded

focus
ON   Personalizing the Victims

Innocent victims trigger more compassion if personalized. In a week when a soon-forgotten earthquake in Iran kills 3,000 people, one small boy dies, trapped in a well shaft in Italy, and the whole world grieves. Concerned that the projected death statistics of a nuclear war are impersonal to the point of being incomprehensible, international law professor Roger Fisher proposed a way to personalize the victims:

> It so happens that a young man, usually a navy officer, accompanies the president wherever he goes. This young man has a black attachè case which contains the codes that are needed to fire nuclear weapons.
>
> I can see the president at a staff meeting considering nuclear war as an abstract question. He might conclude, "On SIOP Plan One, the decision is affirmative. Communicate the Alpha line XYZ." Such jargon keeps what is involved at a distance.

My suggestion, then, is quite simple. Put that needed code number in a little capsule and implant that capsule right next to the heart of a volunteer. The volunteer will carry with him a big, heavy butcher knife as he accompanies the president. If ever the president wants to fire nuclear weapons, the only way he can do so is by first, with his own hands, killing one human being.

"George," the president would say, "I'm sorry, but tens of millions must die." The president then would have to look at someone and realize what death is—what an *innocent* death is. Blood on the White House carpet: it's reality brought home.

When I suggested this to friends in the Pentagon, they said, "My God, that's terrible. Having to kill someone would distort the president's judgment. He might never push the button."

Source: Adapted from "Preventing Nuclear War" by Roger Fisher, *Bulletin of the Atomic Scientists,* March 1981, pp. 11–17.

---

data automatically, the "teacher" should just go ahead. After the experimenter left, another person, who had been assigned a clerical role (actually a second confederate), assumed command. The clerk "decided" that the shock should be increased one level for each wrong answer and instructed the teacher accordingly. Now 80 percent of the teachers refused to comply fully. The confederate, feigning disgust at this defiance, sat down in front of the shock generator and tried to take over the teacher's role. At that point most of the defiant participants protested. Some tried to unplug the generator. One large man lifted the zealous confederate from his chair and threw him across the room. This rebellion against an illegitimate authority contrasted sharply with the deferential politeness usually shown the experimenter.

It also contrasts with the behavior of hospital nurses who in one study were called by an unknown physician and ordered to administer an obvious drug overdose (Hofling & others, 1966). The researchers told one group of nurses and nursing students about the experiment and asked how they would react. Nearly all said they would not have followed the order. One said she would have replied, "I'm sorry, sir, but I am not authorized to give any medication without a written order, especially one so large over the usual dose and one that I'm unfamiliar with. If it were possible, I would be glad to do it, but this is against hospital policy and my own ethical standards." Nevertheless, when 22 other nurses were actually given the phoned-in overdose order, all but one obeyed without delay (until being intercepted on their way to the patient). Although not all nurses are so compliant (Krackow & Blass, 1995; Rank & Jacobson, 1977), these nurses were following a familiar script: Doctor (a legitimate authority) orders; nurse obeys.

Compliance with legitimate authority was also apparent in the strange case of the "rectal ear ache" (Cohen & Davis, 1981). A doctor ordered eardrops for a patient suffering infection in the right ear. On the prescription, the doctor abbreviated "place in right ear" as "place in R ear." Reading the order, the compliant nurse put the required drops in the compliant patient's rectum.

Given orders, most soldiers will torch people's homes or kill—behaviors that in other contexts they would consider immoral.

The compliant nurse might empathize with the reported 70 fast-food restaurant managers in 30 states who, between 1995 and 2006, complied with orders from a self-described authority, usually posing as a police officer (ABC News, 2004; Snopes, 2008; Wikipedia, 2008). The supposed officer described a generic employee or customer. Once the manager had identified someone fitting the description, the authoritative-sounding caller gave an order to stripsearch the person to see if he or she had stolen property. One male Taco Bell manager in Arizona pulled aside a 17-year-old female customer who fit the description and, with the caller giving orders, carried out a search that included body cavities. After forcing a 19-year-old female employee to strip against her will, a South Dakota restaurant manager explained that "I never wanted to do it. . . . I was just doing what he told me to do." The manager feared that disobedience might mean losing his job or going to jail, explained his defense lawyer.

In another incident, a McDonald's manager received a call from an "Officer Scott" who described an employee he said was suspected of purse stealing. The female manager brought an 18-year-old woman who fit the description into the office and followed a series of orders to have her empty her pockets and successive pieces of clothing. Over her 3½ hours of humiliating detention, the requests became progressively more bizarre, including sexual contact with a male. The traumatized teen sued McDonald's, claiming they had not adequately forewarned staff of the scam, and was awarded $6.1 million (CNN, 2007).

INSTITUTIONAL AUTHORITY

If the prestige of the authority is that important, then perhaps the institutional prestige of Yale University legitimized the Milgram experiment commands. In postexperimental interviews, many participants said that had it not been for Yale's reputation, they would not have obeyed. To see whether that was true, Milgram moved the experiment to less prestigious Bridgeport, Connecticut. He set himself up in a modest commercial building as the "Research Associates of Bridgeport." When the "learner-has-a-heart-condition" experiment was run with the same personnel, what percentage of the men do you suppose fully obeyed? Although the obedience rate (48 percent) was still remarkably high, it was significantly lower than the 65 percent rate at Yale.

In everyday life, too, authorities backed by institutions wield social power. Robert Ornstein (1991) tells of a psychiatrist friend who was called to the edge of a cliff above San Mateo, California, where one of his patients, Alfred, was threatening to jump. When the psychiatrist's reasoned reassurance failed to dislodge Alfred, the psychiatrist could only hope that a police crisis expert would soon arrive.

THE inside STORY

Stanley Milgram on Obedience

While working for Solomon E. Asch, I wondered whether his conformity experiments could be made more humanly significant. First, I imagined an experiment similar to Asch's, except that the group induced the person to deliver shocks to a protesting victim. But a control was needed to see how much shock a person would give in the absence of group pressure. Someone, presumably the experimenter, would have to instruct the subject to give the shocks. But now a new question arose: Just how far would a person go when ordered to administer such shocks? In my mind, the issue had shifted to the willingness of people to comply with destructive orders. It was an exciting moment for me. I realized that this simple question was both humanly important and capable of being precisely answered.

The laboratory procedure gave scientific expression to a more general concern about authority, a concern forced upon members of my generation, in particular upon Jews such as myself, by the atrocities of World War II. The impact of the Holocaust on my own psyche energized my interest in obedience and shaped the particular form in which it was examined.

Source: Abridged from the original for this book and from Milgram, 1977, with permission of Alexandra Milgram.

Stanley Milgram (1933–1984)

Although no expert came, another police officer, unaware of the drama, happened onto the scene, took out his power bullhorn, and yelled at the assembled cliffside group: "Who's the ass who left that Pontiac station wagon double-parked out there in the middle of the road? I almost hit it. Move it *now,* whoever you are." Hearing the message, Alfred obediently got down at once, moved the car, and then without a word got into the police cruiser for a trip to the nearby hospital.

"If the commander-in-chief tells this lieutenant colonel to go stand in the corner and sit on his head, I will do so."
—*OLIVER NORTH, 1987*

THE LIBERATING EFFECTS OF GROUP INFLUENCE

These classic experiments give us a negative view of conformity. But conformity can also be constructive. The heroic firefighters who rushed into the flaming World Trade Center towers were "incredibly brave," note social psychologists Susan Fiske, Lasana Harris, and Amy Cuddy (2004), but they were also "partly obeying their superiors, partly conforming to extraordinary group loyalty." Consider, too, the occasional liberating effect of conformity. Perhaps you can recall a time you felt justifiably angry at an unfair teacher but you hesitated to object. Then one or two other students spoke up about the unfair practices, and you followed their example, which had a liberating effect. Milgram captured this liberating effect of conformity by placing the teacher with two confederates who were to help conduct the procedure. During the experiment, both confederates defied the experimenter, who then ordered the real participant to continue alone. Did he? No. Ninety percent liberated themselves by conforming to the defiant confederates.

Reflections on the Classic Studies

The common response to Milgram's results is to note their counterparts in recent history: the "I was only following orders" defenses of Adolf Eichmann in Nazi Germany; of American Lieutenant William Calley, who in 1968 directed the unprovoked slaughter of hundreds of Vietnamese in the village of My Lai; and of the "ethnic cleansings" occurring in Iraq, Rwanda, Bosnia, and Kosovo.

Soldiers are trained to obey superiors. Thus, one participant in the My Lai massacre recalled:

The United States military now trains soldiers to disobey inappropriate, unlawful orders.

[Lieutenant Calley] told me to start shooting. So I started shooting, I poured about four clips into the group. . . . They were begging and saying, "No, no." And the mothers were hugging their children and. . . . Well, we kept right on firing. They was waving their arms and begging. (Wallace, 1969)

The "safe" scientific contexts of the obedience experiments differ from the wartime contexts. Moreover, much of the mockery and brutality of war and genocide goes beyond obedience (Miller, 2004). Some of those who implemented the Holocaust were "willing executioners" who hardly needed to be commanded to kill (Goldhagen, 1996).

The obedience experiments also differ from the other conformity experiments in the strength of the social pressure: Obedience is explicitly commanded. Without the coercion, people did not act cruelly. Yet both the Asch and the Milgram experiments share certain commonalities. They showed how compliance can take precedence over moral sense. They succeeded in pressuring people to go against their own consciences. They did more than teach an academic lesson; they sensitized us to moral conflicts in our own lives. And they illustrated and affirmed some familiar social psychological principles: the link between *behavior and attitudes* and the *power of the situation*.

BEHAVIOR AND ATTITUDES

In Chapter 4 we noted that attitudes fail to determine behavior when external influences override inner convictions. These experiments vividly illustrate that principle. When responding alone, Asch's participants nearly always gave the correct answer. It was another matter when they stood alone against a group.

In the obedience experiments, a powerful social pressure (the experimenter's commands) overcame a weaker one (the remote victim's pleas). Torn between the pleas of the victim and the orders of the experimenter, between the desire to avoid doing harm and the desire to be a good participant, a surprising number of people chose to obey.

Why were the participants unable to disengage themselves? Imagine yourself as the teacher in yet another version of Milgram's experiment (one he never conducted). Assume that when the learner gives the first wrong answer, the experimenter asks you to zap him with 330 volts. After flicking the switch, you hear the learner scream, complain of a heart disturbance, and plead for mercy. Do you continue?

"Maybe I was too patriotic." So said ex-torturer Jeffrey Benzien, shown here demonstrating the "wet bag" technique to South Africa's Truth and Reconciliation Commission. He would place a cloth over victims' heads, bringing them to the terrifying brink of asphyxiation over and over again. Such terror tactics were used by the former security police to get an accused person to disclose, for example, where guns were hidden. "I did terrible things," Benzien admitted with apologies to his victims, though he claimed only to be following orders.

I think not. Recall the step-by-step entrapment of the foot-in-the-door phenomenon (Chapter 4) as we compare this hypothetical experiment to what Milgram's participants experienced. Their first commitment was mild—15 volts—and it elicited no protest. By the time they delivered 75 volts and heard the learner's first groan, they already had complied 5 times, and the next request was to deliver only slightly more. By the time they delivered 330 volts, the participants had complied 22 times and reduced some of their dissonance. They were therefore in a different psychological state from that of someone beginning the experiment at that point. Ditto the fast-food restaurant managers in the strip-search scam, after they had complied with initially reasonable-seeming orders from a supposed authority. As we saw in Chapter 4, external behavior and internal disposition can feed each other, sometimes in an escalating spiral. Thus, reported Milgram (1974, p. 10):

> Many subjects harshly devalue the victim as a consequence of acting against him. Such comments as, "He was so stupid and stubborn he deserved to get shocked," were common. Once having acted against the victim, these subjects found it necessary to view him as an unworthy individual, whose punishment was made inevitable by his own deficiencies of intellect and character.

During the early 1970s, Greece's military junta used this "blame-the-victim" process to train torturers (Haritos-Fatouros, 1988, 2002; Staub, 1989, 2003). There, as in the earlier training of SS officers in Nazi Germany, the military selected candidates based on their respect for and submission to authority. But such tendencies alone do not a torturer make. Thus, they would first assign the trainee to guard prisoners, then to participate in arrest squads, then to hit prisoners, then to observe torture, and only then to practice it. Step by step, an obedient but otherwise decent person evolved into an agent of cruelty. Compliance bred acceptance.

As a Holocaust survivor, University of Massachusetts social psychologist Ervin Staub knows too well the forces that can transform citizens into agents of death. From his study of human genocide across the world, Staub (2003) shows where gradually increasing aggression can lead. Too often, criticism produces contempt, which licenses cruelty, which, when justified, leads to brutality, then killing, then systematic killing. Evolving attitudes both follow and justify actions. Staub's disturbing conclusion: "Human beings have the capacity to come to experience killing other people as nothing extraordinary" (1989, p. 13).

But humans also have a capacity for heroism. During the Nazi Holocaust, the French village of Le Chambon sheltered 5,000 Jews and other refugees destined for deportation to Germany. The villagers were mostly Protestants whose own authorities, their pastors, had taught them to "resist whenever our adversaries will demand of us obedience contrary to the orders of the Gospel" (Rochat, 1993; Rochat & Modigliani, 1995). Ordered to divulge the locations of sheltered Jews, the head pastor modeled disobedience: "I don't know of Jews, I only know of human beings." Without knowing how terrible the war would be, the resisters, beginning in 1940, made an initial commitment and then—supported by their beliefs, by their own authorities, and by one another—remained defiant till the village's liberation in 1944. Here and elsewhere, the ultimate response to Nazi occupation came early. Initial helping heightened commitment, leading to more helping.

THE POWER OF THE SITUATION

The most important lesson of Chapter 5—that culture is a powerful shaper of lives—and this chapter's most important lesson—that immediate situational forces are just as powerful—reveal the strength of the social context. To feel this for yourself, imagine violating some minor norms: standing up in the middle of a class;

"Men's actions are too strong for them. Show me a man who had acted and who had not been the victim and slave of his action."

—RALPH WALDO EMERSON, REPRESENTATIVE MEN: GOETHE, 1850

Even in an individualistic culture, few of us desire to challenge our culture's clearest norms, as did Stephen Gough while walking the length of Britain naked (apart from hat, socks, boots, and a rucksack). Starting in June 2003, he made it from Lands End, England's most southerly point, to John O'Groats, Scotland's most northerly mainland point. During his 7-month, 847-mile trek he was arrested 15 times and spent about five months behind bars. "My naked activism is firstly and most importantly about me standing up for myself, a declaration of myself as a beautiful human being," Gough (2003) declared from his website.

singing out loud in a restaurant; playing golf in a suit. In trying to break with social constraints, we suddenly realize how strong they are.

The students in one Pennsylvania State University experiment found it surprisingly difficult to violate the norm of being "nice" rather than confrontational. Participants imagined themselves discussing with three others whom to select for survival on a desert island. They were asked to imagine one of the others, a man, injecting three sexist comments, such as, "I think we need more women on the island to keep the men satisfied." How would they react to such sexist remarks? Only 5 percent predicted they would ignore each of the comments or wait to see how others reacted. But when Janet Swim and Lauri Hyers (1999) engaged other students in discussions where such comments were actually made by a male confederate, 55 percent (not 5 percent) said nothing. Likewise, although people predict they would be upset by witnessing a person making a racial slur—and would avoid picking the racist person as a partner in an experiment—those actually experiencing such an event typically exhibit indifference (Kawakami & others, 2009). These experiments demonstrate the power of normative pressures and how hard it is to predict behavior, even our own behavior.

Milgram's experiments also offer a lesson about evil. In horror movies and suspense novels, evil results from a few bad apples, a few depraved killers. In real life we similarly think of Hitler's extermination of Jews, of Saddam Hussein's extermination of Kurds, of Osama bin Laden's plotting terror. But evil also results from social forces—from the heat, humidity, and disease that help make a whole barrel of apples go bad. The American military police, whose abuse of Iraqi prisoners at Abu Ghraib prison horrified the world, were under stress, taunted by many of those they had come to save, angered by comrades' deaths, overdue to return home, and under lax supervision—an evil situation that produced evil behavior (Fiske & others, 2004). Situations can induce ordinary people to capitulate to cruelty.

This is especially true when, as happens often in complex societies, the most terrible evil evolves from a sequence of small evils. German civil servants surprised Nazi leaders with their willingness to handle the paperwork of the Holocaust. They were not killing Jews, of course; they were merely pushing paper (Silver & Geller, 1978). When fragmented, evil becomes easier. Milgram studied this compartmentalization of evil by involving yet another 40 men more indirectly. With someone else triggering the shock, they had only to administer the learning test. Now, 37 of the 40 fully complied.

So it is in our everyday lives: The drift toward evil usually comes in small increments, without any conscious intent to do evil. Procrastination involves a similar unintended drift, toward self-harm (Sabini & Silver, 1982). A student knows the deadline for a term paper weeks ahead. Each diversion from work on the paper—a video game here, a TV program there—seems harmless enough. Yet gradually the student veers toward not doing the paper without ever consciously deciding not to do it.

It is tempting to assume that Eichmann and the Auschwitz death camp commanders were uncivilized monsters. Indeed, their evil was fueled by virulent anti-Semitism. And the social situation alone does not explain why, in the same neighborhood or death camp, some personalities displayed vicious cruelty and others heroic kindness. Still, the commanders would not have stood out to us as monsters. After a hard day's work, they would relax by listening to Beethoven and Schubert. Of the 14 men who formulated the Final Solution leading to the Nazi Holocaust, 8 had European university doctorates (Patterson, 1996). Like most other Nazis, Eichmann himself was outwardly indistinguishable from common people with ordinary jobs (Arendt, 1963; Zillmer & others, 1995). Mohamed Atta, the leader of the 9/11 attacks, reportedly had been a "good boy" and an excellent student from a healthy family. Zacarias Moussaoui, the would-be twentieth 9/11 attacker, had been very polite when applying for flight lessons and buying knives. He called women "ma'am." The pilot of the second plane to hit the World Trade Center was

"The social psychology of this century reveals a major lesson: Often it is not so much the kind of person a man is as the kind of situation in which he finds himself that determines how he will act."
—STANLEY MILGRAM, OBEDIENCE TO AUTHORITY, 1974

"History, despite its wrenching pain, cannot be unlived, and if faced with courage, need not be lived again."
—MAYA ANGELOU, PRESIDENTIAL INAUGURAL POEM, JANUARY 20, 1993

"I would say, on the basis of having observed a thousand people . . . that if a system of death camps were set up in the United States of the sort we had seen in Nazi Germany, one would be able to find sufficient personnel for those camps in any medium-sized American town."
—STANLEY MILGRAM, ON CBS'S 60 MINUTES, 1979

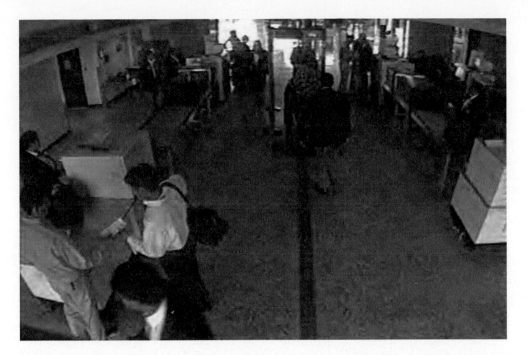

The "unexceptional" 9/11 terrorists. Hijackers Nawaf al-Hazmi (blue shirt) and Salem al-Hazmi (white shirt) were normal-looking, normal-acting passengers as they went through Dulles Airport security on September 11, 2001.

said to be an amiable, "laid-back" fellow, much like the "intelligent, friendly, and 'very courteous'" pilot of the plane that dove into the Pentagon. If these men had lived next door to us, they would hardly have fit our image of evil monsters. They were "unexceptional" people (McDermott, 2005).

As Milgram noted (1974, p. 6), "The most fundamental lesson of our study is that ordinary people, simply doing their jobs, and without any particular hostility on their part, can become agents in a terrible destructive process." As Mister Rogers often reminded his preschool television audience, "Good people sometimes do bad things." Under the sway of evil forces, even nice people are sometimes corrupted as they construct moral rationalizations for immoral behavior (Tsang, 2002). So it is that ordinary soldiers may, in the end, follow orders to shoot defenseless civilians; admired political leaders may lead their citizens into ill-fated wars; ordinary employees may follow instructions to produce and distribute harmful, degrading products; and ordinary group members may heed commands to brutally haze initiates.

So, does a situational analysis of harm-doing exonerate harm-doers? Does it absolve them of responsibility? In laypeople's minds, the answer is to some extent yes, notes Arthur Miller (2006). But the psychologists who study the roots of evil insist otherwise. To explain is not to excuse. To understand is not to forgive. You can forgive someone whose behavior you don't understand, and you can understand someone whom you do not forgive. Moreover, adds James Waller (2002), "When we understand the ordinariness of extraordinary evil, we will be less surprised by evil, less likely to be unwitting contributors to evil, and perhaps better equipped to forestall evil."

Finally, a comment on the experimental method used in conformity research (see synopsis, Table 6.1): Conformity situations in the laboratory differ from those in everyday life. How often are we asked to judge line lengths or administer shock? But as combustion is similar for a burning match and a forest fire, so we assume that psychological processes in the laboratory and in everyday life are similar (Milgram, 1974). We must be careful in generalizing from the simplicity of a burning match to the complexity of a forest fire. Yet controlled experiments on burning matches can give us insights into combustion that we cannot gain by observing forest fires. So, too, the social-psychological experiment offers insights into behavior not readily revealed in everyday life. The experimental situation is unique, but so is every

TABLE :: 6.1 Summary of Classic Obedience Studies

Topic	Researcher	Method	Real-Life Example
Norm formation	Sherif	Assessing suggestibility regarding seeming movement of light	Interpreting events differently after hearing from others; appreciating a tasty food that others love
Conformity	Asch	Agreement with others' obviously wrong perceptual judgments	Doing as others do; fads such as tattoos
Obedience	Milgram	Complying with commands to shock another	Soldiers or employees following questionable orders

social situation. By testing with a variety of unique tasks, and by repeating experiments at different times and places, researchers probe for the common principles that lie beneath the surface diversity.

The classic conformity experiments answered some questions but raised others: Sometimes people conform; sometimes they do not. (1) *When* do they conform? (2) *Why* do people conform? Why don't they ignore the group and "to their own selves be true"? (3) Is there a type of *person* who is likely to conform? In the next section we will take these questions one at a time.

Summing Up: What Are the Classic Conformity and Obedience Studies?

Three classic sets of experiments illustrate how researchers have studied conformity.

- Muzafer Sherif observed that others' judgments influenced people's estimates of the movement of a point of light that actually did not move. Norms for "proper" answers emerged and survived both over long periods of time and through succeeding generations of research participants.

- Solomon Asch had people listen to others' judgments of which of three comparison lines was equal to a standard line and then make the same judgment themselves. When the others unanimously gave a wrong answer, the participants conformed 37 percent of the time.

- Stanley Milgram's obedience experiments elicited an extreme form of compliance. Under optimum

conditions—a legitimate, close-at-hand commander, a remote victim, and no one else to exemplify disobedience—65 percent of his adult male participants fully obeyed instructions to deliver what were supposedly traumatizing electric shocks to a screaming, innocent victim in an adjacent room.

- These classic experiments expose the potency of several phenomena. Behavior and attitudes are mutually reinforcing, enabling a small act of evil to foster the attitude that leads to a bigger evil act. The power of the situation is seen when good people, faced with dire circumstances, commit reprehensible acts (although dire situations may produce heroism in others).

What Predicts Conformity?

Some situations trigger much conformity, others little conformity. If you wanted to produce maximum conformity, what conditions would you choose?

Social psychologists wondered: If even Asch's noncoercive, unambiguous situation could elicit a 37 percent conformity rate, would other settings produce even more? Researchers soon discovered that conformity did grow if the judgments

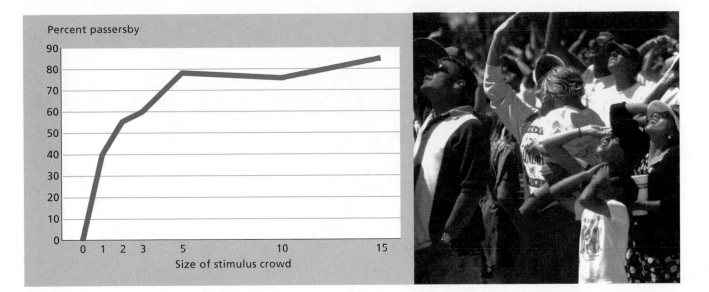

FIGURE :: 6.6

Group Size and Conformity

The percentage of passersby who imitated a group looking upward increased as group size increased to 5 persons.

Source: Data from Milgram, Bickman, & Berkowitz, 1969.

were difficult or if the participants felt incompetent. The more insecure we are about our judgments, the more influenced we are by others.

Group attributes also matter. Conformity is highest when the group has three or more people and is unanimous, cohesive, and high in status. Conformity is also highest when the response is public and made without prior commitment. Let's look at each of these conditions.

Group Size

In laboratory experiments, a small group can have a large effect. Asch and other researchers found that 3 to 5 people will elicit much more conformity than just 1 or 2. Increasing the number of people beyond 5 yields diminishing returns (Gerard & others, 1968; Rosenberg, 1961). In a field experiment, Milgram and his colleagues (1969) had 1, 2, 3, 5, 10, or 15 people pause on a busy New York City sidewalk and look up. As Figure 6.6 shows, the percentage of passersby who also looked up increased as the number looking up increased from 1 to 5 persons.

The way the group is "packaged" also makes a difference. Rutgers University researcher David Wilder (1977) gave students a jury case. Before giving their own judgments, the students watched videotapes of four confederates giving their judgments. When the confederates were presented as two independent groups of two people, the participants conformed more than when the four confederates presented their judgments as a single group. Similarly, two groups of three people elicited more conformity than one group of six, and three groups of two people elicited even more. Evidently, the agreement of independent small groups makes a position more credible.

Unanimity

Imagine yourself in a conformity experiment in which all but one of the people responding before you give the same wrong answer. Would the example of this one nonconforming confederate be as liberating as it was for the individuals in Milgram's obedience experiment? Several experiments reveal that someone who

FIGURE :: 6.7

The Effect of Unanimity on Conformity

When someone giving correct answers punctures the group's unanimity, individuals conform only one-fourth as often.

Source: From Asch, 1955.

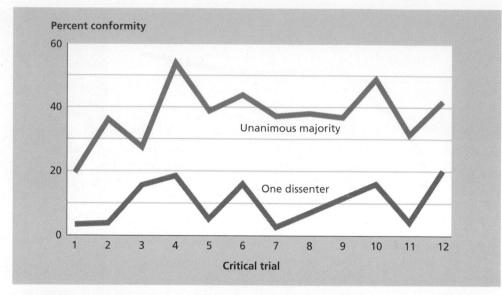

It is difficult to stand alone as a minority of one. But doing so sometimes makes a hero, as was the lone dissenting jury member played by Henry Fonda in the classic movie *12 Angry Men.*

"My opinion, my conviction, gains infinitely in strength and success, the moment a second mind has adopted it."
—*NOVALIS, FRAGMENT*

punctures a group's unanimity deflates its social power (Allen & Levine, 1969; Asch, 1955; Morris & Miller, 1975). As Figure 6.7 illustrates, people will usually voice their own convictions if just one other person has also differed from the majority. The participants in such experiments often later say they felt warm toward and close to their nonconforming ally. Yet they deny that the ally influenced them: "I would have answered just the same if he weren't there."

It's difficult to be a minority of one; few juries are hung because of one dissenting juror. And only 1 in 10 U.S. Supreme Court decisions over the last half-century has had a lone dissenter; most have been unanimous or a 5–4 split (Granberg & Bartels, 2005).

Conformity experiments teach the practical lesson that it is easier to stand up for something if you can find someone else to stand up with you. Many religious groups recognize this. Following the example of Jesus, who sent his disciples out in pairs, the Mormons send two missionaries into a neighborhood together. The support of the one comrade greatly increases a person's social courage.

Observing someone else's dissent—even when it is wrong—can increase our own independence. Charlan Nemeth and Cynthia Chiles (1988) discovered this after having people observe a lone individual in a group of four misjudge blue stimuli as green. Although the dissenter was wrong, once they had observed him the observers were more likely to exhibit their own form of independence: 76 percent of the time they correctly labeled red slides "red" even when everyone else was incorrectly calling them "orange." Participants who had no opportunity to observe the "green" dissenter conformed 70 percent of the time.

Cohesion

A minority opinion from someone outside the groups we identify with—from someone at another college or of a different religion—sways us less than the same minority opinion from someone within our group (Clark & Maass, 1988). A heterosexual arguing for gay rights would sway heterosexuals more effectively than would a homosexual. People even comply more readily with requests from those said to share their birthday, their first name, or features of their fingerprint (Burger & others, 2004; Silvia, 2005).

The more **cohesive** a group is, the more power it gains over its members. In college sororities, for example, friends tend to share binge-eating tendencies, especially as they grow closer (Crandall, 1988). People within an ethnic group may feel a similar "own-group conformity pressure"—to talk, act, and dress as "we" do. Blacks who "act White" or Whites who "act Black" may be mocked by their peers (Contrada & others, 2000).

In experiments, too, group members who feel attracted to the group are more responsive to its influence (Berkowitz, 1954; Lott & Lott, 1961; Sakurai, 1975). They do not like disagreeing with other group members. Fearing rejection by group members whom they like, they allow them a certain power (Hogg, 2001). In his *Essay Concerning Human Understanding*, the seventeenth-century philosopher John Locke recognized the cohesiveness factor: "Nor is there one in ten thousand who is stiff and insensible enough to bear up under the constant dislike and condemnation of his own club."

Our inclination to go with our group—to think what it thinks and do what it does—surfaced in one experiment as people reported greater liking for a piece of music that was said to be liked by people akin to themselves (but *dis*liked the music more when it was liked by someone *un*like themselves [Hilmert & others, 2006]). Cohesion-fed conformity also appears in college dorms, where students' attitudes over time become more similar to those living near them (Cullum & Harton, 2007).

And it has tragically appeared in massacres, as men have been unwilling to separate themselves from their close comrades, even when killing was not something they would have done apart from their group. Historian Christopher Browning (1992) recalls the nearly 500-man German Reserve Police Battalion 101 being awakened in Poland one morning in July 1942. Their well-liked commander nervously explained that they had been ordered to send the male adults from the 1,800 Jews in a nearby village to a work camp, and to shoot the women, children, and elderly. With obvious discomfort over this task, he offered to let any of the older men who did not feel up to the task to step out. Only a dozen did. The rest participated, with many of them being physically sick with disgust afterwards.

In post-war testimonies from some 125 men, most of whom were middle-aged family men, anti-Semitism did not explain their actions. Rather, reported Browning, they were constrained by the power of cohesion: Don't break ranks. The men felt a "strong urge not to separate themselves from the group by stepping out" (p. 71).

Status

As you might suspect, higher-status people tend to have more impact (Driskell & Mullen, 1990). Junior group members—even junior social psychologists—acknowledge more conformity to their group than do senior group members (Jetten & others, 2006). Or consider this: Studies of jaywalking behavior, conducted with the

cohesiveness
A "we feeling"; the extent to which members of a group are bound together, such as by attraction for one another.

unwitting aid of nearly 24,000 pedestrians, reveal that the baseline jaywalking rate of 25 percent decreases to 17 percent in the presence of a nonjaywalking confederate and increases to 44 percent in the presence of another jaywalker (Mullen & others, 1990). The nonjaywalker best discourages jaywalking when well dressed. Clothes seem to "make the person" in Australia, too. Michael Walker, Susan Harriman, and Stuart Costello (1980) found that Sydney pedestrians were more compliant when approached by a well-dressed survey taker than one who was poorly dressed.

Milgram (1974) reported that in his obedience experiments, people of lower status accepted the experimenter's commands more readily than people of higher status. After delivering 450 volts, a 37-year-old welder turned to the higher-status experimenter and deferentially asked, "Where do we go from here, Professor?" (p. 46). Another participant, a divinity school professor who disobeyed at 150 volts, said, "I don't understand why the experiment is placed above this person's life" and plied the experimenter with questions about "the ethics of this thing" (p. 48).

Public Response

One of the first questions researchers sought to answer was this: Would people conform more in their public responses than in their private opinions? Or would they wobble more in their private opinions but be unwilling to conform publicly, lest they appear wishy-washy? The answer is now clear: In experiments, people conform more when they must respond in front of others rather than writing their answers privately. Asch's participants, after hearing others respond, were less influenced by group pressure if they could write answers that only the experimenter would see. It is much easier to stand up for what we believe in the privacy of the voting booth than before a group.

Prior Commitment

In 1980 Genuine Risk became the second filly ever to win the Kentucky Derby. In her next race, the Preakness, she came off the last turn gaining on the leader, Codex, a colt. As they came out of the turn neck and neck, Codex moved sideways toward Genuine Risk, causing her to hesitate and giving him a narrow victory. Had Codex brushed Genuine Risk? Had his jockey even whipped Genuine Risk in the face? The race referees huddled. After a brief deliberation they judged that no foul had occurred and confirmed Codex as the winner. The decision caused an uproar. Televised instant replays showed that Codex had indeed brushed Genuine Risk, the sentimental favorite. A protest was filed. The officials reconsidered their decision, but they did not change it.

Did their declared judgment immediately after the race affect officials' openness toward reaching a different decision later? We will never know for sure. We can, however, put people through a laboratory version of this event—with and without the immediate commitment—and observe whether the commitment makes a difference. Again, imagine yourself in an Asch-type experiment. The experimenter displays the lines and asks you to respond first. After you give your judgment and then hear everyone else disagree, the experimenter offers you an opportunity to reconsider. In the face of group pressure, do you now back down?

Did Codex brush against Genuine Risk? Once race referees publicly announced their decision, no amount of evidence could budge them.

People almost never do (Deutsch & Gerard, 1955). Once having made a public commitment, they stick to it. At most, they will change their judgments in later situations (Saltz-stein & Sandberg, 1979). We may therefore expect that judges of diving or gymnastic competitions, for example, will seldom change their ratings after seeing the other judges' ratings, although they might adjust their later performance ratings.

Prior commitments restrain persuasion, too. When simulated juries make decisions, hung verdicts are more likely in cases when jurors are polled by a show of hands rather than by secret ballot (Kerr & MacCoun, 1985). Making a public commitment makes people hesitant to back down.

"All right! Have it your own way. It was a ball."

Prior commitment: Once they commit themselves to a position, people seldom yield to social pressure. Real umpires and referees rarely reverse their initial judgments.

Smart persuaders know this. Salespeople ask questions that prompt us to make statements for, rather than against, what they are marketing. Environmentalists ask people to commit themselves to recycling, energy conservation, or bus riding. That's because behavior then changes more than when environmental appeals are heard without inviting a commitment (Katzev & Wang, 1994). Teens 14 to 17 who make a public virginity-till-marriage pledge reportedly become somewhat more likely to remain sexually abstinent, or to delay intercourse, than similar teens who don't make the pledge (Bearman & Brückner, 2001; Brückner & Bearman, 2005). (If they violate their pledge they are, however, somewhat less likely to use a condom.)

"Those who never retract their opinions love themselves more than they love truth."

—JOUBERT, PENSÈES

Summing Up: What Predicts Conformity?

- Using conformity testing procedures, experimenters have explored the circumstances that produce conformity. Certain situations appear to be especially powerful. For example, conformity is affected by the characteristics of the group: People conform most when three or more people, or groups, model the behavior or belief.
- Conformity is reduced if the modeled behavior or belief is not unanimous.

- Conformity is enhanced by group cohesion.
- The higher the status of those modeling the behavior or belief, the greater likelihood of conformity.
- People also conform most when their responses are public (in the presence of the group).
- A prior commitment to a certain behavior or belief increases the likelihood that a person will stick with that commitment rather than conform.

Why Conform?

What two forms of social influence explain why people will conform to others?

"Do you see yonder cloud that's almost in the shape of a camel?" asks Shakespeare's Hamlet of Polonius. "'Tis like a camel indeed," replies Polonius. "Methinks it is a weasel," says Hamlet a moment later. "It is backed like a weasel," acknowledges Polonius. "Or like a whale?" wonders Hamlet. "Very like a whale," agrees Polonius. Question: Why does Polonius so readily agree every time Hamlet changes his mind?

Or consider this nonfictional situation: There I was, an American attending my first lecture during an extended visit at a German university. As the lecturer finished, I lifted my hands to join in the clapping. But rather than clap, the other people began rapping the tables with their knuckles. What did this mean? Did they disapprove of the speech? Surely, not everyone would be so openly rude to a visiting dignitary. Nor did their faces express displeasure. No, I realized, this must be a German ovation. Whereupon, I added my knuckles to the chorus.

What prompted this conformity? Why had I not clapped even while the others rapped? Why did Polonius so readily echo Hamlet's words? There are two possibilities: A person may bow to the group (a) to be accepted and avoid rejection or (b) to obtain important information. Morton Deutsch and Harold Gerard (1955) named these two possibilities **normative influence** and **informational influence.** The first springs from our desire to be *liked,* and the second from our desire to be *right.*

Normative influence is "going along with the crowd" to avoid rejection, to stay in people's good graces, or to gain their approval. Perhaps the subordinate Polonius was willing to change his mind and agree with Hamlet, the higher-status Prince of Denmark, to curry favor.

normative influence
Conformity based on a person's desire to fulfill others' expectations, often to gain acceptance.

informational influence
Conformity occurring when people accept evidence about reality provided by other people.

In the laboratory and in everyday life, groups often reject those who deviate consistently (Miller & Anderson, 1979; Schachter, 1951). That's a lesson learned by a media studies professor who became an outcast while playing the online game "City of Heroes" (Vargas, 2009). The professor, with whom I empathize because (I am not making this up) we share the same name—David Myers—played by the rules but did not conform to the customs. Much as drivers who go 50 in a 70 mph zone are disliked for violating norms but not rules, Myers was derided with instant messages: "I hope your mother gets cancer." "EVERYONE HATES YOU." "If you kill me one more time I will come and kill you for real and I am not kidding."

As most of us know, social rejection is painful; when we deviate from group norms, we often pay an emotional price. Brain scans show that group judgments differing from one's own activate a brain area that also is active when one feels the pain of bad betting decisions (Klucharev & others, 2009). Gerard (1999) recalls that in one of his conformity experiments an initially friendly participant became upset, asked to leave the room, and returned looking

sick and visibly shaken. I became worried and suggested that we discontinue the session. He absolutely refused to stop and continued through all 36 trials, not yielding to the others on a single trial. After the experiment was over and I explained the subterfuge to him, his entire body relaxed and he sighed with relief. Color returned to his face. I asked him why he had left the room. "To vomit," he said. He did not yield, but at what a price! He wanted so much to be accepted and liked by the others and was afraid he would not be because he had stood his ground against them. There you have normative pressure operating with a vengeance.

Sometimes the high price of deviation compels people to support what they do not believe in or at least to suppress their disagreement. "I was afraid that Leideritz and others would think I was a coward," reported one German officer, explaining his reluctance to dissent from mass executions (Waller, 2002). Fearing a courtmartial for disobedience, some of the soldiers at My Lai participated in the massacre. Normative influence leads to compliance especially for people who have recently seen others ridiculed, or who are seeking to climb a status ladder (Hollander, 1958; Janes & Olson, 2000). As John F. Kennedy (1956) recalled, "'The way to get along,' I was told when I entered Congress, 'is to go along'" (p. 4).

Normative influence often sways us without our awareness. When a research team led by Jessica Nolan (2008) asked 810 Californians what influenced their energy conservation, people rated environmental protection and saving money ahead of other people doing it. Yet it was their beliefs about how often their neighbors tried to conserve that best predicted their own self-reported conservation. And in a follow-up study, it was door-hung normative messages, such as "99% of people in your community reported turning off unnecessary lights to save energy," that produced the greatest drop in electricity use.

Informational influence, on the other hand, leads people to privately accept others' influence. Viewing a changing cloud shape, Polonius may actually see what Hamlet helps him see. When reality is ambiguous, as it was for participants in the autokinetic situation, other people can be a valuable source of information. The individual may reason, "I can't tell how far the light is moving. But this guy seems to know."

Social influence on evaluations of political debates: Normative or informational influence? As people watched the 2008 American presidential debates on CNN, they also viewed real-time scoring from reporters, pundits, and (at the bottom of the screen) from a focus group of undecided voters, whose responses to various arguments were averaged and displayed as moving lines. Research suggests that, more than they suppose, people may be influenced by viewing other people's negative or positive reactions to each candidate (Fein & others, 2007).

Our friends have extra influence on us for informational as well as normative reasons (Denrell, 2008; Denrell & Le Mens, 2007). If our friend buys a particular car and takes us to a particular restaurant, we will gain information that may lead us to like what our friend likes—even if we don't care what our friend likes. Our friends influence the experiences that inform our attitudes.

To discover what the brain is doing when people experience an Asch-type conformity experiment, an Emory University neuroscience team put participants in a functional magnetic resonance imaging (fMRI) brain scanner while having them answer perceptual questions after hearing others' responses (Berns & others, 2005). (The task involved mentally rotating a figure to find its match among several possibilities.) When the participants conformed to a wrong answer, the brain regions dedicated to perception became active. And when they went *against* the group, brain regions associated with emotion became active. These results suggest that when people conform, their perceptions may be genuinely influenced.

So, concern for *social image* produces *normative influence*. The desire to be *correct* produces *informational influence*. In day-to-day life, normative and informational influence often occur together. I was not about to be the only person in that German lecture hall clapping (normative influence). Yet the others' behavior also showed me the appropriate way to express my appreciation (informational influence).

Conformity experiments have sometimes isolated either normative or informational influence. Conformity is greater when people respond publicly before a group; this surely reflects normative influence (because people receive the same information whether they respond publicly or privately). On the other hand, conformity is greater when participants feel incompetent, when the task is difficult, and when the individuals care about being right—all signs of informational influence.

Chimpanzees, like humans, have been observed to ape their peers. They may copy tool use or food-washing habits observed in role models. And once they have observed and picked up a cultural way of doing something—perhaps a technique for scooping up tasty ants with a stick—they persist.

Summing Up: Why Conform?

- Experiments reveal two reasons people conform. *Normative influence* results from a person's desire for acceptance: We want to be liked. The tendency to conform more when responding publicly reflects normative influence.

- *Informational influence* results from others' providing evidence about reality. The tendency to conform more on difficult decision-making tasks reflects informational influence: We want to be right.

Who Conforms?

Conformity varies not only with situations but also with persons. How much so? And in what social contexts do personality traits shine through?

Are some people generally more susceptible (or should I say, more open) to social influence? Among your friends, can you identify some who are "conformists" and others who are "independent"? In their search for the conformer, researchers have focused on three predictors: personality, culture, and social roles.

Personality

During the late 1960s and 1970s, researchers observed only weak connections between personal characteristics and social behaviors such as conformity (Mischel, 1968). In contrast with the demonstrable power of situational factors, personality scores were poor predictors of individuals' behavior. If you wanted to know how conforming or aggressive or helpful someone was going to be, it seemed you were better off knowing about the situation than the person's psychological test scores. As Milgram (1974) concluded: "I am certain that there is a complex personality basis to obedience and disobedience. But I know we have not found it" (p. 205).

During the 1980s, the idea that personal dispositions make little difference prompted personality researchers to pinpoint the circumstances under which traits *do* predict behavior. Their research affirms a principle that we met in Chapter 4: Although internal factors (attitudes, traits) seldom precisely predict a specific action,

Personality effects loom larger when we note people's differing reactions to the same situation, as when one person reacts with terror and another with delight to a roller coaster ride.

they better predict a person's *average* behavior across many situations (Epstein, 1980; Rushton & others, 1983). An analogy may help: Just as your response to a single test item is hard to predict, so is your behavior in a single situation. And just as your total score across the many items of a test is more predictable, so is your total conformity (or outgoingness or aggressiveness) across many situations.

Personality also predicts behavior better when social influences are weak. Milgram's obedience experiments created "strong" situations; their clear-cut demands made it difficult for personality differences to operate. Even so, Milgram's participants differed widely in how obedient they were, and there is good reason to suspect that sometimes his participants' hostility, respect for authority, and concern for meeting expectations affected their obedience (Blass, 1990, 1991). And in "weaker" situations—as when two strangers sit in a waiting room with no cues to guide their behavior—individual personalities are free to shine (Ickes & others, 1982; Monson & others, 1982). Even temporary moods matter. Positive moods, which induce more superficial information processing, tend to enhance conformity, negative moods to reduce conformity (Tong & others, 2008).

But even in strong situations, individuals differ. An Army report on the Abu Ghraib prison abuse praised three men who, despite threats of ridicule and court-martial, stood apart from their comrades (O'Connor, 2004). Lt. David Sutton terminated one incident and alerted his commanders. "I don't want to judge, but yes, I witnessed something inappropriate and I reported it," said Sutton. Navy dog handler William Kimbro resisted "significant pressure" to participate in "improper interrogations." And Specialist Joseph Darby blew the whistle, giving military police the evidence that raised the alarm. Darby, called a "rat" by some, received death threats for his dissent and was given military protection. But back home, his mother joined others in applauding: "Honey, I'm so proud of you because you did the good thing and good always triumphs over evil, and the truth will always set you free" (ABC News, December 2004).

The pendulum of professional opinion swings. Without discounting the undeniable power of the social forces recognized in the 1960s and 1970s, the pendulum has swung back toward an appreciation of individual personality and its genetic predispositions. Like the attitude researchers we considered earlier, personality researchers are clarifying and reaffirming the connection between who we are and what we do. Thanks to their efforts, today's social psychologists now agree with pioneering

"I don't want to get adjusted to this world."
—*WOODY GUTHRIE*

theorist Kurt Lewin's (1936) dictum: "Every psychological event depends upon the state of the person and at the same time on the environment, although their relative importance is different in different cases" (p. 12).

Culture

When researchers in Australia, Austria, Germany, Italy, Jordan, South Africa, Spain, and the United States repeated the obedience experiments, how do you think the results compared with those with American participants? The obedience rates were similar, or even higher—85 percent in Munich (Blass, 2000).

Does cultural background help predict how *conforming* people will be? Indeed it does. James Whittaker and Robert Meade (1967) repeated Asch's conformity experiment in several countries and found similar conformity rates in most—31 percent in Lebanon, 32 percent in Hong Kong, 34 percent in Brazil—but 51 percent among the Bantu of Zimbabwe, a tribe with strong sanctions for nonconformity. When Milgram (1961) used a different conformity procedure to compare Norwegian and French students, he consistently found the French students to be less conforming. An analysis by Rod Bond and Peter Smith (1996) of 133 studies in 17 countries showed how cultural values influence conformity. Compared with people in individualistic countries, those in collectivist countries (where harmony is prized and connections help define the self) are more responsive to others' influence. In individualist countries, university students see themselves as more nonconforming than others in their consumer purchases and political views—as individuals amid the sheep (Pronin & others, 2007).

Cultural differences also exist within any country. For example, in five studies, Nicole Stephens and her co-researchers (2007) found that working-class people tend to prefer similarity to others while middle-class people more strongly preferred to see themselves as unique individuals. In an experiment, people chose a pen from among five green and orange pens (with three or four of one color). Of university students from working-class backgrounds, 72 percent picked one from the majority color, as did 44 percent of those from middle-class backgrounds (with a college-graduate parent). Those from working-class backgrounds also came to like their chosen pen more after seeing someone else make the same choice. They responded more positively to a friend's knowingly buying the same car they had just bought. And they were also more likely to prefer visual images that they knew others had chosen.

In addition, cultures may change over time. Replications of Asch's experiment with university students in Britain, Canada, and the United States sometimes trigger less conformity than Asch observed two or three decades earlier (Lalancette & Standing, 1990; Larsen, 1974, 1990; Nicholson & others, 1985; Perrin & Spencer, 1981). So conformity and obedience are universal phenomena, yet they vary across cultures and eras.

Social Roles

> All the world's a stage,
> And all the men and women merely players:
> They have their exits and their entrances;
> And one man in his time plays many parts.
> —William Shakespeare

Role theorists assume, as did William Shakespeare's character Jaques in *As You Like It*, that social life is like acting on a theatrical stage, with all its scenes, masks, and scripts. And those roles have much to do with conformity. Social roles allow some freedom of interpretation to those who act them out, but some aspects of any role *must* be performed. A student must at least show up for exams, turn in papers, and maintain some minimum grade point average.

When only a few norms are associated with a social category (for example, riders on an escalator should stand to the right and walk to the left), we do not regard the

Heiress Patricia Hearst as "Tanya" the revolutionary and as a suburban socialite.

position as a social role. It takes a whole cluster of norms to define a role. I could readily generate a long list of norms to which I conform in my role as a professor or as a father. Although I may acquire my particular image by violating the least important norms (valuing efficiency, I rarely arrive early for anything), violating my role's most important norms (failing to meet classes, abusing my children) could have led to my being fired or having my children removed from my care.

Roles have powerful effects. In Chapter 4 we noted that we tend to absorb our roles. On a first date or on a new job, you may act the role self-consciously. As you internalize the role, self-consciousness subsides. What felt awkward now feels genuine.

That is the experience of many immigrants, Peace Corps workers, and international students and executives. After arriving in a new country, it takes time to learn how to talk and act appropriately in the new context—to conform, as I did with the Germans who rapped their knuckles on their desks. And the almost universal experience of those who repatriate back to their home country is reentry distress (Sussman, 2000). In ways one may not have been aware of, the process of conforming will have shifted one's behavior, values, and identity to accommodate a different place. One must "re-conform" to one's former roles before being back in sync.

The case of kidnapped newspaper heiress Patricia Hearst illustrates the power of role playing. In 1974, when she was 19, Hearst was kidnapped by some young revolutionaries who called themselves the Symbionese Liberation Army (SLA). Soon Hearst publicly announced that she had joined her captors and renounced her former life, her wealthy parents, and her fiancé. She asked that people "try to understand the changes I've gone through." Twelve days later, a bank camera recorded her participation in an SLA armed holdup.

Nineteen months later, Hearst was apprehended. After two years' incarceration and "deprogramming," she resumed her role as an heiress, marrying "well" and becoming a suburban Connecticut mother and author who devotes much of her time to charitable causes (Johnson, 1988; Schiffman, 1999). If Patricia Hearst had really been a "closet" revolutionary all along, or had she merely obeyed her captors to escape punishment, people could have understood her actions. What they could not understand (and what therefore made this one of the biggest news stories of the 1970s) was that, as Philip Brickman (1979) wrote, "she could really be an heiress, really a revolutionary, and then perhaps really an heiress again." Surely, a role shift on this scale could not happen to you or me—or could it?

Yes and no. As we saw earlier in this chapter, our actions depend not only on the power of the situation but also on our personalities. Not everyone responds in the same way to pressure to conform. In Patricia Hearst's predicament, you or I might respond differently. Nevertheless, we have seen that social situations can move most "normal" people to behave in "abnormal" ways. This is clear from those experiments that put well-intentioned people in bad situations to see whether good or evil prevails. To a dismaying extent, evil wins. Nice guys often don't finish nice.

ROLE REVERSAL

"Great Spirit, grant that I may not criticize my neighbor until I have walked for a moon in his moccasins."
—NATIVE AMERICAN PRAYER

Role playing can also be a positive force. By intentionally playing a new role and conforming to its expectations, people sometimes change themselves or empathize with people whose roles differ from their own.

Roles often come in pairs defined by relationships—parent and child, teacher and student, doctor and patient, employer and employee. Role reversals can help each understand the other. A negotiator or a group leader can therefore create better communication by having the two sides reverse roles, with each arguing the other's position. Or each side can be asked to restate the other party's point (to the other's satisfaction) before replying. The next time you get into a difficult argument with a friend or parent, try to restate the other person's perceptions and feelings before going on with your own. This intentional, temporary conformity may repair your relationship.

So far in this chapter, we have discussed classic studies of conformity and obedience, identified the factors that predict conformity, and considered who conforms and why. Remember that our primary quest in social psychology is not to catalog differences but to identify universal principles of behavior.

Social roles will always vary with culture, but the processes by which those roles influence behavior vary much less. People in Nigeria and Japan define teen roles differently from people in Europe and North America, but in all cultures role expectations guide the conformity found in social relations.

Summing Up: Who Conforms?

- The question "Who conforms?" has produced few definitive answers. Personality scores are poor predictors of specific acts of conformity but better predictors of average conformity. Trait effects are strongest in "weak" situations where social forces do not overwhelm individual differences.

- Although conformity and obedience are universal, different cultures socialize people to be more or less socially responsive.
- Social roles involve a certain degree of conformity, and conforming to expectations is an important task when stepping into a new social role.

Do We Ever Want to Be Different?

Will people ever actively resist social pressure? When compelled to do A, will they instead do Z? What would motivate such anticonformity?

This chapter emphasizes the power of social forces. It is therefore fitting that we conclude by again reminding ourselves of the power of the person. We are not just billiard balls moving where pushed. We may act according to our own values, independently of the forces that push upon us. Knowing that someone is trying to coerce us may even prompt us to react in the *opposite* direction.

"To do just the opposite is also a form of imitation."
—LICHTENBERG, APHORISMEN, 1764–1799

Reactance

Individuals value their sense of freedom and self-efficacy. When blatant social pressure threatens their sense of freedom, they often rebel. Think of Romeo and Juliet, whose love was intensified by their families' opposition. Or think of children asserting their freedom and independence by doing the opposite of what their parents ask. Savvy parents therefore offer their children choices instead of commands: "It's time to clean up: Do you want a bath or a shower?"

Reactance.

The theory of psychological **reactance**—that people act to protect their sense of freedom—is supported by experiments showing that attempts to restrict a person's freedom often produce an anticonformity "boomerang effect" (Brehm & Brehm, 1981; Nail & others, 2000). In one field experiment, many nongeeky students stopped wearing a "Livestrong" wristband when nearby geeky academic students started wearing the band (Berger & Heath, 2008). Likewise, rich Brits dissociated themselves from a dissimilar group when they stopped wearing Burberry caps after they caught on among soccer hooligans (Clevstrom & Passariello, 2006).

Reactance may contribute to underage drinking. A survey of 18- to 24-year-olds by the Canadian Centre on Substance Abuse (1997) revealed that 69 percent of those over the legal drinking age (21) had been drunk in the last year, as had 77 percent of those *under* 21. In the United States, a survey of students on 56 campuses revealed a 25 percent rate of alcohol abstinence among students of legal drinking age (21) but only a 19 percent abstinence rate among students under 21 (Engs & Hanson, 1989).

Asserting Uniqueness

Imagine a world of complete conformity, where there were no differences among people. Would such a world be a happy place? If nonconformity can create discomfort, can sameness create comfort?

People feel uncomfortable when they appear too different from others. But in individualistic Western cultures they also feel uncomfortable when they appear exactly like everyone else. As experiments by C. R. Snyder and Howard Fromkin (1980) have shown, people feel better when they see themselves as moderately unique. Moreover, they act in ways that will assert their individuality. In one experiment, Snyder (1980) led Purdue University students to believe that their "10 most important attitudes" were either distinct from or nearly identical to the attitudes of 10,000 other students. When they next participated in a conformity experiment, those deprived of their feeling of uniqueness were the ones most likely to assert their individuality by nonconformity. Moreover, individuals who have the highest "need for uniqueness" tend to be the least responsive to majority influence (Imhoff & Erb, 2009).

reactance
A motive to protect or restore one's sense of freedom. Reactance arises when someone threatens our freedom of action.

Reactance at work? Underage students have been found to be less often abstinent and more often drinking to excess than students over the legal drinking age.

When body tattoos come to be perceived as pack behavior—as displaying conformity rather than individuality—we may expect their popularity to decline.

"When I'm in America, I have no doubt I'm a Jew, but I have strong doubts about whether I'm really an American. And when I get to Israel, I know I'm an American, but I have strong doubts about whether I'm a Jew."

—*LESLIE FIEDLER*, FIEDLER ON THE ROOF, *1991*

"Self-consciousness, the recognition of a creature by itself as a 'self,' [cannot] exist except in contrast with an 'other,' a something which is not the self."

—*C. S. LEWIS*, THE PROBLEM OF PAIN, *1940*

Both social influence and the desire for uniqueness appear in popular baby names. People seeking less commonplace names often hit upon the same ones at the same time. Among the top 10 U.S. girls' baby names for 2007 were Isabella (2), Madison (5), and Olivia (7). Those who in the 1960s broke out of the pack by naming their baby Rebecca, thinking they were bucking convention, soon discovered their choice was part of a new pack, notes Peggy Orenstein (2003). Hillary, a popular late '80s, early '90s name, became less original-seeming and less frequent (even among her admirers) after Hillary Clinton became famous. Although the popularity of such names then fades, observes Orenstein, it may resurface with a future generation. Max, Rose, and Sophie sound like the roster of a retirement home—or a primary school.

Seeing oneself as unique also appears in people's "spontaneous self-concepts." William McGuire and his Yale University colleagues (McGuire & others, 1979; McGuire & Padawer-Singer, 1978) report that when children are invited to "tell us about yourself," they are most likely to mention their distinctive attributes. Foreign-born children are more likely than others to mention their birthplace. Redheads are more likely than black- and brown-haired children to volunteer their hair color. Light and heavy children are the most likely to refer to their body weight. Minority children are the most likely to mention their race.

Likewise, we become more keenly aware of our gender when we are with people of the other gender (Cota & Dion, 1986). When I attended an American Psychological Association meeting with 10 others—all women, as it happened—I immediately was aware of my gender. As we took a break at the end of the second day, I joked that the line would be short at my bathroom, triggering the woman sitting next to me to notice what hadn't crossed her mind—the group's gender makeup.

The principle, says McGuire, is that "one is conscious of oneself insofar as, and in the ways that, one is different." Thus, "If I am a Black woman in a group of White women, I tend to think of myself as a Black; if I move to a group of Black men, my blackness loses salience and I become more conscious of being a woman" (McGuire & others, 1978). This insight helps us understand why White people who grow up amid non-White people tend to have a strong White identity, why gays may be more conscious of their sexual identity than straights, and why any minority group tends to be conscious of its distinctiveness and how the surrounding culture relates to it (Knowles & Peng, 2005). The majority group, being less conscious of race, may see the minority group as hypersensitive. When occasionally living in Scotland, where my American accent marks me as a foreigner, I am conscious of my national identity and sensitive to how others react to it.

When the people of two cultures are nearly identical, they still will notice their differences, however small. Even trivial distinctions may provoke scorn and conflict. Jonathan Swift satirized the phenomenon in *Gulliver's Travels* with the story of the

Little-Endians' war against the Big-Endians. Their difference: The Little-Endians preferred to break their eggs on the small end, the Big-Endians on the large end. On a world scale, the differences may not seem great between Sunni and Shia, Hutus and Tutsis, or Catholic and Protestant Northern Irish. But anyone who reads the news knows that these small differences have meant big conflicts (Rothbart & Taylor, 1992). Rivalry is often most intense when the other group closely resembles you.

Asserting our uniqueness. Though not wishing to be greatly deviant, most of us express our distinctiveness through our personal styles and dress.

So, although we do not like being greatly deviant, we are, ironically, all alike in wanting to feel distinctive and in noticing how we are distinctive. (In thinking you are different, you are like everyone else.) But as research on the self-serving bias (Chapter 2) makes clear, it is not just any kind of distinctiveness we seek but distinctiveness in the right direction. Our quest is not merely to be different from the average, but *better* than average.

Summing Up: Do We Ever Want to Be Different?

- Social psychology's emphasis on the power of social pressure must be joined by a complementary emphasis on the power of the person. We are not puppets. When social coercion becomes blatant, people often experience *reactance*—a motivation to defy the coercion in order to maintain their sense of freedom.

- We are not comfortable being too different from a group, but neither do we want to appear the same as everyone else. Thus, we act in ways that preserve our sense of uniqueness and individuality. In a group, we are most conscious of how we differ from the others.

POSTSCRIPT: On Being an Individual within Community

Do your own thing. Question authority. If it feels good, do it. Follow your bliss. Don't conform. Think for yourself. Be true to yourself. You owe it to yourself.

We hear words like those over and again *if* we live in an individualistic Western nation, such as those of Western Europe, Australia, New Zealand, Canada, or, especially, the United States. The unchallenged assumption that individualism is good and conformity is bad is what Chapter 1 called a "social representation," a collectively shared idea. Our mythical cultural heroes—from Sherlock Holmes to Luke Skywalker to Neo of the *Matrix* trilogy—often stand up against institutional rules. Individualists assume the preeminence of individual rights and celebrate the one who stands against the group.

In 1831 the French writer Alexis de Tocqueville coined the term "individualism" after traveling in America. Individualists, he noted, owe no one "anything and hardly expect anything from anybody. They form the habit of thinking of themselves in isolation and imagine that their whole destiny is in their hands." A century and a half later, psychotherapist Fritz Perls (1972) epitomized this radical individualism in his "Gestalt prayer":

> I do my thing, and you do your thing.
> I am not in this world to live up to your expectations.
> And you are not in this world to live up to mine.

Psychologist Carl Rogers (1985) agreed: "The only question which matters is, 'Am I living in a way which is deeply satisfying to me, and which truly expresses me?'"

As we noted in Chapter 2, that is hardly the only question that matters to people in many other cultures, including those of Asia, South America, and most of Africa. Where *community* is prized, conformity is accepted. Schoolchildren often display their solidarity by wearing uniforms; many workers do the same. To maintain harmony, confrontation and dissent are muted. "The stake that stands out gets pounded down," say the Japanese. South Africans have a word that expresses human connection. *Ubuntu*, explained Desmond Tutu (1999), conveys the idea that "my humanity is caught up by, is inextricably bound up in, yours." *Umuntu ngumuntu ngabantu*, says a Zulu maxim: "A person is a person through other persons."

Amitai Etzioni (1993), a past president of the American Sociological Association, urges us toward a "communitarian" individualism that balances our nonconformist individualism with a spirit of community. Fellow sociologist Robert Bellah

(1996) concurs. "Communitarianism is based on the value of the sacredness of the individual," he explains. But it also "affirms the central value of solidarity . . . that we become who we are through our relationships."

As Westerners in various nations, most readers of this book enjoy the benefits of nonconformist individualism. Communitarians remind us that we also are social creatures having a basic need to belong. Conformity is neither all bad nor all good. We therefore do well to balance our "me" and our "we," our needs for independence and for attachment, our individuality and our social identity.

Making the Social Connection

In this chapter we examined the influences that cause people to conform, one of which is group pressure. To see a video of teen girls discussing how group pressure influences their body image, go to the Online Learning Center for this book. This chapter also described Ervin Staub's work on obedience and cruelty. Is obedience to authority a key factor in genocide? Watch the video of Staub exploring this question and see what you think.

"To swallow and follow, whether old doctrine or new propaganda, is a weakness still dominating the human mind."

—Charlotte Perkins Gilman, *Human Work*, 1904

"Remember that to change thy mind and to follow him that sets thee right, is to be none the less a free agent."

—Marcus Aurelius Antoninus, *Meditations*, viii. 16, 121–180

What paths lead to persuasion?

What are the elements of persuasion?

Extreme persuasion: How do cults indoctrinate?

How can persuasion be resisted?

Postscript: Being open but not naive

Joseph Goebbels, Germany's Minister for National Enlightenment and Propaganda from 1933 to 1945, understood the power of persuasion. Given control of publications, radio programs, motion pictures, and the arts, he undertook to persuade Germans to accept Nazi ideology in general and anti-Semitism in particular. His colleague Julius Streicher published a weekly anti-Semitic newspaper, *Der Stürmer*, the only paper read cover to cover by Adolf Hitler. Streicher also published anti-Semitic children's books and, with Goebbels, spoke at the mass rallies that became part of the Nazi propaganda machine.

How effective were Goebbels, Streicher, and other Nazi propagandists? Did they, as the Allies alleged at Streicher's Nuremberg trial, "inject poison into the minds of millions and millions" (Bytwerk, 1976)?

Most Germans were not persuaded to express raging hatred for the Jews. But many were. Others became sympathetic to measures such as firing Jewish university professors, boycotting Jewish-owned businesses, and, eventually, sending Jews to concentration camps. Most other Germans became either sufficiently uncertain or sufficiently intimidated to condone the regime's massive genocidal program, or at least to allow it to happen. Without the complicity of millions of people, there would have been no Holocaust (Goldhagen, 1996).

persuasion

The process by which a message induces change in beliefs, attitudes, or behaviors.

"Speech has power. Words do not fade. What starts out as a sound ends in a deed."

—RABBI ABRAHAM HESCHEL, 1961

The powers of **persuasion** were apparent more recently in what a Pew survey (2003) called the "rift between Americans and Western Europeans" over the Iraq war. Surveys shortly before the war revealed that Americans favored military action against Iraq by about two to one, while Europeans were opposing it by the same margin (Burkholder, 2003; Moore, 2003; Pew, 2003). Once the war began, Americans' support for the war rose, for a time, to more than three to one (Newport & others, 2003). Except for Israel, people surveyed in all other countries were opposed to the attack.

Without taking sides regarding the wisdom of the war—that debate we can leave to history—we can surely agree on this: The huge opinion gap between Americans and the citizens of other countries reflected persuasion. What persuaded most Americans to favor the war? What persuaded most people elsewhere to oppose it?

Attitudes were being shaped, at least in part, by persuasive messages in the U.S. media that led half of Americans to believe that Saddam Hussein was directly involved in the 9/11 attacks and four in five to falsely believe that weapons of mass destruction would be found (Duffy, 2003; Gallup, 2003; Newport & others, 2003). Sociologist James Davison Hunter (2002) notes that culture-shaping usually occurs top-down, as cultural elites control the dissemination of information and ideas. Thus, Americans, and people elsewhere, learned about and watched two different wars (della Cava, 2003; Friedman, 2003; Goldsmith, 2003; Krugman, 2003; *Tomorrow,* 2003). Depending on the country where you lived and the media available to you, you may have heard about "America's liberation of Iraq" or "America's invasion of Iraq."

In the view of many Americans, the other nations' media combined a pervasive anti-American bias with a blindness to the threat posed by Saddam. To many people elsewhere, the "embedded" American media were biased in favor of the military. Regardless of where bias lay or whose perspective was better informed, this much seems clear: Depending on where they lived, people were given (and discussed and believed) differing information. Persuasion matters.

Persuasive forces also have been harnessed to promote healthier living. Thanks partly to health-promotion campaigns, the Centers for Disease Control reports that the American cigarette smoking rate has plunged to 21 percent, half the rate of 40 years ago. *Statistics Canada* reports a similar smoking decline in Canada. And the rate of new U.S. collegians reporting abstinence from beer has increased—from 25 percent in 1981 to 41 percent in 2007 (Pryor & others, 2007).

As these examples show, efforts to persuade are sometimes diabolical, sometimes controversial, and sometimes beneficial. Persuasion is neither inherently good nor bad. It is a message's purpose and content that elicit judgments of good or bad. The bad we call "propaganda." The good we call "education." Education is more factually based and less coercive than propaganda. Yet generally we call it "education" when we believe it, "propaganda" when we don't (Lumsden & others, 1980).

A case in point: For three decades, Al Gore has sought to explain "an inconvenient truth" that few wanted to hear. By spewing massive carbon dioxide into the atmosphere, humanity is threatening its future. A growing scientific consensus, he reports, predicts resulting climate warming, melting icecaps, rising seas, more extreme

Persuasion is everywhere. When we approve of it, we may call it "education."

weather, and millions of resulting deaths. With his traveling show (and resulting movie, book, and seven-continent Live Earth concert), and through the Alliance for Climate Protection, Gore's ambition is nothing less than what James Traub (2007) calls a "program of mass persuasion." "The central challenge," Gore explained to Traub, "is to expand the limits of what's now considered politically possible. The outer boundary of what's considered plausible today still falls far short of the near boundary of what would actually solve the crisis." Still, thanks to growing evidence and public awareness of climate change, he foresees a sudden, "nonlinear" shift in public opinion.

Is the mass persuasion mission of Al Gore, the Alliance for Climate Protection, and other kindred spirits education? Or is it propaganda? Our opinions have to come from somewhere. Persuasion—whether it be education or propaganda—is therefore inevitable. Indeed, persuasion is everywhere—at the heart of politics, marketing, courtship, parenting, negotiation, evangelism, and courtroom decision making. Social psychologists therefore seek to understand what leads to effective, long-lasting attitude change. What factors affect persuasion? As persuaders, how can we most effectively "educate" others?

> "A fanatic is one who can't change his mind and won't change the subject."
> —*WINSTON CHURCHILL, 1954*

Imagine that you are a marketing or advertising executive. Or imagine that you are a preacher, trying to increase love and charity among your parishioners. Or imagine that you want to promote energy conservation, to encourage breastfeeding, or to campaign for a political candidate. What could you do to make yourself and your message persuasive? And if you are wary of being influenced, to what tactics should you be alert?

To answer such questions, social psychologists usually study persuasion the way some geologists study erosion—by observing the effects of various factors in brief, controlled experiments. The effects are small and are most potent on weak attitudes that don't touch our values. Yet they enable us to understand how, given enough time, such factors could produce big effects.

What Paths Lead to Persuasion?

What two paths lead to influence? What type of cognitive processing does each involve—and with what effects?

While serving as chief psychologist for the U.S. War Department during World War II, Yale professor Carl Hovland and his colleagues (1949) supported the war effort by studying persuasion. Hoping to boost soldier morale, the Hovland team studied the effects of training films and historical documentaries on new recruits' attitudes toward the war. Back at Yale after the war, they continued studying what makes a message persuasive. Their research manipulated factors related to the communicator, the content of the message, the channel of communication, and the audience.

Researchers at Ohio State University then suggested that people's thoughts in response to persuasive messages also matter. If a message is clear but unconvincing, then you will easily counterargue the message and won' t be persuaded. If the message offers convincing arguments, then your thoughts will be more favorable and you will most likely be persuaded. This "cognitive response" approach helps us understand why persuasion occurs more in some situations than in others.

As shown in Figure 7.1, persuasion entails clearing several hurdles. Any factors that help people clear the hurdles in the persuasion process increase the likelihood of persuasion. For example, if an attractive source increases your attention to a message, then the message should have a better chance of persuading you.

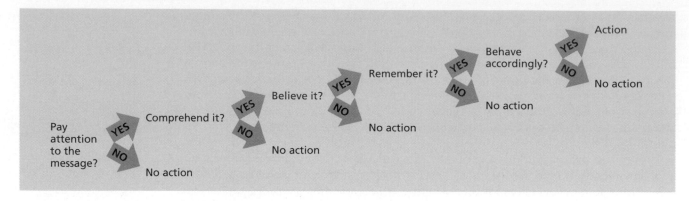

FIGURE :: 7.1

The Hurdles of the Persuasion Process

To elicit action, a persuasive message must clear several hurdles. What is crucial, however, is not so much remembering the message itself as remembering one's own thoughts in response.

Source: Adapted from W. J. McGuire. "An Information-Processing Model of Advertising Effectiveness," in *Behavioral and Management Sciences in Marketing,* H. L. Davis and A. J. Silk, eds. Copyright © 1978. Reprinted by permission of John Wiley & Sons.

The Central Route

Richard Petty and John Cacioppo (Cass-ee-OH-poh) (1986; Petty & Briñol, 2008) and Alice Eagly and Shelly Chaiken (1993, 1998) took this one step further. They theorized that persuasion is likely to occur via one of two routes. When people are motivated and able to think about an issue, they are likely to take the **central route to persuasion**—focusing on the arguments. If those arguments are strong and compelling, persuasion is likely. If the message offers only weak arguments, thoughtful people will notice that the arguments aren't very compelling and will counterargue.

The Peripheral Route

But sometimes the strength of the arguments doesn't matter. Sometimes we're not motivated enough or able to think carefully. If we're distracted, uninvolved, or just plain busy, we may not take the time to reflect on the message's content. Rather than noticing whether the arguments are particularly compelling, we might follow the **peripheral route to persuasion**—focusing on cues that trigger automatic acceptance without much thinking. In these situations, easily understood familiar statements are more persuasive than novel statements with the same meaning. Thus, for uninvolved or distracted people, "Don't put all your eggs in one basket" has more impact than "Don't risk everything on a single venture" (Howard, 1997).

Smart advertisers adapt ads to their consumers' thinking. They do so for good reason. Much of consumer behavior—such as one's spontaneous decision, while shopping, to pick up some ice cream of a particular brand—is made unthinkingly (Dijksterhuis & others, 2005). Something as minor as German music may lead customers to buy German wine, whereas others, hearing French music, reach for French wine (North & others, 1997). Billboards and television commercials—media that consumers are able to take in for only brief amounts of time—therefore use the peripheral route, with visual images as peripheral cues. Instead of providing arguments in favor of smoking, cigarette ads associate the product with images of beauty and pleasure. So do soft-drink ads that promote "the real thing" with images of youth, vitality, and happy polar bears. On the other hand, magazine computer ads (which interested, logical consumers may pore over for

---

central route to persuasion

Occurs when interested people focus on the arguments and respond with favorable thoughts.

peripheral route to persuasion

Occurs when people are influenced by incidental cues, such as a speaker's attractiveness.

"All effective propaganda must be limited to a very few points and must harp on these in slogans until the last member of the public understands."

—ADOLF HITLER, MEIN KAMPF, 1926

some time) seldom feature Hollywood stars or great athletes. Instead they offer customers information on competitive features and prices.

These two routes to persuasion—one explicit and reflective, the other more implicit and automatic—were a forerunner to today's "dual processing" models of the human mind. Central route processing often swiftly changes explicit attitudes. Peripheral route processing more slowly builds implicit attitudes, through repeated associations between an attitude object and an emotion (Petty & Briñol, 2008).

Different Paths for Different Purposes

The ultimate goal of the advertiser, the preacher, and even the teacher is not just to have people pay attention to the message and move on. Typically, the goal is behavior change (buying a product, loving one's neighbor, or studying more effectively). Are the two routes to persuasion equally likely to fulfill that goal? Petty and his colleagues (1995) note how central route processing can lead to more enduring change than does the peripheral route. When people are thinking carefully and mentally elaborating on issues, they rely not just on the strength of persuasive appeals but on their own thoughts in response as well. It's not so much the arguments that are persuasive as the way they get people thinking. And when people think deeply rather than superficially, any changed attitude will more likely persist, resist attack, and influence behavior (Petty & others, 1995; Verplanken, 1991).

Persuasion via the peripheral route often produces superficial and temporary attitude change. As sex educators know, changing attitudes is easier than changing behavior. Studies assessing the effectiveness of abstinence education find some increase in attitudes supporting abstinence but little long-term impact on sexual behavior (Hauser, 2005). Likewise, HIV prevention education tends to have more effect on attitudes toward condoms than on condom use (Albarracin & others, 2003). In both cases, changing behavior as well as attitudes seems to require people's actively processing and rehearsing their own convictions. (Stay tuned for an example of how health educators have successfully engaged young teens in smoking-prevention training.)

None of us has the time to thoughtfully analyze all issues. Often we take the peripheral route, by using simple rule-of-thumb heuristics, such as "trust the experts" or "long messages are credible" (Chaiken & Maheswaran, 1994). Residents of my community once voted on a complicated issue involving the legal ownership of our local hospital. I didn't have the time or the interest to study that question myself (I had this book to write). But I noted that referendum supporters were all people I either liked or regarded as experts. So I used a simple heuristic—friends and experts can be trusted—and voted accordingly. We all make snap judgments using such heuristics: If a speaker is articulate and appealing, has apparently good motives, and has several arguments (or better, if the different arguments come from different sources), we usually take the easy peripheral route and accept the message without much thought (Figure 7.2).

Summing Up: What Paths Lead to Persuasion?

- Sometimes persuasion occurs as people focus on arguments and respond with favorable thoughts. Such systematic, or "central route," persuasion occurs when people are naturally analytical or involved in the issue.

- When issues don't engage systematic thinking, persuasion may occur through a faster, "peripheral route," as people use heuristics or incidental cues to make snap judgments.

- Central route persuasion, being more thoughtful and less superficial, is more durable and more likely to influence behavior.

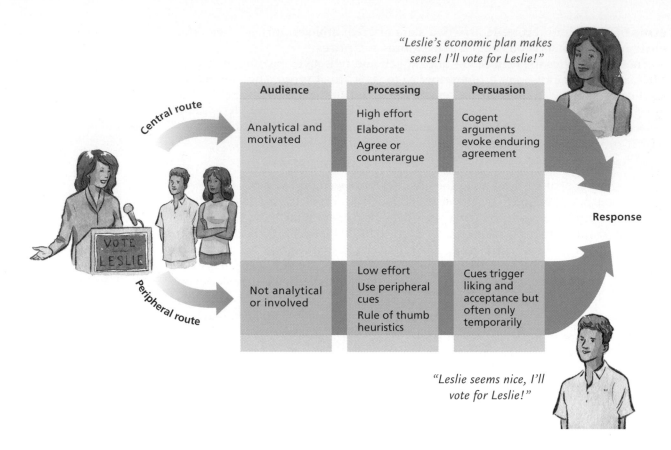

FIGURE :: 7.2

The Central and Peripheral Routes to Persuasion

Computer ads typically take the central route, by assuming their audience wants to systematically compare features and prices. Soft-drink ads usually take the peripheral route, by merely associating their product with glamour, pleasure, and good moods. Central route processing more often produces enduring attitude change.

What Are the Elements of Persuasion?

Among the ingredients of persuasion explored by social psychologists are these four: (1) the communicator, (2) the message, (3) how the message is communicated, and (4) the audience. In other words, __who__ says __what__, by what __method__, to __whom__? How do these factors affect the likelihood that we will take either the central or the peripheral route to persuasion?

Who Says? The Communicator

Imagine the following scene: I. M. Wright, a middle-aged American, is watching the evening news. In the first segment, a small group of radicals is shown burning an American flag. As they do, one shouts through a bullhorn that whenever any government becomes oppressive, "it is the Right of the People to alter or to abolish it. . . . It is their right, it is their duty, to throw off such government!" Angered, Mr. Wright mutters to his wife, "It's sickening to hear them spouting that Communist line." In the next segment, a presidential candidate speaking before an antitax rally declares, "Thrift should be the guiding principle in our government expenditure. It should be made clear to all government workers that corruption and waste are very great crimes." An obviously pleased Mr. Wright relaxes and smiles: "Now that's the kind of good sense we need. That's my kinda guy."

Now switch the scene. Imagine Mr. Wright hearing the same revolutionary line about "the Right of the People" at a July 4 oration of the Declaration of Independence (from which the line comes) and hearing a Communist speaker read the thrift sentence from *Quotations from Chairman Mao Zedong* (from which it comes). Would he now react differently?

Social psychologists have found that who is saying something does affect how an audience receives it. In one experiment, when the Socialist and Liberal leaders in the Dutch parliament argued identical positions using the same words, each was most effective with members of his own party (Wiegman, 1985). It's not just the message that matters, but also who says it. What makes one communicator more persuasive than another?

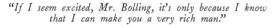

"If I seem excited, Mr. Bolling, it's only because I know that I can make you a very rich man."

Effective persuaders know how to convey a message effectively.

CREDIBILITY

Any of us would find a statement about the benefits of exercise more believable if it came from the Royal Society or National Academy of Sciences rather than from a tabloid newspaper. But the effects of source **credibility** (perceived expertise and trustworthiness) diminish after a month or so. If a credible person's message is persuasive, its impact may fade as its source is forgotten or dissociated from the message. And the impact of a noncredible person may correspondingly increase over time if people remember the message better than the reason for discounting it (Cook & Flay, 1978; Gruder & others, 1978; Pratkanis & others, 1988). This delayed persuasion, after people forget the source or its connection with the message, is called the **sleeper effect.**

PERCEIVED EXPERTISE   How does one become an authoritative "expert"? One way is to begin by saying things the audience agrees with, which makes one seem smart. Another is to be introduced as someone who is *knowledgeable* on the topic. A message about toothbrushing from "Dr. James Rundle of the Canadian Dental Association" is more convincing than the same message from "Jim Rundle, a local high school student who did a project with some of his classmates on dental hygiene" (Olson & Cal, 1984). After spending more than a decade studying high school marijuana use, University of Michigan researchers concluded that scare messages from unreliable sources did not affect marijuana use during the 1960s and 1970s. From a credible source, however, scientific reports of the biological and psychological results of long-term marijuana use "can play an important role in reducing . . . drug use" (Bachman & others, 1988).

Another way to appear credible is to *speak confidently*. Bonnie Erickson and her collaborators (1978) had University of North Carolina students evaluate courtroom testimony given in a straightforward manner or in a more hesitant manner. For example:

QUESTION: Approximately how long did you stay there before the ambulance arrived?

ANSWER: *[Straightforward]* Twenty minutes. Long enough to help get Mrs. David straightened out.
[Hesitating] Oh, it seems like it was about uh, twenty minutes. Just long enough to help my friend Mrs. David, you know, get straightened out.

credibility
Believability. A credible communicator is perceived as both expert and trustworthy.

sleeper effect
A delayed impact of a message that occurs when an initially discounted message becomes effective, as we remember the message but forget the reason for discounting it.

"Believe an expert."
—*VIRGIL,* AENEID, 19 B.C.

The students found the straightforward witnesses much more competent and credible.

PERCEIVED TRUSTWORTHINESS   Speech style also affects a speaker's apparent trustworthiness. Gordon Hemsley and Anthony Doob (1978) found that if videotaped witnesses looked their questioner *straight in the eye* instead of gazing downward, they impressed people as more believable.

Trustworthiness is also higher if the audience believes the communicator is *not trying to persuade* them. In an experimental version of what later became the "hidden-camera" method of television advertising, Elaine Hatfield and Leon Festinger (Walster & Festinger, 1962) had some Stanford University undergraduates eavesdrop on graduate students' conversations. (What they actually heard was a tape recording.) When the conversational topic was relevant to the eavesdroppers (having to do with campus regulations), the speakers had more influence if the listeners presumed the speakers were unaware of the eavesdropping. After all, if people think no one is listening, why would they be less than fully honest?

We also perceive as sincere those who *argue against their own self-interest.* Alice Eagly, Wendy Wood, and Shelly Chaiken (1978) presented University of Massachusetts students with a speech attacking a company's pollution of a river. When they said the speech was given by a political candidate with a business background or to an audience of company supporters, it seemed unbiased and was persuasive. When the same antibusiness speech was supposedly given to environmentalists by a pro-environment politician, listeners could attribute the politician's arguments to personal bias or to the audience. Being willing to suffer for one's beliefs—which Gandhi, Martin Luther King, Jr., and other great leaders have done—also helps convince people of one's sincerity (Knight & Weiss, 1980).

Norman Miller and his colleagues (1976) at the University of Southern California found that perceptions of trustworthiness and credibility also increase when people *talk fast.* People who listened to tape-recorded messages rated fast speakers (about 190 words per minute) as more objective, intelligent, and knowledgeable than slow speakers (about 110 words per minute). They also found the more rapid speakers more persuasive. John F. Kennedy, an exceptionally effective public speaker, sometimes spoke in bursts approaching 300 words per minute.

Some television ads are obviously constructed to make the communicator appear both expert and trustworthy. A drug company may peddle its pain reliever using a speaker in a white lab coat, who declares confidently that most doctors recommend their key ingredient (which is merely aspirin). Given such peripheral cues, people who don't care enough to analyze the evidence may automatically infer that the product is special. Other ads seem not to use the credibility principle. It's not primarily for his expertise about sports apparel that Nike paid Tiger Woods $100 million to appear in its ads.

Clearly, communicators gain credibility if they appear to be expert and trustworthy (Pornpitakpan, 2004). When we know in advance that a source is credible, we think more favorable thoughts in response to the message. If we learn the source *after* a message generates favorable thoughts, high credibility strengthens our confidence in our thinking, which also strengthens the persuasive impact of the message (Briñol & others, 2002, 2004; Tormala & others, 2006).

ATTRACTIVENESS AND LIKING

attractiveness
Having qualities that appeal to an audience. An appealing communicator (often someone similar to the audience) is most persuasive on matters of subjective preference.

Most of us deny that endorsements by star athletes and entertainers affect us. We know that stars are seldom knowledgeable about the products they endorse. Besides, we know the intent is to persuade us; we don't just accidentally eavesdrop on Jennifer Lopez discussing clothes or fragrances. Such ads are based on another characteristic of an effective communicator: **attractiveness.**

We may think we are not influenced by attractiveness or likability, but researchers have found otherwise. We're more likely to respond to those we like, a phenomenon

TABLE :: 7.1 Six Persuasion Principles

In his book *Influence: Science and Practice,* persuasion researcher Robert Cialdini (2000) illustrates six principles that underlie human relationships and human influence. (This chapter describes the first two.)

Principle	Application
Authority: People defer to credible experts.	Establish your expertise; identify problems you have solved and people you have served.
Liking: People respond more affirmatively to those they like.	Win friends and influence people. Create bonds based on similar interests, praise freely.
Social proof: People allow the example of others to validate how to think, feel, and act.	Use "peer power"—have respected others lead the way.
Reciprocity: People feel obliged to repay in kind what they've received.	Be generous with your time and resources. What goes around, comes around.
Consistency: People tend to honor their public commitments.	Have others write or voice their intentions. Don't say "Please do this by . . ." Instead, elicit a "yes" by asking.
Scarcity: People prize what's scarce.	Highlight genuinely exclusive information or opportunities.

well known to those organizing charitable solicitations, and candy sales. Even a mere fleeting conversation with someone is enough to increase our liking for that person, and our responsiveness to his or her influence (Burger & others, 2001). Our liking may open us up to the communicator's arguments (central route persuasion), or it may trigger positive associations when we see the product later (peripheral route persuasion). As with credibility, the liking-begets-persuasion principle suggests applications (Table 7.1).

Attractiveness comes in several forms. *Physical attractiveness* is one. Arguments, especially emotional ones, are often more influential when they come from people we consider beautiful (Chaiken, 1979; Dion & Stein, 1978; Pallak & others, 1983).

Similarity is another. As Chapter 11 will emphasize, we tend to like people who are like us. We also are influenced by them, a fact that has been harnessed by a successful antismoking campaign that features youth appealing to other youth through ads that challenge the tobacco industry about its destructiveness and its marketing practices (Krisberg, 2004). People who *act* as we do, subtly mimicking our postures, are likewise more influential. Thus salespeople are sometimes taught to "mimic and mirror": If the customer's arms or legs are crossed, cross yours; if she smiles, smile back. (See "Research Close-Up: Experimenting with a Virtual Social Reality.")

Another example: Theodore Dembroski, Thomas Lasater, and Albert Ramirez (1978) gave African American junior high students an audiotaped appeal for proper dental care. When a dentist assessed the cleanliness of their teeth the next day, those who heard the appeal from an African American dentist (whose face they were shown) had cleaner teeth. As a general rule, people respond better to a message that comes from someone in their group (Van Knippenberg & Wilke, 1992; Wilder, 1990).

Is similarity, as in this instance, more important than credibility? Sometimes yes, sometimes no. Timothy Brock (1965) found paint store customers more influenced by the testimony of a similarly ordinary person who had recently bought the same amount of paint they planned to buy than by an expert who had recently purchased 20 times as much. But recall that when discussing dental hygiene, a leading dentist (a dissimilar but expert source) was more persuasive than a student (a similar but inexpert source).

Such seemingly contradictory findings bring out the scientific detective in us. They suggest that an undiscovered factor is at work—that similarity is more

research CLOSE-UP

Experimenting with a Virtual Social Reality

University of California, Santa Barbara social psychologist Jim Blascovich developed a new interest shortly after walking into a colleague's virtual reality lab. Wearing a headset, Blascovich found himself facing a plank across a virtual deep pit. Although he knew that the room had no pit, he couldn't suppress his fear and bring himself to walk the plank.

The experience triggered a thought: Might social psychologists have a use for virtual environments? Might they offer people real-seeming experiences that the researcher could control and manipulate? Might this allow social psychologists to study conformity? to enable physically remote people to interact in a virtual meeting? to observe people's responses to another's physical deformity? to explore persuasion?

The experimental power of virtual human interaction is shown in an experiment by Blascovich's former associate, Jeremy Bailenson, in collaboration with graduate student Nick Yee. At Stanford University's Virtual Human Interaction Lab, 69 student volunteers fitted with a 3-D virtual reality headset found themselves across the table from a virtual human—a computer-generated man or woman who delivered a three-minute pitch for a university security policy that required students to carry an ID at all times.

The digital person featured realistic-looking lips that moved, eyes that blinked, and a head that swayed. For half the participants, those movements mimicked, with a four-second delay, the student's movements. If the student tilted her head and looked up, the digital chameleon would do the same. Earlier experiments with real humans had found that such mimicry fosters liking, by suggesting empathy and rapport (see Chapter 11). In Bailenson and Yee's (2005) experiment, students with a mimicking rather than a nonmimicking digital companion similarly liked the partner more. They also found the mimicker more interesting, honest, and persuasive; they paid better attention to it (looking away less often); and they were somewhat more likely to agree with the message.

For Blascovich (2002), such studies illustrate the potential of virtual social realities. Creating stimuli that imply others' presence "costs less, requires less effort, and, quite important, provides a greater degree of experimental control than creating stimuli based on the actual presence of others." People, even trained confederates, are difficult to control. Digital people can be perfectly controlled. And exact replications become possible.

Experimenting with a virtual social reality. In an experiment by Jeremy Bailenson and Nick Yee, a person whose expressions and movements echoed one's own was both liked and persuasive.

important given the presence of factor X, and credibility is more important given the absence of factor X. Factor X, as George Goethals and Erick Nelson (1973) discovered, is whether the topic is more one of *subjective preference* or *objective reality*. When the choice concerns matters of personal value, taste, or way of life, *similar* communicators have the most influence. But on judgments of fact—Does Sydney have less rainfall than London?—confirmation of belief by a *dissimilar* person does more to boost confidence. A dissimilar person provides a more independent judgment.

Attractive communicators, such as Serena and Venus Williams endorsing Reebok and Puma, often trigger peripheral route persuasion. We associate their message or product with our good feelings toward the communicator, and we approve and believe.

What Is Said? The Message Content

It matters not only who says something but also *what* that person says. If you were to help organize an appeal to get people to vote for school taxes or to stop smoking or to give money to world hunger relief, you might wonder how best to promote central route persuasion. Common sense could lead you to either side of these questions:

- Is a logical message more persuasive—or one that arouses emotion?
- Will you get more opinion change by advocating a position only slightly discrepant from the listeners' existing opinions or by advocating an extreme point of view?
- Should the message express your side only, or should it acknowledge and refute the opposing views?
- If people are to present both sides—say, in successive talks at a community meeting or in a political debate—is there an advantage to going first or last?

Let's take these questions one at a time.

REASON VERSUS EMOTION

Suppose you were campaigning in support of world hunger relief. Would you best itemize your arguments and cite an array of impressive statistics? Or would you be more effective presenting an emotional approach—perhaps the compelling story of one starving child? Of course, an argument can be both reasonable and emotional. You can marry passion and logic. Still, which is *more* influential—reason or emotion? Was Shakespeare's Lysander right: "The will of man is by his reason sway'd"? Or was Lord Chesterfield's advice wiser: "Address yourself generally to the senses, to the heart, and to the weaknesses of mankind, but rarely to their reason"?

The answer: It depends on the audience. Well-educated or analytical people are responsive to rational appeals (Cacioppo & others, 1983, 1996; Hovland & others, 1949). Thoughtful, involved audiences often travel the central route; they are more responsive to reasoned arguments. Uninterested audiences more often travel the peripheral route; they are more affected by their liking of the communicator (Chaiken, 1980; Petty & others, 1981).

To judge from interviews before major elections, many voters are uninvolved. As we might therefore expect, Americans' voting preferences have been more

"The truth is always the strongest argument."
—*SOPHOCLES*, PHAEDRA, 496–406 B.C.

"Opinion is ultimately determined by the feelings and not the intellect."
—*HERBERT SPENCER*, SOCIAL STATICS, 1851

FIGURE :: 7.3

People who snacked as they read were more persuaded than those who read without snacking.

Source: Data from Janis, Kaye, & Kirschner, 1965.

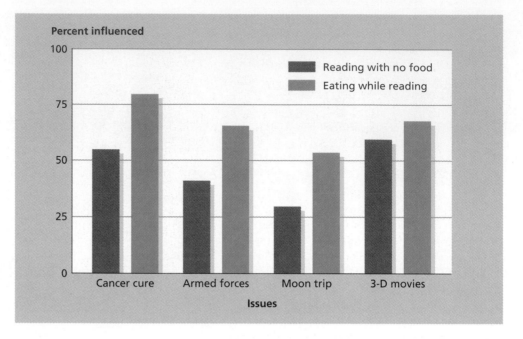

predictable from emotional reactions to the candidates than from their beliefs about the candidates' traits and likely behaviors (Abelson & others, 1982). In the 2004 U.S. presidential election, many Americans who agreed more with Democratic candidate John Kerry nevertheless liked George W. Bush better (seeing him as more decisive and as "someone you admire")—and voted for him.

It also matters how people's attitudes were formed. When people's initial attitudes are formed primarily through emotion, they are more persuaded by later emotional appeals; when their initial attitudes are formed primarily through reason, they are more persuaded by later intellectual arguments (Edwards, 1990; Fabrigar & Petty, 1999). New emotions may sway an emotion-based attitude. But to change an information-based attitude, more information may be needed.

THE EFFECT OF GOOD FEELINGS Messages also become more persuasive through association with good feelings. Irving Janis and his colleagues (1965; Dabbs & Janis, 1965) found that Yale students were more convinced by persuasive messages if they were allowed to enjoy peanuts and Pepsi while reading the messages (Figure 7.3). Similarly, Mark Galizio and Clyde Hendrick (1972) found that Kent State University students were more persuaded by folk-song lyrics accompanied by pleasant guitar music than they were by unaccompanied lyrics. There is, it seems, something to be gained from conducting business over sumptuous lunches with soft background music.

Good feelings often enhance persuasion, partly by enhancing positive thinking and partly by linking good feelings with the message (Petty & others, 1993). As we noted in Chapter 3, people who are in a good mood view the world through rose-colored glasses. But they also make faster, more impulsive decisions; they rely more on peripheral cues (Bodenhausen, 1993; Braverman, 2005; Moons & Mackie, 2007). Unhappy people ruminate more before reacting, so they are less easily swayed by weak arguments. (They also *produce* more cogent persuasive messages [Forgas, 2007].) Thus, if you can't make a strong case, you might want to put your audience in a good mood and hope they'll feel good about your message without thinking too much about it.

THE EFFECT OF AROUSING FEAR Messages can also be effective by evoking negative emotions. When persuading people to cut down on smoking, get a tetanus shot, or drive carefully, a fear-arousing message can be potent (de Hoog & others, 2007; Muller & Johnson, 1990). By requiring cigarette makers to include graphic representations of the hazards of smoking on each pack of cigarettes, the Canadian government assumed—correctly, it turns out—that showing cigarette smokers the horrible things that can happen to smokers adds to persuasiveness (O'Hegarty & others, 2007; Peters & others, 2007; Stark & others, 2008). But how much fear should you arouse? Should you evoke just a little fear, lest people become so frightened that they tune out your painful message? Or should you try to scare the daylights out of them? Experiments by Howard Leventhal (1970), by Ronald Rogers and his collaborators (Robberson & Rogers, 1988), and by Natascha de Hoog and her colleagues (2007) show that, often, the more frightened and vulnerable people feel, the more they respond.

The effectiveness of fear-arousing communications is being applied in ads discouraging not only smoking but also risky sexual behaviors and drinking and driving. When Claude Levy-Leboyer (1988) found that attitudes toward alcohol and drinking habits among French youth were changed effectively by fear-arousing pictures, the French government incorporated such pictures into its TV spots.

"If the jury had been sequestered in a nicer hotel, this would probably never have happened."

Good feelings help create positive attitudes.
© The New Yorker Collection, 1997, Frank Cotham, from cartoonbank.com. All Rights Reserved.

Canadian cigarette warnings, sampled here, use fear-arousal.

An effective antismoking ad campaign offered graphic "truth" ads. In one, vans pull up outside an unnamed corporate tobacco office. Teens pile out and unload 1,200 body bags covering two city blocks. As a curious corporate suit peers out a window above, a teen shouts into a loudspeaker: "Do you know how many people tobacco kills every day? . . . . We're going to leave these here for you, so you can see what 1,200 people actually look like" (Nicholson, 2007). While teens who viewed a simultaneous cerebral Philip Morris ad (lecturing, "Think. Don't Smoke") were not less likely to smoke, those viewing the more dramatic and edgy ad became significantly less inclined to smoke (Farrelly & others, 2002, 2008).

Fear-arousing communications have also been used to increase people's detection behaviors, such as getting mammograms, doing breast or testicular self-exams, and checking for signs of skin cancer. Sara Banks, Peter Salovey, and their colleagues (1995) had women aged 40–66 who had not obtained mammograms view an educational video on mammography. Of those who received a positively framed message (emphasizing that getting a mammogram can save your life through early detection), only half got a mammogram within 12 months. Of those who received a fear-framed message (emphasizing that not getting a mammogram can cost you your life), two-thirds got a mammogram within 12 months.

Anxiety-creating health messages about, say, the risks of high cholesterol can increase people's intentions to eat a low-fat, low-cholesterol diet (Millar & Millar, 1996). To have one's fears aroused is to become more intensely interested in information about a disease, and in ways to prevent it (Das & others, 2003; Ruiter & others, 2001). Fear-framed messages work better when trying to prevent a bad outcome (such as cancer) than when trying to promote a good outcome (such as fitness) (Lee & Aaker, 2004).

Playing on fear won't always make a message more potent, though. Many people who have been made afraid of AIDS are *not* abstaining from sex or using condoms. Many people who have been made to fear an early death from smoking continue to smoke. When the fear pertains to a pleasurable activity, notes Elliot Aronson (1997), the result often is not behavioral change but denial. People may engage in denial because, when they aren't told how to avoid the danger, frightening messages can be overwhelming (Leventhal, 1970; Rogers & Mewborn, 1976).

For that reason, fear-arousing messages are more effective if they lead people not only to fear the severity and likelihood of a threatened event but also to perceive a solution and feel capable of implementing it (DeVos-Comby & Salovey, 2002; Maddux & Rogers, 1983; Ruiter & others, 2001). Many ads designed to reduce sexual risks will aim both to arouse fear—"AIDS kills"—and to offer a protective strategy: Abstain, or wear a condom, or save sex for a committed relationship.

Vivid propaganda often exploits fears. When feeling frightened or threatened, people tend to become more responsive to a controversial, charismatic leader (Gordijn & Stapel, 2008). The Nazi newspaper *Der Stürmer* aroused fear with hundreds of unsubstantiated anecdotes about Jews who were said to have ground rats to make hash, seduced non-Jewish women, and cheated families out of their life savings. Streicher's appeals, like most Nazi propaganda, were emotional, not logical. The appeals also gave clear, specific instructions on how to combat "the danger": They listed Jewish businesses so readers would avoid them, encouraged readers to submit for publication the names of Germans who patronized Jewish shops and professionals, and directed readers to compile lists of Jews in their area (Bytwerk & Brooks, 1980).

DISCREPANCY

Picture the following scene: Nicole arrives home on spring vacation and hopes to convert her portly, middle-aged father to her new "health-fitness lifestyle." She runs five miles a day. Her father says his idea of exercise is "channel surfing." Nicole thinks, "Would I be more likely to get Dad off his duff by urging him to try a modest exercise program, say a daily walk, or by trying to get him involved in something strenuous, say a program of calisthenics and running? Maybe if I asked him

Al Gore to presenters of his climate change film: "You're telling some not only inconvenient truths but hard truths, and it can be scary as hell. You're not going to get people to go with you if you scare them with fear."

—*QUOTED BY POOLEY (2007)*

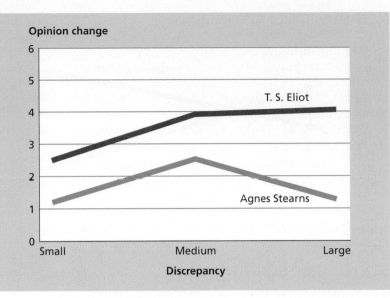

FIGURE :: 7.4

Discrepancy Interacts with Communicator Credibility

Only a highly credible communicator maintains effectiveness when arguing an extreme position.

Source: Data from Aronson, Turner, & Carlsmith, 1963.

to take up a rigorous exercise program, he would compromise and at least take up something worthwhile. But then again maybe he'd write me off and do nothing."

Like Nicole, social psychologists can reason either way. Disagreement produces discomfort, and discomfort prompts people to change their opinions. (Recall from Chapter 4 the effects of dissonance.) So perhaps greater disagreement will produce more change. Then again, a communicator who proclaims an uncomfortable message may be discredited. People who disagree with conclusions drawn by a newscaster rate the newscaster as more biased, inaccurate, and untrustworthy. People are more open to conclusions within their range of acceptability (Liberman & Chaiken, 1992; Zanna, 1993). So perhaps greater disagreement will produce less change.

Elliot Aronson, Judith Turner, and Merrill Carlsmith (1963) reasoned that a *credible source*—one hard to discount—would elicit the most opinion change when advocating a position *greatly discrepant* from the recipient's. Sure enough, when credible T. S. Eliot was said to have highly praised a disliked poem, people changed their opinion more than when he gave it faint praise. But when "Agnes Stearns, a student at Mississippi State Teachers College," evaluated a disliked poem, high praise was no more persuasive than faint praise. Thus, as Figure 7.4 shows, discrepancy and credibility *interact:* The effect of a large versus small discrepancy depends on whether the communicator is credible.

So the answer to Nicole's question—"Should I argue an extreme position?"—is, "It depends." Is Nicole in her adoring father's eyes a highly prestigious, authoritative source? If so, Nicole should push for a complete fitness program. If not, Nicole would be wise to make a more modest appeal.

The answer also depends on her father's engagement with the issue. Deeply involved people tend to accept only a narrow range of views. To them, a moderately discrepant message may seem foolishly radical, especially if the message argues an opposing view rather than being a more extreme version of their own view (Pallak & others, 1972; Petty & Cacioppo, 1979; Rhine & Severance, 1970). If Nicole's father has not yet thought or cared much about exercise, she can probably take a more extreme position than if he is strongly committed to not exercising. So, if you are a credible authority and your audience isn't much concerned with your issue, go for it: Advocate a discrepant view.

ONE-SIDED VERSUS TWO-SIDED APPEALS

Persuaders face another practical issue: how to deal with opposing arguments. Once again, common sense offers no clear answer. Acknowledging the opposing arguments might confuse the audience and weaken the case. On the other hand, a message might seem fairer and be more disarming if it recognizes the opposition's arguments.

FIGURE :: 7.5

The Interaction of Initial Opinion with One-versus Two-Sidedness

After Germany's defeat in World War II, American soldiers skeptical of a message suggesting Japan's strength were more persuaded by a two-sided communication. Soldiers initially agreeing with the message were strengthened more by a one-sided message.

Source: Data from Hovland, Lumsdaine, & Sheffield, 1949.

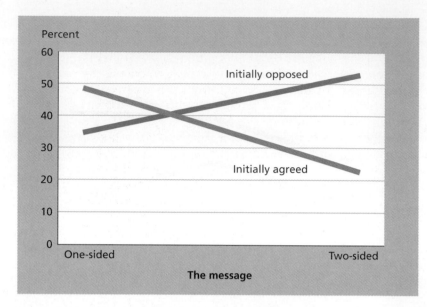

Carol Werner and her colleagues (2002) showed the disarming power of a simple two-sided message in an experiment on aluminum-can recycling. Signs added to wastebaskets in a University of Utah classroom building said, for example, "No Aluminum Cans Please!!!!! Use the Recycler Located on the First Floor, Near the Entrance." When a final persuasive message acknowledged and responded to the main counterargument—"It May Be Inconvenient. But It Is Important!!!!!!!!!!!!"—recycling reached 80 percent (double the rate before any message, and more than in other message conditions).

After Germany's defeat in World War II, the U.S. Army did not want soldiers to relax and think that the still-ongoing war with Japan would become easy. So Carl Hovland and his colleagues (1949) in the Army's Information and Education Division designed two radio broadcasts. Both argued that the Pacific war would last at least two more years. One broadcast was one-sided; it did not acknowledge contradictory arguments, such as the advantage of fighting only one enemy instead of two. The other broadcast was two-sided; it mentioned and responded to the opposing arguments. As Figure 7.5 illustrates, the effectiveness of the message depended on the listener. A one-sided appeal was most effective with those who already agreed. An appeal that acknowledged opposing arguments worked better with those who disagreed.

Experiments also reveal that a two-sided presentation is more persuasive and enduring if people are (or will be) aware of opposing arguments (Jones & Brehm, 1970; Lumsdaine & Janis, 1953). In simulated trials, a defense case becomes more credible when the defense brings up damaging evidence before the prosecution does (Williams & others, 1993). Thus, a political candidate speaking to a politically informed group would indeed be wise to respond to the opposition. So, *if your audience will be exposed to opposing views, offer a two-sided appeal.*

"Opponents fancy they refute us when they repeat their own opinion and pay no attention to ours."
—*GOETHE,* MAXIMS AND REFLECTIONS, 1829

This interaction effect typifies persuasion research. For optimists, positive persuasion works best ("The new plan reduces tuition in exchange for part-time university service"). For pessimists, negative persuasion is more effective ("All students will have to work part-time for the university, lest they pay out-of-state tuition") (Geers & others, 2003). We might wish that persuasion variables had simple effects. (It would make this an easier chapter to study.) Alas, most variables, note Richard Petty and Duane Wegener (1998), "have complex effects—increasing persuasion in some situations and decreasing it in others."

As students and scientists we cherish "Occam's razor"—seeking the simplest possible principles. But if human reality is complex, well, our principles will need to have some complexity as well.

PRIMACY VERSUS RECENCY

Imagine that you are a consultant to a prominent politician who must soon debate another prominent politician over a ballot proposition on bilingual education. Three weeks before the vote, each politician is to appear on the nightly news and present a prepared statement. By the flip of a coin, your side receives the choice of whether to speak first or last. Knowing that you are a former social psychology student, everyone looks to you for advice.

You mentally scan your old books and lecture notes. Would first be better? People's preconceptions control their interpretations. Moreover, a belief, once formed, is difficult to discredit, so going first could give voters ideas that would favorably bias how they perceive and interpret the second speech. Besides, people may pay more attention to what comes first. Then again, people remember recent things better. Might it really be more effective to speak last?

Your first line of reasoning predicts what is most common, a **primacy effect:** Information presented early is most persuasive. First impressions are important. For example, can you sense a difference between these two descriptions?

- John is intelligent, industrious, impulsive, critical, stubborn, and envious.
- John is envious, stubborn, critical, impulsive, industrious, and intelligent.

When Solomon Asch (1946) gave those sentences to college students in New York City, those who read the adjectives in the intelligent-to-envious order rated the person more positively than did those given the envious-to-intelligent order. The earlier information seemed to color their interpretation of the later information, producing the primacy effect.

Some other interesting examples of the primacy effect:

- In some experiments, people have succeeded on a guessing task 50 percent of the time. Those whose successes come early seem more capable than those whose successes come after early failures (Jones & others, 1968; Langer & Roth, 1975; McAndrew, 1981).
- In political polls and in primary election voting, candidates benefit from being listed first on the ballot (Moore, 2004a).
- Norman Miller and Donald Campbell (1959) gave Northwestern University students a condensed transcript from an actual civil trial. They placed the plaintiff's testimony and arguments in one block, those for the defense in another. The students read both blocks. When they returned a week later to declare their opinions, most sided with the information they had read first.

What about the opposite possibility? Would our better memory of recent information ever create a **recency effect?** We have all experienced what the book of Proverbs observed: "The one who first states a case seems right, until the other comes and cross-examines." We know from our experience (as well as from memory experiments) that today's events can temporarily outweigh significant past events. To test this, Miller and Campbell gave another group of students one block of testimony to read. A week later the researchers had them read the second block and then immediately state their opinions. The results were the reverse of the other condition—a recency effect. Apparently the first block of arguments, being a week old, had largely faded from memory.

Forgetting creates the recency effect (1) when enough time separates the two messages *and* (2) when the audience commits itself soon after the second message. When the two messages are back-to-back, followed by a time gap, the primacy effect usually occurs (Figure 7.6). This is especially so when the first message stimulates thinking (Haugtvedt & Wegener, 1994). What advice would you now give to the political debater?

Dana Carney and Mahzarin Banaji (2008) discovered that order can also affect simple preferences. When encountering two people or horses or foods or whatever, people tend to prefer the first presented option. For example, when offered two

primacy effect
Other things being equal, information presented first usually has the most influence.

recency effect
Information presented last sometimes has the most influence. Recency effects are less common than primacy effects.

In 2008, the U.S. Democratic Party convention was immediately followed by the Republican Party convention, after which there was a two-month time gap before the election. If experiments on primacy and recency are applicable, which party would benefit most from this timing?

FIGURE :: 7.6

Primacy Effect versus Recency Effect

When two persuasive messages are back-to-back and the audience then responds at some later time, the first message has the advantage (primacy effect). When the two messages are separated in time and the audience responds soon after the second message, the second message has the advantage (recency effect).

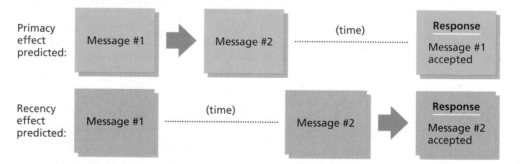

similar-looking pieces of bubble gum, one placed after the other on a white clipboard, 62 percent, when asked to make a snap judgment, chose the first-presented piece. Across four experiments, the findings were consistent: "First is best."

How Is It Said? The Channel of Communication

channel of communication

The way the message is delivered—whether face-to-face, in writing, on film, or in some other way.

For persuasion, there must be communication. And for communication, there must be a **channel**: a face-to-face appeal, a written sign or document, a media advertisement.

Commonsense psychology places faith in the power of written words. How do we try to get people to attend a campus event? We post notices. How do we get drivers to slow down and keep their eyes on the road? We put "Drive Carefully" messages on billboards. How do we discourage students from dropping trash on campus? We post antilitter messages on campus bulletin boards.

ACTIVE EXPERIENCE OR PASSIVE RECEPTION?

Are spoken appeals more persuasive? Not necessarily. Those of us who speak publicly, as teachers or persuaders, often become so enamored of our spoken words that we overestimate their power. Ask college students what aspect of their college experience has been most valuable or what they remember from their first year, and few, I am sad to say, recall the brilliant lectures that we faculty remember giving.

Thomas Crawford (1974) and his associates tested the impact of the spoken word by going to the homes of people from 12 churches shortly before and after they heard sermons opposing racial bigotry and injustice. When asked during the second interview whether they had heard or read anything about racial prejudice or discrimination since the previous interview, only 10 percent recalled the sermons spontaneously. When the remaining 90 percent were asked directly whether their priest had "talked about prejudice or discrimination in the last couple of weeks," more than 30 percent denied hearing such a sermon. The end result: The sermons left racial attitudes unaffected.

When you stop to think about it, an effective preacher has many hurdles to surmount. As Figure 7.1 showed, a persuasive speaker must deliver a message that not only gets attention but also is understandable, convincing, memorable, and compelling. A carefully thought-out appeal must consider each of those steps in the persuasion process.

Consider another well-intentioned effort. At Scripps College in California, a week-long antilitter campaign urged students to "Keep Scripps' campus beautiful," "Let's clean up our trash," and so forth. Such slogans were placed in students' mailboxes each morning and displayed on prominent posters. The day before the campaign began, social psychologist Raymond Paloutzian (1979) placed litter near

a trash can along a well-traveled sidewalk. Then he stepped back to record the behavior of 180 passersby. No one picked up anything. On the last day of the campaign, he repeated the test with 180 more passersby. Did the pedestrians now race one another in their zeal to comply with the appeals? Hardly. Only 2 of the 180 picked up the trash.

Passively received appeals, however, are not always futile. My drugstore sells two brands of aspirin, one heavily advertised and one unadvertised. Apart from slight differences in how fast each tablet crumbles in your mouth, any pharmacist will tell you the two brands are identical. Aspirin is aspirin. Our bodies cannot tell the difference. But our pocketbooks can. The advertised brand sells to millions of people for three times the price of the unadvertised brand.

With such power, can the media help a wealthy political candidate buy an election? In presidential primaries, those who spend the most usually get the most votes (Grush, 1980; Open Secrets, 2005). Advertising exposure helps make an unfamiliar candidate into a familiar one. As we will see in Chapter 11, mere exposure to unfamiliar stimuli breeds liking. Moreover, *mere repetition* can make things

Advertising power. Cigarette advertising campaigns have correlated with teen smoking increases among the targeted gender (Pierce & others, 1994, 1995). This photo shows models practicing the "correct" pucker and blow technique for a 1950s TV ad.

"Ah, that is always the way with you men; you believe nothing the first time, and it is foolish enough to let mere repetition convince you of what you consider in itself unbelievable."

—GEORGE MACDONALD, PHANTASTES, 1858

believable (Moons & others, 2009). People rate trivial statements such as "Mercury has a higher boiling point than copper" as more truthful if they read and rated them a week before.

Researcher Hal Arkes (1990) calls such findings "scary." As political manipulators know, believable lies can displace hard truths. Repeated clichés can cover complex realities. Even repeatedly saying that a consumer claim is *false* can, when the discounting is presented amid other true and false claims, lead older adults later to misremember it as *true* (Skurnik & others, 2005). As they forget the discounting, their lingering familiarity with the claim can make it seem believable. In the political realm, even correct information may fail to discount implanted misinformation (Bullock, 2006; Nyhan & Reifler, 2008). Thus, in the 2008 U.S. presidential election, false rumors—that Obama was a Muslim, that McCain wanted to keep U.S. forces in Iraq for 100 years—resisted efforts at disconfirmation, which sometimes helped make the falsehood seem familiar and thus true.

Mere repetition of a statement also serves to increase its fluency—the ease with which it spills off our tongue—which increases believability (McGlone & Tofighbakhsh, 2000). Other factors, such as rhyming, also increase fluency and believability. "Haste makes waste" may say essentially the same thing as "rushing causes mistakes," but it seems more true. Whatever makes for fluency (familiarity, rhyming) also makes for credibility.

Because passively received appeals are sometimes effective and sometimes not, can we specify in advance the topics on which a persuasive appeal will be successful? There is a simple rule: Persuasion *decreases* as the significance and familiarity of the issue *increase*. On minor issues, such as which brand of aspirin to buy, it's easy to demonstrate the media's power. On more familiar and important issues, such as attitudes about a lengthy and controversial war, persuading people is like trying to push a piano uphill. It is not impossible, but one shove won't do it.

As we saw in Chapter 4, Behavior and Attitudes, active experience also strengthens attitudes. When we act, we amplify the idea behind what we've done, especially when we feel responsible. What is more, attitudes more often endure and influence our behavior when rooted in our own experience. Compared with attitudes formed passively, experience-based attitudes are more confident, more stable, and less vulnerable to attack. These principles are evident in many studies which show that the most effective HIV-prevention interventions not only give people information but also give them behavioral training, such as by practicing assertiveness in refusing sex and using protection (Albarracin & others, 2005).

PERSONAL VERSUS MEDIA INFLUENCE

Persuasion studies demonstrate that the major influence on us is not the media but our contact with people. Modern selling strategies seek to harness the power of word-of-mouth personal influence through "viral marketing," "creating a buzz," and "seeding" sales (Walker, 2004). The *Harry Potter* series was not expected to be a best seller (*Harry Potter and the Sorcerer's Stone* had a first printing of 500 copies). It was kids talking to other kids that made it so.

"You do realize, you will never make a fortune out of writing children's books?"

—J. K. ROWLING'S LITERARY AGENT BEFORE RELEASE OF HARRY POTTER AND THE SORCERER'S STONE

Two classic field experiments illustrate the strength of personal influence. Some years ago, Samuel Eldersveld and Richard Dodge (1954) studied political persuasion in Ann Arbor, Michigan. They divided citizens intending not to vote for a revision of the city charter into three groups. Among those exposed only to what they saw and heard in the mass media, 19 percent changed their minds and voted in favor of the revision on election day. Of a second group, who received four mailings in support of the revision, 45 percent voted for it. Among people in a third group, who were visited personally and given the appeal face-to-face, 75 percent cast their votes for the revision.

In another field experiment, a research team led by John Farquhar and Nathan Maccoby (1977; Maccoby, 1980; Maccoby & Alexander, 1980) tried to reduce the frequency of heart disease among middle-aged adults in three small California

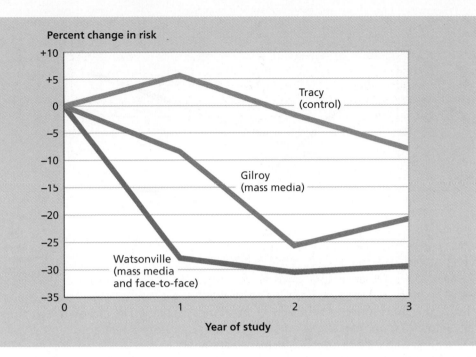

FIGURE :: 7.7

Percentage change from base-line (0) in coronary risk after one, two, or three years of health education.

Source: Data from Maccoby, 1980.

cities. To check the relative effectiveness of personal and media influence, they interviewed and medically examined 1,200 participants before the project began and at the end of each of the following three years. Residents of Tracy, California, received no persuasive appeals other than those occurring in their regular media. In Gilroy, California, a two-year multimedia campaign used TV, radio, newspapers, and direct mail to teach people about coronary risk and what they could do to reduce it. In Watsonville, California, this media campaign was supplemented by personal contacts with two-thirds of those participants whose blood pressure, weight, and age put them in a high-risk group. Using behavior-modification principles, the researchers helped the Watsonville participants set specific goals and reinforced their successes.

As Figure 7.7 shows, after one, two, and three years, the high-risk participants in Tracy (the control town) were at about as much at risk as before. High-risk participants in Gilroy, which was deluged with media appeals, improved their health habits and decreased their risk somewhat. Those in Watsonville, who received personal contacts as well as the media campaign, changed most.

MEDIA INFLUENCE: THE TWO-STEP FLOW   Although face-to-face influence is usually greater than media influence, we should not underestimate the media's power. Those who personally influence our opinions must get their ideas from some source, and often their sources are the media. Elihu Katz (1957) observed that many of the media's effects operate in a **two-step flow of communication:** from media to opinion leaders to the rank and file. In any large group, it is these *opinion leaders* and trendsetters—"the influentials"—that marketers and politicians seek to woo (Keller & Berry, 2003). Opinion leaders are individuals perceived as experts. They may include talk show hosts and editorial columnists; doctors, teachers and scientists; and people in all walks of life who have made it their business to absorb information and to inform their friends and family. If I want to evaluate computer equipment, I defer to the opinions of my sons, who get many of their ideas from the printed page. Sell them and you will sell me.

The two-step flow of information influences the drugs your physician describes, reports a Stanford School of Business research team (Nair & others, 2008). Physicians look to opinion leaders within their social network—often a university hospital–based specialist—when deciding what drugs to favor. For more than 9 in 10

two-step flow of communication
The process by which media influence often occurs through opinion leaders, who in turn influence others.

FIGURE :: 7.8

Easy-to-understand messages are most persuasive when videotaped. Difficult messages are most persuasive when written. Thus, the difficulty of the message interacts with the medium to determine persuasiveness.

Source: Data from Chaiken & Eagly, 1978.

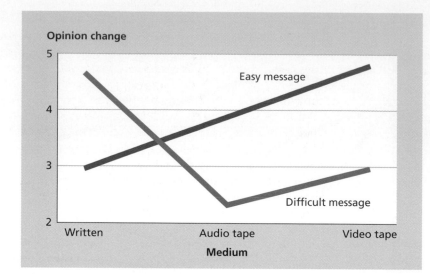

In study after study, most people agree that mass media influence attitudes—other people's attitudes, but not their own (Duck & others, 1995).

physicians, this influence comes through personal contact. The largest drug companies know that opinion leaders drive sales, and therefore target about one-third of their marketing dollars on these influential people.

The two-step flow model reminds us that media influences penetrate the culture in subtle ways. Even if the media had little direct effect on people's attitudes, they could still have a big indirect effect. Those rare children who grow up without watching television do not grow up beyond television's influence. Unless they live as hermits, they will join in TV-imitative play on the schoolground. They will ask their parents for the TV-related toys their friends have. They will beg or demand to watch their friends' favorite programs, and will do so when visiting friends' homes. Parents can just say no, but they cannot switch off television's influence.

COMPARING MEDIA Lumping together all media, from mass mailings to television to podcasting, oversimplifies. Studies comparing different media find that the more lifelike the medium, the more persuasive its message. Thus, the order of persuasiveness seems to be: live (face-to-face), videotaped, audiotaped, and written.

To add to the complexity, messages are best *comprehended* and *recalled* when written. Comprehension is one of the first steps in the persuasion process (recall Figure 7.1). So Shelly Chaiken and Alice Eagly (1976) reasoned that if a message is difficult to comprehend, persuasion should be greatest when the message is written, because readers will be able to work through the message at their own pace. The researchers gave University of Massachusetts students easy or difficult messages in writing, on audiotape, or on videotape. Figure 7.8 displays their results: Difficult messages were indeed most persuasive when written; easy messages, when videotaped. The TV medium takes control of the pacing of the message away from the recipients. By drawing attention to the communicator and away from the message itself, TV also encourages people to focus on peripheral cues, such as the communicator's attractiveness (Chaiken & Eagly, 1983).

To Whom Is It Said? The Audience

As we saw in Chapter 6, people's traits often don't predict their responses to social influence. A particular trait may enhance one step in the persuasion process (Figure 7.1) but work against another. Take self-esteem. People with low self-esteem are often slow to comprehend a message and therefore hard to persuade. Those with high self-esteem may comprehend yet remain confident of their own opinions. The conclusion: People with moderate self-esteem are the easiest to influence (Rhodes & Wood, 1992).

Let's also consider two other audience characteristics: age and thoughtfulness.

HOW OLD ARE THEY?

As evident during the 2008 U.S. presidential campaign—with John McCain the decided favorite of older voters and Barack Obama of younger voters—people's social and political attitudes correlate with their age. Social psychologists offer two possible explanations for age differences. One is a *life cycle explanation:* Attitudes change (for example, become more conservative) as people grow older. The other is a *generational explanation:* Attitudes do *not* change; older people largely hold onto the attitudes they adopted when they were young. Because these attitudes are different from those being adopted by young people today, a generation gap develops.

The evidence mostly supports the generational explanation. In surveys and resurveys of groups of younger and older people over several years, the attitudes of older people usually show less change than do those of young people. As David Sears (1979, 1986) put it, researchers have "almost invariably found generational rather than life cycle effects."

The teens and early twenties are important formative years (Koenig & others, 2008; Krosnick & Alwin, 1989). Attitudes are changeable then, and the attitudes formed tend to stabilize through middle adulthood. Gallup interviews of more than 120,000 people suggest that political attitudes formed at age 18—relatively Republican-favoring during the popular Reagan era, and more Democratic-favoring during the unpopular George W. Bush era—tend to last (Silver, 2009).

Young people might therefore be advised to choose their social influences—the groups they join, the media they imbibe, the roles they adopt—carefully. In analyzing National Opinion Research Center archives, James Davis (2004) discovered, for example, that Americans reaching age 16 during the 1960s have, ever since, been more politically liberal than average. Much as tree rings can, years later, reveal the telltale marks laid down by a drought, so attitudes decades later may reveal the events, such as the Vietnam War and civil rights era of the 1960s, that shaped the adolescent and early-twenties mind. For many people, these years are a critical period for the formation of attitudes and values.

Vermont's Bennington College provides a striking example. During the late 1930s and early 1940s, Bennington students—women from privileged, conservative families—encountered a free-spirited environment led by a left-leaning young faculty. One of those professors, social psychologist Theodore Newcomb, later denied that the faculty was trying to make "good little liberals" out of its students. Yet the students became much more liberal than was typical of those from their social backgrounds. Moreover, attitudes formed at Bennington endured. A half-century later, the Bennington women, now 70ish, voted Democratic by a three-to-one margin in the 1984 presidential election, while other college-educated women who were in their seventies were voting Republican by a three-to-one margin (Alwin & others, 1991). The views embraced at an impressionable time had survived a lifetime of wider experience.

Adolescent and early-adult experiences are formative partly because they make deep and lasting impressions. When Howard Schuman and Jacqueline Scott (1989) asked people to name the one or two most important national or world events of the previous half-century, most recalled events from their teens or early twenties. For those who experienced the Great Depression or World War II as 16- to 24-year-olds, those events overshadowed the civil rights movement and the Kennedy assassination of the early sixties, the Vietnam War and moon landing of the late sixties, and the women's movement of the seventies—all of which were imprinted on the minds of younger people who experienced them as 16- to 24-year-olds. We may therefore expect that today's young adults will include events such as 9/11 and the Iraq war as memorable turning points.

That is not to say that older adults are inflexible. Studies conducted by Norval Glenn in 1980 and 1981 found that most people in their fifties and sixties had more liberal sexual and racial attitudes than they had in their thirties and forties. Given the "sexual revolution" that began in the 1960s and became mainstream in the 1970s, these middle-aged people had apparently changed with the times. Few of us are utterly uninfluenced by changing cultural norms. Moreover, near the end of their lives, older adults may again become more susceptible to attitude change, perhaps because of a decline in the strength of their attitudes (Visser & Krosnick, 1998).

WHAT ARE THEY THINKING?

The crucial aspect of central route persuasion is not the message but the responses it evokes in a person's mind. Our minds are not sponges that soak up whatever pours over them. If the message summons favorable thoughts, it persuades us. If it provokes us to think of contrary arguments, we remain unpersuaded.

FOREWARNED IS FOREARMED—IF YOU CARE ENOUGH TO COUNTER-ARGUE What circumstances breed counterargument? One is knowing that someone is going to try to persuade you. If you had to tell your family that you wanted to drop out of school, you would likely anticipate their pleading with you to stay. So you might develop a list of arguments to counter every conceivable argument they might make.

Jonathan Freedman and David Sears (1965) demonstrated the difficulty of trying to persuade people under such circumstances. They warned one group of California high schoolers that they were going to hear a talk: "Why Teenagers Should Not Be Allowed to Drive." Those forewarned did not budge in their opinions. Others, not forewarned, did budge. In courtrooms, too, defense attorneys sometimes forewarn juries about prosecution evidence to come. With mock juries, such "stealing thunder" neutralizes its impact (Dolnik & others, 2003).

DISTRACTION DISARMS COUNTERARGUING Persuasion is also enhanced by a distraction that inhibits counterarguing (Festinger & Maccoby, 1964; Keating & Brock, 1974; Osterhouse & Brock, 1970). Political ads often use this technique. The words promote the candidate, and the visual images keep us occupied so we don't analyze the words. Distraction is especially effective when the message is simple (Harkins & Petty, 1981; Regan & Cheng, 1973). Sometimes, though, distraction precludes our processing an ad. That helps explain why ads viewed during violent or sexual TV programs are so often unremembered and ineffective (Bushman, 2005, 2007).

UNINVOLVED AUDIENCES USE PERIPHERAL CUES Recall the two routes to persuasion—the central route of systematic thinking and the peripheral route of heuristic cues. Like a road that winds through a small town, the central route has starts and stops as the mind analyzes arguments and formulates responses. Like the freeway that bypasses the town, the peripheral route speeds people to their destination. Analytical people—those with a high **need for cognition**—enjoy thinking carefully and prefer central routes (Cacioppo & others, 1996). People who like to conserve their mental resources—those with a low need for cognition—are quicker to respond to such peripheral cues as the communicator's attractiveness and the pleasantness of the surroundings.

This simple theory—that *what we think in response to a message is crucial*, especially if we are motivated and able to think about it—has generated many predictions, most of which have been confirmed by Petty, Cacioppo, and others (Axsom & others, 1987; Haddock & others, 2008; Harkins & Petty, 1987). Many experiments have explored ways to stimulate people's thinking

- by using *rhetorical questions.*
- by presenting *multiple speakers* (for example, having each of three speakers give one argument instead of one speaker giving three).
- by making people *feel responsible* for evaluating or passing along the message.
- by *repeating* the message.
- by getting people's *undistracted attention.*

"To be forewarned and therefore forearmed . . . is eminently rational if our belief is true; but if our belief is a delusion, this same forewarning and forearming would obviously be the method whereby the delusion rendered itself incurable."

—*C. S. LEWIS*, SCREWTAPE PROPOSES A TOAST, 1965

need for cognition
The motivation to think and analyze. Assessed by agreement with items such as "The notion of thinking abstractly is appealing to me" and disagreement with items such as "I only think as hard as I have to."

The consistent finding with each of these techniques: *Stimulating thinking makes strong messages more persuasive and* (because of counterarguing) *weak messages less persuasive.*

The theory also has practical implications. Effective communicators care not only about their images and their messages but also about how their audience is likely to react. The best instructors tend to get students to think actively. They ask rhetorical questions, provide intriguing examples, and challenge students with difficult problems. All these techniques are likely to foster a process that moves information through the central route to persuasion. In classes where the instruction is less engaging, you can provide your own central processing. If you think about the material and elaborate on the arguments, you are likely to do better in the course.

During the final days of a closely contested 1980 U.S. presidential campaign, Ronald Reagan effectively used rhetorical questions to stimulate desired thoughts in voters' minds. His summary statement in the presidential debate began with two potent rhetorical questions that he repeated often during the campaign's remaining week: "Are you better off than you were four years ago? Is it easier for you to go and buy things in the stores than it was four years ago?" Most people answered no, and Reagan, thanks partly to the way he prodded people to take the central route, won by a bigger-than-expected margin.

"Are you better off than you were four years ago?" Ronald Reagan soared to victory with a memorable rhetorical question that triggered voters' thinking.

Summing Up: What Are the Elements of Persuasion?

- What makes persuasion effective? Researchers have explored four factors: the *communicator* (who says it), the *message* (what is said), the *channel* (how it is said), and the *audience* (to whom it is said).

- Credible communicators have the best success in persuading. People who speak unhesitatingly, who talk fast, and who look listeners straight in the eye seem more credible. So are people who argue against their own self-interest. An attractive communicator also is effective on matters of taste and personal values.

- The message itself persuades; associating it with good feelings makes it more convincing. People often make quicker, less reflective judgments while in good moods. Fear-arousing messages can also be effective, especially if the recipients feel vulnerable but can take protective action.

- How discrepant a message should be from an audience's existing opinions depends on the communicator's credibility. And whether a one- or two-sided message is more persuasive depends on whether

the audience already agrees with the message, is unaware of opposing arguments, and is unlikely later to consider the opposition.

- When two sides of an issue are included, the primacy effect often makes the first message more persuasive. If a time gap separates the presentations, the more likely result will be a recency effect in which the second message prevails.

- Another important consideration is how the message is communicated. Usually, face-to-face appeals work best. Print media can be effective for complex messages. And the mass media can be effective when the issue is minor or unfamiliar, and when the media reach opinion leaders.

- Finally, it matters who receives the message. The age of the audience makes a difference; young people's attitudes are more subject to change. What does the audience think while receiving a message? Do they think favorable thoughts? Do they counterargue? Were they forewarned?

Hundreds of thousands of people in recent years have been recruited by members of some 2,500 religious cults, but seldom through an abrupt decision.

© Charles Addams. With permission Tee and Charles Addams Foundation.

"You go on home without me, Irene. I'm going to join this man's cult."

Extreme Persuasion: How Do Cults Indoctrinate?

What persuasion and group influence principles are harnessed by new religious movements ("cults")?

On March 22, 1997, Marshall Herff Applewhite and 37 of his disciples decided the time had come to shed their bodies—mere "containers"—and be whisked up to a UFO trailing the Hale-Bopp Comet, en route to heaven's gate. So they put themselves to sleep by mixing phenobarbital into pudding or applesauce, washing it down with vodka, and then fixing plastic bags over their heads so they would suffocate in their slumber. On that same day, a cottage in the French Canadian village of St. Casimir exploded in an inferno, consuming 5 people—the latest of 74 members of the Order of the Solar Temple to have committed suicide in Canada, Switzerland, and France. All were hoping to be transported to the star Sirius, nine light-years away.

The question on many minds: What persuades people to leave behind their former beliefs and join these mental chain gangs? Should we attribute their strange behaviors to strange personalities? Or do their experiences illustrate the common dynamics of social influence and persuasion?

Bear two things in mind. First, this is hindsight analysis. It uses persuasion principles to explain, after the fact, a troubling social phenomenon. Second, explaining *why* people believe something says nothing about the *truth* of their beliefs. That is a logically separate issue. A psychology of religion might tell us *why* a theist believes in God and an atheist disbelieves, but it cannot tell us who is right. Explaining either belief does nothing to change its validity. Remember that if someone tries to discount your beliefs by saying, "You just believe that because. . . ," you might recall Archbishop William Temple's reply to a questioner who challenged: "Well, of course, Archbishop, the point is that you believe what you believe because of the way you were brought up." To which the archbishop replied: "That is as it may be.

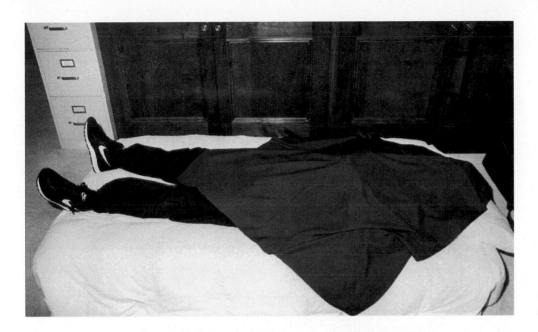

One of 37 suicide victims seeking heaven's gate.

But the fact remains that you believe I believe what I believe because of the way I was brought up, because of the way you were brought up."

In recent decades, several **cults**—which some social scientists prefer to call new religious movements—have gained much publicity: Sun Myung Moon's Unification Church, Jim Jones's People's Temple, David Koresh's Branch Davidians, and Marshall Applewhite's Heaven's Gate.

Sun Myung Moon's mixture of Christianity, anticommunism, and glorification of Moon himself as a new messiah attracted a worldwide following. In response to Moon's declaration "What I wish must be your wish," many people committed themselves and their incomes to the Unification Church.

In 1978 in Guyana, 914 disciples of Jim Jones, who had followed him there from San Francisco, shocked the world when they died by following his order to down a suicidal grape drink laced with tranquilizers, painkillers, and a lethal dose of cyanide.

In 1993 high-school dropout David Koresh used his talent for memorizing Scripture and mesmerizing people to seize control of a faction of the Branch Davidian sect. Over time, members were gradually relieved of their bank accounts and possessions. Koresh also persuaded the men to live celibately while he slept with their wives and daughters, and he convinced his 19 "wives" that they should bear his children. Under siege after a shootout that killed 6 members and 4 federal agents, Koresh told his followers they would soon die and go with him straight to heaven. Federal agents rammed the compound with tanks, hoping to inject tear gas. By the end of the assault, 86 people were consumed in a fire that engulfed the compound.

Marshall Applewhite was not similarly tempted to command sexual favors. Having been fired from two music teaching jobs for affairs with students, he sought sexless devotion by castration, as had 7 of the other 17 Heaven's Gate men who died with him (Chua-Eoan, 1997; Gardner, 1997). While in a psychiatric hospital in 1971, Applewhite had linked up with nurse and astrology dabbler Bonnie Lu Nettles, who gave the intense and charismatic Applewhite a cosmological vision of a route to "the next level." Preaching with passion, he persuaded his followers to renounce families, sex, drugs, and personal money with promises of a spaceship voyage to salvation.

How could these things happen? What persuaded these people to give such total allegiance? Shall we make dispositional explanations—by blaming the victims? Shall we dismiss them as gullible or unbalanced? Or can familiar principles of

cult (also called new religious movement) A group typically characterized by (1) distinctive ritual and beliefs related to its devotion to a god or a person, (2) isolation from the surrounding "evil" culture, and (3) a charismatic leader. (A sect, by contrast, is a spinoff from a major religion.)

conformity, compliance, dissonance, persuasion, and group influence explain their behavior—putting them on common ground with the rest of us who in our own ways are shaped by such forces?

Attitudes Follow Behavior

As Chapter 4 showed over and again, people usually internalize commitments made voluntarily, publicly, and repeatedly. Cult leaders seem to know this.

COMPLIANCE BREEDS ACCEPTANCE

New converts soon learn that membership is no trivial matter. They are quickly made active members of the team. Behavioral rituals, public recruitment, and fund-raising strengthen the initiates' identities as members. As those in social-psychological experiments come to believe in what they bear witness to (Aronson & Mills, 1959; Gerard & Mathewson, 1966), so cult initiates become committed advocates. The greater the personal commitment, the more the need to justify it.

THE FOOT-IN-THE-DOOR PHENOMENON

How are people induced to make a commitment to such a drastic life change? Seldom by an abrupt, conscious decision. One does not just decide, "I'm through with mainstream religion. I'm gonna find a cult." Nor do cult recruiters approach people on the street with, "Hi. I'm a Moonie. Care to join us?" Rather, the recruitment strategy exploits the foot-in-the-door principle. Unification Church recruiters, for example, would invite people to a dinner and then to a weekend of warm fellowship and discussions of philosophies of life. At the weekend retreat, they would encourage the attenders to join them in songs, activities, and discussion. Potential converts were then urged to sign up for longer training retreats. The pattern in cults is for the activities to become gradually more arduous, culminating in having recruits solicit contributions and attempt to convert others.

Once converts have entered the cult, they find that monetary offerings are at first voluntary, then mandatory. Jim Jones eventually inaugurated a required 10-percent-of-income contribution, which soon increased to 25 percent. Finally, he ordered members to turn over to him everything they owned. Workloads also became progressively more demanding. Former cult member Grace Stoen recalls the gradual progress:

> Nothing was ever done drastically. That's how Jim Jones got away with so much. You slowly gave up things and slowly had to put up with more, but it was always done very gradually. It was amazing, because you would sit up sometimes and say, wow, I really have given up a lot. I really am putting up with a lot. But he did it so slowly that you figured, I've made it this far, what the hell is the difference? (Conway & Siegelman, 1979, p. 236)

Persuasive Elements

We can also analyze cult persuasion using the factors discussed in this chapter (and summarized in Figure 7.9): *Who* (the communicator) said *what* (the message) to *whom* (the audience)?

FIGURE :: 7.9

Variables Known to Affect the Impact of Persuasive Communications

In real life, these variables may interact; the effect of one may depend on the level of another.

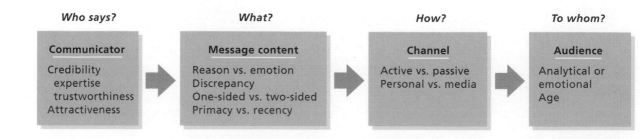

Who says?	*What?*	*How?*	*To whom?*
Communicator	**Message content**	**Channel**	**Audience**
Credibility expertise trustworthiness Attractiveness	Reason vs. emotion Discrepancy One-sided vs. two-sided Primacy vs. recency	Active vs. passive Personal vs. media	Analytical or emotional Age

THE COMMUNICATOR

Successful cults typically have a charismatic leader—someone who attracts and directs the members. As in experiments on persuasion, a credible communicator is someone the audience perceives as expert and trustworthy—for example, as "Father" Moon.

Jim Jones used "psychic readings" to establish his credibility. Newcomers were asked to identify themselves as they entered the church before services. Then one of his aides would quickly call the person's home and say, "Hi. We're doing a survey, and we'd like to ask you some questions." During the service, one ex-member recalled, Jones would call out the person's name and say

> Have you ever seen me before? Well, you live in such and such a place, your phone number is such and such, and in your living room you've got this, that, and the other, and on your sofa you've got such and such a pillow. . . . Now do you remember me ever being in your house? (Conway & Siegelman, 1979, p. 234)

Trust is another aspect of credibility. Cult researcher Margaret Singer (1979) noted that middle-class Caucasian youths are more vulnerable to recruitment because they are more trusting. They lack the "street smarts" of lower-class youths (who know how to resist a hustle) and the wariness of upper-class youths (who have been warned of kidnappers since childhood). Many cult members have been recruited by friends or relatives, people they trust (Stark & Bainbridge, 1980).

THE MESSAGE

The vivid, emotional messages and the warmth and acceptance with which the group showers lonely or depressed people can be strikingly appealing: Trust the master, join the family; we have the answer, the "one way." The message echoes through channels as varied as lectures, small-group discussions, and direct social pressure.

THE AUDIENCE

Recruits are often young people under 25, still at that comparatively open age before attitudes and values stabilize. Some, such as the followers of Jim Jones, are less educated people who like the message's simplicity and find it difficult to counterargue. But most are educated, middle-class people who, taken by the ideals, overlook the contradictions in those who profess selflessness and practice greed, who pretend concern and behave indifferently.

Potential converts are often at turning points in their lives, facing personal crises, or vacationing or living away from home. They have needs; the cult offers them an answer (Lofland & Stark, 1965; Singer, 1979). Gail Maeder joined Heaven's Gate after her T-shirt shop had failed. David Moore joined when he was 19, just out of high school, and searching for direction. Times of social and economic upheaval are especially conducive to someone who can make apparent simple sense out of the confusion (O'Dea, 1968; Sales, 1972).

Most of those who have carried out suicide bombings in the Middle East (and other places such as Bali, Madrid, and London) were, likewise, young men at the transition between adolescence and adult maturity. Like cult recruits, they come under the influence of authoritative, religiously oriented communicators. These compelling voices indoctrinate them into seeing themselves as "living martyrs" whose fleeting moment of self-destruction will be their portal into bliss and heroism. To overcome the will to survive, each candidate makes public commitments—creating a will, writing goodbye letters, making a farewell video—that create a psychological point of no return (Kruglanski & Golec de Zavala, 2005). All of this typically transpires in the relative isolation of small cells, with group influences that fan hatred for the enemy.

Military training creates cohesion and commitment through some of the same tactics used by leaders of new religious movements, fraternities, and therapeutic communities.

"Avoid *'Total Situations'* where you lose contact with your social support and informational networks. Never allow yourself to be cut off emotionally from your familiar and trusted reference groups of family, friends, neighbors, co-workers—do not accept putdowns against them."

—PHILLIP ZIMBARDO AND CINCY X. WANG, "DR. Z'S 20 HINTS ABOUT RESISTING UNWANTED INFLUENCES ON YOU," 2007

Group Effects

Cults also illustrate the next chapter's theme: the power of a group to shape members' views and behavior. The cult typically separates members from their previous social support systems and isolates them with other cult members. There may then occur what Rodney Stark and William Bainbridge (1980) call a "social implosion": External ties weaken until the group collapses inward socially, each person engaging only with other group members. Cut off from families and former friends, they lose access to counterarguments. The group now offers identity and defines reality. Because the cult frowns on or punishes disagreements, the apparent consensus helps eliminate any lingering doubts. Moreover, stress and emotional arousal narrow attention, making people "more susceptible to poorly supported arguments, social pressure, and the temptation to derogate nongroup members" (Baron, 2000).

Marshall Applewhite and Bonnie Nettles at first formed their own group of two, reinforcing each other's aberrant thinking—a phenomenon that psychiatrists call *folie à deux* (French for "insanity of two"). As others joined them, the group's social isolation facilitated peculiar thinking. As Internet conspiracy theory groups illustrate, virtual groups can likewise foster paranoia. Heaven's Gate was skilled in Internet recruiting.

These techniques—increasing behavioral commitments, persuasion, and group isolation—do not, however, have unlimited power. The Unification Church successfully recruited fewer than 1 in 10 people who attended its workshops (Ennis & Verrilli, 1989). Most who joined Heaven's Gate left before that fateful day. David Koresh ruled with a mix of persuasion, intimidation, and violence. As Jim Jones made his demands more extreme, he, too, increasingly had to control people with intimidation. He used threats of harm to those who fled the community, beatings for noncompliance, and drugs to neutralize disagreeable members. By the end, he was as much an arm twister as a mind bender.

Some of these cult influence techniques bear similarities to techniques used by more benign, widely accepted groups. Buddhist and Catholic monasteries, for example, have cloistered adherents with kindred spirits. Fraternity and sorority members have reported that the initial "love bombing" of potential cult recruits is not unlike their own "rush" period. Members lavish prospective pledges with attention and make them feel special. During the pledge period, new members are somewhat isolated, cut off from old friends who did not pledge. They spend time studying the history and rules of their new group. They suffer and commit time on its behalf. They are expected to comply with all its demands. The result is usually a committed new member.

Much the same is true of some therapeutic communities for recovering drug and alcohol abusers. Zealous self-help groups form a cohesive "social cocoon," have intense beliefs, and exert a profound influence on members' behavior (Galanter, 1989, 1990).

Another constructive use of persuasion is in counseling and psychotherapy, which social-counseling psychologist Stanley Strong views "as a branch of applied social psychology" (1978, p. 101). Like Strong, psychiatrist Jerome Frank (1974, 1982) recognized years ago that it takes persuasion to change self-defeating attitudes and behaviors. Frank noted that the psychotherapy setting, like cults and zealous self-help groups, provides (1) a supportive, confiding social relationship, (2) an offer of expertise and hope, (3) a special rationale or myth that explains one's difficulties and offers a new perspective, and (4) a set of rituals and learning experiences that promises a new sense of peace and happiness.

I choose the examples of fraternities, sororities, self-help groups, and psychotherapy not to disparage them but to illustrate two concluding observations. First, if we attribute new religious movements to the leader's mystical force or to the followers' peculiar weaknesses, we may delude ourselves into thinking we are immune to social control techniques. In truth, our own groups—and countless political leaders, educators, and other persuaders—successfully use many of these same tactics on us. Between education and indoctrination, enlightenment and propaganda, conversion and coercion, therapy and mind control, there is but a blurry line.

Second, the fact that Jim Jones and other cult leaders abused the power of persuasion does not mean persuasion is intrinsically bad. Nuclear power enables us to light up homes or wipe out cities. Sexual power enables us to express and celebrate committed love or exploit people for selfish gratification. Similarly, persuasive power enables us to enlighten or deceive, to promote health or to sell addictive drugs, to advance peace or stir up hatred. Knowing that these powers can be harnessed for evil purposes should alert us, as scientists and citizens, to guard against their immoral use. But the powers themselves are neither inherently evil nor inherently good; it is how we use them that determines whether their effect is destructive or constructive. Condemning persuasion because of deceit is like condemning eating because of gluttony.

Summing Up: Extreme Persuasion: How Do Cults Indoctrinate?

The successes of religious cults provide an opportunity to see powerful persuasion processes at work. It appears that their success has resulted from three general techniques:

- Eliciting behavioral commitments (as described in Chapter 4)
- Applying principles of effective persuasion (this chapter)
- Isolating members in like-minded groups (to be discussed in Chapter 8)

How Can Persuasion Be Resisted?

Having perused the "weapons of influence," we consider some tactics for resisting influence. How might we prepare people to resist unwanted persuasion?

Martial arts trainers devote as much time teaching defensive blocks, deflections, and parries as they do teaching attack. "On the social influence battlefield," note Brad Sagarin and his colleagues (2002), researchers have focused more on persuasive attack than on defense. Being persuaded comes naturally, Daniel Gilbert and his colleagues (1990, 1993) report. It is easier to accept persuasive messages than to doubt them. To *understand* an assertion (say, that lead pencils are a health hazard) is to *believe* it—at least temporarily, until one actively undoes the initial, automatic acceptance. If a distracting event prevents the undoing, the acceptance lingers.

Still, blessed with logic, information, and motivation, we do resist falsehoods. If the credible-seeming repair person's uniform and the doctor's title have intimidated us into unthinking agreement, we can rethink our habitual responses to authority. We can seek more information before committing time or money. We can question what we don't understand.

Strengthening Personal Commitment

Chapter 6 presented another way to resist: Before encountering others' judgments, make a public commitment to your position. Having stood up for your convictions, you will become less susceptible (or, should we say, less "open") to what others have to say. In mock civil trials, straw polls of jurors can foster a hardening of expressed positions, leading to more deadlocks (Davis & others, 1993).

CHALLENGING BELIEFS

How might we stimulate people to commit themselves? From his experiments, Charles Kiesler (1971) offered one possible way: Mildly attack their position. Kiesler found that when committed people were attacked strongly enough to cause them to react, but not so strongly as to overwhelm them, they became even more committed. Kiesler explained: "When you attack committed people and your attack is of inadequate strength, you drive them to even more extreme behaviors in defense of their previous commitment" (p. 88). Perhaps you can recall that happening in an argument, as those involved escalated their rhetoric, committing themselves to increasingly extreme positions.

DEVELOPING COUNTERARGUMENTS

There is a second reason a mild attack might build resistance. Like inoculations against disease, even weak arguments will prompt counterarguments, which are then available for a stronger attack. William McGuire (1964) documented this in a series of experiments. McGuire wondered: Could we inoculate people against persuasion much as we inoculate them against a virus? Is there such a thing as **attitude inoculation**? Could we take people raised in a "germ-free ideological environment"—people who hold some unquestioned belief—and stimulate their mental defenses? And would subjecting them to a small dose of belief-threatening material inoculate them against later persuasion?

attitude inoculation
Exposing people to weak attacks upon their attitudes so that when stronger attacks come, they will have refutations available.

That is what McGuire did. First, he found some cultural truisms, such as "It's a good idea to brush your teeth after every meal if at all possible." He then showed that people were vulnerable to a powerful, credible assault upon those truisms (for example, prestigious authorities were said to have discovered that too much toothbrushing can damage one's gums). If, however, before having their belief attacked, they were "immunized" by first receiving a small challenge to their belief, *and* if they read or wrote an essay in refutation of this mild attack, then they were better able to resist the powerful attack.

Remember that effective inoculation stimulates but does not overwhelm our defenses. Follow-up experiments show that when people resist but feel they've done so poorly—with weak counterarguments—their attitudes weaken and they become more vulnerable to a follow-up appeal (Tormala & others, 2006). Resisting persuasion also drains energy from our self-control system. Thus, soon after resisting, or while weakened by tiredness or other self-control efforts such as dieting, we may become worn down and more susceptible to persuasion (Burkley, 2008).

THE inside STORY

I confess to having felt like Mr. Clean when doing this immunization work because I was studying how to help people resist being manipulated. Then, after our research was published, an advertising executive called and said, "Very interesting, Professor: I was delighted to read about it." Somewhat righteously, I replied, "Very nice of you to say that Mr. Executive, but I'm really on the other side. You're trying to persuade people, and I'm trying to make them more resistant." "Oh, don't underrate yourself, Professor," he said. "We can use what you're doing to diminish the effect of our competitors' ads." And sure enough, it has become almost standard for advertisers to mention other brands and deflate their claims.

William McGuire (1925–2007)
Yale University

A "poison parasite" ad.

Robert Cialdini and his colleagues (2003) agree that appropriate counterarguments are a great way to resist persuasion. But they wondered how to bring them to mind in response to an opponent's ads. The answer, they suggest, is a "poison parasite" defense—one that combines a poison (strong counterarguments) with a parasite (retrieval cues that bring those arguments to mind when seeing the opponent's ads). In their studies, participants who viewed a familiar political ad were least persuaded by it when they had earlier seen counterarguments overlaid on a replica of the ad. Seeing the ad again thus also brought to mind the puncturing counterarguments. Antismoking ads have effectively done this, for example, by re-creating a "Marlboro Man" commercial set in the rugged outdoors but now showing a coughing, decrepit cowboy.

Real-Life Applications: Inoculation Programs

Could attitude inoculation work outside the laboratory by preparing people to resist unwanted persuasion? Applied research on smoking prevention and consumer education offers encouraging answers.

INOCULATING CHILDREN AGAINST PEER PRESSURE TO SMOKE

In a demonstration of how laboratory research findings can lead to practical applications, a research team led by Alfred McAlister (1980) had high school students "inoculate" seventh-graders against peer pressures to smoke. The seventh-graders

FIGURE :: 7.10

The percentage of cigarette smokers at an "inoculated" junior high school was much less than at a matched control school using a more typical smoking education program.

Source: Data from McAlister & others, 1980; Telch & others, 1981.

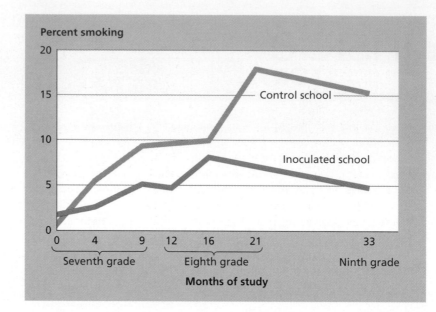

were taught to respond to advertisements implying that liberated women smoke by saying, "She's not really liberated if she is hooked on tobacco." They also acted in role plays in which, after being called "chicken" for not taking a cigarette, they answered with statements such as "I'd be a real chicken if I smoked just to impress you." After several of these sessions during the seventh and eighth grades, the inoculated students were half as likely to begin smoking as were uninoculated students at another junior high school that had an identical parental smoking rate (Figure 7.10).

Other research teams have confirmed that inoculation procedures, sometimes supplemented by other life skill training, reduce teen smoking (Botvin & others, 1995, 2008; Evans & others, 1984; Flay & others, 1985). Most newer efforts emphasize strategies for resisting social pressure. One study exposed sixth- to eighth-graders to antismoking films or to information about smoking, together with role plays of student-generated ways of refusing a cigarette (Hirschman & Leventhal, 1989). A year and a half later, 31 percent of those who watched the antismoking films had taken up smoking. Among those who role-played refusing, only 19 percent had begun smoking.

Antismoking and drug education programs apply other persuasion principles, too. They use attractive peers to communicate information. They trigger the students' own cognitive processing ("Here's something you might want to think about"). They get the students to make a public commitment (by making a rational decision about smoking and then announcing it, along with their reasoning, to their classmates). Some of these smoking-prevention programs require only two to six hours of class, using prepared printed materials or videotapes. Today any school district or teacher wishing to use the social-psychological approach to smoking prevention can do so easily, inexpensively, and with the hope of significant reductions in future smoking rates and associated health costs.

INOCULATING CHILDREN AGAINST THE INFLUENCE OF ADVERTISING

"In general, my children refuse to eat anything that hasn't danced on television."

—*ERMA BOMBECK*

Belgium, Denmark, Greece, Ireland, Italy, and Sweden all restrict advertising that targets children (McGuire, 2002). In the United States, notes Robert Levine in *The Power of Persuasion: How We're Bought and Sold,* the average child sees over 10,000 commercials a year. "Two decades ago," he notes, "children drank twice as much milk as soda. Thanks to advertising, the ratio is now reversed" (2003, p. 16).

Smokers often develop an "initial brand choice" in their teens, said a 1981 report from researchers at Philip Morris (FTC, 2003). "Today's teenager is tomorrow's potential regular customer, and the overwhelming majority of smokers first begin

Children are the advertiser's dream. Researchers have therefore studied ways to inoculate children against the more than 10,000 ads they see each year, many as they are glued to a TV set.

to smoke while still in their teens" (Lichtblau, 2003). That explains why some cigarette and smokeless tobacco companies aggressively market to college and university students, by advertising, by sponsoring parties, and by offering free cigarettes (usually in situations where students are also drinking), all as part of their marketing of nicotine to "entry level" smokers (Farrell, 2005).

Hoping to restrain advertising's influence, researchers have studied how to immunize young children against the effects of television commercials. Their research was prompted partly by studies showing that children, especially those under age 8, (1) have trouble distinguishing commercials from programs and fail to grasp their persuasive intent, (2) trust television advertising rather indiscriminately, and (3) desire and badger their parents for advertised products (Adler & others, 1980; Feshbach, 1980; Palmer & Dorr, 1980). Children, it seems, are an advertiser's dream: gullible, vulnerable, and an easy sell.

Armed with these findings, citizens' groups have given the advertisers of such products a chewing out (Moody, 1980): "When a sophisticated advertiser spends millions to sell unsophisticated, trusting children an unhealthy product, this can only be called exploitation." In "Mothers' Statement to Advertisers" (Motherhood Project, 2001), a broad coalition of women echoed this outrage:

> For us, our children are priceless gifts. For you, our children are customers, and childhood is a "market segment" to be exploited. . . . The line between meeting and creating consumer needs and desire is increasingly being crossed, as your battery of highly trained and creative experts study, analyze, persuade, and manipulate our children. . . . The driving messages are "You deserve a break today," "Have it your way," "Follow your instincts. Obey your thirst," "Just Do It," "No Boundaries," "Got the Urge?" These [exemplify] the dominant message of advertising and marketing: that life is about selfishness, instant gratification, and materialism.

On the other side are the commercial interests. They claim that ads allow parents to teach their children consumer skills and, more important, finance children's television programs. In the United States, the Federal Trade Commission has been in the middle, pushed by research findings and political pressures while trying to decide whether to place new constraints on TV ads for unhealthy foods and for R-rated movies aimed at underage youth.

Meanwhile, researchers have found that inner-city seventh-graders who are able to think critically about ads—who have "media resistance skills"—also better resist peer pressure as eighth-graders and are less likely to drink alcohol as ninth-graders (Epstein & Botvin, 2008). Researchers have also wondered whether children can

"When it comes to targeting kid consumers, we at General Mills follow the Procter and Gamble model of 'cradle to grave.'. . . We believe in getting them early and having them for life."

—*WAYNE CHILICKI, GENERAL MILLS (QUOTED BY MOTHERHOOD PROJECT, 2001)*

be taught to resist deceptive ads. In one such effort, a team of investigators led by Norma Feshbach (1980; Cohen, 1980) gave small groups of Los Angeles–area elementary school children three half-hour lessons in analyzing commercials. The children were inoculated by viewing ads and discussing them. For example, after viewing a toy ad, they were immediately given the toy and challenged to make it do what they had just seen in the commercial. Such experiences helped breed a more realistic understanding of commercials.

Consumer advocates worry that inoculation may be insufficient. Better to clean the air than to wear gas masks. It is no surprise, then, that parents resent it when advertisers market products to children, then place them on lower store shelves where kids will see them, pick them up, and nag and whine until sometimes wearing the parent down. For that reason, urges the "Mothers' Code for Advertisers," there should be no advertising in schools, no targeting children under 8, no product placements in movies and programs targeting children and adolescents, and no ads directed at children and adolescents "that promote an ethic of selfishness and a focus on instant gratification" (Motherhood Project, 2001).

Implications of Attitude Inoculation

The best way to build resistance to brainwashing probably is not just stronger indoctrination into one's current beliefs. If parents are worried that their children might become members of a cult, they might better teach their children about the various cults and prepare them to counter persuasive appeals.

For the same reason, religious educators should be wary of creating a "germ-free ideological environment" in their churches and schools. People who live amid diverse views become more discerning and more likely to modify their views in response to strong but not weak arguments (Levitan & Visser, 2008). Also, a challenge to one's views, if refuted, is more likely to solidify one's position than to undermine it, particularly if the threatening material can be examined with like-minded others (Visser & Mirabile, 2004). Cults apply this principle by forewarning members of how families and friends will attack the cult's beliefs. When the expected challenge comes, the member is armed with counterarguments.

Another implication is that, for the persuader, an ineffective appeal can be worse than none. Can you see why? Those who reject an appeal are inoculated against further appeals. Consider an experiment in which Susan Darley and Joel Cooper (1972) invited students to write essays advocating a strict dress code. Because that was against the students' own positions and the essays were to be published, all chose *not* to write the essay—even those offered money to do so. After turning down the money, they became even more extreme and confident in their anti–dress code opinions. Those who have rejected initial appeals to quit smoking may likewise become immune to further appeals. Ineffective persuasion, by stimulating the listener's defenses, may be counterproductive. It may "harden the heart" against later appeals.

Summing Up: How Can Persuasion Be Resisted?

- How do people resist persuasion? A *prior public commitment* to one's own position, stimulated perhaps by a mild attack on the position, breeds resistance to later persuasion.

- A mild attack can also serve as an *inoculation*, stimulating one to develop counterarguments that will then be available if and when a strong attack comes.

- This implies, paradoxically, that one way to strengthen existing attitudes is to challenge them, though the challenge must not be so strong as to overwhelm them.

POSTSCRIPT: Being Open but Not Naive

As recipients of persuasion, our human task is to live in the land between gullibility and cynicism. Some people say that being persuadable is a weakness. "Think for yourself," we are urged. But is being closed to informational influence a virtue, or is it the mark of a fanatic? How can we live with humility and openness to others and yet be critical consumers of persuasive appeals?

To be open, we can assume that every person we meet is, in some ways, our superior. Each person I encounter has some expertise that exceeds my own and thus has something to teach me. As we connect, I hope to learn from this person and perhaps to reciprocate by sharing my knowledge.

To be critical thinkers, we might take a cue from inoculation research. Do you want to build your resistance to false messages without becoming closed to valid messages? Be an active listener. Force yourself to counterargue. Don't just listen; react. After hearing a political speech, discuss it with others. If the message cannot withstand careful analysis, so much the worse for it. If it can, its effect on you will be that much more enduring.

Making the Social Connection

This chapter highlights Richard Petty's ideas about persuasion through his theory and research. We also reported Petty's ideas about dissonance in Chapter 4, Behavior and Attitudes. Go to the Online Learning Center to view Richard Petty on the central and peripheral routes to persuasion.

Group Influence

"Never doubt that a small group of thoughtful, committed citizens can change the world."

—Anthropologist Margaret Mead

Tawna is nearing the end of her daily run. Her mind prods her to keep going; her body begs her to walk the remaining six blocks. She compromises and does a slow jog home. The next day conditions are identical, except that two friends run with her. Tawna runs her route two minutes faster. She wonders, "Did I run better merely because Gail and Sonja went along? Would I always run better if in a group?"

At almost every turn, we are involved in groups. Our world contains not only 6.8 billion individuals, but 193 nation-states, 4 million local communities, 20 million economic organizations, and hundreds of millions of other formal and informal groups—couples having dinner, housemates hanging out, soldiers plotting strategy. How do such groups influence individuals?

Group interactions often have dramatic effects. Intellectual college students hang out with other intellectuals, and they strengthen one another's intellectual interests. Deviant youth hang out with other deviant youth, amplifying one another's antisocial tendencies. But *how* do these groups affect attitudes? And what influences lead groups to make smart and dumb decisions?

Individuals also influence their groups. As the 1957 classic film *12 Angry Men* opens, 12 wary murder trial jurors file into the jury room. It is a hot day. The tired jurors are close to agreement and eager for a quick verdict convicting a teenage boy of knifing his father. But one maverick, played by Henry Fonda, refuses to vote guilty. As the heated deliberation proceeds, the jurors one by one change their minds until they reach a unanimous verdict: "Not guilty." In real trials, a lone individual seldom sways the entire group. Yet history is made by minorities that sway majorities. What helps make a minority—or a leader—persuasive?

We will examine these intriguing phenomena of group influence one at a time. But first things first: What is a group and why do groups exist?

What Is a Group?

The answer to this question seems self-evident—until several people compare their definitions. Are jogging partners a group? Are airplane passengers a group? Is a group a set of people who identify with one another, who sense they belong together? Is a group those who share common goals and rely on one another? Does a group form when individuals become organized? when their relationships with one another continue over time? These are among the social psychological definitions of a group (McGrath, 1984).

group
Two or more people who, for longer than a few moments, interact with and influence one another and perceive one another as "us."

Group dynamics expert Marvin Shaw (1981) argued that all groups have one thing in common: Their members interact. Therefore, he defines a **group** as two or more people who interact and influence one another. Moreover, notes Australian National University social psychologist John Turner (1987), groups perceive themselves as "us" in contrast to "them." A pair of jogging companions, then, would indeed constitute a group. Different groups help us meet different human needs—to *affiliate* (to belong to and connect with others), to *achieve*, and to gain a social *identity* (Johnson & others, 2006).

By Shaw's definition, students working individually in a computer room would not be a group. Although physically together, they are more a collection of individuals than an interacting group (though each may be part of a group with dispersed others in an online chat room). The distinction between collections of unrelated individuals in a computer lab and the more influential group behavior among interacting individuals sometimes blurs. People who are merely in one another's presence do sometimes influence one another. At a football game, they may perceive themselves as "us" fans in contrast with "them" who root for the other team.

In this chapter we consider three examples of such collective influence: *social facilitation, social loafing,* and *deindividuation.* These three phenomena can occur with minimal interaction (in what we call "minimal group situations"). Then we consider three examples of social influence in interacting groups: *group polarization, groupthink,* and *minority influence.*

Summing Up: What Is a Group?

- A group exists when two or more people interact for more than a few moments, affect one another in some way, and think of themselves as "us."

Social Facilitation: How Are We Affected by the Presence of Others?

Let's explore social psychology's most elementary question: Are we affected by the mere presence of another person? "Mere presence" means people are not competing, do not reward or punish, and in fact do nothing except be present as a passive *audience or as **co-actors**. Would the mere presence of others affect a person's jogging, eating, typing, or exam performance? The search for the answer is a scientific mystery story.*

co-actors
Co-participants working individually on a noncompetitive activity.

The Mere Presence of Others

More than a century ago, Norman Triplett (1898), a psychologist interested in bicycle racing, noticed that cyclists' times were faster when they raced together than when each one raced alone against the clock. Before he peddled his hunch (that others' presence boosts performance), Triplett conducted one of social psychology's first laboratory experiments. Children told to wind string on a fishing reel as rapidly as possible wound faster when they worked with co-actors than when they worked alone.

Ensuing experiments found that others' presence improves the speed with which people do simple multiplication problems and cross out designated letters. It also improves the accuracy with which people perform simple motor tasks, such as keeping a metal stick in contact with a dime-sized disk on a moving turntable (F. H. Allport, 1920; Dashiell, 1930; Travis, 1925). This **social facilitation** effect also occurs with animals. In the presence of others of their species, ants excavate more sand, chickens eat more grain, and sexually active rat pairs mate more often (Bayer, 1929; Chen, 1937; Larsson, 1956).

social facilitation
(1) Original meaning: the tendency of people to perform simple or well-learned tasks better when others are present. (2) Current meaning: the strengthening of dominant (prevalent, likely) responses in the presence of others.

But wait: Other studies revealed that on some tasks the presence of others *hinders* performance. In the presence of others, cockroaches, parakeets, and green finches learn mazes more slowly (Allee & Masure, 1936; Gates & Allee, 1933; Klopfer, 1958). This disruptive effect also occurs with people. Others' presence diminishes efficiency at learning nonsense syllables, completing a maze, and performing complex multiplication problems (Dashiell, 1930; Pessin, 1933; Pessin & Husband, 1933).

Saying that the presence of others sometimes facilitates performance and sometimes hinders it is about as satisfying as the typical Scottish weather forecast—predicting that it might be sunny but then again it might rain. By 1940 research activity in this area had ground to a halt, and it lay dormant for 25 years until awakened by the touch of a new idea.

Social psychologist Robert Zajonc (pronounced *Zy-ence*, rhymes with *science*) wondered whether these seemingly contradictory findings could be reconciled. As often happens at creative moments in science, Zajonc (1965) used one field of research to illuminate another. The illumination came from a well-established principle in experimental psychology: Arousal enhances whatever response tendency is dominant. Increased arousal enhances performance on easy tasks for which the most likely—"dominant"—response is correct. People solve easy anagrams, such as *akec*, fastest when they are aroused. On complex tasks, for which the correct answer is not dominant, increased arousal promotes *incorrect* responding. On harder anagrams, such as *theloacco*, people do worse when anxious.

Could this principle solve the mystery of social facilitation? It seemed reasonable to assume that others' presence will arouse or energize people (Mullen & others, 1997); most of us can recall feeling tense or excited in front of an audience. If social arousal facilitates dominant responses, it should *boost performance on easy tasks* and *hurt performance on difficult tasks*.

Social facilitation: Do you ride faster when bicycling with others?

FIGURE :: 8.1

The Effects of Social Arousal

Robert Zajonc reconciled apparently conflicting findings by proposing that arousal from others' presence strengthens dominant responses (the correct responses only on easy or well-learned tasks).

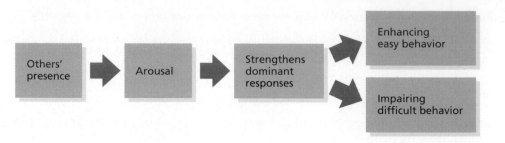

"Mere social contact begets . . . a stimulation of the animal spirits that heightens the efficiency of each individual workman."

—*KARL MARX, DAS KAPITAL, 1867*

"Discovery consists of seeing what everybody has seen and thinking what nobody had thought."

—*ALBERT VON SZENT-GYÖRGYI, THE SCIENTIST SPECULATES, 1962*

With that explanation, the confusing results made sense. Winding fishing reels, doing simple multiplication problems, and eating were all easy tasks for which the responses were well learned or naturally dominant. Sure enough, having others around boosted performance. Learning new material, doing a maze, and solving complex math problems were more difficult tasks for which the correct responses were initially less probable. In these cases, the presence of others increased the number of *incorrect* responses on these tasks. The same general rule—*arousal facilitates dominant responses*—worked in both cases (Figure 8.1). Suddenly, what had looked like contradictory results no longer seemed contradictory.

Zajonc's solution, so simple and elegant, left other social psychologists thinking what Thomas H. Huxley thought after first reading Darwin's *On the Origin of Species:* "How extremely stupid not to have thought of that!" It seemed obvious—once Zajonc had pointed it out. Perhaps, however, the pieces fit so neatly only through the spectacles of hindsight. Would the solution survive direct experimental tests?

After almost 300 studies, conducted with the help of more than 25,000 volunteers, the solution has survived (Bond & Titus, 1983; Guerin, 1993, 1999). Social arousal facilitates dominant responses, whether right or wrong. For example, Peter Hunt and Joseph Hillery (1973) found that in others' presence, students took less time to learn a simple maze and more time to learn a complex one (just as the cockroaches do!). And James Michaels and his collaborators (1982) found that good pool players in a student union (who had made 71 percent of their shots while being unobtrusively observed) did even better (80 percent) when four observers came up to watch them play. Poor shooters (who had previously averaged 36 percent) did even worse (25 percent) when closely observed.

Athletes, actors, and musicians perform well-practiced skills, which helps explain why they often perform best when energized by the responses of a supportive audience. Studies of more than 80,000 college and professional athletic events in Canada, the United States, and England reveal that home teams win about 6 in 10 games (somewhat fewer for baseball and football, somewhat more for basketball and soccer, but consistently more than half [Table 8.1]). The home advantage may, however, also stem from the players' familiarity with their home environment, less travel fatigue, feelings of dominance derived from territorial control, or increased team identity when cheered by fans (Zillmann & Paulus, 1993).

Crowding: The Presence of Many Others

So people do respond to others' presence. But does the presence of observers always arouse people? In times of stress, a comrade can be comforting. Nevertheless, with others present, people perspire more, breathe faster, tense their muscles more, and have higher blood pressure and a faster heart rate (Geen & Gange, 1983; Moore & Baron, 1983). Even a supportive audience may elicit poorer performance on challenging tasks (Butler & Baumeister, 1998). Having your entire extended family attend your first piano recital probably won't boost your performance.

TABLE :: 8.1 Home Advantage in Major Team Sports

Sport	Games Studied	Percentage of Home Games Won
Baseball	135,665	54.3
Football	2,592	57.3
Ice hockey	4,322	61.1
Basketball	13,596	64.4
Soccer	37,202	69.0

The effect of others' presence increases with their number (Jackson & Latané, 1981; Knowles, 1983). Sometimes the arousal and self-conscious attention created by a large audience interferes even with well-learned, automatic behaviors, such as speaking. Given *extreme* pressure, we're vulnerable to "choking." Stutterers tend to stutter more in front of larger audiences than when speaking to just one or two people (Mullen, 1986).

Being *in* a crowd also intensifies positive or negative reactions. When they sit close together, friendly people are liked even more, and *unfriendly* people are *disliked* even more (Schiffenbauer & Schiavo, 1976; Storms & Thomas, 1977). In experiments with Columbia University students and with Ontario Science Center visitors, Jonathan Freedman and his co-workers (1979, 1980) had an accomplice listen to a humorous tape or watch a movie with other participants. When they all sat close together, the accomplice could more readily induce the individuals to laugh and clap. As theater directors and sports fans know, and as researchers have confirmed, a "good house" is a full house (Aiello & others, 1983; Worchel & Brown, 1984)

Perhaps you've noticed that a class of 35 students feels more warm and lively in a room that seats just 35 than when spread around a room that seats 100. When others are close by, we are more likely to notice and join in their laughter or clapping. But crowding also enhances arousal, as Gary Evans (1979) found. He tested 10-person groups of University of Massachusetts students, either in a room 20 by 30 feet or in one 8 by 12 feet. Compared with those in the large room, those densely packed had higher pulse rates and blood pressure (indicating arousal). On difficult tasks they made more errors, an effect of crowding replicated by Dinesh Nagar and Janak Pandey (1987) with university students in India. Crowding, then, has a similar effect to being observed by a crowd: it enhances arousal, which facilitates dominant responses.

Heightened arousal in crowded homes also tends to increase stress. Crowding produces less distress in homes divided into many spaces, however, enabling people to withdraw in privacy (Evans & others, 1996, 2000).

Why Are We Aroused in the Presence of Others?

What you do well, you will be energized to do best in front of others (unless you become hyperaroused and self-conscious). What you find difficult may seem impossible in the same circumstances. What is it about other people that creates arousal? Evidence supports three possible factors (Aiello & Douthitt, 2001; Feinberg & Aiello, 2006): evaluation apprehension, distraction, and mere presence.

A good house is a full house, as James Maas's Cornell University introductory psychology students experienced in this 2,000-seat auditorium. If the class had 100 students meeting in this large space, it would feel much less energized.

EVALUATION APPREHENSION

**evaluation
apprehension**
Concern for how others are
evaluating us.

Nickolas Cottrell surmised that observers make us apprehensive because we wonder how they are evaluating us. To test whether **evaluation apprehension** exists, Cottrell and his associates (1968) blindfolded observers, supposedly in preparation for a perception experiment. In contrast to the effect of the watching audience, the mere presence of these blindfolded people did *not* boost well-practiced responses.

Other experiments confirmed Cottrell's conclusion: The enhancement of dominant responses is strongest when people think they are being evaluated. In one experiment, individuals running on a University of California at Santa Barbara jogging path sped up as they came upon a woman seated on the grass—*if* she was facing them rather than sitting with her back turned (Worringham & Messick, 1983).

Evaluation apprehension also helps explain

- why people perform best when their co-actor is slightly superior (Seta, 1982).
- why arousal lessens when a high-status group is diluted by adding people whose opinions don't matter to us (Seta & Seta, 1992).
- why people who worry most about what others think are the ones most affected by their presence (Gastorf & others, 1980; Geen & Gange, 1983).
- why social facilitation effects are greatest when the others are unfamiliar and hard to keep an eye on (Guerin & Innes, 1982).

The self-consciousness we feel when being evaluated can also interfere with behaviors that we perform best automatically (Mullen & Baumeister, 1987). If self-conscious basketball players analyze their body movements while shooting critical free throws, they are more likely to miss.

DRIVEN BY DISTRACTION

Glenn Sanders, Robert Baron, and Danny Moore (1978; Baron, 1986) carried evaluation apprehension a step further. They theorized that when we wonder how co-actors are doing or how an audience is reacting, we become distracted. This *conflict* between paying attention to others and paying attention to the task overloads our cognitive system, causing arousal. We are "driven by distraction." This arousal comes not just from the presence of another person but even from a nonhuman distraction, such as bursts of light (Sanders, 1981a, 1981b).

MERE PRESENCE

Zajonc, however, believes that the mere presence of others produces some arousal even without evaluation apprehension or arousing distraction. Recall that facilitation effects also occur with nonhuman animals. This hints at an innate social arousal mechanism common to much of the zoological world. (Animals probably are not consciously worrying about how other animals are evaluating them.) At the human level, most runners are energized when running with someone else, even one who neither competes nor evaluates.

This is a good time to remind ourselves that a good theory is a scientific shorthand: It simplifies and summarizes a variety of observations. Social facilitation theory does this well. It is a simple summary of many research findings. A good theory also offers clear predictions that (1) help confirm or modify the theory, (2) guide new exploration, and (3) suggest practical applications. Social facilitation theory has definitely generated the first two types of prediction: (1) The basics of the theory (that the presence of others is arousing and that this social arousal enhances dominant responses) have been confirmed, and (2) the theory has brought new life to a long-dormant field of research.

Are there (3) some practical applications? We can make some educated guesses. As Figure 8.2 shows, many new office buildings have replaced private offices with

FIGURE :: 8.2

In the "open-office plan," people work in the presence of others. How might this affect worker efficiency?

Source: Photo courtesy of Herman Miller Inc.

large, open areas divided by low partitions. Might the resulting awareness of others' presence help boost the performance of well-learned tasks but disrupt creative thinking on complex tasks? Can you think of other possible applications?

Summing Up: Social Facilitation: How Are We Affected by the Presence of Others?

- Social psychology's most elementary issue concerns the mere presence of others. Some early experiments on this question found that performance improved with observers or co-actors present. Others found that the presence of others can hurt performance. Robert Zajonc reconciled those findings by applying a well-known principle from experimental psychology: Arousal facilitates dominant responses. Because the presence of others is arousing, the presence of observers or co-actors boosts performance on easy tasks (for which the correct response is dominant) and hinders performance on difficult tasks (for which incorrect responses are dominant).

- Being in a crowd, or in crowded conditions, is similarly arousing and facilitates dominant responses.

- But why are we aroused by others' presence? Experiments suggest that the arousal stems partly from evaluation apprehension and partly from distraction—a conflict between paying attention to others and concentrating on the task. Other experiments, including some with animals, suggest that the presence of others can be arousing even when we are not evaluated or distracted.

Social Loafing: Do Individuals Exert Less Effort in a Group?

In a team tug-of-war, will eight people on a side exert as much force as the sum of their best efforts in individual tugs-of-war? If not, why not? What level of individual effort can we expect from members of work groups?

The Rope-Pulling
Apparatus

People in the first position pulled
less hard when they thought
people behind them were also
pulling.

Source: Data from Ingham,
Levinger, Graves, & Peckham,
1974. Photo by Alan G. Ingham.

Social facilitation usually occurs when people work toward individual goals
and when their efforts, whether winding fishing reels or solving math problems,
can be individually evaluated. These situations parallel some everyday work situations, but not those in which people pool their efforts toward a *common* goal and
where individuals are *not* accountable for their efforts. A team tug-of-war provides
one such example. Organizational fund-raising—pooling candy sale proceeds to
pay for the class trip—provides another. So does a class group project on which all
students get the same grade. On such "additive tasks"—tasks where the group's
achievement depends on the sum of the individual efforts—will team spirit boost
productivity? Will bricklayers lay bricks faster when working as a team than when
working alone? One way to attack such questions is with laboratory simulations.

Many Hands Make Light Work

Nearly a century ago, French engineer Max Ringelmann (reported by Kravitz &
Martin, 1986) found that the collective effort of tug-of-war teams was but half the
sum of the individual efforts. Contrary to the presumption that "in unity there is
strength," this suggested that group members may actually be *less* motivated when
performing additive tasks. Maybe, though, poor performance stemmed from poor
coordination—people pulling a rope in slightly different directions at slightly different times. A group of Massachusetts researchers led by Alan Ingham (1974) cleverly eliminated that problem by making individuals think others were pulling with
them, when in fact they were pulling alone. Blindfolded participants were assigned
the first position in the apparatus shown in Figure 8.3 and told, "Pull as hard as you
can." They pulled 18 percent harder when they knew they were pulling alone than
when they believed that behind them two to five people were also pulling.

Researchers Bibb Latané, Kipling Williams, and Stephen Harkins (1979; Harkins
& others, 1980) kept their ears open for other ways to investigate this phenomenon,
which they labeled **social loafing.** They observed that the noise produced by six
people shouting or clapping "as loud as you can" was less than three times that
produced by one person alone. Like the tug-of-war task, however, noisemaking is
vulnerable to group inefficiency. So Latané and his associates followed Ingham's
example by leading their Ohio State University participants to believe others were
shouting or clapping with them, when in fact they were doing so alone.

Their method was to blindfold six people, seat them in a semicircle, and have
them put on headphones, over which they were blasted with the sound of people
shouting or clapping. People could not hear their own shouting or clapping, much
less that of others. On various trials they were instructed to shout or clap either

social loafing

The tendency for people to
exert less effort when they
pool their efforts toward a
common goal than when they
are individually accountable.

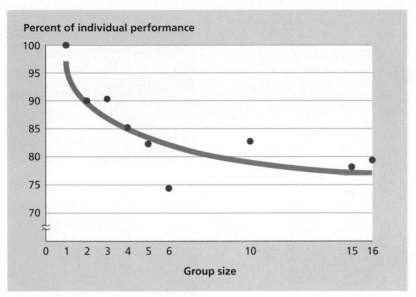

FIGURE :: 8.4

Effort Decreases as
Group Size Increases

A statistical digest of 49 studies,
involving more than 4,000 participants, revealed that effort
decreases (loafing increases)
as the size of the group
increases. Each dot represents
the aggregate data from one
of these studies.

Source: From K. D. Williams,
J. M. Jackson, & S. J. Karau, in
*Social Dilemmas: Perspectives
on Individuals and Groups,* edited
by D. A. Schroeder. Copyright ©
1992 by Praeger Publishers.
Reprinted with permission of
Greenwood Publishing Group,
Inc., Westport, CT.

alone or along with the group. People who were told about this experiment guessed the participants would shout louder when with others, because they would be less inhibited (Harkins, 1981). The actual result? Social loafing: When the participants believed five others were also either shouting or clapping, they produced one-third less noise than when they thought themselves alone. Social loafing occurred even when the participants were high school cheerleaders who believed themselves to be cheering together rather than alone (Hardy & Latané, 1986).

Curiously, those who clapped both alone and in groups did not view themselves as loafing; they perceived themselves as clapping equally in both situations. This parallels what happens when students work on group projects for a shared grade. Williams reports that all agree loafing occurs—but no one admits to doing the loafing.

John Sweeney (1973), a political scientist interested in the policy implications of social loafing, observed the phenomenon in an experiment at the University of Texas. Students pumped exercise bicycles more energetically (as measured by electrical output) when they knew they were being individually monitored than when they thought their output was being pooled with that of other riders. In the group condition, people were tempted to **free-ride** on the group effort.

In this and 160 other studies (Karau & Williams, 1993, and Figure 8.4), we see a twist on one of the psychological forces that makes for social facilitation: evaluation apprehension. In the social loafing experiments, individuals believed they were evaluated only when they acted alone. The group situation (rope pulling, shouting, and so forth) *decreased* evaluation apprehension. When people are not accountable and cannot evaluate their own efforts, responsibility is diffused across all group members (Harkins & Jackson, 1985; Kerr & Bruun, 1981). By contrast, the social facilitation experiments *increased* exposure to evaluation. When made the center of attention, people self-consciously monitor their behavior (Mullen & Baumeister, 1987). So, when being observed *increases* evaluation concerns, social facilitation occurs; when being lost in a crowd *decreases* evaluation concerns, social loafing occurs (Figure 8.5).

To motivate group members, one strategy is to make individual performance identifiable. Some football coaches do this by filming and evaluating each player individually. Whether in a group or not, people exert more effort when their outputs are individually identifiable: University swim team members swim faster in intrasquad relay races when someone monitors and announces their individual times (Williams & others, 1989).

free riders
People who benefit from the
group but give little in return.

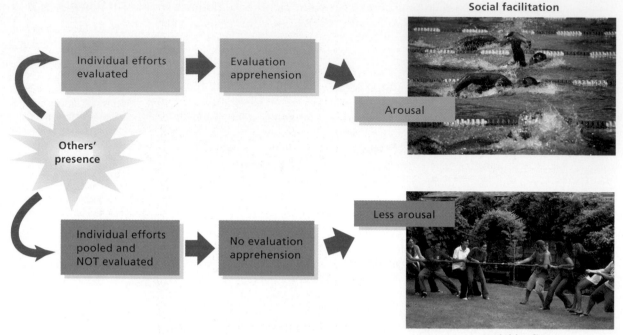

Social facilitation

Individual efforts evaluated → Evaluation apprehension →

Others' presence

Arousal

Less arousal

Individual efforts pooled and NOT evaluated → No evaluation apprehension →

Social loafing

FIGURE :: 8.5

Social Facilitation or Social Loafing?

When individuals cannot be evaluated or held accountable, loafing becomes more likely. An individual swimmer is evaluated on her ability to win the race. In tug-of-war, no single person on the team is held accountable, so any one member might relax or loaf.

Social Loafing in Everyday Life

How widespread is social loafing? In the laboratory the phenomenon occurs not only among people who are pulling ropes, cycling, shouting, and clapping but also among those who are pumping water or air, evaluating poems or editorials, producing ideas, typing, and detecting signals. Do these consistent results generalize to everyday worker productivity?

In one small experiment, assembly-line workers produced 16 percent more product when their individual output was identified, even though they knew their pay would not be affected (Faulkner & Williams, 1996). And consider: A key job in a pickle factory once was picking the right size dill pickle halves off the conveyor belt and stuffing them into jars. Unfortunately, workers were tempted to stuff any size pickle in, because their output was not identifiable (the jars went into a common hopper before reaching the quality-control section). Williams, Harkins, and Latané (1981) note that research on social loafing suggests "making individual production identifiable, and raises the question: 'How many pickles could a pickle packer pack if pickle packers were only paid for properly packed pickles?'"

Researchers have also found evidence of social loafing in varied cultures, particularly by assessing agricultural output in formerly communist countries. On their collective farms under communism, Russian peasants worked one field one day, another field the next, with little direct responsibility for any given plot. For their own use, they were given small private plots. One analysis found that the private plots occupied 1 percent of the agricultural land, yet produced 27 percent of the Soviet farm output (H. Smith, 1976). In communist Hungary, private plots accounted for only 13 percent of the farmland but produced one-third of the output (Spivak, 1979). When China began allowing farmers to sell food grown in excess of that owed to the state, food production jumped 8 percent per year—2.5 times the annual increase in the preceding 26 years (Church, 1986). In an effort to tie rewards to productive effort, today's Russia is "decollectivizing" many of its farms (Kramer, 2008).

What about collectivist cultures under noncommunist regimes? Latané and his co-researchers (Gabrenya & others, 1985) repeated their sound-production experiments in Japan, Thailand, Taiwan, India, and Malaysia. Their findings? Social loafing was evident in all those countries, too. Seventeen later studies in Asia reveal that people in collectivist cultures do, however, exhibit less social loafing than do people in individualist cultures (Karau & Williams, 1993; Kugihara, 1999). As we noted in Chapter 2, loyalty to family and work groups runs strong in collectivist cultures. Likewise, women (as Chapter 5 explained) tend to be less individualistic than men—and to exhibit less social loafing.

In North America, workers who do not pay dues or volunteer time to their unions or professional associations nevertheless are usually happy to accept the benefits those organizations provide. So, too, are public television viewers who don't respond to their station's fund drives. This hints at another possible explanation of social loafing. When rewards are divided equally, regardless of how much one contributes to the group, any individual gets more reward per unit of effort by free-riding on the group. So people may be motivated to slack off when their efforts are not individually monitored and rewarded. Situations that welcome free riders can therefore be, in the words of one commune member, a "paradise for parasites."

But surely collective effort does not always lead to slacking off. Sometimes the goal is so compelling and maximum output from everyone is so essential that team spirit maintains or intensifies effort. In an Olympic crew race, will the individual rowers in an eight-person crew pull their oars with less effort than those in a one- or two-person crew?

The evidence assures us they will not. People in groups loaf less when the task is *challenging, appealing,* or *involving* (Karau & Williams, 1993). On challenging tasks, people may perceive their efforts as indispensable (Harkins & Petty, 1982; Kerr, 1983; Kerr & others, 2007). When people see others in their group as unreliable or as unable to contribute much, they work harder (Plaks & Higgins, 2000; Williams & Karau, 1991). But, in many situations, so do less capable individuals as they strive to keep up with others' greater productivity (Weber & Hertel, 2007). Adding incentives or challenging a group to strive for certain standards also promotes collective effort (Harkins & Szymanski, 1989; Shepperd & Wright, 1989). Group members will work hard when convinced that high effort will bring rewards (Shepperd & Taylor, 1999).

Groups also loaf less when their members are *friends* or they feel identified with or indispensable to their group (Davis & Greenlees, 1992; Gockel & others, 2008; Karau & Williams, 1997; Worchel & others, 1998). Even just expecting to interact with someone again serves to increase effort on team projects (Groenenboom & others, 2001). Collaborate on a class project with others whom you will be seeing often and you will probably feel more motivated than you would if you never expected to see them again. Latané notes that Israel's communal kibbutz farms have actually outproduced Israel's noncollective farms (Leon, 1969). Cohesiveness intensifies effort.

These findings parallel those from studies of everyday work groups. When groups are given challenging objectives, when they are rewarded for group success, and when there is a spirit of commitment to the "team," group members work hard (Hackman, 1986). Keeping work groups small can also

Teamwork at the Charles River regatta in Boston. Social loafing occurs when people work in groups but without individual accountability—unless the task is challenging, appealing, or involving and the group members are friends.

help members believe their contributions are indispensable (Comer, 1995). Although social loafing is common when group members work without individual accountability, many hands need not always make light work.

Summing Up: Social Loafing: Do Individuals Exert Less Effort in a Group?

- Social facilitation researchers study people's performance on tasks where they can be evaluated individually. However, in many work situations, people pool their efforts and work toward a common goal without individual accountability.
- Group members often work less hard when performing such "additive tasks." This finding parallels

everyday situations where diffused responsibility tempts individual group members to free-ride on the group's effort.

- People may, however, put forth even more effort in a group when the goal is important, rewards are significant, and team spirit exists.

Deindividuation: When Do People Lose Their Sense of Self in Groups?

Group situations may cause people to lose self-awareness, with resulting loss of individuality and self-restraint. What circumstances trigger such "deindividuation"?

In April 2003, in the wake of American troops entering Iraq's cities, looters—"liberated" from the scrutiny of Saddam Hussein's police—ran rampant. Hospitals lost beds. The National Library lost tens of thousands of old manuscripts and lay in smoldering ruins. Universities lost computers, chairs, even lightbulbs. The National Museum in Baghdad had 15,000 objects stolen—most of what had not previously been removed to safekeeping (Burns, 2003a, 2003b; Lawler, 2003c; Polk & Schuster, 2005). "Not since the Spanish conquistadors ravaged the Aztec and Inca cultures has so much been lost so quickly," reported *Science* (Lawler, 2003a). "They came in mobs: A group of 50 would come, then would go, and another would come," explained one university dean (Lawler, 2003b). Such reports had the rest of the world wondering: What happened to the looters' sense of morality? Why did such behavior erupt? And why was it not anticipated?

Apparently acting without their normal conscience, people looted Iraqi institutions after the toppling of Saddam Hussein's regime.

Doing Together What We Would Not Do Alone

As we have seen, social facilitation experiments show that groups can arouse people, and social loafing experiments show that groups can diffuse responsibility. When arousal and diffused responsibility combine and normal inhibitions diminish, the results may be startling. People may commit acts that range from a mild lessening of restraint (throwing food in the dining hall, snarling at a referee, screaming during a rock concert) to impulsive self-gratification (group vandalism, orgies, thefts) to destructive social explosions (police brutality, riots, lynchings).

These unrestrained behaviors have something in common: They are somehow provoked by the power of a group. Groups can generate a sense of excitement, of being caught up in something bigger than one's self. It is harder to imagine a single rock fan screaming deliriously at a private rock concert, or a single police officer beating a defenseless offender or suspect. In group situations, people are more likely to abandon normal restraints, to lose their sense of individual identity, to become responsive to group or crowd norms—in a word, to become what Leon Festinger, Albert Pepitone, and Theodore Newcomb (1952) labeled **deindividuated.** What circumstances elicit this psychological state?

GROUP SIZE

A group has the power not only to arouse its members but also to render them unidentifiable. The snarling crowd hides the snarling basketball fan. A lynch mob enables its members to believe they will not be prosecuted; they perceive the action as the *group's*. Looters, made faceless by the mob, are freed to loot. In an analysis of 21 instances in which crowds were present as someone threatened to jump from a building or a bridge, Leon Mann (1981) found that when the crowd was small and exposed by daylight, people usually did not try to bait the person with cries of "Jump!" But when a large crowd or the cover of night gave people anonymity, the crowd usually did bait and jeer.

Brian Mullen (1986) reported a similar effect associated with lynch mobs: The bigger the mob, the more its members lose self-awareness and become willing to commit atrocities, such as burning, lacerating, or dismembering the victim.

In each of these examples, from sports crowds to lynch mobs, evaluation apprehension plummets. People's attention is focused on the situation, not on themselves. And because "everyone is doing it," all can attribute their behavior to the situation rather than to their own choices.

PHYSICAL ANONYMITY

How can we be sure that the effect of crowds means greater anonymity? We can't. But we can experiment with anonymity to see if it actually lessens inhibitions. Philip Zimbardo (1970, 2002) got the idea for such an experiment from his undergraduate students, who questioned how good boys in William Golding's *Lord of the Flies* could so suddenly become monsters after painting their faces. To experiment with such anonymity, he dressed New York University women in identical white coats and hoods, rather like Ku Klux Klan members (Figure 8.6). Asked to deliver electric shocks to a woman, they pressed the shock button twice as long as did women who were unconcealed and wearing large name tags.

deindividuation
Loss of self-awareness and evaluation apprehension; occurs in group situations that foster responsiveness to group norms, good or bad.

"A mob is a society of bodies voluntarily bereaving themselves of reason."
—*RALPH WALDO EMERSON, "COMPENSATION," ESSAYS, FIRST SERIES, 1841*

FIGURE :: 8.6

In Philip Zimbardo's deindividuation research, anonymous women delivered more shock to helpless victims than did identifiable women.

FIGURE :: 8.7

Children were more likely to transgress by taking extra Halloween candy when in a group, when anonymous, and, especially, when deindividuated by the combination of group immersion and anonymity.

Source: Data from Diener & others, 1976.

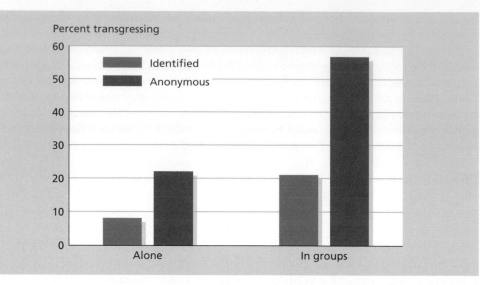

The Internet offers similar anonymity. Millions of those who were aghast at the looting by the Baghdad mobs were on those very days anonymously pirating music tracks using file-sharing software. With so many doing it, and with so little concern about being caught, downloading someone's copyright-protected property and then offloading it to an MP3 player just didn't seem terribly immoral. When compared with face-to-face conversations, the anonymity offered by chat rooms, newsgroups, and listservs also has been observed to foster higher levels of hostile, uninhibited "flaming" behavior (Douglas & McGarty, 2001).

In several recent cases on the Internet, anonymous online bystanders have egged on people threatening suicide, sometimes with live video feeding the scene to scores of people. Online communities "are like the crowd outside the building with the guy on the ledge," noted an analyst of technology's social effects, Jeffrey Cole. Sometimes a caring person tried to talk the person down, while others, in effect, chanted, "Jump, jump." "The anonymous nature of these communities only emboldens the meanness or callousness of the people on these sites," Cole adds (quoted by Stelter, 2008).

Testing deindividuation on the streets, Patricia Ellison, John Govern, and their colleagues (1995) had a confederate driver stop at a red light and wait for 12 seconds whenever she was followed by a convertible or a 4 × 4 vehicle. While enduring the wait, she recorded any horn-honking (a mild aggressive act) by the car behind. Compared with drivers of convertibles and 4 × 4s with the car tops down, those who were relatively anonymous (with the tops up) honked one-third sooner, twice as often, and for nearly twice as long.

A research team led by Ed Diener (1976) cleverly demonstrated the effect both of being in a group *and* of being physically anonymous. At Halloween, they observed 1,352 Seattle children trick-or-treating. As the children, either alone or in groups, approached 1 of 27 homes scattered throughout the city, an experimenter greeted them warmly, invited them to "take *one* of the candies," and then left the candy unattended. Hidden observers noted that children in groups were more than twice as likely to take extra candy as solo children. Also, children who had been asked their names and where they lived were less than half as likely to transgress as those who were left anonymous. As Figure 8.7 shows, the transgression rate varied dramatically with the situation. When they were deindividuated both by group immersion and by anonymity, most children stole extra candy.

Those studies make me wonder about the effect of wearing uniforms. Preparing for battle, warriors in some tribal cultures (like rabid fans of some sports teams) depersonalize themselves with body and face paints or special masks. After the battle, some cultures kill, torture, or mutilate any remaining enemies; other cultures take prisoners alive. Robert Watson (1973) scrutinized anthropological files and discovered this: The cultures with depersonalized warriors were also the cultures that brutalized their enemies. In Northern Ireland, 206 of 500 violent attacks studied by Andrew Silke (2003) were conducted by attackers who wore masks, hoods, or other face disguises. Compared with undisguised attackers, these anonymous attackers inflicted more serious injuries, attacked more people, and committed more vandalism.

Does becoming physically anonymous *always* unleash our worst impulses? Fortunately, no. In all these situations, people were responding to clear antisocial cues. Robert Johnson and Leslie Downing (1979) point out that the Klan-like outfits worn by Zimbardo's participants may have been stimulus cues for hostility. In an experiment at the University of Georgia, women put on nurses' uniforms before deciding how much shock someone should receive. When those wearing the nurses' uniforms were made anonymous, they became *less* aggressive in administering shocks than when their names and personal identities were stressed. From their analysis of 60 deindividuation studies, Tom Postmes and Russell Spears (1998; Reicher & others, 1995) concluded that being anonymous makes one less self-conscious, more group-conscious, and more responsive to cues present in the situation, whether negative (Klan uniforms) or positive (nurses' uniforms).

AROUSING AND DISTRACTING ACTIVITIES

Aggressive outbursts by large groups often are preceded by minor actions that arouse and divert people's attention. Group shouting, chanting, clapping, or dancing serve both to hype people up and to reduce self-consciousness. One observer of a Unification Church ritual recalls how the "choo-choo" chant helped deindividuate:

> All the brothers and sisters joined hands and chanted with increasing intensity, choo-choo-choo, Choo-choo-choo, CHOO-CHOO-CHOO! YEA! YEA! POWW!!! The act made us a group, as though in some strange way we had all experienced something important together. The power of the choo-choo frightened me, but it made me feel more comfortable and there was something very relaxing about building up the energy and releasing it. (Zimbardo & others, 1977, p. 186)

Ed Diener's experiments (1976, 1979) have shown that activities such as throwing rocks and group singing can set the stage for more disinhibited behavior. There is a self-reinforcing pleasure in acting impulsively while observing others doing likewise. When we see others act as we are acting, we think they feel as we do, which reinforces our own feelings (Orive, 1984). Moreover, impulsive group action absorbs our attention. When we yell at the referee, we are not thinking about our values; we are reacting to the immediate situation. Later, when we stop to think about what we have done or said, we sometimes feel chagrined. Sometimes. At other times we *seek* deindividuating group experiences—dances, worship experiences, group encounters—where we can enjoy intense positive feelings and closeness to others.

Diminished Self-Awareness

Group experiences that diminish self-consciousness tend to disconnect behavior from attitudes. Research by Ed Diener (1980) and Steven Prentice-Dunn and Ronald Rogers (1980, 1989) revealed that unself-conscious, deindividuated people are less restrained, less self-regulated, more likely to act without thinking about their own values, and more responsive to the situation. Those findings complement and reinforce the experiments on *self-awareness* (Chapter 3).

Self-awareness is the opposite of deindividuation. Those made self-aware, by acting in front of a mirror or a TV camera, exhibit *increased* self-control, and their actions more clearly reflect their attitudes. In front of a mirror, people taste-testing cream cheese varieties eat less of the high-fat variety (Sentyrz & Bushman, 1998).

"Attending a service in the Gothic cathedral, we have the sensation of being enclosed and steeped in an integral universe, and of losing a prickly sense of self in the community of worshipers."
—YI-FU TUAN, 1982

Soccer fans after a 1985 riot and the collapse of a wall that killed 39 people in Brussels. The soccer hooligans are often likable as individuals, reported one English journalist who ran with them for eight years, but demonic in a crowd (Buford, 1992).

People made self-aware are also less likely to cheat (Beaman & others, 1979; Diener & Wallbom, 1976). So are those who generally have a strong sense of themselves as distinct and independent (Nadler & others, 1982). In Japan, where (mirror or no mirror) people more often imagine how they might look to others, people are no more likely to cheat when not in front of a mirror (Heine & others, 2008). The principle: People who are self-conscious, or who are temporarily made so, exhibit greater consistency between their words outside a situation and their deeds in it.

We can apply those findings to many situations in everyday life. Circumstances that decrease self-awareness, as alcohol consumption does, increase deindividuation (Hull & others, 1983). Deindividuation decreases in circumstances that increase self-awareness: mirrors and cameras, small towns, bright lights, large name tags, undistracted quiet, individual clothes and houses (Ickes & others, 1978). When a teenager leaves for a party, a parent's parting advice could well be "Have fun, and remember who you are." In other words, enjoy being with the group, but be self-aware; maintain your personal identity; be wary of deindividuation.

Summing Up: Deindividuation: When Do People Lose Their Sense of Self in Groups?

- When high levels of social arousal combine with diffused responsibility, people may abandon their normal restraints and lose their sense of individuality.

- Such deindividuation is especially likely when people are in a large group, are physically anonymous, and are aroused and distracted.

- The resulting diminished self-awareness and self-restraint tend to increase people's responsiveness to the immediate situation, be it negative or positive. Deindividuation is less likely when self-awareness is high.

Group Polarization: Do Groups Intensify Our Opinions?

Many conflicts grow as people on both sides talk mostly with like-minded others. Does interaction with like-minded people amplify preexisting attitudes? If so, why?

Which effect—good or bad—does group interaction more often have? Police brutality and mob violence demonstrate its destructive potential. Yet support-group leaders, management consultants, and educational theorists proclaim group interaction's benefits, and social and religious movements urge their members to strengthen their identities by fellowship with like-minded others.

Studies of people in small groups have produced a principle that helps explain both bad and good outcomes: Group discussion often strengthens members' initial inclinations. The unfolding of this research on **group polarization** illustrates the process of inquiry—how an interesting discovery often leads researchers to hasty and erroneous conclusions, which ultimately are replaced with more accurate conclusions. This is a scientific mystery I can discuss firsthand, having been one of the detectives.

group polarization
Group-produced enhancement of members' preexisting tendencies; a strengthening of the members' average tendency, not a split within the group.

The Case of the "Risky Shift"

More than 300 studies began with a surprising finding by James Stoner (1961), then an MIT graduate student. For his master's thesis in management, Stoner tested the commonly held belief that groups are more cautious than individuals. He posed decision dilemmas in which the participant's task was to advise imagined characters how much risk to take. Put yourself in the participant's shoes: What advice would you give the character in this situation?[1]

> Helen is a writer who is said to have considerable creative talent but who so far has been earning a comfortable living by writing cheap westerns. Recently she has come up with an idea for a potentially significant novel. If it could be written and accepted, it might have considerable literary impact and be a big boost to her career. On the other hand, if she cannot work out her idea or if the novel is a flop, she will have expended considerable time and energy without remuneration.
>
> Imagine that you are advising Helen. Please check the *lowest* probability that you would consider acceptable for Helen to attempt to write the novel.
>
> Helen should attempt to write the novel if the chances that the novel will be a success are at least
>
> ____ 1 in 10
> ____ 2 in 10
> ____ 3 in 10
> ____ 4 in 10
> ____ 5 in 10
> ____ 6 in 10
> ____ 7 in 10
> ____ 8 in 10
> ____ 9 in 10
> ____ 10 in 10 (Place a check here if you think Helen should attempt the novel only
>   if it is certain that the novel will be a success.)

After making your decision, guess what this book's average reader would advise.

Having marked their advice on a dozen items, five or so individuals would then discuss and reach agreement on each item. How do you think the group decisions compared with the average decision before the discussions? Would the groups be likely to take greater risks, be more cautious, or stay the same?

To everyone's amazement, the group decisions were usually riskier. Dubbed the "risky shift phenomenon," this finding set off a wave of group risk-taking studies. These revealed that risky shift occurs not only when a group decides by consensus; after a brief discussion, individuals, too, will alter their decisions. What is more, researchers successfully repeated Stoner's finding with people of varying ages and occupations in a dozen nations.

During discussion, opinions converged. Curiously, however, the point toward which they converged was usually a lower (riskier) number than their initial average.

---

[1] This item, constructed for my own research, illustrates the sort of decision dilemma posed by Stoner.

Here was a delightful puzzle. The small risky shift effect was reliable, unexpected, and without any immediately obvious explanation. What group influences produce such an effect? And how widespread is it? Do discussions in juries, business committees, and military organizations also promote risk taking? Does this explain why teenage reckless driving, as measured by death rates, nearly doubles when a 16- or 17-year-old driver has two teenage passengers rather than none (Chen & others, 2000)?

After several years of study, we discovered that the risky shift was not universal. We could write decision dilemmas on which people became more *cautious* after discussion. One of these featured "Roger," a young married man with two school-age children and a secure but low-paying job. Roger can afford life's necessities but few of its luxuries. He hears that the stock of a relatively unknown company may soon triple in value if its new product is favorably received or decline considerably if it does not sell. Roger has no savings. To invest in the company, he is considering selling his life insurance policy.

Can you see a general principle that predicts both the tendency to give riskier advice after discussing Helen's situation and more cautious advice after discussing Roger's? If you are like most people, you would advise Helen to take a greater risk than Roger, even before talking with others. It turns out there is a strong tendency for discussion to accentuate these initial leanings; groups discussing the "Roger" dilemma became more risk-averse than they were before discussion.

Do Groups Intensify Opinions?

Realizing that this group phenomenon was not a consistent shift toward increased risk, we reconceived the phenomenon as a tendency for group discussion to *enhance* group members' initial leanings. This idea led investigators to propose what French researchers Serge Moscovici and Marisa Zavalloni (1969) called group polarization: *Discussion typically strengthens the average inclination of group members.*

GROUP POLARIZATION EXPERIMENTS

This new view of the changes induced by group discussion prompted experimenters to have people discuss attitude statements that most of them favored or most of them opposed. Would talking in groups enhance their shared initial inclinations as it did with the decision dilemmas? In groups, would risk takers take bigger risks, bigots become more hostile, and givers become more generous? That's what the group polarization hypothesis predicts (Figure 8.8).

Dozens of studies confirm group polarization.

- Moscovici and Zavalloni (1969) observed that discussion enhanced French students' initially positive attitude toward their president and negative attitude toward Americans.

FIGURE :: 8.8

Group Polarization

The group polarization hypothesis predicts that discussion will strengthen an attitude shared by group members.

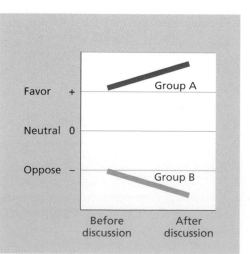

- Mititoshi Isozaki (1984) found that Japanese university students gave more pronounced judgments of "guilty" after discussing a traffic case. When jury members are inclined to award damages, the group award similarly tends to exceed that preferred by the median jury member (Sunstein, 2007a).

- Markus Brauer and his co-workers (2001) found that French students' dislike for certain other people was exacerbated after discussing their shared negative impressions.

Another research strategy has been to pick issues on which opinions are divided and then isolate people who hold the same view. Does discussion with like-minded people strengthen shared views? Does it magnify the attitude gap that separates the two sides?

George Bishop and I wondered. So we set up groups of relatively prejudiced and unprejudiced high school students and asked them to respond—before and after discussion—to issues involving racial attitudes, such as property rights versus open housing (Myers & Bishop, 1970). We found that the discussions among like-minded students did indeed increase the initial gap between the two groups (Figure 8.9).

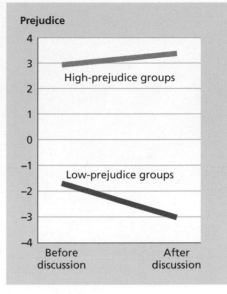

FIGURE :: 8.9

Discussion increased polarization between homogeneous groups of high- and low-prejudice high school students. Talking over racial issues increased prejudice in a high-prejudice group and decreased it in a low-prejudice group.

Source: Data from Myers & Bishop, 1970.

GROUP POLARIZATION IN EVERYDAY LIFE

In everyday life people associate mostly with others whose attitudes are similar to their own. (See Chapter 11, or just look at your own circle of friends.) Does everyday group interaction with like-minded friends intensify shared attitudes? Do nerds become nerdier and jocks jockier?

It happens. The self-segregation of boys into all-male groups and of girls into all-female groups accentuates over time their initially modest gender differences, notes Eleanor Maccoby (2002). Boys with boys become gradually more competitive and action oriented in their play and fictional fare, and girls with girls become more relationally oriented. On U.S. federal appellate court cases, "Republican-appointed judges tend to vote like Republicans and Democratic-appointed judges tend to vote like Democrats," David Schkade and Cass Sunstein (2003) have observed. But such tendencies are accentuated when among like-minded judges. "A Republican appointee sitting with two other Republicans votes far more conservatively than when the same judge sits with at least one Democratic appointee. A Democratic appointee, meanwhile, shows the same tendency in the opposite ideological direction."

GROUP POLARIZATION IN SCHOOLS   Another real-life parallel to the laboratory phenomenon is what education researchers have called the "accentuation" effect: Over time, initial differences among groups of college students become accentuated. If the first-year students at college X are initially more intellectual than the students at college Y, that gap is likely to increase by the time they graduate. Likewise, compared with fraternity and sorority members, independents tend to have more liberal political attitudes, a difference that grows with time in college (Pascarella & Terenzini, 1991). Researchers believe this results partly from group members reinforcing shared inclinations.

GROUP POLARIZATION IN COMMUNITIES   Polarization also occurs in communities, as people self-segregate. "Crunchy places . . . attract crunchy types and become crunchier," observes David Brooks (2005). "Conservative places . . . attract conservatives and become more so." Neighborhoods become echo chambers, with opinions richocheting off kindred-spirited friends. One experiment assembled small groups of Coloradoans in liberal Boulder and conservative Colorado Springs. The discussions increased agreement within small groups about global warming, affirmative action, and same-sex unions. Nevertheless, those in Boulder generally converged further left and those in Colorado Springs further right (Schkade & others, 2007).

"What explains the rise of fascism in the 1930s? The emergence of student radicalism in the 1960s? The growth of Islamic terrorism in the 1990s? . . . The unifying theme is simple: *When people find themselves in groups of like-minded types, they are especially likely to move to extremes.* [This] is the phenomenon of *group polarization.*"

—*CASS SUNSTEIN,* GOING TO EXTREMES, *2009*

Animal gangs. The pack is more than the sum of the wolves.

In two trials, South African courts reduced sentences after learning how social-psychological phenomena, including deindividuation and group polarization, led crowd members to commit murderous acts (Colman, 1991). What do you think: Should courts consider social-psychological phenomena as possible extenuating circumstances?

In the United States, the end result has become a more divided country. The percentage of landslide counties—those voting 60 percent or more for one presidential candidate—nearly doubled between 1976 and 2000 (Bishop, 2004). The percentage of entering collegians declaring themselves as politically "middle of the road" dropped from 60 percent in 1983 to 45 in 2005, with corresponding increases in those declaring themselves on the right or the left (Pryor & others, 2005). On campuses, the clustering of students into mostly White sororities and fraternities and into ethnic minority student organizations tends to strengthen social identities and to increase antagonisms among the social groups (Sidanius & others, 2004).

In laboratory studies the competitive relationships and mistrust that individuals often display when playing games with one another often worsen when the players are groups (Winquist & Larson, 2004). During actual community conflicts, like-minded people associate increasingly with one another, amplifying their shared tendencies. Gang delinquency emerges from a process of mutual reinforcement within neighborhood gangs, whose members share attributes and hostilities (Cartwright, 1975). If "a second out-of-control 15-year-old moves in [on your block]," surmises David Lykken (1997), "the mischief they get into as a team is likely to be more than merely double what the first would do on his own. . . . A gang is more dangerous than the sum of its individual parts." Indeed, "unsupervised peer groups" are "the strongest predictor" of a neighborhood's crime victimization rate, report Bonita Veysey and Steven Messner (1999). Moreover, experimental interventions that take delinquent adolescents and group them with other delinquents actually—no surprise to any group polarization researcher—increase the rate of problem behavior (Dishion & others, 1999).

GROUP POLARIZATION ON THE INTERNET

E-mail, blogs, and electronic chat rooms offer a potential new medium for like-minded people to find one another and for group interaction. On MySpace, there are tens of thousands of groups of kindred spirits discussing religion, politics, hobbies, cars, music, and you name it. The Internet's countless virtual groups enable peacemakers and neo-Nazis, geeks and goths, conspiracy

"Before the Internet, I just assumed I was the only one, and kept more or less to myself."

focus
ON   Group Polarization

Shakespeare portrayed the polarizing power of the like-minded group in this dialogue of Julius Caesar's followers:

> **Antony:** Kind souls, what weep you when you but behold Our Caesar's vesture wounded? Look you here. Here is himself, marr'd, as you see, with traitors.
>
> **First Citizen:** O piteous spectacle!
>
> **Second Citizen:** O noble Caesar!
>
> **Third Citizen:** O woeful day!
>
> **Fourth Citizen:** O traitors, villains!
>
> **First Citizen:** O most bloody sight!
>
> **Second Citizen:** We will be revenged!
>
> **All:** Revenge! About! Seek! Burn! Fire! Kill! Slay! Let not a traitor live!

Source: From *Julius Caesar* by William Shakespeare, Act III, Scene ii, lines 199–209.

theorists and cancer survivors to isolate themselves with like-minded others and find support for their shared concerns, interests, and suspicions (Gerstenfeld & others, 2003; McKenna & Bargh, 1998, 2000; Sunstein, 2001). Without the nonverbal nuances of face-to-face contact, will such discussions produce group polarization? Will peacemakers become more pacifistic and militia members more terror prone? E-mail, Google, and chat rooms "make it much easier for small groups to rally like-minded people, crystallize diffuse hatreds and mobilize lethal force," observes Robert Wright (2003). As broadband spreads, Internet-spawned polarization will increase, he speculates. "Ever seen one of Osama bin Laden's recruiting videos? They're very effective, and they'll reach their targeted audience much more efficiently via broadband." According to one University of Haifa analysis, terrorist websites—which grew from a dozen in 1997 to some 4,700 at the end of 2005—have increased more than four times faster than the total number of websites (Ariza, 2006).

GROUP POLARIZATION IN TERRORIST ORGANIZATIONS From their analysis of terrorist organizations around the world, Clark McCauley and Mary Segal (1987; McCauley, 2002) note that terrorism does not erupt suddenly. Rather, it arises among people whose shared grievances bring them together. As they interact in isolation from moderating influences, they become progressively more extreme. The social amplifier brings the signal in more strongly. The result is violent acts that the individuals, apart from the group, would never have committed.

For example, the 9/11 terrorists were bred by a long process that engaged the polarizing effect of interaction among the like-minded. The process of becoming a terrorist, noted a National Research Council panel, isolates individuals from other belief systems, dehumanizes potential targets, and tolerates no dissent (Smelser & Mitchell, 2002). Over time, group members come to categorize the world as "us" and "them" (Moghaddam, 2005; Qirko, 2004). Ariel Merari (2002), an investigator of Middle Eastern and Sri Lankan suicide terrorism, believes the key to creating a terrorist suicide is the group process. "To the best of my knowledge, there has not been a single case of suicide terrorism which was done on a personal whim."

According to one analysis of terrorists who were members of the Salafi Jihad—an Islamic fundamentalist movement, of which al Qaeda is a part—70 percent joined while living as expatriates. After moving to foreign places in search of jobs or education, they became mindful of their Muslim identity and often gravitated to mosques and moved in with other expatriate Muslims, who sometimes recruited them into cell groups that provided "mutual emotional and social support" and "development of a common identity" (Sageman, 2004).

Massacres, similarly, have been found to be group phenomena. The violence is enabled and escalated by the killers egging one another on (Zajonc, 2000). It is difficult to influence someone once "in the pressure cooker of the terrorist group," notes Jerrold Post (2005) after interviewing many accused terrorists. "In the long run, the most effective antiterrorist policy is one that inhibits potential recruits from joining in the first place."

Explaining Polarization

Why do groups adopt stances that are more exaggerated than that of their average individual member? Researchers hoped that solving the mystery of group polarization might provide some insights into group influence. Solving small puzzles sometimes provides clues for solving larger ones.

Among several proposed theories of group polarization, two have survived scientific scrutiny. One deals with the arguments presented during a discussion, the other with how members of a group view themselves vis-à-vis the other members. The first idea is an example of what Chapter 6 called *informational influence* (influence that results from accepting evidence about reality). The second is an example of *normative influence* (influence based on a person's desire to be accepted or admired by others).

INFORMATIONAL INFLUENCE

According to the best-supported explanation, group discussion elicits a pooling of ideas, most of which favor the dominant viewpoint. Some discussed ideas are common knowledge to group members (Gigone & Hastie, 1993; Larson & others, 1994; Stasser, 1991). Other ideas may include persuasive arguments that some group members had not previously considered. When discussing Helen the writer, someone may say, "Helen should go for it, because she has little to lose. If her novel flops, she can always go back to writing cheap westerns." Such statements often entangle information about the person's *arguments* with cues concerning the person's *position* on the issue. But when people hear relevant arguments without learning the specific stands other people assume, they still shift their positions (Burnstein & Vinokur, 1977; Hinsz & others, 1997). *Arguments*, in and of themselves, matter.

But there's more to attitude change than merely hearing someone else's arguments. *Active participation* in discussion produces more attitude change than does passive listening. Participants and observers hear the same ideas, but when participants express them in their own words, the verbal commitment magnifies the impact. The more group members repeat one another's ideas, the more they rehearse and validate them (Brauer & others, 1995).

This illustrates a point made in Chapter 7. People's minds are not just blank tablets for persuaders to write upon. With central route persuasion, what people think in response to a message is crucial. Indeed, just thinking about an issue for a couple of minutes can strengthen opinions (Tesser & others, 1995). (Perhaps you can recall your feelings becoming polarized as you merely ruminated about someone you disliked, or liked.) Even just *expecting* to discuss an issue with an equally expert person holding an opposing view can motivate people to marshal their arguments and thus to adopt a more extreme position (Fitzpatrick & Eagly, 1981).

NORMATIVE INFLUENCE

A second explanation of polarization involves comparison with others. As Leon Festinger (1954) argued in his influential theory of **social comparison,** we humans want to evaluate our opinions and abilities by comparing our views with others'. We are most persuaded by people in our "reference groups"—groups we identify

"If you have an apple and I have an apple and we exchange apples, then you and I will still each have one apple. But if you have an idea and I have an idea and we exchange these ideas, then each of us will have two ideas."

—*ATTRIBUTED TO GEORGE BERNARD SHAW (1856–1950)*

social comparison
Evaluating one's opinions and abilities by comparing oneself with others.

with (Abrams & others, 1990; Hogg & others, 1990). Moreover, wanting people to like us, we may express stronger opinions after discovering that others share our views.

When we ask people (as I asked you earlier) to predict how others would respond to items such as the "Helen" dilemma, they typically exhibit **pluralistic ignorance:** They don't realize how strongly others support the socially preferred tendency (in this case, writing the novel). A typical person will advise writing the novel even if its chance of success is only 4 in 10 but will estimate that most other people would require 5 or 6 in 10. (This finding is reminiscent of the self-serving bias: People tend to view themselves as better-than-average embodiments of socially desirable traits and attitudes.) When the discussion begins, most people discover they are not outshining the others as they had supposed. In fact, some others are ahead of them, having taken an even stronger position in favor of writing the novel. No longer restrained by a misperceived group norm, they are liberated to voice their preferences more strongly.

Perhaps you can recall a time when you and someone else wanted to go out with each other but each of you feared to make the first move, presuming the other probably did not have a reciprocal interest. Such pluralistic ignorance impedes the start-up of relationships (Vorauer & Ratner, 1996).

Or perhaps you can recall a time when you and others were guarded and reserved in a group, until someone broke the ice and said, "Well, to be perfectly honest, I think. . . ." Soon you were all surprised to discover strong support for your shared views. Sometimes when a professor asks if anyone has any questions, no one will respond, leading each student to infer that he or she is the only one confused. All presume that fear of embarrassment explains their own silence but that everyone else's silence means they understand the material.

Dale Miller and Cathy McFarland (1987) bottled this familiar phenomenon in a laboratory experiment. They asked people to read an incomprehensible article and to seek help if they ran into "any really serious problems in understanding the paper." Although none of the individuals sought help, they presumed *other* people would not be similarly restrained by fear of embarrassment. Thus, they wrongly inferred that people who didn't seek help didn't need any. To overcome such pluralistic ignorance, someone must break the ice and enable others to reveal and reinforce their shared reactions.

This social comparison theory prompted experiments that exposed people to others' positions but not to their arguments. This is roughly the experience we have when reading the results of an opinion poll or of exit polling on election day. When people learn others' positions—without prior commitment and without discussion or sharing of arguments—will they adjust their responses to maintain a socially favorable position? As Figure 8.10 illustrates, they will. This comparison-based polarization is usually less than that produced by a lively discussion. Still, it's surprising that, instead of simply conforming to the group average, people often go it one better.

Merely learning others' choices also contributes to the bandwagon effect that creates blockbuster songs, books, and movies. Sociologist Matthew Salganik and his colleagues (2006) experimented with the phenomenon by engaging 14,341 Internet participants in listening to and, if they wished, downloading previously unknown songs. The researchers randomly assigned some participants to a condition that disclosed previous participants' download choices. Among those given that information, popular songs became more popular and unpopular songs became less popular.

Group polarization research illustrates the complexity of social-psychological inquiry. Much as we like our explanations of a phenomenon to be simple, one explanation seldom accounts for all the data. Because people are complex, more than one factor frequently influences an outcome. In group discussions, persuasive arguments predominate on issues that have a factual element ("Is she guilty of the

pluralistic ignorance
A false impression of what most other people are thinking or feeling, or how they are responding.

FIGURE :: 8.10

On "risky" dilemma items (such as the case of Helen), mere exposure to others' judgments enhanced individuals' risk-prone tendencies. On "cautious" dilemma items (such as the case of Roger), exposure to others' judgments enhanced their cautiousness.

Source: Data from Myers, 1978.

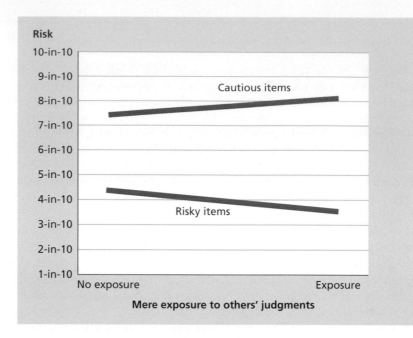

crime?"). Social comparison sways responses on value-laden judgments ("How long a sentence should she serve?") (Kaplan, 1989). On the many issues that have both factual and value-laden aspects, the two factors work together. Discovering that others share one's feelings (social comparison) unleashes arguments (informational influence) supporting what everyone secretly favors.

Summing Up: Group Polarization: Do Groups Intensify Our Opinions?

- Potentially positive and negative results arise from group discussion. While trying to understand the curious finding that group discussion enhanced risk taking, investigators discovered that discussion actually tends to strengthen whatever is the initially dominant point of view, whether risky or cautious.

- In everyday situations, too, group interaction tends to intensify opinions. This *group polarization* phenomenon provided a window through which researchers could observe group influence.

- Experiments confirmed two group influences: *informational* and *normative*. The information gleaned from a discussion mostly favors the initially preferred alternative, thus reinforcing support for it.

Groupthink: Do Groups Hinder or Assist Good Decisions?

When do group influences hinder good decisions? When do groups promote good decisions, and how can we lead groups to make optimal decisions?

Do the social-psychological phenomena we have been considering in these first eight chapters occur in sophisticated groups such as corporate boards or the president's cabinet? Is there likely to be self-justification? self-serving bias? a cohesive "we feeling" promoting conformity and stifling dissent? public commitment producing resistance to change? group polarization? Social psychologist Irving Janis (1971, 1982) wondered whether such phenomena might help explain good and bad group decisions made by some twentieth-century American presidents and

THE inside STORY

Irving Janis on Groupthink

The idea of *groupthink* hit me while reading Arthur Schlesinger's account of how the Kennedy administration decided to invade the Bay of Pigs. At first, I was puzzled: How could bright, shrewd people like John F. Kennedy and his advisers be taken in by the CIA's stupid, patchwork plan? I began to wonder whether some kind of psychological contagion had interfered, such as social conformity or the concurrence-seeking that I had observed in cohesive small groups. Further study (initially aided by my daughter Charlotte's work on a high school term paper) convinced me that subtle group processes had hampered their carefully appraising the risks and debating the issues. When I then analyzed other U.S. foreign policy fiascos and the Watergate coverup, I found the same detrimental group processes at work.

Irving Janis (1918–1990)

their advisers. To find out, he analyzed the decision-making procedures that led to several major fiascos:

- *Pearl Harbor.* In the weeks preceding the December 1941 Pearl Harbor attack that put the United States into World War II, military commanders in Hawaii received a steady stream of information about Japan's preparations for an attack on the United States somewhere in the Pacific. Then military intelligence lost radio contact with Japanese aircraft carriers, which had begun moving straight for Hawaii. Air reconnaissance could have spotted the carriers or at least provided a few minutes' warning. But complacent commanders decided against such precautions. The result: No alert was sounded until the attack on a virtually defenseless base was under way. The loss: 18 ships, 170 planes, and 2,400 lives.

- *The Bay of Pigs Invasion.* In 1961 President John Kennedy and his advisers tried to overthrow Fidel Castro by invading Cuba with 1,400 CIA-trained Cuban exiles. Nearly all the invaders were soon killed or captured, the United States was humiliated, and Cuba allied itself more closely with the former U.S.S.R. After learning the outcome, Kennedy wondered aloud, "How could we have been so stupid?"

- *The Vietnam War.* From 1964 to 1967 President Lyndon Johnson and his "Tuesday lunch group" of policy advisers escalated the war in Vietnam on the assumption that U.S. aerial bombardment, defoliation, and search-and-destroy missions would bring North Vietnam to the peace table with the appreciative support of the South Vietnamese populace. They continued the escalation despite warnings from government intelligence experts and nearly all U.S. allies. The resulting disaster cost more than 58,000 American and 1 million Vietnamese lives, polarized Americans, drove the president from office, and created huge budget deficits that helped fuel inflation in the 1970s.

Janis believed those blunders were bred by the tendency of decision-making groups to suppress dissent in the interest of group harmony, a phenomenon he called **groupthink.** (See "The Inside Story: Irving Janis on Groupthink.") In work groups, camaraderie boosts productivity (Mullen & Copper, 1994). Moreover, team spirit is good for morale. But when making decisions, close-knit groups may pay a price. Janis believed that the soil from which groupthink sprouts includes

- an amiable, *cohesive* group.
- relative *isolation* of the group from dissenting viewpoints.
- a *directive leader* who signals what decision he or she favors.

groupthink
"The mode of thinking that persons engage in when concurrence-seeking becomes so dominant in a cohesive in-group that it tends to override realistic appraisal of alternative courses of action."—Irving Janis (1971)

When planning the ill-fated Bay of Pigs invasion, the newly elected President Kennedy and his advisers enjoyed a strong esprit de corps. Arguments critical of the plan were suppressed or excluded, and the president soon endorsed the invasion.

Symptoms of Groupthink

From historical records and the memoirs of participants and observers, Janis identified eight groupthink symptoms. These symptoms are a collective form of dissonance reduction that surfaces as group members try to maintain their positive group feeling when facing a threat (Turner & others, 1992, 1994).

The first two groupthink symptoms lead group members to *overestimate their group's might and right.*

- *An illusion of invulnerability.* The groups Janis studied all developed an excessive optimism that blinded them to warnings of danger. Told that his forces had lost radio contact with the Japanese carriers, Admiral Kimmel, the chief naval officer at Pearl Harbor, joked that maybe the Japanese were about to round Honolulu's Diamond Head. They actually were, but Kimmel's laughing at the idea dismissed the very possibility of its being true.

- *Unquestioned belief in the group's morality.* Group members assume the inherent morality of their group and ignore ethical and moral issues. The Kennedy group knew that adviser Arthur Schlesinger, Jr., and Senator J. William Fulbright had moral reservations about invading a small, neighboring country. But the group never entertained or discussed those moral qualms.

Group members also become *closed-minded.*

- *Rationalization.* The groups discount challenges by collectively justifying their decisions. President Johnson's Tuesday lunch group spent far more time rationalizing (explaining and justifying) than reflecting upon and rethinking prior decisions to escalate. Each initiative became an action to defend and justify.

- *Stereotyped view of opponent.* Participants in these groupthink tanks consider their enemies too evil to negotiate with or too weak and unintelligent to defend themselves against the planned initiative. The Kennedy group convinced itself that Castro's military was so weak and his popular support so shallow that a single brigade could easily overturn his regime.

Finally, the group suffers from pressures toward *uniformity.*

- *Conformity pressure.* Group members rebuffed those who raised doubts about the group's assumptions and plans, at times not by argument but by personal sarcasm. Once, when President Johnson's assistant Bill Moyers arrived at a meeting, the president derided him with, "Well, here comes Mr. Stop-the-Bombing." Faced with such ridicule, most people fall into line.

"All those in favor say 'Aye.'"
"Aye."
"Aye."
"Aye."
"Aye."
"Aye."
"Aye."

Self-censorship contributes to an illusion of unanimity.

- *Self-censorship.* Since disagreements were often uncomfortable and the groups seemed in consensus, members withheld or discounted their misgivings. In the months following the Bay of Pigs invasion, Arthur Schlesinger (1965, p. 255) reproached himself "for having kept so silent during those crucial discussions in the Cabinet Room, though my feelings of guilt were tempered by the knowledge that a course of objection would have accomplished little save to gain me a name as a nuisance."

- *Illusion of unanimity.* Self-censorship and pressure not to puncture the consensus create an illusion of unanimity. What is more, the apparent consensus confirms the group's decision. This appearance of consensus was evident in the Pearl Harbor, Bay of Pigs, and Vietnam fiascos and in other fiascos before and since. Albert Speer (1971), an adviser to Adolf Hitler, described the atmosphere around Hitler as one where pressure to conform suppressed all deviation. The absence of dissent created an illusion of unanimity:

  > In normal circumstances people who turn their backs on reality are soon set straight by the mockery and criticism of those around them, which makes them aware they have lost credibility. In the Third Reich there were no such correctives, especially for those who belonged to the upper stratum. On the contrary, every self-deception was multiplied as in a hall of distorting mirrors, becoming a repeatedly confirmed picture of a fantastical dream world which no longer bore any relationship to the grim outside world. In those mirrors I could see nothing but my own face reproduced many times over. No external factors disturbed the uniformity of hundreds of unchanging faces, all mine. (p. 379)

- *Mindguards.* Some members protect the group from information that would call into question the effectiveness or morality of its decisions. Before the Bay of Pigs invasion, Robert Kennedy took Schlesinger aside and told him, "Don't push it any further." Secretary of State Dean Rusk withheld diplomatic and intelligence experts' warnings against the invasion. They thus served as the president's "mindguards," protecting him from disagreeable facts rather than physical harm.

Groupthink symptoms can produce a failure to seek and discuss contrary information and alternative possibilities (Figure 8.11). When a leader promotes an idea and when a group insulates itself from dissenting views, groupthink may produce defective decisions (McCauley, 1989).

People "are never so likely to settle a question rightly as when they discuss it freely."
—*JOHN STUART MILL, ON LIBERTY, 1859*

"There was a serious flaw in the decision-making process."
—*REPORT OF THE PRESIDENTIAL COMMISSION ON THE SPACE SHUTTLE CHALLENGER ACCIDENT, 1986*

Groupthink on a Titanic scale. Despite four messages of possible icebergs ahead, Captain Edward Smith—a directive and respected leader—kept his ship sailing at full speed into the night. There was an illusion of invulnerability (many believed the ship to be unsinkable). There was conformity pressure (crew mates chided the lookout for not being able to use his naked eye and dismissed his misgivings). And there was mindguarding (a *Titanic* telegraph operator failed to pass the last and most complete iceberg warning to Captain Smith).

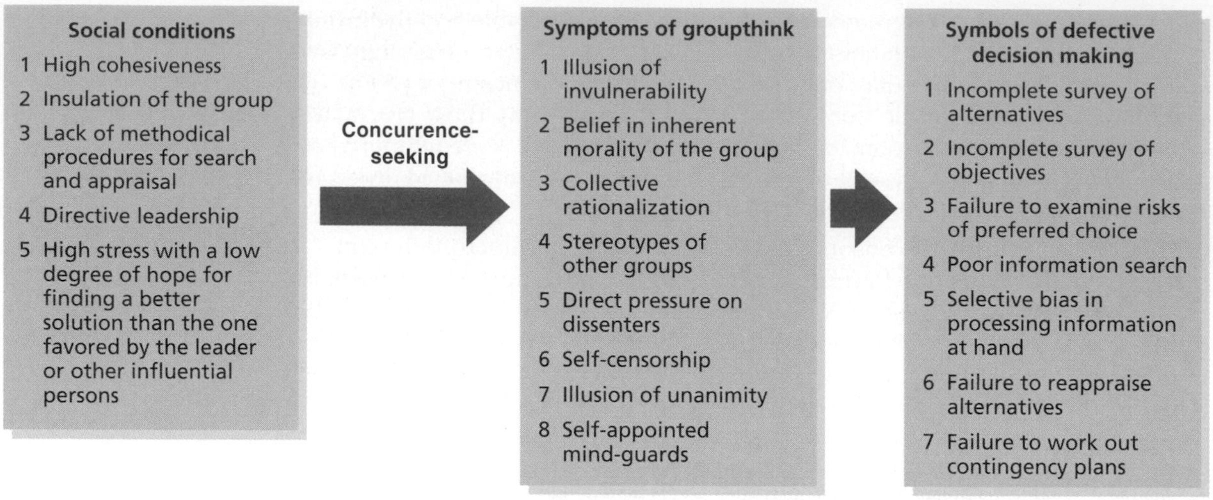

Social conditions
1 High cohesiveness
2 Insulation of the group
3 Lack of methodical procedures for search and appraisal
4 Directive leadership
5 High stress with a low degree of hope for finding a better solution than the one favored by the leader or other influential persons
Concurrence-seeking
Symptoms of groupthink
1 Illusion of invulnerability
2 Belief in inherent morality of the group
3 Collective rationalization
4 Stereotypes of other groups
5 Direct pressure on dissenters
6 Self-censorship
7 Illusion of unanimity
8 Self-appointed mind-guards
Symbols of defective decision making
1 Incomplete survey of alternatives
2 Incomplete survey of objectives
3 Failure to examine risks of preferred choice
4 Poor information search
5 Selective bias in processing information at hand
6 Failure to reappraise alternatives
7 Failure to work out contingency plans

FIGURE :: 8.11

Theoretical Analysis of Groupthink

Source: Janis & Mann, 1977, p. 132.

"History will remember both that the president failed to hear the warning bells and that many others failed to ring them loudly enough."
—NEW YORK TIMES *EDITORIAL, DECEMBER 1, 2006*

British psychologists Ben Newell and David Lagnado (2003) believe groupthink symptoms may have also contributed to the Iraq war. They and others contended that both Saddam Hussein and George W. Bush surrounded themselves with like-minded advisers and intimidated opposing voices into silence. Moreover, they each received filtered information that mostly supported their assumptions—Iraq's expressed assumption that the invading force could be resisted; and the United States' assumption that Iraq had weapons of mass destruction, that its people would welcome invading soldiers as liberators, and that a short, peaceful occupation would soon lead to a thriving democracy.

Critiquing Groupthink

Although Janis's ideas and observations have received enormous attention, some researchers are skeptical (Fuller & Aldag, 1998; t'Hart, 1998). The evidence was retrospective, so Janis could pick supporting cases. Follow-up experiments have supported aspects of Janis's theory:

- Directive leadership is indeed associated with poorer decisions, because subordinates sometimes feel too weak or insecure to speak up (Granstrom & Stiwne, 1998; McCauley, 1998).
- Groups do prefer supporting over challenging information (Schulz-Hardt & others, 2000).
- When members look to a group for acceptance, approval, and social identity, they may suppress disagreeable thoughts (Hogg & Hains, 1998; Turner & Pratkanis, 1997).
- Groups with diverse perspectives outperform groups of like-minded experts (Nemeth & Ormiston, 2007; Page, 2007). Engaging people who think differently from you can make you feel uncomfortable. But compared with comfortably homogeneous groups, diverse groups tend to produce more ideas and greater creativity.
- In discussion, information that is shared by group members does tend to dominate and crowd out unshared information, meaning that groups often do not benefit from all that their members know (Sunstein & Hastie, 2008).

Yet friendships need not breed groupthink (Esser, 1998; Mullen & others, 1994). In a secure, highly cohesive group (say, a family), committed members will often care enough to voice disagreement (Packer, 2009). The norms of a cohesive group can favor either consensus, which can lead to groupthink, or critical analysis, which prevents it (Postmes & others, 2001). When academic colleagues in a close-knit department share their draft manuscripts with one another, they *want* critique: "Do what you can to save me from my own mistakes." In a free-spirited atmosphere, cohesion can enhance effective teamwork, too.

Moreover, when Philip Tetlock and his colleagues (1992) looked at a broader sample of historical episodes, it became clear that even good group procedures sometimes yield ill-fated decisions. As President Carter and his advisers plotted their humiliating attempt to rescue American hostages in Iran in 1980, they welcomed different views and realistically considered the perils. Had it not been for a helicopter problem, the rescue might have succeeded. (Carter later reflected that had he sent in one more helicopter, he would have been reelected president.) To reword Mister Rogers, sometimes good groups do bad things.

Reflecting on the critiques of groupthink, Paul Paulus (1998) reminds us of Leon Festinger's (1987) observation that the only unchanging theory is an untestable one. "If a theory is at all testable, it will not remain unchanged. It has to change. All theories are wrong." Thus, said Festinger, we shouldn't ask whether a theory is right or wrong but, rather, "how much of the empirical realm can it handle and how must it be modified." Irving Janis, having tested and modified his own theory before his death in 1990, would surely have welcomed others continuing to reshape it. In science that is how we grope our way toward truth—by testing our ideas against reality, revising them, and then testing them some more.

Preventing Groupthink

Flawed group dynamics help explain many failed decisions; sometimes too many cooks spoil the broth. However, given open leadership, a cohesive team spirit can improve decisions. Sometimes two or more heads are better than one.

In search of conditions that breed good decisions, Janis also analyzed two successful ventures: the Truman administration's formulation of the Marshall Plan for getting Europe back on its feet after World War II and the Kennedy administration's handling of the former U.S.S.R.'s attempts to install missile bases in Cuba in 1962. Janis's (1982) recommendations for preventing groupthink incorporate many of the effective group procedures used in both cases:

- Be impartial—do not endorse any position.
- Encourage critical evaluation; assign a "devil's advocate." Better yet, welcome the input of a genuine dissenter, which does even more to stimulate original thinking and to open a group to opposing views, report Charlan Nemeth and her colleagues (2001a, 2001b).
- Occasionally subdivide the group, then reunite to air differences.
- Welcome critiques from outside experts and associates.
- Before implementing, call a "second-chance" meeting to air any lingering doubts.

When such steps are taken, group decisions may take longer to make, yet ultimately prove less defective and more effective.

Group Problem Solving

Not every group decision is flawed by groupthink. Under some conditions two or more heads really are better than one. In work settings such as operating rooms

"Truth springs from argument amongst friends."
—*PHILOSOPHER DAVID HUME, 1711–1776*

"One of the dangers in the White House, based on my reading of history, is that you get wrapped up in group-think and everybody agrees with everything and there's no discussion and there are no dissenting views. So I'm going to be welcoming a vigorous debate inside the White House."
—*BARACK OBAMA, AT A DECEMBER 1, 2008, PRESS CONFERENCE*

and executive boardrooms, team decisions surpass individual decisions when the discussion values each person's skills and knowledge and draws out their varied information (Mesmer-Magnus & DeChurch, 2009).

Patrick Laughlin and John Adamopoulos (1980; Laughlin, 1996; Laughlin & others, 2003) have shown the wisdom of groups with various intellectual tasks. Consider one of their analogy problems:

Assertion is to *disproved* as *action* is to
  a. *hindered*
  b. *opposed*
  c. *illegal*
  d. *precipitate*
  e. *thwarted*

Most college students miss this question when answering alone, but answer correctly (thwarted) after discussion. Moreover, Laughlin finds that if just two members of a six-person group are initially correct, two-thirds of the time they convince all the others. If only one person is correct, this "minority of one" almost three-fourths of the time fails to convince the group. And when given tricky logic problems, three, four, or five heads are better than two (Laughlin & others, 2006).

Dell Warnick and Glenn Sanders (1980) and Verlin Hinsz (1990) confirmed that several heads can be better than one when they studied the accuracy of eyewitness reports of a videotaped crime or job interview. Interacting groups of eyewitnesses gave accounts that were much more accurate than those provided by the average isolated individual. Several heads critiquing one another can also allow the group to avoid some forms of cognitive bias and produce some higher-quality ideas (McGlynn & others, 1995; Wright & others, 1990). In science, the benefits of diverse minds collaborating has led to more and more "team science"—to an increasing proportion of scientific publication, especially highly cited publication, by multi-author teams (Cacioppo, 2007).

But contrary to the popular idea that face-to-face brainstorming generates more creative ideas than do the same people working alone, researchers agree it isn't so (Paulus & others, 1995, 1997, 1998, 2000; Stroebe & Diehl, 1994). And contrary to the popular idea that brainstorming is most productive when the brainstormers are admonished "not to criticize," encouraging people to debate ideas appears to stimulate ideas and to extend creative thinking beyond the brainstorming session (Nemeth & others, 2004).

People *feel* more productive when generating ideas in groups (partly because people disproportionately credit themselves for the ideas that come out). But time and again researchers have found that people working alone usually will generate *more* good ideas than will the same people in a group (Nijstad & others, 2006; Rietzschel & others, 2006). Large brainstorming groups are especially inefficient. In accord with social loafing theory, large groups cause some individuals to free-ride on others' efforts. In accord with normative influence theory, they cause others to feel apprehensive about voicing oddball ideas. And they cause "production blocking"—losing one's ideas while awaiting a turn to speak (Nijstad & Stroebe, 2006). As James Watson and Francis Crick demonstrated in discovering DNA, challenging two-person conversations can more effectively engage creative thinking. Watson later recalled that he and Crick benefited from *not* being the most brilliant people seeking to crack the genetic code. The most brilliant researcher "was so intelligent that she rarely sought advice" (quoted by Cialdini, 2005). If you are (and regard yourself as) the most gifted person, why seek others' input? Like Watson and Crick, psychologists Daniel Kahneman and the late Amos Tversky similarly collaborated in their exploration of intuition and its influence on economic decision making. (See Chapter 3 and "The Inside Story: Behind a Nobel Prize.")

THE inside STORY

Behind a Nobel Prize: Two Minds Are Better Than One

In the Spring of 1969, Amos Tversky, my younger colleague at the Hebrew University of Jerusalem, and I met over lunch and shared our own recurrent errors of judgment. From there were born our studies of human intuition.

I had enjoyed collaboration before, but this was magical. Amos was very smart, and also very funny. We could spend hours of solid work in continuous mirth. His work was always characterized by confidence and by a crisp elegance, and it was a joy to find those characteristics now attached to my ideas as well. As we were writing our first paper, I was conscious of how much better it was than the more hesitant piece I would have written by myself.

All our ideas were jointly owned. We did almost all the work on our joint projects while physically together, including the drafting of questionnaires and papers. Our principle was to discuss every disagreement until it had been resolved to our mutual satisfaction.

Some of the greatest joys of our collaboration—and probably much of its success—came from our ability to elaborate on each other's nascent thoughts: If I expressed a half-formed idea, I knew that Amos would be there to understand it, probably more clearly than I did, and that if it had merit, he would see it.

Amos and I shared the wonder of together owning a goose that could lay golden eggs—a joint mind that was better than our separate minds. We were a team, and we remained in that mode for well over a decade. The Nobel Prize was awarded for work that we produced during that period of intense collaboration.

Daniel Kahneman,
Princeton University,
Nobel Laureate, 2002

However, Vincent Brown and Paul Paulus (2002) have identified three ways to enhance group brainstorming:

- *Combine group and solitary brainstorming.* Group brainstorming is most productive when it *precedes* solo brainstorming. With new categories primed by the group brainstorming, individuals' ideas can continue flowing without being impeded by the group context that allows only one person to speak at a time.

- *Have group members interact by writing.* Another way to take advantage of group priming, without being impeded by the one-at-a-time rule, is to have group members write and read, rather than speak and listen. Brown and Paulus describe this process of passing notes and adding ideas, which has everyone active at once, as "brainwriting."

- *Incorporate electronic brainstorming.* There is a potentially more efficient way to avoid the verbal traffic jams of traditional group brainstorming in larger groups: Let individuals produce and read ideas on networked computers.

So, when group members freely combine their creative ideas and varied insights, the frequent result is not groupthink but group problem solving. The wisdom of groups is evident in everyday life as well as in the laboratory:

- *Weather forecasting.* "Two forecasters will come up with a forecast that is more accurate than either would have come up with working alone," reports Joel Myers (1997), president of the largest private forecasting service.

- *Google.* Google has become a dominant search engine by harnessing what James Surowiecki (2004) calls *The Wisdom of Crowds.* Google interprets a link to Page X as a vote for Page X, and weights most heavily links from pages that are themselves highly ranked. Harnessing the democratic character of the Web, Google often takes less than one-tenth of a second to lead you right to what you want.
- *Game shows.* For a befuddled contestant on *Who Wants to Be a Millionaire,* a valuable lifeline was to "ask the audience," which usually offered wisdom superior to the contestant's intuition. This is because the average judgment from a crowd of people typically errs less than does the average judgment by individuals.
- *The "crowd within."* Likewise, the average of different guesses from the same persons tends to surpass the person's individual guesses (Herzog & Hertwig, 2009). Edward Vul and Harold Pashler (2008) discovered this when asking people to guess the correct answers to factual questions such as "What percentage of the world's airports are in the United States?" Then the researchers asked their participants to make a second guess, either immediately or three weeks later. The result? "You can gain about 1/10th as much from asking yourself the same question twice as you can from getting a second opinion from someone else, but if you wait 3 weeks, the benefit of re-asking yourself the same question rises to 1/3 the value of a second opinion."
- *Prediction markets.* In U.S. presidential elections since 1988, the final public opinion polls have provided a good gauge to the election result. An even better predictor, however, has been the Iowa Election Market. Taking everything (including polls) into account, people buy and sell shares in candidates. Other prediction markets have harnessed collective wisdom in gauging the likelihood of other events, such as an avian flu epidemic (Arrow & others, 2008; Stix, 2008).

Thus, we can conclude that when information from many, diverse people is combined, all of us together can become smarter than almost any of us alone. We're in some ways like a flock of geese, no one of which has a perfect navigational sense. Nevertheless, by staying close to one another, a group of geese can navigate accurately. The flock is smarter than the bird.

Summing Up: Groupthink: Do Groups Hinder or Assist Good Decisions?

- Analysis of several international fiascos indicates that group cohesion can override realistic appraisal of a situation. This is especially true when group members strongly desire unity, when they are isolated from opposing ideas, and when the leader signals what he or she wants from the group.
- Symptomatic of this overriding concern for harmony, labeled groupthink, are (1) an illusion of invulnerability, (2) rationalization, (3) unquestioned belief in the group's morality, (4) stereotyped views of the opposition, (5) pressure to conform, (6) self-censorship of misgivings, (7) an illusion of unanimity, and (8) "mindguards" who protect the group from unpleasant information. Critics have noted that some aspects of Janis's groupthink model (such

as directive leadership) seem more implicated in flawed decisions than others (such as cohesiveness).

- Both in experiments and in actual history, however, groups sometimes decide wisely. These cases suggest ways to prevent groupthink: upholding impartiality, encouraging "devil's advocate" positions, subdividing and then reuniting to discuss a decision, seeking outside input, and having a "second-chance" meeting before implementing a decision.
- Research on group problem solving suggests that groups can be more accurate than individuals; groups also generate more and better ideas if the group is small or if, in a large group, individual brainstorming follows the group session.

The Influence of the Minority: How Do Individuals Influence the Group?

Groups influence individuals. But when—and how—do individuals influence their groups? What makes some individuals effective?

Each chapter in this social influence unit concludes with a reminder of our power as individuals. We have seen that

- cultural situations mold us, but we also help create and choose these situations.
- pressures to conform sometimes overwhelm our better judgment, but blatant pressure motivates reactance; we assert our individuality and freedom.
- persuasive forces are powerful, but we can resist persuasion by making public commitments and by anticipating persuasive appeals.

This chapter has emphasized group influences on the individual, so we conclude by seeing how individuals can influence their groups.

At this chapter's beginning, we considered the film *12 Angry Men*, in which a lone juror eventually wins over 11 others. That's a rare occurrence in a jury room, yet in most social movements a small minority will sway, and then eventually become, the majority. "All history," wrote Ralph Waldo Emerson, "is a record of the power of minorities, and of minorities of one." Think of Copernicus and Galileo, of Martin Luther King, Jr., of Susan B. Anthony. The American civil rights movement was ignited by the refusal of one African American woman, Rosa Parks, to relinquish her seat on a bus in Montgomery, Alabama. Technological history has also been made by innovative minorities. As Robert Fulton developed his steamboat—"Fulton's Folly"—he endured constant derision: "Never did a single encouraging remark, a bright hope, a warm wish, cross my path" (Cantril & Bumstead, 1960). Indeed, if minority viewpoints never prevailed, history would be static and nothing would ever change.

What makes a minority persuasive? What might Arthur Schlesinger have done to get the Kennedy group to consider his doubts about the Bay of Pigs invasion? Experiments initiated by Serge Moscovici in Paris have identified several determinants of minority influence: *consistency, self-confidence,* and *defection*.

(Note: "Minority influence" refers to minority *opinions,* not to ethnic minorities.)

Consistency

More influential than a minority that wavers is a minority that sticks to its position. Moscovici and his associates (1969; Moscovici, 1985) found that if a minority of participants consistently judges blue slides as green, members of the majority will occasionally agree. But if the minority wavers, saying "blue" to one-third of the blue slides and "green" to the rest, virtually no one in the majority will ever agree with "green."

Experiments show—and experience confirms—that nonconformity, especially persistent nonconformity, is often painful, and that being a minority in a group can be unpleasant (Levine, 1989; Lücken & Simon, 2005). That helps explain a *minority slowness effect*—a tendency for people with minority views to express them less quickly than do people in the majority (Bassili, 2003). If you set out to be Emerson's minority of one, prepare yourself for ridicule—especially when you argue an issue that's personally relevant to the majority and when the group wants to settle an issue by reaching consensus (Kameda & Sugimori, 1993; Kruglanski & Webster, 1991; Trost & others, 1992). People may attribute your dissent to psychological peculiarities (Papastamou & Mugny, 1990). When Charlan Nemeth (1979) planted a

"If the single man plant himself indomitably on his instincts, and there abide, the huge world will come round to him."

—*RALPH WALDO EMERSON, NATURE, ADDRESS, AND LECTURES: THE AMERICAN SCHOLAR, 1849* minority of two within a simulated jury and had them oppose the majority's opinions, the duo was inevitably disliked.

Nevertheless, the majority acknowledged that the persistence of the two did more than anything else to make them rethink their positions. Compared to majority influence that often triggers unthinking agreement, minority influence stimulates a deeper processing of arguments, often with increased creativity (Kenworthy & others, 2008; Martin & others, 2007, 2008).

University students who have racially diverse friends, or who are exposed to racial diversity in discussion groups, display less simplistic thinking (Antonio & others, 2004). With dissent from within one's own group, people take in more information, think about it in new ways, and often make better decisions (Page, 2007). Believing that one need not win friends to influence people, Nemeth quotes Oscar Wilde: "We dislike arguments of any kind; they are always vulgar, and often convincing."

Some successful companies have recognized the creativity and innovation sometimes stimulated by minority perspectives, which may contribute new ideas and stimulate colleagues to think in fresh ways. 3M, which has been famed for valuing "respect for individual initiative," has welcomed employees spending time on wild ideas. The Post-it® note's adhesive was a failed attempt by Spencer Silver to develop a super-strong glue. Art Fry, after having trouble marking his church choir hymnal with pieces of paper, thought, "What I need is a bookmark with Spence's adhesive along the edge." Even so, this was a minority view that eventually won over a skeptical marketing department (Nemeth, 1997).

Self-Confidence

Consistency and persistence convey self-confidence. Furthermore, Nemeth and Joel Wachtler (1974) reported that any behavior by a minority that conveys self-confidence—for example, taking the head seat at the table—tends to raise self-doubts among the majority. By being firm and forceful, the minority's apparent self-assurance may prompt the majority to reconsider its position. This is especially so on matters of opinion rather than fact. Based on their research at Italy's University of Padova, Anne Maass and her colleagues (1996) report that minorities are less persuasive when answering a question of fact ("from which country does Italy import most of its raw oil?") than attitude ("from which country should Italy import most of its raw oil?").

Defections from the Majority

A persistent minority punctures any illusion of unanimity. When a minority consistently doubts the majority wisdom, majority members become freer to express their own doubts and may even switch to the minority position. But what about a lone defector, someone who initially agreed with the majority but then reconsidered and dissented? In research with University of Pittsburgh students, John Levine (1989) found that a minority person who had defected from the majority was even more persuasive than a consistent minority voice. In her jury-simulation experiments, Nemeth found that—not unlike the *12 Angry Men* scenario—once defections begin, others often soon follow, initiating a snowball effect.

Are these factors that strengthen minority influence unique to minorities? Sharon Wolf and Bibb Latané (1985; Wolf, 1987) and Russell Clark (1995) believe not. They argue that the same social forces work for both majorities and minorities. Informational influence (via persuasive arguments) and normative influence (via social comparison) fuel both group polarization and minority influence. And if consistency, self-confidence, and defections from the other side strengthen the minority, such variables also strengthen a majority. The social impact of any position, majority or minority, depends on the strength, immediacy, and number of those who support it.

Anne Maass and Russell Clark (1984, 1986) agree with Moscovici, however, that minorities are more likely than majorities to convert people to *accepting* their views. And from their analyses of how groups evolve over time, John Levine and Richard Moreland (1985) conclude that new recruits to a group exert a different type of minority influence than do longtime members. Newcomers exert influence through the attention they receive and the group awareness they trigger in the old-timers. Established members feel freer to dissent and to exert leadership.

There is a delightful irony in this new emphasis on how individuals can influence the group. Until recently, the idea that the minority could sway the majority was itself a minority view in social psychology. Nevertheless, by arguing consistently and forcefully, Moscovici, Nemeth, Maass, Clark, and others have convinced the majority of group influence researchers that minority influence is a phenomenon worthy of study. And the way that several of these minority influence researchers came by their interests should, perhaps, not surprise us. Anne Maass (1998) became interested in how minorities could effect social change after growing up in postwar Germany and hearing her grandmother's personal accounts of fascism. Charlan Nemeth (1999) developed her interest while she was a visiting professor in Europe "working with Henri Tajfel and Serge Moscovici. The three of us were 'outsiders'—I an American Roman Catholic female in Europe, they having survived World War II as Eastern European Jews. Sensitivity to the value and the struggles of the minority perspective came to dominate our work."

Is Leadership Minority Influence?

In 1910 the Norwegians and the English engaged in an epic race to the South Pole. The Norwegians, effectively led by Roald Amundsen, made it. The English, ineptly led by Robert Falcon Scott, did not; Scott and three team members died. Amundsen illustrated the power of **leadership,** the process by which individuals mobilize and guide groups. The presidency of George W. Bush illustrates "the power of one," observes Michael Kinsley (2003). "Before Bush brought it up [there was] no popular passion" for the idea "that Saddam was a terrible threat and had to go. . . . You could call this many things, but one of them is leadership. If real leadership means leading people where they don't want to go, George W. Bush has shown himself to be a real leader."

Some leaders are formally appointed or elected; others emerge informally as the group interacts. What makes for good leadership often depends on the situation—the best person to lead the engineering team may not make the best leader of the sales force. Some people excel at **task leadership**—at organizing work, setting standards, and focusing on goal attainment. Others excel at **social leadership**—at building teamwork, mediating conflicts, and being supportive.

Task leaders generally have a directive style—one that can work well if the leader is bright enough to give good orders (Fiedler, 1987). Being goal oriented, such leaders also keep the group's attention and effort focused on its mission. Experiments show that the combination of specific, challenging goals and periodic progress reports helps motivate high achievement (Locke & Latham, 1990).

Social leaders generally have a democratic style—one that delegates authority, welcomes input from team members, and, as we have seen, helps prevent groupthink. Many experiments reveal that social leadership is good for morale. Group members usually feel more satisfied when they participate in making decisions (Spector, 1986; Vanderslice & others, 1987). Given control over their tasks, workers also become more motivated to achieve (Burger, 1987).

People tend to respond more positively to a decision if they are given a chance to voice their opinions during the decision-making process (van den Bos & Spruijt, 2002). People who value good group feeling and take pride in achievement therefore thrive under democratic leadership and participative management,

leadership
The process by which certain group members motivate and guide the group.

task leadership
Leadership that organizes work, sets standards, and focuses on goals.

social leadership
Leadership that builds teamwork, mediates conflict, and offers support.

Participative management, illustrated in this "quality circle," requires democratic rather than autocratic leaders.

a management style common in Sweden and Japan (Naylor, 1990; Sundstrom & others, 1990). Women more often than men exhibit a democratic leadership style (Eagly & Johnson, 1990).

The once-popular "great person" theory of leadership—that all great leaders share certain traits—has fallen into disrepute. Effective leadership styles, we now know, vary with the situations. Subordinates who know what they are doing may resent working under task leadership, whereas those who don't may welcome it. Recently, however, social psychologists have again wondered if there might be qualities that mark a good leader in many situations (Hogan & others, 1994). British social psychologists Peter Smith and Monir Tayeb (1989) report that studies done in India, Taiwan, and Iran have found that the most effective supervisors in coal mines, banks, and government offices score high on tests of *both* task and social leadership. They are actively concerned with how work is progressing *and* sensitive to the needs of their subordinates.

Studies also reveal that many effective leaders of laboratory groups, work teams, and large corporations exhibit the behaviors that help make a minority view persuasive. Such leaders engender trust by *consistently* sticking to their goals. And they often exude a *self-confident* charisma that kindles the allegiance of their followers (Bennis, 1984; House & Singh, 1987). Charismatic leaders typically have a compelling *vision* of some desired state of affairs, an ability to *communicate* that to others in clear and simple language, and enough optimism and faith in their group to *inspire* others to follow.

In one analysis of 50 Dutch companies, the highest morale was at firms with chief executives who most inspired their colleagues "to transcend their own self-interests for the sake of the collective" (de Hoogh & others, 2004). Leadership of this kind—**transformational leadership**—motivates others to identify with and commit themselves to the group's mission. Transformational leaders—many of whom are charismatic, energetic, self-confident extraverts—articulate high standards, inspire people to share their vision, and offer personal attention (Bono & Judge, 2004). In organizations, the frequent result of such leadership is a more engaged, trusting, and effective workforce (Turner & others, 2002).

To be sure, groups also influence their leaders. Sometimes those at the front of the herd have simply sensed where it is already heading. Political candidates know how to read the opinion polls. Someone who typifies the group's views is more likely to be selected as a leader; a leader who deviates too radically from the group's standards may be rejected (Hogg & others, 1998). Smart leaders usually remain with the

transformational leadership
Leadership that, enabled by a leader's vision and inspiration, exerts significant influence.

focus
ON   Transformational Community Leadership

As a striking example of transformational (consistent, self-confident, inspirational) leadership, consider Walt and Mildred Woodward, the owners and editors of the newspaper on Bainbridge Island, Washington, during World War II and in the two decades after. It was from Bainbridge that, on March 30, 1942, the first of nearly 120,000 West Coast people of Japanese descent were relocated to internment camps. With six days' notice and under armed guard, they boarded a ferry and were sent away, leaving behind on the dock tearful friends and neighbors (one of whom was their insurance agent, my father). "Where, in the face of their fine record since December 7 [Pearl Harbor Day], in the face of their rights of citizenship, in the face of their own relatives being drafted and enlisting in our Army, in the face of American decency, is there any excuse for this high-handed, much-too-short evacuation order?" editorialized the Woodwards (1942) in their *Bainbridge Review*. Throughout the war, the Woodwards, alone among West Coast newspaper editors, continued to voice opposition to the internment. They also recruited their former part-time employee, Paul Ohtaki, to write a weekly column bringing news of the displaced islanders. Stories by Ohtaki and others of "Pneumonia Hits 'Grandpa Koura'" and "First Island Baby at Manzanar Born" reminded those back home of their absent neighbors and prepared the way for their eventual welcome home—a contrast to the prejudice that greeted their return to other West Coast communities where newspapers supported the internment and fostered hostility toward the Japanese.

After enduring some vitriolic opposition, the Woodwards lived to receive many honors for their courage, which was dramatized in the book and movie *Snow Falling on Cedars*. At the March 30, 2004, groundbreaking for a national memorial on the ferry departure site, former internee and Bainbridge Island Japanese American Community president Frank Kitamoto declared that "this memorial is also for Walt and Millie Woodward, for Ken Myers, for Genevive Williams . . . and the many others who supported us," and who challenged the forced removal at the risk of being called unpatriotic. "Walt Woodward said if we can suspend the Bill of Rights for Japanese Americans it can be suspended for fat Americans or blue-eyed

In March of 1942, 274 Bainbridge Islanders became the first of some 120,000 Japanese Americans and Japanese immigrants interned during World War II. Sixty-two years later, ground was broken for a national memorial (*Nidoto Nai Yoni*—Let It Not Happen Again), remembering the internees and the transformational leaders who supported them and prepared for their welcome home.

Americans." Reflecting on the Woodwards' transformational leadership, cub reporter Ohtaki (1999) observed that "on Bainbridge Island there was none of the hostility to the returning Japanese that you saw in other places, and I think that's in large part because of the Woodwards." When, later, he asked the Woodwards, "Why did you do this, when you could have dropped it and not suffered the anger of some of your readers?" they would always answer, "It was the right thing to do."

majority and spend their influence prudently. In rare circumstances, the right traits matched with the right situation yield history-making greatness, notes Dean Keith Simonton (1994). To have a Winston Churchill or a Margaret Thatcher, a Thomas Jefferson or a Karl Marx, a Napoleon or an Adolf Hitler, an Abraham Lincoln or a Martin Luther King, Jr., takes the right person in the right place at the right time.

When an apt combination of intelligence, skill, determination, self-confidence, and social charisma meets a rare opportunity, the result is sometimes a championship, a Nobel Prize, or a social revolution.

Summing Up: The Influence of the Minority: How Do Individuals Influence the Group?

- Although a majority opinion often prevails, sometimes a minority can influence and even overturn a majority position. Even if the majority does not adopt the minority's views, the minority's speaking up can increase the majority's self-doubts and prompt it to consider other alternatives, often leading to better, more creative decisions.

- In experiments, a minority is most influential when it is consistent and persistent in its views, when its actions convey self-confidence, and after it begins to elicit some defections from the majority.

- Through their task and social leadership, formal and informal group leaders exert disproportionate influence. Those who consistently press toward their goals and exude a self-confident charisma often engender trust and inspire others to follow.

POSTSCRIPT: Are Groups Bad for Us?

A selective reading of this chapter could, I must admit, leave readers with the impression that, on balance, groups are bad. In groups we become more aroused, more stressed, more tense, more error-prone on complex tasks. Submerged in a group that gives us anonymity, we have a tendency to loaf or have our worst impulses unleashed by deindividuation. Police brutality, lynchings, gang destruction, and terrorism are all group phenomena. Discussion in groups often polarizes our views, enhancing mutual racism or hostility. It may also suppress dissent, creating a homogenized groupthink that produces disastrous decisions. No wonder we celebrate those individuals—minorities of one—who, alone against a group, have stood up for truth and justice. Groups, it seems, are ba-a-a-d.

All that is true, but it's only half the truth. The other half is that, as social animals, we are group-dwelling creatures. Like our distant ancestors, we depend on one another for sustenance, support, and security. Moreover, when our individual tendencies are positive, group interaction accentuates our best. In groups, runners run faster, audiences laugh louder, and givers become more generous. In self-help groups, people strengthen their resolve to stop drinking, lose weight, and study harder. In kindred-spirited groups, people expand their spiritual consciousness. "A devout communing on spiritual things sometimes greatly helps the health of the soul," observed fifteenth-century cleric Thomas à Kempis, especially when people of faith "meet and speak and commune together."

Depending on which tendency a group is magnifying or disinhibiting, groups can be very, very bad or very, very good. So we had best choose our groups wisely and intentionally.

Making the Social Connection

In this chapter we discussed group polarization and whether groups intensify opinions. This phenomenon will also be covered in Chapter 15 when we look at juries and how they make decisions. Can you think of other situations where group polarization might be in effect? Go to the Online Learning Center for this book to view a clip about cliques and the influence of the group.

Social
part **three**
Relations

Social psychology is the scientific study of how people think about, influence, and relate to one another. Having explored how we *think about* (Part One) and *influence* (Part Two) one another, we now consider how we *relate* to one another. Our feelings and actions toward people are sometimes negative, sometimes positive. Chapters 9, "Prejudice: Disliking Others," and 10, "Aggression: Hurting Others," examine the nastier aspects of human relations: Why do we dislike, even despise, one another? Why and when do we hurt one another? Then in Chapters 11, "Attraction and Intimacy: Liking and Loving Others," and 12, "Helping," we explore the nicer aspects: Why do we like or love particular people? When will we offer help to friends or strangers? Last, in Chapter 13, "Conflict and Peacemaking," we consider how social conflicts develop and how they can be justly and amicably resolved.

CHAPTER

9 Prejudice

DISLIKING OTHERS

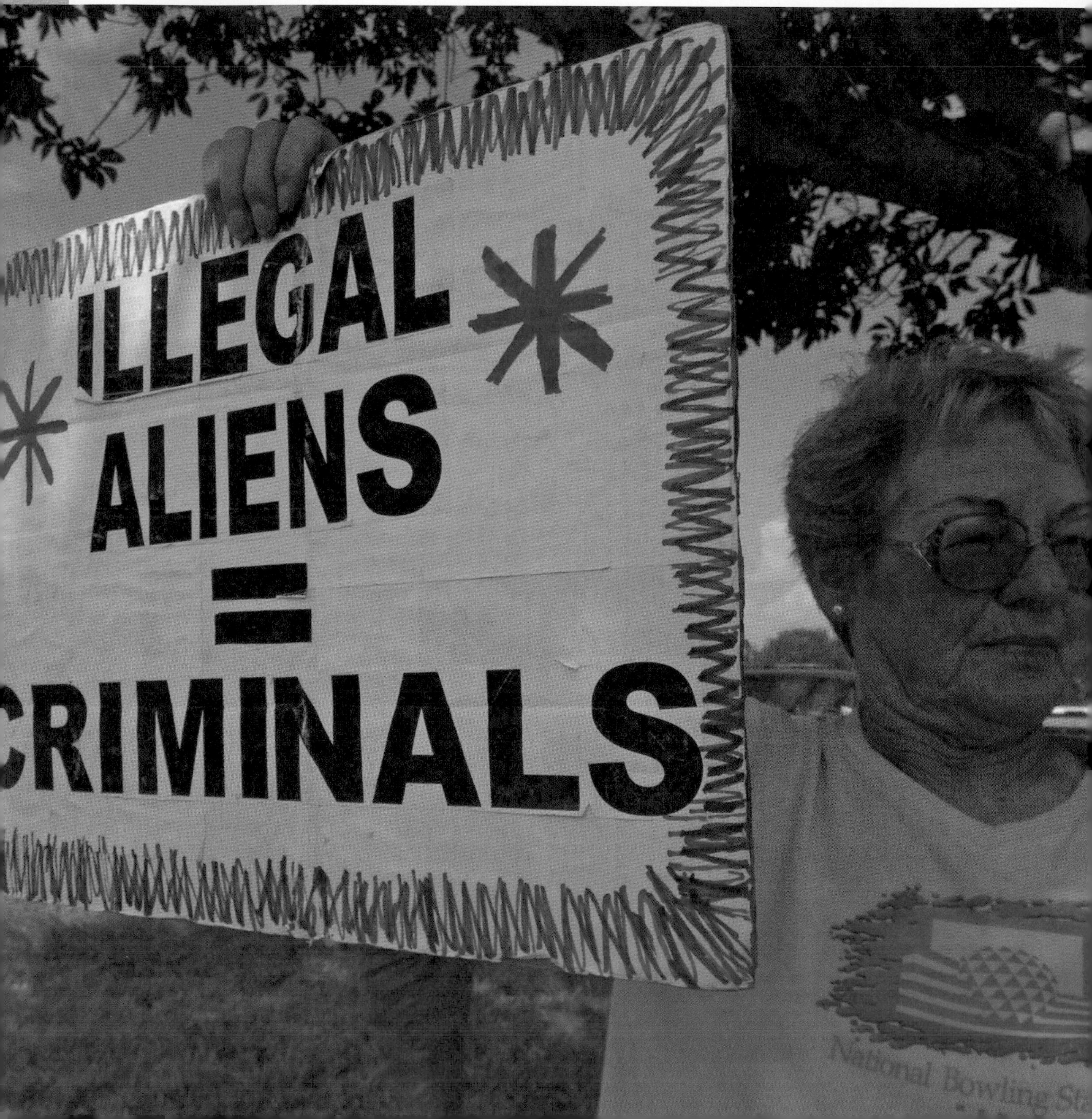

"Prejudice. A vagrant opinion without visible means of support."

—Ambrose Bierce, *The Devil's Dictionary*, 1911

What is the nature and power of prejudice?

What are the social sources of prejudice?

What are the motivational sources of prejudice?

What are the cognitive sources of prejudice?

What are the consequences of prejudice?

Postscript: Can we reduce prejudice?

Prejudice comes in many forms—for our own group and against some other group: "northeastern liberals" or "southern rednecks," against Arab "terrorists" or American "infidels," against people who are short or fat or homely.

Consider some striking examples:

- *Religion.* After 9/11 and the Iraq war, 4 in 10 Americans admitted "some feelings of prejudice against Muslims" and about half of non-Muslims in western Europe perceived Muslims negatively and as "violent" (Pew, 2008; Saad, 2006; Wike & Grim, 2007). Muslims reciprocated the negativity, with most in Jordan, Turkey, Egypt, and even Britain seeing Westerners as "greedy" and "immoral."

- *Obesity.* When seeking love and employment, overweight people—especially White women—face slim prospects. In correlational studies, overweight people marry less often, gain entry to less-desirable jobs, and make less money (Swami & others, 2008). In experiments where some people are made to appear overweight, they are perceived as less attractive, intelligent, happy, self-disciplined, and successful (Gortmaker & others, 1993; Hebl & Heatherton, 1998; Pingitore & others, 1994). Weight discrimination, in fact, exceeds race or gender discrimination and occurs at every employment stage—hiring, placement, promotion, compensations, discipline, and discharge (Roehling, 2000). Negative assumptions about and discrimination against overweight people help explain why overweight women and obese men seldom (relative to their numbers in the general population) become the CEOs of large corporations (Roehling & others, 2008, 2009).

- *Sexual orientation.* Many gay youth—two-thirds of gay secondary school students in one national British survey—report experiencing homophobic bullying (Hunt & Jensen, 2007). And one in five British lesbian and gay adults report having been victimized by aggressive harassment, insults, or physical assaults (Dick, 2008). In a U.S. national survey, 20 percent of gay, lesbian, and bisexual persons reported having experienced a personal or property crime based on their sexual orientation, and half reported experiencing verbal harassment (Herek, 2009).

- *Age.* People's perceptions of the elderly—as generally kind but frail, incompetent, and unproductive—predispose patronizing behavior, such as baby-talk speech that leads elderly people to feel less competent and act less capably (Bugental & Hehman, 2007).

- *Immigrants.* A fast-growing research literature documents anti-immigrant prejudice among Germans toward Turks, the French toward North Africans, the British toward West Indians and Pakistanis, and Americans toward Latin American immigrants (Pettigrew, 2006). As we will see, the same factors that feed racial and gender prejudice also feed dislike of immigrants (Pettigrew & others, 2008; Zick & others, 2008).

What Is the Nature and Power of Prejudice?

How is "prejudice" distinct from "stereotyping," "discrimination," "racism," and "sexism"? Are stereotypes necessarily false or malicious? What forms does prejudice assume today?

Defining Prejudice

prejudice
A preconceived negative judgment of a group and its individual members.

Prejudice, stereotyping, discrimination, racism, sexism—the terms often overlap. Let's clarify them. Each of the situations just described involved a negative evaluation of some group. And that is the essence of **prejudice:** a preconceived negative judgment of a group and its individual members. (Some prejudice definitions include *positive* judgments, but nearly all uses of "prejudice" refer to *negative* ones— what Gordon Allport termed in his classic book, *The Nature of Prejudice,* "an antipathy based upon a faulty and inflexible generalization" [1954, p. 9].)

Prejudice is an attitude. As we saw in Chapter 4, an attitude is a distinct combination of feelings, inclinations to act, and beliefs. It can be easily remembered as the ABCs of attitudes: *a*ffect (feelings), *b*ehavior tendency (inclination to act), and *c*ognition (beliefs). A prejudiced person may *dislike* those different from self and *behave* in a discriminatory manner, *believing* them ignorant and dangerous. Like many attitudes, prejudice is complex. For example, it may include a component of patronizing affection that serves to keep the target disadvantaged.

The negative evaluations that mark prejudice often are supported by negative beliefs, called **stereotypes.** To stereotype is to generalize. To simplify the world, we generalize: The British are reserved. Americans are outgoing. Professors are absentminded. Here are some widely shared stereotypes uncovered in research:

stereotype
A belief about the personal attributes of a group of people. Stereotypes are sometimes overgeneralized, inaccurate, and resistant to new information.

- During the 1980s, women who assumed the title of "Ms." were seen as more assertive and ambitious than those who called themselves "Miss" or "Mrs." (Dion, 1987; Dion & Cota, 1991; Dion & Schuller, 1991). Now that "Ms." is the standard female title, the stereotype has shifted. It's married women who keep their own surnames that are seen as assertive and ambitious (Crawford & others, 1998; Etaugh & others, 1999).

- Public opinion surveys reveal that Europeans have had definite ideas about other Europeans. They have seen the Germans as relatively hardworking, the French as pleasure-loving, the British as cool and unexcitable, the Italians as amorous, and the Dutch as reliable. (One expects these findings to be reliable, considering that they come from Willem Koomen and Michiel Bähler, 1996, at the University of Amsterdam.)

- Europeans also view southern Europeans as more emotional and less efficient than northern Europeans (Linssen & Hagendoorn, 1994). The stereotype of the southerner as more expressive even holds within countries: James Pennebaker and his colleagues (1996) report that across 20 Northern Hemisphere countries (but not in 6 Southern Hemisphere countries), southerners within a country are perceived as more expressive than northerners.

Familiar stereotypes: "Heaven is a place with an American house, Chinese food, British police, a German car, and French art. Hell is a place with a Japanese house, Chinese police, British food, German art, and a French car."
—ANONYMOUS, AS REPORTED BY YUEH-TING LEE (1996)

Such generalizations can be more or less true (and are not always negative). The elderly *are* more frail. Southern countries in the Northern Hemisphere do have higher rates of violence. People living in the south in those countries do report being more expressive than those in the northern regions of their country. Teachers' stereotypes of achievement differences in students from different gender, ethnic, and class backgrounds tend to mirror reality (Madon & others, 1998). "Stereotypes," note Lee Jussim, Clark McCauley, and Yueh-Ting Lee (1995), "may be positive or negative, accurate or inaccurate." An accurate stereotype may even be desirable. We call it "sensitivity to diversity" or "cultural awareness in a multicultural world." To stereotype the British as more concerned about punctuality than Mexicans is to understand what to expect and how to get along with others in each culture.

The problem with stereotypes arises when they are *overgeneralized* or just plain wrong. To presume that most American welfare clients are African American is to overgeneralize, because it just isn't so. University students' stereotypes of members of particular fraternities (as preferring, say, foreign language to economics, or softball to tennis) contain a germ of truth but are overblown. Individuals within the stereotyped group vary more than expected (Brodt & Ross, 1998).

Prejudice is a negative *attitude;* **discrimination** is negative *behavior.* Discriminatory behavior often has its source in prejudicial attitudes (Dovidio & others, 1996; Wagner & others, 2008). Such was evident when researchers analyzed the responses to 1,115 identically worded e-mails sent to Los Angeles area landlords regarding vacant apartments. Encouraging replies came back to 89 percent of notes signed "Patrick McDougall," to 66 percent from "Said Al-Rahman," and to 56 percent from "Tyrell Jackson" (Carpusor & Loges, 2006).

discrimination
Unjustified negative behavior toward a group or its members.

racism

(1) An individual's prejudicial attitudes and discriminatory behavior toward people of a given race, or (2) institutional practices (even if not motivated by prejudice) that subordinate people of a given race.

sexism

(1) An individual's prejudicial attitudes and discriminatory behavior toward people of a given sex, or (2) institutional practices (even if not motivated by prejudice) that subordinate people of a given sex.

As Chapter 4 emphasized, however, attitudes and behavior are often loosely linked. Prejudiced attitudes need not breed hostile acts, nor does all oppression spring from prejudice. **Racism** and **sexism** are institutional practices that discriminate, even when there is no prejudicial intent. If word-of-mouth hiring practices in an all-White business have the effect of excluding potential non-White employees, the practice could be called racist—even if an employer intended no discrimination.

Prejudice: Subtle and Overt

Prejudice provides one of the best examples of our *dual attitude* system (Chapter 2). We can have different explicit (conscious) and implicit (automatic) attitudes toward the same target, as shown by 500 studies using the "Implicit Association Test" (Carpenter, 2008). The test, which Chapter 2 introduced and which has been taken online by some 6 million people, assesses "implicit cognition"—what you know without knowing that you know (Greenwald & others, 2008). It does so by measuring people's speed of associations. Much as we more quickly associate a hammer with a nail than with a pail, so the test can measure how speedily we associate "White" with "good" versus "Black" with "good." Thus, we may retain from childhood a habitual, automatic fear or dislike of people for whom we now express respect and admiration. Although explicit attitudes may change dramatically with education, implicit attitudes may linger, changing only as we form new habits through practice (Kawakami & others, 2000).

A raft of experiments—by researchers at Ohio State University and the University of Wisconsin (Devine & Sharp, 2008), Yale and Harvard universities (Banaji, 2004), Indiana University (Fazio, 2007), the University of Colorado (Wittenbrink, 2007; Wittenbrink & others, 1997), the University of Washington (Greenwald & others, 2000), the University of Virginia (Nosek & others, 2007), and New York University (Bargh & Chartrand, 1999)—have confirmed that prejudiced and stereotypic evaluations can occur outside people's awareness. Some of these studies briefly flash words or faces that "prime" (automatically activate) stereotypes for some racial, gender, or age group. Without their awareness, the participants' activated stereotypes may then bias their behavior. Having been primed with images associated with African Americans, for example, they may then react with more hostility to an experimenter's (intentionally) annoying request.

Keeping in mind the distinction between conscious, explicit prejudice and unconscious, implicit prejudice, let's examine two common forms of prejudice: racial prejudice and gender prejudice.

Racial Prejudice

In the context of the world, every race is a minority. Non-Hispanic Whites, for example, are only one-fifth of the world's people and will be one-eighth within another half-century. Thanks to mobility and migration over the past two centuries, the world's races now intermingle, in relations that are sometimes hostile, sometimes amiable.

To a molecular biologist, skin color is a trivial human characteristic, one controlled by a minuscule genetic difference. Moreover, nature doesn't cluster races in neatly defined categories. It is people, not nature, who label Barack Obama, the son of a White woman, as "Black," and who sometimes label Tiger Woods "African American" (his ancestry is 25 percent African) or "Asian American" (he is also 25 percent Thai and 25 percent Chinese)—or even as Native American or Dutch (he is one-eighth each).

Most folks see prejudice—in other people. In one Gallup poll, White Americans estimated 44 percent of their peers to be high in prejudice (5 or higher on a

10-point scale). How many gave themselves a high score? Just 14 percent (Whitman, 1998).

IS RACIAL PREJUDICE DISAPPEARING?

Which is right: people's perceptions of high prejudice in others, or their perceptions of low prejudice in themselves? And is racial prejudice becoming a thing of the past?

Explicit prejudicial attitudes can change very quickly. In 1942 most Americans agreed, "There should be separate sections for Negroes on streetcars and buses" (Hyman & Sheatsley, 1956). Today the question would seem bizarre, because such blatant prejudice has nearly disappeared. In 1942 fewer than a third of all Whites (only 1 in 50 in the South) supported school integration; by 1980, support for it was 90 percent. Considering what a thin slice of history is covered by the years since 1942 or even since slavery was practiced, the changes are dramatic. In Britain, overt racial prejudice, as expressed in opposition to interracial marriage or having an ethnic minority boss, has similarly plummeted, especially among younger adults (Ford, 2008).

African Americans' attitudes also have changed since the 1940s, when Kenneth Clark and Mamie Clark (1947) demonstrated that many held anti-Black prejudices. In making its historic 1954 decision declaring segregated schools unconstitutional, the Supreme Court found it noteworthy that when the Clarks gave African American children a choice between Black dolls and White dolls, most chose the White. In studies from the 1950s through the 1970s, Black children were increasingly likely to prefer Black dolls. And adult Blacks came to view Blacks and Whites as similar in traits such as intelligence, laziness, and dependability (Jackman & Senter, 1981; Smedley & Bayton, 1978).

People of different races also now share many of the same attitudes and aspirations, notes Amitai Etzioni (1999). More than 9 in 10 Blacks and Whites say they could vote for a Black presidential candidate. More than 8 in 10 in both groups agree that "to graduate from high school, students should be required to understand the common history and ideas that tie all Americans together." Similar proportions in the two groups seek "fair treatment for all, without prejudice or discrimination." And about two-thirds of both groups agree that moral and ethical standards have been in decline. Thanks to such shared ideals, notes Etzioni, most Western democracies have been spared the ethnic tribalism that has torn apart places such as Kosovo and Rwanda.

Shall we conclude, then, that racial prejudice is extinct in countries such as the United States, Britain, and Canada? Not if we consider the 7,772 perpetrators of reported hate crime incidents during 2006 (FBI, 2008). Not if we consider the small proportion of Whites who, as Figure 9.1 shows, would not vote for a Black presidential candidate. Not if we consider the 6 percent greater support that Obama would likely have received in 2008, according to one statistical analysis of voter racial and political attitudes, if there had been no White racial prejudice (Fournier & Tompson, 2008).

So, how great is the progress toward racial equality? In the United States, Whites tend to compare the present with the oppressive past and to perceive swift and radical progress. Blacks tend to compare the present with their ideal world, which has not yet been realized, and to percive somewhat less progress (Eibach & Ehrlinger, 2006).

"I'm a 'Cablinasian.'" Tiger Woods, 1997 (describing his *Ca*ucasian, *Bl*ack, *In*dian, and *Asian* ancestry).

"I cannot let the moment of rejoicing pass without entering in the record my profound appreciation of your part in setting straight the course of American history."
—*LETTER TO KENNETH CLARK, FROM CITY COLLEGE OF NEW YORK PRESIDENT BUELL GALLAGHER, AFTER THE 1954 SUPREME COURT SCHOOL DESEGREGATION DECISION*

Psychologists usually capitalize Black and White to emphasize that these are socially applied race labels, not literal color labels for persons of African and European ancestry.

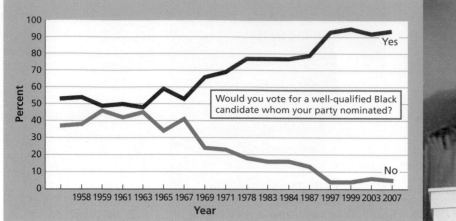

Would you vote for a well-qualified Black candidate whom your party nominated?

FIGURE :: 9.1

Changing Racial Attitudes of White Americans from 1958 to 2007

Abraham Lincoln's ghostly embrace of Barack Obama visualized the Obama mantra: "Change we can believe in." Two days later, Obama stood on steps built by the hands of slaves, placed his hand on a Bible last used in Lincoln's own inauguration, and spoke "a most sacred oath"—in a place, he reflected, where his "father less than 60 years ago might not have been served at a local restaurant."

Source: Data from Gallup Polls (brain.gallup.com).

SUBTLE FORMS OF PREJUDICE

Prejudice in subtle forms is even more widespread. Some experiments have assessed people's *behavior* toward Blacks and Whites. As we will see in Chapter 12, Whites are equally helpful to any person in need—except when the needy person is remote (say, a wrong-number caller with an apparent Black accent who needs a message relayed). Likewise, when asked to use electric shocks to "teach" a task, White people have given no more (if anything, less) shock to a Black than to a White person—except when they were angered or when the recipient couldn't retaliate or know who did it (Crosby & others, 1980; Rogers & Prentice-Dunn, 1981).

Thus, prejudiced attitudes and discriminatory behavior surface when they can hide behind the screen of some other motive. In Australia, Britain, France, Germany, and the Netherlands, blatant prejudice is being replaced by subtle prejudice (exaggerating ethnic differences, feeling less admiration and affection for immigrant minorities, rejecting them for supposedly nonracial reasons) (Pedersen & Walker, 1997; Tropp & Pettigrew, 2005a). Some researchers call such subtle prejudice "modern racism" or "cultural racism." Modern prejudice often appears subtly, in our preferences for what is familiar, similar, and comfortable (Dovidio & others, 1992; Esses & others, 1993a; Gaertner & Dovidio, 2005).

On paper-and-pencil questionnaires, Janet Swim and her co-researchers (1995, 1997) have found a subtle ("modern")

Although prejudice dies last in socially intimate contacts, interracial marriage has increased in most countries, and 77 percent of Americans now approve of "marriage between Blacks and Whites"—a sharp increase from the 4 percent who approved in 1958 (Carroll, 2007).

sexism that parallels subtle ("modern") racism. Both forms appear in denials of discrimination and in antagonism toward efforts to promote equality (as in agreeing with a statement such as "Women are getting too demanding in their push for equal rights").

We can also detect bias in behavior:

- One research team led by Ian Ayres (1991) visited 90 Chicago-area car dealers, using a uniform strategy to negotiate the lowest price on a new car that cost the dealer about $11,000. White males were given a final price that averaged $11,362, White females were given an average price of $11,504, the average price for Black males was $11,783, and for Black females it was $12,237—almost 8 percent higher than the average for White males.

- To test for possible labor market discrimination, M.I.T. researchers sent 5,000 résumés out in response to 1,300 varied employment ads (Bertrand & Mullainathan, 2003). Applicants randomly assigned White names (Emily, Greg) received one callback for every 10 résumés sent. Those given Black names (Lakisha, Jamal) received one callback for every 15 résumés sent.

- In one analysis of traffic stops, African Americans and Latinos were four times more likely than Whites to be searched, twice as likely to be arrested, and three times more likely to be handcuffed and to have excessive force used against them (Lichtblau, 2005).

Modern prejudice even appears as a race sensitivity that leads to exaggerated reactions to isolated minority persons—overpraising their accomplishments, overcriticizing their mistakes, and failing to warn Black students, as they would White students, about potential academic difficulty (Crosby & Monin, 2007; Fiske, 1989; Hart & Morry, 1997; Hass & others, 1991). It also appears as patronization. For example, Kent Harber (1998) gave White students at Stanford University a poorly written essay to evaluate. When the students thought the writer was Black, they rated it *higher* than when they were led to think the author was White, and they rarely offered harsh criticisms. The evaluators, perhaps wanting to avoid the appearance of bias, patronized the Black essayists with lower standards. Such "inflated praise and insufficient criticism" may hinder minority student achievement, Harber noted.

In several American states Black motorists have represented a minority of the drivers and speeders on interstate highways, yet they have been most often stopped and searched by state police (Lamberth, 1998; Staples, 1999a, 1999b). In one New Jersey Turnpike study, Blacks made up 13.5 percent of the car occupants, 15 percent of the speeders, and 35 percent of the drivers stopped.

AUTOMATIC PREJUDICE

How widespread are automatic prejudiced reactions to African Americans? Experiments have shown such reactions in varied contexts. For example, in clever experiments by Anthony Greenwald and his colleagues (1998, 2000), 9 in 10 White people took longer to identify pleasant words (such as *peace* and *paradise*) as "good" when associated with Black rather than White faces. The participants consciously expressed little or no prejudice; their bias was unconscious and unintended. Moreover, report Kurt Hugenberg and Galen Bodenhausen (2003), the more strongly people exhibit such implicit prejudice, the readier they are to perceive anger in Black faces (Figure 9.2).

Critics note that unconscious *associations* may only indicate cultural assumptions, perhaps without *prejudice* (which involves negative feelings and action tendencies). But some studies find that implicit bias can leak into behavior:

- In a Swedish study, a measure of implicit biases against Arab-Muslims predicted the likelihood of 193 corporate employers not interviewing applicants with Muslim names (Rooth, 2007).

- In a medical study of 287 physicians, those exhibiting the most implicit racial bias were the least likely to recommend clot-busting drugs for a Black patient described as complaining of chest pain (Green & others, 2007).

- In a study of 44 Australian drug and alcohol nurses, those displaying the most implicit bias against drug users were also the most likely, when facing job stress, to want a different job (von Hippel & others, 2008).

Some people more quickly learn positive associations (and more slowly learn negative associations) to neutral stimuli. Such people tend to exhibit little implicit racial bias (Livingston & Drwecki, 2007).

FIGURE :: 9.2

Facing Prejudice

Where does the anger disappear? Kurt Hugenberg and Galen Bodenhausen showed university students a movie of faces morphing from angry to happy. Those who had scored as most prejudiced (on an implicit racial attitudes test) perceived anger lingering more in ambiguous Black than White faces.

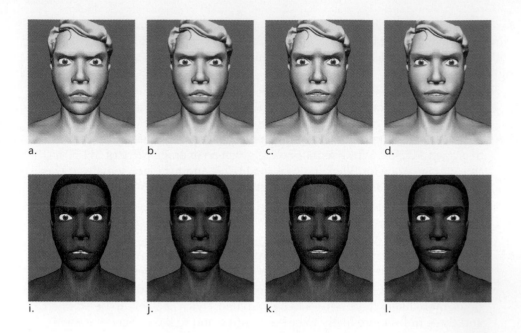

"I cannot totally grasp all that I am. . . . For that darkness is lamentable in which the possibilities in me are hidden from myself."

—*ST. AUGUSTINE,*
CONFESSIONS, A.D. 398

In some situations, automatic, implicit prejudice can have life or death consequences. In separate experiments, Joshua Correll and his co-workers (2002, 2006, 2007) and Anthony Greenwald and his co-workers (2003) invited people to press buttons quickly to "shoot" or "not shoot" men who suddenly appeared on-screen holding either a gun or a harmless object such as a flashlight or a bottle. The participants (both Blacks and Whites, in one of the studies) more often mistakenly shot harmless targets who were Black. In the aftermath of London police shooting dead a man who *looked* Muslim, researchers also found Australians more ready to shoot someone wearing Muslim headgear (Unkelbach & others, 2008). If we implicitly associate a particular ethnic group with danger, then faces from that group will tend to capture our attention and trigger arousal (Donders & others, 2008; Dotsch & Wigboldus, 2008; Trawalter & others, 2008).

In a related series of studies, Keith Payne (2001, 2006) and Charles Judd and colleagues (2004) found that when primed with a Black rather than a White face, people think guns: They more quickly recognize a gun and they more often mistake a

Automatic prejudice. When Joshua Correll and his colleagues invited people to react quickly to people holding either a gun or a harmless object, race influenced perceptions and reactions.

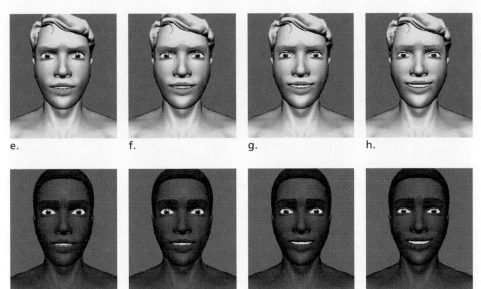

tool, such as a wrench, for a gun. Even when race does not bias perception, it may bias reaction—as people require more or less evidence before firing (Klauer & Voss, 2008).

Jennifer Eberhardt and her colleagues (2004) demonstrated that the reverse effect can occur as well. Exposing people to weapons makes them pay more attention to faces of African Americans and even makes police officers more likely to judge stereotypical-looking African Americans as criminals. These studies help explain why Amadou Diallo (a Black immigrant in New York City) was shot 41 times by police officers for removing his wallet from his pocket.

It also appears that different brain regions are involved in automatic and consciously controlled stereotyping (Correll & others, 2006; Cunningham & others, 2004; Eberhardt, 2005). Pictures of outgroups that elicit the most disgust (such as drug addicts and the homeless) elicit brain activity in areas associated with disgust and avoidance (Harris & Fiske, 2006). This suggests that automatic prejudices involve primitive regions of the brain associated with fear, such as the amygdala, whereas controlled processing is more closely associated with the frontal cortex, which enables conscious thinking. We also use different bits of our frontal lobes when thinking about ourselves or groups we identify with, versus when thinking about people that we perceive as dissimilar to us (Jenkins & others, 2008; Mitchell & others, 2006).

Even the social scientists who study prejudice seem vulnerable to automatic prejudice, note Anthony Greenwald and Eric Schuh (1994). They analyzed biases in authors' citations of social science articles by people with selected non-Jewish names (Erickson, McBride, etc.) and Jewish names (Goldstein, Siegel, etc.). Their analysis of nearly 30,000 citations, including 17,000 citations of prejudice research, found something remarkable: Compared with Jewish authors, non-Jewish authors had 40 percent higher odds of citing non-Jewish names. (Greenwald and Schuh could not determine whether Jewish authors were overciting their Jewish colleagues or whether non-Jewish authors were overciting their non-Jewish colleagues, or both.)

Gender Prejudice

How pervasive is prejudice against women? In Chapter 5 we examined gender-role norms—people's ideas about how women and men *ought* to behave. Here we consider gender *stereotypes*—people's beliefs about how women and men *do* behave. Norms are *pre*scriptive; stereotypes are *de*scriptive.

GENDER STEREOTYPES

"All the pursuits of men are the pursuits of women also, and in all of them a woman is only a lesser man."

—*PLATO*, *REPUBLIC*, *360 B.C.*

From research on stereotypes, two conclusions are indisputable: Strong gender stereotypes exist, and, as often happens, members of the stereotyped group accept the stereotypes. Men and women agree that you *can* judge the book by its sexual cover. In one survey, Mary Jackman and Mary Senter (1981) found that gender stereotypes were much stronger than racial stereotypes. For example, only 22 percent of men thought the two sexes equally "emotional." Of the remaining 78 percent, those who believed females were more emotional outnumbered those who thought males were by 15 to 1. And what did the women believe? To within 1 percentage point, their responses were identical.

Remember that stereotypes are generalizations about a group of people and may be true, false, or overgeneralized from a kernel of truth. In Chapter 5 we noted that the average man and woman do differ somewhat in social connectedness, empathy, social power, aggressiveness, and sexual initiative (though not in intelligence). Do we then conclude that gender stereotypes are accurate? Sometimes stereotypes exaggerate differences. But not always, observed Janet Swim (1994). She found that Pennsylvania State University students' stereotypes of men's and women's restlessness, nonverbal sensitivity, aggressiveness, and so forth were reasonable approximations of actual gender differences. Moreover, such stereotypes have persisted across time and culture. Averaging data from 27 countries, John Williams and his colleagues (1999, 2000) found that folks everywhere perceive women as more agreeable, men as more outgoing. The persistence and omnipresence of gender stereotypes leads some evolutionary psychologists to believe they reflect innate, stable reality (Lueptow & others, 1995).

Stereotypes (beliefs) are not prejudices (attitudes). Stereotypes may support prejudice. Yet one might believe, without prejudice, that men and women are "different yet equal." Let us therefore see how researchers probe for gender prejudice.

SEXISM: BENEVOLENT AND HOSTILE

Judging from what people tell survey researchers, attitudes toward women have changed as rapidly as racial attitudes. As Figure 9.3 shows, the percent of Americans willing to vote for a female presidential candidate has roughly paralleled the increased percent willing to vote for a Black candidate. In 1967, 56 percent of first-year American college students agreed that "the activities of married women are best confined to the home and family"; by 2002, only 22 percent agreed (Astin & others, 1987; Sax & others, 2002). Thereafter, the question no longer seemed worth asking, and in 2008, conservatives cheered what they once would have questioned: the nomination of working mother-of-five Governor Sarah Palin as Republican vice presidential nominee.

"Women are wonderful primarily because they are [perceived as] so nice. [Men are] perceived as superior to women in agentic [competitive, dominant] attributes that are viewed as equipping people for success in paid work, especially in male-dominated occupations."

—*ALICE EAGLY (1994)*

Alice Eagly and her associates (1991) and Geoffrey Haddock and Mark Zanna (1994) also report that people don't respond to women with gut-level negative emotions as they do to certain other groups. Most people like women more than men. They perceive women as more understanding, kind, and helpful. A *favorable* stereotype, which Eagly (1994) dubs the *women-are-wonderful effect*, results in a favorable attitude.

But gender attitudes often are ambivalent, report Peter Glick, Susan Fiske, and their colleagues (1996, 2007) from their surveys of 15,000 people in 19 nations. They frequently mix a *benevolent sexism* ("Women have a superior moral sensibility") with *hostile sexism* ("Once a man commits, she puts him on a tight leash").

Stereotypes about men also come in contrasting pairs. Glick and his colleagues (Glick & others, 2004) report ambivalent sexism toward men—with *benevolent* attitudes of men as powerful and *hostile* attitudes that characterized men as immoral. People who endorse benevolent sexism toward women also tend to endorse benevolent sexism toward men. These complementary ambivalent sexist views of men and women may serve to justify the status quo in gender relations (Jost & Kay, 2005).

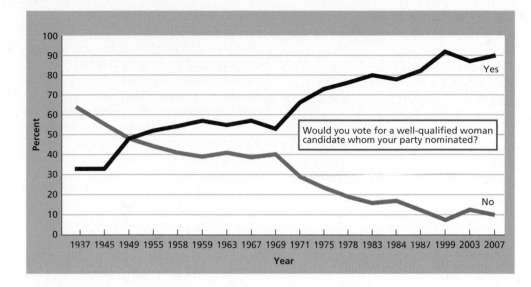

FIGURE :: 9.3

Changing Gender Attitudes from 1958 to 2007

Source: Data from Gallup Polls (brain.gallup.com).

The chart shows the question: "Would you vote for a well-qualified woman candidate whom your party nominated?" plotting Percent (y-axis, 0 to 100) against Year (x-axis: 1937, 1945, 1949, 1955, 1958, 1959, 1963, 1967, 1969, 1971, 1975, 1978, 1983, 1984, 1987, 1999, 2003, 2007). The "Yes" line rises from about 33% to about 90%, and the "No" line falls from about 63% to about 10%.

GENDER DISCRIMINATION

Being male isn't all roses. Compared to women, men are three times more likely to commit suicide and be murdered. They are nearly all the battlefield and death row casualties. They die five years sooner. And males represent the majority with mental retardation or autism, as well as students in special education programs (Baumeister, 2007; S. Pinker, 2008).

Second, one heavily publicized finding of discrimination against women came from a 1968 study in which Philip Goldberg gave women students at Connecticut College several short articles and asked them to judge the value of each. Sometimes a given article was attributed to a male author (for example, John T. McKay) and sometimes to a female author (for example, Joan T. McKay). In general, the articles received lower ratings when attributed to a female. That's right: Women discriminated against women.

Eager to demonstrate the subtle reality of gender discrimination, I obtained Goldberg's materials in 1980 and repeated the experiment with my own students. They (women and men) showed no such tendency to deprecate women's work. So Janet Swim, Eugene Borgida, Geoffrey Maruyama, and I (1989) searched the literature and corresponded with investigators to learn all we could about studies of gender bias in the evaluation of men's and women's work. To our surprise, the biases that occasionally surfaced were as often against men as women. But the most common result across 104 studies involving almost 20,000 people was *no difference*. On most comparisons, judgments of someone's work were unaffected by whether the work was attributed to a female or a male. Summarizing other studies of people's evaluations of women and men as leaders, professors, and so forth, Alice Eagly (1994) concluded, "Experiments have *not* demonstrated any *overall* tendency to devalue women's work."

Is gender bias fast becoming extinct in Western countries? Has the women's movement nearly completed its work? As with racial prejudice, blatant gender prejudice is dying, but subtle bias lives.

One such bias can be seen in analysis of birth announcements (Gonzalez & Koestner, 2005). Parents announce the birth of their baby boys with more pride than the birth of their baby girls. In contrast, they announce the birth of their baby girls with more happiness than the birth of their baby boys. It seems that even at birth, parents are already describing their boys in terms of status and their girls in terms of relationships.

Question: *"Misogyny" is the hatred of women. What is the corresponding word for the hatred of men?*

Answer: *In most dictionaries, no such word exists.*

"And just why do we always call my income the second income?"

Gender prejudice gets expressed subtly.

In the world beyond democratic Western countries, gender discrimination looms even larger. Two-thirds of the world's unschooled children are girls (United Nations, 1991). In some countries, discrimination extends to violence, even to being prosecuted for adultery after being raped or to being doused with kerosene and set ablaze by dissatisfied husbands (UN, 2006).

But the biggest violence against women may occur prenatally. Around the world, people tend to prefer having baby boys. In the United States in 1941, 38 percent of expectant parents said they preferred a boy if they could have only one child; 24 percent preferred a girl; and 23 percent said they had no preference. In 2003 the answers were virtually unchanged with 38 percent still preferring a boy (Lyons, 2003; Simmons, 2000). With the widespread use of ultrasound to determine the sex of a fetus and the growing availability of abortion, these preferences are affecting the number of boys and girls. A recent census in China revealed 118 newborn boys for every 100 girls—leading to projections of a surplus of 40 million males unable to find mates (AP, 2007a). Such unbalanced sex ratios historically have had social consequences, with a male excess (as in frontier towns, immigrant ghettos, and mining camps) predicting more traditional gender roles and higher violence rates (Guttentag & Secord, 1983; Hvistendahl, 2008). Similar imbalances exist in Taiwan (119 boys to 100 girls), Singapore (118 to 100), and parts of India (120 to 100). The net result is tens of millions of "missing women."

To conclude, overt prejudice against people of color and against women is far less common today than it was in the mid-twentieth century. Nevertheless, techniques that are sensitive to subtle prejudice still detect widespread bias. And in parts of the world, gender prejudice makes for misery. Therefore, we need to look carefully and closely at the social, emotional, and cognitive sources of prejudice.

Summing Up: What Is the Nature and Power of Prejudice?

- *Prejudice* is a preconceived negative *attitude*. *Stereotypes* are *beliefs* about another group—beliefs that may be accurate, inaccurate, or overgeneralized but based on a kernel of truth. Discrimination is unjustified negative *behavior*. *Racism* and *sexism* may refer to individuals' prejudicial attitudes or discriminatory behavior, or to oppressive institutional practices (even if not intentionally prejudicial).

- Prejudice exists in subtle and unconscious guises as well as overt, conscious forms. Researchers have devised subtle survey questions and indirect methods for assessing people's attitudes and behavior to detect unconscious prejudice.

- Racial prejudice against Blacks in the United States was widely accepted until the 1960s; since that time it has become far less prevalent, but it still exists.

- Similarly, prejudice against women has lessened in recent decades. Nevertheless, strong gender stereotypes and a fair amount of gender bias are still found in the United States and, to a greater degree, around the world.

What Are the Social Sources of Prejudice?

What social conditions breed prejudice? How does society maintain prejudice?

Prejudice springs from several sources. It may arise from differences in social status and people's desires to justify and maintain those differences. It may also be learned from our parents as we are socialized about what differences matter between people. Our social institutions, too, may function to maintain and support prejudice. Consider first how prejudice can function to defend self-esteem and social position.

Social Inequalities: Unequal Status and Prejudice

A principle to remember: *Unequal status breeds prejudice.* Masters view slaves as lazy, irresponsible, lacking ambition—as having just those traits that justify the slavery. Historians debate the forces that create unequal status. But once those inequalities exist, prejudice helps justify the economic and social superiority of those who have wealth and power. Tell me the economic relationship between two groups and I'll predict the intergroup attitudes.

Historical examples abound. Where slavery was practiced, prejudice ran strong. Nineteenth-century politicians justified imperial expansion by describing exploited colonized people as "inferior," "requiring protection," and a "burden" to be borne (G. W. Allport, 1958, pp. 204–205). Six decades ago, sociologist Helen Mayer Hacker (1951) noted how stereotypes of Blacks and women helped rationalize the inferior status of each: Many people thought both groups were mentally slow, emotional and primitive, and "contented" with their subordinate role. Blacks were "inferior"; women were "weak." Blacks were all right in their place; women's place was in the home.

Theresa Vescio and her colleagues (2005) tested that reasoning. They found that powerful men who stereotype their female subordinates give them plenty of praise, but fewer resources, thus undermining their performance. This sort of patronizing allows the men to maintain their positions of power. In the laboratory, too, patronizing benevolent sexism (statements implying that women, as the weaker sex, need support) has undermined women's cognitive performance by planting intrusive thoughts—self-doubts, preoccupations, and decreased self-esteem (Dardenne & others, 2007).

Peter Glick and Susan Fiske's distinction between "hostile" and "benevolent" sexism extends to other prejudices. We see other groups as competent or as likable, but often not as both. These two culturally universal dimensions of social perception—likability (warmth) and competence—were illustrated by one European's comment that "Germans love Italians, but don't admire them. Italians admire Germans, but don't love them" (Cuddy & others, 2009). We typically *respect* the competence of those high in status and *like* those who agreeably accept a lower status. In the United States, report Fiske and her colleagues (1999), Asians, Jews, Germans, nontraditional women, and assertive African Americans and gay men tend to be respected but not so well liked. Traditionally subordinate African Americans and Hispanics, traditional women, less masculine gay men, and people with disabilities tend to be seen as less competent but liked for their emotional, spiritual, artistic, or athletic qualities.

Some people notice and justify status differences. Those high in **social dominance orientation** tend to view people in terms of hierarchies. They like their own social groups to be high-status—they prefer being on the top. Being in a dominant, high-status position also tends to promote this orientation (Guimond & others, 2003).

"Prejudice is never easy unless it can pass itself off for reason."

—*WILLIAM HAZLITT (1778–1830), "ON PREJUDICE"*

social dominance orientation
A motivation to have one's group dominate other social groups.

Jim Sidanius, Felicia Pratto, and their colleagues (Pratto & others, 1994; Sidanius & others, 2004; Sidanius & Pratto, 1999) argue that this desire to be on top leads people high in social dominance to embrace prejudice and to support political positions that justify prejudice. Indeed, people high in social dominance orientation often support policies that maintain hierarchies such as tax cuts for the well-off, and they often oppose policies that undermine hierarchy, such as affirmative action. People high in social dominance orientation also prefer professions, such as politics and business, that increase their status and maintain hierarchies. They avoid jobs, such as social work, that undermine hierarchies. Status may breed prejudice, but some people more than others seek and try to maintain status.

Socialization

Prejudice springs from unequal status and from other social sources, including our acquired values and attitudes. The influence of family socialization appears in children's prejudices, which often mirror those perceived in their mothers (Castelli & others, 2007). Even children's implicit racial attitudes reflect their parents' explicit prejudice (Sinclair & others, 2004). Our families and cultures pass on all kinds of information—how to find mates, drive cars, and divide the household labors, and whom to distrust and dislike.

THE AUTHORITARIAN PERSONALITY

ethnocentric
Believing in the superiority of one's own ethnic and cultural group, and having a corresponding disdain for all other groups.

authoritarian personality
A personality that is disposed to favor obedience to authority and intolerance of outgroups and those lower in status.

In the 1940s University of California, Berkeley researchers—two of whom had fled Nazi Germany—set out on an urgent research mission: to uncover the psychological roots of an anti-Semitism so poisonous that it caused the slaughter of millions of Jews and turned many millions of Europeans into indifferent spectators. In studies of American adults, Theodor Adorno and his colleagues (1950) discovered that hostility toward Jews often coexisted with hostility toward other minorities. In those who were strongly prejudiced, prejudice appeared to be not specific to one group but an entire way of thinking about those who are "different." Moreover, these judgmental, **ethnocentric** people shared certain tendencies: an intolerance for weakness, a punitive attitude, and a submissive respect for their ingroup's authorities, as reflected in their agreement with such statements as "Obedience and respect for authority are the most important virtues children should learn." From those findings, Adorno and his colleagues (1950) theorized an **authoritarian personality** that is particularly prone to engage in prejudice and stereotyping.

Inquiry into authoritarian people's early lives revealed that, as children, they often faced harsh discipline. That supposedly led them to repress their hostilities and impulses and to "project" them onto outgroups. The insecurity of authoritarian children seemed to predispose them toward an excessive concern with power and status and an inflexible right-wrong way of thinking that made ambiguity difficult to tolerate. Such people therefore tended to be submissive to those with power over them and aggressive or punitive toward those whom they considered beneath them.

Scholars criticized the research for focusing on right-wing authoritarianism and overlooking dogmatic authoritarianism of the left. Still, its main conclusion has survived: Authoritarian tendencies, sometimes reflected in ethnic tensions, surge during threatening times of economic recession and social upheaval (Doty & others, 1991; Sales, 1973). In contemporary Russia, individuals scoring high in authoritarianism have tended to support a return to Marxist-Leninist ideology and to oppose democratic reform (McFarland & others, 1992, 1996).

Moreover, contemporary studies of right-wing authoritarians by University of Manitoba psychologist Bob Altemeyer (1988, 1992) confirm that there *are* individuals whose fears and hostilities surface as prejudice. Their feelings of moral superiority may go hand in hand with brutality toward perceived inferiors.

Different forms of prejudice—toward Blacks, gays and lesbians, women, Muslims, immigrants, the homeless—*do* tend to coexist in the same individuals (Zick

& others, 2008). As Altemeyer concludes, right-wing authoritarians tend to be "equal opportunity bigots."

Particularly striking are people high in social dominance orientation and authoritarian personality. Altemeyer (2004) reports that these "Double Highs" are, not surprisingly, "among the most prejudiced persons in our society." What is perhaps most surprising and more troubling is that they seem to display the worst qualities of each type of personality, striving for status often in manipulative ways while being dogmatic and ethnocentric. Altemeyer argues that although these people are relatively rare, they are predisposed to be leaders of hate groups.

Although authoritarianism and social dominance orientation can co-exist, it appears that they have different ideological bases. Authoritarianism appears more related to concern with security and control, whereas social dominance orientation appears more related to one's group status (Cohrs & others, 2005). For example, one analysis compared how these two constructs related to support for the war in Iraq. Authoritarianism led to support for the war by intensifying the perceived threat to the United States posed by Iraq. Social dominance orientation increased support by reducing concern with the possible loss of life. Both constructs led to greater support by boosting prejudice (McFarland, 2005).

RELIGION AND PREJUDICE

Those who benefit from social inequalities while avowing that "all are created equal" need to justify keeping things the way they are. What could be a more powerful justification than to believe that God has ordained the existing social order? For all sorts of cruel deeds, noted William James, "piety is the mask" (1902, p. 264).

In almost every country, leaders invoke religion to sanctify the present order. The use of religion to support injustice helps explain a consistent pair of findings concerning North American Christianity: (1) church members express more racial prejudice than nonmembers, and (2) those professing traditional or fundamentalist Christian beliefs express more prejudice than those professing more progressive beliefs (Altemeyer & Hunsberger, 1992; Batson & others, 1993; Woodberry & Smith, 1998).

Knowing the correlation between two variables—religion and prejudice—tells us nothing about their causal connection. Consider three possibilities:

- There may be *no connection* at all. Perhaps people with less education are both more fundamentalist and more prejudiced. (In one study of 7,070 Brits, those scoring high on IQ tests at age 10 expressed more nontraditional and anti-racist views at age 30 [Deary & others, 2008].)
- Perhaps *prejudice causes religion,* by leading people to create religious ideas to support their prejudices.
- Or perhaps *religion causes prejudice,* by leading people to believe that because all individuals possess free will, impoverished minorities have themselves to blame for their status.

If indeed religion causes prejudice, then more religious church members should also be more prejudiced. But three other findings consistently indicate otherwise.

- Among church members, faithful church attenders were, in 24 out of 26 comparisons, less prejudiced than occasional attenders (Batson & Ventis, 1982).
- Gordon Allport and Michael Ross (1967) found that those for whom religion is an end in itself (those who agree, for example, with the statement "My religious beliefs are what really lie behind my whole approach to life") express *less* prejudice than those for whom religion is more a means to other ends (who agree "A primary reason for my interest in religion is that my church is a congenial social activity"). And those who score highest on Gallup's "spiritual commitment" index are more welcoming of a person of another race moving in next door (Gallup & Jones, 1992).

- Protestant ministers and Roman Catholic priests gave more support to the civil rights movement than did laypeople (Fichter, 1968; Hadden, 1969). In Germany, 45 percent of clergy in 1934 had aligned themselves with the Confessing Church, which was organized to oppose the Nazi regime (Reed, 1989).

What, then, is the relationship between religion and prejudice? The answer we get depends on *how* we ask the question. If we define religiousness as church membership or willingness to agree at least superficially with traditional beliefs, then the more religious people are the more racially prejudiced. Bigots often rationalize bigotry with religion. But if we assess depth of religious commitment in any of several other ways, then the very devout are less prejudiced—hence the religious roots of the modern civil rights movement, among whose leaders were many ministers and priests. It was Thomas Clarkson and William Wilberforce's faith-inspired values ("Love your neighbor as yourself") that, two centuries ago, motivated their successful campaign to end the British Empire's slave trade and the practice of slavery. As Gordon Allport concluded, "The role of religion is paradoxical. It makes prejudice and it unmakes prejudice" (1958, p. 413).

> "We have just enough religion to make us hate, but not enough to make us love one another."
>
> —JONATHAN SWIFT, THOUGHTS ON VARIOUS SUBJECTS, *1706*

CONFORMITY

Once established, prejudice is maintained largely by inertia. If prejudice is socially accepted, many people will follow the path of least resistance and conform to the fashion. They will act not so much out of a need to hate as out of a need to be liked and accepted. Thus, people become more likely to favor (or oppose) discrimination after hearing someone else do so, and they are less supportive of women after hearing sexist humor (Ford & others, 2008; Zitek & Hebl, 2007).

Thomas Pettigrew's (1958) studies of Whites in South Africa and the American South revealed that during the 1950s, those who conformed most to other social norms were also most prejudiced; those who were less conforming mirrored less of the surrounding prejudice. The price of nonconformity was painfully clear to the ministers of Little Rock, Arkansas, where the U.S. Supreme Court's 1954 school desegregation decision was implemented. Most ministers privately favored integration but feared that advocating it openly would decrease membership and financial contributions (Campbell & Pettigrew, 1959). Or consider the Indiana steelworkers and West Virginia coal miners of the same era. In the mills and the mines, the workers accepted integration. In the neighborhoods, the norm was rigid segregation (Minard, 1952; Reitzes, 1953). Prejudice was clearly not a manifestation of "sick" personalities but simply of the social norms.

Conformity also maintains gender prejudice. "If we have come to think that the nursery and the kitchen are the natural sphere of a woman," wrote George Bernard Shaw in an 1891 essay, "we have done so exactly as English children come to think that a cage is the natural sphere of a parrot—because they have never seen one anywhere else." Children who *have* seen women elsewhere—children of employed women—have less stereotyped views of men and women (Hoffman, 1977).

In all this, there is a message of hope. If prejudice is not deeply ingrained in personality, then as fashions change and new norms evolve, prejudice can diminish. And so it has.

Institutional Supports

Social institutions (schools, government, the media) may bolster prejudice through overt policies such as segregation, or by passively reinforcing the status quo. Until the 1970s many banks routinely denied mortgages to unmarried women and to minority applicants, with the result that most homeowners were White married couples. Similarly, political leaders may both reflect and reinforce prevailing attitudes.

When Arkansas Governor Orville Faubus in 1957 barred the doors of Central High School in Little Rock to prevent integration, he was both representing his constituents and lending legitimacy to their views.

Schools are one of the institutions most prone to reinforce dominant cultural attitudes. An analysis of stories in 134 children's readers written before 1970 found that male characters outnumbered female characters three to one (Women on Words and Images, 1972). Who was portrayed as showing initiative, bravery, and competence? Note the answer in this excerpt from the classic *Dick and Jane* children's reader: Jane, sprawled out on the sidewalk, her roller skates beside her, listens as Mark explains to his mother:

"She cannot skate," said Mark.
"I can help her."
"I want to help her."
"Look at her, Mother."
"Just look at her."
"She's just like a girl."
"She gives up."

Institutional supports for prejudice, like that reader, are often unintended and unnoticed. Not until the 1970s, when changing ideas about males and females brought new perceptions of such portrayals, was this blatant (to us) stereotyping widely noticed and changed.

What contemporary examples of institutionalized biases still go unnoticed? Here is one that most of us failed to notice, although it was right before our eyes: By examining 1,750 photographs of people in magazines and newspapers, Dane Archer and his associates (1983) discovered that about two-thirds of the average male photo, but less than half of the average female photo, was devoted to the face. As Archer widened his search, he discovered that such "face-ism" is common. He found it in the periodicals of 11 other countries, in 920 portraits gathered from the artwork of six centuries, and in the amateur drawings of students at the University of California, Santa Cruz. Georgia Nigro and her colleagues (1988) confirmed the face-ism phenomenon in more magazines, including *Ms.*

The researchers suspect that the visual prominence given the faces of men and the bodies of women both

Unintended bias: Is lighter skin "normal"?

Face-ism: Male photos in the media more often show just the face.

reflects and perpetuates gender bias. In research in Germany, Norbert Schwarz and Eva Kurz (1989) confirmed that people whose faces are prominent in photos seem more intelligent and ambitious. But better a whole-body depiction than none at all. When Ruth Thibodeau (1989) examined the previous 42 years of *New Yorker* cartoons, she could find only a single instance in which an African American appeared in a cartoon unrelated to race. (Even today, because so few syndicated cartoons show diversity, it is easier to depict diversity in this book's photos than in its cartoons.)

Films and television programs also embody and reinforce prevailing cultural attitudes. The muddleheaded, wide-eyed African American butlers and maids in 1930s movies helped perpetuate the stereotypes they reflected. Today many people find such images offensive, yet even a modern TV comedy skit of a crime-prone African American can later make another African American who is accused of assault seem more guilty (Ford, 1997). Violent rap music from Black artists leads both Black and White listeners to stereotype Blacks as having violent dispositions (Johnson & others, 2000). And sexual rap music depictions of promiscuous Black females reduce listeners' support for Black pregnant women in need (Johnson & others, 2009).

Summing Up: What Are the Social Sources of Prejudice?

- The social situation breeds and maintains prejudice in several ways. A group that enjoys social and economic superiority will often use prejudicial beliefs to justify its privileged position.
- Children are also brought up in ways that foster or reduce prejudice. The family, religious communities, and the broader society can sustain or reduce prejudices.
- Social institutions (government, schools, the media) also support prejudice, sometimes through overt policies and sometimes through unintentional inertia.

What Are the Motivational Sources of Prejudice?

Prejudice may be bred by social situations, but motivation underlies both the hostilities of prejudice and the desire to be unbiased. Frustration can feed prejudice, as can the desire to see one's group as superior. But at times, people are also motivated to avoid prejudice.

Frustration and Aggression: The Scapegoat Theory

As we will see in Chapter 10, pain and frustration (the blocking of a goal) often evoke hostility. When the cause of our frustration is intimidating or unknown, we often redirect our hostility. This phenomenon of "displaced aggression" may have contributed to the lynchings of African Americans in the South after the Civil War. Between 1882 and 1930, more lynchings occurred in years when cotton prices were low and economic frustration was therefore presumably high (Hepworth & West, 1988; Hovland & Sears, 1940). Hate crimes seem not to have fluctuated with unemployment in recent decades (Green & others, 1998). However, when living standards are rising, societies tend to be more open to diversity and to the passage and enforcement of antidiscrimination laws (Frank, 1999). Ethnic peace is easier to maintain during prosperous times.

Targets for displaced aggression vary. Following their defeat in World War I and their country's subsequent economic chaos, many Germans saw Jews as villains. Long before Hitler came to power, one German leader explained: "The Jew is just convenient. . . . If there were no Jews, the anti-Semites would have to invent them" (quoted by G. W. Allport, 1958, p. 325). In earlier centuries people vented their fear and hostility on witches, whom they sometimes burned or drowned in public. In our time, it was those Americans who felt more anger than fear after the 9/11 attack who expressed greater intolerance toward immigrants and Middle Easterners (Skitka & others, 2004). Passions provoke prejudice.

Competition is an important source of frustration that can fuel prejudice. When two groups compete for jobs, housing, or social prestige, one group's goal fulfillment can become the other group's frustration. Thus, the **realistic group conflict theory** suggests that prejudice arises when groups compete for scarce resources (Maddux & others, 2008; Riek & others, 2006; Sassenberg & others, 2007). A corresponding ecological principle, Gause's law, states that maximum competition will exist between species with identical needs.

In Western Europe, for example, some people agree, "Over the last five years people like yourself have been economically worse off than most [name of country's minority group]." These frustrated people also express relatively high levels of blatant prejudice (Pettigrew & Meertens, 1995; Pettigrew & others, 2008). In Canada, opposition to immigration since 1975 has gone up and down with the unemployment rate (Palmer, 1996). In the United States, concerns about immigrants taking jobs are greatest among those with the lowest incomes (AP/Ipsos, 2006; Pew, 2006). Likewise, the strongest anti-Black prejudice has occurred among Whites who are closest to Blacks on the socioeconomic ladder (Greeley & Sheatsley, 1971; Pettigrew, 1978; Tumin, 1958). When interests clash, prejudice may be the result.

"And now at this point in the meeting I'd like to shift the blame away from me and onto someone else."

Scapegoats provide an outlet for frustrations and hostilities.
© The New Yorker Collection, 1985, Michael Maslin, from cartoonbank.com. All Rights Reserved.

realistic group conflict theory
The theory that prejudice arises from competition between groups for scarce resources.

"Whoever is dissatisfied with himself is continually ready for revenge."
—NIETZSCHE, THE GAY SCIENCE, *1882–1887*

Social Identity Theory: Feeling Superior to Others

Humans are a group-bound species. Our ancestral history prepares us to feed and protect ourselves—to live—in groups. Humans cheer for their groups, kill for their groups, die for their groups. Not surprisingly, we also define ourselves by our groups, note Australian social psychologists John Turner (1981, 2001, 2004),

social identity

The "we" aspect of our self-concept; the part of our answer to "Who am I?" that comes from our group memberships.

Michael Hogg (1992, 2006, 2008), and their colleagues. Self-concept—our sense of who we are—contains not just a *personal identity* (our sense of our personal attributes and attitudes) but also a **social identity** (Chen & others, 2006). Fiona identifies herself as a woman, an Aussie, a Labourite, a University of New South Wales student, a member of the MacDonald family. We carry such social identities like playing cards, playing them when appropriate. Prime American students to think of themselves as "Americans" and they will display heightened anger and disrespect toward Muslims; prime their "student" identity and they will instead display heightened anger toward police (Ray & others, 2008).

Working with the late British social psychologist Henri Tajfel, a Polish native who lost family and friends in the Holocaust and then devoted much of his career to studying ethnic hatred, Turner proposed *social identity theory*. Turner and Tajfel observed the following:

ingroup

"Us"—a group of people who share a sense of belonging, a feeling of common identity.

- *We categorize:* We find it useful to put people, ourselves included, into categories. To label someone as a Hindu, a Scot, or a bus driver is a shorthand way of saying some other things about the person.
- *We identify:* We associate ourselves with certain groups (our **ingroups**), and gain self-esteem by doing so.
- *We compare:* We contrast our groups with other groups (**outgroups**), with a favorable bias toward our own group.

outgroup

"Them"—a group that people perceive as distinctively different from or apart from their ingroup.

We evaluate ourselves partly by our group memberships. Having a sense of "we-ness" strengthens our self-concepts. It *feels* good. We seek not only *respect* for ourselves but also *pride* in our groups (Smith & Tyler, 1997). Moreover, seeing our groups as superior helps us feel even better. It's as if we all think, "I am an X [name your group]. X is good. Therefore, I am good."

Lacking a positive personal identity, people often seek self-esteem by identifying with a group. Thus, many disadvantaged youths find pride, power, security, and identity in gang affiliations. When people's personal and social identities become fused—when the boundary between self and group blurs—they become more willing to fight or die for their group (Swann & others, 2009). Many superpatriots, for example, define themselves by their national identities (Staub, 1997, 2005). And many people at loose ends find identity in their associations with new religious movements, self-help groups, or fraternal clubs (Figure 9.4).

Because of our social identifications, we conform to our group norms. We sacrifice ourselves for team, family, nation. And the more important our social identity and the more strongly attached we feel to a group, the more we react prejudicially to threats from another group (Crocker & Luhtanen, 1990; Hinkle & others, 1992). Israeli historian and former Jerusalem deputy mayor Meron Benvenisti (1988) reported that among Jerusalem's Jews and Arabs, social identity has been so central to self-concept that it constantly reminds them of who they are not. Thus, on the integrated street where he lived, his own children—to his dismay—"have not acquired a single Arab friend."

INGROUP BIAS

The group definition of who you are—your gender, race, religion, marital status, academic major—implies a definition of who you are not. The circle that includes "us" (the ingroup) excludes "them" (the outgroup). The more that ethnic Turks in the Netherlands see themselves as Turks or as Muslims, the less they see themselves as Dutch (Verkuyten & Yildiz, 2007).

ingroup bias

The tendency to favor one's own group.

The mere experience of being formed into groups may promote **ingroup bias.** Ask children, "Which are better, the children in your school or the children at [another school nearby]?" Virtually all will say their own school has the better children.

For adults, too, the closer to home, the better things seem. More than 80 percent of both Whites and Blacks say race relations are generally good in their own

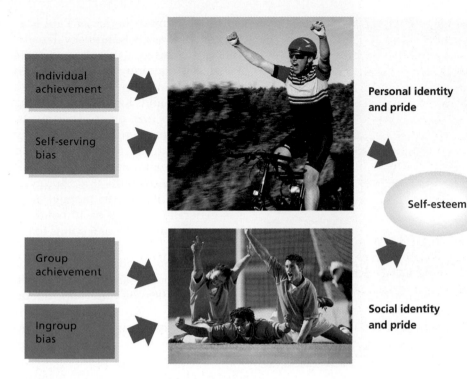

neighborhoods, but fewer than 60 percent see relations as generally good in the country as a whole (Sack & Elder, 2000). Merely sharing a birthday with someone creates enough of a bond to evoke heightened cooperation in a laboratory experiment (Miller & others, 1998).

INGROUP BIAS SUPPORTS A POSITIVE SELF-CONCEPT   Ingroup bias is one more example of the human quest for a positive self-concept (Chapter 2). When our group has been successful, we can make ourselves feel better by identifying more strongly with it. College students whose team has just been victorious frequently report, "*We* won." After their team's defeat, though, students are more likely to say, "*They* lost." Basking in the reflected glory of a successful ingroup is strongest among those who have just experienced an ego blow, such as learning they did poorly on a "creativity test" (Cialdini & others, 1976). We can also bask in the reflected glory of a friend's achievement—except when the friend outperforms us on something pertinent to our identity (Tesser & others, 1988). If you think of yourself as an outstanding psychology student, you will likely take more pleasure in a friend's excellence in mathematics.

INGROUP BIAS FEEDS FAVORITISM   We are so group-conscious that, given any excuse to think of ourselves as a group, we will do so—and we will then exhibit ingroup bias. Even forming conspicuous groups on no logical basis—say, merely by composing groups X and Y with the flip of a coin—will produce some ingroup bias (Billig & Tajfel, 1973; Brewer & Silver, 1978; Locksley & others, 1980). In Kurt Vonnegut's novel *Slapstick*, computers gave everyone a new middle name; all "Daffodil-11s" then felt unity with one another and distance from "Raspberry-13s." The self-serving bias (Chapter 2) rides again, enabling people to achieve a more positive social identity: "We" are better than "they," even when "we" and "they" are defined randomly!

In a series of experiments, Tajfel and Michael Billig (1974; Tajfel, 1970, 1981, 1982) further explored how little it takes to provoke favoritism toward *us* and unfairness toward *them*. In one study, Tajfel and Billig had individual British teenagers evaluate modern abstract paintings and then told them that they and some other

"There is a tendency to define one's own group positively in order to evaluate oneself positively."
—*JOHN C. TURNER (1984)*

Basking in reflected glory. After Jamaican-Canadian sprinter Ben Johnson won the Olympic 100-meter race, Canadian media described this victory by a "Canadian." After Johnson's gold medal was taken away because of steroid use, Canadian media then emphasized his "Jamaican" identity (Stelzl & others, 2008).

"Nationality is a sense of belonging and a sense of place—a pleasure in your history, in the peculiarities of your people's behaviour, in the music and the familiar sounds of the world around you. I don't think a particular culture is better. I just think it's a culture you are more at home with."

—*BILL WILSON, SCOTTISH NATIONALIST PARTY ACTIVIST, 2003*

Something favored by an "outgroup" may be cast in a negative light.

"*Uh-oh! They seem to have loved it!*"

teens had favored the art of Paul Klee over that of Wassily Kandinsky. Finally, without ever meeting the other members of their Klee-favoring group, each teen divided some money among members of the Klee- and Kandinsky-favoring groups. In this and other experiments, defining groups even in this trivial way produced ingroup favoritism. David Wilder (1981) summarized the typical result: "When given the opportunity to divide 15 points [worth money], subjects generally award 9 or 10 points to their own group and 5 or 6 points to the other group."

We are more prone to ingroup bias when our group is small and lower in status relative to the outgroup (Ellemers & others, 1997; Mullen & others, 1992). When we're part of a small group surrounded by a larger group, we are more conscious of our group membership; when our ingroup is the majority, we think less about it. To be a foreign student, to be gay or lesbian, or to be of a minority race or gender at some social gathering is to feel one's social identity more keenly and to react accordingly.

MUST INGROUP LIKING FOSTER OUTGROUP DISLIKING? Does ingroup bias reflect (1) liking for the ingroup, (2) dislike for the outgroup, or both? Does ethnic pride cause prejudice? Does a strong feminist identity lead feminists to dislike nonfeminists? Does loyalty to a particular fraternity or sorority lead its members to deprecate independents and members of other fraternities and sororities? Or is (1) true: people merely favor their own group without any animosity toward others?

Experiments support both (1) and (2). Outgroup stereotypes prosper when people feel their ingroup identity keenly, such as when they are with other ingroup members (Wilder & Shapiro, 1991). At a club meeting, we sense most strongly our differences from those in another club. When anticipating bias against our group, we more strongly disparage the outgroup (Vivian & Berkowitz, 1993).

We also ascribe uniquely human emotions (love, hope, contempt, resentment) to ingroup members, and are more reluctant to see such human emotions in outgroup members (Demoulin & others, 2008; Leyens & others, 2003, 2007). There is a long history of denying human attributes to outgroups—a process called "infrahumanization." European explorers pictured many of the peoples they encountered as savages ruled by animal instinct. "Africans have been likened to apes, Jews to vermin, and immigrants to parasites," note Australian social psychologists Stephen Loughman and Nick Haslam (2007).

Yet ingroup bias results at least as much from perceiving that one's own group is good (Brewer, 2007) as from a sense that other groups are bad (Rosenbaum & Holtz, 1985). Even when there is no "them" (imagine yourself bonding with a handful of fellow survivors on a deserted island), one can come to love "us" (Gaertner & others, 2006). So it seems that positive feelings for our own groups need not be mirrored by equally strong negative feelings for outgroups.

NEED FOR STATUS, SELF-REGARD, AND BELONGING

Status is relative: To perceive ourselves as having status, we need people below us. Thus, one psychological benefit of prejudice, or of any status system, is a feeling of superiority. Most of us can recall a time when we took secret satisfaction in another's failure—perhaps seeing a brother or sister punished or a classmate failing a test. In Europe and North America, prejudice is often greater among those low or slipping on the socioeconomic ladder and among those whose positive self-image is being threatened (Lemyre & Smith, 1985; Pettigrew & others, 1998; Thompson & Crocker, 1985). In one study, members of lower-status sororities were more disparaging of other sororities than were members of higher-status sororities (Crocker & others, 1987). Perhaps people whose status is secure have less need to feel superior.

In study after study, thinking about your own mortality—by writing a short essay on dying and the emotions aroused by thinking about death—provokes enough insecurity to intensify ingroup favoritism and outgroup prejudice (Greenberg & others, 1990, 1994; Harmon-Jones & others, 1996; Schimel & others 1999; Solomon & others, 2000). One study found that among Whites, thinking about death can even promote liking for racists who argue for their group's superiority (Greenberg & others, 2001, 2008). With death on their minds, people exhibit **terror management.** They shield themselves from the threat of their own death by derogating those who further arouse their anxiety by challenging their worldviews. When people are

Father, Mother, and Me,
  sister and Auntie say
All the people like us are
  We, and every one else
  is They.
And They live over the
  sea, While We live over
  the way.
But would you believe it?
  They look upon We
As only a sort of They!
—RUDYARD KIPLING, 1926
(QUOTED BY MULLEN, 1991)

"By exciting emulation and comparisons of superiority, you lay the foundation of lasting mischief; you make brothers and sisters hate each other."
—SAMUEL JOHNSON, QUOTED IN JAMES BOSWELL'S LIFE OF SAMUEL JOHNSON, 1791

terror management According to "terror management theory," people's self-protective emotional and cognitive responses (including adhering more strongly to their cultural worldviews and prejudices) when confronted with reminders of their mortality.

The curse of cliques? Did the tendency of high school students to form ingroups and disparage outgroups—jocks, preppies, goths, geeks—contribute to a tribal atmosphere that helped form the context for school massacres, like the one at Colorado's Columbine High School being remembered here, or elsewhere?

"It's not enough that we succeed. Cats must also fail."

already feeling vulnerable about their mortality, prejudice helps bolster a threatened belief system. Thinking about death can also, however, lead people to pursue communal feelings such as togetherness and altruism (McGregor & others, 2001).

Reminding people of their death can also affect support for important public policies. Before the 2004 presidential election, giving people cues related to death—including asking them to recall their emotions related to the 9/11 attack, or subliminally exposing them to 9/11 related pictures—increased support for President George W. Bush and his anti-terrorism policies (Landau & others, 2004). In Iran, reminders of death increased college students' support for suicide attacks against the United States (Pyszczynski & others, 2006).

All this suggests that a man who doubts his own strength and independence might, by proclaiming women to be pitifully weak and dependent, boost his masculine image. Indeed, when Joel Grube, Randy Kleinhesselink, and Kathleen Kearney (1982) had Washington State University men view young women's videotaped job interviews, men with low self-acceptance disliked strong, nontraditional women. Men with high self-acceptance preferred them. Experiments confirm the connection between self-image and prejudice: Affirm people and they will evaluate an outgroup more positively; threaten their self-esteem and they will restore it by denigrating an outgroup (Fein & Spencer, 1997; Spencer & others, 1998).

An Arizona State University research team argues that the nature of an outgroup threat influences perceptions of the outgroup (Cottrell & Neuberg, 2005; Maner & others, 2005). For example, when the safety of one's ingroup is threatened, people will be vigilant for signs of outgroup anger. When the researchers activated self-protection concerns (for example, by having participants view scary movie clips), they found that White people perceived greater anger in African American male and Arab faces.

Despised outgroups can also serve to strengthen the ingroup. As we will explore further in Chapter 13, the perception of a common enemy unites a group. School spirit is seldom so strong as when the game is with the archrival. The sense of comradeship among workers is often highest when they all feel a common antagonism toward management. To solidify the Nazi hold over Germany, Hitler used the "Jewish menace." But when the need to belong is met, people become more accepting of outgroups, report Mario Mikulincer and Phillip Shaver (2001). They subliminally primed some Israeli students with words that fostered a sense of belonging (*love, support, hug*) and others with neutral words. The students then read an essay that was supposedly written by a fellow Jewish student and another by an Arab student. When primed with neutral words, the Israeli students evaluated the supposed Israeli student's essay as superior to the supposed Arab student's essay. When the participants were primed with a sense of belonging, that bias disappeared.

Motivation to Avoid Prejudice

Motivations not only lead people to be prejudiced but also lead people to avoid prejudice. Try as we might to suppress unwanted thoughts—thoughts about food, thoughts about romance with a friend's partner, judgmental thoughts about another group—they sometimes refuse to go away (Macrae & others, 1994; Wegner & Erber, 1992). This is especially so for older adults, and people under alcohol's influence who lose some of their ability to inhibit unwanted thoughts and therefore to suppress old stereotypes (Bartholow & others, 2006; von Hippel & others,

2000). Patricia Devine and her colleagues (1989, 2000, 2005) report that people low and high in prejudice sometimes have similar automatic prejudicial responses. The result: Unwanted (dissonant) thoughts and feelings often persist. Breaking the prejudice habit is not easy.

In real life, encountering a minority person may trigger a knee-jerk stereotype. Those with accepting and those with disapproving attitudes toward homosexuals may both feel uncomfortable sitting with a gay male on a bus seat (Monteith, 1993). Encountering an unfamiliar Black male, people—even those who pride themselves on not being prejudiced—may respond warily. Seeking not to appear prejudiced, they may divert their attention away from the person (Richeson & Trawalter, 2008).

In one experiment by E. J. Vanman and colleagues (1990), White people viewed slides of White and Black people, imagined themselves interacting with them, and rated their probable liking of the person. Although the participants saw themselves liking the Black more than the White persons, their facial muscles told a different story. Instruments revealed that when a Black face appeared, there tended to be more activity in frowning than smiling muscles. An emotion processing center in the brain also becomes more active as a person views an unfamiliar person of another race (Hart & others, 2000).

Researchers who study stereotyping contend, however, that prejudicial reactions are not inevitable (Crandall & Eshelman, 2003; Kunda & Spencer, 2003). The motivation to avoid prejudice can lead people to modify their thoughts and actions. Aware of the gap between how they *should* feel and how they *do* feel, self-conscious people will feel guilt and try to inhibit their prejudicial response (Bodenhausen & Macrae, 1998; Dasgupta & Rivera, 2006; Zuwerink & others, 1996). Even automatic prejudices subside, note Devine and her colleagues (2005), when people's motivation to avoid prejudice is internal (because prejudice is wrong) rather than external (because they don't want others to think badly of them).

The moral: Overcoming what Devine calls "the prejudice habit" isn't easy. If you find yourself reacting with knee-jerk presumptions or feelings, don't despair; that's not unusual. It's what you do with that awareness that matters. Do you let those feelings hijack your behavior? Or do you compensate by monitoring and correcting your behavior in future situations?

Summing Up: What Are the Motivational Sources of Prejudice?

- People's motivations affect prejudice. Frustration breeds hostility, which people sometimes vent on scapegoats and sometimes express more directly against competing groups.

- People also are motivated to view themselves and their groups as superior to other groups. Even trivial group memberships lead people to favor their group over others. A threat to self-image heightens such ingroup favoritism, as does the need to belong.

- On a more positive note, if people are motivated to avoid prejudice, they can break the prejudice habit.

What Are the Cognitive Sources of Prejudice?

To understand stereotyping and prejudice, it also helps to remember how our minds work. How does the way we think about the world, and simplify it, influence our stereotypes? And how do our stereotypes affect our judgments?

FIGURE :: 9.5

Number of Psychological Articles Mentioning "Stereotypes" (or Derivative Word), by Decade

Source: PsycINFO.

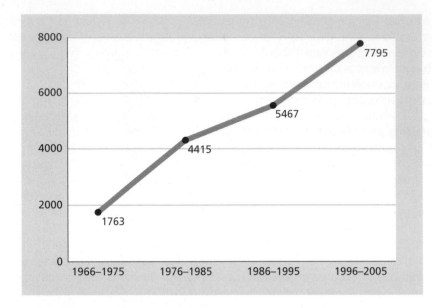

A newer look at prejudice, fueled by a surge in studies of stereotyping (Figure 9.5), applies new research on social thinking. The basic point is this: Stereotyped beliefs and prejudiced attitudes exist not only because of social conditioning and because they enable people to displace hostilities, but also as by-products of normal thinking processes. Many stereotypes spring less from malice of the heart than the machinery of the mind. Like perceptual illusions, which are by-products of our knack for interpreting the world, stereotypes can be by-products of how we simplify our complex worlds.

Categorization: Classifying People into Groups

One way we simplify our environment is to *categorize*—to organize the world by clustering objects into groups (Macrae & Bodenhausen, 2000, 2001). A biologist classifies plants and animals. A human classifies people. Having done so, we think about them more easily. If persons in a group share some similarities—if most MENSA members are smart, most basketball players are tall—knowing their group memberships can provide useful information with minimal effort (Macrae & others, 1994). Stereotypes sometimes offer "a beneficial ratio of information gained to effort expended" (Sherman & others, 1998). Stereotypes represent cognitive efficiency. They are energy-saving schemes for making speedy judgments and predicting how others will think and act.

SPONTANEOUS CATEGORIZATION

We find it especially easy and efficient to rely on stereotypes when we are

- pressed for time (Kaplan & others, 1993).
- preoccupied (Gilbert & Hixon, 1991).
- tired (Bodenhausen, 1990).
- emotionally aroused (Esses & others, 1993b; Stroessner & Mackie, 1993).
- too young to appreciate diversity (Biernat, 1991).

Ethnicity and sex are powerful ways of categorizing people. Imagine Tom, a 45-year-old African American Atlanta real estate agent. I suspect that your image of "Black male" predominates over the categories "middle-aged," "businessperson," and "American southerner."

Experiments expose our spontaneous categorization of people by race. Much as we organize what is actually a color continuum into what we perceive as distinct colors such as red, blue, and green, so we cannot resist categorizing people into groups. We label people of widely varying ancestry as simply "Black" or "White," as if such categories were black and white. When individuals view different people making statements, they often forget who said what, yet they remember the race of the person who made each statement (Hewstone & others, 1991; Stroessner & others, 1990; Taylor & others, 1978). By itself, such categorization is not prejudice, but it does provide a foundation for prejudice.

In fact, it's necessary for prejudice. Social identity theory implies that those who feel their social identity keenly will concern themselves with correctly categorizing people as *us* or *them*. To test that prediction, Jim Blascovich and his co-researchers (1997) compared racially prejudiced people (who feel their racial identity keenly) with nonprejudiced people. Both groups were equally speedy at classifying white, black, and gray ovals. But how much time did each group take to categorize *people* by race? Especially when shown faces whose race was somewhat ambiguous (Figure 9.6), prejudiced people took longer, with more apparent concern for classifying people as either "us" (one's own race) or "them" (another race). Prejudice requires racial categorization.

FIGURE :: 9.6

Racial Categorization

Quickly: What race is this person? Less prejudiced people respond more quickly, with less apparent concern with possibly misclassifying someone (as if thinking, "who cares?").

PERCEIVED SIMILARITIES AND DIFFERENCES

Picture the following objects: apples, chairs, pencils.

There is a strong tendency to see objects within a group as being more uniform than they really are. Were your apples all red? Your chairs all straight-backed? Your pencils all yellow? Once we classify two days in the same month, they seem more alike, temperature-wise, than the same interval across months. People guess the eight-day average temperature difference between, say, November 15 and 23 to be less than the eight-day difference between November 30 and December 8 (Krueger & Clement, 1994).

It's the same with people. Once we assign people to groups—athletes, drama majors, math professors—we are likely to exaggerate the similarities within the groups and the differences between them (S. E. Taylor, 1981; Wilder, 1978). Mere division into groups can create an **outgroup homogeneity effect**—a sense that *they* are "all alike" and different from "us" and "our" group (Ostrom & Sedikides, 1992). As we generally like people we perceive as similar to us and dislike those we perceive as different, the result is a tendency toward ingroup bias (Byrne & Wong, 1962; Rokeach & Mezei, 1966; Stein & others, 1965).

The mere fact of a group decision can also lead outsiders to overestimate a group's unanimity. If a conservative wins a national election by a slim majority, observers infer that "the people have turned conservative." If a liberal won by an equally slim margin, voter attitudes would barely differ, but observers would now attribute a "liberal mood" to the country. Whether a decision is made by majority rule or by a designated group executive, people tend to presume that it reflects the entire group's attitudes (Allison & others, 1985 to 1996). In the 1994 U.S. elections, Republicans captured the Congress with 53 percent of the votes (in an election in

outgroup homogeneity effect

Perception of outgroup members as more similar to one another than are ingroup members. Thus "they are alike; we are diverse."

which most adults did not vote)—producing what commentators described as a "revolution," a "landslide," a "sea change" in American politics. Even the 2000 U.S. presidential election, a virtual draw, was interpreted as a repudiation of the losing candidate, Al Gore, who actually received more votes.

When the group is our own, we are more likely to see diversity:

* Many non-Europeans see the Swiss as a fairly homogeneous people. But to the people of Switzerland, the Swiss are diverse, encompassing French-, German-, Italian-, and Romansh-speaking groups.
* Many Anglo Americans lump "Latinos" together. Mexican Americans, Cuban Americans, and Puerto Ricans—among many others—see important differences (Huddy & Virtanen, 1995).
* Sorority sisters perceive the members of any other sorority as less diverse than the members of their own (Park & Rothbart, 1982).

"Women are more like each other than men [are]"

—LORD (NOT LADY) CHESTERFIELD

In general, the greater our familiarity with a social group, the more we see its diversity (Brown & Wootton-Millward, 1993; Linville & others, 1989). The less our familiarity, the more we stereotype. Also, the smaller and less powerful the group, the less we attend to them and the more we stereotype (Fiske, 1993; Hancock & Rhodes, 2008; Mullen & Hu, 1989).

Perhaps you have noticed: *They*—the members of any racial group other than your own—even *look* alike. Many of us can recall embarrassing ourselves by confusing two people of another racial group, prompting the person we've misnamed to say, "You think we all look alike." Experiments by John Brigham, June Chance, Alvin Goldstein, and Roy Malpass in the United States and by Hayden Ellis in Scotland reveal that people of other races do in fact *seem* to look more alike than do people of one's own race (Chance & Goldstein, 1981, 1996; Ellis, 1981; Meissner & Brigham, 2001). When White students are shown faces of a few White and a few Black individuals and then asked to pick those individuals out of a photographic lineup, they show an **own-race bias:** They more accurately recognize the White faces than the Black, and they often falsely recognize Black faces never before seen.

own-race bias

The tendency for people to more accurately recognize faces of their own race. (Also called the *cross-race effect* or *other-race effect*.)

As Figure 9.7 illustrates, Blacks more easily recognize another Black than they do a White (Bothwell & others, 1989). Similarly, Hispanics more readily recognize another Hispanic whom they saw a couple of hours earlier than they do an equally slightly familiar Anglo (Platz & Hosch, 1988). Likewise, British South Asians are quicker than White Brits to recognize South Asian faces (Walker & Hewstone, 2008). And 10- to 15-year-old Turkish children are quicker than Austrian children to recognize Turkish faces (Sporer & others, 2007). Even infants as young as 9 months display better own-race recognition of faces (Kelly & others, 2005, 2007).

FIGURE :: 9.7

The Own-Race Bias

White subjects more accurately recognize the faces of Whites than of Blacks; Black subjects more accurately recognize the faces of Blacks than of Whites.

Source: From P. G. Devine & R. S. Malpass, 1985.

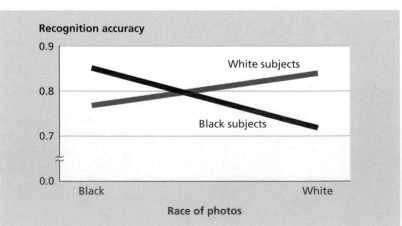

It's true outside the laboratory as well, as Daniel Wright and his colleagues (2001) found after either a Black or a White researcher approached Black and White people in South African and English shopping malls. When later asked to identify the researcher from lineups, people better recognized those of their own race. Follow-up research also reveals an "own-age bias": People more accurately recognize people similar to their own age (Wright & Stroud, 2002). It's not that we cannot perceive differences among faces of another group. Rather, when looking at a face from another racial group we often attend, first, to group ("that man is Black") rather than to individual features. When viewing someone of our own group, we are less attentive to the race category and more attentive to individual details (Bernstein & others, 2007; Hugenberg & others, 2007; Shriver & others, 2008). Indeed, our attending to someone's being in a different social category may also be contributing to a parallel *own-age bias*—the tendency for both children and older adults to more accurately identify faces from their own age groups (Anastasi & Rhodes, 2005, 2006). (Perhaps you have noticed that senior citizens look more alike than do your fellow students?)

Distinctiveness: Perceiving People Who Stand Out

Other ways we perceive our worlds also breed stereotypes. Distinctive people and vivid or extreme occurrences often capture attention and distort judgments.

DISTINCTIVE PEOPLE

Have you ever found yourself in a situation where you were the only person of your gender, race, or nationality? If so, your difference from the others probably made you more noticeable and the object of more attention. A Black in an otherwise White group, a man in an otherwise female group, or a woman in an otherwise male group seems more prominent and influential and to have exaggerated good and bad qualities (Crocker & McGraw, 1984; S. E. Taylor & others, 1979). When someone in a group is made conspicuous, we tend to see that person as causing whatever happens (Taylor & Fiske, 1978). If we are positioned to look at Joe, even if Joe is merely an average group member, Joe will seem to have a greater-than-average influence on the group.

Have you noticed that people also define you by your most distinctive traits and behaviors? Tell people about someone who is a skydiver and a tennis player, report Lori Nelson and Dale Miller (1995), and they will think of the person as a skydiver. Asked to choose a gift book for the person, they will pick a skydiving book over a tennis book. A person who has both a pet snake and a pet dog is seen more as a snake owner than a dog owner.

People also take note of those who violate expectations (Bettencourt & others, 1997). "Like a flower blooming in winter, intellect is more readily noticed where it is not expected," reflected Stephen Carter (1993, p. 54) on his own experience as an African American intellectual. Such perceived distinctiveness makes it easier for highly capable job applicants from low-status groups to get noticed, though they also must work harder to prove that their abilities are genuine (Biernat & Kobrynowicz, 1997).

Ellen Langer and Lois Imber (1980) cleverly demonstrated the attention paid to distinctive people. They asked Harvard

Distinctive people, such as Houston Rockets 7'6" player Yao Ming, draw attention.

students to watch a video of a man reading. The students paid closer attention when they were led to think he was out of the ordinary—a cancer patient, a homosexual, or a millionaire. They noticed characteristics that other viewers ignored, and their evaluation of him was more extreme. Those who thought the man was a cancer patient noticed distinctive facial characteristics and bodily movements and thus perceived him to be much more "different from most people" than did the other viewers. The extra attention we pay to distinctive people creates an illusion that they differ from others more than they really do. If people thought you had the IQ of a genius, they would probably notice things about you that otherwise would pass unnoticed.

DISTINCTIVENESS FEEDS SELF-CONSCIOUSNESS When surrounded by Whites, Blacks sometimes detect people reacting to their distinctiveness. Many report being stared or glared at, being subject to insensitive comments, and receiving bad service (Swim & others, 1998). Sometimes, however, we misperceive others as reacting to our distinctiveness. At Dartmouth College, researchers Robert Kleck and Angelo Strenta (1980) discovered this when they led college women to feel disfigured. The women thought the purpose of the experiment was to assess how someone would react to a facial scar created with theatrical makeup; the scar was on the right cheek, running from the ear to the mouth. Actually, the purpose was to see how the women themselves, when made to feel deviant, would perceive others' behavior toward them. After applying the makeup, the experimenter gave each woman a small hand mirror so she could see the authentic-looking scar. When she put the mirror down, he then applied some "moisturizer" to "keep the makeup from cracking." What the "moisturizer" really did was remove the scar.

The scene that followed was poignant. A young woman, feeling terribly self-conscious about her supposedly disfigured face, talked with another woman who saw no such disfigurement and knew nothing of what had gone on before. If you have ever felt similarly self-conscious—perhaps about a physical handicap, acne, even just a bad hair day—then perhaps you can sympathize with the self-conscious woman. Compared with women who were led to believe their conversational partners merely thought they had an allergy, the " disfigured" women became acutely sensitive to how their partners were looking at them. They rated their partners as more tense, distant, and patronizing. Observers who later analyzed videotapes of how the partners treated "disfigured" persons could find no such differences in treatment. Self-conscious about being different, the "disfigured" women had misinterpreted mannerisms and comments they would otherwise not have noticed.

Self-conscious interactions between a majority and a minority person can therefore feel tense even when both are well intentioned (Devine & others, 1996). Tom, who is known to be gay, meets tolerant Bill, who is straight and wants to respond without prejudice. But feeling unsure of himself, Bill holds back a bit. Tom, expecting negative attitudes from most people, misreads Bill's hesitancy as hostility and responds with a seeming chip on his shoulder.

Anyone can experience this phenomenon. Majority group members (in one study, White residents of Manitoba) often have beliefs—"meta-stereotypes"—about how minorities stereotype them (Vorauer & others, 1998). Even relatively unprejudiced Canadian Whites, Israeli Jews, or American Christians may sense that outgroup minorities stereotype them as prejudiced, arrogant, or patronizing. If George worries that Gamal perceives him as "your typical educated racist," he may be on guard when talking with Gamal.

stigma consciousness
A person's expectation of being victimized by prejudice or discrimination.

STIGMA CONSCIOUSNESS People vary in **stigma consciousness**—in how much they expect others to stereotype them. Gays and lesbians, for example, differ in how much they suppose others "interpret all my behaviors" in terms of their homosexuality (Lewis & others, 2006; Pinel, 1999, 2004).

Seeing oneself as a victim of pervasive prejudice has its ups and downs (Branscombe & others, 1999; Dion, 1998). The downside is that those who perceive

Self-consciousness about being different affects how we interpret others' behavior.

themselves as frequent victims live with the stress of presumed stereotypes and antagonism, and therefore experience lower well-being. While living in Europe, stigma-conscious Americans—Americans who perceive Europeans as resenting them—live more fretfully than those who feel accepted.

The upside is that perceptions of prejudice buffer individual self-esteem. If someone is nasty, "Well, it's not directed at me personally." Moreover, perceived prejudice and discrimination enhance our feelings of social identity and prepare us to join in collective social action.

VIVID CASES

Our minds also use distinctive cases as a shortcut to judging groups. Are the Japanese good baseball players? "Well, there's Ichiro Suzuki and Hideki Matsui and Kosuke Fukudome. Yeah, I'd say so." Note the thought processes at work here: Given limited experience with a particular social group, we recall examples of it and generalize from those (Sherman, 1996). Moreover, encountering an example of a negative stereotype (say, a hostile Black) can prime the stereotype, leading us to minimize contact with the group (Henderson-King & Nisbett, 1996).

Such generalizing from a single case can cause problems. Vivid instances, though more available in memory, seldom represent the larger group. Exceptional athletes, though distinctive and memorable, are not the best basis for judging the distribution of athletic talent among an entire group.

Those in a numerical minority, being more distinctive, also may be numerically overestimated by the majority. What proportion of your country's population would you say is Muslim? People in non-Muslim countries often overestimate this proportion. (In the United States, a Pew Research Center [2007a] study reported that 0.6 percent of the population were Muslim.)

Or consider a 1990 Gallup poll report that the average American greatly overestimated the U.S. Black population and Hispanic population (Figure 9.8). A more recent Gallup poll found the average American thinking 21 percent of men were gay and 22 percent of women were lesbian (Robinson, 2002). Repeated surveys suggest that actually about 3 or 4 percent of men and 1 or 2 percent of women have a same-sex orientation (National Center for Health Statistics, 1991; Smith, 1998; Tarmann, 2002).

FIGURE :: 9.8

Overestimating
Minority Populations

Source: 1990 Gallup Poll (Gates, 1993).

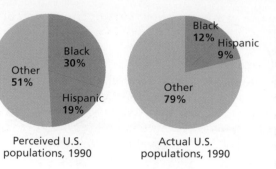

Perceived U.S.
populations, 1990

Actual U.S.
populations, 1990

Myron Rothbart and his colleagues (1978) showed how distinctive cases also fuel stereotypes. They had University of Oregon students view 50 slides, each of which stated a man's height. For one group of students, 10 of the men were slightly over 6 feet (up to 6 feet, 4 inches). For other students, these 10 men were well over 6 feet (up to 6 feet, 11 inches). When asked later how many of the men were over 6 feet, those given the moderately tall examples recalled 5 percent too many. Those given the extremely tall examples recalled 50 percent too many. In a follow-up experiment, students read descriptions of the actions of 50 men, 10 of whom had committed either nonviolent crimes, such as forgery, or violent crimes, such as rape. Of those shown the list with the violent crimes, most overestimated the number of criminal acts.

DISTINCTIVE EVENTS

Stereotypes assume a correlation between group membership and individuals' presumed characteristics ("Italians are emotional," "Jews are shrewd," "Accountants are perfectionists"). Even under the best of conditions, our attentiveness to unusual occurrences can create illusory correlations. Because we are sensitive to distinctive events, the co-occurrence of two such events is especially noticeable—more noticeable than each of the times the unusual events do *not* occur together.

David Hamilton and Robert Gifford (1976) demonstrated illusory correlation in a classic experiment. They showed students slides in which various people, members of "Group A" or "Group B," were said to have done something desirable or undesirable. For example, "John, a member of Group A, visited a sick friend in the hospital." Twice as many statements described members of Group A as Group B, but both groups did nine desirable acts for every four undesirable behaviors. Since both Group B and the undesirable acts were less frequent, their co-occurrence—for example, "Allen, a member of Group B, dented the fender of a parked car and didn't leave his name"—was an unusual combination that caught people's attention. The students therefore overestimated the frequency with which the "minority" group (B) acted undesirably, and they judged Group B more harshly.

Remember, Group A members outnumbered Group B members two to one, and Group B members committed undesirable acts in the same *proportion* as Group A members (thus, they committed only half as many). Moreover, the students had no preexisting biases for or against Group B, and they received the information more systematically than daily experience ever offers it. Although researchers debate why it happens, they agree that illusory correlation occurs and provides yet another source for the formation of racial stereotypes (Berndsen & others, 2002). Thus, the features that most distinguish a minority from a majority are those that become associated with it (Sherman & others, 2009). Your ethnic or social group may be like other groups in most ways, but people will notice how it differs.

In experiments, even single co-occurrences of an unusual act by someone in an atypical group—"Ben, a Jehovah's Witness, owns a pet sloth"—can embed illusory correlations in people's minds (Risen & others, 2007). This enables the mass media to feed illusory correlations. When a self-described homosexual person murders or sexually abuses someone, homosexuality is often mentioned. When a heterosexual does the same, the person's sexual orientation is seldom mentioned. Likewise, when ex-mental patients Mark Chapman and John Hinckley, Jr., shot John Lennon and President Reagan, respectively, the assailants' mental histories commanded attention. Assassins and mental hospitalization are both relatively infrequent, making the combination especially newsworthy. Such reporting adds to the illusion of a large correlation between (1) violent tendencies and (2) homosexuality or mental hospitalization.

Unlike the students who judged Groups A and B, we often have preexisting biases. David Hamilton's further research with Terrence Rose (1980) revealed that our preexisting stereotypes can lead us to "see" correlations that aren't there. The researchers had University of California at Santa Barbara students read sentences in which various adjectives described the members of different occupational groups ("Juan, an accountant, is timid and thoughtful"). In actuality, each occupation was described equally often by each adjective; accountants, doctors, and salespeople were equally often timid, wealthy, and talkative. The students, however, *thought* they had more often read descriptions of timid accountants, wealthy doctors, and talkative salespeople. Their stereotyping led them to perceive correlations that weren't there, thus helping to perpetuate the stereotypes.

Attribution: Is It a Just World?

In explaining others' actions, we frequently commit the fundamental attribution error that was discussed in Chapter 3: We attribute others' behavior so much to their inner dispositions that we discount important situational forces. The error occurs partly because our attention focuses on the person, not on the situation. A person's race or sex is vivid and gets attention; the situational forces working upon that person are usually less visible. Slavery was often overlooked as an explanation for slave behavior; the behavior was instead attributed to the slaves' own nature. Until recently, the same was true of how we explained the perceived differences between women and men. Because gender-role constraints were hard to see, we attributed men's and women's behavior solely to their innate dispositions. The more people assume that human traits are fixed dispositions, the stronger are their stereotypes and the greater their acceptance of racial inequities (Levy & others, 1998; Williams & Eberhardt, 2008).

GROUP-SERVING BIAS

Thomas Pettigrew (1979, 1980) showed how attribution errors bias people's explanations of group members' behaviors. We grant members of our own group the benefit of the doubt: "She donated because she has a good heart; he refused because he's using every penny to help support his mother." When explaining acts by members of other groups, we more often assume the worst: "She donated to gain favor; he refused because he's selfish." In one classic study, the light shove that Whites perceived as mere "horsing around" when done by another White became a "violent gesture" when done by a Black (Duncan, 1976).

Positive behavior by outgroup members is more often dismissed. It may be seen as a "special case" ("He is certainly bright and hardworking—not at all like other . . ."), as owing to luck or some special advantage ("She probably got admitted just because her med school had to fill its quota for women applicants"), as demanded by the situation ("Under the circumstances, what could the cheap Scot do but pay the whole check?"), or as attributable to extra effort ("Asian students get better grades because they're so compulsive"). Disadvantaged groups and groups that stress modesty (such as the Chinese) exhibit less of this **group-serving bias** (Fletcher & Ward, 1989; Heine & Lehman, 1997; Jackson & others, 1993).

The group-serving bias can subtly color our language. A team of University of Padua (Italy) researchers led by Anne Maass (1995, 1999) has found that positive behaviors by another ingroup member are often described as general dispositions (for example, "Karen is helpful"). When performed by an outgroup member, the same behavior is often described as a specific, isolated act ("Carmen opened the door for the man with the cane"). With negative behavior, the specificity reverses:

group-serving bias
Explaining away outgroup members' positive behaviors; also attributing negative behaviors to their dispositions (while excusing such behavior by one's own group).

Just-world thinking? Some people argued against giving legal rights to American prisoners in the Guantanamo Bay detention camp that housed alleged combatants from Afghanistan and Iraq. One argument was that these people would not be confined there if they had not done horrendous things, so why allow them to argue their innocence in U.S. courts?

"Eric shoved her" (an isolated act by an ingroup member) but "Enrique was aggressive" (an outgroup member's general disposition). Maass calls this group-serving bias the *linguistic intergroup bias.*

Earlier we noted that blaming the victim can justify the blamer's own superior status (Table 9.1). Blaming occurs as people attribute an outgroup's failures to its members' flawed dispositions, notes Miles Hewstone (1990): "They fail because they're stupid; we fail because we didn't try." If women, Blacks, or Jews have been abused, they must somehow have brought it on themselves. When the British made a group of German civilians walk through the Bergen-Belsen concentration camp at the close of World War II, one German responded: "What terrible criminals these prisoners must have been to receive such treatment." (Such group-serving bias illustrates the motivations that underlie prejudice, as well as the cognition. Motivation and cognition, emotion and thinking, are inseparable.)

THE JUST-WORLD PHENOMENON

In a series of experiments conducted at the universities of Waterloo and Kentucky, Melvin Lerner and his colleagues (Lerner, 1980; Lerner & Miller, 1978) discovered that merely *observing* another innocent person being victimized is enough to make the victim seem less worthy.

Lerner (1980) noted that such disparaging of hapless victims results from the human need to believe that "I am a just person living in a just world, a world where people get what they deserve." From early childhood, he argues, we are taught that good is rewarded and evil punished. Hard work and virtue pay dividends; laziness and immorality do not. From this it is but a short leap to assuming that those who flourish must be good and those who suffer must deserve their fate.

Numerous studies have confirmed this **just-world phenomenon** (Hafer & Bègue, 2005). Imagine that you, along with some others, are participating in one of Lerner's

just-world phenomenon

The tendency of people to believe that the world is just and that people therefore get what they deserve and deserve what they get.

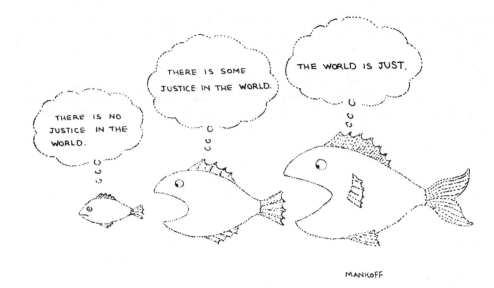

TABLE :: 9.1 How Self-Enhancing Social Identities Support Stereotypes

	Ingroup	Outgroup
Attitude	Favoritism	Denigration
Perceptions	Heterogeneity (we differ)	Homogeneity (they're alike)
Attributions for negative behavior	To situations	To dispositions

studies—supposedly on the perception of emotional cues (Lerner & Simmons, 1966). One of the participants, a confederate, is selected by lottery to perform a memory task. This person receives painful shocks whenever she gives a wrong answer. You and the others note her emotional responses.

After watching the victim receive these apparently painful shocks, the experimenter asks you to evaluate her. How would you respond? With compassionate sympathy? We might expect so. As Ralph Waldo Emerson wrote, "The martyr cannot be dishonored." On the contrary, in these experiments the martyrs *were* dishonored. When observers were powerless to alter the victim's fate, they often rejected and devalued the victim. Juvenal, the Roman satirist, anticipated these results: "The Roman mob follows after Fortune . . . and hates those who have been condemned."

Linda Carli and her colleagues (1989, 1999) report that the just-world phenomenon colors our impressions of rape victims. Carli had people read detailed descriptions of interactions between a man and a woman. In one scenario, a woman and her boss meet for dinner, go to his home, and each have a glass of wine. Some read this scenario with a happy ending: "Then he led me to the couch. He held my hand and asked me to marry him." In hindsight, people find the ending unsurprising and admire the man's and woman's character traits. Others read the same scenario with a terrible ending: "But then he became very rough and pushed me onto the couch. He held me down on the couch and raped me." Given this ending, people see the rape as inevitable and blame the woman for provocative behavior that seems faultless in the first scenario.

This line of research suggests that people are indifferent to social injustice not because they have no concern for justice but because they see no injustice. Those who assume a just world believe that rape victims must have behaved seductively

The classic illustration of "just-world thinking" comes from the Old Testament story of Job, a good person who suffers terrible misfortune. Job's friends surmise that, this being a just world, Job must have done something wicked to elicit such terrible suffering.

(Borgida & Brekke, 1985), that battered spouses must have provoked their beatings (Summers & Feldman, 1984), that poor people don't deserve better (Furnham & Gunter, 1984), and that sick people are responsible for their illnesses (Gruman & Sloan, 1983). Such beliefs enable successful people to reassure themselves that they, too, deserve what they have. The wealthy and healthy can see their own good fortune, and others' misfortune, as justly deserved. Linking good fortune with virtue and misfortune with moral failure enables the fortunate to feel pride and to avoid responsibility for the unfortunate.

People loathe a loser even when the loser's misfortune quite obviously stems substantially from bad luck. Children, for example, tend to view lucky others—such as someone who has found money on a sidewalk—as more likely than unlucky children to do good things and be a nice person (Olson & others, 2008). Adults *know* that gambling outcomes are just good or bad luck and should not affect their evaluations of the gambler. Still, they can't resist playing Monday-morning quarterback—judging people by their results. Ignoring the fact that reasonable decisions can bring bad results, they judge losers as less competent (Baron & Hershey, 1988). Lawyers and stock market investors may similarly judge themselves by their outcomes, becoming smug after successes and self-reproachful after failures. Talent and initiative matter. But the just-world assumption discounts the uncontrollable factors that can derail good efforts even by talented people.

Summing Up: What Are the Cognitive Sources of Prejudice?

- Recent research shows how the stereotyping that underlies prejudice is a by-product of our thinking—our ways of simplifying the world. Clustering people into categories exaggerates the uniformity within a group and the differences between groups.

- A distinctive individual, such as a lone minority person, has a compelling quality that makes us aware of differences that would otherwise go unnoticed. The occurrence of two distinctive events (for example, a minority person committing an unusual crime) helps create an *illusory correlation* between people and behavior. Attributing others' behavior to their dispositions can lead to the *group-serving bias:* assigning outgroup members' negative behavior to their natural character while explaining away their positive behaviors.

- Blaming the victim results from the common presumption that because this is a just world, people get what they deserve.

What Are the Consequences of Prejudice?

Beyond the causes of prejudice, it is important to examine its consequences. Stereotypes can be self-perpetuating—their existence can prevent their change. Stereotypes can also create their own reality. Even if they are initially untrue, their existence can make them become true. The negative allegations of prejudice can also undermine people's performance and affect how people interpret discrimination.

Self-Perpetuating Stereotypes

Prejudice is preconceived judgment. Prejudgments are inevitable: None of us is a dispassionate bookkeeper of social happenings, tallying evidence for and against our biases.

Prejudgments guide our attention and our memories. People who accept gender stereotypes often misrecall their own school grades in stereotype-consistent ways. For example, women often recall receiving worse math grades and better arts grades than were actually the case (Chatard & others, 2007).

Moreover, once we judge an item as belonging to a category such as a particular race or sex, our memory for it later shifts toward the features we associate with that category. Johanne Huart and his colleagues (2005) demonstrated this by showing Belgian university students a face that was a blend of 70 percent of the features of a typical male and 30 percent female (or vice versa). Later, those shown the 70 percent male face recalled seeing a male (as you might expect), but also misrecalled the face as being even more prototypically male (as, say, the 80 percent male face shown in Figure 9.9).

Prejudgments are self-perpetuating. Whenever a member of a group behaves as expected, we duly note the fact; our prior belief is confirmed. When a member of a group behaves inconsistently with our expectation, we may interpret or explain away the behavior as due to special circumstances (Crocker & others, 1983). The contrast to a stereotype can also make someone seem exceptional. Telling some people that "Maria played basketball" and others that "Mark played basketball" may make Maria seem more athletic than Mark (Biernat, 2003). Stereotypes therefore influence how we construe someone's behavior (Kunda & Sherman-Williams, 1993; Sanbonmatsu & others, 1994; Stangor & McMillan, 1992). Prime White folks with negative media images of Black folks (for example, looting after Hurricane Katrina) and the activated stereotype may be poisonous. In one experiment, such images produced reduced empathy for other Black people in need (Johnson & others, 2008).

Perhaps you, too, can recall a time when, try as you might, you could not overcome someone's opinion of you, a time when no matter what you did you were misinterpreted. Misinterpretations are likely when someone *expects* an unpleasant encounter with you (Wilder & Shapiro, 1989). William Ickes and his colleagues (1982) demonstrated this in an experiment with pairs of college-age men. As the men arrived, the experimenters falsely forewarned one member of each pair that the other person was "one of the unfriendliest people I've talked to lately." The two were then introduced and left alone together for five minutes. Students in another condition of the experiment were led to think the other participant was exceptionally friendly.

Those in both conditions were friendly to the new acquaintance. In fact, those who expected him to be *un*friendly went out of their way to be friendly, and their smiles and other friendly behaviors elicited a warm response. But unlike the positively biased students, those expecting an unfriendly person attributed this reciprocal friendliness to their own "kid-gloves" treatment of him. They afterward expressed more mistrust and dislike for the person and rated his behavior as less friendly. Despite their partner's actual friendliness, the negative bias induced these students to "see" hostilities lurking beneath his "forced smiles." They would never have seen it if they hadn't believed it.

We do notice information that is strikingly inconsistent with a stereotype, but even that information has less impact than might be expected. When

> "Labels act like shrieking sirens, deafening us to all finer discriminations that we might otherwise perceive."
> —*GORDON ALLPORT*, THE NATURE OF PREJUDICE, *1954*

When people violate our stereotypes, we salvage the stereotype by splitting off a new subgroup stereotype, such as "senior Olympians."

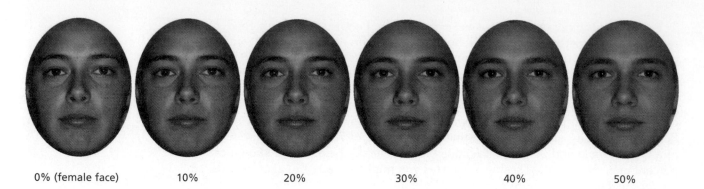

| 0% (female face) | 10% | 20% | 30% | 40% | 50% |

FIGURE :: 9.9

Categorization Influences Memories

Shown a face that was 70 percent male, people usually classified the person as a male, and then recollected the face as more male-typical than it was (Huart & others, 2005).

---

subtyping

Accommodating individuals who deviate from one's stereotype by thinking of them as "exceptions to the rule."

subgrouping

Accommodating individuals who deviate from one's stereotype by forming a new stereotype about this subset of the group.

---

we focus on an atypical example, we can salvage the stereotype by splitting off a new category (Brewer & Gaertner, 2004; Hewstone, 1994; Kunda & Oleson, 1995, 1997). The positive image that British schoolchildren form of their friendly school police officers (whom they perceive as a special category) doesn't improve their image of police officers in general (Hewstone & others, 1992). This **subtyping**— seeing people who deviate as exceptions—helps maintain the stereotype that police officers are unfriendly and dangerous. A different way to accommodate the inconsistent information is to form a new stereotype for those who don't fit. Recognizing that the stereotype does not apply for everyone in the category, homeowners who have "desirable" Black neighbors can form a new and different stereotype of "professional, middle-class Blacks." This **subgrouping**—forming a subgroup stereotype—tends to lead to modest change in the stereotype as the stereotype becomes more differentiated (Richards & Hewstone, 2001). Subtypes are exceptions to the group; subgroups are acknowledged as a part of the overall group.

Discrimination's Impact: The Self-Fulfilling Prophecy

Attitudes may coincide with the social hierarchy not only as a rationalization for it but also because discrimination affects its victims. "One's reputation," wrote Gordon Allport, "cannot be hammered, hammered, hammered into one's head without doing something to one's character" (1958, p. 139). If we could snap our fingers and end all discrimination, it would be naive for the White majority to say to Blacks, "The tough times are over, folks! You can now all be attaché-carrying executives and professionals." When the oppression ends, its effects linger, like a societal hangover.

In *The Nature of Prejudice*, Allport catalogued 15 possible effects of victimization. Allport believed these reactions were reducible to two basic types—those that involve blaming oneself (withdrawal, self-hate, aggression against one's own group) and those that involve blaming external causes (fighting back, suspiciousness, increased group pride). If victimization takes a toll—say, higher rates of crime—people can use the result to justify the discrimination: "If we let those people in our nice neighborhood, property values will plummet."

Does discrimination indeed affect its victims? We must be careful not to overstate the point. The soul and style of Black culture is for many a proud heritage, not just a response to victimization (Jones, 2003). Nevertheless, social beliefs *can* be self-confirming, as demonstrated in a clever pair of experiments by Carl Word, Mark Zanna, and Joel Cooper (1974). In the first experiment, Princeton University

---

"It is understandable that the suppressed people should develop an intense hostility towards a culture whose existence they make possible by their work, but in whose wealth they have too small a share."

—*SIGMUND FREUD*, THE FUTURE OF AN ILLUSION, *1927*

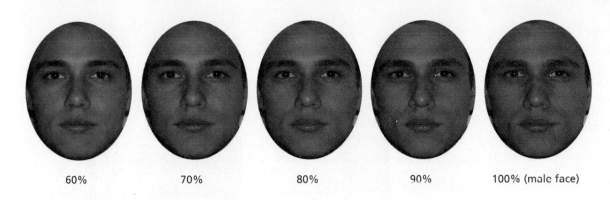

| 60% | 70% | 80% | 90% | 100% (male face) |

White male volunteers interviewed White and Black research assistants posing as job applicants. When the applicant was Black, the interviewers sat farther away, ended the interview 25 percent sooner, and made 50 percent more speech errors than when the applicant was White. Imagine being interviewed by someone who sat at a distance, stammered, and ended the interview rather quickly. Would it affect your performance or your feelings about the interviewer?

To find out, the researchers conducted a second experiment in which trained interviewers treated people as the interviewers in the first experiment had treated either the White or the Black applicants. When videotapes of the interviews were later rated, those who were treated like the Blacks in the first experiment seemed more nervous and less effective. Moreover, the interviewees could themselves sense a difference; those treated the way the Blacks had been treated judged their interviewers to be less adequate and less friendly. The experimenters concluded part of "the 'problem' of Black performance resides . . . within the interaction setting itself." As with other self-fulfilling prophecies (recall Chapter 3), prejudice affects its targets.

> "If we foresee evil in our fellow man, we tend to provoke it; if good, we elicit it."
> —*GORDON ALLPORT, THE NATURE OF PREJUDICE, 1958*

Stereotype Threat

Just being sensitive to prejudice is enough to make us self-conscious when living as a numerical minority—perhaps as a Black person in a White community or as a White person in a Black community. And as with other circumstances that siphon off our mental energy and attention, the result can be diminished mental and physical stamina (Inzlicht & others, 2006). Placed in a situation where others expect you to perform poorly, your anxiety may also cause you to confirm the belief. I am a short guy in my 60s. When I join a pickup basketball game with bigger, younger players, I presume that they expect me to be a detriment to their team, and that tends to undermine my confidence and performance. Claude Steele and his colleagues call this phenomenon **stereotype threat**—a self-confirming apprehension that one will be evaluated based on a negative stereotype (Steele, 1997; Steele & others, 2002; see also reducingstereotypethreat.org).

In several experiments, Steven Spencer, Claude Steele, and Diane Quinn (1999) gave a very difficult math test to men and women students who had similar math backgrounds. When told that there were *no* gender differences on the test and no evaluation of any group stereotype, the women's performance consistently equaled the men's. Told that there *was* a gender difference, the women dramatically confirmed the stereotype (Figure 9.10). Frustrated by the extremely difficult test questions, they apparently felt added apprehension, which undermined their performances.

The media can provoke stereotype threat. Paul Davies and his colleagues (2002, 2005) had women and men watch a series of commercials expecting that they would be tested for their memory of details. For half the participants, the commercials contained only neutral stimuli; for the other half, some of the commercials contained

stereotype threat
A disruptive concern, when facing a negative stereotype, that one will be evaluated based on a negative stereotype. Unlike self-fulfilling prophecies that hammer one's reputation into one's self-concept, stereotype threat situations have immediate effects.

> "Math class is tough!"
> —*"TEEN TALK" BARBIE DOLL (LATER REMOVED FROM THE MARKET)*

FIGURE :: 9.10

Stereotype Vulnerability and Women's Math Performance

Steven Spencer, Claude Steele, and Diane Quinn (1999) gave equally capable men and women a difficult math test. When participants were led to believe there were gender differences on the test, women scored lower than men. When the threat of confirming the stereotype was removed (when gender differences were not expected), women did just as well as men.

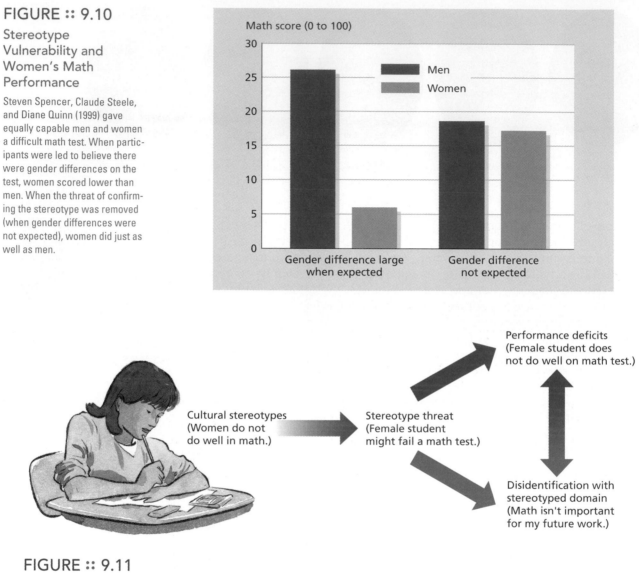

FIGURE :: 9.11

Stereotype Threat

Threat from facing a negative stereotype can produce performance deficits and disidentification.

images of "airheaded" women. After seeing the stereotypic images, women not only performed worse than men on a math test but also reported less interest in obtaining a math or science major or entering a math or science career.

Might racial stereotypes be similarly self-fulfilling? Steele and Joshua Aronson (1995) gave difficult verbal abilities tests to Whites and Blacks. Blacks underperformed Whites only when taking the tests under conditions high in stereotype threat. Jeff Stone and his colleagues (1999) report that stereotype threat affects athletic performance, too. Blacks did worse than usual when a golf task was framed as a test of "sports intelligence," and Whites did worse when it was a test of "natural athletic ability." "When people are reminded of a negative stereotype about themselves—'White men can't jump' or 'Black men can't think'—it can adversely affect performance," Stone (2000) surmised.

If you tell students they are at risk of failure (as is often suggested by minority support programs), the stereotype may erode their performance, says Steele (1997). It may cause them to "disidentify" with school and seek self-esteem elsewhere (Figure 9.11). Indeed, as African American students move from eighth to tenth

THE inside STORY

Claude Steele on Stereotype Threat

During a committee meeting on campus diversity at the University of Michigan in the late 1980s, I noticed an interesting fact: At every level of entering SAT score, minority students were getting lower college grades than their nonminority counterparts. Soon, Steven Spencer, Joshua Aronson, and I found that this was a national phenomenon; it happened at most colleges and it happened to other groups whose abilities were negatively stereotyped, such as women in advanced math classes. This underperformance wasn't caused by group differences in preparation. It happened at all levels of preparation (as measured by SATs).

Eventually, we produced this underperformance in the laboratory by simply having motivated people perform a difficult task in a domain where their group was negatively stereotyped. We also found that we could eliminate this underperformance by making the same task irrelevant to the stereotype, by removing the "stereotype threat," as we had come to call it. This latter finding spawned more research: figuring out how to reduce stereotype threat and its ill effects. Through this work, we have gained an appreciation for two big things: first, the importance of life context in shaping psychological functioning, and second, the importance of social identities like age, race, and gender in shaping that context.

Claude Steele

grade, there has been a weakening connection between their school performance and self-esteem (Osborne, 1995). Moreover, students who are led to think they have benefited from gender- or race-based preferences in gaining admission to a college or an academic group tend to underperform those who are led to feel competent (Brown & others, 2000).

Better, therefore, to challenge students to believe in their potential, observes Steele. In another of his research team's experiments, Black students responded well to criticism of their writing when also told, "I wouldn't go to the trouble of giving you this feedback if I didn't think, based on what I've read in your letter, that you are capable of meeting the higher standard that I mentioned" (Cohen & others, 1999).

How does stereotype threat undermine performance? It does so in three ways, contend Topni Schmader, Michael Johns, and Chad Forbes (2008):

- *Stress.* fMRI brain scans suggest that the stress of stereotype threat impairs brain activity associated with mathematical processing and increases activity in areas associated with emotion processing (Derks & others, 2008; Krendl & others, 2008; Wraga & others, 2007).
- *Self-monitoring.* Worrying about making mistakes disrupts focused attention (Keller & Dauenheimer, 2003; Seibt & Forster, 2004).
- *Suppressing unwanted thoughts and emotions.* The effort required to regulate one's thinking takes energy and disrupts working memory (Bonnot & Croizet, 2007).

If stereotype threats can disrupt performance, could positive stereotypes enhance it? Margaret Shih, Todd Pittinsky, and Nalini Ambady (1999) confirmed that possibility. When Asian American females were asked biographical questions that reminded them of their gender identity before taking a math test, their performance plunged (compared with a control group). When similarly reminded of their Asian identity, their performance rose. Negative stereotypes disrupt performance, and positive stereotypes, it seems, facilitate performance (Rydell & others, 2009).

Do Stereotypes Bias Judgments of Individuals?

Yes, stereotypes bias judgments, but here is some good news: *People often evaluate individuals more positively than the groups they compose* (Miller & Felicio, 1990). Anne Locksley, Eugene Borgida, and Nancy Brekke have found that once someone knows a person, "stereotypes may have minimal, if any, impact on judgments about that person" (Borgida & others, 1981; Locksley & others, 1980, 1982). They discovered this by giving University of Minnesota students anecdotal information about recent incidents in the life of "Nancy." In a supposed transcript of a telephone conversation, Nancy told a friend how she responded to three different situations (for example, being harassed by a seedy character while shopping). Some of the students read transcripts portraying Nancy responding assertively (telling the seedy character to leave); others read a report of passive responses (simply ignoring the character until he finally drifts away). Still other students received the same information, except that the person was named "Paul" instead of Nancy. A day later the students predicted how Nancy (or Paul) would respond to other situations.

Did knowing the person's gender have any effect on those predictions? None at all. Expectations of the person's assertiveness were influenced solely by what the students had learned about that individual the day before. Even their judgments of masculinity and femininity were unaffected by knowing the person's gender. Gender stereotypes had been left on the shelf; the students evaluated Nancy and Paul as individuals.

An important principle discussed in Chapter 3 explains this finding. Given (1) general (base-rate) information about a group and (2) trivial but vivid information about a particular group member, the vivid information usually overwhelms the effect of the general information. This is especially so when the person doesn't fit our image of the typical group member (Fein & Hilton, 1992; Lord & others, 1991). For example, imagine yourself being told how most people in a conformity experiment actually behaved and then viewing a brief interview with one of the supposed participants. Would you react like the typical viewer—by guessing the person's behavior from the interview, ignoring the base-rate information on how most people actually behaved?

People often believe such stereotypes, yet ignore them when given personalized, anecdotal information. Thus, many people believe "politicians are crooks" but "our Senator Jones has integrity." No wonder many people have a low opinion of politicians yet usually vote to reelect their own representatives. And no wonder some White Americans who felt general distrust of Black people came to trust and support a Black presidential candidate as they came to know him.

These findings resolve a puzzling set of findings considered early in this chapter. We know that gender stereotypes (1) are strong yet (2) have little effect on people's judgments of work attributed to a man or a woman. Now we see why. People may have strong gender stereotypes, yet ignore them when judging a particular individual.

People sometimes maintain general prejudices (such as against gays and lesbians) without applying their prejudice to particular individuals whom they know and respect, such as Ellen DeGeneres.

STRONG STEREOTYPES MATTER

However, *strong* and seemingly relevant stereotypes do color our judgments of individuals (Krueger & Rothbart, 1988). When Thomas Nelson, Monica Biernat, and Melvin Manis (1990) had students estimate the heights of individually pictured men and women, they judged the individual men as taller than the women—even when their heights were equal, even when they were told that sex didn't predict height in this sample, and even when they were offered cash rewards for accuracy.

In a follow-up study, Nelson, Michele Acker, and Manis (1996) showed University of Michigan students photos of other students from the university's engineering and nursing schools, along with descriptions of each student's interests. Even when informed that the sample contained an equal number of males and females from each school, the same description was judged more likely to come from a nursing student when attached to a female face. Thus, even when a strong gender stereotype is known to be irrelevant, it has an irresistible force.

STEREOTYPES BIAS INTERPRETATIONS

Stereotypes also color how we interpret events, note David Dunning and David Sherman (1997). If people are told, "Some felt the politician's statements were untrue," they will infer that the politician was lying. If told, "Some felt the physicist's statements were untrue," they infer only that the physicist was mistaken. When told two people had an altercation, people perceive it as a fistfight if told it involved two lumberjacks, but as a verbal spat if told it involved two marriage counselors. A person concerned about her physical condition seems vain if she is a model but health conscious if she is a triathlete. As a prison guides and constrains its inmates, conclude Dunning and Sherman, the "cognitive prison" of our stereotypes guides and constrains our impressions.

Sometimes we make judgments, or begin interacting with someone, with little to go on but our stereotype. In such cases stereotypes can strongly bias our interpretations and memories of people. For example, Charles Bond and his colleagues (1988) found that after getting to know their patients, White psychiatric nurses put Black and White patients in physical restraints equally often. But they restrained *incoming* Black patients more often than their White counterparts. With little else to go on, stereotypes mattered.

Such bias can also operate more subtly. In an experiment by John Darley and Paget Gross (1983), Princeton University students viewed a videotape of a fourth-grade girl, Hannah. The tape depicted her either in a depressed urban neighborhood, supposedly the child of lower-class parents, or in an affluent suburban setting, the child of professional parents. Asked to guess Hannah's ability level in various subjects, both groups of viewers refused to use Hannah's class background to prejudge her ability level; each group rated her ability level at her grade level.

Other students also viewed a second videotape, showing Hannah taking an oral achievement test in which she got some questions right and some wrong. Those who had previously been introduced to professional-class Hannah judged her answers as showing high ability and later recalled her getting most questions right; those who had met lower-class Hannah judged her ability as below grade level and recalled her missing almost half the questions. But remember: The second videotape was *identical* for the two groups. So we see that when stereotypes are strong and the information about someone is ambiguous (unlike the cases of Nancy and Paul), stereotypes can *subtly* bias our judgments of individuals.

Finally, we evaluate people more extremely when their behavior violates our stereotypes (Bettencourt & others, 1997). A woman who rebukes someone cutting in front of her in a movie line ("Shouldn't you go to the end of the line?") may seem more assertive than a man who reacts similarly (Manis & others, 1988). Aided by the testimony of social psychologist Susan Fiske and her colleagues (1991), the U.S.

Supreme Court saw such stereotyping at work when Price Waterhouse, one of the nation's top accounting firms, denied Ann Hopkins's promotion to partner. Among the 88 candidates for promotion, Hopkins, the only woman, was number one in the amount of business she brought in to the company and, according to testimony, was hardworking and exacting. But others testified that Hopkins needed a "course at charm school," where she could learn to "walk more femininely, talk more femininely, dress more femininely. . . ." After reflecting on the case and on stereotyping research, the Supreme Court in 1989 decided that encouraging men, but not women, to be aggressive, is to act "on the basis of gender":

> We sit not to determine whether Ms. Hopkins is nice, but to decide whether the partners reacted negatively to her personality because she is a woman. . . . An employer who objects to aggressiveness in women but whose positions require this trait places women in an intolerable Catch 22: out of a job if they behave aggressively and out of a job if they don't.

Summing Up: What Are the Consequences of Prejudice?

- Prejudice and stereotyping have important consequences, especially when strongly held, when judging unknown individuals, and when deciding policies regarding whole groups.

- Once formed, stereotypes tend to perpetuate themselves and resist change. They also create their own realities through self-fulfilling prophecies.

- Prejudice can also undermine people's performance through stereotype threat, by making people apprehensive that others will view them stereotypically.

- Stereotypes, especially when strong, can predispose how we perceive people and interpret events.

POSTSCRIPT: Can We Reduce Prejudice?

Social psychologists have been more successful in explaining prejudice than in alleviating it. Because prejudice results from many interrelated factors, there is no simple remedy. Nevertheless, we can now anticipate techniques for reducing prejudice (discussed further in chapters to come): If unequal status breeds prejudice, then we can seek to create cooperative, equal-status relationships. If prejudice rationalizes discriminatory behavior, then we can mandate nondiscrimination. If social institutions support prejudice, then we can pull out those supports (for example, persuade the media to model interracial harmony). If outgroups seem more unlike one's own group than they really are, then we can make efforts to personalize their members. If automatic prejudices lead us to engage in behaviors that make us feel guilty, then we can use that guilt to motivate ourselves to break the prejudice habit.

Since the end of World War II in 1945, a number of those antidotes have been applied, and racial and gender prejudices have indeed diminished. Social-psychological research also has helped break down discriminatory barriers. "We risked a lot by testifying on Ann Hopkins's behalf, no doubt about it," Susan Fiske (1999) later wrote.

> As far as we knew, no one had ever introduced the social psychology of stereotyping in a gender case before. . . . If we succeeded, we would get the latest stereotyping research out of the dusty journals and into the muddy trenches of legal debate, where it might be useful. If we failed, we might hurt the client, slander social psychology, and damage my reputation as a scientist. At the time I had no idea that the testimony would eventually make it successfully through the Supreme Court.

It now remains to be seen whether, during this century, progress will continue . . . or whether, as could easily happen in a time of increasing population and diminishing resources, antagonisms will again erupt into open hostility.

 ## Making the Social Connection

In this chapter we explored how prejudice can be both subtle and overt. The Online Learning Center for this book presents a video on interracial marriage that explores this phenomenon. Another issue in this chapter is Claude Steele's concept of stereotype threat. Have you ever been concerned that you were being stereotyped? Watch the video of Steele explaining his theory to learn more. Finally, watch the third video to understand the impact of prejudice on its targets.

Aggression

HURTING OTHERS

"Our behavior toward each other is the strangest, most unpredictable, and most unaccountable of all the phenomena with which we are obliged to live. In all of nature, there is nothing so threatening to humanity as humanity itself."

—Lewis Thomas (1981)

Although Woody Allen's tongue-in-cheek prediction that "by 1990 kidnapping will be the dominant mode of social interaction" went unfulfilled, the years since have hardly been serene. The horror of 9/11 may have been the most dramatic recent violence, but in terms of human lives, it was not the most catastrophic. About the same time, the human carnage from tribal warfare in the Congo was claiming an estimated 3 million lives, some of the victims hacked to death with machetes, many others dying of starvation and disease after fleeing in terror from their villages (Sengupta, 2003). In neighboring Rwanda, where some 750,000 people—including more than half the Tutsi population—were slaughtered in the genocidal summer of 1994, residents are all too familiar with this human capacity for carnage (Dutton & others, 2005; Staub, 1999). So are the people of the Congo, where 5 million people have died war-related deaths in the last decade, and the people of Sudan, where war and genocide have claimed 2.5 million people (Clooney & others, 2008). The Iraq war, by one estimate in a leading medical journal, killed some 650,000 civilians (Burnham & others, 2006).

Worldwide, more than $3 billion per day is spent on arms and armies—$3 billion that could feed, educate, and protect the environment of the world's impoverished millions. During the last century,

FIGURE :: 10.1

The Bloodiest Century

Twentieth-century humanity was the most educated, and homicidal, in history (data from Renner, 1999). Adding in genocides and human-made famines, there were approximately 182 million "deaths by mass unpleasantness" (White, 2000). By the century's end, such deaths were declining (Human Security Centre, 2005).

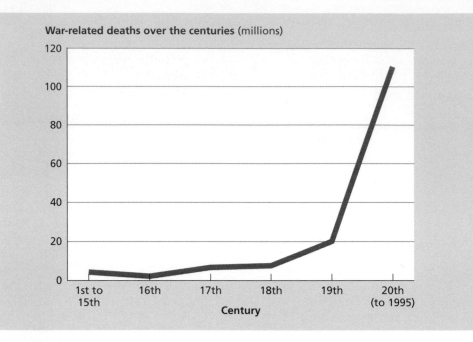

War-related deaths over the centuries (millions)

some 250 wars killed 110 million people, enough to populate a "nation of the dead" with more than the combined population of France, Belgium, the Netherlands, Denmark, Finland, Norway, and Sweden (Figure 10.1). The tolls came not only from the world wars but also from genocides, including the 1915 to 1923 genocide of 1 million Armenians by the Ottoman Empire, the slaughter of some 250,000 Chinese in Nanking after it had surrendered to Japanese troops in 1937, the 1971 Pakistani genocide of 3 million Bangladeshis, and the 1.5 million Cambodians murdered in a reign of terror starting in 1975 (Dutton & others, 2005; Sternberg, 2003). As Hitler's genocide of millions of Jews, Stalin's genocide of millions of Russians, Mao's genocide of millions of Chinese, and the genocide of millions of Native Americans from the time of Columbus through the nineteenth century make plain, the human potential for extraordinary cruelty crosses cultures and races.

Are we like the mythical Minotaur, half human, half beast? What explains that midsummer day in 1941 when the non-Jewish half of the Polish town of Jebwabne murdered the other half in a macabre frenzy of violence, leaving only a dozen or so survivors among the 1,600 Jews (Gross, 2001)? What explains such monstrous behavior? In this chapter we ask four more-specific questions:

- Is aggression biologically predisposed, or do we learn it?

- What circumstances prompt hostile outbursts?

- Do the media influence aggression?

- How might we reduce aggression?

First, however, we need to clarify the term "aggression."

What Is Aggression?

The original Thugs, members of a sect in northern India, were aggressing when between 1550 and 1850 they strangled more than 2 million people and claimed to do so in the service of the goddess Kali. But people also use "aggressive" to describe a dynamic salesperson. Social psychologists distinguish such self-assured, energetic, go-getting behavior from behavior that hurts, harms, or destroys. The former is assertiveness, the latter aggression.

For our discussion in this chapter, we will define **aggression** as physical or verbal behavior intended to cause harm. This definition excludes unintentional harm such as auto accidents or sidewalk collisions; it also excludes actions that may involve pain as an unavoidable side effect of helping someone, such as dental treatments or—in the extreme—assisted suicide. It includes kicks and slaps, threats and insults, even gossip or snide "digs." It includes decisions during experiments about how much to hurt someone, such as how much electric shock to impose. It also includes destroying property, lying, and other behavior whose goal is to hurt.

The definition covers two distinct types of aggression. Animals exhibit *social* aggression, characterized by displays of rage; and *silent* aggression, as when a predator stalks its prey. Social and silent aggression involve separate brain regions. In humans, psychologists label the two types "hostile" and "instrumental" aggression. **Hostile aggression** springs from anger; its goal is to injure. **Instrumental aggression** aims to injure, too—but only as a means to some other end.

Most terrorism is instrumental aggression. "What nearly all suicide terrorist campaigns have in common is a specific secular and strategic goal," concludes Robert Pape (2003) after studying all suicide bombings from 1980 to 2001. That goal is "to compel liberal democracies to withdraw military forces from territory that the terrorists consider to be their homeland." Terrorism is rarely committed by someone with a psychological pathology, note Arie Kruglanski and Shira Fishman (2006). Rather, it is a strategic tool used during conflict. In explaining the aim of the 9/11 attacks, Osama bin Laden noted that for a cost of only $500,000 they inflicted $500 billion worth of damage to the American economy (Zakaria, 008).

Most wars are instrumental aggression. In 2003, American and British leaders justified attacking Iraq not as a hostile effort to kill Iraqis but as an instrumental act of liberation and of self-defense against presumed weapons of mass destruction. Hostile aggression is "hot"; instrumental aggression is "cool."

Most murders, however, are hostile aggression. Approximately half erupt from arguments, and others result from romantic triangles, or from brawls while under the influence of alcohol or drugs (Ash, 1999). Such murders are impulsive, emotional outbursts, which helps explain why data from 110 nations show that a death penalty has not resulted in fewer homicides (Costanzo, 1998; Wilkes, 1987). Some murders and many other violent acts of retribution and sexual coercion, however, are instrumental (Felson, 2000). Most of Chicago's more than 1,000 murders carried out by organized crime during the prohibition era and the years following were cool and calculated.

aggression
Physical or verbal behavior intended to hurt someone.

hostile aggression
Aggression driven by anger and performed as an end in itself. (Also called *affective aggression*.)

instrumental aggression
Aggression that is a means to some other end.

"Of course, we'll never actually use it against a potential enemy, but it will allow us to negotiate from a position of strength."

Humanity has armed its capacity for destruction without comparably arming its capacity for the inhibition of aggression.
Reprinted with permission of General Media Magazines.

What Are Some Theories of Aggression?

In analyzing causes of hostile and instrumental aggression, social psychologists have focused on three big ideas: (1) There is a biologically rooted aggressive drive; (2) aggression is a natural response to frustration; and (3) aggressive behavior is learned.

Aggression as a Biological Phenomenon

Philosophers have debated whether our human nature is fundamentally that of a benign, contented, "noble savage" or that of a brute. The first view, argued by the eighteenth-century French philosopher Jean-Jacques Rousseau (1712–1778), blames society, not human nature, for social evils. The second idea, associated with the English philosopher Thomas Hobbes (1588–1679), credits society for restraining the human brute. In the twentieth century, the "brutish" view—that aggressive drive is inborn and thus inevitable—was argued by Sigmund Freud in Vienna and Konrad Lorenz in Germany.

INSTINCT THEORY AND EVOLUTIONARY PSYCHOLOGY

Freud speculated that human aggression springs from a self-destructive impulse. It redirects toward others the energy of a primitive death urge (the "death instinct"). Lorenz, an animal behavior expert, saw aggression as adaptive rather than self-destructive. The two agreed that aggressive energy is **instinctive** (unlearned and universal). If not discharged, it supposedly builds up until it explodes or until an appropriate stimulus "releases" it, like a mouse releasing a mousetrap.

instinctive behavior
An innate, unlearned behavior pattern exhibited by all members of a species.

The idea that aggression is an instinct collapsed as the list of supposed human instincts grew to include nearly every conceivable human behavior. Nearly 6,000 supposed instincts were enumerated in one 1924 survey of social science books (Barash, 1979). The social scientists had tried to *explain* social behavior by *naming* it. It's tempting to play this explaining-by-naming game: "Why do sheep stay together?" "Because of their herd instinct." "How do you know they have a herd instinct?" "Just look at them: They're always together!"

Instinct theory also fails to account for the variations in aggressiveness from person to person and culture to culture. How would a shared human instinct for aggression explain the difference between the peaceful Iroquois before White invaders came and the hostile Iroquois after the invasion (Hornstein, 1976)? Although aggression is biologically influenced, the human propensity to aggress does not qualify as instinctive behavior.

Our distant ancestors nevertheless sometimes found aggression adaptive, note evolutionary psychologists David Buss and Todd Shackelford (1997). Aggressive behavior was a strategy for gaining resources, defending against attack, intimidating or eliminating male rivals for females, and deterring mates from sexual infidelity. In some preindustrial societies, being a good warrior made for higher status and reproductive opportunities (Roach, 1998). The adaptive value of aggression, Buss and Shackelford believe, helps explain the relatively high levels of male-male aggression across human history. "This does not imply . . . that men have an 'aggression instinct' in the sense of some pent-up energy that must be released. Rather, men have inherited from their successful ancestors psychological mechanisms" that improve their odds of contributing their genes to future generations.

NEURAL INFLUENCES

Because aggression is a complex behavior, no one spot in the brain controls it. But researchers have found neural systems in both animals and humans that facilitate aggression. When the scientists activate these brain areas, hostility increases; when they deactivate them, hostility decreases. Docile animals can thus be provoked into rage, and raging animals into submission.

In one experiment, researchers placed an electrode in an aggression-inhibiting area of a domineering monkey's brain. A smaller monkey, given a button that activated the electrode, learned to push it every time the tyrant monkey became intimidating. Brain activation works with humans, too. After receiving painless electrical stimulation in her amygdala (a part of the brain core), one woman became enraged and smashed her guitar against the wall, barely missing her psychiatrist's head (Moyer, 1976, 1983).

Does this mean that violent people's brains are in some way abnormal? To find out, Adrian Raine and his colleagues (1998, 2000, 2005, 2008) used brain scans to measure brain activity in murderers and to measure the amount of gray matter in men with antisocial conduct disorder. They found that the prefrontal cortex, which acts like an emergency brake on deeper brain areas involved in aggressive behavior, was 14 percent less active than normal in murderers (excluding those who had been abused by their parents) and 15 percent smaller in the antisocial men. As other studies of murderers and death-row inmates confirm, abnormal brains can contribute to abnormally aggressive behavior (Davidson & others, 2000; Lewis, 1998; Pincus, 2001).

GENETIC INFLUENCES

Heredity influences the neural system's sensitivity to aggressive cues. It has long been known that animals can be bred for aggressiveness. Sometimes this is done for practical purposes (the breeding of fighting cocks). Sometimes breeding is done for research. Finnish psychologist Kirsti Lagerspetz (1979) took normal albino mice and bred the most aggressive ones together; she did the same with the least aggressive ones. After repeating the procedure for 26 generations, she had one set of fierce mice and one set of placid mice.

Aggressiveness also varies among primates and humans (Asher, 1987; Bettencourt & others, 2006; Denson & others, 2006; Olweus, 1979). Our temperaments—how intense and reactive we are—are partly brought with us into the world, influenced by our sympathetic nervous system's reactivity (Kagan, 1989; Wilkowski & Robinson, 2008). A person's temperament, observed in infancy, usually endures (Larsen & Diener, 1987; Wilson & Matheny, 1986). A child who is nonaggressive at age 8 will very likely still be a nonaggressive person at age 48 (Huesmann & others, 2003). Thus, identical twins, when asked separately, are more likely than fraternal twins to agree on whether they have "a violent temper" or have gotten into fights (Rowe & others, 1999; Rushton & others, 1986). Of convicted criminals who are twins, fully half of their identical twins (but only one in five fraternal twins) also have criminal records (Raine, 1993, 2008).

Long-term studies following several hundred New Zealand children reveal

Genes predispose the pit bull's aggressiveness.

Alcohol and sexual assault. "Ordinary men who drank too much," was the *New York Times* description of the mob that openly assaulted some 50 women attending a June 2000 NYC parade. "Stoked with booze, they worked up from hooting at women, to grabbing them, to drenching them with water and pulling off their tops and pants" (Staples, 2000).

that a recipe for aggressive behavior combines a gene that alters neurotransmitter balance with childhood maltreatment (Caspi & others, 2002; Moffitt & others, 2003). Neither "bad" genes nor a "bad" environment alone predispose later aggressiveness and antisocial behavior; rather, genes predispose some children to be more sensitive and responsive to maltreatment. Nature and nurture interact.

BIOCHEMICAL INFLUENCES

Blood chemistry also influences neural sensitivity to aggressive stimulation.

ALCOHOL Both laboratory experiments and police data indicate that alcohol unleashes aggression when people are provoked (Bushman, 1993; Taylor & Chermack, 1993; Testa, 2002). Consider:

- In experiments, when asked to think back on relationship conflicts, intoxicated people administer stronger shocks and feel angrier than do sober people (MacDonald & others, 2000).
- In 65 percent of homicides and 55 percent of in-home fights and assaults, the assailant and/or the victim had been drinking (American Psychological Association, 1993).
- If spouse-battering alcoholics cease their problem drinking after treatment, their violent behavior typically ceases (Murphy & O'Farrell, 1996).

Alcohol enhances aggressiveness by reducing people's self-awareness, by focusing their attention on a provocation, and by people's mentally associating alcohol with aggression (Bartholow & Heinz, 2006; Giancola & Corman, 2007; Ito & others, 1996). Alcohol deindividuates, and it disinhibits.

TESTOSTERONE Hormonal influences appear to be much stronger in lower animals than in humans. But human aggressiveness does correlate with the male sex hormone, testosterone. Consider:

- Drugs that diminish testosterone levels in violent human males will subdue their aggressive tendencies.
- After people reach age 25, their testosterone levels and rates of violent crime decrease together.
- Testosterone levels tend to be higher among prisoners convicted of planned and unprovoked violent crimes than of nonviolent crimes (Dabbs, 1992; Dabbs & others, 1995, 1997, 2001).
- Among the normal range of teen boys and adult men, those with high testosterone levels are more prone to delinquency, hard drug use, and aggressive responses to provocation (Archer, 1991; Dabbs & Morris, 1990; Olweus & others, 1988).
- When given a dose of testosterone, women become less attuned to another's aggression-deterring threat signal (van Honk & Schutter, 2007).
- After handling a gun, people's testosterone levels rise, and the more their testosterone rises the more hot sauce they will impose on another (Klinesmith & others, 2006).
- In men, testosterone increases the facial width-to-height ratio. And sure enough, in the laboratory, men with relatively wider faces display more aggression. Ditto in the hockey rink, where collegiate and professional hockey players with relatively wide faces spend more time in the penalty box (Carré & McCormick, 2008).

"We could avoid two-thirds of all crime simply by putting all able-bodied young men in cryogenic sleep from the age of 12 through 28."
—*DAVID LYKKEN*, THE ANTISOCIAL PERSONALITIES, *1995*

Testosterone, said James Dabbs (2000), "is a small molecule with large effects." Injecting a man with testosterone won't automatically make him aggressive, yet men with low testosterone are somewhat less likely to react aggressively when provoked (Geen, 1998). Testosterone is roughly like battery power. Only if the battery levels are very low will things noticeably slow down.

LOW SEROTONIN   Another culprit often found at the scene of violence is a low level of the neurotransmitter serotonin, for which the impulse-controlling frontal lobes have many receptors. In both primates and humans, low serotonin is often found among violence-prone children and adults (Bernhardt, 1997; Mehlman & others, 1994; Wright, 1995). Moreover, lowering people's serotonin levels in the laboratory increases their response to aversive events and their willingness to deliver supposed electric shocks or to retaliate against unfairness (Crockett & others, 2008).

BIOLOGY AND BEHAVIOR INTERACT   It is important to remember that the traffic between testosterone, serotonin, and behavior flows both ways. Testosterone, for example, may facilitate dominance and aggressiveness, but dominating or defeating behavior also boosts testosterone levels (Mazur & Booth, 1998). After a World Cup soccer match or a big basketball game between archrivals, testosterone levels rise in the winning fans and fall in the losing fans (Bernhardt & others, 1998). The phenomenon also occurs in the laboratory, where socially anxious men exhibit a pronounced drop in their testosterone level after losing a rigged face-to-face competition (Maner & others, 2008). Testosterone surges, plus celebration-related drinking, probably explain the finding of Cardiff University researchers that fans of *winning* rather than losing soccer and rugby teams commit more postgame assaults (Sivarajasingam & others, 2005).

So, neural, genetic, and biochemical influences predispose some people to react aggressively to conflict and provocation. But is aggression so much a part of human nature that it makes peace unattainable? The American Psychological Association and the International Council of Psychologists have joined other organizations in endorsing a statement on violence developed by scientists from a dozen nations (Adams, 1991): "It is scientifically incorrect [to say that] war or any other violent behavior is genetically programmed into our human nature [or that] war is caused by 'instinct' or any single motivation." Thus, there are, as we will see, ways to reduce human aggression.

Aggression as a Response to Frustration

It is a warm evening. Tired and thirsty after two hours of studying, you borrow some change from a friend and head for the nearest soft-drink machine. As the machine devours the change, you can almost taste the cold, refreshing cola. But when you push the button, nothing happens. You push it again. Then you flip the coin return button. Still nothing. Again, you hit the buttons. You slam the machine. Alas, no money and no drink. You stomp back to your studies, empty-handed and shortchanged. Should your roommate beware? Are you now more likely to say or do something hurtful?

One of the first psychological theories of aggression, the popular **frustration-aggression theory,** answered yes. "Frustration always leads to some form of aggression," said John Dollard and his colleagues (1939, p. 1). **Frustration** is anything (such as the malfunctioning vending machine) that blocks our attaining a goal. Frustration grows when our motivation to achieve a goal is very strong, when we expected gratification, and when the blocking is complete. When Rupert Brown and his colleagues (2001) surveyed British ferry passengers heading to France, they found much higher than normal aggressive attitudes on a day when French fishing boats blockaded the port, preventing their travel. Blocked from obtaining their goal, the passengers became more likely (in responding to various vignettes) to agree with an insult toward a French person who had spilled coffee.

Some violent sex offenders, wishing to free themselves of persistent, damaging impulses and to reduce their prison terms, have requested castration. Should their requests be granted? If so, and if they are deemed no longer at risk to commit sexual violence, should their prison terms be reduced or eliminated?

frustration-aggression theory
The theory that frustration triggers a readiness to aggress.

frustration
The blocking of goal-directed behavior.

FIGURE :: 10.2

The Classic Frustration-Aggression Theory

Frustration creates a motive to aggress. Fear of punishment or disapproval for aggressing against the source of frustration may cause the aggressive drive to be displaced against some other target or even redirected against oneself.

Source: Based on Dollard & others, 1939, and Miller, 1941.

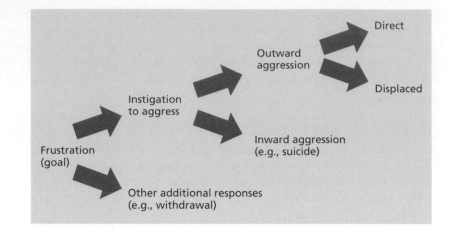

displacement

The redirection of aggression to a target other than the source of the frustration. Generally, the new target is a safer or more socially acceptable target.

As Figure 10.2 suggests, the aggressive energy need not explode directly against its source. We learn to inhibit direct retaliation, especially when others might disapprove or punish; instead, we *displace* our hostilities to safer targets. **Displacement** occurs in an old anecdote about a man who, humiliated by his boss, berates his wife, who yells at their son, who kicks the dog, which bites the mail carrier (who goes home and berates his wife . . .). In experiments and in real life, displaced aggression is most likely when the target shares some similarity to the instigator and does some minor irritating act that unleashes the displaced aggression (Marcus-Newhall & others, 2000; Miller & others, 2003; Pedersen & others, 2000). When a person is harboring anger from a prior provocation, even a trivial offense—one that would normally produce no response—may elicit an explosive overreaction (as you may realize if you have ever yelled at your roommate after losing money in a malfunctioning vending machine).

In one experiment, Eduardo Vasquez and his co-researchers (2005) provoked some University of Southern California students (but not others) by having an experimenter insult their performance on an anagram-solving test. Shortly afterward, the students had to decide how long another supposed student should be required to immerse his or her hand in painful cold water while completing a task. When the supposed student committed a trivial offense—by giving a mild insult—the previously provoked participants responded punitively, by recommending a longer cold-water treatment than did the unprovoked participants. This phenomenon of displaced aggression helps us understand, notes Vasquez, why a previously provoked and still-angry person might respond to mild highway offenses with road rage, or react to spousal criticism with spouse abuse. It also helps explain why frustrated major league baseball pitchers, in one analysis of nearly 5 million at-bats from 74,197 games since 1960, were most likely to hit batters after the batter hit a home run the last time at bat, or after the previous batter did so (Timmerman, 2007).

Various commentators have observed that the understandably intense American anger over 9/11 contributed to the eagerness to attack Iraq. Americans were looking for an outlet for their rage and found one in an evil tyrant, Saddam Hussein, who was once their ally. "The 'real reason' for this war," noted Thomas Friedman (2003), "was that after 9/11 America needed to hit someone in the Arab-Muslim world. . . . We hit Saddam for one simple reason: because we could, and because he deserved it, and because

Frustration-triggered aggression sometimes appears as road rage. Road rage is fed by perceptions of hostile intentions from other drivers, as when one is cut off in traffic (Britt & Garrity, 2006).

FIGURE :: 10.3

A Simplified Synopsis
of Leonard Berkowitz's
Revised Frustration-
Aggression Theory

he was right in the heart of that world." One of the war's advocates, Vice President Richard Cheney (2003), seemed to concur. When asked why most others in the world disagreed with America's launching war, he replied, "They didn't experience 9/11."

FRUSTRATION-AGGRESSION THEORY REVISED

Laboratory tests of the frustration-aggression theory have produced mixed results: Sometimes frustration increased aggressiveness, sometimes not. For example, if the frustration was understandable—if, as in one experiment, a confederate disrupted a group's problem solving because his hearing aid malfunctioned (rather than just because he wasn't paying attention)—then frustration led to irritation, not aggression (Burnstein & Worchel, 1962).

Leonard Berkowitz (1978, 1989) realized that the original theory overstated the frustration-aggression connection, so he revised it. Berkowitz theorized that frustration produces *anger,* an emotional readiness to aggress. Anger arises when someone who frustrates us could have chosen to act otherwise (Averill, 1983; Weiner, 1981).

A frustrated person is especially likely to lash out when aggressive cues pull the cork, releasing bottled-up anger (Figure 10.3). Sometimes the cork will blow without such cues. But, as we will see, cues associated with aggression amplify aggression (Carlson & others, 1990).

Terrorists understand the anger-eliciting effect of their actions. Social psychologists Clark McCauley (2004) and Richard Wagner (2006) note that terrorists sometimes aim to commit an act that will induce a strong and angry enemy to overreact, producing effects that ultimately serve the terrorists' interests.

Frustration may be unrelated to deprivation. The most sexually frustrated people are probably not celibate. The most economically frustrated people may not be the impoverished residents of African shantytowns. During the 1930s depression, when economic misery was widespread, violent crime was not notably high. Likewise, Palestinian suicide bombers have not been the most deprived of Palestinians. Like Northern Ireland's IRA, Italy's Red Brigades, and Germany's Bader-Meinhof gang, they are mostly middle class (Krueger, 2007a, 2007b; Pettigrew, 2003). So, too, were the 9/11 terrorists, who were professionally trained and world-traveled. Contrary to the myth that terrorists attack us as a response to their desperate poverty, collective humiliation and lack of civil liberties feed terrorism far more than does absolute deprivation.

The point is not that deprivation and social injustice are irrelevant to social unrest, but that *frustration arises from the gap between expectations and attainments.* When your expectations are fulfilled by your attainments, and when your desires are reachable at your income, you feel satisfied rather than frustrated (Solberg & others, 2002).

RELATIVE DEPRIVATION

Frustration is often compounded when we compare ourselves with others. Workers' feelings of well-being depend on whether their compensation compares favorably with that of others in their line of work (Yuchtman, 1976). A raise in salary for a city's police officers, while temporarily lifting their morale, may deflate that of the firefighters.

Note that frustration-aggression theory *is designed to explain hostile aggression, not instrumental aggression.*

"The war on terrorism will not be won until we have come to grips with the problem of poverty, and thus the sources of discontent."
—*FORMER WORLD BANK PRESIDENT JAMES WOLFENSOHN*

"Evils which are patiently endured when they seem inevitable become intolerable when once the idea of escape from them is suggested."
—*ALEXIS DE TOCQUEVILLE, 1856*

relative deprivation
The perception that one is less well-off than others with whom one compares oneself.

"A house may be large or small; as long as the surrounding houses are equally small, it satisfies all social demands for a dwelling. But let a palace arise beside the little house, and it shrinks from a little house into a hut."
—KARL MARX

"Woman's discontent increases in exact proportion to her development."
—ELIZABETH CADY STANTON, 1815–1902, AMERICAN SUFFRAGIST

Such feelings, called **relative deprivation,** explain why happiness tends to be lower and crime rates higher in communities and nations with large income inequality (Hagerty, 2000; Kawachi & others, 1999). And it explains why the former East Germans revolted against their communist regime: They had a higher standard of living than some Western European countries, but a frustratingly lower one than their West German neighbors (Baron & others, 1992).

The term *relative deprivation* was coined by researchers studying the satisfaction felt by American soldiers in World War II (Merton & Kitt, 1950; Stouffer & others, 1949). Ironically, those in the air corps felt *more* frustrated about their own rate of promotion than those in the military police, for whom promotions were slower. The air corps' promotion rate was rapid, and most air corps personnel probably perceived themselves as better than the average air corps member (the self-serving bias). Thus, their aspirations soared higher than their achievements. The result? Frustration.

One possible source of such frustration today is the affluence depicted in television programs and commercials. In cultures where television is a universal appliance, it helps turn absolute deprivation (lacking what others have) into relative deprivation (feeling deprived). Karen Hennigan and her co-workers (1982) analyzed crime rates in American cities around the time television was introduced. In 34 cities where television ownership became widespread in 1951, the 1951 larceny theft rate (for crimes such as shoplifting and bicycle stealing) took an observable jump. In 34 other cities, where a government freeze had delayed the introduction of television until 1955, a similar jump in the theft rate occurred—in 1955.

Aggression as Learned Social Behavior

Theories of aggression based on instinct and frustration assume that hostile urges erupt from inner emotions, which naturally "push" aggression from within. Social psychologists contend that learning also "pulls" aggression out of us.

THE REWARDS OF AGGRESSION

By experience and by observing others, we learn that aggression often pays. Experiments have transformed animals from docile creatures into ferocious fighters. Severe defeats, on the other hand, create submissiveness (Ginsburg & Allee, 1942; Kahn, 1951; Scott & Marston, 1953).

People, too, can learn the rewards of aggression. A child whose aggressive acts successfully intimidate other children will likely become increasingly aggressive (Patterson & others, 1967). Aggressive hockey players—the ones sent most often to the penalty box for rough play—score more goals than nonaggressive players (McCarthy & Kelly, 1978a, 1978b). Canadian teenage hockey players whose fathers applaud physically aggressive play show the most aggressive attitudes and style of play (Ennis & Zanna, 1991). In the waters off Somalia, paying ransom to hijackers of ships—a reported $150 million in 2008 (BBC, 2008)—rewarded the pirates, thus fueling further hijackings. In these cases, aggression is instrumental in achieving certain rewards.

The same is true of terrorist acts, which enable powerless people to garner widespread attention. "The primary targets of suicide-bombing attacks are not those who are injured but those who are made to witness it through media coverage," note Paul Marsden and Sharon Attia (2005). Terrorism's purpose is, with the help of media amplification, to terrorize. "Kill one, frighten ten thousand," asserts an ancient Chinese proverb. Deprived of what Margaret Thatcher called "the oxygen of publicity," terrorism would surely diminish, concluded Jeffrey Rubin (1986). It's like the 1970s incidents of naked spectators "streaking" onto football fields for a few seconds of television exposure. Once the networks decided to ignore the incidents, the phenomenon ended.

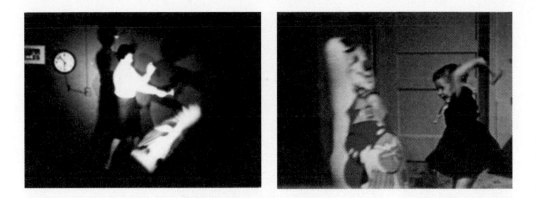

In Bandura's famous experiment, children exposed to an adult's aggression against a Bobo doll became likely to reproduce the observed aggression.

OBSERVATIONAL LEARNING

Albert Bandura (1997) proposed a **social learning theory** of aggression. He believes that we learn aggression not only by experiencing its payoffs but also by observing others. As with most social behaviors, we acquire aggression by watching others act and noting the consequences.

Picture this scene from one of Bandura's experiments (Bandura & others, 1961). A preschool child is put to work on an interesting art activity. An adult is in another part of the room, where there are Tinker Toys, a mallet, and a big, inflated "Bobo" doll. After a minute of working with the Tinker Toys, the adult gets up and for almost 10 minutes attacks the inflated doll. She pounds it with the mallet, kicks it, and throws it, while yelling, "Sock him in the nose. . . . Knock him down. . . . Kick him."

After observing this outburst, the child is taken to a different room with many very attractive toys. But after two minutes the experimenter interrupts, saying these are her best toys and she must "save them for the other children." The frustrated child now goes into yet another room with various toys designed for aggressive and nonaggressive play, two of which are a Bobo doll and a mallet.

Seldom did children who were not exposed to the aggressive adult model display any aggressive play or talk. Although frustrated, they nevertheless played calmly. Those who had observed the aggressive adult were many times more likely to pick up the mallet and lash out at the doll. Watching the adult's aggressive behavior lowered their inhibitions. Moreover, the children often reproduced the model's specific acts and said her words. Observing aggressive behavior had both lowered their inhibitions and taught them ways to aggress.

Bandura (1979) believes that everyday life exposes us to aggressive models in the family, in one's subculture, and, as we will see, in the mass media.

THE FAMILY   Physically aggressive children tend to have had physically punitive parents, who disciplined them by modeling aggression with screaming, slapping, and beating (Patterson & others, 1982). These parents often had parents who were themselves physically punitive (Bandura & Walters, 1959; Straus & Gelles, 1980). Such punitive behavior may escalate into abuse, and although most abused children do not become criminals or abusive parents, 30 percent do later abuse their own children—four times the general population rate (Kaufman & Zigler, 1987; Widom, 1989). Violence often begets violence.

Family influence also appears in higher violence rates in cultures and in families with absentee fathers (Triandis, 1994). David Lykken (2000) computed that American children reared without fathers are about seven times more likely to be abused, to drop out of school, to become runaways, to become unmarried teenage parents, and to commit violent crimes. The correlation between parental absence (usually father absence) and violence holds across races, income levels, education, and locations (Staub, 1996; Zill, 1988). Moreover, in one British study that followed more

social learning theory
The theory that we learn social behavior by observing and imitating and by being rewarded and punished.

A peaceable kingdom. In 2008, a man was convicted of murder in Scotland's Orkney Islands—the second murder conviction since the 1800s.

than 10,000 individuals for 33 years since their birth in 1958, the risk of problems such as aggressive behavior increased following a parental breakup during middle childhood (Cherlin & others, 1998).

The point is not that children from father-absent homes are doomed to become delinquent or violent; in fact, nurtured by a caring mother and extended family, most such children thrive. The point is also not that father absence causes violence; we don't know that it does. The point is simply that there is a correlation: Where and when fathers are absent, the violence risk increases.

THE CULTURE The social environment outside the home also provides models. In communities where "macho" images are admired, aggression is readily transmitted to new generations (Cartwright, 1975; Short, 1969). The violent subculture of teenage gangs, for instance, provides its junior members with aggressive models. Among Chicago adolescents who are otherwise equally at risk for violence, those who have observed gun violence are at doubled risk for violent behavior (Bingenheimer & others, 2005).

The broader culture also matters. Show social psychologists a man from a nondemocratic culture that has great economic inequality, that prepares men to be warriors, and that has engaged in war, and they will show you someone who is predisposed to aggressive behavior (Bond, 2004).

Richard Nisbett (1990, 1993) and Dov Cohen (1996, 1998) have explored the subculture effect. Within the United States, they report, the sober, cooperative White folk who settled New England and the Middle Atlantic region produced a different culture from that of the swashbuckling, honor-preserving White folk (many of them my own Scots-Irish ancestral cousins) who settled much of the South. The former were farmer-artisans; the latter, more aggressive hunters and herders. To the present day, American cities and areas populated by southerners have higher than average White homicide rates. Not surprisingly, southern males are also more likely than northern males to perceive their peers as supporting aggressive responses (Vandello & others, 2008).

People learn aggressive responses both by experience and by observing aggressive models. But when will aggressive responses actually occur? Bandura (1979) contended that aggressive acts are motivated by a variety of aversive experiences— frustration, pain, insults (Figure 10.4). Such experiences arouse us emotionally. But

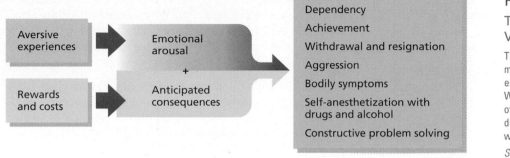

FIGURE :: 10.4

The Social Learning View of Aggression

The emotional arousal stemming from an aversive experience motivates aggression. Whether aggression or some other response actually occurs depends on what consequences we have learned to expect.

Source. Based on Bandura, 1979, 1997.

whether we act aggressively depends on the consequences we anticipate. Aggression is most likely when we are aroused and it seems safe and rewarding to aggress.

Summing Up: What Are Some Theories of Aggression?

- Aggression (defined as verbal or physical behavior intended to cause harm) manifests itself in two forms: *hostile aggression,* which springs from emotions such as anger, and *instrumental aggression,* which aims to injure as a means to some other end.

- There are three broad theories of aggression. The *instinct* view, most commonly associated with Sigmund Freud and Konrad Lorenz, contended that aggressive energy will accumulate from within, like water accumulating behind a dam. Although the available evidence offers little support for that view, aggression is biologically influenced by heredity, blood chemistry, and the brain.

- According to the second view, *frustration* causes anger and hostility. Given aggressive cues, that anger may provoke aggression. Frustration stems not from deprivation itself but from the gap between expectations and achievements.

- The *social learning* view presents aggression as learned behavior. By experience and by observing others' success, we sometimes learn that aggression pays. Social learning enables family and subcultural influences on aggression, as well as media influences (which we will discuss in the next section).

What Are Some Influences on Aggression?

Under what conditions do we aggress? In the previous section, we examined some theories of aggression. Now we dig deeper and examine some specific influences: aversive incidents, arousal, the media, and the group context.

Aversive Incidents

Recipes for aggression often include some type of aversive experience: pain, uncomfortable heat, an attack, or overcrowding.

PAIN

Researcher Nathan Azrin (1967) was doing experiments with laboratory rats in a cage wired to deliver electric shocks to the animals' feet. Azrin wanted to know if switching off the shocks would reinforce two rats' positive interactions with each other. He planned to turn on the shock and then, once the rats approached each other, cut off the pain. To his great surprise, the experiment proved impossible. As soon as the rats felt pain, they attacked each other, before the experimenter could switch off the shock. The greater the shock (and pain), the more violent the attack.

Today's ethical guidelines restrict researchers' use of painful stimuli.

Is this true of rats alone? The researchers found that with a wide variety of species, the cruelty the animals imposed on each other matched zap for zap the cruelty imposed on them. As Azrin (1967) explained, the pain-attack response occurred

> in many different strains of rats. Then we found that shock produced attack when pairs of the following species were caged together: some kinds of mice, hamsters, opossums, raccoons, marmosets, foxes, nutria, cats, snapping turtles, squirrel monkeys, ferrets, red squirrels, bantam roosters, alligators, crayfish, amphiuma (an amphibian), and several species of snakes including the boa constrictor, rattlesnake, brown rat-snake, cottonmouth, copperhead, and black snake. The shock-attack reaction was clearly present in many very different kinds of creatures. In all the species in which shock produced attack it was fast and consistent, in the same "push-button" manner as with the rats.

The animals were not choosy about their targets. They would attack animals of their own species and also those of a different species, or stuffed dolls, or even tennis balls.

The researchers also varied the source of pain. They found that not just shocks induced attack; intense heat and "psychological pain"—for example, suddenly not rewarding hungry pigeons that have been trained to expect a grain reward after pecking at a disk—brought the same reaction as shocks. This "psychological pain" is, of course, frustration.

Pain heightens aggressiveness in humans, too. Many of us can recall such a reaction after stubbing a toe or suffering a headache. Leonard Berkowitz and his associates demonstrated this by having University of Wisconsin students hold one hand in either lukewarm water or painfully cold water. Those whose hands were submerged in the cold water reported feeling more irritable and more annoyed, and they were more willing to blast another person with unpleasant noise. In view of such results, Berkowitz (1983, 1989, 1998) proposed that aversive stimulation rather than frustration is the basic trigger of hostile aggression. Frustration is certainly one important type of unpleasantness. But any aversive event, whether a dashed expectation, a personal insult, or physical pain, can incite an emotional outburst. Even the torment of a depressed state increases the likelihood of hostile, aggressive behavior.

HEAT

People have theorized for centuries about the effect of climate on human action. Hippocrates (ca. 460–377 B.C.) compared the civilized Greece of his day with the savagery in the region further north (what is now Germany and Switzerland) and decided that northern Europe's harsh climate was to blame. More than a millennium later, the English attributed their "superior" culture to England's ideal climate. French thinkers proclaimed the same for France. Because climate remains relatively steady while cultural traits change over time, the climate theory of culture obviously has limited validity.

Temporary climate variations can, however, affect behavior. Offensive odors, cigarette smoke, and air pollution have all been linked with aggressive behavior (Rotton & Frey, 1985). But the most-studied environmental irritant is heat. William Griffitt (1970; Griffitt & Veitch, 1971) found that compared with students who answered questionnaires in a

Pain attack. Frustrated after losing the first two rounds of his 1997 heavyweight championship fight with Evander Holyfield, and feeling pain from an accidental head butt, Mike Tyson reacts by biting off part of Holyfield's ear.

Los Angeles, May 1993. Riots are more likely during hot summer weather.

room with a normal temperature, those who did so in an uncomfortably hot room (over 90°F) reported feeling more tired and aggressive and expressed more hostility toward a stranger. Follow-up experiments revealed that heat also triggers retaliative actions (Bell, 1980; Rule & others, 1987).

Does uncomfortable heat increase aggression in the real world as well as in the laboratory? Consider:

- In heat-stricken Phoenix, Arizona, drivers without air-conditioning have been more likely to honk at a stalled car (Kenrick & MacFarlane, 1986).
- During the 1986 to 1988 major league baseball seasons, the number of batters hit by a pitch was two-thirds greater for games played above 90°F than for games played below 80°F (Reifman & others, 1991). Pitchers weren't wilder on hot days—they had no more walks or wild pitches. They just clobbered more batters.
- The riots that broke out in 79 U.S. cities between 1967 and 1971 occurred on more hot than cool days; none of them happened in winter.
- Studies in six cities have found that when the weather is hot, violent crimes are more likely (Anderson & Anderson, 1984; Cohn, 1993; Cotton, 1981, 1986; Harries & Stadler, 1988; Rotton & Frey, 1985).
- Across the Northern Hemisphere, it is not only hotter days that have more violent crimes, but also hotter seasons of the year, hotter summers, hotter years, hotter cities, and hotter regions (Anderson & Anderson, 1998; Anderson & others, 2000). Anderson and his colleagues project that if a 4-degree-Fahrenheit (about 2°C) global warming occurs, the United States alone will annually see at least 50,000 more serious assaults.

Do these real-world findings show that heat discomfort directly fuels aggressiveness? Although the conclusion appears plausible, these *correlations* between temperature and aggression don't prove it. People certainly could be more irritable in hot, sticky weather. And in the laboratory, hot temperatures do increase arousal and hostile thoughts and feelings (Anderson & others, 1999). There may be other contributing factors, though. Maybe hot summer evenings drive people into the streets. There, other group influence factors may well take over. Then again (researchers are debating this), maybe there comes a point where stifling heat suppresses violence (Bell, 2005; Bushman & others, 2005a, 2005b; Cohn & Rotton, 2005).

"I pray thee, good Mercutio, let's retire; The day is hot, the Capulets abroad, And, if we meet, we shall not 'scape a brawl, For now, these hot days, is the mad blood stirring."
—*SHAKESPEARE*, ROMEO AND JULIET

ATTACKS

Being attacked or insulted by another is especially conducive to aggression. Several experiments, including one at Osaka University by Kennichi Ohbuchi and Toshihiro Kambara (1985), confirm that intentional attacks breed retaliatory attacks. In most of these experiments, one person competes with another in a reaction-time contest. After each test trial, the winner chooses how much shock to give the loser. Actually, each person is playing a programmed opponent, who steadily escalates the amount of shock. Do the real participants respond charitably? Hardly. Extracting "an eye for an eye" is the more likely response.

Arousal

So far we have seen that various aversive stimulations can arouse anger. Do other types of arousal, such as those that accompany exercise or sexual excitement, have a similar effect? Imagine that Lourdes, having just finished a stimulating short run, comes home to discover that her date for the evening has called and left word that he has made other plans. Will Lourdes more likely explode in fury after her run than if she discovered the same message after awakening from a nap? Or, since she has just exercised, will her aggression be exorcised? To discover the answer, consider how we interpret and label our bodily states.

In a famous experiment, Stanley Schachter and Jerome Singer (1962) found we can experience an aroused bodily state in different ways. They aroused University of Minnesota men by injecting adrenaline. The drug produced body flushing, heart palpitation, and more rapid breathing. When forewarned that the drug would produce those effects, the men felt little emotion, even when waiting with either a hostile or a euphoric person. Of course, they could readily attribute their bodily sensations to the drug. Schachter and Singer led another group of men to believe the drug produced no such side effects. Then they, too, were placed in the company of a hostile or a euphoric person. How did they feel and act? They were angered when with the hostile person, amused when with the person who was euphoric. The principle seemed to be: *A given state of bodily arousal feeds one emotion or another, depending on how the person interprets and labels the arousal.*

Other experiments indicate that arousal is not as emotionally undifferentiated as Schachter believed. Yet being physically stirred up does intensify just about any emotion (Reisenzein, 1983). For example, Paul Biner (1991) reports that people find radio static unpleasant, *especially* when they are aroused by bright lighting. And Dolf Zillmann (1988), Jennings Bryant, and their collaborators found that people who have just pumped an exercise bike or watched a film of a Beatles rock concert find it easy to misattribute their arousal to a provocation. They then retaliate with heightened aggression. Although common sense might lead us to assume that Lourdes's run would have drained her aggressive tensions, enabling her to accept bad news calmly, these studies show that *arousal feeds emotions.*

Sexual arousal and other forms of arousal, such as anger, can therefore amplify one another (Zillmann, 1989). Love is never so passionate as after a fight or a fright. In the laboratory, erotic stimuli are more arousing to people who have just been frightened. Similarly, the arousal of a roller-coaster ride may spill over into romantic feeling for one's partner.

A frustrating, hot, or insulting situation heightens arousal. When it does, the arousal, combined with hostile thoughts and feelings, may form a recipe for aggressive behavior (Figure 10.5).

Aggression Cues

As we noted when considering the frustration-aggression hypothesis, violence is more likely when aggressive cues release pent-up anger. Leonard Berkowitz (1968, 1981, 1995) and others have found that the sight of a weapon is such a cue. In one

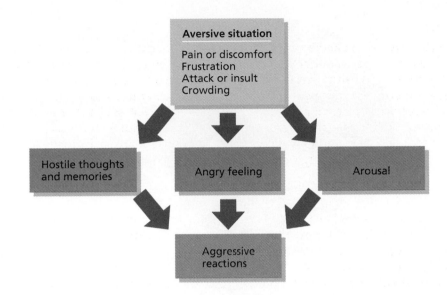

FIGURE :: 10.5

Elements of Hostile Aggression

An aversive situation can trigger aggression by provoking hostile cognitions, hostile feelings, and arousal. These reactions make us more likely to perceive harmful intent and to react aggressively.

Source: Simplified from Anderson, Deuser, & DeNeve, 1995.

experiment, children who had just played with toy guns became more willing to knock down another child's blocks. In another, angered University of Wisconsin men gave more electric shocks to their tormenter when a rifle and a revolver (supposedly left over from a previous experiment) were nearby than when badminton rackets had been left behind (Berkowitz & LePage, 1967). Guns prime hostile thoughts and punitive judgments (Anderson & others, 1998; Dienstbier & others, 1998). What's within sight is within mind. This is especially so when a weapon is perceived as an instrument of violence rather than a recreational item. For hunters, seeing a hunting rifle does not prime aggressive thoughts, though it does for nonhunters (Bartholow & others, 2004).

Berkowitz was not surprised that in the United States, a country with some 200 million privately owned guns, half of all murders are committed with handguns, or that handguns in homes are far more likely to kill household members than intruders. "Guns not only permit violence," he reported, "they can stimulate it as well. The finger pulls the trigger, but the trigger may also be pulling the finger."

Berkowitz is further unsurprised that countries that ban handguns have lower murder rates. Compared with the United States, Britain has one-fourth as many people and one-sixteenth as many murders. The United States has 10,000 handgun homicides a year; Australia has about a dozen, Britain two dozen, and Canada 100. When Washington, D.C., adopted a law restricting handgun possession, the numbers of gun-related murders and suicides each abruptly dropped about 25 percent. No changes occurred in other methods of murder and suicide, nor did adjacent areas outside the reach of this law experience any such declines (Loftin & others, 1991).

Researchers also have examined risks of violence in homes with and without guns. This is controversial research, because such homes may differ in many ways. One study sponsored by the Centers for Disease Control compared gun owners and nonowners of the same gender, race, age, and neighborhood. The ironic and tragic result was that those who kept a gun in the home (often for protection) were 2.7 times as likely to be murdered—nearly always by a family member or a close acquaintance (Kellermann, 1997; Kellermann & others, 1993). Another study found that the risk of suicide in homes with guns was 5 times as high as in homes without them (Taubes, 1992). A newer national study found a slightly weaker, but still significant, link between guns and homicide or suicide. Compared with others of the same gender, age, and race, people with guns at home were 41 percent as likely to be homicide victims and 3.4 times as likely to die of suicide (Wiebe, 2003). A gun in the home has often meant the difference between a fight and a funeral, or between suffering and suicide.

2006 Gallup survey of Americans: "Do you think having a gun in the house makes it a safer place to be or a more dangerous place to be?"
Safer: 47%
More dangerous: 43%
Depends, or no opinion: 10%

Weapons Used to Commit Murder in the United States in 2002

Source: FBI Uniform Crime Reports.

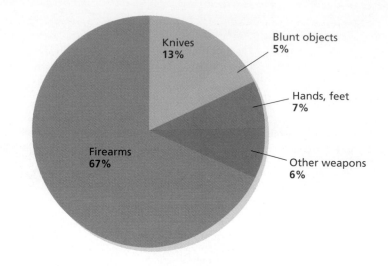

Guns not only serve as aggression cues but also put psychological distance between aggressor and victim. As Milgram's obedience studies taught us, remoteness from the victim facilitates cruelty. A knife can kill someone, but a knife attack requires a great deal more personal contact than pulling a trigger from a distance (Figure 10.6).

Media Influences: Pornography and Sexual Violence

The quintupled juvenile violent crime arrest rate reported by the FBI between 1960 and the early 1990s prompted social psychologists to wonder: Why the change? What social forces caused the mushrooming violence?

Alcohol contributes to aggression, but alcohol use had not dramatically changed since 1960. Similarly, other biological influences (testosterone, genes, neurotransmitters) had not undergone any major change. Might the surging violence instead have been fueled by the growth in individualism and materialism? by the growing gap between the powerful rich and the powerless poor? by the decline in two-parent families and the increase in absent fathers? by the media's increasing modeling of unrestrained sexuality and violence?

The last question arises because the increased rates of criminal violence, including sexual coercion, coincided with the increased availability of violent and sexual material in the media that started during the "sexual revolution" of the 1960s. Is the historical correlation a coincidence? To find out, researchers have explored the social consequences of pornography (which *Webster's* defines as erotic depictions intended to excite sexual arousal) and the effects of modeling violence in movies and on television.

In the United States, pornography has become a bigger business than professional football, basketball, and baseball combined, thanks to some $13 billion a year spent on the industry's cable and satellite networks, on its theaters and pay-per-view movies, and on in-room hotel movies, phone sex, sex magazines, and Internet sites (National Research Council, 2002; Richtel, 2007). Surveys of Australian and American teens and university students reveal that males' viewing of X-rated films and Internet pornography is several times higher than females' (Carroll & others, 2008; Flood, 2007; Wolak & others, 2007).

Social-psychological research on pornography has focused mostly on depictions of sexual violence, which is commonplace in twenty-first-century top-renting adult videos (Sun & others, 2008). A typical sexually violent episode finds a man forcing himself upon a woman. She at first resists and tries to fight off her attacker.

Gradually she becomes sexually aroused, and her resistance melts. By the end she is in ecstasy, pleading for more. We have all viewed or read nonpornographic versions of this sequence: She resists, he persists. Dashing man grabs and forcibly kisses protesting woman. Within moments, the arms that were pushing him away are clutching him tight, her resistance overwhelmed by her unleashed passion. In *Gone With the Wind*, Scarlett O'Hara is carried to bed protesting and kicking and wakes up singing.

Social psychologists report that viewing such fictional scenes of a man overpowering and arousing a woman can (a) distort one's perceptions of how women actually respond to sexual coercion and (b) increase men's aggression against women.

DISTORTED PERCEPTIONS OF SEXUAL REALITY

Does viewing sexual violence reinforce the "rape myth"—that some women would welcome sexual assault and that "no doesn't really mean no"? Researchers have observed a correlation between amount of TV viewing and rape myth acceptance (Kahlor & Morrison, 2007). To explore the relationship experimentally, Neil Malamuth and James Check (1981) showed University of Manitoba men either two nonsexual movies or two movies depicting a man sexually overcoming a woman. A week later, when surveyed by a different experimenter, those who saw the films with mild sexual violence were more accepting of violence against women.

Other studies confirm that exposure to pornography increases acceptance of the rape myth (Oddone-Paolucci & others, 2000). For example, while spending three evenings watching sexually violent movies, male viewers in an experiment by Charles Mullin and Daniel Linz (1995) became progressively less bothered by the raping and slashing. Compared with others not exposed to the films, three days later they expressed less sympathy for domestic violence victims, and they rated the victims' injuries as less severe. In fact, said researchers Edward Donnerstein, Daniel Linz, and Steven Penrod (1987), what better way for an evil character to get people to react calmly to the torture and mutilation of women than to show a gradually escalating series of such films?

Note that the sexual message (that many women enjoy being "taken") was subtle and unlikely to elicit counterarguing. Given frequent media images of women's resistance melting in the arms of a forceful man, we shouldn't be surprised that even women often believe that some *other* woman might enjoy being sexually overpowered—though virtually none think it of themselves (Malamuth & others, 1980).

"Pornography that portrays sexual aggression as pleasurable for the victim increases the acceptance of the use of coercion in sexual relations."
—*SOCIAL SCIENCE CONSENSUS AT SURGEON GENERAL'S WORKSHOP ON PORNOGRAPHY AND PUBLIC HEALTH (KOOP, 1987)*

AGGRESSION AGAINST WOMEN

CORRELATIONAL STUDIES Evidence also suggests that pornography contributes to men's actual aggression toward women (Kingston & others, 2009). Correlational studies raise that possibility. John Court (1985) noted that across the world, as pornography became more widely available during the 1960s and 1970s, the rate of reported rapes sharply increased—except in countries and areas where pornography was controlled. In Hawaii the number of reported rapes rose ninefold between 1960 and 1974, dropped when restraints on pornography were temporarily imposed, and rose again

Did Ted Bundy's (1989) comments on the eve of his execution for a series of rape-murders acknowledge pornography's toll or make it a handy excuse? "The most damaging kinds of pornography [involve] sexual violence. Like an addiction, you keep craving something that is harder, harder, something which, which gives you a greater sense of excitement. Until you reach a point where the pornography only goes so far, you reach that jumping off point where you begin to wonder if maybe actually doing it would give you that which is beyond just reading it or looking at it."

FIGURE :: 10.7

After viewing an aggressive-erotic film, college men delivered stronger shocks than before, especially to a woman.

Source: Data from Donnerstein, 1980.

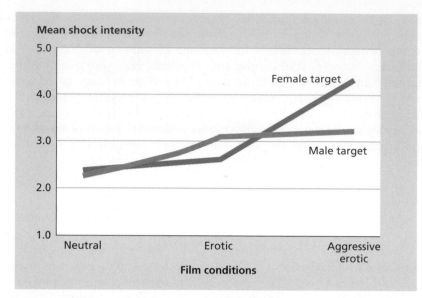

when the restraints were lifted. But there are counterexamples. Japan has had widely available violent pornography and a low rape rate. In the United States, the reported rape rate has not increased since 1995 despite the mushrooming of Internet pornography.

In another correlational study, Larry Baron and Murray Straus (1984) discovered that the sales of sexually explicit magazines (such as *Hustler* and *Playboy*) in the 50 states correlated with state rape rates, even after controlling for other factors, such as the percentage of young males in each state. Alaska ranked first in sex magazine sales and first in rape. On both measures, Nevada was second.

When interviewed, Canadian and American sexual offenders commonly acknowledge pornography use. William Marshall (1989) reported that Ontario rapists and child molesters used pornography much more than men who were not sexual offenders. A follow-up study of 341 Canadian child molesters found this to be true even after controlling for other sexual abuse predictors (Kingston & others, 2008). Studies of serial killers (by the FBI) and of child sex abusers (by the Los Angeles Police Department) also reported considerable exposure to pornography (Bennett, 1991; Ressler & others, 1988). And among university men, high pornography consumption has predicted sexual aggressiveness even after controlling for other predictors of antisocial behavior, such as general hostility (Vega & Malamuth, 2007).

Repeated exposure to erotic films featuring quick, uncommitted sex also tends to

- *decrease attraction for one's partner*
- *increase acceptance of extramarital sex and of women's sexual submission to men*
- *increase men's perceiving women in sexual terms*

(Source: See Myers, 2000a)

EXPERIMENTAL STUDIES   Although limited to the sorts of short-term behaviors that can be studied in the laboratory, controlled experiments reveal what correlational studies cannot: cause and effect. A consensus statement by 21 leading social scientists summed up the results: "Exposure to violent pornography increases punitive behavior toward women" (Koop, 1987). One of those social scientists, Edward Donnerstein (1980), had shown 120 University of Wisconsin men a neutral, an erotic, or an aggressive-erotic (rape) film. Then the men, supposedly as part of another experiment, "taught" a male or female confederate some nonsense syllables by choosing how much shock to administer for incorrect answers. The men who had watched the rape film administered markedly stronger shocks (Figure 10.7), especially when angered and with a female victim.

If the ethics of conducting such experiments trouble you, rest assured that these researchers appreciate the controversial and powerful experience they are giving participants. Only after giving their knowing consent do people participate. Moreover, after the experiment, researchers effectively debunk any myths the films communicated (Check & Malamuth, 1984).

TABLE :: 10.1 Percentage of Women Reporting Rape Experiences in Five Countries

Country	Sample of Women	Completed and Attempted Rape
Canada	Student sample at 95 colleges and universities	23% rape or sexual assault
Germany	Berlin late adolescents	17% criminal sexual violence
New Zealand	Sample of psychology students	25%
United Kingdom	Student sample at 22 universities	19%
United States	Representative sample at 32 colleges and universities	28%
Seoul, Korea	Adult women	22%

Source: Studies reported by Koss, Heise, and Russo (1994) and Krahé (1998).

Justification for this experimentation is not only scientific but also humanitarian. In a nationally representative survey of 9,684 American adults, 11 percent of women reported experiencing forced sex at some time in their lives (Basile & others, 2007; CDC, 2008).

Surveys in other industrialized countries offer similar results (Table 10.1). Three in four stranger rapes and nearly all acquaintance rapes went unreported to police. Thus, the official rape rate greatly underestimates the actual rape rate.

Women are most at risk when encountering men who exhibit the promiscuous behavior and hostile attitudes pornography cultivates (Figure 10.8).

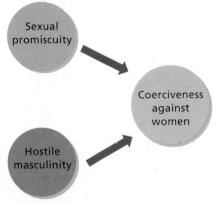

FIGURE :: 10.8

Sexually Aggressive Men

Men who sexually coerce women often combine a history of impersonal sex with hostile masculinity, reports Neil Malamuth (1996, 2003; Jacques-Tiura & others, 2007).

MEDIA AWARENESS EDUCATION

As most Germans quietly tolerated the degrading anti-Semitic images that fed the Holocaust, so most people today tolerate media images of women that feed sexual harassment, abuse, and rape. Should such portrayals that demean or violate women be restrained by law?

In the contest of individual versus collective rights, most people in Western nations side with individual rights. As an alternative to censorship, many psychologists favor "media awareness training." Pornography researchers have successfully resensitized and educated participants to women's actual responses to sexual violence. Could educators similarly promote critical viewing skills? By sensitizing people to the portrayal of women that predominates in pornography and to issues of sexual harassment and violence, it should be possible to debunk the myth that women enjoy being coerced. "Our utopian and perhaps naive hope," wrote Edward Donnerstein, Daniel Linz, and Steven Penrod (1987, p. 196), "is that in the end the truth revealed through good science will prevail and the public will be convinced that these images not only demean those portrayed but also those who view them."

Is such a hope naive? Consider: Without a ban on cigarettes, the number of U.S. smokers dropped from 42 percent in 1965 to 21 percent in 2004 (CDC, 2005). Without censorship of racism, once-common media images of African Americans

"What we're trying to do is raise the level of awareness of violence against women and pornography to at least the level of awareness of racist and Ku Klux Klan literature."

—GLORIA STEINEM (1988)

"The average U.S. household has more televisions (2.73) than people (2.6)."

—TIME, 2007

as childlike, superstitious buffoons have nearly disappeared. As public consciousness changed, scriptwriters, producers, and media executives shunned exploitative images of minorities. Will we one day look back with embarrassment on the time when movies entertained people with scenes of mayhem, mutilation, and sexual coercion?

Media Influences: Television

We have seen that watching an aggressive model attack a Bobo doll can unleash children's aggressive urges and teach them new ways to aggress. And we have seen that after viewing movies depicting sexual violence, many angry men will act more violently toward women. Does everyday television viewing have any similar effects?

Although very recent data are scarce (funding for media monitoring waned after the early 1990s), these facts about television watching remain: Today, in much of the industrialized world, nearly all households (99.2 percent in Australia, for example) have a TV set, more than have telephones (Trewin, 2001). Most homes have more than one set, which helps explain why parents and children often give differing reports of what the children are watching (Donnerstein, 1998).

In the average U.S. home, the TV is on eight hours a day, with individual household members averaging about three hours. Thanks to digital video recorders (DVRs) that allow people to "time-shift" their TV watching, Americans in 2008 watched more TV than ever before (Nielsen, 2008a, 2008b). Women watch more than men, non-Whites more than Whites, retired people more than those in school or working, and the less educated more than the highly educated (Comstock & Scharrer, 1999, Nielsen, 2008a). For the most part, these facts about Americans' viewing habits have also characterized Europeans, Australians, and Japanese (Murray & Kippax, 1979).

During all those hours, what social behaviors are modeled? From 1994 to 1997, bleary-eyed employees of the National Television Violence Study (1997) analyzed some 10,000 programs from the major networks and cable channels. Their findings? Six in 10 programs contained violence ("physically compelling action that threatens to hurt or kill, or actual hurting or killing"). During fistfights, people who went down usually shook it off and came back stronger—unlike most real fistfights that last one punch (often resulting in a broken jaw or hand). In 73 percent of violent scenes, the aggressors went unpunished. In 58 percent, the victim was not shown to experience pain. In children's programs, only 5 percent of violence was shown to have any long-term consequences; two-thirds depicted violence as funny. To adults, violence seems less violent when humorous (Kirsh, 2006).

What does it add up to? All told, television beams its electromagnetic waves into children's eyeballs for more growing-up hours than they spend in school. More hours, in fact, than they spend in any other waking activity. By the end of elementary school, the average child has witnessed some 8,000 TV murders and 100,000 other violent acts (Huston & others, 1992). According to one content analysis, American prime-time violence increased 75 percent between 1998 and the 2005–2006 season, which averaged 4.41 violent events per hour (PTC, 2007). Reflecting on his 22 years of cruelty counting, media researcher George Gerbner (1994) lamented: "Humankind has had more bloodthirsty eras but none as filled with *images* of violence as the present. We are awash in a tide of violent representations the world has never seen . . . drenching every home with graphic scenes of expertly choreographed brutality."

Does prime-time crime stimulate the behavior it depicts? Or, as viewers vicariously participate in aggressive acts, do the shows drain off aggressive energy? The latter idea, a variation on the **catharsis** hypothesis, maintains that watching violent drama enables people to release their pent-up hostilities. Defenders of the media cite this theory frequently and remind us that violence predates television. In an

catharsis
Emotional release. The catharsis view of aggression is that aggressive drive is reduced when one "releases" aggressive energy, either by acting aggressively or by fantasizing aggression.

imaginary debate with one of television's critics, the medium's defender might argue: "Television played no role in the genocides of Jews and Native Americans. Television just reflects and caters to our tastes." "Agreed," responds the critic, "but it's also true that during America's TV age, reported violent crime increased several times faster than the population rate. Surely you don't mean the popular arts are mere passive reflections, without any power to influence public consciousness, or that advertisers' belief in the medium's power is an illusion." The defender replies: "The violence epidemic results from many factors. TV may even reduce aggression by keeping people off the streets and by offering them a harmless opportunity to vent their aggression."

Studies of television viewing and aggression aim to identify effects more subtle and pervasive than the occasional "copycat" murders that capture public attention. They ask: How does television affect viewers' *behavior* and viewers' *thinking*?

TELEVISION'S EFFECTS ON BEHAVIOR

Do viewers imitate violent models? Examples abound of actual criminals reenacting television crimes. In one survey of 208 prison convicts, 9 of 10 admitted learning new criminal tricks by watching crime programs. Four out of 10 said they had attempted specific crimes seen on television (*TV Guide*, 1977).

CORRELATING TV VIEWING AND BEHAVIOR Crime stories are not scientific evidence. Researchers therefore use correlational and experimental studies to examine the effects of viewing violence. One technique, commonly used with schoolchildren, correlates their TV watching with their aggressiveness. The frequent result: The more violent the content of the child's TV viewing, the more aggressive the child (Eron, 1987; Turner & others, 1986). The relationship is modest but consistently found in North America, Europe, and Australia. And it extends to devious "indirect aggression." British girls who most often view programs that model gossiping, backbiting, and social exclusion also more often display such behavior (Coyne & Archer, 2005).

Can we conclude, then, that a diet of violent TV fuels aggression? Perhaps you are already thinking that because this is a correlational study, the cause-effect relation could also work in the opposite direction. Maybe aggressive children prefer aggressive programs. Or maybe some underlying third factor, such as lower intelligence, predisposes some children to prefer both aggressive programs and aggressive behavior.

Researchers have developed two ways to test these alternative explanations. They test the "hidden third factor" explanation by statistically pulling out the influence of some of these possible factors. For example, William Belson (1978; Muson, 1978) studied 1,565 London boys. Compared with those who watched little violence, those who watched a great deal (especially realistic rather than cartoon violence) admitted to 50 percent more violent acts during the preceding six months (for example, vandalizing a public telephone). Belson also examined 22 likely third factors, such as family size. The "heavy violence" and "light violence" viewers still differed after the researchers equated them with respect to potential third factors. So Belson surmised that the heavy viewers were indeed more violent *because* of their TV exposure.

Similarly, Leonard Eron and Rowell Huesmann (1980, 1985) found that violence viewing among 875 8-year-olds correlated with aggressiveness even after statistically pulling out several obvious possible third factors. Moreover, when they restudied those individuals as 19-year-olds, they discovered that viewing violence at age 8 modestly predicted aggressiveness at age 19, but that aggressiveness at age 8 did *not* predict viewing violence at age 19. Aggression followed viewing, not the reverse. Moreover, by age 30, those who had watched the most violence in childhood were more likely than others to have been convicted of a crime (Figure 10.9).

"One of television's great contributions is that it brought murder back into the home where it belongs. Seeing a murder on television can be good therapy. It can help work off one's antagonisms."

—*ALFRED HITCHCOCK*

FIGURE :: 10.9

Children's Television Viewing and Later Criminal Activity

Violence viewing at age 8 was a predictor of a serious criminal offense by age 30.

Source: Data from Eron and Huesmann (1984).

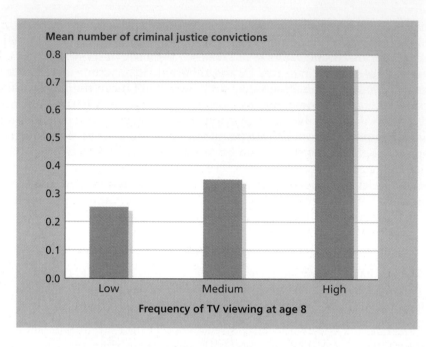

Follow-up studies have confirmed these findings in various ways, including these:

- Correlating 8-year-olds' violence viewing with their later likelihood of adult spouse abuse (Huesmann & others, 1984, 2003)
- Correlating adolescents' violence viewing with their later likelihood of assault, robbery, and threats of injury (Johnson & others, 2002)
- Correlating elementary schoolchildren's violent media exposure with how often they got into fights when restudied two to six months later (Gentile & others, 2004)

In all these studies, the investigators were careful to adjust for likely "third factors" such as preexisting lower intelligence or hostility.

Another fact to ponder: Where television goes, increased violence follows. Even murder rates increase when and where television comes. In Canada and the United States, the homicide rate doubled between 1957 and 1974 as violent television spread. In census regions where television came later, the homicide rate jumped later, too. In South Africa, where television was not introduced until 1975, a similar near doubling of the White homicide rate did not begin until after 1975 (Centerwall, 1989). And in a closely studied remote Canadian town where television came late, playground aggression doubled soon after (Williams, 1986).

Notice that these studies illustrate how researchers are now using correlational findings to *suggest* cause and effect. Yet an infinite number of possible third factors could be creating a merely coincidental relation between viewing violence and practicing aggression. Fortunately, the experimental method can control these extraneous factors. If we randomly assign some children to watch a violent film and others a nonviolent film, any later aggression difference between the two groups will be due to the only factor that distinguishes them: what they watched.

TV VIEWING EXPERIMENTS The trailblazing Bobo-doll experiments by Albert Bandura and Richard Walters (1963) sometimes had young children view the adult pounding the inflated doll on film instead of observing it live—with much the same effect. Then Leonard Berkowitz and Russell Geen (1966) found that angered college students who viewed a violent film acted more aggressively than did similarly angered students who viewed nonaggressive films. These laboratory experiments, coupled with growing public concern, were sufficient to prompt the U.S. Surgeon General to commission 50 new research studies during the early 1970s. By and large, those studies, and more than 100 later ones, confirmed that viewing violence amplifies aggression (Anderson & others, 2003).

For example, research teams led by Ross Parke (1977) in the United States and Jacques Leyens (1975) in Belgium showed institutionalized American and Belgian delinquent boys a series of either aggressive or nonaggressive commercial films. Their consistent finding: "Exposure to movie violence . . . led to an increase in viewer aggression." Compared with the week preceding the film series, physical attacks increased sharply in cottages where boys were viewing violent films. Dolf Zillmann and James Weaver (1999) similarly exposed men and women, on four consecutive days, to violent or nonviolent feature films. When participating in a different project on the fifth day, those exposed to the violent films were more hostile to the research assistant.

The aggression provoked in these experiments is not assault and battery; it's more on the scale of a shove in the lunch line, a cruel comment, a threatening gesture. Nevertheless, the convergence of evidence is striking. "The irrefutable conclusion," said a 1993 American Psychological Association youth violence commission, is "that viewing violence increases violence." This is especially so among people with aggressive tendencies and when an attractive person commits justified, realistic violence that goes unpunished and that shows no pain or harm (Comstock, 2008; Gentile & others, 2007; Zillmann & Weaver, 2007).

All in all, conclude researchers Brad Bushman and Craig Anderson (2001), violence viewing's effect on aggression surpasses the effect of passive smoking on lung cancer, calcium intake on bone mass, and homework on academic achievement. As with smoking and cancer, not everyone shows the effect, which in some recent studies is actually quite modest, note Christopher Ferguson and John Kilburn (2009). Moreover, as media executives and some researchers remind us, other factors matter as well (Gunter, 2008). But the evidence is now "overwhelming," say Bushman and Anderson: "Exposure to media violence causes significant increases in aggression." The research base is large, the methods diverse, and the overall findings consistent, echo a National Institute of Mental Health task force of leading media violence researchers (Anderson & others, 2003). "Our indepth review . . . reveals unequivocal evidence that exposure to media violence can increase the likelihood of aggressive and violent behavior in both immediate and long-term contexts."

WHY DOES TV VIEWING AFFECT BEHAVIOR? Given the convergence of correlational and experimental evidence, researchers have explored *why* viewing violence has this effect. Consider three possibilities (Geen & Thomas, 1986). One is the *arousal* it produces (Mueller & others, 1983; Zillmann, 1989). As we noted earlier, arousal tends to spill over: One type of arousal energizes other behaviors.

Other research shows that viewing violence *disinhibits*. In Bandura's experiment, the adult's punching of the Bobo doll seemed to make outbursts legitimate and to lower the children's inhibitions. Viewing violence primes the viewer for aggressive behavior by activating violence-related thoughts (Berkowitz, 1984; Bushman & Geen, 1990; Josephson, 1987). Listening to music with sexually violent lyrics seems to have a similar effect (Barongan & Hall, 1995; Johnson & others, 1995; Pritchard, 1998).

Media portrayals also evoke *imitation*. The children in Bandura's experiments reenacted the specific behaviors they had witnessed. The commercial television industry is hard-pressed to dispute that television leads viewers to imitate what they have seen: Its advertisers model consumption. Are media executives right, however, to argue that TV merely holds a mirror to a violent society? that art imitates life? and that the "reel" world therefore shows us the real world? Actually, on TV programs, acts of assault have outnumbered affectionate acts four to one. In other ways as well, television models an unreal world.

"Then shall we simply allow our children to listen to any story anyone happens to make up, and so receive into their minds ideas often the very opposite of those we shall think they ought to have when they are grown up?"
—PLATO, THE REPUBLIC, 360 B.C.

"High exposure to media violence is a major contributing cause of the high rate of violence in modern U.S. society."
—SOCIAL PSYCHOLOGIST CRAIG A. ANDERSON, TESTIFYING TO THE U.S. SENATE COMMERCE, SCIENCE, AND TRANSPORTATION COMMITTEE, MARCH 21, 2000

prosocial behavior
Positive, constructive, helpful social behavior; the opposite of antisocial behavior.

But there is good news here, too. If the ways of relating and problem solving modeled on television do trigger imitation, especially among young viewers, then TV modeling of **prosocial behavior** should be socially beneficial. In Chapter 12 we will explore how television's subtle influence can indeed teach children positive lessons in behavior.

TELEVISION'S EFFECTS ON THINKING

We have focused on television's effect on behavior, but researchers have also examined the cognitive effects of viewing violence: Does prolonged viewing *desensitize* us to cruelty? Does it give us mental *scripts* for how to act? Does it distort our *perceptions* of reality? Does it *prime* aggressive thoughts?

DESENSITIZATION   Repeat an emotion-arousing stimulus, such as an obscene word, over and over. What happens? The emotional response will "extinguish." After witnessing thousands of acts of cruelty, there is good reason to expect a similar emotional numbing. The most common response might well become, "Doesn't bother me at all." Such a response is precisely what Victor Cline and his colleagues (1973) observed when they measured the physiological arousal of 121 Utah boys who watched a brutal boxing match. Compared with boys who watched little television, the responses of those who watched habitually were more a shrug than a concern.

"Fifty years of research on the effect of TV violence on children leads to the inescapable conclusion that viewing media violence is related to increases in aggressive attitudes, values, and behaviors."

—JOHN P. MURRAY (2008)

Of course, these boys might differ in ways other than television viewing. But in experiments on the effects of viewing sexual violence, similar desensitization—a sort of psychic numbness—occurs when young men view "slasher" films. Moreover, experiments by Ronald Drabman and Margaret Thomas (1974, 1975, 1976) confirmed that such viewing breeds a more blasé reaction when later viewing a brawl or observing two children fighting. In one survey of 5,456 middle-school students, exposure to movies with brutality was widespread (Sargent & others, 2002). Two-thirds had seen *Scream*. Such viewing patterns help explain why, despite the portrayals of extreme violence (or, should we say, *because* of it), Gallup youth surveys show that the percentage of 13- to 17-year-olds feeling there was too much movie violence has declined, from 42 percent in 1977 to 27 percent in 2003.

As television and movies have become more sexually explicit—the number of prime-time American TV scenes involving sexual talk or behavior nearly doubled between 1998 and 2005 (Kaiser, 2005)—teen concern about media sex depictions has similarly declined. Today's teens "appear to have become considerably more desensitized to graphic depictions of violence and sex than their parents were at their age," concludes Gallup researcher Josephine Mazzuca (2002). Media portrayals desensitize.

social scripts
Culturally provided mental instructions for how to act in various situations.

SOCIAL SCRIPTS   When we find ourselves in new situations, uncertain how to act, we rely on **social scripts**—culturally provided mental instructions for how to act. After so many action films, youngsters may acquire a script that is played when they face real-life conflicts. Challenged, they may "act like a man" by intimidating or eliminating the threat. Likewise, after witnessing innumerable sexual innuendoes and acts on TV and in music lyrics—mostly involving impulsive or short-term relationships—youths may acquire sexual scripts they later enact in real-life relationships (Escobar-Chaves & Anderson, 2008; Fischer & Greitemeyer, 2006; Kunkel, 2001). Thus, the more sexual content that adolescents view (even when controlling for other predictors of early sexual activity), the more likely they are to perceive their peers as sexually active, to develop sexually permissive attitudes, and to experience early intercourse (Escobar-Chaves & others, 2005; Martino & others, 2005). Media portrayals implant social scripts.

"We don't teach our children that healthy relationships involve drunken, naked parties in a hot tub with strangers—but that's what they see when they turn on 'The Real World.' When they're fed a steady diet of these depictions over and over again from the time they're very young, this behavior becomes acceptable—even normal."

—U.S. SENATOR BARACK OBAMA, 2005

ALTERED PERCEPTIONS   Does television's fictional world also mold our conceptions of the real world? George Gerbner and his University of Pennsylvania associates (1979, 1994) suspected this is television's most potent effect. Their surveys of both adolescents and adults showed that heavy viewers (four hours a day or more) are more likely than light viewers (two hours or fewer) to exaggerate the frequency of violence in the world around them and to fear being personally assaulted. Similar feelings of vulnerability have been expressed by South African women after viewing violence against women (Reid & Finchilescu, 1995). A national survey of American 7- to 11-year-old children found that heavy viewers were more likely than light viewers to admit fears "that somebody bad might get into your house" or that "when you go outside, somebody might hurt you" (Peterson & Zill, 1981). For those who watch much television, the world becomes a scary place. Media portrayals shape perceptions of reality.

COGNITIVE PRIMING New evidence also reveals that watching violent videos primes networks of aggressive-related ideas (Bushman, 1998). After viewing violence, people offer more hostile explanations for others' behavior (was the shove intentional?). They interpret spoken homonyms with the more aggressive meaning (interpreting "punch" as a hit rather than a drink). And they recognize aggressive words more quickly. Media portrayals prime thinking.

Perhaps television's biggest effect relates not to its quality but to its quantity. Compared with more active recreation, TV watching sucks people's energy and dampens their moods (Kubey & Csikszentmihalyi, 2002). Moreover, TV annually replaces in people's lives a thousand or more hours of other activities. If, like most others, you have spent a thousand-plus hours per year watching TV, think how you might have used that time if there were no television. What difference would that have made in who you are today? In seeking to explain the post-1960 decline in civic activities and organizational memberships, Robert Putnam (2000) reported that every added hour a day spent watching TV competes with civic participation. Television steals time from club meetings, volunteering, congregational activities, and political engagement.

People who watch many hours of television see the world as a dangerous place.

© 2009 Tom Tomorrow. Reprinted with permission of Dan Perkins.

"The more fully that any given generation was exposed to television in its formative years, the lower its civic engagement [its rate of voting, joining, meeting, giving, and volunteering]."
—*ROBERT PUTNAM*, BOWLING ALONE, *2000*

Media Influences: Video Games

The scientific debate over the effects of media violence "is basically over," contend Douglas Gentile and Craig Anderson (2003; Anderson & Gentile, 2008). Researchers are now shifting their attention to video games, which have exploded in popularity and are exploding with increasing brutality. Educational research shows that "video games are excellent teaching tools," note Gentile and Anderson. "If health video games can successfully teach health behaviors, and flight simulator video games can teach people how to fly, then what should we expect violent murder-simulating games to teach?"

THE GAMES KIDS PLAY

In 2010 the video-game industry celebrated its thirty-eighth birthday. Since the first video game in 1972, we have moved from electronic Ping-Pong to splatter games (Anderson & others, 2007). By the turn of the twenty-first century, Americans were purchasing some 200 million games a year, with the average girl playing 6 hours a

"We had an internal rule that we wouldn't allow violence against people."
—*NOLAN BUSHNELL*, ATARI FOUNDER

week and the average boy 12 hours (Gentile & others, 2004). Today's mass-murder simulators are not obscure games. In one survey of fourth-graders, 59 percent of girls and 73 percent of boys reported their favorite games as violent ones (Anderson, 2003, 2004). Games rated "M" (mature) are supposedly intended for sale only to those 17 and older but often are marketed to those younger. The Federal Trade Commission found that in four out of five attempts, underage children could easily purchase them (Pereira, 2003).

In the popular *Grand Theft Auto: San Andreas,* youth are invited to play psychopath, notes Gentile (2004). "You can run down pedestrians with the car, you can do carjackings, you can do drive-by shootings, you can run down to the red-light district, pick up a prostitute, have sex with her in your car, and then kill her to get your money back." In effective 3D graphics, you can knock people over, stomp on them until they cough up blood, and watch them die. And as research by Susan Persky and James Blascovich (2005) demonstrates, virtual-reality games promise even more realism, engagement, and impact.

EFFECTS OF THE GAMES KIDS PLAY

Concerns about violent video games heightened after teen assassins in separate incidents in Kentucky, Arkansas, and Colorado enacted the horrific violence they had so often played on-screen. People wondered: What do youth learn from endless hours of role-playing attacking and dismembering people?

Most smokers don't die of lung cancer. Most abused children don't become abusive. And most people who spend hundreds of hours rehearsing human slaughter live gentle lives. This enables video-game defenders, like tobacco and TV interests, to say their products are harmless. "There is absolutely no evidence, none, that playing a violent game leads to aggressive behavior," contended Doug Lowenstein (2000), president of the Interactive Digital Software Association. Gentile and Anderson nevertheless offer some reasons why violent game playing *might* have a more toxic effect than watching violent television. With game playing, players

- identify with, and play the role of, a violent character.
- actively rehearse violence, not just passively watch it.
- engage in the whole sequence of enacting violence—selecting victims, acquiring weapons and ammunition, stalking the victim, aiming the weapon, pulling the trigger.
- are engaged with continual violence and threats of attack.
- repeat violent behaviors over and over.
- are rewarded for effective aggression.

For such reasons, military organizations often prepare soldiers to fire in combat (which many in World War II reportedly were hesitant to do) by engaging them with attack-simulation games.

But what does the available research actually find? Craig Anderson (2003, 2004; Anderson & others, 2004, 2007) offers statistical digests of three dozen available studies that reveal five consistent effects. Playing violent video games, more than playing nonviolent games,

- *increases arousal.* Heart rate and blood pressure rise.
- *increases aggressive thinking.* For example, Brad Bushman and Anderson (2002) found that after playing games such as *Duke Nukem* and *Mortal Kombat,* university students became more likely to guess that a man whose car was just rear-ended would respond aggressively, by using abusive language, kicking out a window, or starting a fight.
- *increases aggressive feelings.* Frustration levels rise, as does expressed hostility, although the hostile feelings subside within a few minutes after ending game play (Barlett & others, 2009).

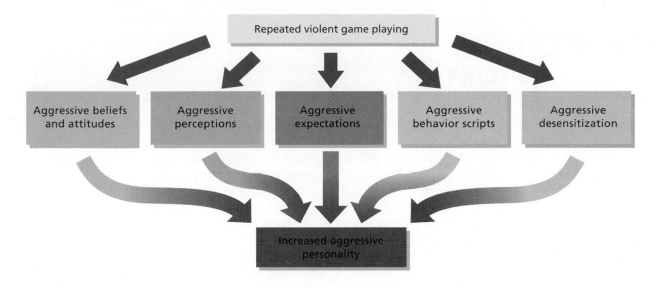

FIGURE :: 10.10

Violent Video-Game Influences on Aggressive Tendencies

Source: Adapted from Craig A. Anderson and Brad J. Bushman (2001).

- *increases aggressive behaviors.* After violent game play, children and youth play more aggressively with their peers, get into more arguments with their teachers, and participate in more fights. The effect occurs inside and outside the laboratory, across self-reports, teacher reports, and parent reports, and for reasons illustrated in Figure 10.10. Is this merely because naturally hostile kids are drawn to such games? No, even when controlling for personality and temperament, exposure to video-game violence increases aggressive behavior (Bartholow & others, 2005). Moreover, observed Douglas Gentile and his co-researchers (2004) from a study of young adolescents, even among those who scored low in hostility, the percent of heavy violent gamers who got into fights was ten times the 4 percent involved in fights among their nongaming counterparts. And after they start playing the violent games, previously nonhostile kids become more likely to have fights. In Japan, too, playing violent video games early in a school year predicts physical aggressiveness later in the year, even after controlling for gender and prior aggressiveness (Anderson & others, 2008).

- *decreases prosocial behaviors.* After violent video-game playing, people become slower to help a person whimpering in the hallway outside and slower to offer help to peers. On a later monetary decision-making task, they become more likely to exploit rather than to trust and cooperate with a partner (Sheese & Graziano, 2005). They also, as revealed by decreased brain activity associated with emotion, become *desensitized* to violence (Bartholow & others, 2006; Carnagey & others, 2007).

Moreover, the more violent the games played, the bigger the effects. The bloodier the game (for example, the higher the blood level setting in one experiment with *Mortal Combat* players) the greater the gamer's after-game hostility and arousal (Barlett & others, 2008). Video games *have* become more violent, which helps explain why newer studies find the biggest effects. Although much remains to be learned, these studies indicate that, contrary to the catharsis hypothesis—as exemplified by one civil liberties author who speculates that violent games may have a "calming effect" on violent tendencies (Heins, 2004)—practicing violence breeds rather than releases violence.

THE inside STORY

Craig Anderson on Video-Game Violence

Understanding the clearly harmful effects being documented by TV/film violence researchers, I was disturbed as I noticed the increasing violence in video games. With one of my graduate students, Karen Dill, I therefore began correlational and experimental investigations that intersected with growing public concern and led to my testifying before a U.S. Senate subcommittee and consulting for a wide array of government and public policy groups, including parent and child advocacy organizations.

Although it is gratifying to see one's research have a positive impact, the video-game industry has gone to great lengths to dismiss the research, much as 30 years ago cigarette manufacturers ridiculed basic medical research by asking how many Marlboros a lab rat had to smoke before contracting cancer. I also get some pretty nasty mail from gamers, and the volume of requests for information led me to offer resources and answers at www.psychology.iastate.edu/faculty/caa.

Many people believe that the best way to enhance understanding of a complicated topic is to find people who will give opposite views and give each "side" equal time. Media violence news stories typically give equal time to industry representatives and their preferred "experts" along with reassuring words from a carefree 4-year-old, which can leave the impression that we know less than we do. If all the experts in a given area agree, does this idea of "fairness" and "balance" make sense? Or should we expect that legitimate experts will have published peer-reviewed original research articles on the issue at hand?

Craig A. Anderson,
Iowa State University

> "It is hard to measure the increasing acceptance of brutality in American life, but its evidence is everywhere, starting with the video games of killing that are a principal entertainment of boys."
>
> —SUSAN SONTAG,
> REGARDING THE TORTURE
> OF OTHERS, 2004

As a concerned scientist, Anderson (2003, 2004) therefore encourages parents to discover what their kids are ingesting and to ensure that their media diet, as least in their own home, is healthy. Parents may not be able to control what their child watches, plays, and eats in someone else's home. Nor can they control the media's effect on their children's peer culture. (That is why advising parents to "just say no" is naive.) But parents can oversee consumption in their own home and provide increased time for alternative activities. Networking with other parents can build a kid-friendly neighborhood. And schools can help by providing media awareness education.

Group Influences

We have considered what provokes *individuals* to aggress. If frustrations, insults, and aggressive models heighten the aggressive tendencies of isolated people, then such factors are likely to prompt the same reaction in groups. As a riot begins, aggressive acts often spread rapidly after the "trigger" example of one antagonistic person. Seeing looters freely helping themselves to TV sets, normally law-abiding bystanders may drop their moral inhibitions and imitate.

Groups can amplify aggressive reactions partly by diffusing responsibility. Decisions to attack in war typically are made by strategists remote from the front lines. They give orders, but others carry them out. Does such distancing make it easier to recommend aggression?

Jacquelyn Gaebelein and Anthony Mander (1978) simulated that situation in the laboratory. They asked their University of North Carolina, Greensboro, students to *shock* someone or to *advise* someone how much shock to administer. When the recipient was innocent of any provocation, as are most victims of mass aggression, the advisers recommended more shock than given by the frontline participants, who felt more directly responsible for any hurt.

Diffusion of responsibility increases not only with distance but also with numbers. (Recall from Chapter 8 the phenomenon of deindividuation.) Brian Mullen (1986) analyzed information from 60 lynchings occurring between 1899 and 1946 and made an interesting discovery: The greater the number of people in a lynch mob, the more vicious the murder and mutilation.

Through social "contagion," groups magnify aggressive tendencies, much as they polarize other tendencies. Examples are youth gangs, soccer fans, rapacious soldiers, urban rioters, and what Scandinavians call "mobbing"—school-children in groups repeatedly harassing or attacking an insecure, weak schoolmate (Lagerspetz & others, 1982). Mobbing is a group activity.

Social contagion. When 17 juvenile, orphaned male bull elephants were relocated during the mid-1990s to a South African park, they became an out-of-control adolescent gang and killed 40 white rhinoceros. In 1998, concerned park officials relocated 6 older, stronger bull elephants into their midst. The result: The rampaging soon quieted down (Slotow & others, 2000). One of these dominant bulls, at left, faces down several of the juveniles.

Youths sharing antisocial tendencies and lacking close family bonds and expectations of academic success may find social identity in a gang. As group identity develops, conformity pressures and deindividuation increase (Staub, 1996). Self-identity diminishes as members give themselves over to the group, often feeling a satisfying oneness with the others. The frequent result is social contagion—group-fed arousal, disinhibition, and polarization. As gang expert Arnold Goldstein (1994) observed, until gang members marry out, age out, get a job, go to prison, or die, they hang out. They define their turf, display their colors, challenge rivals, and sometimes commit delinquent acts and fight over drugs, territory, honor, women, or insults.

The twentieth-century massacres that claimed over 150 million lives were "not the sums of individual actions," notes Robert Zajonc (2000). *"Genocide is not the plural of homicide."* Massacres are *social* phenomena fed by "moral imperatives"—a collective mentality (including images, rhetoric, and ideology) that mobilizes a group or a culture for extraordinary actions. The massacres of Rwanda's Tutsis, of Europe's Jews, and of America's native population were collective phenomena requiring widespread support, organization, and participation. Before launching the genocidal initiative, Rwanda's Hutu government and business leaders bought and distributed 2 million Chinese machetes. Over three months, the Hutu attackers reportedly would get up, eat a hearty breakfast, gather together, and then go hunt their former neighbors who had fled. They would hack to death anyone they found, then return home, wash, and socialize over a few beers (Dalrymple, 2007; Hatzfeld, 2007).

Experiments in Israel by Yoram Jaffe and Yoel Yinon (1983) confirm that groups can amplify aggressive tendencies. In one, university men angered by a supposed fellow participant retaliated with decisions to give much stronger shocks when in groups than when alone. In another experiment (Jaffe & others, 1981), people decided, either alone or in groups, how much punishing shock to give someone for incorrect answers on a task. As Figure 10.11 shows, individuals gave progressively more of the assumed shock as the experiment proceeded, and group decision making magnified this individual tendency. When circumstances provoke an individual's aggressive reaction, the addition of group interaction will often amplify it. (See "Research Close-Up: When Provoked, Are Groups More Aggressive Than Individuals?")

Aggression studies provide an apt opportunity to ask how well social psychology's laboratory findings generalize to everyday life. Do the circumstances that trigger someone to deliver electric shock or allocate hot sauce really tell us anything about the circumstances that trigger verbal abuse or a punch in the face? Craig Anderson and Brad Bushman (1997; Bushman & Anderson, 1998) note that social psychologists have studied aggression in both the laboratory and everyday worlds, and the findings are strikingly consistent. In *both* contexts, increased aggression is predicted by the following:

"The worst barbarity of war is that it forces men collectively to commit acts against which individually they would revolt with their whole being."
—*ELLEN KEY*, WAR, PEACE, AND THE FUTURE, *1916*

FIGURE :: 10.11

Group-Enhanced Aggression

When individuals chose how much shock to administer as punishment for wrong answers, they escalated the shock level as the experiment proceeded. Group decision making further polarized this tendency.

Source: Data from Jaffe & others, 1981.

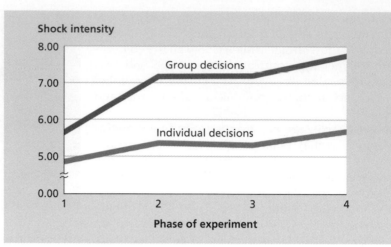

research CLOSE-UP

When Provoked, Are Groups More Aggressive Than Individuals?

Aggression researchers are noted for their creative methods for measuring aggression, which in various experiments has involved such tactics as administering shock, blasting sound, and hurting people's feelings. Holly McGregor and her colleagues (1998) took their cue from a cook's arrest for assault after lacing two police officers' food with Tabasco sauce, and from child abuse cases in which parents have force-fed hot sauce to their children. This inspired the idea of measuring aggression by having people decide how much hot sauce someone else must consume.

That is what Gettysburg College psychologist Bruce Meier and North Dakota State University psychologist Verlin Hinsz (2004) did when comparing aggressive behavior by groups and individuals. They told participants, either as individuals or in groups of three, that they were studying the relationship between personality and food preferences, and that they would be tasting and rating hot sauce. The experimenter explained that he needed to remain blind as to how much hot sauce each individual or group would be consuming and so needed the participants to choose the portion. After having the participants sample the intense hot sauce using a wooden stick, the experimenter left to collect the hot sauce that another individual or group had supposedly selected. He returned with a cup filled with 48 grams of the sauce, which each participant expected later to consume. The participants, in turn, were now to spoon as much or as little hot sauce as they wished into a cup for the supposed other people to consume. (In reality, no participant was forced to consume anything.)

The striking result, seen in Table 10.2, was that groups retaliated by dishing out 24 percent more hot sauce than did individuals, and that group targets were dished 24 percent more than were individuals. Thus, given toxic circumstances, interaction with a group (as a source or target) amplifies individual aggressive tendencies. This finding was particularly evident in the intergroup condition. Group members, after each receiving a nasty 48 grams of hot sauce, retaliated by dishing out 93 grams of hot sauce for each member of the group that had given them hot sauce. Apparently, surmised Meier and Hinsz, groups not only respond more aggressively to provocation but also perceive more hostility from other groups than they do from individuals.

TABLE :: 10.2 Mean Amount of Hot Sauce Dished Out (grams)

SOURCE	TARGET	
	Individual	Group
Individual	58.2	71.0
Group	71.1	92.9

Source: Meier & Hinsz, 2004.

- Male actors
- Aggressive or anger-prone personalities
- Alcohol use
- Violence viewing
- Anonymity
- Provocation
- The presence of weapons
- Group interaction

The laboratory allows us to test and revise theories under controlled conditions. Real-world events inspire ideas and provide the venue for applying our theories. Aggression research illustrates how the interplay between studies in the controlled lab and the complex real world advances psychology's contribution to human welfare. Hunches gained from everyday experience inspire theories, which stimulate laboratory research, which then deepens our understanding and our ability to apply psychology to real problems.

Summing Up: What Are Some Influences on Aggression?

- Many factors exert influence on aggression. One factor is aversive experiences, which include not only frustrations but also discomfort, pain, and personal attacks, both physical and verbal.

- Arousal from almost any source, even physical exercise or sexual stimulation, can be transformed into other emotions such as anger.

- Aggression cues, such as the presence of a gun, increase the likelihood of aggressive behavior.

- Viewing violence (1) breeds a modest increase in *aggressive behavior*, especially in people who are provoked, (2) *desensitizes* viewers to aggression, and (3) alters their *perceptions* of reality. These findings parallel the results of research on the effects of viewing violent pornography, which can increase men's aggression against women and distort their perceptions of women's responses to sexual coercion.

- Television permeates the daily life of millions of people and portrays considerable violence. Correlational and experimental studies converge on the conclusion that heavy exposure to televised violence correlates with aggressive behavior.

- Repeatedly playing violent video games may increase aggressive thinking, feelings, and behavior even more than television or movies do, as the experience involves much more active participation than those other media.

- Much aggression is committed by groups. Circumstances that provoke individuals may also provoke groups. By diffusing responsibility and polarizing actions, group situations amplify aggressive reactions.

How Can Aggression Be Reduced?

We have examined instinct, frustration-aggression, and social learning theories of aggression, and we have scrutinized biological and social influences on aggression. How, then, can we reduce aggression? Do theory and research suggest ways to control aggression?

Catharsis?

"Youngsters should be taught to vent their anger." So advised Ann Landers (1969). If a person "bottles up his rage, we have to find an outlet. We have to give him an opportunity of letting off steam." So asserted the once prominent psychiatrist

Fritz Perls (1973). "Some expression of prejudice . . . lets off steam . . . it can siphon off conflict through words, rather than actions," argued Andrew Sullivan (1999) in a *New York Times Magazine* article on hate crimes. Such statements assume the "hydraulic model," which implies accumulated aggressive energy, like dammed-up water, needs a release.

The concept of catharsis is usually credited to Aristotle. Although Aristotle actually said nothing about aggression, he did argue that we can purge emotions by experiencing them and that viewing the classic tragedies therefore enabled a catharsis (purging) of pity and fear. To have an emotion excited, he believed, is to have that emotion released (Butcher, 1951). The catharsis hypothesis has been extended to include the emotional release supposedly obtained not only by observing drama but also through our recalling and reliving past events, through our expressing emotions, and through our actions.

Assuming that aggressive action or fantasy drains pent-up aggression, some therapists and group leaders have encouraged people to ventilate suppressed aggression by acting it out—by whopping one another with foam bats or beating a bed with a tennis racket while screaming. If led to believe that catharsis effectively vents emotions, people will react more aggressively to an insult as a way to improve their mood (Bushman & others, 2001). Some psychologists, believing that catharsis is therapeutic, advise parents to encourage children's release of emotional tension through aggressive play.

Many laypeople have also bought the catharsis idea, as reflected in their nearly two-to-one agreement with the statement "Sexual materials provide an outlet for bottled-up impulses" (Niemi & others, 1989). But then other national surveys reveal that most Americans also agree, "Sexual materials lead people to commit rape." So is the catharsis approach valid or not?

Consider: If viewing erotica provides an outlet for sexual impulses, places with high consumption of sex magazines should have low rape rates. After viewing erotica people should experience diminished sexual desire and men should be less likely to view and treat women as sexual objects. But studies show the opposites are true (Kelley & others, 1989; McKenzie-Mohr & Zanna, 1990). Sexually explicit videos are an aphrodisiac; they feed sexual fantasies that fuel a variety of sexual behaviors.

The near consensus among social psychologists is that—contrary to what Freud, Lorenz, and their followers supposed—viewing or participating in violence fails to produce catharsis (Geen & Quanty, 1977). Actually, notes researcher Brad Bushman (2002), "Venting to reduce anger is like using gasoline to put out a fire." For example, Robert Arms and his associates report that Canadian and American spectators of football, wrestling, and hockey games exhibit *more* hostility after viewing the event than before (Arms & others, 1979; Goldstein & Arms, 1971; Russell, 1983). Not even war seems to purge aggressive feelings. After a war, a nation's murder rate has tended to jump (Archer & Gartner, 1976).

In laboratory tests of catharsis, Brad Bushman (2002) invited angered participants to hit a punching bag while either ruminating about the person who angered them or thinking about becoming physically fit. A third group did not hit the punching bag. When given a chance to administer loud blasts of noise to the person who angered them, people in the punching bag plus rumination condition felt angrier and were most aggressive. Moreover, doing nothing at all more effectively reduced aggression than did "blowing off steam" by hitting the bag.

In some real-life experiments, too, aggressing has led to heightened aggression. Ebbe Ebbesen and his co-researchers (1975) interviewed 100 engineers and technicians shortly after they were angered by layoff notices. Some were asked questions that gave them an opportunity to express hostility against their employer or supervisors—for example, "What instances can you think of where the company has not been fair with you?" Afterward, they answered a questionnaire assessing attitudes toward the company and the supervisors. Did the previous opportunity to "vent"

"It is time to put a bullet, once and for all, through the heart of the catharsis hypothesis. The belief that observing violence (or 'ventilating it') gets rid of hostilities has virtually never been supported by research."
—CAROL TAVRIS (1988, p. 194)

"He who gives way to violent gestures will increase his rage."
—CHARLES DARWIN, THE EXPRESSION OF EMOTION IN MAN AND ANIMALS, 1872

or "drain off" their hostility reduce it? To the contrary, their hostility increased. Expressing hostility bred more hostility.

Sound familiar? Recall from Chapter 4 that cruel acts beget cruel attitudes. Furthermore, as we noted in analyzing Stanley Milgram's obedience experiments, little aggressive acts can breed their own justification. People derogate their victims, rationalizing further aggression.

Retaliation may, in the short run, reduce tension and even provide pleasure (Ramirez & others, 2005). But in the long run it fuels more negative feelings. When people who have been provoked hit a punching bag, even when they believe it will be cathartic, the effect is the opposite—leading them to exhibit *more* cruelty, report Bushman and his colleagues (1999, 2000, 2001). "It's like the old joke," reflected Bushman (1999). "How do you get to Carnegie Hall? Practice, practice, practice. How do you become a very angry person? The answer is the same. Practice, practice, practice."

Should we therefore bottle up anger and aggressive urges? Silent sulking is hardly more effective, because it allows us to continue reciting our grievances as we conduct conversations in our heads. Bushman and his colleagues (2005) experimented with the toxic effect of such rumination. After being provoked by an obnoxious experimenter with insults such as "Can't you follow directions? Speak louder!" half were given a distraction (by being asked to write an essay about their campus landscape), and half were induced to ruminate (by writing an essay about their experiences as a research participant). Next, they were mildly insulted by a supposed fellow participant (actually a confederate), to whom they responded by prescribing a hot sauce dose this person would have to consume. The distracted participants, their anger now abated, prescribed only a mild dose. The still-seething ruminators displaced their aggressive urge and prescribed twice as much.

Fortunately, there are nonaggressive ways to express our feelings and to inform others how their behavior affects us. Across cultures, those who reframe accusatory "you" messages as "I" messages—"I feel angry about what you said," or, "I get irritated when you leave dirty dishes"—communicate their feelings in a way that better enables the other person to make a positive response (Kubany & others, 1995). We can be assertive without being aggressive.

A Social Learning Approach

If aggressive behavior is learned, then there is hope for its control. Let us briefly review factors that influence aggression and speculate how to counteract them.

Aversive experiences such as frustrated expectations and personal attacks predispose hostile aggression. So it is wise to refrain from planting false, unreachable expectations in people's minds. Anticipated rewards and costs influence instrumental aggression. This suggests that we should reward cooperative, nonaggressive behavior.

In experiments, children become less aggressive when caregivers ignore their aggressive behavior and reinforce their nonaggressive behavior (Hamblin & others, 1969). Punishing the aggressor is less consistently effective. Threatened punishment deters aggression only under ideal conditions: when the punishment is strong, prompt, and sure; when it is combined with reward for the desired behavior; and when the recipient is not angry (R. A. Baron, 1977).

Moreover, there are limits to punishment's effectiveness. Most homicide is impulsive, hot aggression—the result of an argument, an insult, or an attack. If mortal aggression were cool and instrumental, we could hope that waiting until it happens and severely punishing the criminal afterward would deter such acts. In that world, states that impose the death penalty might have a lower murder rate than states without the death penalty. But in our world of hot homicide, that is not so (Costanzo, 1998). As John Darley and Adam Alter (2009) note, "A remarkable amount of crime is committed by impulsive individuals, frequently young males, who are frequently drunk or high on drugs, and who often are in packs of similar and similarly mindless young men." No wonder, they say, that trying to reduce crime by increasing sentences has proven so fruitless, while on-the-street policing that produces more arrests has produced encouraging results, such as a 50 percent drop in gun-related crimes in some cities.

Thus, we must *prevent* aggression before it happens. We must teach nonaggressive conflict-resolution strategies. When psychologists Sandra Jo Wilson and Mark Lipsey (2005) assembled data from 249 studies of school violence prevention programs, they found encouraging results, especially for programs focused on selected "problem" students. After being taught problem-solving skills, emotion-control strategies, and conflict resolution techniques, the typical 20 percent of students engaging in some violent or disruptive behavior in a typical school year was reduced to 13 percent.

Physical punishment can also have negative side effects. Punishment is aversive stimulation; it models the behavior it seeks to prevent. And it is coercive (recall that we seldom internalize actions coerced with strong external justifications). These are reasons why violent teenagers and child-abusing parents so often come from homes where discipline took the form of harsh physical punishment.

To foster a gentler world, we could model and reward sensitivity and cooperation from an early age, perhaps by training parents how to discipline without violence. Training programs encourage parents to reinforce desirable behaviors and to frame statements positively ("When you finish cleaning your room, you can go play," rather than, "If you don't clean your room, you're grounded"). One "aggression-replacement program" has reduced rearrest rates of juvenile offenders and gang members by teaching the youths and their parents communication skills, training them to control anger, and raising their level of moral reasoning (Goldstein & others, 1998).

If observing aggressive models lowers inhibitions and elicits imitation, then we might also reduce brutal, dehumanizing portrayals in films and on television—steps comparable to those already taken to reduce racist and sexist portrayals. We can also inoculate children against the effects of media violence. Wondering if the TV networks would ever "face the facts and change their programming," Eron and Huesmann (1984) taught 170 Oak Park, Illinois, children that television portrays the world unrealistically, that aggression is less common and less effective than TV suggests, and that aggressive behavior is undesirable. (Drawing upon attitude research, Eron and Huesmann encouraged children to draw these inferences themselves and to attribute their expressed criticisms of television to their own convictions.) When restudied two years later, these children were less influenced by TV violence than were untrained children. In a more recent study, Stanford University used 18 classroom lessons to persuade children to simply reduce their TV watching and video-game playing (Robinson & others, 2001). They reduced their TV viewing by a third—and the children's aggressive behavior at school dropped 25 percent compared with children in a control school.

Aggressive stimuli also trigger aggression. This suggests reducing the availability of weapons such as handguns. In 1974, Jamaica implemented a sweeping anti-crime program that included strict gun control and censorship of gun scenes from television and movies (Diener & Crandall, 1979).

Suggestions such as these can help us minimize aggression. But given the complexity of aggression's causes and the difficulty of controlling them, who can feel the optimism expressed by Andrew Carnegie's forecast that in the twentieth century, "To kill a man will be considered as disgusting as we in this day consider it disgusting to eat one." Since Carnegie uttered those words in 1900, some 200 million human beings have been killed. It is a sad irony that although today we understand human aggression better than ever before, humanity's inhumanity endures. Nevertheless, cultures can change. "The Vikings slaughtered and plundered," notes science writer Natalie Angier. "Their descendants in Sweden haven't fought a war in nearly 200 years."

Summing Up: How Can Aggression Be Reduced?

- How can we minimize aggression? Contrary to the catharsis hypothesis, expressing aggression by catharsis tends to breed further aggression, not reduce it.

- The social learning approach suggests controlling aggression by counteracting the factors that provoke it: by reducing aversive stimulation, by rewarding and modeling nonaggression, and by eliciting reactions incompatible with aggression.

POSTSCRIPT: Reforming a Violent Culture

In 1960 the United States (apologies to readers elsewhere, but we Americans do have a special problem with violence) had 3.3 police officers for every reported violent crime. In 1993 we had 3.5 crimes for every police officer (Walinsky, 1995). Since then, the crime rate has lessened, thanks partly to the incarceration of six times as many people today as in 1960. Still, on my small campus, which required no campus police in 1960, we now employ six full-time and seven part-time officers, and we offer a nightly shuttle service to transport students around campus.

Americans' ideas for protecting ourselves abound:

- Buy a gun for self-protection. (We have . . . 211 million guns . . . which puts one at tripled risk of being murdered, often by a family member, and at fivefold increased risk of suicide [Taubes, 1992]. Safer nations, such as Canada and Britain, mandate domestic disarmament.)
- Build more prisons. (We have, but until recently crime continued to escalate. Moreover, the social and fiscal costs of incarcerating more than 2 million people, mostly men, are enormous.)
- Impose a "three strikes and you're out" requirement of lifetime incarceration for those convicted of three violent crimes. (But are we really ready to pay for all the new prisons—and prison hospitals and nursing homes—we would need to house and care for aging former muggers?)
- Deter brutal crime and eliminate the worst offenders as some countries do—by executing the offenders. To show that killing people is wrong—kill people who kill people. (But nearly all the cities and states with the dozen highest violent-crime rates already have the death penalty. Because most homicide is impulsive or under the influence of drugs or alcohol, murderers rarely calculate consequences.)

What matters more than a punishment's severity is its certainty. The National Research Council (1993) reports that a 50 percent increase in the probability of apprehension and incarceration reduces subsequent crime twice as much as does doubling incarceration duration. Even so, former FBI director Louis Freeh (1993) was skeptical that tougher or swifter punishment is the ultimate answer: "The frightening level of lawlessness which has come upon us like a plague is more than a law enforcement problem. The crime and disorder which flow from hopeless poverty, unloved children, and drug abuse can't be solved merely by bottomless prisons, mandatory sentencing, and more police." Reacting to crime after it happens is the social equivalent of Band-Aids on bullet wounds.

An alternative approach is suggested by a story about the rescue of a drowning person from a rushing river. Having successfully administered first aid, the rescuer spots another struggling person and pulls her out, too. After a half dozen repetitions, the rescuer suddenly turns and starts running away while the river sweeps yet another floundering person into view. "Aren't you going to rescue that fellow?" asks a bystander. "Heck no," the rescuer shouts. "I'm going upstream to find out what's pushing all these people in."

To be sure, we need police, prisons, and social workers, all of whom help us deal with the social pathologies that plague us. It's fine to swat the mosquitoes, but better if we can drain the swamps—by infusing our culture with nonviolent ideals, challenging the social toxins that corrupt youth, and renewing the moral roots of character.

Making the Social Connection

Aggression, as this chapter illustrates, includes varied verbal and physical behaviors that intend to cause harm to another. On the Online Learning Center for this book, University of Illinois psychologist Dorothy Espelage illustrates such behaviors as she discusses "Characteristics of Children Who Bully." Bullying includes verbal teasing and name-calling, physical shoving and hitting, and social rejection and exclusion. She describes children who engage in such behaviors and how teachers can prevent these behaviors.

Attraction and Intimacy

LIKING AND LOVING OTHERS

"I get by with a little help from my friends."

—John Lennon and Paul McCartney, Sgt. Pepper's Lonely
Hearts Club Band, 1967

Our lifelong dependence on one another puts relationships at the core of our existence. In your beginning there very likely was an attraction—the attraction between a particular man and a particular woman. Aristotle called humans "the social animal." Indeed, we have what today's social psychologists call a **need to belong**—to connect with others in enduring, close relationships.

Social psychologists Roy Baumeister and Mark Leary (1995) illustrate the power of social attachments:

- For our ancestors, mutual attachments enabled group survival. When hunting game or erecting shelter, 10 hands were better than 2.

- For heterosexual women and men, the bonds of love can lead to children, whose survival chances are boosted by the nurturing of two bonded parents who support each other.

- For children and their caregivers, social attachments enhance survival. Unexplainably separated from each other, parent and toddler may both panic until reunited in a tight embrace. Reared under extreme neglect or in institutions without belonging to anybody, children become pathetic, anxious creatures.

- For university students, relationships consume much of life. How much of your waking life is spent talking with people? One

need to belong
A motivation to bond with others in relationships that provide ongoing, positive interactions.

sampling of 10,000 tape recordings of half-minute slices of students' waking hours (using belt-worn recorders) found them talking to someone 28 percent of the time—and that doesn't count the time they spent listening to someone (Mehl & Pennebaker, 2003). In 2008, the average American 13- to 17-year-old sent or received 1,742 text messages per month (Steinhauer & Holson, 2008).

- For people everywhere (no matter their sexual orientation), actual and hoped-for close relationships can dominate thinking and emotions. Finding a supportive person in whom we can confide, we feel accepted and prized. Falling in love, we feel irrepressible joy. When relationships with partners, family, and friends are healthy, self-esteem—a barometer of our relationships—rides high (Denissen & others, 2008). Longing for acceptance and love, we spend billions on cosmetics, clothes, and diets. Even seemingly dismissive people relish being accepted (Carvallo & Gabriel, 2006).

- Exiled, imprisoned, or in solitary confinement, people ache for their own people and places. Rejected, we are at risk for depression (Nolan & others, 2003). Time passes more slowly and life seems less meaningful (Twenge & others, 2003). When queried three months after arriving on a large university campus, many international students, like some homesick domestic students, report declining feelings of well-being (Cemalcilar & Falbo, 2008).

"There's no question in my mind about what stands at the heart of the communication revolution—the human desire to connect."
—*JOSH SILVERMAN, PRESIDENT OF SKYPE, 2009*

- For the jilted, the widowed, and the sojourner in a strange place, the loss of social bonds triggers pain, loneliness, or withdrawal. Losing a close relationship, adults feel jealous, distraught, or bereaved, as well as more mindful of death and the fragility of life. After relocating, people—especially those with the strongest need to belong—typically feel homesick (Watt & Badger, 2009).

- Reminders of death in turn heighten our need to belong, to be with others, and to hold close those we love (Mikulincer & others, 2003; Wisman & Koole, 2003). Facing the terror of 9/11, millions of Americans called and connected with loved ones. Likewise, the shocking death of a classmate, a co-worker, or a family member brings people together, their differences no longer mattering.

We are, indeed, social animals. We need to belong. As with other motivations, thwarting the need to belong intensifies it; satisfying the need reduces the motivation (DeWall & others, 2009). And as Chapter 14 confirms, when we do belong—when we feel supported by close, intimate relationships—we tend to be healthier and happier. Satisfy the need to belong in balance with two other human needs—to feel *autonomy* and *competence*—and the typical result is a deep sense of well-being (Deci & Ryan, 2002; Patrick & others, 2007; Sheldon & Niemiec, 2006). Happiness is feeling connected, free, and capable.

Social psychologist Kipling Williams (2002, 2007) has explored what happens when our need to belong is thwarted by *ostracism* (acts of excluding or ignoring).

Humans in all cultures, whether in schools, workplaces, or homes, use ostracism to regulate social behavior. Some of us know what it is like to be shunned—to be avoided, met with averted eyes, or given the silent treatment. People (women especially) respond to ostracism with depressed mood, anxiety, hurt feelings, efforts to restore relationships, and eventual withdrawal. The silent treatment is "emotional abuse" and "a terrible, terrible weapon to use," say those who have experienced it from a family member or a co-worker. In experiments, people who are left out of a simple game of ball tossing feel deflated and stressed.

A recipe for violence: an unstable disposition plus ostracism. Mark Leary, Robin Kowalski, and their colleagues (2003) report that in all but 2 of 15 school shootings from 1995 to 2001, such as by Eric Harris and Dylan Klebold at Columbine High School, the assailants had experienced ostracism.

Sometimes deflation turns nasty. In several studies, Jean Twenge and her collaborators (2001, 2002, 2007; DeWall & others, 2009; Leary & others, 2006) gave some people an experience of being socially included. Others experienced temporary exclusion: They were told (based on a personality test) either that they "were likely to end up alone later in life" or that others whom they'd met didn't want them in their group. Those led to feel excluded became not only more likely to engage in self-defeating behaviors, such as underperforming on an aptitude test, but also less able to regulate their behavior (they drank less of a healthy but bad-tasting drink and ate more unhealthy but good-tasting cookies). And they became more likely to disparage or deliver a blast of noise to someone who had insulted them. If a small laboratory experience of being "voted off the island" could produce such aggression, noted the researchers, one wonders what aggressive tendencies "might arise from a series of important rejections or chronic exclusion."

Williams and his colleagues (2000) were surprised to discover that even "cyberostracism" by faceless people whom one will never meet takes a toll. (Perhaps you have experienced this when feeling ignored in a chat room or when your e-mail is not answered.) The researchers had 1,486 participants from 62 countries play a Web-based game of throwing a flying disc with two others (actually computer-generated fellow players). Those ostracized by the other players experienced poorer moods and became more likely to conform to others' wrong judgments on a subsequent perceptual task. Exclusion hurts longest for anxious people, and hurts even when it's by a disliked outgroup—Australian KKK members in one experiment (Gonsalkorale & Williams, 2006; Zadro & others, 2006).

Williams and four of his colleagues (2000) even found ostracism stressful when each of them was ignored for an agreed-upon day by the unresponsive four others. Contrary to their expectations that this would be a laughter-filled role-playing game, the simulated ostracism disrupted work, interfered with pleasant social functioning, and "caused temporary concern, anxiety, paranoia, and general fragility of spirit." To thwart our deep need to belong is to unsettle our life.

Given the dramatic effects of rejection in experiments, what do you expect are the long-term effects of chronic rejection?

Ostracized people exhibit heightened activity in a brain cortex area that also is activated in response to physical pain (Figure 11.1). Other evidence confirms the convergence of social and physical pain in humans and other animals (MacDonald & Leary, 2005).

Asked to recall a time when they were socially excluded—perhaps left alone in the dorm when others went out—people in one experiment even perceived the room temperature as five degrees colder than did those asked to recall a social acceptance experience (Zhong & Leonardelli, 2008). Such recollections come easily:

FIGURE :: 11.1

The Pain of Rejection

Naomi Eisenberger, Matthew Lieberman, and Kipling Williams (2003) reported that social ostracism evokes a brain response similar to that triggered by physical pain.

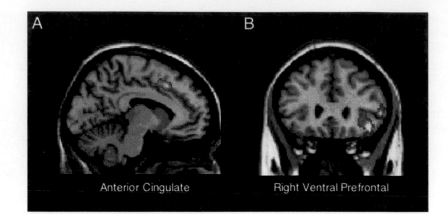

A

B

Anterior Cingulate

Right Ventral Prefrontal

People remember and relive past social pain more easily than past physical pain (Chen & others, 2008). Ostracism, it seems, is a real pain.

Roy Baumeister (2005) finds a silver lining in the rejection research. When recently excluded people experience a safe opportunity to make a new friend, they "seem willing and even eager to take it." They become more attentive to smiling, accepting faces (DeWall & others, 2009). An exclusion experience also triggers increased mimicry of others' behavior as a nonconscious effort to build rapport (Lakin & others, 2008). And at a societal level, notes Baumeister, meeting the need to belong should pay dividends.

> My colleagues in sociology have pointed out that minority groups who feel excluded show many of the same patterns that our laboratory manipulations elicit: high rates of aggression and antisocial behavior, decreased willingness to cooperate and obey rules, poorer intellectual performance, more self-destructive acts, short-term focus, and the like. Possibly if we can promote a more inclusive society, in which more people feel themselves to be accepted as valued members, some of these tragic patterns could be reduced.

What Leads to Friendship and Attraction?

What factors nurture liking and loving? Let's start with those that help initiate attraction: proximity, physical attractiveness, similarity, and feeling liked.

"I cannot tell how my ankles bend, nor whence the cause of my faintest wish, Nor the cause of the friendship I emit, nor the cause of the friendship I take again."

—*WALT WHITMAN,*
SONG OF MYSELF, 1855

What predisposes one person to like, or to love, another? Few questions about human nature arouse greater interest. The ways affections flourish and fade form the stuff and fluff of soap operas, popular music, novels, and much of our everyday conversation. Long before I knew there was a field such as social psychology, I had memorized Dale Carnegie's recipe for *How to Win Friends and Influence People*.

So much has been written about liking and loving that almost every conceivable explanation—and its opposite—has already been proposed. For most people—and for you—what factors nurture liking and loving?

- Does absence make the heart grow fonder? Or is someone who is out of sight also out of mind?
- Is it likes that attract? Or opposites?
- How much do good looks matter?
- What has fostered your close relationships?

Let's start with those factors that help a friendship begin and then consider those that sustain and deepen a relationship, thus satisfying our need to belong.

Proximity

One powerful predictor of whether any two people are friends is sheer **proximity.** Proximity can also breed hostility; most assaults and murders involve people living close together. But much more often, proximity kindles liking. Mitja Back and his University of Leipzig colleagues (2008) confirmed this by randomly assigning students to seats at their first class meeting, and then having each make a brief self-introduction to the whole class. One year after this one-time seating assignment, students reported greater friendship with those who just happened, during that first class gathering, to be seated next to or near them.

Close relationships with friends and family contribute to health and happiness.

Though it may seem trivial to those pondering the mysterious origins of romantic love, sociologists long ago found that most people marry someone who lives in the same neighborhood, or works at the same company or job, or sits in the same class, or visits the same favorite place (Bossard, 1932; Burr, 1973; Clarke, 1952; McPherson & others, 2001). In a Pew survey (2006) of people married or in long-term relationships, 38 percent met at work or at school, and some of the rest met when their paths crossed in their neighborhood, church, or gym, or while growing up. Look around. If you marry, it may well be to someone who has lived or worked or studied within walking distance.

INTERACTION

Even more significant than geographic distance is "functional distance"—how often people's paths cross. We frequently become friends with those who use the same entrances, parking lots, and recreation areas. Randomly assigned college roommates, who interact frequently, are far more likely to become good friends than enemies (Newcomb, 1961). At the college where I teach, men and women once lived on opposite sides of the campus. They understandably bemoaned the lack of cross-sex friendships. Now that they live in gender-integrated residence halls and share common sidewalks, lounges, and laundry facilities, friendships between men and women are far more frequent. Interaction enables people to explore their similarities, to sense one another's liking, and to perceive themselves as part of a social unit (Arkin & Burger, 1980).

So if you're new in town and want to make friends, try to get an apartment near the mailboxes, a desk near the coffeepot, a parking spot near the main buildings. Such is the architecture of friendship.

The chance nature of such contacts helps explain a surprising finding. Consider: If you had an identical twin who became engaged to someone, wouldn't you (being in so many ways similar to

proximity
Geographical nearness. Proximity (more precisely, "functional distance") powerfully predicts liking.

"I do not believe that friends are necessarily the people you like best, they are merely the people who got there first."
—SIR PETER USTINOV,
DEAR ME, 1979

"Sometimes I think you only married me because I lived next door!"

Feeling close to those close by: People often become attached to, and sometimes fall in love with, familiar co-workers.

your twin) expect to share your twin's attraction to that person? But no, reported researchers David Lykken and Auke Tellegen (1993); only half of identical twins recall really liking their twin's selection, and only 5 percent said, "I could have fallen for my twin's fiancé." Romantic love is often rather like ducklings' imprinting, surmised Lykken and Tellegen. With repeated exposure to and interaction with someone, our infatuation may fix on almost anyone who has roughly similar characteristics and who reciprocates our affection. (Later research has shown that identical twins' spouses do, however, tend to have fairly similar personalities [Rushton & Bons, 2005].)

"When I'm not near the one I love, I love the one I'm near."

—E. Y. HARBURG, FINIAN'S RAINBOW, LONDON: CHAPPELL MUSIC, 1947

Why does proximity breed liking? One factor is availability; obviously there are fewer opportunities to get to know someone who attends a different school or lives in another town. But there is more to it than that. Most people like their roommates, or those one door away, better than those two doors away. Those just a few doors away, or even a floor below, hardly live at an inconvenient distance. Moreover, those close by are potential enemies as well as friends. So why does proximity encourage affection more often than animosity?

ANTICIPATION OF INTERACTION

Proximity enables people to discover commonalities and exchange rewards. But merely *anticipating* interaction also boosts liking. John Darley and Ellen Berscheid (1967) discovered this when they gave University of Minnesota women ambiguous information about two other women, one of whom they expected to talk with intimately. Asked how much they liked each one, the women preferred the person they expected to meet. Expecting to date someone similarly boosts liking (Berscheid & others, 1976). Even voters on the losing side of an election will find their opinions of the winning candidate—whom they are now stuck with—rising (Gilbert & others, 1998).

The phenomenon is adaptive. Anticipatory liking—expecting that someone will be pleasant and compatible—increases the chance of forming a rewarding relationship (Klein & Kunda, 1992; Knight & Vallacher, 1981; Miller & Marks, 1982). It's a good thing that we are biased to like those we often see, for our lives are filled with relationships with people

"If I weren't so fond of you, I'd probably be really fond of someone else."

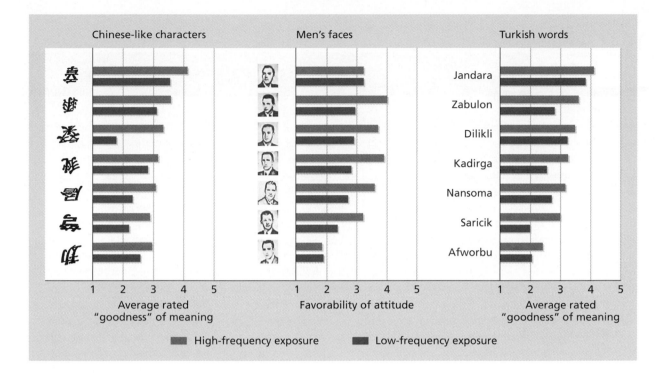

FIGURE :: 11.2

The Mere-Exposure Effect

Students rated stimuli—a sample of which is shown here—more positively after being shown them repeatedly.

Source: From Zajonc, 1968.

whom we may not have chosen but with whom we need to have continuing interactions—roommates, siblings, grandparents, teachers, classmates, co-workers. Liking such people is surely conducive to better relationships with them, which in turn makes for happier, more productive living.

MERE EXPOSURE

Proximity leads to liking not only because it enables interaction and anticipatory liking but also for another reason: More than 200 experiments reveal that, contrary to an old proverb, familiarity does not breed contempt. Rather, it fosters fondness (Bornstein, 1989, 1999). **Mere exposure** to all sorts of novel stimuli—nonsense syllables, Chinese calligraphy characters, musical selections, faces—boosts people's ratings of them. Do the supposed Turkish words *nansoma, saricik,* and *afworbu* mean something better or something worse than the words *iktitaf, biwojni,* and *kadirga?* University of Michigan students tested by Robert Zajonc (1968, 1970) preferred whichever of these words they had seen most frequently. The more times they had seen a meaningless word or a Chinese ideograph, the more likely they were to say it meant something good (Figure 11.2). I've tested this idea with my own students. Periodically flash certain nonsense words on a screen. By the end of the semester, students will rate those "words" more positively than other nonsense words they have never before seen.

Or consider: What are your favorite letters of the alphabet? People of differing nationalities, languages, and ages prefer the letters appearing in their own names and those that frequently appear in their own languages (Hoorens & others, 1990, 1993; Kitayama & Karasawa, 1997; Nuttin, 1987). French students rate capital W, the least frequent letter in French, as their least favorite letter. Japanese students

mere-exposure effect
The tendency for novel stimuli to be liked more or rated more positively after the rater has been repeatedly exposed to them.

focus
ON
Liking Things Associated with Oneself

We humans love to feel good about ourselves, and generally we do. Not only are we prone to self-serving bias (Chapter 2), we also exhibit what Brett Pelham, Matthew Mirenberg, and John Jones (2002) call *implicit egotism:* We like what we associate with ourselves.

That includes the letters of our name, but also the people, places, and things that we unconsciously connect with ourselves (Jones & others, 2002; Koole & others, 2001). If a stranger's or politician's face is morphed to include features of our own, we like the new face better (Bailenson & others, 2009; DeBruine, 2004). We are also more attracted to people whose arbitrary experimental code number resembles our birth date, and we are even disproportionately likely to marry someone whose first or last name resembles our own, such as by starting with the same letter (Jones & others, 2004).

Such preferences appear to subtly influence other major life decisions as well, including our locations and careers, report Pelham and his colleagues. Philadelphia, being larger than Jacksonville, has 2.2 times as many men named Jack. But it has 10.4 times as many people named Philip. Likewise, Virginia Beach has a disproportionate number of people named Virginia.

Does this merely reflect the influence of one's place when naming one's baby? Are people in Georgia, for example, more likely to name their babies George or Georgia? That may be so, but it doesn't explain why states tend to have a relative excess of people whose *last* names are similar to the state names. California, for example, has a disproportionate number of people whose names begin with Cali (as in Califano). Likewise, major Canadian cities tend to have larger-than-expected numbers of people whose last names overlap with the city names. Toronto has a marked excess of people whose names begin with Tor.

Moreover, women named "Georgia" are disproportionately likely to *move* to Georgia, as do Virginias to Virginia. Such mobility could help explain why St. Louis has a 49 percent excess (relative to the national proportion) of men named Louis, and why people named Hill, Park, Beach, Lake, or Rock are disproportionately likely to live in cities with names (such as Park City) that include their names. "People are attracted to places that resemble their names," surmise Pelham, Mirenberg, and Jones.

Weirder yet—I am not making this up—people seem to prefer careers related to their names. Across the United States, Jerry, Dennis, and Walter are equally popular names (0.42 percent of people carry each of these names). Yet America's dentists are almost twice as likely to be named Dennis as Jerry or Walter. There also are 2.5 times as many dentists named Denise as there are with the equally popular name Beverly or Tammy. People named George or Geoffrey are overrepresented among geoscientists (geologists, geophysicists, and geochemists). And in the 2000 presidential campaign, people with last names beginning with B and G were disproportionately likely to contribute to the campaigns of Bush and Gore, respectively.

Reading about implicit egotism–based preferences gives me pause: Has this anything to do with why I enjoyed that trip to Fort Myers? Why I've written about moods, the media, and marriage? Why I collaborated with Professor Murdoch? If so, does this also explain why it was Suzie who sold seashells by the seashore?

How much do you like your name? In six studies, Jochen Gebauer and his colleagues (2008) report that liking of one's own name is a reliable indicator of both implicit and explicit self-esteem.

prefer not only letters from their names but also numbers corresponding to their birth dates. This "name letter effect" reflects more than mere exposure, however—see "Focus On: Liking Things Associated with Oneself."

The mere-exposure effect violates the commonsense prediction of boredom—*decreased* interest—regarding repeatedly heard music or tasted foods (Kahneman & Snell, 1992). Unless the repetitions are incessant ("Even the best song becomes tiresome if heard too often," says a Korean proverb), familiarity usually doesn't breed contempt, it increases liking. When completed in 1889, the Eiffel Tower in Paris was mocked as grotesque (Harrison, 1977). Today it is the beloved symbol of Paris.

So, do visitors to the Louvre in Paris really adore the *Mona Lisa* for the artistry it displays, or are they simply delighted to find a familiar face? It might be both: To know her is to like her. Eddie Harmon-Jones and John Allen (2001) explored this phenomenon experimentally. When they showed people a woman's face, their cheek (smiling) muscles typically became more active with repeated viewings. Mere exposure breeds pleasant feelings.

Zajonc and his co-workers William Kunst-Wilson and Richard Moreland reported that even exposure *without awareness* leads to liking (Kunst-Wilson & Zajonc, 1980; Moreland & Zajonc, 1977; Wilson, 1979). In fact, mere exposure has an even stronger effect when people receive stimuli without awareness (Bornstein & D'Agostino, 1992). In one experiment, women students using headphones listened in one ear to a prose passage. They also repeated the words out loud and compared them with a written version to check for errors. Meanwhile, brief, novel melodies played in the other ear. This procedure focused attention on the verbal material and away from the tunes. Later, when the women heard the tunes interspersed among similar ones not previously played, they did not recognize them. Nevertheless, they *liked best* the tunes they had previously heard.

Note that conscious judgments about the stimuli in these experiments provided fewer clues to what people had heard or seen than did their instant feelings. You can probably recall immediately and intuitively liking or disliking something or someone without consciously knowing why. Zajonc (1980) argues that *emotions are often more instantaneous than thinking.* Zajonc's rather astonishing idea—that emotions are semi-independent of thinking ("affect may precede cognition")—has found support in recent brain research. Emotion and cognition are enabled by distinct brain regions. Lesion a monkey's amygdala (the emotion-related brain structure) and its emotional responses will be impaired, but its cognitive functions will be intact. Lesion its hippocampus (a memory-related structure) and its cognition will be impaired, but its emotional responses remain intact (Zola-Morgan & others, 1991).

The mere-exposure effect has "enormous adaptive significance," notes Zajonc (1998). It is a "hardwired" phenomenon that predisposes our attractions and attachments. It helped our ancestors categorize things and people as either familiar and safe, or unfamiliar and possibly dangerous. The mere-exposure effect colors our evaluations of others: We like familiar people (Swap, 1977). It works the other way around, too: People we like (for example, smiling rather than unsmiling strangers) seem more familiar (Garcia-Marques & others, 2004).

The phenomenon's negative side, as we noted in Chapter 9, is our wariness of the unfamiliar—which may explain the automatic, unconscious prejudice people often feel when confronting those who are different. Fearful or prejudicial feelings are not always expressions of stereotyped beliefs; sometimes the beliefs arise later as justifications for intuitive feelings. Infants as young as 3 months exhibit an own-race preference: If surrounded by others of their race, they prefer to gaze at faces of their own familiar race (Bar-Haim & others, 2006; Kelly & others, 2005, 2007).

We even like ourselves better when we are the way we're used to seeing ourselves. In a delightful experiment, Theodore Mita, Marshall Dermer, and Jeffrey Knight (1977) photographed women students at the University of Wisconsin, Milwaukee, and later showed each one her actual picture along with a mirror image of it. Asked which picture they liked better, most preferred the mirror image—the image they were used to seeing. (No wonder our photographs never look quite right.) When close friends of the women were shown the same two pictures, they preferred the true picture—the image *they* were used to seeing.

Advertisers and politicians exploit this phenomenon. When people have no strong feelings about a product or a candidate, repetition alone can increase sales or votes (McCullough & Ostrom, 1974; Winter, 1973). After endless repetition of a commercial, shoppers often have an unthinking, automatic, favorable response to the product. If candidates are relatively unknown, those with the most media exposure usually win (Patterson, 1980; Schaffner & others, 1981). Political strategists who understand the mere-exposure effect have replaced reasoned argument with brief ads that hammer home a candidate's name and sound-bite message.

The respected chief of the Washington State Supreme Court, Keith Callow, learned this lesson when in 1990 he lost to a seemingly hopeless opponent, Charles

The mere-exposure effect. If she is like most of us, German chancellor Angela Merkel may prefer her familiar mirror-image (left), which she sees each morning while brushing her teeth, to her actual image (right).

Johnson. Johnson, an unknown attorney who handled minor criminal cases and divorces, filed for the seat on the principle that judges "need to be challenged." Neither man campaigned, and the media ignored the race. On election day, the two candidates' names appeared without any identification—just one name next to the other. The result: a 53 percent to 47 percent Johnson victory. "There are a lot more Johnsons out there than Callows," offered the ousted judge afterward to a stunned legal community. Indeed, the state's largest newspaper counted 27 Charles Johnsons in its local phone book. There was Charles Johnson, the local judge. And, in a nearby city, there was television anchorman Charles Johnson, whose broadcasts were seen on statewide cable TV. Forced to choose between two unknown names, many voters preferred the comfortable, familiar name of Charles Johnson.

Physical Attractiveness

What do (or did) you seek in a potential date? Sincerity? Character? Humor? Good looks? Sophisticated, intelligent people are unconcerned with such superficial qualities as good looks; they know "beauty is only skin deep" and "you can't judge a book by its cover." At least, they know that's how they *ought* to feel. As Cicero counseled, "Resist appearance."

"We should look to the mind, and not to the outward appearances."
—AESOP, FABLES

Attractiveness and dating. For Internet dating customers, looks are part of what is offered and sought.

The belief that looks are unimportant may be another instance of how we deny real influences upon us, for there is now a file cabinet full of research studies showing that appearance *does* matter. The consistency and pervasiveness of this effect is astonishing. Good looks are a great asset.

ATTRACTIVENESS AND DATING

Like it or not, a young woman's physical attractiveness is a moderately good predictor of how frequently she dates, and a young man's attractiveness is a modestly good predictor of how frequently he dates (Berscheid & others, 1971; Krebs & Adinolfi, 1975; Reis & others, 1980, 1982; Walster & others, 1966). Moreover, women more than men say they would prefer a mate who's homely and warm over one who's attractive and cold (Fletcher & others, 2004). In a

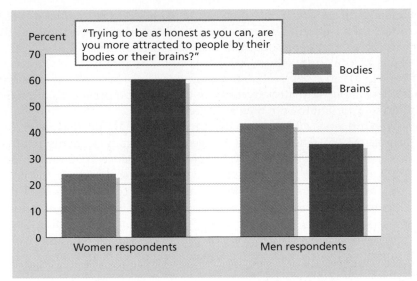

FIGURE :: 11.3

What Women and Men
Report Finding Most
Attractive

Source: Fox News/Opinion
Dynamics Poll of registered
voters, 1999.

worldwide BBC Internet survey of nearly 220,000 people, men more than women ranked attractiveness as important in a mate, while women more than men assigned importance to honesty, humor, kindness, and dependability (Lippa, 2007).

Do such self-reports imply, as many have surmised, that women are better at following Cicero's advice? Or that nothing has changed since 1930, when the English philosopher Bertrand Russell (1930, p. 139) wrote, "On the whole women tend to love men for their character while men tend to love women for their appearance"? Or does it merely reflect the fact that men more often do the inviting? If women were to indicate their preferences among various men, would looks be as important to them as to men?

To see whether men are indeed more influenced by looks, researchers have provided heterosexual male and female students with information about someone of the other sex, including the person's picture. Or they have briefly introduced a man and a woman and later asked each about their interest in dating the other. In such experiments, men do put somewhat more value on opposite-sex physical attractiveness, as they do in opinion polls (Figure 11.3) (Feingold, 1990, 1991; Sprecher & others, 1994). Perhaps sensing this, women worry more about their appearance and constitute nearly 90 percent of cosmetic surgery patients (ASAPS, 2005). Women also better recall others' appearance, as when asked "Was the person on the right wearing black shoes?" or when asked to recall someone's clothing or hair (Mast & Hall, 2006).

Women respond to men's looks. In one ambitious study, Elaine Hatfield and her co-workers (1966) matched 752 University of Minnesota first-year students for a "Welcome Week" matching dance. The researchers gave each student personality and aptitude tests but then matched the couples randomly. On the night of the dance, the couples danced and talked for two and one-half hours and then took a brief intermission to evaluate their dates. How well did the personality and aptitude tests predict attraction? Did people like someone better who was high in self-esteem, or low in anxiety, or different from themselves in outgoingness? The researchers examined a long list of possibilities. But so far as they could determine, only one thing mattered: how physically attractive the person was (as previously rated by the researchers). The more attractive a woman was, the more the man liked her and wanted to date her again. And the more attractive the man was, the more the woman liked him and wanted to date him again. Pretty pleases.

More recent studies have gathered data from speed-dating evenings, during which people interact with a succession of potential dates for only a few minutes

"Personal beauty is a greater
recommendation than any
letter of introduction."
—ARISTOTLE, *DIOGENES
LAERTIUS*

each and later indicate which ones they would like to see again (mutual "yes's" are given contact information). The procedure is rooted in research showing that we can form durable impressions of others based on seconds-long "thin slices" of their social behavior (Ambady & others, 2000). In speed-dating research by Paul Eastwick and Eli Finkel (2008a, 2008b), men more than women presumed the importance of a potential date's physical attractiveness; but in reality, a prospect's attractiveness was similarly important to both men and women.

Looks even influence voting, or so it seems from a study by Alexander Todorov and colleagues (2005). They showed Princeton University students photographs of the two major candidates in 95 U.S. Senate races since 2000 and in 600 U.S. House of Representatives races. Based on looks alone, the students (by preferring competent-looking over more baby-faced candidates) correctly guessed the winners of 72 percent of the Senate and 67 percent of the House races. In a follow-up study Joan Chiao and her co-researchers (2008) confirmed the finding that voters prefer competent-looking candidates. But gender also mattered: Men were more likely to vote for physically attractive female candidates, and women were more likely to vote for approachable-looking male candidates.

THE MATCHING PHENOMENON

Not everyone can end up paired with someone stunningly attractive. So how do people pair off? Judging from research by Bernard Murstein (1986) and others, they get real. They pair off with people who are about as attractive as they are. Several studies have found a strong correspondence between the rated attractiveness of husbands and wives, of dating partners, and even of those within particular fraternities (Feingold, 1988; Montoya, 2008). People tend to select as friends, and especially to marry, those who are a "good match" not only to their level of intelligence but also to their level of attractiveness.

Experiments confirm this **matching phenomenon.** When choosing whom to approach, knowing the other is free to say yes or no, people often approach someone whose attractiveness roughly matches (or not too greatly exceeds) their own (Berscheid & others, 1971; Huston, 1973; Stroebe & others, 1971). They seek out someone who seems desirable, but are mindful of the limits of their own desirability. Good physical matches may be conducive to good relationships, reported Gregory White (1980) from a study of UCLA dating couples. Those who were most similar in physical attractiveness were most likely, nine months later, to have fallen more deeply in love.

Perhaps this research prompts you to think of happy couples who differ in perceived "hotness." In such cases, the less attractive person often has compensating qualities. Each partner brings assets to the social marketplace, and the value of the respective assets creates an equitable match. Personal advertisements and self-presentations to online dating services exhibit this exchange of assets (Cicerello &

> "If you would marry wisely, marry your equal."
>
> —OVID, 43 B.C.–A.D. 17

matching phenomenon
The tendency for men and women to choose as partners those who are a "good match" in attractiveness and other traits.

DILBERT © Scott Adams/Distributed by United Features Syndicate, Inc.

Asset matching. High-status Rolling Stones guitarist Keith Richards has been married to supermodel Patti Hansen, 19 years his junior, since 1983.

Sheehan, 1995; Hitsch & others, 2006; Koestner & Wheeler, 1988; Rajecki & others, 1991). Men typically offer wealth or status and seek youth and attractiveness; women more often do the reverse: "Attractive, bright woman, 26, slender, seeks warm, professional male." Men who advertise their income and education, and women who advertise their youth and looks, receive more responses to their ads (Baize & Schroeder, 1995). The asset-matching process helps explain why beautiful young women often marry older men of higher social status (Elder, 1969; Kanazawa & Kovar, 2004).

Of course, given the combination of self-serving bias (Chapter 2), repeated exposure to one's own face, and strategic self-presentation, we can expect most people to report positive self-images. And so it was for participants in one study of some 22,000 people who completed self-descriptions for one online dating service (Hitsch & others, 2006). Sixty-seven percent of men and 72 percent of women rated themselves as having "above average" or "very good" looks. Only 1 percent estimated their looks as "less than average." Nearly all the rest said they looked "like anyone else walking down the street."

"Love is often nothing but a favorable exchange between two people who get the most of what they can expect, considering their value on the personality market."
—*ERICH FROMM*, THE SANE SOCIETY, *1955*

THE PHYSICAL-ATTRACTIVENESS STEREOTYPE

Does the attractiveness effect spring entirely from sexual attractiveness? Clearly not, as Vicky Houston and Ray Bull (1994) discovered when they used a makeup artist to give an otherwise attractive accomplice an apparently scarred, bruised, or birthmarked face. When riding on a Glasgow commuter rail line, people of both sexes avoided sitting next to the accomplice when she appeared facially disfigured. Moreover, much as adults are biased toward attractive adults, young children are biased toward attractive children (Dion, 1973; Dion & Berscheid, 1974; Langlois & others, 2000). To judge from how long they gaze at someone, even 3-month-old infants prefer attractive faces (Langlois & others, 1987).

Adults show a similar bias when judging children. Margaret Clifford and Elaine Hatfield (Clifford & Walster, 1973) gave Missouri fifth-grade teachers identical information about a boy or a girl, but with the photograph of an attractive or an unattractive child attached. The teachers perceived the attractive child as more intelligent and successful in school. Think of yourself as a playground supervisor having to discipline an unruly child. Might you, like the women studied by Karen Dion (1972), show less warmth and tact to an unattractive child? The sad truth is that most of us assume what we might call a "Bart Simpson effect"—that homely children are less able and socially competent than their beautiful peers.

What is more, we assume that beautiful people possess certain desirable traits. Other things being equal, we guess beautiful people are happier, sexually warmer, and more outgoing, intelligent, and successful—though not more honest or concerned for others (Eagly & others, 1991; Feingold, 1992b; Jackson & others, 1995).

physical-attractiveness stereotype

The presumption that physically attractive people possess other socially desirable traits as well: What is beautiful is good.

Added together, the findings define a **physical-attractiveness stereotype:** What is beautiful is good. Children learn the stereotype quite early—and one of the ways they learn it is through stories told to them by adults. Snow White and Cinderella are beautiful—and kind. The witch and the stepsisters are ugly—and wicked. "If you want to be loved by somebody who isn't already in your family, it doesn't hurt to be beautiful," surmised one 8-year-old girl. Or as one kindergarten girl put it when asked what it means to be pretty, "It's like to be a princess. Everybody loves you" (Dion, 1979). Think of the public's widespread admiration of Princess Diana and criticism of Prince Charles's second wife, the former Camilla Parker-Bowles.

If physical attractiveness is that important, then permanently changing people's attractiveness should change the way others react to them. But is it ethical to alter someone's looks? Such manipulations are performed millions of times a year by cosmetic surgeons and orthodontists. With teeth straightened and whitened, hair replaced and dyed, face lifted, fat liposuctioned, and breasts enlarged, lifted, or reduced, most self-dissatisfied people do express satisfaction with the results of their procedures, though some unhappy patients seek out repeat procedures (Honigman & others, 2004).

"Even virtue is fairer in a fair body."

—VIRGIL, AENEID, 1ST CENTURY B.C.

To examine the effect of such alterations on others, Michael Kalick (1977) had Harvard students rate their impressions of eight women based on profile photographs taken before or after cosmetic surgery. Not only did they judge the women as more physically attractive after the surgery but also as kinder, more sensitive, more sexually warm and responsive, more likable, and so on.

FIRST IMPRESSIONS   To say that attractiveness is important, other things being equal, is not to say that physical appearance always outranks other qualities. Some people more than others judge people by their looks (Livingston, 2001). Moreover, attractiveness most affects first impressions. But first impressions are important—and have become more so as societies become increasingly mobile and urbanized and as contacts with people become more fleeting (Berscheid, 1981). Your Facebook self-presentation starts with . . . your face.

Though interviewers may deny it, attractiveness and grooming affect first impressions in job interviews (Cash & Janda, 1984; Mack & Rainey, 1990; Marvelle & Green, 1980). People rate new products more favorably when they are associated with attractive inventors (Baron & others, 2006). Such impressions help explain why attractive people and tall people have more prestigious jobs and make more money (Engemann & Owyang, 2003; Persico & others, 2004).

Patricia Roszell and her colleagues (1990) looked at the incomes of a national sample of Canadians whom interviewers had rated on a 1 (homely)-to-5 (strikingly attractive) scale. They found that for each additional scale unit of rated attractiveness, people earned, on average, an additional $1,988 annually. Irene Hanson Frieze and her associates (1991) did the same analysis with 737 MBA graduates after rating them on a similar 1-to-5 scale using student yearbook photos. For each additional scale unit of rated attractiveness, men earned an added $2,600 and women earned an added $2,150.

The speed with which first impressions form, and their influence on thinking, helps explain why pretty prospers. Even a .013 second exposure—too brief to discern a face—is enough to enable people to guess a face's attractiveness (Olson & Marshuetz, 2005). Moreover, when categorizing subsequent words as either good or bad, an attractive face predisposes people to categorize good words faster. Pretty is perceived promptly and primes positive processing.

THE inside STORY

I vividly remember the afternoon I began to appreciate the far-reaching implications of physical attractiveness. Graduate student Karen Dion (now a professor at the University of Toronto) learned that some researchers at our Institute of Child Development had collected popularity ratings from nursery school children and taken a photo of each child. Although teachers and caregivers of children had persuaded us that "all children are beautiful" and no physical-attractiveness discriminations could be made, Dion suggested we instruct some people to rate each child's looks and that we correlate these with popularity. After doing so, we realized our long shot had hit home: Attractive children were popular children. Indeed, the effect was far more potent than we and others had assumed, with a host of implications that investigators are still tracing.

Ellen Berscheid,
University of Minnesota

IS THE "BEAUTIFUL IS GOOD" STEREOTYPE ACCURATE?

Do beautiful people indeed have desirable traits? For centuries, those who considered themselves serious scientists thought so when they sought to identify physical traits (shifty eyes, a weak chin) that would predict criminal behavior. Or, on the other hand, was Leo Tolstoy correct when he wrote that it's "a strange illusion . . . to suppose that beauty is goodness"? There is some truth to the stereotype. Attractive children and young adults are somewhat more relaxed, outgoing, and socially polished (Feingold, 1992b; Langlois & others, 2000). William Goldman and Philip Lewis (1977) demonstrated this by having 60 University of Georgia men call and talk for five minutes with each of three women students. Afterward the men and women rated the most attractive of their unseen telephone partners as somewhat more socially skillful and likable. Physically attractive individuals tend also to be more popular, more outgoing, and more gender typed—more traditionally masculine if male, more feminine if female (Langlois & others, 1996).

These small average differences between attractive and unattractive people probably result from self-fulfilling prophecies. Attractive people are valued and favored, so many develop more social self-confidence. (Recall from Chapter 2 an experiment in which men evoked a warm response from unseen women they *thought* were attractive.) By that analysis, what's crucial to your social skill is not how you look but how people treat you and how you feel about yourself—whether you accept yourself, like yourself, and feel comfortable with yourself.

WHO IS ATTRACTIVE?

I have described attractiveness as if it were an objective quality like height, which some people have more of, some less. Strictly speaking, attractiveness is whatever the people of any given place and time find attractive. This, of course, varies. The beauty standards by which Miss Universe is judged hardly apply even to the whole planet. People in various places and times have pierced noses, lengthened necks, dyed hair, whitened teeth, painted skin, gorged themselves to become voluptuous, starved to become thin, and bound themselves with leather corsets to make their breasts seem small—or used silicone and padded bras to make them seem big. For cultures with scarce resources and for poor or hungry people, plumpness seems attractive; for cultures and individuals with abundant resources, beauty more often

Standards of beauty differ from culture to culture. Yet some people are considered attractive throughout most of the world.

equals slimness (Nelson & Morrison, 2005). Moreover, attractiveness influences life outcomes less in cultures where relationships are based more on kinship or social arrangement than on personal choice (Anderson & others, 2008). Despite such variations, there remains "strong agreement both within and across cultures about who is and who is not attractive," note Judith Langlois and her colleagues (2000).

In 2007, U.S. plastic surgeons performed nearly 12 million cosmetic procedures, 91 percent of which were on women (surgery.org, 2008).

To be really attractive is, ironically, to be perfectly average (Rhodes, 2006). Research teams led by Langlois and Lorri Roggman (1990, 1994) at the University of Texas and Anthony Little and David Perrett (2002), working with Ian Penton-Voak at the University of St. Andrews, have digitized multiple faces and averaged them using a computer. Inevitably, people find the composite faces more appealing than almost all the actual faces (Figure 11.4). As this suggests, attractive faces are also perceived as more alike than unattractive faces (Potter & others, 2006). There are more ways to be homely than beautiful. With both humans and animals, averaged looks best embody prototypes (for your typical man, woman, dog, or whatever), and thus are easy for the brain to process and categorize, notes Jamin Halberstadt (2006). Perfectly average is easy on the eyes (and brain).

Computer-averaged faces and bodies also tend to be perfectly symmetrical—another characteristic of strikingly attractive (and reproductively successful) people (Brown & others, 2008; Gangestad & Thornhill, 1997). Research teams led by Gillian Rhodes (1999, 2006) and by Ian Penton-Voak (2001) have shown that if you could merge either half of your face with its mirror image—thus forming a perfectly symmetrical new face—you would boost your looks. Averaging a number of such attractive, symmetrical faces produces an even better looking face.

EVOLUTION AND ATTRACTION   Psychologists working from the evolutionary perspective explain the human preference for attractive partners in terms of reproductive strategy (Chapter 5). They assume that beauty signals biologically important information: health, youth, and fertility. Over time, men who preferred fertile-looking women outreproduced those who were as happy to mate with postmenopausal females. That, David Buss (1989) believes, explains why the males he studied in 37 cultures—from Australia to Zambia—did indeed prefer youthful female characteristics that signify reproductive capacity.

"Power is the greatest aphrodisiac."
—HENRY KISSINGER, 1971

Evolutionary psychologists also assume that evolution predisposes women to favor male traits that signify an ability to provide and protect resources. No wonder physically attractive females tend to marry high-status males, and men compete with such determination to display status by achieving fame and fortune. In

FIGURE :: 11.4

Who's the Fairest of Them All?

Each year's selection of "Miss Germany" provides one country's answer. A University of Regensburg student research team, working with a German television channel, offered an alternative. Christof Braun and his compatriots (Gruendl, 2005) photographed the twenty-two 2002 "Queen of Beauty" finalists, without makeup and with hair tied back, and then created a "Virtual Miss Germany" that was the blended composite of them all. When adults in a local shopping mall were shown the finalists and the Virtual Miss Germany, they easily rated Virtual Miss Germany as the most attractive of them all. Although the winning real Miss Germany may have been disappointed by the news that everyone preferred her virtual competitor to herself, she can reassure herself that she will never meet her virtual competitor.

screening potential mates, report Norman Li and his fellow researchers (2002), men require a modicum of physical attractiveness, women require status and resources, and both welcome kindness and intelligence.

Evolutionary psychologists have also explored men's and women's response to other cues to reproductive success. Judging from glamor models and beauty pageant winners, men everywhere have felt most attracted to women whose waists are 30 percent narrower than their hips—a shape associated with peak sexual fertility (Singh, 1993, 1995; Singh & Randall, 2007; Streeter & McBurney, 2003). Circumstances that reduce a woman's fertility—malnutrition, pregnancy, menopause—also change her shape.

When judging males as potential marriage partners, women, too, prefer a male waist-to-hip ratio suggesting health and vigor. They rate muscular men as sexier, and muscular men do feel sexier and report more lifetime sex partners (Frederick & Haselton, 2007). This makes evolutionary sense, notes Jared Diamond (1996): A muscular hunk was more likely than a scrawny fellow to gather food, build houses, and defeat rivals. But today's women prefer men with high incomes even more (Singh, 1995).

During ovulation, women show heightened preference for men with masculinized features (Gangestad & others, 2004; Macrae & others, 2002). One study found that, when ovulating, young women tend to wear and prefer more revealing outfits than when infertile (Figure 11.5). In another study, ovulating lap dancers averaged $70 in tips per hour—double the $35 of those who were menstruating (Miller & others, 2007).

So, in every culture the beauty business is a big and growing business. Asians, Britons, Germans, and Americans are all seeking cosmetic surgery in rapidly increasing numbers (Wall, 2002). Beverly Hills now has twice as many plastic surgeons as pediatricians (*People*, 2003). Modern, affluent people with cracked or discolored teeth fix them. More and more, so do people with wrinkles and flab.

We are, evolutionary psychologists suggest, driven by primal attractions. Like eating and breathing, attraction and mating are too important to leave to the whims of culture.

SOCIAL COMPARISON   Although our mating psychology has biological wisdom, attraction is not all hardwired. What's attractive to you also depends on your comparison standards.

"Women in the '50s vacuumed. Women in the '00s *are* vacuumed. Our Hoovers have turned on us!"
—NEW YORK TIMES COLUMNIST MAUREEN DOWD ON LIPOSUCTION (JANUARY 19, 2000)

FIGURE :: 11.5

Fertility and Dress

In a University of Texas study by Kristina Durante and her colleagues (2008), sexually uninhibited women tended to wear more revealing clothes on high-fertility days of their cycle and to imagine (through sketches on a paper doll) wearing more revealing outfits to a party. Shown here are examples of an outfit drawn by the same participant at low fertility (at left) and high fertility (at right).

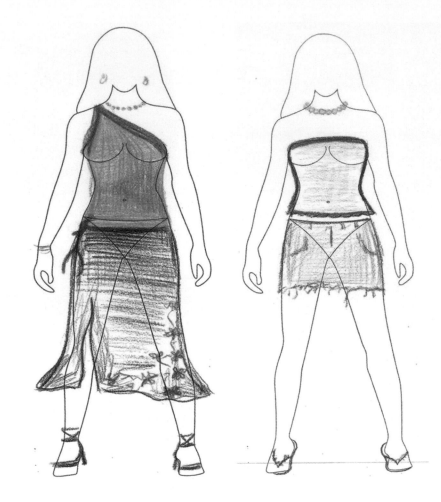

Extreme makeover (as illustrated by these before (1997) and after (2005) photos of actress/comedian Kathy Griffin). If you imperfectly meet your culture's beauty standard, you can accept yourself, imperfections and all. Or you can paralyze wrinkle-causing muscles, suck away fat, and reshape your nose with a makeover. Question: Where would you draw the line between appropriate self-improvement and self-indulgent vanity? To what extent should we accept ourselves rather than change our (unacceptable) selves? Would you support shaping up by losing weight? acne treatments? braces to align crooked teeth? a chin tuck? a nose job? breast enlargement? an extreme makeover?

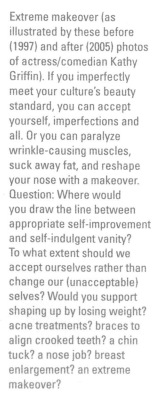

MAXINE by Marian Henley

Douglas Kenrick and Sara Gutierres (1980) had male confederates interrupt Montana State University men in their dormitory rooms and explain, "We have a friend coming to town this week and we want to fix him up with a date, but we can't decide whether to fix him up with her or not, so we decided to conduct a survey.... We want you to give us your vote on how attractive you think she is ... on a scale of 1 to 7." Shown a picture of an average young woman, those who had just been watching *Charlie's Angels* (a television show featuring three beautiful women) rated her less attractive than those who hadn't.

Laboratory experiments confirm this "contrast effect." To men who have recently been gazing at centerfolds, average women or even their own wives tend to seem less attractive (Kenrick & others, 1989). Viewing pornographic films simulating passionate sex similarly decreases satisfaction with one's own partner (Zillmann, 1989). Being sexually aroused may *temporarily* make a person of the other sex seem more attractive. But the lingering effect of exposure to perfect "10s," or of unrealistic sexual depictions, is to make one's own partner seem less appealing—more like a "6" than an "8."

It works the same way with our self-perceptions. After viewing a superattractive person of the same gender, people rate themselves as being *less* attractive than after viewing a homely person (Brown & others, 1992; Thornton & Maurice, 1997). This appears especially true for women. A man's viewing sculpted muscular male bodies in men's magazines can heighten a feeling of inadequacy (Aubrey & Taylor, 2009). But the social comparison effect appears greatest for women. Seeing other fit and attractive women tends to diminish satisfaction with one's own body, and being dissatisfied with one's body makes one especially sensitive to and deflated by exposure to super-attractive women (Trampe & others, 2007).

Men's self-rated desirability is also deflated by exposure to more dominant, successful men. Thanks to modern media, we may see in an hour "dozens of individuals who are more attractive and more successful than any of our ancestors would have seen in a year, or even a lifetime," note Sara Gutierres and her co-researchers (1999). Such extraordinary comparison standards trick us into devaluing our potential mates and ourselves and spending billions on cosmetics, diet aids, and plastic surgery. But even after another 12 million annual cosmetic procedures, there may be no net gain in human satisfaction. If others get their teeth straightened, capped, and whitened and you don't, the social comparison may leave you more dissatisfied with your normal, natural teeth than you would have been if you were surrounded by peers whose teeth were also natural.

THE ATTRACTIVENESS OF THOSE WE LOVE   Let's conclude our discussion of attractiveness on an upbeat note. First, a 17-year-old girl's facial attractiveness is a surprisingly weak predictor of her attractiveness at ages 30 and 50. Sometimes

"Love is only a dirty trick played on us to achieve a continuation of the species."
—*NOVELIST W. SOMERSET MAUGHAM, 1874–1965*

"Do I love you because you are beautiful, or are you beautiful because I love you?"
—*PRINCE CHARMING, IN RODGERS & HAMMERSTEIN'S CINDERELLA*

Bizarro by Dan Piraro

ANNOUNCING an INCREDIBLE ALTERNATIVE to COSMETIC SURGERY!!
MORE PERMANENT! LESS EXPENSIVE & PAINFUL!

BEFORE   AFTER

FOR INFORMATION, CALL *The American Psychological Assoc.*

Warm and likable people seem more attractive.

BIZZARO (New) © Dan Piraro, King Features Syndicate.

an average-looking adolescent, especially one with a warm, attractive personality, becomes a quite attractive middle-aged adult (Zebrowitz & others, 1993, 1998).

Second, not only do we perceive attractive people as likable, we also perceive likable people as attractive. Perhaps you can recall individuals who, as you grew to like them, became more attractive. Their physical imperfections were no longer so noticeable. Alan Gross and Christine Crofton (1977; see also Lewandowski & others, 2007) had students view someone's photograph after reading a favorable or an unfavorable description of the person's personality. Those portrayed as warm, helpful, and considerate also *looked* more attractive. It may be true, then, that "handsome is as handsome does." Discovering someone's similarities to us also makes the person seem more attractive (Beaman & Klentz, 1983; Klentz & others, 1987).

Moreover, love sees loveliness: The more in love a woman is with a man, the more physically attractive she finds him (Price & others, 1974). And the more in love people are, the less attractive they find all others of the opposite sex (Johnson & Rusbult, 1989; Simpson & others, 1990). "The grass may be greener on the other side," note Rowland Miller and Jeffry Simpson (1990), "but happy gardeners are less likely to notice." Beauty really *is*, to some extent, in the eye of the beholder.

Similarity versus Complementarity

From our discussion so far, one might surmise Leo Tolstoy was entirely correct: "Love depends . . . on frequent meetings, and on the style in which the hair is done up, and on the color and cut of the dress." As people get to know one another, however, other factors influence whether acquaintance develops into friendship.

DO BIRDS OF A FEATHER FLOCK TOGETHER?

"Can two walk together except they be agreed?"

—AMOS 3:3

Of this much we may be sure: Birds that flock together are of a feather. Friends, engaged couples, and spouses are far more likely than randomly paired people to share common attitudes, beliefs, and values. Furthermore, the greater the similarity between husband and wife, the happier they are and the less likely they are to divorce (Byrne, 1971; Caspi & Herbener, 1990). Such correlational findings are intriguing. But cause and effect remain an enigma. Does similarity lead to liking? Or does liking lead to similarity?

LIKENESS BEGETS LIKING To discern cause and effect, we experiment. Imagine that at a campus party Lakesha gets involved in a long discussion of politics, religion, and personal likes and dislikes with Les and Lon. She and Les discover

Henry James's description of novelist George Eliot (the pen name of Mary Ann Evans): "She is magnificently ugly—deliciously hideous. She has a low forehead, a dull grey eye, a vast pendulous nose, a huge mouth, full of uneven teeth, and a chin and jawbone qui n'en finissent pas. . . . Now in this vast ugliness resides a most powerful beauty which, in a very few minutes, steals forth and charms the mind, so that you end as I ended, in falling in love with her."

they agree on almost everything, she and Lon on few things. Afterward, she reflects: "Les is really intelligent . . . and so likable. I hope we meet again." In experiments, Donn Byrne (1971) and his colleagues captured the essence of Lakesha's experience. Over and over again, they found that the more similar someone's attitudes are to your own, the more likable you will find the person. Likeness produces liking not only for college students but also for children and the elderly, for people of various occupations, and for those in various cultures. When others think as we do, we not only appreciate their attitudes but also make positive inferences about their character (Montoya & Horton, 2004).

The likeness-leads-to-liking effect has been tested in real-life situations by noting who comes to like whom.

- At the University of Michigan, Theodore Newcomb (1961) studied two groups of 17 unacquainted male transfer students. After 13 weeks of boardinghouse life, those whose agreement was initially highest were most likely to have formed close friendships. One group of friends was composed of 5 liberal arts students, each a political liberal with strong intellectual interests. Another was made up of 3 conservative veterans who were all enrolled in the engineering college.

- At two of Hong Kong's universities, Royce Lee and Michael Bond (1996) found that roommate friendships flourished over a six-month period when roommates shared values and personality traits, but more so when they perceived their roommates as similar. As so often happens, reality matters, but perception matters more.

- People like not only those who think as they do but also those who act as they do. Subtle mimicry fosters fondness. Have you noticed that when someone nods their head as you do and echoes your thoughts, you feel a certain rapport and liking? That's a common experience, report Rick van Baaren and his colleagues (2003a, 2003b), and one result is higher tips for Dutch restaurant servers who mimic their customers by merely repeating their order. Natural mimicry increases rapport, note Jessica Lakin and Tanya Chartrand (2003), and desire for rapport increases mimicry.

- When Peter Buston and Stephen Emlen (2003) surveyed nearly 1,000 college-age people, they found that the desire for similar mates far outweighed the desire for beautiful mates. Attractive people sought attractive mates. Wealthy people wanted mates with money. Family-oriented people desired family-oriented mates.

- Studies of newlyweds reveal that similar attitudes, traits, and values help bring couples together and predict their satisfaction (Gaunt, 2006; Gonzaga & others, 2007; Luo & Klohnen, 2005). That is the basis of one psychologist-founded Internet dating site, which claims to match singles using the similarities that mark happy couples (Carter & Snow, 2004; Warren, 2005).

"Actually, Lou, I think it was more than just my being in the right place at the right time. I think it was my being the right race, the right religion, the right sex, the right socioeconomic group, having the right accent, the right clothes, going to the right schools . . ."

The most appealing people are those most like us.

"And they are friends who have come to regard the same things as good and the same things as evil, they who are friends of the same people, and they who are the enemies of the same people. . . . We like those who resemble us, and are engaged in the same pursuits."

—*ARISTOTLE, RHETORIC, 4TH CENTURY B.C.*

So similarity breeds content. Birds of a feather *do* flock together. Surely you have noticed this upon discovering a special someone who shares your ideas, values, and desires, a soul mate who likes the same music, the same activities, even the same foods you do.

DISSIMILARITY BREEDS DISLIKE   We have a bias—the false consensus bias—toward assuming that others share our attitudes. Getting to know someone—and discovering that the person is actually dissimilar—tends to decrease liking (Norton & others, 2007). If those dissimilar attitudes pertain to our strong moral convictions, we dislike and distance ourselves from them all the more (Skitka & others, 2005). People in one political party often are not so much fond of fellow party members as they are disdainful of the opposition (Hoyle, 1993; Rosenbaum, 1986). Straight men often disdain gay men, who are doubly dissimilar to themselves—in perceived gender traits and sexuality (Lehavot & Lambert, 2007).

In general, dissimilar attitudes depress liking more than similar attitudes enhance it (Singh & Ho, 2000; Singh & Teob, 1999). Within their own groups, where they expect similarity, people find it especially hard to like someone with dissimilar

"We've learned so much from each other that you remind me of me."

views (Chen & Kenrick, 2002). That perhaps explains why dating partners and roommates become more similar over time in their emotional responses to events and in their attitudes (Anderson & others, 2003; Davis & Rusbult, 2001). "Attitude alignment" helps promote and sustain close relationships, a phenomenon that can lead partners to overestimate their attitude similarities (Kenny & Acitelli, 2001; Murray & others, 2002).

Whether people perceive those of another race as similar or dissimilar influences their racial attitudes. Wherever one group of people regards another as "other"—as creatures who speak differently, live differently, think differently—the potential for conflict is high. In fact, except for intimate relationships such as dating, the perception of like minds seems more important for attraction than like skins. Most Whites have expressed more liking for, and willingness to work with, a like-minded Black than a dissimilarly minded White (Insko & others, 1983; Rokeach, 1968). The more that Whites presume that Blacks support their values, the more positive their racial attitudes (Biernat & others, 1996).

"Cultural racism" persists, argues social psychologist James Jones (1988, 2003, 2004), because cultural differences are a fact of life. Black culture tends to be present-oriented, spontaneously expressive, spiritual, and emotionally driven. White culture tends to be more future-oriented, materialistic, and achievement-driven. Rather than trying to eliminate such differences, says Jones, we might better appreciate what they "contribute to the cultural fabric of a multicultural society." There are situations in which expressiveness is advantageous and situations in which future orientation is advantageous. Each culture has much to learn from the other. In countries such as Canada, Britain, and the United States, where migration and differing birthrates make for growing diversity, educating people to respect and enjoy those who differ is a major challenge. Given increasing cultural diversity and given our natural wariness of differences, this may in fact be the major social challenge of our time. (See "The Inside Story: James Jones on Cultural Diversity.")

THE inside STORY

James Jones on Cultural Diversity

As a Yale graduate student I was invited to write a book on prejudice. Wanting to take readers past the individual blame aspect of prejudice, I entitled the volume *Prejudice and Racism* and explained how race problems are embedded in society. Prejudice is ultimately not a race problem but a culture problem. European- and African-heritage cultures differ, and their differences are the soil from which springs cultural racism—the intolerance of those whose culture differs. In today's world of ethnic mixing, we must learn to accept our cultural diversity even as we seek unifying ideals.

James Jones,
University of Delaware

DO OPPOSITES ATTRACT?

Are we not also attracted to people who in some ways *differ* from ourselves, in ways that complement our own characteristics? We are attracted to people whose scent suggests dissimilar enough genes to prevent inbreeding and offspring with weakened immune systems (Garver-Apgar & others, 2006). But what about attitudes and behavioral traits? Researchers have explored that question by comparing not only friends' and spouses' attitudes and beliefs but also their ages, religions, races, smoking behaviors, economic levels, educations, height, intelligence, and appearance. In all these ways and more, similarity still prevails (Buss, 1985; Kandel, 1978). Smart birds flock together. So do rich birds, Protestant birds, tall birds, pretty birds.

Still we resist: Are we not attracted to people whose needs and personalities complement our own? Would a sadist and a masochist find true love? Even the *Reader's Digest* has told us that "opposites attract. . . . Socializers pair with loners, novelty-lovers with those who dislike change, free spenders with scrimpers, risk-takers with the very cautious" (Jacoby, 1986). Sociologist Robert Winch (1958) reasoned that the needs of an outgoing and domineering person would naturally complement those of someone who is shy and submissive. The logic seems compelling, and most of us can think of couples who view their differences as complementary: "My husband and I are perfect for each other. I'm Aquarius—a decisive person. He's Libra—can't make decisions. But he's always happy to go along with arrangements I make."

Given the idea's persuasiveness, the inability of researchers to confirm it is astonishing. For example, most people feel attracted to expressive, outgoing people (Friedman & others, 1988). Would this be especially so when one is down in the dumps? Do depressed people seek those whose gaiety will cheer them up? To the contrary, it is nondepressed people who most prefer the company of happy people (Locke & Horowitz, 1990; Rosenblatt & Greenberg, 1988, 1991; Wenzlaff & Prohaska, 1989). When you're feeling blue, another's bubbly personality can be aggravating. The contrast effect that makes average people feel homely in the company of beautiful people also makes sad people more conscious of their misery in the company of cheerful people.

Some **complementarity** may evolve as a relationship progresses (even a relationship between identical twins). Yet people seem slightly more prone to like and to marry those whose needs and personalities are *similar* (Botwin & others, 1997; Buss, 1984; Fishbein & Thelen, 1981a, 1981b; Nias, 1979). Perhaps one day we will discover some ways (other than heterosexuality) in which differences commonly breed liking. Dominance/submissiveness may be one such way (Dryer & Horowitz, 1997; Markey & Kurtz, 2006). And we tend not to feel attracted to those who show our own worst traits (Schimel & others, 2000). But researcher David Buss (1985) doubts complementarity: "The tendency of opposites to marry, or mate . . . has never been reliably demonstrated, with the single exception of sex."

complementarity
The popularly supposed tendency, in a relationship between two people, for each to complete what is missing in the other.

Liking Those Who Like Us

Liking is usually mutual. Proximity and attractiveness influence our initial attraction to someone, and similarity influences longer-term attraction as well. If we have a deep need to belong and to feel liked and accepted, would we not also take a liking to those who like us? Are the best friendships mutual admiration societies? Indeed, one person's liking for another does predict the other's liking in return (Kenny & Nasby, 1980; Montoya & Insko, 2008).

But does one person's liking another *cause* the other to return the appreciation? People's reports of how they fell in love suggest so (Aron & others, 1989). Discovering that an appealing someone really likes you seems to awaken romantic feelings. Experiments confirm it: Those told that certain others like or admire them usually feel a reciprocal affection (Berscheid & Walster, 1978). And all the better, one speed dating experiment suggests, when someone likes you especially, more than others (Eastwick & others, 2007).

"The average man is more interested in a woman who is interested in him than he is in a woman with beautiful legs."
—*ACTRESS MARLENE DIETRICH (1901–1992)*

focus ON

Bad Is Stronger Than Good

Dissimilar attitudes, we have noted, turn us off to others more than similar attitudes turn us on. And others' criticism captures our attention and affects our emotions more than does their praise. Roy Baumeister, Ellen Bratslavsky, Catrin Finkenauer, and Kathleen Vohs (2001) say this is just the tip of an iceberg: "In everyday life, bad events have stronger and more lasting consequences than comparable good events." Consider:

- Destructive acts harm close relationships more than constructive acts build them. (Cruel words linger after kind ones have been forgotten.)

- Bad moods affect our thinking and memory more than do good moods. (Despite our natural optimism, it's easier to recall past bad emotional events than good ones.)

- There are more words for negative than positive emotions, and people asked to think of emotion words mostly come up with negative words. (*Sadness, anger,* and *fear* are the three most common.)

- Single bad events (traumas) have more lasting effects than single very good events. (A death triggers more search for meaning than does a birth.)

- Routine bad events receive more attention and trigger more rumination than do routine good events. (Losing money upsets people more than gaining the same amount of money makes them happy.)

- Very bad family environments override the genetic influence on intelligence more than do very good family environments. (Bad parents can make their genetically bright children less intelligent; good parents are less able to make their unintelligent children smarter.)

- A bad reputation is easier to acquire, and harder to shed, than a good one. (A single act of lying can destroy one's reputation for integrity.)

- Poor health decreases happiness more than good health increases it. (Pain produces misery far more than comfort produces joy.)

The power of the bad prepares us to deal with threats and protects us from death and disability. For survival, bad can be badder than good is good. The importance of the bad is one likely reason why the first century of psychology focused so much more on the bad than on the good. From its start until 2009, Psyc INFO (a guide to psychology's literature) had, at my last count, 15,818 articles mentioning anger, 98,268 mentioning anxiety, and 127,876 mentioning depression. There were 17 articles on these topics for every 1 dealing with the positive emotions of joy (1,950), life satisfaction (6,664), or happiness (6,401). Similarly, "fear" (32,686 articles) has triumphed over "courage" (1,623). The strength of the bad is "perhaps the best reason for a positive psychology movement," Baumeister and his colleagues surmise. To overcome the strength of individual bad events, "human life needs far more good than bad."

"Well—and I'm not just saying this because you're my husband—it stinks."

And consider this finding by Ellen Berscheid and her colleagues (1969): Students like another student who says eight positive things about them better than one who says seven positive things and one negative thing. We are sensitive to the slightest hint of criticism. Writer Larry L. King speaks for many in noting, "I have discovered over the years that good reviews strangely fail to make the author feel as good as bad reviews make him feel bad."

Whether we are judging ourselves or others, negative information carries more weight because, being less usual, it grabs more attention (Yzerbyt & Leyens, 1991). People's votes are more influenced by their impressions of presidential candidates' weaknesses than by their impressions of strengths (Klein, 1991), a phenomenon that has not been lost on those who design negative campaigns. It's a general rule of life, note Roy Baumeister and his colleagues (2001): Bad is stronger than good. (See "Focus On: Bad Is Stronger Than Good.")

Our liking for those we perceive as liking us was recognized long ago. Observers from the ancient philosopher Hecato ("If you wish to be loved, love") to Ralph Waldo Emerson ("The only way to have a friend is to be one") to Dale Carnegie ("Dole out praise lavishly") anticipated the findings. What they did not anticipate was the precise conditions under which the principle works.

ATTRIBUTION

As we've seen, flattery *will* get you somewhere. But not everywhere. If praise clearly violates what we know is true—if someone says, "Your hair looks great," when we haven't washed it in three days—we may lose respect for the flatterer and wonder whether the compliment springs from ulterior motives (Shrauger, 1975). Thus, we often perceive criticism to be more sincere than praise (Coleman & others, 1987). In fact, when someone prefaces a statement with "To be honest," we know we are about to hear a criticism.

Laboratory experiments reveal something we've noted in previous chapters: Our reactions depend on our attributions. Do we attribute the flattery to **ingratiation**—to a self-serving strategy? Is the person trying to get us to buy something, to acquiesce sexually, to do a favor? If so, both the flatterer and the praise lose appeal (Gordon, 1996; Jones, 1964). But if there is no apparent ulterior motive, then we warmly receive both flattery and flatterer.

ingratiation
The use of strategies, such as flattery, by which people seek to gain another's favor.

"If 60,000 people tell me they loved a show, then one walks past and says it sucked, that's the comment I'll hear."
—*MUSICIAN DAVE MATTHEWS, 2000*

SELF-ESTEEM AND ATTRACTION

Elaine Hatfield (Walster, 1965) wondered if another's approval is especially rewarding after we have been deprived of approval, much as eating is most rewarding when we're hungry. To test that idea, she gave some Stanford University women either very favorable or very unfavorable analyses of their personalities, affirming some and wounding others. Then she asked them to evaluate several people, including an attractive male confederate who just before the experiment had struck up a warm conversation with each woman and had asked each for a date. (Not one turned him down.) Which women do you suppose most liked the man? It was those whose self-esteem had been temporarily shattered and who were presumably hungry for social approval. (After this experiment Hatfield spent almost an hour talking with each woman and explaining the experiment. She reports that, in the end, none remained disturbed by the temporary ego blow or the broken date.)

This helps explain why people sometimes fall passionately in love on the rebound, after an ego-bruising rejection. Unfortunately, however, low-self-esteem individuals tend to underestimate how much their partner appreciates them. They also have less generous views of their partner and therefore feel less happy with the relationship (Murray & others, 2000). If you feel down about yourself, you will likely feel pessimistic about your relationships. Feel good about yourself and you're more likely to feel confident of your dating partner's or spouse's regard.

GAINING ANOTHER'S ESTEEM

If approval that comes after disapproval is powerfully rewarding, then would we most like someone who liked us after initially disliking us? Or would we most like someone who liked us from the start (and therefore gave us more total approval)? Ray is in a small discussion class with his roommate's cousin, Sophia. After the first week of classes, Ray learns via his "pipeline" that Sophia thinks him rather shallow. As the semester progresses, he learns that Sophia's opinion of him is steadily rising; gradually she comes to view him as bright, thoughtful, and charming. Would Ray like Sophia more if she had thought well of him from the beginning? If Ray is simply counting the number of approving comments he receives, then the answer will be yes. But if, after her initial disapproval, Sophia's rewards become more potent, Ray then might like her better than if she had been consistently affirming.

To see which is more often true, Elliot Aronson and Darwyn Linder (1965) captured the essence of Ray's experience in a clever experiment. They "allowed"

"Hatred which is entirely conquered by love passes into love, and love on that account is greater than if it had not been preceded by hatred."

—BENEDICT SPINOZA, ETHICS, 1677

80 University of Minnesota women to overhear a sequence of evaluations of themselves by another woman. Some women heard consistently positive things about themselves, some consistently negative. Others heard evaluations that changed either from negative to positive (like Sophia's evaluations of Ray) or from positive to negative. In this and other experiments, the target person was especially well liked when the individual experienced a gain in the other's esteem, especially when the gain occurred gradually and reversed the earlier criticism (Aronson & Mettee, 1974; Clore & others, 1975). Perhaps Sophia's nice words have more credibility coming after her not-so-nice words. Or perhaps after being withheld, they are especially gratifying.

Aronson speculated that constant approval can lose value. When a husband says for the five-hundredth time, "Gee, honey, you look great," the words carry far less impact than were he now to say, "Gee, honey, you look awful in that dress." A loved one you've doted on is hard to reward but easy to hurt. This suggests that an open, honest relationship—one where people enjoy one another's esteem and acceptance yet are honest—is more likely to offer continuing rewards than one dulled by the suppression of unpleasant emotions, one in which people try only, as Dale Carnegie advised, to "lavish praise." Aronson (1988) put it this way:

> As a relationship ripens toward greater intimacy, what becomes increasingly important is authenticity—our ability to give up trying to make a good impression and begin to reveal things about ourselves that are honest even if unsavory. . . . If two people are genuinely fond of each other, they will have a more satisfying and exciting relationship over a longer period of time if they are able to express both positive and negative feelings than if they are completely "nice" to each other at all times. (p. 323)

In most social interactions, we self-censor our negative feelings. Thus, note William Swann and his colleagues (1991), some people receive no corrective feedback. Living in a world of pleasant illusion, they continue to act in ways that alienate their would-be friends. A true friend is one who can let us in on bad news.

"It takes your enemy and your friend, working together, to hurt you to the heart; the enemy to slander you and the friend to get the news to you."

—MARK TWAIN, PUDD'NHEAD WILSON'S NEW CALENDAR, 1897

"No one is perfect until you fall in love with them."

—ANDY ROONEY

Someone who really loves us will be honest with us but will also tend to see us through rose-colored glasses. When Sandra Murray and her co-workers (1996a, 1996b, 1997) studied dating and married couples, they found that the happiest (and those who became happier with time) were those who idealized each other, who even saw their partners more positively than their partners saw themselves. When we're in love, we're biased to find those we love not only physically attractive but socially attractive, and we're happy to have our partners view us with a similar positive bias (Boyes & Fletcher, 2007). Moreover, the most satisfied married couples tend to have idealized one another as newlyweds and to approach problems without immediately criticizing their partners and finding fault (Karney & Bradbury, 1997; Miller & others, 2006). Honesty has its place in a good relationship, but so does a presumption of the other's basic goodness.

Relationship Rewards

Asked why they are friends with someone or why they were attracted to their partners, most people can readily answer. "I like Carol because she's warm, witty, and well-read." What that explanation leaves out—and what social psychologists believe is most important—is ourselves. Attraction involves the one who is attracted as well as the attractor. Thus, a more psychologically accurate answer might be, "I like Carol because of how I feel when I'm with her." We are attracted to those we find it satisfying and gratifying to be with. Attraction is in the eye (and brain) of the beholder.

The point can be expressed as a simple **reward theory of attraction:** Those who reward us, or whom we associate with rewards, we like. If a relationship gives us more rewards than costs, we will like it and will wish it to continue. This will be especially true if the relationship is more profitable than alternative relationships (Rusbult, 1980). Mutual attraction flourishes when each meets the other's unmet needs (Byers & Wang, 2004). In his 1665 book of *Maxims,* La Rochefoucauld

reward theory of attraction

The theory that we like those whose behavior is rewarding to us or whom we associate with rewarding events.

Experimenter   Person A   Person B

FIGURE :: 11.6

Liking by Association

After interacting with a friendly experimenter, people preferred someone who looked like her (Person A) to one who didn't (Person B). After interacting with an unfriendly experimenter, people avoided the woman who resembled her (Lewicki, 1985).

conjectured, "Friendship is a scheme for the mutual exchange of personal advantages and favors whereby self-esteem may profit."

We not only like people who are rewarding to be with but also, according to the second version of the reward principle, like those we associate with good feelings. According to theorists Donn Byrne and Gerald Clore (1970), Albert Lott and Bernice Lott (1974), and Jan DeHouwer and colleagues (2001), conditioning creates positive feelings toward things and people linked with rewarding events. When, after a strenuous week, we relax in front of a fire, enjoying good food, drink, and music, we will likely feel a special warmth toward those around us. We are less likely to take a liking to someone we meet while suffering a splitting headache.

Pawel Lewicki (1985) tested this liking-by-association principle. In one experiment, University of Warsaw students were virtually 50-50 in choosing which of two pictured women (A or B in Figure 11.6) looked friendlier. Other students, having interacted with a warm, friendly experimenter who resembled woman A, chose woman A by a 6-to-1 margin. In a follow-up study, the experimenter acted *un*friendly toward half the participants. When these individuals later had to turn in their data to one of two women, they nearly always *avoided* the one who resembled the experimenter. (Perhaps you can recall a time when you reacted positively or negatively to someone who reminded you of someone else.)

Other experiments confirm this phenomenon of liking—and disliking—by association. In one, college students who evaluated strangers in a pleasant room liked them better than those who evaluated them in an uncomfortably hot room (Griffitt, 1970). In another, people evaluated photographs of other people while in either an elegant, sumptuously furnished room or a shabby, dirty room (Maslow & Mintz, 1956). Again, the good feelings evoked by the elegant surroundings transferred to the people being rated. Elaine Hatfield and William Walster (1978) found a practical tip in these research studies: "Romantic dinners, trips to the theatre, evenings at home together, and vacations never stop being important. . . . If your relationship is to survive, it's important that you *both* continue to associate your relationship with good things."

This simple theory of attraction—we like those who reward us and those we associate with rewards—helps us understand why people everywhere feel attracted to those who are warm, trustworthy, and responsive (Fletcher & others, 1999; Regan,

Our liking and disliking of people is influenced by the events with which they are associated.

Copyright © Mell Lazarus. By permission of Mell Lazarus and Creators Syndicate, Inc.

1998; Wojciszke & others, 1998). The reward theory also helps explain some of the influences on attraction:

- *Proximity* is rewarding. It costs less time and effort to receive friendship's benefits with someone who lives or works close by.
- We like *attractive* people because we perceive that they offer other desirable traits and because we benefit by associating with them.
- If others have *similar* opinions, we feel rewarded because we presume that they like us in return. Moreover, those who share our views help validate them. We especially like people if we have successfully converted them to our way of thinking (Lombardo & others, 1972; Riordan, 1980; Sigall, 1970).
- We like to be liked and love to be loved. Thus, liking is usually *mutual*. We like those who like us.

Summing Up: What Leads to Friendship and Attraction?

- The best predictor of whether any two people are friends is their sheer proximity to each other. Proximity is conducive to repeated exposure and interaction, which enables us to discover similarities and to feel each other's liking.
- A second determinant of initial attraction is physical attractiveness. Both in laboratory studies and in field experiments involving blind dates, college students tend to prefer attractive people. In everyday life, however, people tend to choose someone whose attractiveness roughly matches their own (or who, if less attractive, has other compensating

qualities). Positive attributions about attractive people define a physical-attractiveness stereotype—an assumption that what is beautiful is good.
- Liking is greatly aided by similarity of attitudes, beliefs, and values. Likeness leads to liking; opposites rarely attract.
- We are also likely to develop friendships with people who *like us*.
- According to the reward theory of attraction, we like people whose behavior we find rewarding, or whom we associate with rewarding events.

What Is Love?

What is this thing called "love"? Can passionate love endure? If not, what can replace it?

Loving is more complex than liking and thus more difficult to measure, more perplexing to study. People yearn for it, live for it, die for it. Yet only in the last couple of decades has loving become a serious topic in social psychology.

Most attraction researchers have studied what is most easily studied—responses during brief encounters between strangers. The influences on our initial liking of another—proximity, attractiveness, similarity, being liked, and other rewarding traits—also influence our long-term, close relationships. The impressions that dating couples quickly form of each other therefore provide a clue to their long-term future (Berg, 1984; Berg & McQuinn, 1986). Indeed, if North American romances flourished *randomly,* without regard to proximity and similarity, then most Catholics (being a minority) would marry Protestants, most Blacks would marry Whites, and college graduates would be as apt to marry high school dropouts as fellow graduates.

So first impressions are important. Nevertheless, long-term loving is not merely an intensification of initial liking. Social psychologists have therefore shifted their attention toward the study of enduring, close relationships.

Passionate Love

The first step in scientifically studying romantic love, as in studying any variable, is to decide how to define and measure it. We have ways to measure aggression, altruism, prejudice, and liking—but how do we measure love?

"How do I love thee? Let me count the ways," wrote Elizabeth Barrett Browning. Social scientists have counted various ways. Psychologist Robert Sternberg (1998) views love as a triangle consisting of three components: passion, intimacy, and commitment (Figure 11.7).

Some elements of love are common to all loving relationships: mutual understanding, giving and receiving support, enjoying the loved one's company. Some elements are distinctive. If we experience passionate love, we express it physically, we expect the relationship to be exclusive, and we are intensely fascinated with our partner. You can see it in our eyes.

Zick Rubin (1973) confirmed this. He administered a love scale to hundreds of University of Michigan dating couples. Later, from behind a one-way mirror in a laboratory waiting room, he clocked eye contact among "weak-love" and "strong-love" couples. His result will not surprise you: The strong-love couples gave themselves away by gazing long into each other's eyes. When talking, they also nod their head, smile naturally, and lean forward, Gian Gonzaga and others (2001) have observed.

Passionate love is emotional, exciting, intense. Elaine Hatfield (1988) defined it as *"a state of intense longing for union with another"* (p. 193). If reciprocated, one feels fulfilled and joyous; if not, one feels empty or despairing. Like other forms of

"Love is nature's way of giving a reason to be living."
—PAUL WEBSTER, "LOVE IS A MANY SPLENDORED THING," 1955

passionate love
A state of intense longing for union with another. Passionate lovers are absorbed in each other, feel ecstatic at attaining their partner's love, and are disconsolate on losing it.

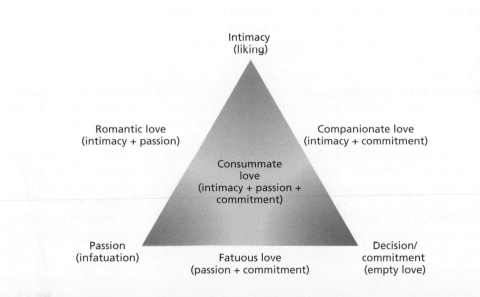

FIGURE :: 11.7

Robert Sternberg's (1988) Conception of Kinds of Loving as Combinations of Three Basic Components of Love

Researchers report that sustained eye contact, nodding, and smiling are indicators of passionate love.

emotional excitement, passionate love involves a roller coaster of elation and gloom, tingling exhilaration and dejected misery. "We are never so defenseless against suffering as when we love," observed Freud. Passionate love preoccupies the lover with thoughts of the other—as Robert Graves put it in his poem "Symptoms of Love": "Listening for a knock; waiting for a sign."

Passionate love is what you feel when you not only love someone but also are "in love" with him or her. As Sarah Meyers and Ellen Berscheid (1997) note, we understand that someone who says, "I love you, but I'm not in love with you" means to say, "I like you. I care about you. I think you're marvelous. But I don't feel sexually attracted to you." I feel friendship but not passion.

A THEORY OF PASSIONATE LOVE

To explain passionate love, Hatfield notes that a given state of arousal can be steered into any of several emotions, depending on how we attribute the arousal. An emotion involves both body and mind—both arousal and the way we interpret and label that arousal. Imagine yourself with pounding heart and trembling hands: Are you experiencing fear, anxiety, joy? Physiologically, one emotion is quite similar to another. You may therefore experience the arousal as joy if you are in a euphoric situation, anger if your environment is hostile, and passionate love if the situation is romantic. In this view, passionate love is the psychological experience of being biologically aroused by someone we find attractive.

If indeed passion is a revved-up state that's labeled "love," then whatever revs one up should intensify feelings of love. In several experiments, college men aroused sexually by reading or viewing erotic materials had a heightened response to a woman—for example, by scoring much higher on a love scale when describing their girlfriend (Carducci & others, 1978; Dermer & Pyszczynski, 1978; Stephan & others, 1971). Proponents of the **two-factor theory of emotion,** developed by Stanley Schachter and Jerome Singer (1962), argue that when the revved-up men responded to a woman, they easily misattributed some of their own arousal to her.

two-factor theory of emotion

Arousal × its label = emotion.

According to this theory, being aroused by *any* source should intensify passionate feelings—provided that the mind is free to attribute some of the arousal to a romantic stimulus. In a dramatic demonstration of this phenomenon, Donald Dutton and Arthur Aron (1974) had an attractive young woman approach individual young men as they crossed a narrow, wobbly, 450-foot-long suspension walkway hanging 230 feet above British Columbia's rocky Capilano River. The woman asked each man to help her fill out a class questionnaire. When he had finished, she scribbled her name and phone number and invited him to call if he wanted to hear more about the project. Most accepted the phone number, and half who did so called. By contrast, men approached by the woman on a low, solid bridge, rarely called. Once again, physical arousal accentuated romantic responses.

Scary movies, roller-coaster rides, and physical exercise have the same effect, especially to those we find attractive (Foster & others, 1998; White & Kight, 1984). The effect holds true with married couples, too. Those who do exciting activities together report the best relationships. And after doing an arousing rather than a mundane laboratory task (roughly the equivalent of a three-legged race on their hands and knees), couples also reported higher satisfaction with their overall relationship (Aron & others, 2000). Adrenaline makes the heart grow fonder.

As this suggests, passionate love is a biological as well as a psychological phenomenon. Research by social psychologist Arthur Aron and his colleagues (2005) indicates that passionate love engages dopamine-rich brain areas associated with reward (Figure 11.8).

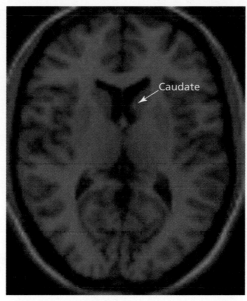

FIGURE :: 11.8

This Is Your Brain on Love

MRI scans from young adults intensely in love revealed areas, such as the caudate nucleus, which became more active when gazing at the loved-one's photo (but not when gazing at the photo of another acquaintance).

Source: Aron & others, 2005.

"The 'adrenaline' associated with a wide variety of highs can spill over and make passion more passionate. (Sort of a 'Better loving through chemistry' phenomenon.)"

—*ELAINE HATFIELD AND RICHARD RAPSON (1987)*

VARIATIONS IN LOVE: CULTURE AND GENDER

There is always a temptation to assume that most others share our feelings and ideas. We assume, for example, that love is a precondition for marriage. Most cultures—89 percent in one analysis of 166 cultures—do have a concept of romantic love, as reflected in flirtation or couples running off together (Jankowiak & Fischer, 1992). But in some cultures, notably those practicing arranged marriages, love tends to follow rather than to precede marriage. Even in the individualistic United States as recently as the 1960s, only 24 percent of college women and 65 percent of college men considered (as do nearly all collegians today) love to be the basis of marriage (Reis & Aron, 2008).

Do males and females differ in how they experience passionate love? Studies of men and women falling in and out of love reveal some surprises. Most people, including the writer of the following letter to a newspaper advice columnist, suppose that women fall in love more readily:

> Dear Dr. Brothers:
>   Do you think it's effeminate for a 19-year-old guy to fall in love so hard it's like the whole world's turned around? I think I'm really crazy because this has happened several times now and love just seems to hit me on the head from nowhere . . . My father says this is the way girls fall in love and that it doesn't happen this way with guys—at least it's not supposed to. I can't change how I am in this way but it kind of worries me.—P.T. (quoted by Dion & Dion, 1985)

P.T. would be reassured by the repeated finding that it is actually men who tend to fall in love more readily (Dion & Dion, 1985; Peplau & Gordon, 1985). Men also seem to fall out of love more slowly and are less likely than women to break up a premarital romance. Once in love, however, women are typically as emotionally involved as their partners, or more so. They are more likely to report feeling euphoric and "giddy and carefree," as if they were "floating on a cloud." Women are also somewhat more likely than men to focus on the intimacy of the friendship and on their concern for their partner. Men are more likely than women to think about the playful and physical aspects of the relationship (Hendrick & Hendrick, 1995).

"When in doubt, Sis, you've got to listen to your heart. If it's going thump, thump, thump, slow and steady, you've got the wrong guy."

companionate love
The affection we feel for those with whom our lives are deeply intertwined.

Companionate Love

Although passionate love burns hot, it eventually simmers down. The longer a relationship endures, the fewer its emotional ups and downs (Berscheid & others, 1989). The high of romance may be sustained for a few months, even a couple of years. But no high lasts forever. "When you're in love it's the most glorious two-and-a-half days of your life," jests comedian Richard Lewis. The novelty, the intense absorption in the other, the thrill of the romance, the giddy "floating on a cloud" feeling, fades. After two years of marriage, spouses express affection about half as often as when they were newlyweds (Huston & Chorost, 1994). About four years after marriage, the divorce rate peaks in cultures worldwide (Fisher, 1994). If a close relationship is to endure, it will settle to a steadier but still warm afterglow that Hatfield calls **companionate love.**

Unlike the wild emotions of passionate love, companionate love is lower key; it's a deep, affectionate attachment. It activates different parts of the brain (Aron & others, 2005). And it is just as real. Nisa, a !Kung San woman of the African Kalahari Desert, explains: "When two people are first together, their hearts are on fire and their passion is very great. After a while, the fire cools and that's how it stays. They continue to love each other, but it's in a different way—warm and dependable" (Shostak, 1981).

It won't surprise those who know the rock song "Addicted to Love" to find out that the flow and ebb of romantic love follows the pattern of addictions to coffee, alcohol, and other drugs. At first, a drug gives a big kick, perhaps a high. With repetition, opponent emotions gain strength and tolerance develops. An amount that once was highly stimulating no longer gives a thrill. Stopping the substance, however, does not return you to where you started. Rather, it triggers withdrawal symptoms—malaise, depression, the blahs. The same often happens in love. The passionate high is fated to become lukewarm. The no-longer-romantic relationship becomes taken for granted—until it ends. Then the jilted lover, the widower, the divorcé, are surprised at how empty life now seems without the person they long ago stopped feeling passionately attached to. Having focused on what was not working, they stopped noticing what was (Carlson & Hatfield, 1992).

Unlike passionate love, companionate love can last a lifetime.

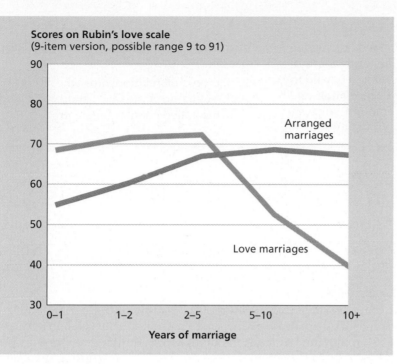

FIGURE :: 11.9

Romantic Love between Partners in Arranged or Love Marriages in Jaipur, India

Source: Data from Gupta & Singh, 1982.

The cooling of passionate love over time and the growing importance of other factors, such as shared values, can be seen in the feelings of those who enter arranged versus love-based marriages in India. Usha Gupta and Pushpa Singh (1982) asked 50 couples in Jaipur, India, to complete a love scale. They found that those who married for love reported diminishing feelings of love after a five-year newlywed period. By contrast, those in arranged marriages reported *more* love if their marriage was five or more years old (Figure 11.9; for other data on the seeming success of arranged marriages, see J. E. Myers & others, 2005, and Yelsma & Athappilly, 1988).

The cooling of intense romantic love often triggers a period of disillusion, especially among those who believe that romantic love is essential both for a marriage and for its continuation. Jeffry Simpson, Bruce Campbell, and Ellen Berscheid (1986) suspect "the sharp rise in the divorce rate in the past two decades is linked, at least in part, to the growing importance of intense positive emotional experiences (e.g., romantic love) in people's lives, experiences that may be particularly difficult to sustain over time." Compared with North Americans, Asians tend to focus less on personal feelings and more on the practical aspects of social attachments (Dion & Dion, 1988; Sprecher & others, 1994, 2002). Thus, they are less vulnerable to disillusionment. Asians are also less prone to the self-focused individualism that in the long run can undermine a relationship and lead to divorce (Dion & Dion, 1991, 1996; Triandis & others, 1988).

The decline in intense mutual fascination may be natural and adaptive for species survival. The result of passionate love frequently is children, whose survival is aided by the parents' waning obsession with each other (Kenrick & Trost, 1987). Nevertheless, for those married more than 20 years, some of the lost romantic feeling is often renewed as the family nest empties and the parents are once again free to focus their attention on each other (Hatfield & Sprecher, 1986; White & Edwards, 1990). "No man or woman really knows what love is until they have been married a quarter of a century," said Mark Twain. If the relationship has been intimate, mutually rewarding, and rooted in a shared life history, companionate love deepens.

"Don't it always seem to go
That you don't know what you've got till it's gone."
—*JONI MITCHELL,*
"BIG YELLOW TAXI," 1970

"Grow old along with me!
The best is yet to be."
—*ROBERT BROWNING*

Summing Up: What Is Love?

- Researchers have characterized love as having components of intimacy, passion, and commitment. Passionate love is experienced as a bewildering confusion of ecstasy and anxiety, elation and pain. The two-factor theory of emotion suggests that in a romantic context, arousal from any source, even painful experiences, can be steered into passion.

- In the best of relationships, the initial passionate high settles to a steadier, more affectionate relationship called companionate love.

What Enables Close Relationships?

What factors influence the ups and downs of our close relationships? Let's consider three factors: attachment styles, equity, and self-disclosure.

Attachment

Love is a biological imperative. We are social creatures, destined to bond with others. Our need to belong is adaptive. Cooperation promotes survival. In solo combat, our ancestors were not the toughest predators; but as hunter-gatherers, and in fending off predators, they gained strength from numbers. Because group dwellers survived and reproduced, we today carry genes that predispose us to form such bonds.

Researchers have found that different forms of a particular gene predict mammalian pair bonding. In the mouse-like prairie vole, and in humans, injections of hormones such as oxytocin (which is released in females during nursing and during mating) and vasopressin produce good feelings that trigger male-female bonding (Donaldson & Young, 2008; Young, 2009). In humans, genes associated with vasopressin activity predict marital stability (Walum & others, 2008). Such is the biology of enduring love.

Our infant dependency strengthens our human bonds. Soon after birth we exhibit various social responses—love, fear, anger. But the first and greatest of these is love. As babies, we almost immediately prefer familiar faces and voices. We coo and smile when our parents give us attention. By around 8 months, we crawl toward mother or father and typically let out a wail when separated from them. Reunited, we cling. By keeping infants close to their caregivers, strong social attachment serves as a powerful survival impulse.

Deprived of familiar attachments, sometimes under conditions of extreme neglect, children may become withdrawn, frightened, silent. After studying the mental health of homeless children for the World Health Organization, psychiatrist John Bowlby (1980, p. 442) reflected, "Intimate attachments to other human beings are the hub around which a person's life revolves. . . . From these intimate attachments [people draw] strength and enjoyment of life."

Researchers have compared the nature of attachment and love in various close relationships—between parents and children, between friends, and between spouses or lovers (Davis, 1985; Maxwell, 1985; Sternberg & Grajek, 1984). Some elements are common to all loving attachments: mutual understanding, giving and receiving support, valuing and enjoying being with the loved one. Passionate love is, however, spiced with some added features: physical affection, an expectation of exclusiveness, and an intense fascination with the loved one.

Passionate love is not just for lovers. The intense love of parent and infant for each other qualifies as a form of passionate love, even to the point of engaging brain areas akin to those enabling passionate romantic love. Phillip Shaver and his co-workers (1988) note that year-old infants, like young adult lovers, welcome physical affection, feel distress when separated, express intense affection when reunited, and take great pleasure in the significant other's attention and approval. Knowing that infants

Attachment, especially to caretakers, is a powerful survival impulse.

vary in their styles of relating to caregivers, Shaver and Cindy Hazan (1993, 1994) wondered whether infant attachment styles might carry over to adult relationships.

ATTACHMENT STYLES

About 7 in 10 infants, and nearly that many adults, exhibit **secure attachment** (Baldwin & others, 1996; Jones & Cunningham, 1996; Mickelson & others, 1997). When placed as infants in a strange situation (usually a laboratory playroom), they play comfortably in their mother's presence, happily exploring this strange environment. If she leaves, they become distressed; when she returns, they run to her, hold her, then relax and return to exploring and playing (Ainsworth, 1973, 1979). This trusting attachment style, many researchers believe, forms a working model of intimacy—a blueprint for one's adult intimate relationships, in which underlying trust sustains relationships through times of conflict (Miller & Rempel, 2004). Secure adults find it easy to get close to others and don't fret about getting too dependent or being abandoned. As lovers, they enjoy sexuality within the context of a secure, committed relationship. And their relationships tend to be satisfying and enduring (Feeney, 1996; Feeney & Noller, 1990; Simpson & others, 1992).

Kim Bartholomew and Leonard Horowitz (1991) proposed an influential attachment model that classifies people's attachment styles according to their images of self (positive or negative) and of others (positive or negative). Secure people have a positive image of both self and others (Table 11.1). They sense their own worth and lovability, and expect that others will accept and respond to their love.

secure attachment
Attachments rooted in trust and marked by intimacy.

TABLE :: 11.1 Attachment Styles

Kim Bartholomew and Leonard Horowitz (1991) proposed four distinct attachment styles based on a person's ideas of self and others.

		Model of Self	
		Positive	**Negative**
Model of Others	**Positive**	Secure	Preoccupied
	Negative	Dismissive	Fearful

"My preference is for someone who's afraid of closeness, like me."

People with the **preoccupied attachment** style (also called *anxious-ambivalent*) have positive expectations of others but a sense of their own unworthiness. In the strange situation, anxious-ambivalent infants are more likely to cling tightly to their mother. If she leaves, they cry; when she returns, they may be indifferent or hostile. As adults, anxious-ambivalent individuals are less trusting, and therefore more possessive and jealous. They may break up repeatedly with the same person. When discussing conflicts, they get emotional and often angry (Cassidy, 2000; Simpson & others, 1996). By contrast, friends who support each others' freedom and acknowledge each others' perspectives usually have a satisfying relationship (Deci & others, 2006).

People with negative views of others exhibit either the **dismissive** or the **fearful attachment** style; the two styles share the characteristic of *avoidance*. Although internally aroused, avoidant infants reveal little distress during separation or clinging upon reunion. As adults, avoidant people tend to be less invested in relationships and more likely to leave them. They also are more likely to engage in one-night stands of sex without love. Examples of the two styles might be "I want to keep my options open" (dismissing) and "I am uncomfortable getting close to others" (fearful).

Some researchers attribute these varying attachment styles, which have been studied across 62 cultures (Schmitt & others, 2004), to parental responsiveness. Cindy Hazan (2004) sums up the idea: "Early attachment experiences form the basis of *internal working models* or characteristic ways of thinking about relationships." Thus, sensitive, responsive mothers—mothers who engender a sense of basic trust in the world's reliability—typically have securely attached infants, observed Mary Ainsworth (1979) and Erik Erikson (1963). In fact, one study of 100 Israeli grandmother-daughter-granddaughter threesomes found intergenerational consistency of attachment styles (Besser & Priel, 2005). And youths who have experienced nurturant and involved parenting tend later to have warm and supportive relationships with their romantic partners (Conger & others, 2000).

Other researchers believe attachment styles may reflect inherited temperament (Gillath & others, 2008; Harris, 1998). A gene that predisposes prairie voles to cuddle and mate for life (and has the same effect on laboratory mice genetically engineered to have the gene) has varying human forms. One is more commonly found in faithful, married men, another in those who are unmarried or unfaithful (Caldwell & others, 2008; Walum & others, 2008). Moreover, teens who are prone to anger and anxiety tend to have, as young adults, more fragile relationships (Donnellan & others, 2005). For better or for worse, early attachment styles do seem to lay a foundation for future relationships.

preoccupied attachment
Attachments marked by a sense of one's own unworthiness and anxiety, ambivalence, and possessiveness.

dismissive attachment
An avoidant relationship style marked by distrust of others.

fearful attachment
An avoidant relationship style marked by fear of rejection.

equity
A condition in which the outcomes people receive from a relationship are proportional to what they contribute to it. Note: Equitable outcomes needn't always be equal outcomes.

Equity

If each partner pursues his or her personal desires willy-nilly, the relationship will die. Therefore, our society teaches us to exchange rewards by what Elaine Hatfield, William Walster, and Ellen Berscheid (1978) have called an **equity** principle of attraction: What you and your partner get out of a relationship should be proportional to what you each put into it. If two people receive equal outcomes, they should contribute equally; otherwise one or the other will feel it is unfair. If both feel their outcomes correspond to the assets and efforts each contributes, then both perceive equity.

Strangers and casual acquaintances maintain equity by exchanging benefits: You lend me your class notes; later, I'll lend you mine. I invite you to my party; you invite me to yours. Those in an enduring relationship, including roommates and those in love, do not feel bound to trade similar benefits—notes for notes, parties for parties (Berg, 1984). They feel freer to maintain equity by exchanging a variety of benefits ("When you drop by to lend me your notes, why don't you stay for dinner?") and eventually to stop keeping track of who owes whom.

LONG-TERM EQUITY

Is it crass to suppose that friendship and love are rooted in an equitable exchange of rewards? Don't we sometimes give in response to a loved one's need, without expecting anything in return? Indeed, those involved in an equitable, long-term relationship are unconcerned with short-term equity. Margaret Clark and Judson Mills (1979, 1993; Clark, 1984, 1986) have argued that people even take pains to *avoid* calculating any exchange benefits. When we help a good friend, we do not want instant repayment. If someone invites us for dinner, we wait before reciprocating, lest the person attribute the motive for our return invitation to be merely paying off a social debt. True friends tune into one another's needs even when reciprocation is impossible (Clark & others, 1986, 1989). Similarly, happily married people tend not to keep score of how much they are giving and getting (Buunk & Van Yperen, 1991). As people observe their partners being self-giving, their sense of trust grows (Wieselquist & others, 1999).

> "Love is the most subtle kind of self-interest."
> —HOLBROOK JOHNSON

In experiments with University of Maryland students, Clark and Mills confirmed that not being calculating is a mark of friendship. Tit-for-tat exchanges boosted people's liking when the relationship was relatively formal but diminished liking when the two sought friendship. Clark and Mills surmise that marriage contracts, in which each partner specifies what is expected from the other, would more likely undermine than enhance love. Only when the other's positive behavior is voluntary can we attribute it to love.

Previously we noted an equity principle at work in the matching phenomenon: People usually bring equal assets to romantic relationships. Often they are matched for attractiveness, status, and so forth. If they are mismatched in one area, such as attractiveness, they tend to be mismatched in some other area, such as status. But in total assets, they are an equitable match. No one says, and few even think, "I'll trade you my good looks for your big income." But especially in relationships that last, equity is the rule.

PERCEIVED EQUITY AND SATISFACTION

In one Pew Research Center (2007b) survey, "sharing household chores" ranked third (after "faithfulness" and a "happy sexual relationship") among nine things that people saw as marks of successful marriages. Indeed, those in an equitable relationship are typically content (Fletcher & others, 1987; Hatfield & others, 1985; Van Yperen & Buunk, 1990). Those who perceive their relationship as inequitable feel discomfort: The one who has the better deal may feel guilty and the one who senses a raw deal may feel strong irritation. (Given the self-serving bias—most husbands perceive themselves as contributing more housework than their wives credit them for—the person who is "overbenefited" is less sensitive to the inequity.)

Robert Schafer and Patricia Keith (1980) surveyed several hundred married couples of all ages, noting those who felt their marriages were somewhat unfair because one spouse contributed too little to the cooking, housekeeping, parenting,

FIGURE :: 11.10

Perceived inequities trigger marital distress, which fosters the perception of inequities.

Source: Adapted from Grote & Clark, 2001.

or providing. Inequity took its toll: Those who perceived inequity also felt more distressed and depressed. During the child-rearing years, when wives often feel underbenefited and husbands overbenefited, marital satisfaction tends to dip. During the honeymoon and empty-nest stages, spouses are more likely to perceive equity and to feel satisfaction with their marriages (Feeney & others, 1994). When both partners freely give and receive, and make decisions together, the odds of sustained, satisfying love are good.

Perceived inequity triggers marital distress, agree Nancy Grote and Margaret Clark (2001) from their tracking of married couples over time. But they also report that the traffic between inequity and distress runs both ways: Marital distress exacerbates the perception of unfairness (Figure 11.10).

Self-Disclosure

Deep, companionate relationships are intimate. They enable us to be known as we truly are and to feel accepted. We discover this delicious experience in a good marriage or a close friendship—a relationship where trust displaces anxiety and where we are free to open ourselves without fear of losing the other's affection (Holmes & Rempel, 1989). Such relationships are characterized by what the late Sidney Jourard called **self-disclosure** (Derlega & others, 1993). As a relationship grows, self-disclosing partners reveal more and more of themselves to each other; their knowledge of each other penetrates to deeper and deeper levels. In relationships that flourish, much of this self-disclosure shares successes and triumphs, and mutual delight over good happenings (Gable & others, 2006).

Research studies find that most of us enjoy this intimacy. We feel pleased when a normally reserved person says that something about us "made me feel like opening up" and shares confidential information (Archer & Cook, 1986; D. Taylor & others, 1981). It's gratifying to be singled out for another's disclosure. Not only do we like those who disclose, we also disclose to those whom we like. And after disclosing to them, we like them more (Collins & Miller, 1994). Lacking opportunities for intimate disclosure, we experience the pain of loneliness (Berg & Peplau, 1982; Solano & others, 1982).

Experiments have probed both the *causes* and the *effects* of self-disclosure. When are people most willing to disclose intimate information concerning "what you like and don't like about yourself" or "what you're most ashamed and most proud of"? And what effects do such revelations have on those who reveal and receive them?

The most reliable finding is the **disclosure reciprocity** effect: Disclosure begets disclosure (Berg, 1987; Miller, 1990; Reis & Shaver, 1988). We reveal more to those who have been open with us. But intimate disclosure is seldom instant. (If it is, the person may seem indiscreet and unstable.) Appropriate intimacy progresses like a dance: I reveal a little, you reveal a little—but not too much. You then reveal more, and I reciprocate.

For those in love, deepening intimacy is exciting. "Rising intimacy will create a strong sense of passion," note Roy Baumeister and Ellen Bratslavsky (1999). This helps explain why those who remarry after the loss of a spouse tend to begin the new marriage with an increased frequency of sex, and why passion often rides highest when intimacy is restored following severe conflict.

Some people—most of them women—are especially skilled "openers"; they easily elicit intimate disclosures from others, even from those who normally don't reveal very much of themselves (Miller & others, 1983; Pegalis & others, 1994; Shaffer & others, 1996). Such people tend to be good listeners. During conversation they maintain attentive facial expressions and appear to be comfortably enjoying themselves (Purvis & others, 1984). They may also express interest by uttering

self-disclosure
Revealing intimate aspects of oneself to others.

disclosure reciprocity
The tendency for one person's intimacy of self-disclosure to match that of a conversational partner.

supportive phrases while their conversational partner is speaking. They are what psychologist Carl Rogers (1980) called "growth-promoting" listeners—people who are genuine in revealing their own feelings, who are accepting of others' feelings, and who are empathic, sensitive, reflective listeners.

What are the effects of such self-disclosure? Humanistic psychologist Sidney Jourard (1964) argued that dropping our masks, letting ourselves be known as we are, nurtures love. He presumed that it is gratifying to open up to another and then to receive the trust another implies by being open with us. People feel better on days when they have disclosed something significant about themselves, such as their being lesbian or gay, and feel worse when concealing their identity (Beals & others, 2009). Having an intimate friend with whom we can discuss threats to our self-image seems to help us survive stress (Swann & Predmore, 1985). A true friendship is a special relationship that helps us cope with our other relationships. "When I am with my friend," reflected the Roman playwright Seneca, "methinks I am alone, and as much at liberty to speak anything as to think it." At its best, marriage is such a friendship, sealed by commitment.

Intimate self-disclosure is also one of companionate love's delights. The most self-revealing dating and married couples tend to enjoy the most satisfying and enduring relationships (Berg & McQuinn, 1986; Hendrick & others, 1988; Sprecher, 1987). For example, in a study of newlywed couples that were all equally in love, those who most deeply and accurately knew each other were most likely to enjoy enduring love (Neff & Karney, 2005). Married partners who most strongly agree that "I try to share my most intimate thoughts and feelings with my partner" tend to have the most satisfying marriages (Sanderson & Cantor, 2001).

In a Gallup national marriage survey, 75 percent of those who prayed with their spouses (and 57 percent of those who didn't) reported their marriages as very happy (Greeley, 1991). Among believers, shared prayer from the heart is a humbling, intimate, soulful exposure. Those who pray together also more often say they discuss their marriages together, respect their spouses, and rate their spouses as skilled lovers.

Researchers have also found that women are often more willing to disclose their fears and weaknesses than are men (Cunningham, 1981). As feminist writer Kate Millett (1975) put it, "Women express, men repress." Nevertheless, men today, particularly men with egalitarian gender-role attitudes, seem increasingly willing to reveal intimate feelings and to enjoy the satisfactions that accompany a relationship of mutual trust and self-disclosure. And that, say Arthur Aron and Elaine Aron (1994), is the essence of love—two selves connecting, disclosing, and identifying with each other; two selves, each retaining their individuality, yet sharing activities, delighting in similarities, and mutually supporting. The result for many romantic partners is "self-other integration": intertwined self-concepts (Slotter & Gardner, 2009; Figure 11.11).

That being so, might we cultivate closeness by experiences that mirror the escalating closeness of budding friendships? The Arons and their collaborators (1997) wondered. They paired volunteer students who were strangers to each other for 45 minutes. For the first 15 minutes, they shared thoughts on a list of personal but low-intimacy topics such as "When did you last sing to yourself?" The next 15 minutes were spent on more intimate topics such as "What is your most treasured memory?" The last 15 minutes invited even more self-disclosure, with questions such as "Complete this sentence: 'I wish I had someone with whom I could share . . .'" and "When did you last cry in front of another person? By yourself?"

"What is a Friend? I will tell you. It is a person with whom you dare to be yourself."
—FRANK CRANE,
A DEFINITION OF FRIENDSHIP

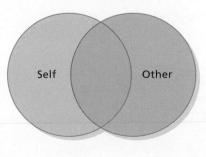

FIGURE :: 11.11

Love: An Overlapping of Selves—You Become Part of Me, I Part of You

Source: From A. L. Weber and J. Harvey, *Perspective on Close Relationships.* Published by Allyn & Bacon, Boston, MA. Copyright © 1994 by Pearson Education. Reprinted by permission of the publishers.

Compared with control participants who spent the 45 minutes in small talk ("What was your high school like?" "What is your favorite holiday?"), those who experienced the escalating self-disclosure ended the hour feeling remarkably close to their conversation partners—in fact, "closer than the closest relationship in the lives of 30 percent of similar students," reported the researchers. These relationships surely were not yet marked by the loyalty and commitment of true friendship. Nevertheless, the experiment provides a striking demonstration of how readily a sense of closeness to others can grow, given open self-disclosure—which can also occur via the Internet. (See "Focus On: Does the Internet Create Intimacy or Isolation?")

To promote self-disclosure in ongoing dating relationships, Richard Slatcher and James Pennebaker (2006) invited one member of 86 couples to spend 20 minutes on each of three days writing their deepest thoughts and feelings about the relationship (or, in a control condition, writing merely about their daily activities). Those who pondered and journaled their feelings expressed more emotion to their partners in the days following. Three months later, 77 percent were still dating (compared with 52 percent in the control group).

focus ON

Does the Internet Create Intimacy or Isolation?

As a reader of this college text, you are almost surely one of the world's 1.5 billion (as of 2008) Internet users. It took the telephone seven decades to go from 1 percent to 75 percent penetration of North American households. Internet access reached 75 percent penetration in about seven years (Putnam, 2000). You and half of European Union citizens, 3 in 4 Americans, and more than 4 in 5 Canadians and Australians enjoy e-mail, Web surfing, and perhaps participating in listservs, news groups, or chat rooms (Internetworldstats.com).

What do you think: Is computer-mediated communication within virtual communities a poor substitute for in-person relationships? Or is it a wonderful way to widen our social circles? Does the Internet do more to connect people or to drain time from face-to-face relationships? Consider the emerging debate.

Point: The Internet, like the printing press and the telephone, expands communication, and communication enables relationships. Printing reduced face-to-face storytelling and the telephone reduced face-to-face chats, but both enable us to reach and be reached by people without limitations of time and distance. Social relations involve networking, and the Net is the ultimate network. It enables efficient networking with family, friends, and kindred spirits—including people we otherwise never would have found, be they fellow MS patients, St. Nicholas collectors, or Harry Potter fans.

Counterpoint: True, but computer communication is impoverished. It lacks the nuances of eye-to-eye contact punctuated with nonverbal cues and physical touches. Except for simple emoticons—such as a :-)

"On the Internet, nobody knows you're a dog."

The Internet allows people to feign who they really aren't.

for an unnuanced smile—electronic messages are devoid of gestures, facial expressions, and tones of voice. No wonder it's so easy to misread them. The absence of expressive e-motion makes for ambiguous emotion.

For example, vocal nuances can signal whether a statement is serious, kidding, or sarcastic. Research by Justin Kruger and his colleagues (2006) shows that communicators often think their "just kidding" intent is equally clear, whether e-mailed or spoken. Actually, when e-mailed it often isn't. Thanks also to one's anonymity in virtual discussions, the result is sometimes a hostile "flame war."

The Internet, like television, diverts time from real relationships. Internet romances are not the developmental equivalent of real dating. Cybersex is artificial intimacy. Individualized web-based entertainment displaces getting together for bridge. Such artificiality and isolation is regrettable, because our ancestral history predisposes our needing real-time relationships, replete with smirks and smiles. No wonder that a Stanford University survey found that 25 percent of more than 4,000 adults surveyed reported that their time online had reduced time spent in person and on the phone with family and friends (Nie & Erbring, 2000).

Point: But most folks don't perceive the Internet to be isolating. Another national survey found that "Internet users in general—and online women in particular—believe that their use of e-mail has strengthened their relationships and increased their contact with relatives and friends" (Pew, 2000). Internet use may displace in-person intimacy, but it also displaces television watching. If one-click cyber-shopping is bad for your local bookstore, it frees time for relationships. Telecommuting does the same, enabling people to work from home and thereby spend more time with their families.

And why say that computer-formed relationships are unreal? On the Internet your looks and location cease to matter. Your appearance, age, and race don't deter people from relating to you based on what's more genuinely important—your shared interests and values. In workplace and professional networks, computer-mediated discussions are less influenced by status and are therefore more candid and equally participatory. Computer-mediated communication fosters more spontaneous self-disclosure than face-to-face conversation (Joinson, 2001).

Most Internet flirtations go nowhere. "Everyone I know who has tried online dating . . . agrees that we loathe spending (wasting?) hours gabbing to someone and then meeting him and realizing that he is a creep," observed one Toronto woman (Dicum, 2003). Nevertheless, friendships and romantic relationships that form on the Internet are more likely than in-person relationships to last for at least two years, report Katelyn McKenna and John Bargh, and their colleagues (Bargh & others, 2002, 2004; McKenna & Bargh, 1998, 2000; McKenna & others, 2002). In one experiment, they found that people disclosed more, with greater honesty and less posturing, when they met people online. They also felt more liking for people with whom they conversed online for 20 minutes than for those met for the same time face-to-face. This was true even when they unknowingly met the very same person in both contexts. People surveyed similarly feel that Internet friendships are as real, important, and close as offline relationships.

No wonder a Pew survey (2006) of Internet users who are single and looking for romance found that 74 percent used the Internet to further their romantic interests and that 37 percent had gone to an online dating website. One popular Internet matchmaking site claimed, by 2008, 17 million participants and $200 million in annual revenues (Cullen & Masters, 2008). Although published data on the effectiveness of online matchmaking is sparse, efforts are under way to harvest data from hundreds of questions put to thousands of couples to see which combinations of answers might help predict enduring partnerships (Epstein, 2007; Tierney, 2008).

Counterpoint: The Internet allows people to be who they really are, but also to feign who they really aren't, sometimes in the interests of sexual exploitation. Internet sexual media, like other forms of pornography, likely serve to distort people's perceptions of sexual reality, decrease the attractiveness of their real-life partner, prime men to perceive women in sexual terms, make sexual coercion seem more trivial, provide mental scripts for how to act in sexual situations, increase arousal, and lead to disinhibition and imitation of loveless sexual behaviors.

Finally, suggests Robert Putnam (2000), the social benefits of computer-mediated communication are constrained by two other realities: The "digital divide" accentuates social and educational inequalities between the haves and the have-nots. Although "cyberbalkanization" enables those of us with hearing loss to network, it also enables White supremacists to find one another. The digital divide may be remedied with lowering computer prices and increasing public access locations. The balkanization is intrinsic to the medium.

As the debate over the Internet's social consequences continues, "the most important question," says Putnam (p. 180), will be "not what the Internet will do to us, but what we will do with it? . . . How can we harness this promising technology for thickening community ties? How can we develop the technology to enhance social presence, social feedback, and social cues? How can we use the prospect of fast, cheap communication to enhance the now fraying fabric of our real communities?"

Summing Up: What Enables Close Relationships?

- From infancy to old age, attachments are central to human life. Secure attachments, as in an enduring marriage, mark happy lives.

- Companionate love is most likely to endure when both partners feel the partnership is equitable, with both perceiving themselves receiving from the relationship in proportion to what they contribute to it.

- One reward of companionate love is the opportunity for intimate self-disclosure, a state achieved gradually as each partner reciprocates the other's increasing openness.

How Do Relationships End?

Often love dies. What factors predict marital dissolution? How do couples typically detach from or renew their relationships?

In 1971 a man wrote a love poem to his bride, slipped it into a bottle, and dropped it into the Pacific Ocean between Seattle and Hawaii. A decade later, a jogger found it on a Guam beach:

> If, by the time this letter reaches you, I am old and gray, I know that our love will be as fresh as it is today.
>
> It may take a week or it may take years for this note to find you. . . . If this should never reach you, it will still be written in my heart that I will go to extreme means to prove my love for you. Your husband, Bob.

The woman to whom the love note was addressed was reached by phone. When the note was read to her she burst out laughing. And the more she heard, the harder she laughed. "We're divorced," she finally said, and slammed down the phone.

So it often goes. Smart brains can make dumb decisions. Comparing their unsatisfying relationship with the support and affection they imagine are available elsewhere, people are divorcing more often—at nearly double the 1960 rate. Each year, Canada and the United States record one divorce for every two marriages. As economic and social barriers to divorce weakened during the 1960s and 1970s, thanks partly to women's increasing employment, divorce rates rose. "We are living longer, but loving more briefly," quipped Os Guiness (1993, p. 309).

Britain's royal House of Windsor knows well the hazards of modern marriage. The fairy-tale marriages of Princess Margaret, Princess Anne, Prince Charles, and Prince Andrew all crumbled, smiles replaced with stony stares. Shortly after her 1986 marriage to Prince Andrew, Sarah Ferguson gushed, "I love his wit, his charm, his looks. I worship him." Andrew reciprocated her euphoria: "She is the best thing in my life." Six years later, Andrew, having decided her friends were "philistines," and Sarah, having derided Andrew's boorish behavior as "terribly gauche," called it quits (*Time,* 1992).

Divorce

Divorce rates have varied widely by country, ranging from .01 percent of the population annually in Bolivia, the Philippines, and Spain to .54 percent in the world's most divorce-prone country, the United States. To predict a culture's divorce rates, it helps to know its values (Triandis, 1994). Individualistic cultures (where love is a feeling and people ask, "What does my heart say?") have more divorce than do communal cultures (where love entails obligation and people ask, "What will other people say?"). Individualists marry "for as long as we both shall love," collectivists more often for life. Individualists expect more passion and personal fulfillment

> "When I was a young man, I vowed never to marry until I found the ideal woman. Well I found her—but alas, she was waiting for the ideal man."
>
> —FRENCH STATESMAN ROBERT SCHUMAN (1886–1963)

in a marriage, which puts greater pressure on the relationship (Dion & Dion, 1993). "Keeping romance alive" was rated as important to a good marriage by 78 percent of American women surveyed and 29 percent of Japanese women (*American Enterprise*, 1992).

Even in Western society, however, those who enter relationships with a long-term orientation and an intention to persist do experience healthier, less turbulent, and more durable partnerships (Arriaga, 2001; Arriaga & Agnew, 2001). Enduring

"*Don't you understand? I love you! I need you! I want to spend the rest of my vacation with you!*"

relationships are rooted in enduring love and satisfaction, but also in fear of the termination cost, a sense of moral obligation, and inattention to possible alternative partners (Adams & Jones, 1997; Maner & others, 2009; Miller, 1997).

Those whose commitment to a union outlasts the desires that gave birth to it will endure times of conflict and unhappiness. One national survey found that 86 percent of those who were unhappily married but who stayed with the marriage were, when reinterviewed five years later, now mostly "very" or "quite" happy with their marriages (Popenoe, 2002). By contrast, "narcissists"—those more focused on their own desires and image—enter relationships with less commitment and less likelihood of long-term relational success (Campbell & Foster, 2002).

Risk of divorce also depends on who marries whom (Fergusson & others, 1984; Myers, 2000a; Tzeng, 1992). People usually stay married if they

- married after age 20.
- both grew up in stable, two-parent homes.
- dated for a long while before marriage.
- are well and similarly educated.
- enjoy a stable income from a good job.
- live in a small town or on a farm.
- did not cohabit or become pregnant before marriage.
- are religiously committed.
- are of similar age, faith, and education.

None of those predictors, by itself, is essential to a stable marriage. Moreover, they are correlates of enduring marriages, not necessarily causes. But if none of those things is true for someone, marital breakdown is an almost sure bet. If all are true, they are very likely to stay together until death. The English perhaps had it right when, several centuries ago, they presumed that the temporary intoxication of passionate love was a foolish basis for permanent marital decisions. Better, they felt, to choose a mate based on stable friendship and compatible backgrounds, interests, habits, and values (Stone, 1977).

The Detachment Process

Severing bonds produces a predictable sequence of agitated preoccupation with the lost partner, followed by deep sadness and, eventually, the beginnings of emotional detachment, a return to normal living, and a renewed sense of self (Hazan & Shaver, 1994; Lewandowski & Bizzoco, 2007). Even newly separated couples who have long ago ceased feeling affection are often surprised at their desire to be near the former partner. Deep and long-standing attachments seldom break quickly; detaching is a process, not an event.

"Passionate love is in many ways an altered state of consciousness. . . . In many states today, there are laws that a person must not be in an intoxicated condition when marrying. But passionate love is a kind of intoxication."

—ROY BAUMEISTER, MEANINGS OF LIFE, *1991*

FIGURE :: 11.12

National Opinion
Research Center
Surveys of 23,076
Married Americans,
1972–2004

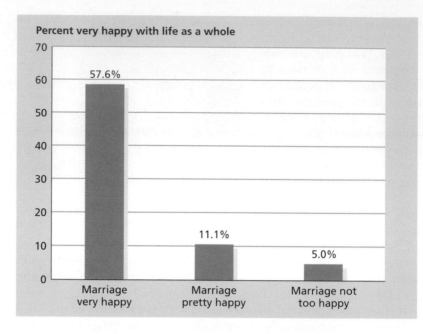

Among dating couples, the closer and longer the relationship and the fewer the available alternatives, the more painful the breakup (Simpson, 1987). Surprisingly, Roy Baumeister and Sara Wotman (1992) report that, months or years later, people recall more pain over spurning someone's love than over having been spurned. Their distress arises from guilt over hurting someone, from upset over the heartbroken lover's persistence, or from uncertainty over how to respond. Among married couples, breakup has additional costs: shocked parents and friends, guilt over broken vows, anguish over reduced household income, and possibly restricted parental rights. Still, each year millions of couples are willing to pay such costs to extricate themselves from what they perceive as the greater costs of continuing a painful, unrewarding relationship. Such costs include, in one study of 328 married couples, a tenfold increase in depression symptoms when a marriage is marked by discord rather than satisfaction (O'Leary & others, 1994). When, however, a marriage is "very happy," life as a whole usually seems "very happy" (Figure 11.12).

When relationships suffer, those without better alternatives or who feel invested in a relationship (through time, energy, mutual friends, possessions, and perhaps children) will seek alternatives to exiting the relationship. Caryl Rusbult and her colleagues (1986, 1987, 1998) have explored three ways of coping with a failing relationship (Table 11.2). Some people exhibit *loyalty*—by waiting for conditions to improve. The problems are too painful to confront and the risks of separation are too great, so the loyal partner perseveres, hoping the good old days will return. Others (especially men) exhibit *neglect*; they ignore the partner and allow the relationship to deteriorate. With painful dissatisfactions ignored, an insidious

TABLE :: 11.2 Responses to Relationship Distress

	Passive	Active
Constructive	*Loyalty:* Await improvement	*Voice:* Seek to improve relationships
Destructive	*Neglect:* Ignore the partner	*Exit:* End the relationship

Source: Rusbult & others, 1986, 1987, 1998, 2001.

emotional uncoupling ensues as the partners talk less and begin redefining their lives without each other. Still others will *voice* their concerns and take active steps to improve the relationship by discussing problems, seeking advice, and attempting to change.

Study after study—in fact, 115 studies of 45,000 couples—reveal that unhappy couples disagree, command, criticize, and put down. Happy couples more often agree, approve, assent, and laugh (Karney & Bradbury, 1995; Noller & Fitzpatrick, 1990). After observing 2,000 couples, John Gottman (1994, 1998) noted that healthy marriages were not necessarily devoid of conflict. Rather, they were marked by an ability to reconcile differences and to overbalance criticism with affection. In successful marriages, positive interactions (smiling, touching, complimenting, laughing) outnumbered negative interactions (sarcasm, disapproval, insults) by at least a five-to-one ratio.

It's not distress and arguments that predict divorce, add Ted Huston and colleagues (2001) from their following of newlyweds through time. (Most newlyweds experience conflict.) Rather, it's coldness, disillusionment, and hopelessness that predict a dim marital future. This is especially so, observed William Swann and his associates (2003, 2006), when inhibited men are coupled with critical women.

Successful couples have learned, sometimes aided by communication training, to restrain the poisonous put-downs and gut-level reactions. They fight fairly (by stating feelings without insulting). They depersonalize conflict with comments such as "I know it's not your fault" (Markman & others, 1988; Notarius & Markman, 1993; Yovetich & Rusbult, 1994). Would unhappy relationships get better if the partners agreed to *act* more as happy couples do—by complaining and criticizing less? by affirming and agreeing more? by setting aside times to voice their concerns? by praying or playing together daily? As attitudes trail behaviors, do affections trail actions?

Joan Kellerman, James Lewis, and James Laird (1989) wondered. They knew that among couples passionately in love, eye gazing is typically prolonged and mutual (Rubin, 1973). Would intimate eye gazing similarly stir feelings between those not in love (much as 45 minutes of escalating self-disclosure evoked feelings of closeness among those unacquainted students)? To find out, they asked unacquainted male-female pairs to gaze intently for two minutes either at each other's hands or into each other's eyes. When they separated, the eye gazers reported a tingle of attraction and affection toward each other. Simulating love had begun to stir it.

By enacting and expressing love, researcher Robert Sternberg (1988) believes the passion of initial romance can evolve into enduring love:

> "Living happily ever after" need not be a myth, but if it is to be a reality, the happiness must be based upon different configurations of mutual feelings at various times in a relationship. Couples who expect their passion to last forever, or their intimacy to remain unchallenged, are in for disappointment. . . . We must constantly work at understanding, building, and rebuilding our loving relationships. Relationships are constructions, and they decay over time if they are not maintained and improved. We cannot expect a relationship simply to take care of itself, any more than we can expect that of a building. Rather, we must take responsibility for making our relationships the best they can be.

Summing Up: How Do Relationships End?

- Often love does not endure. As divorce rates rose in the twentieth century, researchers discerned predictors of marital dissolution. One predictor is an individualistic culture that values feelings over commitment; other factors include the couple's age, education, values, and similarity.

- Researchers are also identifying the process through which couples either detach or rebuild their relationships. And they are identifying the positive and nondefensive communication styles that mark healthy, stable marriages.

POSTSCRIPT: Making Love

Two facts of contemporary life seem beyond dispute: First, *close, enduring relationships are hallmarks of a happy life.* In National Opinion Research Center surveys of 43,295 Americans since 1972, 40 percent of married adults, 23 percent of those never married, 20 percent of the divorced, and 16 percent of the separated declared their lives "very happy." Similar results come from national surveys in Canada and Europe (Inglehart, 1990).

Second, *close, enduring relationships are in decline.* Compared with a half century ago, people today more often move, live alone, divorce, and have a succession of relationships.

Given the psychological ingredients of marital happiness—kindred minds, social and sexual intimacy, equitable giving and receiving of emotional and material resources—it becomes possible to contest the French saying "Love makes the time pass and time makes love pass." But it takes effort to stem love's decay. It takes effort to carve out time each day to talk over the day's happenings. It takes effort to forgo nagging and bickering and instead to disclose and hear each other's hurts, concerns, and dreams. It takes effort to make a relationship into "a classless utopia of social equality" (Sarnoff & Sarnoff, 1989), in which both partners freely give and receive, share decision making, and enjoy life together.

By minding our close relationships, sustained satisfaction is possible, note John Harvey and Julia Omarzu (1997). Australian relationships researcher Patricia Noller (1996) concurs: "Mature love . . . love that sustains marriage and family as it creates an environment in which individual family members can grow . . . is sustained by beliefs that love involves acknowledging and accepting differences and weaknesses; that love involves an internal decision to love another person and a long-term commitment to maintain that love; and finally that love is controllable and needs to be nurtured and nourished by the lovers."

For those who commit themselves to creating an equitable, intimate, mutually supportive relationship, there may come the security, and the joy, of enduring, companionate love. When someone "loves you for a long, long time," explained the wise, old Skin Horse to the Velveteen Rabbit, "not just to play with, but REALLY loves you, then you become Real. . . ."

> "Does it happen all at once, like being wound up," [the rabbit] asked, "or bit by bit?"
>
> "It doesn't happen all at once," said the Skin Horse. "You become. It takes a long time. That's why it doesn't often happen to people who break easily, or have sharp edges, or who have to be carefully kept. Generally, by the time you are Real, most of your hair has been loved off, and your eyes drop out and you get loose in the joints and very shabby. But these things don't matter at all, because once you are Real you can't be ugly, except to people who don't understand."

Making the Social Connection

The Online Learning Center for this book includes a video on each of three important topics from this chapter. The first video presents David Buss discussing his ideas about the evolutionary psychology of physical attractiveness. Next is a video on love in late adulthood: how might attraction and intimacy be different in a mature couple as opposed to a pair of teenagers or young adults? Finally, recall this chapter's discussion of the ending of relationships. In this chapter's third video, Robert Emery reports on research to identify trends in divorce.

"Love cures people—both the ones who give it and the ones who receive it."

—Psychiatrist Karl Meninger, 1893–1990

On a hillside in Jerusalem, hundreds of trees form the Garden of the Righteous Among the Nations. Beneath each tree is a plaque with the name of a European Christian who gave refuge to one or more Jews during the Nazi Holocaust. These "righteous Gentiles" knew that if the refugees were discovered, Nazi policy dictated that host and refugee would suffer a common fate. Many did (Hellman, 1980; Wiesel, 1985). Countless more rescuers remain nameless. For every Jew who survived the war in Nazi territory, dozens of people often acted heroically. Orchestra conductor Konrad Latte, one of 2,000 Jews who lived out the war in Berlin, was saved by the heroism of 50 Germans who served as his protectors (Schneider, 2000).

One hero who did not survive was Jane Haining, a Church of Scotland missionary who was matron at a school for 400 mostly Jewish girls. On the eve of war, the church, fearing her safety, ordered her to return home. She refused, saying, "If these children need me in days of sunshine, how much more do they need me in days of darkness?" (Barnes, 2008; Brown, 2008). Indeed, she reportedly cut up her leather luggage to make soles for her girls' shoes. In April 1944 Haining accused a cook of eating sparse food rations intended for her girls. The cook, a Nazi party member, denounced her to the Gestapo, who arrested her for having worked among the Jews and having wept to

The Wall of Honor in the Garden of the Righteous, Jerusalem, honors more than 16,000 rescuers as "Righteous Among the Nations." Most were humble people who saw their own behavior as mere common decency (Rochat & Modigliani, 1995).

see her girls forced to wear yellow stars. A few weeks later she was sent to Auschwitz, where she suffered the same fate as millions of Jews.

On 9/11 and in the days that followed, one coordinated act of evil triggered innumerable acts of kindness. Multitudes of donors overwhelmed blood banks, food banks, and clothing banks. Some were self-sacrificially altruistic during the crisis. After the World Trade Center's North Tower was struck, Ed Emery gathered five Fiduciary Trust colleagues on the South Tower's ninetieth floor, escorted them down 12 floors, got them on a packed express elevator, let the doors close in front of him, and then headed back up to the ninety-seventh floor, hoping to evacuate six more colleagues who were backing up the computers. Alas, when moments later his own building was struck beneath him, his fate was sealed.

Nearby, his colleague Edward McNally was thinking of how, in his last moments, he could help his loved ones. As the floor began buckling, he called his wife, Liz, and recited life insurance policies and bonuses. "He said I meant the world to him, and he loved me," Mrs. McNally later recalled as they exchanged their final goodbyes (New York Times, 2002). But her phone rang one more time. It was her husband again, telling her he had booked them on a trip to Rome for her fortieth birthday. "Liz, you have to cancel that."

Less dramatic acts of comforting, caring, and compassion abound: Without asking anything in return, people offer directions, donate money, give blood, volunteer time.

Good Samaritan, Fernand Schultz-Wettel

- Why, and when, will people help?

- Who will help?

- What can be done to lessen indifference and increase helping?

Those are this chapter's primary questions.

Altruism is selfishness in reverse. An altruistic person is concerned and helpful even when no benefits are offered or expected in return. Jesus' parable of the Good Samaritan provides the classic illustration:

> A man was going down from Jerusalem to Jericho, and fell into the hands of robbers, who stripped him, beat him, and went away, leaving him half dead. Now by chance a priest was going down that road; and when he saw him, he passed by on the other side. So likewise a Levite, when he came to the place and saw him, passed by on the other side. But a Samaritan while traveling came near him; and when he saw him, he was moved with pity. He went to him and bandaged his wounds, having poured oil and wine on them. Then he put him on his own animal, brought him to an inn, and took care of him. The next day he took out two denarii, gave them to the innkeeper, and said, "Take care of him; and when I come back, I will repay you whatever more you spend." (Luke 10:30–35, NRSV)

The Samaritan story illustrates altruism. Filled with compassion, he is motivated to give a stranger time, energy, and money while expecting neither repayment nor appreciation.

altruism
A motive to increase another's welfare without conscious regard for one's self-interests.

Why Do We Help?

To study helping acts, social psychologists identify circumstances in which people perform such deeds. Before looking at what the experiments reveal, let's consider what might motivate helping.

Social Exchange and Social Norms

Several theories of helping agree that, in the long run, helping behavior benefits the giver as well as the receiver. One explanation assumes that human interactions are guided by "social economics." We exchange not only material goods and money but also social goods—love, services, information, status (Foa & Foa, 1975). In doing so, we aim to minimize costs and maximize rewards. **Social-exchange theory** does not contend that we consciously monitor costs and rewards, only that such considerations predict our behavior.

Suppose your campus is having a blood drive and someone asks you to participate. Might you not implicitly weigh the *costs* of donating (needle prick, time, fatigue) against those of not donating (guilt, disapproval)? Might you not also weigh the *benefits* of donating (feeling good about helping someone, free refreshments) against those of not donating (saving the time, discomfort, and anxiety)? According

social-exchange theory
The theory that human interactions are transactions that aim to maximize one's rewards and minimize one's costs.

"Hey, there's Sara, padding her college-entrance résumé!"

to social-exchange theory—supported by studies of Wisconsin blood donors by Jane Allyn Piliavin and her research team (1982, 2003)—such subtle calculations precede decisions to help or not.

REWARDS

Rewards that motivate helping may be external or internal. When businesses donate money to improve their corporate images or when someone offers a ride hoping to receive appreciation or friendship, the reward is external. We give to get. Thus, we are most eager to help someone attractive to us, someone whose approval we desire (Krebs, 1970; Unger, 1979). In experiments, and in everyday life, public generosity boosts one's status, while selfish behavior can lead to punishment (Hardy & Van Vugt, 2006; Henrich and others, 2006).

Rewards may also be internal. Helping also increases our sense of self-worth. Nearly all blood donors in Jane Piliavin's research agreed that giving blood "makes you feel good about yourself" and "gives you a feeling of self-satisfaction." Indeed, "Give blood," advises an old Red Cross poster. "All you'll feel is good." Feeling good helps explain why people far from home will do kindnesses for strangers whom they will never see again.

Helping's boost to self-worth explains why so many people feel good after doing good. One month-long study of 85 couples found that giving emotional support to one's partner was positive for the *giver*; giving support boosted the giver's mood (Gleason & others, 2003). Piliavin (2003) and Susan Andersen (1998) point to dozens of studies showing that youth engaged in community service projects, school-based "service learning," or tutoring children develop social skills and positive social values. They are at markedly less risk for delinquency, pregnancy, and school dropout and are more likely to become engaged citizens. Volunteering likewise benefits morale and health. Bereaved spouses recover from their depressed feelings faster when they are engaged in helping others (Brown & others, 2008). Those who do good tend to do well.

Ditto for giving money. Making donations activates brain areas linked with reward (Harbaugh & others, 2007). Generous people are happier than those whose spending is self-focused. In one experiment, people received an envelope with cash that some were instructed to spend on themselves, while others were directed to spend on other people. At the day's end, the happiest people were those assigned to the spend-it-on-others condition (Dunn & others, 2008).

This cost-benefit analysis can seem demeaning. In defense of the theory, however, is it not a credit to humanity that helping can be inherently rewarding? that much of our behavior is not antisocial but "prosocial"? that we can find fulfillment in the giving of love? How much worse if we gained pleasure only by serving ourselves.

"True," some readers may reply. "Still, reward theories imply that a helpful act is never truly altruistic—that we merely call it 'altruistic' when its rewards are inconspicuous. If we help the screaming woman so we can gain social approval, relieve our distress, prevent guilt, or boost our self-image, is it really altruistic?" That argument is reminiscent of B. F. Skinner's (1971) analysis of helping. We credit people

"Men do not value a good deed unless it brings a reward."

—*OVID*, EPISTULAE EX PONTO, *10* A.D.

THE inside STORY

Dennis Krebs on Life Experience and Professional Interests

At age 14, I was traumatized when my family moved from Vancouver, B.C., to California. I fell from president of my junior high school to an object of social ridicule because of my clothes, accent, and behavior. The fighting skills I had acquired boxing soon generated a quite different reputation from the one I enjoyed in Canada. I sank lower and lower until, after several visits to juvenile detention homes, I was arrested and convicted for driving under the influence of drugs. I escaped from jail, hitchhiked to a logging camp in Oregon, and eventually made my way back to British Columbia. I was admitted to university on probation, graduated at the top of my class, won a Woodrow Wilson Fellowship, and was accepted to a psychology doctoral program at Harvard.

Attending Harvard required moving back to the United States. Concerned about my escapee record in California, I turned myself in and suffered through the ensuing publicity. I was pardoned, in large part because of the tremendous support I received from many people. After three years at Harvard, I was hired as an assistant professor. Eventually I returned to British Columbia to chair the Psychology Department at Simon Fraser University.

Though it makes me somewhat uncomfortable, I disclose this history as a way of encouraging people with two strikes against them to remain in the game. A great deal of the energy I have invested in understanding morality has stemmed from a need to understand why I went wrong, and my interest in altruism has been fueled by the generosity of those who helped me overcome my past.

Dennis Krebs,
Simon Fraser University

for their good deeds, said Skinner, only when we can't explain them. We attribute their behavior to their inner dispositions only when we lack external explanations. When the external causes are obvious, we credit the causes, not the person.

There is, however, a weakness in reward theory. It easily degenerates into explaining-by-naming. If someone volunteers for the Big Sister tutor program, it is tempting to "explain" her compassionate action by the satisfaction it brings her. But such after-the-fact naming of rewards creates a circular explanation: "Why did she volunteer?" "Because of the inner rewards." "How do you know there are inner rewards?" "Why else would she have volunteered?" Because of this circular reasoning, **egoism**—the idea that self-interest motivates all behavior—has fallen into disrepute.

To escape the circularity, we must define the rewards and the costs independently of the helping behavior. If social approval motivates helping, then in experiments we should find that when approval follows helping, helping increases. And it does (Staub, 1978).

INTERNAL REWARDS

So far, we have mostly considered the external rewards of helping. We also need to consider internal factors, such as the helper's emotional state or personal traits.

The benefits of helping include internal self-rewards. Near someone in distress, we may feel distress. A woman's scream outside your window arouses and distresses you. If you cannot reduce your arousal by interpreting the scream as a playful shriek, then you may investigate or give aid, thereby reducing your distress (Piliavin & Piliavin, 1973). Altruism researcher Dennis Krebs (1975) found that Harvard University men whose physiological responses and self-reports revealed the most arousal in response to another's distress also gave the most help to the person.

"For it is in giving that we receive."
—*SAINT FRANCIS OF ASSISI, 1181–1226*

egoism
A motive (supposedly underlying all behavior) to increase one's own welfare. The opposite of altruism, which aims to increase another's welfare.

GUILT Distress is not the only negative emotion we act to reduce. Throughout recorded history, guilt has been a painful emotion, so painful that we will act in ways that avoid guilt feelings. As Everett Sanderson remarked after heroically saving a child who had fallen onto subway tracks in front of an approaching train, "If I hadn't tried to save that little girl, if I had just stood there like the others, I would have died inside. I would have been no good to myself from then on."

Cultures have institutionalized ways to relieve guilt: animal and human sacrifices, offerings of grain and money, penitent behavior, confession, denial. In ancient Israel, the sins of the people were periodically laid on a "scapegoat" animal that was then led into the wilderness to carry away the people's guilt.

To examine the consequences of guilt, social psychologists have induced people to transgress: to lie, to deliver shock, to knock over a table loaded with alphabetized cards, to break a machine, to cheat. Afterward, the guilt-laden participants may be offered a way to relieve their guilt: by confessing, by disparaging the one harmed, or by doing a good deed to offset the bad one. The results are remarkably consistent: People will do whatever can be done to expunge the guilt, relieve their bad feelings, and restore their self-image.

Picture yourself as a participant in one such experiment conducted with Mississippi State University students by David McMillen and James Austin (1971). You and another student, each seeking to earn credit toward a course requirement, arrive for the experiment. Soon after, a confederate enters, portraying himself as a previous participant looking for a lost book. He strikes up a conversation in which he mentions that the experiment involves taking a multiple-choice test, for which most of the correct answers are "B." After the accomplice departs, the experimenter arrives, explains the experiment, and then asks, "Have either of you been in this experiment before or heard anything about it?"

Would you lie? The behavior of those who have gone before you in this experiment—100 percent of whom told the little lie—suggests that you would. After you have taken the test (without receiving any feedback on it), the experimenter says: "You are free to leave. However, if you have some spare time, I could use your help in scoring some questionnaires." Assuming you have told the lie, do you think you would now be more willing to volunteer some time? The answer again is yes. On average, those who had not been induced to lie volunteered only two minutes of time. Those who had lied were apparently eager to redeem their self-images; on average they offered a whopping 63 minutes. One moral of this experiment was well expressed by a 7-year-old girl, who, in one of our own experiments, wrote: "Don't Lie or youl Live with gilt" (and you will feel a need to relieve it).

Our eagerness to do good after doing bad reflects our need to reduce *private* guilt and restore a shaken self-image. It also reflects our desire to reclaim a positive *public* image. We are more likely to redeem ourselves with helpful behavior when other people know about our misdeeds (Carlsmith & Gross, 1969).

All in all, guilt leads to much good. By motivating people to confess, apologize, help, and avoid repeated harm, guilt boosts sensitivity and sustains close relationships.

Among adults, the inner rewards of altruism—feeling good about oneself after donating blood or helping pick up someone's dropped materials—can offset other negative moods as well (Cialdini, Kenrick, & Baumann, 1981; Williamson & Clark, 1989). Thus, when an adult is in a guilty, a sad, or an otherwise negative mood, a helpful deed (or any other mood-improving experience) helps neutralize the bad feelings.

EXCEPTIONS TO THE FEEL BAD–DO GOOD SCENARIO Among well-socialized adults, should we always expect to find the "feel bad–do good" phenomenon? No. In Chapter 10 we saw that one negative mood, anger, produces anything but compassion. Another exception is profound grief. People who suffer the loss of a spouse or a child, whether through death or separation, often undergo a period of intense self-preoccupation, which restrains giving to others (Aderman & Berkowitz, 1983; Gibbons & Wicklund, 1982).

In a powerful laboratory simulation of self-focused grief, William Thompson, Claudia Cowan, and David Rosenhan (1980) had Stanford University students listen privately to a taped description of a person (whom they were to imagine was their best friend of the other sex) dying of cancer. The experiment focused some students' attention on their own worry and grief:

> He (she) could die and you would lose him, never be able to talk to him again. Or worse, he could die slowly. You would know every minute could be your last time together. For months you would have to be cheerful for him while you were sad. You would have to watch him die in pieces, until the last piece finally went, and you would be alone.

For others, it focused their attention on the friend:

> He spends his time lying in bed, waiting
> those interminable hours, just waiting and hoping for something to happen. Anything. He tells you that it's not knowing that is the hardest.

Schoolchildren packing toy donations for the needy. As children mature, they usually come to take pleasure in being helpful to others.

The researchers report that regardless of which tape the participants heard, they were profoundly moved and sobered by the experience, yet not the least regretful of participating (although some participants who in a control condition listened to a boring tape were regretful). Did their moods affect their helpfulness? When immediately thereafter they were given a chance to help a graduate student with her research anonymously, 25 percent of those whose attention had been self-focused helped. Of those whose attention was other-focused, 83 percent helped. The two groups were equally touched, but only the other-focused participants found helping someone especially rewarding. In short, the feel bad–do good effect occurs with people whose attention is on others, people for whom altruism is therefore rewarding (Barnett & others, 1980; McMillen & others, 1977). If they are not self-preoccupied by depression or grief, sad people are sensitive, helpful people.

FEEL GOOD, DO GOOD   Are happy people unhelpful? Quite the contrary. There are few more consistent findings in psychology: Happy people are helpful people. This effect occurs with both children and adults, regardless of whether the good mood comes from a success, from thinking happy thoughts, or from any of several other positive experiences (Salovey & others, 1991). One woman recalled her experience after falling in love:

> At the office, I could hardly keep from shouting out how deliriously happy I felt. The work was easy; things that had annoyed me on previous occasions were taken in stride. And I had strong impulses to help others; I wanted to share my joy. When Mary's type-writer broke down, I virtually sprang to my feet to assist. Mary! My former "enemy"! (Tennov, 1979, p. 22)

In experiments on happiness and helpfulness, the person who is helped may be someone seeking a donation, an experimenter seeking help with paperwork, or a woman who drops papers. Here are three examples.

"It's curious how, when you're in love, you yearn to go about doing acts of kindness to everybody."
—P. G. WODEHOUSE, THE MATING SEASON, 1949

In Sydney, Australia, Joseph Forgas and his colleagues (2008) had a confederate offer either a mood-boosting compliment to a Target department store salesperson or a neutral or mood-deflating comment. Moments later, a second confederate, who was "blind" to the mood-induction condition, sought the employee's help in locating a nonexistent item. Among less-experienced staff (who lacked a practiced routine for answering such requests), those receiving the mood boost made the greatest effort to help.

In Opole, Poland, Dariusz Dolinski and Richard Nawrat (1998) found that a positive mood of relief can dramatically boost helping. Imagine yourself as one of their unwitting subjects. After illegally parking your car for a few moments, you return to discover what looks like a ticket under your windshield wiper (where parking tickets are placed). Groaning inwardly, you pick up the apparent ticket, and then are much relieved to discover it is only an ad (or a blood drive appeal). Moments later, a university student approaches you and asks you to spend 15 minutes answering questions—to "help me complete my M.A. thesis." Would your positive, relieved mood make you more likely to help? Indeed, 62 percent of people whose fear had just turned to relief agreed willingly. That was nearly double the number who did so when no ticketlike paper was left or when it was left on the car door (not a place for a ticket).

In the United States, Alice Isen, Margaret Clark, and Mark Schwartz (1976) had a confederate call people who had received a free sample of stationery 0 to 20 minutes earlier. The confederate said she had used her last dime to dial this (supposedly wrong) number and asked each person to relay a message by phone. As Figure 12.1 shows, the individuals' willingness to relay the phone message rose during the 5 minutes afterward. Then, as the good mood wore off, helpfulness dropped.

If sad people are sometimes extra helpful, how can it be that happy people are also helpful? Experiments reveal that several factors are at work (Carlson & others, 1988). Helping softens a bad mood and sustains a good mood. (Perhaps you can recall feeling good after giving someone directions.) A positive mood is, in turn, conducive to positive thoughts and positive self-esteem, which predispose us to positive behavior (Berkowitz, 1987; Cunningham & others, 1990; Isen & others, 1978). In a good mood—after being given a gift or while feeling the warm glow of success—people are more likely to have positive thoughts and associations with being helpful. Positive thinkers are likely to be positive actors.

FIGURE :: 12.1

Percentage of Those Willing to Relay a Phone Message 0 to 20 Minutes after Receiving a Free Sample

Of control subjects who did not receive a gift, only 10 percent helped.

Source: Data from Isen & others, 1976.

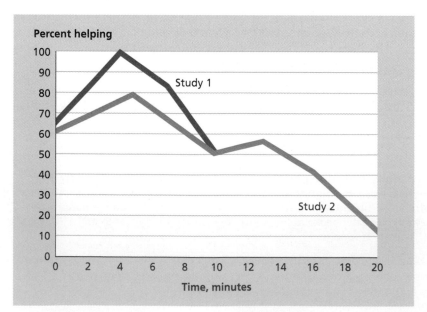

SOCIAL NORMS

Often we help others not because we have calculated consciously that such behavior is in our self-interest but because of a subtler form of self-interest: because something tells us we *ought* to. We ought to help a new neighbor move in. We ought to return the wallet we found. We ought to protect our combat buddies from harm. Norms, the *oughts* of our lives, are social expectations. They *prescribe* proper behavior. Researchers who study helping behavior have identified two social norms that motivate altruism: the reciprocity norm and the social-responsibility norm.

THE RECIPROCITY NORM   Sociologist Alvin Gouldner (1960) contended that one universal moral code is a **reciprocity norm:** *To those who help us, we should return help, not harm.* Gouldner believed this norm is as universal as the incest taboo. We "invest" in others and expect dividends. Politicians know that the one who gives a favor can later expect a favor. Mail surveys and solicitations sometimes include a little gift of money or personalized address labels, assuming some people will reciprocate the favor. The reciprocity norm even applies in marriage. At times, one may give more than one receives, but in the long run, the exchange should balance out. In all such interactions, to receive without giving in return violates the reciprocity norm.

Reciprocity within social networks helps define the **social capital**—the supportive connections, information flow, trust, and cooperative actions—that keep a community healthy. Neighbors keeping an eye on one another's homes is social capital in action.

The norm operates most effectively as people respond publicly to deeds earlier done to them. In laboratory games as in everyday life, fleeting one-shot encounters produce greater selfishness than sustained relationships. But even when people respond anonymously, they sometimes do the right thing and repay the good done to them. (Burger & others, 2009). In one experiment, Mark Whatley and his colleagues (1999) found that university students more willingly made a charity pledge when it was the charity of someone who had previously bought them some candy (Figure 12.2).

When people cannot reciprocate, they may feel threatened and demeaned by accepting aid. Thus, proud, high-self-esteem people are often reluctant to seek help (Nadler & Fisher, 1986). Receiving unsolicited help can take one's self-esteem down a notch (Schneider & others, 1996; Shell & Eisenberg, 1992). Studies have found this can happen to beneficiaries of affirmative action, especially when affirmative action fails to affirm the person's competence and chances for future success (Pratkanis & Turner, 1996).

THE SOCIAL-RESPONSIBILITY NORM
The reciprocity norm reminds us to balance giving and receiving in social relations. If the only norm were reciprocity, however, the Samaritan would not have been the Good Samaritan. In the parable, Jesus obviously had something more humanitarian in mind, something made explicit in another of his teachings: "If you love those who love you [the reciprocity norm], what right have you to claim any credit? . . . I say to you, love your enemies" (Matthew 5:46, 44).

With people who clearly are dependent and unable to reciprocate, such as children, the severely impoverished, and those with

reciprocity norm
An expectation that people will help, not hurt, those who have helped them.

"If you don't go to somebody's funeral, they won't come to yours."
—*YOGI BERRA*

social capital
The mutual support and cooperation enabled by a social network.

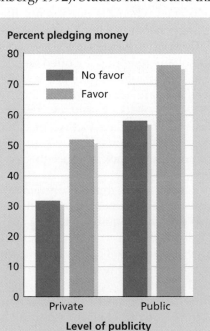

Percent pledging money

FIGURE :: 12.2

Private and Public Reciprocation of a Favor

People were more willing to pledge to an experimental confederate's charity if the confederate had done a small favor for them earlier, especially when their reciprocation was made known to the confederate.
Source: From Whatley & others, 1999.

Following Pakistan's devastating 2005 earthquake, the social-responsibility norm engaged helping behaviors.

social-responsibility norm
An expectation that people will help those needing help.

disabilities, another social norm motivates our helping. The **social-responsibility norm** is the belief that people should help those who need help, without regard to future exchanges (Berkowitz, 1972; Schwartz, 1975). The norm motivates people to retrieve a dropped book for a person on crutches, for example. In India, a relatively collectivist culture, people support the social-responsibility norm more strongly than in the individualist West (Baron & Miller, 2000). They voice an obligation to help even when the need is not life-threatening or the needy person—perhaps a stranger needing a bone marrow transplant—is outside their family circle.

Even when helpers in Western countries remain anonymous and have no expectation of any reward, they often help needy people (Shotland & Stebbins, 1983). However, they usually apply the social-responsibility norm selectively to those whose need appears not to be due to their own negligence. Especially among political conservatives (Skitka & Tetlock, 1993), the norm seems to be: Give people what they deserve. If they are victims of circumstance, such as natural disaster, then by all means be generous. If they seem to have created their own problems (by laziness, immorality, or lack of foresight, for example), then, the norm suggests, they don't deserve help.

Responses are thus closely tied to *attributions*. If we attribute the need to an uncontrollable predicament, we help. If we attribute the need to the person's choices, fairness does not require us to help; we say it's the person's own fault (Weiner, 1980). Attributions affect public policy as well as individual helping decisions. Many Americans in 2008 opposed government help for the country's failing automakers, which were held responsible for their own short-sighted decisions.

The key, say Udo Rudolph and colleagues (2004) from their review of more than three dozen pertinent studies, is whether your attributions evoke sympathy, which in turn motivates helping (Figure 12.3).

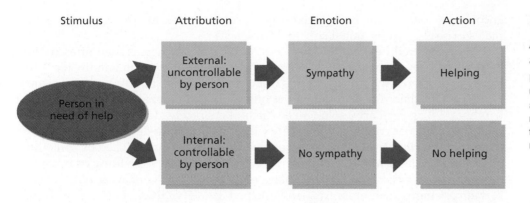

Stimulus   Attribution   Emotion   Action

Person in need of help

External: uncontrollable by person → Sympathy → Helping

Internal: controllable by person → No sympathy → No helping

FIGURE :: 12.3
Attributions and Helping

In this model, proposed by German researcher Udo Rudolph and colleagues (2004), helping is mediated by people's explanations of the predicament and their resulting degree of sympathy.

When the *Titanic* sank, 70 percent of the females and 20 percent of the males survived. The chances of survival were 2.5 times better for a first- than a third-class passenger. Yet, thanks to gender norms for altruism, the survival odds were better for third-class passengers who were women (47 percent) than for first-class passengers who were men (31 percent).

Imagine yourself as one of the University of Wisconsin students in a study by Richard Barnes, William Ickes, and Robert Kidd (1979). You receive a call from "Tony Freeman," who explains that he is in your introductory psychology class. He says that he needs help for the upcoming exam and that he has gotten your name from the class roster. "I don't know. I just don't seem to take good notes in there," Tony explains. "I know I can, but sometimes I just don't feel like it, so most of the notes I have aren't very good to study with." How sympathetic would you feel toward Tony? How much of a sacrifice would you make to lend him your notes? If you are like the students in this experiment, you would probably be much less inclined to help than if Tony had explained that his troubles were beyond his control. Thus, the social-responsibility norm compels us to help those most in need and those most deserving.

GENDER AND RECEIVING HELP If, indeed, perception of another's need strongly determines one's willingness to help, will women, if perceived as less competent and more dependent, receive more help than men? That is indeed the case. Alice Eagly and Maureen Crowley (1986) located 35 studies that compared help received by male or female victims. (Virtually all the studies involved short-term encounters with strangers in need—the very situations in which people expect males to be chivalrous, note Eagly and Crowley.)

Women offered help equally to males and females, whereas men offered more help when the persons in need were females. Several experiments in the 1970s found that women with disabled cars (for example, with a flat tire) got many more offers of help than did men (Penner & others, 1973; Pomazal & Clore, 1973; West & others, 1975). Similarly, solo female hitchhikers received far more offers of help than solo males or couples (Pomazal & Clore, 1973; M. Snyder & others, 1974). Of course, men's chivalry toward lone women may have been motivated by something other than altruism. Mating motives not only increase men's spending on conspicuous luxuries, they also motivate displays of heroism (Griskevicius & others, 2007). Not surprisingly, men more frequently helped attractive than unattractive women (Mims & others, 1975; Stroufe & others, 1977; West & Brown, 1975).

Women not only receive more offers of help in certain situations but also seek more help (Addis & Mahalik, 2003). They are twice as likely to seek medical and psychiatric help. They are the majority of callers to radio counseling programs and clients of college counseling centers. They more often welcome help from friends. Arie Nadler (1991), a Tel Aviv University expert on help seeking, attributes this to gender differences in independence versus interdependence (Chapter 5).

Evolutionary Psychology

Another explanation of helping comes from evolutionary theory. As you may recall from Chapters 5 and 11, evolutionary psychology contends that life's essence is gene survival. Our genes drive us in adaptive ways that have maximized their chance of survival. When our ancestors died, their genes lived on, predisposing us to behave in ways that will spread them into the future.

"Fallen heroes do not have children. If self-sacrifice results in fewer descendants, the genes that allow heroes to be created can be expected to disappear gradually from the population."

—*E. O. WILSON*, ON HUMAN NATURE, 1978

As suggested by the title of Richard Dawkins's (1976) popular book *The Selfish Gene*, evolutionary psychology offers a humbling human image—one that psychologist Donald Campbell (1975a, 1975b) called a biological reaffirmation of a deep, self-serving "original sin." Genes that predispose individuals to self-sacrifice in the interests of strangers' welfare would not survive in the evolutionary competition. Genetic selfishness should, however, predispose us toward two specific types of selfless or even self-sacrificial helping: kin protection and reciprocity.

KIN PROTECTION

Our genes dispose us to care for relatives. Thus, one form of self-sacrifice that *would* increase gene survival is devotion to one's children. Compared with neglectful parents, parents who put their children's welfare ahead of their own are more likely to pass their genes on. As evolutionary psychologist David Barash (1979, p. 153) wrote, "Genes help themselves by being nice to themselves, even if they are enclosed in different bodies." Genetic egoism (at the biological level) fosters parental altruism (at the psychological level). Although evolution favors self-sacrifice for one's children, children have less at stake in the survival of their parents' genes. Thus, according to the theory, parents will generally be more devoted to their children than their children are to them.

kin selection
The idea that evolution has selected altruism toward one's close relatives to enhance the survival of mutually shared genes.

Other relatives share genes in proportion to their biological closeness. You share one-half your genes with your brothers and sisters, one-eighth with your cousins. **Kin selection**—favoritism toward those who share our genes—led the evolutionary biologist J. B. S. Haldane to jest that although he would not give up his life for his brother, he would sacrifice himself for *three* brothers—or for nine cousins. Haldane would not have been surprised that genetic relatedness predicts helping and that genetically identical twins are noticeably more mutually supportive than fraternal twins (Segal, 1984; Stewart-Williams, 2007). In one laboratory game experiment, identical twins were half again as likely as fraternal twins to cooperate with their twin for a shared gain when playing for money (Segal & Hershberger, 1999).

The point is not that we calculate genetic relatedness before helping but that nature (as well as culture) programs us to care about close relatives. When Carlos Rogers of the Toronto Raptors NBA basketball team volunteered to end his career and donate a kidney to his sister (who died before she could receive it), people applauded his self-sacrificial love. But such acts for close kin are not totally unexpected. What we do not expect (and therefore honor) is the altruism of those who risk themselves to save a stranger.

We share common genes with many besides our relatives. Blue-eyed people share particular genes with other blue-eyed people. How do we detect the people in which copies of our genes occur most abundantly? As the blue-eyes example suggests, one clue lies in physical similarities. Also, in evolutionary history, genes were shared more with neighbors than with foreigners. Are we therefore biologically biased to be more helpful to those who look similar to us and those who live near us? In the aftermath of natural disasters and other life-and-death situations, the order of who gets helped would not surprise an evolutionary psychologist: the children before the old, family members before friends, neighbors before strangers (Burnstein & others, 1994; Form & Nosow, 1958). Helping stays close to home.

Some evolutionary psychologists note that kin selection predisposes ethnic ingroup favoritism—the root of countless historical and contemporary conflicts (Rushton, 1991). E. O. Wilson (1978) noted that kin selection is "the enemy of civilization. If human beings are to a large extent guided . . . to favor their own relatives and tribe, only a limited amount of global harmony is possible" (p. 167).

RECIPROCITY

Genetic self-interest also predicts reciprocity. An organism helps another, biologist Robert Trivers argued, because it expects help in return (Binham, 1980). The giver expects later to be the getter. Failure to reciprocate gets punished. The cheat, the turncoat, and the traitor are universally despised.

Reciprocity works best in small, isolated groups, groups in which one will often see the people for whom one does favors. Sociable female baboons—those who groom and stay in close contact with their peers—gain a reproductive advantage: Their infants more often live to see a first birthday (Silk & others, 2003). If a vampire bat has gone a day or two without food, it asks a well-fed nestmate to regurgitate food for a meal (Wilkinson, 1990). The donor bat does so willingly, losing fewer hours till starvation than the recipient gains. But such favors occur only among familiar nestmates who share in the give-and-take. Those who always take and never give, and those who have no relationship with the donor bat, go hungry. It pays to have friends.

For similar reasons, reciprocity among humans is stronger in rural villages than in big cities. Small schools, towns, churches, work teams, and dorms are all conducive to a community spirit in which people care for one another. Compared with people in small-town or rural environments, those in big cities are less willing to relay a phone message, less likely to mail "lost" letters, less cooperative with survey interviewers, less helpful to a lost child, and less willing to do small favors (Hedge & Yousif, 1992; Steblay, 1987).

If individual self-interest inevitably wins in genetic competition, then why will we help strangers? Why will we help those whose limited resources or abilities preclude their reciprocating? And what causes soldiers to throw themselves on grenades? One answer, initially favored by Darwin (then discounted by selfish-gene theorists, but now back again) is *group selection:* When groups are in competition, groups of mutually supportive altruists outlast groups of nonaltruists (Krebs, 1998; McAndrew, 2002; Wilson & Wilson, 2008). This is most dramatically evident with the social insects, who function like cells in a body. Bees and ants will labor sacrificially for their colony's survival. To a much lesser extent, humans exhibit ingroup loyalty by sacrificing to support "us," sometimes against "them." Natural selection

"Let's say you're walking by a pond and there's a drowning baby. If you said, 'I've just paid $200 for these shoes and the water would ruin them, so I won't save the baby,' you'd be an awful, horrible person. But there are millions of children around the world in the same situation, where just a little money for medicine or food could save their lives. And yet we don't consider ourselves monsters for having this dinner rather than giving the money to Oxfam. Why is that?"

—PHILOSOPHER-PSYCHOLOGIST JOSHUA GREENE (QUOTED BY ZIMMER, 2004).

"Just as nature is said to abhor a vacuum, so it abhors true altruism. Society, on the other hand, adores it."

—EVOLUTIONARY PSYCHOLO-GIST DAVID BARASH, "THE CONFLICTING PRESSURES OF SELFISHNESS AND ALTRUISM," 2003

TABLE :: 12.1 Comparing Theories of Altruism

How Is Altruism Explained?

Theory	Level of Explanation	Externally Rewarded Helping	Intrinsic Helping
Social-exchange	Psychological	External rewards for helping	Distress → inner rewards for helping
Social norms	Sociological	Reciprocity norm	Social-responsibility norm
Evolutionary	Biological	Reciprocity	Kin selection

is therefore "multilevel," say some researchers (Mirsky, 2009). It operates at *both* individual and group levels.

Donald Campbell (1975a, 1975b) offered another basis for unreciprocated altruism: Human societies evolved ethical and religious rules that serve as brakes on the biological bias toward self-interest. Commandments such as "love your neighbor as yourself" admonish us to balance self-concern with concern for the group, and so contribute to the survival of the group. Richard Dawkins (1976) offered a similar conclusion: "Let us try to *teach* generosity and altruism, because we are born selfish. Let us understand what our selfish genes are up to, because we may then at least have the chance to upset their designs, something no other species has ever aspired to" (p. 3).

Comparing and Evaluating Theories of Helping

By now you perhaps have noticed similarities among the social-exchange, social norm, and evolutionary views of altruism. As Table 12.1 shows, each proposes two types of prosocial behavior: a tit-for-tat reciprocal exchange and a more unconditional helpfulness. They do so at three complementary levels of explanation. If the evolutionary view is correct, then our genetic predispositions *should* manifest themselves in psychological and sociological phenomena.

Each theory appeals to logic. Yet each is vulnerable to charges of being speculative and after the fact. When we start with a known effect (the give-and-take of everyday life) and explain it by conjecturing a social-exchange process, a "reciprocity norm," or an evolutionary origin, we might merely be explaining-by-naming. The argument that a behavior occurs because of its survival function is hard to disprove. With hindsight it's easy to think it had to be that way. If we can explain *any* conceivable behavior after the fact as the result of a social exchange, a norm, or natural selection, then we cannot disprove the theories. Each theory's task is therefore to generate predictions that enable us to test it.

An effective theory also provides a coherent scheme for summarizing a variety of observations. With this criterion, our three altruism theories get higher marks. Each offers us a broad perspective that illuminates both enduring commitments and spontaneous help.

Genuine Altruism

My town, Holland, Michigan, has a corporation with several thousand employees that, for most of the last half-century, annually gave away 10 percent of its pretax profits with one stipulation: The gift was always anonymous. In a nearby city, anonymous donors in 2005 pledged to provide Michigan public university or community college costs—ranging from 65 to 100 percent depending on length of residence—for *all* Kalamazoo public schools graduates. Are such anonymous benefactors—along with lifesaving heroes, everyday blood donors, and Peace Corps volunteers—ever motivated by an ultimate goal of selfless concern for others? Or is their ultimate goal some form of self-benefit, such as gaining a reward, avoiding punishment and guilt, or relieving distress?

"Are you all right, Mister? Is there anything I can do?"

"Young man, you're the only one who bothered to stop! I'm a millionaire and I'm going to give you five thousand dollars!"

We never know what benefits may come from helping someone in distress.

Abraham Lincoln illustrated the philosophical issue in a conversation with another passenger in a horse-drawn coach. After Lincoln argued that selfishness prompts all good deeds, he noticed a sow making a terrible noise. Her piglets had gotten into a marshy pond and were in danger of drowning. Lincoln called the coach to a halt, jumped out, ran back, and lifted the little pigs to safety. Upon his return, his companion remarked, "Now, Abe, where does selfishness come in on this little episode?" "Why, bless your soul, Ed, that was the very essence of selfishness. I should have had no peace of mind all day had I gone and left that suffering old sow worrying over those pigs. I did it to get peace of mind, don't you see?" (Sharp, cited by Batson & others, 1986). Until recently, psychologists would have sided with Lincoln.

Helpfulness so reliably makes helpers feel better that Daniel Batson (2006; Batson & others, 2008) has devoted much of his career to discerning whether helpfulness also contains a streak of genuine altruism. Batson theorizes that our willingness to help is influenced by both self-serving and selfless considerations (Figure 12.4). Distress over someone's suffering motivates us to relieve our upset, either by escaping the distressing situation (like the priest and the Levite) or by helping (like the Samaritan). But especially when we feel securely attached to someone, report both Batson and a team of attachment researchers led by Mario Mikulincer (2005), we also feel **empathy.** Loving parents suffer when their children suffer and rejoice over their children's joys—an empathy lacking in child abusers and other perpetrators of cruelty (Miller & Eisenberg, 1988). We also feel empathy for those with whom we identify. In September 1997 millions of people who never came within miles of England's Princess Diana (but who felt as if they knew her after hundreds of tabloid stories and 44 *People* magazine cover articles) wept for her and her motherless sons—but shed no tears for the nearly 1 million faceless Rwandans murdered or having died in squalid refugee camps since 1994.

When we feel empathy, we focus not so much on our own distress as on the sufferer. Genuine sympathy and compassion motivate us to help others for their own

empathy
The vicarious experience of another's feelings; putting oneself in another's shoes.

"When people ask me how I'm doing, I say, 'I'm only as good as my most sad child.'"
—*MICHELLE OBAMA, OCTOBER 24, 2008*

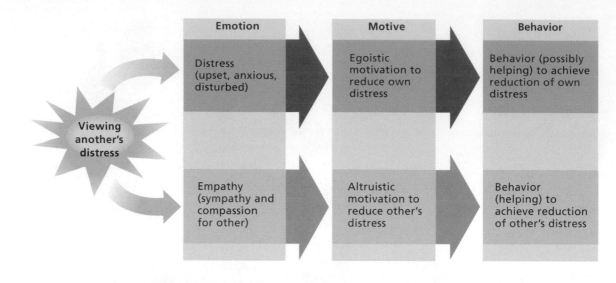

Emotion	Motive	Behavior
Distress (upset, anxious, disturbed)	Egoistic motivation to reduce own distress	Behavior (possibly helping) to achieve reduction of own distress
Empathy (sympathy and compassion for other)	Altruistic motivation to reduce other's distress	Behavior (helping) to achieve reduction of other's distress

Viewing another's distress

FIGURE :: 12.4

Egoistic and Altruistic Routes to Helping

Viewing another's distress can evoke a mixture of self-focused distress and other-focused empathy. Researchers agree that distress triggers egoistic motives. But they debate whether empathy can trigger a pure altruistic motive.

Source: Adapted from Batson, Fultz, & Schoenrade, 1987.

sakes. When we value another's welfare, perceive the person as in need, and take the person's perspective, we feel empathic concern (Batson & others, 2007).

In humans, empathy comes naturally. Even day-old infants cry more when they hear another infant cry (Hoffman, 1981). In hospital nurseries, one baby's crying sometimes evokes a chorus of crying. Most 18-month-old infants, after observing an unfamiliar adult accidentally drop a marker or clothespin and have trouble reaching it, will readily help (Warneken & Tomasello, 2006). To some, this suggests that humans are hardwired for empathy. Primates and even mice also display empathy, indicating that the building blocks of altruism predate humanity (de Waal, 2005, 2007, 2008; Langford & others, 2006). In one classic experiment, most rhesus monkeys refused to operate a device that gained them food if it would cause another monkey to receive an electric shock (Masserman & others, 1964).

Often distress and empathy together motivate responses to a crisis. In 1983, people watched on television as an Australian bushfire wiped out hundreds of homes near Melbourne. Afterward, Paul Amato (1986) studied donations of money and goods. He found that those who felt angry or indifferent gave less than those who felt either distressed (shocked and sickened) or empathic (sympathetic and worried for the victims).

To separate egoistic distress reduction from empathy-based altruism, Batson's research group conducted studies that aroused feelings of empathy. Then the researchers noted whether the aroused people would reduce their own distress by escaping the situation or whether they would go out of their way to aid the person. The results were consistent: With their empathy aroused, people usually helped.

In one of these experiments, Batson and his associates (1981) had University of Kansas women observe a young woman suffering while she supposedly received electric shocks. During a pause in the experiment, the obviously upset victim explained to the experimenter that a childhood fall against an electric fence left her acutely sensitive to shocks. The experimenter suggested that perhaps the observer (the actual participant in this experiment) might trade places and take the remaining shocks for her. Previously, half of these actual participants had been led to believe the suffering person was a kindred spirit on matters of values and interests (thus arousing their empathy). Some also were led to believe that their part in the

Might genuine altruism motivate an international health educator leading exercise with children in Uganda? Daniel Batson believes it might.

experiment was completed, so that in any case they were done observing the woman's suffering. Nevertheless, their empathy aroused, virtually all willingly offered to substitute for the victim.

Is this genuine altruism? Mark Schaller and Robert Cialdini (1988) doubted it. Feeling empathy for a sufferer makes one sad, they noted. In one of their experiments, they led people to believe that their sadness was going to be relieved by a different sort of mood-boosting experience—listening to a comedy tape. Under such conditions, people who felt empathy were not especially helpful. Schaller and Cialdini concluded that if we feel empathy but know that something else will make us feel better, we aren't as likely to help.

Everyone agrees that some helpful acts are either obviously egoistic (done to gain external rewards or avoid punishment) or subtly egoistic (done to gain internal rewards or relieve inner distress). Is there a third type of helpfulness—a genuine altruism that aims simply to increase another's welfare (producing happiness for oneself merely as a by-product)? Is empathy-based helping a source of such altruism? Cialdini (1991) and his colleagues Mark Schaller and Jim Fultz have doubted it. They note that no experiment rules out all possible egoistic explanations for helpfulness.

But other findings suggest that genuine altruism does exist: With their empathy aroused, people will help even when they believe no one will know about their helping. Their concern continues until someone *has* been helped (Fultz & others, 1986). If their efforts to help are unsuccessful, they feel bad even if the failure is not their fault (Batson & Weeks, 1996). And people will sometimes persist in wanting to help a suffering person even when they believe their own distressed mood arises from a "mood-fixing" drug (Schroeder & others, 1988).

After 25 such experiments testing egoism versus altruistic empathy, Batson (2001, 2006) and others (Dovidio, 1991; Staub, 1991) believe that sometimes people do focus on others' welfare, not on their own. Batson, a former philosophy and theology student, had begun his research feeling "excited to think that if we could ascertain whether people's concerned reactions were genuine, and not simply a subtle form of selfishness, then we could shed new light on a basic issue regarding

"The measure of our character is what we would do if we were never found out."
—PARAPHRASED FROM THOMAS MACAULAY

focus
ON

The Benefits—and the Costs—of Empathy-Induced Altruism

People do most of what they do, including much of what they do for others, for their own benefit, acknowledge University of Kansas altruism researcher Daniel Batson and his colleagues (2004). But egoism is not the whole story of helping, they believe; there is also a genuine altruism rooted in empathy, in feelings of sympathy and compassion for others' welfare. We are supremely social creatures. Consider:

Empathy-induced altruism

- *produces sensitive helping.* Where there is empathy, it's not just the thought that counts—it's alleviating the other's suffering.
- *inhibits aggression.* Show Batson someone who feels empathy for a target of potential aggression and he'll show you someone who's unlikely to favor attack— someone who's as likely to forgive as to harbor anger. In general, women report more empathic feelings than men, and they are less likely to support war and other forms of aggression (Jones, 2003).
- *increases cooperation.* In laboratory experiments, Batson and Nadia Ahmad found that people in potential conflict are more trusting and cooperative when they feel empathy for the other. Personalizing an outgroup, by getting to know people in it, helps people understand their perspective.
- *improves attitudes toward stigmatized groups.* Take others' perspective, allow yourself to feel what they feel, and you may become more supportive of others like them (the homeless, those with AIDS, or even convicted criminals).

But empathy-induced altruism comes with liabilities, notes the Batson group.

- *It can be harmful.* People who risk their lives on behalf of others sometimes lose them. People who seek to do good can also do harm, sometimes by unintentionally humiliating or demotivating the recipient.
- *It can't address all needs.* It's easier to feel empathy for a needy individual than, say, for Mother Earth, whose environment is being stripped and warmed at the peril of our descendants.
- *It burns out.* Feeling others' pain is painful, which may cause us to avoid situations that evoke our empathy, or to experience "burnout" or "compassion fatigue."
- *It can feed favoritism, injustice, and indifference to the larger common good.* Empathy, being particular, produces partiality—toward a single child or family or pet. Moral principles, being universal, produce concern for unseen others as well. Empathy-based estate planning bequeaths inheritances to particular loved ones. Morality-based estate planning is more inclusive. When their empathy for someone is aroused, people will violate their own standards of fairness and justice by giving that person favored treatment (Batson & others, 1997; Oceja, 2008). Ironically, note Batson and his colleagues (1999), empathy-induced altruism can therefore "pose a powerful threat to the common good [by leading] me to narrow my focus of concern to those for whom I especially care—the needing friend—and in so doing to lose sight of the bleeding crowd." No wonder charity so often stays close to home.

"As I see it, there are two great forces of human nature: self-interest, and caring for others."

—BILL GATES, "A NEW APPROACH TO CAPITALISM IN THE TWENTY-FIRST CENTURY," 2008

human nature" (1999a). Two decades later he believes he has his answer. Genuine "empathy-induced altruism is part of human nature" (1999b). And that, says Batson, raises the hope—confirmed by research—that inducing empathy might improve attitudes toward stigmatized people: people with AIDS, the homeless, the imprisoned, and other minorities. (See "Focus On: The Benefit—and the Costs—of Empathy-Induced Altruism.")

During the Vietnam War, 63 soldiers received Medals of Honor for using their bodies to shield their buddies from exploding devices (Hunt, 1990). Most were in close-knit combat groups. Most threw themselves on live hand grenades. In doing so, 59 sacrificed their lives. So did several Iraq war soldiers, such as Corporal Jason Dunham, whose family in 2007 received his Medal of Honor after he threw himself on a grenade to save his unit. Unlike other altruists, such as the 50,000 Gentiles now believed to have rescued 200,000 Jews from the Nazis, these soldiers had no time to reflect on the shame of cowardice or the eternal rewards of self-sacrifice. Yet something drove them to act.

Summing Up: Why Do We Help?

- Three theories explain helping behavior. The social-exchange theory assumes that helping, like other social behaviors, is motivated by a desire to maximize rewards, which may be external or internal. Thus, after wrongdoing, people often become more willing to offer help. Sad people also tend to be helpful. Finally, there is a striking feel good–do good effect: Happy people are helpful people. Social norms also mandate helping. The reciprocity norm stimulates us to help those who have helped us. The social-responsibility norm beckons us to help needy people, even if they cannot reciprocate, as long as they are deserving. Women in crisis, partly because they may be seen as more needy, receive more offers of help than men, especially from men.

- Evolutionary psychology assumes two types of helping: devotion to kin and reciprocity. Most evolutionary psychologists, however, believe that the genes of selfish individuals are more likely to survive than the genes of self-sacrificing individuals. Thus, selfishness is our natural tendency and society must therefore teach helping.

- We can evaluate these three theories according to the ways in which they characterize prosocial behavior as based on tit-for-tat exchange and/or unconditional helpfulness. Each can be criticized for using speculative or after-the-fact reasoning, but they do provide a coherent scheme for summarizing observations of prosocial behavior.

- In addition to helping that is motivated by external and internal rewards, and the evading of punishment or distress, there appears also to be a genuine, empathy-based altruism. With their empathy aroused, many people are motivated to assist others in need or distress, even when their helping is anonymous or their own mood will be unaffected.

When Will We Help?

What circumstances prompt people to help, or not to help? How and why is helping influenced by the number and behavior of other bystanders? by mood states? by traits and values?

On March 13, 1964, 28-year-old bar manager Kitty Genovese was set upon by a knife-wielding attacker as she returned from work to her Queens, New York, apartment house at 3:00 A.M. Her screams of terror and pleas for help—"Oh my God, he stabbed me! Please help me! Please help me!"—aroused some of her neighbors (38 of them, according to an initial *New York Times* report). Some supposedly came to their windows and caught fleeting glimpses as the attacker left and returned to attack again. Not until her attacker finally departed did anyone call the police. Soon after, Kitty Genovese died.

A later analysis disputed the initial report that 38 witnesses observed the murder yet remained inactive (Manning & others, 2007). Nevertheless, the story helped inspire research on bystander inaction, which was illustrated in other incidents:

- Seventeen-year-old Andrew Mormille was knifed in the stomach as he rode the subway home. After his attackers left the car, 11 other riders watched the young man bleed to death.
- Eleanor Bradley tripped and broke her leg while shopping. Dazed and in pain, she pleaded for help. For 40 minutes, the stream of sidewalk pedestrians simply parted and flowed around her. Finally, a cab driver helped her to a doctor (Darley & Latané, 1968).
- As more than a million locals and tourists mingled in the warm sun during and after a June 2000 parade alongside New York's Central Park, a pack of alcohol-fueled young men became sexually aggressive—groping, and in some cases stripping, 60 women. In the days that followed, media attention focused on the mob psychology behind this sexual aggression and on police inaction (at least two victims had approached nearby police, who failed to respond). But what about the thousands of milling people? Why did they tolerate this? Among the many bystanders with cell phones, why did not one person call 911 (Dateline, 2000)?

Bystander inaction. What influences our interpretations of a scene such as this, and our decisions to help or not to help?

What is shocking is not that in these cases some people failed to help, but that in each of these groups (of 11, hundreds, and thousands) almost 100 percent of onlookers failed to respond. Why? In the same or similar situations, would you or I react as they did?

Social psychologists were curious and concerned about bystanders' lack of involvement. So they undertook experiments to identify when people will help in an emergency. Then they broadened the question to "Who is likely to help in non-emergencies—by such deeds as giving money, donating blood, or contributing time?" Let's examine these experiments by looking first at the *circumstances* that enhance helpfulness and then at the *people* who help.

Number of Bystanders

Bystander passivity during emergencies has prompted social commentators to lament people's "alienation," "apathy," "indifference," and "unconscious sadistic impulses." By attributing the nonintervention to the bystanders' dispositions, we can reassure ourselves that, as caring people, we would have helped. But were the bystanders such inhuman characters?

Social psychologists Bibb Latané and John Darley (1970) were unconvinced. They staged ingenious emergencies and found that a single situational factor—the presence of other bystanders—greatly decreased intervention. By 1980 they had conducted four dozen experiments that compared help given by bystanders who perceived themselves to be either alone or with others. Given unrestricted communication among the bystanders, a person was at least as likely to be helped by a lone bystander as when observed by several bystanders (Latané & Nida, 1981; Stalder, 2008). In Internet communication, too, people are more likely to respond helpfully to a request for help (such as from someone seeking the link to the campus library) if they believe they alone (and not several others as well) have received it (Blair & others, 2005).

Sometimes the victim was actually less likely to get help when many people were around. When Latané, James Dabbs (1975), and 145 collaborators "accidentally" dropped coins or pencils during 1,497 elevator rides, they were helped 40 percent of the time when one other person was on the elevator and less than 20 percent of the time when there were six passengers.

Why does the presence of other bystanders sometimes inhibit helping? Latané and Darley surmised that as the number of bystanders increases, any given bystander is less likely to *notice* the incident, less likely to *interpret* the incident as a problem or an emergency, and less likely to *assume responsibility* for taking action (Figure 12.5).

NOTICING

Twenty minutes after Eleanor Bradley has fallen and broken her leg on a crowded city sidewalk, you come along. Your eyes are on the backs of the pedestrians in front of you (it is bad manners to stare at those you pass) and your private thoughts are on the day's events. Would you therefore be less likely to notice the injured woman than if the sidewalk were virtually deserted?

To find out, Latané and Darley (1968) had Columbia University men fill out a questionnaire in a room, either by themselves or with two strangers. While they were working (and being observed through a one-way mirror), there was a staged emergency: Smoke poured into the room through a wall vent. Solitary students, who often glanced idly about the room while working, noticed the smoke almost immediately—usually in less than 5 seconds. Those in groups kept their eyes on their work. It typically took them about 20 seconds to notice the smoke.

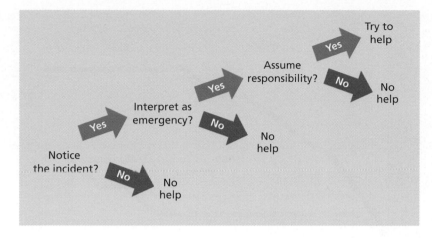

FIGURE :: 12.5

Latané and Darley's
Decision Tree

Only one path up the tree leads to
helping. At each fork of the path,
the presence of other bystanders may divert a person down a
branch toward not helping.

Source: Adapted from Darley &
Latané, 1968.

INTERPRETING

Once we notice an ambiguous event, we must interpret it. Put yourself in the room filling with smoke. Though worried, you don't want to embarrass yourself by appearing flustered. You glance at the others. They look calm, indifferent. Assuming everything must be okay, you shrug it off and go back to work. Then one of the others notices the smoke and, noting your apparent unconcern, reacts similarly. This is yet another example of informational influence (Chapter 6). Each person uses others' behavior as clues to reality. Such misinterpretations can contribute to a delayed response to actual fires in offices, restaurants, and other multiple-occupancy settings (Canter & others, 1980).

The misinterpretations are fed by what Thomas Gilovich, Kenneth Savitsky, and Victoria Husted Medvec (1998) call an *illusion of transparency*—a tendency to overestimate others' ability to "read" our internal states. (See the Research Close-Up in Chapter 2.) In their experiments, people facing an emergency presumed their concern was more visible than it was. More than we usually suppose, our concern or alarm is opaque. Keenly aware of our emotions, we presume they leak out and that others see right through us. Sometimes others do read our emotions, but often we keep our cool quite effectively. The result is what Chapter 8 called "pluralistic ignorance"—ignorance that others are thinking and feeling what we are. In emergencies, each person may think, "I'm very concerned," but perceive others as calm—"so maybe it's not an emergency."

So it happened in Latané and Darley's experiment. When those working alone noticed the smoke, they usually hesitated a moment, then got up, walked over to the vent, felt, sniffed, and waved at the smoke, hesitated again, and then went to report it. In dramatic contrast, those in groups of 3 did not move. Among the 24 men in eight groups, only 1 person reported the smoke within the first four minutes (Figure 12.6). By the end of the six-minute experiment, the smoke was so thick it was obscuring the men's vision and they were rubbing their eyes and coughing. Still, in only three of the eight groups did even a single person leave to report the problem.

Equally interesting the group's passivity affected its members' interpretations. What caused the smoke? "A leak in the air conditioning." "Chemistry labs in the building." "Steam pipes." "Truth gas." Not one said, "Fire." The group members, by serving as nonresponsive models, influenced one another's interpretation of the situation.

That experimental dilemma parallels real-life dilemmas we all face. Are the shrieks outside merely playful antics or the desperate screams of someone being assaulted? Is the boys' scuffling a friendly tussle or a vicious fight? Is the person slumped in the doorway sleeping, high on drugs, or seriously ill, perhaps in a diabetic coma? That surely was the question confronting those who passed by Sidney Brookins (AP, 1993).

FIGURE :: 12.6

The Smoke-Filled-Room Experiment

Smoke pouring into the testing room was much more likely to be reported by individuals working alone than by three-person groups.

Source: Data from Darley & Latané, 1968.

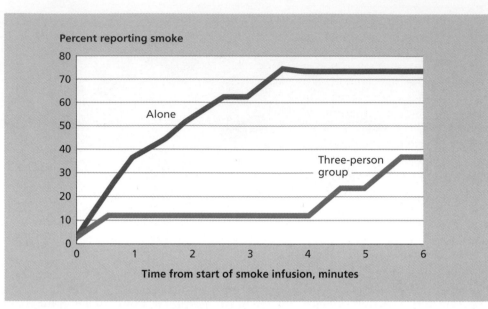

Percent reporting smoke

Alone

Three-person group

Time from start of smoke infusion, minutes

THE inside STORY

John M. Darley on Bystander Reactions

Shocked by the Kitty Genovese murder, Bibb Latané and I met over dinner and began to analyze the bystanders' reactions. Being social psychologists, we thought not about the personality flaws of the "apathetic" individuals, but rather about how anyone in that situation might react as did these people. By the time we finished our dinner, we had formulated several factors that together could lead to the surprising result: no one helping. Then we set about conducting experiments that isolated each factor and demonstrated its importance in an emergency situation.

John M. Darley, Princeton University

Brookins, who had suffered a concussion when beaten, died after lying near the door to a Minneapolis apartment house for two days. That may also have been the question for the Internet chat room members who in 2003 watched via webcam as 21-year-old Brandon Vedas took an overdose of drugs and died. As his life ebbed, his audience, which was left to wonder whether he was putting on an act, failed to decipher available clues to his whereabouts and to contact police (Nichols, 2003).

Unlike the smoke-filled-room experiment, each of these everyday situations involves another in desperate need. To see if the same **bystander effect** occurs in such situations, Latané and Judith Rodin (1969) staged an experiment around a woman in distress. A female researcher set Columbia University men to work on a questionnaire and then left through a curtained doorway to work in an adjacent office. Four minutes later she could be heard (from a tape recorder) climbing on a chair to reach some papers. This was followed by a scream and a loud crash as the chair collapsed and she fell to the floor. "Oh, my God, my foot . . . I . . . I . . . can't move it," she sobbed. "Oh . . . my ankle . . . I . . . can't get this . . . thing . . . off me." Only after two minutes of moaning did she manage to make it out her office door.

Seventy percent of those who were alone when they overheard the "accident" came into the room or called out to offer help. Among pairs of strangers confronting the emergency, only 40 percent of the time did either person offer help. Those who did nothing apparently interpreted the situation as a non-emergency.

bystander effect
The finding that a person is less likely to provide help when there are other bystanders.

"A mild sprain," said some. "I didn't want to embarrass her," explained others. This again demonstrates the bystander effect. As the number of people known to be aware of an emergency increases, any given person becomes less likely to help. For the victim, there is no safety in numbers.

People's interpretations also affect their reactions to street crimes. In staging physical fights between a man and a woman, Lance Shotland and Margaret Straw (1976) found that bystanders intervened 65 percent of the time when the woman shouted, "Get away from me; I don't know you," but only 19 percent of the time when she shouted, "Get away from me; I don't know why I ever married you." Assumed spouse abuse, it seems, just doesn't trigger as much intervention as stranger abuse.

Interpretations matter. Is this man locked out of his car or is he a burglar? Our interpretation affects our response.

ASSUMING RESPONSIBILITY

Failing to notice and misinterpretation are not the bystander effect's only causes. Sometimes an emergency is obvious. According to initial reports, those who saw and heard Kitty Genovese's pleas for help correctly interpreted what was happening. But the lights and silhouetted figures in neighboring windows told them that others were also watching. That diffused the responsibility for action.

Few of us have observed a murder. But all of us have at times been slower to react to a need when others were present. Passing a stranded motorist on a busy highway, we are less likely to offer help than on a country road. To explore bystander inaction in clear emergencies, Darley and Latané (1968) simulated the Genovese drama. They placed people in separate rooms from which the participants would hear a victim crying for help. To create that situation, Darley and Latané asked some New York University students to discuss their problems with university life over a laboratory intercom. The researchers told the students that to guarantee their anonymity, no one would be visible, nor would the experimenter eavesdrop. During the ensuing discussion, when the experimenter turned his microphone on, the participants heard one person lapse into a seizure. With increasing intensity and speech difficulty, he pleaded for someone to help.

Of those led to believe there were no other listeners, 85 percent left their room to seek help. Of those who believed four others also overheard the victim, only 31 percent went for help. Were those who didn't respond apathetic and indifferent? When the experimenter came in to end the experiment, most immediately expressed concern. Many had trembling hands and sweating palms. They believed an emergency had occurred but were undecided whether to act.

After the smoke-filled room, the woman-in-distress, and the seizure experiments, Latané and Darley asked the participants whether the presence of others had influenced them. We know the others had a dramatic

In Thirty-Eight Witnesses, *A. M. Rosenthal reflects on the Kitty Genovese murder and asks how far away one must be from a known murder to be absolved of responsibility. A block? A mile? A thousand miles?*

Responsibility diffusion. The nine paparazzi photographers on the scene immediately after the Princess Diana car accident all had cell phones. With one exception, none called for help. Their almost unanimous explanation was that they assumed "someone else" had already called (Sancton, 1997).

effect. Yet the participants almost invariably denied the influence. They typically replied, "I was aware of the others, but I would have reacted just the same if they weren't there." That response reinforces a familiar point: *We often do not know why we do what we do.* That is why experiments are revealing. A survey of uninvolved bystanders following a real emergency would have left the bystander effect hidden.

Urban dwellers are seldom alone in public places, which helps account for why city people often are less helpful than country people. "Compassion fatigue" and "sensory overload" from encountering so many needy people further restrain helping in large cities across the world (Levine & others, 1994; Yousif & Korte, 1995). In large cities, bystanders are also more often strangers—whose increasing numbers depress helping. When bystanders are friends or people who share a group identity, increased numbers may, instead, increase helping (Levine & Crowther, 2008).

Nations, too, have often been bystanders to catastrophes, even to genocide. As 800,000 people were murdered in Rwanda, we all stood by. And in this new century, we stood by again during the human slaughter in Sudan's Darfur region. "With many potential actors, each feels less responsible," notes Ervin Staub (1997). "It's not our responsibility," say the leaders of unaffected nations. Psychologist Peter Suedfeld (2000)—like Staub, a Holocaust survivor—notes that the diffusion of responsibility also helps explain "why the vast majority of European citizens stood idly by during the persecution, removal, and killing of their Jewish compatriots."

REVISITING RESEARCH ETHICS

These experiments raise an ethical issue. Is it right to force unwitting people to overhear someone's apparent collapse? Were the researchers in the seizure experiment ethical when they forced people to decide whether to interrupt their discussion to report the problem? Would you object to being in such a study? Note that it would have been impossible to get your "informed consent"; doing so would have destroyed the experiment's cover.

The researchers were always careful to debrief the laboratory participants. After explaining the seizure experiment, probably the most stressful, the experimenter gave the participants a questionnaire. One hundred percent said the deception was justified and that they would be willing to take part in similar experiments in the future. None reported feeling angry at the experimenter. Other researchers confirm that the overwhelming majority of participants in such experiments say that their participation was both instructive and ethically justified (Schwartz & Gottlieb, 1981). In field experiments, an accomplice assisted the victim if no one else did, thus reassuring bystanders that the problem was being dealt with.

Remember that the social psychologist has a twofold ethical obligation: to protect the participants and to enhance human welfare by discovering influences upon human behavior. Such discoveries can alert us to unwanted influences and show us how we might exert positive influences. The ethical principle seems to be: After protecting participants' welfare, social psychologists fulfill their responsibility to society by giving us insight into our behavior.

Helping When Someone Else Does

If observing aggressive models can heighten aggression (Chapter 10) and if unresponsive models can heighten nonresponding, then will helpful models promote helping? Imagine hearing a crash followed by sobs and moans. If another bystander said, "Uh-oh. This is an emergency! We've got to do something," would it stimulate others to help?

The evidence is clear: Prosocial models do promote altruism. Some examples:

- James Bryan and Mary Ann Test (1967) found that Los Angeles drivers were more likely to offer help to a female driver with a flat tire if a quarter mile earlier they had witnessed someone helping another woman change a tire.
- In another experiment, Bryan and Test observed that New Jersey Christmas shoppers were more likely to drop money in a Salvation Army kettle if they had just seen someone else do the same.
- Philippe Rushton and Anne Campbell (1977) found British adults more willing to donate blood if they were approached after observing a confederate consent to donating.
- A glimpse of extraordinary human kindness and charity—such as I gave you in the examples of heroic altruism at this chapter's outset—often triggers what Jonathan Haidt (2003) calls *elevation*, "a distinctive feeling in the chest of warmth and expansion" that may provoke chills, tears, and throat clenching. Such elevation often inspires people to become more self-giving.

Models sometimes, however, contradict in practice what they preach. Parents may tell their children, "Do as I say, not as I do." Experiments show that children learn moral judgments both from what they hear preached and from what they see practiced (Rice & Grusec, 1975; Rushton, 1975). When exposed to hypocrites, they imitate: They say what the model says and do what the model does.

> "We are, in truth, more than half what we are by imitation. The great point is, to choose good models and to study them with care."
>
> —LORD CHESTERFIELD, LETTERS, JANUARY 18, 1750

Time Pressures

Darley and Batson (1973) discerned another determinant of helping in the Good Samaritan parable. The priest and the Levite were both busy, important people, probably hurrying to their duties. The lowly Samaritan surely was less pressed for time. To see whether people in a hurry would behave as the priest and the Levite did, Darley and Batson cleverly staged the situation described in the parable.

After collecting their thoughts before recording a brief extemporaneous talk (which, for half the participants, was actually on the Good Samaritan parable), Princeton Theological Seminary students were directed to a recording studio in an adjacent building. En route, they passed a man sitting slumped in a doorway, head down, coughing and groaning. Some of the students had been sent off nonchalantly: "It will be a few minutes before they're ready for you, but you might as well head on over." Of those, almost two-thirds stopped to offer help. Others were told, "Oh, you're late. They were expecting you a few minutes ago . . . so you'd better hurry." Of these, only 10 percent offered help.

Reflecting on these findings, Darley and Batson remarked:

A person not in a hurry may stop and offer help to a person in distress. A person in a hurry is likely to keep going. Ironically, he is likely to keep going even if he is hurrying to speak on the parable of the Good Samaritan, thus inadvertently confirming the point of the parable. (Indeed, on several occasions, a seminary student going to give his talk on the parable of the Good Samaritan literally stepped over the victim as he hurried on his way!)

Are we being unfair to the seminary students, who were, after all, hurrying to *help* the experimenter? Perhaps they keenly felt the social-responsibility norm but found it pulling them two ways—toward the experimenter and toward the victim. In another enactment of the Good Samaritan situation, Batson and his associates (1978) directed 40 University of Kansas students to an experiment in another building. Half were told they were late, half that they had plenty of time. Half of each of

FIGURE :: 12.7

Mismatched Needs and Donations

Similarity, along with proximity and the vivid portrayals of victims, helps explain why victims of some calamities (such as Hurricane Katrina and the 9/11 attacks) generate a huge outpouring of donations, while other, much greater, problems such as malaria receive far less attention and response (Loewenstein & Small, 2007; Spence, 2006).

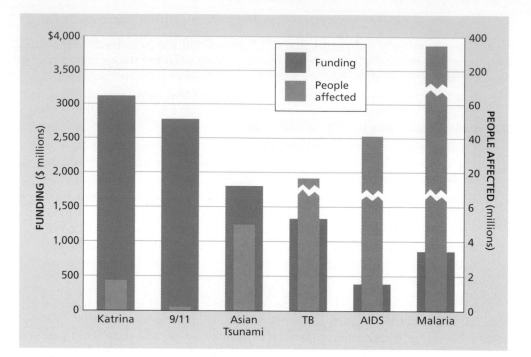

these groups thought their participation was vitally important to the experimenter; half thought it was not essential. The results: Those leisurely on their way to an unimportant appointment usually stopped to help. But people seldom stopped to help if, like the White Rabbit in *Alice's Adventures in Wonderland,* they were late for a very important date.

Can we conclude that those who were rushed were callous? Did the seminarians notice the victim's distress and then consciously choose to ignore it? No. Harried, preoccupied, rushing to help the experimenter, they simply did not take time to tune in to the person in need. As social psychologists have so often observed, their behavior was influenced more by context than by conviction.

Similarity

Because similarity is conducive to liking (Chapter 11), and liking is conducive to helping, we are more empathic and helpful toward those *similar* to us (Miller & others, 2001). The similarity bias applies to both dress and beliefs. Tim Emswiller and his fellow researchers (1971) had confederates, dressed either conservatively or in counterculture garb, approach "conservative" and "hip" Purdue University students seeking a dime for a phone call. Fewer than half the students did the favor for those dressed differently from themselves. Two-thirds did so for those dressed similarly. Likewise, Scottish shoppers in a more antigay era were less willing to make change for someone if the person wore a T-shirt with a pro-gay slogan (Gray & others, 1991). See also Figure 12.7 and "Research Close-Up: Ingroup Similarity and Helping."

No face is more familiar than one's own. That explains why, when Lisa DeBruine (2002) had McMaster University students play an interactive game with a supposed other player, they were more trusting and generous when the other person's pictured face had some features of their own face morphed into it (Figure 12.10). In me I trust. Even just sharing a birthday, a first name, or a fingerprint pattern leads people to respond more to a request for help (Burger & others, 2004).

Does the similarity bias extend to race? During the 1970s, researchers explored that question with confusing results:

research
CLOSE-UP
Ingroup Similarity and Helping

Likeness breeds liking, and liking elicits helping. So, do people offer more help to others who display similarities to themselves? To explore the similarity-helping relationship, Mark Levine, Amy Prosser, and David Evans at Lancaster University joined with Stephen Reicher at St. Andrews University (2005) to study the behavior of some Lancaster students who earlier had identified themselves as fans of the nearby Manchester United soccer football team. Taking their cue from John Darley and Daniel Batson's (1973) famous Good Samaritan experiment, they directed each newly arrived participant to the laboratory in an adjacent building. En route, a confederate jogger—wearing a shirt from either Manchester United or rival Liverpool—seemingly slipped on a grass bank just in front of them, grasped his ankle, and groaned in apparent pain. As Figure 12.8 shows, the Manchester fans routinely paused to offer help to their fellow Manchester supporter but usually did not offer such help to a supposed Liverpool supporter.

But, the researchers wondered, what if we remind Manchester fans of the identity they share with Liverpool supporters—as football fans rather than as detractors

who scorn football fans as violent hooligans? So they repeated the experiment, but with one difference: Before participants witnessed the jogger's fall, the researcher explained that the study concerned the positive aspects of being a football fan. Given that only a small minority of fans are troublemakers, this research aimed to explore what fans get out of their love for "the beautiful game." Now a jogger wearing a football club shirt, whether for Manchester or Liverpool, became one of "us fans." And as Figure 12.9 shows, the grimacing jogger was helped regardless of which team he supported—and more so than if wearing a plain shirt.

The principle in the two cases is the same, notes the Lancaster research team: People are predisposed to help their fellow group members, whether those are defined more narrowly (as "us Manchester fans") or more inclusively (as "us football fans"). If even rival fans can be persuaded to help one another if they think about what unites them, then surely other antagonists can as well. One way to increase people's willingness to help others is to promote social identities that are inclusive rather than exclusive.

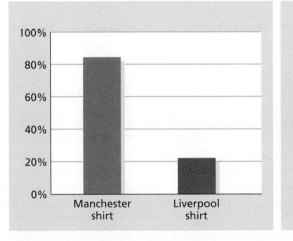

FIGURE :: 12.8

Percent of Manchester United Fans Who Helped Victim Wearing Manchester or Liverpool Shirt

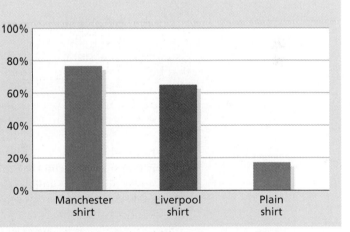

FIGURE :: 12.9

Common Fan Identity Condition: Percent of Manchester United Fans Who Helped Victim Wearing Manchester or Liverpool Shirt

- Some studies found a same-race bias (Benson & others, 1976; Clark, 1974; Franklin, 1974; Gaertner, 1973; Gaertner & Bickman, 1971; Sissons, 1981).
- Others found no bias (Gaertner, 1975; Lerner & Frank, 1974; Wilson & Donnerstein, 1979; Wispe & Freshley, 1971).
- Still others—especially those involving face-to-face situations—found a bias toward helping those of a different race (Dutton, 1971, 1973; Dutton & Lake, 1973; Katz & others, 1975).

FIGURE :: 12.10

Similarity Breeds Cooperation

Lisa DeBruine (2002) morphed participants' faces (left) with strangers' faces (right) to make the composite center faces— toward whom the participants were more generous than toward the stranger.

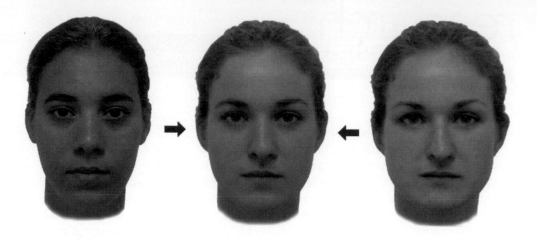

Is there a general rule that resolves these seemingly contradictory findings?

Few people want to appear prejudiced. Perhaps, then, people favor their own race but keep that bias secret to preserve a positive image. If so, the same-race bias should appear only when people can attribute failure to help to nonrace factors. That is what happened in experiments by Samuel Gaertner and John Dovidio (1977, 1986). For example, University of Delaware White women were less willing to help a Black than a White woman in distress *if* their responsibility could be diffused among the bystanders ("I didn't help the Black woman because there were others who could"). When there were no other bystanders, the women were equally helpful to the Black and the White women. The rule seems to be: When norms for appropriate behavior are well defined, Whites don't discriminate; when norms are ambiguous or conflicting, racial similarity may bias responses (Saucier & others, 2005).

For me, the laboratory came to life one night as I walked from a dinner meeting in Washington, D.C., to my hotel. On a deserted sidewalk, a well-dressed, distraught-seeming man about my age approached me and begged for a dollar. He explained that he had just come over from London and, after visiting the Holocaust Museum, had accidentally left his wallet in a taxi. So here he was, stranded and needing a $24 taxi fare to a friend's home in suburban D.C.

"So how's one dollar going to get you there?" I asked.

"I asked people for more, but no one would help me," he nearly sobbed, "so I thought maybe if I asked for less I could collect taxi fare."

"But why not take the Metro?" I challenged.

"It stops about five miles from Greenbriar, where I need to go," he explained. "Oh my, how am I ever going to get there? If you could help me out, I will mail you back the money on Monday."

Here I was, as if a participant in an on-the-street altruism experiment. Having grown up in a city, and as a frequent visitor to New York and Chicago, I am accustomed to panhandling and have never rewarded it. But I also consider myself a caring person. Moreover, this fellow was unlike any panhandler I had ever met. He was dressed sharply. He was intelligent. He had a convincing story. And he looked like me! If he's lying, he's a slimeball, I said to myself, and giving him money would be stupid, naive, and rewarding slimeballism. If he's a truth-teller and I turn my back on him, then *I'm* a slimeball.

He had asked for $1. I gave him $30, along with my name and address, which he took gratefully, and disappeared into the night.

As I walked on, I began to suspect—correctly as it turned out—that I had been a patsy. Having lived in Britain, why had I not tested his knowledge of England? Why had I not taken him to a phone booth to call his friend? Why had I at least not offered to pay a taxi driver and send him on his way, rather than give him the money? And why, after a lifetime of resisting scams, had I succumbed to this one?

Sheepishly, because I like to think myself not influenced by ethnic stereotypes, I had to admit that it was not only his socially skilled, personal approach but also the mere fact of his similarity to me.

Summing Up: When Will We Help?

- Several situational influences work to inhibit or to encourage altruism. As the number of bystanders at an emergency increases, any given bystander is (1) less likely to notice the incident, (2) less likely to interpret it as an emergency, and (3) less likely to assume responsibility. Experiments on helping behavior pose an ethical dilemma but fulfill the researcher's mandate to enhance human life by uncovering important influences on behavior.

- When are people most likely to help? One circumstance is when they have just observed someone else helping.

- Another circumstance that promotes helping is having at least a little spare time; those in a hurry are less likely to help.

- We tend to help those whom we perceive as being similar to us.

Who Will Help?

We have considered internal influences on the decision to help (such as guilt and mood) and external influences as well (such as social norms, number of bystanders, time pressures, and similarity). We also need to consider the helpers' dispositions, including, for example, their personality traits and religious values.

Personality Traits

Surely some traits must distinguish the Mother Teresa types from others. Faced with identical situations, some people will respond helpfully, while others won't bother. Who are the likely helpers?

For many years social psychologists were unable to discover a single personality trait that predicted helping with anything close to the predictive power of situational, guilt, and mood factors. Modest relationships were found between helping and certain personality variables, such as a need for social approval. But by and large, personality tests were unable to identify the helpers. Studies of rescuers of Jews in Nazi Europe reveal a similar conclusion: Although the social context clearly influenced willingness to help, there was no definable set of altruistic personality traits (Darley, 1995).

If that finding has a familiar ring, it could be from a similar conclusion by conformity researchers (Chapter 6): Conformity, too, seemed more influenced by the situation than by measurable personality traits. Perhaps, though, you recall from Chapter 2 that who we are does affect what we do. Attitude and trait measures seldom predict a *specific* act, which is what most experiments on altruism measure (in contrast with the lifelong altruism of a Mother Teresa). But they predict average behavior across many situations more accurately.

Personality researchers have responded to the challenge. First, they have found *individual differences* in helpfulness and shown that those differences persist over time and are noticed by one's peers (Hampson, 1984; Penner, 2002; Rushton & others, 1981). Some people are reliably more helpful.

Second, researchers are gathering clues to the *network of traits* that predispose a person to helpfulness. Those high in positive emotionality, empathy, and self-efficacy are most likely to be concerned and helpful (Eisenberg & others, 1991; Krueger & others, 2001; Walker & Frimer, 2007).

"There are . . . reasons why personality should be rather unimportant in determining people's reactions to the emergency. For one thing, the situational forces affecting a person's decision are so strong."
—BIBB LATANÉ AND JOHN DARLEY (1970, P. 115)

Third, personality influences how particular people react to *particular situations* (Carlo & others, 1991; Romer & others, 1986; Wilson & Petruska, 1984). Those high in self-monitoring are attuned to others' expectations and are therefore helpful *if* they think helpfulness will be socially rewarded (White & Gerstein, 1987). Others' opinions matter less to internally guided, low-self-monitoring people.

Gender

The interaction of person and situation also appears in 172 studies that have compared the helpfulness of nearly 50,000 male and female individuals. After analyzing these results, Alice Eagly and Maureen Crowley (1986) reported that when faced with potentially dangerous situations in which strangers need help (such as with a flat tire or a fall in a subway), men more often help. (Eagly and Crowley also report that among 6,767 individuals who have received the Carnegie medal for heroism in saving human life, 90 percent have been men.)

In safer situations, such as volunteering to help with an experiment or spend time with children with developmental disabilities, women are slightly more likely to help. In a UCLA survey of 272,036 entering American collegians, 63 percent of men—and 75 percent of women—rated "helping others in difficulty" as "very important" or "essential" (Pryor & others, 2007). Women also have been as likely as, or more likely than, men to risk death as Holocaust rescuers, to donate a kidney, and to volunteer with the Peace Corps and Doctors of the World (Becker & Eagly, 2004). Thus, the gender difference interacts with (depends on) the situation. Faced with a friend's problems, women respond with greater empathy and spend more time helping (George & others, 1998).

Religious Faith

In 1943, with Nazi submarines sinking ships faster than the Allied forces could replace them, the troop ship SS *Dorchester* steamed out of New York harbor with 902 men headed for Greenland (Elliott, 1989; Kurzman, 2004; Parachin, 1992). Among those leaving anxious families behind were four chaplains: Methodist preacher George Fox, Rabbi Alexander Goode, Catholic priest John Washington, and Reformed Church minister Clark Poling. Some 150 miles from their destination, on a moonless night, *U-boat 456* caught the *Dorchester* in its cross hairs. Within moments of the torpedo's impact, stunned men were pouring out of their bunks as the ship began listing. With power cut off, the ship's radio was useless; its escort vessels, unaware of the unfolding tragedy, pushed on in the darkness. On board, chaos reigned as panicky men came up from the hold without life jackets and leapt into overcrowded lifeboats.

As the four chaplains arrived on the steeply sloping deck, they began guiding the men to their boat stations. They opened a storage locker, distributed life jackets, and coaxed the men over the side. When Petty Officer John Mahoney turned back to retrieve his gloves, Rabbi Goode responded, "Never mind. I have two pairs." Only later did Mahoney realize that the Rabbi was not conveniently carrying an extra pair; he was giving up his own.

In the icy, oil-smeared water, as Private William Bednar heard the chaplains preaching courage he found the strength to swim out from under the ship until reaching a life raft. Still on board, Grady Clark watched in awe as the chaplains handed out the last life jacket and then, with ultimate selflessness, gave away their own. As Clark slipped into the waters, he looked back at an unforgettable sight: The four chaplains were standing—their arms linked—praying, in Latin, Hebrew, and English. Other men joined them in a huddle as the *Dorchester* slid beneath the sea. "It was the finest thing I have ever seen or hope to see this side of heaven," said John Ladd, another of the 230 survivors.

Does the chaplains' heroic example rightly imply that faith promotes courage and caring? The world's four largest religions—Christianity, Islam, Hinduism, and

The four chaplains' ultimate selflessness inspired this painting, which hangs in Valley Forge, Pennsylvania's Chapel of the Four Chaplains.

Buddhism—all teach compassion and charity (Steffen & Masters, 2005). But do their followers walk the talk?

Consider, first, what happens when people are subtly "primed" with either materialistic or spiritual thoughts. With money on their minds—after unscrambling text that included words such as *salary* or after seeing a poster with currency on it—people were less helpful to a confused person and less generous when asked to donate to help needy students (Vohs & others, 2006, 2008). With God on their minds—after unscrambling sentences with words such as *spirit, divine, God,* and *sacred*—people become much more generous in their donations (Pichon & others, 2007; Shariff & Norenzayan, 2007).

Consider also the many studies of spontaneous helping. Confronted with a minor emergency, intrinsically religious people are only slightly more responsive (Trimble, 1993). More recently, researchers are also exploring planned helping—the sort of sustained helping provided by AIDS volunteers, Big Brother and Big Sister helpers, and supporters of campus service organizations. It is when making intentional choices about long-term helping that religious faith better predicts altruism.

From their analyses of why people volunteer, as when befriending AIDS patients, Mark Snyder, Allen Omoto, and Gil Clary (Clary & Snyder, 1993, 1995, 1999; Clary & others, 1998) have discerned multiple motivations. Some are rooted in rewards—seeking to join a group, gain approval, enhance job prospects, reduce guilt, learn skills, or boost self-esteem. Others help to act upon their religious or humanitarian values and concern for others.

In studies of college students and the general public, those religiously committed have reported volunteering more hours—as tutors, relief workers, and campaigners for social justice—than have the religiously uncommitted (Benson & others, 1980; Hansen & others, 1995; Penner, 2002). Among Americans whom the Gallup Poll classifies as "engaged" with a faith community, the median person reports volunteering two hours per week; the median disengaged person reports volunteering zero hours per week (Winseman, 2005). Worldwide surveys confirm the correlation between faith engagement and volunteering. One analysis of 117,007 people responding to World Values Surveys in 53 countries reported that twice-weekly

FIGURE :: 12.11

Helping and Religious Engagement

Worldwide, report Gallup researchers Brett Pelham and Steve Crabtree (2008), highly religious people are more likely to report having given away money in the last month, and also to report having volunteered and helped a stranger. Highly religious said religion is important in their daily life and attended a service in the last week. Less religious are all others.

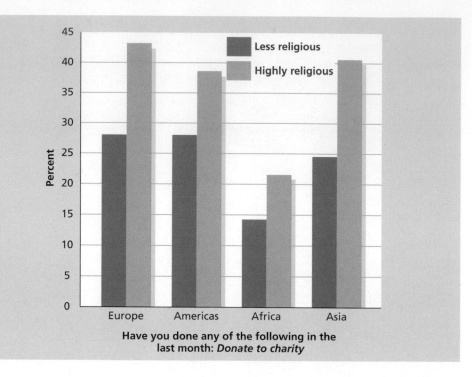

Have you done any of the following in the last month: *Donate to charity*

religious attenders "are more than five times more likely to volunteer" than nonattenders (Ruiter & De Graaf, 2006).

Moreover, Sam Levenson's jest—"When it comes to giving, some people stop at nothing"—is seldom true of church and synagogue members. In a Gallup survey, Americans who said they never attended church or synagogue reported giving away 1.1 percent of their incomes (Hodgkinson & others, 1990). Weekly attenders were two and a half times as generous. This 24 percent of the population gave 48 percent of all charitable contributions; the other three-quarters of Americans gave the remaining half. Follow-up surveys, including a massive Gallup World Survey of 2,000 or more people in each of 140 countries, confirm the faith and philanthropy correlation. Despite having lower incomes, highly religious people (who reported that religion is important to their daily lives and that they had attended a religious service in the prior week) reported markedly higher than average rates of charitable giving, volunteerism, and helping a stranger in the previous month (Figure 12.11).

Do the religious links with planned helping extend similarly to other communal organizations? Robert Putnam (2000) analyzed national survey data from 22 types of organizations, including hobby clubs, professional associations, self-help groups, and service clubs. "It was membership in religious groups," he reports, "that was most closely associated with other forms of civic involvement, like voting, jury service, community projects, talking with neighbors, and giving to charity" (p. 67).

"Religion is the mother of philanthropy."

—FRANK EMERSON ANDREWS, ATTITUDES TOWARD GIVING, 1953

Summing Up: Who Will Help?

- In contrast with altruism's potent situational and mood determinants, personality test scores have served as only modest predictors of helping. However, new evidence indicates that some people are consistently more helpful than others.

- The effect of personality or gender may depend on the situation. Men, for example, have been observed to help more in dangerous situations, women as volunteers.

- Religious faith predicts long-term altruism, as reflected in volunteerism and charitable contributions.

How Can We Increase Helping?

To increase helping, can we reverse the factors that inhibit helping? Or can we teach norms of helping and socialize people to see themselves as helpful?

As social scientists, our goal is to understand human behavior, thus also suggesting ways to improve it. So, how might we apply research-based understanding to increase helping? One way to promote altruism is to reverse those factors that inhibit it. Given that hurried, preoccupied people are less likely to help, can we think of ways to slow people down and turn their attention outward? If the presence of others diminishes each bystander's sense of responsibility, how can we enhance responsibility?

Reduce Ambiguity, Increase Responsibility

If Latané and Darley's decision tree (see Figure 12.5) describes the dilemmas bystanders face, then helping should increase if we can prompt people to correctly *interpret an incident* and to *assume responsibility*. Leonard Bickman and his colleagues (1975, 1977, 1979) tested that presumption in a series of experiments on crime reporting. In each, they staged a shoplifting incident in a supermarket or bookstore. In some of the stores, they placed signs aimed at sensitizing bystanders to shoplifting and informing them how to report it. The researchers found that the signs had little effect. In other cases, witnesses heard a bystander interpret the incident: "Say, look at her. She's shoplifting. She put that into her purse." (The bystander then left to look for a lost child.) Still others heard this person add, "We saw it. We should report it. It's our responsibility." Both comments substantially boosted reporting of the crime.

The potency of personal influence is no longer in doubt. Robert Foss (1978) surveyed several hundred blood donors and found that neophyte donors, unlike veterans, were usually there at someone's personal invitation. Leonard Jason and his collaborators (1984) confirmed that personal appeals for blood donation are much more effective than posters and media announcements—if the personal appeals come from friends. But even strangers' direct appeals can be surprisingly effective. That's what Francis Flynn and Vanessa Lake (2008) found when they had Columbia University students ask strangers to take 5 to 10 minutes to complete a questionnaire. They guessed they'd have to ask four people for every person who would agree. In reality, half of the people agreed when asked directly. Likewise, strangers were more agreeable than expected when asked "Can I use your cell phone to make a call?" and when asked "Can you show me where the [campus] gym is?" and "Will you walk me there?"

Personalized nonverbal appeals can also be effective. Mark Snyder and his coworkers (1974; Omoto & Snyder, 2002) found that hitchhikers doubled their number of ride offers by looking drivers straight in the eye, and that most AIDS volunteers got involved through someone's personal influence. A personal approach, as my panhandler knew, makes one feel less anonymous, more responsible.

Henry Solomon and Linda Solomon (1978; Solomon & others, 1981) explored ways to reduce anonymity. They found that bystanders who had identified themselves to one another—by name, age, and so forth—were more likely to offer aid to a sick person than were anonymous bystanders. Similarly, when a female experimenter caught the eye of another shopper and gave her a warm smile before stepping on an elevator, that shopper was far more likely than other shoppers to offer help when the experimenter later said, "Damn. I've left my glasses. Can anyone tell me what floor the umbrellas are on?" Even a trivial momentary conversation with someone ("Excuse me, aren't you Suzie Spear's sister?" "No, I'm not") dramatically increased the person's later helpfulness.

Helpfulness also increases when one expects to meet the victim and other witnesses again. Using a laboratory intercom system, Jody Gottlieb and Charles Carver

(1980) led University of Miami students to believe they were discussing problems of college living with other students. (Actually, the other discussants were tape-recorded.) When one of the supposed fellow discussants had a choking fit and cried out for help, she was helped most quickly by those who believed they would soon be meeting the discussants face-to-face. In short, anything that personalizes bystanders—a personal request, eye contact, stating one's name, anticipation of interaction—increases willingness to help. In experiments, restaurant patrons have tipped more when their servers introduced themselves by name, wrote friendly messages on checks, touched guests on the arm or shoulder, and sat or squatted at the table during the service encounter (Leodoro & Lynn, 2007).

Personal treatment makes bystanders more self-aware and therefore more attuned to their own altruistic ideals. Recall from earlier chapters that people made self-aware by acting in front of a mirror or a TV camera exhibit increased consistency between attitudes and actions. By contrast, "deindividuated" people are less responsible. Thus, circumstances that promote self-awareness—name tags, being watched and evaluated, undistracted quiet—should also increase helping.

Shelley Duval, Virginia Duval, and Robert Neely (1979) confirmed this. They showed some University of Southern California women their own images on a TV screen or had them complete biographical questionnaires just before giving them a chance to contribute time and money to people in need. Those made self-aware contributed more. Similarly, pedestrians who have just had their pictures taken by someone became more likely to help another pedestrian pick up dropped envelopes (Hoover & others, 1983). And among those who had just seen themselves in a mirror, 70 percent of Italian pedestrians helped a stranger by mailing a postcard, as did 13 percent of others approached (Abbate & others, 2006). Self-aware people more often put their ideals into practice.

Guilt and Concern for Self-Image

Earlier we noted that people who feel guilty will act to reduce guilt and restore their self-worth. Can heightening people's awareness of their transgressions therefore increase their desire to help? Have university students think about their past transgressions and they become more likely to agree to volunteer to help with a school project—though the volunteering boost lessens if they are also given a chance to wash their hands, an act that seemingly cleanses some of the evoked guilty feelings (Zhong & Liljenquist, 2006).

A Reed College research team led by Richard Katzev (1978) experimented with guilt-induced helping in everyday contexts. When visitors to the Portland Art Museum disobeyed a "Please do not touch" sign, experimenters reprimanded some of them: "Please don't touch the objects. If everyone touches them, they will deteriorate." Likewise, when visitors to the Portland Zoo fed unauthorized food to the bears, some of them were admonished with, "Hey, don't feed unauthorized food to the animals. Don't you know it could hurt them?" In both cases, 58 percent of the now guilt-laden individuals shortly thereafter offered help to another experimenter who had "accidentally" dropped something. Of those not reprimanded, only one-third helped. Guilt-laden people are helpful people.

That was my experience recently, after passing a man struggling to get up from a busy city sidewalk as I raced to catch a train. His glazed eyes brought to mind the many drunken people I had assisted during my college days as an emergency room attendant. Or . . . I wondered after walking by . . . was he actually experiencing a health crisis? Plagued by guilt, I picked up sidewalk litter, offered my train seat to an elderly couple looking for seats together, and vowed that the next time I faced uncertainty in an unfamiliar city I would think to call 911.

People also care about their public images. When Robert Cialdini and his colleagues (1975) asked some of their Arizona State University students to chaperone delinquent children on a zoo trip, only 32 percent agreed to do so. With other students

Door-in-the-face technique.
HI & LOIS © King Features Syndicate.

the questioner first made a very large request—that the students commit two years as volunteer counselors to delinquent children. After getting the **door-in-the-face** in response to this request (all refused), the questioner then counteroffered with the chaperoning request, saying, in effect, "OK, if you won't do that, would you do just this much?" With this technique, nearly twice as many—56 percent— agreed to help.

Cialdini and David Schroeder (1976) offer another practical way to trigger concern for self-image: Ask for a contribution so small that it's hard to say no without feeling like a Scrooge. Cialdini (1995) discovered this when a United Way canvasser came to his door. As she solicited his contribution, he was mentally preparing his refusal—until she said magic words that demolished his financial excuse: "Even a penny will help." "I had been neatly finessed into compliance," recalled Cialdini. "And there was another interesting feature of our exchange as well. When I stopped coughing (I really had choked on my attempted rejection), I gave her not the penny she had mentioned but the amount I usually allot to legitimate charity solicitors. At that, she thanked me, smiled innocently, and moved on."

Was Cialdini's response atypical? To find out, he and Schroeder had a solicitor approach suburbanites. When the solicitor said, "I'm collecting money for the American Cancer Society," 29 percent contributed an average of $1.44 each. When the solicitor added, "Even a penny will help," 50 percent contributed an average of $1.54 each. When James Weyant (1984) repeated this experiment, he found similar results: The "even a penny will help" boosted the number contributing from 39 to 57 percent. And when 6,000 people were solicited by mail for the American Cancer Society, those asked for small amounts were more likely to give—and gave no less on average—than those asked for larger amounts (Weyant & Smith, 1987). When previous donors are approached, bigger requests (within reason) do elicit bigger donations (Doob & McLaughlin, 1989). But with door-to-door solicitation, there is more success with requests for small contributions, which are difficult to turn down and still allow the person to maintain an altruistic self-image.

Labeling people as helpful can also strengthen a helpful self-image. After they had made charitable contributions, Robert Kraut (1973) told some Connecticut women, "You are a generous person." Two weeks later, these women were more willing than those not so labeled to contribute to a different charity.

Socializing Altruism

If we can learn altruism, then how might we socialize it? Here are five ways (Figure 12.12).

TEACHING MORAL INCLUSION

Rescuers of Jews in Nazi Europe, leaders of the antislavery movement, and medical missionaries shared at least one common trait: They were *morally inclusive.* Their moral concern encircled people who differed from themselves. One rescuer faked a pregnancy on behalf of a pregnant hidden Jew—thus including the soon-to-be-born child within the circle of her own children's identities (Fogelman, 1994).

door-in-the-face technique
A strategy for gaining a concession. After someone first turns down a large request (the door-in-the-face), the same requester counteroffers with a more reasonable request.

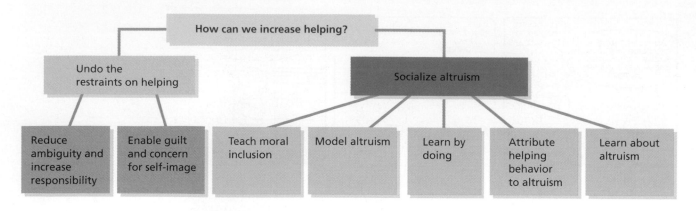

FIGURE :: 12.12

Practical Ways to Increase Helping

moral exclusion
The perception of certain individuals or groups as outside the boundary within which one applies moral values and rules of fairness. Moral inclusion is regarding others as within one's circle of moral concern.

Moral exclusion—omitting certain people from one's circle of moral concern—has the opposite effect. It justifies all sorts of harm, from discrimination to genocide (Opotow, 1990; Staub, 2005a; Tyler & Lind, 1990). Exploitation or cruelty becomes acceptable, even appropriate, toward those whom we regard as undeserving or as nonpersons (and also toward animals outside one's circle of concern). The Nazis excluded Jews from their moral community. Anyone who participates in enslavement, death squads, or torture practices a similar exclusion. To a lesser extent, moral exclusion describes those of us who concentrate our concerns, favors, and financial inheritance upon "our people" (for example, our children) to the exclusion of others.

It also describes restrictions in the public empathy for the human costs of war. Reported war deaths are typically "our deaths." Many Americans, for example, know that some 58,000 Americans died in the Vietnam War (their 58,248 names are inscribed on the Vietnam War Memorial). But few Americans know that the war also left some 2 million Vietnamese dead. During the recent Iraq war, news of American fatalities—more than 4,000 by the beginning of 2009—caused much more concern than the little-known number of Iraqi deaths, for which a low range of estimates published by leading medical journals was more than 150,000 (Alkhuzai & others, 2008).

We easily become numbed by impersonal big numbers of outgroup fatalities, note Paul Slovic (2007) and Elizabeth Dunn and Claire Ashton-James (2008). People presume that they would be more upset about a hurricane that killed 5,000 rather than 50 people. But whether Dunn and Ashton-James told people that Hurricane Katrina claimed 50, 500, 1,000, or 5,000 lives, their sadness was unaffected by the number. Ditto for the scale of other tragedies, including a forest fire in Spain and the war in Iraq. "If I look at the mass I will never act," said Mother Teresa. "If I look at the one, I will."

A first step toward socializing altruism is therefore to counter the natural ingroup bias favoring kin and tribe by personalizing and broadening the range of people whose well-being should concern us. Daniel Batson (1983) notes how religious teachings do this. They extend the reach of kin-linked altruism by urging "brotherly and sisterly" love toward all "children of God" in the whole human "family." If everyone is part of our family, then everyone has a moral claim on us. The boundaries between "we" and "they" fade. Inviting advantaged people to put themselves in others' shoes, to imagine how they feel, also helps (Batson & others, 2003). To "do unto others as you would have them do unto you," one must take the others' perspective.

"We consider humankind our family."

—*PARLIAMENT OF THE WORLD RELIGIONS, TOWARDS A GLOBAL ETHIC, 1993*

MODELING ALTRUISM

Earlier we noted that seeing unresponsive bystanders makes us less likely to help. People reared by extremely punitive parents, as were many delinquents and chronic criminals, also show much less of the empathy and principled caring that typifies altruists.

If we see or read about someone helping, we are more likely to offer assistance. It's better, find Robert Cialdini and his co-workers (2003), *not* to publicize rampant tax cheating, littering, and teen drinking, and instead to emphasize—to define a norm of—people's widespread honesty, cleanliness, and abstinence. In one experiment, they asked visitors not to remove petrified wood from along the paths of the Petrified Forest National Park. Some were also told that "past visitors have removed the petrified wood." Other people who were told that "past visitors have left the petrified wood" to preserve the park were much less likely to pick up samples placed along a path.

Modeling effects were also apparent within the families of European Christians who risked their lives to rescue Jews and of American civil rights activists. These exceptional altruists typically reported having warm and close relationships with at least one parent who was, similarly, a strong "moralist" or committed to humanitarian causes (London, 1970; Oliner & Oliner, 1988; Rosenhan, 1970). Their families—and often their friends and churches—had taught them the norm of helping and caring for others. This "prosocial value orientation" led them to include people from other groups in their circle of moral concern and to feel responsible for others' welfare, noted altruism researcher Ervin Staub (1989, 1991, 1992).

Staub (1999) knows of what he speaks: "As a young Jewish child in Budapest I survived the Holocaust, the destruction of most European Jews by Nazi Germany and its allies. My life was saved by a Christian woman who repeatedly endangered her life to help me and my family, and by Raoul Wallenberg, the Swede who came to Budapest and with courage, brilliance, and complete commitment saved the lives of tens of thousands of Jews destined for the gas chambers. These two heroes were not passive bystanders, and my work is one of the ways for me not to be one." (See "Focus On: Behavior and Attitudes among Rescuers of Jews.")

Do television's positive models promote helping, much as its aggressive portrayals promote aggression? Prosocial TV models have actually had even greater effects than antisocial models. Susan Hearold (1986) statistically combined 108 comparisons of prosocial programs with neutral programs or no program. She found that, on average, "If the viewer watched prosocial programs instead of neutral programs, he would [at least temporarily] be elevated from the 50th to the 74th percentile in prosocial behavior—typically altruism."

In one such study, researchers Lynette Friedrich and Aletha Stein (1973; Stein & Friedrich, 1972) showed preschool children *Mister Rogers' Neighborhood* episodes each day for four weeks as part of their nursery school program. (*Mister Rogers' Neighborhood* aims to enhance young children's social and emotional development.) During the viewing period, children from less educated homes became more cooperative, helpful, and likely to state their feelings. In a follow-up study, kindergartners who viewed four *Mister Rogers'* programs were able to state the show's prosocial content, both on a test and in puppet play (Friedrich & Stein, 1975; also Coates & others, 1976).

Other media also effectively model prosocial behavior. Recent studies show positive effects on attitudes or behavior from playing prosocial video games and listening to prosocial music lyrics (Gentile & others, 2009; Greitemeyer, 2009).

"Children can learn to be altruistic, friendly and self-controlled by looking at television programs depicting such behavior patterns."
—*NATIONAL INSTITUTE OF MENTAL HEALTH, TELEVISION AND BEHAVIOR, 1982*

LEARNING BY DOING

Ervin Staub (2005b) has shown that just as immoral behavior fuels immoral attitudes, so helping increases future helping. Children and adults learn by doing. In a series of studies with children near age 12, Staub and his students found that after

focus ON

Behavior and Attitudes among Rescuers of Jews

Goodness, like evil, often evolves in small steps. The Gentiles who saved Jews often began with a small commitment—to hide someone for a day or two. Having taken that step, they began to see themselves differently, as people who help. Then they became more intensely involved. Given control of a confiscated Jewish-owned factory, Oskar Schindler began by doing small favors for his Jewish workers, who were earning him handsome profits. Gradually, he took greater and greater risks to protect them. He got permission to set up workers' housing next to the factory. He rescued individuals separated from their families and reunited loved ones. Finally, as the Russians advanced, he saved some 1,200 Jews by setting up a fake factory in his hometown and taking along his entire group of "skilled workers" to staff it.

Others, such as Raoul Wallenberg, began by agreeing to a personal request for help and ended up repeatedly risking their lives. Wallenberg became Swedish ambassador to Hungary, where he saved tens of thousands of Hungarian Jews from extermination at Auschwitz. One of those given protective identity papers was 6-year-old Ervin Staub, now a University of Massachusetts social psychologist whose experience set him on a lifelong mission to understand why some people perpetrate evil, some stand by, and some help.

Munich, 1948. Oskar Schindler with some of the Jews he saved from the Nazis during World War II.
Source: Rappoport & Kren, 1993.

children were induced to make toys for hospitalized children or for an art teacher, they became more helpful. So were children after teaching younger children to make puzzles or use first aid.

When children act helpfully, they develop helping-related values, beliefs, and skills, notes Staub. Helping also helps satisfy their needs for a positive self-concept. On a larger scale, "service learning" and volunteer programs woven into a school curriculum have been shown to increase later citizen involvement, social responsibility, cooperation, and leadership (Andersen, 1998; Putnam, 2000). Attitudes follow behavior. Helpful actions therefore promote the self-perception that one is caring and helpful, which in turn promotes further helping.

ATTRIBUTING HELPFUL BEHAVIOR TO ALTRUISTIC MOTIVES

overjustification effect

The result of bribing people to do what they already like doing; they may then see their actions as externally controlled rather than intrinsically appealing.

Another clue to socializing altruism comes from research on what Chapter 4 called the **overjustification effect:** When the justification for an act is more than sufficient, the person may attribute the act to the extrinsic justification rather than to an inner motive. Rewarding people for doing what they would do anyway therefore undermines intrinsic motivation. We can state the principle positively: By providing people with just enough justification to prompt a good deed (weaning them from bribes and threats), we may increase their pleasure in doing such deeds on their own.

Daniel Batson and his associates (1978, 1979) put the overjustification phenomenon to work. In several experiments, they found that University of Kansas students felt most altruistic after they agreed to help someone without payment or implied social pressure. When pay had been offered or social pressures were present, people felt less altruistic after helping.

In another experiment, the researchers led students to attribute a helpful act to compliance ("I guess we really don't have a choice") or to compassion ("The guy really needs help"). Later, when the students were asked to volunteer their time to a local service agency, 25 percent of those who had been led to perceive their previous helpfulness as mere compliance now volunteered; of those led to see themselves as compassionate, 60 percent volunteered. The moral? When people wonder, "Why am I helping?" it's best if the circumstances enable them to answer, "Because help was needed, and I am a caring, giving, helpful person."

Although rewards undermine intrinsic motivation when they function as controlling bribes, an unanticipated compliment can make people feel competent and worthy. When Joel is coerced with "If you quit being chicken and give blood, we'll win the fraternity prize for most donations," he isn't likely to attribute his donation to altruism. When Jocelyn is rewarded with "That's terrific that you'd choose to take an hour out of such a busy week to give blood," she's more likely to walk away with an altruistic self-image—and thus to contribute again (Piliavin & others, 1982; Thomas & Batson, 1981; Thomas & others, 1981).

To predispose more people to help in situations where most don't, it can also pay to induce a tentative positive commitment, from which people may infer their own helpfulness. Delia Cioffi and Randy Garner (1998) observed that only about 5 percent of students responded to a campus blood drive after receiving an e-mail announcement a week ahead. They asked other students to reply to the announcement with a yes "if you think you probably will donate." Of those, 29 percent did reply and the actual donation rate was 8 percent. They asked a third group to reply with a no if they did *not* anticipate donating. Now 71 percent implied they might give (by not replying). Imagine yourself in this third group. Might you have decided not to say no because, after all, you *are* a caring person so there's a chance you might give? And might that thought have opened you to persuasion as you encountered campus posters and flyers during the ensuing week? That apparently is what happened, because 12 percent of these students—more than twice the normal rate—showed up to offer their blood.

Inferring that one is a helpful person seems also to have happened when Dariusz Dolinski (2000) stopped pedestrians on the streets of Wroclaw, Poland, and asked them for directions to a nonexistent "Zubrzyckiego Street" or to an illegible address. Everyone tried unsuccessfully to help. After doing so, about two-thirds (twice the number of those not given the opportunity to try to help) agreed when asked by someone 100 meters farther down the road to watch their heavy bag or bicycle for five minutes.

LEARNING ABOUT ALTRUISM

Researchers have found another way to boost altruism, one that provides a happy conclusion to this chapter. Some social psychologists worry that as people become more aware of social psychology's findings, their behavior may change, thus invalidating the findings (Gergen, 1982). Will learning about the factors that inhibit altruism reduce their influence? Sometimes, such "enlightenment" is not our problem but one of our goals.

Experiments with University of Montana students by Arthur Beaman and his colleagues (1978) revealed that once people understand why the presence of bystanders inhibits helping, they become more likely to help in group situations. The researchers used a lecture to inform some students how bystander inaction can affect the interpretation of an emergency and feelings of responsibility. Other students heard either a different lecture or no lecture at all. Two weeks later, as part of a different experiment in a different location, the participants found themselves walking (with an unresponsive confederate) past someone slumped over or past a person sprawled beneath a bicycle. Of those who had not heard the helping lecture, a fourth paused to offer help; twice as many of those "enlightened" did so.

Having read this chapter, perhaps you, too, have changed. As you come to understand what influences people's responses, will your attitudes and your behavior be the same?

Summing Up: How Can We Increase Helping?

Research suggests that we can enhance helpfulness in three ways.

- First, we can reverse those factors that inhibit helping. We can take steps to reduce the ambiguity of an emergency, to make a personal appeal, and to increase feelings of responsibility.

- Second, we can even use reprimands or the door-in-the-face technique to evoke guilt feelings or a concern for self-image.

- Third, we can teach altruism. Research into television's portrayals of prosocial models shows the medium's power to teach positive behavior. Children who

view helpful behavior tend to act helpfully. If we want to promote altruistic behavior, we should remember the overjustification effect: When we coerce good deeds, intrinsic love of the activity often diminishes. If we provide people with enough justification for them to decide to do good, but not much more, they will attribute their behavior to their own altruistic motivation and henceforth be more willing to help. Learning about altruism, as you have just done, can also prepare people to perceive and respond to others' needs.

POSTSCRIPT: Taking Social Psychology into Life

Those of us who research, teach, and write about social psychology do so believing that our work matters. It engages humanly significant phenomena. Studying social psychology can therefore expand our thinking and prepare us to live and act with greater awareness and compassion, or so we presume.

How good it feels, then, when students and former students confirm our presumptions with stories of how they have related social psychology to their lives. Shortly before I wrote the last paragraph, a former student, now living in Washington, D.C., stopped by. She mentioned that she recently found herself part of a stream of pedestrians striding past a man lying unconscious on the sidewalk. "It took my mind back to our social psych class and the accounts of why people fail to help in such situations. Then I thought, 'Well, if I just walk by, too, who's going to help him?'" So she made a call to an emergency help number and waited with the victim—and other bystanders who now joined her—until help arrived.

Making the Social Connection

As part of this chapter's exploration of helping, we engaged John Darley's classic research on the bystander effect. The chapter on prejudice (Chapter 9) introduced Darley's work on how stereotypes can subtly bias our judgments of individuals. Why does the presence of others inhibit people's helping? Go to the Online Learning Center for this book to watch Darley describe his research.

Conflict and Peacemaking

"If you want peace, work for justice."

—Pope Paul VI

There is a speech that has been spoken in many languages by the leaders of many countries. It goes like this: "The intentions of our country are entirely peaceful. Yet, we are also aware that other nations, with their new weapons, threaten us. Thus we must defend ourselves against attack. By so doing, we shall protect our way of life and preserve the peace" (Richardson, 1960). Almost every nation claims concern only for peace but, mistrusting other nations, arms itself in self-defense. The result is a world that has been spending $2 billion per day on arms and armies while hundreds of millions die of malnutrition and untreated disease.

The elements of such **conflict** (a perceived incompatibility of actions or goals) are similar at many levels: conflict between nations in an arms race, between religious factions disputing points of doctrine, between corporate executives and workers disputing salaries, and between bickering spouses. People in conflict perceive that one side's gain is the other's loss:

- "We want peace and security." "So do we, but you threaten us."

- "I'd like the music off." "I'd like it on."

- "We want more pay." "We can't afford to give it to you."

As civil rights leaders know, creatively managed conflicts can have constructive outcomes.

conflict
A perceived incompatibility of actions or goals.

peace
A condition marked by low levels of hostility and aggression and by mutually beneficial relationships.

Sometimes the result is that everybody loses, as when a salary cap impasse between National Hockey League owners and players caused the 2005 season to be cancelled.

A relationship or an organization without conflict is probably apathetic. Conflict signifies involvement, commitment, and caring. If conflict is understood and recognized, it can end oppression and stimulate renewed and improved human relations. Without conflict, people seldom face and resolve their problems.

Genuine **peace** is more than the suppression of open conflict, more than a fragile, superficial calm. Peace is the outcome of a creatively managed conflict. Peace is the parties reconciling their perceived differences and reaching genuine accord. "We got our increased pay. You got your increased profit. Now each of us is helping the other achieve the organization's goals." Peace, says peace researcher Royce Anderson (2004), "is a condition in which individuals, families, groups, communities, and/or nations experience low levels of violence and engage in mutually harmonious relationships."

In this chapter we explore conflict and peacemaking by asking what factors create or exacerbate conflict, and what factors contribute to peace:

- What social situations feed conflict?
- How do misperceptions fuel conflict?
- Does contact with the other side reduce conflict?
- When do cooperation, communication, and mediation enable reconciliation?

What Creates Conflict?

Social-psychological studies have identified several ingredients of conflict. What's striking (and what simplifies our task) is that these ingredients are common to all levels of social conflict, whether international, intergroup, or interpersonal.

Social Dilemmas

Several of the problems that most threaten our human future—nuclear arms, climate change, overpopulation, natural-resource depletion—arise as various parties pursue their self-interests, ironically, to their collective detriment. One individual may think, "It would cost me a lot to buy expensive greenhouse emission controls.

Besides, the greenhouse gases I personally generate are trivial." Many others reason similarly, and the result is a warning climate, rising seas, and more extreme weather.

In some societies, parents benefit by having many children who can assist with the family tasks and provide security in their old age. But when most families have many children generation after generation, the result is the collective devastation of overpopulation. Choices that are individually rewarding become collectively punishing. We therefore have a dilemma: How can we reconcile individual self-interest with communal well-being?

To isolate and study that dilemma, social psychologists have used laboratory games that expose the heart of many real social conflicts. "Social psychologists who study conflict are in much the same position as the astronomers," noted conflict researcher Morton Deutsch (1999). "We cannot conduct true experiments with large-scale social events. But we can identify the conceptual similarities between the large scale and the small, as the astronomers have between the planets and Newton's apple. That is why the games people play as subjects in our laboratory may advance our understanding of war, peace, and social justice."

Let's consider two laboratory games that are each an example of a **social trap:** the Prisoner's Dilemma and the Tragedy of the Commons.

THE PRISONER'S DILEMMA

This dilemma derives from an anecdote concerning two suspects being questioned separately by the district attorney (DA) (Rapoport, 1960). The DA knows they are jointly guilty but has only enough evidence to convict them of a lesser offense. So the DA creates an incentive for each one to confess privately:

- If Prisoner A confesses and Prisoner B doesn't, the DA will grant immunity to A, and will use A's confession to convict B of a maximum offense (and vice versa if B confesses and A doesn't).
- If both confess, each will receive a moderate sentence.
- If neither prisoner confesses, each will be convicted of a lesser crime and receive a light sentence.

The matrix of Figure 13.1 summarizes the choices. If you were a prisoner faced with such a dilemma, with no chance to talk to the other prisoner, would you confess?

social trap
A situation in which the conflicting parties, by each rationally pursuing its self-interest, become caught in mutually destructive behavior. Examples include the Prisoner's Dilemma and the Tragedy of the Commons.

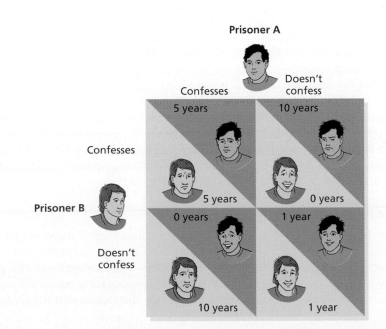

FIGURE :: 13.1

The Classic Prisoner's Dilemma

In each box, the number above the diagonal is prisoner A's outcome. Thus, if both prisoners confess, both get five years. If neither confesses, each gets a year. If one confesses, that prisoner is set free in exchange for evidence used to convict the other of a crime bringing a 10-year sentence. If you were one of the prisoners, unable to communicate with your fellow prisoner, would you confess?

FIGURE :: 13.2

Laboratory Version of the Prisoner's Dilemma

The numbers represent some reward, such as money. In each box, the number above the diagonal lines is the outcome for person A. Unlike the classic Prisoner's Dilemma (a one-shot decision), most laboratory versions involve repeated plays.

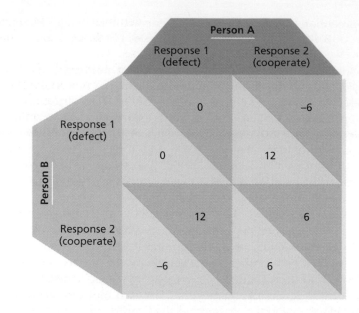

Many people say they would confess to be granted immunity, even though mutual *non*confession elicits lighter sentences than mutual confession. Perhaps this is because (as shown in the Figure 13.1 matrix) no matter what the other prisoner decides, each is better off confessing than being convicted individually. If the other also confesses, the sentence is moderate rather than severe. If the other does not confess, one goes free.

In some 2,000 studies (Dawes, 1991), university students have faced variations of the Prisoner's Dilemma with the choices being to defect or to cooperate, and the outcomes not being prison terms but chips, money, or course points. As Figure 13.2 illustrates, on any given decision, a person is better off defecting (because such behavior exploits the other's cooperation or protects against the other's exploitation). However—and here's the rub—by not cooperating, both parties end up far worse off than if they had trusted each other and thus had gained a joint profit. This dilemma often traps each one in a maddening predicament in which both realize they *could* mutually profit. But unable to communicate and mistrusting each other, they often become "locked in" to not cooperating.

Punishing another's lack of cooperation might seem like a smart strategy, but in the laboratory it can have counterproductive effects (Dreber & others, 2008). Punishment typically triggers retaliation, which means that those who punish tend to escalate conflict, worsening their outcomes, while nice guys finish first. What punishers see as a defensive reaction, recipients see as an aggressive escalation (Anderson & others, 2008). When hitting back, they may hit harder while seeing themselves as merely returning tit for tat. In one experiment, London volunteers used a mechanical device to press back on another's finger after receiving pressure on their own. While seeking to reciprocate with the same degree of pressure, they typically responded with 40 percent more force. Thus, touches soon escalated to hard presses, much like a child saying "I just touched him, and then he hit me!" (Shergill & others, 2003).

THE TRAGEDY OF THE COMMONS

Many social dilemmas involve more than two parties. Global warming stems from deforestation and from the carbon dioxide emitted by cars, furnaces, and coal-fired power plants. Each gas-guzzling SUV contributes infinitesimally to the problem, and the harm each does is diffused over many people. To model such social predicaments, researchers have developed laboratory dilemmas that involve multiple people.

A metaphor for the insidious nature of social dilemmas is what ecologist Garrett Hardin (1968) called the **Tragedy of the Commons.** He derived the name from the centrally located grassy pasture in old English towns.

In today's world the "commons" can be air, water, fish, cookies, or any shared and limited resource. If all use the resource in moderation, it may replenish itself as rapidly as it's harvested. The grass will grow, the fish will reproduce, and the cookie jar will be restocked. If not, there occurs a tragedy of the commons. Imagine 100 farmers surrounding a commons capable of sustaining 100 cows. When each grazes one cow, the common feeding ground is optimally used. But then a farmer reasons, "If I put a second cow in the pasture, I'll double my output, minus the mere 1 percent overgrazing" and adds a second cow. So does each of the other farmers. The inevitable result? The Tragedy of the Commons—a mud field.

Likewise, environmental pollution is the sum of many minor pollutions, each of which benefits the individual polluters much more than they could benefit themselves (and the environment) if they stopped polluting. We litter public places—dorm lounges, parks, zoos—while keeping our personal spaces clean. We deplete our natural resources because the immediate personal benefits of, say, taking a long, hot shower outweigh the seemingly inconsequential costs. Whalers knew others would exploit the whales if they didn't and that taking a few whales would hardly diminish the species. Therein lies the tragedy. Everybody's business (conservation) becomes nobody's business.

Is such individualism uniquely American? Kaori Sato (1987) gave students in a more collective culture, Japan, opportunities to harvest—for actual money—trees from a simulated forest. The students shared equally the costs of planting the forest, and the result was like those in Western cultures. More than half the trees were harvested before they had grown to the most profitable size.

Sato's forest reminds me of our home's cookie jar, which was restocked once a week. What we *should* have done was conserve cookies so that each day we could each enjoy two or three. But lacking regulation and fearing that other family members would soon deplete the resource, what we actually did was maximize our individual cookie consumption by downing one after the other. The result: Within 24 hours the cookie glut would often end, the jar sitting empty for the rest of the week.

When resources are not partitioned, people often consume more than they realize (Herlocker & others, 1997). As a bowl of mashed potatoes is passed around a table of 10, the first few diners are more likely to scoop out a disproportionate share than when a platter of 10 chicken drumsticks is passed.

The Prisoner's Dilemma and the Tragedy of the Commons games have several similar features.

> **Tragedy of the Commons**
>
> The "commons" is any shared resource, including air, water, energy sources, and food supplies. The tragedy occurs when individuals consume more than their share, with the cost of their doing so dispersed among all, causing the ultimate collapse—the tragedy—of the commons.

THE FUNDAMENTAL ATTRIBUTION ERROR

First, both games tempt people to *explain their own behavior situationally* ("I had to protect myself against exploitation by my opponent") and to explain their partners' behavior dispositionally ("she was greedy," "he was untrustworthy"). Most never realize that their counterparts are viewing them with the same fundamental attribution error (Gifford & Hine, 1997; Hine & Gifford, 1996). People with self-inflating, self-focused narcissistic tendencies are especially unlikely to empathize with others' perspectives (Campbell & others, 2005).

EVOLVING MOTIVES

Second, *motives often change.* At first, people are eager to make some easy money, then to minimize their losses, and finally to save face and avoid defeat (Brockner & others, 1982; Teger, 1980). These shifting motives are strikingly similar to the shifting motives during the buildup of the 1960s Vietnam War. At first, President Johnson's speeches expressed concern for democracy, freedom, and justice. As the conflict escalated, his concern became protecting America's honor and avoiding

When, after their 1980–1988 war, more than a million casualties, and ruined economies, Iran and Iraq finally laid down their arms, the border over which they had fought was exactly the same as when they started.

© Steve Benson. Used by permission of Steve Benson and Creators Syndicate, Inc.

the national humiliation of losing a war. A similar shift occurred during the war in Iraq, which was initially proposed as a response to supposed weapons of mass destruction.

OUTCOMES NEED NOT SUM TO ZERO

non-zero-sum games
Games in which outcomes need not sum to zero. With cooperation, both can win; with competition, both can lose. (Also called *mixed-motive situations*.)

Third, most real-life conflicts, like the Prisoner's Dilemma and the Tragedy of the Commons, are **non-zero-sum games.** The two sides' profits and losses need not add up to zero. Both can win; both can lose. Each game pits the immediate interests of individuals against the well-being of the group. Each is a diabolical social trap that shows how, even when each individual behaves "rationally," harm can result. No malicious person planned for the earth's atmosphere to be warmed by a blanket of carbon dioxide.

Not all self-serving behavior leads to collective doom. In a plentiful commons—as in the world of the eighteenth-century capitalist economist Adam Smith (1776, p. 18)—individuals who seek to maximize their own profit may also give the community what it needs: "It is not from the benevolence of the butcher, the brewer, or the baker, that we expect our dinner," he observed, "but from their regard to their own interest."

RESOLVING SOCIAL DILEMMAS

Faced with social traps, how can we induce people to cooperate for their mutual betterment? Research with the laboratory dilemmas reveals several ways (Gifford & Hine, 1997).

"Like the old buffalo hunters, fishermen have a personal incentive to make as much as they can this year, even if they're destroying their own profession in the process."

—*JOHN TIERNEY, "WHERE THE TUNA ROAM," 2006*

REGULATION If taxes were entirely voluntary, how many would pay their full share? Modern societies do not depend on charity to pay for schools, parks, and social and military security. We also develop rules to safeguard our common good. Fishing and hunting have long been regulated by local seasons and limits; at the global level, an International Whaling Commission sets an agreed-upon "harvest" that enables whales to regenerate. Likewise, where fishing industries, such as the Alaskan halibut fishery, have implemented "catch shares"—guaranteeing each fisher a percentage of each year's allowable catch—competition and overfishing have been greatly reduced (Costello & others, 2008).

Small is cooperative. On the isle of Muck, off Scotland's west coast, Constable Lawrence MacEwan has had an easy time policing the island's residents, recently numbering 33. Over his 40 years on the job, there has never been a crime (*Scottish Life*, 2001).

In everyday life, however, regulation has costs—costs of administering and enforcing the regulations, costs of diminished personal freedom. A volatile political question thus arises: At what point does a regulation's cost exceed its benefits?

SMALL IS BEAUTIFUL   There is another way to resolve social dilemmas: Make the group small. In a small commons, each person feels more responsible and effective (Kerr, 1989). As a group grows larger, people become more likely to think, "I couldn't have made a difference anyway"—a common excuse for noncooperation (Kerr & Kaufman-Gilliland, 1997).

In small groups, people also feel more identified with a group's success. Anything else that enhances group identity will also increase cooperation. Even just a few minutes of discussion or just believing that one shares similarities with others in the group can increase "we feeling" and cooperation (Brewer, 1987; Orbell & others, 1988). Residential stability also strengthens communal identity and pro-community behavior, including even baseball attendance independent of a team's record (Oishi & others, 2007).

In small groups—as opposed to large ones—individuals are less likely to take more than their equal share of available resources (Allison & others, 1992). On the Pacific Northwest island where I grew up, our small neighborhood shared a communal water supply. On hot summer days when the reservoir ran low, a light came on, signaling our 15 families to conserve. Recognizing our responsibility to one another, and feeling that our conservation really mattered, each of us conserved. Never did the reservoir run dry.

In a much larger commons—say, a city—voluntary conservation is less successful. Because the harm one does diffuses across many others, each individual can rationalize away personal accountability. Some political theorists and social psychologists therefore argue that, where feasible, the commons should be divided into smaller territories (Edney, 1980). In his 1902 *Mutual Aid,* the Russian revolutionary Pyotr Kropotkin set down a vision of small communities rather than central government making consensus decisions for the benefit of all (Gould, 1988).

Evolutionary psychologist Robin Dunbar (1996) notes that hunter-gatherer societies often travel together as groups of 30 to 35 people, and that tribal villages and clans often have averaged about 150 people—enough to afford mutual support and protection but not more people than one can monitor. This seemingly natural group size is also, he believes, the optimum size for business organizations, religious congregations, and military fighting units.

"For that which is common to the greatest number has the least care bestowed upon it."
—ARISTOTLE

COMMUNICATION To resolve a social dilemma, people must communicate. In the laboratory as in real life, group communication sometimes degenerates into threats and name-calling (Deutsch & Krauss, 1960). More often, communication enables people to cooperate (Bornstein & others, 1988, 1989). Discussing the dilemma forges a group identity, which enhances concern for everyone's welfare. It devises group norms and consensus expectations and puts pressure on members to follow them. Especially when people are face-to-face, it enables them to commit themselves to cooperation (Bouas & Komorita, 1996; Drolet & Morris, 2000; Kerr & others, 1994, 1997; Pruitt, 1998).

A clever experiment by Robyn Dawes (1980, 1994) illustrates the importance of communication. Imagine that an experimenter offered you and six strangers a choice: You can each have $6, or you can donate your $6 to the others. If you give away your money, the experimenter will double your gift. No one will be told whether you chose to give or keep your $6. Thus, if all seven give, everyone pockets $12. If you alone keep your $6 and all the others give theirs, you pocket $18. If you give and the others keep, you pocket nothing. In this experiment, cooperation is mutually advantageous, but it requires risk. Dawes found that, without discussion, about 30 percent of people gave. With discussion, in which they could establish trust and cooperation, about 80 percent gave.

Open, clear, forthright communication between two parties reduces mistrust. Without communication, those who expect others not to cooperate will usually refuse to cooperate themselves (Messé & Sivacek, 1979; Pruitt & Kimmel, 1977). One who mistrusts is almost sure to be uncooperative (to protect against exploitation). Noncooperation, in turn, feeds further mistrust ("What else could I do? It's a dog-eat-dog world"). In experiments, communication reduces mistrust, enabling people to reach agreements that lead to their common betterment.

> "My own belief is that Russian and Chinese behavior is as much influenced by suspicion of our intentions as ours is by suspicion of theirs. This would mean that we have great influence on their behavior—that, by treating them as hostile, we assure their hostility."
>
> —U.S. SENATOR J. WILLIAM FULBRIGHT (1971)

CHANGING THE PAYOFFS Laboratory cooperation rises when experimenters change the payoff matrix to reward cooperation and punish exploitation (Komorita & Barth, 1985; Pruitt & Rubin, 1986). Changing payoffs also helps resolve actual dilemmas. In some cities, freeways clog and skies smog because people prefer the convenience of driving themselves directly to work. Each knows that one more car does not add noticeably to the congestion and pollution. To alter the personal cost-benefit calculations, many cities now give carpoolers incentives, such as designated freeway lanes or reduced tolls.

To change behavior, many cities have changed the payoff matrix. Fast carpool-only lanes increase the benefits of carpooling and the costs of driving alone.

APPEALS TO ALTRUISTIC NORMS In Chapter 12 we saw how increasing people's feelings of responsibility for others boosts altruism. So, will appeals to altruistic motives prompt people to act for the common good?

The evidence is mixed. On the one hand, just *knowing* the dire consequences of noncooperation has little effect. In laboratory games, people realize that their self-serving choices are mutually destructive, yet they continue to make them. Outside the laboratory, warnings of doom and appeals to conserve have brought little response. Shortly after taking office in 1976, President Carter declared that America's response to the energy crisis should be "the moral equivalent of war" and urged conservation. The following summer, Americans consumed more gasoline than ever before. At the beginning of this new century, people knew that global warming was under way—and were buying gas-slurping SUVs in record numbers. As we have seen many times in this book, attitudes sometimes fail to influence behavior. *Knowing* what is good does not necessarily lead to *doing* what is good.

Still, most people do adhere to norms of social responsibility, reciprocity, equity, and keeping one's commitments (Kerr, 1992). The problem is how to tap such feelings. One way is through the influence of a charismatic leader who inspires others to cooperate (De Cremer, 2002). Another way is by defining situations in ways that imply cooperative norms. Lee Ross and Andrew Ward (1996) invited Stanford dormitory advisers to nominate male students whom they thought especially likely to cooperate and others whom they thought likely to defect while playing a Prisoner's Dilemma game. In reality, the two groups of students were equally likely to cooperate. What affected cooperation dramatically—in this and follow-up research (Liberman & others, 2004)—was whether the researchers labeled the simulation the "Wall Street Game" (in which case one-third of the participants cooperated) or the "Community Game" (with two-thirds cooperating).

Communication can also activate altruistic norms. When permitted to communicate, participants in laboratory games frequently appeal to the social-responsibility norm: "If you defect on the rest of us, you're going to have to live with it for the rest of your life" (Dawes & others, 1977). Noting that, researcher Robyn Dawes (1980) and his associates gave participants a short sermon about group benefits, exploitation, and ethics. Then the participants played a dilemma game. The sermon worked: People chose to forgo immediate personal gain for the common good. (Recall, too, from Chapter 12, the disproportionate volunteerism and charitable contributions by people who regularly hear sermons in churches and synagogues.)

Could such appeals work in large-scale dilemmas? Jeffery Scott Mio and his colleagues (1993) found that after reading about the commons dilemma (as you have), theater patrons littered less than patrons who read about voting. Moreover, when cooperation obviously serves the public good, one can usefully appeal to the social-responsibility norm (Lynn & Oldenquist, 1986). For example, if people believe public transportation saves time, they will be more likely to use it if they also believe it reduces pollution (Van Vugt & others, 1996). In the 1960s struggle for civil rights, many marchers willingly agreed, for the sake of the larger group, to suffer harassment, beatings, and jail. In wartime, people make great personal sacrifices for the good of their group. As Winston Churchill said of the Battle of Britain, the actions of the Royal Air Force pilots were genuinely altruistic: A great many people owed a great deal to those who flew into battle knowing there was a high probability—70 percent for those on a standard tour of duty—that they would not return (Levinson, 1950).

> "Never in the field of human conflict was so much owed by so many to so few."
> —*SIR WINSTON CHURCHILL, HOUSE OF COMMONS, AUGUST 20, 1940*

To summarize, we can minimize destructive entrapment in social dilemmas by establishing rules that regulate self-serving behavior, by keeping groups small, by enabling people to communicate, by changing payoffs to make cooperation more rewarding, and by invoking compelling altruistic norms.

Competition

Hostilities often arise when groups compete for scarce jobs, housing, or resources. When interests clash, conflict erupts—a phenomenon Chapter 9 identified as *realistic group conflict*. As one Algerian immigrant to France explained after Muslim youth rioted in dozens of French cities in the autumn of 2005, "There is no exit, no factories, no jobs for them. They see too much injustice" (Sciolino, 2005).

To experiment on competition's effect, we could randomly divide people into two groups, have the groups compete for a scarce resource, and note what happens. That is precisely what Muzafer Sherif (1966) and his colleagues did in a dramatic series of experiments with typical 11- and 12-year-old boys. The inspiration for those experiments dated back to Sherif's witnessing, as a teenager, Greek troops invading his Turkish province in 1919.

Competition kindles conflict. Here, in Sherif's Robber's Cave experiment, one group of boys raids the bunkhouse of another.

They started killing people right and left. [That] made a great impression on me. There and then I became interested in understanding why these things were happening among human beings. . . . I wanted to learn whatever science or specialization was needed to understand this intergroup savagery. (quoted by Aron & Aron, 1989, p. 131)

After studying the social roots of savagery, Sherif introduced the seeming essentials into several three-week summer camping experiences. In one such study, he divided 22 unacquainted Oklahoma City boys into two groups, took them to a Boy Scout camp in separate buses, and settled them in bunkhouses about a half-mile apart at Oklahoma's Robber's Cave State Park. For most of the first week, each group was unaware of the other's existence. By cooperating in various activities—preparing meals, camping out, fixing up a swimming hole, building a rope bridge—each group soon became close-knit. They gave themselves names: "Rattlers" and "Eagles." Typifying the good feeling, a sign appeared in one cabin: "Home Sweet Home."

Group identity thus established, the stage was set for the conflict. Near the first week's end, the Rattlers discovered the Eagles "on 'our' baseball field." When the camp staff then proposed a tournament of competitive activities between the two groups (baseball games, tugs-of-war, cabin inspections, treasure hunts, and so forth), both groups responded enthusiastically. This was win-lose competition. The spoils (medals, knives) would all go to the tournament victor.

The result? The camp gradually degenerated into open warfare. It was like a scene from William Golding's novel *Lord of the Flies*, which depicts the social disintegration of boys marooned on an island. In Sherif's study, the conflict began with each side calling the other names during the competitive activities. Soon it escalated to dining hall "garbage wars," flag burnings, cabin ransackings, even fistfights. Asked to describe the other group, the boys said they were "sneaky," "smart alecks," "stinkers," but referring to their own group as "brave," "tough," "friendly."

Little-known fact: How did Sherif unobtrusively observe the boys without inhibiting their behavior? He became the camp maintenance man (Williams, 2002).

The win-lose competition had produced intense conflict, negative images of the outgroup, and strong ingroup cohesiveness and pride. Group polarization no doubt exacerbated the conflict. In competition-fostering situations, groups behave more competitively than do individuals (Wildschut & others, 2003, 2007). Men, especially, get caught up in intergroup competition (Van Vugt & others, 2007).

All of this occurred without any cultural, physical, or economic differences between the two groups and with boys who were their communities' "cream of the crop." Sherif noted that, had we visited the camp at that point, we would have concluded these "were wicked, disturbed, and vicious bunches of youngsters" (1966, p. 85). Actually, their evil behavior was triggered by an evil situation.

Competition breeds such conflict, later research has shown, especially when (a) people perceive that resources such as money, jobs, or power are limited and available on a zero-sum basis (others' gain is one's loss), and (b) a distinct outgroup stands out as a potential competitor (Esses & others, 2005). Thus, those who see immigrants as competing for their own jobs will tend to express negative attitudes toward immigrants and immigration.

Fortunately, as we will see, Sherif not only made strangers into enemies; he then also made the enemies into friends.

Perceived Injustice

"That's unfair!" "What a ripoff!" "We deserve better!" Such comments typify conflicts bred by perceived injustice. But what is "justice"? According to some social-psychological theorists, people perceive justice as equity—the distribution of rewards in proportion to individuals' contributions (Walster & others, 1978). If you and I have a relationship (employer-employee, teacher-student, husband-wife, colleague-colleague), it is equitable if

$$\frac{\text{My outcomes}}{\text{My inputs}} = \frac{\text{Your outcomes}}{\text{Your inputs}}$$

If you contribute more and benefit less than I do, you will feel exploited and irritated; I may feel exploitative and guilty. Chances are, though, that you will be more sensitive to the inequity than I will (Greenberg, 1986; Messick & Sentis, 1979).

We may agree with the equity principle's definition of justice yet disagree on whether our relationship is equitable. If two people are colleagues, what will each consider a relevant input? The one who is older may favor basing pay on seniority, the other on current productivity. Given such a disagreement, whose definition is likely to prevail? More often than not, those with social power convince themselves and others that they deserve what they're getting (Mikula, 1984). This has been called a "golden" rule: Whoever has the gold makes the rules.

And how do those who are exploited react? Elaine Hatfield, William Walster, and Ellen Berscheid (1978) detected three possibilities. They can *accept* and justify their inferior position ("We're poor but we're happy"). They can *demand compensation*, perhaps by harassing, embarrassing, even cheating their exploiter. If all else fails, they may try to restore equity by *retaliating*.

Critics argue that equity is not the only conceivable definition of justice. (Pause a moment: Can you imagine any other?) Edward Sampson (1975) argued that equity theorists wrongly assume that the economic principles that guide Western, capitalist nations are universal. Some noncapitalist cultures define justice not as equity but as *equality* or even *fulfillment of need*: "From each according to his abilities, to each according to his needs" (Karl Marx). Compared with individualistic Americans, people socialized under the influence of collectivist cultures, such as China and India, define justice more as equality or need fulfillment (Hui & others, 1991; Leung & Bond, 1984; Murphy-Berman & others, 1984).

On what basis *should* rewards be distributed? Merit? Equality? Need? Some combination of those? Political philosopher John Rawls (1971) invited us to consider a future in which our own place on the economic ladder is unknown. Which standard of justice would we prefer? Gregory Mitchell and his colleagues (1993) report that students want some reward for productivity but also, should they find themselves at the bottom, enough priority placed on equality to meet their own needs.

Misperception

Recall that conflict is a *perceived* incompatibility of actions or goals. Many conflicts contain but a small core of truly incompatible goals; the bigger problem is the misperceptions of the other's motives and goals. The Eagles and the Rattlers did indeed

"Do unto others 20% better than you would expect them to do unto you, to correct for subjective error."
—LINUS PAULING (1962)

"Solutions to the distribution problem are nontrivial. Children fight, colleagues complain, group members resign, tempers flare, and nations battle over issues of fairness. As parents, employers, teachers, and presidents know, the most frequent response to an allocation decision is 'not fair.'"
—ARNOLD KAHN & WILLIAM GAEDDERT (1985)

FIGURE :: 13.3

Many conflicts contain a core of truly incompatible goals surrounded by a larger exterior of misperceptions.

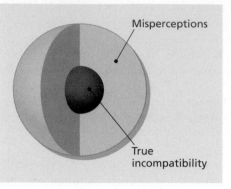

have some genuinely incompatible aims. But their perceptions subjectively magnified their differences (Figure 13.3).

In earlier chapters we considered the seeds of such misperception. The *self-serving bias* leads individuals and groups to accept credit for their good deeds and shirk responsibility for bad deeds, without according others the same benefit of the doubt. A tendency to *self-justify* inclines people to deny the wrong of their evil acts ("You call that hitting? I hardly touched him!"). Thanks to the *fundamental attribution error*, each side sees the other's hostility as reflecting an evil disposition. One then filters the information and interprets it to fit one's *preconceptions*. Groups frequently *polarize* these self-serving, self-justifying, biasing tendencies. One symptom of *groupthink* is the tendency to perceive one's own group as moral and strong, the opposition as evil and weak. Acts of terrorism that in most people's eyes are despicable brutality are seen by others as "holy war." Indeed, the mere fact of being in a group triggers an *ingroup bias.* And negative *stereotypes* of the outgroup, once formed, are often resistant to contradictory evidence.

So it should not surprise us, though it should sober us, to discover that people in conflict—people everywhere—form distorted images of one another. Wherever in the world you live, was it not true that when your country was last at war it clothed itself in moral virtue? that it prepared for war by demonizing the enemy? that most of its people accepted their government's case for war and rallied 'round its flag? Show social psychologists Ervin Staub and Daniel Bar-Tal (2003) a group in intractable conflict and they will show you a group that

- sees its own goals as supremely important.
- takes pride in "us" and devalues "them."
- believes itself victimized.
- elevates patriotism, solidarity, and loyalty to their group's needs.
- celebrates self-sacrifice and suppresses criticism.

"Aggression breeds patriotism, and patriotism curbs dissent."

—*MAUREEN DOWD, 2003*

Although one side to a conflict may indeed be acting with greater moral virtue, the point is that enemy images are fairly predictable. Even the types of misperception are intriguingly predictable.

MIRROR-IMAGE PERCEPTIONS

To a striking degree, the misperceptions of those in conflict are mutual. People in conflict attribute similar virtues to themselves and vices to the other. When the American psychologist Urie Bronfenbrenner (1961) visited the Soviet Union in 1960 and conversed with many ordinary citizens in Russian, he was astonished to hear them saying the same things about America that Americans were saying about Russia. The Russians said that the U.S. government was militarily aggressive; that it exploited and deluded the American people; that in diplomacy it was not to be trusted. "Slowly and painfully, it forced itself upon one that the Russians' distorted picture of us was curiously similar to our view of them—a mirror image."

Analyses of American and Russian perceptions by psychologists (Tobin & Eagles, 1992; White, 1984) and political scientists (Jervis, 1985) revealed that mirror-image perceptions persisted into the 1980s. The same action (patrolling the other's coast with submarines, selling arms to smaller nations) seemed more hostile when *they* did it.

When two sides have clashing perceptions, at least one of the two is misperceiving the other. And when such misperceptions exist, noted Bronfenbrenner,

Self-confirming, mirror-image perceptions are a hallmark of intense conflict, as in the former Yugoslavia.

"It is a psychological phenomenon without parallel in the gravity of its consequences . . . for *it is characteristic of such images that they are self-confirming*." If A expects B to be hostile, A may treat B in such a way that B fulfills A's expectations, thus beginning a vicious circle (Kennedy & Pronin, 2008). Morton Deutsch (1986) explained:

> You hear the false rumor that a friend is saying nasty things about you; you snub him; he then badmouths you, confirming your expectation. Similarly, if the policymakers of East and West believe that war is likely and either attempts to increase its military security vis-à-vis the other, the other's response will justify the initial move.

Negative **mirror-image perceptions** have been an obstacle to peace in many places:

- Both sides of the Arab-Israeli conflict insisted that "we" are motivated by our need to protect our security and our territory, whereas "they" want to obliterate us and gobble up our land. "We" are the indigenous people here, "they" are the invaders. "We" are the victims; "they" are the aggressors" (Bar-Tal, 2004; Heradstveit, 1979; Kelmom, 2007). Given such intense mistrust, negotiation is difficult.

- At Northern Ireland's University of Ulster, J. A. Hunter and his colleagues (1991) showed Catholic and Protestant students videos of a Protestant attack at a Catholic funeral and a Catholic attack at a Protestant funeral. Most students attributed the other side's attack to "bloodthirsty" motives but its own side's attack to retaliation or self-defense.

- Terrorism is in the eye of the beholder. In the Middle East, a public opinion survey found 98 percent of Palestinians agreeing that the killing of 29 Palestinians by an assault-rifle-bearing Israeli at a mosque constituted terrorism, and 82 percent *dis*agreed that the killing of 21 Israeli youths by a Palestinian suicide-bombing constituted terrorism (Kruglanski & Fishman, 2006). Israelis likewise have responded to violence with intensified perceptions of Palestinian evil intent (Bar-Tal, 2004).

Such conflicts, notes Philip Zimbardo (2004a), engage "a two-category world— of good people, like US, and of bad people, like THEM." "In fact," note Daniel

mirror-image perceptions
Reciprocal views of each other often held by parties in conflict; for example, each may view itself as moral and peace-loving and the other as evil and aggressive.

Mirror-image perceptions fuel conflict. In the 2000 U.S. presidential election recount in Florida, each side's supporters said, "We only want a fair and accurate ballot count. The other side is trying to steal the election."

"A successful war on terrorism demands an understanding of how so much of the world has come to dislike America. When people who are born with the same human nature as you and I grow up to commit suicide bombings—or applaud them—there must be a reason."

—ROBERT WRIGHT, "TWO YEARS LATER, A THOUSAND YEARS AGO," 2003

Kahneman and Jonathan Renshon (2007), all the biases uncovered in 40 years of psychological research are conducive to war. They "incline national leaders to exaggerate the evil intentions of adversaries, to misjudge how adversaries perceive them, to be overly sanguine when hostilities start, and overly reluctant to make necessary concessions in negotiations."

Opposing sides in a conflict tend to exaggerate their differences. On issues such as immigration and affirmative action, proponents aren't as liberal and opponents aren't as conservative as their adversaries suppose (Sherman & others, 2003). Opposing sides also tend to have a "bias blind spot," notes Cynthia McPherson Frantz (2006). They see their own understandings as not influenced by their liking or disliking for others, while seeing those who disagree with them as unfair and biased. Moreover, partisans tend to perceive a rival as especially disagreeing with their own core values (Chambers & Melnyk, 2006).

John Chambers, Robert Baron, and Mary Inman (2006) confirmed misperceptions on issues related to abortion and politics. Partisans perceived exaggerated differences from their adversaries, who actually agreed with them more often than they supposed. From such exaggerated perceptions of the other's position arise culture wars. Ralph White (1996, 1998) reports that the Serbs started the war in Bosnia partly out of an exaggerated fear of the relatively secularized Bosnian Muslims, whose beliefs they wrongly associated with Middle Eastern Islamic fundamentalism and fanatical terrorism. Resolving conflict involves abandoning such exaggerated perceptions and coming to understand the other's mind. But that isn't easy, notes Robert Wright (2003): "Putting yourself in the shoes of people who do things you find abhorrent may be the hardest moral exercise there is."

Destructive mirror-image perceptions also operate in conflicts between small groups and between individuals. As we saw in the dilemma games, both parties may say, "We want to cooperate. But *their* refusal to cooperate forces *us* to react defensively." In a study of executives, Kenneth Thomas and Louis Pondy (1977) uncovered such attributions. Asked to describe a significant recent conflict, only 12 percent felt the other party was cooperative; 74 percent perceived themselves as cooperative. The typical executive explained that he or she had "suggested," "informed," and "recommended," whereas the antagonist had "demanded," "disagreed with everything I said," and "refused."

Group conflicts are often fueled by an illusion that the enemy's top leaders are evil but their people, though controlled and manipulated, are pro-us. This *evil leader–good people* perception characterized Americans' and Russians' views of each other during the Cold War. The United States entered the Vietnam War believing that in areas dominated by the Communist Vietcong "terrorists," many of the people were allies-in-waiting. As suppressed information later revealed, those beliefs were mere wishful thinking. In 2003 the United States began the Iraq war presuming the

"The American people are good, but the leaders are bad."

—BAGHDAD GROCER ADUL GESAN AFTER 1998 AMERICAN BOMBING OF IRAQ

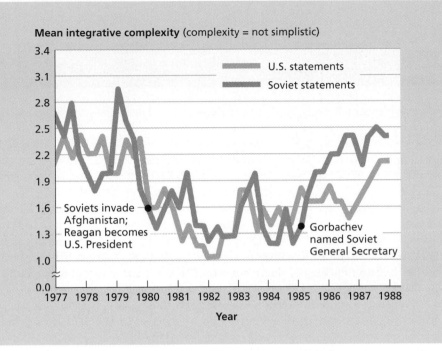

FIGURE :: 13.4

Complexity of Official
U.S. and Soviet Policy
Statements, 1977–1986

Source: From Tetlock, 1988.

existence of "a vast underground network that would rise in support of coalition forces to assist security and law enforcement" (Phillips, 2003). Alas, the network didn't materialize, and the resulting postwar security vacuum enabled looting, sabotage, persistent attacks on American forces, and increasing attacks from an insurgency determined to drive Western interests from the country.

SIMPLISTIC THINKING

When tension rises—as happens during an international crisis—rational thinking becomes more difficult (Janis, 1989). Views of the enemy become more simplistic and stereotyped, and seat-of-the-pants judgments become more likely. Even the mere expectation of conflict can serve to freeze thinking and impede creative problem solving (Carnevale & Probst, 1998). Social psychologist Philip Tetlock (1988) observed inflexible thinking when he analyzed the complexity of Russian and American rhetoric since 1945. During the Berlin blockade, the Korean War, and the Russian invasion of Afghanistan, political statements became simplified into stark, good-versus-bad terms. At other times—notably after Mikhail Gorbachev became the Soviet general secretary (Figure 13.4)—political statements acknowledged that each country's motives are complex.

Researchers have also analyzed political rhetoric preceding the outset of major wars, surprise military attacks, Middle Eastern conflicts, and revolutions (Conway & others, 2001). In nearly every case, attacking leaders displayed increasingly simplistic we-are-good/they-are-bad thinking immediately prior to their aggressive action. But shifts *away* from simplistic rhetoric typically preceded new U.S.-Russian agreements, reported Tetlock. His optimism was confirmed when President Reagan in 1988 traveled to Moscow to sign the American-Russian intermediate-range nuclear force (INF) treaty, and then Gorbachev visited New York and told the United Nations that he would remove 500,000 Soviet troops from Eastern Europe:

> I would like to believe that our hopes will be matched by our joint effort to put an end to an era of wars, confrontation and regional conflicts, to aggressions against nature, to the terror of hunger and poverty as well as to political terrorism. This is our common goal and we can only reach it together.

research CLOSE-UP

Misperception and War

Most research that I report in this book offers numerical data drawn from observations of people's behavior, cognitions, and attitudes as exhibited in laboratory experiments or in surveys. But there are other ways to do research. Some social psychologists, especially in Europe, analyze natural human discourse; they study written texts or spoken conversation to glimpse how people interpret and construct the events of their lives (Edwards & Potter, 2005). Others have analyzed human behavior in historical contexts, as did Irving Janis (1972) in exploring groupthink in historical fiascoes and Philip Tetlock (2005) in exploring the judgment failures of supposed political experts.

In what was arguably social psychology's longest career, Ralph K. White, legendary for his late 1930s studies of democratic versus autocratic leadership (with pioneering social psychologists Kurt Lewin and Ronald Lippitt), published in 2004—at age 97—a capstone article summarizing his earlier analyses (1968, 1984, 1986) of how misperceptions feed war. In reviewing 10 wars from the last century, White reported that each was marked by at least one of three misperceptions: *underestimating* the strength of one's enemy, *rationalizing* one's own

motives and behavior, and, especially, *demonizing* the enemy.

Underestimating one's adversary, he observed, emboldened Hitler to attack Russia, Japan to attack the United States, and the United States to enter the Korean and Vietnam wars. And rationalization of one's own actions and demonization of the adversary are the hallmark of war. In the early twenty-first century as the United States and Iraq talked of war, each said the other was "evil." To George W. Bush, Saddam Hussein was a "murderous tyrant" and a "madman" who threatened the civilized world with weapons of mass destruction. To Iraq's government, the Bush government was a "gang of evil" that "threatens the world with their evil schemes and lusts for Middle Eastern oil" (Zajonc, 2003).

The truth need not lie midway between such clashing perceptions. Yet "valid perception is an antidote to hate," concluded White as he reflected on his lifetime as a peace psychologist. Empathy—accurately perceiving the other's thoughts and feelings—is "one of the most important factors for preventing war. . . . Empathy can help two or more nations avoid the dangers of misperception that lead to the wars most would prefer not to fight."

SHIFTING PERCEPTIONS

If misperceptions accompany conflict, then they should appear and disappear as conflicts wax and wane. And they do, with startling regularity. The same processes that create the enemy's image can reverse that image when the enemy becomes an ally. Thus, the "bloodthirsty, cruel, treacherous, buck-toothed little Japs" of World War II soon became—in North American minds (Gallup, 1972) and in the media—our "intelligent, hard-working, self-disciplined, resourceful allies."

The Germans, who after two world wars were hated, then admired, and then again hated, were once again admired—apparently no longer plagued by what earlier was presumed to be cruelty in their national character. So long as Iraq was attacking unpopular Iran, even while using chemical weapons to massacre its own Kurds, many nations supported it. Our enemy's enemy is our friend. When Iraq ended its war with Iran and invaded oil-rich Kuwait, Iraq's behavior suddenly became "barbaric." Images of our enemies change with amazing ease.

The extent of misperceptions during conflict provides a chilling reminder that people need not be insane or abnormally malicious to form these distorted images of their antagonists. When we experience conflict with another nation, another group, or simply a roommate or a parent, we readily misperceive our own motives and actions as good and the other's as evil. And just as readily, our antagonists form a mirror-image perception of us.

So, with the antagonists trapped in a social dilemma, competing for scarce resources, or perceiving injustice, the conflict continues until something enables both parties to peel away their misperceptions and work at reconciling their actual differences. Good advice, then, is this: When in conflict, do not assume that the other fails to share your values and morality. Rather, compare perceptions, assuming that the other is likely perceiving the situation differently.

Summing Up: What Creates Conflict?

- Whenever two or more people, groups, or nations interact, their perceived needs and goals may conflict. Many social dilemmas arise as people pursue individual self-interest to their collective detriment. Two laboratory games, the Prisoner's Dilemma and the Tragedy of the Commons, exemplify such dilemmas. In real life we can avoid such traps by establishing rules that regulate self-serving behavior; by keeping social groups small so people feel responsibility for one another; by enabling communication, thus reducing mistrust; by changing payoffs to make cooperation more rewarding; and by invoking altruistic norms.

- When people compete for scarce resources, human relations often sink into prejudice and hostility. In his famous experiments, Muzafer Sherif found that win-lose competition quickly made strangers into enemies, triggering outright warfare even among normally upstanding boys.

- Conflicts also arise when people feel unjustly treated. According to equity theory, people define justice as the distribution of rewards in proportion to one's contributions. Conflicts occur when people disagree on the extent of their contributions and thus on the equity of their outcomes.

- Conflicts frequently contain a small core of truly incompatible goals, surrounded by a thick layer of misperceptions of the adversary's motives and goals. Often, conflicting parties have mirror-image perceptions. When both sides believe "We are peace-loving—they are hostile," each may treat the other in ways that provoke confirmation of its expectations. International conflicts are sometimes also fed by an evil leader–good people illusion.

How Can Peace Be Achieved?

Although toxic forces can breed destructive conflict, we can harness other forces to bring conflict to a constructive resolution. What are these ingredients of peace and harmony?

We have seen how conflicts are ignited by social traps, competition, perceived injustices, and misperceptions. Although the picture is grim, it is not hopeless. Sometimes closed fists become open arms as hostilities evolve into friendship. Social psychologists have focused on four strategies for helping enemies become comrades. We can remember these as the four Cs of peacemaking: contact, cooperation, communication, and conciliation.

> "We know more about war than we do about peace—more about killing than we know about living."
>
> *—GENERAL OMAR BRADLEY, 1893–1981, FORMER U.S. ARMY CHIEF OF STAFF*

Contact

Might putting two conflicting individuals or groups into close contact enable them to know and like each other? We have seen why it might not: In Chapter 3, we saw how negative expectations can bias judgments and create self-fulfilling prophecies. When tensions run high, contact may fuel a fight.

But we also saw, in Chapter 11, that proximity—and the accompanying interaction, anticipation of interaction, and mere exposure—boosts liking. In Chapter 4, we noted how blatant racial prejudice declined following desegregation, showing that *attitudes follow behavior.* If this social-psychological principle now seems obvious, remember: That's how things usually seem once you know them. To the U.S. Supreme Court in 1896, the idea that desegregated behavior might reduce prejudicial attitudes was anything but obvious. What seemed obvious at the time was "that legislation is powerless to eradicate racial instincts" (*Plessy v. Ferguson*).

A recent meta-analysis supports the argument that, in general, contact predicts tolerance. In a painstakingly complete analysis, Linda Tropp and Thomas Pettigrew (2005a; Pettigrew & Tropp, 2006, 2008) assembled data from 516 studies of 250,555 people in 38 nations. In 94 percent of studies, *increased contact predicted decreased prejudice.* This is especially so for majority group attitudes toward minorities (Tropp & Pettigrew, 2005b).

Newer studies confirm the correlation between contact and positive attitudes. For example, the more interracial contact South African Blacks and Whites have, the more sympathetic their policy attitudes are to those of the other group (Dixon & others, 2007). Even vicarious indirect contact, via story reading or through a friend's having an outgroup friend, tends to reduce prejudice (Cameron & Rutland, 2006; Pettigrew & others, 2007; Turner & others, 2007a, 2007b, 2008). This indirect contact effect, also called "the extended-contact effect," can help spread more positive attitudes through a peer group.

We can also observe that in the United States, segregation and expressed prejudice have diminished together since the 1960s. But was interracial contact the *cause* of these improved attitudes? Were those who actually experienced desegregation affected by it?

DOES DESEGREGATION IMPROVE RACIAL ATTITUDES?

School desegregation has produced measurable benefits, such as leading more Blacks to attend and succeed in college (Stephan, 1988). Does desegregation of schools, neighborhoods, and workplaces also produce favorable social results? The evidence is mixed.

On the one hand, many studies conducted during and shortly after desegregation found Whites' attitudes toward Blacks improving markedly. Whether the people were department store clerks and customers, merchant marines, government workers, police officers, neighbors, or students, racial contact led to diminished prejudice (Amir, 1969; Pettigrew, 1969). For example, near the end of World War II, the U.S. Army partially desegregated some of its rifle companies (Stouffer & others, 1949). When asked their opinions of such desegregation, 11 percent of the White soldiers in segregated companies approved. Of those in desegregated companies, 60 percent approved.

When Morton Deutsch and Mary Collins (1951) took advantage of a made-to-order natural experiment, they observed similar results. In accord with state law, New York City desegregated its public housing units; it assigned families to apartments without regard to race. In a similar development across the river in Newark, New Jersey, Blacks and Whites were assigned to separate buildings. When surveyed, White women in the desegregated development were far more likely to favor interracial housing and to say their attitudes toward Blacks had improved. Exaggerated stereotypes had wilted in the face of reality. As one woman put it, "I've really come to like it. I see they're just as human as we are."

Findings such as those influenced the Supreme Court's 1954 decision to desegregate U.S. schools and helped fuel the civil rights movement of the 1960s (Pettigrew, 1986, 2004). Yet initial studies of the effects of school desegregation were less encouraging. After reviewing all the available studies, Walter Stephan (1986) concluded that racial attitudes had been little affected by desegregation. For Blacks, the noticeable consequence of desegregated schooling was less on attitudes than on their increased likelihood of attending integrated (or predominantly White) colleges, living in integrated neighborhoods, and working in integrated settings.

Likewise, many student exchange programs have had less-than-hoped-for positive effects on student attitudes toward their host countries. For example, when eager American students study in France, often living with other Americans as they do so, their stereotypes of the French have tended not to improve (Stroebe & others, 1988). Contact also failed to allay the loathing of Rwandan Tutsis by their Hutu neighbors or to eliminate the sexism of many men living and working in constant contact with women. When interactions are negative, contact *increases* prejudice (Pettigrew, 2008).

Thus, we can see that sometimes desegregation improves racial attitudes; and sometimes—especially when there is anxiety or perceived threat (Pettigrew, 2004)—it doesn't. Such disagreements excite the scientist's detective spirit. What explains the difference? So far, we've been lumping all kinds of desegregation together. Actual desegregation occurs in many ways and under vastly different conditions.

FIGURE :: 13.5

Desegregation Needn't
Mean Contact

After this Scottburgh, South
Africa, beach became "open"
and desegregated in the new
South Africa, Blacks (represented
by red dots), Whites (blue dots),
and Indians (yellow dots) tended
to cluster with their own race.

Source: From Dixon & Durrheim,
2003.

WHEN DOES DESEGREGATION IMPROVE RACIAL ATTITUDES?

Might the frequency of interracial contact be a factor? Indeed it seems to be. Researchers have gone into dozens of desegregated schools and observed with whom children of a given race eat, talk, and loiter. Race influences contact. Whites disproportionately associate with Whites, Blacks with Blacks (Schofield, 1982, 1986). In one study of Dartmouth University e-mail exchanges, Black students, though only 7 percent of students, sent 44 percent of their e-mails to other Black students (Sacerdote & Marmaros, 2005).

The same self-imposed segregation was evident in a South African desegregated beach, as John Dixon and Kevin Durrheim (2003) discovered when they recorded the location of Black, White, and Indian beachgoers one midsummer (December 30th) afternoon (Figure 13.5). Desegregated neighborhoods, cafeterias, and restaurants, too, may fail to produce integrated interactions (Clack & others, 2005; Dixon & others, 2005a, 2005b).

In one study that tracked the attitudes of more than 1,600 European students, over time, contact did serve to reduce prejudice, but prejudice also minimized contact (Binder, 2009). Anxiety as well as prejudice helps explain why participants in interracial relationships (when students are paired as roommates or as partners in an experiment) may engage in less intimate self-disclosure than those in same-race relationships (Johnson & others, 2009; Trail & others, 2009).

Efforts to facilitate contact sometimes help, but sometimes fall flat. "We had one day when some of the Protestant schools came over," explained one Catholic youngster after a Northern Ireland school exchange (Cairns & Hewstone, 2002). "It was supposed to be like . . . mixing, but there was very little mixing. It wasn't because we didn't want to; it was just really awkward." The lack of mixing stems partly from "pluralistic ignorance": Many Whites and Blacks say they would like more contact but misperceive that the other does not reciprocate their feelings. (See "Research Close-Up: Relationships That Might Have Been.")

research CLOSE-UP

Relationships That Might Have Been

Perhaps you can recall a time when you really would have liked to reach out to someone. Maybe it was someone to whom you felt attracted. But doubting that your feelings were reciprocated, you didn't risk rebuff. Or maybe it was someone of another race whom you wanted to welcome to the open seat at your dining hall or library table. But you worried that the person might be wary of sitting with you. It's likely that on some such occasions the other person actually reciprocated your openness to connecting but assumed that your distance signified indifference or even prejudice. Alas, thanks to what Chapter 8 called "pluralistic ignorance"—shared false impressions of another's feelings—you passed like ships in the night.

Studies by University of Manitoba psychologist Jacquie Vorauer (2001, 2005; Vorauer & Sakamoto, 2006) illuminate this phenomenon. In their new relationships, people often overestimate the transparency of their feelings, Vorauer reports. Presuming that their feelings are leaking out, they experience the "illusion of transparency" we discussed in Chapter 2. Thus, they may assume that their body language conveys their romantic interest, when actually the intended recipient never gets the message. If the other person actually shares the positive feelings, and is similarly overestimating his or her own transparency, then the possibility of a relationship is quenched.

The same phenomenon, Vorauer reports, often occurs with low-prejudice people who actually would love more friendships with those outside their racial or social group. If Whites presume that Blacks think them prejudiced, and if Blacks presume that Whites stereotype them, then both will feel anxious about making the first move. Such anxiety is "a central factor" in South Africa's "continuing informal segregation," reports Gillian Finchilescu (2005).

Seeking to replicate and extend Vorauer's work, Nicole Shelton and Jennifer Richeson (2005; Richeson & Shelton, 2008) undertook a coordinated series of surveys and behavioral tests.

In their first study, University of Massachusetts White students viewed themselves as having more-than-average interest in cross-racial contacts and friendships, and they perceived White students in general as more eager for such than were Black students. Black students had mirror-image views—seeing themselves as more eager for such than were White students. "I want to have friendships across racial lines," thought the typical student. "But those in the other racial group don't share my desire for such."

Would this pluralistic ignorance generalize to a more specific setting? To find out, Shelton and Richeson's second study asked White Princeton students to imagine how they would react upon entering their dining hall and noticing several Black (or White) "students who live near you sitting together." How interested would you be in joining them? And how likely is it that one of them would beckon you to join them? Again, Whites believed that they more than those of the other race would be interested in the contact.

And how do people explain failures to make interracial contact? In their third study, Shelton and Richeson invited Princeton White and Black students to contemplate a dining hall situation in which they notice a table with familiar-looking students of the other race but neither they nor the seated students reach out to the other. The study participants, regardless of race, attributed their own inaction in such a situation primarily to fear of rejection, and more often attributed the seated students' inaction to lack of interest. In a fourth study at Dartmouth University, Shelton and Richeson replicated this study with different instructions but similar results.

Would this pluralistic ignorance phenomenon extend to other real-life settings, and to contact with a single other person? In Study 5, Shelton and Richeson invited Princeton students, both Black and White, to a study of "friendship formation." After participants had filled out some background information, the experimenter took their picture, attached it to background information, ostensibly took it to the room of a supposed fellow participant, and then returned with the other person's sheet and photo—showing a person of the same sex but the other race. The participants were then asked, "To what extent are you concerned about being accepted by the other participant?" and "How likely is it that the other person won't want you as a friend?" Regardless of their race, the participants guessed that they, more than the other-race fellow participant, were interested in friendship but worried about rejection.

Do these social misperceptions constrain actual interracial contact? In a sixth study, Shelton and Richeson confirmed that White Princeton students who were most prone to pluralistic ignorance—to presuming that they feared interracial rejection more than did Black students—were also the most likely to experience diminishing cross-racial contacts in the ensuing seven weeks.

Vorauer, Shelton, and Richeson are not contending that misperceptions alone impede romances and cross-racial friendships. But misperceptions do restrain people from risking an overture. Understanding this phenomenon—recognizing that others' coolness may actually reflect motives and feelings similar to our own—may help us reach out to others, and sometimes to transform potential friendships into real ones.

THE inside STORY

During the initial stages of our collaboration, we spent more time simply listening to each other talk about the stress associated with being assistant professors than actually thinking about research ideas, though ideas generally sprang from those conversations. During one of these supportive phone conversations, we started to talk about the classes we were teaching and ideas for lectures that we could use. (Nicole was teaching social stigma, and Jennifer was teaching intergroup relations.) We soon realized that we had noticed that both White and ethnic minority students in our classes often indicated that they genuinely wanted to interact with people outside of their ethnic group but were afraid that they would not be accepted. However, they did not think people of other ethnic groups had the same fears; they assumed that members of other groups simply did not want to connect. This sounded very much like Dale Miller's work on pluralistic ignorance. Over the course of a few weeks, we designed a series of studies to explore pluralistic ignorance in the context of interracial interactions.

Since the publication of our article, we have had researchers tell us that we should use our work in new student orientation sessions in order to reduce students' fears about reaching across racial lines. We are delighted that when we present this work in our courses, students of all racial backgrounds tell us that it indeed has opened their eyes about making the first move to develop interracial friendships.

Nicole Shelton,
Princeton University

Jennifer Richeson,
Northwestern University

FRIENDSHIP   In contrast, the more encouraging older studies of store clerks, soldiers, and housing project neighbors involved considerable interracial contact, more than enough to reduce the anxiety that marks initial intergroup contact. Other studies involving prolonged, personal contact—between Black and White prison inmates, between Black and White girls in an interracial summer camp, between Black and White university roommates, and between Black, Colored, and White South Africans—show similar benefits (Clore & others, 1978; Foley, 1976; Holtman & others, 2005; Van Laar & others, 2005). Among American students who have studied in Germany or in Britain, the more their contact with host country people, the more positive their attitudes (Stangor & others, 1996). In experiments, those who form *friendships* with outgroup members develop more positive attitudes toward the outgroup (Pettigrew & Tropp, 2000; Wright & others, 1997). It's not just head knowledge of other people that matters; it's also the *emotional* ties that form with intimate friendships and interracial roommate pairings that serve to reduce anxiety and increase empathy (Pettigrew & Tropp, 2000, 2008; Shook & Fazio, 2008).

The diminishing anxiety that accompanies friendly outgroup interactions is a biological event: It is measurable as decreased stress hormone reactivity in cross-ethnic contexts (Page-Gould & others, 2008).

"Group salience" (visibility) also helps bridge divides between people. If you forever think of that friend solely as an individual, your affective ties may not generalize to other members of the friend's group (Miller, 2002). Ideally, then, we should form trusting friendships across group lines but also recognize that the friend represents those in another group—with whom we turn out to have much in common (Brown & others, 2007).

We will be most likely to befriend people who differ from us if their outgroup identity is initially minimized—if we see them as essentially like us rather than feeling threatened by their being different. If our liking for our new friends is to generalize to others, their group identity must at some point become salient. So, to reduce prejudice and conflict, we had best initially minimize group diversity, then acknowledge it, then transcend it.

Surveys of nearly 4,000 Europeans reveal that friendship is a key to successful contact: If you have a minority group friend, you become much more likely to express sympathy and support for the friend's group, and even somewhat more support for immigration by that group. It's true of West Germans' attitudes toward Turks, French people's attitudes toward Asians and North Africans, Netherlanders' attitudes toward Surinamers and Turks, British attitudes toward West Indians and Asians, and Northern Ireland Protestants' and Catholics' attitudes toward each other (Brown & others, 1999; Hamberger & Hewstone, 1997; Paolini & others, 2004; Pettigrew, 1997). Likewise, antigay feeling is lower among people who know gays personally (Herek, 1993; Hodson & others, 2009; Vonofakou & others, 2007). In one U.S. survey, 55 percent of those who knowingly had a gay family member or close friend supported gay marriage—double the 25 percent support among those who didn't (Neidorf & Morin, 2007).

EQUAL-STATUS CONTACT The social psychologists who advocated desegregation never claimed that all contact would improve attitudes. They expected poor results when contacts were competitive, unsupported by authorities, and unequal (Pettigrew, 1988; Stephan, 1987). Before 1954 many prejudiced Whites had frequent contacts with Blacks—as shoeshine men and domestic workers. As we saw in Chapter 9, such unequal contacts breed attitudes that merely justify the continuation of inequality. So it's important that the contact be **equal-status contact,** like that between the store clerks, the soldiers, the neighbors, the prisoners, and the summer campers.

In colleges and universities, informal interactions enabled by classroom ethnic diversity pay dividends for all students, report University of Michigan researcher Patricia Gurin and colleagues from national collegiate surveys (2002). Such interactions tend to be intellectually growth-promoting and to foster greater acceptance of difference. Such findings informed a U.S. Supreme Court 2003 decision that racial diversity is a compelling interest of higher education and may be a criterion in admissions.

equal-status contact
Contact on an equal basis. Just as a relationship between people of unequal status breeds attitudes consistent with their relationship, so do relationships between those of equal status. Thus, to reduce prejudice, interracial contact should be between persons equal in status.

Cooperation

Although equal-status contact can help, it is sometimes not enough. It didn't help when Muzafer Sherif stopped the Eagles versus Rattlers competition and brought the groups together for noncompetitive activities, such as watching movies, shooting off fireworks, and eating. By that time, their hostility was so strong that mere contact only provided opportunities for taunts and attacks. When an Eagle was bumped by a Rattler, his fellow Eagles urged him to "brush off the dirt." Desegregating the two groups hardly promoted their social integration.

Given entrenched hostility, what can a peacemaker do? Think back to the successful and the unsuccessful desegregation efforts. The army's racial mixing of rifle companies not only brought Blacks and Whites into equal-status contact but also made them interdependent. Together, they were fighting a common enemy, striving toward a shared goal.

Does that suggest a second factor that predicts whether the effect of desegregation will be favorable? Does competitive contact divide and *cooperative* contact unite? Consider what happens to people who together face a common predicament. In conflicts at all levels, from couples to rival teams to nations, shared threats and common goals breed unity.

COMMON EXTERNAL THREATS BUILD COHESIVENESS

Together with others, have you ever been caught in a blizzard, punished by a teacher, or persecuted and ridiculed because of your social, racial, or religious identity? If so, you may recall feeling close to those with whom you shared the predicament. Perhaps previous social barriers were dropped as you helped one another dig out of the snow or struggled to cope with your common enemy.

Such friendliness is common among those who experience a shared threat. John Lanzetta (1955) observed this when he put four-man groups of naval ROTC cadets to work on problem-solving tasks and then began informing them over a loudspeaker that their answers were wrong, their productivity inexcusably low, their thinking stupid. Other groups did not receive this harassment. Lanzetta observed that the group members under duress became friendlier to one another, more cooperative, less argumentative, less competitive. They were in it together. And the result was a cohesive spirit.

Having a common enemy unified the groups of competing boys in Sherif's camping experiments—and in many subsequent experiments (Dion, 1979). Just being reminded of an outgroup (say, a rival school) heightens people's responsiveness to their own group (Wilder & Shapiro, 1984). When keenly conscious of who "they" are, we also know who "we" are.

Shared predicaments trigger cooperation, as these Wal-Mart workers on strike in Germany demonstrate.

When facing a well-defined external threat during wartime, we-feeling soars. The membership of civic organizations mushrooms (Putnam, 2000). Citizens unite behind their leader and support their troops. This was dramatically evident after the catastrophe of 9/11 and the threats of further terrorist attacks. In New York City, "old racial antagonisms have dissolved," reported the *New York Times* (Sengupta, 2001). "I just thought of myself as Black," said 18-year-old Louis Johnson, reflecting on life before 9/11. "But now I feel like I'm an American, more than ever." One sampling of conversation on 9/11, and another of New York Mayor Giuliani's press conferences before and after 9/11, found a doubled rate of the word "we" (Liehr & others, 2004; Pennebaker & Lay, 2002).

George W. Bush's job performance ratings reflected this threat-bred spirit of unity. Just before 9/11, a mere 51 percent of Americans approved of his presidential performance. Just after, an exceptional 90 percent approved. In the public eye, the mediocre president of 9/10 had become the exalted president of 9/12—"our leader" in the fight against "those who hate us." Thereafter, his ratings gradually declined but then jumped again as the war against Iraq began (Figure 13.6). When Florette Cohen and her colleagues (2005) asked American students to reflect on the events of 9/11 (rather than on an upcoming exam), they become more likely to agree that "I endorse the actions of President Bush and the members of his administration who have taken bold action in Iraq."

Leaders may even *create* a threatening external enemy as a technique for building group cohesiveness. George Orwell's novel *1984* illustrates the tactic: The leader of the protagonist nation uses border conflicts with the other two major powers to lessen internal strife. From time to time the enemy shifts, but there is always an enemy. Indeed, the nation seems to *need* an enemy. For the world, for a nation, for a group, having a common enemy is powerfully unifying. Thus, we can expect that Protestant-Catholic religious differences that feel great in Northern Ireland or South America will feel more negligible to those living under Islamic regimes. Likewise, Sunni and Shia Islamic differences that feel great in Iraq will not seem so great to Muslims in countries where both must cope with anti-Muslim attitudes.

Simultaneous external threats were also breeding unity elsewhere in the world. Palestinian suicide bombers in Israel rallied partisan Jews behind Prime Minister Ariel Sharon and his government, while the Israeli Defense Force killing of Palestinians and destruction of their property united Muslim factions in their animosity toward Sharon (Pettigrew, 2003). And after the United States attacked Iraq, Pew Research Center (2003) polls of Indonesian and Jordanian Muslims found rising

"I couldn't help but say to [Mr. Gorbachev], just think how easy his task and mine might be in these meetings that we held if suddenly there was a threat to this world from some other species from another planet. [We'd] find out once and for all that we really are all human beings here on this earth together."
—RONALD REAGAN, DECEMBER 4, 1985, SPEECH

"There's an enemy out there."
—GEORGE W. BUSH, 2005

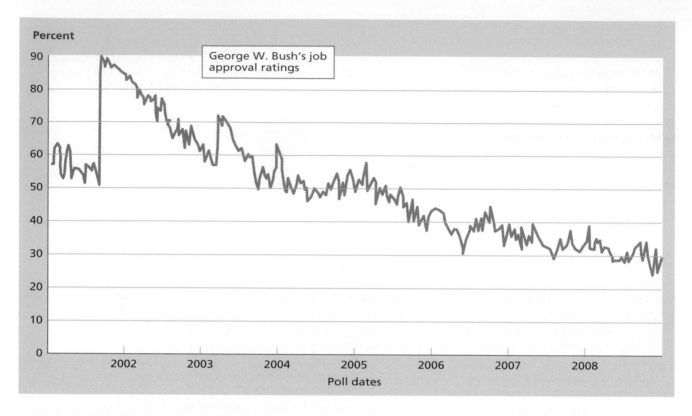

Percent

FIGURE :: 13.6

External Threats Breed Internal Unity

As the ups and downs of President George Bush's approval ratings illustrate, national conflicts mold public attitudes (Gallup, 2006).

anti-Americanism. The 53 percent of Jordanians who expressed a positive view of Americans in the summer of 2002 plummeted to 18 percent shortly after the war. "Before the war, I would have said that if Osama (bin Laden) was responsible for the two towers, we would not be proud of it," said one Syrian 21-year-old Islamic law student. "But if he did it now we would be proud of him" (Rubin, 2003).

focus ON   Why Do We Care Who Wins?

Why, for sports fans everywhere, does it matter who wins? Why does it matter to New Yorkers whether two dozen of George Steinbrenner's multimillionaire temporary employees, most born in other states or countries, win the World Series? During the annual NCAA basketball "March Madness," why do perfectly normal adults become insanely supportive of their team, and depressed when it loses? And why for that ultimate sporting event, World Cup Football, do soccer fans worldwide dream of their country victorious?

Theory and evidence indicate that the roots of rivalry run deep. There's something primal at work when the crowd erupts as the two rivals take the floor for a basketball game. There's something tribal at work during the ensuing two hours of passion, all in response to the ups and downs of a mere orange leather sphere. Our ancestors, living in a world where neighboring tribes occasionally raided and pillaged one another's camps, knew that there was safety in solidarity. (Those who didn't band together left fewer descendants.) Whether hunting, defending, or attacking, more hands were better than 2. Dividing the world into "us" and "them" entails significant costs, such as racism and war, but also provides the benefits of communal solidarity. To identify us and them, our ancestors—not so far removed from today's rabid fans—dressed or painted themselves in group-specific costumes and colors.

As social animals, we live in groups, cheer on our groups, kill for our groups, die for our groups. We also define ourselves by our groups. Our self-concept—our sense of who we are—consists not only of our personal attributes and attitudes but also of our social identity. Our social identities—our knowing who "we" are—strengthens self-concept and pride, especially when perceiving that "we" are superior. Lacking a positive individual identity, many youths find pride, power, and identity in gangs. Many patriots define themselves by their national identities.

The group definition of who we *are* also implies who we are *not*. Many social-psychological experiments reveal that being formed into groups—even arbitrary groups—promotes "ingroup bias." Cluster people into groups defined by nothing more than their birth date or even the last digit of their driver's license and they'll feel a certain kinship with their number mates, and will show them favoritism. So strong is our group consciousness that "we" seem better than "they" even when "we" and "they" are defined randomly.

As post-9/11 America illustrates, group solidarity soars when people face a common enemy. As Muzafer Sherif's Robber's Camp experiment vividly demonstrated, competition creates enemies. Fueled by competition and unleashed by the anonymity of a crowd, passions can culminate in sport's worst moments—fans taunting opponents, screaming at umpires, even pelting referees with beer bottles.

Group identification soars further with success. Fans find self-respect by their personal achievements but also, in at least small measure, by their association with the victorious athletes when their team wins. Queried after a big football victory, university students commonly report that "*we* won" (Cialdini & others, 1976). As we noted in Chapter 9, they bask in reflected glory. Asked the outcome after a defeat, students more often distance themselves from the team by saying, "*They* lost."

Ironically, we often reserve our most intense passions for rivals most similar to us. Freud long ago recognized that animosities formed around small differences: "Of two neighbouring towns, each is the other's most jealous rival; every little canton looks down upon the others with contempt. Closely related races keep one another at arm's length; the South German cannot endure the North German, the Englishman casts every kind of aspersion upon the Scot, the Spaniard despises the Portuguese."

As an occasional resident of Scotland, I've witnessed many examples of the *Xenophobe's Guide to the Scots* observation—that Scots divide non-Scots "into two main groups: (1) The English; (2) The Rest." As rabid Chicago Cubs fans are happy if either the Cubs win or the White Sox lose, so ardent New Zealand soccer fans root for New Zealand and whoever is playing Australia (Halberstadt & others, 2006). Rabid fans of Scottish soccer likewise rejoice in either a Scotland victory or an England defeat. "Phew! They Lost," rejoiced one Scottish tabloid front-page headline after England's 1996 Euro Cup defeat—by Germany, no less.

Group identity feeds, and is fed by, competition.

Might the world likewise find unity if facing a common enemy? On September 21, 1987, President Ronald Reagan observed, "In our obsession with antagonisms of the moment, we often forget how much unites all the members of humanity. Perhaps we need some outside, universal threat to recognize this common bond." Two decades later, Al Gore (2007) agreed, suggesting that, with the specter of climate change, "We—all of us—now face a universal threat. Though it is not from outside this world, it is nevertheless cosmic in scale."

FIGURE :: 13.7

After competition, the Eagles and the Rattlers rated each other unfavorably. After they worked cooperatively to achieve super-ordinate goals, hostility dropped sharply.

Source: Data from Sherif, 1966, p. 84.

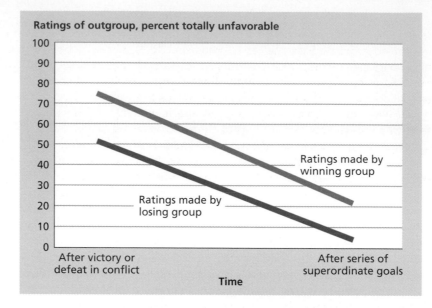

Ratings of outgroup, percent totally unfavorable

Ratings made by winning group

Ratings made by losing group

After victory or defeat in conflict

After series of superordinate goals

Time

SUPERORDINATE GOALS FOSTER COOPERATION

superordinate goal

A shared goal that necessitates cooperative effort; a goal that overrides people's differences from one another.

Closely related to the unifying power of an external threat is the unifying power of **superordinate goals,** goals that unite all in a group and require cooperative effort. To promote harmony among his warring campers, Sherif introduced such goals. He created a problem with the camp water supply, necessitating both groups' cooperation to restore the water. Given an opportunity to rent a movie, one expensive enough to require the joint resources of the two groups, they again cooperated. When a truck "broke down" on a camp excursion, a staff member casually left the tug-of-war rope nearby, prompting one boy to suggest that they all pull the truck to get it started. When it started, a backslapping celebration ensued over their victorious "tug-of-war against the truck."

After working together to achieve such superordinate goals, the boys ate together and enjoyed themselves around a campfire. Friendships sprouted across group lines. Hostilities plummeted (Figure 13.7). On the last day, the boys decided to travel home together on one bus. During the trip they no longer sat by groups. As the bus approached Oklahoma City and home, they, as one, spontaneously sang "Oklahoma" and then bade their friends farewell. With isolation and competition, Sherif made strangers into bitter enemies. With superordinate goals, he made enemies into friends.

Are Sherif's experiments mere child's play? Or can pulling together to achieve superordinate goals be similarly beneficial with adults in conflict? Robert Blake and Jane Mouton (1979) wondered. So in a series of two-week experiments involving more than 1,000 executives in 150 different groups, they re-created the essential features of the situation experienced by the Rattlers and the Eagles. Each group first engaged in activities by itself, then competed with another group, and then cooperated with the other group in working toward jointly chosen superordinate goals. Their results provided "unequivocal evidence that adult reactions parallel those of Sherif's younger subjects."

Extending those findings, John Dovidio, Samuel Gaertner, and their collaborators (2005) report that working cooperatively has especially favorable effects under conditions that lead people to define a new, inclusive group that dissolves their former subgroups. Old feelings of bias against another group diminish when members of the two groups sit alternately around a table (rather than on opposite sides), give their new group a single name, and then work together under conditions that foster a good mood. "Us" and "them" become "we." To combat Germany, Italy, and Japan during World War II, the United States and the former USSR, along with other nations, formed one united group named the Allies. So long as the superordinate goal of defeating a common enemy lasted, so did supportive U.S. attitudes toward the Russians. Economic interdependence through international trade also motivates peace. "Where goods cross frontiers, armies won't," notes Michael Shermer (2006). With so much of China's economy now interwoven with Western economies, their economic interdependence diminishes the likelihood of war between China and the West.

The cooperative efforts by the Rattlers and the Eagles ended in success. Would the same harmony have emerged if the water had remained off, the movie unaffordable, the truck still stalled? Likely not. In experiments with University of Virginia students, Stephen Worchel and his associates (1977, 1978, 1980) confirmed that *successful* cooperation between two groups boosts their attraction for each other. If previously conflicting groups *fail* in a cooperative effort, however, and if conditions allow them to attribute their failure to each other, the conflict may worsen. Sherif's groups were already feeling hostile to each other. Thus, failure to raise sufficient funds for the movie might have been attributed to one group's "stinginess" and "selfishness." That would have exacerbated rather than alleviated their conflict.

Promoting "common ingroup identity." The banning of gang colors and the common European practice of school uniforms—an increasing trend in the United States, as well—aim to change "us" and "them" to "we."

COOPERATIVE LEARNING IMPROVES RACIAL ATTITUDES

So far we have noted the apparently meager social benefits of typical school desegregation (especially if unaccompanied by the emotional bonds of friendship and by equal-status relationships). And we have noted the apparently dramatic social benefits of successful, cooperative contacts between members of rival groups. Could putting those two findings together suggest a constructive alternative to traditional desegregation practices? Several independent research teams speculated yes. Each wondered whether, without compromising academic achievement, we could promote interracial friendships by replacing competitive learning situations with cooperative ones. Given the diversity of their methods—all involving students on integrated study teams, sometimes in competition with other teams—the results are striking and heartening.

Are students who participate in existing cooperative activities, such as interracial athletic teams and class projects, less prejudiced? In one recent experiment, White youth on two- to three-week Outward Bound expeditions (involving intimate contact and cooperation) expressed improved attitudes toward Blacks a month after the expedition *if* they had been randomly assigned to an interracial expedition group (Green & Wong, 2008).

Robert Slavin and Nancy Madden (1979) analyzed survey data from 2,400 students in 71 American high schools and found similarly encouraging results. Those of different races who play and work together are more likely to report having friends of another race and to express positive racial attitudes. Charles Green and his colleagues (1988) confirmed this in a study of 3,200 Florida middle-school students. Compared with students at traditional, competitive schools, those at schools with interracial learning "teams" had more positive racial attitudes.

From this correlational finding, can we conclude that cooperative interracial activity improves racial attitudes? The way to find out is to experiment. Randomly designate some students, but not others, to work together in racially mixed

Interracial cooperation—on athletic teams, in class projects and extracurricular activities—melts differences and improves racial attitudes. White teen athletes who play cooperative team sports (such as basketball) with Black teammates express more liking and support for Blacks than do their counterparts involved in individual sports (such as wrestling) (Brown & others, 2003).

groups. Slavin (1985; Slavin & others, 2003) and his colleagues divided classes into interracial teams, each composed of four or five students from all achievement levels. Team members sat together, studied a variety of subjects together, and at the end of each week competed with the other teams in a class tournament. All members contributed to their team's score by doing well, sometimes by competing with other students whose recent achievements were similar to their own, sometimes by competing with their own previous scores. Everyone had a chance to succeed. Moreover, team members were motivated to help one another prepare for the weekly tournament—by drilling each other on fractions, spelling, or historical events—whatever was the next event. Rather than isolating students from one another, team competition brought them into closer contact and drew out mutual support.

Another research team, led by Elliot Aronson (2004; Aronson & Gonzalez, 1988), elicited similar group cooperation with a "jigsaw" technique. In experiments in Texas and California elementary schools, the researchers assigned children to racially and academically diverse six-member groups. The subject was then divided into six parts, with each student becoming the expert on his or her part. In a unit on Chile, one student might be the expert on Chile's history, another on its geography, another on its culture. First, the various "historians," "geographers," and so forth got together to master their material. Then they returned to the home groups to teach it to their classmates. Each group member held, so to speak, a piece of the jigsaw.

Self-confident students therefore had to listen to and learn from reticent students, who in turn soon realized they had something important to offer their peers. Other research teams—led by David Johnson and Roger Johnson (1987, 2003, 2004) at the University of Minnesota, Elizabeth Cohen (1980) at Stanford University, Shlomo Sharan and Yael Sharan (1976, 1994) at Tel Aviv University, and Stuart Cook (1985) at the University of Colorado—have devised additional methods for cooperative learning. Studies (148 of them across eleven countries) show that adolescents, too, have more positive peer relationships and may even achieve more when working cooperatively rather than competitively (Roseth & others, 2008).

From all of this research, what can we conclude? With cooperative learning, students learn not only the material but other lessons as well. Cooperative learning, say Slavin and Cooper (1999), promotes "the academic achievement of all students while simultaneously improving intergroup relations." Aronson reported that

"This was truly an exciting event. My students and I had found a way to make desegregation work the way it was intended to work!"

—ELLIOT ARONSON,
"DRIFTING MY OWN WAY,"
2003

Cooperation and peace. Researchers have identified more than 40 peaceful societies—societies where people live with no, or virtually no, recorded instances of violence. An analysis of 25 of these societies, including the Amish shown here, reveals that most base their worldviews on cooperation rather than competition (Bonta, 1997).

"children in the interdependent, jigsaw classrooms grow to like each other better, develop a greater liking for school, and develop greater self-esteem than children in traditional classrooms" (1980, p. 232).

Cross-racial friendships also begin to blossom. The exam scores of minority students improve (perhaps because academic achievement is now peer supported). After the experiments are over, many teachers continue using cooperative learning (D. W. Johnson & others, 1981; Slavin, 1990). "It is clear," wrote race-relations expert John McConahay (1981), that cooperative learning "is the most effective practice for improving race relations in desegregated schools that we know of to date."

Should we have "known it all along"? At the time of the 1954 Supreme Court decision, Gordon Allport spoke for many social psychologists in predicting, "Prejudice . . . may be reduced by equal status contact between majority and minority groups in the pursuit of common goals" (1954, p. 281). Cooperative learning experiments confirmed Allport's insight, making Robert Slavin and his colleagues (1985, 2003) optimistic: "Thirty years after Allport laid out the basic principles operationalized in cooperative learning methods, we finally have practical, proven methods for implementing contact theory in the desegregated classroom. . . . Research on cooperative learning is one of the greatest success stories in the history of educational research."

So, cooperative, equal-status contacts exert a positive influence on boy campers, industrial executives, college students, and schoolchildren. Does the principle extend to all levels of human relations? Are families unified by pulling together to farm the land, restore an old house, or sail a sloop? Are communal identities forged by barn raisings, group singing, or cheering on the football team? Is international understanding bred by international collaboration in science and space, by joint efforts to feed the world and conserve resources, by friendly personal contacts between people of different nations? Indications are that the answer to all of those questions is yes (Brewer & Miller, 1988; Desforges & others, 1991, 1997; Deutsch, 1985, 1994). Thus, an important challenge facing our divided world is to identify and agree on our superordinate goals and to structure cooperative efforts to achieve them.

focus
ON

Branch Rickey, Jackie Robinson, and the Integration of Baseball

On April 10, 1947, nineteen words that forever changed the face of baseball would also put social-psychological principles to the test. In the sixth inning of a Brooklyn Dodgers exhibition game with their top minor league club, the Montreal Royals' radio announcer Red Barber read a statement from Dodger president Branch Rickey: "The Brooklyn Dodgers today purchased the contract of Jackie Roosevelt Robinson from the Montreal Royals. He will report immediately." Five days later, Robinson became the first African American since 1887 to play major league baseball. In the fall, Dodger fans realized their dreams of going to the World Series. Robinson, after enduring racial taunts, beanballs, and spikes, was voted *Sporting News* rookie of the year and in a poll finished second to Bing Crosby as the most popular man in America. Baseball's racial barrier was forever broken.

Motivated by both his Methodist morality and a drive for baseball success, Rickey had been planning the move for some time, report social psychologists Anthony Pratkanis and Marlene Turner (1994a, 1994b). Three years earlier, Rickey had been asked by the sociologist-chair of the Mayor's Committee on Unity to desegregate his team. His response was to ask for time (so the hiring would not be attributed to pressure) and for advice on how best to do it. In 1945 Rickey was the only owner voting against keeping Blacks out of baseball. In 1947 he made his move using these principles identified by Pratkanis and Turner:

- *Create a perception that change is inevitable.* Leave little possibility that protest or resistance can turn back the clock. The announcer Red Barber, a traditional southerner, recalled that in 1945 Rickey took him to lunch and explained very slowly and strongly that his scouts were searching for "the first black player I can put on the white Dodgers. I don't know who he is or where he is, but, he is coming." An angered Barber at first intended to quit, but in time decided to accept the inevitable and keep the world's "best sports announcing job." Rickey was equally matter-of-fact with the players in 1947, offering to trade any player who didn't want to play with Robinson.

- *Establish equal-status contact with a superordinate goal.* One sociologist explained to Rickey that when relationships focus on an overarching goal, such as

winning the pennant, "the people involved would adjust appropriately." One of the players who had been initially opposed later helped Robinson with his hitting, explaining, "When you're on a team, you got to pull together to win."

- *Puncture the norm of prejudice.* Rickey led the way, but others helped. Team leader, shortstop Pee Wee Reese, a southerner, set a pattern of sitting and eating with Robinson. One day in Cincinnati, as the crowd was hurling slurs—"get the nigger off the field"—Reese left his shortstop position, walked over to Robinson at first base, smiled and spoke to him, and then—with a hushed crowd watching—put his arm around Robinson's shoulder.

- *Cut short the spiral of violence by practicing nonviolence.* Rickey, wanting "a ballplayer with guts enough not to fight back," role-played for Robinson the kind of insults and dirty play he would experience and gained Robinson's commitment not to return violence with violence. When Robinson was taunted and spiked, he left the responses to his teammates. Team cohesion was thereby increased.

Robinson and Bob Feller later became the first players in baseball history elected to the Hall of Fame in their first year of eligibility. As he received the award, Robinson asked three persons to stand beside him: his mother, Mallie; his wife, Rachel; and his friend Branch Rickey.

Jackie Robinson and Branch Rickey

GROUP AND SUPERORDINATE IDENTITIES

In everyday life, we often reconcile multiple identities (Gaertner & others, 2000, 2001; Hewstone & Greenland, 2000; Huo & others, 1996). We acknowledge our sub-group identity (as parent or child) and then transcend it (sensing our superordinate identity as a family). Pride in our ethnic heritage can complement our larger communal or national identity. Being mindful of our *multiple* social identities that we partially share with anyone else enables social cohesion (Brewer & Pierce, 2005; Crisp & Hewstone, 1999, 2000). "I am many things, some of which you are, too."

But in ethnically diverse cultures, how do people balance their ethnic identities with their national identities? They may have what identity researcher Jean Phinney (1990) calls a "bicultural" identity, one that identifies with both the ethnic culture and the larger culture. Ethnically conscious Asians living in England may also feel strongly British (Hutnik, 1985). French Canadians who identify with their ethnic roots may or may not also feel strongly Canadian (Driedger, 1975). Hispanic Americans who retain a strong sense of their "Cubanness" (or of their Mexican or Puerto Rican heritage) may feel strongly American (Roger & others, 1991). As W. E. B. DuBois (1903, p. 17) explained in *The Souls of Black Folk*, "The American Negro [longs] . . . to be both a Negro and an American." In 2008 U.S. presidential primary contests, Latinos and Asians largely favored Hillary Clinton over the Black candidate, Barack Obama. But if their ethnic identity was shifted—if induced in experiments to think of themselves as "non-White"—they became more likely to vote for the non-White Obama (Zhong & others, 2008).

Over time, identification with a new culture often grows. Former East and West Germans come to see themselves as "German" (Kessler & Mummendey, 2001). The children of Chinese immigrants to Australia and the United States feel their Chinese identity somewhat less keenly, and their new national identity more strongly, than do immigrants who were born in China (Rosenthal & Feldman, 1992). Often, however, the *grand*children of immigrants feel more comfortable identifying with their ethnicity (Triandis, 1994).

Researchers have wondered whether pride in one's group competes with identification with the larger culture. As we noted in Chapter 9, we evaluate ourselves partly in terms of our social identities. Seeing our own group (our school, our employer, our family, our race, our nation) as good helps us feel good about ourselves. A positive ethnic identity can therefore contribute to positive self-esteem. So can a positive mainstream culture identity. "Marginal" people, who have neither a strong ethnic nor a strong mainstream cultural identity (Table 13.1), often have low self-esteem. Bicultural people, who affirm both identities, typically have a strongly positive self-concept (Phinney, 1990). Often, they alternate between their two cultures, adapting their language and behavior to whichever group they are with (LaFromboise & others, 1993).

Debate continues over the ideals of multiculturalism (celebrating differences) versus assimilation (meshing one's values and habits with the prevailing culture). On one side are those who believe, as the Department of Canadian Heritage (2006) has declared, that "multiculturalism ensures that all citizens can keep their identities,

"Most of us have overlapping identities which unite us with very different groups. We can love what we are, without hating what—and who—we are not. We can thrive in our own tradition, even as we learn from others, and come to respect their teachings."
—KOFI ANNAN, NOBEL PEACE PRIZE LECTURE, 2001

TABLE :: 13.1 Ethnic and Cultural Identity

Identification with Majority Group	Identification with Ethnic Group	
	Strong	Weak
Strong	Bicultural	Assimilated
Weak	Separated	Marginal

A difficult balancing act. These ethnically conscious French Canadians—supporting Bill 101 "live French in Quebec"—may or may not also feel strongly Canadian. As countries become more ethnically diverse, people debate how we can build societies that are both plural and unified.

can take pride in their ancestry and have a sense of belonging. Acceptance gives Canadians a feeling of security and self-confidence, making them open to and accepting of diverse cultures." On the other side are those who concur with Britain's Commission for Racial Equality chair, Trevor Phillips (2004), in worrying that multiculturalism separates people rather than encouraging common values, a view that inspired the Rwandan government to adopt the official view that "there is no ethnicity here. We are all Rwandan." In the aftermath of Rwanda's ethnic bloodbath, government documents and government-controlled radio and newspapers have ceased mentioning Hutu and Tutsi (Lacey, 2004).

In the space between multiculturalism and assimilation lies "diversity within unity," a perspective advocated by sociologist Amitai Etzioni and others (2005). "It presumes that all members of a given society will fully respect and adhere to those basic values and institutions that are considered part of the basic shared framework of the society. At the same time, every group in society is free to maintain its distinct subculture—those policies, habits, and institutions that do not conflict with the shared core."

By forging unifying ideals, immigrant countries such as the United States, Canada, and Australia have avoided ethnic wars. In these countries, Irish and Italians, Swedes and Scots, Asians and Africans seldom kill in defense of their ethnic identities. Nevertheless, even the immigrant nations struggle between separation and wholeness, between people's pride in their distinct heritage and unity as one nation, between acknowledging the reality of diversity and questing for shared values. The ideal of diversity within unity forms the United States motto: *E pluribus unum*. Out of many, one.

Communication

Conflicting parties have other ways to resolve their differences. When husband and wife, or labor and management, or nation X and nation Y disagree, they can **bargain** with each other directly. They can ask a third party to **mediate** by making suggestions and facilitating their negotiations. Or they can **arbitrate** by submitting their disagreement to someone who will study the issues and impose a settlement.

BARGAINING

If you want to buy or sell a new car, are you better off adopting a tough bargaining stance—opening with an extreme offer so that splitting the difference will yield a favorable result? Or are you better off beginning with a sincere "good-faith" offer?

Experiments suggest no simple answer. On the one hand, those who demand more will often get more. Robert Cialdini, Leonard Bickman, and John Cacioppo (1979) provide a typical result: In a control condition, they approached various Chevrolet dealers and asked the price of a new Monte Carlo sports coupe with designated options. In an experimental condition, they approached other dealers and first struck a tougher bargaining stance, asking for and rejecting a price on a *different* car ("I need a lower price than that. That's a lot"). When they then asked

bargaining
Seeking an agreement to a conflict through direct negotiation between parties.

mediation
An attempt by a neutral third party to resolve a conflict by facilitating communication and offering suggestions.

arbitration
Resolution of a conflict by a neutral third party who studies both sides and imposes a settlement.

the price of the Monte Carlo, exactly as in the control condition, they received offers that averaged some $200 lower.

Tough bargaining may lower the other party's expectations, making the other side willing to settle for less (Yukl, 1974). But toughness can sometimes backfire. Many a conflict is not over a pie of fixed size but over a pie that shrinks if the conflict continues. Negotiators often fail to realize their common interests; in fact, about 20 percent of the time they negotiate "lose-lose" agreements that are mutually costly (Thompson & Hrebec, 1996).

A time delay is often a lose-lose scenario. When a strike is prolonged, both labor and management lose. Being tough is another potential lose-lose scenario. If the other party responds with an equally tough stance, both may be locked into positions from which neither can back down without losing face. In the weeks before the 1991 Persian Gulf War, the first President Bush threatened, in the full glare of publicity, to "kick Saddam's ass." Saddam Hussein, no less macho, threatened to make "infidel" Americans "swim in their own blood." After such belligerent statements, it was difficult for each side to evade war and save face.

MEDIATION

A third-party mediator may offer suggestions that enable conflicting parties to make concessions and still save face (Pruitt, 1998). If my concession can be attributed to a mediator, who is gaining an equal concession from my antagonist, then neither of us will be viewed as weakly caving in to the other's demands.

TURNING WIN-LOSE INTO WIN-WIN   Mediators also help resolve conflicts by facilitating constructive communication. Their first task is to help the parties rethink the conflict and gain information about the others' interests (Thompson, 1998). Typically, people on both sides have a competitive "win-lose" orientation: They are successful if their opponent is unhappy with the result, and unsuccessful if their opponent is pleased (Thompson & others, 1995). The mediator aims to replace this win-lose orientation with a cooperative "win-win" orientation, by prodding both sides to set aside their conflicting demands and instead to think about each other's underlying needs, interests, and goals. In experiments, Leigh Thompson (1990a, 1990b) found that, with experience, negotiators become better able to make mutually beneficial trade-offs and thus to achieve win-win resolutions.

A classic story of such a resolution concerns the two sisters who quarreled over an orange (Follett, 1940). Finally they compromised and split the orange in half, whereupon one sister squeezed her half for juice while the other used the peel to make a cake. In experiments at the State University of New York at Buffalo, Dean Pruitt and his associates induced bargainers to search for **integrative agreements** (Johnson & Johnson, 2003; Pruitt & Lewis, 1975, 1977). If the sisters had each explained *why* they wanted the orange, they very likely would have agreed to share it, giving one sister all the juice and the other all the peel. This is an example of an integrative agreement. Compared with compromises, in which each party sacrifices something important, integrative agreements are more enduring. Because they are mutually rewarding, they also lead to better ongoing relationships (Pruitt, 1986).

integrative agreements
Win-win agreements that reconcile both parties' interests to their mutual benefit.

UNRAVELING MISPERCEPTIONS WITH CONTROLLED COMMUNICATIONS   Communication often helps reduce self-fulfilling misperceptions. Perhaps you can recall experiences similar to that of this college student:

> Often, after a prolonged period of little communication, I perceive Martha's silence as a sign of her dislike for me. She, in turn, thinks that my quietness is a result of my being mad at her. My silence induces her silence, which makes me even more silent . . . until this snowballing effect is broken by some occurrence that makes it necessary for us to interact. And the communication then unravels all the misinterpretations we had made about one another.

The outcome of such conflicts often depends on *how* people communicate their feelings to one another. Roger Knudson and his colleagues (1980) invited

TABLE :: 13.2 How Couples Can Fight Constructively

Do Not	Do
• evade the argument, give the silent treatment, or walk out on it	• clearly define the issue and repeat the other's arguments in your own words
• use your intimate knowledge of the other person to hit below the belt and humiliate	• divulge your positive and negative feelings
• bring in unrelated issues	• welcome feedback about your behavior
• feign agreement while harboring resentment	• clarify where you agree and disagree and what matters most to each of you
• tell the other party how she or he is feeling	• ask questions that help the other find words to express the concern
• attack indirectly by criticizing someone or something the other person values	• wait for spontaneous explosions to subside, without retaliating
• undermine the other by intensifying his or her insecurity or threatening disaster	• offer positive suggestions for mutual improvement

married couples to come to the University of Illinois psychology laboratory and relive, through role playing, one of their past conflicts. Before, during, and after their conversation (which often generated as much emotion as the actual previous conflict), the couples were observed closely and questioned. Couples who evaded the issue—by failing to make their positions clear or failing to acknowledge their spouse's position—left with the illusion that they were more in harmony and agreement than they really were. Often, they came to believe they now agreed more when actually they agreed less. In contrast, those who engaged the issue—by making their positions clear and by taking one another's views into account—achieved more actual agreement and gained more accurate information about one another's perceptions. That helps explain why couples who communicate their concerns directly and openly are usually happily married (Grush & Glidden, 1987).

Such findings have triggered programs that train couples and children how to manage conflicts constructively (Horowitz and Boardman, 1994). If managed constructively, conflict provides opportunities for reconciliation and more genuine harmony. Psychologists Ian Gotlib and Catherine Colby (1988) offer advice on how to avoid destructive quarrels and how to have good quarrels (Table 13.2). Children, for example, learn that conflict is normal, that people can learn to get along with those who are different, that most disputes can be resolved with two winners, and that nonviolent communication strategies are an alternative to a world of bullies and victims. This "violence prevention curriculum . . . is not about passivity," notes Deborah Prothrow-Stith (1991, p. 183). "It is about using anger not to hurt oneself or one's peers, but to change the world."

David Johnson and Roger Johnson (1995, 2000, 2003) put first- through ninth-grade children through about a dozen hours of conflict resolution training in six schools, with very heartening results. Before the training, most students were involved in daily conflicts—put-downs and teasing, playground turn-taking conflicts, conflicts over possessions—conflicts that nearly always also resulted in a winner and a loser. After training, the children more often found win-win solutions, better mediated friends' conflicts, and retained and applied their new skills in and out of school throughout the school year. When implemented with

Communication facilitators work to break down barriers, as in this diversity training exercise for teenagers.

a whole student body, the result is a more peaceful student community and increased academic achievement.

Conflict researchers report that a key factor is *trust* (Noor & others, 2008; Ross & Ward, 1995). If you believe the other person is well intentioned, you are then more likely to divulge your needs and concerns. Lacking trust, you may fear that being open will give the other party information that might be used against you. Even simple behaviors can enhance trust. In experiments, negotiators who were instructed to mimic the others' mannerisms, as naturally empathic people in close relationships often do, elicited more trust and greater discovery of compatible interests and mutually satisfying deals (Maddux & others, 2008).

When the two parties mistrust each other and communicate unproductively, a third-party mediator—a marriage counselor, a labor mediator, a diplomat— sometimes helps. Often the mediator is someone trusted by both sides. In the 1980s it took an Algerian Muslim to mediate the conflict between Iran and Iraq, and the pope to resolve a geographical dispute between Argentina and Chile (Carnevale & Choi, 2000).

After coaxing the conflicting parties to rethink their perceived win-lose conflict, the mediator often has each party identify and rank its goals. When goals are compatible, the ranking procedure makes it easier for each to concede on less important goals so that both achieve their chief goals (Erickson & others, 1974; Schulz & Pruitt, 1978). South Africa achieved internal peace when Black and White South Africans granted each other's top priorities—replacing apartheid with majority rule and safeguarding the security, welfare, and rights of Whites (Kelman, 1998).

Once labor and management both believe that management's goal of higher productivity and profit is compatible with labor's goal of better wages and working conditions, they can begin to work for an integrative win-win solution. If workers will forgo benefits that are moderately beneficial to them but very costly to management (perhaps company-provided dental care), and if management will forgo moderately valuable arrangements that workers very much resent (perhaps inflexibility

"[There is] a psychological barrier between us, a barrier of suspicion, a barrier of rejection; a barrier of fear, of deception, a barrier of hallucination. . . ."

—*EGYPTIAN PRESIDENT ANWAR AL-SADAT, TO THE ISRAELI KNESSET, 1977* of working hours), then both sides may gain (Ross & Ward, 1995). Rather than seeing itself as making a concession, each side can see the negotiation as an effort to exchange bargaining chips for things more valued.

When the parties then convene to communicate directly, they are usually not set loose in the hope that, eyeball-to-eyeball, the conflict will resolve itself. In the midst of a threatening, stressful conflict, emotions often disrupt the ability to understand the other party's point of view. Although happiness and gratitude can increase trust, anger decreases it (Dunn & Schweitzer, 2005). Communication may thus become most difficult just when it is most needed (Tetlock, 1985).

The mediator will often structure the encounter to help each party understand and feel understood by the other. The mediator may ask the conflicting parties to restrict their arguments to statements of fact, including statements of how they feel and how they respond when the other acts in a given way: "I enjoy music. But when you play it loud, I find it hard to concentrate. That makes me crabby." Also, the mediator may ask people to reverse roles and argue the other's position or to imagine and explain what the other person is experiencing. (Experiments show that inducing empathy decreases stereotyping and increases cooperation [Batson & Moran, 1999; Galinsky & Moskowitz, 2000].) Or the mediator may have them restate one another's positions before replying with their own: "It annoys you when I play my music and you're trying to study."

Neutral third parties may also suggest mutually agreeable proposals that would be dismissed—"reactively devalued"—if offered by either side. Constance Stillinger and her colleagues (1991) found that a nuclear disarmament proposal that Americans dismissed when attributed to the former Soviet Union seemed more acceptable when attributed to a neutral third party. Likewise, people will often reactively devalue a concession offered by an adversary ("they must not value it"); the same concession may seem more than a token gesture when suggested by a third party.

These peacemaking principles—based partly on laboratory experiments, partly on practical experience—have helped mediate both international and industrial conflicts (Blake & Mouton, 1962, 1979; Fisher, 1994; Wehr, 1979). One small team of Arab and Jewish Americans, led by social psychologist Herbert Kelman (1997, 2007, 2008), has conducted workshops bringing together influential Arabs and Israelis. Another social psychologist team, led by Ervin Staub and Laurie Ann Pearlman (2005a, 2005b; 2009), worked in Rwanda between 1999 and 2003 by training facilitators and journalists to understand and write about Rwanda's traumas in ways that promote healing and reconciliation. Using methods such as those we've considered, Kelman and colleagues counter misperceptions and have participants seek creative solutions for their common good. Isolated, the participants are free to speak directly to their adversaries without fear that their constituents are second-guessing what they are saying. The result? Those from both sides typically come to understand the other's perspective and how the other side responds to their own group's actions.

ARBITRATION

Some conflicts are so intractable, the underlying interests so divergent, that a mutually satisfactory resolution is unattainable. In Bosnia and Kosovo, both Serbs and Muslims could not have jurisdiction over the same homelands. In a divorce dispute over custody of a child, both parents cannot enjoy full custody. In those and many other cases (disputes over tenants' repair bills, athletes' wages, and national territories), a third-party mediator may—or may not—help resolve the conflict.

If not, the parties may turn to *arbitration* by having the mediator or another third party *impose* a settlement. Disputants usually prefer to settle their differences without arbitration so that they retain control over the outcome. Neil McGillicuddy and others (1987) observed this preference in an experiment involving disputants

"In the research on the effects of mediation, one finding stands out: The worse the state of the parties' relationship is with one another, the dimmer the prospects that mediation will be successful."
—KENNETH KRESSEL & DEAN PRUITT (1985)

coming to a dispute settlement center. When people knew they would face an arbitrated settlement if mediation failed, they tried harder to resolve the problem, exhibited less hostility, and thus were more likely to reach agreement.

In cases where differences seem large and irreconcilable, the prospect of arbitration may cause the disputants to freeze their positions, hoping to gain an advantage when the arbitrator chooses a compromise. To combat that tendency, some disputes, such as those involving salaries of individual baseball players, are settled with "final-offer arbitration," in which the third party chooses one of the two final offers. Final-offer arbitration motivates each party to make a reasonable proposal.

Typically, however, the final offer is not as reasonable as it would be if each party, free of self-serving bias, saw its own proposal through others' eyes. Negotiation researchers report that most disputants are made stubborn by "optimistic overconfidence" (Kahneman & Tversky, 1995). Successful mediation is hindered when, as often happens, both parties believe they have a two-thirds chance of winning a final-offer arbitration (Bazerman, 1986, 1990).

Conciliation

Sometimes tension and suspicion run so high that even communication, let alone resolution, becomes all but impossible. Each party may threaten, coerce, or retaliate against the other. Unfortunately, such acts tend to be reciprocated, escalating the conflict. So, would a strategy of appeasing the other party by being unconditionally cooperative produce a satisfying result? Often not. In laboratory games, those who are 100 percent cooperative often are exploited. Politically, a one-sided pacifism is usually out of the question.

GRIT

Social psychologist Charles Osgood (1962, 1980) advocated a third alternative, one that is conciliatory yet strong enough to discourage exploitation. Osgood called it "graduated and reciprocated initiatives in tension reduction." He nicknamed it **GRIT**, a label that suggests the determination it requires. GRIT aims to reverse the "conflict spiral" by triggering reciprocal de-escalation. To do so, it draws upon social-psychological concepts, such as the norm of reciprocity and the attribution of motives.

GRIT requires one side to initiate a few small de-escalatory actions, after *announcing a conciliatory intent*. The initiator states its desire to reduce tension, declares each conciliatory act before making it, and invites the adversary to reciprocate. Such announcements create a framework that helps the adversary correctly interpret what otherwise might be seen as weak or tricky actions. They also bring public pressure to bear on the adversary to follow the reciprocity norm.

Next, the initiator establishes credibility and genuineness by carrying out, exactly as announced, several verifiable *conciliatory acts*. This intensifies the pressure to reciprocate. Making conciliatory acts diverse—perhaps offering medical help, closing a military base, and lifting a trade ban—keeps the initiator from making a significant sacrifice in any one area and leaves the adversary freer to choose its own

"Don't worry, dear—it's just a *peace* offensive."

GRIT
Acronym for "graduated and reciprocated initiatives in tension reduction"—a strategy designed to de-escalate international tensions.

People perceive that they respond more favorably to conciliation but that others might be responsive to coercion.

means of reciprocation. If the adversary reciprocates voluntarily, its own conciliatory behavior may soften its attitudes.

GRIT *is* conciliatory. But it is not "surrender on the installment plan." The remaining aspects of the plan protect each side's self-interest by *maintaining retaliatory capability*. The initial conciliatory steps entail some small risk but do not jeopardize either one's security; rather, they are calculated to begin edging both sides down the tension ladder. If one side takes an aggressive action, the other side reciprocates in kind, making clear it will not tolerate exploitation. Yet the reciprocal act is not an overresponse that would re-escalate the conflict. If the adversary offers its own conciliatory acts, these, too, are matched or even slightly exceeded. Morton Deutsch (1993) captured the spirit of GRIT in advising negotiators to be "'firm, fair, and friendly': *firm* in resisting intimidation, exploitation, and dirty tricks; *fair* in holding to one's moral principles and not reciprocating the other's immoral behavior despite his or her provocations; and *friendly* in the sense that one is willing to initiate and reciprocate cooperation."

Does GRIT really work? In a lengthy series of experiments at Ohio University, Svenn Lindskold and his associates (1976 to 1988) found "strong support for the various steps in the GRIT proposal." In laboratory games, announcing cooperative intent *does* boost cooperation. Repeated conciliatory or generous acts *do* breed greater trust (Klapwijk & Van Lange, 2009). Maintaining an equality of power *does* protect against exploitation.

Lindskold was not contending that the world of the laboratory experiment mirrors the more complex world of everyday life. Rather, experiments enable us to formulate and verify powerful theoretical principles, such as the reciprocity norm and the self-serving bias. As Lindskold (1981) noted, "It is the theories, not the individual experiments, that are used to interpret the world."

REAL-WORLD APPLICATIONS

GRIT-like strategies have occasionally been tried outside the laboratory, with promising results. During the Berlin crisis of the early 1960s, U.S. and Russian tanks faced each other barrel to barrel. The crisis was defused when the Americans pulled back their tanks step-by-step. At each step, the Russians reciprocated. Similarly, in the 1970s small concessions by Israel and Egypt (for example, Israel allowing Egypt to open up the Suez Canal, Egypt allowing ships bound for Israel to pass through) helped reduce tension to a point where the negotiations became possible (Rubin, 1981).

To many, the most significant attempt at GRIT was the so-called Kennedy experiment (Etzioni, 1967). On June 10, 1963, President Kennedy gave a major speech, "A Strategy for Peace." He noted that "Our problems are man-made . . . and can be solved by man," and then announced his first conciliatory act: The United States was stopping all atmospheric nuclear tests and would not resume them unless another country did. Kennedy's entire speech was published in the Soviet press. Five days later Premier Khrushchev reciprocated, announcing he had halted production of strategic bombers. There soon followed further reciprocal gestures: The United States agreed to sell wheat to Russia, the Russians agreed to a "hot line" between the two countries, and the two countries soon achieved a test-ban treaty. For a time, these conciliatory initiatives eased relations between the two countries.

Might conciliatory efforts also help reduce tension between individuals? There is every reason to expect so. When a relationship is strained and communication nonexistent, it sometimes takes only a conciliatory gesture—a soft answer, a warm smile, a gentle touch—for both parties to begin easing down the tension ladder, to a rung where contact, cooperation, and communication again become possible.

"I am not suggesting that principles of individual behavior can be applied to the behavior of nations in any direct, simpleminded fashion. What I am trying to suggest is that such principles may provide us with hunches about international behavior that can be tested against experience in the larger arena."

—*CHARLES E. OSGOOD (1966)*

Summing Up: How Can Peace Be Achieved?

- Although conflicts are readily kindled and fueled by social dilemmas, competition, and misperceptions, some equally powerful forces, such as *contact, cooperation, communication,* and *conciliation,* can transform hostility into harmony. Despite some encouraging early studies, other studies show that mere contact (such as mere desegregation in schools) has little effect upon racial attitudes. But when contact encourages emotional ties with individuals identified with an outgroup and when it is structured to convey *equal status,* hostilities often lessen.

- Contacts are especially beneficial when people work together to overcome a common threat or to achieve a superordinate goal. Taking their cue from experiments on *cooperative contact,* several research teams have replaced competitive classroom learning situations with opportunities for cooperative learning, with heartening results.

- Conflicting parties often have difficulty communicating. A *third-party mediator* can promote communication by prodding the antagonists to replace their competitive win-lose view of their conflict with a more cooperative win-win orientation. Mediators can also structure communications that will peel away misperceptions and increase mutual understanding and trust. When a negotiated settlement is not reached, the conflicting parties may defer the outcome to an *arbitrator,* who either dictates a settlement or selects one of the two final offers.

- Sometimes tensions run so high that genuine communication is impossible. In such cases, small conciliatory gestures by one party may elicit reciprocal conciliatory acts by the other party. One such conciliatory strategy, GRIT (graduated and reciprocated initiatives in tension reduction), aims to alleviate tense international situations. Those who mediate tense labor-management and international conflicts sometimes use another peacemaking strategy. They instruct the participants, as this chapter instructed you, in the dynamics of conflict and peacemaking in the hope that understanding can help former adversaries establish and enjoy peaceful, rewarding relationships.

POSTSCRIPT: The Conflict between Individual and Communal Rights

Many social conflicts are a contest between individual and collective rights. One person's right to own handguns conflicts with a neighborhood's right to safe streets. One person's right to smoke conflicts with others' rights to a smoke-free environment. One industrialist's right to do unregulated business conflicts with a community's right to clean air.

Hoping to blend the best of individualist and collectivist values, some social scientists—myself included—have advocated a communitarian synthesis that aims to balance individual rights with the collective right to communal well-being. Communitarians welcome incentives for individual initiative and appreciate why Marxist economies have crumbled. "If I were, let's say, in Albania at this moment," said communitarian sociologist Amitai Etzioni (1991), "I probably would argue that there's too much community and not enough individual rights." But communitarians also question the other extreme—the rugged individualism and self-indulgence of the 1960s ("Do your own thing"), the 1970s (the "Me decade"), the 1980s ("Greed is good"), and the 1990s ("Follow your bliss"). Unrestrained personal freedom, they say, destroys a culture's social fabric; unregulated commercial freedom, they add, has plundered our shared environment and produced the 2008 economic collapse. Echoing the French Revolutionists, their motto might well be "liberty, equality, *and* fraternity."

During the last half-century, Western individualism has intensified. Parents have become more likely to prize independence and self-reliance in their children, and are less concerned with obedience (Alwin, 1990; Remley, 1988). Clothing and grooming styles have become more diverse, personal freedoms have increased, and common values have waned (Putnam, 2000; Schlesinger, 1991).

"This is the age of the individual."

—*PRESIDENT RONALD REAGAN, ADDRESS ON WALL STREET, 1982*

"There is no society. There are only individuals and their families."

—*PRIME MINISTER MARGARET THATCHER, AFTER HER THIRD ELECTION*

Communitarians are not advocating a nostalgia trip—a return, for example, to the more restrictive and unequal gender roles of the 1950s. Rather, they propose a middle ground between the individualism of the West and the collectivism of the East, between the macho independence traditionally associated with males and the caregiving connectedness traditionally associated with females, between concerns for individual rights and for communal well-being, between liberty and fraternity, between me-thinking and we-thinking.

As with luggage searches at airports, smoking bans on planes, and sobriety checkpoints and speed limits on highways, societies are accepting some adjustments to individual rights in order to protect the public good. Environmental restraints on individual freedoms (to pollute, to whale, to deforest) similarly exchange certain short-term liberties for long-term communal gain. Some individualists warn that such constraints on individual liberties may plunge us down a slippery slope leading to the loss of more important liberties. If today we let them search our luggage, tomorrow they'll be knocking down the doors of our houses. If today we censor cigarette ads or pornography on television, tomorrow they'll be removing books from our libraries. If today we ban handguns, tomorrow they'll take our hunting rifles. In protecting the interests of the majority, do we risk suppressing the basic rights of minorities? Communitarians reply that if we don't balance concern for individual rights with concern for our collective well-being, we risk worse civic disorder, which in turn *will* fuel cries for an autocratic crackdown.

This much is sure: As the conflict between individual and collective rights continues, cross-cultural and gender scholarship can illuminate alternative cultural values and make visible our own assumed values.

 ## Making the Social Connection

As we saw in this chapter, perceived injustice can be a source of conflict. Go to the Online Learning Center for this book to watch a video in which a lesbian couple discuss how they felt conflicted about a perceived injustice and resolved the issue. The second video for this chapter presents Elliot Aronson describing his jigsaw classroom technique for effective learning and social integration.

Applying part **four** Social Psychology

Throughout this book, I have linked the laboratory to life by relating social psychology's principles and findings to everyday happenings. Now, in three short, concluding chapters, we will recall a number of these principles and apply them in distinct practical contexts. Chapter 14, "Social Psychology in the Clinic," applies social psychology to evaluating and promoting mental and physical health. Chapter 15, "Social Psychology in Court," explores the social thinking of and social influences on jurors and juries. Chapter 16, "Social Psychology and the Sustainable Future," explores how social-psychological principles might help avert the ecological crisis that threatens to engulf us as a result of increasing population, consumption, and climate change.

CHAPTER

14

Social
Psychology
in the
Clinic

"Life does not consist mainly, or even largely, of facts and happenings. It consists mainly of the storm of thoughts that are forever blowing through one's mind."

—Mark Twain, 1835–1910

If you are a typical college student, you may occasionally feel mildly depressed. Perhaps you have at times felt dissatisfied with life, discouraged about the future, sad, lacking appetite and energy, unable to concentrate, perhaps even wondering if life is worth living. Maybe disappointing grades have seemed to jeopardize your career goals. Perhaps the breakup of a relationship has left you in despair. At such times, you may fall into self-focused brooding that only worsens your feelings. In one survey of 90,000 American collegians, 44 percent reported that during the last school year they had at some point felt "so depressed it was difficult to function" (ACHA, 2006). For some 10 percent of men and nearly twice that many women, life's down times are not just temporary blue moods in response to bad events; rather, they define a major depressive episode that lasts for weeks without any obvious cause.

Among the many thriving areas of applied social psychology is one that relates social psychology's concepts to depression; to other problems such as loneliness, anxiety, and physical illness; and to happiness and well-being. This bridge-building research between social psychology and **clinical psychology** seeks answers to four important questions:

• As laypeople or as professional psychologists, how can we improve our judgments and predictions about others?

clinical psychology
The study, assessment, and treatment of people with psychological difficulties.

- How do the ways in which we think about self and others fuel problems such as depression, loneliness, anxiety, and ill health?

- How might people reverse these maladaptive thought patterns?

- What part do close, supportive relationships play in health and happiness?

What Influences the Accuracy of Clinical Judgments?

Do the influences on our social judgment (discussed in Chapters 2 through 4) also affect clinicians' judgments of clients? If so, what biases should clinicians and their clients be wary of?

A parole board talks with a convicted rapist and ponders whether to release him. A clinical psychologist ponders whether her patient is seriously suicidal. A physician notes a patient's symptoms and decides whether to recommend an invasive test. A school social worker ponders whether a child's overheard threat was a macho joke, a onetime outburst, or a signal indicating a potential school assassin.

All these professionals must decide whether to make their judgments subjectively or objectively. Should they listen to their gut instincts, their hunches, their inner wisdom? Or should they rely on the wisdom embedded in formulas, statistical analyses, and computerized predictions?

In the contest between heart and head, most psychological clinicians vote with their hearts. They listen to the whispers from their experience, a still small voice that clues them. They prefer not to let cold calculations decide the futures of warm human beings. As Figure 14.1 indicates, they are far more likely than nonclinical (and more research-oriented) psychologists to welcome nonscientific "ways of knowing." Feelings trump formulas.

Clinical judgments are also *social* judgments, notes social-clinical psychologist James Maddux (2008). The social construction of mental illness works like this, he says: Someone observes a pattern of atypical or unwanted thinking and acting. A powerful group sees the desirability or profitability of diagnosing and treating this problem, and thus gives it a name. News about this disease spreads, and people

"To free a man of error is to give, not to take away. Knowledge that a thing is false is a truth."
—*ARTHUR SCHOPENHAUER, 1788–1860*

FIGURE :: 14.1

Clinical Intuition

When Narina Nunez, Debra Ann Poole, and Amina Memon (2003) surveyed a national sample of clinical and nonclinical psychologists, they discovered "two cultures"—one mostly skeptical of "alternative ways of knowing," the other mostly accepting.

Source: From Nunez, Poole, & Memon, 2003.

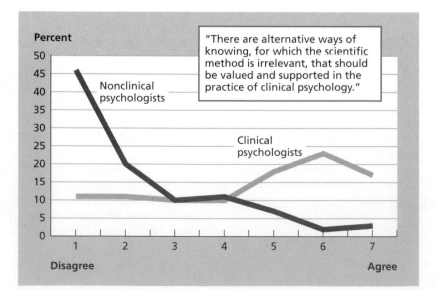

begin seeing it in themselves or family members. And thus is born Body Dysmorphic Disorder (for those preoccupied with an appearance defect), Oppositional Defiant Disorder (for toddlers throwing tantrums), Hypoactive Sexual Desire Disorder (for those not wanting sex often enough), or Orgasmic Disorder (for those having orgasms too late or too soon). "The science of medicine is not diminished by acknowledging that the notions of *health* and *illness* are socially constructed," notes Maddux, "nor is the science of economics diminished by acknowledging that the notions of *poverty* and *wealth* are socially constructed."

As social phenomena, clinical judgments are thus vulnerable to illusory correlations, overconfidence bred by hindsight, and self-confirming diagnoses (Garb, 2005; Maddux, 1993). Let's see why alerting mental health workers to how people form impressions (and misimpressions) might help avert serious misjudgments (McFall, 1991, 2000).

Illusory Correlations

As we saw in Chapter 1, a given correlation may or may not be meaningful; it depends how statistically common the correlation is. For example, if two of your friends have blue eyes and are gay, does that mean that all gay people have blue eyes? Of course not. But someone who is unaware of illusory correlations might think so.

As we noted in Chapter 3, it's tempting to see correlations where none exist. If we expect two things to be associated—if, for example, we believe that premonitions predict events—it's easy to perceive illusory correlations. Even when shown random data, we may notice and remember instances when premonitions and events are coincidentally related, and soon forget all the instances when premonitions aren't borne out and when events happen without a prior premonition.

Clinicians, like all of us, may perceive illusory correlations. If expecting particular responses to Rorschach inkblots to be more common among people with a sexual disorder, they may, in reflecting on their experience, believe they have witnessed such associations. To discover when such a perception is an illusory correlation, psychological science offers a simple method: Have one clinician administer and interpret the test. Have another clinician assess the same person's traits or symptoms. Repeat this process with many people. The proof of the pudding is in the eating: Are test outcomes in fact correlated with reported symptoms? Some tests are indeed predictive. Others, such as the Rorschach inkblots and the Draw-a-Person test, have correlations far weaker than their users suppose (Lilienfeld & others, 2000, 2005).

Why, then, do clinicians continue to express confidence in uninformative or ambiguous tests? Pioneering experiments by Loren Chapman and Jean Chapman (1969, 1971) helped us see why. They invited both college students and professional clinicians to study some test performances and diagnoses. If the students or clinicians *expected* a particular association they generally *perceived* it, regardless of whether the data were supportive. For example, clinicians who believed that only suspicious people draw peculiar eyes on the Draw-a-Person test perceived such a relationship—even when shown cases in which suspicious people drew peculiar eyes less often than nonsuspicious people. If they believed in a connection, they were more likely to notice confirming instances.

In fairness to clinicians, illusory thinking also occurs among political analysts, historians, sportscasters, personnel directors, stockbrokers, and many other professionals, including research psychologists. As a researcher, I have often been unaware of the shortcomings of my theoretical analyses. I so eagerly presume that my idea of truth is *the* truth that, no matter how hard I try, I cannot see my own error. During the last 40 years, I have read dozens of reviews of my own manuscripts and have been a reviewer for dozens of others. My experience is that it is far easier to spot someone else's sloppy thinking than to perceive one's own.

"No one can see his own errors."

—*PSALM 19:12*

20/20 hindsight. Kurt Cobain, member of the rock group Nirvana, whose songs often expressed depressed, suicidal thinking. Should others have used such signs to predict or prevent his suicide?

Hindsight and Overconfidence

If someone we know commits suicide, how do we react? One common reaction is to think that we, or those close to the person, should have been able to predict and therefore to prevent the suicide: "We should have known!" In hindsight, we can see the suicidal signs and the pleas for help. One experiment gave participants a description of a depressed person. Some participants were told that the person subsequently committed suicide; other participants were not told this. Compared with those not informed of the suicide, those who had been informed became more likely to say they "would have expected" it (Goggin & Range, 1985). Moreover, those told of the suicide viewed the victim's family more negatively. After a tragedy, an I-should-have-known-it-all-along phenomenon can leave family, friends, and therapists feeling guilty.

David Rosenhan (1973) and seven associates provided a striking example of potential error in after-the-fact explanations. To test mental health workers' clinical insights, they each made an appointment with a different mental hospital admissions office and complained of "hearing voices." Apart from giving false names and vocations, they reported their life histories and emotional states honestly and exhibited no further symptoms. Most were diagnosed as schizophrenic and remained hospitalized for two to three weeks. Hospital clinicians then searched for early incidents in the pseudopatients' life histories and hospital behavior that "confirmed" and "explained" the diagnosis. Rosenhan tells of one pseudopatient who truthfully explained to the interviewer that he had a close childhood relationship with his mother but was rather remote from his father. During adolescence and beyond, however, his father became a close friend while his relationship with his mother cooled. His present relationship with his wife was characteristically close and warm. Apart from occasional angry exchanges, friction was minimal. The children had rarely been spanked.

The interviewer, "knowing" the person suffered from schizophrenia, explained the problem this way:

> This white 39-year-old male . . . manifests a long history of considerable ambivalence in close relationships, which begins in early childhood. A warm relationship with his mother cools during his adolescence. A distant relationship to his father is described as becoming very intense. Affective stability is absent. His attempts to control emotionality with his wife and children are punctuated by angry outbursts and, in the case of the children, spankings. And while he says that he has several good friends, one senses considerable ambivalence embedded in those relationships also.

Rosenhan later told some staff members (who had heard about his controversial experiment but doubted such mistakes could occur in their hospital) that during the next three months one or more pseudopatients would seek admission to their hospital. After the three months, he asked the staff to guess which of the 193 patients admitted during that time were really pseudopatients. Of the 193 new patients, 41 were believed by at least one staff member to be pseudopatients. Actually, there were none.

Self-Confirming Diagnoses

So far we've seen that mental health clinicians sometimes perceive illusory correlations and that hindsight explanations can err. A third problem with clinical judgment is that patients may also supply information that fulfills clinicians' expectations. To get a feel for how this phenomenon might be tested experimentally, imagine yourself on a blind date with someone who has been told that you are an uninhibited, outgoing person. To see whether this is true, your date slips questions into the conversation, such as "Have you ever done anything crazy in front of other people?" As you answer such questions, will you reveal a different "you" than if your date had been told you were shy and reserved?

In a clever series of experiments at the University of Minnesota, Mark Snyder (1984), in collaboration with William Swann and others, gave interviewers some hypotheses to test concerning individuals' traits. Snyder and Swann found that people often test for a trait by looking for information that confirms it. As in the blind-date example, if people are trying to find out if someone is an extravert, they often solicit instances of extraversion ("What would you do if you wanted to liven things up at a party?"). Testing for introversion, they are more likely to ask, "What factors make it hard for you to really open up to people?" In response, those probed for extraversion seem more sociable, and those probed for introversion seem more shy. Our assumptions and expectations about another help create the kind of person we see.

At Indiana University, Russell Fazio and his colleagues (1981) reproduced this finding and also discovered that those asked the "extraverted" questions later perceived themselves as actually more outgoing than those asked the introverted questions. Moreover, they really became noticeably more outgoing. An accomplice of the experimenter later met each participant in a waiting room and 70 percent of the time guessed correctly from the person's behavior which condition the person had come from.

In other experiments, Snyder and his colleagues (1982) tried to get people to search for behaviors that would *disconfirm* the trait they were testing. In one experiment, they told the interviewers, "It is relevant and informative to find out ways in which the person . . . may not be like the stereotype." In another experiment, Snyder (1981) offered "$25 to the person who develops the set of questions that tell the most about . . . the interviewee." Still, confirmation bias persisted: People resisted choosing "introverted" questions when testing for extraversion.

On the basis of Snyder's experiments, can you see why the behaviors of people undergoing psychotherapy come to fit their therapists' theories (Whitman & others, 1963)? When Harold Renaud and Floyd Estess (1961) conducted life-history interviews of 100 healthy, successful adult men, they were startled to discover that their subjects' childhood experiences were loaded with "traumatic events," tense relations with certain people, and bad decisions by their parents—the very factors usually used to explain psychiatric problems. If therapists go fishing for traumas in early childhood experiences, they will often find them. Thus, surmised Snyder (1981):

> The psychiatrist who believes (erroneously) that adult gay males had bad childhood relationships with their mothers may meticulously probe for recalled (or fabricated) signs of tension between their gay clients and their mothers, but neglect to so carefully interrogate their heterosexual clients about their maternal relationships. No doubt, any individual could recall some friction with his or her mother, however minor or isolated the incidents.

"As is your sort of mind, So is your sort of search: You'll find What you desire."
—*ROBERT BROWNING, 1812–1889*

Clinical versus Statistical Prediction

It will come as no surprise, given these hindsight- and diagnosis-confirming tendencies, that most clinicians and interviewers express more confidence in their intuitive assessments than in statistical data (such as using past grades and aptitude scores to predict success in graduate or professional school). Yet when researchers pit statistical prediction against intuitive prediction, the statistics usually win. Statistical predictions are indeed unreliable, but human intuition—even expert intuition—is even more unreliable (Faust & Ziskin, 1988; Meehl, 1954; Swets & others, 2000).

Three decades after demonstrating the superiority of statistical over intuitive prediction, Paul Meehl (1986) found the evidence stronger than ever:

> There is no controversy in social science which shows [so many] studies coming out so uniformly in the same direction as this one . . . When you are pushing 90 investigations, predicting everything from the outcome of football games to the diagnosis of liver disease and when you can hardly come up with a half dozen studies showing even a weak tendency in favor of the clinician, it is time to draw a practical conclusion.

"A very bright young man who is likely to succeed in life. He is intelligent enough to achieve lofty goals as long as he stays on task and remains motivated."

—PROBATION OFFICER'S CLINICAL INTUITION IN RESPONSE TO ERIC HARRIS'S "HOMICIDAL THOUGHTS"—2½ MONTHS BEFORE HE COMMITTED THE COLUMBINE HIGH SCHOOL MASSACRE

One University of Minnesota research team conducted an all-encompassing digest ("meta-analysis") of 134 studies predicting human behavior or making psychological or medical diagnoses and prognoses (Grove & others, 2000). In only 8 of the studies, which were conducted mostly in medical, mental health, or education settings, did clinical prediction surpass "mechanical" (statistical) prediction. In eight times as many (63 studies), statistical prediction fared better. (The rest were a virtual draw.) Ah, but would clinicians fare differently when given the opportunity for a firsthand clinical interview? Yes, report the researchers: Allowed interviews, the clinicians fared substantially *worse*. "It is fair to say that 'the ball is in the clinicians' court,'" the researchers concluded. "Given the overall deficit in clinicians' accuracy relative to mechanical prediction, the burden falls on advocates of clinical prediction to show that clinicians' predictions are more [accurate or cost-effective]."

What if we combined statistical prediction with clinical intuition? What if we gave professional clinicians the statistical prediction of someone's future academic performance or risk of parole violation or suicide and asked them to refine or improve on the prediction? Alas, in the few studies where that has been done, prediction was better if the "improvements" were ignored (Dawes, 1994).

Why then do so many clinicians continue to interpret Rorschach inkblot tests and offer intuitive predictions about parolees, suicide risks, and likelihood of child abuse? Partly out of sheer ignorance, said Meehl, but also partly out of "mistaken conceptions of ethics":

> If I try to forecast something important about a college student, or a criminal, or a depressed patient by inefficient rather than efficient means, meanwhile charging this person or the taxpayer 10 times as much money as I would need to achieve greater predictive accuracy, that is not a sound ethical practice. That it feels better, warmer, and cuddlier to me as predictor is a shabby excuse indeed.

"The effect of Meehl's work on clinical practice in the mental health area can be summed up in a single word: Zilch. He was honored, elected to the presidency of [the American Psychological Association] at a very young age in 1962, recently elected to the National Academy of Sciences, and ignored."

—ROBYN M. DAWES (1989)

Such words are shocking. Did Meehl (who did not completely dismiss clinical expertise) underestimate experts' intuitions? To see why his findings are apparently valid, consider the assessment of human potential by graduate admissions interviewers. Dawes (1976) explained why statistical prediction is so often superior to an interviewer's intuition when predicting certain outcomes such as graduate school success:

> What makes us think that we can do a better job of selection by interviewing (students) for a half hour, than we can by adding together relevant (standardized) variables, such as undergraduate GPA, GRE score, and perhaps ratings of letters of recommendation? The most reasonable explanation to me lies in our overevaluation of our cognitive capacity. And it is really cognitive conceit. Consider, for example, what goes into a GPA. Because for most graduate applicants it is based on at least 3½ years of undergraduate study, it is a composite measure arising from a minimum of 28 courses and possibly, with the popularity of the quarter system, as many as 50 . . . Yet you

focus
ON
A Physician's View

Reading this book helps me understand the human behaviors I observe in my work as a cancer specialist and as medical director of a large staff of physicians. A few examples:

Reviews of medical records illustrate the "I-knew-it-all-along phenomenon." Physician reviewers who assess the medical records of their colleagues often believe, in hindsight, that problems such as cancer or appendicitis should clearly have been recognized and treated much more quickly. Once you know the correct diagnosis, it's easy to look back and interpret the early symptoms accordingly.

For many physicians I have known, the intrinsic motives behind their entering the profession—to help people, to be scientifically stimulated—soon become "overjustified" by the high pay. Before long, the joy is lost. The extrinsic rewards become the reason to practice, and the physician, having lost the altruistic motives, works to increase "success," measured in income.

"Self-serving bias" is ever present. We physicians gladly accept personal credit when things go well. When they don't—when the patient is misdiagnosed or doesn't get well or dies—we attribute the failure elsewhere. We were given inadequate information or the case was ill-fated from the beginning.

I also observe many examples of "belief perseverance." Even when presented with the documented facts about, say, how AIDS is transmitted, people will strangely persist in wrongly believing that it is just a "gay" disease or that they should fear catching it from mosquito bites. It makes me wonder: How can I more effectively persuade people of what they need to know and act upon?

Indeed, as I observe medical attitudes and decision making I feel myself submerged in a giant practical laboratory of social psychology. To understand the goings-on around me, I find social psychological insights invaluable and would strongly advise premed students to study the field.

Burton F. VanderLaan,
Chicago, Illinois

---

and I, looking at a folder or interviewing someone for a half hour, are supposed to be able to form a better impression than one based on 3½ years of the cumulative evaluations of 20–40 different professors. . . . Finally, if we do wish to ignore GPA, it appears that the only reason for doing so is believing that the candidate is particularly brilliant even though his or her record may not show it. What better evidence for such brilliance can we have than a score on a carefully devised aptitude test? Do we really think we are better equipped to assess such aptitude than is the Educational Testing Service, whatever its faults?

The bottom line, contends Dawes (2005) after three decades pressing his point, is that, lacking evidence, using clinical intuition rather than statistical prediction "is simply unethical."

Implications for Better Clinical Practice

Professional clinicians are human; they are "vulnerable to insidious errors and biases," concluded James Maddux (1993). They are, as we have seen,

- frequently the victims of illusory correlation.
- too readily convinced of their own after-the-fact analyses.

When evaluating clients, mental health workers, like all of us, are vulnerable to cognitive illusions.

- unaware that erroneous diagnoses can be self-confirming.
- likely to overestimate their clinical intuition.

The implications for mental health workers are easily stated: Be mindful that clients' verbal agreement with what you say does not prove its validity. Beware of the tendency to see relationships that you expect to see or that are supported by striking examples readily available in your memory. Rely on your notes more than on your memory. Recognize that hindsight is seductive: It can lead you to feel overconfident and sometimes to judge yourself too harshly for not having foreseen outcomes. Guard against the tendency to ask questions that assume your preconceptions are correct; consider opposing ideas and test them, too (Garb, 1994).

Summing Up: What Influences the Accuracy of Clinical Judgments?

- As psychiatrists and clinical psychologists diagnose and treat their clients, they may perceive *illusory correlations*.

- *Hindsight* explanations of people's difficulties are sometimes too easy. Indeed, after-the-fact explaining can breed overconfidence in clinical judgment.

- When interacting with clients, erroneous diagnoses are sometimes *self-confirming*, because interviewers tend to seek and recall information that verifies what they are looking for.

- Research on the errors that so easily creep into intuitive judgments illustrates the need for rigorous testing of intuitive conclusions and the use of statistics to make predictions.

- The scientific method cannot answer all questions and is itself vulnerable to bias. Thankfully, however, it can help us sift truth from falsehood if we are aware of the biases that tend to cloud judgments that are made "from the heart."

What Cognitive Processes Accompany Behavior Problems?

One of psychology's most intriguing research frontiers concerns the cognitive processes that accompany psychological disorders. What are the memories, attributions, and expectations of depressed, lonely, shy, or illness-prone people?

Depression

People who feel depressed tend to think in negative terms. They view life through dark-colored glasses. With seriously depressed people—those who are feeling worthless, lethargic, uninterested in friends and family, and unable to sleep or eat normally—the negative thinking is self-defeating. Their intensely pessimistic outlook leads them to magnify every bad experience and minimize every good one. They may view advice to "count your blessings" or "look on the bright side" as hopelessly unrealistic. As one depressed young woman reported, "The real me is worthless and inadequate. I can't move forward with my work because I become frozen with doubt" (Burns, 1980, p. 29).

DISTORTION OR REALISM?

Are all depressed people unrealistically negative? To find out, Lauren Alloy and Lyn Abramson (1979; Alloy & others, 2004) studied college students who were either mildly depressed or not depressed. They had the students press a button and observe whether the button controlled a light coming on. Surprisingly, the

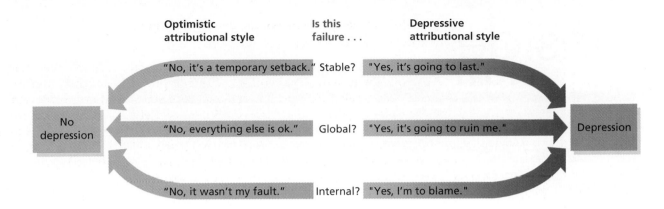

FIGURE :: 14.2

Depressive Explanatory Style

Depression is linked with a negative, pessimistic way of explaining and interpreting failures.

depressed students were quite accurate in estimating their degree of control. It was the nondepressives whose judgments were distorted; they exaggerated the extent of their control. Despite their self-preoccupation, mildly depressed people also are more attuned to others' feelings (Harkness & others, 2005).

This surprising phenomenon of **depressive realism,** nicknamed the "sadder-but-wiser effect," shows up in various judgments of one's control or skill (Ackermann & DeRubeis, 1991; Alloy & others, 1990). Shelley Taylor (1989, p. 214) explains:

> Normal people exaggerate how competent and well liked they are. Depressed people do not. Normal people remember their past behavior with a rosy glow. Depressed people [unless severely depressed] are more evenhanded in recalling their successes and failures. Normal people describe themselves primarily positively. Depressed people describe both their positive and negative qualities. Normal people take credit for successful outcomes and tend to deny responsibility for failure. Depressed people accept responsibility for both success and failure. Normal people exaggerate the control they have over what goes on around them. Depressed people are less vulnerable to the illusion of control. Normal people believe to an unrealistic degree that the future holds a bounty of good things and few bad things. Depressed people are more realistic in their perceptions of the future. In fact, on virtually every point on which normal people show enhanced self-regard, illusions of control, and unrealistic visions of the future, depressed people fail to show the same biases. "Sadder but wiser" does indeed appear to apply to depression.

Underlying the thinking of depressed people are their attributions of responsibility. Consider: If you fail an exam and blame yourself, you may conclude that you are stupid or lazy; consequently, you may feel depressed. If you attribute the failure to an unfair exam or to other circumstances beyond your control, you may feel angry. In over 100 studies involving 15,000 subjects, depressed people have been more likely than nondepressed people to exhibit a negative **explanatory style** (Haeffel & others, 2008; Peterson & Steen, 2002; Sweeney & others, 1986). As shown in Figure 14.2, this explanatory style attributes failure and setbacks to causes that are *stable* ("It's going to last forever"), *global* ("It's going to affect everything I do"), and *internal* ("It's all my fault"). The result of this pessimistic, overgeneralized, self-blaming thinking, say Abramson and her colleagues (1989), is a depressing sense of hopelessness.

IS NEGATIVE THINKING A CAUSE OR A RESULT OF DEPRESSION?

The cognitive accompaniments of depression raise a chicken-and-egg question: Do depressed moods cause negative thinking, or does negative thinking cause depression?

depressive realism
The tendency of mildly depressed people to make accurate rather than self-serving judgments, attributions, and predictions.

"Life is the art of being well deceived."
—WILLIAM HAZLITT, 1778–1830

explanatory style
One's habitual way of explaining life events. A negative, pessimistic, depressive explanatory style attributes failure to stable, global, and internal causes.

THE inside STORY

Shelley Taylor on Positive Illusions

Some years ago, I was conducting interviews with people who had cancer for a study on adjustment to intensely stressful events. I was surprised to learn that, for some people, the cancer experience actually seemed to have brought benefits, as well as the expected liabilities. Many people told me that they thought they were better people for the experience, they felt they were better adjusted to cancer than other people, they believed that they could exert control over their cancer in the future, and they believed their futures would be cancer-free, even when we knew from their medical histories that their cancers were likely to recur.

As a result, I became fascinated by how people can construe even the worst of situations as good, and I've studied these "positive illusions" ever since. Through our research, we learned quickly that you don't have to experience a trauma to demonstrate positive illusions. Most

people, including the majority of college students, think of themselves as somewhat better than average, as more in control of the circumstances around them than may actually be true, and as likely to experience more positive future outcomes in life than may be realistic. These illusions are not a sign of maladjustment—quite the contrary. Good mental health may depend on the ability to see things as somewhat better than they are and to find benefits even when things seem most bleak.

Shelley Taylor,
UCLA

DEPRESSED MOODS CAUSE NEGATIVE THINKING   As we saw in Chapter 3, our moods color our thinking. When we *feel* happy, we *think* happy. We see and recall a good world. But let our mood turn gloomy, and our thoughts switch to a different track. Off come the rose-colored glasses; on come the dark glasses. Now the bad mood primes our recollections of negative events (Bower, 1987; Johnson & Magaro, 1987). Our relationships seem to sour, our self-images tarnish, our hopes for the future dim, people's behavior seems more sinister (Brown & Taylor, 1986; Mayer & Salovey, 1987). As depression increases, memories and expectations plummet; when depression lifts, thinking brightens (Barnett & Gotlib, 1988; Kuiper & Higgins, 1985). As an example, *currently* depressed people recall their parents as having been rejecting and punitive. But *formerly* depressed people recall their parents in the same positive terms as do never-depressed people (Lewinsohn & Rosenbaum, 1987). Thus, when you hear depressed people trashing their parents, remember: Moods modify memories.

By studying Indiana University basketball fans, Edward Hirt and his colleagues (1992) demonstrated that even a temporary bad mood can darken our thinking. After the fans were either depressed by watching their team lose or elated by a victory, the researchers asked them to predict the team's future performance, and their own. After a loss, people offered bleaker assessments not only of the team's future but also of their own likely performance at throwing darts, solving anagrams, and getting a date. When things aren't going our way, it may seem as though they never will.

A depressed mood also affects behavior. When depressed, we tend to be withdrawn, glum, and quick to complain. Stephen Strack and James Coyne (1983) found that depressed people were realistic in thinking that others didn't appreciate their behavior; their pessimism and bad moods can even trigger social rejection (Carver & others, 1994). Depressed behavior can also trigger reciprocal depression in others. College students who have depressed roommates tend to become a little depressed themselves (Burchill & Stiles, 1988; Joiner, 1994; Sanislow & others, 1989). In dating couples, too, depression is often contagious (Katz & others, 1999). (Better news

"To the man who is enthusiastic and optimistic, if what is to come should be pleasant, it seems both likely to come about and likely to be good, while to the indifferent or depressed man it seems the opposite."

—*ARISTOTLE, THE ART OF RHETORIC, 4TH CENTURY B.C.*

comes from a study that followed nearly 5,000 residents of one Massachussetts city for 20 years. Happiness also is contagious. When surrounded by happy people, people become more likely to be happy in the future [Fowler & Christakis, 2008].)

We can see, then, that being depressed has cognitive and behavioral effects. Does it also work the other way around: Does depression have cognitive *origins?*

NEGATIVE THINKING CAUSES DEPRESSED MOODS Depression is natural when experiencing severe stress—losing a job, getting divorced or rejected, or suffering any experi-

Stresses challenge some people and defeat others. Researchers have sought to understand the "explanatory style" that makes some people more vulnerable to depression.

ence that disrupts our sense of who we are and why we are worthy human beings (Hamilton & others, 1993; Kendler & others, 1993). The brooding that comes with this short-term depression can be adaptive. Much as nausea and pain protect the body from toxins, so depression protects us, by slowing us down, causing us to reassess, and then redirecting our energy in new ways (Watkins, 2008). Insights gained during times of depressed inactivity may later result in better strategies for interacting with the world. But depression-prone people respond to bad events with intense rumination and self-blame (Mor & Winquist, 2002; Pyszczynski & others, 1991). Their self-esteem fluctuates more rapidly up with boosts and down with threats (Butler & others, 1994).

Why are some people so affected by *minor* stresses? Evidence suggests that when stress-induced rumination is filtered through a negative explanatory style, the frequent outcome is depression (Robinson & Alloy, 2003). Colin Sacks and Daphne Bugental (1987) asked some young women to get acquainted with a stranger who sometimes acted cold and unfriendly, creating an awkward social situation. Unlike optimistic women, those with a pessimistic explanatory style—who characteristically offer stable, global, and internal attributions for bad events—reacted to the social failure by feeling depressed. Moreover, they then behaved more antagonistically toward the next people they met. Their negative thinking led to a negative mood, which then led to negative behavior.

Such depressing rumination is more common among women, reports Susan Nolen-Hoeksema (2003). When trouble strikes, men tend to act, women tend to think—and often to "overthink," she reports. And that helps explain why, beginning in adolescence, women have, compared with men, a doubled risk of depression (Hyde & others, 2008).

Outside the laboratory, studies of children, teenagers, and adults confirm that those with the pessimistic explanatory style are more likely to become depressed when bad things happen. One study monitored university students every six weeks for two-and-a-half years (Alloy & others, 1999). Only 1 percent of those who began college with optimistic thinking styles had a first depressive episode, but 17 percent of those with pessimistic thinking styles did. "A recipe for severe depression is preexisting pessimism encountering failure," notes Martin Seligman (1991, p. 78). Moreover, patients who end therapy no longer feeling depressed but retaining a negative explanatory style tend to relapse as bad events occur (Seligman, 1992). If those with a more optimistic explanatory style relapse, they often recover quickly (Metalsky & others, 1993; Needles & Abramson, 1990).

Researcher Peter Lewinsohn and his colleagues (1985) have assembled these findings into a coherent psychological understanding of depression. The negative

The Vicious Circle
of Depression

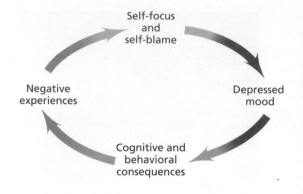

self-image, attributions, and expectations of a depressed person are, they report, an essential link in a vicious circle that is triggered by negative experience—perhaps academic or vocational failure, family conflict, or social rejection (Figure 14.3). Such ruminations create a depressed mood that alters drastically the way a person thinks and acts, which then fuels further negative experiences, self-blame, and depressed mood. In experiments, mildly depressed people's moods brighten when a task diverts their attention to something external (Nix & others, 1995). Depression is therefore *both* a cause and a result of negative cognitions.

Martin Seligman (1991, 1998, 2002) believes that self-focus and self-blame help explain the near-epidemic levels of depression in the Western world today. In North America, for example, young adults today are three times as likely as their grandparents to have suffered depression—despite their grandparents' experiencing a lower standard of living and greater hardship (Cross-National Collaborative Group, 1992; Swindle & others, 2000). Seligman believes that the decline of religion and family, plus the growth of individualism, breeds hopelessness and self-blame when things don't go well. Failed courses, careers, and marriages produce despair when we stand alone, with nothing and no one to fall back on. If, as a macho *Fortune* ad declared, you can "make it on your own," on "your own drive, your own guts, your own energy, your own ambition," then whose fault is it if you *don't* make it? In non-Western cultures, where close-knit relationships and cooperation are the norm, major depression is less common and less tied to guilt and self-blame over perceived personal failure. In Japan, for example, depressed people instead tend to report feeling shame over letting down their family or co-workers (Draguns, 1990).

These insights into the thinking style linked with depression have prompted social psychologists to study thinking patterns associated with other problems. How do those who are plagued with excessive loneliness, shyness, or substance abuse view themselves? How well do they recall their successes and their failures? To what do they attribute their ups and downs?

Loneliness

If depression is the common cold of psychological disorders, then loneliness is the headache. Loneliness, whether chronic or temporary, is a painful awareness that our social relationships are less numerous or meaningful than we desire. In modern cultures, close social relationships are less numerous. One national survey revealed a one-third drop, over two decades, in the number of people with whom Americans can discuss "important matters." Reflecting on the finding, Robert Putnam (2006) reported that his data likewise reveal "sharp generational differences—baby boomers are more socially marooned than their parents, and the boomers' kids are lonelier still. Is it because of two-career families? Ethnic diversity? The Internet? Suburban sprawl? Everyone has a favorite culprit. Mine is TV, but the jury is still out."

Other researchers have offered different explanations. In a study of Dutch adults, Jenny de Jong-Gierveld (1987) documented the loneliness that unmarried and unattached people are likely to experience. She speculated that the modern emphasis on individual fulfillment and the depreciation of marriage and family life may be "loneliness-provoking" (as well as depression-provoking). Job-related mobility also makes for fewer long-term family and social ties and increased loneliness (Dill & Anderson, 1999).

FEELING LONELY AND EXCLUDED

But loneliness need not coincide with aloneness. One can feel lonely in the middle of a party. "In America, there is loneliness but no solitude," lamented Mary Pipher (2002). "There are crowds but no community." In Los Angeles, observed her daughter, "There are 10 million people around me but nobody knows my name." Lacking social connections, and feeling lonely (or when made to feel so in an experiment), people may compensate by seeing humanlike qualities in things, animals, and supernatural beings, with which they find companionship (Epley & others, 2008).

"Enemies, yes, but doesn't your moat also keep out love?"

One can be utterly alone—as I am while writing these words in the solitude of an isolated turret office at a British university 5,000 miles from home—without feeling lonely. To feel lonely is to feel excluded from a group, unloved by those around you, unable to share your private concerns, different and alienated from those in your surroundings (Beck & Young, 1978; Davis & Franzoi, 1986). It is also to be at increased risk for high blood pressure and heart disease, and thus accelerated physical decline with age (Hawkley & Cacioppo, 2007). In *Loneliness: Human Nature and the Need for Social Connection*, John Cacioppo and William Patrick (2008) explain other physical and emotional effects of loneliness, which affects stress hormones and immune activity. Loneliness—which may be evoked by an icy stare or a cold shoulder—even feels, quite literally, cold. When recalling an experience of exclusion, people estimate a lower room temperature than when thinking of being included. After being excluded in a little ball game, people show a heightened preference for warm foods and drinks (Zhong & Leonardelli, 2008).

Adolescents more than adults experience loneliness (Heinrich & Gullone, 2006). When beeped by an electronic pager at various times during a week and asked to record what they were doing and how they felt, adolescents more often than adults reported feeling lonely when alone (Larsen & others, 1982). Males and females feel lonely under somewhat different circumstances—males when isolated from group interaction, females when deprived of close one-to-one relationships (Berg & McQuinn, 1988; Stokes & Levin, 1986). Men's relationships, it is said, tend to be side-by-side; women's relationships tend to be face-to-face. One exception: After divorce, men tend to feel lonelier than do women (Dykstra & Fokkema, 2007). But for all people, including those recently widowed, the loss of a person to whom one has been attached can produce unavoidable feelings of loneliness (Stroebe & others, 1996).

Such feelings can be adaptive. The path of loneliness signals people to seek social connections, which facilitate survival. Even when loneliness triggers nostalgia—a longing for the past—it serves to remind people of their social connections (Zhou & others, 2008).

PERCEIVING OTHERS NEGATIVELY

Like depressed people, chronically lonely people seem caught in a vicious circle of self-defeating social thinking and social behaviors. They have some of the negative explanatory style of the depressed; they perceive their interactions as making a poor impression, blame themselves for their poor social relationships, and see most things as beyond their control (Anderson & others, 1994; Christensen & Kashy, 1998; Snodgrass, 1987). Moreover, they perceive others in negative ways. When paired with a stranger of the same gender or with a first-year college roommate, lonely students are more likely to perceive the other person negatively (Jones & others, 1981; Wittenberg & Reis, 1986). As Figure 14.4 illustrates, loneliness, depression, and shyness sometimes feed one another.

These negative views may both reflect and color the lonely person's experience. Believing in their social unworthiness and feeling pessimistic about others

FIGURE :: 14.4

The Interplay
of Chronic Shyness,
Loneliness, and
Depression

Solid arrows indicate primary
cause-effect direction, as summarized by Jody Dill and Craig
Anderson (1999). Dotted lines
indicate additional effects.

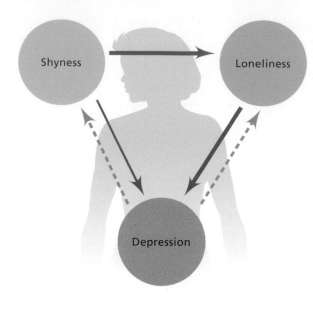

inhibit lonely people from acting to reduce their loneliness.
Lonely people often find it hard
to introduce themselves, make
phone calls, and participate in
groups (Nurmi & others, 1996,
1997; Rook, 1984; Spitzberg &
Hurt, 1987). Yet, like mildly depressed people, they are attuned to others and skilled at
recognizing emotional expression (Gardner & others, 2005).
Like depression, loneliness is
genetically influenced; identical twins are much more likely
than fraternal twins to share
moderate to extreme loneliness
(Boomsma & others, 2006).

Anxiety and Shyness

Shyness is a form of social anxiety characterized by self-consciousness and worry
about what others think (Anderson & Harvey, 1988; Asendorpf, 1987; Carver &
Scheier, 1986). Being interviewed for a much-wanted job, dating someone for the
first time, stepping into a roomful of strangers, performing before an important audience, or giving a speech (one of the most common phobias) can make almost anyone feel anxious. But some people feel anxious in almost any situation in which they
may feel they are being evaluated, such as having a casual lunch with a co-worker.
For these people, anxiety is more a personality trait than a temporary state.

DOUBTING OUR ABILITY IN SOCIAL SITUATIONS

What causes us to feel anxious in social situations? Why are some people shack-
led in the prison of their own social anxiety? Barry Schlenker and Mark Leary
(1982, 1985; Leary & Kowalski, 1995) answer those questions by applying self-
presentation theory. As you may recall from Chapters 2 and 4, self-presentation
theory assumes that we are eager to present ourselves in
ways that make a good impression. The implications for
social anxiety are straightforward: *We feel anxious when we
are motivated to impress others but have self-doubts.* This simple
principle helps explain a variety of research findings, each
of which may ring true in your own experience. We feel
most anxious when we are

Self-disclosure in relationships, and a positive explanatory
style help protect people from feelings of loneliness.

- with powerful, high-status people—people whose
  impressions of us matter.
- in an evaluative context, such as when making a first
  impression on the parents of one's fiancé.
- self-conscious (as shy people often are), with our
  attention focused on ourselves and how we are
  coming across.
- focused on something central to our self-image, as
  when a college professor presents ideas before peers
  at a professional convention.
- in novel or unstructured situations, such as a first
  school dance or first formal dinner, where we are
  unsure of the social rules.

For most people, the tendency in all such situations is to be cautiously self-protective: to talk less; to avoid topics that reveal one's ignorance; to be guarded about oneself; to be unassertive, agreeable, and smiling. Ironically, such anxious concern with making a good impression often makes a bad impression (Broome & Wegner, 1994; Meleshko & Alden, 1993). With time, however, shy people often become well liked. Their lack of egotism, their modesty, sensitivity, and discretion wear well (Gough & Thorne, 1986; Paulhus & Morgan, 1997; Shepperd & others, 1995).

OVERPERSONALIZING SITUATIONS

Compared with unshy people, shy, self-conscious people (whose numbers include many adolescents) see incidental events as somehow relevant to themselves (Fenigstein, 1984; Fenigstein & Vanable, 1992). Shy, anxious people overpersonalize situations, a tendency that breeds anxious concern and, in extreme cases, paranoia. They also overestimate the extent to which other people are watching and evaluating them. If their hair won't comb right or they have a facial blemish, they assume everyone else notices and judges them accordingly. Shy people may even be conscious of their self-consciousness. They wish they could stop worrying about blushing, about what others are thinking, or about what to say next.

When a person is eager to impress important people, social anxiety is natural.

To reduce social anxiety, some people turn to alcohol. Alcohol lowers anxiety and reduces self-consciousness (Hull & Young, 1983). Thus, chronically self-conscious people are especially likely to drink following a failure. If recovering from alcoholism, they are more likely than those low in self-consciousness to relapse when they again experience stress or failure.

Symptoms as diverse as anxiety and alcohol abuse can also serve a self-handicapping function. Labeling oneself as anxious, shy, depressed, or under the influence of alcohol can provide an excuse for failure (Snyder & Smith, 1986). Behind a barricade of symptoms, the person's ego stands secure. "Why don't I date? Because I'm shy, so people don't easily get to know the real me." The symptom is an unconscious strategic ploy to explain away negative outcomes.

What if we were to remove the need for such a ploy by providing people with a handy alternative explanation for their anxiety and therefore for possible failure? Would a shy person no longer need to be shy? That is precisely what Susan Brodt and Philip Zimbardo (1981) found when they brought shy and not-shy college women to the laboratory and had them converse with a handsome male who posed as another participant. Before the conversation, the women were cooped up in a small chamber and blasted with loud noise. Some of the shy women (but not others) were told that the noise would leave them with a pounding heart, a common symptom of social anxiety. Thus, when these women later talked with the man, they could attribute their pounding hearts and any conversational difficulties to the noise, not to their shyness or social inadequacy. Compared with the shy women who were not given this handy explanation for their pounding hearts, these women were no longer so shy. They talked fluently once the conversation got going and asked questions of the man. In fact, unlike the other shy women (whom the man could easily spot as shy), these women were to him indistinguishable from the not-shy women.

Health, Illness, and Death

In the industrialized world, at least half of all deaths are linked with behavior—with consuming cigarettes, alcohol, drugs, and harmful foods; with reactions to stress; with lack of exercise and not following a doctor's advice. Efforts to study and change these behavioral contributions to illness helped create a new interdisciplinary field called **behavioral medicine.** Psychology's contribution to this interdisciplinary science is its subfield, **health psychology.** Health psychologists study how people respond to illness symptoms and how emotions and explanations influence health.

behavioral medicine
An interdisciplinary field that integrates and applies behavioral and medical knowledge about health and disease.

health psychology
The study of the psychological roots of health and illness. Offers psychology's contribution to behavioral medicine.

REACTIONS TO ILLNESS

How do people decide whether they are ill? How do they explain their symptoms? What influences their willingness to seek and follow treatment?

NOTICING SYMPTOMS   Chances are you have recently experienced at least one of these physical complaints: headache, stomachache, nasal congestion, sore muscles, ringing in the ears, excess perspiration, cold hands, racing heart, dizziness, stiff joints, and diarrhea or constipation (Pennebaker, 1982). Such symptoms require interpretation. Are they meaningless? Or are you coming down with something that requires medical attention? Hardly a week goes by without our playing doctor by self-diagnosing some symptom.

Noticing and interpreting our body's signals is like noticing and interpreting how our car is running. Unless the signals are loud and clear, we often miss them. Most of us cannot tell whether a car needs an oil change merely by listening to its engine. Similarly, most of us are not astute judges of our heart rate, blood-sugar level, or blood pressure. People guess their blood pressure based on how they feel, which often is unrelated to their actual blood pressure (Baumann & Leventhal, 1985). Furthermore, the early signs of many illnesses, including cancer and heart disease, are subtle and easy to miss.

EXPLAINING SYMPTOMS: AM I SICK?   With more serious aches and pains, the questions become more specific—and more critical. Does the small cyst match our idea of a malignant lump? Is the stomachache bad enough to be appendicitis? Is the pain in the chest area merely—as many heart attack victims suppose—a muscle spasm? Indeed, reports the National Institutes of Health, most heart attack victims wait too long before seeking medical help. What factors influence how we explain symptoms?

Once we notice symptoms, we interpret them using familiar disease schemas (Bishop, 1991). In medical schools, this can have amusing results. As part of their training, medical students learn the symptoms associated with various diseases. Because they also experience various symptoms, they sometimes attribute their symptoms to recently learned disease schemas. ("Maybe this wheeze is the beginning of pneumonia.") As you may have discovered, psychology students are prone to this effect as they read about psychological disorders.

DO I NEED TREATMENT?   Once people notice a symptom and interpret it as possibly serious, several factors influence their decision to seek medical care. People more often seek treatment if they believe their symptoms have a physical rather than a psychological cause (Bishop, 1987). They may delay seeking help, however, if they feel embarrassed, if they think the likely benefits of medical attention won't justify the cost and inconvenience, or if they want to avoid a possibly devastating diagnosis.

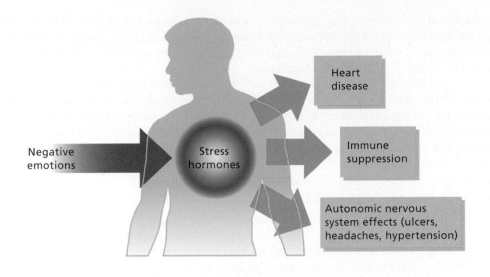

FIGURE :: 14.5

Stress-caused negative emotions may have various effects on health. This is especially so for depressed or anger-prone people.

The U.S. National Center for Health Statistics (NCHS) reports a gender difference in decisions to seek medical treatment: Compared with men, women report more symptoms, use more prescription and nonprescription drugs, and visit physicians twice as often for preventive care (NCHS, 2008). Women also visit psychotherapists 50 percent more often (Olfson & Pincus, 1994).

So, are women more often sick? Apparently not. In fact, men may be more disease-prone. Among other problems, men have higher rates of hypertension, ulcers, and cancer, as well as shorter life expectancies. So why are women more likely to see a doctor? Perhaps women are more attentive to their internal states. Perhaps they are less reluctant to admit "weakness" and seek help (Bishop, 1984).

Patients are more willing to follow treatment instructions when they have warm relationships with their doctors, when they help plan their treatment, and when options are framed attractively. People are more likely to elect an operation when given "a 40 percent chance of surviving" than when given "a 60 percent chance of not surviving" (Rothman & Salovey, 1997; Wilson & others, 1987). Such "gain-framed" messages also persuade more people to use sunscreen, eschew cigarettes, and get HIV tests (Detweiler & others, 1999; Salovey & others, 2002; Schneider & others, 2000). Better to tell people that "sunscreen maintains healthy, young-looking skin" than to tell them that "not using sunscreen decreases your chances of healthy, young-looking skin."

EMOTIONS AND ILLNESS

Do our emotions predict our susceptibility to heart disease, stroke, cancer, and other ailments (Figure 14.5)? Consider the following.

Heart disease has been linked with a competitive, impatient, and—the aspect that matters most—*anger-prone* personality (Kupper & Denollet, 2007; Williams, 1993). Under stress, reactive, anger-prone "Type A" people secrete more of the stress hormones believed to accelerate the buildup of plaque on the walls of the heart's arteries.

Depression also increases the risk of various ailments. Mildly depressed people are more vulnerable to heart disease, even after controlling for differences in smoking and other disease-related factors (Anda & others, 1993). The year after a heart attack, depressed people have a doubled risk of further heart problems (Frasure-Smith & others, 1995, 1999, 2005). The toxicity of negative emotions contributes to the high rate of depression and anxiety among chronically ill people (Cohen & Rodriguez, 1995). The association between depression and heart disease may result from stress-related inflammation of the arteries (Matthews, 2005; Miller & Blackwell, 2006). Stress hormones enhance protein production that contributes to inflammation, which helps fight infections. But inflammation also can exacerbate asthma, clogged arteries, and depression.

George Vaillant (1997) witnessed the effect of distress when he followed a group of male Harvard alumni from midlife into old age. Of those whom at age 52 he classified as "squares" (having never abused alcohol, used tranquilizers, or seen a psychiatrist), only 5 percent had died by age 75. Of those classified as "distressed" (who had abused alcohol and either used tranquilizers or seen a psychiatrist), 38 percent had died.

OPTIMISM AND HEALTH

Stories abound of people who take a sudden turn for the worse when something makes them lose hope, or who suddenly improve when hope is renewed. As cancer attacks the liver of 9-year-old Jeff, his doctors fear the worst. But Jeff remains optimistic. He is determined to grow up to be a cancer research scientist. One day Jeff is elated. A specialist who has taken a long-distance interest in his case is planning to stop off while on a cross-country trip. There is so much Jeff wants to tell the doctor and to show him from the diary he has kept since he got sick. On the anticipated day, fog blankets his city. The doctor's plane is diverted to another city, from which the doctor flies on to his final destination. Hearing the news, Jeff cries quietly. The next morning, pneumonia and fever have developed, and Jeff lies listless. By evening he is in a coma. The next afternoon he dies (Visintainer & Seligman, 1983).

Understanding the links between attitudes and disease requires more than dramatic true stories. If hopelessness coincides with cancer, we are left to wonder: Does cancer breed hopelessness, or does hopelessness also hinder resistance to cancer? To resolve this chicken-and-egg riddle, researchers have (1) experimentally created hopelessness by subjecting organisms to uncontrollable stresses and (2) correlated the hopeless explanatory style with future illnesses.

STRESS AND ILLNESS   The clearest indication of the effects of hopelessness—what Chapter 2 labels *learned helplessness*—comes from experiments that subject animals to mild but uncontrollable electric shocks, loud noises, or crowding. Such experiences do not cause diseases such as cancer, but they do lower the body's resistance. Rats injected with live cancer cells more often develop and die of tumors if they also receive inescapable shocks than if they receive escapable shocks or no shocks. Moreover, compared with juvenile rats given controllable shocks, those given uncontrollable shocks are twice as likely in adulthood to develop tumors if given cancer cells and another round of shocks (Visintainer & Seligman, 1985). Animals that have learned helplessness react more passively, and blood tests reveal a weakened immune response.

It's a big leap from rats to humans. But a growing body of evidence reveals that people who undergo highly stressful experiences become more vulnerable to disease (Segerstrom & Miller, 2004). Stress doesn't make us sick, but it does divert energy from our disease-fighting immune system, leaving us more vulnerable to infections and malignancy (Cohen, 2002, 2004). The death of a spouse, the stress of a space flight landing, even the strain of an exam week have all been associated with depressed immune defenses (Jemmott & Locke, 1984).

Consider:

- Stress magnifies the severity of symptoms experienced by volunteers who are knowingly infected with a cold virus (Cohen & others, 2003, 2006; Dixon, 1986).
- Newlywed couples who became angry while discussing problems suffered more immune system suppression the next day (Kiecolt-Glaser & others, 1993). When people are stressed by marital conflict, laboratory puncture wounds take a day or two longer to heal (Kiecolt-Glaser & others, 2005).

The Delany sisters, both over 100, attributed their longevity to a positive outlook on life.

- Compared with nonprocrastinating students, carefree procrastinators reported lower stress and illness early in a semester but higher stress and illness late in the term. (Which of these students sounds like you?) Overall, the self-defeating procrastinators also were sicker and got lower grades (Tice & Baumeister, 1997).

EXPLANATORY STYLE AND ILLNESS   If uncontrollable stress affects health, depresses immune functioning, and generates a passive, hopeless resignation, then will people who exhibit such pessimism be more vulnerable to illness? Several studies have confirmed that a pessimistic style of explaining bad events (saying, "It's going to last, it's going to undermine everything, and it's my fault") makes illness more likely. Christopher Peterson and Martin Seligman (1987) studied the press quotations of 94 members of baseball's Hall of Fame and gauged how often they offered pessimistic (stable, global, internal) explanations for bad events, such as losing big games. Those who routinely did so tended to die at somewhat younger ages. Optimists—who offered stable, global, and internal explanations for *good* events—usually outlived the pessimists.

Other studies have followed lives through time:

- Harvard graduates who expressed the most optimism in 1946 were the healthiest when restudied 34 years later (Peterson & others, 1988).
- One Dutch research team followed 941 older adults for nearly a decade (Giltay & others, 2004, 2007). Among those in the upper optimism quartile only 30 percent died, compared with 57 percent of those in the lower optimism quartile.
- Catholic nuns who expressed the most positive feelings at an average age of 22 outlived their more dour counterparts by an average 7 years over the ensuing half-century and more (Danner & others, 2001).

It is important to note, however, that healthy behaviors—exercise, good nutrition, not smoking, not drinking to excess—are essential contributors to the longevity of many optimists (Peterson & Bossio, 2000; Whooley & others, 2008).

From their own studies, researchers Howard Tennen and Glenn Affleck (1987) agree that a positive, hopeful explanatory style is generally good medicine. The healing power of positive belief is evident in the well-known *placebo effect*, referring to the healing power of *believing* that one is getting an effective treatment. (If you *think* a treatment is going to be effective, it just may be—even if it's actually inert.)

Tennen and Affleck also remind us that every silver lining has a cloud. Optimists may see themselves as invulnerable and thus fail to take sensible precautions; for example, those who smoke cigarettes optimistically underestimate the risks involved (Segerstrom & others, 1993). And when things go wrong in a big way—when the optimist encounters a devastating illness—adversity can be shattering. Optimism is good for health. But remember: Even optimists have a mortality rate of 100 percent.

Summing Up: What Cognitive Processes Accompany Behavior Problems?

- Social psychologists are actively exploring the attributions and expectations of depressed, lonely, socially anxious, and physically ill people. Depressed people have a *negative explanatory style,* interpreting negative events as being stable, global, and internally caused. Despite their more negative judgments, mildly depressed people in laboratory tests tend to be surprisingly realistic. Depression can be a vicious circle in which negative thoughts elicit self-defeating behaviors and vice versa.

- Loneliness involves feelings of isolation or not fitting in, and is common in individualistic societies. Like depression, it can be a vicious circle in which feelings of aloofness lead to socially undesirable behaviors.

- Most people experience anxiety in situations where they are being evaluated, but shy individuals are extremely prone to anxiety even in friendly, casual situations. This can be another vicious circle in which anxious feelings elicit awkward, off-putting behavior.

- The mushrooming field of health psychology is exploring how people decide they are ill, how they explain their symptoms, and when they seek and follow treatment. It also is exploring the effects of negative emotions and the links among illness, stress, and a pessimistic explanatory style.

What Are Some Social-Psychological Approaches to Treatment?

We have considered patterns of thinking that are linked with problems in living, ranging from serious depression to extreme shyness to physical illness. Do these maladaptive thought patterns suggest any treatments?

There is no social-psychological therapy. But therapy is a social encounter, and social psychologists have suggested how their principles might be integrated into existing treatment techniques (Forsyth & Leary, 1997; Strong & others, 1992). Consider three approaches, discussed below.

Inducing Internal Change through External Behavior

In Chapter 4 we reviewed a broad range of evidence for a simple but powerful principle: Our actions affect our attitudes. The roles we play, the things we say and do, and the decisions we make influence who we are.

Consistent with this attitudes-follow-behavior principle, several psychotherapy techniques prescribe action.

- Behavior therapists try to shape behavior on the theory that the client's inner disposition will also change after the behavior changes.

- In assertiveness training, the individual may first role-play assertiveness in a supportive context, then gradually implement assertive behaviors in everyday life.

- Rational-emotive therapy assumes that we generate our own emotions; clients receive "homework" assignments to talk and act in new ways that will generate new emotions: Challenge that overbearing relative. Stop telling yourself you're an unattractive person and ask someone out.
- Self-help groups subtly induce participants to behave in new ways in front of the group—to express anger, cry, act with high self-esteem, express positive feelings.

All these techniques share a common assumption: If we cannot directly control our feelings by sheer willpower, we can influence them indirectly through our behavior.

Experiments confirm that what we say about ourselves can affect how we feel. In one experiment, students were induced to write self-laudatory essays (Mirels & McPeek, 1977). These students, more than others who wrote essays about a current social issue, later expressed higher self-esteem when rating themselves privately for a different experimenter. In several more experiments, Edward Jones and his associates (1981; Rhodewalt & Agustsdottir, 1986) influenced students to present themselves to an interviewer in either self-enhancing or self-deprecating ways. Again, the public displays—whether upbeat or downbeat—carried over to later self-esteem. Saying is believing, even when we talk about ourselves.

In this experiment and many others, people internalize their behavior most when they perceive some choice. For example, Pamela Mendonca and Sharon Brehm (1983) invited one group of overweight children who were about to begin a weight-loss program to choose the treatment they preferred. Then they reminded them periodically that they had chosen their treatment. Other children who simultaneously experienced the same eight-week program were given no choice. Those who felt responsible for their treatment had lost more weight both at the end of the eight-week program and three months later.

Breaking Vicious Circles

If depression, loneliness, and social anxiety maintain themselves through a vicious circle of negative experiences, negative thinking, and self-defeating behavior, it should be possible to break the circle at any of several points—by changing the environment, by training the person to behave more constructively, by reversing negative thinking. And it is. Several therapy methods help free people from depression's vicious circle.

SOCIAL SKILLS TRAINING

Depression, loneliness, and shyness are not just problems in someone's mind. To be around a depressed person for any length of time can be irritating and depressing. As lonely and shy people suspect, they may indeed come across poorly in social situations. In these cases, social skills training may help. By observing and then practicing new behaviors in safe situations, the person may develop the confidence to behave more effectively in other situations.

As the person begins to enjoy the rewards of behaving more skillfully, a more positive self-perception develops. Frances Haemmerlie and Robert Montgomery (1982, 1984, 1986) demonstrated this in several heartwarming studies with shy, anxious college students. Those who are inexperienced and nervous around those of the other sex may say to themselves, "I don't date much, so I must be socially inadequate, so I shouldn't try reaching out to anyone." To reverse this negative sequence, Haemmerlie and Montgomery enticed such students into pleasant interactions with people of the other sex.

In one experiment, college men completed social anxiety questionnaires and then came to the laboratory on two different days. Each day they enjoyed 12-minute conversations with each of six young women. The men thought the women were also participants. Actually, the women were confederates who had been asked to carry on a natural, positive, friendly conversation with each of the men.

Social skills training: When shy, anxious people first observe, then rehearse, then try out more assertive behaviors in real situations, their social skills often improve.

The effect of these two-and-a-half hours of conversation was remarkable. As one participant wrote afterward, "I had never met so many girls that I could have a good conversation with. After a few girls, my confidence grew to the point where I didn't notice being nervous like I once did." Such comments were supported by a variety of measures. Unlike men in a control condition, those who experienced the conversations reported considerably less female-related anxiety when retested one week and six months later. Placed alone in a room with an attractive female stranger, they also became much more likely to start a conversation. Outside the laboratory they actually began occasional dating.

Haemmerlie and Montgomery note that not only did all this occur without any counseling but also it may very well have occurred *because* there was no counseling. Having behaved successfully on their own, the men could now perceive themselves as socially competent. Although seven months later the researchers did debrief the participants, by that time the men had presumably enjoyed enough social success to maintain their internal attributions for success. "Nothing succeeds like success," concluded Haemmerlie (1987)—"as long as there are no external factors present that the client can use as an excuse for that success!"

EXPLANATORY STYLE THERAPY

The vicious circles that maintain depression, loneliness, and shyness can be broken by social skills training, by positive experiences that alter self-perceptions, *and* by changing negative thought patterns. Some people have good social skills, but their experiences with hypercritical friends and family have convinced them otherwise. For such people it may be enough to help them reverse their negative beliefs about themselves and their futures. Among the cognitive therapies with this aim is an *explanatory style therapy* proposed by social psychologists (Abramson, 1988; Gillham & others, 2000; Greenberg & others, 1992).

One such program taught depressed college students to change their typical attributions. Mary Anne Layden (1982) first explained the advantages of making attributions more like those of the typical nondepressed person (by accepting credit for successes and seeing how circumstances can make things go wrong). After assigning a variety of tasks, she helped the students see how they typically interpreted success and failure. Then came the treatment phase: Layden instructed them to keep a diary of daily successes and failures, noting how they contributed to their own successes and noting external reasons for their failures. When retested after a month of this attributional retraining and compared with an untreated control group, their self-esteem had risen and their attributional style had become more positive. The more their explanatory style improved, the more their depression lifted. By changing their attributions, they had changed their emotions.

Maintaining Change through Internal Attributions for Success

Two of the principles considered so far—that internal change may follow behavior change and that changed self-perceptions and self-attributions can help break a vicious circle—converge on a corollary principle: Once improvement is achieved, it endures best if people attribute it to factors under their own control rather than to a treatment program.

As a rule, coercive techniques trigger the most dramatic and immediate behavior changes (Brehm & Smith, 1986). By making the unwanted behavior extremely costly or embarrassing and the healthier behavior extremely rewarding, a therapist may achieve impressive results. The problem, as 40 years of social-psychological research reminds us, is that coerced changes in behavior soon wane.

Consider the experience of Marta, who is concerned with her mild obesity and frustrated with her inability to do anything about it. Marta is considering several commercial weight-control programs. Each claims it achieves the best results. She chooses one and is ordered onto a strict 1,200-calorie-a-day diet. Moreover, she is required to record and report her calorie intake each day and to come in once a week and be weighed so she and her instructor can know precisely how she is doing. Confident of the program's value and not wanting to embarrass herself, Marta adheres to the program and is delighted to find the unwanted pounds gradually disappearing. "This unique program really does work!" Marta tells herself as she reaches her target weight.

Sadly, however, after graduating from the program, Marta experiences the fate of most weight-control graduates (Jeffery & others, 2000): She regains the lost weight. On the street, she sees her instructor approaching. Embarrassed, she moves to the other side of the sidewalk and looks away. Alas, she is recognized by the instructor, who warmly invites her back into "the program." Admitting that the program achieved good results for her the first time, Marta grants her need of it and agrees to return, beginning a second round of yo-yo dieting.

Marta's experience typifies that of the participants in several weight-control experiments, including one by Janet Sonne and Dean Janoff (1979). Half the participants were led, like Marta, to attribute their changed eating behavior to the program. The others were led to credit their own efforts. Both groups lost weight during the program. But when reweighed 11 weeks later, those in the self-control condition had maintained the weight loss better. These people, like those in the shy-man-meets-women study described earlier, illustrate the benefits of self-efficacy. Having learned to cope successfully and believing that *they did it*, they felt more confident and were more effective.

Having emphasized what changed behavior and thought patterns can accomplish, we do well to remind ourselves of their limits. Social skills training and positive thinking cannot transform us into consistent winners who are loved and admired by everyone. Furthermore, temporary depression, loneliness, and shyness are perfectly appropriate responses to profoundly bad events. It is when such feelings exist chronically and without any discernible cause that there is reason for concern and a need to change the self-defeating thoughts and behaviors.

Using Therapy as Social Influence

Psychologists more and more accept the idea that social influence—one person affecting another—is at the heart of therapy. Stanley Strong (1991) offers a prototypical example: A thirtyish woman comes to a therapist complaining of depression.

The therapist gently probes her feelings and her situation. She explains her helplessness and her husband's demands. Although admiring her devotion, the therapist helps her see how she takes responsibility for her husband's problems. She protests. But the therapist persists. In time, she realizes that her husband may not be as fragile as she presumed. She begins to see how she can respect both her husband and herself. With the therapist, she plans strategies for each new week. At the end of a long stream of reciprocal influences between therapist and client, she emerges no longer depressed and equipped with new ways of behaving.

Early analyses of psychotherapeutic influence focused on how therapists establish credible expertise and trustworthiness and how their credibility enhances their influence (Strong, 1968). Later analyses focused less on the therapist than on how the interaction affects the client's thinking (Cacioppo & others, 1991; McNeill & Stoltenberg, 1988; Neimeyer & others, 1991). Peripheral cues, such as therapist credibility, may open the door for ideas that the therapist can now get the client to think about. But the thoughtful central route to persuasion provides the most enduring attitude and behavior change. Therapists should therefore aim not to elicit a client's superficial agreement with their expert judgment but to change the client's own thinking.

Fortunately, most clients entering therapy are motivated to take the central route—to think deeply about their problems under the therapist's guidance. The therapist's task is to offer arguments and raise questions calculated to elicit favorable thoughts. The therapist's insights matter less than the thoughts they evoke in the client. The therapist needs to put things in ways that a client can hear and understand, comments that will prompt agreement rather than counterargument, and that will allow time and space for the client to reflect. Questions such as "How do you respond to what I just said?" can stimulate the client's thinking.

Martin Heesacker (1989) illustrates with the case of Dave, a 35-year-old male graduate student. Having seen what Dave denied—an underlying substance abuse problem—the counselor drew on his knowledge of Dave, an intellectual person who liked hard evidence, in persuading him to accept the diagnosis and join a treatment-support group. The counselor said, "OK, if my diagnosis is wrong, I'll be glad to change it. But let's go through a list of the characteristics of a substance abuser to check out my accuracy." The counselor then went through each criterion slowly, giving Dave time to think about each point. As he finished, Dave sat back and exclaimed, "I don't believe it: I'm a damned alcoholic."

In his 1620 *Pensées*, the philosopher Pascal foresaw this principle: "People are usually more convinced by reasons they discover themselves than by those found by others." It's a principle worth remembering.

Summing Up: What Are Some Social-Psychological Approaches to Treatment?

- Changes in external behavior can trigger internal change.

- A self-defeating cycle of negative attitudes and behaviors can be broken by training more skillful behavior, by positive experiences that alter self-perceptions, and by changing negative thought patterns.

- Improved states are best maintained after treatment if people attribute their improvement to internal factors under their continued control rather than to the treatment program itself.

- Mental health workers also are recognizing that changing clients' attitudes and behaviors requires persuasion. Therapists, aided by their image as expert, trustworthy communicators, aim to stimulate healthier thinking by offering cogent arguments and raising questions.

How Do Social Relationships Support Health and Well-Being?

There is one other major topic in the social psychology of mental and physical well-being. Supportive close relationships—feeling liked, affirmed, and encouraged by intimate friends and family—predict both health and happiness.

Our relationships are fraught with stress. "Hell is others," wrote Jean-Paul Sartre. When Peter Warr and Roy Payne (1982) asked a representative sample of British adults what, if anything, had emotionally strained them the day before, "family" was their most frequent answer. And stress, as we have seen, aggravates health problems such as coronary heart disease, hypertension, and suppression of our disease-fighting immune system.

Still, on balance, close relationships contribute less to illness than to health and happiness. Asked what prompted yesterday's times of pleasure, the same British sample, by an even larger margin, again answered "family." Close relationships provide our greatest heartaches, but also our greatest joys.

Close Relationships and Health

Eight extensive investigations, each interviewing thousands of people across several years, have reached a common conclusion: Close relationships predict health (Berkman, 1995; Ryff & Singer, 2000). Health risks are greater among lonely people, who often experience more stress, sleep less well, and commit suicide more often (Cacioppo & Patrick, 2008). Compared with those who have few social ties, those who have close relationships with friends, kin, or other members of close-knit religious or community organizations are less likely to die prematurely. Outgoing, affectionate, relationship-oriented people not only have more friends, but also are less susceptible to cold viruses with which an experimenter injects them (Figure 14.6; Cohen & others, 1997, 2003).

Married people also tend to live healthier, longer lives than their unmarried counterparts. The National Center for Health Statistics (2004) reports that people,

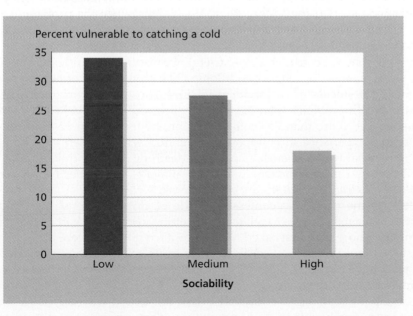

FIGURE :: 14.6

Rate of Colds by Sociability

After a cold virus injection, highly sociable people were less vulnerable to catching colds.

Source: From Cohen & others, 2003.

regardless of age, sex, race, and income, tend to be healthier if married. Married folks experience less pain from headaches and backaches, suffer less stress, and drink and smoke less. One experiment subjected married women to the threat of electric ankle shocks as they lay in an fMRI brain scanning machine (Coan & others, 2006). Meanwhile, some of the women held their husband's hand, some held an anonymous person's hand, and some held no hand at all. While awaiting the shocks, the threat-responsive areas of the women's brains were less active if they held their husband's hand. Consistent with findings that it's happy, supportive marriages that are conducive to health (De Vogli & others, 2007), the soothing hand-holding benefit was greatest for those reporting the happiest marriages.

Giving social support also matters. In one five-year study of 423 elderly married couples, those who gave the most social support (from rides and errands for friends and neighbors to emotional support of their spouse) enjoyed greater longevity, even after controlling for age, sex, initial health, and economic status (Brown & others, 2003). Especially among women, suggests a Finnish study that tracked more than 700 people's illnesses, it is better to give than only to receive (Väänänen & others, 2005).

Moreover, losing social ties heightens the risk of disease.

- A Finnish study of 96,000 newly widowed people found their risk of death doubled in the week following their partner's death (Kaprio & others, 1987).
- A National Academy of Sciences study revealed that recently widowed people become more vulnerable to disease and death (Dohrenwend & others, 1982).
- A study of 30,000 men revealed that when a marriage ends, men drink and smoke more and eat fewer vegetables and more fried foods (Eng & others, 2001).

CONFIDING AND HEALTH

So there is a link between social support and health. Why? Perhaps those who enjoy close relationships eat better, exercise more, and smoke and drink less. Perhaps friends and family help bolster our self-esteem. Perhaps a supportive network helps us evaluate and overcome stressful events (Taylor & others, 1997). In more than 80 studies, social support has been linked with better-functioning cardiovascular and immune systems (Uchino & others, 1996). Thus, when we are wounded by someone's dislike or the loss of a job, a friend's advice, help, and reassurance may indeed be good medicine (Cutrona, 1986; Rook, 1987). Even when the problem isn't mentioned, friends provide us with distraction and a sense that, come what may, we're accepted, liked, and respected.

With someone we consider a close friend, we also may confide painful feelings. In one study, James Pennebaker and Robin O'Heeron (1984) contacted the surviving spouses of suicide or car accident victims. Those who bore their grief alone had more health problems than those who expressed it openly. When Pennebaker (1990) surveyed more than 700 college women, he found 1 in 12 reported a traumatic sexual experience in childhood. Compared with women who had experienced nonsexual traumas, such as parental death or divorce, the sexually abused women reported more headaches, stomach ailments, and other health problems, *especially if they had kept their history of abuse secret.*

To isolate the confiding, confessional side of close relationships, Pennebaker asked the bereaved spouses to relate the upsetting events that had been preying on their minds. Those they first asked to describe a trivial event were physically tense. They stayed tense until they confided their troubles. Then they relaxed. Writing about personal traumas in a diary also seems to help. When volunteers in another experiment did so, they had fewer health problems during the next six months. One participant explained, "Although I have not talked with anyone about what I wrote, I was finally able to deal with it, work through the pain instead of trying

"Friendship is a sovereign antidote against all calamities."
—SENECA, 5 B.C.–A.D. 65

to block it out. Now it doesn't hurt to think about it." Even if it's only "talking to my diary," and even if the writing is about one's future dreams and life goals, it helps to be able to confide (Burton & King, 2008; King, 2001; Lyubomirsky & others, 2006).

Other experiments confirm the benefits of engaging with others rather than suppressing stressful experiences. In one, Stephen Lepore and his colleagues (2000) had students view a stressful slide show and video on the Holocaust and either talk about it immediately afterward or not. Two days later, those who talked were experiencing less stress and fewer intrusive thoughts.

POVERTY, INEQUALITY, AND HEALTH

We have seen connections between health and the feelings of control that accompany a positive explanatory style. And we have seen connections between health and social support. Feelings of control and support together with health care and nutritional factors help explain why economic status correlates with longevity. Recall from Chapter 1 the study of old grave markers in Glasgow, Scotland: Those with the costliest, highest pillars (indicating affluence) tended to have lived the longest (Carroll & others, 1994). Still today, in Scotland, the United States, and Canada, poorer people are at greater risk for premature death. Poverty predicts perishing. Wealthy predicts healthy.

The correlation between poverty and ill health could run either way. Bad health isn't good for one's income. But most evidence indicates that the arrow runs from poverty toward ill health (Sapolsky, 2005). So how *does* poverty "get under the skin"? The answers include (a) reduced access to quality health care, (b) unhealthier lifestyles (smoking is much more common among less educated and lower-income people), and, to a striking extent, (c) increased stress. To be poor is to be at risk for increased stress, negative emotions, and a toxic environment (Adler & Snibbe, 2003; Chen, 2004; Gallo & Matthews, 2003). To be poor is to more often be sleep-deprived after working a second job, earning paychecks that don't cover the bills,

Wealthy and healthy. A 2008 *Scotsman* article illustrated the striking disparity in life expectancy in lower-income Calton, on the east end of Glasgow, and in affluent Lenzie, eight miles away.

commuting on crowded public transit, living in a high-pollution area, and doing hard labor that's controlled by someone else. Even among primates, those with the least control—at the bottom of the social pecking order—are most vulnerable when exposed to a coldlike virus (Cohen & others, 1997).

Poverty and its associated stresses help explain the lower life expectancy of disadvantaged minorities. In the United States, for example, at birth the average White person has a life expectancy of 78 years, the average Black person 73 years (CDC, 2005). Poverty also helps explain a curious but oft-reported correlation between intelligence and health. Edinburgh University researcher Ian Deary (2005) and his colleagues observed this correlation after stumbling across data from an intelligence test administered on June 1, 1932, to virtually all Scots born in 1921. When they searched Scotland's death records, they found, as have researchers in other countries since, that "whether you live to collect your old-age pension depends in part on your IQ at age 11. You just can't keep a good predictor down." Partly, the low-intelligence risk factor—which is roughly equivalent to that of obesity or high blood pressure, he reports—is due to the low-IQ persons having been less likely to cease smoking after its risks became known, and therefore more likely to die of lung cancer. Poverty-related stresses and lack of control also contribute, he notes.

People also die younger in regions with great income inequality (Kawachi & others, 1999; Lynch & others, 1998; Marmot & Wilkinson, 1999). People in Britain and the United States have larger income disparities and lower life expectancies than people in Japan and Sweden. Where inequality has grown over the last decade, as in Eastern Europe and Russia, life expectancy has been at the falling end of the teeter-totter.

Is inequality merely an indicator of poverty? The mixed evidence indicates that poverty matters but that inequality matters, too. John Lynch and his colleagues (1998, 2000) report that people at every income level are at greater risk of early death if they live in a community with great income inequality. It's not just being poor, it's also *feeling* poor, relative to one's surroundings, that proves toxic. And that, Robert Sapolsky (2005) suggests, helps explain why the United States, which has the greatest income inequality of Westernized nations, simultaneously ranks number 1 in the world on health care expenditures and number 29 on life expectancy.

Close Relationships and Happiness

Confiding painful feelings is good not only for the body but for the soul as well. That's the conclusion of studies showing that people are happier when supported by a network of friends and family.

"Woe to him who is alone when he falls and has not another to lift him up."
—*ECCLESIASTES 4:10b*

Some studies, summarized in Chapter 2, compare people in a competitive, individualistic culture, such as the United States, Canada, and Australia, with those in collectivist cultures, such as Japan and many developing countries. Individualistic cultures offer independence, privacy, and pride in personal achievements. Collectivist cultures, with their tighter social bonds, offer protection from loneliness, alienation, divorce, and stress-related diseases.

FRIENDSHIPS AND HAPPINESS

Other studies compare individuals with few or many close relationships. Being attached to friends with whom we can share intimate thoughts has two effects, observed the seventeenth-century philosopher Francis Bacon. "It redoubleth joys, and cutteth griefs in half." So it seems from answers to a question asked of Americans by the National Opinion Research Center: "Looking back over the last six months, who are the people with whom you discussed matters important to you?" Compared with those who could name five or six such intimates, those who could name no such person were twice as likely to report being "not very happy."

Other findings confirm the importance of social networks. Across the life span, friendships foster self-esteem and well-being (Hartup & Stevens, 1997). For example,

- The happiest university students are those who feel satisfied with their love life (Emmons & others, 1983).

- Those who enjoy close relationships cope better with a variety of stresses, including bereavement, rape, job loss, and illness (Abbey & Andrews, 1985; Perlman & Rook, 1987).

- Among 800 alumni of Hobart and William Smith colleges surveyed by Wesley Perkins, those who preferred having very close friends and a close marriage to having a high income and occupational success and prestige were twice as likely as their former classmates to describe themselves as "fairly" or "very" happy (Perkins, 1991). When asked "What is necessary for your happiness?" or "What is it that makes your life meaningful?" most people mention—before anything else—satisfying close relationships with family, friends, or romantic partners (Berscheid, 1985; Berscheid & Peplau, 1983). Happiness hits close to home.

> "The sun looks down on nothing half so good as a household laughing together over a meal."
> —C. S. LEWIS, "MEMBERSHIP," 1949

MARITAL ATTACHMENT AND HAPPINESS

For more than 9 in 10 people worldwide, one eventual example of a close relationship has been marriage. Does marriage correlate positively with happiness? Or is there more happiness in the pleasure-seeking single life than in the "bondage," "chains," and "yoke" of marriage?

A mountain of data reveals that most people are happier attached than unattached. Survey after survey of many tens of thousands of Europeans and Americans has produced a consistent result: Compared with those single or widowed, and especially compared with those divorced or separated, married people report being happier and more satisfied with life (Gove & others, 1990; Inglehart, 1990). In representative surveys of 46,000 Americans since 1972, for example, 23 percent of never-married adults, but 40 percent of married adults, have reported being "very happy". This marriage-happiness link occurs across ethnic groups (Parker & others, 1995). Lesbian couples, too, report greater well-being than those who are alone (Peplau & Fingerhut, 2007). This is but one illustration of what social psychologist Bella DePaulo (2006) documents: There are multiple ways to satisfy the human need to belong. Nevertheless, there are few stronger predictors of happiness than a close, nurturing, equitable, intimate, lifelong companionship with one's best friend.

Is marriage, as is so often supposed, more strongly associated with men's happiness than women's? Given women's greater contribution to household work and to supportive nurturing, we might expect so. The married versus never-married happiness gap, however, is only slightly greater among men than women. In European surveys and in a statistical digest of 93 other studies, the marital happiness gap is virtually identical for men and women (Inglehart, 1990; Wood & others, 1989). Although a bad marriage is often more depressing to a woman than to a man, the myth that single women are happier than married women can be laid to rest. Throughout the Western world, married people of both sexes report more happiness than those never married, divorced, or separated.

More important than being married, however, is the marriage's quality. People who say their marriages are satisfying—who find themselves still in love with their partners—rarely report being unhappy, discontented with life, or depressed. Fortunately, most married people *do* declare their marriages happy ones. In the National Opinion Research Center surveys, almost two-thirds say their marriages are "very happy." Three out of four say their spouses are their best friends. Four out of five people say they would marry the same people again. As a consequence, most such people feel quite happy with life as a whole.

FIGURE :: 14.7

Marital Status and
Depression

A National Institute of Mental
Health survey of psychological
disorders found depression rates
two to four times greater for
adults not married.

Source: Data from Robins &
Regier, 1991, p. 72.

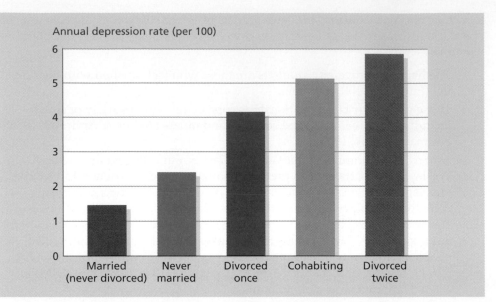

Why are married people generally happier? Does marriage promote happiness, or is it the other way around—does happiness promote marriage? Are happy people more appealing as marriage partners? Do depressed people more often stay single or suffer divorce (Figure 14.7)? Certainly, happy people are more fun to be with. They are also more outgoing, trusting, compassionate, and focused on others (Myers, 1993). Unhappy people, as we have noted, are more often socially rejected. Depression often triggers marital stress, which deepens the depression (Davila & others, 1997). So, positive, happy people do more readily form happy relationships.

But "the prevailing opinion of researchers," reports University of Oslo sociologist Arne Mastekaasa (1995), is that the marriage-happiness connection is "mainly due" to the beneficial effects of marriage. Put on your thinking cap: If the happiest people marry sooner and more often, then as people age (and progressively less happy people move into marriage), the average happiness of both married and never-married people should decline. (The older, less happy newlyweds would pull down the average happiness of married people, and the unmarried group would be more and more left with the unhappy people.) But the data do not support that prediction. This suggests that marital intimacy does—for most people—pay emotional dividends. A Rutgers University team that followed 1,380 New Jersey adults over 15 years concurs (Horwitz & others, 1997). The tendency for married people to be less depressed occurs even after controlling for premarital happiness.

Marriage enhances happiness for at least two reasons. First, married people are more likely to enjoy an enduring, supportive, intimate relationship and are less likely to suffer loneliness. No wonder male medical students in a study by UCLA's Robert Coombs survived medical school with less stress and anxiety if they were married (Coombs, 1991). A good marriage gives each partner a dependable companion, a lover, a friend.

There is a second, more prosaic, reason why marriage promotes happiness, or at least buffers us from misery. Marriage offers the roles of spouse and parent, which can provide additional sources of self-esteem (Crosby, 1987). It is true that multiple roles can multiply stress. Our circuits can and do overload. Yet each role also provides rewards, status, avenues to enrichment, and escape from stress faced in other parts of one's life. A self with many identities is like a mansion with many rooms. When fire struck one wing of Windsor Castle, most of the castle still remained for royals and tourists to enjoy. When our personal identity stands on several legs, it, too, holds up under the loss of any one. If I mess up at work, well, I can tell myself I'm still a good husband and father, and, in the final analysis, these parts of me are what matter most.

Summing Up: How Do Social Relationships Support Health and Well-Being?

- Health and happiness are influenced not only by social cognition but also by social relations. People who enjoy close, supportive relationships are at less risk for illness and premature death. Such relationships help people cope with stress, especially by enabling people to confide their intimate emotions.

- Close relationships also foster happiness. People who have intimate, long-term attachments with friends and family members cope better with loss and report greater happiness. Compared with unmarried adults, those who are married, for example, are much more likely to report being very happy and are at less risk for depression. This appears due both to the greater social success of happy people and to the well-being engendered by a supportive life companion.

POSTSCRIPT: Enhancing Happiness

Several years ago I wrote a book, *The Pursuit of Happiness*, that reported key findings from new research studies of happiness. When the editors wanted to subtitle the book *What Makes People Happy?* I cautioned them: That's not a question this or any book can answer. What we have learned is simply what correlates with—and therefore predicts—happiness. Thus, the book's revised subtitle was *Who Is Happy—and Why?*

Nevertheless, in 400 subsequent media interviews concerning happiness, the most frequent question has been "What can people do to be happy?" Without claiming any easy formula for health and happiness, I assembled 10 research-based points to ponder:

1. *Realize that enduring happiness doesn't come from "making it."* People adapt to changing circumstances—even to wealth or a disability. Thus, wealth is like health: Its utter absence breeds misery, but having it (or any circumstance we long for) doesn't guarantee happiness.

2. *Take control of your time.* Happy people feel in control of their lives, often aided by mastering their use of time. It helps to set goals and break them into daily aims. Although we often overestimate how much we will accomplish in any given day (leaving us frustrated), we generally underestimate how much we can accomplish in a year, given just a little progress every day.

3. *Act happy.* We can sometimes act ourselves into a frame of mind. Manipulated into a smiling expression, people feel better; when they scowl, the whole world seems to scowl back. So put on a happy face. Talk as if you feel positive self-esteem, are optimistic, and are outgoing. Going through the motions can trigger the emotions.

4. *Seek work and leisure that engage your skills.* Happy people often are in a zone called "flow"—absorbed in a task that challenges them without overwhelming them. The most expensive forms of leisure (sitting on a yacht) often provide less flow experience than gardening, socializing, or craft work.

5. *Join the "movement" movement.* An avalanche of research reveals that aerobic exercise not only promotes health and energy but also is an antidote for mild depression and anxiety. Sound minds reside in sound bodies.

6. *Give your body the sleep it wants.* Happy people live active, vigorous lives yet reserve time for renewing sleep and solitude. Many people suffer from a sleep debt, with resulting fatigue, diminished alertness, and gloomy moods.

7. *Give priority to close relationships.* Intimate friendships with those who care deeply about you can help you weather difficult times. Confiding is good for soul and body. Resolve to nurture your closest relationships: to *not* take those closest to you for granted, to display to them the sort of kindness that you display to others, to affirm them, to share, and to play together. To rejuvenate your affections, resolve in such ways to *act* lovingly.

8. *Focus beyond the self.* Reach out to those in need. Happiness increases helpfulness. (Those who feel good do good.) But doing good also makes one feel good.

9. *Keep a gratitude journal.* Those who pause each day to reflect on some positive aspect of their lives (their health, friends, family, freedom, education, senses, natural surroundings, and so on) experience heightened well-being.

10. *Nurture your spiritual self.* For many people, faith provides a support community, a reason to focus beyond self, and a sense of purpose and hope. Study after study finds that actively religious people are happier and that they cope better with crises.

Making the Social Connection

In this chapter we discussed moods and mood disorders. How does spending time alone affect our moods? And is negative thinking a cause of depression, or one of its effects? View the videos on the Online Learning Center for this book and consider these questions.

CHAPTER

15

Social Psychology in Court

> "A courtroom is a battleground where lawyers compete for the minds of jurors."
>
> —James Randi, 1999

It was the most publicized criminal case in human history: Football hero, actor, and broadcaster O. J. Simpson was accused of brutally murdering his estranged wife and her male acquaintance. The evidence was compelling, the prosecution argued. Simpson's behavior fit a long-standing pattern of spouse abuse and threats of violence. Blood tests confirmed that his blood was at the crime scene and his victim's blood was on his glove, his car, even on a sock in his bedroom. His travels the night of the murder and the way he fled when arrest was imminent were, prosecutors said, additional indicators of his guilt.

Simpson's defense attorneys responded that racial prejudice may have motivated the officer who allegedly found the bloody glove at Simpson's estate. Moreover, they said, Simpson could not receive a fair trial. Would the jurors—10 of whom were women—be kindly disposed to a man alleged to have abused and murdered a woman? And how likely was it that jurors could heed the judge's instructions to ignore prejudicial pretrial publicity?

The case raised other questions that have been examined in social-psychological experiments:

- There were no eyewitnesses to this crime. How influential is eyewitness testimony? How trustworthy are eyewitness recollections? What makes a credible witness?

- Simpson was handsome, rich, famous, and widely admired. Can jurors ignore, as they should, a defendant's attractiveness and social status?

- How well do jurors comprehend important information, such as statistical probabilities involved in DNA blood tests?

- The jury in the criminal case was composed mostly of women and Blacks, but it also included two men, one Hispanic, and two non-Hispanic Whites. In the follow-up civil trial, in which Simpson was sued for damages, the jury had nine Whites. Do jurors' characteristics bias their verdicts? If so, can lawyers use the jury selection process to stack a jury in their favor?

- In cases such as this, a 12-member jury deliberates before delivering a verdict. During deliberations, how do jurors influence one another? Can a minority win over the majority? Do 12-member juries reach the same decisions as 6-member juries?

Such questions fascinate lawyers, judges, and defendants. And they are questions to which social psychology can suggest answers, as law schools have recognized by hiring professors of "law and social science" and as trial lawyers have recognized when hiring psychological consultants.

We can think of a courtroom as a miniature social world, one that magnifies everyday social processes with major consequences for those involved. In criminal cases, psychological factors may influence decisions involving arrest, interrogation, prosecution, plea bargaining, sentencing, and parole. Whether a case reaches a jury verdict or not, the social dynamics of the courtroom matter. Let's therefore consider two sets of factors that have been heavily researched: (1) *eyewitness testimony* and its influence on judgments of a defendant, and (2) characteristics of *jurors* as individuals and as a group.

"What are you—some kind of justice freak?"

How Reliable Is Eyewitness Testimony?

As the courtroom drama unfolds, jurors hear testimony, form impressions of the defendant, listen to instructions from the judge, and render a verdict. Let's take these steps one at a time, starting with eyewitness testimony.

Although never in trouble with the law, Kirk Bloodsworth was convicted for the sexual assault and slaying of a 9-year-old girl after five eyewitnesses identified him at his trial. During his two years on death row and seven more under a sentence of life imprisonment, he maintained his innocence. Then DNA testing proved it was not his semen on the girl's underwear. Released from prison, he still lived under a cloud of doubt until in 2003, 19 years after his death sentence, DNA testing identified the actual killer (Wells & others, 2006).

The Power of Persuasive Eyewitnesses

In Chapter 3 we noted that vivid anecdotes and personal testimonies can be powerfully persuasive, often more so than compelling but abstract information. There's no better way to end an argument than to say, "I saw it with my own eyes!"

Memory researcher Elizabeth Loftus (1974, 1979) found that those who had "seen" were indeed believed, even when their testimony was shown to be useless. When students were presented with a hypothetical robbery-murder case with circumstantial evidence but no eyewitness testimony, only 18 percent voted for conviction. Other students received the same information but with the addition of a single eyewitness. Now, knowing that someone had declared, "That's the one!" 72 percent voted for conviction. For a third group, the defense attorney discredited that testimony (the witness had 20/400 vision and was not wearing glasses). Did that discrediting reduce the effect of the testimony? In this case, not much: 68 percent still voted for conviction.

Later experiments revealed that discrediting may reduce somewhat the number of guilty votes (Whitley, 1987). But unless contradicted by another eyewitness, a vivid eyewitness account is difficult to erase from jurors' minds (Leippe, 1985). That helps explain why, compared with criminal cases lacking eyewitness testimony (such as the O. J. case), those that have eyewitness testimony (such as the Bloodsworth case) are more likely to produce convictions (Visher, 1987).

Can't jurors spot erroneous testimony? To find out, Gary Wells, R. C. L. Lindsay, and their colleagues staged hundreds of eyewitnessed thefts of a calculator at the University of Alberta. Afterward, they asked each eyewitness to identify the culprit from a photo lineup. Other people, acting as jurors, observed the eyewitnesses being questioned and then evaluated their testimony. Are incorrect eyewitnesses believed less often than those who are accurate? As it happened, both correct and incorrect eyewitnesses were believed 80 percent of the time (Wells &

"As it turned out, my battery of lawyers was no match for their battery of eyewitnesses."

The innocent James Newsome (left) mistakenly identified by eyewitnesses, and the actual culprit (right).

others, 1979). That led the researchers to speculate that "human observers have absolutely no ability to discern eyewitnesses who have mistakenly identified an innocent person" (Wells & others, 1980).

In a follow-up experiment, Lindsay, Wells, and Carolyn Rumpel (1981) staged the theft under conditions that sometimes allowed witnesses a good long look at the thief and sometimes didn't. The jurors believed the witnesses more when conditions were good. But even when conditions were so poor that two-thirds of the witnesses had actually misidentified an innocent person, 62 percent of the jurors still usually believed the witnesses.

Wells and Michael Leippe (1981) found that jurors are more skeptical of eyewitnesses whose memory of trivial details is poor—though these tend to be the most *accurate* witnesses. Jurors think a witness who can remember that there were three pictures hanging in the room must have "really been paying attention" (Bell & Loftus, 1988, 1989). Actually, those who pay attention to surrounding details are *less* likely to attend to the culprit's face.

The persuasive power of three eyewitnesses sent Chicagoan James Newsome, who had never been arrested before, to prison on a life sentence for supposedly gunning down a convenience store owner. Fifteen years later he was released, after fingerprint technology revealed the real culprit to be Dennis Emerson, a career criminal who was three inches taller and had longer hair (*Chicago Tribune*, 2002).

When Eyes Deceive

Is eyewitness testimony often inaccurate? Stories abound of innocent people who have wasted years in prison because of the testimony of eyewitnesses who were sincerely wrong (Brandon & Davies, 1973; Doyle, 2005; Wells & others, 2006). Seventy years ago, Yale law professor Edwin Borchard (1932) documented 65 convictions of people whose innocence was later proven (and who were released after receiving clemency or being acquitted after a new trial). Most resulted from mistaken identifications, and some were narrowly saved from execution. In modern times, among the first 130 convictions overturned by DNA evidence, 78 percent were wrongful convictions influenced by mistaken eyewitnesses (Stambor, 2006). Another analysis estimated that 0.5 percent of 1.5 million American criminal convictions each year err, with roughly 4,500 of these 7,500 wrongful convictions based on mistaken identification (Cutler & Penrod, 1995).

To assess the accuracy of eyewitness recollections, we need to learn their overall rates of "hits" and "misses." One way for researchers to gather such information is to stage crimes comparable to those in everyday life and then solicit eyewitness reports.

Over the last century this has been done many times in Europe and elsewhere, sometimes with disconcerting results (Sporer, 2008). For example, at California State University, Hayward, 141 students witnessed an "assault" on a professor. Seven weeks later, when Robert Buckhout (1974) asked them to identify the assailant from a group of six photographs, 60 percent chose an innocent person. No wonder eyewitnesses to actual crimes sometimes disagree about what they saw. Later studies have confirmed that eyewitnesses often are more confident than correct. For example, Brian Bornstein and Douglas Zickafoose (1999) found that students felt, on average, 74 percent sure of their later recollections of a classroom visitor but were only 55 percent correct.

"Certitude is not the test of certainty."

—*OLIVER WENDELL HOLMES,*
COLLECTED LEGAL PAPERS

Three studies of live lineups conducted in England and Wales show remarkable consistency. Roughly 40 percent of witnesses identified the suspect. Forty percent made no identification. And, despite having been cautioned that the person they witnessed might not be in the lineup, 20 percent made a mistaken identification (Valentine & others, 2003).

FIGURE :: 15.1

Sometimes Believing Is Seeing

Cultural expectations affect perceiving, remembering, and reporting. In a 1947 experiment on rumor transmission, Gordon Allport and Leo Postman showed people this picture of a White man holding a razor blade and then had them tell a second person about it, who then told a third person, and so on. After six tellings, the razor blade in the White man's hand usually shifted to the Black man's.

Source: Allport, G. W. and L. Postman, Figure from *The Psychology of Rumor* by Gordon W. Allport and Leo Postman, copyright © 1947 and renewed 1975 by the Estate of Gordon Allport. Illustration copyright © Graphic Presentation Services. Reprinted by permission of Robert Allport.

Eyewitness recall of detail is sometimes impressive. When John Yuille and Judith Cutshall (1986) studied accounts of a midafternoon murder on a busy Burnaby, British Columbia, street, they found that eyewitnesses' recall for detail was 80 percent accurate.

Of course, some witnesses are more confident than others. Wells and his colleagues report (2002, 2006) that it's the confident witnesses whom jurors find most believable. Unless their credibility is punctured by an obvious error, confident witnesses seem more credible (Tenney & others, 2007). In the convictions overturned by DNA evidence, the eyewitnesses proved persuasive because of their great but mistaken confidence in their identifications of the perpetrator. So it is disconcerting that unless conditions are very favorable, as when the culprit is very distinctive-looking, the certainty of witnesses often bears only a modest relation to their accuracy. Yet some people—whether right or wrong—chronically express themselves more assertively. And that, says Michael Leippe (1994), explains why mistaken eyewitnesses are so often persuasive.

This finding would surely come as a surprise to members of the 1972 U.S. Supreme Court. In a judgment that established the position of the U.S. judiciary system regarding eyewitness identifications, the Court, we now realize, goofed. It declared that among the factors to be considered in determining accuracy is "the level of certainty demonstrated by the witness" (Wells & Murray, 1983).

Errors sneak into our perceptions and our memories because our minds are not videotape machines. Many errors are quite understandable, as revealed by "change blindness" experiments in which people fail to detect that an innocent person entering a scene differs from another person exiting the scene (Davis & others, 2008). People are quite good at recognizing a pictured face when later shown the same picture alongside a new face. But University of Stirling face researcher Vicki Bruce (1998) was surprised to discover that subtle differences in views, expressions, or lighting "are hard for human vision to deal with." We construct our memories based partly on what we perceived at the time and partly on our expectations, beliefs, and current knowledge (Figures 15.1 and 15.2).

The strong emotions that accompany witnessed crimes and traumas may further corrupt eyewitness memories. In one experiment, visitors wore heart rate monitors while in the London Dungeon's Horror Labyrinth. Those exhibiting the most emotion later made the most mistakes in identifying someone they had encountered (Valentine & Mesout, 2009).

Charles Morgan and his team of Yale colleagues and military psychologists (2004) documented the effect of stress on memory with more than 500 soldiers at survival schools—mock prisoner of war camps that were training the soldiers to withstand deprivation of food and sleep, combined with intense, confrontational interrogation, resulting in a high heart rate and a flood of stress hormones. A day after release from the camp, when the participants were asked to identify their intimidating

FIGURE :: 15.2

Expectations Affect
Perception

Is the drawing on the far right a
face or figure?

Source: From Fisher, 1968,
adapted by Loftus, 1979b. Drawing by Anne Canevari Green.

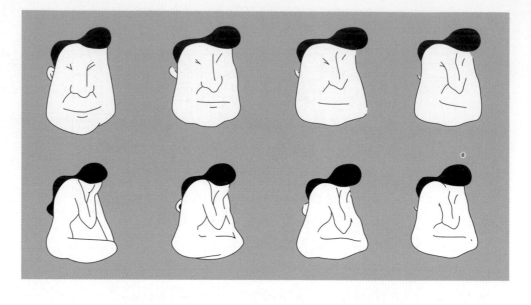

*Recall from Chapter 9
the "own-race bias"—the
tendency to more accurately
recognize faces of one's own
race.*

interrogators from a 15-person lineup, only 30 percent could do so, although 62 percent could recall a low-stress interrogator. Thus, concluded the researchers, "contrary
to the popular conception that most people would never forget the face of a clearly
seen individual who had physically confronted them and threatened them for more
than 30 minutes, [many] were unable to correctly identify their perpetrator." As
illustrated in "Focus On: Eyewitness Testimony," we are most at risk for false recollections made with high confidence with faces of another race (Brigham & others,
2006; Meissner & others, 2005).

The Misinformation Effect

Elizabeth Loftus and her associates (1978) provided a dramatic demonstration of
memory construction. They showed University of Washington students 30 slides
depicting successive stages of an automobile-pedestrian accident. One critical slide
showed a red Datsun stopped at a stop sign or a yield sign. Afterward they asked
half the students, among other questions, "Did another car pass the red Datsun
while it was stopped at the stop sign?" They asked the other half the same question, but with the words "stop sign" replaced by "yield sign." Later, all viewed
both slides in Figure 15.3 and recalled which one they had seen previously. Those
who had been asked the question consistent with what they had seen were 75 percent correct. Those previously asked the misleading question were only 41 percent
correct; more often than not, they denied seeing what they had actually seen and
instead "remembered" the picture they had never seen!

misinformation effect
Incorporating "misinformation"
into one's memory of the event
after witnessing an event
and receiving misleading
information about it.

In other studies of this **misinformation effect,** Loftus (1979a, 1979b, 2001) found
that after suggestive questions, witnesses may believe that a red light was actually
green or that a robber had a mustache when he didn't. When questioning eyewitnesses, police and attorneys commonly ask questions framed by their own understanding of what happened. So it is troubling to discover how easily witnesses
incorporate misleading information into their memories, especially when they
believe the questioner is well informed and when suggestive questions are repeated
(Smith & Ellsworth, 1987; Zaragoza & Mitchell, 1996).

It also is troubling to realize that false memories feel and look like real memories.
They can be as persuasive as real memories—convincingly sincere, yet sincerely
wrong. This is true of young children (who are especially susceptible to misinformation) as well as adults. Stephen Ceci and Maggie Bruck (1993a, 1993b, 1995) demonstrated children's suggestibility by telling children, once a week for 10 weeks,
"Think real hard, and tell me if this ever happened to you." For example, "Can you
remember going to the hospital with the mousetrap on your finger?" Remarkably,

focus
ON   Eyewitness Testimony

In 1984, I was a 22-year-old college student with a perfect GPA and a bright future. One dark night someone broke into my apartment, put a knife to my throat, and raped me.

During my ordeal I was determined that if, by the grace of God, I should live, I was going to make sure that my rapist was caught and punished. My mind quickly separated me from my body and began recording every detail of my attacker. I carefully studied his face: noting his hairline, his brow, his chin. I listened hard to his voice, his speech, his words. I looked for scars, for tattoos, for anything that would help me identify him. Then, after what seemed like an eternity, and in a brief moment when my rapist let down his guard, I fled from my apartment in the early morning wrapped only in a blanket. I had survived.

Later that day I began the painstaking process of trying to bring my attacker to justice. For hours I sat with a police artist and meticulously looked through books filled with hundreds of noses, eyes, eyebrows, hairlines, nostrils, and lips—reliving the attack again and again in the minute details that together made up his composite sketch. The next day the newspaper carried my rapist's image on the front page. There was a lead. The case had its first suspect. Several days later I sat before a series of photographs and picked out my attacker. I got him. I knew he was the man. I was completely confident. I was sure.

When the case went to trial six months later, I took the witness stand, put my hand on the Bible, and swore to "tell the whole truth and nothing but the truth." Based on my eyewitness testimony Ronald Junior Cotton was sentenced to prison for life. Ronald Cotton was never going see the light of day again. Ronald Cotton would never rape another woman again.

During a 1987 retrial hearing the defense brought forward another inmate, Bobby Poole, who had bragged of raping me. In court, he denied raping me. When asked if I had ever seen this man, I emphatically answered that I had never seen him before in my life. Another victim agreed. Ronald Cotton was resentenced to two life sentences with no chance for parole.

In 1995, 11 years after I had first identified Ronald Cotton as my rapist, I was asked if I would consent to a blood sample so that DNA tests could be run on evidence from the rape. I agreed because I knew that Ronald Cotton had raped me and DNA was only going to confirm that. That test would put to rest any future appeals brought on Cotton's behalf.

I will never forget the day I learned the DNA results. I stood in my kitchen as the detective and district attorney told me: "Ronald Cotton didn't rape you. It was Bobby Poole." Their words struck me like a thunderbolt. The man I was convinced I never saw before in my life was the man who held a knife to my throat, who hurt me, who raped me, who crushed my spirit, who robbed me of my soul. The man I was positive did all those things and whose face continued to haunt me at night was innocent.

Ronald Cotton was released from prison after serving 11 years, becoming the first convicted felon in North Carolina exonerated through DNA testing. Bobby Poole, serving a life sentence of his own and dying of cancer, confessed to the rapes without remorse.

Ronald Cotton and I now shared something in the brutal crime that had pitted us against each other for years—we were both victims. My part in his conviction, though, filled me with guilt and shame. We were the same age, so I knew what he had missed during those 11 years in prison. I had had the opportunity to move on and begin to heal. To graduate from college. To find trust and love in marriage. To find self-confidence in work. And to find the hope of a bright future in the gifts of my beautiful children. Ronald Cotton, on the other hand, spent those years alone defending himself from the violence that punctuated his life in prison.

Sometime after Ronald Cotton's release I requested a meeting through our attorneys so that I might say I was sorry and seek his forgiveness. In the end, Ron and I finally found total freedom through forgiveness. I will forever look back now through our unlikely friendship, thankful that in Ron's case of mistaken identity, I wasn't dead wrong.

Jennifer Thompson talks with Ronald Cotton after his release.

Jennifer Thompson,
North Carolina, USA

FIGURE :: 15.3

The Misinformation Effect

When shown one of these two pictures and then asked a question suggesting the sign from the other photo, most people later "remembered" seeing the sign they had never actually seen.

Source: From Loftus, Miller, & Burns, 1978. Photos courtesy of Elizabeth Loftus.

when later interviewed by a new adult who asked the same question, 58 percent of preschoolers produced false and often detailed stories about the fictitious event. One boy explained that his brother had pushed him into a basement woodpile, where his finger got stuck in the trap. "And then we went to the hospital, and my mommy, daddy, and Colin drove me there, to the hospital in our van, because it was far away. And the doctor put a bandage on this finger."

Given such vivid stories, professional psychologists were often fooled. They could not reliably separate real from false memories—nor could the children. Told the incident never actually happened, some protested. "But it really did happen. I remember it!" For Bruck and Ceci (1999, 2004), such findings raise the possibility of false accusations, as in alleged child sex abuse cases where children's memories may have been contaminated by repeated suggestive questioning and where there is no corroborating evidence. Given suggestive interview questions, Bruck and Ceci report, most preschoolers and many older children will produce false reports such as seeing a thief steal food in their day-care center.

Even among American and British university students, imagining childhood events, such as breaking a window with their hand or having a nurse remove a skin sample, led one-fourth to recall that the imagined event actually happened (Garry

& others, 1996; Mazzoni & Memom, 2003). This "imagination inflation" happens partly because visualizing something activates similar areas in the brain as does actually experiencing it (Gonsalves & others, 2004).

Retelling

Retelling events commits people to their recollections, accurate or not. An accurate retelling helps them later resist misleading suggestions (Bregman & McAllister, 1982). Other times, the more we retell a story, the more we convince ourselves of a false-hood. Wells, Ferguson, and Lindsay (1981) demonstrated this by having eyewitnesses to a staged theft rehearse their answers to questions before taking the witness stand. Doing so increased the confidence of those who were wrong and thus made jurors who heard their false testimony more likely to convict the innocent person.

In Chapter 4 we noted that we often adjust what we say to please our listeners. Moreover, having done so, we come to believe the altered message. Imagine witnessing an argument that erupts into a fight in which one person injures the other. Afterward, the injured party sues. Before the trial, a smooth lawyer for one of the two parties interviews you. Might you slightly adjust your testimony, giving a version of the fight that supports this lawyer's client? If you did so, might your later recollections in court be similarly slanted?

Blair Sheppard and Neil Vidmar (1980) report that the answer to both questions is yes. At the University of Western Ontario, they had some students serve as witnesses to a fight and others as lawyers and judges. When interviewed by lawyers for the defendant, the witnesses later gave the judge testimony that was more favorable to the defendant. In a follow-up experiment, Vidmar and Nancy Laird (1983) noted that witnesses did not omit important facts from their testimony; they just changed their tone of voice and choice of words depending on whether they thought they were witnesses for the defendant or for the plaintiff. Even this was enough to bias the impressions of those who heard the testimony. So it's not only suggestive questions that can distort eyewitness recollections but also their own retellings, which may be adjusted subtly to suit their audience.

Reducing Error

Given these error-prone tendencies, what constructive steps can be taken to increase the accuracy of eyewitnesses and jurors? Former U.S. Attorney General Janet Reno wondered, as had Canada's Law Reform Commission a decade earlier, and she invited Gary Wells to share suggestions. Afterward, the Department of Justice convened a panel of researchers, attorneys, and law enforcement officers to hammer out *Eyewitness Evidence: A Guide for Law Enforcement* (Technical Working Group, 1999; Wells & others, 2000). Their suggestions parallel many of those from a recent Canadian review of eyewitness identification procedures (Yarmey, 2003a). They include ways to (a) train police interviewers and (b) administer lineups. Doing so supports a "forensic science of mind." It seeks to preserve rather than contaminate the eyewitness memory aspect of the crime scene.

> "Witnesses probably ought to be taking a more realistic oath: 'Do you swear to tell the truth, the whole truth, or whatever it is you think you remember?'"
>
> —ELIZABETH F. LOFTUS, "MEMORY IN CANADIAN COURTS OF LAW," 2003

TRAIN POLICE INTERVIEWERS

When Ronald Fisher and his co-workers (1987, 1989) examined tape-recorded interviews of eyewitnesses conducted by experienced Florida police detectives, they found a typical pattern. Following an open-ended beginning ("Tell me what you recall"), the detectives would occasionally interrupt with follow-up questions, including questions eliciting terse answers ("How tall was he?").

The *Eyewitness Evidence* guide instructs interviewers to begin by allowing eye-witnesses to offer their own unprompted recollections. The recollections will be most complete if the interviewer jogs the memory by first guiding people to recon-struct the setting. Have them visualize the scene and what they were thinking and feeling at the time. Even showing pictures of the setting—of, say, the store checkout

research CLOSE-UP

Feedback to Witnesses

Eyewitness to a crime on viewing a lineup: "Oh, my God . . . I don't know . . . It's one of those two . . . but I don't know . . . Oh, man . . . the guy a little bit taller than number two . . . It's one of those two, but I don't know. . . ."

Months later at trial: "You were positive it was number two? It wasn't a maybe?"

Eyewitness's answer: "There was no maybe about it . . . I was absolutely positive."

(*Missouri v. Hutching,* 1994, reported by Wells & Bradfield, 1998)

What explains witnesses misrecalling their original uncertainty? Gary Wells and Amy Bradfield (1998, 1999) wondered. Research had shown that one's confidence gains a boost from (a) learning that another witness has fingered the same person, (b) being asked the same question repeatedly, and (c) preparing for cross-examination (Lüüs & Wells, 1994; Shaw, 1996; Wells & others, 1981). Might the lineup interviewer's feedback also influence not just confidence but also recollections of earlier confidence ("I knew it all along")?

To find out, Wells and Bradfield conducted two experiments in which 352 Iowa State University students viewed a grainy security camera video of a man entering a store. Moments later, off camera, he murders a security guard. The students then viewed the photo spread from the actual criminal case, minus the gunman's photo, and were asked to identify the gunman. All 352 students made a false identification, following which the experimenter gave confirming feedback ("Good. You identified the actual suspect"), disconfirming feedback ("Actually, the suspect was number____"), or no feedback. Finally, all were later asked, "At the time that you identified the person in the photo spread, how certain were you that the person you identified from the photos was the gunman that you saw in the video?" (from 1, not at all certain, to 7, totally certain).

The experiment produced two striking results: First, the effect of the experimenter's casual comment was huge. In the confirming feedback condition, 58 percent of the eyewitnesses rated their certainty as 6 or 7 when making their initial judgments—4 times the 14 percent who said the same in the no-feedback condition and 11 times the 5 percent in the disconfirming condition. We shouldn't be surprised that witnesses' postfeedback confidence would be raised by confirming feedback, but those were their recollections of how confident they felt *before* they received any feedback.

It wasn't obvious to the participants that their judgments were affected, for the second rather amazing finding is that

FIGURE :: 15.4

Recalled Certainty of Eyewitnesses' False Identification after Receiving Confirming or Disconfirming Feedback (Experiment 2)

Note that participants who said feedback did not influence them were influenced no less.

Source: Data from Wells & Bradfield, 1998.

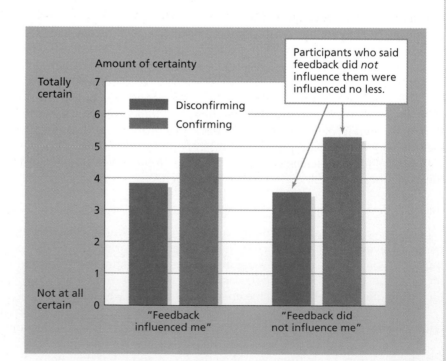

when asked if the feedback had influenced their answers, 58 percent said no. Moreover, as a group, those who felt uninfluenced were influenced just as much as those who said they were (Figure 15.4).

This phenomenon—increased witness confidence after supportive feedback—is both big and reliable enough, across many studies, to have gained a name: the *post-identification feedback effect* (Douglass & Steblay, 2006; Jones & others, 2008; Wright & Skagerberg, 2007). It is understandable that eyewitnesses would be curious about the accuracy of their recollections, and that interrogators would want to satisfy their curiosity ("you did identify the actual suspect"). But the possible later effect of inflated eyewitness confidence points to the need to keep interrogators blind (ignorant) of which person is the suspect.

The inability of eyewitnesses to appreciate the post-identification feedback effect points to a lesson that runs deeper than jury research. Once again we see why we need social-psychological research. As social psychologists have so often found—recall Milgram's obedience experiments—simply asking people how they would act, or asking what explains their actions, sometimes gives us wrong answers. Benjamin Franklin was right: "There are three things extremely hard, Steel, a Diamond, and to know one's self." That is why we need not only to do surveys that ask people to explain themselves but also experiments in which we see what they actually do.

lane with a clerk standing where she was robbed—can promote accurate recall (Cutler & Penrod, 1988). After giving witnesses ample, uninterrupted time to report everything that comes to mind, the interviewer then jogs their memory with evocative questions ("Was there anything unusual about the voice? Was there anything unusual about the person's appearance or clothing?").

When Fisher and his colleagues (1989, 1994) trained detectives to question in this way, the information they elicited from eyewitnesses increased 50 percent without increasing the false memory rate. A later statistical summary of 42 studies confirmed that this "cognitive interview" substantially increases details recalled, with no loss in accuracy (Kohnken & others, 1999). In response to such results, most police agencies in North America and all of them in England and Wales have adopted the cognitive interview procedure (Geiselman, 1996; Kebbell & others, 1999). The FBI now includes the procedure in its training program (Bower, 1997). (The procedure also shows promise for enhancing information gathered in oral histories and medical surveys.)

Interviewers on memory reconnaissance missions must be careful to keep their questions free of hidden assumptions. Loftus and Guido Zanni (1975) found that questions such as "Did you see the broken headlight?" triggered twice as many "memories" of nonexistent events as did questions without the hidden assumption: "Did you see a broken headlight?"

Flooding eyewitnesses with an array of mug shots also reduces accuracy in later identifying the culprit (Brigham & Cairns, 1988). Errors are especially likely when the witness has to stop, think, and analytically compare faces. Witnesses who help build a face composite later have more difficulty identifying the actual face from a lineup (Wells & others, 2005). Verbally describing a robber's face also disrupts later recognition of it from a photographic lineup. Some researchers think this "verbal overshadowing" occurs because one's memory for the face accommodates the verbal depiction; others believe that the word-based description replaces the unconscious perception or makes it inaccessible (Fallshore & Schooler, 1995; Meissner & others, 2001; Schooler, 2002).

Accurate identifications tend to be automatic and effortless. The right face just pops out (Dunning & Stern, 1994). In studies by David Dunning and Scott Perretta (2002), eyewitnesses who make their identifications in less than 10 to 12 seconds were nearly 90 percent accurate; those taking longer were only about 50 percent accurate. Although other studies challenge a neat 10- to 12-second rule, they confirm that quicker identifications are generally more accurate (Weber & others, 2004). For example, when Tim Valentine and his co-workers (2003) analyzed 640 eyewitness viewings of London police lineups they, too, found that nearly 9 in 10 "fast" identifications were of the actual suspect, as were fewer than 4 in 10 slower identifications.

THE FAR SIDE® By GARY LARSON

"That's him! That's the one! ... I'd recognize that silly little hat anywhere!"

Lineup fairness? From the suspect's perspective a lineup is fair, note John Brigham, David Ready, and Stacy Spier (1990), when "the other lineup members are reasonably similar in general appearance to the suspect."

Younger eyewitnesses, and those who had viewed the culprit for more than a minute, were also more accurate than older eyewitnesses and those who had less than a minute's exposure.

MINIMIZE FALSE LINEUP IDENTIFICATIONS

The case of Ron Shatford illustrates how the composition of a police lineup can promote misidentification (Doob & Kirshenbaum, 1973). After a suburban Toronto department store robbery, the cashier involved could recall only that the culprit was not wearing a tie and was "very neatly dressed and rather good looking." When police put the good-looking Shatford in a lineup with 11 unattractive men, all of whom wore ties, the cashier readily identified him as the culprit. Only after he had served 15 months of a long sentence did another person confess, allowing Shatford to be retried and found not guilty.

Gary Wells (1984, 1993, 2005, 2008) and the *Eyewitness Evidence* guide report that one way to reduce misidentifications is to remind witnesses that the person they saw may or may not be in the lineup. Alternatively, give eyewitnesses a "blank" lineup that contains no suspects and screen out those who make false identifications. Those who do not make such errors turn out to be more accurate when they later face the actual lineup.

Dozens of studies in Europe, North America, Australia, and South Africa show that mistakes also subside when witnesses simply make individual yes or no judgments in response to a *sequence* of people (Lindsay & Wells, 1985; Meissner & others, 2005; Steblay & others, 2001). A simultaneous lineup tempts people to pick the person who, among the lineup members, most resembles the perpetrator. Witnesses viewing just one suspect at a time are less likely to make false identifications. If witnesses view a group of photos or people simultaneously, they are more likely to choose whoever most resembles the culprit. (When not given a same-race lineup, witnesses may pick someone of the culprit's race, especially when it's a different race from their own [Wells & Olson, 2001].) With a "sequential lineup," eyewitnesses compare each person with their memory of the culprit and make an absolute decision—match or no-match (Gronlund, 2004a, 2004b).

These no-cost procedures make police lineups more like good experiments. They contain a *control group* (a no-suspect lineup or a lineup in which mock witnesses try to guess the suspect based merely on a general description). They have an experimenter who is *blind* to the hypothesis (and who therefore won't welcome an expected identification while asking "Might it be anyone else?" in response to a different identification). Questions are *scripted and neutral,* so they don't subtly demand a particular response (the procedure doesn't imply the culprit is in the lineup). And they prohibit confidence-inflating post-lineup comments ("you got him") prior to trial testimony. Such procedures greatly reduce the natural human confirmation bias (having an idea and seeking confirming evidence). Lineups can also now be effectively administered by computers (MacLin & others, 2005).

Although procedures such as double-blind testing are common in psychological science, they are still uncommon in criminal procedures (Wells & Olson, 2003). But

TABLE :: 15.1 Influences on Eyewitness Testimony

Phenomenon	Eyewitness Experts Agreeing*	Jurors Agreeing*
Question wording. An eyewitness's testimony about an event can be affected by how the questions put to that eyewitness are worded.	98%	85%
Lineup instructions. Police instructions can affect an eyewitness's willingness to make an identification.	98%	41%
Confidence malleability. An eyewitness's confidence can be influenced by factors that are unrelated to identification accuracy.	95%	50%
Mug-shot-induced bias. Exposure to mug shots of a suspect increases the likelihood that the witness will later choose that suspect in a lineup.	95%	59%
Postevent information. Eyewitnesses' testimony about an event often reflects not only what they actually saw but also information they obtained later on.	94%	60%
Attitudes and expectations. An eyewitness's perception and memory of an event may be affected by his or her attitudes and expectations.	92%	81%
Cross-race bias. Eyewitnesses are more accurate when identifying members of their own race than members of other races.	90%	47%
Accuracy versus confidence. An eyewitness's confidence is not a good predictor of his or her identification accuracy.	87%	38%

*"This phenomenon is reliable enough for psychologists to present it in courtroom testimony."

Source: Experts from S. M. Kassin, V. A. Tubb, H. M. Hosch, & A. Memon (2001). Jurors from T. R. Benton, D. F. Ross, E. Bradshaw, W. N. Thomas, & G. S. Bradshaw (2006).

their time may be coming. New Jersey's attorney general has mandated statewide blind testing (to avoid steering witnesses toward suspects) and sequential lineups (to minimize simply comparing people and choosing the person who most resembles the one they saw commit a crime) (Kolata & Peterson, 2001; Wells & others, 2002). Police might also use a new procedure tested by Sean Pryke, Rod Lindsay, and colleagues (2004). They invited students to identify a prior class visitor from multiple lineups that separately presented face, body, and voice samples. Their finding: An eyewitness who consistently identified the same suspect—by face, by body, and by voice—was nearly always an accurate eyewitness.

EDUCATE JURORS

Do jurors evaluate eyewitness testimony rationally? Do they understand how the circumstances of a lineup determine its reliability? Do they know whether or not to take an eyewitness's self-confidence into account? Do they realize how memory can be influenced—by earlier misleading questions, by stress at the time of the incident, by the interval between the event and the questioning, by whether the suspect is the same or a different race, by whether recall of other details is sharp or hazy? Studies in Canada, Great Britain, and the United States reveal that jurors fail to fully appreciate most of these factors, all of which are known to influence eyewitness testimony (Cutler & others, 1988; Devenport & others, 2002; Noon & Hollin, 1987; Wells & Turtle, 1987; Yarmey, 2003a, 2003b).

To educate jurors, experts now are asked frequently (usually by defense attorneys) to testify about eyewitness testimony. Their aim is to offer jurors the sort of information you have been reading about to help them evaluate the testimony of both prosecution and defense witnesses. Table 15.1, drawn from a survey of 64 researchers on eyewitness testimony, lists some of the most agreed-upon phenomena. A follow-up survey compared their understandings with those of 111 jurors sampled in Tennessee.

When taught the conditions under which eyewitness accounts are trustworthy, jurors become more discerning (Cutler & others, 1989; Devenport & others, 2002; Wells, 1986). Moreover, attorneys and judges are recognizing the importance of some of these factors when deciding when to ask for or permit suppression of lineup evidence (Stinson & others, 1996, 1997).

Summing Up: How Reliable Is Eyewitness Testimony?

- In hundreds of experiments, social psychologists have found that the accuracy of eyewitness testimony can be impaired by a host of factors involving the ways people form judgments and memories.

- Some eyewitnesses express themselves more assertively than others. The assertive witness is more likely to be believed, although assertiveness is actually a trait of the witness that does not reflect the certainty of the information.

- The human eye is not a video camera; it is vulnerable to variations in light, angle, and other changes that impair recognition of a face.

- When false information is given to a witness, the misinformation effect may result in the witness coming to believe that the false information is true.

- As the sequence of events in a crime is told repeatedly, errors may creep in and become embraced by the witness as part of the true account.

- To reduce such errors, interviewers are advised to let the witness tell what he or she remembers without interruption, and to encourage the witness to visualize the scene of the incident and the emotional state the witness was in when the incident occurred.

- Educating jurors about the pitfalls of eyewitness testimony can improve the way testimony is received and, ultimately, the accuracy of the verdict.

What Other Factors Influence Juror Judgments?

Are the defendant's attractiveness and similarity to jurors likely to bias them? How faithfully do jurors follow judges' instructions?

The Defendant's Characteristics

According to the famed trial lawyer Clarence Darrow (1933), jurors seldom convict a person they like or acquit one they dislike. He argued that the main job of the trial lawyer is to make a jury like the defendant. Was he right? And is it true, as Darrow also said, that "facts regarding the crime are relatively unimportant"?

Darrow overstated the case. One classic study of more than 3,500 criminal cases and 4,000 civil cases found that four times in five the judge agreed with the jury's decision (Kalven & Zeisel, 1966). Although both may have been wrong, the evidence usually is clear enough that jurors can set aside their biases, focus on the facts, and agree on a verdict (Saks & Hastie, 1978; Visher, 1987). Facts do matter.

Nevertheless, when jurors are asked to make social judgments—would this defendant intentionally commit *this* offense?—facts are not all that matter. As we noted in Chapter 7, communicators are more persuasive if they seem credible and attractive. Jurors cannot help forming impressions of the defendant. Can they put those impressions aside and decide the case based on the facts alone?

To judge from the more lenient treatment often received by high-status defendants (McGillis, 1979), bias lingers. But actual cases vary in so many ways—in the type of crime, in the status, age, gender, and race of the defendant—that it's hard to isolate the factors that influence jurors. So experimenters have controlled such factors by giving mock jurors the same basic facts of a case while varying, say, the defendant's attractiveness or similarity to the jurors.

PHYSICAL ATTRACTIVENESS

In Chapter 11 we noted a physical attractiveness stereotype: Beautiful people seem like good people. Michael Efran (1974) wondered whether that stereotype would bias students' judgments of someone accused of cheating. He asked some of his University of Toronto students whether attractiveness should affect presumption of guilt. They answered, "No, it shouldn't." But did it? Yes. When Efran gave other students a description of the case with a photograph of either an attractive or an unattractive defendant, they judged the more attractive as less guilty and recommended that person for lesser punishment.

Other experimenters have confirmed that when the evidence is meager or ambiguous, justice is not blind to a defendant's looks (Mazzella & Feingold, 1994). O. J. Simpson's being, as one prospective juror put it, "a hunk of a fellow," probably did not hurt his case. Diane Berry and Leslie Zebrowitz-McArthur (1988) discovered this when they asked people to judge the guilt of baby-faced and mature-faced defendants. Baby-faced adults (people with large, round eyes and small chins) seemed more naive and were found guilty more often of crimes of mere negligence but less often of intentional criminal acts. If convicted, unattractive people also strike people as more dangerous, especially if they are sexual offenders (Esses & Webster, 1988).

THE FAR SIDE® BY GARY LARSON

© 1980 FarWorks, Inc. All Rights Reserved/Dist. by Creators Syndicate

"And so I ask the jury—is that the face of a mass murderer?"

Other things being equal, people often judge physically appealing defendants more leniently.

In a mammoth experiment conducted with BBC Television, Richard Wiseman (1998) showed viewers evidence about a burglary, with just one variation. Some viewers saw the defendant played by an actor that fit what a panel of 100 people judged as the stereotypical criminal—unattractive, crooked nose, small eyes. Among 64,000 people phoning in their verdict, 41 percent judged him guilty. British viewers elsewhere saw an attractive, baby-faced defendant with large blue eyes. Only 31 percent found him guilty.

To see if these findings extend to the real world, Chris Downs and Phillip Lyons (1991) asked police escorts to rate the physical attractiveness of 1,742 defendants appearing before 40 Texas judges in misdemeanor cases. Whether the misdemeanor was serious (such as forgery), moderate (such as harassment), or minor (such as public intoxication), the judges set higher bails and fines for less attractive defendants (Figure 15.5). What explains this dramatic effect? Are unattractive people also lower in status? Are they indeed more likely to flee or to commit another crime, as the judges perhaps suppose? Or do judges simply ignore the Roman statesman Cicero's advice: "The final good and the supreme duty of the wise man is to resist appearance."

SIMILARITY TO THE JURORS

If Clarence Darrow was even partly right in his declaration that liking or disliking a defendant colors judgments, then other factors that influence liking should also matter. Among such influences is the principle, noted in Chapter 11, that likeness

FIGURE :: 15.5

Attractiveness and Legal Judgments

Texas Gulf Coast judges set higher bails and fines for less attractive defendants.

Source: Data from Downs & Lyons, 1991.

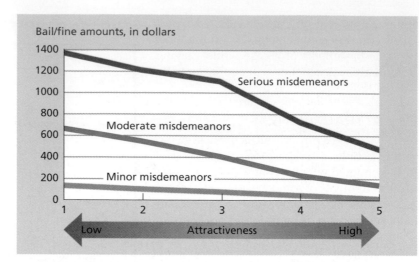

(similarity) leads to liking. When people pretend they are jurors, they are indeed more sympathetic to a defendant who shares their attitudes, religion, race, or (in cases of sexual assault) gender (Selby & others, 1977; Towson & Zanna, 1983; Ugwue-gbu, 1979). Juror racial bias is usually small, but jurors do exhibit some tendency to treat racial outgroups less favorably (Mitchell & others, 2005).

Some examples:

- Paul Amato (1979) had Australian students read evidence concerning a left- or right-wing person accused of a politically motivated burglary. The students judged less guilt when the defendant's political views were similar to their own.

- When Cookie Stephan and Walter Stephan (1986) had English-speaking people judge someone accused of assault, they were more likely to think the person not guilty if the defendant's testimony was in English, rather than translated from Spanish or Thai.

- When a defendant's race fits a crime stereotype—say, a White defendant charged with embezzlement or a Black defendant charged with auto theft—mock jurors offer more negative verdicts and punishments (Jones & Kaplan, 2003; Mazzella & Feingold, 1994). Whites who espouse nonprejudiced views are more likely to demonstrate racial bias in trials where race issues are not blatant (Sommers & Ellsworth, 2000, 2001).

    In actual capital cases, reports Craig Haney (1991), data "show that Blacks are overpunished as defendants or under-valued as victims, or both." One analysis of 80,000 criminal convictions during 1992 and 1993 found that U.S. federal judges—only 5 percent of whom were Black—sentenced Blacks to 10 percent longer sentences than Whites when comparing cases with the same seriousness and criminal history (Associated Press, 1995). Likewise, Blacks who kill Whites are more often sentenced to death than Whites who kill Blacks (Butterfield, 2001).

There were differences within each race in perceptions of Simpson's guilt or innocence. White women whose identity focused on gender were especially likely to think Simpson guilty. African Americans for whom race was central to their identity were especially likely to think him innocent (Fairchild & Cowan, 1997; Newman & others, 1997).

"You look like this sketch of someone who's thinking about committing a crime."

In two recent studies, harsher sentences are also given those who look more stereotypically Black. Irene Blair and her colleagues (2004) found that, given similar criminal histories, Black and White inmates in Florida receive similar sentences—but that within each race, those with more "Afrocentric" facial features are given longer sentences. And Jennifer Eberhardt and her co-researchers (2006) report that over a two-decade period, Black males convicted of murdering a White person were doubly likely to be sentenced to death if they had more stereotypically Afrocentric features (58 percent versus 24 percent for Blacks with features less Afrocentric than average.)

"I'm going to have to recuse myself."

So it seems we are more sympathetic toward a defendant with whom we can identify. If we think we wouldn't have committed that criminal act, we may assume that someone like us is also unlikely to have done it. That helps explain why, in acquaintance-rape trials, men more often than women judge the defendant not guilty (Fischer, 1997). That also helps explain why a national survey before the O. J. Simpson trial got under way found that 77 percent of Whites, but only 45 percent of Blacks, saw the case against him as at least "fairly strong" (Smolowe, 1994).

Ideally, jurors would leave their biases outside the courtroom and begin a trial with open minds. So implies the Sixth Amendment to the U.S. Constitution: "The accused shall enjoy the right to a speedy and public trial by impartial jury." In its concern for objectivity, the judicial system is similar to science. Both scientists and jurors are supposed to sift and weigh the evidence. Both the courts and science have rules about what evidence is relevant. Both keep careful records and assume that others given the same evidence would decide similarly.

When the evidence is clear and individuals focus on it (as when they reread and debate the meaning of testimony), their biases are indeed minimal (Kaplan & Schersching, 1980). The quality of the evidence matters more than the prejudices of the individual jurors.

The Judge's Instructions

All of us can recall courtroom dramas in which an attorney exclaimed, "Your honor, I object!" whereupon the judge sustains the objection and instructs the jury to ignore the other attorney's suggestive question or the witness's remark. How effective are such instructions?

Nearly all states in the United States now have "rape shield" statutes that prohibit or limit testimony concerning the victim's prior sexual activity. Such testimony, though irrelevant to the case at hand, tends to make jurors more sympathetic to the accused rapist's claim that the woman consented to sex (Borgida, 1981; Cann & others, 1979). If such reliable, illegal, or prejudicial testimony is nevertheless slipped in by the defense or blurted out by a witness, will jurors follow a judge's instruction to ignore it? And is it enough for the judge to remind jurors, "The issue is not whether you like or dislike the defendant but whether the defendant committed the offense"?

"The jury will disregard the witness's last remarks."

It is not easy for jurors to erase inadmissible testimony from memory.

reactance
A motive to protect or restore one's sense of freedom. Reactance arises when someone threatens our freedom of action.

Very possibly not. Several experimenters report that jurors show concern for due process (Fleming & others, 1999) but that they find it hard to ignore inadmissible evidence, such as the defendant's previous convictions. In one study, Stanley Sue, Ronald Smith, and Cathy Caldwell (1973) gave University of Washington students a description of a grocery store robbery-murder and a summary of the prosecution's case and the defense's case. When the prosecution's case was weak, no one judged the defendant guilty. When a tape recording of an incriminating phone call made by the defendant was added to the weak case, about one-third judged the person guilty. The judge's instructions that the tape was not legal evidence and should be ignored did nothing to erase the effect of the damaging testimony.

Indeed, Sharon Wolf and David Montgomery (1977) found that a judge's order to ignore testimony—"It must play no role in your consideration of the case. You have no choice but to disregard it"—can even boomerang, adding to the testimony's impact. Perhaps such statements create **reactance** in the jurors. Or perhaps they sensitize jurors to the inadmissible testimony, as when I warn you not to notice your nose as you finish this sentence. Judges can more easily strike inadmissible testimony from the court records than from the jurors' minds. As trial lawyers sometimes say, "You can't unring a bell."

This is especially so with emotional information (Edwards & Bryan, 1997). When jurors are told vividly about a defendant's record ("hacking up a woman"), a judge's instructions to ignore are more likely to boomerang than when the inadmissible information is less emotional ("assault with a deadly weapon"). Even if jurors later claim to have ignored the inadmissible information, it may alter how they construe other information.

Pretrial publicity also is hard for jurors to ignore, especially in studies with real jurors and serious crimes (Steblay & others, 1999). In one large-scale experiment, Geoffrey Kramer and his colleagues (1990) exposed nearly 800 mock jurors (most from actual jury rolls) to incriminating news reports about the past convictions of a man accused of robbing a supermarket. After the jurors viewed a videotaped reenactment of the trial, they either did or did not hear the judge's instructions to disregard the pretrial publicity. The effect of the judicial admonition was nil.

People whose opinions are biased by pretrial publicity typically deny its effect on them, and that denial makes it hard to eliminate biased jurors (Moran & Cutler, 1991). In experiments, even getting mock jurors to pledge their impartiality and their

Will jurors clear their minds of pretrial publicity that might bias their evaluation of evidence? Although jurors will deny being biased, experiments have shown otherwise.

willingness to disregard prior information has not eliminated the pretrial publicity effect (Dexter & others, 1992). O. J. Simpson's attorneys, it seems, had reason to worry about the enormous pretrial publicity. And the trial judge had reason to order jurors not to view pertinent media publicity and to sequester them during the trial.

Judges can hope, with some support from available research, that during deliberation, jurors who bring up inadmissible evidence will be chastised for doing so, and that jury group verdicts may therefore be less influenced by such evidence (London & Nunez, 2000). To minimize the effects of inadmissible testimony, judges also can forewarn jurors that certain types of evidence, such as a rape victim's sexual history, are irrelevant. Once jurors form impressions based on such evidence, a judge's admonitions have much less effect (Borgida & White, 1980; Kassin & Wrightsman, 1979). Thus, reports Vicki Smith (1991), a pretrial training session pays dividends. Teaching jurors legal procedures and standards of proof improves their understanding of the trial procedure and their willingness to withhold judgment until after they have heard all the trial information.

Better yet, judges could cut inadmissible testimony before the jurors hear it—by videotaping testimonies and removing the inadmissible parts. Live and videotaped testimonies have much the same impact as do live and videotaped lineups (Cutler & others, 1989; Miller & Fontes, 1979). Perhaps courtrooms of the future will have life-size television monitors. Critics object that the procedure prevents jurors from observing how the defendant and others react to the witness. Proponents argue that videotaping not only enables the judge to edit out inadmissible testimony but also speeds up the trial and allows witnesses to talk about crucial events before memories fade.

Additional Factors

We have considered three courtroom factors—eyewitness testimony, the defendant's characteristics, and the judge's instructions. Researchers are also studying the influence of other factors. For example, at Michigan State University, Norbert Kerr and his colleagues (1978, 1981, 1982) studied these issues: Does a severe potential punishment (for example, a death penalty) make jurors less willing to convict—and was it therefore strategic for the Los Angeles prosecutors not to seek the death penalty for O. J. Simpson? Do experienced jurors' judgments differ from those of novice jurors? Are defendants judged more harshly when the *victim* is attractive or has suffered greatly? Kerr's research suggests that the answer to all three questions is yes.

Experiments by Mark Alicke and Teresa Davis (1989) and by Michael Enzle and Wendy Hawkins (1992) confirm that jurors' judgments of blame and punishment can be affected by the victim's characteristics—even when the defendant is unaware of such. Consider the 1984 case of the "subway vigilante" Bernard Goetz. When four teens approached Goetz for $5 on a New York subway, the frightened Goetz pulled out a loaded gun and shot each of them, leaving one partly paralyzed. When Goetz was charged with attempted homicide, there was an outcry of public support for him based partly on the disclosure that the youths had extensive criminal records and that three of them were carrying concealed, sharpened screwdrivers. Although Goetz didn't know any of this, he was acquitted of the attempted homicide charge and convicted only of illegal firearm possession.

Summing Up: What Other Factors Influence Juror Judgments?

- The facts of a case are usually compelling enough that jurors can lay aside their biases and render a fair judgment. When the evidence is ambiguous, however, jurors are more likely to interpret it with their preconceived biases and to feel sympathetic to a defendant who is attractive or similar to themselves.
- When jurors are exposed to damaging pretrial publicity or to inadmissible evidence, will they follow a judge's instruction to ignore it? In simulated trials, the judge's orders were sometimes followed, but often, especially when the judge's admonition came *after* an impression was made, they were not.
- Researchers have also explored the influence of other factors, such as the severity of the potential sentence and various characteristics of the victim.

What Influences the Individual Juror?

Verdicts depend on what happens in the courtroom—the eyewitness testimonies, the defendant's characteristics, the judge's instructions. But verdicts also depend on how the individual jurors process information.

Courtroom influences on "the average juror" are worth pondering. But no juror is the average juror; each carries into the courthouse individual attitudes and personalities. And when they deliberate, jurors influence one another. So two key questions are (1) How are verdicts influenced by individual jurors' dispositions? and (2) How are verdicts influenced by jurors' group deliberation?

Juror Comprehension

To gain insight into juror comprehension, Nancy Pennington and Reid Hastie (1993) had mock jurors, sampled from courthouse jury pools, view reenactments of actual trials. In making their decisions, the jurors first constructed a story that made sense of all the evidence. After observing one murder trial, for example, some jurors concluded that a quarrel made the defendant angry, triggering him to get a knife, search for the victim, and stab him to death. Others surmised that the frightened defendant picked up a knife that he used to defend himself when he later encountered the victim. When jurors begin deliberating, they often discover that others have constructed different stories. This implies—and research confirms—that jurors are best persuaded when attorneys present evidence in narrative fashion—a story. In felony cases, where the national conviction rate is 80 percent, the prosecution case more often than the defense case follows a narrative structure.

UNDERSTANDING INSTRUCTIONS

Next, the jurors must grasp the judge's instructions concerning the available verdict categories. For those instructions to be effective, jurors must first understand them. Study after study has found that many people do not understand the standard legalese of judicial instructions. Depending on the type of case, a jury may be told that the standard of proof is a "preponderance of the evidence," "clear and convincing evidence," or "beyond a reasonable doubt." Such statements may have one meaning for the legal community and different meanings in the minds of jurors (Kagehiro, 1990; Wright & Hall, 2007).

A judge may also remind jurors to avoid premature conclusions as they weigh each new item of presented evidence. But research with both college students and mock jurors chosen from actual prospective jury pools shows that warm-blooded human beings do form premature opinions, and those leanings do influence how they interpret new information (Carlson & Russo, 2001).

After observing actual cases and later interviewing the jurors, Stephen Adler (1994) found "lots of sincere, serious people who—for a variety of reasons—were missing key points, focusing on irrelevant issues, succumbing to barely recognized prejudices, failing to see through the cheapest appeals to sympathy or hate, and generally botching the job."

"Your Honor, we're going to go with the prosecution's spin."

Effective prosecutors offer jurors plausible stories.

In 1990 Imelda Marcos, widow of Philippine dictator Ferdinand Marcos, was tried for transferring hundreds of millions of dollars of Philippine money into American banks for her own use. During jury selection, lawyers eliminated anyone who was aware of her role in her husband's dictatorship. Ill-equipped to follow the complex money transactions, those who made it onto the jury fell back on sympathy for Mrs. Marcos, a former beauty queen who appeared in court dressed in black, clutching her rosaries, and wiping away tears (Adler, 1994).

UNDERSTANDING STATISTICAL INFORMATION

Tests on blood found at the scene where O. J. Simpson's ex-wife and her fellow victim were murdered revealed bloodstains that matched Simpson's mix of blood proteins but not the victims'. Learning that only 1 in 200 people share this blood type, some people assumed the chances were 99.5 percent that Simpson was the culprit. But 1 in 200 means the culprit could be any one of at least 40,000 people in the Los Angeles area, noted the defense. Faced with such arguments, three in five people will discount the relevance of the blood-type evidence, report William Thompson and Edward Schumann (1987). Actually, both attorneys were wrong. The evidence is relevant because few of the other 40,000 people can reasonably be considered suspects. But the 99.5 percent argument ignores the fact that the defendant was charged partly because his blood type matched.

When a more precise DNA match with Simpson's blood was found, prosecutors contended that the chance of such

Faced with an incomprehensibly complex accounting of Imelda Marcos's alleged thefts of public money, jurors fell back on their intuitive assessments of the seemingly devout and sincere woman and found her not guilty.

Alan Dershowitz, an O. J. Simpson defense attorney, argued to the media that only 1 in 1,000 men who abuse their wives later murder them. More relevant, replied critics, is the probability that a husband is guilty given that (a) he abused his wife, and (b) his wife was murdered. From available data, Jon Merz and Jonathan Caulkins (1995) calculated that probability as .81.

a match was 1 in 170 million, and the defense showed that experts disagreed about the reliability of DNA testing. For one thing, defendants for whom there is an incriminating DNA match seem less likely to be guilty when they are from a big city, where someone else might have the matching DNA (Koehler & Maachi, 2004).

But Gary Wells (1992) and Keith Niedermeier and colleagues (1999) report that even when people (including experienced trial judges) understand naked statistical probabilities, they may be unpersuaded. Told that 80 percent of the tires of the Blue Bus Co. but only 20 percent of the alternative Grey Bus Co. match the tracks of a bus that killed a dog, people seldom convict the Blue Co. The naked numbers allow a plausible alternative scenario—that the accident was caused by one of 20 percent of Grey buses. Told that an eyewitness identified the bus as blue, people usually will convict, even if the eyewitness was shown to be only 80 percent accurate in making such identifications. The plausible alternative scenario in the first case creates a psychological difference between saying there is an 80 percent chance that something is true and saying that something is true based on 80 percent reliable evidence.

Naked numbers, it seems, must be supported by a convincing story. Thus, reports Wells, one Toronto mother lost a paternity suit seeking child support from her child's alleged father despite a blood test showing a 99.8 percent probability that the man was her child's father. She lost after the man took the stand and persuasively denied the allegation. But a persuasive story without forensic evidence may also seem unconvincing. Some psychologists believe this is especially so for viewers of the television show *CSI*, many of whom have unreasonable expectations of the quantity and quality of physical evidence (Houck, 2006; Winter & York, 2007).

INCREASING JURORS' UNDERSTANDING

Understanding how jurors misconstrue judicial instructions and statistical information is a first step toward better decisions. A next step might be giving jurors access to transcripts rather than forcing them to rely on their memories in processing complex information (Bourgeois & others, 1993). A further step would be devising and testing clearer, more effective ways to present information—a task on which several social psychologists have worked. For example, when a judge quantifies the required standard of proof (as, say, 51, 71, or 91 percent certainty), jurors understand and respond appropriately (Kagehiro, 1990).

And surely there must be a simpler way to tell jurors, as required by the Illinois Death Penalty Act, not to impose the death sentence in murder cases when there are justifying circumstances: "If you do not unanimously find from your consideration of all the evidence that there are no mitigating factors sufficient to preclude imposition of a death sentence, then you should sign the verdict requiring the court to impose a sentence other than death" (Diamond, 1993). When jurors are given instructions rewritten into simple language, they are less susceptible to the judge's biases (Halverson & others, 1997).

Phoebe Ellsworth and Robert Mauro (1998) sum up the dismal conclusions of jury researchers: "Legal instructions are typically delivered in a manner likely to frustrate the most conscientious attempts at understanding . . . The language is technical and . . . no attempt is made either to assess jurors' mistaken preconceptions about the law or to provide any kind of useful education."

Jury Selection

Given the variations among individual jurors, can trial lawyers use the jury selection process to stack juries in their favor? Legal folklore suggests that sometimes they can. One president of the Association of Trial Lawyers of America boldly proclaimed, "Trial attorneys are acutely attuned to the nuances of human behavior, which enables them to detect the minutest traces of bias or inability to reach an appropriate decision" (Bigam, 1977).

Mindful that people's assessments of others are error-prone, social psychologists doubt that attorneys come equipped with fine-tuned social Geiger counters. In some 6,000 American trials a year, consultants—some of them social scientists in the American Society of Trial Consultants—help lawyers pick juries and plot strategy (Gavzer, 1997; Hutson, 2007; Miller, 2001). In several celebrated trials, survey researchers have used "scientific jury selection" to help attorneys weed out those likely to be unsympathetic. One famous trial involved two of President Nixon's former cabinet members, conservatives John Mitchell and Maurice Stans. A survey revealed that from the defense's viewpoint the worst possible juror was "a liberal, Jewish, Democrat who reads the *New York Times* or the *Post,* listens to Walter Cronkite, is interested in political affairs, and is well-informed about Watergate" (Zeisel & Diamond, 1976). Of the first nine trials, relying on "scientific" selection methods, the defense won seven (Hans & Vidmar, 1981; Wrightsman, 1978). (However, we can't know how many of those nine would have been won anyway, without scientific juror selection.)

O. J. Simpson attorneys in the criminal trial also used a jury selection consultant—and won (Lafferty, 1994). Meeting the press after the not-guilty verdict, Simpson's attorney immediately thanked the jury selection consultant.

Many trial attorneys have now used scientific jury selection to identify questions they can use to exclude those biased against their clients, and most report satisfaction with the results (Gayoso & others, 1991; Moran & others, 1994). Most jurors, when asked by a judge to "raise your hand if you've read anything about this case that would prejudice you," don't directly acknowledge their preconceptions. It takes further questioning to reveal them. For example, if the judge allows an attorney to check prospective jurors' attitudes toward drugs, the attorney can often guess their verdicts in a drug-trafficking case (Moran & others, 1990). Likewise, people who acknowledge they "don't put much faith in the testimony of psychiatrists" are less likely to accept an insanity defense (Cutler & others, 1992).

> "Beware of the Lutherans, especially the Scandinavians; they are almost always sure to convict."
> —CLARENCE DARROW, "HOW TO PICK A JURY," 1936

Individuals react differently to specific features of a case. Racial prejudice becomes relevant in racially charged cases; gender seems linked with verdicts only in rape and battered-woman cases; belief in personal responsibility versus corporate responsibility relates to personal injury awards in suits against businesses (Ellsworth & Mauro, 1998).

Despite the excitement—and ethical concern—about scientific jury selection, experiments reveal that attitudes and personal characteristics don't always predict verdicts. There are "no magic questions to be asked of prospective jurors, not even a guarantee that a particular survey will detect useful attitude-behavior or personality-behavior relationships," cautioned Steven Penrod and Brian Cutler (1987). Researchers Michael Saks and Reid Hastie (1978) agreed: "The studies are unanimous in showing that evidence is a substantially more potent determinant of jurors' verdicts than the individual characteristics of jurors" (p. 68). "The best conclusion is that there are cases where jury-selection consultants can make a difference but such cases are few and far between," add Neil Kressel and Dorit Kressel (2002). In courtrooms, jurors' public pledge of fairness and the judge's instruction to "be fair" strongly commit most jurors to the norm of fairness.

Ditto for judges. At her Senate confirmation hearing, the first Hispanic U.S. Supreme Court Justice, Sonia Sotomayor, assured her skeptical questioners that she would follow the law without influence from her background and identity. But complete neutrality is an ideal that even judges seldom attain (as illustrated by the 5-to-4 Supreme Court vote that decided the contested 2000 U.S. presidential election for Republican George W. Bush, with conservative and liberal judges voting in opposition).

"Death-Qualified" Jurors

A *close* case can, however, be decided by who is selected for the jury. In criminal cases, people who do not oppose the death penalty—and who therefore are eligible to serve when a death sentence is possible—are more prone to favor the prosecution, to feel that courts coddle criminals, and to oppose protecting the constitutional rights of defendants (Bersoff, 1987). Simply put, these "death-qualified" jurors are more concerned with crime control and less concerned with due process of law. When a court dismisses potential jurors who have moral scruples against the death penalty—something O. J. Simpson's prosecutors chose not to do—it constructs a jury that is more likely to vote guilty.

On this issue, social scientists are in "virtual unanimity . . . about the biasing effects of death qualification," reports Craig Haney (1993). The research record is "unified," reports Phoebe Ellsworth (1985, p. 46): "Defendants in capital-punishment cases do assume the extra handicap of juries predisposed to find them guilty." What is more, conviction-prone jurors tend also to be more authoritarian—more rigid, punitive, closed to mitigating circumstances, and contemptuous of those of lower status (Gerbasi & others, 1977; Luginbuhl & Middendorf, 1988; Moran & Comfort, 1982, 1986; Werner & others, 1982).

Because the legal system operates on tradition and precedent, such research findings only slowly alter judicial practice. In 1986 the U.S. Supreme Court, in a split decision, overturned a lower-court ruling that death-qualified jurors are indeed a biased sample. Ellsworth (1989) believes the Court in this case disregarded the compelling and consistent evidence partly because of its "ideological commitment to capital punishment" and partly because of the havoc that would result if the convictions of thousands of people on death row had to be reconsidered. The solution, should the Court ever wish to adopt it for future cases, is to convene separate juries to (a) decide guilt in capital murder cases, and, given a guilty verdict, to (b) hear additional evidence on factors motivating the murder and to decide between death or imprisonment.

But a deeper issue is at stake here: whether the death penalty itself falls under the U.S. Constitution's ban on "cruel and unusual punishment." As readers in Canada, Australia, New Zealand, Western Europe, and most of South America know, their countries prohibit capital punishment. There, as in the United States, public attitudes tend to support the prevailing practice (Costanzo, 1997). But American pro-capital punishment attitudes seem to be softening. After reaching 80 percent in 1994, support fell to 64 percent in 2007 (Ruby, 2007).

In wrestling with the punishment, U.S. courts have considered whether courts inflict the penalty arbitrarily, whether they apply it with racial bias, and whether legal killing deters illegal killing. The social science answers to these questions are clear, note social psychologists Mark Costanzo (1997) and Craig Haney and Deana Logan (1994). Consider the deterrence issue. States with a death penalty do not have lower homicide rates. Homicide rates have not dropped when states have initiated the death penalty, and they have not risen when states have abolished it. When committing a crime of passion, people don't pause to calculate the consequences (which include life in prison without parole

> "The kind of juror who would be unperturbed by the prospect of sending a man to his death . . . is the kind of juror who would too readily ignore the presumption of the defendant's innocence, accept the prosecution's version of the facts, and return a verdict of guilty."
>
> —WITHERSPOON v. ILLINOIS, 1968

> "Ninety percent of all known executions are carried out in just four countries: China, Iran, Saudi Arabia, and the United States."
>
> —*JIMMY CARTER*, OUR ENDANGERED VALUES, 2005

Guilty. Jury selection criteria may yield conviction-prone jurors.

as another potent deterrent). Moreover, the death penalty is applied inconsistently (in Texas 40 times as often as in New York). And it is applied more often with poor defendants, who often receive a weak defense (*Economist*, 2000). Nevertheless, the Supreme Court has determined that admitting only death-qualified jurors provides a representative jury of one's peers and that "the death penalty undoubtedly is a significant deterrent."

Humanitarian considerations aside, say the appalled social scientists, what is the rationale for clinging to cherished assumptions and intuitions in the face of contradictory evidence? Why not put our cultural ideas to the test? If they find support, so much the better for them. If they crash against a wall of contradictory evidence, so much the worse for them. Such are the ideals of critical thinking that fuel both psychological science and civil democracy.

Average homicide rate per 100,000

• *for entire United States: 9*
• *for death-penalty states: 9.3*

(*Source:* Scientific American, *February 2001*)

Summing Up: What Influences the Individual Juror?

• Social psychologists are interested in not only the interactions among witnesses, judges, and juries, but also what happens within and between individual jurors. One major concern is jurors' ability to comprehend evidence, especially when it involves statistics indicating the probability that a given person committed the crime.

• Trial lawyers often use jury consultants to help them select jurors most sympathetic to their case. People who are aware of pretrial publicity, for example, may be disqualified from serving.

• In cases where the death penalty may be applied, lawyers can disqualify any prospective juror who opposes the death penalty on principle. Social psychology research argues that this in itself produces a biased jury, but the Supreme Court has ruled otherwise.

How Do Group Influences Affect Juries?

What influences how individual jurors' prejudgments coalesce into a group decision?

Imagine a jury that has just finished a trial and has entered the jury room to begin its deliberations. Researchers Harry Kalven and Hans Zeisel (1966) reported that chances are about two in three that the jurors will *not* agree initially on a verdict. Yet, after discussion, 95 percent emerge with a consensus. Obviously, group influence has occurred.

In the United States, 300,000 times a year small groups sampled from the 3 million people called for jury duty convene to seek a group decision (Kagehiro, 1990). Are they and juries elsewhere subject to the social influences that mold other decision groups—to patterns of majority and minority influence? to group polarization? to groupthink? Let's start with a simple question: If we knew the jurors' initial leanings, could we predict their verdict?

The law prohibits observation of actual juries. So researchers simulate the jury process by presenting a case to mock juries and having them deliberate as a real jury would. In a series of such studies at the University of Illinois, James Davis, Robert Holt, Norbert Kerr, and Garold Stasser tested various mathematical schemes for predicting group decisions, including decisions by mock juries (Davis & others, 1975, 1977, 1989; Kerr & others, 1976). Will some mathematical combination of initial decisions predict the final group decision? Davis and his colleagues found that the scheme that predicts best varies according to the nature of the case. But in several experiments, a "two-thirds-majority" scheme fared best: The group verdict was

FIGURE :: 15.6

Group Polarization in Juries

In highly realistic simulations of a murder trial, 828 Massachusetts jurors stated their initial verdict preferences, then deliberated the case for periods ranging from three hours to five days. Deliberation strengthened initial tendencies that favored the prosecution.

Source: From Hastie & others, 1983.

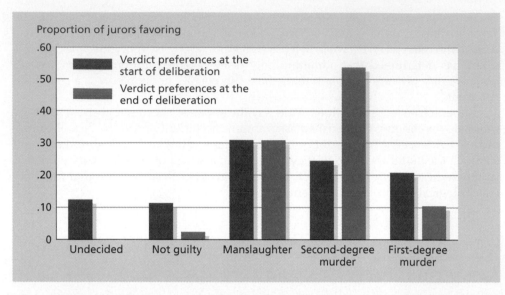

usually the alternative favored by at least two-thirds of the jurors at the outset. Without such a majority, a hung jury was likely.

Likewise, in Kalven and Zeisel's survey of juries, 9 in 10 reached the verdict favored by the majority on the first ballot. Although you or I might fantasize about someday being the courageous lone juror who sways the majority, the fact is that it seldom happens.

Minority Influence

Seldom, yet sometimes, what was initially a minority opinion prevails. A typical 12-person jury is like a typical small college class: The three quietest people rarely talk and the three most vocal people contribute more than half the talking (Hastie & others, 1983). In the Mitchell-Stans trial, the four jurors who favored acquittal persisted, were vocal, and eventually prevailed. From the research on minority influence, we know that jurors in the minority will be most persuasive when they are consistent, persistent, and self-confident. This is especially so if they can begin to trigger some defections from the majority (Gordijn & others, 2002; Kerr, 1981b).

Group Polarization

Jury deliberation shifts people's opinions in other intriguing ways as well. In experiments, deliberation often magnifies initial sentiments. For example, Robert Bray and Audrey Noble (1978) had University of Kentucky students listen to a 30-minute tape of a murder trial. Then, assuming the defendant was found guilty, they recommended a prison sentence. Groups of high authoritarians initially recommended strong punishments (56 years) and after deliberation were even more punitive (68 years). The low-authoritarian groups were initially more lenient (38 years) and after deliberation became more so (29 years). By contrast, group diversity often moderates judgments. Compared with Whites who judge Black defendants on all-White mock juries, those serving on racially mixed mock juries enter deliberation expressing more leniency and during the deliberation exhibit openness to a wider range of information (Sommers, 2006).

Confirmation that group polarization can occur in juries comes from an ambitious study in which Reid Hastie, Steven Penrod, and Nancy Pennington (1983) put together 69 twelve-person juries from Massachusetts citizens on jury duty. Each jury was shown a reenactment of an actual murder case, with roles played by an experienced judge and actual attorneys. Then they were given unlimited time to deliberate the case in a jury room. As Figure 15.6 shows, the evidence

research
CLOSE-UP

Group Polarization in a Natural Court Setting

In simulated juries, deliberation often amplifies jurors' individual inclinations. Does such group polarization occur in actual courts? Cass Sunstein, David Schkade, and Lisa Ellman (2004) show us how researchers can harvest data from natural settings when exploring social-psychological phenomena. Their data were 14,874 votes by judges on 4,958 three-judge U.S. circuit court panels. (On these federal "Courts of Appeals," an appeal is almost always heard by three of the court's judges.)

Sunstein, a behavioral science–oriented law professor, and his colleagues first asked whether a judge's votes tended to reflect the ideology of the Republican or Democratic president who appointed them. Indeed, when voting on ideologically tinged cases involving affirmative action, environmental regulation, campaign finance, and abortion, Democratic-appointed judges more often supported the liberal position than did Republican-appointed judges. No surprise there. That's what presidents and their party members assume when seeking congressional approval of their kindred-spirited judicial nominees.

Would such tendencies be amplified when the panel had three judges appointed by the same party? Would three Republican appointed judges be even more often conservative than the average Republican appointee?

And would three Democratic-appointed judges be more often liberal than the average Democrat appointee? Or would judges vote their convictions uninfluenced by their fellow panelists? Table 15.2 presents their findings.

Note that when three appointees from the same party formed a panel (RRR or DDD), they became more likely to vote their party's ideological preference than did the average individual judge. The polarization exhibited by like-minded threesomes was, the Sunstein team reported, "confirmed in many areas, including affirmative action, campaign finance, sex discrimination, sexual harassment, piercing the corporate veil, disability discrimination, race discrimination, and review of environmental regulations" (though not in the politically volatile cases of abortion and capital punishment, where judges voted their well-formed convictions).

Sunstein and his colleagues offer an example: If all three judges "believe that an affirmative action program is unconstitutional, and no other judge is available to argue on its behalf, then the exchange of arguments in the room will suggest that the program is genuinely unconstitutional." This is group polarization in action, they conclude—an example of "one of the most striking findings in modern social science: Groups of like-minded people tend to go to extremes."

TABLE :: 15.2 Proportion of "Liberal" Voting by Individual Judges and by Three-Judge Panels

Examples of Case Type	Individual Judges' Votes Party*		Individual Judges' Votes, by Panel Composition			
	R	D	RRR	RRD	RDD	DDD
Campaign finance	.28	.46	.23	.30	.35	.80
Affirmative action	.48	.74	.37	.50	.83	.85
Environmental	.46	.64	.27	.55	.62	.72
Sex discrimination	.35	.51	.31	.38	.49	.75
Average across 13 case types	.38	.51	.34	.39	.50	.61

* R = Republican appointee; D = Democratic appointee.

was incriminating: Four out of five jurors voted guilty before deliberation but felt unsure enough that a weak verdict of manslaughter was their most popular preference. After deliberation, nearly all agreed the accused was guilty, and most now preferred a stronger verdict—second-degree murder. Through deliberation, their initial leanings had grown stronger.

Leniency

In many experiments, one other curious effect of deliberation has surfaced: Especially when the evidence is not highly incriminating, deliberating jurors often become more lenient (MacCoun & Kerr, 1988). This qualifies the "two-thirds-majority-rules" finding, for if even a bare majority initially favors *acquittal*, it usually will prevail (Stasser & others, 1981). Moreover, a minority that favors acquittal stands a better chance of prevailing than one that favors conviction (Tindale & others, 1990).

Once again, a survey of actual juries confirms the laboratory results. Kalven and Zeisel (1966) report that in those cases where the majority does not prevail, it usually shifts to acquittal (as in the Mitchell-Stans trial). When a judge disagrees with the jury's decision, it is usually because the jury acquits someone the judge would have convicted.

Might "informational influence" (stemming from others' persuasive arguments) account for the increased leniency? The "innocent-unless-proved-guilty" and "proof-beyond-a-reasonable-doubt" rules put the burden of proof on those who favor conviction. Perhaps this makes evidence of the defendant's innocence more persuasive. Or perhaps "normative influence" creates the leniency effect, as jurors who view themselves as fair-minded confront other jurors who are even more concerned with protecting a possibly innocent defendant.

"It is better that ten guilty persons escape than one innocent suffer."

—WILLIAM BLACKSTONE, 1769

Are Twelve Heads Better Than One?

In Chapter 8 we saw that on thought problems where there is an objective right answer, group judgments surpass those by most individuals. Does the same hold true in juries? When deliberating, jurors exert normative pressure by trying to shift others' judgments by the sheer weight of their own. But they also share information, thus enlarging one another's understanding. So, does informational influence produce superior collective judgment?

The evidence, though meager, is partially encouraging. Groups recall information from a trial better than do their individual members (Vollrath & others, 1989). Deliberation also tends to cancel out certain biases and draws jurors' attention away from their own prejudgments and to the evidence. Twelve heads can be, it seems, better than one.

Are Six Heads as Good as Twelve?

In keeping with their British heritage, juries in the United States and Canada have traditionally been composed of 12 people whose task is to reach consensus—a unanimous verdict. However, in several cases appealed during the early 1970s, the U.S. Supreme Court modified that requirement. It declared that in civil cases and state criminal cases not potentially involving a death penalty, courts could use 6-person juries. Moreover, the Court affirmed a state's right to allow less than unanimous verdicts, even upholding one Louisiana conviction based on a 9-to-3 vote (Tanke & Tanke, 1979). There is no reason to suppose, argued the Court, that smaller juries, or juries not required to reach consensus, will deliberate or decide differently from the traditional jury.

The Court's assumptions triggered an avalanche of criticism from both legal scholars and social psychologists (Saks, 1974, 1996). Some criticisms were matters of simple statistics. For example, if 10 percent of a community's total jury pool is Black, then 72 percent of 12-member juries but only 47 percent of 6-member juries may be expected to have at least one Black person. So smaller juries may be less likely to reflect a community's diversity.

And if, in a given case, one-sixth of the jurors initially favor acquittal, that would be a single individual in a 6-member jury and 2 people in a 12-member jury. The Court assumed that, psychologically, the two situations would be identical. But as you may recall from our discussion of conformity, resisting group pressure is far more difficult for a minority of one than for a minority of two. Psychologically speaking, a jury split 10 to 2 is not equivalent to a jury split 5 to 1. Not surprisingly, then, 12-person juries are twice as likely as 6-person juries to have hung verdicts (Ellsworth & Mauro, 1998; Saks & Marti, 1997).

Jury researcher Michael Saks (1998) sums up the research findings: "Larger juries are more likely than smaller juries to contain members of minority groups, more accurately recall trial testimony, give more time to deliberation, hang more often, and appear more likely to reach 'correct' verdicts."

In 1978, after some of these studies were reported, the Supreme Court rejected Georgia's 5-member juries (although it still retains the 6-member jury). Announcing the Court's decision, Justice Harry Blackmun drew upon both the logical and the experimental data to argue that 5-person juries would be less representative, less reliable, less accurate (Grofman, 1980). Ironically, many of these data actually involved comparisons of 6- versus 12-member juries, and thus also argued against the 6-member jury. But having made and defended a public commitment to the 6-member jury, the Court was not convinced that the same arguments applied (Tanke & Tanke, 1979).

From Lab to Life: Simulated and Real Juries

Perhaps while reading this chapter, you have wondered what some critics (Tapp, 1980; Vidmar, 1979) have wondered: Isn't there an enormous gulf between college students discussing a hypothetical case and real jurors deliberating a real person's fate? Indeed there is. It is one thing to ponder a pretend decision, given minimal information, and quite another to agonize over the complexities and profound consequences of an actual case. So Reid Hastie, Martin Kaplan, James Davis, Eugene Borgida, and others have asked their participants, who sometimes are drawn from actual juror pools, to view enactments of actual trials. The enactments are so realistic that sometimes participants forget the trial they are watching on television is staged (Thompson & others, 1981).

Student mock jurors become engaged, too. "As I eavesdropped on the mock juries," recalls researcher Norbert Kerr (1999), "I became fascinated by the jurors' insightful arguments, their mix of amazing recollections and memory fabrications, their prejudices, their attempts to persuade or coerce, and their occasional courage in standing alone. Here brought to life before me were so many of the psychological processes I had been studying! Although our student jurors understood they were only simulating a real trial, they really cared about reaching a fair verdict."

The U.S. Supreme Court (1986) debated the usefulness of jury research in its decision regarding the use of "death-qualified" jurors in capital punishment cases. Defendants have a constitutional "right to a fair trial and an impartial jury whose composition is not biased toward the prosecution." The dissenting judges argued that this right is violated when jurors include only those who accept the death penalty. Their argument, they said, was based chiefly on "the essential unanimity of the results obtained by researchers using diverse subjects and varied methodologies." The majority of the judges, however, declared their "serious doubts about the value of these studies in predicting the behavior of actual jurors." The dissenting judges replied that the courts have not allowed experiments with actual juries; thus, "defendants claiming prejudice from death qualification should not be denied recourse to the only available means of proving their case."

Researchers also defend the laboratory simulations by noting that the laboratory offers a practical, inexpensive method of studying important issues under controlled conditions (Dillehay & Nietzel, 1980; Kerr & Bray, 2005). As researchers have begun testing them in more realistic situations, findings from the laboratory studies have often held up quite well. No one contends that the simplified world of the jury

Hung juries are rarely a problem. Among 59,511 U.S. federal court criminal trials during one 13-year period, 2.5 percent ended in a hung jury, as did a mere 0.6 percent of 67,992 federal civil trials (Saks, 1998).

"We have considered [the social science studies] carefully because they provide the only basis, besides judicial hunch, for a decision about whether smaller and smaller juries will be able to fulfill the purposes and functions of the Sixth Amendment."
—*JUSTICE HARRY BLACKMUN, BALLEW v. GEORGIA, 1978*

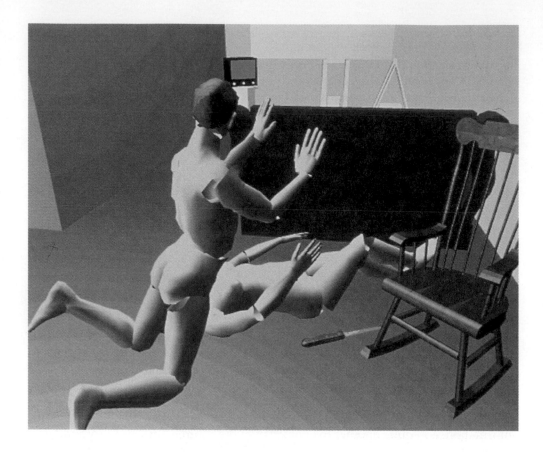

Attorneys are using new technology to present crime stories in ways jurors can easily grasp, as in this computer simulation of a homicide generated on the basis of forensic evidence.

experiment mirrors the complex world of the real courtroom. Rather, the experiments help us formulate theories with which we interpret the complex world.

Come to think of it, are these jury simulations any different from social psychology's other experiments, all of which create simplified versions of complex realities? By varying just one or two factors at a time in this simulated reality, the experimenter pinpoints how changes in one or two aspects of a situation can affect us. And that is the essence of social psychology's experimental method.

Summing Up: How Do Group Influences Affect Juries?

- Juries are groups, and they are swayed by the same influences that bear upon other types of groups. For example, the most vocal members of a jury tend to do most of the talking and the quietest members say little.

- As a jury deliberates, opposing views may become more entrenched and polarized.

- Especially when evidence is not highly incriminating, deliberation may make jurors more lenient than they originally were.

- The 12-member jury is a tradition stemming from English Common Law. Researchers find that a jury this size allows for reasonable diversity among jurors, a mix of opinions and orientations, and better recall of information.

- Researchers have also examined and questioned the assumptions underlying several recent U.S. Supreme Court decisions permitting smaller juries and nonunanimous juries.

- Simulated juries are not real juries, so we must be cautious in generalizing research findings to actual courtrooms. Yet, like all experiments in social psychology, laboratory jury experiments help us formulate theories and principles that we can use to interpret the more complex world of everyday life.

POSTSCRIPT: Thinking Smart with Psychological Science

An intellectually fashionable idea, sometimes called "postmodernism," contends that truth is socially constructed; knowledge always reflects the cultures that form it. Indeed, as we have often noted in this book, we do often follow our hunches, our biases, our cultural bent. Social scientists are not immune to confirmation bias, belief perseverance, overconfidence, and the biasing power of preconceptions. Our preconceived ideas and values guide our theory development, our interpretations, our topics of choice, and our language.

Being mindful of hidden values within psychological science should motivate us to clean the cloudy spectacles through which we view the world. Mindful of our vulnerability to bias and error, we can steer between the two extremes—of being naive about a value-laden psychology that pretends to be value-neutral, or of being tempted to an unrestrained subjectivism that dismisses evidence as nothing but collected biases. In the spirit of humility, we can put testable ideas to the test. If we think capital punishment does (or does not) deter crime more than other available punishments, we can utter our personal opinions, as has the U.S. Supreme Court. Or we can ask whether states with a death penalty have lower homicide rates, whether their rates have dropped after instituting the death penalty, and whether they have risen when abandoning the penalty.

As we have seen, the Court considered pertinent social science evidence when disallowing five-member juries and ending school desegregation. But it has discounted research when offering opinions as to whether the death penalty deters crime, whether society views execution as what the U.S. Constitution prohibits ("cruel and unusual punishment"), whether courts inflict the penalty arbitrarily, whether they apply it with racial bias, and whether potential jurors selected by virtue of their accepting capital punishment are biased toward conviction.

Beliefs and values do guide the perceptions of judges as well as scientists and laypeople. And that is why we need to think smarter—to rein in our hunches and biases by testing them against available evidence. If our beliefs find support, so much the better for them. If not, so much the worse for them. That's the humble spirit that underlies both psychological science and everyday critical thinking.

Making the Social Connection

This chapter discussed the accuracy of our memories, specifically the memories of eyewitnesses to a crime. When a child is an eyewitness, should he or she be called to testify in court, and how reliable are children's memories for reporting what they saw? For that matter, how reliable are adults' memories? Consider these questions as you watch the videos Children's Eyewitness Testimony and When Eyes Deceive on the Online Learning Center for this book.

Social Psychology and the Sustainable Future

"Can we move nations and people in the direction of sustainability? Such a move would be a modification of society comparable in scale to only two other changes: the Agricultural Revolution and the Industrial Revolution of the past two centuries. Those revolutions were gradual, spontaneous, and largely unconscious. This one will have to be a fully conscious operation. . . . If we actually do it, the undertaking will be absolutely unique in humanity's stay on the Earth."

—William D. Ruckelshaus, Former Environmental Protection Agency director "Toward a Sustainable World,"1989

Despite the recent economic recession, life for most people in Western countries is good. Today the average North American enjoys luxuries unknown even to royalty in centuries past: hot showers, flush toilets, central air-conditioning, microwave ovens, jet travel, wintertime fresh fruit, big-screen digital television, e-mail, and Post-it notes. But on the horizon, beyond the sunny skies of comfort and convenience, dark clouds of an environmental disaster are gathering. In scientific meetings hosted by the United Nations, Britain's Royal Society, and the U.S. National Academy of Sciences, a consensus has emerged: Increasing population and increasing consumption have combined to overshoot the earth's ecological carrying capacity (Figure 16.1).

FIGURE :: 16.1

The Ecological Overshoot

The human demand for things such as land, timber, fish, and fuels is increasingly exceeding the earth's regenerative capacity.

Source: World Wildlife Fund *Living Planet Report 2008.*

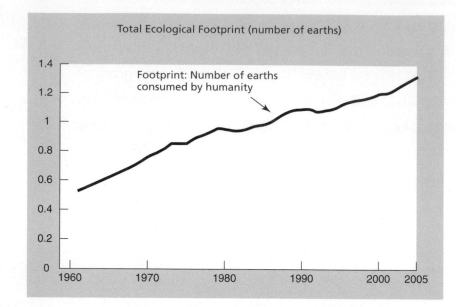

Total Ecological Footprint (number of earths)

Footprint: Number of earths consumed by humanity

An Environmental Call to Action

Although these are, materially, the best of times for many people on earth, humanity is creating a climate change that may, if human behavior does not change, become a weapon of mass destruction.

In 1950 the earth carried 2.5 billion people and 50 million cars (N. Myers, 2000). Today, reports the UN and World Bank, it has nearly 7 billion people and 600 million cars. The greenhouse gases emitted by motor vehicles, along with the burning of coal and oil to generate electricity and heat buildings, are changing the earth's climate. The latest Intergovernmental Panel on Climate Change (2007) report—a consensus statement of expert scientists from 40 countries—expresses greater confidence than any of its prior reports that human activity is dangerously warming the planet (Kerr, 2007a).

In follow-up statements, many scientists argued that the consensus warning is too cautious. Given the decades needed to implement new energy technologies, and given the built-in time lags between our actions and future consequences, the need for action is urgent, they say (Kerr, 2007b). The accelerating melting of the world's great ice sheets caused NASA's climate scientist James Hansen to worry that the sea level could rise a disastrous several meters by this century's end (Kerr, 2007d). In 2008, the American Geophysical Union (the world's largest scientific association of earth and space scientists) strengthened its statement of concern to warn that "The Earth's climate is now clearly out of balance and is warming," as is evident from increased atmospheric, land, and ocean temperatures—the nine warmest years on record have occurred since 1998 (Revkin, 2008)—and from the resulting melting glaciers and sea ice, and changing rainfall distribution and length of seasons.

"The consequences of the past century's temperature increase," notes *Science* editor Donald Kennedy (2006), "are becoming dramatically apparent in the increased frequency of extreme weather events." With the changing climate, hurricanes and heat waves, droughts and floods are becoming more common and extreme weather-related insurance payouts are rising (Rohter, 2004). As precipitation falls more as rain and less as snow, the likely result will be more floods in rainy seasons and less melting snow and glaciers for rivers during dry seasons.

"We're toast if we don't get on a very different path."
—NASA CLIMATE SCIENTIST JAMES HANSEN TO ASSOCIATED PRESS, 2008

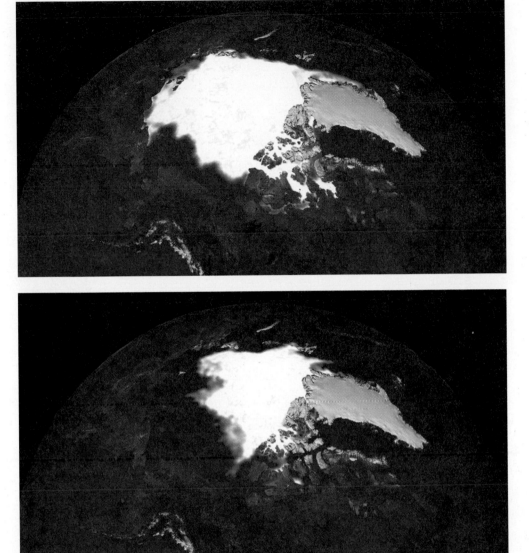

Melting of Arctic Sea ice. From 1979, when Arctic Sea ice was first measured, to 2007, the ice pack declined 43 percent (Kerr, 2007c).

It's a national security issue, say some: Terrorist bombs and global warming are both weapons of mass destruction. "If we learned that Al Qaeda was secretly developing a new terrorist technique that could disrupt water supplies around the globe, force tens of millions from their homes and potentially endanger our entire planet, we would be aroused into a frenzy and deploy every possible asset to neutralize the threat," observed essayist Nicholas Kristof (2007). "Yet that is precisely the threat that we're creating ourselves, with our greenhouse gases."

Global warming is also causing environmental destruction. Trees and shrubs are invading the North American tundra, crowding out tundra species. Plants and animals are gradually migrating toward the poles and toward higher elevations, interfering with polar and alpine ecosystems. Sub-Saharan African agricultural and grazing lands are gradually turning into desert. Such ecological changes can set off conflict and war, notes Jeffrey Sachs (2006): The deadly carnage in Darfur, Sudan, has roots in rainfall decline. Climate matters.

As the earth's population increases, the demand increases for resources to produce food, clothing, and shelter. Most of the world's original forest cover has been taken down, and what remains in the tropics is being cleared for agriculture,

FIGURE :: 16.2

World Population
Growth

Source: Population Reference
Bureau, 2006.

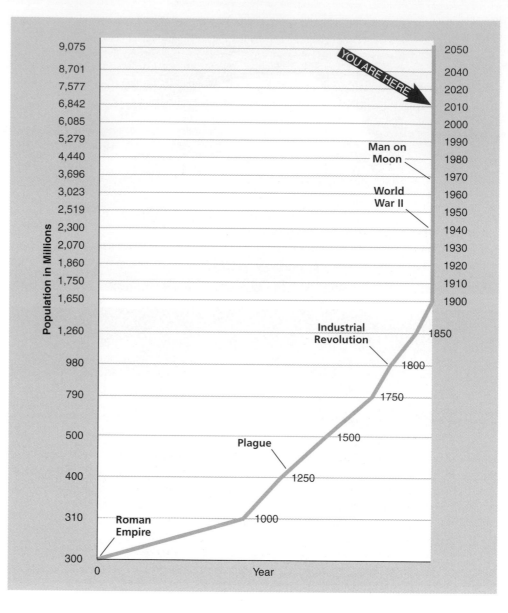

Between now and 2050, the projected 2.6 billion population increase exceeds the world's entire population in 1950, and nearly all this increase is expected in the world's poorest countries. Fifty-one countries, including Germany, Italy, and Japan, are expected to lose population (Cohen, 2005).

livestock grazing, logging, and settlements. With deforestation come soil erosion, diminished absorption of greenhouse gases, greater extremes of rainfall and temperature resulting in periodic floods and droughts, and the devastation of many animal species. A growing population's appetite for fish, together with ecosystem destruction, has also led to decreasing annual catches of most major fish species. Stocks of wild salmon, Atlantic cod, haddock, herring, and other species have suffered major depletion.

With consumption and population both destined to increase (despite falling birth rates—see Figure 16.2), further pollution, global warming, and environmental destruction seem inevitable. The simple, stubborn fact is that the earth cannot indefinitely support developed countries' current rate of consumption, much less the projected increase in consumption as less-developed countries such as China and India attain higher living standards. For the human species to survive and flourish, some things must change.

So why is global warming not a hotter topic? Why have Americans been much less concerned about global warming than Canadians and Europeans (Ipsos, 2007; Pew, 2006)? Why are only one-third of Americans "very worried" that ocean levels will rise and that flooding and droughts will become more common (Saad, 2007)? Is it, as Gallup researcher Lydia Saad (2003) believes, because on a chilly winter day "'global warming' may sound, well, appealing"? Might people be more concerned if it was framed as "global heating"? Recall from earlier chapters that labels matter; language shapes thought. Whether we describe someone who responds to others as "conforming" or as "sensitive" shapes our perceptions and our attitudes.

"One day fairly soon we will all go belly up like guppies in a neglected fishbowl. I suggest an epitaph for the whole planet: . . . 'We could have saved it, but we were too darn cheap and lazy.'"

—KURT VONNEGUT, "NOTES FROM MY BED OF GLOOM,"
1990

Summing Up: An Environmental Call to Action

- Residents of the world's developed nations enjoy the comfort and convenience of technological innovations not dreamed of a century ago.

- Yet scientists report that we are imperiled by a global crisis. Exploding population and increasing consumption have together exceeded the earth's carrying capacity and produced the serious inter-related problems of pollution, global warming, and environmental destruction.

Enabling Sustainable Living

Although increasing population and consumption have overshot the world's carrying capacity, new technologies together with reduced consumption may enable sustainable living.

What shall we do? Eat, drink, and be merry, for tomorrow is doom? Behave as have so many participants in prisoners' dilemma games, by pursuing self interest to our collective detriment? ("Heck, on a global scale, my consumption is infinitesimal; it makes my life comfortable and costs the world practically nothing.") Wring our hands, dreading that fertility plus prosperity equals calamity, and vow never to bring children into a doomed world?

Those more optimistic about the future see two routes to sustainable lifestyles: (a) increasing technological efficiency and agricultural productivity, and (b) moderating consumption and decreasing population.

New Technologies

One component in a sustainable future is improved technologies. Today's new refrigerators consume half the energy of those sold a decade ago (Heap & Comim, 2005). We have replaced many incandescent bulbs with energy-saving ones, replaced printed and delivered letters and catalogs with e-mail and e-commerce, and replaced many commuter miles driven with telecommuting.

There is also good news about cars. Today's middle-aged adults drive cars that get twice the mileage and produce a twentieth of the pollution of the ones they drove as teenagers. For the future, we have hybrid cars, which conserve gasoline by using an electric power cell.

Does the convenience of a ready-made beverage justify the resources consumed idling in line?

Plausible future technologies include diodes that emit light for 20 years without bulbs; ultrasound washing machines that consume no water, heat, or soap; reusable and compostable plastics; cars running on fuel cells that combine hydrogen and oxygen and produce water exhaust; lightweight materials stronger than steel; roofs and roads that double as solar energy collectors; and heated and cooled chairs that provide personal comfort with less heating and cooling of rooms (N. Myers, 2000; Zhang & others, 2007).

Given the speed of innovation (who could have imagined today's world a century ago?), the future will surely bring solutions that we aren't yet imagining. Surely, say the optimists, the future will bring increased material well-being for more people requiring many fewer raw materials and creating much less polluting waste.

Reducing Consumption

The second component of a sustainable future is controlling consumption. Though accounting for only 5 percent of the world's population, the United States consumes 26 percent of the world's energy (USGS, 2006). Unless we argue that today's less-developed countries are somehow less deserving of an improved standard of living, we must anticipate that their consumption will increase. As it does, the United States and other developed countries must consume less. If world economic growth enabled all countries to match Americans' present car ownership, the number of cars would multiply more than 10 times—to over 6 billion cars (N. Myers, 2000).

Thanks to family planning efforts, the world's population growth rate has decelerated, especially in developed nations. Even in less-developed countries, when food security has improved and women have become educated and empowered, birth rates have fallen. But if birth rates everywhere instantly fell to a replacement level of 2.1 children per woman, the lingering momentum of population growth, fueled by the bulge of younger humans, would continue for years to come.

Given that humans have already overshot the earth's carrying capacity, consumption must also moderate. With our material appetites continually swelling—as more people seek personal computers, air-conditioning, jet travel—what can be done to moderate consumption by those who can afford to overconsume?

One way is through public policies that harness the motivating power of incentives. As a general rule, we get less of what we tax, and more of what we reward. Many cities are using tax monies to build bike lanes and subsidize improved mass transportation, thus encouraging alternatives to cars. On jammed highways, many regions have created high-occupancy vehicle lanes that reward carpooling and penalize driving solo. U.S. consumers who buy hybrid cars are eligible for tax rebates, and some states allow hybrid drivers to use carpool lanes without a passenger in the car. Gregg Easterbrook (2004) notes that if the United States had raised its gasoline tax by 50 cents a decade ago, as was proposed, the country would now have smaller, more fuel-efficient cars (as do the Europeans, with their higher petrol taxes) and would therefore import less oil. This, in turn, would have led to lower oil consumption, less global warming, lower gas prices, and a smaller trade deficit weighing down the economy.

Another way to encourage greener homes and businesses is to harness the power of immediate feedback by installing "smart meters" that provide a continuous readout of electricity use and its cost. Turn off a computer monitor or the lights in an empty room, and the meter displays the decreased wattage. Turn on the air-conditioning, and the usage and cost are immediately known. In Britain, where smart meters are being installed in businesses, Conservative Party leader David Cameron has supported a plan to have them installed in all homes. "Smart meters have the power to revolutionize people's relationship with the energy they use," he said to Parliament (Rosenthal, 2008).

Support for new energy policies will require a shift in public consciousness not unlike that occurring during the 1960s civil rights movement and the 1970s

Living within Environmental Limits
Respecting the limits of the planet's environment, resources and biodiversity—to improve our environment and ensure that the natural resources needed for life are unimpaired and remain so for future generations.

Ensuring a Strong, Healthy and Just Society
Meeting the diverse needs of all people in existing and future communities, promoting personal well-being, social cohesion and inclusion, and creating equal opportunity for all.

Achieving a Sustainable Economy
Building a strong, stable and sustainable economy which provides prosperity and opportunities for all, and in which environmental and social costs fall on those who impose them (Polluter Pays), and efficient resource use is incentivised.

Using Sound Science Responsibly
Ensuring policy is developed and implemented on the basis of strong scientific evidence, whilst taking into account scientific uncertainty (through the Precautionary Principle) as well as public attitudes and values.

Promoting Good Governance
Actively promoting effective, participative systems of governance in all levels of society—engaging people's creativity, energy, and diversity.

FIGURE :: 16.3

The "Shared UK Principles of Sustainable Development"

The British government defines sustainable development as development that meets present needs without compromising future generations' abilities to meet their needs. "We want to live within environmental limits and achieve a just society, and we will do so by means of sustainable economy, good governance, and sound science." Social psychology's contribution will be to help influence behaviors that enable people to live within environmental limits and to enjoy personal and social well-being.

Source: www.sustainable-development.gov.uk, 2005.

women's movement. What's needed, contend Al Gore and the Alliance for Climate Protection, is mass persuasion. Yale University environmental science dean James Gustave Speth (2008) is calling for a "new consciousness" in which people

- see humanity as part of nature,
- see nature as having intrinsic value that we must steward,
- value the future and its inhabitants as well as our present,
- appreciate our human interdependence, by thinking "we" and not just "me,"
- define quality of life in relational and spiritual rather than materialistic terms, and
- value equity, justice, and the human community.

"I still say it will lead to global warming."

© 2007 Shapiro. Reprinted by permission of Mike Shapiro.

As the earth's atmosphere heats up and petroleum and other fossil fuels become scarce, such a shift is inevitable, eventually. Is there any hope that human priorities might shift from accumulating money to finding meaning, and from aggressive consumption to nurturing connections? The British government's plan for achieving sustainable development includes an emphasis on promoting personal well-being and social health (Figure 16.3). Perhaps social psychology can help point the way to greater well-being, by documenting *materialism*, by informing people that *economic growth does not automatically improve human morale,* and by helping people understand *why materialism and money fail to satisfy.*

Summing Up: Enabling Sustainable Living

- Humanity can prepare for a sustainable future by increasing technological efficiency.

- We can also create incentives and change actions and attitudes to control population and moderate consumption. Attending to concepts in social psychology

that address our attitudes and our behaviors may help accomplish those objectives. Rapid cultural change has happened in the last 40 years, and there is hope that in response to the global crisis it can happen again.

The Social Psychology of Materialism and Wealth

What might social psychology contribute to our understanding of changing materialism? To what extent do money and consumption buy happiness? And why do materialism and economic growth not bring enduringly greater satisfaction?

Does money buy happiness? Few of us would answer yes. But ask a different question—"Would a *little* more money make you a *little* happier?"—and most of us will say yes. There is, we believe, a connection between wealth and well-being. That belief feeds what Juliet Schor (1998) calls the "cycle of work and spend"—working more to buy more.

Increased Materialism

Although the earth asks that we live more lightly upon it, materialism has surged, most clearly in the United States. According to one Gallup poll (1990), 1 in 2 women, 2 in 3 men, and 4 in 5 people earning more than $75,000 a year would like to be rich—although, considering that half the world's people live on less than $2 a day, an income of $75,000 means they are already fabulously rich (Shah, 2005). Think of it as today's American dream: life, liberty, and the purchase of happiness.

Such materialism surged during the 1970s and 1980s. The most dramatic evidence comes from the UCLA/American Council on Education annual survey of nearly a quarter million entering collegians. The proportion considering it "very important or essential" that they become "very well off financially" rose from 39 percent in 1970 to 74 percent in 2007 (Figure 16.4). Those proportions virtually flip-flopped with those who considered it very important to "develop a meaningful philosophy of life." Materialism was up, spirituality down.

What a change in values! Among 19 listed objectives, new American collegians in most recent years have ranked becoming "very well off financially" number 1. That outranks not only developing a life philosophy but also "becoming an authority in my own field," "helping others in difficulty," and "raising a family."

Wealth and Well-Being

Does sustainable consumption indeed enable "the good life?" Does being well-off produce—or at least correlate with—psychological well-being? Would people be happier if they could exchange a simple lifestyle for one with palatial

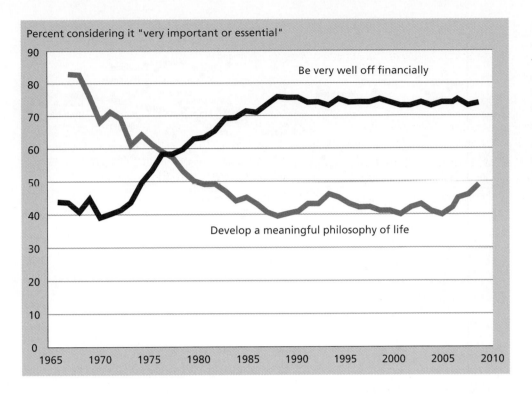

Percent considering it "very important or essential"

Be very well off financially

Develop a meaningful philosophy of life

FIGURE :: 16.4

Changing Materialism, from Annual Surveys of More than 200,000 Entering U.S. Collegians (total sample 13 million students)

Source: Data from Dey, Astin, & Korn, 1991, and subsequent annual reports.

surroundings, ski vacations in the Alps, and executive-class travel? Would you be happier if you won a sweepstakes and could choose from its suggested indulgences: a 40-foot yacht, deluxe motor home, designer wardrobe, luxury car, or private housekeeper? Social-psychological theory and evidence offer some answers.

We can observe the traffic between wealth and well-being by asking, first, if *rich nations are happier.* There is, indeed, some correlation between national wealth and well-being (measured as self-reported happiness and life satisfaction). The Scandinavians have been mostly prosperous and satisfied; the Bulgarians are neither (Figure 16.5). But once nations reach about $10,000 GNP per person, which was roughly the economic level of Ireland before its recent economic surge, higher levels of national wealth are not predictive of increased well-being. Better to be Irish than Bulgarian. But happiness is about the same whether one is an average Irish person or an average Norwegian (with more than double the Irish purchasing power) (Inglehart, 1990, 1997, 2009).

We can ask, second, whether within any given nation, *rich people are happier.* In poor countries—where low income threatens basic needs—being relatively well-off does predict greater well-being (Howell & Howell, 2008). In affluent countries, where most can afford life's necessities, affluence still matters—partly because people with more money perceive more control over their lives (Johnson & Krueger, 2006). But compared with poor countries, income matters. Once a comfortable income level is reached, more and more money produces diminishing long-term returns. World values researcher Ronald Inglehart (1990, p. 242) therefore found the income-happiness correlation to be "surprisingly weak."

Even the super-rich—the *Forbes* 100 wealthiest Americans—have reported only slightly greater happiness than average (Diener & others, 1985). And even winning a state lottery seems not to enduringly elevate well-being (Brickman & others, 1978). Such jolts of joy have "a short half-life," notes Richard Ryan (1999).

We can ask, third, whether, over time, a culture's *happiness rises with its affluence.* Does our collective well-being float upward with a rising economic tide?

"I always in the back of my mind figured a lot of money will buy you a little bit of happiness. But it's not really true."

—GOOGLE BILLIONAIRE CO-FOUNDER SERGEY BRIN, 2006

FIGURE :: 16.5

National Wealth and Well-Being, from 1995 World Bank Data and the 2000 World Values Survey

Subjective well-being index combines happiness and life satisfaction (average of percentage rating themselves as [a] "very happy" or "happy" minus percentage "unhappy," and as [b] 7 or above on a 10-point life satisfaction scale minus percentage rating themselves at 4 or below).

Source: Ronald Inglehart, 2006.

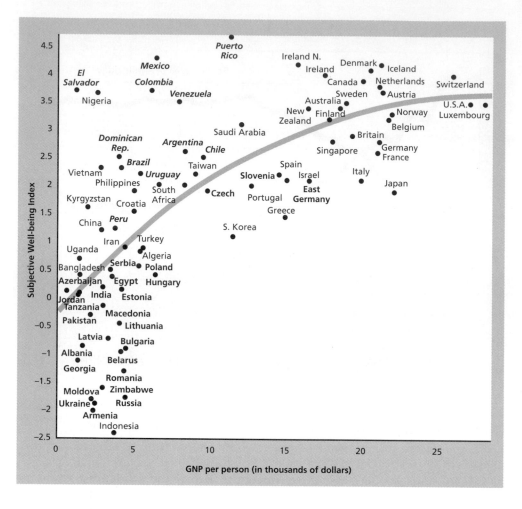

In 1957, as economist John Kenneth Galbraith was describing the United States as *The Affluent Society,* Americans' per-person income was (in 2000 dollars) about $9,000. Today, as Figure 16.6 indicates, the United States is a doubly affluent society. Although this rising tide has lifted the yachts faster than the dinghies, nearly all boats have risen. With double the spending power, thanks partly to the surge in married women's employment, we now own twice as many cars per person, eat out twice as often, and are supported by a whole new world of technology. Since 1960 we have also seen the proportion of households with dishwashers rise from 7 to 60 percent, with clothes dryers rise from 20 to 74 percent, and with air-conditioning rise from 15 to 86 percent (Bureau of the Census, 2009).

So, believing that it's "very important" to "be very well-off financially," and having become better off financially, are today's Americans happier? Are they happier with espresso coffee, caller ID, camera cell phones, and suitcases on wheels than before?

They are not. Since 1957 the number of Americans who say they are "very happy" has declined slightly: from 35 to 32 percent. Twice as rich and apparently no happier. Meanwhile, the divorce rate has doubled, the teen suicide rate has more than doubled, and more people than ever (especially teens and young adults) are depressed.

We might call this soaring wealth and shrinking spirit "the American paradox." More than ever, we have big houses and broken homes, high incomes and low morale, more comfortable cars and more road rage. We excel at making a living but often fail at making a life. We celebrate our prosperity but yearn for purpose. We cherish our freedoms but long for connection. In an age of plenty, we feel spiritual hunger (Myers, 2000a).

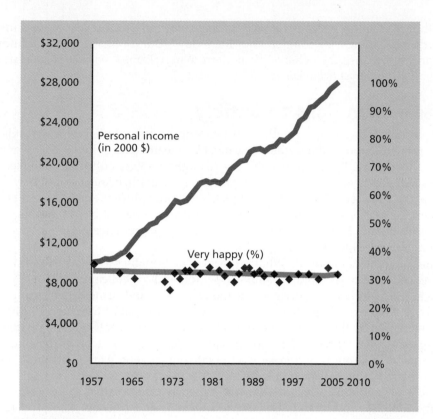

FIGURE :: 16.6

Has Economic Growth Advanced Human Morale?

While inflation-adjusted income has risen, self-reported happiness has not.

Source: Happiness data from General Social Surveys, National Opinion Research Center, University of Chicago. Income data from Bureau of the Census (1975) and *Economic Indicators.*

Today's material comforts in China: people shopping for laptops and other increasingly valuable goods. Despite increasing incomes, the percentage of Chinese who feel satisfied with their lives has declined.

It is hard to avoid a startling conclusion: Our becoming much better-off over the last five decades has not been accompanied by one iota of increased subjective well-being. The same has been true of the European countries and Japan, reports Richard Easterlin (1995). In Britain, for example, great increases in the percent of households with cars, central heating, and telephones have not been accompanied by increased happiness. After a decade of extraordinary economic growth in China—from few owning a phone and 40 percent owning a color television to most people now having such things—Gallup surveys revealed a *decreasing* proportion of people satisfied "with the way things are going in your life today" (Burkholder, 2005). The findings are startling because they challenge modern materialism: *Economic growth has provided no apparent boost to human morale.*

Materialism Fails to Satisfy

It is striking that economic growth in affluent countries has failed to satisfy. It is further striking that individuals who strive most for wealth tend to live with lower well-being. This finding "comes through very strongly in every culture I've looked at," reports Richard Ryan (1999). Seek extrinsic goals—wealth, beauty, popularity—and you may find anxiety, depression, and psychosomatic ills (Eckersley, 2005; Sheldon & others, 2004). Those who instead strive for intrinsic goals such as "intimacy, personal growth, and contribution to the community" experience a higher quality of life, concludes Tim Kasser (2000, 2002).

Pause a moment and think: What is the most personally satisfying event that you experienced in the last month? Kennon Sheldon and his colleagues (2001) put that question (and similar questions about the last week and semester) to samples of university students. Then they asked them to rate the extent to which 10 different needs were met by the satisfying event. The students rated self-esteem, relatedness (feeling connected with others), and autonomy (feeling in control) as the emotional needs that most strongly accompanied the satisfying event. At the bottom of the list of factors predicting satisfaction were money and luxury.

People who identify themselves with expensive possessions experience fewer positive moods, report Emily Solberg, Ed Diener, and Michael Robinson (2003). Such materialists tend to report a relatively large gap between what they want and what they have, and to enjoy fewer close, fulfilling relationships. The challenge for healthy nations, then, is to foster improving standards of living without encouraging a materialism and consumerism that displaces the deep need to belong.

But why do yesterday's luxuries, such as air-conditioning and television, so quickly become today's requirements? Two principles drive this psychology of consumption.

> "Why do you spend your money for that which is not bread, and your labor for that which does not satisfy?"
>
> —ISAIAH 55:2

OUR HUMAN CAPACITY FOR ADAPTATION

adaptation-level phenomenon
The tendency to adapt to a given level of stimulation and thus to notice and react to changes from that level.

The **adaptation-level phenomenon** is our tendency to judge our experience (for example, of sounds, temperatures, or income) relative to a neutral level defined by our prior experience. We adjust our neutral levels—the points at which sounds seem neither loud nor soft, temperatures neither hot nor cold, events neither pleasant nor unpleasant—on the basis of our experience. We then notice and react to up or down changes from those levels.

Thus, as our achievements rise above past levels, we feel successful and satisfied. As our social prestige, income, or in-home technology improves, we feel pleasure.

Could Lucy ever experience enough "ups"? Not according to the adaptation-level phenomenon.
PEANUTS © United Features Syndicate, Inc.

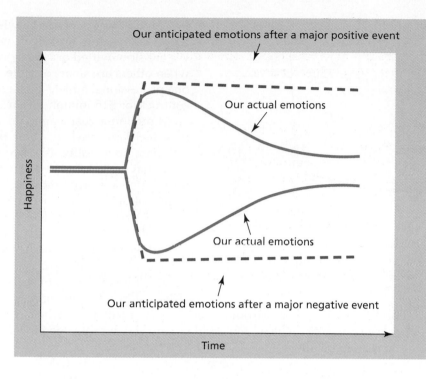

FIGURE :: 16.7

The Impact Bias

As explained in Chapter 2, people generally overestimate the enduring impact of significant positive and negative life events.

Source: Figure inspired by de Botton, 2004.

Before long, however, we adapt. What once felt good comes to register as neutral, and what formerly was neutral now feels like deprivation.

Would it ever, then, be possible to create a social paradise? Donald Campbell (1975b) answered no: If you woke up tomorrow to your utopia—perhaps a world with no bills, no ills, someone who loves you unreservedly—you would feel euphoric, for a time. Yet before long, you would recalibrate your adaptation level and again sometimes feel gratified (when achievements surpass expectations), sometimes feel deprived (when they fall below), and sometimes feel neutral.

To be sure, adaptation to some events, such as the death of a spouse, may be incomplete, as the sense of loss lingers (Diener & others, 2006). Yet, as Chapter 2 explained, we generally underestimate our adaptive capacity. People have difficulty predicting the intensity and duration of their future positive and negative emotions (Wilson & Gilbert, 2003; Figure 16.7). The elation from getting what we want—riches, top exam scores, the Chicago Cubs winning the World Series— evaporates more rapidly than we expect. We also sometimes "miswant." When first-year university students predicted their satisfaction with various housing possibilities shortly before entering their school's housing lottery, they focused on physical features. "I'll be happiest in a beautiful and well-located dorm," many students seemed to think. But they were wrong. When contacted a year later, it was the social features, such as a sense of community, that predicted happiness, report Elizabeth Dunn and her colleagues (2003). Likewise, Leaf Van Boven and Thomas Gilovich (2003) report from their surveys and experiments that positive *experiences* (often social experiences) leave us happier. The best things in life are not things.

OUR WANTING TO COMPARE

Much of life revolves around **social comparison,** a point made by the old joke about two hikers who meet a bear. One reaches into his backpack and pulls out a pair of sneakers. "Why bother putting those on?" asks the other. "You can't outrun a bear." "I don't have to outrun the bear," answers the first. "I just have to outrun you."

Similarly, happiness is relative to our comparisons with others, especially those within our own groups (Lyubomirsky, 2001; Zagefka & Brown, 2005). Whether we

social comparison
Evaluating one's abilities and opinions by comparing oneself with others.

Social comparisons foster feelings.

"O.K., if you can't see your way to giving me a pay raise, how about giving Parkerson a pay cut?"

feel good or bad depends on whom we're comparing ourselves with. We are slow-witted or clumsy only when others are smart or agile. Let one professional athlete sign a new contract for $15 million a year and an $8-million-a-year teammate may now feel less satisfied. "Our poverty became a reality. Not because of our having less, but by our neighbors having more," recalled Will Campbell in *Brother to a Dragonfly.* (See "Focus On: Social Comparison, Belonging, and Happiness.")

Further feeding our luxury fever is the tendency to compare upward: As we climb the ladder of success or affluence, we mostly compare ourselves with peers who are at or above our current level, not with those who have less. People living in communities where a few residents are very wealthy tend to feel less satisfied as they compare upward.

The U.S. rich-poor gap has grown, observes Michael Hagerty (2000). Even in China, income inequality has grown. This helps explain why rising affluence has not produced increased happiness. Rising income inequality, notes Hagerty, makes for more people who have rich neighbors. Television's modeling of the lifestyles of the wealthy also serves to accentuate feelings of "relative deprivation" and desires for more (Schor, 1998).

The adaptation-level and social comparison phenomena give us pause. They imply that the quest for happiness through material achievement requires continually expanding affluence. But the good news is that adaptation to simpler lives can also happen. If we shrink our consumption by choice or by necessity, we will initially feel a pinch, but it will pass. "Weeping may tarry for the night, but joy comes with the morning," reflected the Psalmist. Indeed, thanks to our capacity to adapt and to adjust comparisons, the emotional impact of significant life events—losing a job or even a disabling accident—dissipates sooner than most people suppose (Gilbert & others, 1998).

focus ON

Social Comparison, Belonging, and Happiness

Mfezy was born in a South African village. She grew up in a family where there was no money for luxuries, yet she never felt herself to be poor. What she did know, from early childhood, was the truth of the Xhosa saying— "Umntu ngumtu ngaabantu," which translated means "a person is made by other people."

When Mfezy wanted to start a master's degree in psychology at Rhodes University, she was asked at an interview about how, coming from such a poor background herself, she could understand better-off people. She replied that she did not come from a "poor" background.

The word "poor" was, she felt, only attached as a label by better-off people. She told her interviewers that the village community that she came from was all family. Every woman in the community was like a mother to her. Each carried responsibility for her well-being. She felt held in a wide love. In such a situation how could she be "poor"? Mfezy did not seek to romanticize poverty in any way, yet neither had she felt "poor"—even in times of hardship.

Source: From Peter Millar's *Guguletu Journal,* The Iona Community.

Toward Sustainability and Survival

As individuals and as a global society, we face difficult social and political issues. How might a democratic society induce people to adopt values that emphasize happiness over materialism? How might a market economy mix incentives for prosperity with restraints that preserve a habitable planet? To what extent can we depend on technological innovations, such as alternative energy sources, to reduce our ecological footprints? And in the meantime, to what extent does the superordinate goal of preserving the earth for our grandchildren call us each to limit our own liberties—our freedom to drive, burn, and dump whatever we wish?

A shift to postmaterialist values will gain momentum as people, governments, and corporations take these steps:

- Face the implications of population and consumption growth for pollution, climate change, and environmental destruction
- Realize that materialist values make for *less* happy lives
- Identify and promote the things in life that matter more than economic growth

"If the world is to change for the better it must have a change in human consciousness," said Czech poet-president Vaclav Havel (1990). We must discover "a deeper sense of responsibility toward the world, which means responsibility toward something higher than self." If people came to believe that stacks of unplayed CDs, closets full of seldom-worn clothes, and garages with luxury cars do not define the good life, then might a shift in consciousness become possible? Instead of being an indicator of social status, might conspicuous consumption become gauche?

Social psychology's contribution to a sustainable and survivable future will come partly through its consciousness-transforming insights into adaptation and comparison. These insights also come from experiments that lower people's comparison standards and thereby cool luxury fever and renew contentment. In two such experiments, Marshall Dermer and his colleagues (1979) put university women through imaginative exercises in deprivation. After viewing depictions of the grimness of Milwaukee life in 1900, or after imagining and writing about being burned and disfigured, the women expressed greater satisfaction with their own lives.

> "All our wants, beyond those which a very moderate income will supply, are purely imaginary."
> —*HENRY ST. JOHN, LETTER TO SWIFT, 1719*

Close, supportive relationships are a key element in well-being.

In another experiment, Jennifer Crocker and Lisa Gallo (1985) found that people who five times completed the sentence "I'm glad I'm not a . . ." afterward felt less depressed and more satisfied with their lives than did those who completed sentences beginning "I wish I were a. . . ." Realizing that others have it worse helps us count our blessings. "I cried because I had no shoes," says a Persian proverb, "until I met a man who had no feet." *Downward* social comparison facilitates contentment.

Downward comparison to a hypothetical worse-off self also enhances contentment. In one experiment, Minkyung Koo and her colleagues (2008) invited people to write about how they might never have met their romantic partner. Compared to others who wrote about meeting their partner, those who imagined not having the relationship expressed more satisfaction with it. Can you likewise imagine how some good things in *your* life might never have happened? It's very easy for me to imagine not having chanced into an acquaintance that led to an invitation to author this book. Just thinking about that reminds me to count my blessings.

Social psychology also contributes to a sustainable and survivable future through its explorations of the good life. If materialism does not enhance life quality, what does?

- *Close, supportive relationships.* As we saw in Chapter 11, our deep need to belong is satisfied by close, supportive relationships. People who are supported by intimate friendships or a committed marriage are much more likely to declare themselves "very happy."

- *Faith communities* and voluntary organizations are often a source of such connections, as well as of meaning and hope. That helps explain a finding from National Opinion Research Center surveys of 46,000 Americans since 1972: 27 percent of those rarely or never attending religious services declared themselves very happy, as did 48 percent of those attending multiple times weekly.

- *Positive thinking habits.* Optimism, self-esteem, perceived control, and extraversion also mark happy experiences and happy lives.

- *Flow.* Work and leisure experiences that engage one's skills mark happy lives. Between the anxiety of being overwhelmed and stressed, and the apathy of being underwhelmed and bored, notes Mihaly Csikszentmihalyi (1990, 1999), lies a zone in which people experience *flow*, an optimal state in which, absorbed in an activity, we lose consciousness of self and time. When their experience is sampled using electronic pagers, people report greatest enjoyment not when mindlessly passive but when unselfconsciously absorbed in a mindful challenge. In fact, the less expensive (and generally more involving) a leisure activity, the *happier* people are while doing it. Most people are happier gardening than powerboating, talking to friends than watching TV. Low-consumption recreations prove most satisfying.

"We have failed to see how our economy, our environment and our society are all one. And that delivering the best possible quality of life for us all means more than concentrating solely on economic growth."
—*PRIME MINISTER TONY BLAIR, FOREWORD TO A BETTER QUALITY OF LIFE, 1999*

That is good news indeed. Those things that make for the genuinely good life—close relationships, social networks based on belief, positive thinking habits, engaging activity—are enduringly sustainable. And that is an idea close to the heart of Jigme Singye Wangchuk, King of Bhutan. "Gross national happiness is more important than gross national product," he believes. Writing from the Center of Bhutan Studies in Bhutan, Sander Tideman (2003) explains: "Gross National Happiness . . . aims to promote real progress and sustainability by measuring the quality of life, rather than the mere sum of production and consumption." Now other nations, too, are assessing national quality of life. (See "Research Close-Up: Measuring National Well-Being.")

research
CLOSE-UP

Measuring National Well-Being

"A city is successful not when it's rich, but when its people are happy." So believes Bogotá, Colombia, former mayor Enrique Peñalosa, in explaining his campaign to improve his city's quality of life—by building schools and increasing school enrollment 34 percent, building or rebuilding more than 1,200 parks, creating an effective transit system, and reducing the murder rate dramatically (Gardner & Assadourian, 2004).

Peñalosa's idea of national success is shared by a growing number of social scientists and government planners. In Britain, the New Economic Foundation has developed a "Measure of Domestic Progress" that tracks national social health and has published a *Well-Being Manifesto for a Flourishing Society.* The foundation's motto: "We believe in economics as if people and the planet mattered." To assess national progress, they urge, we should measure not just financial progress but also the kinds of growth that enhance people's life satisfaction and happiness.

British economist Andrew Oswald (2006), one of a new breed of economists who study the relationships between economic and psychological well-being, notes that "economists' faith in the value of growth is diminishing. That is a good thing and will slowly make its way into the minds of tomorrow's politicians."

Leading the way toward new ways of assessing human progress are the newly developed "Guidelines for National Indicators of Subjective Well-Being and Ill-Being" developed by University of Illinois psychologist Ed Diener (2005; Diener & others, 2008, 2009) and signed by four dozen of the world's leading researchers (Figure 16.8). It notes that "global measures of subjective well-being, such as assessments of life satisfaction and happiness, can be useful for policy debates," such as by detecting the human effects of any policy interventions. More specifically, questions are now available for assessing these indicators:

- *Positive emotions,* including those involving low arousal (contentment), moderate arousal (pleasure), and high arousal (euphoria), and those involving positive responses to others (affection) and to activities (interest and engagement).

- *Negative emotions,* including anger, sadness, anxiety, stress, frustration, envy, guilt and shame, loneliness, and helplessness. Measures may ask people to recall or record the frequency of their experiencing positive and negative emotions.

- *Happiness,* which often is taken to mean a general positive mood, such as indicated by people's answers to a widely used survey question: "Taking all things together, how would you say things are these days— would you say that you are very happy, pretty happy, or not too happy?"

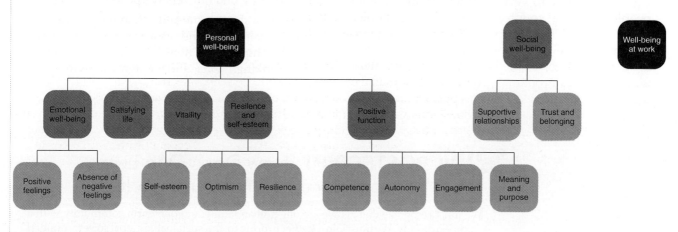

FIGURE :: 16.8

Components of Well-Being

In its 2009 *National Accounts of Well-Being* report, Britain's New Economic Foundation urges governments to "directly measure people's subjective well-being: their experiences, feelings and perceptions of how their lives are going." What matters, this think tank argues, is not so much people's economic level as their experienced quality of life. Categories for assessing national well-being include personal well-being, social well-being, and work-related well-being:

(continued)

- *Life satisfaction*, which engages people in appraising their life as a whole.
- *Domain satisfactions*, which invites people to indicate their satisfaction with their physical health, work, leisure, relationships, family, and community.
- *Quality of life*, a broader concept that includes one's environment and health, and one's perceptions of such.

Many of these indicators are part of worldwide Gallup surveys of well-being in more than 130 countries encompassing more than 95 percent of the world's people (Gallup News, 2007; Harter & Gurley, 2008). The surveys compare countries (revealing, for example, that people in some high-income countries such as Israel and Saudi Arabia report lower levels of positive emotion than people in some low-income countries such as Kenya and India). Gallup also is conducting a massive 25-year survey of the health and well-being of U.S. residents, with 250 interviewers conducting a thousand surveys a day, seven days a week. The result is a daily snapshot of American well-being—of people's happiness, stress, anger, sleep, money worries, laughter, socializing, work, and much more. Although the project was recently launched, researchers have already identified the best days of the year (largely weekends and holidays) and monitored the short-term emotional impact of economic ups and downs. And with 300,000+ respondents a year, any subgroup of 1 percent of the population will have some 3,000 respondents included, thus enabling researchers to compare people in very specific occupations, locales, religions, and ethnic groups.

Summing Up: The Social Psychology of Materialism and Wealth

- To judge from the expressed values of college students and the "luxury fever" that marked late-twentieth-century America, today's Americans—and to a lesser extent people in other Western countries—live in a highly materialistic age.
- People in rich nations report greater happiness and life satisfaction than those in poor nations (though with diminishing returns as one moves from moderately to very wealthy countries). Rich people within a country are somewhat happier than working-class people, though again more and more money provides diminishing returns (as evident in studies of the super-rich and of lottery winners). Does economic growth over time make people happier? Not at all, it seems from the slight decline in self-reported happiness and the increasing rate of depression during the post-1960 years of increasing affluence.

- Two principles help explain why materialism fails to satisfy: the adaptation-level phenomenon and social comparison. When incomes and consumption rise, we soon adapt. And comparing ourselves with others, we may find our relative position unchanged.

- To build a sustainable and satisfying future, we can individually seek and, as a society, promote close relationships, social networks based on belief, positive thinking habits, and engaging activity.

POSTSCRIPT: How Does One Live Responsibly in the Modern World?

We must recognize that . . . we are one human family and one Earth community with a common destiny. We must join together to bring forth a sustainable global society founded on respect for nature, universal human rights, economic justice, and a culture of peace. Towards this end, it is imperative that we, the peoples of the Earth, declare our responsibility to one another, to the greater community of life, and to future generations.

—Preamble, The Earth Charter, www.earthcharter.org

Reading and writing about population growth, global warming, materialism, consumption, adaptation, comparison, and sustainability provokes my reflection: Am I part of the answer or part of the problem? I can talk a good line. But do I walk my own talk?

If I'm to be honest, my record is mixed.

I ride a bike to work year-round. But I also flew 80,000 miles last year on fuel-guzzling jets.

I have insulated my 108-year-old home, installed an efficient furnace, and turned the winter daytime thermostat down to 67. But having grown up in a cool summer climate, I can't imagine living without my air-conditioning on sweltering summer days.

To control greenhouse gas production, I routinely turn off lights and the computer monitor when away from my office and have planted trees around my house. But I've helped finance South American deforestation with the imported beef I've dined on and the coffee I've sipped.

I applauded in 1973 when the United States established an energy-conserving 55 mph national maximum speed limit and was disappointed when it was abandoned in 1995. But now that drivers on the highway around my town are back up to 70 mph, I drive no less than 70 mph—even with (blush) no other cars in sight.

At my house we recycle all our home paper, cans, and bottles. But each week we receive enough mail, newspapers, and periodicals to fill a three-cubic-foot paper recycling bin.

Not bad, I tell myself. But it's hardly a bold response to the looming crisis. Our great-grandchildren will not thrive on this planet if all of today's 7 billion humans (much less all of tomorrow's 9 billion) were to demand a similar-sized ecological footprint.

How, then, does one participate in the modern world, welcoming its beauties and conveniences, yet remain mindful of our environmental legacy? Even the leaders of the simpler-living movement—who also flew gas-guzzling jets to the three conferences we attended together in luxurious surroundings—struggle with how to live responsibly in the modern world.

So what do you think? What regulations do you favor or oppose? Higher fuel efficiency requirements for cars and trucks? Auto pollution checks? Leaf-burning bans to reduce smog? If you live in a country where high fuel taxes motivate people to drive small fuel-efficient cars, do you wish you could have the much lower fuel taxes and cheaper petrol that have enabled Americans to drive big cars? If you are an American, would you favor higher gasoline and oil taxes to help conserve resources and restrain global warming?

How likely is it that humanity will be able to curb global warming and resource depletion? If the biologist E. O. Wilson (2002) is right to speculate that humans evolved to commit themselves only to their small piece of geography, their own kin, and their own time, can we hope that our species will exhibit "extended altruism" by caring for our distant descendants? Will today's envied "lifestyles of the rich and famous" become gauche in a future where sustainability becomes necessity? Or will people's concern for themselves and for displaying the symbols of success always trump their concerns for their unseen great-grandchildren?

"The great dilemma of environmental reasoning stems from this conflict between short-term and long-term values."

—E. O. WILSON, THE FUTURE OF LIFE, 2002

Making the Social Connection

In this chapter we've discussed ways in which social psychology can encourage the development of new technologies and reduce consumption among residents of developed countries. We've also seen the social-psychological evidence that material wealth does not buy happiness or well-being.

One factor that does boost people's well-being is experiencing "flow" as they focus on a challenge that engages their skills. The Online Learning Center for this book offers an example: a group of adventure racers realizing their potential as they hike, canoe, rappel, swim, and climb a 335-mile trek through treacherous terrain.

Epilogue

If you have read this entire book, your introduction to social psychology is complete. In the Preface I offered my hope that this book "would be at once solidly scientific and warmly human, factually rigorous and intellectually provocative." You, not I, are the judge of whether that goal has been achieved. But I can tell you that giving away the discipline has been a joy for me as your author. If receiving my gift has brought you any measure of pleasure, stimulation, and enrichment, then my joy is compounded.

A knowledge of social psychology, I do believe, has the power to restrain intuition with critical thinking, illusion with understanding, and judgmentalism with compassion. In these 16 chapters, we have assembled social psychology's insights into belief and persuasion, love and hate, conformity and independence. We have glimpsed incomplete answers to intriguing questions: How do our attitudes feed and get fed by our actions? What leads people sometimes to hurt and sometimes to help one another? What kindles social conflict, and how can we transform closed fists into helping hands? Answering such questions expands our minds. And, "once expanded to the dimensions of a larger idea," noted Oliver Wendell Holmes, the mind "never returns to its original size." Such has been my experience, and perhaps yours, as you, through this and other courses, become an educated person.

David G. Myers
davidmyers.org

References

Abbate, C. S., Isgro, A., Wicklund, R. A., & Boca, S. (2006). A field experiment on perspective-taking, helping, and self-awareness. *Basic and Applied Social Psychology, 28*, 283–287.

Abbey, A. (1987). Misperceptions of friendly behavior as sexual interest: A survey of naturally occurring incidents. *Psychology of Women Quarterly, 11*, 173–194.

Abbey, A. (1991). Misperception as an antecedent of acquaintance rape: A consequence of ambiguity in communication between women and men. In A. Parrot (Ed.), *Acquaintance rape*. New York: John Wiley.

Abbey, A., & Andrews, F. M. (1985). Modeling the psychological determinants of life quality. *Social Indicators Research, 16*, 1–34.

Abbey, A., McAuslan, P., & Ross, L. T. (1998). Sexual assault perpetration by college men: The role of alcohol, misperception of sexual intent, and sexual beliefs and experiences. *Journal of Social and Clinical Psychology, 17*, 167–195.

ABC News. (2004, December 28). Whistle-blower revealed abuse at Abu Ghraib prison (abcnews.go.com).

ABC News. (2004, March 31). Bizarre hoax leads to strip searches (abcnews.go.com).

Abelson, R. (1972). Are attitudes necessary? In B. T. King & E. McGinnies (Eds.), *Attitudes, conflict and social change*. New York: Academic Press.

Abelson, R. P., Kinder, D. R., Peters, M. D., & Fiske, S. T. (1982). Affective and semantic components in political person perception. *Journal of Personality and Social Psychology, 42*, 619–630.

Abrams, D., Wetherell, M., Cochrane, S., Hogg, M. A., & Turner, J. C. (1990). Knowing what to think by knowing who you are: Self-categorization and the nature of norm formation, conformity and group polarization. *British Journal of Social Psychology, 29*, 97–119.

Abramson, L. Y. (Ed.). (1988). *Social cognition and clinical psychology: A synthesis*. New York: Guilford.

Abramson, L. Y., Metalsky, G. I., & Alloy, L. B. (1989). Hopelessness depression: A theory-based subtype. *Psychological Review, 96*, 358–372.

Acitelli, L. K., & Antonucci, T. C. (1994). Gender differences in the link between marital support and satisfaction in older couples. *Journal of Personality and Social Psychology, 67*, 688–698.

Ackermann, R., & DeRubeis, R. J. (1991). Is depressive realism real? *Clinical Psychology Review, 11*, 565–584.

Adair, J. G., Dushenko, T. W., & Lindsay, R. C. L. (1985). Ethical regulations and their impact on research practice. *American Psychologist, 40*, 59–72.

Adams, D. (Ed.). (1991). *The Seville statement on violence: Preparing the ground for the constructing of peace*. UNESCO.

Adams, G., Garcia, D. M., Purdie-Vaughns, V., & Steele, C. M. (2006). The detrimental effects of a suggestion of sexism in an instruction situation. *Journal of Experimental Social Psychology, 42*, 602–615.

Adams, J. M., & Jones, W. H. (1997). The conceptualization of marital commitment: An integrative analysis. *Journal of Personality and Social Psychology, 72*, 1177–1196.

Addis, M. E., & Mahalik, J. R. (2003). Men, masculinity, and the contexts of help seeking. *American Psychologist, 58*, 5–14.

Aderman, D., & Berkowitz, L. (1983). Self-concern and the unwillingness to be helpful. *Social Psychology Quarterly, 46*, 293–301.

Adler, N. E., & Snibbe, A. C. (2003). The role of psychosocial processes in explaining the gradient between socioeconomic status and health. *Current Directions in Psychological Science, 12*, 119–123.

Adler, N. E., Boyce, T., Chesney, M. A., Cohen, S., Folkman, S., Kahn, R. L., & Syme, S. L. (1993). Socioeconomic inequalities in health: No easy solution. *Journal of the American Medical Association, 269*, 3140–3145.

Adler, N. E., Boyce, T., Chesney, M. A., Cohen, S., Folkman, S., Kahn, R. L., & Syme, S. L. (1994). Socioeconomic status and health: The challenge of the gradient. *American Psychologist, 49*, 15–24.

Adler, R. P., Lesser, G. S., Meringoff, L. K., Robertson, T. S., & Ward, S. (1980). *The effects of television advertising on children*. Lexington, MA: Lexington Books.

Adler, S. J. (1994). *The jury*. New York: Times Books.

Adorno, T., Frenkel-Brunswik, E., Levinson, D., & Sanford, R. N. (1950). *The authoritarian personality*. New York: Harper.

Agthe, M., Spörrle, M., & Försterling, F. (2008). Success attributions and more: Multidimensional extensions of the sexual attribution bias to failure attributions, social emotions, and the desire for social interaction. *Personality and Social Psychology Bulletin, 34*, 1627–1638.

Aiello, J. R., & Douthitt, E. Z. (2001). Social facilitation from Triplett to electronic performance monitoring. *Group Dynamics: Theory, Research, and Practice, 5*, 163–180.

Aiello, J. R., Thompson, D. E., & Brodzinsky, D. M. (1983). How funny is crowding anyway? Effects of room size, group size, and the introduction of humor. *Basic and Applied Social Psychology, 4*, 193–207.

Ainsworth, M. D. S. (1973). The development of infant-mother attachment. In B. Caldwell & H. Ricciuti (Eds.), *Review of child development research* (Vol. 3). Chicago: University of Chicago Press.

Ainsworth, M. D. S. (1979). Infant-mother attachment. *American Psychologist, 34*, 932–937.

Ajzen, I., & Fishbein, M. (1977). Attitude-behavior relations: A theoretical analysis and review of empirical research. *Psychological Bulletin, 84*, 888–918.

Ajzen, I., & Fishbein, M. (2005). The influence of attitudes on behavior. In D. Albarracin, B. T. Johnson, & M. P. Zanna (Eds.), *The handbook of attitudes*. Mahwah, NJ: Erlbaum.

Albarracin, D., Gillette, J. C., Ho, M-H., Earl, A. N., Glasman, L. R., & Durantini, M. R. (2005). A test of major assumptions about behavior change: A comprehensive look at the effects of passive and active HIV-prevention interventions since the beginning of the epidemic. *Psychological Bulletin, 131*, 856–897.

Albarracin, D., Johnson, B. T., Fishbein, M., & Muellerleile, P. A. (2001). Theories of reasoned action and planned behavior as models of condom use: A meta-analysis. *Psychological Bulletin, 127*, 142–161.

Albarracin, D., McNatt, P. S., Klein, C. T. F., Ho, R. M., Mitchell, A. L., & Kumkale, G. T. (2003). Persuasive communications to change actions: An analysis of behavioral and cognitive impact in HIV prevention. *Health Psychology, 22*, 166–177.

Alicke, M. D., & Davis, T. L. (1989). The role of *a posteriori* victim information in judgments of blame and sanction. *Journal of Experimental Social Psychology, 25*, 362–377.

Alkhuzai, A. H., & 18 others. (2008). Violence-related mortality in Iraq from 2002 to 2006. *New England Journal of Medicine*, **358**, 484–493.

Allee, W. C., & Masure, R. M. (1936). A comparison of maze behavior in paired and isolated shell-parakeets (*Melopsittacus undulatus Shaw*) in a two-alley problem box. *Journal of Comparative Psychology*, **22**, 131–155.

Allen, V. L., & Levine, J. M. (1969). Consensus and conformity. *Journal of Experimental Social Psychology*, **5**, 389–399.

Allison, S. T., Beggan, J. K., McDonald, R. A., & Rettew, M. L. (1995). The belief in majority determination of group decision outcomes. *Basic and Applied Social Psychology*, **16**, 367–382.

Allison, S. T., Jordan, M. R., & Yeatts, C. E. (1992). A cluster-analytic approach toward identifying the structure and content of human decision making. *Human Relations*, **45**, 49–72.

Allison, S. T., Mackie, D. M., & Messick, D. M. (1996). Outcome biases in social perception: Implications for dispositional inference, attitude change, stereotyping, and social behavior. *Advances in Experimental Social Psychology*, **28**, 53–93.

Allison, S. T., Mackie, D. M., Muller, M. M., & Worth, L. T. (1993). Sequential correspondence biases and perceptions of change: The Castro studies revisited. *Personality and Social Psychology Bulletin*, **19**, 151–157.

Allison, S. T., McQueen, L. R., & Schaerfl, L. M. (1992). Social decision making processes and the equal partitionment of shared resources. *Journal of Experimental Social Psychology*, **28**, 23–42.

Allison, S. T., & Messick, D. M. (1985). The group attribution error. *Journal of Experimental Social Psychology*, **21**, 563–579.

Allison, S. T., & Messick, D. M. (1987). From individual inputs to group outputs, and back again: Group processes and inferences about members. In C. Hendrick (Ed.), *Group processes: Review of personality and social psychology* (Vol. 8). Newbury Park, CA: Sage.

Allison, S. T., Messick, D. M., & Goethals, G. R. (1989). On being better but not smarter than others: The Muhammad Ali effect. *Social Cognition*, **7**, 275–296.

Allison, S. T., Worth, L. T., & King, M. W. C. (1990). Group decisions as social inference heuristics. *Journal of Personality and Social Psychology*, **58**, 801–811.

Alloy, L. B., & Abramson, L. Y. (1979). Judgment of contingency in depressed and nondepressed students: Sadder but wiser? *Journal of Experimental Psychology: General*, **108**, 441–485.

Alloy, L., Abramson, L. Y., Gibb, B. E., Crossfield, A. G., Pieracci, A. M., Spasojevic, J., & Steinberg, J. A. (2004). Developmental antecedents of cognitive vulnerability to depression: Review of findings from the cognitive vulnerability to depression project. *Journal of Cognitive Psychotherapy*, **18**, 115–133.

Alloy, L. B., Abramson, L. Y., Whitehouse, W. G., Hogan, M. E., Tashman, N. A., Steinberg, D. L., Rose, D. T., & Donovan, P. (1999). Depressogenic cognitive styles: Predictive validity, information processing and personality characteristics, and developmental origins. *Behaviour Research and Therapy*, **37**, 503–531.

Alloy, L. B., Albright, J. S., Abramson, L. Y., & Dykman, B. M. (1990). Depressive realism and nondepressive optimistic illusions: The role of the self. In R. E. Ingram (Ed.), *Contemporary psychological approaches to depression: Theory, research and treatment*. New York: Plenum.

Allport, F. H. (1920). The influence of the group upon association and thought. *Journal of Experimental Psychology*, **3**, 159–182.

Allport, G. (1954). *The nature of prejudice*. Cambridge, MA: Addison-Wesley.

Allport, G. W. (1958). *The nature of prejudice* (abridged). Garden City, NY: Anchor Books.

Allport, G. W., & Ross, J. M. (1967). Personal religious orientation and prejudice. *Journal of Personality and Social Psychology*, **5**, 432–443.

Altemeyer, R. (1988). *Enemies of freedom: Understanding right-wing authoritarianism*. San Francisco: Jossey-Bass.

Altemeyer, R. (1992). Six studies of right-wing authoritarianism among American state legislators. Unpublished manuscript, University of Manitoba.

Altemeyer, R. (2004). Highly dominating, highly authoritarian personalities. *Journal of Social Psychology*, **144**, 421–447.

Altemeyer, R., & Hunsberger, B. (1992). Authoritarianism, religious fundamentalism, quest, and prejudice. *International Journal for the Psychology of Religion*, **2**, 113–133.

Altman, I., & Vinsel, A. M. (1978). Personal space: An analysis of E. T. Hall's proxemics framework. In I. Altman & J. Wohlwill (Eds.), *Human behavior and the environment*. New York: Plenum.

Alwin, D. F. (1990). Historical changes in parental orientations to children. In N. Mandell (Ed.), *Sociological studies of child development* (Vol. 3). Greenwich, CT: JAI Press.

Alwin, D. F., Cohen, R. L., & Newcomb, T. M. (1991). *Political attitudes over the life span: The Bennington women after fifty years*. Madison:: University of Wisconsin Press.

Amato, P. R. (1979). Juror-defendant similarity and the assessment of guilt in politically motivated crimes. *Australian Journal of Psychology*, **31**, 79–88.

Amato, P. R. (1986). Emotional arousal and helping behavior in a real-life emergency. *Journal of Applied Social Psychology*, **16**, 633–641.

Ambady, N., Bernieri, F. J., & Richeson, J. A. (2000). Toward a histology of social behavior: Judgmental accuracy from thin slices of the behavioral stream. In M. P. Zanna (Ed.), *Advances in Experimental Social Psychology*, **32**, 201–271.

Ambady, N., & Rosenthal, R. (1992). Thin slices of expressive behavior as predictors of interpersonal consequences: A meta-analysis. *Psychological Bulletin*, **111**, 256–274.

Ambady, N., & Rosenthal, R. (1993). Half a minute: Predicting teacher evaluations from thin slices of nonverbal behavior and physical attractiveness. *Journal of Personality and Social Psychology*, **64**, 431–441.

American Enterprises. (1992, January/ February). Women, men, marriages and ministers, p. 106.

American Medical Association (AMA). (2004, November 11). Women lead in number of medical school applications. *Voice* (ama-assn.org).

American Psychological Association. (1993). *Violence and youth: Psychology's response. Volume I: Summary report of the American Psychological Assocation Commission on Violence and Youth*. Washington DC: Public Interest Directorate, American Psychological Association.

American Psychological Association. (2002). *Ethical principles of psychologists and code of conduct 2002*. Washington, DC: APA (www.apa.org/ethics/ code2002.html).

Amir, Y. (1969). Contact hypothesis in ethnic relations. *Psychological Bulletin*, **71**, 319–342.

Anastasi, J. S., & Rhodes, M. G. (2005). An own-age bias in face recognition for children and older adults. *Psychonomic Bulletin & Review*, **12**, 1043–1047.

Anastasi, J. S., & Rhodes, M. G. (2006). Evidence for an own-age bias in face recognition. *North American Journal of Psychology*, **8**, 237–252.

Anda, R., Williamson, D., Jones, D., Macera, C., Eaker, E., Glassman, A., & Marks, J. (1993). Depressed affect, hopelessness, and the risk of ischemic heart disease in a cohort of U.S. adults. *Epidemiology*, **4**, 285–294.

Andersen, S. M. (1998). Service Learning: A National Strategy for Youth Development. A Position Paper issued by the Task Force on Education Policy. Washington, DC: Institute for Communitarian Policy Studies, George Washington University.

Andersen, S. M., & Chen, S. (2002). The relational self: An interpersonal social-cognitive theory. *Psychological Review*, **109**, 619–645.

Anderson, C., Keltner, D., & John, O. P. (2003). Emotional convergence between people over time. *Journal of Personality and Social Psychology*, **84**, 1054–1068.

Anderson, C., Srivastava, S., Beer, J. S., Spataro, S. E., & Chatman, J. A. (2006). Knowing your place: Self-perceptions of status in face-to-face groups. *Journal of Personality and Social Psychology*, **91**, 1094–1110.

Anderson, C. A. (1982). Inoculation and counter-explanation: Debiasing techniques in the perseverance of social theories. *Social Cognition*, **1**, 126–139.

Anderson, C. A. (2003). Video games and aggressive behavior. In D. Ravitch and J. P. Viteritti (Eds.), *Kids stuff: Marking violence and vulgarity in the popular culture*. Baltimore, MD: Johns Hopkins University Press.

Anderson, C. A. (2004). An update on the effects of violent video games. *Journal of Adolescence*, **27**, 113–122.

Anderson, C. A., & Anderson, D. C. (1984). Ambient temperature and violent crime: Tests of the linear and curvilinear hypotheses. *Journal of Personality and Social Psychology*, **46**, 91–97.

Anderson, C. A., & Anderson, K. B. (1998). Temperature and aggression: Paradox, controversy, and a (fairly) clear picture. In R. G. Geen & E. Donnerstein (Eds.), *Human aggression: Theories, research, and implications for social policy*. San Diego: Academic Press.

Anderson, C. A., Anderson, K. B., Dorr, N., DeNeve, K. M., & Flanagan, M. (2000). Temperature and aggression. In M. P. Zanna (Ed.), *Advances in Experimental Social Psychology*. San Diego: Academic Press.

Anderson, C. A., Benjamin, A. J., Jr., & Bartholow, B. D. (1998). Does the gun pull the trigger? Automatic priming effects of weapon pictures and weapon names. *Psychological Science*, **9**, 308–314.

Anderson, C. A., Berkowitz, L., Donnerstein, E., Huesmann, L. R., Johnson, J. D., Linz, D., Malamuth, N. M., & Wartella, E. (2003). The influence of media violence on youth. *Psychological Science in the Public Interest*, **4**(3), 81–110.

Anderson, C. A., Buckley, K. E., & Carnagey, N. L. (2008). Creating your own hostile environment: A laboratory examination of trait aggressiveness and the violence escalation cycle. *Personality and Social Psychology Bulletin*, **34**, 462–473.

Anderson, C. A., & Bushman, B. J. (1997). External validity of "trivial" experiments: The case of laboratory aggression. *Review of General Psychology*, **1**, 19–41.

Anderson, C. A., & Bushman, B. J. (2001). Effects of violent video games on aggressive behavior, aggressive cognition, aggressive affect, physiological arousal, and prosocial behavior: A meta-analytic review of the scientific literature. *Psychological Science*, **12**, 353–359.

Anderson, C. A., Carnagey, N. L., Flanagan, M., benjamin, A. J., Jr., Eubanks, J., & Valentine, J. C. (2004). Violent video games: Specific effects of violent content on aggressive thoughts and behavior. *Advances in Experimental Social Psychology*, **36**, 199–249.

Anderson, C. A., Deuser, W. E., & DeNeve, K. M. (1995). Hot temperatures, hostile affect, hostile cognition, and arousal: Tests of a general model of affective aggression. *Personality and Social Psychology Bulletin*, **21**, 434–448.

Anderson, C. A., & Gentile, D. A. (2008). Media violence, aggression, and public policy. In E. Borgida & S. Fiske (Eds.), *Beyond common sense: Psychological science in the courtroom*. Malden, MA: Blackwell.

Anderson, C. A., Gentile, D. A., & Buckley, K. E. (2007). *Violent video game effects on children and adolescents: Theory, research, and public policy*. New York: Oxford University Press.

Anderson, C. A., & Harvey, R. J. (1988). Discriminating between problems in living: An examination of measures of depression, loneliness, shyness, and social anxiety. *Journal of Social and Clinical Psychology*, **6**, 482–491.

Anderson, C. A., Horowitz, L. M., & French, R. D. (1983). Attributional style of lonely and depressed people. *Journal of Personality and Social Psychology*, **45**, 127–136.

Anderson, C. A., Lepper, M. R., & Ross, L. (1980). Perseverance of social theories: The role of explanation in the persistence of discredited information. *Journal of Personality and Social Psychology*, **39**, 1037–1049.

Anderson, C. A., Lindsay, J. J., & Bushman, B. J. (1999). Research in the psychological laboratory: Truth or triviality? *Current Directions in Psychological Science*, **8**, 3–9.

Anderson, C. A., Miller, R. S., Riger, A. L., Dill, J. C., & Sedikides, C. (1994). Behavioral and characterological attributional styles as predictors of depression and loneliness: Review, refinement, and test. *Journal of Personality and Social Psychology*, **66**, 549–558.

Anderson, C. A., Sakamoto, A., Gentile, D. A., Ihori, N., Shibuya, A., Yukawa, S., Naito, M., & Kobayashi, K. (2008). Longitudinal effects of violent video games on aggression in Japan and the United States. *Pediatrics*, **122**, e1067–e1072.

Anderson, C. A., & Sechler, E. S. (1986). Effects of explanation and counterexplanation on the development and use of social theories. *Journal of Personality and Social Psychology*, **50**, 24–34.

Anderson, R. (2004). A definition of peace. *Peace and Conflict*, **10**, 101–116.

Anderson, S. L., Adams, G., & Plaut, V. C. (2008). The cultural grounding of personal relationship: The importance of attractiveness in everyday life. *Journal of Personality and Social Psychology*, **95**, 352–368.

Antonio, A. L., Chang, M. J., Hakuta, K., Kenny, D. A., Levin, S., & Milem, J. F. (2004). Effects of racial diversity on complex thinking in college students. *Psychological Science*, **15**, 507–510.

AP/Ipsos. (2006, May 4). Associated Press/Ipsos Poll data reported by personal correspondence with Michael Gross.

Archer, D., & Gartner, R. (1976). Violent acts and violent times: A comparative approach to postwar homicide rates. *American Sociological Review*, **41**, 937–963.

Archer, D., Iritani, B., Kimes, D. B., & Barrios, M. (1983). Face-ism: Five studies of sex differences in facial prominence. *Journal of Personality and Social Psychology*, **45**, 725–735.

Archer, J. (1991). The influence of testosterone on human aggression. *British Journal of Psychology*, **82**, 1–28.

Archer, J. (2000). Sex differences in aggression between heterosexual partners: A meta-analytic review. *Psychological Bulletin*, **126**, 651–680.

Archer, J. (2004). Sex differences in aggression in real-world settings: A meta-analytic review. *Review of General Psychology*, **8**, 291–322.

Archer, J. (2007). A cross-cultural perspective on physical aggression between partners. *Issues in Forensic Psychology*, No. 6, 125–131.

Archer, R. L., & Cook, C. E. (1986). Personalistic self-disclosure and attraction: Basis for relationship or scarce resource. *Social Psychology Quarterly*, **49**, 268–272.

Arendt, H. (1963). *Eichmann in Jerusalem: A report on the banality of evil*. New York: Viking.

Argyle, M., & Henderson M. (1985). *The anatomy of relationships.* London: Heinemann.

Argyle, M., Shimoda, K., & Little, B. (1978). Variance due to persons and situations in England and Japan. *British Journal of Social and Clinical Psychology,* **17,** 335–337.

Ariza, L. M. (2006, January). Virtual Jihad: The Internet as the ideal terrorism recruiting tool. *Scientific American,* pp. 18–21.

Arkes, H. R. (1990). Some practical judgment/decision making research. Paper presented at the American Psychological Association convention.

Arkes, H. R., & Tewtlock, P. E. (2004). Attributions of implicit prejudice, or "would Jesse Jackson 'fail' the implicit association test?" *Psychological Inquiry,* **15,** 257–278.

Arkin, R. M., Appleman, A., & Burger, J. M. (1980). Social anxiety, self-presentation, and the self-serving bias in causal attribution. *Journal of Personality and Social Psychology,* **38,** 23–35.

Arkin, R. M., & Burger, J. M. (1980). Effects of unit relation tendencies on interpersonal attraction. *Social Psychology Quarterly,* **43,** 380–391.

Arkin, R. M., Lake, E. A., & Baumgardner, A. H. (1986). Shyness and self-presentation. In W. H. Jones, J. M. Cheek, & S. R. Briggs (Eds.), *Shyness: Perspectives on research and treatment.* New York: Plenum.

Armitage, C. J., & Conner, M. (2001). Efficacy of the theory of planned behaviour: A meta-analytic review. *British Journal of Social Psychology,* **40,** 471–499.

Armor, D. A., & Sackett, A. M. (2006). Accuracy, error, and bias in predictions for real versus hypothetical events. *Journal of Personality and Social Psychology,* **91,** 583–600.

Armor, D. A., & Taylor, S. E. (1996). Situated optimism: Specific outcome expectancies and self-regulation. In M. P. Zanna (Ed.), *Advances in experimental social psychology* (Vol. 30). San Diego: Academic Press.

Arms, R. L., Russell, G. W., & Sandilands, M. L. (1979). Effects on the hostility of spectators of viewing aggressive sports. *Social Psychology Quarterly,* **42,** 275–279.

Aron, A., & Aron, E. (1989). *The heart of social psychology,* 2nd ed. Lexington, MA: Lexington Books.

Aron, A., & Aron, E. N. (1994). Love. In A. L. Weber & J. H. Harvey (Eds.), *Perspective on close relationships.* Boston: Allyn & Bacon.

Aron, A., Dutton, D. G., Aron, E. N., & Iverson, A. (1989). Experiences of falling in love. *Journal of Social and Personal Relationships,* **6,** 243–257.

Aron, A., Fisher, H., Mashek, D. J., Strong, G., Li, H., & Brown, L. L. (2005).

Reward, motivation, and emotion systems associated with early-stage intense romantic love. *Journal of Neurophysiology,* **94,** 327–337.

Aron, A., Melinat, E., Aron, E. N., Vallone, R. D., & Bator, R. J. (1997). The experimental generation of interpersonal closeness: A procedure and some preliminary findings. *Personality and Social Psychology Bulletin,* **23,** 363–377.

Aron, A., Norman, C. C., Aron, E. N., McKenna, C., & Heyman, R. E. (2000). Couples' shared participation in novel and arousing activities and experienced relationship quality. *Journal of Personality and Social Psychology,* **78,** 273–284.

Aronson, E. (1980). *The social animal.* 3rd edition. New York: Freeman.

Aronson, E. (1988). *The social animal.* 5th edition. New York: Freeman.

Aronson, E. (1997). Bring the family address to American Psychological Society annual convention, reported in *APS Observer,* July/August, pp. 17, 34, 35.

Aronson, E. (2004). Reducing hostility and building compassion: Lessons from the jigsaw classroom. In A. G. Miller (Ed.), *The social psychology of good and evil.* New York: Guilford.

Aronson, E., Brewer, M., & Carlsmith, J. M. (1985). Experimentation in social psychology. In G. Lindzey & E. Aronson (Eds.), *Handbook of social psychology* (Vol. 1). Hillsdale, NJ: Erlbaum.

Aronson, E., & Gonzalez, A. (1988). Desegregation, jigsaw, and the Mexican-American experience. In P. A. Katz & D. Taylor (Eds.), *Towards the elimination of racism: Profiles in controversy.* New York: Plenum.

Aronson, E., & Linder, D. (1965). Gain and loss of esteem as determinants of interpersonal attractiveness. *Journal of Experimental Social Psychology,* **1,** 156–171.

Aronson, E., & Mettee, D. R. (1974). Affective reactions to appraisal from others. *Foundations of interpersonal attraction.* New York: Academic Press.

Aronson, E., & Mills, J. (1959). The effect of severity of initiation on liking for a group. *Journal of Abnormal and Social Psychology,* **59,** 177–181.

Aronson, E., Turner, J. A., & Carlsmith, J. M. (1963). Communicator credibility and communicator discrepancy as determinants of opinion change. *Journal of Abnormal and Social Psychology,* **67,** 31–36.

Arora, R. (2005). China's "Gen Y" bucks tradition. Gallup Poll, http://www.gallup.com/poll/15934/Chinas-Gen-Bucks-Tradition.aspx. Viewed online 1/22/09.

Arriaga, X. B. (2001). The ups and downs of dating: Fluctuations in satisfaction in newly formed romantic

relationships. *Journal of Personality and Social Psychology,* **80,** 754–765.

Arriaga, X. B., & Agnew, C. R. (2001). Being committed: Affective, cognitive, and conative components of relationship commitment. *Personality and Social Psychology Bulletin,* **27,** 1190–1203.

Arrow, K. J., & 21 others. (2008). The promise of prediction markets. *Science,* **320,** 877–878.

ASAPS. (2005). Cosmetic surgery quick facts: 2004 ASAPS statistics. The American Society for Aesthetic Plastic Surgery (www.surgery.org).

Asch, S. E. (1946). Forming impressions of personality. *Journal of Abnormal and Social Psychology,* **41,** 258–290.

Asch, S. E. (1955, November). Opinions and social pressure. *Scientific American,* pp. 31–35.

Asendorpf, J. B. (1987). Videotape reconstruction of emotions and cognitions related to shyness. *Journal of Personality and Social Psychology,* **53,** 541–549.

Ash, R. (1999). *The top 10 of everything 2000.* New York: DK Publishing.

Asher, J. (1987, April). Born to be shy? *Psychology Today,* pp. 56–64.

Associated Press (AP). (1993, June 10). Walking past a dying man. *New York Times* (via Associated Press).

Associated Press (AP). (1995, September 25). Blacks are given tougher sentences, analysis shows. *Grand Rapids Press,* p. A3.

Associated Press (AP). (2007a, January 12). China facing major gender imbalance. Associated Press release.

Associated Press (AP). (2007b, January 15). Kids copying execution accidentally hang selves. *Grand Rapids Press,* p. A3.

Astin, A. W., Green, K. C., Korn, W. S., & Schalit, M. (1987). *The American freshman: National norms for Fall 1987.* Los Angeles: Higher Education Research Institute, UCLA.

Aubrey, J. S., & Taylor, L. D. (2009). The role of lad magazines in priming men's chronic and temporary appearance-related schemata: An investigation of longitudinal and experimental findings. *Human Communication Research,* **35,** 28–58.

Augoustinos, M., & Innes, J. M. (1990). Towards an integration of social representations and social schema theory. *British Journal of Social Psychology,* **29,** 213–231.

Averill, J. R. (1983). Studies on anger and aggression: Implications for theories of emotion. *American Psychologist,* **38,** 1145–1160.

Axsom, D., Yates, S., & Chaiken, S. (1987). Audience response as a heuristic cue in persuasion. *Journal of Personality and Social Psychology,* **53,** 30–40.

Ayres, I. (1991). Fair driving: Gender and race discrimination in retail car negotiations. *Harvard Law Review,* **104,** 817–872.

Azrin, N. H. (1967, May). Pain and aggression. *Psychology Today,* pp. 27–33.

Baars, B. J., & McGovern, K. A. (1994). Consciousness. In V. Ramachandran (Ed.), *Encyclopedia of Human Behavior.* Orlando, FL: Academic Press.

Babad, E., Bernieri, F., & Rosenthal, R. (1991). Students as judges of teachers' verbal and nonverbal behavior. *American Educational Research Journal,* **28,** 211–234.

Babad, E., Hills, M., & O'Driscoll, M. (1992). Factors influencing wishful thinking and predictions of election outcomes. *Basic and Applied Social Psychology,* **13,** 461–476.

Bachman, J. G., Johnston, L. D., O'Malley, P. M., & Humphrey, R. N. (1988). Explaining the recent decline in marijuana use: Differentiating the effects of perceived risks, disapproval, and general lifestyle factors. *Journal of Health and Social Behavior,* **29,** 92–112.

Bachman, J. G., & O'Malley, P. M. (1977). Self-esteem in young men: A longitudinal analysis of the impact of educational and occupational attainment. *Journal of Personality and Social Psychology,* **35,** 365–380.

Back, M. D., Schmukle, S. C., & Egloff, B. (2008). Becoming friends by chance. *Psychological Science,* **19,** 439–440.

Bailenson, J. N., Iyengar, S., Yee, N., & Collins, N. (2009). Facial similarity between voters and candidates causes influence. *Public Opinion Quarterly.*

Bailenson, J. N., & Yee, N. (2005). Digital chameleons: Automatic assimilation of nonverbal gestures in immersive virtual environments. *Psychological Science,* **16,** 814–819.

Bailey, J. M., Gaulin, S., Agyei, Y., & Gladue, B. A. (1994). Effects of gender and sexual orientation on evolutionary relevant aspects of human mating psychology. *Journal of Personality and Social Psychology,* **66,** 1081–1093.

Bailey, J. M., Kirk, K. M., Zhu, G., Dunne, M. P., & Martin, N. G. (2000). Do individual differences in sociosexuality represent genetic or environmentally contingent strategies? Evidence from the Australian Twin Registry. *Journal of Personality and Social Psychology,* **78,** 537–545.

Baize, H. R., Jr., & Schroeder, J. E. (1995). Personality and mate selection in personal ads: Evolutionary preferences in a public mate selection process. *Journal of Social Behavior and Personality,* **10,** 517–536.

Baldwin, M. W., Keelan, J. P. R., Fehr, B., Enns, V., & Koh-Rangarajoo, E. (1996). Social-cognitive conceptualization of attachment working models: Availability and accessibility effects. *Journal of Personality and Social Psychology,* **71,** 94–109.

Banaji, M. R. (2004). The opposite of a great truth is also true: Homage of Koan #7. In J. T. Jost, M. R. Banaji, & D. A. Prentice (Eds.), *Perspectivism in social psychology: The yin and yang of scientific progress.* Washington, DC: American Psychological Association.

Bandura, A. (1979). The social learning perspective: Mechanisms of aggression. In H. Toch (Ed.), *Psychology of crime and criminal justice.* New York: Holt, Rinehart & Winston.

Bandura, A. (1997). *Self-efficacy: The exercise of control.* New York: Freeman.

Bandura, A. (2000). Social cognitive theory: An agentic perspective. *Annual Review of Psychology,* **52,** 1–26.

Bandura, A. (2004). Swimming against the mainstream: The early years from chilly tributary to transformative mainstream. *Behaviour Research and Therapy,* **42,** 613–630.

Bandura, A. (2008). Reconstrual of "free will" from the agentic perspective of social cognitive theory. In J. Baer, J. C. Kaufman, & R. F. Baumeister (Eds.), *Are we free? Psychology and free will.* New York: Oxford University Press.

Bandura, A., Pastorelli, C., Barbaranelli, C., & Caprara, G. V. (1999). Self-efficacy pathways to childhood depression. *Journal of Personality and Social Psychology,* **76,** 258–269.

Bandura, A., Ross, D., & Ross, S. A. (1961). Transmission of aggression through imitation of aggressive models. *Journal of Abnormal and Social Psychology,* **63,** 575–582.

Bandura, A., & Walters, R. H. (1959). *Adolescent aggression.* New York: Ronald Press.

Bandura, A., & Walters, R. H. (1963). *Social learning and personality development.* New York: Holt, Rinehart & Winston.

Banks, S. M., Salovey, P., Greener, S., Rothman, A. J., Moyer, A., Beauvais, J., & Epel, E. (1995). The effects of message framing on mammography utilization. *Health Psychology,* **14,** 178–184.

Barash, D. (1979). *The whisperings within.* New York: Harper & Row.

Barash, D. P. (2003, November 7). Unreason's seductive charms. *Chronicle of Higher Education* (www.chronicle.com/free/v50/i11/11b00601.htm).

Barber, B. M., & Odean, T. (2001a). Boys will be boys: Gender, overconfidence and common stock investment. *Quarterly Journal of Economics,* **116,** 261–292.

Barber, B. M., & Odean, T. (2001b). The Internet and the investor. *Journal of Economic Perspectives,* **15,** 41–54.

Barber, N. (2000). On the relationship between country sex ratios and teen pregnancy rates: A replication. *Cross-Cultural Research,* **34,** 327–333.

Bargh, J. A. (2006). What have we been priming all these years? On the development, mechanisms, and ecology of nonconscious social behavior. *European Journal of Social Psychology,* **36,** 147–168.

Bargh, J. A., & Chartrand, T. L. (1999). The unbearable automaticity of being. *American Psychologist,* **54,** 462–479.

Bargh, J. A., Chen, M., & Burrows, L. (1996). Automaticity and social behavior: Direct effects of trait construct and stereotype activation, *Journal of Personality and Social Psychology,* **43,** 437–449.

Bargh, J. A., & Ferguson, M. J. (2000). Beyond behaviorism: On the automaticity of higher mental processes. *Psychological Bulletin,* **126,** 925–945.

Bargh, J. A., & McKenna, K. Y. A. (2004). The Internet and social life. *Annual Review of Psychology,* **55,** 573–590.

Bargh, J. A., McKenna, K. Y. A., & Fitzsimons, G. M. (2002). Can you see the real me? Activation and expression of the "true self" on the Internet. *Journal of Social Issues,* **58,** 33–48.

Bargh, J. A., & Raymond, P. (1995). The naive misuse of power: Nonconscious sources of sexual harassment. *Journal of Social Issues,* **51,** 85–96.

Bar-Haim, Y., Ziv, T., Lamy, D., & Hodes, R. M. (2006). Nature and nurture in own-race face processing. *Psychological Science,* **17,** 159–163.

Barlett, C., Branch, O., Rodeheffer, C., & Harris, R. (2009). How long do the short-term violent video game effects last? *Aggressive Behavior,* **35,** 225–236.

Barlett, C. P., Harris, R. J., & Bruey, C. (2008). The effect of the amount of blood in a violence video game on aggression, hostility, and arousal. *Journal of Experimental Social Psychology,* **44,** 539–546.

Barnes, E. (2008, August 24). Scots heroine of Auschwitz who gave her life for young Jews. *Scotland on Sunday,* p. 3.

Barnes, R. D., Ickes, W., & Kidd, R. F. (1979). Effects of the perceived intentionality and stability of another's dependency on helping behavior. *Personality and Social Psychology Bulletin,* **5,** 367–372.

Barnett, M. A., King, L. M., Howard, J. A., & Melton, E. M. (1980). Experiencing negative affect about self or other: Effects on helping behavior in children and adults. Paper presented at the Midwestern Psychological Association convention.

Barnett, P. A., & Gotlib, I. H. (1988). Psychosocial functioning and depression: Distinguishing among antecedents, concomitants, and consequences. *Psychological Bulletin, 104,* 97–126.

Baron, J., & Hershey, J. C. (1988). Outcome bias in decision evaluation. *Journal of Personality and Social Psychology, 54,* 569–579.

Baron, J., & Miller, J. G. (2000). Limiting the scope of moral obligations to help: A cross-cultural investigation. *Journal of Cross-Cultural Psychology, 31,* 703–725.

Baron, L., & Straus, M. A. (1984). Sexual stratification, pornography, and rape in the United States. In N. M. Malamuth & E. Donnerstein (Eds.), *Pornography and sexual aggression.* New York: Academic Press.

Baron, R. A. (1977). *Human aggression.* New York: Plenum.

Baron, R. A., Markman, G. D., & Bollinger, M. (2006). Exporting social psychology: Effects of attractiveness on perceptions of entrepreneurs, their ideas for new products, and their financial success. *Journal of Applied Social Psychology, 36,* 467–492.

Baron, R. S. (1986). Distraction-conflict theory: Progress and problems. In L. Berkowitz (Ed.), *Advances in experimental social psychology,* Orlando, FL: Academic Press.

Baron, R. S. (2000). Arousal, capacity, and intense indoctrination. *Personality and Social Psychology Review, 4,* 238–254.

Baron, R. S., Kerr, N. L., & Miller, N. (1992). *Group process, group decision, group action.* Pacific Grove, CA: Brooks/Cole.

Baron-Cohen, S. (2004). *The essential difference: Men, women, and the extreme male brain.* London: Penguin Books.

Baron-Cohen, S. (2005). Sex differences in the brain: Implications for explaining autism. *Science, 310,* 819–823.

Barongan, C., & Hall, G. C. N. (1995). The influence of misogynous rap music on sexual aggression against women. *Psychology of Women Quarterly, 19,* 195–207.

Barry, D. (1995, January). Bored stiff. *Funny Times,* p. 5.

Barry, D. (1998). *Dave Barry turns 50.* New York: Crown.

Bar-Tal, D. (2004). The necessity of observing real life situations: Palestinian-Israeli violence as a laboratory for learning about social behaviour. *European Journal of Social Psychology, 34,* 677–701.

Bartholomew, K., & Horowitz, L. (1991). Attachment styles among young adults: A test of a four-category model. *Journal of Personality and Social Psychology, 61,* 226–244.

Bartholomew, R. E., & Goode, E. (2000, May/June). Mass delusions and hysterias: Highlights from the past millennium. *Skeptical Inquirer,* pp. 20–28.

Bartholow, B. C., Anderson, C. A., Carnagey, N. L., & Benjamin, A.J., Jr. (2004). Interactive effects of life experience and situational cues on aggression: The weapons priming effect in hunters and nonhunters. *Journal of Experimental Social Psychology, 41,* 48–60.

Bartholow, B. C., & Heinz, A. (2006). Alcohol and aggression without consumption: Alcohol cues, aggressive thoughts, and hostile perception bias. *Psychological Science, 17,* 30–37.

Bartholow, B. C., Sestir, M. A., & Davis, E. B. (2005). Correlates and consequences of exposure to video game violence: Hostile personality, empathy, and aggressive behavior. *Personality and Social Psychology Bulletin, 31,* 1573–1586.

Bartholow, B. D., Bushman, B. J., & Sestir, M. A. (2006). Chronic violent video game exposure and desensitization: Behavioral and event-related brain potential data. *Journal of Experimental Social Psychology, 42*(4), 532–539.

Barzun, J. (1975). *Simple and direct.* New York: Harper & Row, pp. 173–174.

Basile, K. C., Chen, J., Lynberg, M. C., & Saltzman, L. E. (2007). Prevalence and characteristics of sexual violence victimization. *Violence and Victims, 22,* 437–448.

Bassili, J. N. (2003). The minority slowness effect: Subtle inhibitions in the expression of views not shared by others. *Journal of Personality and Social Psychology, 84,* 261–276.

Bastian, B., & Haslam, N. (2006). Psychological essentialism and stereotype endorsement. *Journal of Experimental Social Psychology, 42,* 228–235.

Batson, C. D. (1983). Sociobiology and the role of religion in promoting prosocial behavior: An alternative view. *Journal of Personality and Social Psychology, 45,* 1380–1385.

Batson, C. D. (1999a). Behind the scenes. In D. G. Myers, *Social psychology,* 6th edition. New York: McGraw-Hill.

Batson, C. D. (1999b). Addressing the altruism question experimentally. Paper presented at a Templeton Foundation/Fetzer Institute Symposium on Empathy, Altruism, and Agape, Cambridge, MA.

Batson, C. D. (2001). Addressing the altruism question experimentally. In S. G. Post, L. B. Underwood, J. P. Schloss, & W. B. Hurlbut (Eds.), *Altruism and altruistic love: Science, philosophy, and religion in dialogue.* New York: Oxford University Press.

Batson, C. D. (2006). "Not all self-interest after all": Economics of empathy-induced altruism. In D. De Cremer, M. Zeelenberg, & J. K. Murnighan (Eds.), *Social psychology and economics.* Mahwah, NJ: Erlbaum.

Batson, C. D., Ahmad, N., Powell, A. A., & Stocks, E. L. (2008). Prosocial motivation. In J. Y. Shah & W. L. Gardner (Eds.), *Handbook of motivation science.* New York: Guilford.

Batson, C. D., Ahmad, N., & Stocks, E. L. (2004). Benefits and liabilities of empathy-induced altruism. In A. G. Miller (Ed.), *The social psychology of good and evil.* New York: Guilford.

Batson, C. D., Ahmad, N., Yin, J., Bedell, S. J., Johnson, J. W., Templin, C. M., & Whiteside, A. (1999). Two threats to the common good: Self-interested egoism and empathy-induced altruism. *Personality and Social Psychology Bulletin, 25,* 3–16.

Batson, C. D., Bolen, M. H., Cross, J. A., & Neuringer-Benefiel, H. E. (1986). Where is the altruism in the altruistic personality? *Journal of Personality and Social Psychology, 50,* 212–220.

Batson, C. D., Coke, J. S., Jasnoski, M. L., & Hanson, M. (1978). Buying kindness: Effect of an extrinsic incentive for helping on perceived altruism. *Personality and Social Psychology Bulletin, 4,* 86–91.

Batson, C. D., Duncan, B. D., Ackerman, P., Buckley, T., & Birch, K. (1981). Is empathic emotion a source of altruistic motivation? *Journal of Personality and Social Psychology, 40,* 290–302.

Batson, C. D., Eklund, J. H., Chermok, V. L., Hoyt, J. L., & Ortiz, B. G. (2007). An additional antecedent of empathic concern: Valuing the welfare of the person in need. *Journal of Personality and Social Psychology, 93,* 65–74.

Batson, C. D., Fultz, J., & Schoenrade, P. A. (1987). Distress and empathy: Two qualitatively distinct vicarious emotions with different motivational consequences. *Journal of Personality, 55,* 19–40.

Batson, C. D., Harris, A. C., McCaul, K. D., Davis, M., & Schmidt, T. (1979). Compassion or compliance: Alternative dispositional attributions for one's helping behavior. *Social Psychology Quarterly, 42,* 405–409.

Batson, C. D., Kobrynowicz, D., Dinnerstein, J. L., Kampf, H. C., & Wilson, A. D. (1997). In a very different voice: Unmasking moral hypocrisy. *Journal of Personality and Social Psychology, 72,* 1335–1348.

Batson, C. D., Lishner, D. A., Carpenter, A., Dulin, L., Harjusola-Webb, S., Stocks, E. L., Gale, S., Hassan, O., & Sampat, B. (2003). ". . . As you would have them do unto you": Does imagining yourself in the other's place stimulate moral action? *Personality and Social Psychology Bulletin, 29,* 1190–1201.

Batson, C. D., & Moran, T. (1999). Empathy-induced altruism in a prisoner's dilemma. *European Journal of Social Psychology, 29,* 909–924.

Batson, C. D., Sager, K., Garst, E., Kang, M., Rubchinsky, K., & Dawson, K. (1997). Is empathy-induced helping due to self-other merging? *Journal of Personality and Social Psychology, 73,* 495–509.

Batson, C. D., Schoenrade, P., & Ventis, W. L. (1993). *Religion and the individual: A social-psychological perspective.* New York: Oxford University Press.

Batson, C. D., Sympson, S. C., Hindman, J. L., Decruz, P., Todd, R. M., Jennings, G., & Burris, C. T. (1996). "I've been there, too": Effect on empathy of prior experience with a need. *Personality and Social Psychology Bulletin, 22,* 474–482.

Batson, C. D., & Thompson, E. R. (2001). Why don't moral people act morally? Motivational considerations. *Current Directions in Psychological Science, 10,* 54–57.

Batson, C. D., Thompson, E. R., & Chen, H. (2002). Moral hypocrisy: Addressing some alternatives. *Journal of Personality and Social Psychology, 83,* 330–339.

Batson, C. D., Thompson, E. R., Seuferling, G., Whitney, H., & Strongman, J. A. (1999). Moral hypocrisy: Appearing moral to oneself without being so. *Journal of Personality and Social Psychology, 77,* 525–537.

Batson, C. D., & Ventis, W. L. (1982). *The religious experience: A social psychological perspective.* New York: Oxford University Press.

Batson, C. D., & Weeks, J. L. (1996). Mood effects of unsuccessful helping: Another test of the empathy-altruism hypothesis. *Personality and Social Psychology Bulletin, 22,* 148–157.

Baumann, L. J., & Leventhal, H. (1985). "I can tell when my blood pressure is up, can't I?" *Health Psychology, 4,* 203–218.

Baumeister, R. (1996). Should schools try to boost self-esteem? Beware the dark side. *American Educator, 20,* 14–19, 43.

Baumeister, R. (2005). Rejected and alone. *The Psychologist, 18,* 732–735.

Baumeister, R. (2007). Is there anything good about men? Address to the American Psychological Association convention.

Baumeister, R. F. (2005). *The cultural animal: Human nature, meaning, and social life.* New York: Oxford University Press.

Baumeister, R. F., & Bratslavsky, E. (1999). Passion, intimacy, and time: Passionate love as a function of change in intimacy. *Personality and Social Psychology Review, 3,* 49–67.

Baumeister, R. F., Bratslavsky, E., Finkenauer, C., & Vohs, D. K. (2001). Bad is stronger than good. *Review of General Psychology, 5,* 323–370.

Baumeister, R. F., Bratslavsky, E., Muraven, M., & Tice, D. M. (1998). Ego depletion: Is the active self a limited resource? *Journal of Personality and Social Psychology, 74,* 1252–1265.

Baumeister, R. F., Campbell, J. D., Krueger, J. I., & Vohs, K. D. (2003). Does high self-esteem cause better performance, interpersonal success, happiness, or healthier lifestyles? *Psychological Science in the Public Interest, 4*(1), 1–44.

Baumeister, R. F., Catanese, K. R., & Vohs, K. D. (2001). Is there a gender difference in strength of sex drive? Theoretical views, conceptual distinctions, and a review of relevant evidence. *Personality and Social Psychology Review, 5,* 242–273.

Baumeister, R. F., Chesner, S. P., Senders, P. S., & Tice, D. M. (1988). Who's in charge here? Group leaders do lend help in emergencies. *Personality and Social Psychology Bulletin, 14,* 17–22.

Baumeister, R. F., & Exline, J. J. (2000). Self-control, morality, and human strength. *Journal of Social and Clinical Psychology, 19,* 29–42.

Baumeister, R. F., & Leary, M. R. (1995). The need to belong: Desire for interpersonal attachment as a fundamental human motivation. *Psychological Bulletin, 117,* 497–529.

Baumeister, R. F., Muraven, M., & Tice, D. M. (2000). Ego depletion: A resource model of volition, self-regulation, and controlled processing. *Social Cognition, 18,* 130–150.

Baumeister, R. F., & Scher, S. J. (1988). Self-defeating behavior patterns among normal individuals: Review and analysis of common self-destructive tendencies. *Psychological Bulletin, 104,* 3–22.

Baumeister, R. F., & Vohs, K. (2004). Sexual economics: Sex as female resource for social exchange in heterosexual interactions. *Personality and Social Psychology Bulletin, 8,* 339–363.

Baumeister, R. F., & Wotman, S. R. (1992). *Breaking hearts: The two sides of unrequited love.* New York: Guilford.

Baumgardner, A. H., & Brownlee, E. A. (1987). Strategic failure in social interaction: Evidence for expectancy disconfirmation process. *Journal of Personality and Social Psychology, 52,* 525–535.

Baumhart, R. (1968). *An honest profit.* New York: Holt, Rinehart & Winston.

Baxter, T. L., & Goldberg, L. R. (1987). Perceived behavioral consistency underlying trait attributions to oneself and another: An extension of the actor-observer effect. *Personality and Social Psychology Bulletin, 13,* 437–447.

Bayer, E. (1929). Beitrage zur zeikomponenten theorie des hungers. *Zeitschrift fur Psychologie, 112,* 1–54.

Bazerman, M. H. (1986, June). Why negotiations go wrong. *Psychology Today,* pp. 54–58.

Bazerman, M. H. (1990). *Judgment in managerial decision making,* 2nd edition. New York: John Wiley.

BBC (2008, November 21). Pirates "gained $150m this year" (news.bbc.co.uk).

Beals, K. P., Peplau, L. A., & Gable, S. L. (2009). Stigma management and well-being: The role of perceived social support, emotional processing, and suppression. *Personality and Social Psychology Bulletin, 35,* 867–879.

Beaman, A. L., Barnes, P. J., Klentz, B., & McQuirk, B. (1978). Increasing helping rates through information dissemination: Teaching pays. *Personality and Social Psychology Bulletin, 4,* 406–411.

Beaman, A. L., & Klentz, B. (1983). The supposed physical attractiveness bias against supporters of the women's movement: A meta-analysis. *Personality and Social Psychology Bulletin, 9,* 544–550.

Beaman, A. L., Klentz, B., Diener, E., & Svanum, S. (1979). Self-awareness and transgression in children: Two field studies. *Journal of Personality and Social Psychology, 37,* 1835–1846.

Bearman, P. S., & Brueckner, H. (2001). Promising the future: Virginity pledges and first intercourse. *American Journal of Sociology, 106,* 859–912.

Beaulieu, C. M. J. (2004). Intercultural study of personal space: A case study. *Journal of Applied Social Psychology, 34,* 794–805.

Beck, A. T., & Young, J. E. (1978, September). College blues. *Psychology Today,* pp. 80–92.

Becker, S. W., & Eagly, A. H. (2004). The heroism of women and men. *American Psychologist, 59,* 163–178.

Bell, B. E., & Loftus, E. F. (1988). Degree of detail of eyewitness testimony and mock juror judgments. *Journal of Applied Social Psychology, 18,* 1171–1192.

Bell, B. E., & Loftus, E. F. (1989). Trivial persuasion in the courtroom: The power of (a few) minor details. *Journal of Personality and Social Psychology, 56,* 669–679.

Bell, P. A. (1980). Effects of heat, noise, and provocation on retaliatory evaluative behavior. *Journal of Social Psychology, 110,* 97–100.

Bell, P. A. (2005). Reanalysis and perspective in the heat-aggression debate. *Journal of Personality and Social Psychology*, **89**, 71–73.

Bellah, R. N. (1995/1996, Winter). Community properly understood: A defense of "democratic communitarianism." *The Responsive Community*, pp. 49–54.

Belluck, P. (2008, June 15). Gay couples find marriage is a mixed bag. *New York Times* (www.nytimes.com).

Belson, W. A. (1978). *Television violence and the adolescent boy.* Westmead, England: Saxon House, Teakfield Ltd.

Bem, D. J. (1972). Self-perception theory. In L. Berkowitz (Ed.), *Advances in experimental social psychology* (Vol. 6). New York: Academic Press.

Bem, D. J., & McConnell, H. K. (1970). Testing the self-perception explanation of dissonance phenomena: On the salience of premanipulation attitudes. *Journal of Personality and Social Psychology*, **14**, 23–31.

Bennett, R. (1991, February). Pornography and extrafamilial child sexual abuse: Examining the relationship. Unpublished manuscript, Los Angeles Police Department Sexually Exploited Child Unit.

Bennis, W. (1984). Transformative power and leadership. In T. J. Sergiovani & J. E. Corbally (Eds.), *Leadership and organizational culture.* Urbana: University of Illinois Press.

Benson, P. L., Dehority, J., Garman, L., Hanson, E., Hochschwender, M., Lebold, C., Rohr, R., & Sullivan, J. (1980). Intrapersonal correlates of nonspontaneous helping behavior. *Journal of Social Psychology*, **110**, 87–95.

Benson, P. L., Karabenick, S. A., & Lerner, R. M. (1976). Pretty pleases: The effects of physical attractiveness, race, and sex on receiving help. *Journal of Experimental Social Psychology*, **12**, 409–415.

Benton, T. R., Ross, D. F., Bradshaw, E., Thomas, W. N., & Bradshaw, G. S. (2006). Eyewitness memory is still not common sense: Comparing jurors, judges and law enforcement to eyewitness experts. *Applied Cognitive Psychology*, **20**, 115–129.

Benvenisti, M. (1988, October 16). Growing up in Jerusalem. *New York Times Magazine*, pp. 34–37.

Berg, J. H. (1984). Development of friendship between roommates. *Journal of Personality and Social Psychology*, **46**, 346–356.

Berg, J. H. (1987). Responsiveness and self-disclosure. In V. J. Derlega & J. H. Berg (Eds.), *Self-disclosure: Theory, research, and therapy.* New York: Plenum.

Berg, J. H., & McQuinn, R. D. (1986). Attraction and exchange in continuing and noncontinuing dating relationships. *Journal of Personality and Social Psychology*, **50**, 942–952.

Berg, J. H., & McQuinn, R. D. (1988). Loneliness and aspects of social support networks. Unpublished manuscript, University of Mississippi.

Berg, J. H., & Peplau, L. A. (1982). Loneliness: The relationship of self-disclosure and androgyny. *Personality and Social Psychology Bulletin*, **8**, 624–630.

Berger, J., & Heath, C. (2008). Who drives divergence? Identity signaling, outgroup dissimilarity, and the abandonment of cultural tastes. *Journal of Personality and Social Psychology*, **95**, 593–607.

Berglas, S., & Jones, E. E. (1978). Drug choice as a self-handicapping strategy in response to noncontingent success. *Journal of Personality and Social Psychology*, **36**, 405–417.

Berkman, L. F. (1995). The role of social relations in health promotion. *Psychosomatic Medicine*, **57**, 245–254.

Berkowitz, L. (1954). Group standards, cohesiveness, and productivity. *Human Relations*, **7**, 509–519.

Berkowitz, L. (1968, September). Impulse, aggression and the gun. *Psychology Today*, pp. 18–22.

Berkowitz, L. (1972). Social norms, feelings, and other factors affecting helping and altruism. In L. Berkowitz (Ed.), *Advances in experimental social psychology* (Vol. 6). New York: Academic Press.

Berkowitz, L. (1978). Whatever happened to the frustration-aggression hypothesis? *American Behavioral Scientists*, **21**, 691–708.

Berkowitz, L. (1981, June). How guns control us. *Psychology Today*, pp. 11–12.

Berkowitz, L. (1983). Aversively stimulated aggression: Some parallels and differences in research with animals and humans. *American Psychologist*, **38**, 1135–1144.

Berkowitz, L. (1984). Some effects of thoughts on anti- and prosocial influences of media events: A cognitive-neoassociation analysis, *Psychological Bulletin*, **95**, 410–427.

Berkowitz, L. (1987). Mood, self-awareness, and willingness to help. *Journal of Personality and Social Psychology*, **52**, 721–729.

Berkowitz, L. (1989). Frustration-aggression hypothesis: Examination and reformulation. *Psychological Bulletin*, **106**, 59–73.

Berkowitz, L. (1995). A career on aggression. In G. G. Brannigan & M. R. Merrens (Eds.), *The social psychologists: Research adventures.* New York: McGraw-Hill.

Berkowitz, L. (1998). Affective aggression: The role of stress, pain, and negative affect. In R. G. Geen & E. Donnerstein (Eds.), *Human aggression: Theories, research, and implications for social policy.* San Diego: Academic Press.

Berkowitz, L., & Geen, R. G. (1966). Film violence and the cue properties of available targets. *Journal of Personality and Social Psychology*, **3**, 525–530.

Berkowitz, L., & LePage, A. (1967). Weapons as aggression-eliciting stimuli. *Journal of Personality and Social Psychology*, **7**, 202–207.

Berndsen, M., Spears, R., van der Plight, J., & McGarty, C. (2002). Illusory correlation and stereotype formation: Making sense of group differences and cognitive biases. In C. McGarty, V. Y. Yzerbyt, & R. Spears (Eds.), *Stereotypes as explanations: The formation of meaningful beliefs about social groups.* New York: Cambridge University Press.

Bernhardt, P. C. (1997). Influences of serotonin and testosterone in aggression and dominance: Convergence with social psychology. *Current Directions in Psychology*, **6**, 44–48.

Bernhardt, P. C., Dabbs, J. M., Jr., Fielden, J. A., & Lutter, C. D. (1998). Testosterone changes during vicarious experiences of winning and losing among fans at sporting events. *Physiology and Behavior*, **65**, 59–62.

Berns, G. S., Chappelow, J., Zink, C. F., Pagnoni, G., Martin-Skurski, M. E., & Richards, J. (2005). Neurobiological correlates of social conformity and independence during mental rotation. *Biological Psychiatry*, **58**, 245–253.

Bernstein, M. J., Young, S. G., & Hugenberg, K. (2007). The cross-category effect. Mere social categorization is sufficient to elicit an own-group bias in face recognition. *Psychological Science*, **18**, 706–712.

Berry, D. S., & Zebrowitz-McArthur, L. (1988). What's in a face: Facial maturity and the attribution of legal responsibility. *Personality and Social Psychology Bulletin*, **14**, 23–33.

Berscheid, E. (1981). An overview of the psychological effects of physical attractiveness and some comments upon the psychological effects of knowledge of the effects of physical attractiveness. In W. Lucker, K. Ribbens, & J. A. McNamera (Eds.), *Logical aspects of facial form (craniofacial growth series).* Ann Arbor: University of Michigan Press.

Berscheid, E. (1985). Interpersonal attraction. In G. Lindzey & E. Aronson (Eds.), *The handbook of social psychology.* New York: Random House.

Berscheid, E. (1999). The greening of relationship science. *American Psychologist*, **54**, 260–266.

Berscheid, E., Boye, D., & Walster (Hatfield), E. (1968). Retaliation as a means of restoring equity. *Journal of Personality and Social Psychology, 10,* 370–376.

Berscheid, E., Dion, K., Walster (Hatfield), E., & Walster, G. W. (1971). Physical attractiveness and dating choice: A test of the matching hypothesis. *Journal of Experimental Social Psychology, 7,* 173–189.

Berscheid, E., Graziano, W., Monson, T., & Dermer, M. (1976). Outcome dependency: Attention, attribution, and attraction. *Journal of Personality and Social Psychology, 34,* 978–989.

Berscheid, E., & Peplau, L. A. (1983). The emerging science of relationships. In H. H. Kelley, E. Berscheid, A. Christensen, J. H. Harvey, T. L. Huston, G. Levinger, E. McClintock, L. A. Peplau, & D. R. Peterson (Eds.), *Close relationships.* New York: Freeman.

Berscheid, E., Snyder, M., & Omoto, A. M. (1989). Issues in studying close relationships: Conceptualizing and measuring closeness. In C. Hendrick (Ed.), *Review of personality and social psychology* (Vol. 10). Newbury Park, CA: Sage.

Berscheid, E., & Walster (Hatfield), E. (1978). *Interpersonal attraction.* Reading, MA: Addison-Wesley.

Berscheid, E., Walster, G. W., & Hatfield (was Walster), E. (1969). Effects of accuracy and positivity of evaluation on liking for the evaluator. Unpublished manuscript. Summarized by E. Berscheid and E. Walster (Hatfield) (1978), *Interpersonal attraction.* Reading, MA: Addison-Wesley.

Bersoff, D. N. (1987). Social science data and the Supreme Court: Lockhart as a case in point. *American Psychologist, 42,* 52–58.

Bertrand, M., & Mullainathan, S. (2003). Are Emily and Greg more employable than Lakisha and Jamal? A field experiment on labor market discrimination. Massachusetts Institute of Technology, Department of Economics, Working Paper 03-22.

Besser, A., & Priel, B. (2005). The apple does not fall far from the tree: Attachment styles and personality vulnerabilities to depression in three generations of women. *Personality and Social Psychology Bulletin, 31,* 1052–1073.

Bettencourt, B. A., Dill, K. E., Greathouse, S. A., Charlton, K., & Mulholland, A. (1997). Evaluations of ingroup and outgroup members: The role of category-based expectancy violation. *Journal of Experimental Social Psychology, 33,* 244–275.

Bettencourt, B. A., & Kernahan, C. (1997). A meta-analysis of aggression in the presence of violent cues: Effects of gender differences and aversive provocation. *Aggressive Behavior, 23,* 447–456.

Bettencourt, B. A., Talley, A., Benjamin, A. J., & Valentine, J. (2006). Personality and aggressive behavior under provoking and neutral conditions: A meta-analytic review. *Psychological Bulletin, 132,* 751–777.

Bianchi, S. M., Milkie, M. A., Sayer, L. C., & Robinson, J. P. (2000). Is anyone doing the housework? Trends in the gender division of household labor. *Social Forces, 79,* 191–228.

Bickman, L. (1975). Bystander intervention in a crime: The effect of a mass-media campaign. *Journal of Applied Social Psychology, 5,* 296–302.

Bickman, L. (1979). Interpersonal influence and the reporting of a crime. *Personality and Social Psychology Bulletin, 5,* 32–35.

Bickman, L., & Green, S. K. (1977). Situational cues and crime reporting: Do signs make a difference? *Journal of Applied Social Psychology, 7,* 1–18.

Biernat, M. (1991). Gender stereotypes and the relationship between masculinity and femininity: A developmental analysis. *Journal of Personality and Social Psychology, 61,* 351–365.

Biernat, M. (2003). Toward a broader view of social stereotyping. *American Psychologist, 58,* 1019–1027.

Biernat, M., & Kobrynowicz, D. (1997). Gender- and race-based standards of competence: Lower minimum standards but higher ability standards for devalued groups. *Journal of Personality and Social Psychology, 72,* 544–557.

Biernat, M., Vescio, T. K., & Green, M. L. (1996). Selective self-stereotyping. *Journal of Personality and Social Psychology, 71,* 1194–1209.

Bigam, R. G. (1977, March). Voir dire: The attorney's job. *Trial 13,* p. 3. Cited by G. Bermant & J. Shepard in "The voir dire examination, juror challenges, and adversary advocacy." In B. D. Sales (Ed.), *Perspectives in law and psychology, Vol. II: The trial process.* New York: Plenum Press, 1981.

Billig, M., & Tajfel, H. (1973). Social categorization and similarity in intergroup behaviour. *European Journal of Social Psychology, 3,* 27–52.

Binder, J., Zagefka, H., Brown, R., Funke, F., Kessler, T., Mummendey, A., Maquil, A., Demoulin, S., & Leyens, J-P. (2009). Does contact reduce prejudice or does prejudice reduce contact? A longitudinal test of the contact hypothesis among majority and minority groups in three European countries. *Journal of Personality and Social Psychology, 96,* 843–856.

Biner, P. M. (1991). Effects of lighting-induced arousal on the magnitude of goal valence. *Personality and Social Psychology Bulletin, 17,* 219–226.

Bingenheimer, J. B., Brennan, R. T., & Earls, F. J. (2005). Firearm violence exposure and serious violent behavior. *Science, 308,* 1323–1326.

Binham, R. (1980, March–April). Trivers in Jamaica. *Science, 80,* 57–67.

Bishop, B. (2004, April 4). The schism in U.S. politics begins at home: Growing gaps found from county to county in presidential race. *American-Statesman* (and personal correspondence, November 22, 2004).

Bishop, G. D. (1984). Gender, role, and illness behavior in a military population. *Health Psychology, 3,* 519–534.

Bishop, G. D. (1987). Lay conceptions of physical symptoms. *Journal of Applied Social Psychology, 17,* 127–146.

Bishop, G. D. (1991). Understanding the understanding of illness: Lay disease representations. In J. A. Skelton & R. T. Croyle (Eds.), *Mental representation in health and illness.* New York: Springer-Verlag.

Björkqvist, K. (1994). Sex differences in physical, verbal, and indirect aggression: A review of recent research. *Sex Roles, 30,* 177–188.

Blackburn, R. T., Pellino, G. R., Boberg, A., & O'Connell, C. (1980). Are instructional improvement programs off target? *Current Issues in Higher Education, 1,* 31–48.

Blair, C. A., Thompson, L. F., & Wuensch, K. L. (2005). Electronic helping behavior: The virtual presence of others makes a difference. *Basic and Applied Social Psychology, 27,* 171–178.

Blair, I. V., Judd, C. M., & Chapleau, K. M. (2004). The influence of Afrocentric facial features in criminal sentencing. *Psychological Science, 15,* 674–679.

Blake, R. R., & Mouton, J. S. (1962). The intergroup dynamics of win-lose conflict and problem-solving collaboration in union-management relations. In M. Sherif (Ed.), *Intergroup relations and leadership.* New York: Wiley.

Blake, R. R., & Mouton, J. S. (1979). Intergroup problem solving in organizations: From theory to practice. In W. G. Austin and S. Worchel (Eds.), *The social psychology of intergroup relations.* Monterey, CA: Brooks/Cole.

Blanchard, F. A., & Cook, S. W. (1976). Effects of helping a less competent member of a cooperating interracial group on the development of interpersonal attraction. *Journal of Personality and Social Psychology, 34,* 1245–1255.

Blank, H., Fischer, V., & Erdfelder, E. (2003). Hindsight bias in political elections. *Memory, 11,* 491–504.

Blank, H., Nestler, S., von Collani, G., & Fischer, V. (2008). How many hindsight biases are there? *Cognition, 106,* 1408–1440.

Blanton, H., Jaccard, J., Christie, C., & Gonzales, P. M. (2007). Plausible assumptions, questionable assumptions and post hoc rationalizations: Will the real IAT please stand up? *Journal of Experimental Social Psychology*, **43**, 399–409.

Blanton, H., Jaccard, J., Gonzales, P. M., & Christie, C. (2006). Decoding the implicit association test: Implications for criterion prediction. *Journal of Experimental Social Psychology*, **42**, 192–212.

Blanton, H., Pelham, B. W., DeHart, T., & Carvallo, M. (2001). Overconfidence as dissonance reduction. *Journal of Experimental Social Psychology*, **37**, 373–385.

Blascovich, J. (2002). Social influence within immersive virtual environments. In R. Schroeder (Ed.), *The social life of avatars*. New York: Springer-Verlag.

Blascovich, J., Wyer, N. A., Swart, L. A., & Kibler, J. L. (1997). Racism and racial categorization. *Journal of Personality and Social Psychology*, **72**, 1364–1372.

Blass, T. (1990). Psychological approaches to the Holocaust: Review and evaluation. Paper presented to the American Psychological Association convention.

Blass, T. (1991). Understanding behavior in the Milgram obedience experiment: The role of personality, situations, and their interactions. *Journal of Personality and Social Psychology*, **60**, 398–413.

Blass, T. (1996). Stanley Milgram: A life of inventiveness and controversy. In G. A. Kimble, C. A. Boneau, & M. Wertheimer (Eds.). *Portraits of pioneers in psychology* (Vol. II). Washington, DC: American Psychological Association.

Blass, T. (1999). The Milgram paradigm after 35 years: Some things we now know about obedience to authority. *Journal of Applied Social Psychology*, **29**, 955–978.

Blass, T. (2000). The Milgram paradigm after 35 years: Some things we now know about obedience to authority. In T. Blass (Ed.), *Obedience to authority: Current perspectives on the Milgram paradigm*. Mahwah, NJ: Erlbaum.

Block, J., & Funder, D. C. (1986). Social roles and social perception: Individual differences in attribution and error. *Journal of Personality and Social Psychology*, **51**, 1200–1207.

Blundell, W. E. (1986). *Storyteller step by step: A guide to better feature writing*. New York: Dow Jones. Cited by S. H. Stocking & P. H. Gross (1989), *How do journalists think? A proposal for the study of cognitive bias in newsmaking*. Bloomington, IN: ERIC Clearinghouse on Reading and Communication

Skills, Smith Research Center, Indiana University.

Boden, J. M., Fergusson, D. M., & Horwood, L. J. (2007). Self-esteem and violence: Testing links between adolescent self-esteem and later hostilty and violent behavior. *Social Psychiatry and Psychiatric Empidemiology*, **42**, 881–891.

Boden, J. M., Fergusson, D. M., & Horwood, L. J. (2008). Does adolescent self-esteem predict later life outcomes? A test of the causal role of self-esteem. *Development and Psychopathology*, **20**, 319–339.

Bodenhausen, G. V. (1990). Stereotypes as judgmental heuristics: Evidence of circadian variations in discrimination. *Psychological Science*, **1**, 319–322.

Bodenhausen, G. V. (1993). Emotions, arousal, and stereotypic judgments: A heuristic model of affect and stereotyping. In D. M. Mackie & D. L. Hamilton (Eds.), *Affect, cognition, and stereotyping: Interactive processes in group perception*. San Diego: Academic Press.

Bodenhausen, G. V., & Macrae, C. N. (1998). Stereotype activation and inhibition. In R. S. Wyer, Jr., *Stereotype activation and inhibition: Advances in social cognition* (Vol. 11). Mahwah, NJ: Erlbaum.

Bodenhausen, G. V., Sheppard, L. A., & Kramer, G. F. (1994). Negative affect and social judgment: The differential impact of anger and sadness. *European Journal of Social Psychology*, **24**, 45–62.

Boggiano, A. K., Barrett, M., Weiher, A. W., McClelland, G. H., & Lusk, C. M. (1987). Use of the maximal-operant principle to motivate children's intrinsic interest. *Journal of Personality and Social Psychology*, **53**, 866–879.

Boggiano, A. K., Harackiewicz, J. M., Bessette, J. M., & Main, D. S. (1985). Increasing children's interest through performance-contingent reward. *Social Cognition*, **3**, 400–411.

Boggiano, A. K., & Pittman, T. S. (Eds.) (1992). *Achievement and motivation: A social-developmental perspective. Cambridge studies in social and emotional development* (pp. 37–53). New York: Cambridge University Press.

Boggiano, A. K., & Ruble, D. N. (1985). Children's responses to evaluative feedback. In R. Schwarzer (Ed.), *Self-related cognitions in anxiety and motivation*. Hillsdale, NJ: Erlbaum.

Bohner, G., Bless, H., Schwarz, N., & Strack, F. (1988). What triggers causal attributions? The impact of valence and subjective probability. *European Journal of Social Psychology*, **18**, 335–345.

Bonanno, G. A., Rennicke, C., & Dekel, S. (2005). Self-enhancement among high-exposure survivors of the September 11th terrorist attack: Resilience or social maladjustment?

Journal of Personality and Social Psychology, **88**, 984–998.

Bond, C. F., Jr., DiCandia, C. G., & MacKinnon, J. R. (1988). Responses to violence in a psychiatric setting: The role of patient's race. *Personality and Social Psychology Bulletin*, **14**, 448–458.

Bond, C. F., Jr., & Titus, L. J. (1983). Social facilitation: A meta-analysis of 241 studies. *Psychological Bulletin*, **94**, 265–292.

Bond, M. H. (2004). Culture and aggression: From context to coercion. *Personality and Social Psychology Review*, **8**, 62–78.

Bond, R., & Smith, P. B. (1996). Culture and conformity: A meta-analysis of studies using Asch's (1952b, 1956) line judgment task. *Psychological Bulletin*, **119**, 111–137.

Bonnot, V., & Croizet, J-C. (2007). Stereotype internalization and women's math performance: The role of interference in working memory. *Journal of Experimental Social Psychology*, **43**, 857–866.

Bono, J. E., & Judge, T. A. (2004). Personality and transformational and transactional leadership: A meta-analysis. *Journal of Applied Psychology*, **89**, 901–910.

Bonta, B. D. (1997). Cooperation and competition in peaceful societies. *Psychological Bulletin*, **121**, 299–320.

Boomsma, D. I., Cacioppo, J. T., Slagboom, P. E., & Posthuma, D. (2006). Genetic linkage and association analysis for loneliness in Dutch twin and sibling pairs points to a region on chromosome 12q23-24. *Behavior Genetics*, **36**, 137–146.

Borchard, E. M. (1932). *Convicting the innocent: Errors of criminal justice*. New Haven: Yale University Press. Cited by E. R. Hilgard & E. F. Loftus (1979), Effective interrogation of the eyewitness. *International Journal of Clinical and Experimental Hypnosis*, **17**, 342–359.

Borgida, E. (1981). Legal reform of rape laws. In L. Bickman (Ed.), *Applied social psychology annual* (Vol. 2, pp. 211–241). Beverly Hills, CA: Sage.

Borgida, E., & Brekke, N. (1985). Psychelegal research on rape trials. In A. W. Burgess (Ed.), *Rape and sexual assault: A research handbook*. New York: Garland.

Borgida, E., Locksley, A., & Brekke, N. (1981). Social stereotypes and social judgment. In N. Cantor & J. Kihlstrom (Eds.), *Cognition, social interaction, and personality*. Hillsdale, NJ: Erlbaum.

Borgida, E., & White, P. (1980). Judgmental bias and legal reform. Unpublished manuscript, University of Minnesota.

Borkenau, P., & Liebler, A. (1993). Convergence of stranger ratings of personality and intelligence with self-ratings, partner ratings, and measured intelligence. *Journal of Personality and Social Psychology, 65,* 546–553.

Bornstein, B. H., & Zicafoose, D. J. (1999). "I know I know it, I know I saw it": The stability of the confidence-accuracy relationship across domains. *Journal of Experimental Psychology: Applied, 5,* 76–88.

Bornstein, G., & Rapoport, A. (1988). Intergroup competition for the provision of step-level public goods: Effects of preplay communication. *European Journal of Social Psychology, 18,* 125–142.

Bornstein, G., Rapoport, A., Kerpel, L., & Katz, T. (1989). Within- and between-group communication in intergroup competition for public goods. *Journal of Experimental Social Psychology, 25,* 422–436.

Bornstein, R. F. (1989). Exposure and affect: Overview and meta-analysis of research, 1968–1987. *Psychological Bulletin, 106,* 265–289.

Bornstein, R. F. (1999). Source amnesia, misattribution, and the power of unconscious perceptions and memories. *Psychoanalytic Psychology, 16,* 155–178.

Bornstein, R. F., & D'Agostino, P. R. (1992). Stimulus recognition and the mere exposure effect. *Journal of Personality and Social Psychology, 63,* 545–552.

Bornstein, R. F., Galley, D. J., Leone, D. R., & Kale, A. R. (1991). The temporal stability of ratings of parents: Test-retest reliability and influence of parental contact. *Journal of Social Behavior and Personality, 6,* 641–649.

Bossard, J. H. S. (1932). Residential propinquity as a factor in marriage selection. *American Journal of Sociology, 38,* 219–224.

Bothwell, R. K., Brigham, J. C., & Malpass, R. S. (1989). Cross-racial identification. *Personality and Social Psychology Bulletin, 15,* 19–25.

Botvin, G. J., Epstein, J. A., & Griffin, K. W. (2008). A social influence model of alcohol use for inner-city adolescents: Family drinking, perceived drinking norms, and perceived social benefits of drinking. *Journal of Studies on Alcohol and Drugs, 69,* 397–405.

Botvin, G. J., Schinke, S., & Orlandi, M. A. (1995). School-based health promotion: Substance abuse and sexual behavior. *Applied & Preventive Psychology, 4,* 167–184.

Botwin, M. D., Buss, D. M., & Shackelford, T. K. (1997). Personality and mate preferences: Five factors in mate selection and marital satisfaction. *Journal of Personality, 65,* 107–136.

Bouas, K. S., & Komorita, S. S. (1996). Group discussion and cooperation in social dilemmas. *Personality and Social Psychology Bulletin, 22,* 1144–1150.

Bourgeois, M. J., Horowitz, I. A., & Lee, L. F. (1993). Effects of technicality and access to trial transcripts on verdicts and information processing in a civil trial. *Personality and Social Psychology Bulletin, 19,* 219–226.

Bowen, E. (1988, April 4). Whatever became of Honest Abe? *Time.*

Bower, B. (1997). Thanks for the memories: Scientists evaluate interviewing tactics for boosting eyewitness recall. *Science, 151,* 246–247.

Bower, G. H. (1987). Commentary on mood and memory. *Behavioral Research and Therapy, 25,* 443–455.

Bowlby, J. (1980). *Loss, sadness and depression, Vol. III of Attachment and loss.* London: Basic Books.

Boyatzis, C. J., Matillo, G. M., & Nesbitt, K. M. (1995). Effects of the "Mighty Morphin Power Rangers" on children's aggression with peers. *Child Study Journal, 25,* 45–55.

Boyes, A. D., & Fletcher, G. J. O. (2007). Metaperceptions of bias in intimate relationships. *Journal of Personality and Social Psychology, 92,* 286–306.

Bradley, W., & Mannell, R. C. (1984). Sensitivity of intrinsic motivation to reward procedure instructions. *Personality and Social Psychology Bulletin, 10,* 426–431.

Brandon, R., & Davies, C. (1973). *Wrongful imprisonment: Mistaken convictions and their consequences.* Hamden, CT: Archon Books.

Branscombe, N. R., Schmitt, M. T., & Harvey, R. D. (1999). Perceiving pervasive discrimination among African Americans: Implications for group identification and well-being. *Journal of Personality and Social Psychology, 77,* 135–149.

Brauer, M., Judd, C. M., & Gliner, M. D. (1995). The effects of repeated expressions on attitude polarization during group discussions. *Journal of Personality and Social Psychology, 68,* 1014–1029.

Brauer, M., Judd, C. M., & Jacquelin, V. (2001). The communication of social stereotypes: The effects of group discussion and information distribution on stereotypic appraisals. *Journal of Personality and Social Psychology, 81,* 463–475.

Braverman, J. (2005). The effect of mood on detection of covariation. *Personality and Social Psychology Bulletin, 31,* 1487–1497.

Bray, R. M., & Noble, A. M. (1978). Authoritarianism and decisions of mock juries: Evidence of jury bias and group polarization. *Journal of Personality and Social Psychology, 36,* 1424–1430.

Bregman, N. J., & McAllister, H. A. (1982). Eyewitness testimony: The role of commitment in increasing reliability. *Social Psychology Quarterly, 45,* 181–184.

Brehm, J. W. (1956). Post-decision changes in desirability of alternatives. *Journal of Abnormal Social Psychology, 52,* 384–389.

Brehm, J. W. (1999). Would the real dissonance theory please stand up? Paper presented to the American Psychological Society convention.

Brehm, S., & Brehm, J. W. (1981). *Psychological reactance: A theory of freedom and control.* New York: Academic Press.

Brehm, S. S., & Smith, T. W. (1986). Social psychological approaches to psychotherapy and behavior change. In S. L. Garfield & A. F. Bergin (Eds.), *Handbook of psychotherapy and behavior change,* 3rd edition. New York: Wiley.

Brenner, S. N., & Molander, E. A. (1977, January–February). Is the ethics of business changing? *Harvard Business Review,* pp. 57–71.

Brewer, M. B. (1987). Collective decisions. *Social Science, 72,* 140–143.

Brewer, M. B. (2007). The importance of being *we:* Human nature and intergroup relations. *American Psychologist, 62,* 726–738.

Brewer, M. B., & Gaertner, S. L. (2004). Toward reduction of prejudice: Intergroup contact and social categorization. In M. B. Brewer & M. Hewstone (Eds.), *Self and social identity.* Malden, MA: Blackwell.

Brewer, M. B., & Miller, N. (1988). Contact and cooperation: When do they work? In P. A. Katz & D. Taylor (Eds.), *Towards the elimination of racism: Profiles in controversy.* New York: Plenum.

Brewer, M. B., & Pierce, K. P. (2005). Social identity complexity and outgroup tolerance. *Personality and Social Psychology Bulletin, 31,* 428–437.

Brewer, M. B., & Silver, M. (1978). In-group bias as a function of task characteristics. *European Journal of Social Psychology, 8,* 393–400.

Brickman, P. (1978). Is it real? In J. Harvey, W. Ickes, & R. Kidd (Eds.), *New directions in attribution research* (Vol. 2). Hillsdale, NJ: Erlbaum.

Brickman, P., Coates, D. & Janoff-Bulman, R. J. (1978). Lottery winners and accident victims: Is happiness relative? *Journal of Personality and Social Psychology, 36,* 917–927.

Brigham, J. C., Bennett, L. B., Meissner, C. A., & Mitchell, T. L. (2006). The influence of race on eyewitness testimony. In R. Lindsay, M. Toglia, D. Ross, & J. D. Read (Eds.), *Handbook of eyewitness psychology.* Mahwah, NJ: Erlbaum.

Brigham, J. C., & Cairns, D. L. (1988). The effect of mugshot inspections on eyewitness identification accuracy. *Journal of Applied Social Psychology, 18,* 1394–1410.

Brigham, J. C., Ready, D. J., & Spier, S. A. (1990). Standards for evaluating the fairness of photograph lineups. *Basic and Applied Social Psychology, 11,* 149–163.

Briñol, P., Petty, R. E., & Tormala, Z. L. (2004). Self-validation of cognitive responses to advertisements. *Journal of Consumer Research, 30,* 559–573.

Briñol, P., Tormala, Z. L., & Petty, R. E. (2002). Source credibility as a determinant of self-validation effects in persuasion. Poster presented at the European Association of Experimental Social Psychology, San Sebastian, Spain.

British Psychological Society (2000). *Code of conduct, ethical principles and guidelines.* Leicester, UK: British Psychological Society (www.bps.org.uk/documents/Code.pdf).

Britt, T. W., & Garrity, M. J. (2006). Attributions and personality as predictors of the road rage response. *British Journal of Social Psychology, 45,* 127–147.

Brock, T. C. (1965). Communicator-recipient similarity and decision change. *Journal of Personality and Social Psychology, 1,* 650–654.

Brockner, J., & Hulton, A. J. B. (1978). How to reverse the vicious cycle of low self-esteem: The importance of attentional focus. *Journal of Experimental Social Psychology, 14,* 564–578.

Brockner, J., Rubin, J. Z., Fine, J., Hamilton, T. P., Thomas, B., & Turetsky, B. (1982). Factors affecting entrapment in escalating conflicts: The importance of timing. *Journal of Research in Personality, 16,* 247–266.

Brodt, S. E., & Ross, L. D. (1998). The role of stereotyping in overconfident social prediction. *Social Cognition, 16,* 228–252.

Brodt, S. E., & Zimbardo, P. G. (1981). Modifying shyness-related social behavior through symptom misattribution. *Journal of Personality and Social Psychology, 41,* 437–449.

Bronfenbrenner, U. (1961). The mirror image in Soviet-American relations. *Journal of Social Issues, 17*(3), 45–56.

Brooks, D. (2004, June 5). Circling the wagons. *New York Times* (www.nytimes.com).

Brooks, D. (2005, August 10). All cultures are not equal. *New York Times* (www.nytimes.com).

Broome, A., & Wegner, D. M. (1994). Some positive effects of releasing socially anxious people from the need to please. Paper presented to the American Psychological Society convention.

Brown, D. E. (1991). *Human universals.* New York: McGraw-Hill.

Brown, D. E. (2000). Human universals and their implications. In N. Roughley (Ed.), *Being humans: Anthropological universality and particularity in transdisciplinary perspectives.* New York: Walter de Gruyter.

Brown, G. (2008). *Wartime courage: Stories of extraordinary bravery in World War II.* London: Bloomsbury.

Brown, H. J., Jr. (1990). *P.S. I love you.* Nashville: Rutledge Hill.

Brown, J. D., & Dutton, K. A. (1994). From the top down: Self-esteem and self-evaluation. Unpublished manuscript, University of Washington.

Brown, J. D., Novick, N. J., Lord, K. A., & Richards, J. M. (1992). When Gulliver travels: Social context, psychological closeness, and self-appraisals. *Journal of Personality and Social Psychology, 62,* 717–727.

Brown, J. D., & Taylor, S. E. (1986). Affect and the processing of personal information: Evidence for mood-activated self-schemata. *Journal of Experimental Social Psychology, 22,* 436–452.

Brown, K. T., Brown, T. N., Jackson, J. S., Sellers, R. M., & Manuel, W. J. (2003). Teammates on and off the field? Contact with Black teammates and the racial attitudes of White student athletes. *Journal of Applied Social Psychology, 33,* 1379–1403.

Brown, R. (1965). *Social psychology.* New York: Free Press.

Brown, R. (1987). Theory of politeness: An exemplary case. Paper presented to the Society of Experimental Social Psychology meeting. Cited by R. O. Kroker & L. A. Wood (1992), Are the rules of address universal? IV: Comparison of Chinese, Korean, Greek, and German usage. *Journal of Cross-Cultural Psychology, 23,* 148–162.

Brown, R., Eller, A., Leeds, S., & Stace, K. (2007). Intergroup contact and intergroup attitudes: A longitudinal study. *European Journal of Social Psychology, 37,* 692–703.

Brown, R., Maras, P., Masser, B., Vivian, J., & Hewstone, M. (2001). Life on the ocean wave: Testing some intergroup hypotheses in a naturalistic setting. *Group Processes and Intergroup Relations, 4,* 81–97.

Brown, R., Vivian, J., & Hewstone, M. (1999). Changing attitudes through intergroup contact: The effects of group membership salience. *European Journal of Social Psychology, 29,* 741–764.

Brown, R., & Wootton-Millward, L. (1993). Perceptions of group homogeneity during group formation and change. *Social Cognition, 11,* 126–149.

Brown, R. P., Charnsangavej, T., Keough, K. A., Newman, M. L., & Rentfrom, P. J. (2000). Putting the "affirm" into affirmative action: Preferential selection and academic performance. *Journal of Personality and Social Psychology, 79,* 736–747.

Brown, S. L., Brown, R. M., House, J. S., & Smith, D. M. (2008). Coping with spousal loss: Potential buffering effects of self-reported helping behavior. *Personality and Social Psychology Bulletin, 34,* 849–861.

Brown, S. L., Nesse, R. M., Vinokur, A. D., & Smith, D. M. (2003). Providing social support may be more beneficial than receiving it. *Psychological Science, 14,* 320–327.

Brown, V. R., & Paulus, P. B. (2002). Making group brainstorming more effective: Recommendations from an associative memory perspective. *Current Directions in Psychological Science, 11,* 208–212.

Brown, W. M., Price, M. E., Kang, J., Pound, N., Zhao, Y., & Yu, H. (2008). Fluctuating asymmetry and preferences for sex-typical bodily characteristics. *Proceedings of the National Academy of Sciences, 105,* 12938–12943 (pnas.org).

Browning, C. R. (1992). *Ordinary men: Reserve Police Battalion 101 and the final solution in Poland.* New York: HarperCollins.

Bruce, V. (1998, July). Identifying people caught on video. *The Psychologist,* pp. 331–335.

Bruck, M., & Ceci, S. J. (1999). The suggestibility of children's memory. *Annual Review of Psychology, 50,* 419–439.

Bruck, M., & Ceci, S. (2004). Forensic developmental psychology: Unveiling four common misconceptions. *Current Directions in Psychological Science, 15,* 229–232.

Brückner, H., & Bearman, P. (2005). After the promise: The STD consequences of adolescent virginity pledges. *Journal of Adolescent Health, 36,* 271–278.

Bryan, J. H., & Test, M. A. (1967). Models and helping: Naturalistic studies in aiding behavior. *Journal of Personality and Social Psychology, 6,* 400–407.

Buckhout, R. (1974, December). Eyewitness testimony. *Scientific American,* pp. 23–31.

Buehler, R., & Griffin, D. (2003). Planning, personality, and prediction: The role of future focus in optimistic time predictions. *Organizational Behavior and Human Decision Processes, 92,* 80–90.

Buehler, R., Griffin, D., & Ross, M. (1994). Exploring the "planning fallacy": When people underestimate their task completion times. *Journal of Personality and Social Psychology, 67,* 366–381.

Buehler, R., Griffin, D., & Ross, M. (2002). Inside the planning fallacy: The causes and consequences of optimistic time predictions. In T. Gilovich, D. Griffin, & D. Kahneman (Eds.),

Heuristics and biases: The psychology of intuitive judgment. Cambridge: Cambridge University Press.

Buehler, R., Messervey, D., & Griffin, D. (2005). Collaborative planning and prediction: Does group discussion affect optimistic biases in estimation? *Organizational Behavior and Human Decision Processes, 97,* 47–63.

Buffardi, L. E., & Campbell, W. K. (2008). Narcissism and social networking websites. *Personality and Social Psychology Bulletin, 34,* 1303–1314.

Buford, B. (1992). *Among the thugs.* New York: Norton.

Bugental, D. B., & Hehman, J. A. (2007). Ageism: A review of research and policy implications. *Social Issues and Policy Review, 1,* 173–216.

Buller, D. J. (2005). *Adapting minds: Evolutionary psychology and the persistent quest for human nature.* Cambridge, MA: MIT Press.

Buller, D. J. (2009, January). Four fallacies of pop evolutionary psychology. *Scientific American,* pp. 74–81.

Bullock, J. (2006, March 17). The enduring importance of false political beliefs. Paper presented at the annual meeting of the Western Political Science Association, Albuquerque (www.allacademic.com/meta/p97459_index.html).

Burchill, S. A. L., & Stiles, W. B. (1988). Interactions of depressed college students with their roommates: Not necessarily negative. *Journal of Personality and Social Psychology, 55,* 410–419.

Bureau of the Census. (1975). *Historical abstract of the United States: Colonial times to 1970.* Washington, DC: Superintendent of Documents.

Bureau of the Census. (1993, May 4). Voting survey, reported by Associated Press.

Bureau of the Census. (2009). *The 2009 statistical abstract* (Table 946; www.census.gov).

Burger, J. M. (1987). Increased performance with increased personal control: A self-presentation interpretation. *Journal of Experimental Social Psychology, 23,* 350–360.

Burger, J. M. (1991). Changes in attributions over time: The ephemeral fundamental attribution error. *Social Cognition, 9,* 182–193.

Burger, J. M. (2009, January). Replicating Milgram: Would people still obey today? *American Psychologist, 64,* 1–11.

Burger, J. M., & Burns, L. (1988). The illusion of unique invulnerability and the use of effective contraception. *Personality and Social Psychology Bulletin, 14,* 264–270.

Burger, J. M., & Guadagno, R. E. (2003). Self-concept clarity and the foot-in-the-door procedure. *Basic and Applied Social Psychology, 25,* 79–86.

Burger, J. M., Messian, N., Patel, S., del Prade, A., & Anderson, C. (2004). What a coincidence! The effects of incidental similarity on compliance. *Personality and Social Psychology Bulletin, 30,* 35–43.

Burger, J. M., & Palmer, M. L. (1991). Changes in and generalization of unrealistic optimism following experiences with stressful events: Reactions to the 1989 California earthquake. *Personality and Social Psychology Bulletin, 18,* 39–43.

Burger, J. M., & Pavelich, J. L. (1994). Attributions for presidential elections: The situational shift over time. *Basic and Applied Social Psychology, 15,* 359–371.

Burger, J. M., Sanchez, J., Imberi, J. E., & Grande, L. R. (2009). The norm of reciprocity as an internalized social norm: Returning favors even when no one finds out. *Social Influence, 4,* 11–17.

Burger, J. M., Soroka, S., Gonzago, K., Murphy, E., & Somervell, E. (2001). The effect of fleeting attraction on compliance to requests. *Personality and Social Psychology Bulletin, 27,* 1578–1586.

Burkholder, R. (2003, February 14). Unwilling coalition? Majorities in Britain, Canada oppose military action in Iraq. *Gallup Poll Tuesday Briefing* (www.gallup.com/poll).

Burkholder, R. (2005, January 11). Chinese far wealthier than a decade ago, but are they happier? Gallup Poll (www.poll.gallup.com).

Burkley, E. (2008). The role of self-control in resistance to persuasion. *Personality and Social Psychology Bulletin, 34,* 419–431.

Burn, S. M. (1992). Locus of control, attributions, and helplessness in the homeless. *Journal of Applied Social psychology, 22,* 1161–1174.

Burnham, G., Lafta, R., Doocy, S., & Roberts, L. (2006). Mortality after the 2003 invasion of Iraq: A cross-sectional cluster sample survey. *Lancet, 368,* 1421–1428.

Burns, D. D. (1980). *Feeling good: The new mood therapy.* New York: Signet.

Burns, J. F. (2003a, April 13). Pillagers strip Iraqi museum of its treasure. *New York Times* (www.nytimes.com).

Burns, J. F. (2003b, April 14). Baghdad residents begin a long climb to an ordered city. *New York Times* (www.nytimes.com).

Burnstein, E., Crandall, R., & Kitayama, S. (1994). Some neo-Darwinian decision rules for altruism: Weighing cues for inclusive fitness as a function of the biological importance of the decision.

Journal of Personality and Social Psychology, 67, 773–789.

Burnstein, E., & Vinokur, A. (1977). Persuasive argumentation and social comparison as determinants of attitude polarization. *Journal of Experimental Social Psychology, 13,* 315–332.

Burnstein, E., & Worchel, P. (1962). Arbitrariness of frustration and its consequences for aggression in a social situation. *Journal of Personality, 30,* 528–540.

Burr, W. R. (1973). *Theory construction and the sociology of the family.* New York: Wiley.

Burson, K. A., Larrick, R. P., & Klayman, J. (2006). Skilled or unskilled, but still unaware of it: How perceptions of difficulty drive miscalibration in relative comparisons. *Journal of Personality and Social Psychology, 90,* 60–77.

Burton, C. M., & King, L. A. (2008). Effects of (very) brief writing on health: The two-minute miracle. *British Journal of Health Psychology, 13,* 9–14.

Bush, G. W. (2005, December 12). Address to the World Affairs Council of Philadelphia. Quote by CNN.com, Bush: Iraqi democracy making progress.

Bush, G. W. (2006). Quoted by David Brooks, Ends without means. *New York Times,* September 14, 2006 (www.nytimes.com).

Bush, G. W. (2008). Quoted by Terence Hunt, AP White House correspondent, Bush says Iraq war was worth it. Yahoo! News (news.yahoo.com).

Bushman, B. J. (1993). Human aggression while under the influence of alcohol and other drugs: An integrative research review. *Current Directions in Psychological Science, 2,* 148–152.

Bushman, B. J. (1998). Priming effects of media violence on the accessibility of aggressive constructs in memory. *Personality and Social Psychology Bulletin, 24,* 537–545.

Bushman, B. J. (2002). Does venting anger feed or extinguish the flame? Catharsis, rumination, distraction, anger, and aggressive responding. *Personality and Social Psychology Bulletin, 28,* 724–731.

Bushman, B. J. (2005). Violence and sex in television programs do not sell products in advertisements. *Psychological Science, 16,* 702–708.

Bushman, B. J. (2007). That was a great commercial, but what were they selling? Effects of violence and sex on memory for products in television commercials. *Journal of Applied Social Psychology, 37,* 1784–1796.

Bushman, B. J., & Anderson, C. A. (1998). Methodology in the study of aggression: Integrating experimental and nonexperimental findings. In R. Geen & E. Donnerstein (Eds.), *Human aggression: Theories, research and implications for policy.* San Diego: Academic Press.

Bushman, B. J., & Anderson, C. A. (2001). Media violence and the American public: Scientific facts versus media misinformation. *American Psychologist, 56,* 477–489.

Bushman, B. J., & Anderson, C. A. (2002). Violent video games and hostile expectations: A test of the general aggression model. *Personality and Social Psychology Bulletin, 28,* 1679–1686.

Bushman, B. J., & Baumeister, R. (1998). Threatened egotism, narcissism, self-esteem, and direct and displaced aggression: Does self-love or self-hate lead to violence? *Journal of Personality and Social Psychology, 75,* 219–229.

Bushman, B. J., & Baumeister, R. F. (2002). Does self-love or self-hate lead to violence? *Journal of Research in Personality, 36,* 543–545.

Bushman, B. J., Baumeister, R. F., & Phillips, C. M. (2001). Do people aggress to improve their mood? Catharsis beliefs, affect regulation opportunity, and aggressive responding. *Journal of Personality and Social Psychology, 81,* 17–32.

Bushman, B. J., Baumeister, R. F., & Stack, A. D. (1999). Catharsis, aggression, and persuasive influence: Self-fulfilling or self-defeating prophecies? *Journal of Personality and Social Psychology, 76,* 367–376.

Bushman, B. J., Baumeister, R. F., Thomaes, S., Ryu, E., Begeer, S., & West, S. G. (2009). Looking again, and harder, for a link between low self-esteem and aggression. *Journal of Personality,* published online February 2, 2009.

Bushman, B. J., & Bonacci, A. M. (2002). Violence and sex impair memory for television ads. *Journal of Applied Psychology, 87,* 557–564.

Bushman, B. J., & Bonacci, A. M. (2004). You've got mail: Using e-mail to examine the effect of prejudiced attitudes on discrimination against Arabs. *Journal of Experimental Social Psychology, 40,* 753–759.

Bushman, B. J., Bonacci, A. M., Pedersen, W. C., Vasquez, E. A., & Miller, N. (2005). Chewing on it can chew you up: Effects of rumination on triggered displaced aggression. *Journal of Personality and Social Psychology, 88,* 969–983.

Bushman, B. J., & Geen, R. G. (1990). Role of cognitive-emotional mediators and individual differences in the effects of media violence on aggression. *Journal of Personality and Social Psychology, 58,* 156–163.

Bushman, B. J., Wang, M. C., & Anderson, C. A. (2005a). Is the curve relating temperature to aggression linear or curvilinear? Assaults and temperature in Minneapolis reexamined. *Journal of Personality and Social Psychology, 89,* 62–66.

Bushman, B. J., Wang, M. C., & Anderson, C. A. (2005b). Is the curve relating temperature to aggression linear or curvilinear? A response to Bell (2005) and to Cohn and Rotton (2005). *Journal of Personality and Social Psychology, 89,* 74–77.

Buss, D. M. (1984). Toward a psychology of person-environment (PE) correlation: The role of spouse selection. *Journal of Personality and Social Psychology, 47,* 361–377.

Buss, D. M. (1985). Human mate selection. *American Scientist, 73,* 47–51.

Buss, D. M. (1989). Sex differences in human mate preferences: Evolutionary hypotheses tested in 37 cultures. *Behavioral and Brain Sciences, 12,* 1–49.

Buss, D. M. (1994a). *The evolution of desire: Strategies of human mating.* New York: Basic Books.

Buss, D. M. (1994b). The strategies of human mating. *American Scientist, 82,* 238–249.

Buss, D. M. (1995a). Evolutionary psychology: A new paradigm for psychological science. *Psychological Inquiry, 6,* 1–30.

Buss, D. M. (1995b). Psychological sex differences: Origins through sexual selection. *American Psychologist, 50,* 164–168.

Buss, D. M. (1999). Behind the scenes. In D. G. Myers, *Social psychology,* 6th edition. New York: McGraw-Hill.

Buss, D. M. (2007). The evolution of human mating strategies: Consequences for conflict and cooperation. In S. W. Gangestad & J. A. Simpson (Eds.), *The evolution of mind: Fundamental questions and controversies.* New York: Guilford.

Buss, D. M. (Ed.). (2005). *The handbook of evolutionary psychology.* New York: Wiley.

Buss, D. M., & Shackelford, T. K. (1997). Human aggression in evolutionary psychological perspective. *Clinical Psychology Review, 17,* 605–619.

Buston, P. M., & Emlen, S. T. (2003). Cognitive processes underlying human mate choice: The relationship between self-perception and mate preference in Western society. *Proceedings of the National Academy of Sciences, 100,* 8805–8810.

Butcher, S. H. (1951). *Aristotle's theory of poetry and fine art.* New York: Dover.

Butler, A. C., Hokanson, J. E., & Flynn, H. A. (1994). A comparison of self-esteem lability and low trait

self-esteem as vulnerability factors for depression. *Journal of Personality and Social Psychology, 66,* 166–177.

Butler, J. L., & Baumeister, R. F. (1998). The trouble with friendly faces: Skilled performance with a supportive audience. *Journal of Personality and Social Psychology, 75,* 1213–1230.

Butterfield, F. (2001, April 20). Victims' race affects decisions on killers' sentence, study finds. *New York Times,* p. A10.

Butz, D. A., & Plant, E. A. (2006). Perceiving outgroup members as unresponsive: Implications for approach-related emotions, intentions, and behavior. *Journal of Personality and Social Psychology, 91,* 1066–1079.

Buunk, B. P., & van der Eijnden, R. J. J. M. (1997). Perceived prevalence, perceived superiority, and relationship satisfaction: Most relationships are good, but ours is the best. *Personality and Social Psychology Bulletin, 23,* 219–228.

Buunk, B. P., & Van Yperen, N. W. (1991). Referential comparisons, relational comparisons, and exchange orientation: Their relation to marital satisfaction. *Personality and Social Psychology Bulletin, 17,* 709–717.

Byers, S., & Wang, A. (2004). Understanding sexuality in close relationships from the social exchange perspective. In J. H. Harvey, A. Wenzel, & S. Sprecher (Eds.), *The handbook of sexuality in close relationships.* Mahwah, NJ: Erlbaum.

Byrne, D. (1971). *The attraction paradigm.* New York: Academic Press.

Byrne, D., & Clore, G. L. (1970). A reinforcement model of evaluative responses. *Personality: An International Journal, 1,* 103–128.

Byrne, D., & Wong, T. J. (1962). Racial prejudice, interpersonal attraction, and assumed dissimilarity of attitudes. *Journal of Abnormal and Social Psychology, 65,* 246–253.

Byrnes, J. P., Miller, D. C., & Schafer, W. D. (1999). Gender differences in risk taking: A meta-analysis. *Psychological Bulletin, 125,* 367–383.

Bytwerk, R. L. (1976). Julius Streicher and the impact of *Der Stürmer. Wiener Library Bulletin, 29,* 41–46.

Bytwerk, R. L., & Brooks, R. D. (1980). Julius Streicher and the rhetorical foundations of the holocaust. Paper presented to the Central States Speech Association convention.

Cacioppo, J. T. (2007, October). The rise in collaborative science. *Association for Psychological Science Observer,* pp. 52–53.

Cacioppo, J. T., & 18 others. (2007). Social neuroscience: Progress and implications for mental health. *Perspectives on Psychological Science, 2,* 99–123.

Cacioppo, J. T., Claiborn, C. D., Petty, R. E., & Heesacker, M. (1991). General framework for the study of attitude change in psychotherapy. In C. R. Snyder & D. R. Forsyth (Eds.), *Handbook of social and clinical psychology.* New York: Pergamon.

Cacioppo, J. T., & Patrick, W. (2008). *Loneliness: Human nature and the need for social connection.* New York: Norton.

Cacioppo, J. T., & Petty, R. E. (1981). Electromyograms as measures of extent and affectivity of information processing. *American Psychologist, 36*, 441–456.

Cacioppo, J. T., & Petty, R. E. (1986). Social processes. In M. G. H. Coles, E. Donchin, & S. W. Porges (Eds.), *Psychophysiology.* New York: Guilford.

Cacioppo, J. T., Petty, R. E., Feinstein, J. A., & Jarvis, W. B. G. (1996). Dispositional differences in cognitive motivation: The life and times of individuals varying in need for cognition. *Psychological Bulletin, 119*, 197–253.

Cacioppo, J. T., Petty, R. E., & Morris, K. J. (1983). Effects of need for cognition on message evaluation, recall, and persuasion. *Journal of Personality and Social Psychology, 45*, 805–818.

Cairns, E., & Hewstone, M. (2002). The impact of peacemaking in Northern Ireland on intergroup behavior. In S. Gabi & B. Nevo (Eds.), *Peace education: The concept, principles, and practices around the world.* Mahwah, NJ: Erlbaum.

Caldwell, H. K., Lee, H-J., MacBeth, A. H., & Young, W. S. (2008). Vasopressin: Behavioral roles of an "original" neuropeptide. *Progress in Neurobiology, 84*, 1–24.

Cameron, L., & Rutland, A. (2006). Extended contact through story reading in school: Reducing children's prejudice toward the disabled. *Journal of Social Issues, 62*, 469–488.

Campbell, D. T. (1975a). The conflict between social and biological evolution and the concept of original sin. *Zygon, 10*, 234–249.

Campbell, D. T. (1975b). On the conflicts between biological and social evolution and between psychology and moral tradition. *American Psychologist, 30*, 1103–1126.

Campbell, E. Q., & Pettigrew, T. F. (1959). Racial and moral crisis: The role of Little Rock ministers. *American Journal of Sociology, 64*, 509–516.

Campbell, W. K. (2005). *When you love a man who loves himself.* Chicago: Sourcebooks.

Campbell, W. K., Bosson, J. K., Goheen, T. W., Lakey, C. E., & Kernis, M. H. (2007). Do narcissists dislike themselves "deep down inside"? *Psychological Science, 18*, 227–229.

Campbell, W. K., Bush, C. P., Brunell, A. B., & Shelton, J. (2005). Understanding the social costs of narcissism: The case of the tragedy of the commons. *Personality and Social Psychology Bulletin, 31*, 1358–1368.

Campbell, W. K., & Foster, C. A. (2002). Narcissism and commitment in romantic relationships: An investment model analysis. *Personality and Social Psychology Bulletin, 28*, 484–495.

Campbell, W. K., Rudich, E., & Sedikides, C. (2002). Narcissism, self-esteem, and the positivity of self-views: Two portraits of self-love. *Personality and Social Psychology Bulletin, 28*, 358–368.

Campbell, W. K., & Sedikides, C. (1999). Self-threat magnifies the self-serving bias: A meta-analytic integration. *Review of General Psychology, 3*, 23–43.

Canadian Centre on Substance Abuse (1997). *Canadian profile: Alcohol, tobacco, and other drugs.* Ottawa: Canadian Centre on Substance Abuse.

Canadian Psychological Association (2000). *Canadian code of ethics for psychologists.* Ottawa: Canadian Psychological Association (www.cpa .ca/ethics2000.html).

Cann, A., Calhoun, L. G., & Selby, J. W. (1979). Attributing responsibility to the victim of rape: Influence of information regarding past sexual experience. *Human Relations, 32*, 57–67.

Canter, D., Breaux, J., & Sime, J. (1980). Domestic, multiple occupancy, and hospital fires. In D. Canter (Ed.), *Fires and human behavior.* Hoboken, NJ: Wiley.

Cantril, H., & Bumstead, C. H. (1960). *Reflections on the human venture.* New York: New York University Press.

Caputo, D., & Dunning, D. (2005). What you don't know: The role played by errors of omission in imperfect self-assessments. *Journal of Experimental Social Psychology, 41*, 488–505.

Carducci, B. J., Cosby, P. C., & Ward, D. D. (1978). Sexual arousal and interpersonal evaluations. *Journal of Experimental Social Psychology, 14*, 449–457.

Carli, L. L. (1999). Cognitive reconstruction, hindsight, and reactions to victims and perpetrators. *Personality and Social Psychology Bulletin, 25*, 966–979.

Carli, L. L., & Leonard, J. B. (1989). The effect of hindsight on victim derogation. *Journal of Social and Clinical Psychology, 8*, 331–343.

Carlo, G., Eisenberg, N., Troyer, D., Switzer, G., & Speer, A. L. (1991). The altruistic personality: In what contexts is it apparent? *Journal of Personality and Social Psychology, 61*, 450–458.

Carlsmith, J. M., & Gross, A. E. (1969). Some effects of guilt on compliance. *Journal of Personality and Social Psychology, 11*, 232–239.

Carlson, J., & Hatfield, E. (1992). *The psychology of emotion.* Fort Worth, TX: Holt, Rinehart & Winston.

Carlson, K. A., & Russo, J. E. (2001). Biased interpretation of evidence by mock jurors. *Journal of Experimental Psychology: Applied, 7*, 91–103.

Carlson, M., Charlin, V., & Miller, N. (1988). Positive mood and helping behavior: A test of six hypotheses. *Journal of Personality and Social Psychology, 55*, 211–229.

Carlson, M., Marcus-Newhall, A., & Miller, N. (1990). Effects of situational aggression cues: A quantitative review. *Journal of Personality and Social Psychology, 58*, 622–633.

Carlston, D. E., & Shovar, N. (1983). Effects of performance attributions on others' perceptions of the attributor. *Journal of Personality and Social Psychology, 44*, 515–525.

Carlston, D. E., & Skowronski, J. J. (2005). Linking versus thinking: Evidence for the different associative and attributional bases of spontaneous trait transference and spontaneous trait inference. *Journal of Personality and Social Psychology, 89*, 884–898.

Carlton-Ford, S., Ender, M., & Tabatabai, A. (2008). Iraqi adolescents: Self-regard, self-derogation, and perceived threat in war. *Journal of Adolescence, 31*, 53–75.

Carnagey, N. L., Anderson, C. A., & Bushman, B. J. (2007). The effect of video game violence on physiological desensitization to real-life violence. *Journal of Experimental Social Psychology, 43*, 489–496.

Carnahan, T., & McFarland, S. (2007). Revisiting the Stanford Prison Experiment: Could participant self-selection have led to the cruelty? *Personality and Social Psychology Bulletin, 33*, 603–614.

Carnevale, P. J., & Choi, D-W. (2000). Culture in the mediation of international disputes. *International Journal of Psychology, 35*, 105–110.

Carnevale, P. J., & Probst, T. M. (1998). Social values and social conflict in creative problem solving and categorization. *Journal of Personality and Social Psychology, 74*, 1300–1309.

Carney, D. R., & Banaji, M. R. (2008). First is best. Unpublished manuscript, Harvard University.

Carpusor, A. G., & Loges, W. E. (2006). Rental discrimination and ethnicity in names. *Journal of Applied Social Psychology, 36*, 934–952.

Carré, J. M., & McCormick, C. M. (2008). In your face: Facial metrics predict aggressiveness behaviour in the laboratory and in varsity and professional hockey players. *Proceedings of the Royal Society B, 275,* 2651–2656.

Carroll, D., Davey Smith, G., & Bennett, P. (1994, March). Health and socio-economic status. *The Psychologist,* pp. 122–125.

Carroll, J. (2007, August 16). Most Americans approve of interracial marriages. Gallup News Service (www.gallup.com).

Carroll, J. S., Padilla-Walker, L. M., Nelson, L. J., Olson, C. D., Barry, C. M., & Madsen, S. D. (2008). Generation XXX: Pornography acceptance and use among emerging adults. *Journal of Adolescent Research, 23,* 6–30.

Carter, S. L. (1993). *Reflections of an affirmative action baby.* New York: Basic Books.

Carter, S., & Snow, C. (2004, May). Helping singles enter better marriages using predictive models of marital success. Presented to the American Psychological Society convention.

Cartwright, D. S. (1975). The nature of gangs. In D. S. Cartwright, B. Tomson, & H. Schwartz (Eds.), *Gang delinquency.* Monterey, CA: Brooks/ Cole.

Carvallo, M., & Gabriel, S. (2006). No man is an island: The need to belong and dismissing avoidant attachment style. *Personality and Social Psychology Bulletin, 32,* 697–709.

Carver, C. S., Kus, L. A., & Scheier, M. F. (1994). Effect of good versus bad mood and optimistic versus pessimistic outlook on social acceptance versus rejection. *Journal of Social and Clinical Psychology, 13,* 138–151.

Carver, C. S., & Scheier, M. F. (1978). Self-focusing effects of dispositional self-consciousness, mirror presence, and audience presence. *Journal of Personality and Social Psychology, 36,* 324–332.

Carver, C. S., & Scheier, M. F. (1981). *Attention and self-regulation.* New York: Springer-Verlag.

Carver, C. S., & Scheier, M. F. (1986). Analyzing shyness: A specific application of broader self-regulatory principles. In W. H. Jones, J. M. Cheek, & S. R. Briggs (Eds.), *Shyness: Perspectives on research and treatment.* New York: Plenum.

Cash, T. F., & Janda, L. H. (1984, December). The eye of the beholder. *Psychology Today,* pp. 46–52.

Caspi, A., & Herbener, E. S. (1990). Continuity and change: Assortative marriage and the consistency of personality in adulthood. *Journal of Personality and Social Psychology, 58,* 250–258.

Caspi, A., McClay, J., Moffitt, T., Mill, J., Martin, J., Craig, I. W., Taylor, A., & Poulton, R. (2002). Role of genotype in the cycle of violence in maltreated children. *Science, 297,* 851–854.

Caspi, A., Sugden, K., Moffitt, T. E., Taylor, A., Craig, I. W., Harrington, H. L., McClay, J., Mill, J., Martin, J., Braithwaite, A., & Poulton, R. (2003). Influence of life stress on depression: Moderation by a polymorphism in the 5-HTT gene. *Science, 30,* 386–389.

Cassidy, J. (2000). Adult romantic attachments: A developmental perspective on individual differences. *Review of General Psychology Special Issue: Adult attachment, 4,* 111–131.

Castelli, L., Carraro, L., Tomelleri, S., & Amari, A. (2007). White children's alignment to the perceived racial attitudes of the parents: Closer to the mother than father. *British Journal of Developmental Psychology, 25,* 353–357.

Ceci, S. J., & Bruck, M. (1993a). Child witnesses: Translating research into policy. *Social Policy Report* (Society for Research in Child Development), *7*(3), 1–30.

Ceci, S. J., & Bruck, M. (1993b). Suggestibility of the child witness: A historical review and synthesis. *Psychological Bulletin, 113,* 403–439.

Ceci, S. J., & Bruck, M. (1995). *Jeopardy in the courtroom: A scientific analysis of children's testimony.* Washington, DC: American Psychological Association.

Cemalcilar, Z., & Falbo, T. (2008). A longitudinal study of the adaptation of international students in the United States. *Journal of Cross-Cultural Psychology, 39,* 799–804.

Centers for Disease Control (CDC). (2005, February 28). Deaths: Preliminary data for 2003. *National Vital Statistics Reports, 53,* No. 15 (by D. L. Hoyert, H-C. Kung, & B. L. Smith), Centers for Disease Control and Prevention, National Center for Health Statistics.

Centers for Disease Control (CDC). (2005, November 11). Cigarette smoking among adults in the United States. *Morbidity and Mortality Weekly Report, 54*(44), 1121–1124.

Centers for Disease Control (CDC). (2008, Spring). Sexual violence: Facts at a glance. Centers for Disease Control and Prevention (www.cdc .gov/injury).

Centerwall, B. S. (1989). Exposure to television as a risk factor for violence. *American Journal of Epidemiology, 129,* 643–652.

Chaiken, S. (1979). Communicator physical attractiveness and persuasion. *Journal of Personality and Social Psychology, 37,* 1387–1397.

Chaiken, S. (1980). Heuristic versus systematic information processing and the use of source versus message cues in persuasion. *Journal of Personality and Social Psychology, 39,* 752–766.

Chaiken, S., & Eagly, A. H. (1976). Communication modality as a determinant of message persuasiveness and message comprehensibility. *Journal of Personality and Social Psychology, 34,* 605–614.

Chaiken, S., & Eagly, A. H. (1983). Communication modality as a determinant of persuasion: The role of communicator salience. *Journal of Personality and Social Psychology, 45,* 241–256.

Chaiken, S., & Maheswaran, D. (1994). Neuristic processing can bias systematic processing: Effects of source credibility, argument ambiguity, and task importance on attitude judgment. *Journal of Personality and Social Psychology, 66,* 460–473.

Chambers, J. R., Baron, R. S., & Inman, M. L. (2006). Misperceptions in intergroup conflict: Disagreeing about what we disagree about. *Psychological Science, 17,* 38–45.

Chambers, J. R., & Melnyk, D. (2006). Why do I hate thee? Conflict misperceptions and intergroup mistrust. *Personality and Social Psychology Bulletin, 32,* 1295–1311.

Chambers, J. R., & Windschitl, P. D. (2004). Biases in social comparative judgments: The role of nonmotivated factors in above-average and comparative-optimism effects. *Psychological Bulletin, 130,* 813–838.

Chance, J. E., & Goldstein, A. G. (1981). Depth of processing in response to own- and other-race faces. *Personality and Social Psychology Bulletin, 7,* 475–480.

Chance, J. E., Goldstein, A. G. (1996). The other-race effect and eyewitness identification. In S. L. Sporer (Ed.), *Psychological issues in eyewitness identification* (pp. 153–176). Mahwah, NJ: Erlbaum.

Chandler, J., & Schwarz, N. (2009). How extending your middle finger affects your perception of others: Learned movements influence concept accessibility. *Journal of Experimental Social Psychology, 45,* 123–128.

Chapman, L. J., & Chapman, J. P. (1969). Genesis of popular but erroneous psychodiagnostic observations. *Journal of Abnormal Psychology, 74,* 272–280.

Chapman, L. J., & Chapman, J. P. (1971, November). Test results are what you think they are. *Psychology Today,* pp. 18–22, 106–107.

Chartrand, T. L., & Bargh, J. A. (1999). The chameleon effect: The perception-behavior link and social interaction. *Journal of Personality and Social Psychology, 76,* 893–910.

Chatard, A., Guimond, S., & Selimbegovic, L. (2007). "How good are you in math?" The effect of gender stereotypes on students' recollection of their school marks. *Journal of Experimental Social Psychology, 43,* 1017–1024.

Check, J., & Malamuth, N. (1984). Can there be positive effects of participation in pornography experiments? *Journal of Sex Research, 20,* 14–31.

Chen, E. (2004). Why socioeconomic status affects the health of children: A psychosocial perspective. *Current Directions in Psychological Science, 13,* 112–115.

Chen, F. F., & Kenrick, D. T. (2002). Repulsion or attraction? Group membership and assumed attitude similarity. *Journal of Personality and Social Psychology, 83,* 111–125.

Chen, L.-H., Baker, S. P., Braver, E. R., & Li, G. (2000). Carrying passengers as a risk factor for crashes fatal to 16- and 17-year-old drivers. *Journal of the American Medical Association, 283,* 1578–1582.

Chen, S. C. (1937). Social modification of the activity of ants in nest-building. *Physiological Zoology, 10,* 420–436.

Chen, S., Boucher, H. C., & Tapias, M. P. (2006). The relational self revealed: Integrative conceptualization and implications for interpersonal life. *Psychological Bulletin, 132,* 151–179.

Chen, Z., Williams, K. D., Fitness, J., & Newton, N. C. (2008). When hurt will not heal: Exploring the capacity to relive social and physical pain. *Psychological Science, 19,* 789–795.

Cheney, R. (2003, March 16). Comments on Face the Nation, CBS News.

Cherlin, A. J., Chase-Lansdale, P. L., & McRae, C. (1998). Effects of parental divorce on mental health throughout the life course. *American Sociological Review, 63,* 239–249.

Chiao, J. Y., Bowman, N. E., & Gill, H. (2008) The political gender gap: Gender bias in facial inferences that predict voting behavior. *PLoS One* **3**(10): e3666. (doi:10.1371/journal.pone.0003666).

Chicago Tribune. (2002, September 30). When believing isn't seeing (www .chicagotribune.com).

Chodorow, N. J. (1978). *The reproduction of mother: Psychoanalysis and the sociology of gender.* Berkeley, CA: University of California Press.

Chodorow, N. J. (1989). *Feminism and psychoanalytic theory.* New Haven, CT: Yale University Press.

Choi, I., & Choi, Y. (2002). Culture and self-concept flexibility. *Personality & Social Psychology Bulletin, 28,* 1508–1517.

Choi, I., Nisbett, R. E., & Norenzayan, A. (1999). Causal attribution across cultures: Variation and universality. *Psychological Bulletin, 125,* 47–63.

Christensen, P. N., & Kashy, D. A. (1998). Perceptions of and by lonely people in initial social interaction. *Personality and Social Psychology Bulletin, 24,* 322–329.

Chua, H. F., Boland, J. E., & Nisbett, R. E. (2005). Cultural variation in eye movements during scene perception. *Proceedings of the National Academy of Sciences, 102,* 12629–12633.

Chua-Eoan, H. (1997, April 7). Imprisoned by his own passions. *Time,* pp. 40–42.

Church, G. J. (1986, January 6). China. *Time,* pp. 6–19.

Cialdini, R. B. (1984). *Influence: How and why people agree to things.* New York: William Morrow.

Cialdini, R. B. (1988). *Influence: Science and practice.* Glenview, IL: Scott, Foresman/Little, Brown.

Cialdini, R. B. (1991). Altruism or egoism? That is (still) the question. *Psychological Inquiry, 2,* 124–126.

Cialdini, R. B. (1995). A full-cycle approach to social psychology. In G. G. Brannigan & M. R. Merrens (Eds.), *The social psychologists: Research adventures.* New York: McGraw-Hill.

Cialdini, R. B. (2000). *Influence: Science and practice,* 4th edition. Boston: Allyn & Bacon.

Cialdini, R. B. (2005). Basic social influence is underestimated. *Psychological Inquiry, 16,* 158–161.

Cialdini, R. B., Bickman, L., & Cacioppo, J. T. (1979). An example of consumeristic social psychology: Bargaining tough in the new car showroom. *Journal of Applied Social Psychology, 9,* 115–126.

Cialdini, R. B., Borden, R. J., Thorne, A., Walker, M. R., Freeman, S., & Sloan, L. R. (1976). Basking in reflected glory: Three (football) field studies. *Journal of Personality and Social Psychology, 39,* 406–415.

Cialdini, R. B., Cacioppo, J. T., Bassett, R., & Miller, J. A. (1978). Lowball procedure for producing compliance: Commitment then cost. *Journal of Personality and Social Psychology, 36,* 463–476.

Cialdini, R. B., Demaine, L. J., Barrett, D. W., Sagarin, B. J., & Rhoads, K. L. V. (2003). The poison parasite defense: A strategy for sapping a stronger opponent's persuasive strength. Unpublished manuscript, Arizona State University.

Cialdini, R. B., Kenrick, D. T., & Baumann, D. J. (1981). Effects of mood on prosocial behavior in children and adults. In N. Eisenberg-Berg (Ed.), *The development of prosocial behavior.* New York: Academic Press.

Cialdini, R. B., & Schroeder, D. A. (1976). Increasing compliance by legitimizing paltry contributions: When even a penny helps. *Journal of Personality and Social Psychology, 34,* 599–604.

Cialdini, R. B., Vincent, J. E., Lewis, S. K., Catalan, J., Wheeler, D., & Danby, B. L. (1975). Reciprocal concessions procedure for inducing compliance: The door-in-the-face technique. *Journal of Personality and Social Psychology, 31,* 206–215.

Cicerello, A., & Sheehan, E. P. (1995). Personal advertisements: A content analysis. *Journal of Social Behavior and Personality, 10,* 751–756.

Cioffi, D., & Garner, R. (1998). The effect of response options on decisions and subsequent behavior: Sometimes inaction is better. *Personality and Social Psychology Bulletin, 24,* 463–472.

Clack, B., Dixon, J., & Tredoux, C. (2005). Eating together apart: Patterns of segregation in a multi-ethnic cafeteria. *Journal of Community and Applied Social Psychology, 15,* 1–16.

Clancy, S. M., & Dollinger, S. J. (1993). Photographic depictions of the self: Gender and age differences in social connectedness. *Sex Roles, 29,* 477–495.

Clark, K., & Clark, M. (1947). Racial identification and preference in Negro children. In T. M. Newcomb & E. L. Hartley (Eds.), *Readings in social psychology.* New York: Holt.

Clark, M. S. (1984). Record keeping in two types of relationships. *Journal of Personality and Social Psychology, 47,* 549–557.

Clark, M. S. (1986). Evidence for the effectiveness of manipulations of desire for communal versus exchange relationships. *Personality and Social Psychology Bulletin, 12,* 414–425.

Clark, M. S., & Bennett, M. E. (1992). Research on relationships: Implications for mental health. In D. Ruble & P. Costanzo (Eds.), *The social psychology of mental health.* New York: Guilford.

Clark, M. S., & Mills, J. (1979). Interpersonal attraction in exchange and communal relationships. *Journal of Personality and Social Psychology, 37,* 12–24.

Clark, M. S., & Mills, J. (1993). The difference between communal and exchange relationships: What it is and is not. *Personality and Social Psychology Bulletin, 19,* 684–691.

Clark, M. S., Mills, J., & Corcoran, D. (1989). Keeping track of needs and inputs of friends and strangers. *Personality and Social Psychology Bulletin, 15,* 533–542.

Clark, M. S., Mills, J., & Powell, M. C. (1986). Keeping track of needs in communal and exchange relationships. *Journal of Personality and Social Psychology, 51,* 333–338.

Clark, R. D., III. (1974). Effects of sex and race on helping behavior in a nonreactive setting. *Representative Research in Social Psychology, 5,* 1–6.

Clark, R. D., III. (1995). A few parallels between group polarization and minority influence. In S. Moscovici, H. Mucchi-Faina, & A. Maass (Eds.), *Minority influence*. Chicago: Nelson-Hall.

Clark, R. D., III, & Maass, S. A. (1988). The role of social categorization and perceived source credibility in minority influence. *European Journal of Social Psychology, 18,* 381–394.

Clarke, A. C. (1952). An examination of the operation of residual propinquity as a factor in mate selection. *American Sociological Review, 27,* 17–22.

Clarke, V. (2003, March 25). Quoted in "Street fighting: A volatile enemy." *Wall Street Journal*, pp. A1, A13.

Clary, E. G., & Snyder, M. (1993). Persuasive communications strategies for recruiting volunteers. In D. R. Young, R. M. Hollister, & V. A. Hodgkinson (Eds.), *Governing, leading, and managing nonprofit orgnaizations*. San Francisco: Jossey-Bass.

Clary, E. G., & Snyder, M. (1995). Motivations for volunteering and giving: A functional approach. In C. H. Hamilton & W. E. Ilchman (Eds.), *Cultures of giving II: How heritage, gender, wealth, and values influence philanthropy*. Bloomington, IN: Indiana University Center on Philanthropy.

Clary, E. G., & Snyder, M. (1999). The motivations to volunteer: Theoretical and practical considerations. *Current Directions in Psychological Science, 8,* 156–159.

Clary, E. G., Snyder, M., Ridge, R. D., Copeland, J., Stukas, A. A., Haugen, J., & Miene, P. (1998). Understanding and assessing the motivations of volunteers: A functional approach. *Journal of Personality and Social Psychology, 74,* 1516–1531.

Cleghorn, R. (1980, October 31). ABC News, meet the Literary Digest. *Detroit Free Press*.

Clevstrom, J., & Passariello, C. (2006, August 18). No kicks from "champagne." *Wall Street Journal*, p. A11.

Clifford, M. M., & Walster, E. H. (1973). The effect of physical attractiveness on teacher expectation. *Sociology of Education, 46,* 248–258.

Cline, V. B., Croft, R. G., & Courrier, S. (1973). Desensitization of children to television violence. *Journal of Personality and Social Psychology, 27,* 360–365.

Clooney, G., Pressman, D., & Prednergast, J. (2008, November 22–23). Obama's opportunity to help Africa. *Wall Street Journal*, p. A13.

Clore, G. L., Bray, R. M., Itkin, S. M., & Murphy, P. (1978). Interracial attitudes and behavior at a summer camp. *Journal of Personality and Social Psychology, 36,* 107–116.

Clore, G. L., Wiggins, N. H., & Itkin, G. (1975). Gain and loss in attraction: Attributions from nonverbal behavior. *Journal of Personality and Social Psychology, 31,* 706–712.

CNN. (2007, October 6). Jury awards $6.1 million in McDonald's strip search case (www.cnn.com).

Coan, J. A., Schaefer, H. S., & Davidson, R. J. (2006). Lending a hand: Social regulation of the neural response to threat. *Psychological Science, 17,* 1032–1039.

Coates, B., Pusser, H. E., & Goodman, I. (1976). The influence of "Sesame Street" and "Mister Rogers' Neighborhood" on children's social behavior in the preschool. *Child Development, 47,* 138–144.

Coats, E. J., & Feldman, R. S. (1996). Gender differences in nonverbal correlates of social status. *Personality and Social Psychology Bulletin, 22,* 1014–1022.

Codol, J.-P. (1976). On the so-called superior conformity of the self behavior: Twenty experimental investigations. *European Journal of Social Psychology, 5,* 457–501.

Cohen, D. (1996). Law, social policy, and violence: The impact of regional cultures. *Journal of Personality and Social Psychology, 70,* 961–978.

Cohen, D. (1998). Culture, social organization, and patterns of violence. *Journal of Personality and Social Psychology, 75,* 408–419.

Cohen, E. G. (1980). Design and redesign of the desegregated school: Problems of status, power and conflict. In W. G. Stephan & J. R. Feagin (Eds.), *School desegregation: Past, present, and future*. New York: Plenum.

Cohen, F., Ogilvie, D. M., Solomon, S., Greenberg, J., & Pyszczynski, T. (2005). American roulette: The effect of reminders of death on support for George W. Bush in the 2004 presidential election. *Analyses of Social Issues and Public Policy, 5*(1), 177–187.

Cohen, G. L., Steele, C. M., & Ross, L. D. (1999). The mentor's dilemma: Providing critical feedback across the racial divide. *Personality and Social Psychology Bulletin, 25,* 1302–1318.

Cohen, J. E. (2005, September). Human population grows up. *Scientific American*, pp. 48–55.

Cohen, M., & Davis, N. (1981). *Medication errors: Causes and prevention*. Philadelphia: G. F. Stickley Co. Cited by R. B. Cialdini (1989), Agents of influence: Bunglers, smugglers, and sleuths. Paper presented at the American Psychological Association convention.

Cohen, S. (1980). Training to understand TV advertising: Effects and some policy implications. Paper presented at the American Psychological Association convention.

Cohen, S. (2002). Psychosocial stress, social networks, and susceptibility to infection. In H. G. Koenig & H. J. Cohen (Eds.), *The link between religion and health: Psychoneuroimmunology and the faith factor*. New York: Oxford University Press.

Cohen, S. (2004). Social relationships and health. *American Psychologist, 59,* 676–684.

Cohen, S., & Rodriguez, M. S. (1995). Pathways linking affective disturbances and physical disorders. *Health Psychology, 14,* 374–380.

Cohen, S., Doyle, W. J., Skoner, D. P., Rabin, B. S., & Gwaltney, J. M., Jr. (1997). Social ties and susceptibility to the common cold. *Journal of the American Medical Association, 277,* 1940–1944.

Cohen, S., Doyle, W. J., Turner, R., Alper, C. M., & Skoner, D. P. (2003). Sociability and susceptibility to the common cold. *Psychological Science, 14,* 389–395.

Cohn, E. G. (1993). The prediction of police calls for service: The influence of weather and temporal variables on rape and domestic violence. *Environmental Psychology, 13,* 71–83.

Cohn, E. G., & Rotton, J. (2005). The curve is still out there: A reply to Bushman, Wang, and Anderson (2005), Is the curve relating temperature to aggression linear or curvilinear? *Journal of Personality and Social Psychology, 89,* 67–70.

Cohrs, J. C., Moschner, B., Maes, J., & Kielmann, S. (2005). The motivational bases of right-wing authoritarianism and social dominance orientation: Relations to values and attitudes in the aftermath of September 11, 2001. *Personality and Social Psychology Bulletin, 31,* 1425–1434.

Colarelli, S. M., Spranger, J. L., Hechanova, M. R. (2006). Women, power, and sex composition in small groups: An evolutionary perspective. *Journal of Organizational Behavior Special Issue: Darwinian Perspectives on Behavior in Organizations, 27,* 163–184.

Coleman, L. M., Jussim, L., & Abraham, J. (1987). Students' reactions to teachers' evaluations: The unique impact of negative feedback. *Journal of Applied Social Psychology, 17,* 1051–1070.

Collins, N. L., & Miller, L. C. (1994). Self-disclosure and liking: A meta-analytic review. *Psychological Bulletin, 116,* 457–475.

Colman, A. M. (1991). Crowd psychology in South African murder trials. *American Psychologist, 46,* 1071–1079. See also A. M. Colman (1991), Psychological evidence in South

African murder trials. *The Psychologist*, **14**, 482–486.

Comer, D. R. (1995). A model of social loafing in a real work group. *Human Relations*, **48**, 647–667.

Comstock, G. (2008). A sociological perspective on television violence and aggression. *American Behavioral Scientist*, **51**, 1184–1211.

Comstock, G., & Scharrer, E. (1999). *Television: What's on, who's watching and what it means*. San Diego: Academic Press.

Conger, R. D., Cui, M., Bryant, C. M., & Elder, G. H. (2000). Competence in early adult romantic relationships: A developmental perspective on family influences. *Journal of Personality and Social Psychology*, **79**, 224–237.

Contrada, R. J., Ashmore, R. D., Gary, M. L., Coups, E., Egeth, J. D., Sewell, A., Ewell, K., Goyal, T. M., & Chasse, V. (2000). Ethnicity-related sources of stress and their effects on well-being. *Current Directions in Psychological Science*, **9**, 136–139.

Conway, F., & Siegelman, J. (1979). *Snapping: America's epidemic of sudden personality change*. New York: Delta Books.

Conway, L. G., III, Suedfeld, P., & Tetlock, P. E. (2001). Integrative complexity and political decisions that lead to war or peace. In D. J. Christie, R. V. Wagner, & D. Winter (Eds.), *Peace, conflict, and violence: Peace psychology for the 21st century*. Englewood Cliffs, NJ: Prentice-Hall.

Conway, M., & Ross, M. (1986). Remembering one's own past: The construction of personal histories. In R. Sorrentino & E. T. Higgins (Eds.), *Handbook of motivation and cognition*. New York: Guilford.

Cook, S. W. (1985). Experimenting on social issues: The case of school desegregation. *American Psychologist*, **40**, 452–460.

Cook, T. D., & Flay, B. R. (1978). The persistence of experimentally induced attitude change. In L. Berkowitz (Ed.), *Advances in experimental social psychology* (Vol. 11). New York: Academic Press.

Cooley, C. H. (1902). *Human nature and the social order*. New York: Schocken Books.

Coombs, R. H. (1991, January). Marital status and personal well-being: A literature review. *Family Relations*, **40**, 97–102.

Cooper, H. (1983). Teacher expectation effects. In L. Bickman (Ed.), *Applied social psychology annual* (Vol. 4). Beverly Hills, CA: Sage.

Cooper, J. (1999). Unwanted consequences and the self: In search of the motivation for dissonance reduction. In E. Harmon-Jones & J. Mills (Eds.), *Cognitive dissonance: Progress on a pivotal theory in social psychology*. Washington, DC: American Psychological Association.

Correll, J., Park, B., Judd, C. M., & Wittenbrink, B. (2002). The police officer's dilemma: Using ethnicity to disambiguate potentially threatening individuals. *Journal of Personality and Social Psychology*, **83**, 1314-1329.

Correll, J., Park, B., Judd, C. M., & Wittenbrink, B. (2007). The influence of stereotypes on decisions to shoot. *European Journal of Social Psychology*, **37**, 1102–1117.

Correll, J., Park, B., Judd, C. M., Wittenbrink, B., Sadler, M. S., & Keesee, T. (2007). Across the thin blue line: Police officers and racial bias in the decision to shoot. *Journal of Personality and Social Psychology*, **92**, 1006–1023.

Correll, J., Urland, G. R., & Ito, T. A. (2006). Event-related potentials and the decision to shoot: The role of threat perception and cognitive control. *Journal of Experimental Social Psychology*, **42**, 120–128.

Costanzo, M. (1997). *Just revenge: Costs and consequences of the death penalty*. New York: St. Martin's.

Costanzo, M. (1998). *Just revenge*. New York: St. Martins.

Costello, C., Gaines, S. D., & Lynham, J. (2008). Can catch shares prevent fisheries' collapse? *Science*, **321**, 1678–1682.

Cota, A. A., & Dion, K. L. (1986). Salience of gender and sex composition of ad hoc groups: An experimental test of distinctiveness theory. *Journal of Personality and Social Psychology*, **50**, 770–776.

Cotton, J. L. (1981). Ambient temperature and violent crime. Paper presented at the Midwestern Psychological Association convention.

Cotton, J. L. (1986). Ambient temperature and violent crime. *Journal of Applied Social Psychology*, **16**, 786–801.

Cottrell, C. A., & Neuberg, S. L. (2005). Different emotional reactions to different groups: A sociofunctional threat-based approach to "prejudice." *Journal of Personality and Social Psychology*, **88**, 770–789.

Cottrell, N. B., Wack, D. L., Sekerak, G. J., & Rittle, R. M. (1968). Social facilitation of dominant responses by the presence of an audience and the mere presence of others. *Journal of Personality and Social Psychology*, **9**, 245–250.

Court, J. H. (1985). Sex and violence: A ripple effect. In N. M. Malamuth & E. Donnerstein (Eds.), *Pornography and sexual aggression*. New York: Academic Press.

Cousins, N. (1978, September 16). The taxpayers revolt: Act two. *Saturday Review*, p. 56.

Coyne, S. M., & Archer, J. (2005). The relationship between indirect and physical aggression on television and in real life. *Social Development*, **14**, 324–338.

Crabb, P. B., & Bielawski, D. (1994). The social representation of material culture and gender in children's books. *Sex Roles*, **30**, 69–79.

Crabtree, S. (2002, January 22). Gender roles reflected in teen tech use. *Gallup Tuesday Briefing* (www.gallup.com).

Crandall, C. S. (1988). Social contagion of binge eating. *Journal of Personality and Social Psychology*, **55**, 588–598.

Crandall, C. S., & Eshleman, A. (2003). A justification–suppression model of the expression and experience of prejudice. *Psychological Bulletin*, **129**, 414–446.

Crano, W. D., & Mellon, P. M. (1978). Causal influence of teachers' expectations on children's academic performance: A cross-legged panel analysis. *Journal of Educational Psychology*, **70**, 39–49.

Crawford, M., Stark, A. C., & Renner, C. H. (1998). The meaning of Ms.: Social assimilation of a gender concept. *Psychology of Women Quarterly*, **22**, 197–208.

Crawford, T. J. (1974). Sermons on racial tolerance and the parish neighborhood context. *Journal of Applied Social Psychology*, **4**, 1–23.

Crisp, R. J., & Hewstone, M. (1999). Differential evaluation of crossed category groups: Patterns, processes, and reducing intergroup bias. *Group Processes & Intergroup Relations*, **2**, 307–333.

Crisp, R. J., & Hewstone, M. (2000). Multiple categorization and social identity. In D. Capozza & R. Brown (Eds.), *Social identity theory: Trends in theory and research*. Beverly Hills, CA: Sage.

Crocker, J. (1981). Judgment of covariation by social perceivers. *Psychological Bulletin*, **90**, 272–292.

Crocker, J. (2002). The costs of seeking self-esteem. *Journal of Social Issues*, **58**, 597–615.

Crocker, J., & Gallo, L. (1985). The self-enhancing effect of downward comparison. Paper presented at the American Psychological Association convention.

Crocker, J., Hannah, D. B., & Weber, R. (1983). Personal memory and causal attributions. *Journal of Personality and Social Psychology*, **44**, 55–56.

Crocker, J., & Knight, K. M. (2005). Contingencies of self-worth. *Current Directions in Psychological Science*, **14**, 200–203.

Crocker, J., & Luhtanen, R. (1990). Collective self-esteem and ingroup bias. *Journal of Personality and Social Psychology*, **58**, 60–67.

Crocker, J., & Luhtanen, R. (2003). Level of self-esteem and contingencies of self-worth: Unique effects on academic, social, and financial problems in college students. *Personality and Social Psychology Bulletin, 29,* 701–712.

Crocker, J., & McGraw, K. M. (1984). What's good for the goose is not good for the gander: Solo status as an obstacle to occupational achievement for males and females. *American Behavioral Scientist, 27,* 357–370.

Crocker, J., & Park, L. E. (2004). The costly pursuit of self-esteem. *Psychological Bulletin, 130,* 392–414.

Crocker, J., Thompson, L. L., McGraw, K. M., & Ingerman, C. (1987). Downward comparison, prejudice, and evaluations of others: Effects of self-esteem and threat. *Journal of Personality and Social Psychology, 52,* 907–916.

Crocker, J., & Wolfe, C. (2001). Contingencies of self-worth. *Psychological Review.*

Crockett, M. J., Clark, L., Tabibnia, G., Lieberman, M. D., & Robbins, T. W. (2008). Serotonin modulates behavioral reactions to unfairness. *Science, 320,* 1739.

Crosby, F. J. (Ed.) (1987). *Spouse, parent, worker: On gender and multiple roles.* New Haven, CT: Yale University Press.

Crosby, F., Bromley, S., & Saxe, L. (1980). Recent unobtrusive studies of black and white discrimination and prejudice: A literature review. *Psychological Bulletin, 87,* 546–563.

Crosby, J. R., & Monin, B. (2007). Failure to warn: How student race affects warnings of potential academic difficulty. *Journal of Experimental Social Psychology, 43,* 663–670.

Cross, P. (1977, Spring). Not *can* but *will* college teaching be improved? *New Directions for Higher Education,* No. 17, pp. 1–15.

Cross, S. E., Liao, M-H., & Josephs, R. (1992). A cross-cultural test of the self-evaluation maintenance model. Paper presented at the American Psychological Association convention.

Crossen, C. (1993). *Tainted truth: The manipulation of face in America.* New York: Simon & Schuster.

Cross-National Collaborative Group. (1992). The changing rate of major depression. *Journal of the American Medical Association, 268,* 3098–3105.

Croxton, J. S., Eddy, T., & Morrow, N. (1984). Memory biases in the reconstruction of interpersonal encounters. *Journal of Social and Clinical Psychology, 2,* 348–354.

Croyle, R. T., & Cooper, J. (1983). Dissonance arousal: Physiological evidence. *Journal of Personality and Social Psychology, 45,* 782–791.

Csikszentmihalyi, M. (1990). *Flow: The psychology of optimal experience.* New York: Harper & Row.

Csikszentmihalyi, M. (1999). If we are so rich, why aren't we happy? *American Psychologist, 54,* 821–827.

Cuddy, A. J. C., & 23 others. (2009). Stereotype content model across cultures: Towards universal similarities and some differences. *British Journal of Social Psychology, 48,* 1–33.

Cullen, L. T., & Masters, C. (2008, January 28). We just clicked. *Time,* pp. 86–89.

Cullum, J., & Harton, H. C. (2007). Cultural evolution: Interpersonal influence, issue importance, and the development of shared attitudes in college residence halls. *Personality and Social Psychology Bulletin, 33,* 1327–1339.

Cunningham, J. D. (1981). Self-disclosure intimacy: Sex, sex-of-target, cross-national, and generational differences. *Personality and Social Psychology Bulletin, 7,* 314–319.

Cunningham, M. R., Shaffer, D. R., Barbee, A. P., Wolff, P. L., & Kelley, D. J. (1990). Separate processes in the relation of elation and depression to helping: Social versus personal concerns. *Journal of Experimental Social Psychology, 26,* 13–33.

Cunningham, W. A., Johnson, M. K., Raye, C. L., Gatenby, J. C., Gore, J. C., & Banaji, M. R. (2004). Separable neural components in the processing of black and white faces. *Psychological Science, 15,* 806–813.

Cutler, B. L., Moran, G., & Narvy, D. J. (1992). Jury selection in insanity defense cases. *Journal of Research in Personality, 26,* 165–182.

Cutler, B. L., & Penrod, S. D. (1988a). Context reinstatement and eyewitness identification. In G. M. Davies & D. M. Thomson (Eds.), *Context reinstatement and eyewitness identification.* New York: Wiley.

Cutler, B. L., & Penrod, S. D. (1988b). Improving the reliability of eyewitness identification: Lineup construction and presentation. *Journal of Applied Psychology, 73,* 281–290.

Cutler, B. L., & Penrod, S. D. (1995). Mistaken identification: The eyewitness, psychology, and the law. New York: Cambridge University Press.

Cutler, B. L., Penrod, S. D., & Dexter, H. R. (1989). The eyewitness, the expert psychologist and the jury. *Law and Human Behavior, 13,* 311–332.

Cutler, B. L., Penrod, S. D., & Stuve, T. E. (1988). Juror decision making in eyewitness identification cases. *Law and Human Behavior, 12,* 41–55.

Cutrona, C. E. (1986). Behavioral manifestations of social support: A microanalytic investigation. *Journal of Personality and Social Psychology, 51,* 201–208.

Cynkar, A. (2007, June). The changing gender composition of psychology. *Monitor on Psychology, 38,* 46–47.

Dabbs, J. M., Jr. (1992). Testosterone measurements in social and clinical psychology. *Journal of Social and Clinical Psychology, 11,* 302–321.

Dabbs, J. M., Jr. (2000). Heroes, rogues, and lovers : Testosterone and behavior. New York: McGraw-Hill.

Dabbs, J. M., Jr., Carr, T. S., Frady, R. L., & Riad, J. K. (1995). Testosterone, crime, and misbehavior among 692 male prison inmates. *Personality and Individual Differences, 18,* 627–633.

Dabbs, J. M., Jr., & Janis, I. L. (1965). Why does eating while reading facilitate opinion change? An experimental inquiry. *Journal of Experimental Social Psychology, 1,* 133–144.

Dabbs, J. M., Jr., & Morris, R. (1990). Testosterone, social class, and antisocial behavior in a sample of 4,462 men. *Psychological Science, 1,* 209–211.

Dabbs, J. M., Jr., Riad, J. K., & Chance, S. E. (2001). Testosterone and ruthless homicide. *Personality and Individual Differences, 31,* 599–603.

Dabbs, J. M., Jr., Strong, R., & Milun, R. (1997). Exploring the mind of testosterone: A beeper study. *Journal of Research in Personality, 31,* 577–588.

Dalrymple, T. (2007). On evil. *New English Review* (www.newenglishreview .org).

Damon, W. (1995). *Greater expectations: Overcoming the culture of indulgence in America's homes and schools.* New York: Free Press.

Danner, D. D., Snowdon, D. A., & Friesen, W. V. (2001). Positive emotions in early life and longevity: Findings from the Nun Study. *Journal of Personality and Social Psychology, 80,* 804–813.

Dardenne, B., Dumont, M., & Bollier, T. (2007). Insidious dangers of benevolent sexism: Consequences for women's performance. *Journal of Personality and Social Psychology, 93,* 764–779.

Darley, J. M. (1995). Book review essay. *Political Psychology.*

Darley, J., & Alter, A. (2009). Behavioral issues of punishment and deterrence. In E. Shafir (Ed.), *The behavioral foundations of policy.* Princeton, NJ: Princeton University Press.

Darley, J. M., & Batson, C. D. (1973). From Jerusalem to Jericho: A study of situational and dispositional variables in helping behavior. *Journal of Personality and Social Psychology, 27,* 100–108.

Darley, J. M., & Berscheid, E. (1967). Increased liking as a result of the anticipation of personal contact. *Human Relations, 20,* 29–40.

Darley, J. M., & Gross, P. H. (1983). A hypothesis-confirming bias in labelling effects. *Journal of Personality and Social Psychology, 44,* 20–33.

Darley, J. M., & Latané, B. (1968). Bystander intervention in emergencies: Diffusion of responsibility. *Journal of Personality and Social Psychology, 8,* 377–383.

Darwin, C. (1859/1988). *The origin of species.* Vol. 15 of *The Works of Charles Darwin,* edited by P. H. Barrett & R. B. Freeman. New York: New York University Press.

Das, E. H. H. J., de Wit, J. B. F., & Stroebe, W. (2003). Fear appeals motivate acceptance of action recommendations: Evidence for a positive bias in the processing of persuasive messages. *Personality and Social Psychology Bulletin, 29,* 650–664.

Dasgupta, N., & Rivera, L. M. (2006). From automatic antigay prejudice to behavior: The moderating role of conscious beliefs about gender and behavioral control. *Journal of Personality and Social Psychology, 91,* 268–280.

Dashiell, J. F. (1930). An experimental analysis of some group effects. *Journal of Abnormal and Social Psychology, 25,* 190–199.

Dateline. (2000, June 20). Dateline NBC. New York: NBC.

Davidson, R. J., Putnam, K. M., & Larson, C. L. (2000). Dysfunction in the neural circuitry of emotion regulation—A possible prelude to violence. *Science, 289,* 591–594.

Davies, M. F. (1997). Belief persistence after evidential discrediting: The impact of generated versus provided explanations on the likelihood of discredited outcomes. *Journal of Experimental Social Psychology, 33,* 561–578.

Davies, P. (2004, April 14). Into the 21st century. *Metaviews* (www.metanexus.net).

Davies, P. (2007). *Cosmic jackpot: Why our universe is just right for life.* Boston: Houghton-Mifflin.

Davies, P. G., Spencer, S. J., Quinn, D. M., & Gerhardstein, R. (2002). Consuming images: How television commercials that elicit stereotype threat can restrain women academically and professionally. *Personality and Social Psychology Bulletin, 28,* 1615–1628.

Davies, P. G., Steele, C. M., & Spencer, S. J., (2005). Clearing the air: Identity safety moderates the effects of stereotype threat on women's leadership aspirations. *Journal of Personality and Social Psychology, 88,* 276–287.

Davila, J., Bradbury, T. N., Cohan, C. L., & Tochluk, S. (1997). Marital functioning and depressive symptoms: Evidence for a stress generation model. *Journal of Personality and Social Psychology, 73,* 849–861.

Davis, B. M., & Gilbert, L. A. (1989). Effect of dispositional and situational influences on women's dominance expression in mixed-sex dyads. *Journal of Personality and Social Psychology, 57,* 294–300.

Davis, C. G., Lehman, D. R., Silver, R. C., Wortman, C. B., & Ellard, J. H. (1996). Self-blame following a traumatic event: The role of perceived avoidability. *Personality and Social Psychology Bulletin, 22,* 557–567.

Davis, C. G., Lehman, D. R., Wortman, C. B., Silver, R. C., & Thompson, S. C. (1995). The undoing of traumatic life events. *Personality and Social Psychology Bulletin, 21,* 109–124.

Davis, D., Loftus, E. F., Vanous, S., & Cucciare, M. (2008). "Unconscious transference" can be an instance of "change blindness." *Applied Cognitive Psychology, 22,* 605–623.

Davis, J. A. (2004). Did growing up in the 1960s leave a permanent mark on attitudes and values? Evidence from the GSS. *Public Opinion Quarterly, 68,* 161–183.

Davis, J. H., Kameda, T., Parks, C., Stasson, M., & Zimmerman, S. (1989). Some social mechanics of group decision making: The distribution of opinion, polling sequence, and implications for consensus. *Journal of Personality and Social Psychology, 57,* 1000–1012.

Davis, J. H., Kerr, N. L., Atkin, R. S., Holt, R., & Meek, D. (1975). The decision processes of 6- and 12-person mock juries assigned unanimous and two-thirds majority rules. *Journal of Personality and Social Psychology, 32,* 1–14.

Davis, J. H., Kerr, N. L., Stasser, G., Meek, D., & Holt, R. (1977). Victim consequences, sentence severity, and decision process in mock juries. *Organizational Behavior and Human Performance, 18,* 346–365.

Davis, J. H., Stasson, M. F., Parks, C. D., Hulbert, L., Kameda, T., Zimmerman, S. K., & Ono, K. (1993). Quantitative decisions by groups and individuals: Voting procedures and monetary awards by mock civil juries. *Journal of Experimental Social Psychology, 29,* 326–346.

Davis, J. L., & Rusbult, C. E. (2001). Attitude alignment in close relationships. *Journal of Personality and Social Psychology, 81,* 65–84.

Davis, K. E. (1985, February). Near and dear: Friendship and love compared. *Psychology Today,* pp. 22–30.

Davis, K. E., & Jones, E. E. (1960). Changes in interpersonal perception as a means of reducing cognitive dissonance. *Journal of Abnormal and Social Psychology, 61,* 402–410.

Davis, L., & Greenlees, C. (1992). Social loafing revisited: Factors that mitigate—and reverse— performance loss. Paper presented at the Southwestern Psychological Association convention.

Davis, M. H., & Franzoi, S. L. (1986). Adolescent loneliness, self-disclosure, and private self-consciousness: A longitudinal investigation. *Journal of Personality and Social Psychology, 51,* 595–608.

Dawes, R. (1998, October). The social usefulness of self-esteem: A skeptical view. *Harvard Mental Health Letter,* pp. 4–5.

Dawes, R. M. (1976). Shallow psychology. In J. S. Carroll & J. W. Payne (Eds.), *Cognition and social behavior.* Hillsdale, NJ: Erlbaum.

Dawes, R. M. (1980a). Social dilemmas. *Annual Review of Psychology, 31,* 169–193.

Dawes, R. M. (1980b). You can't systematize human judgment: Dyslexia. In R. A. Shweder (Ed.), *New directions for methodology of social and behavioral science: Fallible judgment in behavioral research.* San Francisco: Jossey-Bass.

Dawes, R. M. (1990). The potential nonfalsity of the false consensus effect. In R. M. Hogarth (Ed.), *Insights in decision making: A tribute to Hillel J. Einhorn.* Chicago: University of Chicago Press.

Dawes, R. M. (1991). Social dilemmas, economic self-interest, and evolutionary theory. In D. R. Brown & J. E. Keith Smith (Eds.), *Frontiers of mathematical psychology: Essays in honor of Clyde Coombs.* New York: Springer-Verlag.

Dawes, R. M. (1994). *House of cards: Psychology and psychotherapy built on myth.* New York: Free Press.

Dawes, R. M. (2005). The ethical implications of Paul Meehl's work on comparing clinical versus actuarial prediction methods. *Journal of Clinical Psychology, 61,* 1245–1255.

Dawes, R. M., McTavish, J., & Shaklee, H. (1977). Behavior, communication, and assumptions about other people's behavior in a commons dilemma situation. *Journal of Personality and Social Psychology, 35,* 1–11.

Dawkins, R. (1976). *The selfish gene.* New York: Oxford University Press.

Dawson, N. V., Arkes, H. R., Siciliano, C., Blinkhorn, R., Lakshmanan, M., & Petrelli, M. (1988). Hindsight bias: An impediment to accurate probability estimation in clinicopathologic conferences. *Medical Decision Making, 8,* 259–264.

de Botton, A. (2004). *Status anxiety.* New York: Pantheon.

De Cremer, D. (2002). Charismatic leadership and cooperation in social dilemmas: A matter of transforming motives? *Journal of Applied Social Psychology, 32,* 997–1016.

De Hoog, N., Stroebe, W., & de Wit, J. B. F. (2007). The impact of vulnerability to and severity of a health risk on processing and acceptance of fear-arousing communications: A meta-analysis. *Review of General Psychology, 11,* 258–285.

de Hoogh, A. H. B., den Hartog, D. N., Koopman, P. L., Thierry, H., van den Berg, P. T., van der Weide, J. G., & Wilderom, C. P. M. (2004). Charismatic leadership, environmental dynamism, and performance. *European Journal of Work and Organisational Psychology, 13,* 447–471.

De Houwer, J., Thomas, S., & Baeyens, F. (2001). Associative learning of likes and dislikes: A review of 25 years of research on human evaluative conditioning. *Psychological Bulletin, 127,* 853–869.

de Jong-Gierveld, J. (1987). Developing and testing a model of loneliness. *Journal of Personality and Social Psychology, 53,* 119–128.

De Vogli, R., Chandola, T., & Marmot, M. G. (2007). Negative aspects of close relationships and heart disease. *Archives of Internal Medicine, 167,* 1951–1957.

de Waal, F. B. M. (2005–2006, Fall–Winter). The evolution of empathy. *Greater Good,* pp. 6–9.

de Waal, F. B. M., Leimgruber, K., & Greenberg, A. R. (2008). Giving is self-rewarding for monkeys. *Proceedings of the National Academy of Sciences, 105,* 13685–13689.

De Wall, C. N., Maner, J. K., & Rouby, D. A. (2009). Social exclusion and early-stage interpersonal perception: Selective attention to signs of acceptance. *Journal of Personality and Social Psychology, 96,* 729–741.

Deary, I. J. (2005). Intelligence, health and death. *Psychologist, 18,* 610–613.

Deary, I. J., Batty, G. D., & Gale, C. R. (2008). Bright children become enlightened adults. *Psychological Science, 19,* 1–6.

Deaux, K., & LaFrance, M. (1998). Gender. In D. Gilbert, S. Fiske, and G. Lindzey (Eds.), *The handbook of social psychology,* 4th edition. Hillsdale, NJ: Erlbaum.

DeBruine, L. M. (2002). Facial resemblance enhances trust. *Proceedings of the Royal Society of London, 269,* 1307–1312.

DeBruine, L. M. (2004). Facial resemblance increases the attractiveness of same-sex faces more than other-sex faces. *Proceedings of the Royal Society of London, B, 271*(1552): 2085–2090.

Decety, J., & Sommerville, J. A. (2003). Shared representations between self and other: A social cognitive neuroscience view. *Trends in Cognitive Sciences, 7,* 527–533.

Deci, E. L., La Guardia, J. G., Moller, A. C., Scheiner, M. J., & Ryan, R. M. (2006). On the benefits of giving as well as receiving autonomy support: Mutuality in close friendships. *Personality and Social Bulletin, 32,* 313–327.

Deci, E. L., & Ryan, R. M. (1985). *Intrinsic motivation and self-determination in human behavior.* New York: Plenum.

Deci, E. L., & Ryan, R. M. (1987). The support of autonomy and the control of behavior. *Journal of Personality and Social Psychology, 53,* 1024–1037.

Deci, E. L., & Ryan, R. M. (1991). A motivational approach to self: Integration in personality. In R. Dienstbier (Ed.) *Perspectives on motivation: Nebraska Symposium on Motivation* (Vol. 38, pp. 237–288). Lincoln, NE: University of Nebraska Press.

Deci, E. L., & Ryan, R. M. (1997). Behaviorists in search of the null: Revisiting the undermining of intrinsic motivation by extrinsic rewards. Unpublished manuscript, University of Rochester.

Deci, E. L., & Ryan, R. M. (Eds.). (2002). *Handbook of self-determination research.* Rochester, NY: University of Rochester Press.

Deci, E. L., & Ryan, R. M. (2008). Facilitating optimal motivation and psychological well-being across life's domains. *Canadian Psychology, 49,* 14–23.

Delgado, J. (1973). In M. Pines, *The brain changers.* New York: Harcourt Brace Jovanovich.

della Cava, M. R. (2003, April 2). Iraq gets sympathetic press around the world. *USA Today* (www.usatoday.com).

Dembroski, T. M., Lasater, T. M., & Ramirez, A. (1978). Communicator similarity, fear-arousing communications, and compliance with health care recommendations. *Journal of Applied Social Psychology, 8,* 254–269.

Denissen, J. J. A., Penke, L., Schmitt, D. P., & van Aken, M. A. G. (2008). Self-esteem reactions to social interactions: Evidence for sociometer mechanisms across days, people, and nations. *Journal of Personality and Social Psychology, 95,* 181–196.

Dennett, D. (2005, December 26). Spiegel interview with evolution philosopher Daniel Dennett: Darwinism completely refutes intelligent design. *Der Spiegel* (www.service.dspiegel.de).

Dennett, D. C. (2005, August 28). Show me the science. *New York Times* (www.nytimes.com).

Denrell, J. (2008). Indirect social influence. *Science, 321,* 47–48.

Denrell, J., & Le Mens, G. (2007). Interdependent sampling and social influence. *Psychological Review, 114,* 398–422.

Denson, T. F., Pedersen, W. C., & Miller, N. (2006). The displaced aggression questionnaire. *Journal of Personality and Social Psychology, 90,* 1032–1051.

Department of Canadian Heritage. (2006). What is multiculturalism? (www.pch.gc.ca).

DePaulo, B. (2006). *Singled out: How singles are stereotyped, stigmatized, and ignored, and still live happily ever after.* New York: St. Martin's.

DePaulo, B. M., Charlton, K., Cooper, H., Lindsay, J. J., & Muhlenbruck, L. (1997). The accuracy-confidence correlation in the detection of deception. *Personality and Social Psychology Review, 1,* 346–357.

Derks, B., Inzlicht, M., & Kang, S. (2008). The neuroscience of stigma and stereotype threat. *Group Processes and Intergroup Relations, 11,* 163–181.

Derlega, V., Metts, S., Petronio, S., & Margulis, S. T. (1993). *Self-disclosure.* Newbury Park, CA: Sage.

Dermer, M., Cohen, S. J., Jacobsen, E., & Anderson, E. A. (1979). Evaluative judgments of aspects of life as a function of vicarious exposure to hedonic extremes. *Journal of Personality and Social Psychology, 37,* 247–260.

Dermer, M., & Pyszczynski, T. A. (1978). Effects of erotica upon men's loving and liking responses for women they love. *Journal of Personality and Social Psychology, 36,* 1302–1309.

Desforges, D. M., Lord, C. G., Pugh, M. A., Sia, T. L., Scarberry, N. C., & Ratcliff, C. D. (1997). Role of group representativeness in the generalization part of the contact hypothesis. *Basic and Applied Social Psychology, 19,* 183–204.

Desforges, D. M., Lord, C. G., Ramsey, S. L., Mason, J. A., Van Leeuwen, M. D., West, S. C., & Lepper, M. R. (1991). Effects of structured cooperative contact on changing negative attitudes toward stigmatized social groups. *Journal of Personality and Social Psychology, 60,* 531–544.

DeSteno, D., Petty, R. E., Wegener, D. T., & Rucker, D. D. (2000). Beyond valence in the perception of likelihood: The role of emotion specificity. *Journal of Personality and Social Psychology, 78,* 397–416.

Detweiler, J. B., Bedell, B. T., Salovey, P., Pronin, E., & Rothman, A. J. (1999). Message framing and sunscreen use: Gain-framed messages motivate beach-goers. *Health Psychology, 18,* 189–196.

Deutsch, M. (1985). *Distributive justice: A social psychological perspective.* New Haven: Yale University Press.

Deutsch, M. (1986). Folie à deux: A psychological perspective on Soviet-American relations. In M. P. Kearns (Ed.), *Persistent patterns and emergent structures in a waning century*. New York: Praeger.

Deutsch, M. (1993). Educating for a peaceful world. *American Psychologist*, 48, 510–517.

Deutsch, M. (1994). Constructive conflict resolution: Principles, training, and research. *Journal of Social Issues*, 50, 13–32.

Deutsch, M. (1999). Behind the scenes. In D. G. Myers, *Social psychology*, 6th edition (p. 519). New York: McGraw-Hill.

Deutsch, M., & Collins, M. E. (1951). *Interracial housing: A psychological evaluation of a social experiment*. Minneapolis: University of Minnesota Press.

Deutsch, M., & Gerard, H. B. (1955). A study of normative and informational social influence upon individual judgment. *Journal of Abnormal and Social Psychology*, 51, 629–636.

Deutsch, M., & Krauss, R. M. (1960). The effect of threat upon interpersonal bargaining. *Journal of Abnormal and Social Psychology*, 61, 181–189.

Devenport, J. L., Stinson, V., Cutler, B. L., & Kravitz, D. A. (2002). How effective are the cross-examination and expert testimony safeguards? Jurors' perceptions of the suggestiveness and fairness of biased lineup procedures. *Journal of Applied Psychology*, 87, 1042–1054.

Devine, P. A., Brodish, A. B., & Vance, S. L. (2005). Self-regulatory processes in interracial interactions: The role of internal and external motivation to respond without prejudice. In J. P. Forgas, K. D. Williams, & S. M. Laham (Eds.), *Social motivation: Conscious and unconscious processes*. New York: Cambridge University Press.

Devine, P. G. (1989). Stereotypes and prejudice: Their automatic and controlled components. *Journal of Personality and Social Psychology*, 56, 5–18.

Devine, P. G., Evett, S. R., & Vasquez-Suson, K. A. (1996). Exploring the interpersonal dynamics of intergroup contact. In R. Sorrentino & E. T. Higgins (Eds.), *Handbook of motivation and cognition: The interpersonal content* (Vol. 3). New York: Guilford.

Devine, P. G., Plant, E. A., & Buswell, B. N. (2000). Breaking the prejudice habit: Progress and obstacles. In S. Oskamp (Ed.), *Reducing prejudice and discrimination*. Mahwah, NJ: Erlbaum.

Devine, P. G., & Sharp, L. B. (2008). Automatic and controlled processes in stereotyping and prejudice. In T. Nelson (Ed.), *Handbook of prejudice, stereotyping, and discrimination*. New York: Psychology Press.

Devos-Comby, L., & Salovey, P. (2002). Applying persuasion strategies to alter HIV-relevant thoughts and behavior. *Review of General Psychology*, 6, 287–304.

DeWall, C. N., Baumeister, R. F., Stillman, T. F., & Gailliot, M. T. (2007). Violence restrained: Effects of self-regulation and its depletion on aggression. *Journal of Experimental Social Psychology*, 43, 62–76.

DeWall, C. N., Baumeister, R. F., & Vohs, K. D. (2008). Satiated with belongingness? Effects of acceptance, rejection, and task framing on self-regulatory performance. *Journal of Personality and Social Psychology*, 95, 1367–1382.

Dexter, H. R., Cutler, B. L., & Moran, G. (1992). A test of voir dire as a remedy for the prejudicial effects of pretrial publicity. *Journal of Applied Social Psychology*, 22, 819–832.

Dey, E. L., Astin, A. W., & Korn, W. S. (1991). *The American freshman: Twenty-five year trends*. Los Angeles: Higher Education Research Institute, UCLA.

Diamond, J. (1996, December). The best ways to sell sex. *Discover*, pp. 78–86.

Diamond, S. S. (1993). Instructing on death: Psychologists, juries, and judges. *American Psychologist*, 48, 423–434.

Dick, S. (2008). *Homophobic hate crime: The Gay British Crime Survey 2008*. Stonewall (www.stonewall.org.uk).

Dicum, J. (2003, November 11). Letter to the editor. *New York Times*, p. A20.

Diekman, A. B., McDonald, M., & Gardner, W. L. (2000). Love means never having to be careful: The relationship between reading romance novels and safe sex behavior. *Psychology of Women Quarterly*, 24, 179–188.

Diekmann, K. A., Samuels, S. M., Ross, L., & Bazerman, M. H. (1997). Self-interest and fairness in problems of resource allocation: Allocators versus recipients. *Journal of Personality and Social Psychology*, 72, 1061–1074.

Diener, E. (1976). Effects of prior destructive behavior, anonymity, and group presence on deindividuation and aggression. *Journal of Personality and Social Psychology*, 33, 497–507.

Diener, E. (1979). Deindividuation, self-awareness, and disinhibition. *Journal of Personality and Social Psychology*, 37, 1160–1171.

Diener, E. (1980). Deindividuation: The absence of self-awareness and self-regulation in group members. In P. Paulus (Ed.), *The psychology of group influence*. Hillsdale, NJ: Erlbaum.

Diener, E. (2005, December 1). Guidelines for national indicators of subjective well-being and ill-being. Department of Psychology, University of Illinois.

Diener, E., & Crandall, R. (1979). An evaluation of the Jamaican anticrime program. *Journal of Applied Social Psychology*, 9, 135–146.

Diener, E., Horwitz, J., & Emmons, R. A. (1985). Happiness of the very wealthy. *Social Indicators*, 16, 263–274.

Diener, E., Kesebir, P., & Lucas, R. (2008). Benefits of accounts of well-being—for societies and for psychological science. *Applied Psychology*, 57, 37–53.

Diener, E., Lucas, R. E., & Schimmack, U. (2009). *Well-being for public policy*. Oxford, UK: Oxford University Press.

Diener, E., Lucas, R. E., & Scollon, C. N. (2006). Beyond the hedonic treadmill: Revising the adaptation theory of well-being. *American Psychologist*, 61, 305–314.

Diener, E., & Wallbom, M. (1976). Effects of self-awareness on antinormative behavior. *Journal of Research in Personality*, 10, 107–111.

Dienstbier, R. A., Roesch, S. C., Mizumoto, A., Hemenover, S. H., Lott, R. C., & Carlo, G. (1998). Effects of weapons on guilt judgments and sentencing recommendations for criminals. *Basic and Applied Social Psychology*, 20, 93–102.

Dijksterhuis, A., Bos, M. W., Nordgren, L. F., & van Baaren, R. B. (2006). Complex choices better made unconsciously? *Science*, 313, 760–761.

Dijksterhuis, A., & Nordgren, L. F. (2006). A theory of unconscious thought. *Perspectives on Psychological Science*, 1, 95–109.

Dijksterhuis, A., Smith, P. K., van Baaren, R. B., & Wigboldus, D. H. J. (2005). The unconscious consumer: Effects of environment on consumer behavior. *Journal of Consumer Psychology*, 15, 193-202.

Dill, J. C., & Anderson, C. A. (1999). Loneliness, shyness, and depression: The etiology and interrelationships of everyday problems in living. In T. Joiner and J. C. Coyne (Eds.) *The interactional nature of depression: Advances in interpersonal approaches*. Washington, DC: American Psychological Association.

Dillehay, R. C., & Nietzel, M. T. (1980). Constructing a science of jury behavior. In L. Wheeler (Ed.), *Review of personality and social psychology* (Vol. 1). Beverly Hills, CA: Sage.

Dindia, K., & Allen, M. (1992). Sex differences in self-disclosure: A meta-analysis. *Psychological Bulletin*, 112, 106–124.

Dion, K. K. (1972). Physical attractiveness and evaluations of children's transgressions. *Journal of Personality and Social Psychology*, 24, 207–213.

Dion, K. K. (1973). Young children's stereotyping of facial attractiveness. *Developmental Psychology*, 9, 183–188.

Dion, K. K., & Berscheid, E. (1974). Physical attractiveness and peer perception among children. *Sociometry, 37*, 1–12.

Dion, K. K., & Dion, K. L. (1985). Personality, gender, and the phenomenology of romantic love. In P. R. Shaver (Ed.), *Review of personality and social psychology* (Vol. 6). Beverly Hills, CA: Sage.

Dion, K. K., & Dion, K. L. (1991). Psychological individualism and romantic love. *Journal of Social Behavior and Personality, 6*, 17–33.

Dion, K. K., & Dion, K. L. (1993). Individualistic and collectivistic perspectives on gender and the cultural context of love and intimacy. *Journal of Social Issues, 49*, 53–69.

Dion, K. K., & Dion, K. L. (1996). Cultural perspectives on romantic love. *Personal Relationships, 3*, 5–17.

Dion, K. K., & Stein, S. (1978). Physical attractiveness and interpersonal influence. *Journal of Experimental Social Psychology, 14*, 97–109.

Dion, K. L. (1979). Intergroup conflict and intragroup cohesiveness. In W. G. Austin & S. Worchel (Eds.), *The social psychology of intergroup relations.* Monterey, CA: Brooks/Cole.

Dion, K. L. (1987). What's in a title? The Ms. stereotype and images of women's titles of address. *Psychology of Women Quarterly, 11*, 21–36.

Dion, K. L. (1998). The social psychology of perceived prejudice and discrimination. Colloquium presentation, Carleton University.

Dion, K. L., & Cota, A. A. (1991). The Ms. stereotype: Its domain and the role of explicitness in title preference. *Psychology of Women Quarterly, 15*, 403–410.

Dion, K. L., & Dion, K. K. (1988). Romantic love: Individual and cultural perspectives. In R. J. Sternberg & M. L. Barnes (Eds.), *The psychology of love.* New Haven, CT: Yale University Press.

Dion, K. L., & Schuller, R. A. (1991). The Ms. stereotype: Its generality and its relation to managerial and marital status stereotypes. *Canadian Journal of Behavioural Science, 23*, 25–40.

Dishion, T. J., McCord, J., & Poulin, F. (1999). When interventions harm: Peer groups and problem behavior. *American Psychologist, 54*, 755–764.

Dixon, B. (1986, April). Dangerous thoughts: How we think and feel can make us sick. *Science 86*, 63–66.

Dixon, J., & Durrheim, K. (2003). Contact and the ecology of racial division: Some varieties of informal segregation. *British Journal of Social Psychology, 42*, 1–23.

Dixon, J., Durrheim, K., & Tredoux, C. (2005). Beyond the optimal contact strategy: A reality check for the contact hypothesis. *American Psychologist, 60*, 697–711.

Dixon, J., Durrheim, K., & Tredoux, C. (2007). Intergroup contact and attitudes toward the principle and practice of racial equality. *Psychological Science, 18*, 867–872.

Dixon, J., Tredoux, C., & Clack, B. (2005). On the micro-ecology of racial division: A neglected dimension of segregation. *South African Journal of Psychology, 35*, 395–411.

Dohrenwend, B., Pearlin, L., Clayton, P., Hamburg, B., Dohrenwend, B. P., Riley, M., & Rose, R. (1982). Report on stress and life events. In G. R. Elliott & C. Eisdorfer (Eds.), *Stress and human health: Analysis and implications of research* (A study by the Institute of Medicine/National Academy of Sciences). New York: Springer.

Dolinski, D. (2000). On inferring one's beliefs from one's attempt and consequences for subsequent compliance. *Journal of Personality and Social Psychology, 78*, 260–272.

Dolinski, D., & Nawrat, R. (1998). "Fear-then-relief" procedure for producing compliance: Beware when the danger is over. *Journal of Experimental Social Psychology, 34*, 27–50.

Dollard, J., Doob, L., Miller, N., Mowrer, O. H., & Sears, R. R. (1939). *Frustration and aggression.* New Haven, CT: Yale University Press.

Dolnik, L., Case, T. I., & Williams, K. D. (2003). Stealing thunder as a courtroom tactic revisited: Processes and boundaries. *Law and Human Behavior, 27*, 265–285.

Donaldson, Z. R., & Young, L. J. (2008). Oxytocin, vasopressin, and the neurogenetics of sociality. *Science, 322*, 900–904.

Donders, N. C., Correll, J., & Wittenbrink, B. (2008). Danger stereotypes predict racially biased attentional allocation. *Journal of Experimental Social Psychology, 44*, 1328–1333.

Donnellan, M. B., Larsen-Rife, D., & Conger, R. D. (2005). Personality, family history, and competence in early adult romantic relationships. *Journal of Personality and Social Psychology, 88*, 562–576.

Donnerstein, E. (1980). Aggressive erotica and violence against women. *Journal of Personality and Social Psychology, 39*, 269–277.

Donnerstein, E., Linz, D., & Penrod, S. (1987). *The question of pornography.* London: Free Press.

Doob, A. N., & Kirshenbaum, H. M. (1973). Bias in police lineups—partial remembering. *Journal of Police Science and Administration, 1*, 287–293.

Doob, A. N., & McLaughlin, D. S. (1989). Ask and you shall be given: Request size and donations to a good cause. *Journal of Applied Social Psychology, 19*, 1049–1056.

Doob, A. N., & Roberts, J. (1988). Public attitudes toward sentencing in Canada. In N. Walker & M. Hough (Eds.), *Sentencing and the public.* London: Gower.

Dotsch, R., & Wigboldus, D. H. J. (2008). Virtual prejudice. *Journal of Experimental Social Psychology, 44*, 1194–1198.

Doty, R. M., Peterson, B. E., & Winter, D. G. (1991). Threat and authoritarianism in the United States, 1978–1987. *Journal of Personality and Social Psychology, 61*, 629–640.

Douglas, K. M., & McGarty, C. (2001). Identifiability and self-presentation: Computer-mediated communication and intergroup interaction. *British Journal of Social Psychology, 40*, 399–416.

Douglass, A. B., & Steblay, N. (2006). Memory distortion in eyewitnesses: A meta-analysis of the post-identification feedback effect. *Applied Cognitive Psychology, 20*, 859–869.

Douglass, F. (1845/1960). *Narrative of the life of Frederick Douglass, an American slave: Written by himself.* (B. Quarles, Ed.). Cambridge, MA: Harvard University Press.

Dovidio, J. F. (1991). The empathy-altruism hypothesis: Paradigm and promise. *Psychological Inquiry, 2*, 126–128.

Dovidio, J. F., Gaertner, S. L., Anastasio, P. A., & Sanitioso, R. (1992). Cognitive and motivational bases of bias: Implications of aversive racism for attitudes toward Hispanics. In S. Knouse, P. Rosenfeld, & A. Culbertson (Eds.), *Hispanics in the workplace.* Newbury Park, CA: Sage.

Dovidio, J. F., Gaertner, S. L., Hodson, G., Houlette, M., & Johnson, K. M. (2005). Social inclusion and exclusion: Recategorization and the perception of intergroup boundaries. In D. Abrams, M. A. Hogg, & J. M. Marques (Eds.), *The social psychology of inclusion and exclusion.* New York: Psychology Press.

Dovidio, J. R., Brigham, J. C., Johnson, B. T., & Gaertner, S. L. (1996). Stereotyping, prejudice, and discrimination: Another look. In N. Macrae, M. Hewstone, & C. Stangor (Eds.), *Stereotypes and stereotyping.* New York: Guilford.

Downs, A. C., & Lyons, P. M. (1991). Natural observations of the links between attractiveness and initial legal judgments. *Personality and Social Psychology Bulletin, 17*, 541–547.

Doyle, J. M. (2005). *True witness: Cops, courts, science, and the battle against misidentification.* New York: Palgrave MacMillan.

Drabman, R. S., & Thomas, M. H. (1974). Does media violence increase children's toleration of real-life aggression? *Developmental Psychology,* **10,** 418–421.

Drabman, R. S., & Thomas, M. H. (1975). Does TV violence breed indifference? *Journal of Communications,* **25**(4), 86–89.

Drabman, R. S., & Thomas, M. H. (1976). Does watching violence on television cause apathy? *Pediatrics,* **57,** 329–331.

Draguns, J. G. (1990). Normal and abnormal behavior in cross-cultural perspective: Specifying the nature of their relationship. *Nebraska Symposium on Motivation 1989,* **37,** 235–277.

Dreber, A., Rand, D. G., Fudenberg, D., & Nowak, M. A. (2008). Winners don't punish. *Nature,* **452,** 348–351.

Driedger, L. (1975). In search of cultural identity factors: A comparison of ethnic students. *Canadian Review of Sociology and Anthropology,* **12,** 150–161.

Driskell, J. E., & Mullen, B. (1990). Status, expectations, and behavior: A meta-analytic review and test of the theory. *Personality and Social Psychology Bulletin,* **16,** 541–553.

Drolet, A. L., & Morris, M. W. (2000). Rapport in conflict resolution: Accounting for how face-to-face contact fosters mutual cooperation in mixed-motive conflicts. *Journal of Experimental Social Psychology,* **36,** 26–50.

Dryer, D. C., & Horowitz, L. M. (1997). When do opposites attract? Interpersonal complementarity versus similarity. *Journal of Personality and Social Psychology,* **72,** 592–603.

DuBois, W. E. B. (1903/1961). *The souls of black folk.* Greenwich, CT: Fawcett Books.

Duck, J. M., Hogg, M. A., & Terry, D. J. (1995). Me, us and them: Political identification and the third-person effect in the 1993 Australian federal election. *European Journal of Social Psychology,* **25,** 195–215.

Duffy, M. (2003, June 9). Weapons of mass disappearance. *Time,* pp. 28-33.

Dunbar, R. (1996). *Grooming, gossip, and the evolution of language.* Cambridge, MA: Harvard University Press.

Duncan, B. L. (1976). Differential social perception and attribution of intergroup violence: Testing the lower limits of stereotyping of blacks. *Journal of Personality and Social Psychology,* **34,** 590–598.

Dunn, E., & Ashton-James, C. (2008). On emotional innumeracy: Predicted and actual affective response to grand-scale tragedies. *Journal of Experimental Social Psychology,* **44,** 692–698.

Dunn, E. W., Aknin, L. B., & Norton, M. I. (2008). Spending money on others promotes happiness. *Science,* **319,** 1687–1688.

Dunn, E. W., Wilson, T. D., & Gilbert, D. T. (2003). Location, location,

location: The misprediction of satisfaction in housing lotteries. *Personality and Social Psychology Bulletin,* **29,** 1421-1432.

Dunn, J. R., & Schweitzer, M. E. (2005). Feeling and believing: The influence of emotion on trust. *Journal of Personality and Social Psychology,* **88,** 736–748.

Dunning, D. (1995). Trait importance and modifiability as factors influencing self-assessment and self-enhancement motives. *Personality and Social Psychology Bulletin,* **21,** 1297–1306.

Dunning, D. (2005). *Self-insight: Roadblocks and detours on the path to knowing thyself.* London: Psychology Press.

Dunning, D. (2006). Strangers to ourselves? *The Psychologist,* **19,** 600–603.

Dunning, D., Griffin, D. W., Milojkovic, J. D., & Ross, L. (1990). The overconfidence effect in social prediction. *Journal of Personality and Social Psychology,* **58,** 568–581.

Dunning, D., Meyerowitz, J. A., & Holzberg, A. D. (1989). Ambiguity and self-evaluation. *Journal of Personality and Social Psychology,* **57,** 1082–1090.

Dunning, D., Perie, M., & Story, A. L. (1991). Self-serving prototypes of social categories. *Journal of Personality and Social Psychology,* **61,** 957–968.

Dunning, D., & Perretta, S. (2002). Automaticity and eyewitness accuracy: A 10- to 12-second rule for distinguishing accurate from inaccurate positive identifications. *Journal of Applied Psychology,* **87,** 951-962.

Dunning, D., & Sherman, D. A. (1997). Stereotypes and tacit inference. *Journal of Personality and Social Psychology,* **73,** 459–471.

Dunning, D., & Stern, L. B. (1994). Distinguishing accurate from inaccurate eyewitness identifications via inquiries about decision processes. *Journal of Personality and Social Psychology,* **67,** 818–835.

Durante, K. M., Li, N. P., & Haselton, M. G. (2008). Changes in women's dress across the ovulatory cycle: Naturalistic and laboratory task-based evidence. *Personality and Social Psychology Bulletin,* **34,** 1451–1460.

Dutton, D. (2006, January 13). Hardwired to seek beauty. *The Australian* (www.theastralian.news.com.au).

Dutton, D. G. (1971). Reactions of restaurateurs to blacks and whites violating restaurant dress regulations. *Canadian Journal of Behavioural Science,* **3,** 298–302.

Dutton, D. G. (1973). Reverse discrimination: The relationship of amount of perceived discrimination toward a minority group and the

behavior of majority group members. *Canadian Journal of Behavioural Science,* **5,** 34–45.

Dutton, D. G., & Aron, A. P. (1974). Some evidence for heightened sexual attraction under conditions of high anxiety. *Journal of Personality and Social Psychology,* **30,** 510–517.

Dutton, D. G., Boyanowsky, E. O., & Bond, M. H. (2005). Extreme mass homicide: From military massacre to genocide. *Aggression and violent behavior,* **10,** 437–473.

Dutton, D. G., & Lake, R. A. (1973). Threat of own prejudice and reverse discrimination in interracial situations. *Journal of Personality and Social Psychology,* **28,** 94–100.

Duval, S., Duval, V. H., & Neely, R. (1979). Self-focus, felt responsibility, and helping behavior. *Journal of Personality and Social Psychology,* **37,** 1769–1778.

Duval, S., & Wicklund, R. A. (1972). *A theory of objective self-awareness.* New York: Academic Press.

Dykstra, P. A., & Fokkema, T. (2007). Social and emotional loneliness among divorced and married men and women: Comparing the deficit and cognitive perspectives. *Basic and Applied Social Psychology,* **29,** 1–12.

Eagly, A. H. (1987). Sex differences in social behavior: A social-role interpretation. Hillsdale, NJ: Erlbaum.

Eagly, A. H. (1994). Are people prejudiced against women? Donald Campbell Award invited address, American Psychological Association convention.

Eagly, A. H., Ashmore, R. D., Makhijani, M. G., & Longo, L. C. (1991). What is beautiful is good, but . . . : A meta-analytic review of research on the physical attractiveness stereotype. *Psychological Bulletin,* **110,** 109–128.

Eagly, A., & Carli, L. (2007). *Through the labyrinth: The truth about how women become leaders.* Cambridge, MA: Harvard University Press.

Eagly, A. H., & Chaiken, S. (1993). *The psychology of attitudes.* San Diego: Harcourt Brace Jovanovich.

Eagly, A. H., & Chaiken, S. (1998). Attitude structure and function. In D. Gilbert, S. Fiske, and G. Lindzey (Eds.), *The handbook of social psychology,* 4th edition. New York: McGraw-Hill.

Eagly, A. H., & Chaiken, S. (2005). Attitude research in the 21st century: The current state of knowledge. In D. Albarracin, B. T. Johnson, & M. P. Zanna (Eds.), *The handbook of attitudes.* Mahwah, NJ: Erlbaum.

Eagly, A. H., & Crowley, M. (1986). Gender and helping behavior: A meta-analytic review of the social psychological literature. *Psychological Bulletin,* **100,** 283–308.

Eagly, A. H., Diekman, A. B., Johannesen-Schmidt, M. C., & Koenig, A. M. (2004). Gender gaps in sociopolitical attitudes: A social psychological analysis. *Journal of Personality and Social Psychology, 87,* 796–816.

Eagly, A. H., & Johnson, B. T. (1990). Gender and leadership style: A meta-analysis. *Psychological Bulletin, 108,* 233–256.

Eagly, A. H., Mladinic, A., & Otto, S. (1991). Are women evaluated more favorably than men? *Psychology of Women Quarterly, 15,* 203–216.

Eagly, A. H., & Wood, W. (1991). Explaining sex differences in social behavior: A meta-analytic perspective. *Personality and Social Psychology Bulletin, 17,* 306–315.

Eagly, A. H., & Wood, W. (1999). The origins of sex differences in human behavior: Evolved dispositions versus social roles. *American Psychologist, 54,* 408–423.

Eagly, A. H., Wood, W., & Chaiken, S. (1978). Casual inferences about communicators and their effect on opinion change. *Journal of Personality and Social Psychology, 36,* 424–435.

Easterbrook, G. (2004, May 25). The 50¢-a-gallon solution. *New York Times* (www.nytimes.com).

Easterlin, R. (1995). Will raising the incomes of all increase the happiness of all? *Journal of Economic Behavior and Organization, 27,* 35–47.

Eastwick, P. W., & Finkel, E. J. (2008a). Speed-dating as a methodological innovation. *The Psychologist, 21,* 402–403.

Eastwick, P. W., & Finkel, E. J. (2008b). Sex differences in mate preferences revisited: Do people know what they initially desire in a romantic partner? *Journal of Personality and Social Psychology, 94,* 245–264.

Eastwick, P. W., Finkel, E. J., Krishnamurti, T., & Loewenstein, G. (2007). Mispredicting distress following romantic breakup: Revealing the time course of the affective forecasting error. *Journal of Experimental Social Psychology, 44,* 800–807.

Eastwick, P. W., Finkel, E. J., Mochon, D., & Ariely, D. (2007). Selective versus unselective romantic desire. *Psychological Science, 18,* 317–319.

Ebbesen, E. B., Duncan, B., & Konecni, V. J. (1975). Effects of content of verbal aggression on future verbal aggression: A field experiment. *Journal of Experimental Social Psychology, 11,* 192–204.

Eberhardt, J. L., (2005). Imaging race. *American Psychologist, 60,* 181–190.

Eberhardt, J. L., Purdie, V. J., Goff, P. A., & Davies, P. G. (2004). Seeing black: Race, crime, and visual processing. *Journal of Personality and Social Psychology, 87,* 876–893.

Eckersley, R. (2005). Is modern Western culture a health hazard? *International Journal of Epidemiology,* published online November 22.

Economist (2000, June 10). America's death-penalty lottery. *The Economist.*

Edney, J. J. (1980). The commons problem: Alternative perspectives. *American Psychologist, 35,* 131–150.

Edwards, C. P. (1991). Behavioral sex differences in children of diverse cultures: The case of nurturance to infants. In M. Pereira & L. Fairbanks (Eds.), *Juveniles: Comparative socioecology.* Oxford: Oxford University Press.

Edwards, D., & Potter, J. (2005). Discursive psychology, mental states and descriptions. In H. te Molder & J. Potter (Eds.), *Conversation and cognition.* New York: Cambridge University Press.

Edwards, K. (1990). The interplay of affect and cognition in attitude formation and change. *Journal of Personality and Social Psychology, 59,* 202–216.

Edwards, K., & Bryan, T. S. (1997). Judgmental biases produced by instructions to disregard: The (paradoxical) case of emotional information. *Personality and Social Psychology Bulletin, 23,* 849–864.

Efran, M. G. (1974). The effect of physical appearance on the judgment of guilt, interpersonal attraction, and severity of recommended punishment in a simulated jury task. *Journal of Research in Personality, 8,* 45–54.

Egan, L. C., Santos, L. R., & Bloom, P. (2007). The origins of cognitive dissonance: Evidence from children and monkeys. *Psychological Science, 18,* 978–983.

Ehrlich, P., & Feldman, M. (2003). Genes and cultures: What creates our behavioral phenome? *Current Anthropology, 44,* 87-95.

Eibach, R. P., & Ehrlinger, J. (2006). "Keep your eyes on the prize": Reference points and racial differences in assessing progress toward equality. *Personality and Social Psychology Bulletin, 32,* 66–77.

Eibach, R. P., Libby, L. K., & Gilovich, T. D. (2003). When change in the self is mistaken for change in the world. *Journal of Personality and Social Psychology, 84,* 917–931.

Eich, E., Reeves, J. L., Jaeger, B., & Graff-Radford, S. B. (1985). Memory for pain: Relation between past and present pain intensity. *Pain, 23,* 375–380.

Eisenberg, N., Fabes, R. A., Schaller, M., Miller, P., Carlo, G., Poulin, R., Shea, C., & Shell, R. (1991). Personality and socialization correlates of vicarious emotional responding. *Journal of Personality and Social Psychology, 61,* 459–470.

Eisenberg, N., & Lennon, R. (1983). Sex differences in empathy and related capacities. *Psychological Bulletin, 94,* 100–131.

Eisenberger, N. I., Lieberman, M. D., & Williams, K. D. (2003). Does rejection hurt? An fMRI study of social exclusion. *Science, 302,* 290–292.

Eisenberger, R., & Rhoades, L. (2001). Incremental effects of reward on creativity. *Journal of Personality and Social Psychology, 81,* 728–741.

Eisenberger, R., Rhoades, L., & Cameron, J. (1999). Does pay for performance increase or decrease perceived self-determination and intrinsic motivation? *Journal of Personality and Social Psychology, 77,* 1026–1040.

Eisenberger, R., & Shanock, L. (2003). Rewards, intrinsic motivation, and creativity: A case study of conceptual and methodological isolation. *Creativity Research Journal, 15,* 121–130.

Eiser, J. R., Sutton, S. R., & Wober, M. (1979). Smoking, seat-belts, and beliefs about health. *Addictive Behaviors, 4,* 331–338.

Elder, G. H., Jr. (1969). Appearance and education in marriage mobility. *American Sociological Review, 34,* 519–533.

Eldersveld, S. J., & Dodge, R. W. (1954). Personal contact or mail propaganda? An experiment in voting turnout and attitude change. In D. Katz, D. Cartwright, S. Eldersveld, & A. M. Lee (Eds.), *Public opinion and propaganda.* New York: Dryden Press.

Ellemers, N., Van Rijswijk, W., Roefs, M., & Simons, C. (1997). Bias in intergroup perceptions: Balancing group identity with social reality. *Personality and Social Psychology Bulletin, 23,* 186–198.

Elliot, A. J., & Devine, P. G. (1994). On the motivational nature of cognitive dissonance: Dissonance as psychological discomfort. *Journal of Personality and Social Psychology, 67,* 382–394.

Elliott, L. (1989, June). Legend of the four chaplains. *Reader's Digest,* pp. 66–70.

Ellis, B. J., & Symons, D. (1990). Sex difference in sexual fantasy: An evolutionary psychological approach. *Journal of Sex Research, 27,* 490–521.

Ellis, H. D. (1981). Theoretical aspects of face recognition. In G. H. Davies, H. D. Ellis, & J. Shepherd (Eds.), *Perceiving and remembering faces.* London: Academic Press.

Ellison, P. A., Govern, J. M., Petri, H. L., & Figler, M. H. (1995). Anonymity and aggressive driving behavior: A field study. *Journal of Social Behavior and Personality, 10,* 265–272.

Ellsworth, P. (1985, July). Juries on trial. *Psychology Today,* pp. 44–46.

Ellsworth, P. (1989, March 6). Supreme Court ignores social science research on capital punishment. Quoted by *Behavior Today,* pp. 7–8.

Ellsworth, P. C., & Mauro, R. (1998). Psychology and law. In D. Gilbert, S. T. Fiske, & G. Lindzey (Eds.), *Handbook of social psychology,* 4th edition. New York: McGraw-Hill.

Elms, A. C. (1995). Obedience in retrospect. *Journal of Social Issues,* **51,** 21–31.

Emmons, R. A., Larsen, R. J., Levine, S., & Diener, E. (1983). Factors predicting satisfaction judgments: A comparative examination. Paper presented at the Midwestern Psychological Association.

Emswiller, T., Deaux, K., & Willits, J. E. (1971). Similarity, sex, and requests for small favors. *Journal of Applied Social Psychology,* **1,** 284–291.

Eng, P. M., Kawachi, I., Fitzmaurice, G., & Rimm, E. B. (2001). Effects of marital transitions on changes in dietary and other health behaviors in men. Paper presented to the American Psychosomatic Society meeting.

Engemann, K. M., & Owyang, M. T. (2003, April). So much for that merit raise: The link between wages and appearance. *The Regional Economist* (www.stlouisfed.org).

Engs, R., & Hanson, D. J. (1989). Reactance theory: A test with collegiate drinking. *Psychological Reports,* **64,** 1083–1086.

Ennis, B. J., & Verrilli, D. B., Jr. (1989). Motion for leave to file brief amicus curiae and brief of Society for the Scientific Study of Religion, American Sociological Association, and others. U.S. Supreme Court Case No. 88–1600, Holy Spirit Association for the Unification of World Christianity, *et al.,* v. David Molko and Tracy Leal. On petition for writ of certiorari to the Supreme Court of California. Washington, DC: Jenner & Block, 21 Dupont Circle NW.

Ennis, R., & Zanna, M. P. (1991). Hockey assault: Constitutive versus normative violations. Paper presented at the Canadian Psychological Association convention.

Enzle, M. E., & Hawkins, W. L. (1992). A priori actor negligence mediates a posteriori outcome. *Journal of Experimental Social Psychology,* **28**(2), 169–185.

Epley, N., Akalis, S., Waytz, A., & Cacioppo, J. T. (2008). Creating social connection through inferential reproduction: Loneliness and perceived agency in gadgets, gods, and greyhounds. *Psychological Science,* **19,** 114–120.

Epley, N., & Dunning, D. (2006). The mixed blessings of self-knowledge in behavioral prediction: Enhanced discrimination but exacerbated bias. *Personality and Social Psychology Bulletin,* **32,** 641–655.

Epley, N., & Huff, C. (1998). Suspicion, affective response, and educational benefit as a result of deception in psychology research. *Personality and Social Psychology Bulletin,* **24,** 759–768.

Epley, N., Savitsky, K., & Kachelski, R. A. (1999, September/October). What every skeptic should know about subliminal persuasion. *Skeptical Inquirer,* pp. 40–45.

Epley, N., & Whitchurch, E. (2008). Mirror, mirror on the wall: Enhancement in self-recognition. *Personality and Social Psychology Bulletin,* **34,** 1159–1170.

Epstein, J. A., & Botvin, G. J. (2008). Media refusal skills and drug skill refusal techniques: What is their relationship with alcohol use among inner-city adolescents? *Addictive Behavior,* **33,** 528–537.

Epstein, R. (2007, February/March). The truth about online dating. *Scientific American Mind,* pp. 28–35.

Epstein, S. (1980). The stability of behavior: II. Implications for psychological research. *American Psychologist,* **35,** 790–806.

Epstude, K., & Roese, N. J. (2008). The functional theory of counterfactual thinking. *Personality and Social Psychology Review,* **12,** 168–192.

Erickson, B., Holmes, J. G., Frey, R., Walker, L., & Thibaut, J. (1974). Functions of a third party in the resolution of conflict: The role of a judge in pretrial conferences. *Journal of Personality and Social Psychology,* **30,** 296–306.

Erickson, B., Lind, E. A. Johnson, B. C., & O'Barr, W. M. (1978). Speech style and impression formation in a court setting: The effects of powerful and powerless speech. *Journal of Experimental Social Psychology,* **14,** 266–279.

Erikson, E. H. (1963). *Childhood and society.* New York: Norton.

Eron, L. D. (1987). The development of aggressive behavior from the perspective of a developing behaviorism. *American Psychologist,* **42,** 425–442.

Eron, L. D., & Huesmann, L. R. (1980). Adolescent aggression and television. *Annals of the New York Academy of Sciences,* **347,** 319–331.

Eron, L. D., & Huesmann, L. R. (1984). The control of aggressive behavior by changes in attitudes, values, and the conditions of learning. In R. J. Blanchard & C. Blanchard (Eds.), *Advances in the study of aggression* (Vol. 1). Orlando, FL: Academic Press.

Eron, L. D., & Huesmann, L. R. (1985). The role of television in the development of prosocial and antisocial behavior. In D. Olweus, M. Radke-Yarrow, and J. Block (Eds.), *Development of antisocial and prosocial behavior.* Orlando, FL: Academic Press.

Escobar-Chaves, S. L., & Anderson, C. A. (2008). Media and risky behaviors. *The Future of Children,* **18,** 147–180.

Escobar-Chaves, S. L., Tortolero, S. R., Markham, C. M., Low, B. J., Eitel, P., & Thickstun, P. (2005). Impact of the media on adolescent sexual attitudes and behaviors. *Pediatrics,* **116,** 303–326.

Esser, J. K. (1998, February–March). Alive and well after 25 years. A review of groupthink research. *Organizational Behavior and Human Decision Processes,* **73,** 116–141.

Esses, V. M., Haddock, G., & Zanna, M. P. (1993a). Values, stereotypes, and emotions as determinants of intergroup attitudes. In D. Mackie & D. Hamilton (Eds.), *Affect, cognition and stereotyping: Interactive processes in intergroup perception.* San Diego, CA: Academic Press.

Esses, V. M., Haddock, G., & Zanna, M. P. (1993b). The role of mood in the expression of intergroup stereotypes. In M. P. Zanna & J. M. Olson (Eds.), *The psychology of prejudice: The Ontario symposium* (Vol. 7). Hillsdale, NJ: Erlbaum.

Esses, V. M., Jackson, L. M., Dovidio, J. F., & Hodson, G. (2005). Instrumental relations among groups: Group competition, conflict, and prejudice. In J. F. Dovidio, P. Glick, & L. A. Rudman (Eds.), *On the nature of prejudice: Fifty years after Allport* (pp. 227–243). Malden, MA: Blackwell.

Esses, V. M., & Webster, C. D. (1988). Physical attractiveness, dangerousness, and the Canadian criminal code. *Journal of Applied Social Psychology,* **18,** 1017–1031.

Etaugh, C. E., Bridges, J. S., Cummings-Hill, M., & Cohen, J. (1999). "Names can never hurt me": The effects of surname use on perceptions of married women. *Psychology of Women Quarterly,* **23,** 819–823.

Etzioni, A. (1967). The Kennedy experiment. *The Western Political Quarterly,* **20,** 361–380.

Etzioni, A. (1991, May–June). The community in an age of individualism (interview). *The Futurist,* pp. 35–39.

Etzioni, A. (1993). *The spirit of community.* New York: Crown.

Etzioni, A. (1999). The monochrome society. *The Public Interest,* **137** (Fall), 42–55.

Etzioni, A. (2005). The diversity within unity platform. Washington, DC: The Communitarian Network.

Evans, G. W. (1979). Behavioral and physiological consequences of crowding in humans. *Journal of Applied Social Psychology, 9,* 27–46.

Evans, G. W., Lepore, S. J., & Allen, K. M. (2000). Cross-cultural differences in tolerance for crowding: Fact or fiction? *Journal of Personality and Social Psychology, 79,* 204–210.

Evans, G. W., Lepore, S. J., & Schroeder, A. (1996). The role of interior design elements in human responses to crowding. *Journal of Personality and Social Psychology, 70,* 41–46.

Evans, R. I., Smith, C. K., & Raines, B. E. (1984). Deterring cigarette smoking in adolescents: A psycho-social-behavioral analysis of an intervention strategy. In A. Baum, J. Singer, & S. Taylor (Eds.), *Handbook of psychology and health: Social psychological aspects of health* (Vol. 4). Hillsdale, NJ: Erlbaum.

Fabrigar, L. R., & Petty, R. E. (1999). The role of the affective and cognitive bases of attitudes in susceptibility to affectively and cognitively based persuasion. *Personality and Social Psychology Bulletin, 25,* 363–381.

Fairchild, H. H., & Cowan, G. (1997). The O. J. Simpson trial: Challenges to science and society. *Journal of Social Issues, 53,* 583–591.

Fallshore, M., & Schooler, J. W. (1995). Verbal vulnerability of perceptual expertise. *Journal of Experimental Psychology: Learning, Memory, and Cognition, 21,* 1608–1623.

Farquhar, J. W., Maccoby, N., Wood, P. D., Alexander, J. K., Breitrose, H., Brown, B. W., Jr., Haskell, W. L., McAlister, A. L., Meyer, A. J., Nash, J. D., & Stern, M. P. (1977, June 4). Community education for cardiovascular health. *Lancet,* 1192–1195.

Farrell, E. F. (2005, March 18). The battle for hearts and lungs. *Chronicle of Higher Education* (www.chronicle.com).

Farrelly, M. C., Davis, K. C., Duke, J., & Messeri, P. (2008, January 17). Sustaining "truth": Changes in youth tobacco attitudes and smoking intentions after three years of a national antismoking campaign. *Health Education Research* (doi:10.1093/her/cym087).

Farrelly, M. C., Healton, C. G., Davis, K. C., Messeri, P., Hersey, J. C., & Haviland, M. L. (2002). Getting to the truth: Evaluating national tobacco countermarketing campaigns. *American Journal of Public Health, 92,* 901–907.

Farris, C., Treat, T. A., Viken, R. J., & McFall, R. M. (2008). Perceptual mechanisms that characterize gender differences in decoding women's sexual intent. *Psychological Science, 19,* 348–354.

Farwell, L., & Weiner, B. (2000). Bleeding hearts and the heartless: Popular perceptions of liberal and conservative ideologies. *Personality and Social Psychology Bulletin, 26,* 845–852.

Faulkner, S. L., & Williams, K. D. (1996). A study of social loafing in industry. Paper presented to the Midwestern Psychological Association convention.

Faust, D., & Ziskin, J. (1988). The expert witness in psychology and psychiatry. *Science, 241,* 31–35.

Fazio, R. (1987). Self-perception theory: A current perspective. In M. P. Zanna, J. M. Olson, & C. P. Herman (Eds.), *Social influence: The Ontario symposium* (Vol. 5). Hillsdale, NJ: Erlbaum.

Fazio. R. H. (2007). Attitudes as object-evaluation associations of varying strength. *Social Cognition, 25,* 603–637.

Fazio, R. H., Effrein, E. A., & Falender, V. J. (1981). Self-perceptions following social interaction. *Journal of Personality and Social Psychology, 41,* 232–242.

Fazio, R. H., Zanna, M. P., & Cooper, J. (1977). Dissonance versus self-perception: An integrative view of each theory's proper domain of application. *Journal of Experimental Social Psychology, 13,* 464–479.

Fazio, R. H., Zanna, M. P., & Cooper, J. (1979). On the relationship of data to theory: A reply to Ronis and Greenwald. *Journal of Experimental Social Psychology, 15,* 70–76.

Feather, N. T. (2005). Social psychology in Australia: Past and present. *International Journal of Psychology, 40,* 263–276.

Federal Bureau of Investigation (FBI). (2008). *Murder offenders by age, sex, and race, 2008.* (Expanded Homicide Data Table 3).

Federal Bureau of Investigation (FBI). (2008). *Uniform crime reports for the United States.* Washington, DC: Federal Bureau of Investigation.

Federal Trade Commission (FTC). (2003, June 12). Federal Trade Commission cigarette report for 2001 (www.ftc.gov/opa/2003/06/2001cigrpt.htm).

Feeney, J. A. (1996). Attachment, caregiving, and marital satisfaction. *Personal Relationships, 3,* 401–416.

Feeney, J. A., & Noller, P. (1990). Attachment style as a predictor of adult romantic relationships. *Journal of Personality and Social Psychology, 58,* 281–291.

Feeney, J., Peterson, C., & Noller, P. (1994). Equity and marital satisfaction over the family life cycle. *Personality Relationships, 1,* 83–99.

Fein, S., Goethals, G. R., & Kugler, M. B. (2007). Social influence on political judgments: The case of presidential debates. *Political Psychology, 28,* 165–192.

Fein, S., & Hilton, J. L. (1992). Attitudes toward groups and behavioral intentions toward individual group members: The impact of nondiagnostic information. *Journal of Experimental Social Psychology, 28,* 101–124.

Fein, S., & Spencer, S. J. (1997). Prejudice as self-image maintenance: Affirming the self through derogating others. *Journal of Personality and Social Psychology, 73,* 31–44.

Feinberg, J. M., & Aiello, J. R. (2006). Social facilitation: A test of competing theories. *Journal of Applied Social Psychology, 36,* 1–23.

Feingold, A. (1988). Matching for attractiveness in romantic partners and same-sex friends: A meta-analysis and theoretical critique. *Psychological Bulletin, 104,* 226–235.

Feingold, A. (1990). Gender differences in effects of physical attractiveness on romantic attraction: A comparison across five research paradigms. *Journal of Personality and Social Psychology, 59,* 981–993.

Feingold, A. (1991). Sex differences in the effects of similarity and physical attractiveness on opposite-sex attraction. *Basic and Applied Social Psychology, 12,* 357–367.

Feingold, A. (1992a). Gender differences in mate selection preferences: A test of the parental investment model. *Psychological Bulletin, 112,* 125–139.

Feingold, A. (1992b). Good-looking people are not what we think. *Psychological Bulletin, 111,* 304–341.

Feldman, R. S., & Prohaska, T. (1979). The student as Pygmalion: Effect of student expectation on the teacher. *Journal of Educational Psychology, 71,* 485–493.

Feldman, R. S., & Theiss, A. J. (1982). The teacher and student as Pygmalions: Joint effects of teacher and student expectations. *Journal of Educational Psychology, 74,* 217–223.

Felson, R. B. (1984). The effect of self-appraisals of ability on academic performance. *Journal of Personality and Social Psychology, 47,* 944–952.

Felson, R. B. (2000). A social psychological approach to interpersonal aggression. In V. B. Van Hasselt & M. Hersen (Eds.), *Aggression and violence: An introductory text.* Boston: Allyn & Bacon.

Fenigstein, A. (1984). Self-consciousness and the overperception of self as a target. *Journal of Personality and Social Psychology, 47,* 860–870.

Fenigstein, A., & Carver, C. S. (1978). Self-focusing effects of heartbeat feedback. *Journal of Personality and Social Psychology, 36,* 1241–1250.

Fenigstein, A., & Vanable, P. A. (1992). Paranoia and self-consciousness. *Journal of Personality and Social Psychology, 62,* 129–138.

Ferguson, C. J., & Kilburn, J. (2009). The public health risks of media violence: A meta-analytic review. *Journal of Pediatrics,* **154**(5), 759–763.

Fergusson, D. M., Horwood, L. J., & Shannon, F. T. (1984). A proportional hazards model of family breakdown. *Journal of Marriage and the Family,* **46,** 539–549.

Feshbach, S. (1980). Television advertising and children: Policy issues and alternatives. Paper presented at the American Psychological Association convention.

Festinger, L. (1954). A theory of social comparison processes. *Human Relations,* **7,** 117–140.

Festinger, L. (1957). *A theory of cognitive dissonance.* Stanford: Stanford University Press.

Festinger, L. (1987). Reflections on cognitive dissonance theory: Thirty years later. Paper presented at the American Psychological Association convention.

Festinger, L., & Carlsmith, J. M. (1959). Cognitive consequences of forced compliance. *Journal of Abnormal and Social Psychology,* **58,** 203–210.

Festinger, L., & Maccoby, N. (1964). On resistance to persuasive communications. *Journal of Abnormal and Social Psychology,* **68,** 359–366.

Festinger, L., Pepitone, A., & Newcomb, T. (1952). Some consequences of deindividuation in a group. *Journal of Abnormal and Social Psychology,* **47,** 382–389.

Feynman, R. (1967). *The character of physical law.* Cambridge, MA: MIT Press.

Fichter, J. (1968). *America's forgotten priests: What are they saying?* New York: Harper.

Fiedler, F. E. (1987, September). When to lead, when to stand back. *Psychology Today,* pp. 26–27.

Fincham, F. D., & Bradbury, T. N. (1993). Marital satisfaction, depression, and attributions: A longitudinal analysis. *Journal of Personality and Social Psychology,* **64,** 442–452.

Finchilescu, G. (2005). Meta-stereotypes may hinder inter-racial contact. *South African Journal of Psychology,* **35,** 460-472.

Findley, M. J., & Cooper, H. M. (1983). Locus of control and academic achievement: A literature review. *Journal of Personality and Social Psychology,* **44,** 419–427.

Finkel, E. J., & Campbell, W. K. (2001). Self-control and accommodation in close relationships: An interdependence analysis. *Journal of Personality and Social Psychology,* **81,** 263–277.

Fischer, G. J. (1997). Gender effects on individual verdicts and on mock jury verdicts in a simulated acquaintance rape trial. *Sex Roles,* **36,** 491–501.

Fischer, K., Egerton, M., Gershuny, J. I., & Robinson, J. P. (2007). Gender convergence in the American Heritage Time Use Study (AHTUS). *Social Indicators Research,* **82,** 1–33.

Fischer, P., & Greitemeyer, T. (2006). Music and aggression: The impact of sexual-aggressive song lyrics on aggression-related thoughts, emotions, and behavior toward the same and the opposite sex. *Personality and Social Psychology Bulletin,* **32,** 1165–1176.

Fischer, R., & Chalmers, A. (2008). Is optimism universal? A meta-analytical investigation of optimism levels across 22 nations. *Personality and Individual Differences,* **45,** 378–382.

Fischhoff, B. (1982). Debiasing. In D. Kahneman, P. Slovic, & A. Tversky (Eds.), *Judgment under uncertainty: Heuristics and biases.* New York: Cambridge University Press.

Fischhoff, B., & Bar-Hillel, M. (1984). Diagnosticity and the base rate effect. *Memory and Cognition,* **12,** 402–410.

Fischtein, D. S., Herold, E. S., & Desmarais, S. (2007). How much does gender explain in sexual attitudes and behaviors? A survey of Canadian adults. *Archives of Sexual Behavior,* **36,** 451–461.

Fishbein, D., & Thelen, M. H. (1981a). Husband-wife similarity and marital satisfaction: A different approach. Paper presented at the Midwestern Psychological Association convention.

Fishbein, D., & Thelen, M. H. (1981b). Psychological factors in mate selection and marital satisfaction: A review (Ms. 2374). *Catalog of Selected Documents in Psychology,* **11,** 84.

Fishbein, M., & Ajzen, I. (1974). Attitudes toward objects as predictive of single and multiple behavioral criteria. *Psychological Review,* **81,** 59–74.

Fisher, H. (1994, April). The nature of romantic love. *Journal of NIH Research,* pp. 59–64.

Fisher, R. J. (1994). Generic principles for resolving intergroup conflict. *Journal of Social Issues,* **50,** 47–66.

Fisher, R. P., Geiselman, R. E., & Amador, M. (1989). Field test of the cognitive interview: Enhancing the recollection of actual victims and witnesses of crime. *Journal of Applied Psychology,* **74,** 722–727.

Fisher, R. P., Geiselman, R. E., & Raymond, D. S. (1987). Critical analysis of police interview techniques. *Journal of Police Science and Administration,* **15,** 177–185.

Fisher, R. P., McCauley, M. R., & Geiselman, R. E. (1994). Improving eyewitness testimony with the Cognitive Interview. In D. F. Ross, J. D. Read, & M. P. Toglia (Eds.), *Adult eyewitness testimony: Current trends and developments.* Cambridge, England: Cambridge University Press.

Fiske, A. P., Kitayama, S., Markus, H. R., & Nisbett, R. E. (1998). The cultural matrix of social psychology. In D. Gilbert, S. Fiske, and G. Lindzey (Eds.), *The handbook of social psychology,* 4th edition. Hillsdale, NJ: Erlbaum.

Fiske, S. T. (1989). Interdependence and stereotyping: From the laboratory to the Supreme Court (and back). Invited address, American Psychological Association convention.

Fiske, S. T. (1992). Thinking is for doing: Portraits of social cognition from daguerreotype to laserphoto. *Journal of Personality and Social Psychology,* **63,** 877–889.

Fiske, S. T. (1993). Controlling other people: The impact of power on stereotyping. *American Psychologist,* **48,** 621–628.

Fiske, S. T. (1999). Behind the scenes. In D. G. Myers, *Social psychology,* 6th edition. New York: McGraw-Hill.

Fiske, S. T. (2004). Mind the gap: In praise of informal sources of formal theory. *Personality and Social Psychology Review,* **8,** 132–137.

Fiske, S. T., Bersoff, D. N., Borgida, E., Deaux, K., & Heilman, M. E. (1991). Social science research on trial: The use of sex stereotyping research in Price Waterhouse *v.* Hopkins. *American Psychologist,* **46,** 1049–1060.

Fiske, S. T., Harris, L. T., & Cuddy, A. J. C. (2004). Why ordinary people torture enemy prisoners. *Science,* **306,** 1482–1483.

Fiske, S. T., Xu, J., Cuddy, A. C., & Glick, P. (1999). (Dis)respecting versus (Dis)liking: Status and interdependence predict ambivalent stereotypes of competence and warmth. *Journal of Social Issues,* **55,** 473–489.

Fitzpatrick, A. R., & Eagly, A. H. (1981). Anticipatory belief polarization as a function of the expertise of a discussion partner. *Personality and Social Psychology Bulletin,* **1,** 636–642.

Flay, B. R., Ryan, K. B., Best, J. A., Brown, K. S., Kersell, M. W., d'Avernas, J. R., & Zanna, M. P. (1985). Are social-psychological smoking prevention programs effective? The Waterloo study. *Journal of Behavioral Medicine,* **8,** 37–59.

Fleming, M. A., Wegener, D. T., & Petty, R. E. (1999). Procedural and legal motivations to correct for perceived judicial biases. *Journal of Experimental Social Psychology,* **35,** 186–203.

Fletcher, G. J. O., Danilovics, P., Fernandez, G., Peterson, D., & Reeder, G. D. (1986). Attributional complexity: An individual differences measure. *Journal of Personality and Social Psychology,* **51,** 875–884.

Fletcher, G. J. O., Fincham, F. D., Cramer, L., & Heron, N. (1987). The role of attributions in the development of dating relationships. *Journal of Personality and Social Psychology,* **53,** 481–489.

Fletcher, G. J. O., Simpson, J. A., Thomas, G., & Giles, L. (1999). Ideals in intimate relationships. *Journal of Personality and Social Psychology, 76,* 72–89.

Fletcher, G. J. O., Tither, J. M., O'Loughlin, C., Friesen, M., & Overall, N. (2004). Warm and homely or cold and beautiful? Sex differences in trading off traits in mate selection. *Personality and Social Psychology Bulletin, 30,* 659–672.

Fletcher, G. J. O., & Ward, C. (1989). Attribution theory and processes: A cross-cultural perspective. In M. H. Bond (Ed.), *The cross-cultural challenge to social psychology.* Newbury Park, CA: Sage.

Flood, M. (2007). Exposure to pornography among youth in Australia. *Journal of Sociology, 43,* 45–60.

Flynn, F. J., & Lake, V. K. B. (2008). If you need help, just ask: Underestimating compliance with direct requests for help. *Journal of Personality and Social Psychology, 95,* 128–143.

Foa, U. G., & Foa, E. B. (1975). *Resource theory of social exchange.* Morristown, NJ: General Learning Press.

Fogelman, E. (1994). *Conscience and courage: Rescuers of Jews during the Holocaust.* New York: Doubleday Anchor.

Foley, L. A. (1976). Personality and situational influences on changes in prejudice: A replication of Cook's railroad game in a prison setting. *Journal of Personality and Social Psychology, 34,* 846–856.

Follett, M. P. (1940). Constructive conflict. In H. C. Metcalf & L. Urwick (Eds.), *Dynamic administration: The collected papers of Mary Parker Follett.* New York: Harper.

Ford, R. (2008). Is racial prejudice declining in Britain? *British Journal of Sociology, 59,* 609–636.

Ford, T. E. (1997). Effects of stereotypical television portrayals of African-Americans on person perception. *Social Psychology Quarterly, 60,* 266–278.

Ford, T. E., Boxer, C. F., Armstrong, J., & Edel, J. R. (2008). More than "just a joke": The prejudice-releasing function of sexist humor. *Personality and Social Psychology Bulletin, 34,* 159–170.

Forgas, J. P. (1999). Behind the scenes. In D. G. Myers, *Social psychology,* 6th edition. New York: McGraw-Hill.

Forgas, J. P. (2007). When sad is better than happy: Negative affect can improve the quality and effectiveness of persuasive messages and social influence strategies. *Journal of Experimental Social Psychology, 43,* 513–528.

Forgas, J. P. (2008). Affect and cognition. *Perspectives on Psychological Science, 3,* 94–101.

Forgas, J. P., Bower, G. H., & Krantz, S. E. (1984). The influence of mood on perceptions of social interactions. *Journal of Experimental Social Psychology, 20,* 497–513.

Forgas, J. P., Dunn, E., & Granland, S. (2008). Are you being served . . . ? An unobtrusive experiment of affective influences on helping in a department store. *European Journal of Social Psychology, 38,* 333–342.

Forgas, J. P., & Moylan, S. (1987). After the movies: Transient mood and social judgments. *Personality and Social Psychology Bulletin, 13,* 467–477.

Form, W. H., & Nosow, S. (1958). *Community in disaster.* New York: Harper.

Forster, E. M. (1976). *Aspects of the novel* (Ed. O. Stallybrass). Harmondsworth: Penguin. (Original work published 1927.)

Forsyth, D. R., Kerr, N. A., Burnette, J. L., & Baumeister, R. F. (2007). Attempting to improve the academic performance of struggling college students by bolstering their self-esteem: An intervention that backfired. *Journal of Social and Clinical Psychology, 26,* 447–459.

Forsyth, D. R., & Leary, M. R. (1997). Achieving the goals of the scientist-practitioner model: The seven interfaces of social and counseling psychology. *The Counseling Psychologist, 25,* 180–200.

Foss, R. D. (1978). The role of social influence in blood donation. Paper presented at the American Psychological Association convention.

Foster, C. A., Witcher, B. S., Campbell, W. K., & Green, J. D. (1998). Arousal and attraction: Evidence for automatic and controlled processes. *Journal of Personality and Social Psychology, 74,* 86–101.

Fournier, R., & Tompson, T. (2008, September 20). Poll: Racial views steer some white Dems away from Obama. Associated Press via news.yahoo.com (data from www.knowledgenetworks.com survey for AP-Yahoo in partnership with Stanford University).

Fowler, J. H., & Christakis, N. A. (2008). Dynamic spread of happiness in a large social network: Longitudinal analysis over 20 years in the Framingham Heart Study. *British Medical Journal, 337* (doi: 10.1136/bmj.a2338).

Frank, J. D. (1974). *Persuasion and healing: A comparative study of psychotherapy.* New York: Schocken.

Frank, J. D. (1982). Therapeutic components shared by all psychotherapies. In J. H. Harvey & M. M. Parks (Eds.), *The master lecture series: Vol. 1. Psychotherapy research and behavior change.* Washington, DC: American Psychological Association.

Frank, R. (1999). *Luxury fever: Why money fails to satisfy in an era of excess.* New York: Free Press.

Frankel, A., & Snyder, M. L. (1987). Egotism among the depressed: When self-protection becomes self-handicapping. Paper presented at the American Psychological Association convention.

Franklin, B. J. (1974). Victim characteristics and helping behavior in a rural southern setting. *Journal of Social Psychology, 93,* 93–100.

Frantz, C. M. (2006). I AM being fair: The bias blind spot as a stumbling block to seeing both sides. *Basic and Applied Social Psychology, 28,* 157–167.

Frasure-Smith, N., & Lespérance, F. (2005). Depression and coronary heart disease: Complex synergism of mind, body, and environment. *Current Directions in Psychological Science, 14,* 39–43.

Frasure-Smith, N., Lesperance, F., Juneau, M., Talajic, M., & Bourassa, M. G. (1999). Gender, depression, and one-year prognosis after myocardial infarction. *Psychosomatic Medicine, 61,* 26–37.

Frasure-Smith, N., Lesperance, F., & Talajic, M. (1995). The impact of negative emotions on prognosis following myocardial infarction: Is it more than depression? *Health Psychology, 14,* 388–398.

Frederick, D. A., & Haselton, M. G. (2007). Why is muscularity sexy? Tests of the fitness indicator hypothesis. *Personality and Social Psychology Bulletin, 8,* 1167–1183.

Freedman, J. L., Birsky, J., & Cavoukian, A. (1980). Environmental determinants of behavioral contagion: Density and number. *Basic and Applied Social Psychology, 1,* 155–161.

Freedman, J. L., & Fraser, S. C. (1966). Compliance without pressure: The foot-in-the-door technique. *Journal of Personality and Social Psychology, 4,* 195–202.

Freedman, J. L., & Perlick, D. (1979). Crowding, contagion, and laughter. *Journal of Experimental Social Psychology, 15,* 295–303.

Freedman, J. L., & Sears, D. O. (1965). Warning, distraction, and resistance to influence. *Journal of Personality and Social Psychology, 1,* 262–266.

Freedman, J. S. (1965). Long-term behavioral effects of cognitive dissonance. *Journal of Experimental Social Psychology, 1,* 145–155.

Freeh, L. (1993, September 1). Inaugural address as FBI director.

Freeman, M. A. (1997). Demographic correlates of individualism and collectivism: A study of social values in Sri Lanka. *Journal of Cross-Cultural Psychology, 28,* 321–341.

French, J. R. P. (1968). The conceptualization and the measurement of mental health in terms of self-identity theory. In S. B. Sells (Ed.), *The definition and measurement of mental health*. Washington, DC: Department of Health, Education, and Welfare. (Cited by M. Rosenberg, 1979, *Conceiving the self*. New York: Basic Books.)

Freund, B., Colgrove, L. A., Burke, B. L., & McLeod, R. (2005). Self-rated driving performance among elderly drivers referred for driving evaluation. *Accident Analysis and Prevention, 37,* 613–618

Friedman, H. S., & DiMatteo, M. R. (1989). *Health psychology*. Englewood Cliffs, NJ: Prentice-Hall.

Friedman, H. S., Riggio, R. E., & Casella, D. F. (1988). Nonverbal skill, personal charisma, and initial attraction. *Personality and Social Psychology Bulletin, 14,* 203–211.

Friedman, R., & Elliot, A. J. (2008). The effect of arm crossing on persistence and performance. *European Journal of Social Psychology, 38,* 449–461.

Friedman, T. L. (2003, April 9). Hold your applause. *New York Times* (www.nytimes.com).

Friedman, T. L. (2003, June 4). Because we could. *New York Times* (www.nytimes.com).

Friedrich, J. (1996). On seeing oneself as less self-serving than others: The ultimate self-serving bias? *Teaching of Psychology, 23,* 107–109.

Friedrich, L. K., & Stein, A. H. (1973). Aggressive and prosocial television programs and the natural behavior of preschool children. *Monographs of the Society of Research in Child Development, 38* (4, Serial No. 151).

Friedrich, L. K., & Stein, A. H. (1975). Prosocial television and young children: The effects of verbal labeling and role playing on learning and behavior. *Child Development, 46,* 27–38.

Frieze, I. H., Olson, J. E., & Russell, J. (1991). Attractiveness and income for men and women in management. *Journal of Applied Social Psychology, 21,* 1039–1057.

Froming, W. J., Walker, G. R., & Lopyan, K. J. (1982). Public and private self-awareness: When personal attitudes conflict with societal expectations. *Journal of Experimental Social Psychology, 18,* 476–487.

Fuller, S. R., & Aldag, R. J. (1998). Organizational Tonypandy: Lessons from a quarter century of the groupthink phenomenon. *Organizational Behavior and Human Decision Processes, 73,* 163–185.

Fultz, J., Batson, C. D., Fortenbach, V. A., McCarthy, P. M., & Varney, L. L. (1986). Social evaluation and the empathy-altruism hypothesis. *Journal of Personality and Social Psychology, 50,* 761–769.

Funder, D. C. (1987). Errors and mistakes: Evaluating the accuracy of social judgment. *Psychological Bulletin, 101,* 75–90.

Furnham, A. (1982). Explanations for unemployment in Britain. *European Journal of Social Psychology, 12,* 335–352.

Furnham, A., & Gunter, B. (1984). Just world beliefs and attitudes towards the poor. *British Journal of Social Psychology, 23,* 265–269.

Gable, S. L., Gonzaga, G. C., & Strachman, A. (2006). Will you be there for me when things go right? Supportive responses to positive event disclosures. *Journal of Personality and Social Psychology, 91,* 904–917.

Gabrenya, W. K., Jr., Wang, Y.-E., & Latané, B. (1985). Social loafing on an optimizing task: Cross-cultural differences among Chinese and Americans. *Journal of Cross-Cultural Psychology, 16,* 223–242.

Gabriel, S., & Gardner, W. L. (1999). Are there "his" and "hers" types of interdependence? The implications of gender differences in collective versus relational interdependence for affect, behavior, and cognition. *Journal of Personality and Social Psychology, 77,* 642–655.

Gächter, S., Renner, E., & Sefton, M. (2008). The long-run benefits of punishment. *Science, 322,* 1510.

Gaebelein, J. W., & Mander, A. (1978). Consequences for targets of aggression as a function of aggressor and instigator roles: Three experiments. *Personality and Social Psychology Bulletin, 4,* 465–468.

Gaertner, L., Iuzzini, J., Witt, M. G., & Oriña, M. M. (2006). Us without them: Evidence for an intragroup origin of positive in-group regard. *Journal of Personality and Social Psychology, 90,* 426-439.

Gaertner, L., Sedikides, C., & Chang, K. (2008). On pancultural self-enhancement: Well-adjusted Taiwanese self-enhance on personally valued traits. *Journal of Cross-Cultural Psychology, 39,* 463–477.

Gaertner, L., Sedikides, C., & Graetz, K. (1999). In search of self-definition: Motivational primacy of the individual self, motivational primacy of the collective self, or contextual primacy? *Journal of Personality and Social Psychology, 76,* 5–18.

Gaertner, S. L. (1973). Helping behavior and racial discrimination among liberals and conservatives. *Journal of Personality and Social Psychology, 25,* 335–341.

Gaertner, S. L. (1975). The role of racial attitudes in helping behavior. *Journal of Social Psychology, 97,* 95–101.

Gaertner, S. L., & Bickman, L. (1971). Effects of race on the elicitation of helping behavior. *Journal of Personality and Social Psychology, 20,* 218–222.

Gaertner, S. L., & Dovidio, J. F. (1977). The subtlety of white racism, arousal, and helping behavior. *Journal of Personality and Social Psychology, 35,* 691–707.

Gaertner, S. L., & Dovidio, J. F. (1986). The aversive form of racism. In J. F. Dovidio & S. L. Gaertner (Eds.), *Prejudice, discrimination, and racism.* Orlando, FL: Academic Press.

Gaertner, S. L., & Dovidio, J. F. (2005). Understanding and addressing contemporary racism: From aversive racism to the Common Ingroup Identity Model. *Journal of Social Issues, 61,* 615–639.

Gaertner, S. L., Dovidio, J. F., Nier, J. A., Banker, B. S., Ward, C. M., Houlette, M., & Loux, S. (2000). The common ingroup identity model for reducing intergroup bias: Progress and challenges. In D. Capozza & R. Brown (Eds.), *Social identity processes: Trends in theory and research.* London: Sage.

Gaertner, S. L., Mann, J., Murrell, A., & Dovidio, J. F. (2001). Reducing intergroup bias: The benefits of recategorization. In M. A. Hogg & D. Abrams (Eds.), *Intergroup relations: Essential readings.* Philadelphia: Psychology Press.

Gailliot, M. T. (2008). Unlocking the energy dynamics of executive function: Linking executive functioning to brain glycogen. *Perspectives on Psychological Science, 3,* 245–263.

Gailliot, M. T., & Baumeister, R. F. (2007). Self-regulation and sexual restraint. Dispositionally and temporarily poor self-regulatory abilities contribute to failures at restraining sexual behavior. *Personality and Social Psychology Bulletin, 33,* 173–186.

Galanter, M. (1989). *Cults: Faith, healing, and coercion.* New York: Oxford University Press.

Galanter, M. (1990). Cults and zealous self-help movements: A psychiatric perspective. *American Journal of Psychiatry, 147,* 543–551.

Galinsky, A. D., & Moskowitz, G. B. (2000). Perspective-taking: Decreasing stereotype expression, stereotype accessibility, and in-group favoritism. *Journal of Personality and Social Psychology, 78,* 708–724.

Galizio, M., & Hendrick, C. (1972). Effect of musical accompaniment on attitude: The guitar as a prop for persuasion. *Journal of Applied Social Psychology, 2,* 350–359.

Gallo, L. C., & Matthews, K. A. (2003). Understanding the association between socioeconomic status and physical health: Do negative emotions play a role? *Psychological Bulletin, 129,* 10–51.

Gallup. (1996). Gallup survey of scientists sampled from the 1995 edition of *American Men and Women of Science*. Reported by National Center for Science Education (www.ncseweb.org).

Gallup. (2005). The gender gap (Iraq war survey, April 29 to May 1; death penalty survey, May 2 to May 5). Gallup Organization (www.gallup.com).

Gallup News. (2007, October 4). Scientists assess global well-being. Gallup Organization (www.gallup.com/poll).

Gallup Organization. (1990). April 19–22 survey reported in *American Enterprise*, September/October 1990, p. 92.

Gallup Organization. (2003, June 10). American public opinion about Iraq. Gallup Poll News Service (www.gallup.com/poll/focus/sr030610.asp).

Gallup Organization. (2003, July 8). American public opinion about Iraq. Gallup Poll News Service (www.gallup.com).

Gallup Poll. (1990, July). Reported by G. Gallup, Jr., & F. Newport, Americans widely disagree on what constitutes "rich." *Gallup Poll Monthly*, pp. 28–36.

Gallup, G. H. (1972). *The Gallup poll: Public opinion 1935–1971* (Vol. 3, pp. 551, 1716). New York: Random House.

Gallup, G. H., Jr., & Jones, T. (1992). *The saints among us*. Harrisburg, PA: Morehouse.

Gallup, G. H., Jr., & Lindsay, D. M. (1999). *Surveying the religious landscape: Trends in U.S. beliefs*. Harrisburg, PA: Morehouse.

Gangestad, S. W., Simpson, J. A., & Cousins, A. J. (2004). Women's preferences for male behavioral displays change across the menstrual cycle. *Psychological Science, 15*, 203–207.

Gangestad, S. W., & Snyder, M. (2000). Self-monitoring: Appraisal and reappraisal. *Psychological Bulletin, 126*, 530–555.

Gangestad, S. W., & Thornhill, R. (1997). Human sexual selection and developmental stability. In J. A. Simpson & D. T. Kenrick (Eds.), *Evolutionary social psychology*. Mahwah, NJ: Erlbaum.

Garb, H. N. (1994). Judgment research: Implications for clinical practice and testimony in court. *Applied and Preventive Psychology, 3*, 173–183.

Garb, H. N. (2005). Clinical judgment and decision making. *Annual Review of Clinical Psychology, 1*, 67–89.

Garcia-Marques, T., Mackie, D. M., Claypool, H. M., & Garcia-Marques, L. (2004). Positivity can cue familiarity. *Personality and Social Psychology Bulletin, 30*, 585–593.

Gardner, G., & Assadourian, E. (2004). Rethinking the good life. Chapter 8 in *State of the World 2004*. Washington, DC: WorldWatch Institute.

Gardner, M. (1997, July/August). Heaven's Gate: The UFO cult of Bo and Peep. *Skeptical Inquirer*, pp. 15–17.

Gardner, W. L., Pickett, L., Jefferis, V., & Knowles, M. (2005). On the outside looking in: Loneliness and social monitoring. *Personality and Social Psychology Bulletin, 31*, 1549–1560.

Garry, M., Manning, C. G., Loftus, E. F., & Sherman, S. J. (1996). Imagination inflation: Imagining a childhood event inflates confidence that it occurred. *Psychonomic Bulletin & Review, 3*, 208–214.

Garver-Apgar, C. E., Gangestad, S. W., Thornhill, R., Miller, R. D., & Olp, J. J. (2006). Major histocompatibility complex alleles, sexual responsivity, and unfaithfulness in romantic couples. *Psychological Science, 17*, 830–834.

Gastorf, J. W., Suls, J., & Sanders, G. S. (1980). Type A coronary-prone behavior pattern and social facilitation. *Journal of Personality and Social Psychology, 8*, 773–780.

Gates, M. F., & Allee, W. C. (1933). Conditioned behavior of isolated and grouped cockroaches on a simple maze. *Journal of Comparative Psychology, 15*, 331–358.

Gaunt, R. (2006). Couple similarity and marital satisfaction: Are similar spouses happier? *Journal of Personality, 74*, 1401–1420.

Gavanski, I., & Hoffman, C. (1987). Awareness of influences on one's own judgments: The roles of covariation detection and attention to the judgment process. *Journal of Personality and Social Psychology, 52*, 453–463.

Gavzer, B. (1997, January 5). Are trial consultants good for justice? *Parade*, p. 20.

Gawande, A. (2002). *Complications: A surgeon's notes on an imperfect science*. New York: Metropolitan Books, Holt.

Gawronski, B., & Bodenhausen, G. V. (2006). Associative and propositional processes in evaluation: An integrative review of implicit and explicit attitude change. *Psychological Bulletin, 132*, 692–731.

Gayoso, A., Cutler, B. L., & Moran, G. (1991). Assessing the value of social scientists as trial consultants: A consumer research approach. Unpublished manuscript, Florida International University.

Gazzaniga, M. S. (1985). *The social brain: Discovering the networks of the mind*. New York: Basic Books.

Gazzaniga, M. S. (1992). *Nature's mind: The biological roots of thinking, emotions, sexuality, language, and intelligence*. New York: Basic Books.

Gazzaniga, M. (1998). *The mind's past*. Berkeley, CA: University of California Press.

Gazzaniga, M. (2008). *Human: The science behind what makes us unique*. New York: Ecco.

Gebauer, J. E., Riketta, M., Broemer, P., & Maio, G. R. (2008). "How much do you like your name?" An implicit measure of global self-esteem. *Journal of Experimental Social Psychology, 44*, 1346–1354.

Geen, R. G. (1998). Aggression and antisocial behavior. In D. Gilbert, S. Fiske, & G. Lindzey (Eds.), *Handbook of social psychology*, 4th edition. New York: McGraw-Hill.

Geen, R. G., & Gange, J. J. (1983). Social facilitation: Drive theory and beyond. In H. H. Blumberg, A. P. Hare, V. Kent, & M. Davies (Eds.), *Small groups and social interaction* (Vol. 1). London: Wiley.

Geen, R. G., & Quanty, M. B. (1977). The catharsis of aggression: An evaluation of a hypothesis. In L. Berkowitz (Ed.), *Advances in experimental social psychology* (Vol. 10). New York: Academic Press.

Geen, R. G., & Thomas, S. L. (1986). The immediate effects of media violence on behavior. *Journal of Social Issues, 42*(3), 7–28.

Geers, A. L., Handley, I. M., & McLarney, A. R. (2003). Discerning the role of optimism in persuasion: The valence-enhancement hypothesis. *Journal of Personality and Social Psychology, 85*, 554–565.

Geiselman, R. E. (1996, May 14). On the use and efficacy of the cognitive interview: Commentary on Memon & Stevenage on witness memory. *Psychology.96.7.11.witness-memory.2.geiselman* (from psyc@phoenix.princeton.edu@ukacr1.bitnet).

Gentile, B. C., Twenge, J. M., & Campbell, W. K. (2009). Birth cohort differences in self-esteem, 1988–2008: A cross-temporal meta-analysis. Unpublished manuscript.

Gentile, D. A. (2004, May 14). Quoted by K. Laurie in *Violent games* (ScienCentral.com).

Gentile, D. A., & Anderson, C. A. (2003). Violent video games: The newest media violence hazard. In D. A. Gentile (Ed.), *Media violence and children*. Westport, CT: Ablex.

Gentile, D. A., Anderson, C. A., Yukawa, S., Ihori, N., Saleem, M., Ming, L. K., Shiuya, A., Liau, A. K., Khoo, A., Bushman, B. J., Buesmann, L. R., & Sakamoto, A. (2009). The effects of prosocial video games on prosocial behaviors: International evidence from correlational, longitudinal, and experimental studies. *Personality* *and Social Psychology Bulletin*, **35**, 752–763.

Gentile, D. A., Lynch, P. J., Linder, J. R., & Walsh, D. A. (2004). The effects of violent video game habits on adolescent hostility, aggressive behaviors, and school performance. *Journal of Adolescence*, **27**, 5–22.

Gentile, D. A., Saleem, M., & Anderson, C. A. (2007). Public policy and the effects of media violence on children. *Social Issues and Policy Review*, **1**, 15–61.

George, D., Carroll, P., Kersnick, R., & Calderon, K. (1998). Gender-related patterns of helping among friends. *Psychology of Women Quarterly*, **22**, 685–704.

Gerard, H. B. (1999). A social psychologist examines his past and looks to the future. In A. Rodrigues & R. Levine (Eds.), *Reflections on 100 years of experimental social psychology*. New York: Basic Books.

Gerard, H. B., & Mathewson, G. C. (1966). The effects of severity of initiation on liking for a group: A replication. *Journal of Experimental Social Psychology*, **2**, 278–287.

Gerard, H. B., Wilhelmy, R. A., & Conolley, E. S. (1968). Conformity and group size. *Journal of Personality and Social Psychology*, **8**, 79–82.

Gerbasi, K. C., Zuckerman, M., & Reis, H. T. (1977). Justice needs a new blindfold: A review of mock jury research. *Psychological Bulletin*, **84**, 323–345.

Gerbner, G. (1994). The politics of media violence: Some reflections. In C. Hamelink & O. Linne (Eds.), *Mass communication research: On problems and policies*. Norwood, NJ: Ablex.

Gerbner, G., Gross, L., Signorielli, N., Morgan, M., & Jackson-Beeck, M. (1979). The demonstration of power: Violence profile No. 10. *Journal of Communication*, **29**, 177–196.

Gergen, K. E. (1982). *Toward transformation in social knowledge*. New York: Springer-Verlag.

Gerrig, R. J., & Prentice, D. A. (1991, September). The representation of fictional information. *Psychological Science*, **2**, 336–340.

Gerstenfeld, P. B., Grant, D. R., & Chiang, C-P. (2003). Hate online: A content analysis of extremist Internet sites. *Analyses of Social Issues and Public Policy*, **3**, 29–44.

Giancola, P. R., & Corman, M. D. (2007). Alcohol and aggression: A test of the attention-allocation model. *Psychological Science*, **18**, 649–655.

Gibbons, F. X. (1978). Sexual standards and reactions to pornography: Enhancing behavioral consistency through self-focused attention. *Journal of Personality and Social Psychology*, **36**, 976–987.

Gibbons, F. X., & Wicklund, R. A. (1982). Self-focused attention and helping behavior. *Journal of Personality and Social Psychology*, **43**, 462–474.

Gibson, B., & Sanbonmatsu, D. M. (2004). Optimism, pessimism, and gambling: The downside of optimism. *Personality and Social Psychology Bulletin*, **30**, 149–160.

Gifford, R., & Hine, D. W. (1997). Toward cooperation in commons dilemmas. *Canadian Journal of Behavioural Science*, **29**, 167 179.

Gigerenzer, G. (2004). Dread risk, September 11, and fatal traffic accidents. *Psychological Science*, **15**, 286–287.

Gigerenzer, G. (2007). *Gut feelings: The intelligence of the unconscious*. New York: Viking.

Gigone, D., & Hastie, R. (1993). The common knowledge effect: Information sharing and group judgment. *Journal of Personality and Social Psychology*, **65**, 959–974.

Gilbert, D. (2007). *Stumbling on happiness*. New York: Knopf.

Gilbert, D. T., & Ebert, J. E. J. (2002). Decisions and revisions: The affective forecasting of escapable outcomes. Unpublished manuscript, Harvard University.

Gilbert, D. T., Giesler, R. B., & Morris, K. A. (1995). When comparisons arise. *Journal of Personality and Social Psychology*, **69**, 227–236.

Gilbert, D. T., & Hixon, J. G. (1991). The trouble of thinking: Activation and application of stereotypic beliefs. *Journal of Personality and Social Psychology*, **60**, 509–517.

Gilbert, D. T., & Jones, E. E. (1986). Perceiver-induced constraint: Interpretations of self-generated reality. *Journal of Personality and Social Psychology*, **50**, 269–280.

Gilbert, D. T., Krull, D. S., & Malone, P. S. (1990). Unbelieving the unbelievable: Some problems in the rejection of false information. *Journal of Personality and Social Psychology*, **59**, 601–613.

Gilbert, D. T., Lieberman, M. D., Morewedge, C. K., & Wilson, T. D. (2004). The peculiar longevity of things not so bad. *Psychological Science*, **15**, 14–19.

Gilbert, D. T., & Malone, P. S. (1995). The correspondence bias. *Psychological Bulletin*, **117**, 21–38.

Gilbert, D. T., Pinel, E. C., Wilson, T. D., Blumberg, S. J., & Wheatley, T. P. (1998). Immune neglect: A source of durability bias in affective forecasting. *Journal of Personality and Social Psychology*, **75**, 617–638.

Gilbert, D. T., Tafarodi, R. W., & Malone, P. S. (1993). You can't not believe everything you read. *Journal of Personality and Social Psychology*, **65**, 221–233.

Gilbert, D. T., & Wilson, T. D. (2000). Miswanting: Some problems in the forecasting of future affective states. In J. Forgas (Ed.), *Feeling and thinking: The role of affect in social cognition*. Cambridge, England: Cambridge University Press.

Gillath, O. M., Shaver, P. R., Baek, J-M., & Chun, D. S. (2008). Genetic correlates of adult attachment. *Personality and Social Psychology Bulletin*, **34**, 1396–1405.

Gillham, J. E., Shatte, A. J., Reivich, K. J., & Seligman, M. E. P. (2000). Optimism, pessimism, and explanatory style. In E. C. Chang (Ed.), *Optimism and pessimism*. Washington, DC: APA Books.

Gilligan, C. (1982). *In a different voice: Psychological theory and women's development*. Cambridge, MA: Harvard University Press.

Gilligan, C., Lyons, N. P., & Hanmer, T. J. (Eds.) (1990). *Making connections: The relational worlds of adolescent girls at Emma Willard School*. Cambridge, MA: Harvard University Press.

Gillis, J. S., & Avis, W. E. (1980). The male-taller norm in mate selection. *Personality and Social Psychology Bulletin*, **6**, 396–401.

Gilovich, T., & Douglas, C. (1986). Biased evaluations of randomly determined gambling outcomes. *Journal of Experimental Social Psychology*, **22**, 228–241.

Gilovich, T., & Eibach, R. (2001). The fundamental attribution error where it really counts. *Psychological Inquiry*, **12**, 23–26.

Gilovich, T., Kerr, M., & Medvec, V. H. (1993). Effect of temporal perspective on subjective confidence. *Journal of Personality and Social Psychology*, **64**, 552–560.

Gilovich, T., & Medvec, V. H. (1994). The temporal pattern to the experience of regret. *Journal of Personality and Social Psychology*, **67**, 357–365.

Gilovich, T., Medvec, V. H., & Savitsky, K. (2000). The spotlight effect in social judgment: An egocentric bias in estimates of the salience of one's own actions and appearance. *Journal of Personality and Social Psychology*, **78**, 211–222.

Gilovich, T., Savitsky, K., & Medvec, V. H. (1998). The illusion of transparency: Biased assessments of others' ability to read one's emotional states. *Journal of Personality and Social Psychology*, **75**, 332–346.

Giltay, E. J., Geleijnse, J. M., Zitman, F. G., Buijsse, B., & Kromhout, D. (2007). Lifestyle and dietary correlates of dispositional optimism in men: The Zutphen Elderly Study. *Journal of Psychosomatic Research*, **63**, 483–490.

Giltay, E. J., Geleijnse, J. M., Zitman, F. G., Hoekstra, T., & Schouten, E. G. (2004). Dispositional optimism and all-cause and cardiovascular mortality in a prospective cohort of elderly Dutch men and women. *Archives of General Psychiatry, 61,* 1126–1135.

Ginsburg, B., & Allee, W. C. (1942). Some effects of conditioning on social dominance and subordination in inbred strains of mice. *Physiological Zoology, 15,* 485–506.

Gladwell, M. (2003, March 10). Connecting the dots: The paradoxes of intelligence reform. *New Yorker,* pp. 83–88.

Glasman, L. R., & Albarracin, D. (2006). Forming attitudes that predict future behavior: A meta-analysis of the attitude-behavior relation. *Psychological Bulletin, 132,* 778–822.

Glass, D. C. (1964). Changes in liking as a means of reducing cognitive discrepancies between self-esteem and aggression. *Journal of Personality, 32,* 531–549.

Gleason, M. E. J., Iida, M., Bolger, N., & Shrout, P. E. (2003). Daily supportive equity in close relationships. *Personality and Social Psychology Bulletin, 29,* 1036–1045.

Glick, P., & others. (2004). Bad but bold: Ambivalent attitudes toward men predict gender inequality in 16 nations. *Journal of Personality and Social Psychology, 86,* 713–728.

Glick, P., & Fiske, S. T. (1996). The ambivalent sexism inventory: Differentiating hostile and benevolent sexism. *Journal of Personality and Social Psychology, 70,* 491–512.

Glick, P., & Fiske, S. T. (2007). Sex discrimination: The psychological approach. In F. J. Crosby, M. S. Stockdale, & S. Ropp (Eds.), *Sex discrimination in the workplace: Multidisciplinary perspectives.* Malden, MA: Blackwell.

Gockel, C., Kerr, N. L., Seok, D-H., & Harris, D. W. (2008). Indispensability and group identification as sources of task motivation. *Journal of Experimental Social Psychology, 44,* 1316–1321.

Goethals, G. R., Messick, D. M., & Allison, S. T. (1991). The uniqueness bias: Studies of constructive social comparison. In J. Suls & T. A. Wills (Eds.), *Social comparison: Contemporary theory and research.* Hillsdale, NJ: Erlbaum.

Goethals, G. R., & Nelson, E. R. (1973). Similarity in the influence process: The belief-value distinction. *Journal of Personality and Social Psychology, 25,* 117–122.

Goggin, W. C., & Range, L. M. (1985). The disadvantages of hindsight in the perception of suicide. *Journal of Social and Clinical Psychology, 3,* 232–237.

Goh, J. O., Chee, M. W., Tan, J. C., Venkatraman, V., Hebrank, A., Leshikar, E. D., Jenkins, L., Sutton, B. P., Gutchess, A. H., & Park, D. C. (2007). Age and culture modulate object processing and object-science binding in the ventral visual area. *Cognitive, Affective & Behavioral Neuroscience, 7,* 44–52.

Goldhagen, D. J. (1996). *Hitler's willing executioners.* New York: Knopf.

Goldman, W., & Lewis, P. (1977). Beautiful is good: Evidence that the physically attractive are more socially skillful. *Journal of Experimental Social Psychology, 13,* 125–130.

Goldsmith, C. (2003, March 25). World media turn wary eye on U.S. *Wall Street Journal,* p. A12.

Goldstein, A. P. (1994). Delinquent gangs. In A. P. Goldstein, B. Harootunian, and J. C. Conoley (Eds.), *Student aggression: Prevention, control, and replacement.* New York: Guilford.

Goldstein, A. P., Glick, B., & Gibbs, J. C. (1998). Aggression replacement training: A comprehensive intervention for aggressive youth (rev. ed.). Champaign, IL: Research Press.

Goldstein, J. H., & Arms, R. L. (1971). Effects of observing athletic contests on hostility. *Sociometry, 34,* 83–90.

Gonsalkorale, K., & Williams, K. D. (2006). The KKK would not let me play: Ostracism even by a despised outgroup hurts. *European Journal of Social Psychology, 36,* 1–11.

Gonsalves, B., Reber, P. J., Gitelman, D. R., Parrish, T. B., Mesulam, M-M., & Paller, K. A. (2004). Neural evidence that vivid imagining can lead to false remembering. *Psychological Science, 15,* 655–659.

Gonzaga, G. C., Campos, B., & Bradbury, T. (2007). Similarity, convergence, and relationship satisfaction in dating and married couples. *Journal of Personality and Social Psychology, 93,* 34–48.

Gonzaga, G., Keltner, D., Londahl, E. A., & Smith, M. D. (2001). Love and the commitment problem in romantic relations and friendship. *Journal of Personality and Social Psychology, 81,* 247–262.

Gonzalez, A. Q., & Koestner, R. (2005). Parental preference for sex of newborn as reflected in positive affect in birth announcements. *Sex Roles, 52,* 407–411.

González-Vallejo, C., Lassiter, G. D., Bellezza, F. S., & Lindberg, M. J. (2008). "Save angels perhaps": A critical examination of unconscious thought theory and the deliberation-without-attention effect. *Review of General Psychology, 12,* 282–296.

Goodhart, D. E. (1986). The effects of positive and negative thinking on performance in an achievement situation. *Journal of Personality and Social Psychology, 51,* 117–124.

Gordijn, E. H., & Stapel, D. A. (2008). When controversial leaders with charisma are effective: The influence of terror on the need for vision and impact of mixed attitudinal messages. *European Journal of Social Psychology, 38,* 389–411.

Gordijn, E. H., De Vries, N. K., & De Dreu, C. K. W. (2002). Minority influence on focal and related attitudes: Change in size, attributions and information processing. *Personality and Social Psychology Bulletin, 28,* 1315–1326.

Gordon, R. A. (1996). Impact of ingratiation on judgments and evaluations: A meta-analytic investigation. *Journal of Personality and Social Psychology, 71,* 54–70.

Gore, A. (2007, July 1). Moving beyond Kyoto. *New York Times* (www.nytimes.com).

Gortmaker, S. L., Must, A., Perrin, J. M., Sobol, A. M., & Dietz, W. H. (1993). Social and economic consequences of overweight in adolescence and young adulthood. *New England Journal of Medicine, 329,* 1008–1012.

Gotlib, I. H., & Colby, C. A. (1988). How to have a good quarrel. In P. Marsh (Ed.), *Eye to eye: How people interact.* Topsfield, MA: Salem House.

Gottlieb, J., & Carver, C. S. (1980). Anticipation of future interaction and the bystander effect. *Journal of Experimental Social Psychology, 16,* 253–260.

Gottman, J. (with N. Silver). (1994). *Why marriages succeed or fail.* New York: Simon & Schuster.

Gottman, J. M. (1998). Psychology and the study of marital processes. *Annual Review of Psychology, 49,* 169–197.

Gough, H. G., & Thorne, A. (1986). Positive, negative, and balanced shyness. In W. H. Jones, J. M. Cheek, & S. R. Briggs (Eds.), *Shyness: Perspectives on research and treatment.* New York: Plenum.

Gough, S. (2003, November 3). My journey so far (www.nakedwalk.alivewww.co.uk/about_me.htm).

Gould, M. S., & Shaffer, D. (1986). The impact of suicide in television movies: Evidence of imitation. *New England Journal of Medicine, 315,* 690–694.

Gould, S. J. (1988, July). Kropotkin was no crackpot. *Natural History,* pp. 12–21.

Gouldner, A. W. (1960). The norm of reciprocity: A preliminary statement. *American Sociological Review, 25,* 161–178.

Gove, W. R., Style, C. B., & Hughes, M. (1990). The effect of marriage on the well-being of adults: A theoretical analysis. *Journal of Family Issues, 11,* 4–35.

Granberg, D., & Bartels, B. (2005). On being a lone dissenter. *Journal of Applied Social Psychology, 35*, 1849–1858.

Granstrom, K., & Stiwne, D. (1998). A bipolar model of groupthink: An expansion of Janis's concept. *Small Group Research, 29*, 32–56.

Gray, C., Russell, P., & Blockley, S. (1991). The effects upon helping behaviour of wearing pro-gay identification. *British Journal of Social Psychology, 30*, 171–178.

Gray, J. D., & Silver, R. C. (1990). Opposite sides of the same coin: Former spouses' divergent perspectives in coping with their divorce. *Journal of Personality and Social Psychology, 59*, 1180–1191.

Graziano, W. G., Jensen-Campbell, L. A., & Finch, J. F. (1997). The self as a mediator between personality and adjustment. *Journal of Personality and Social Psychology, 73*, 392–404.

Greeley, A. M. (1991). *Faithful attraction.* New York: Tor Books.

Greeley, A. M., & Sheatsley, P. B. (1971). Attitudes toward racial integration. *Scientific American, 225*(6), 13–19.

Green, A. R., Carney, D. R., Pallin, D. J., Ngo, L. H., Raymond, K. L., Iezzoni, L. I., & Banaji, M. R. (2007). Implicit bias among physicians and its prediction of thrombolysis decisions for Black and White patients. *Journal of General Internal Medicine, 22*, 1231–1238.

Green, C. W., Adams, A. M., & Turner, C. W. (1988). Development and validation of the school interracial climate scale. *American Journal of Community Psychology, 16*, 241–259.

Green, D. P., Glaser, J., & Rich, A. (1998). From lynching to gay bashing: The elusive connection between economic conditions and hate crime. *Journal of Personality and Social Psychology, 75*, 82–92.

Green, D. P., & Wong, J. S. (2008). Tolerance and the contact hypothesis: A field experiment. In E. Borgida (Ed.), *The political psychology of democratic citizenship.* London: Oxford University Press.

Green, M. C., Strange, J. J., & Brock, T. C. (Eds.). (2002). *Narrative impact: Social and cognitive foundations.* Mahwah, NJ: Erlbaum.

Greenberg, J. (1986). Differential intolerance for inequity from organizational and individual agents. *Journal of Applied Social Psychology, 16*, 191–196.

Greenberg, J. (2008). Understanding the vital human quest for self-esteem. *Perspectives on Psychological Science, 3*, 48–55.

Greenberg, J., Landau, M. J., Kosloff, S., & Solomon, S. (2008). How our dreams of death transcendence breed prejudice, stereotyping, and conflict. In T. Nelson (Ed.), *Handbook of prejudice, stereotyping, and discrimination.* New York: Psychology Press.

Greenberg, J., Pyszczynski, T., Burling, J., & Tibbs, K. (1992). Depression, self-focused attention, and the self-serving attributional bias. *Personality and Individual Differences, 13*, 959–965.

Greenberg, J., Pyszczynski, T., Solomon, S., Rosenblatt, A., Veeder, M., Kirkland, S., & Lyon, D. (1990). Evidence for terror management theory II: The effects of mortality salience on reactions to those who threaten or bolster the cultural worldview. *Journal of Personality and Social Psychology, 58*, 308–318.

Greenberg, J., Pyszczynski, T., Solomon, S., Simon, L., & Breus, M. (1994). Role of consciousness and accessibility of death-related thoughts in mortality salience effects. *Journal of Personality and Social Psychology, 67*, 627–637.

Greenberg, J., Schimel, J., Martens, A., Solomon, S., & Pyszczynski, T. (2001). Sympathy for the devil: Evidence that reminding whites of their mortality promotes more favorable reactions to white racists. *Motivation and Emotion, 25*, 113–133.

Greenberg, J., Solomon, S., & Pyszczynski, T. (1997). Terror management theory of self-esteem and cultural worldviews: Empirical assessments and conceptual refinements. *Advances in Experimental Social Psychology, 29*, 61–142.

Greenwald, A. G. (1975). On the inconclusiveness of crucial cognitive tests of dissonance versus self-perception theories. *Journal of Experimental Social Psychology, 11*, 490–499.

Greenwald, A. G. (1980). The totalitarian ego: Fabrication and revision of personal history. *American Psychologist, 35*, 603–618.

Greenwald, A. G. (1992). New look 3: Unconscious cognition reclaimed. *American Psychologist, 47*, 766–779.

Greenwald, A. G., & Banaji, M. R. (1995). Implicit social cognition: Attitudes, self-esteem, and stereotypes. *Psychological Review, 102*, 4–27.

Greenwald, A. G., Banaji, M. R., Rudman, L. A., Farnham, S. D., Nosek, B. A., & Mellott, D. S. (2002). A unified theory of implicit attitudes, stereotypes, self-esteem, and self-concept. *Psychological Bulletin, 109*, 3–25.

Greenwald, A. G., Banaji, M. R., Rudman, L. A., Farnham, S. D., Nosek, B. A., & Rosier, M. (2000). Prologue to a unified theory of attitudes, stereotypes, and self-concept. In J. P. Forgas (Ed.), *Feeling and thinking: The role of affect in social cognition and behavior.* New York: Cambridge University Press.

Greenwald, A. G., McGhee, D. E., & Schwartz, J. L. K. (1998). Measuring individual differences in implicit cognition: The implicit association test. *Journal of Personality and Social Psychology, 74*, 1464–1480.

Greenwald, A. G., Nosek, B. A., & Banaji, M. R. (2003). Understanding and using the implicit association test: I. An improved scoring algorithm. *Journal of Personality and Social Psychology, 85*, 197–216.

Greenwald, A. G., Poehlman, T. A., Uhlmann, E. L., & Banaji, M. R. (2008). Understanding and using the Implicit Association Test: III. Meta-analysis of predictive validity. *Journal of Personality and Social Psychology, 97*(1), 17–41.

Greitemeyer, T. (2009). Effects of songs with prosocial lyrics on prosocial thoughts, affect, and behavior. *Journal of Experimental Social Psychology, 45*, 186–190.

Griffitt, W. (1970). Environmental effects on interpersonal affective behavior. Ambient effective temperature and attraction. *Journal of Personality and Social Psychology, 15*, 240–244.

Griffitt, W. (1987). Females, males, and sexual responses. In K. Kelley (Ed.), *Females, males, and sexuality: Theories and research.* Albany: State University of New York Press.

Griffitt, W., & Veitch, R. (1971). Hot and crowded: Influences of population density and temperature on interpersonal affective behavior. *Journal of Personality and Social Psychology, 17*, 92–98.

Griskevicius, V., Tybur, J. M., Sundie, J. M., Cialdini, R. B., Miller, G. F., & Kenrick, D. T. (2007). Blatant benevolence and conspicuous consumption: When romantic motives elicit strategic costly signals. *Journal of Personality and Social Psychology, 93*, 85–102.

Groenenboom, A., Wilke, H. A. M., & Wit, A. P. (2001). Will we be working together again? The impact of future interdependence on group members' task motivation. *European Journal of Social Psychology, 31*, 369–378.

Grofman, B. (1980). The slippery slope: Jury size and jury verdict requirements—legal and social science approaches. In B. H. Raven (Ed.), *Policy studies review annual* (Vol. 4). Beverly Hills, CA: Sage.

Gronlund, S. D. (2004a). Sequential lineups: Shift in criterion or decision strategy? *Journal of Applied Psychology, 89*, 362–368.

Gronlund, S. D. (2004b). Sequential lineup advantage: Contributions of distinctiveness and recollection. *Applied Cognitive Psychology, 19,* 23–37.

Gross, A. E., & Crofton, C. (1977). What is good is beautiful. *Sociometry, 40,* 85–90.

Gross, J. T. (2001). *Neighbors: The destruction of the Jewish community in Jedwabne, Poland.* Princeton: Princeton University Press.

Grote, N. K., & Clark, M. S. (2001). Perceiving unfairness in the family: Cause or consequence of marital distress? *Journal of Personality and Social Psychology, 80,* 281–293.

Grove, J. R., Hanrahan, S. J., & McInman, A. (1991). Success/failure bias in attributions across involvement categories in sport. *Personality and Social Psychology Bulletin, 17,* 93–97.

Grove, W. M., Zald, D. H., Lebow, B. S., Snitz, B. E., & Nelson, C. (2000). Clinical versus mechanical prediction: A meta-analysis. *Psychological Assessment, 12,* 19–30.

Grube, J. W., Kleinhesselink, R. R., & Kearney, K. A. (1982). Male self-acceptance and attraction toward women. *Personality and Social Psychology Bulletin, 8,* 107–112.

Gruder, C. L. (1977). Choice of comparison persons in evaluating oneself. In J. M. Suls & R. L. Miller (Eds.), *Social comparison processes.* Washington, DC: Hemisphere.

Gruder, C. L., Cook, T. D., Hennigan, K. M., Flay, B., Alessis, C., & Kalamaj, J. (1978). Empirical tests of the absolute sleeper effect predicted from the discounting cue hypothesis. *Journal of Personality and Social Psychology, 36,* 1061–1074.

Gruendl, M. (2005, accessed December 14). Beautycheck (www.beautycheck.de).

Gruman, J. C., & Sloan, R. P. (1983). Disease as justice: Perceptions of the victims of physical illness. *Basic and Applied Social Psychology, 4,* 39–46.

Grunberger, R. (1971). *The 12-year Reich: A social history of Nazi Germany, 1933–1945.* New York: Holt, Rinehart & Winston.

Grush, J. E. (1980). Impact of candidate expenditures, regionality, and prior outcomes on the 1976 Democratic presidential primaries. *Journal of Personality and Social Psychology, 38,* 337–347.

Grush, J. E., & Glidden, M. V. (1987). Power and satisfaction among distressed and nondistressed couples. Paper presented at the Midwestern Psychological Association convention.

Guéguen, N., & Jacob, C. (2001). Fund-raising on the Web: The effect of an electronic foot-in-the-door on donation. *CyberPsychology and Behavior, 4,* 705–709.

Guerin, B. (1993). *Social facilitation.* Paris: Cambridge University Press.

Guerin, B. (1994). What do people think about the risks of driving? Implications for traffic safety interventions. *Journal of Applied Social Psychology, 24,* 994–1021.

Guerin, B. (1999). Social behaviors as determined by different arrangements of social consequences: Social loafing, social facilitation, deindividuation, and a modified social loafing. *The Psychological Record, 49,* 565–578.

Guerin, B., & Innes, J. M. (1982). Social facilitation and social monitoring: A new look at Zajonc's mere presence hypothesis. *British Journal of Social Psychology, 21,* 7–18.

Guimond, S., Dambrun, N., Michinov, N., & Duarte, S. (2003). Does social dominance generate prejudice? Integrating individual and contextual determinants of intergroup cognitions. *Journal of Personality and Social Psychology, 84,* 697–721.

Guiness, O. (1993). *The American hour: A time of reckoning and the once and future role of faith.* New York: Free Press.

Gundersen, E. (2001, August 1). MTV is a many splintered thing. *USA Today,* p. 1D.

Gunter, B. (2008). Media violence: Is there a case for causality? *American Behavioral Scientist, 51,* 1061–1122.

Gupta, U., & Singh, P. (1982). Exploratory study of love and liking and type of marriages. *Indian Journal of Applied Psychology, 19,* 92–97.

Gurin, P., Dey, E. L., Hurtado, S., & Gurin, G. (2002). Diversity and higher education: Theory and impact on educational outcomes. *Harvard Educational Review, 72,* 330–366.

Gutierres, S. E., Kenrick, D. T., & Partch, J. J. (1999). Beauty, dominance, and the mating game: Contrast effects in self-assessment reflect gender differences in mate selection. *Journal of Personality and Social Psychology, 25,* 1126–1134.

Gutmann, D. (1977). The cross-cultural perspective: Notes toward a comparative psychology of aging. In J. E. Birren & K. Warner Schaie (Eds.), *Handbook of the psychology of aging.* New York: Van Nostrand Reinhold.

Guttentag, M., & Secord, P. F. (1983). *Too many women? The sex ratio question.* Thousand Oaks, CA: Sage.

Hacker, H. M. (1951). Women as a minority group. *Social Forces, 30,* 60–69.

Hackman, J. R. (1986). The design of work teams. In J. Lorsch (Ed.), *Handbook of organizational behavior.* Englewood Cliffs, NJ: Prentice-Hall.

Hadden, J. K. (1969). *The gathering storm in the churches.* Garden City, NY: Doubleday.

Haddock, G., Maio, G. R., Arnold, K., & Huskinson, T. (2008). Should persuasion be affective or cognitive? The moderating effects of need for affect and need for cognition. *Personality and Social Psychology Bulletin, 34,* 769–778.

Haddock, G., & Zanna, M. P. (1994). Preferring "housewives" to "feminists." *Psychology of Women Quarterly, 18,* 25–52.

Haeffel, G. J., Gibb, B. E., Metalsky, G. I., Alloy, L. B., Abramson, L. Y., Hankin, B. L., Joiner, T. E., Jr., & Swendsen, J. D. (2008). Measuring cognitive vulnerability to depression: Development and validation of the cognitive style questionnaire. *Clinical Psychology Review, 28,* 824–836.

Haemmerlie, F. M. (1987). Creating adaptive illusions in counseling and therapy using a self-perception theory perspective. Paper presented at the Midwestern Psychological Association, Chicago.

Haemmerlie, F. M., & Montgomery, R. L. (1982). Self-perception theory and unobtrusively biased interactions: A treatment for heterosocial anxiety. *Journal of Counseling Psychology, 29,* 362–370.

Haemmerlie, F. M., & Montgomery, R. L. (1984). Purposefully biased interventions: Reducing heterosocial anxiety through self-perception theory. *Journal of Personality and Social Psychology, 47,* 900–908.

Haemmerlie, F. M., & Montgomery, R. L. (1986). Self-perception theory and the treatment of shyness. In W. H. Jones, J. M. Cheek, & S. R. Briggs (Eds.), *A sourcebook on shyness: Research and treatment.* New York: Plenum.

Hafer, C. L., & Bègue, L. (2005). Experimental research on just-world theory: Problems, developments, and future challenges. *Psychological Bulletin, 131,* 128–167.

Hafner, H., & Schmidtke, A. (1989). Do televised fictional suicide models produce suicides? In D. R. Pfeffer (Ed.), *Suicide among youth: Perspectives on risk and prevention.* Washington, DC: American Psychiatric Press.

Hagerty, M. R. (2000). Social comparisons of income in one's community: Evidence from national surveys of income and happiness. *Journal of Personality and Social Psychology, 78,* 764–771.

Haidt, J. (2003). The moral emotions. In R. J. Davidson (Ed.). *Handbook of affective sciences.* Oxford: Oxford University Press.

Haidt, J. (2006). *The happiness hypothesis: Finding modern truth in ancient wisdom.* New York: Basic Books.

Halberstadt, A. G., & Saitta, M. B. (1987). Gender, nonverbal behavior, and perceived dominance: A test of the theory. *Journal of Personality and Social Psychology, 53,* 257–272.

Halberstadt, J. (2006). The generality and ultimate origins of the attractiveness of prototypes. *Personality and Social Psychology Review, 10,* 166–183.

Halberstadt, J., & Green, J. (2008). Carryover effects of analytic thought on preference quality. *Journal of Experimental Social Psychology, 44,* 1199–1203.

Halberstadt, J., & Green, J. (2008). Carryover effects of analytic thought on preference quality. *Journal of Experimental Social Psychology, 44,* 1199–1203.

Halberstadt, J., O'Shea, R. P., & Forgas, J. (2006). Outgroup fanship in Australia and New Zealand. *Australian Journal of Psychology, 58,* 159–165.

Hall, J. A. (1984). *Nonverbal sex differences: Communication accuracy and expressive style.* Baltimore: Johns Hopkins University Press.

Hall, J. A., Coats, E. J., & LeBeau, L. S. (2005). Nonverbal behavior and the vertical dimension of social relations: A meta-analysis. *Psychological Bulletin, 131,* 898–924.

Hall, J. A., Rosip, J. C., LeBeau, L. S., Horgan, T. G., & Carter, J. D. (2006). Attributing the sources of accuracy in unequal-power dyadic communication: Who is better and why? *Journal of Experimental Social Psychology, 42,* 18–27.

Hall, T. (1985, June 25). The unconverted: Smoking of cigarettes seems to be becoming a lower-class habit. *Wall Street Journal,* pp. 1, 25.

Halverson, A. M., Hallahan, M., Hart, A. J., & Rosenthal, R. (1997). Reducing the biasing effects of judges' nonverbal behavior with simplified jury instruction. *Journal of Applied Psychology, 82,* 590–598.

Hamberger, J., & Hewstone, M. (1997). Inter-ethnic contact as a predictor of blatant and subtle prejudice: Tests of a model in four West European nations. *British Journal of Social Psychology, 36,* 173–190.

Hamblin, R. L., Buckholdt, D., Bushell, D., Ellis, D., & Feritor, D. (1969). Changing the game from get the teacher to learn. *Transaction,* January, pp. 20–25, 28–31.

Hamilton, D. L., & Gifford, R. K. (1976). Illusory correlation in interpersonal perception: A cognitive basis of stereotypic judgments. *Journal of Experimental Social Psychology, 12,* 392–407.

Hamilton, D. L., & Rose, T. L. (1980). Illusory correlation and the maintenance of stereotypic beliefs. *Journal of Personality and Social Psychology, 39,* 832–845.

Hamilton, V. L., Hoffman, W. S., Broman, C. L., & Rauma, D. (1993). Unemployment, distress, and coping: A panel study of autoworkers. *Journal of Personality and Social Psychology, 65,* 234–247.

Hampson, R. B. (1984). Adolescent prosocial behavior: Peer-group and situational factors associated with helping. *Journal of Personality and Social Psychology, 46,* 153–162.

Hancock, K. J., & Rhodes, G. (2008). Contact, configural coding and the other-race effect in face recognition. *British Journal of Psychology, 99,* 45–56.

Haney, C. (1991). The fourteenth amendment and symbolic legality: Let them eat due process. *Law and Human Behavior, 15,* 183–204.

Haney, C. (1993). Psychology and legal change. *Law and Human Behavior, 17,* 371–398.

Haney, C., & Logan, D. D. (1994). Broken promise: The Supreme Court's response to social science research on capital punishment. *Journal of Social Issues, 50,* 75–101.

Haney, C., & Zimbardo, P. (1998). The past and future of U.S. prison policy: Twenty-five years after the Stanford Prison Experiment. *American Psychologist, 53,* 709–727.

Haney, C., & Zimbardo, P. G. (2009). Persistent dispositionalism in interactionist clothing: Fundamental attribution error in explaining prison abuse. *Personality and Social Psychology Bulletin, 35,* 807–814.

Hans, V. P., & Vidmar, N. (1981). Jury selection. In N. L. Kerr & R. M. Bray (Eds.), *The psychology of the courtroom.* New York: Academic Press.

Hansen, D. E., Vandenberg, B., & Patterson, M. L. (1995). The effects of religious orientation on spontaneous and nonspontaneous helping behaviors. *Personality and Individual Differences, 19,* 101–104.

Harbaugh, W. T., Mayr, U., & Burghart, D. R. (2007). Neural responses to taxation and voluntary giving reveal motives for charitable donations. *Science, 316,* 1622–1625.

Harber, K. D. (1998). Feedback to minorities: Evidence of a positive bias. *Journal of Personality and Social Psychology, 74,* 622–628.

Hardin, G. (1968). The tragedy of the commons. *Science, 162,* 1243–1248.

Hardy, C., & Latané, B. (1986). Social loafing on a cheering task. *Social Science, 71,* 165–172.

Hardy, C. L., & Van Vugt, M. (2006). Nice guys finish first: The competitive altruism hypothesis. *Personality and Social Psychology Bulletin, 32,* 1402–1413.

Haritos-Fatouros, M. (1988). The official torturer: A learning model for obedience to the authority of violence. *Journal of Applied Social Psychology, 18,* 1107–1120.

Haritos-Fatouros, M. (2002). *Psychological origins of institutionalized torture.* New York: Routledge.

Harkins, S. G. (1981). Effects of task difficulty and task responsibility on social loafing. Presentation to the First International Conference on Social Processes in Small Groups, Kill Devil Hills, North Carolina.

Harkins, S. G., & Jackson, J. M. (1985). The role of evaluation in eliminating social loafing. *Personality and Social Psychology Bulletin, 11,* 457–465.

Harkins, S. G., Latané, B., & Williams, K. (1980). Social loafing: Allocating effort or taking it easy? *Journal of Experimental Social Psychology, 16,* 457–465.

Harkins, S. G., & Petty, R. E. (1982). Effects of task difficulty and task uniqueness on social loafing. *Journal of Personality and Social Psychology, 43,* 1214–1229.

Harkins, S. G., & Petty, R. E. (1987). Information utility and the multiple source effect. *Journal of Personality and Social Psychology, 52,* 260–268.

Harkins, S. G., & Szymanski, K. (1989). Social loafing and group evaluation. *Journal of Personality and Social Psychology, 56,* 934–941.

Harkness, K. L., Sabbagh, M. A., Jacobson, J. A., Chowdrey, N. K., & Chen, T. (2005). Enhanced accuracy of mental state decoding in dysphoric college students. *Cognition & Emotion, 19,* 999–1025.

Harmon-Jones, E., & Allen, J. J. B. (2001). The role of affect in the mere exposure effect: Evidence from psychophysiological and individual differences approaches. *Personality and Social Psychology Bulletin, 27,* 889–898.

Harmon-Jones, E., Gerdjikov, T., & Harmon-Jones, C. (2008). The effect of induced compliance on relative left frontal cortical activity: A test of the action-based model of dissonance. *European Journal of Social Psychology, 38,* 35–45.

Harmon-Jones, E., Greenberg, J., Solomon, S., & Simon, L. (1996). The effects of mortality salience on intergroup bias between minimal groups. *European Journal of Social Psychology, 26,* 677–681.

Harries, K. D., & Stadler, S. J. (1988). Heat and violence: New findings from Dallas field data, 1980–1981. *Journal of Applied Social Psychology, 18,* 129–138.

Harris, J. R. (1996). Quoted from an article by Jerome Burne for the *Manchester Observer* (via Harris: 72073.1211@CompuServe.com).

Harris, J. R. (1998). *The nurture assumption.* New York: Free Press.

Harris, J. R. (2007). *No two alike: Human nature and human individuality.* New York: Norton.

Harris, L. T., & Fiske, S. T. (2006). Dehumanizing the lowest of the low: Neuroimaging responses to extreme out-groups. *Psychological Science, 17*(10), 847–853.

Harris, M. J., & Rosenthal, R. (1985). Mediation of interpersonal expectancy effects: 31 meta-analyses. *Psychological Bulletin, 97,* 363–386.

Harris, M. J., & Rosenthal, R. (1986). Four factors in the mediation of teacher expectancy effects. In R. S. Feldman (Ed.), *The social psychology of education.* New York: Cambridge University Press.

Harrison, A. A. (1977). Mere exposure. In L. Berkowitz (Ed.), *Advances in experimental social psychology* (Vol. 10, pp. 39–83). New York: Academic Press.

Hart, A. J., & Morry, M. M. (1997). Trait inferences based on racial and behavioral cues. *Basic and Applied Social Psychology, 19,* 33–48.

Hart, A. J., Whalen, P. J., Shin, L. M., & others. (2000, August). Differential response in the human amygdala to racial outgroup vs. ingroup face stimuli. *Neuroreport: For Rapid Communication of Neuroscience Research, 11,* 2351–2355.

Harter, J. K., & Gurley, V. F. (2008, September). Measuring well-being in the United States. *APS Observer,* pp. 23–26.

Hartup, W. W., & Stevens, N. (1997). Friendships and adaptation in the life course. *Psychological Bulletin, 121,* 355–370.

Harvey, J. H., & Omarzu, J. (1997). Minding the close relationship. *Personality and Social Psychology Review, 1,* 224–240.

Haselton, M. G., & Buss, D. M. (2000). Error management theory: A new perspective on biases in cross-sex mind reading. *Journal of Personality and Social Psychology, 78,* 81–91.

Haselton, M. G., & Nettle, D. (2006). The paranoid optimist: An integrative evolutionary model of cognitive biases. *Personality and Social Psychology Review, 10,* 47–66.

Haslam, S. A., & Reicher, S. (2007). Beyond the banality of evil: Three dynamics of an interactionist social psychology of tyranny. *Personality and Social Psychology Bulletin, 33,* 615–622.

Hass, R. G., Katz, I., Rizzo, N., Bailey, J., & Eisenstadt, D. (1991). Cross-racial appraisal as related to attitude ambivalence and cognitive complexity. *Personality and Social Psychology Bulletin, 17,* 83–92.

Hastie, R., Penrod, S. D., & Pennington, N. (1983). *Inside the jury.* Cambridge, MA: Harvard University Press.

Hastorf, A., & Cantril, H. (1954). They saw a game: A case study. *Journal of Abnormal and Social Psychology, 49,* 129–134.

Hatfield (Walster), E., Aronson, V., Abrahams, D., & Rottman, L. (1966). Importance of physical attractiveness in dating behavior. *Journal of Personality and Social Psychology, 4,* 508–516.

Hatfield (was Walster), E., Walster, G. W., & Berscheid, E. (1978). *Equity: Theory and research.* Boston: Allyn & Bacon.

Hatfield, E. (1988). Passionate and compassionate love. In R. J. Sternberg & M. L. Barnes (Eds.), *The psychology of love.* New Haven, CT: Yale University Press.

Hatfield, E., & Sprecher, S. (1986). *Mirror, mirror: The importance of looks in everyday life.* Albany, NY: SUNY Press.

Hatfield, E., & Walster, G. W. (1978). *A new look at love.* Reading, MA: Addison-Wesley. (Note: originally published as Walster, E., & Walster, G. W.)

Hatfield, E., Cacioppo, J. T., & Rapson, R. (1992). The logic of emotion: Emotional contagion. In M. S. Clark (Ed.), *Review of Personality and Social Psychology.* Newbury Park, CA: Sage.

Hatfield, E., Traupmann, J., Sprecher, S., Utne, M., & Hay, J. (1985). Equity and intimate relations: Recent research. In W. Ickes (Ed.), *Compatible and incompatible relationships.* New York: Springer-Verlag.

Hatzfeld, J. (2007). *Machete season: The killers in Rwanda speak.* New York: Farrar, Straus and Giroux.

Haugtvedt, C. P., & Wegener, D. T. (1994). Message order effects in persuasion: An attitude strength perspective. *Journal of Consumer Research, 21,* 205–218.

Hauser, D. (2005, June 30). Five years of abstinence-only-until-marriage education: Assessing the impact. *Advocates for Youth* (www .advocatesforyouth.org).

Havel, V. (1990). *Disturbing the peace.* New York: Knopf.

Hawkley, L. C., & Cacioppo, J. T. (2007). Aging and loneliness: Downhill quickly? *Current Directions in Psychological Science, 16,* 187–191.

Hazan, C. (2004). Intimate attachment/capacity to love and be loved. In C. Peterson & M. E. P. Seligman (Eds.), *The values in action classification of strengths and virtues.* Washington, DC: American Psychological Association.

Hazan, C., & Shaver, P. R. (1994). Attachment as an organizational framework for research on close relationships. *Psychological Inquiry, 5,* 1–22.

Headey, B., & Wearing, A. (1987). The sense of relative superiority—central to well-being. *Social Indicators Research, 20,* 497–516.

Heap, B., & Comim, F. (2005). Consumption and happiness: Christian values and an approach towards sustainability. Capability and Sustainability Centre, St. Edmund's College, University of Cambridge. Address to Christians in Science annual meeting.

Hearold, S. (1986). A synthesis of 1043 effects of television on social behavior. In G. Comstock (Ed.), *Public communication and behavior* (Vol. 1). Orlando, FL: Academic Press.

Hebl, M. R., & Heatherton, T. F. (1998). The stigma of obesity in women: The difference is black and white. *Personality and Social Psychology Bulletin, 24,* 417–426.

Hedge, A., & Yousif, Y. H. (1992). Effects of urban size, urgency, and cost on helpfulness: A cross-cultural comparison between the United Kingdom and the Sudan. *Journal of Cross-Cultural Psychology, 23,* 107–115.

Heesacker, M. (1989). Counseling and the elaboration likelihood model of attitude change. In J. F. Cruz, R. A. Goncalves, & P. P. Machado (Eds.), *Psychology and education: Investigations and interventions.* (Proceedings of the International Conference on Interventions in Psychology and Education, Porto, Portugal, July 1987.) Porto, Portugal: Portugese Psychological Association.

Heider, F. (1958). *The psychology of interpersonal relations.* New York: Wiley.

Heine, S. J., & Hamamura, T. (2007). In search of East Asian self-enhancement. *Personality and Social Psychology Review, 11,* 4–27.

Heine, S. J., Kitayama, S., Lehman, D. R., Takata, T., Ide, E., Leung, C., & Matsumoto, H. (2001). Divergent consequences of success and failure in Japan and North America: An investigation of self-improving motivations and malleable selves. *Journal of Personality and Social Psychology, 81,* 599–615.

Heine, S. J., & Lehman, D. R. (1997). The cultural construction of self-enhancement: An examination of group-serving biases. *Journal of Personality and Social Psychology, 72,* 1268–1283.

Heine, S. J., Lehman, D. R., Markus, H. R., & Kitayama, S. (1999). Is there a universal need for positive self-regard? *Psychological Review, 106,* 766–794.

Heine, S. J., Takemoto, T., Moskalenko, S., Lasaleta, J., & Heinrich, J. (2008). Mirrors in the head: Cultural variation in objective self-awareness. *Personality and Social Psychology Bulletin, 34,* 879–887.

Heinrich, L. M., & Gullone, E. (2006). The clinical significance of loneliness: A literature review. *Clinical Psychology Review, 26,* 695–718.

Heins, M. (2004, December 14). Quoted by B. Kloza, Violent Christmas games. *ScienCentralNews* (www.sciencecentral.com).

Helgeson, V. S., Cohen, S., & Fritz, H. L. (1998). Social ties and cancer. In P. M. Cinciripini & others (Eds.), *Psychological and behavioral factors in cancer risk.* New York: Oxford University Press.

Hellman, P. (1980). *Avenue of the righteous of nations.* New York: Atheneum.

Helweg-Larsen, M., Cunningham, S. J., Carrico, A., & Pergram, A. M. (2004). To nod or not to nod: An observational study of nonverbal communication and status in female and male college students. *Psychology of Women Quarterly, 28,* 358–361.

Helweg-Larsen, M., & LoMonaco, B. L. (2008). Queuing among U2 fans: Reactions to social norm violations. *Journal of Applied Social Psychology, 38,* 2378–2393.

Hemsley, G. D., & Doob, A. N. (1978). The effect of looking behavior on perceptions of a communicator's credibility. *Journal of Applied Social Psychology, 8,* 136–144.

Henderson-King, E. I., & Nisbett, R. E. (1996). Anti-black prejudice as a function of exposure to the negative behavior of a single black person. *Journal of Personality and Social Psychology, 71,* 654–664.

Hendrick, S. S., & Hendrick, C. (1995). Gender differences and similarities in sex and love. *Personal Relationships, 2,* 55–65.

Hendrick, S. S., Hendrick, C., & Adler, N. L. (1988). Romantic relationships: Love, satisfaction, and staying together. *Journal of Personality and Social Psychology, 54,* 980–988.

Hennigan, K. M., Del Rosario, M. L., Health, L., Cook, T. D., Wharton, J. D., & Calder, B. J. (1982). Impact of the introduction of television on crime in the United States: Empirical findings and theoretical implications. *Journal of Personality and Social Psychology, 42,* 461–477.

Henrich, J., McElreath, R., Barr, A., Ensminger, J., Barrett, C., Bolyanatz, A., Cardenas, J. C., Gurven, M., Gwako, E., Henrich, N., Lerorogol, C., Marlowe, F., Tracer, D., & Ziker, J. (2006). Costly punishment across human societies. *Science, 312,* 1767–1770.

Henslin, M. (1967). Craps and magic. *American Journal of Sociology, 73,* 316–330.

Hepworth, J. T., & West, S. G. (1988). Lynchings and the economy: A time-series reanalysis of Hovland and Sears (1940), *Journal of Personality and Social Psychology, 55,* 239–247.

Heradstveit, D. (1979). *The Arab-Israeli conflict: Psychological obstacles to peace* (Vol. 28). Oslo, Norway: Universitetsforlaget. Distributed by Columbia University Press. Reviewed by R. K. White (1980), *Contemporary Psychology, 25,* 11–12.

Herek, G. (1993). Interpersonal contact and heterosexuals' attitudes toward gay men: Results from a national survey. *Journal of Sex Research, 30,* 239–244.

Herek, G. M. (2009). Hate crimes and stigma-related experiences among sexual minority adults in the United States: Prevalence estimates from a national probability sample. *Journal of Interpersonal Violence, 24*(1), 54–74.

Herlocker, C. E., Allison, S. T., Foubert, J. D., & Beggan, J. K. (1997). Intended and unintended overconsumption of physical, spatial, and temporal resources. *Journal of Personality and Social Psychology, 73,* 992–1004.

Herzog, S. M., & Hertwig, R. (2009). The wisdom of many in one mind: Improving individual judgments with dialectical bootstrapping. *Psychological Science, 20,* 231–237.

Hewstone, M. (1990). The "ultimate attribution error"? A review of the literature on intergroup causal attribution. *European Journal of Social Psychology, 20,* 311–335.

Hewstone, M. (1994). Revision and change of stereotypic beliefs: In search of the elusive subtyping model. In S. Stroebe & M. Hewstone (Eds.), *European review of social psychology* (Vol. 5). Chichester, England: Wiley.

Hewstone, M., & Fincham, F. (1996). Attribution theory and research: Basic issues and applications. In M. Hewstone, W. Stroebe, and G. M. Stephenson (Eds.), *Introduction to social psychology: A European perspective.* Oxford, UK: Blackwell.

Hewstone, M., & Greenland, K. (2000). Intergroup conflict. Unpublished manuscript, Cardiff University.

Hewstone, M., Hantzi, A., & Johnston, L. (1991). Social categorisation and person memory: The pervasiveness of race as an organizing principle. *European Journal of Social Psychology, 21,* 517–528.

Hewstone, M., Hopkins, N., & Routh, D. A. (1992). Cognitive models of stereotype change: Generalization and subtyping in young people's views of the police. *European Journal of Social Psychology, 22,* 219–234.

Higbee, K. L., Millard, R. J., & Folkman, J. R. (1982). Social psychology research during the 1970s: Predominance of experimentation and college students. *Personality and Social Psychology Bulletin, 8,* 180–183.

Higgins, E. T., & McCann, C. D. (1984). Social encoding and subsequent attitudes, impressions and memory: "Context-driven" and motivational aspects of processing. *Journal of Personality and Social Psychology, 47,* 26–39.

Higgins, E. T., & Rholes, W. S. (1978). Saying is believing: Effects of message modification on memory and liking for the person described. *Journal of Experimental Social Psychology, 14,* 363–378.

Hilmert, C. J., Kulik, J. A., & Christenfeld, N. J. S. (2006). Positive and negative opinion modeling: The influence of another's similarity and dissimilarity. *Journal of Personality and Social Psychology, 90,* 440–452.

Hilton, J. L., & von Hippel, W. (1990). The role of consistency in the judgment of stereotype-relevant behaviors. *Personality and Social Psychology Bulletin, 16,* 430–448.

Hine, D. W., & Gifford, R. (1996). Attributions about self and others in commons dilemmas. *European Journal of Social Psychology, 26,* 429–445.

Hines, M. (2004). *Brain gender.* New York: Oxford University Press.

Hinkle, S., Brown, R., & Ely, P. G. (1992). Social identity theory processes: Some limitations and limiting conditions. *Revista de Psicologia Social,* pp. 99–111.

Hinsz, V. B. (1990). Cognitive and consensus processes in group recognition memory performance. *Journal of Personality and Social Psychology, 59,* 705–718.

Hinsz, V. B., Tindale, R. S., & Vollrath, D. A. (1997). The emerging conceptualization of groups as information processors. *Psychological Bulletin, 121,* 43–64.

Hirschman, R. S., & Leventhal, H. (1989). Preventing smoking behavior in school children: An initial test of a cognitive-development program. *Journal of Applied Social Psychology, 19,* 559–583.

Hirt, E. R., & Markman, K. D. (1995). Multiple explanation: A consider-an-alternative strategy for debiasing judgments. *Journal of Personality and Social Psychology, 69,* 1069–1088.

Hirt, E. R., Zillmann, D., Erickson, G. A., & Kennedy, C. (1992). Costs and benefits of allegiance: Changes in fans' self-ascribed competencies after team victory versus defeat. *Journal of Personality and Social Psychology, 63,* 724–738.

Hitsch, G. J., Hortacsu, A., and Ariely, D. (2006, February). What makes you click? Mate preferences and matching outcomes in online dating. MIT Sloan Research Paper No. 4603-06 (ssrn.com/abstract=895442).

Hobden, K. L., & Olson, J. M. (1994). From jest to antipathy: Disparagement humor as a source of dissonance-motivated attitude change. *Basic and Applied Social psychology, 15,* 239–249.

Hodges, B. H., & Geyer, A. L. (2006). A nonconformist account of the Asch experiments: Values, pragmatics, and moral dilemmas. *Personality and Social Psychology Review,* pp. 102–119.

Hodgkinson, V. A., Weitzman, M. S., & Kirsch, A. D. (1990). From commitment to action: How religious involvement affects giving and volunteering. In R. Wuthnow, V. A. Hodgkinson, & Associates (Eds.), *Faith and philanthropy in America: Exploring the role of religion in America's voluntary sector.* San Francisco: Jossey-Bass.

Hodson, G., Harry, H., & Mitchell, A. (2009). Independent benefits of contact and friendship on attitudes toward homosexuals among authoritarians and highly identified heterosexuals. *European Journal of Social Psychology, 39,* 509–525.

Hoffman, L. W. (1977). Changes in family roles, socialization, and sex differences. *American Psychologist, 32,* 644–657.

Hoffman, M. L. (1981). Is altruism part of human nature? *Journal of Personality and Social Psychology, 40,* 121–137.

Hofling, C. K., Brotzman, E., Dairymple, S., Graves, N., & Pierce, C. M. (1966). An experimental study in nurse-physician relationships. *Journal of Nervous and Mental Disease, 143,* 171–180.

Hofmann, W., Gawronski, B., Gschwendner, T., Le, H., & Schmitt, M. (2005). A meta-analysis on the correlation between the implicit association test and explicit self-report measures. *Personality and Social Psychology Bulletin, 31,* 1369–1385.

Hogan, R., Curphy, G. J., & Hogan, J. (1994). What we know about leadership: Effectiveness and personality. *American Psychologist, 49,* 493–504.

Hogg, M. A. (1992). *The social psychology of group cohesiveness: From attraction to social identity.* London: Harvester Wheatsheaf.

Hogg, M. A. (2001). A social identity theory of leadership. *Personality and Social Psychology Review, 5,* 184–200.

Hogg, M. A. (2006). Social identity theory. In P. J. Burke (Ed.), *Contemporary social psychological theories.* Stanford, CA: Stanford University Press.

Hogg, M. A. (2008). Social identity processes and the empowerment of followers. In R. E. Riggio, I. Chaleff, & J. Lipman-Blumen (Eds.), *The art of followership: How great followers create great leaders and organizations.* San Francisco: Jossey-Bass.

Hogg, M. A., & Hains, S. C. (1998). Friendship and group identification: A new look at the role of cohesiveness in groupthink. *European Journal of Social Psychology, 28,* 323–341.

Hogg, M. A., Hains, S. C., & Mason, I. (1998). Identification and leadership in small groups: Salience, frame of reference, and leader stereotypicality effects on leader evaluations. *Journal of Personality and Social Psychology, 75,* 1248–1263.

Hogg, M. A., Turner, J. C., & Davidson, B. (1990). Polarized norms and social frames of reference: A test of the self-categorization theory of group polarization. *Basic and Applied Social Psychology, 11,* 77–100.

Holland, R. W., Hendriks, M., & Aarts, H. (2005). Smells like clean spirit: Nonconscious effect of scent on cognition and behavior. *Psychological Science, 16,* 689–693.

Holland, R. W., Meertens, R. M., & Van Vugt, M. (2002). Dissonance on the road: Self-esteem as a moderator of internal and external self-justification strategies. *Personality and Social Psychology Bulletin, 28,* 1712–1724.

Hollander, E. P. (1958). Conformity, status, and idiosyncrasy credit. *Psychological Review, 65,* 117–127.

Holmberg, D., & Holmes, J. G. (1994). Reconstruction of relationship memories: A mental models approach. In N. Schwarz & S. Sudman (Eds.), *Autobiographical memory and the validity of retrospective reports.* New York: Springer-Verlag.

Holmes, J. G., & Rempel, J. K. (1989). Trust in close relationships. In C. Hendrick (Ed.), *Review of personality and social psychology* (Vol. 10). Newbury Park, CA: Sage.

Holtgraves, T. (1997). Styles of language use: Individual and cultural variability in conversational indirectness. *Journal of Personality and Social Psychology, 73,* 624–637.

Holtman, Z., Louw, J., Tredoux, C., & Carney, T. (2005). Prejudice and social contact in South Africa: A study of integrated schools ten years after apartheid. *South African Journal of Psychology, 35,* 473–493.

Holtzworth, A., & Jacobson, N. S. (1988). An attributional approach to marital dysfunction and therapy. In J. E. Maddux, C. D. Stoltenberg, & R. Rosenwein (Eds.), *Social processes in clinical and counseling psychology.* New York: Springer-Verlag.

Holtzworth-Munroe, A., & Jacobson, N. S. (1985). Causal attributions of married couples: When do they search for causes? What do they conclude when they do? *Journal of Personality and Social Psychology, 48,* 1398–1412.

Honigman, R. J., Phillips, K. A., & Castle, D. J. (2004). A review of psychosocial outcomes for patients seeking cosmetic surgery. *Plastic and Reconstructive Surgery, 113,* 1229–1237.

Hoorens, V. (1993). Self-enhancement and superiority biases in social comparison. In W. Stroebe & M. Hewstone (Eds.), *European review of social psychology* (Vol. 4). Chichester: Wiley.

Hoorens, V. (1995). Self-favoring biases, self-presentation and the self-other asymmetry in social comparison. *Journal of Personality, 63,* 793–819.

Hoorens, V., & Nuttin, J. M. (1993). Overvaluation of own attributes: Mere ownership or subjective frequency? *Social Cognition, 11,* 177–200.

Hoorens, V., Nuttin, J. M., Herman, I. E., & Pavakanun, U. (1990). Mastery pleasure versus mere ownership: A quasi-experimental cross-cultural and cross-alphabetical test of the name letter effect. *European Journal of Social Psychology, 20,* 181–205.

Hoorens, V., Smits, T., & Shepperd, J. A. (2008). Comparative optimism in the spontaneous generation of future life-events. *British Journal of Social Psychology, 47,* 441–451.

Hoover, C. W., Wood, E. E., & Knowles, E. S. (1983). Forms of social awareness and helping. *Journal of Experimental Social Psychology, 19,* 577–590.

Hooykaas, R. (1972). *Religion and the rise of modern science.* Grand Rapids, MI: Eerdmans.

Hormuth, S. E. (1986). Lack of effort as a result of self-focused attention: An attributional ambiguity analysis. *European Journal of Social Psychology, 16,* 181–192.

Hornstein, H. (1976). *Cruelty and kindness.* Englewood Cliffs, NJ: Prentice-Hall.

Horowitz, S. V., & Boardman, S. K. (1994). Managing conflict: Policy and research implications. *Journal of Social Issues, 50,* 197–211.

Horwitz, A. V., White, H. R., & Howell-White, S. (1997). Becoming married and mental health: A longitudinal study of a cohort of young adults. *Journal of Marriage and the Family, 58,* 895–907.

Höss, R. (1959). *Commandant at Auschwitz: Autobiography.* London: Weidenfeld and Nicolson.

Houck, M. M. (2006, July). CSI: Reality. *Scientific American,* pp. 85–89.

House, R. J., & Singh, J. V. (1987). Organizational behavior: Some new directions for I/O psychology. *Annual Review of Psychology, 38,* 669–718.

Houston, V., & Bull, R. (1994). Do people avoid sitting next to someone who is facially disfigured? *European Journal of Social Psychology, 24,* 279–284.

Hovland, C. I., & Sears, R. (1940). Minor studies of aggression: Correlation of lynchings with economic indices. *Journal of Psychology, 9,* 301–310.

Hovland, C. I., Lumsdaine, A. A., & Sheffield, F. D. (1949). *Experiments on mass communication. Studies in social psychology in World War II* (Vol. III). Princeton, NJ: Princeton University Press.

Howard, D. J. (1997). Familiar phrases as peripheral persuasion cues. *Journal of Experimental Social Psychology, 33,* 231–243.

Howell, R. T., & Howell, C. J. (2008). The relation of economic status to subjective well-being in developing countries: A meta-analysis. *Psychological Bulletin, 134,* 536–560.

Hoyle, R. H. (1993). Interpersonal attraction in the absence of explicit attitudinal information. *Social Cognition, 11,* 309–320.

Hsee, C. K., & Hastie, R. (2006). Decision and experience: Why don't we choose what makes us happy? *Trends in Cognitive Sciences, 10,* 31–37.

Huart, J., Corneille, O., & Becquart, E. (2005). Face-based categorization, context-based categorization, and distortions in the recollection of gender ambiguous faces. *Journal of Experimental Social Psychology, 41,* 598–608.

Huddy, L., & Virtanen, S. (1995). Subgroup differentiation and subgroup bias among Latinos as a function of familiarity and positive distinctiveness. *Journal of Personality and Social Psychology, 68,* 97–108.

Huesmann, L. R., Lagerspetz, K., & Eron, L. D. (1984). Intervening variables in the TV violence-aggression relation: Evidence from two countries. *Developmental Psychology, 20,* 746–775.

Huesmann, L. R., Moise-Titus, J., Podolski, C-L., & Eron, L. D. (2003). Longitudinal relations between children's exposure to TV violence and their aggressive and violent behavior in young adulthood: 1977–1992. *Developmental Psychology, 39,* 201–222.

Hugenberg, K. & Bodenhausen, G. V. (2003). Facing prejudice: Implicit prejudice and the perception of facial threat. *Psychological Science, 14,* 640–643.

Hugenberg, K., Miller, J., & Claypool, H. M. (2007). Categorization and individuation in the cross-race recognition deficit: Toward a solution to an insidious problem. *Journal of Experimental Social Psychology, 43,* 334–340.

Hui, C. H., Triandis, H. C., & Yee, C. (1991). Cultural differences in reward allocation: Is collectivism the explanation? *British Journal of Social Psychology, 30,* 145–157.

Hull, J. G., & Young, R. D. (1983). The self-awareness-reducing effects of alcohol consumption: Evidence and implications. In J. Suls & A. G. Greenwald (Eds.), *Psychological perspectives on the self* (Vol. 2). Hillsdale, NJ: Erlbaum.

Hull, J. G., Levenson, R. W., Young, R. D., & Sher, K. J. (1983). Self-awareness-reducing effects of alcohol consumption. *Journal of Personality and Social Psychology, 44,* 461–473.

Human Security Centre. (2005). *The human security report 2005: War and peace in the 21st century.* University of British Columbia.

Hunt, A. R. (2000, June 22). Major progress, inequities cross three generations. *Wall Street Journal,* pp. A9, A14.

Hunt, M. (1990). *The compassionate beast: What science is discovering about the humane side of humankind.* New York: William Morrow.

Hunt, M. (1993). *The story of psychology.* New York: Doubleday.

Hunt, P. J., & Hillery, J. M. (1973). Social facilitation in a location setting: An examination of the effects over learning trials. *Journal of Experimental Social Psychology, 9,* 563–571.

Hunt, R., & Jensen, J. (2007). *The experiences of young gay people in Britain's schools.* Stonewall (www.stonewall.org.uk).

Hunter, J. A., Stringer, M., & Watson, R. P. (1991). Intergroup violence and intergroup attributions. *British Journal of Social Psychology, 30,* 261–266.

Hunter, J. D. (2002, June 21–22). "To change the world." Paper presented to the Board of Directors of The Trinity Forum, Denver, Colorado.

Huo, Y. J., Smith, H. J., Tyler, T. R., & Lind, E. A. (1996). Superordinate identification, subgroup identification, and justice concerns: Is separatism the problem; is assimilation the answer? *Psychological Science, 7,* 40–45.

Huston, A. C., Donnerstein, E., Fairchild, H., Feshbach, N. D., Katz, P. A., & Murray, J. P. (1992). *Big world, small screen: The role of television in American society.* Lincoln, NE: University of Nebraska Press.

Huston, T. L. (1973). Ambiguity of acceptance, social desirability, and dating choice. *Journal of Experimental Social Psychology, 9,* 32–42.

Huston, T. L., & Chorost, A. F. (1994). Behavioral buffers on the effect of negativity on marital satisfaction: A longitudinal study. *Personal Relationships, 1,* 223–239.

Huston, T. L., Niehuis, S., & Smith, S. E. (2001). The early marital roots of conjugal distress and divorce. *Current Directions in Psychological Science, 10,* 116–119.

Hutnik, N. (1985). Aspects of identity in a multi-ethnic society. *New Community, 12,* 298–309.

Hutson, M. (2007, March/April). Unnatural selection. *Psychology Today,* pp. 90–95.

Hvistendahl, M. (2008, July 9). No country for young men. *New Republic* (www.tnr.com).

Hyde, J. S. (2005). The gender similarities hypothesis. *American Psychologist, 60,* 581–592.

Hyde, J. S., Mezulis, A. H., & Abramson, L. Y. (2008). The ABCs of depression: Integrating affective, biological, and cognitive models to explain the emergence of the gender difference in depression. *Psychological Review, 115,* 291–313.

Hyman, H. H., & Sheatsley, P. B. (1956 & 1964). Attitudes toward desegregation. *Scientific American, 195*(6), 35–39, and *211*(1), 16–23.

Hyman, R. (1981). Cold reading: How to convince strangers that you know all about them. In K. Frazier (Ed.), *Paranormal borderlands of science.* Buffalo, NY: Prometheus Books.

Ickes, B. (1980). On disconfirming our perceptions of others. Paper presented at the American Psychological Association convention.

Ickes, W., Layden, M. A., & Barnes, R. D. (1978). Objective self-awareness and individuation: An empirical link. *Journal of Personality, 46,* 146–161.

Ickes, W., Patterson, M. L., Rajecki, D. W., & Tanford, S. (1982). Behavioral and cognitive consequences of reciprocal versus compensatory responses to preinteraction expectancies. *Social Cognition, 1,* 160–190.

Ickes, W., Snyder, M., & Garcia, S. (1997). Personality influences on the choice of situations. In R. Hogan, J. Johnson, & S. Briggs (Eds.), *Handbook of Personality Psychology.* San Diego: Academic Press.

ILO. (1997, December 11). Women's progress in workforce improving worldwide, but occupation segregation still rife. International Labor Association press release (www.ilo.org/public/english/bureau/inf/pr/1997/35.htm).

Imai, Y. (1994). Effects of influencing attempts on the perceptions of powerholders and the powerless. *Journal of Social Behavior and Personality, 9,* 455–468.

Imhoff, R., & Erb, H-P. (2009). What motivates nonconformity? Uniqueness seeking blocks majority influence. *Personality and Social Psychology Bulletin, 35,* 309–320.

Ingham, A. G., Levinger, G., Graves, J., & Peckham, V. (1974). The Ringelmann effect: Studies of group size and group performance. *Journal of Experimental Social Psychology, 10,* 371–384.

Inglehart, M. R., Markus, H., & Brown, D. R. (1989). The effects of possible selves on academic achievement—a panel study. In J. P. Forgas & J. M. Innes (Eds.), *Recent advances in social psychology: An international perspective.* North-Holland: Elsevier Science Publishers.

Inglehart, R. (1990). *Culture shift in advanced industrial society.* Princeton, NJ: Princeton University Press.

Inglehart, R. (1997). *Modernization and postmodernization.* Princeton: Princeton University Press.

Inglehart, R. (2006). Cultural change and democracy in Latin America. In Frances Hagopian (Ed.), *Contemporary Catholicism, religious pluralism and democracy in Latin America.* South Bend: Notre Dame University Press.

Inglehart, R. (2009). Cultural Change and Democracy in Latin America. In Frances Hagopian (Ed.), *Religious pluralism, democracy, and the Catholic Church in Latin America.* South Bend: University of Notre Dame Press.

Inglehart, R., Foa, R., Peterson, C., & Welzel, C. (2008). Development, freedom, and rising happiness: A global perspective (1981–2007). *Perspectives on Psychological Science, 3,* 264–285.

Inglehart, R., & Welzel, C. (2005). *Modernization, cultural change, and democracy: The human development sequence.* New York: Cambridge University Press.

Insko, C. A., Nacoste, R. W., & Moe, J. L. (1983). Belief congruence and racial discrimination: Review of the evidence and critical evaluation. *European Journal of Social Psychology, 13,* 153–174.

Intergovernmental Panel on Climate Change. (2007). Climate change 2007: The physical science basis. Summary for policymakers (www.ipcc.ch).

Inzlicht, M., McKay, L., & Aronson, J. (2006). Stigma as ego depletion: How being the target of prejudice affects self-control. *Psychological Science, 17,* 262–269.

Ipsos. (2007, June 5). Most Canadians (84%) express concern for reducing non-industrial sources of greenhouse gas emissions. Ipsos Reid survey (www.ipsos-na.com).

IPU. (2008). Women in national parliaments: Situation as of 30 April 2008. International Parliamentary Union (www.ipu.org).

Isen, A. M., Clark, M., & Schwartz, M. F. (1976). Duration of the effect of good mood on helping: Footprints on the sands of time. *Journal of Personality and Social Psychology, 34,* 385–393.

Isen, A. M., & Means, B. (1983). The influence of positive affect on decision-making strategy. *Social Cognition, 2,* 28–31.

Isen, A. M., Shalker, T. E., Clark, M., & Karp, L. (1978). Affect, accessibility of material in memory, and behavior:

A cognitive loop. *Journal of Personality and Social Psychology, 36,* 1–12.

Isozaki, M. (1984). The effect of discussion on polarization of judgments. *Japanese Psychological Research, 26,* 187–193.

ISR Newsletter. (1975). Institute for Social Research, University of Michigan, 3(4), 4–7.

Ito, T. A., Miller, N., & Pollock, V. E. (1996). Alcohol and aggression: A meta-analysis on the moderating effects of inhibitory cues, triggering events, and self-focused attention. *Psychological Bulletin, 120,* 60–82.

Iyengar, S. S., & Lepper, M. R. (2000). When choice is demotivating: Can one desire too much of a good thing? *Journal of Personality and Social Psychology, 79,* 995–1006.

Iyengar, S. S., Wells, R. E., & Schwartz, B. (2006). Doing better but feeling worse: Looking for the "best" job undermines satisfaction. *Psychological Science, 17,* 143–150.

Jackman, M. R., & Senter, M. S. (1981). Beliefs about race, gender, and social class different, therefore unequal: Beliefs about trait differences between groups of unequal status. In D. J. Treiman & R. V. Robinson (Eds.), *Research in stratification and mobility* (Vol. 2). Greenwich, CT: JAI Press.

Jackson, J. M., & Latané, B. (1981). All alone in front of all those people: Stage fright as a function of number and type of co-performers and audience. *Journal of Personality and Social Psychology, 40,* 73–85.

Jackson, J. W., Kirby, D., Barnes, L., & Shepard, L. (1993). Institutional racism and pluralistic ignorance: A cross-national comparison. In M. Wievorka (Ed.), *Racisme et modernite.* Paris: Editions la Découverte.

Jackson, L. A., Hunter, J. E., & Hodge, C. N. (1995). Physical attractiveness and intellectual competence: A meta-analytic review. *Social Psychology Quarterly, 58,* 108–123.

Jacobs, R. C., & Campbell, D. T. (1961). The perpetuation of an arbitrary tradition through several generations of a laboratory microculture. *Journal of Abnormal and Social Psychology, 62,* 649–658.

Jacoby, S. (1986, December). When opposites attract. *Reader's Digest,* pp. 95–98.

Jacques-Tiua, A. J., Abbey, A., Parkhill, M. R., & Zawacki, T. (2007). Why do some men misperceive women's sexual intentions more frequently than others do? An application of the confluence model. *Personality and Social Psychology Bulletin, 333,* 1467–1480.

Jaffe, Y., Shapir, N., & Yinon, Y. (1981). Aggression and its escalation. *Journal of Cross-Cultural Psychology, 12,* 21–36.

Jaffe, Y., & Yinon, Y. (1983). Collective aggression: The group-individual paradigm in the study of collective antisocial behavior. In H. H. Blumberg, A. P. Hare, V. Kent, & M. Davies (Eds.), *Small groups and social interaction* (Vol. 1). Cambridge: Wiley.

James, W. (1890, reprinted 1950). *The principles of psychology* (Vol. 2). New York: Dover.

James, W. (1899). Talks to teachers on psychology: And to students on some of life's ideals. New York: Holt, 1922, p. 33. Cited by W. J. McKeachie, Psychology in America's bicentennial year. *American Psychologist, 31,* 819–833.

James, W. (1902, reprinted 1958). *The varieties of religious experience.* New York: Mentor Books.

Jamieson, D. W., Lydon, J. E., Stewart, G., & Zanna, M. P. (1987). Pygmalion revisited: New evidence for student expectancy effects in the classroom. *Journal of Educational Psychology, 79,* 461–466.

Janes, L. M., & Olson, J. M. (2000). Jeer pressure: The behavioral effects of observing ridicule of others. *Personality and Social Psychology Bulletin, 26,* 474–485.

Janis, I. L. (1971, November). Groupthink. *Psychology Today,* pp. 43–46.

Janis, I. L. (1972). *Victims of groupthink.* New York: Houghton Mifflin.

Janis, I. L. (1982). Counteracting the adverse effects of concurrence-seeking in policy-planning groups: Theory and research perspectives. In H. Brandstatter, J. H. Davis, & G. Stocker-Kreichgauer (Eds.), *Group decision making.* New York: Academic Press.

Janis, I. L. (1989). Crucial decisions: Leadership in policymaking and crisis management. New York: Free Press.

Janis, I. L., Kaye, D., & Kirschner, P. (1965). Facilitating effects of eating while reading on responsiveness to persuasive communications. *Journal of Personality and Social Psychology, 1,* 181–186.

Janis, I. L., & Mann, L. (1977). *Decision-making: A psychological analysis of conflict, choice and commitment.* New York: Free Press.

Jankowiak, W. R., & Fischer, E. F. (1992). A cross-cultural perspective on romantic love. *Ethnology, 31,* 149–155.

Jason, L. A., Rose, T., Ferrari, J. R., & Barone, R. (1984). Personal versus impersonal methods for recruiting blood donations. *Journal of Social Psychology, 123,* 139–140.

Jeffery, R. W., Drewnowski, A., Epstein, L. H., Stunkard, A. J., Wilson, G. T., Wing, R. R., & Hill, D. R. (2000). Long-term maintenance of weight loss: Current status. *Health Psychology, 19,* No. 1 (Supplement), 5–16.

Jelalian, E., & Miller, A. G. (1984). The perseverance of beliefs: Conceptual perspectives and research developments. *Journal of Social and Clinical Psychology, 2,* 25–56.

Jellison, J. M., & Green, J. (1981). A self-presentation approach to the fundamental attribution error: The norm of internality. *Journal of Personality and Social Psychology, 40,* 643–649.

Jemmott, J. B., III., & Locke, S. E. (1984). Psychosocial factors, immunologic mediation, and human susceptibility to infectious diseases: How much do we know? *Psychological Bulletin, 95,* 78–108.

Jenkins, A. C., Macrae, C. N., & Mitchell, J. P. (2008). Repetition suppression of ventromedial prefrontal activity during judgments of self and others. *Proceedings of the National Academy of Sciences, 105,* 4507–4512 (www.pnas.org).

Jennings, D. L., Amabile, T. M., & Ross, L. (1982). Informal covariation assessment: Data-based vs theory-based judgments. In D. Kahneman, P. Slovic, & A. Tversky (Eds.), *Judgment under uncertainty: Heuristics and biases.* New York: Cambridge University Press.

Jervis, R. (1985). Perceiving and coping with threat: Psychological perspectives. In R. Jervis, R. N. Lebow, & J. Stein (Eds.), *Psychology and deterrence.* Baltimore: Johns Hopkins University Press.

Jetten, J., Hornsey, M. J., & Adarves-Yorno, I. (2006). When group members admit to being conformist: The role of relative intragroup status in conformity self-reports. *Personality and Social Psychology Bulletin, 32,* 162–173.

John, O. P., & Srivastava, S. (1999). The Big Five trait taxonomy: History, measurement, and theoretical perspectives. In L. A. Pervin & O. P. John (Eds.), *Handbook of personality: Theory and research.* New York: Guilford.

Johnson, A. L., Crawford, M. T., Sherman, S. J., Rutchick, A. M., Hamilton, D. L., Ferreira, M. B., & Petrocelli, J. V. (2006). A functional perspective on group memberships: Differential need fulfilment in group typology. *Journal of Experimental Social Psychology, 42,* 707–719.

Johnson, C. S., Olson, M. A., & Fazio, R. H. (2009). Getting acquainted in interracial interactions: Avoiding intimacy but approaching race. *Personality and Social Psychology Bulletin, 35,* 557–571.

Johnson, D. J., & Rusbult, C. E. (1989). Resisting temptation: Devaluation of alternative partners as a means of maintaining commitment in close relationships. *Journal of Personality and Social Psychology, 57,* 967–980.

Johnson, D. W., & Johnson, R. T. (1987). *Learning together and alone: Cooperative, competitive, and individualistic learning,* 2nd edition. Englewood Cliffs, NJ: Prentice-Hall.

Johnson, D. W., & Johnson, R. T. (1995). Teaching students to be peacemakers: Results of five years of research. *Peace and Conflict: Journal of Peace Psychology, 1,* 417–438.

Johnson, D. W., & Johnson, R. T. (2000). The three Cs of reducing prejudice and discrimination. In S. Oskamp (Ed.), *Reducing prejudice and discrimination.* Mahwah, NJ: Erlbaum.

Johnson, D. W., & Johnson, R. T. (2003a). Field testing integrative negotiations. *Peace and Conflict, 9,* 39–68.

Johnson, D. W., & Johnson, R. T. (2003b). Student motivation in co-operative groups: Social interdependence theory. In R. M. Gillies & A. F. Ashman (Eds.), *Co-operative learning: The social and intellectual outcomes of learning in groups.* New York: Routledge.

Johnson, D. W., & Johnson, R. T. (2004). Cooperation and the use of technology. In D. H. Jonassen (Eds.), *Handbook of research on educational communications and technology,* 2nd edition. Mahwah, NJ: Erlbaum.

Johnson, D. W., Maruyama, G., Johnson, R., Nelson, D., & Skon, L. (1981). Effects of cooperative, competitive, and individualistic goal structures on achievement: A meta-analysis. *Psychological Bulletin, 89,* 47–62.

Johnson, E. J., & Goldstein, D. (2003). Do defaults save lives? *Science, 302,* 1338–1339.

Johnson, J. A. (2007, June 26). Not so situational. Commentary on the SPSP listserv (spsp-discuss@stolaf.edu).

Johnson, J. D., Bushman, B. J., & Dovidio, J. F. (2008). Support for harmful treatment and reduction of empathy toward blacks: "Remnants" of stereotype activation involving Hurricane Katrina and "Lil' Kim." *Journal of Experimental Social Psychology, 44,* 1506–1513.

Johnson, J. D., Jackson, L. A., & Gatto, L. (1995). Violent attitudes and deferred academic aspirations: Deleterious effects of exposure to rap music. *Basic and Applied Social Psychology, 16,* 27–41.

Johnson, J. D., Olivo, N., Gibson, N., Reed, W., & Ashburn-Hardo, L. (2009). Priming media stereotypes reduces support for social welfare policies: The mediating role of empathy. *Personality and Social Psychology Bulletin, 35,* 463–475.

Johnson, J. D., Trawalter, S., & Dovidio, J. F. (2000). Converging interracial consequences of exposure to violent rap music on stereotypical attributions of Blacks. *Journal of Experimental Social Psychology, 36,* 233–251.

Johnson, J. G., Cohen, P., Smailes, E. M., Kasen, S., & Brook, J. S. (2002). Television viewing and aggressive behavior during adolescence and adulthood. *Science, 295,* 2468–2471.

Johnson, M. H., & Magaro, P. A. (1987). Effects of mood and severity on memory processes in depression and mania. *Psychological Bulletin, 101,* 28–40.

Johnson, P. (1988, November 25–27). Hearst seeks pardon. *USA Today,* p. 3A.

Johnson, R. D., & Downing, L. L. (1979). Deindividuation and valence of cues: Effects of prosocial and antisocial behavior. *Journal of Personality and Social Psychology, 37,* 1532–1538.

Johnson, W., & Krueger, R. F. (2006). How money buys happiness: Genetic and environmental processes linking finances and life satisfaction. *Journal of Personality and Social Psychology, 90,* 680–691.

Joiner, T. E., Jr. (1994). Contagious depression: Existence, specificity to depressed symptoms, and the role of reassurance seeking. *Journal of Personality and Social Psychology, 67,* 287–296.

Joiner, T. E., Jr. (1999). The clustering and contagion of suicide. *Current Directions in Psychological Science, 8,* 89–92.

Joinson, A. N. (2001). Self-disclosure in computer-mediated communication: The role of self-awareness and visual anonymity. *European Journal of Social Psychology, 31,* 177–192.

Joly-Mascheroni, R. M., Senju, A., & Shepherd, A. J. (2008). Dogs catch human yawns. *Biology Letters, 4,* 446–448.

Jonas, K. (1992). Modelling and suicide: A test of the Werther effect. *British Journal of Social Psychology, 31,* 295–306.

Jones, C. S., & Kaplan, M. F. (2003). The effects of racially stereotypical crimes on juror decision-making and information-processing strategies. *Basic and Applied Social Psychology, 25,* 1–13.

Jones, E. E. (1964). *Ingratiation.* New York: Appleton-Century-Crofts.

Jones, E. E. (1976). How do people perceive the causes of behavior? *American Scientist, 64,* 300–305.

Jones, E. E., & Davis, K. E. (1965). From acts to dispositions: The attribution process in person perception. In L. Berkowitz (Ed.), *Advances in experimental social psychology* (Vol. 2). New York: Academic Press.

Jones, E. E., & Harris, V. A. (1967). The attribution of attitudes. *Journal of Experimental Social Psychology, 3,* 2–24.

Jones, E. E., & Nisbett, R. E. (1971). *The actor and the observer: Divergent perceptions of the causes of behavior.* Morristown, NJ: General Learning Press.

Jones, E. E., Rhodewalt, F., Berglas, S., & Skelton, J. A. (1981). Effects of strategic self-presentation on subsequent self-esteem. *Journal of Personality and Social Psychology,* **41,** 407–421.

Jones, E. E., Rock, L., Shaver, K. G., Goethals, G. R., & Ward, L. M. (1968). Pattern of performance and ability attribution: An unexpected primacy effect. *Journal of Personality and Social Psychology,* **10,** 317–340.

Jones, E. E., Williams, K. D., & Brewer, N. (2008). "I had a confidence epiphany!" Obstacles to combating post-identification confidence inflation. *Law and Human Behavior,* **32,** 164–176.

Jones, J. M. (1988). Piercing the veil: Bi-cultural strategies for coping with prejudice and racism. Invited address at the national conference "Opening Doors: An Appraisal of Race Relations in America," University of Alabama, June 11.

Jones, J. M. (2003). TRIOS: A psychological theory of the African legacy in American culture. *Journal of Social Issues,* **59,** 217–242.

Jones, J. M. (2003, April 4). Blacks show biggest decline in support for war compared with 1991. Gallup Poll (www.gallup.com).

Jones, J. M. (2004). TRIOS: A model for coping with the universal context of racism? In G. Philogène (Ed.), *Racial identity in context: The legacy of Kenneth B. Clark.* Washington, DC: American Psychological Association.

Jones, J. T., & Cunningham, J. D. (1996). Attachment styles and other predictors of relationship satisfaction in dating couples. *Personal Relationships,* **3,** 387–399.

Jones, J. T., Pelham, B. W., Carvallo, M., & Mirenberg, M. C. (2004). How do I love thee? Let me count the Js: Implicit egotism and interpersonal attraction. *Journal of Personality and Social Psychology,* **87,** 665–683.

Jones, J. T., Pelham, B. W., & Mirenberg, M. C. (2002). Name letter preferences are not merely mere exposure: Implicit egotism as self-regulation. *Journal of Experimental Social Psychology,* **38,** 170–177.

Jones, R. A., & Brehm, J. W. (1970). Persuasiveness of one- and two-sided communications as a function of awareness there are two sides. *Journal of Experimental Social Psychology,* **6,** 47–56.

Jones, T. F., & 7 others. (2000). Mass psychogenic illness attributed to toxic exposure at a high school. *New England Journal of Medicine,* **342,** 96–100.

Jones, W. H., Carpenter, B. N., & Quintana, D. (1985). Personality and interpersonal predictors of loneliness in two cultures. *Journal of Personality and Social Psychology,* **48,** 1503–1511.

Josephson, W. L. (1987). Television violence and children's aggression: Testing the priming, social script, and disinhibition predictions. *Journal of Personality and Social Psychology,* **53,** 882–890.

Jost, J. T., & Kay, A. C. (2005). Exposure to benevolent sexism and complementary gender stereotypes: Consequences for specific and diffuse forms of system justification. *Journal of Personality and Social Psychology,* **88,** 498–509.

Jourard, S. M. (1964), *The transparent self.* Princeton, NJ: Van Nostrand.

Jourden, F. J., & Heath, C. (1996). The evaluation gap in performance perceptions: Illusory perceptions of groups and individuals. *Journal of Applied Psychology,* **81,** 369–379.

Judd, C. M., Blair, I. V., & Chapleau, K. M. (2004). Automatic stereotypes vs. automatic prejudice: Sorting out the possibilities in the Payne (2001) weapon paradigm. *Journal of Experimental Social Psychology,* **40,** 75–81.

Jussim, L. (1986). Self-fulfilling prophecies: A theoretical and integrative review. *Psychological Review,* **93,** 429–445.

Jussim, L. (2005). Accuracy in social perception: Criticisms, controversies, criteria, components and cognitive processes. *Advances in Experimental Social Psychology,* **37,** 1–93.

Jussim, L., & Harber, K. D. (2005). Teacher expectations and self-fulfilling prophecies: Knowns and unknowns, resolved and unresolved controversies. *Personality and Social Psychology Review,* **9,** 131–155.

Jussim, L., McCauley, C. R., & Lee, Y-T. (1995). Introduction: Why study stereotype accuracy and innaccuracy? In Y. T. Lee, L. Jussim, & C. R. McCauley (Eds.), *Stereotypes accuracy: Toward appreciating group differences.* Washington, DC: American Psychological Association.

Kagan, J. (1989). Temperamental contributions to social behavior. *American Psychologist,* **44,** 668–674.

Kagan, J. (2009). Historical selection. *Review of General Psychology,* **13,** 77–88.

Kagehiro, D. K. (1990). Defining the standard of proof in jury instructions. *Psychological Science,* **1,** 194–200.

Kahle, L. R., & Berman, J. (1979). Attitudes cause behaviors: A cross-lagged panel analysis. *Journal of Personality and Social Psychology,* **37,** 315–321.

Kahlor, L., & Morrison, D. (2007). Television viewing and rape myth acceptance among college women. *Sex Roles,* **56,** 729–739.

Kahn, M. W. (1951). The effect of severe defeat at various age levels on the aggressive behavior of mice. *Journal of Genetic Psychology,* **79,** 117–130.

Kahneman, D., & Miller, D. T. (1986). Norm theory: Comparing reality to its alternatives. *Psychological Review,* **93,** 75–88.

Kahneman, D., & Renshon, J. (2007, January/February). Why hawks win. *Foreign Policy* (www.foreignpolicy.com).

Kahneman, D., & Snell, J. (1992). Predicting a changing taste: Do people know what they will like? *Journal of Behavioral Decision Making,* **5,** 187–200.

Kahneman, D., & Tversky, A. (1979). Intuitive prediction: Biases and corrective procedures. *Management Science,* **12,** 313–327.

Kahneman, D., & Tversky, A. (1995). Conflict resolution: A cognitive perspective. In K. Arrow, R. Mnookin, L. Ross, A. Tversky, & R. Wilson (Eds.), *Barriers to the negotiated resolution of conflict.* New York: Norton.

Kaiser Family Foundation. (2001). National survey. Most gays and lesbians see greater acceptance. News release, November 13, 2001 (www.kff.org).

Kaiser Family Foundation. (2005, November 9). *Sex on TV4* (www.kff.org).

Kalick, S. M. (1977). *Plastic surgery, physical appearance, and person perception.* Unpublished doctoral dissertation, Harvard University. Cited by E. Berscheid in An overview of the psychological effects of physical attractiveness and some comments upon the psychological effects of knowledge of the effects of physical attractiveness. In W. Lucker, K. Ribbens, & J. A. McNamera (Eds.), *Logical aspects of facial form* (craniofacial growth series). Ann Arbor: University of Michigan Press, 1981.

Kalven, H., Jr., & Zeisel, H. (1966). *The American jury.* Chicago: University of Chicago Press.

Kameda, T., & Sugimori, S. (1993). Psychological entrapment in group decision making: An assigned decision rule and a groupthink phenomenon. *Journal of Personality and Social Psychology,* **65,** 282–292.

Kammer, D. (1982). Differences in trait ascriptions to self and friend: Unconfounding intensity from variability. *Psychological Reports,* **51,** 99–102.

Kanagawa, C., Cross, S. E., & Markus, H. R. (2001). "Who am I?" The cultural psychology of the conceptual self. *Personality and Social Psychology Bulletin, 27,* 90–103.

Kanazawa, S., & Kovar, J. L. (2004). Why beautiful people are more intelligent. *Intelligence, 32,* 227–243.

Kandel, D. B. (1978). Similarity in real-life adolescent friendship pairs. *Journal of Personality and Social Psychology, 36,* 306–312.

Kanekar, S., & Nazareth, A. (1988). Attributed rape victim's fault as a function of her attractiveness, physical hurt, and emotional disturbance. *Social Behaviour, 3, 37–40.*

Kanten, A. B., & Teigen, K. H. (2008). Better than average and better with time: Relative evaluations of self and others in the past, present, and future. *European Journal of Social Psychology, 38,* 343–353.

Kaplan, M. F. (1989). Task, situational, and personal determinants of influence processes in group decision making. In E. J. Lawler (Ed.), *Advances in group processes* (Vol. 6). Greenwich, CT: JAI Press.

Kaplan, M. F., & Martin, A. M. (2006). *Understanding world jury systems through social psychological research.* Florence, KY: Taylor and Francis.

Kaplan, M. F., & Schersching, C. (1980). Reducing juror bias: An experimental approach. In P. D. Lipsitt & B. D. Sales (Eds.), *New directions in psycholegal research* (pp. 149–170). New York: Van Nostrand Reinhold.

Kaplan, M. F., Wanshula, L. T., & Zanna, M. P. (1993). Time pressure and information integration in social judgment: The effect of need for structure. In O. Svenson & J. Maule (Eds.), *Time pressure and stress in human judgment and decision making.* Cambridge, England: Cambridge University Press.

Kaprio, J., Koskenvuo, M., & Rita, H. (1987). Mortality after bereavement: A prospective study of 95,647 widowed persons. *American Journal of Public Health, 77,* 283–287.

Karau, S. J., & Williams, K. D. (1993). Social loafing: A meta-analytic review and theoretical integration. *Journal of Personality and Social Psychology, 65,* 681–706.

Karau, S. J., & Williams, K. D. (1997). The effects of group cohesiveness on social loafing and compensation. *Group Dynamics: Theory, Research, and Practice, 1,* 156–168.

Karney, B. R., & Bradbury, T. N. (1995). The longitudinal course of marital quality and stability: A review of theory, method, and research. *Psychological Bulletin, 118,* 3–34.

Karney, B. R., & Bradbury, T. N. (1997). Neuroticism, marital interaction, and the trajectory of marital satisfaction. *Journal of Personality and Social Psychology, 72,* 1075–1092.

Kasen, S., Chen, H., Sneed, J., Crawford, T., & Cohen, P. (2006). Social role and birth cohort influences on gender-linked personality traits in women: A 20-year longitudinal analysis. *Journal of Personality and Social Psychology, 91,* 944–958.

Kashima, E. S., & Kashima, Y. (1998). Culture and language: the case of cultural dimensions and personal pronoun use. *Journal of Cross-Cultural Psychology, 29,* 461–486.

Kashima, Y., & Kashima, E. S. (2003). Individualism, GNP, climate, and pronoun drop: Is individualism determined by affluence and climate, or does language use play a role? *Journal of Cross-Cultural Psychology, 34,* 125–134.

Kasser, T. (2000). Two versions of the American dream: Which goals and values make for a high quality of life? In E. Diener and D. Rahtz (Eds.), *Advances in quality of life: Theory and research.* Dordrecht, Netherlands: Kluwer.

Kasser, T. (2002). *The high price of materialism.* Cambridge, MA: MIT Press.

Kassin, S. M., Goldstein, C. C., & Savitsky, K. (2003). Behavioral confirmation in the interrogation room: On the dangers of presuming guilt. *Law and Human Behavior, 27,* 187–203.

Kassin, S. M., Tubb, V. A., Hosch, H. M., & Memon, A. (2001). On the "general acceptance" of eyewitness testimony research: A new survey of the experts. *American Psychologist, 56,* 405–416.

Kassin, S. M., & Wrightsman, L. S. (1979). On the requirements of proof: The timing of judicial instruction and mock juror verdicts. *Journal of Personality and Social Psychology, 37,* 1877–1887.

Katz, E. (1957). The two-step flow of communication: An up-to-date report on a hypothesis. *Public Opinion Quarterly, 21,* 61–78.

Katz, I., Cohen, S., & Glass, D. (1975). Some determinants of cross-racial helping behavior. *Journal of Personality and Social Psychology, 32,* 964–970.

Katz, J., Beach, S. R. H., & Joiner, T. E., Jr. (1999). Contagious depression in dating couples. *Journal of Social and Clinical Psychology, 18,* 1–13.

Katzev, R., Edelsack, L., Steinmetz, G., & Walker, T. (1978). The effect of reprimanding transgressions on subsequent helping behavior: Two field experiments. *Personality and Social Psychology Bulletin, 4,* 126–129.

Katzev, R., & Wang, T. (1994). Can commitment change behavior? A case study of environmental actions. *Journal of Social Behavior and Personality, 9,* 13–26.

Kaufman, J., & Zigler, E. (1987). Do abused children become abusive parents? *American Journal of Orthopsychiatry, 57,* 186–192.

Kawachi, I., Kennedy, B. P., & Wilkinson, R. G. (1999). Crime: Social disorganization and relative deprivation. *Social Science and Medicine, 48,* 719–731.

Kawachi, I., Kennedy, B. P., Wilkinson, R. G., & Kawachi, K. W. (Eds.). (1999). *Society and population health reader: Income inequality and health.* New York: New Press.

Kawakami, K., Dovidio, J. F., Moll, J., Hermsen, S., & Russin, A. (2000). Just say no (to stereotyping): Effects of training in the negation of stereotypic associations on stereotype activation. *Journal of Personality and Social Psychology, 78,* 871–888.

Kawakami, K., Dunn, E., Kiarmali, F., & Dovidio, J. F. (2009). Mispredicting affective and behavioral responses to racism. *Science, 323,* 276–278.

Keating, J. P., & Brock, T. C. (1974). Acceptance of persuasion and the inhibition of counterargumentation under various distraction tasks. *Journal of Experimental Social Psychology, 10,* 301–309.

Kebbell, M. R., Milne, R., & Wagstaff, G. F. (1999). The cognitive interview: A survey of its forensic effectiveness. *Psychology, Crime, and Law, 5,* 101–115.

Keizer, K., Lindenberg, S., & Steg, L. (2008). The spreading of disorder. *Science, 322,* 1681–1685.

Keller, E. B., & Berry, B. (2003). *The influentials: One American in ten tells the other nine how to vote, where to eat, and what to buy.* New York: Free Press.

Keller, J., & Dauenheimer, D. (2003). Stereotype threat in the classroom: Dejection mediates the disrupting threat effect on women's math performance. *Personality and Social Psychology Bulletin, 29,* 371–381.

Kellerman, J., Lewis, J., & Laird, J. D. (1989). Looking and loving: The effects of mutual gaze on feelings of romantic love. *Journal of Research in Personality, 23,* 145–161.

Kellermann, A. L. (1997). Comment: Gunsmoke—changing public attitudes toward smoking and firearms. *American Journal of Public Health, 87,* 910–912.

Kellermann, A. L., & 9 others. (1993). Gun ownership as a risk factor for homicide in the home. *New England Journal of Medicine, 329,* 1984–1991.

Kelley, H. H. (1973). The process of causal attribution. *American Psychologist, 28,* 107–128.

Kelley, H. H., & Stahelski, A. J. (1970). The social interaction basis of cooperators' and competitors' beliefs about others. *Journal of Personality and Social Psychology, 16,* 66–91.

Kelley, K., Dawson, L., & Musialowski, D. M. (1989). Three faces of sexual explicitness: The good, the bad, and the useful. In D. Zillmann & J. Bryant (Eds.), *Pornography: Reesearch advances and policy considerations.* Hillsdale, NJ: Erlbaum.

Kelly, D. J., Liu, S., Ge, L., Quinn, P. C., Slater, A. M., Lee, K., Liu, Q., & Pascalis, O. (2007). Cross-race preferences for same-race faces extended beyond the African versus Caucasian contrast in 3-month-old infants. *Infancy,* **11,** 87–95.

Kelly, D. J., Quinn, P. C., Slater, A. M., Lee, K., Ge, L., & Pascalis, O. (2007). The other-race effect develops during infancy: Evidence of perceptual narrowing. *Psychological Science,* **18,** 1084–1089.

Kelly, D. J., Quinn, P. C., Slater, A. M., Lee, K., Gibson, A., Smith, M., Ge, L., & Y Pascalis, O. (2005). Three-month-olds, but not newborns prefer own-race faces. *Developmental Science,* **8,** F31–F36.

Kelman, H. C. (1997). Group processes in the resolution of international conflicts: Experiences from the Israeli-Palestinian case. *American Psychologist,* **52,** 212–220.

Kelman, H. C. (1998). Building a sustainable peace: The limits of pragmatism in the Israeli-Palestinian negotiations. Address to the American Psychological Association convention.

Kelman, H. C. (2007). The Israeli-Palestinian peace process and its vicissitudes: Insights from attitude theory. *American Psychologist,* **62,** 287–303.

Kelman, H. C. (2008). Evaluating the contributions of interactive problem solving to the resolution of ethnonational conflicts. *Peace and Conflict,* **14,** 29–60.

Kendler, K. S., Neale, M., Kessler, R., Heath, A., & Eaves, L. (1993). A twin study of recent life events and difficulties. *Archives of General Psychiatry,* **50,** 789–796.

Kennedy, D. (2006). New year, new look, old problem. *Science,* **311,** 15.

Kennedy, J. F. (1956). *Profiles in courage.* New York: Harper.

Kennedy, K. A., & Pronin, E. (2008). When disagreement gets ugly: Perceptions of bias and the escalation of conflict. *Personality and Social Psychology Bulletin,* **34,** 833–848.

Kenny, D. A., & Acitelli, L. K. (2001). Accuracy and bias in the perception of the partner in a close relationship. *Journal of Personality and Social Psychology,* **80,** 439–448.

Kenny, D. A., & Nasby, W. (1980). Splitting the reciprocity correlation. *Journal of Personality and Social Psychology,* **38,** 249–256.

Kenrick, D. T. (1987). Gender, genes, and the social environment: A biosocial interactionist perspective. In P. Shaver & C. Hendrick (Eds.), *Sex and gender: Review of personality and social psychology* (Vol. 7). Beverly Hills, CA: Sage.

Kenrick, D. T., & Gutierres, S. E. (1980). Contrast effects and judgments of physical attractiveness: When beauty becomes a social problem. *Journal of Personality and Social Psychology,* **38,** 131–140.

Kenrick, D. T., Gutierres, S. E., & Goldberg, L. L. (1989). Influence of popular erotica on judgments of strangers and mates. *Journal of Experimental Social Psychology,* **25,** 159–167.

Kenrick, D. T., & MacFarlane, S. W. (1986). Ambient temperature and horn-honking: A field study of the heat/aggression relationship. *Environment and Behavior,* **18,** 179–191.

Kenrick, D. T., Nieuweboer, S., & Buunk, A. P. (2009). Universal mechanisms and cultural diversity: Replacing the blank slate with a coloring book. In M. Schaller, A. Norenzayan, S. Heine, T. Yamagishi, & T. Kameda (Eds.), *Evolution, culture, and the human mind.* New York: Psychology Press.

Kenrick, D. T., & Trost, M. R. (1987). A biosocial theory of heterosexual relationships. In K. Kelly (Ed.), *Females, males, and sexuality.* Albany: State University of New York Press.

Kenworthy, J. B., Hewstone, M., Levine, J. M., Martin, R., & Willis, H. (2008). The phenomenology of minority-majority status: Effects of innovation in argument generation. *European Journal of Social Psychology,* **38,** 624–636.

Kernis, M. H. (2003). High self-esteem: A differentiated perspective. In E. C. Chang & L. J. Sanna (Eds.), *Virtue, vice, and personality: The complexity of behavior.* Washington, DC: APA Books.

Kerr, N. (1999). Behind the scenes. In D. G. Myers, *Social psychology,* 6th edition. New York: McGraw-Hill.

Kerr, N. L. (1978). Severity of prescribed penalty and mock jurors' verdicts. *Journal of Personality and Social Psychology,* **36,** 1431–1442.

Kerr, N. L. (1981a). Effects of prior juror experience on juror behavior. *Basic and Applied Social Psychology,* **2,** 175–193.

Kerr, N. L. (1981b). Social transition schemes: Charting the group's road to agreement. *Journal of Personality and Social Psychology,* **41,** 684–702.

Kerr, N. L. (1983). Motivation losses in small groups: A social dilemma analysis. *Journal of Personality and Social Psychology,* **45,** 819–828.

Kerr, N. L. (1989). Illusions of efficacy: The effects of group size on perceived efficacy in social dilemmas. *Journal of Experimental Social Psychology,* **25,** 287–313.

Kerr, N. L. (1992). Norms in social dilemmas. In D. Schroeder (Ed.), *Social dilemmas: Psychological perspectives.* New York: Praeger.

Kerr, N. L., Atkin, R. S., Stasser, G., Meek, D., Holt, R. W., & Davis, J. H. (1976). Guilt beyond a reasonable doubt: Effects of concept definition and assigned decision rule on the judgments of mock jurors. *Journal of Personality and Social Psychology,* **34,** 282–294.

Kerr, N. L., & Bray, R. M. (2005). Simulation, realism, and the study of the jury. In N. Brewer & K. D. Williams (Eds.), *Psychology and law: An empirical perspective.* New York: Guilford.

Kerr, N. L., & Bruun, S. E. (1981). Ringelmann revisted: Alternative explanations for the social loafing effect. *Personality and Social Psychology Bulletin,* **7,** 224–231.

Kerr, N. L., Garst, J., Lewandowski, D. A., & Harris, S. E. (1997). That still, small voice: Commitment to cooperate as an internalized versus a social norm. *Personality and Social Psychology Bulletin,* **23,** 1300–1311.

Kerr, N. L., Harmon, D. L., & Graves, J. K. (1982). Independence of multiple verdicts by jurors and juries. *Journal of Applied Social Psychology,* **12,** 12–29.

Kerr, N. L., & Kaufman-Gilliland, C. M. (1994). Communication, commitment, and cooperation in social dilemmas. *Journal of Personality and Social Psychology,* **66,** 513–529.

Kerr, N. L. & Kaufman-Gilliland, C. M. (1997). ". . . and besides, I probably couldn't have made a difference anyway": Justification of social dilemma defection via perceived self-inefficacy. *Journal of Experimental Social Psychology,* **33,** 211–230.

Kerr, N. L., & MacCoun, R. J. (1985). The effects of jury size and polling method on the process and product of jury deliberation. *Journal of Personality and Social Psychology,* **48,** 349–363.

Kerr, N. L., Messé, L. A., Seok, D-H., Sambolec, E. J., Lount, R. B., Jr., & Park, E. S. (2007). Psychological mechanisms underlying the Köhler motivation gain. *Personality and Social Psychology Bulletin,* **33,** 828–841.

Kerr, R. A. (2007a). Scientists tell policymakers we're all warming the world. *Science,* **315,** 754–757.

Kerr, R. A. (2007b). How urgent is climate change? *Science,* **318,** 1230–1231.

Kerr, R. A. (2007c). Is battered Arctic Sea ice down for the count? *Science,* **318,** 33.

Kerr, R. A. (2007d). Pushing the scary side of global warming. *Science,* **316,** 1412–1415.

Kessler, T., & Mummendey, A. (2001). Is there any scapegoat around? Determinants of intergroup conflicts at different categorization levels. *Journal of Personality and Social Psychology, 81,* 1090–1102.

Kidd, J. B., & Morgan, J. R. (1969). A predictive information system for management. *Operational Research Quarterly, 20,* 149–170.

Kiecolt-Glaser, J. K., Loving, T. J., Stowell, J. R., Malarkey, W. B., Lemeshow, S., Dickinson, S. L., & Glaser, R. (2005). Hostile marital interactions, proinflammatory cytokine production, and wound healing. *Archives of General Psychiatry, 62,* 1377–1384.

Kiecolt-Glaser, J. K., Malarkey, W. B., Chee, M., Newton, T., Cacioppo, J. T., Mao, H-Y., & Glaser, R. (1993). Negative behavior during marital conflict is associated with immunological down-regulation. *Psychosomatic Medicine, 55,* 395–409.

Kiesler, C. A. (1971). *The psychology of commitment: Experiments linking behavior to belief.* New York: Academic Press.

Kihlstrom, J. F. (1994). The social construction of memory. Address to the American Psychological Society convention.

Kihlstrom, J. F., & Cantor, N. (1984). Mental representations of the self. In L. Berkowitz (Ed.), *Advances in experimental social psychology* (Vol. 17). New York: Academic Press.

Kim, H., & Markus, H. R. (1999). Deviance of uniqueness, harmony or conformity? A cultural analysis. *Journal of Personality and Social Psychology, 77,* 785–800.

Kim, H. S., & Sherman, D. K. (2007). "Express yourself": Culture and the effect of self-expression on choice. *Journal of Personality and Social Psychology, 92,* 1–11.

Kimmel, A. J. (1998). In defense of deception. *American Psychologist, 53,* 803–805.

Kinder, D. R., & Sears, D. O. (1985). Public opinion and political action. In G. Lindzey & E. Aronson (Eds.), *The handbook of social psychology,* 3rd edition. New York: Random House.

King, L. A. (2001). The health benefits of writing about life goals. *Personality and Social Psychology Bulletin, 27,* 798–807.

Kingdon, J. W. (1967). Politicans' beliefs about voters. *The American Political Science Review, 61,* 137–145.

Kingston, D. A., Fedoroff, P., Firestone, P., Curry, S., & Bradford, J. M. (2008). Pornography use and sexual aggression: The impact of frequency and type of pornography use on recidivism among sexual offenders. *Aggressive Behavior, 34,* 341–351.

Kingston, D. A., Malamuth, N. M., Federoff, P., & Marshall, W. L. (2009). The importance of individual differences in pornography use: Theoretical perspectives and implications for treating sexual offenders. *Journal of Sex Research, 46,* 216–232.

Kinnier, R. T., & Metha, A. T. (1989). Regrets and priorities at three stages of life. *Counseling and Values, 33,* 182–193.

Kinsley, M. (2003, April 21). The power of one. *Time,* p. 86.

Kirsh, S. J. (2006). Cartoon violence and aggression in youth. *Aggression and Violent Behavior, 11,* 547–557.

Kitayama, S. (1996). The mutual constitution of culture and the self: Implications for emotion. Paper presented at the American Psychological Society convention.

Kitayama, S. (1999). Behind the scenes. In D. G. Myers, *Social Psychology,* 6th edition. New York: McGraw-Hill.

Kitayama, S., & Karasawa, M. (1997). Implicit self-esteem in Japan: Name letters and birthday numbers. *Personality and Social Psychology Bulletin, 23,* 736–742.

Kitayama, S., & Markus, H. R. (1995). Culture and self: Implications for internationalizing psychology. In N. R. Godlberger & J. B. Veroff (Eds.), *The culture and psychology reader.* New York: New York University Press.

Kitayama, S., & Markus, H. R. (2000). The pursuit of happiness and the realization of sympathy: Cultural patterns of self, social relations, and well-being. In E. Diener & E. M. Suh (Eds.), *Subjective well-being across cultures.* Cambridge, MA: MIT Press.

Kite, M. E. (2001). Changing times, changing gender roles: Who do we want women and men to be? In R. K. Unger (Ed.), *Handbook of the psychology of women and gender.* New York: Wiley.

Klaas, E. T. (1978). Psychological effects of immoral actions: The experimental evidence. *Psychological Bulletin, 85,* 756–771.

Klapwijk, A., & Van Lange, P. A. M. (2009). Promoting cooperation and trust in "noisy" situations: The power of generosity. *Journal of Personality and Social Psychology, 96,* 83–103.

Klauer, K. C., & Voss, A. (2008). Effects of race on responses and response latencies in the weapon identification task: A test of six models. *Personality and Social Psychology Bulletin, 34,* 1124–1140.

Kleck, R. E., & Strenta, A. (1980). Perceptions of the impact of negatively valued physical characteristics on social interaction. *Journal of Personality and Social Psychology, 39,* 861–873.

Klein, I., & Snyder, M. (2003). Stereotypes and behavioral confirmation: From interpersonal to intergroup perspectives. *Advances in Experimental Social Psychology, 35,* 153–235.

Klein, J. G. (1991). Negative effects in impression formation: A test in the political arena. *Personality and Social Psychology Bulletin, 17,* 412–418.

Klein, O., Snyder, M., & Livingston, R. W. (2004). Prejudice on the stage: Self-monitoring and the public expression of group attitudes. *British Journal of Social Psychology, 43,* 299–314.

Klein, W. M., & Kunda, Z. (1992). Motivated person perception: Constructing justifications for desired beliefs. *Journal of Experimental Social Psychology, 28,* 145–168.

Kleinke, C. L. (1977). Compliance to requests made by gazing and touching experimenters in field settings. *Journal of Experimental Social Psychology, 13,* 218–223.

Kleinke, C. L., Peterson, T. R., & Rutledge, R. R. (1998). Effects of self-generated facial expressions on mood. *Journal of Personality and Social Psychology, 74,* 272–279.

Klentz, B., Beaman, A. L., Mapelli, S. D., & Ullrich, J. R. (1987). Perceived physical attractiveness of supporters and nonsupporters of the women's movement: An attitude-similarity mediated error (AS-ME). *Personality and Social Psychology Bulletin, 13,* 513–523.

Klinesmith, J., Kasser, T., & McAndrew, F. T. (2006). Guns, testosterone, and aggression. *Psychological Science, 17*(7), 568–571.

Klopfer, P. H. (1958). Influence of social interaction on learning rates in birds. *Science, 128,* 903.

Klucharev, V., Hytönen, K., Rijpkema, M., Smidts, A., & Fernández, G. (2009). Reinforcement learning signal predicts conformity. *Neuron, 61,* 140–151.

Knight, G. P., Fabes, R. A., & Higgins, D. A. (1996). Concerns about drawing causal inferences from meta-analyses: An example in the study of gender differences in aggression. *Psychological Bulletin, 119,* 410–421.

Knight, J. A., & Vallacher, R. R. (1981). Interpersonal engagement in social perception: The consequences of getting into the action. *Journal of Personality and Social Psychology, 40,* 990–999.

Knight, P. A., & Weiss, H. M. (1980). Benefits of suffering: Communicator suffering, benefitting, and influence. Paper presented at the American Psychological Association convention.

Knowles, E. D., & Peng, K. (2005). White selves: Conceptualizing and measuring a dominant-group identity. *Journal of Personality and Social Psychology, 89,* 223–241.

Knowles, E. S. (1983). Social physics and the effects of others: Tests of the effects of audience size and distance on social judgment and behavior. *Journal of Personality and Social Psychology, 45*, 1263–1279.

Knox, R. E., & Inkster, J. A. (1968). Postdecision dissonance at post-time. *Journal of Personality and Social Psychology, 8*, 319–323.

Knudson, R. M., Sommers, A. A., & Golding, S. L. (1980). Interpersonal perception and mode of resolution in marital conflict. *Journal of Personality and Social Psychology, 38*, 751–763.

Koehler, D. J. (1991). Explanation, imagination, and confidence in judgment. *Psychological Bulletin, 110*, 499–519.

Koehler, J. J., & Macchi, L. (2004). Thinking about low-probability events. *Psychological Science, 15*, 540–546.

Koenig, L. B., McGue, M., & Iacono, W. G. (2008). Stability and change in religiousness during emerging adulthood. *Developmental Psychology, 44*, 531–543.

Koestner, R. F. (1993). False consensus effects for the 1992 Canadian referendum. Paper presented at the American Psychological Association convention.

Koestner, R., & Wheeler, L. (1988). Self-presentation in personal advertisements: The influence of implicit notions of attraction and role expectations. *Journal of Social and Personal Relationships, 5*, 149–160.

Kohnken, G., Milne, R., Memon, A., & Bull, R. (1999). The cognitive interview: A meta-analysis. *Psychology, Crime, and Law, 5*, 3–27.

Kolata, G., & Peterson, I. (2001, July 21). New way to insure eyewitnesses can ID the right bad guy. *New York Times* (www.nytimes.com).

Kolivas, E. D., & Gross, A. M. (2007). Assessing sexual aggression: Addressing the gap between rape victimization and perpetration prevalence rates. *Aggression and Violent Behavior, 12*, 315–328.

Komorita, S. S., & Barth, J. M. (1985). Components of reward in social dilemmas. *Journal of Personality and Social Psychology, 48*, 364–373.

Konrad, A. M., Ritchie, J. E., Jr., Lieb, P., & Corrigall, E. (2000). Sex differences and similarities in job attribute preferences: A meta-analysis. *Psychological Bulletin, 126*, 593–641.

Koo, M., Algoe, S. B., Wilson, T. D., & Gilbert, D. T. (2008). It's a wonderful life: Mentally subtracting positive events improves people's affective states, contrary to their affective forecasts. *Journal of Personality and Social Psychology, 95*, 1217–1224.

Koole, S. L., Dijksterhuis, A., & van Knippenberg, A. (2001). What's in a name? Implicit self-esteem and the automatic self. *Journal of Personality and Social Psychology, 80*, 669–685.

Koomen, W., & Bahler, M. (1996). National stereotypes: Common representations and ingroup favouritism. *European Journal of Social Psychology, 26*, 325–331.

Koomen, W., & Dijker, A. J. (1997). Ingroup and outgroup stereotypes and selective processing. *European Journal of Social Psychology, 27*, 589–601.

Koop, C. E. (1987). Report of the Surgeon General's workshop on pornography and public health. *American Psychologist, 42*, 944–945.

Koppel, M., Argamon, S., & Shimoni, A. R. (2002). Automatically categorizing written texts by author gender. *Literary and Linguistic Computing, 17*, 401–412.

Koriat, A., Lichtenstein, S., & Fischhoff, B. (1980). Reasons for confidence. *Journal of Experimental Social Psychology: Human Learning and Memory, 6*, 107–118.

Korn, J. H., & Nicks, S. D. (1993). The rise and decline of deception in social psychology. Poster presented at the American Psychological Society convention.

Koss, M. P., Heise, L., & Russo, N. F. (1994). The global health burden of rape. *Psychology of Women Quarterly, 18*, 509–537.

Krackow, A., & Blass, T. (1995). When nurses obey or defy inappropriate physician orders: Attributional differences. *Journal of Social Behavior and Personality, 10*, 585–594.

Krahé, B. (1998). Sexual aggression among adolescents: Prevalence and predictors in a German sample. *Psychology of Women Quarterly, 22*, 537–554.

Kramer, A. E. (2008, August 32). Russia's collective farms: Hot capitalist property. *New York Times* (www.nytimes.com).

Kramer, G. P., Kerr, N. L., & Carroll, J. S. (1990). Pretrial publicity, judicial remedies, and jury bias. *Law and Human Behavior, 14*, 409–438.

Kraus, S. J. (1995). Attitudes and the prediction of behavior: A meta-analysis of the empirical literature. *Personality and Social Psychology Bulletin, 21*, 58–75.

Kraut, R. E. (1973). Effects of social labeling on giving to charity. *Journal of Experimental Social Psychology, 9*, 551–562.

Kravitz, D. A., & Martin, B. (1986). Ringelmann rediscovered: The original article. *Journal of Personality and Social Psychology, 50*, 936–941.

Krebs, D. (1970). Altruism—An examination of the concept and a review of the literature. *Psychological Bulletin, 73*, 258–302.

Krebs, D. (1975). Empathy and altruism. *Journal of Personality and Social Psychology, 32*, 1134–1146.

Krebs, D. L. (1998). The evolution of moral behaviors. In C. Crawford & D. L. Krebs (Eds.), *Handbook of evolutionary psychology: Ideas, issues, and applications*. Mahwah, NJ: Erlbaum.

Krebs, D., & Adinolfi, A. A. (1975). Physical attractiveness, social relations, and personality style. *Journal of Personality and Social Psychology, 31*, 245–253.

Krendl, A. C., Richeson, J. A., Kelley, W. M., & Heatherton, T. F. (2008). The negative consequences of threat: A functional magnetic resonance imaging investigation of the neural mechanisms underlying women's underperformance in math. *Psychological Science, 19*, 168–175.

Kressel, K., & Pruitt, D. G. (1985). Themes in the mediation of social conflict. *Journal of Social Issues, 41*, 179–198.

Kressel, N. J., & Kressel, D. F. (2002). *Stack and sway: The new science of jury consulting*. Boulder, CO: Westview.

Krisberg, K. (2004). Successful "truth" anti-smoking campaign in funding jeopardy: New commission works to save campaign. *Medscape* (www.medscape.com).

Kristof, N. D. (2007, August 16). The big melt. *New York Times* (www.nytimes.com).

Krizan, Z., & Suls, J. (2008). Losing sight of oneself in the above-average effect: When egocentrism, focalism, and group diffuseness collide. *Journal of Experimental Social Psychology, 44*, 929–942.

Kroger, R. O., & Wood, L. A. (1992). Are the rules of address universal? IV: Comparison of Chinese, Korean, Greek, and German usage. *Journal of Cross-Cultural Psychology, 23*, 148–162.

Krosnick, J. A., & Alwin, D. F. (1989). Aging and susceptibility to attitude change. *Journal of Personality and Social Psychology, 57*, 416–425.

Krosnick, J. A., & Schuman, H. (1988). Attitude intensity, importance, and certainty and susceptibility to response effects. *Journal of Personality and Social Psychology, 54*, 940–952.

Krueger, A. (2007a, November/December). What makes a terrorist. *The American* (www.american.com).

Krueger, A. (2007b). *What makes a terrorist: Economics and the roots of terrorism*. Princeton, NJ: Princeton University Press.

Krueger, J. (1996). Personal beliefs and cultural stereotypes about racial characteristics. *Journal of Personality and Social Psychology, 71*, 536–548.

Krueger, J., & Clement, R. W. (1994a). Memory-based judgments about multiple categories: A revision and extension of Tajfel's accentuation theory. *Journal of Personality and Social Psychology, 67,* 35–47.

Krueger, J., & Clement, R. W. (1994b). The truly false consensus effect: An ineradicable and egocentric bias in social perception. *Journal of Personality and Social Psychology, 67,* 596–610.

Krueger, J., & Rothbart, M. (1988). Use of categorical and individuating information in making inferences about personality. *Journal of Personality and Social Psychology, 55,* 187–195.

Krueger, J. I. (2007). From social projection to social behaviour. *European Review of Social Psychology, 18,* 1–35.

Krueger, J. I., & Funder, D. C. (2003a). Towards a balanced social psychology: Causes, consequences and cures for the problem-seeking approach to social behavior and cognition. *Behavioral and Brain Sciences, 27*(3), 313–327.

Krueger, J. I., & Funder, D. C. (2003b). Social psychology: A field in search of a center. *Behavioral and Brain Sciences, 27*(3), 361–367.

Krueger, R. F., Hicks, B. M., & McGue, M. (2001). Altruism and antisocial behavior: Independent tendencies, unique personality correlates, distinct etiologies. *Psychological Science, 12,* 397–402.

Kruger, J., & Dunning, D. (1999). Unskilled and unaware of it: How difficulties in recognizing one's own incompetence lead to inflated self-assessments. *Journal of Personality and Social Psychology, 77,* 1121–1134.

Kruger, J., & Evans, M. (2004). If you don't want to be late, enumerate: Unpacking reduces the planning fallacy. *Journal of Experimental Social Psychology, 40,* 586–598.

Kruger, J., & Gilovich, T. (1999). "I cynicism" in everyday theories of responsibility assessment: On biased assumptions of bias. *Journal of Personality and Social Psychology, 76,* 743–753.

Kruger, J., Gordon, C. L., & Kuban, J. (2006). Intentions in teasing: When "just kidding" just isn't good enough. *Journal of Personality and Social Psychology, 90,* 412–425.

Kruger, J., & Savitsky, K. (2009). On the genesis of inflated (and deflated) judgments of responsibility. *Organizational Behavior and Human Decision Processes, 108,* 143–152.

Kruger, J., Windschitl, P. D., Burrus, J., Fessel, F., & Chambers, J. R. (2008). The rational side of egocentrism in social comparisons. *Journal of Experimental Social Psychology, 44,* 220–232.

Kruger, J., Wirtz, D., & Miller, D. T. (2005). Counterfactual thinking and the first instinct fallacy. *Journal of Personality and Social Psychology, 88,* 725–735.

Kruglanski, A. W., & Ajzen, I. (1983). Bias and error in human judgment. *European Journal of Social Psychology, 13,* 1–44.

Kruglanski, A. W., & Fishman, S. (2006). The psychology of terrorism: "Syndrome" versus "tool" perspective. *Journal of Terrorism and Political Violence, 18*(2), 193–215.

Kruglanski, A. W., & Golec de Zavala, A. (2005) Individual motivations, the group process and organizational strategies in suicide terrorism. *Psychology and Sociology (Psycologie et sociologie).*

Kruglanski, A. W., & Webster, D. M. (1991). Group members' reactions to opinion deviates and conformists at varying degrees of proximity to decision deadline and of environmental noise. *Journal of Personality and Social Psychology, 61,* 212–225.

Krugman, P. (2003, February 18). Behind the great divide. *New York Times* (www.nytimes.com).

Krull, D. S., Loy, M. H-M., Lin, J., Wang, C-F., Chen, S., & Zhao, X. (1999). The fundamental fundamental attribution error: Correspondence bias in individualist and collectivist cultures. *Personality and Social Psychology Bulletin, 25,* 1208–1219.

Kubany, E. S., Bauer, G. B., Pangilinan, M. E., Muroka, M. Y., & Enriquez, V. G. (1995). Impact of labeled anger and blame in intimate relationships. *Journal of Cross-Cultural Psychology, 26,* 65–83.

Kubey, R., & Csikszentmihalyi, M. (2002, February). Television addiction is no mere metaphor. *Scientific American, 286,* 74–82.

Kugihara, N. (1999). Gender and social loafing in Japan. *Journal of Social Psychology, 139,* 516–526.

Kuiper, N. A., & Higgins, E. T. (1985). Social cognition and depression: A general integrative perspective. *Social Cognition, 3,* 1–15.

Kull, S. (2003, June 4). Quoted in "Many Americans unaware WMD have not been found." Program on International Policy Attitudes (http://pipa.org/whatsnew/html/new_6_04_03.html).

Kunda, Z., & Oleson, K. C. (1995). Maintaining stereotypes in the face of disconfirmation: Constructing grounds for subtyping deviants. *Journal of Personality and Social Psychology, 68,* 565–579.

Kunda, Z., & Oleson, K. C. (1997). When exceptions prove the rule: How extremity of deviance determines the impact of deviant examples on stereotypes. *Journal of Personality and Social Psychology, 72,* 965–979.

Kunda, Z., & Sherman-Williams, B. (1993). Stereotypes and the construal of individuating information. *Personality and Social Psychology Bulletin, 19,* 90–99.

Kunda, Z., & Spencer, S. J. (2003). When do stereotypes come to mind and when do they color judgment? A goal-based theoretical framework for stereotype activation and application. *Psychological Bulletin, 129,* 522–544.

Kunkel, D. (2001, February 4). Sex on TV. Menlo Park, CA: Henry J. Kaiser Family Foundation (www.kff.org).

Kunst-Wilson, W. R., & Zajonc, R. B. (1980). Affective discrimination of stimuli that cannot be recognized. *Science, 207,* 557–558.

Kupper, N., & Denollet, J. (2007). Type D personality as a prognostic factor in heart disease: Assessment and mediating mechanisms. *Journal of Personality Assessment, 89,* 265–276.

Kurzman, D. (2004). *No greater glory: The four immortal chaplains and the sinking of the Dorchester in World War II.* New York: Random House.

Lacey, M. (2004, April 9). A decade after massacres, Rwanda outlaws ethnicity. *New York Times* (www.nytimes.com).

Lafferty, E. (1994, November 14). Now, a jury of his peers. *Time,* p. 64.

LaFrance, M. (1985). Does your smile reveal your status? *Social Science News Letter, 70* (Spring), 15–18.

LaFrance, M., Hecht, M. A., & Paluck, E. L. (2003). The contingent smile: A meta-analysis of sex differences in smiling. *Psychological Bulletin, 129,* 305–334.

LaFromboise, T., Coleman, H. L. K., & Gerton, J. (1993). Psychological impact of biculturalism: Evidence and theory. *Psychological Bulletin, 114,* 395–412.

Lagerspetz, K. (1979). Modification of aggressiveness in mice. In S. Feshbach & A. Fraczek (Eds.), *Aggression and behavior change.* New York: Praeger.

Lagerspetz, K. M. J., Bjorkqvist, K., Berts, M., & King, E. (1982). Group aggression among school children in three schools. *Scandinavian Journal of Psychology, 23,* 45–52.

Laird, J. D. (1974). Self-attribution of emotion: The effects of expressive behavior on the quality of emotional experience. *Journal of Personality and Social Psychology, 29,* 475–486.

Laird, J. D. (1984). The real role of facial response in the experience of emotion: A reply to Tourangeau and Ellsworth, and others. *Journal of Personality and Social Psychology, 47,* 909–917.

Lakin, J. L., & Chartrand, T. L. (2003). Using nonconscious behavioral mimicry to create affiliation and rapport. *Psychological Science, 14,* 334-339.

Lakin, J. L., Chartrand, T. L., & Arkin, R. M. (2008). I am too just like you: Nonconscious mimicry as an automatic behavioral responses to social exclusion. *Psychological Science,* **19,** 816–821.

Lalancette, M-F., & Standing, L. (1990). Asch fails again. *Social Behavior and Personality,* **18,** 7–12.

Lalonde, R. N. (1992). The dynamics of group differentiation in the face of defeat. *Personality and Social Psychology Bulletin,* **18,** 336–342.

Lalwani, A. K., Shavitt, S., & Johnson, T. (2006). What is the relation between cultural orientation and socially desirable responding? *Journal of Personality and Social Psychology,* **90,** 165–178.

Lamal, P. A. (1979). College student common beliefs about psychology. *Teaching of Psychology,* **6,** 155–158.

Lamberth, J. (1998, August 6). Driving while black: A statistician proves that prejudice still rules the road. *Washington Post,* p. C1.

Landau, M. J., Solomon, S., Greenberg, J., Cohen, F., Pyszczynski, T., Arndt, J., Miller, C. H., Ogilvie, D. M., & Cook, A. (2004). Deliver us from evil: The effects of mortality salience and reminders of 9/11 on support for President George W. Bush. *Personality and Social Psychology Bulletin,* **30,** 1136–1150.

Landers, A. (1985, August). Is affection more important than sex? *Reader's Digest,* pp. 44–46.

Landers, S. (1988, July). Sex, drugs 'n' rock: Relation not causal. *APA Monitor,* p. 40.

Laner, M. R., & Ventrone, N. A. (1998). Egalitarian daters/traditionalist dates. *Journal of Family Issues,* **19,** 468–477.

Laner, M. R., & Ventrone, N. A. (2000). Dating scripts revised. *Journal of Family Issues,* **21,** 488–500.

Langer, E. J. (1977). The psychology of chance. *Journal for the Theory of Social Behavior,* **7,** 185–208.

Langer, E. J., & Imber, L. (1980). The role of mindlessness in the perception of deviance. *Journal of Personality and Social Psychology,* **39,** 360–367.

Langer, E. J., & Rodin, J. (1976). The effects of choice and enhanced personal responsibility for the aged: A field experiment in an institutional setting. *Journal of Personality and Social Psychology,* **334,** 191–198.

Langer, E. J., & Roth, J. (1975). Heads I win, tails it's chance: The illusion of control as a function of the sequence of outcomes in a purely chance task. *Journal of Personality and Social Psychology,* **32,** 951–955.

Langford, D. J., Crager, S. E., Shehzad, Z., Smith, S. B., Sotocinal, S. G., Levenstadt, J. S., Chanda, M. L., Levitin, D. J., & Mogil, J. S. (2006). Social modulation of pain as evidence for empathy in mice. *Science,* **312,** 1967–1970.

Langlois, J. H., Kalakanis, L., Rubenstein, A. J., Larson, A., Hallam, M., & Smoot, M. (2000). Maxims or myths of beauty? A meta-analytic and theoretical review. *Psychological Bulletin,* **126,** 390–423.

Langlois, J. H., & Roggman, L. A. (1990). Attractive faces are only average. *Psychological Science,* **1,** 115–121.

Langlois, J. H., Roggman, L. A., Casey, R. J., Ritter, J. M., Rieser-Danner, L. A., & Jenkins, V. Y. (1987). Infant preferences for attractive faces: Rudiments of a stereotype? *Developmental Psychology,* **23,** 363–369.

Langlois, J. H., Roggman, L. A., & Musselman, L. (1994). What is average and what is not average about attractive faces? *Psychological Science,* **5,** 214–220.

Langlois, J., Kalakanis, L., Rubenstein, A., Larson, A., Hallam, M., & Smoot, M. (1996). Maxims and myths of beauty: A meta-analytic and theoretical review. Paper presented to the American Psychological Society convention.

Lanzetta, J. T. (1955). Group behavior under stress. *Human Relations,* **8,** 29–53.

Larsen, K. (1974). Conformity in the Asch experiment. *Journal of Social Psychology,* **94,** 303–304.

Larsen, K. S. (1990). The Asch conformity experiment: Replication and transhistorical comparisons. *Journal of Social Behavior and Personality,* **5(4),** 163–168.

Larsen, R. J., Csikszentmihalyi, N., & Graef, R. (1982). Time alone in daily experience: Loneliness or renewal? In L. A. Peplau & D. Perlman (Eds.), *Loneliness: A sourcebook of current theory, research and therapy.* New York: Wiley.

Larsen, R. J., & Diener, E. (1987). Affect intensity as an individual difference characteristic: A review. *Journal of Research in Personality,* **21,** 1–39.

Larson, J. R., Jr., Foster-Fishman, P. G., & Keys, C. B. (1994). Discussion of shared and unshared information in decision-making groups. *Journal of Personality and Social Psychology,* **67,** 446–461.

Larsson, K. (1956). *Conditioning and sexual behavior in the male albino rat.* Stockholm: Almqvist & Wiksell.

Larwood, L. (1978). Swine flu: A field study of self-serving biases. *Journal of Applied Social Psychology,* **18,** 283–289.

Larwood, L., & Whittaker, W. (1977). Managerial myopia: Self-serving biases in organizational planning. *Journal of Applied Psychology,* **62,** 194–198.

Lassiter, G. D., Diamond, S. S., Schmidt, H. C., & Elek, J. K. (2007). Evaluating videotaped confessions. *Psychological Science,* **18,** 224–226.

Lassiter, G. D., & Dudley, K. A. (1991). The *a priori* value of basic research: The case of videotaped confessions. *Journal of Social Behavior and Personality,* **6,** 7–16.

Lassiter, G. D., Geers, A. L., Handley, I. M., Weiland, P. E., & Munhall, P. J. (2002). Videotaped interrogations and confessions: A simple change in camera perspective alters verdicts in simulated trials. *Journal of Applied Psychology,* **87,** 867–874.

Lassiter, G. D., & Irvine, A. A. (1986). Videotaped confessions: The impact of camera point of view on judgments of coercion. *Journal of Applied Social Psychology,* **16,** 268–276.

Lassiter, G. D., & Munhall, P. J. (2001). The genius effect: Evidence for a nonmotivational interpretation. *Journal of Experimental Social Psychology,* **37,** 349–355.

Lassiter, G. D., Munhall, P. J., Berger, I. P., Weiland, P. E., Handley, I. M., & Geers, A. L. (2005). Attributional complexity and the camera perspective bias in videotaped confessions. *Basic and Applied Social Psychology,* **27,** 27–35.

Latané, B., & Dabbs, J. M., Jr. (1975). Sex, group size and helping in three cities. *Sociometry,* **38,** 180–194.

Latané, B., & Darley, J. M. (1968). Group inhibition of bystander intervention in emergencies. *Journal of Personality and Social Psychology,* **10,** 215–221.

Latané, B., & Darley, J. M. (1970). *The unresponsive bystander: Why doesn't he help?* New York: Appleton-Century-Crofts.

Latané, B., & Nida, S. (1981). Ten years of research on group size and helping. *Psychological Bulletin,* **89,** 308–324.

Latané, B., & Rodin, J. (1969). A lady in distress: Inhibiting effects of friends and strangers on bystander intervention. *Journal of Experimental Social Psychology,* **5,** 189–202.

Latané, B., Williams, K., & Harkins. S. (1979). Many hands make light the work: The causes and consequences of social loafing. *Journal of Personality and Social Psychology,* **37,** 822–832.

Laughlin, P. R. (1996). Group decision making and collective induction. In E. H. Witte & J. H. Davis (Eds.), *Understanding group behavior: Consensual action by small groups.* Mahwah, NJ: Erlbaum.

Laughlin, P. R., & Adamopoulos, J. (1980). Social combination processes and individual learning for six-person cooperative groups on an intellective task. *Journal of Personality and Social Psychology,* **38,** 941–947.

Laughlin, P. R., Hatch, E. C., Silver, J. S., & Boh, L. (2006). Groups perform better than the best individuals on letters-to-numbers problems: Effects of group size. *Journal of Personality and Social Psychology, 90,* 644–651.

Laughlin, P. R., Zander, M. L., Knievel, E. M., & Tan, T. K. (2003). Groups perform better than the best individuals on letters-to-numbers problems: Informative equations and effective strategies. *Journal of Personality and Social Psychology, 85,* 684–694.

Laumann, E. O., Gagnon, J. H., Michael, R. T., & Michaels, S. (1994). *The social organization of sexuality: Sexual practices in the United States.* Chicago: University of Chicago Press.

Lawler, A. (2003a). Iraq's shattered universities. *Science, 300,* 1490–1491.

Lawler, A. (2003b). Mayhem in Mesopotamia. *Science, 301,* 582–588.

Lawler, A. (2003c). Ten millennia of culture pilfered amid Baghdad chaos. *Science, 300,* 402–403.

Layden, M. A. (1982). Attributional therapy. In C. Antaki & C. Brewin (Eds.), *Attributions and psychological change: Applications of attributional theories to clinical and educational practice.* London: Academic Press.

Lazarsfeld, P. F. (1949). *The American soldier*—an expository review. *Public Opinion Quarterly, 13,* 377–404.

Leaper, C., & Ayres, M. M. (2007). A meta-analytic review of gender variations in adults' language use: Talkativeness, affiliative speech and assertive speech. *Personality and Social Psychology Review, 11,* 328–363.

Leary, M. (1994). *Self-presentation: Impression management and interpersonal behavior.* Pacific Grove, CA: Brooks/Cole.

Leary, M. R. (1998). The social and psychological importance of self-esteem. In R. M. Kowalski & M. R. Leary (Eds.), *The social psychology of emotional and behavioral problems.* Washington, DC: American Psychological Association.

Leary, M. R. (1999). The social and psychological importance of self-esteem. In R. M. Kowalski & M. R. Leary (Eds.), *The social psychology of emotional and behavioral problems.* Washington, DC: APA Books.

Leary, M. R. (2001). Social anxiety as an early warning system: A refinement and extension of the self-presentation theory of social anxiety. In S. G. Hofmann & P. M. DiBartolo (Eds.), *From social anxiety to social phobia: Multiple perspectives.* Needham Heights, MA: Allyn & Bacon.

Leary, M. R. (2004a). *The curse of the self: Self-awareness, egotism, and the quality of human life.* New York: Oxford University Press.

Leary, M. R. (2004b). The self we know and the self we show: Self-esteem, self-presentation, and the maintenance of interpersonal relationships. In M. Brewer & M. Hewstone (Eds.), *Emotion and motivation.* Malden, MA: Usishers.

Leary, M. R. (2007). Motivational and emotional aspects of the self. *Annual Review of Psychology, 58,* 317–344.

Leary, M. R., & Kowalski, R. M. (1995). *Social anxiety.* New York: Guilford.

Leary, M. R., Kowalski, R. M., Smith, L., & Phillips, S. (2003). Teasing, rejection, and violence: Case studies of the school shootings. *Aggressive Behavior, 29,* 202–214.

Leary, M. R., Nezlek, J. B., Radford-Davenport, D., Martin, J., & McMullen, A. (1994). Self-presentation in everyday interactions: Effects of target familiarity and gender composition. *Journal of Personality and Social Psychology, 67,* 664–673.

LeDoux, J. (2002). *Synaptic self: How our brains become who we are.* New York: Viking.

Lee, A. Y., & Aaker, J. L. (2004). Bringing the frame into focus: The influence of regulatory fit on processing fluency and persuasion. *Journal of Personality and Social Psychology, 86,* 205–218.

Lee, F., Hallahan, M., & Herzog, T. (1996). Explaining real-life events: How culture and domain shape attributions. *Personality and Social Psychology Bulletin, 22,* 732–741.

Lee, R. Y-P., & Bond, M. H. (1996). How friendship develops out of personality and values: A study of interpersonal attraction in Chinese culture. Unpublished manuscript, Chinese University of Hong Kong.

Lee, Y-S., & Waite, L. J. (2005). Husbands' and wives' time spent on housework: A comparison of measures. *Journal of Marriage and Family, 67,* 328–336.

Lefcourt, H. M. (1982). *Locus of control: Current trends in theory and research.* Hillsdale, NJ: Erlbaum.

Legrain, P. (2003, May 9). Cultural globalization is not Americanization. *Chronicle of Higher Education* (www.chronicle.com/free).

Lehavot, K., & Lambert, A. J. (2007). Toward a greater understanding of antigay prejudice: On the role of sexual orientation and gender role violation. *Basic and Applied Social Psychology, 29,* 279–292.

Lehman, D. R., Lempert, R. O., & Nisbett, R. E. (1988). The effects of graduate training on reasoning: Formal discipline and thinking about everyday-life events. *American Psychologist, 43,* 431–442.

Leippe, M. R. (1985). The influence of eyewitness nonidentification on mock-jurors. *Journal of Applied Social Psychology, 15,* 656–672.

Leippe, M. R. (1994). The appraisal of eyewitness testimony. In D. F. Ross, J. D. Read, & M. P. Toglia (Eds.), *Adult eyewitness testimony: Current trends and developments.* New York: Cambridge.

Lemyre, L., & Smith, P. M. (1985). Intergroup discrimination and self-esteem in the minimal group paradigm. *Journal of Personality and Social Psychology, 49,* 660–670.

Lench, H. C., Quas, J. A., & Edelstein, R. S. (2006). My child is better than average: The extension and restriction of unrealistic optimism. *Journal of Applied Social Psychology, 36,* 2963–2979.

Leodoro, G., & Lynn, M. (2007). The effect of server posture on the tips of Whites and Blacks. *Journal of Applied Social Psychology, 37,* 201–209.

Leon, D. (1969). *The Kibbutz: A new way of life.* London: Pergamon Press. Cited by B. Latané, K. Williams, & S. Harkins (1979), Many hands make light the work: The causes and consequences of social loafing. *Journal of Personality and Social Psychology, 37,* 822–832.

Leone, C. & Hawkins, L. B. (2006). Self-monitoring and close relationships. *Journal of Personality, 74,* 739–778.

Lepore, S. J., Ragan, J. D., & Jones, S. (2000). Talking facilitates cognitive-emotional processes of adaptation to an acute stressor. *Journal of Personality and Social Psychology, 78,* 499–508.

Lepper, M. R., & Greene, D. (Eds.) (1979). *The hidden costs of reward.* Hillsdale, NJ: Erlbaum.

Lerner, M. J. (1980). *The belief in a just world: A fundamental delusion.* New York: Plenum.

Lerner, M. J., & Miller, D. T. (1978). Just world research and the attribution process: Looking back and ahead. *Psychological Bulletin, 85,* 1030–1051.

Lerner, M. J., & Simmons, C. H. (1966). Observer's reaction to the "innocent victim": Compassion or rejection? *Journal of Personality and Social Psychology, 4,* 203–210.

Lerner, M. J., Somers, D. G., Reid, D., Chiriboga, D., & Tierney, M. (1991). Adult children as caregivers: Egocentric biases in judgments of sibling contributions. *The Gerontologist, 31,* 746–755.

Lerner, R. M., & Frank, P. (1974). Relation of race and sex to supermarket helping behavior. *Journal of Social Psychology, 94,* 201–203.

Leshner, A. I. (2005, October). Science and religion should not be adversaries. *APS Observer* (www.psychologicalscience.org).

Leung, K., & Bond, M. H. (1984). The impact of cultural collectivism on reward allocation. *Journal of Personality and Social Psychology, 47,* 793–804.

Leung, K., & Bond, M. H. (2004). Social axioms: A model of social beliefs in multi-cultural perspective. In M. P. Zanna (Ed.), *Advances in Experimental Social Psychology*. San Diego, CA: Academic Press.

Levav, J., & Fitzsimons, G. J. (2006). When questions change behavior: The role of ease of representation. *Psychological Science, 17,* 207–213.

Leventhal, H. (1970). Findings and theory in the study of fear communications. In L. Berkowitz (Ed.), *Advances in experimental social psychology* (Vol. 5). New York: Academic Press.

Levesque, M. J., Nave, C. S., & Lowe, C. A. (2006). Toward an understanding of gender differences in inferring sexual interest. *Psychology of Women Quarterly, 30,* 150–158.

Levine, J. M. (1989). Reaction to opinion deviance in small groups. In P. Paulus (Ed.), *Psychology of group influence: New perspectives*. Hillsdale, NJ: Erlbaum.

Levine, J. M., & Moreland, R. L. (1985). Innovation and socialization in small groups. In S. Moscovici, G. Mugny, & E. Van Avermaet (Eds.), *Perspectives on minority influence*. Cambridge: Cambridge University Press.

Levine, M., & Crowther, S. (2008). The responsive bystander: How social group membership and group size can encourage as well as inhibit bystander intervention. *Journal of Personality and Social Psychology, 95,* 1429–1439.

Levine, M., Prosser, A., Evans, D., & Reicher, S. (2005). Identity and emergency intervention: How social group membership and inclusiveness of group boundaries shape helping behavior. *Personality and Social Psychology Bulletin, 31,* 443–453.

Levine, R. V. (2003). The kindness of strangers. *American Scientist, 91,* 226–233.

Levine, R. V., Martinez, T. S., Brase, G., & Sorenson, K. (1994). Helping in 36 U.S. cities. *Journal of Personality and Social Psychology, 67,* 69–82.

Levinson, H. (1950). *The science of chance: From probability to statistics*. New York: Rinehart.

Levitan, L. C., & Visser, P. S. (2008). The impact of the social context on resistance to persuasion: Effortful versus effortless responses to counter-attitudinal information. *Journal of Experimental Social Psychology, 44,* 640–649.

Levy, B. (1996). Improving memory in old age through implicit self-stereotyping. *Journal of Personality and Social Psychology, 71,* 1092–1107.

Levy, S. R., Stroessner, S. J., & Dweck, C. S. (1998). Stereotype formation and endorsement: The role of implicit theories. *Journal of Personality and Social Psychology, 74,* 1421–1436.

Levy-Leboyer, C. (1988). Success and failure in applying psychology. *American Psychologist, 43,* 779–785.

Lewandowski, G. W., & Bizzoco, N. M. (2007). Addition through subtraction: Growth following the dissolution of a low-quality relationship. *Journal of Positive Psychology, 2,* 40–54.

Lewandowski, G. W., Jr., Aron, A., & Gee, J. (2007). Personality goes a long way: The malleability of opposite-sex physical attractiveness. *Personal Relationships, 14,* 571–585.

Lewandowsky, S., Stritzke, W. G. K., Oberauer, K., & Morales, M. (2005). Memory for fact, fiction, and misinformation: The Iraq War 2003. *Psychological Science, 16,* 190–195.

Lewicki, P. (1985). Nonconscious biasing effects of single instances on subsequent judgments. *Journal of Personality and Social Psychology, 48,* 563–574.

Lewin, K. (1936). *A dynamic theory of personality*. New York: McGraw-Hill.

Lewinsohn, P. M., Hoberman, H., Teri, L., & Hautziner, M. (1985). An integrative theory of depression. In S. Reiss & R. Bootzin (Eds.), *Theoretical issues in behavior therapy*. New York: Academic Press.

Lewinsohn, P. M., & Rosenbaum, M. (1987). Recall of parental behavior by acute depressives, remitted depressives, and nondepressives. *Journal of Personality and Social Psychology, 52,* 611–619.

Lewis, C. S. (1952). *Mere Christianity*. New York: Macmillan.

Lewis, D. O. (1998). *Guilty by reason of insanity*. London: Arrow.

Lewis, R. J., Derlega, V. J., Clarke, E., & Kuang, J. C. (2006). Stigma consciousness, social constraints, and lesbian well-being. *Journal of Counseling Psychology, 53,* 48–56.

Lewis, R. S., Goto, S. G., & Kong, L. L. (2008). Culture and context: East Asian American and European American differences in P3 event-related potentials and self-construal. *Personality and Social Psychology Bulletin, 34,* 623–634.

Leyens, J.-P., Camino, L., Parke, R. D., & Berkowitz, L. (1975). Effects of movie violence on aggression in a field setting as a function of group dominance and cohesion. *Journal of Personality and Social Psychology, 32,* 346–360.

Leyens, J.-P., Cortes, B., Demoulin, S., Dovidio, J. F., Fiske, S. T., Gaunt, R., Paladino, M-P., Rodriquez-Perez, A., Rodriquez-Torrez, R., & Vaes, J. (2003). Emotional prejudice, essentialism, and nationalism. *European Journal of Social Psychology, 33,* 703–717.

Leyens, J-P., Demoulin, S., Vaes, J., Gaunt, R., & Paladino, M. P. (2007). Infra-humanization: The wall of group

differences. *Social Issues and Policy Review, 1,* 139–172.

Li, N. P., Bailey, J. M., Kenrick, D. T., & Linsenmeier, J. A. W. (2002). The necessities and luxuries of mate preferences: Testing the tradeoffs. *Journal of Personality and Social Psychology, 82,* 947–955.

Liberman, A., & Chaiken, S. (1992). Defensive processing of personally relevant health messages. *Personality and Social Psychology Bulletin, 18,* 669–679.

Liberman, V., Samuels, S. M., & Ross, L. (2004). The name of the game: Predictive power of reputations vs. situational labels in determining Prisoner's Dilemma game moves. *Personality and Social Psychology Bulletin, 30,* 1175–1185.

Lichtblau, E. (2003, March 18). U.S. seeks $289 billion in cigarette makers' profits. *New York Times* (www.nytimes.com).

Lichtblau, E. (2005, August 24). Profiling report leads to a demotion. *New York Times* (www.nytimes.com).

Lichtenstein, S., & Fischhoff, B. (1980). Training for calibration. *Organizational Behavior and Human Performance, 26,* 149–171.

Liehr, P., Mehl, M. R., Summers, L. C., & Pennebaker, J. W. (2004). Connecting with others in the midst of stressful upheaval on September 11, 2001. *Applied Nursing Research, 17,* 2–9.

Lilienfeld, S. O., Fowler, K. A., Lohr, J. M., & Lynn, S. J. (2005). Pseudoscience, nonscience, and nonsense in clinical psychology: Dangers and remedies. In R. H. Wright & N. A. Cummings (Eds.), *Destructive trends in mental health: The well-intentioned path to harm*. New York: Routledge.

Lilienfeld, S. O., Wood, J. M., & Garb, H. N. (2000). The scientific status of projective techniques. *Psychological Science in the Public Interest, 1,* 27–66.

Lindsay, R. C. L., & Wells, G. L. (1985). Improving eyewitness identifications from lineups: Simultaneous versus sequential lineup presentation. *Journal of Applied Psychology, 70,* 556–564.

Lindsay, R. C. L., Wells, G. L., & Rumpel, C. H. (1981). Can people detect eyewitness-identification accuracy within and across situations? *Journal of Applied Psychology, 66,* 79–89.

Lindskold, S. (1978). Trust development, the GRIT proposal, and the effects of conciliatory acts on conflict and cooperation. *Psychological Bulletin, 85,* 772–793.

Lindskold, S. (1979a). Conciliation with simultaneous or sequential interaction: Variations in trustworthiness and vulnerability in the prisoner's dilemma. *Journal of Conflict Resolution, 27,* 704–714.

Lindskold, S. (1979b). Managing conflict through announced conciliatory initiatives backed with retaliatory capability. In W. G. Austin & S. Worchel (Eds.), *The social psychology of intergroup relations*. Monterey, CA: Brooks/Cole.

Lindskold, S. (1981). The laboratory evaluation of GRIT: Trust, cooperation, aversion to using conciliation. Paper presented at the American Association for the Advancement of Science convention.

Lindskold, S. (1983). Cooperators, competitors, and response to GRIT. *Journal of Conflict Resolution, 27*, 521–532.

Lindskold, S., & Aronoff, J. R. (1980). Conciliatory strategies and relative power. *Journal of Experimental Social Psychology, 16*, 187–198.

Lindskold, S., Bennett, R., & Wayner, M. (1976). Retaliation level as a foundation for subsequent conciliation. *Behavioral Science, 21*, 13–18.

Lindskold, S., Betz, B., & Walters, P. S. (1986). Transforming competitive or cooperative climate. *Journal of Conflict Resolution, 30*, 99–114.

Lindskold, S., & Collins, M. G. (1978). Inducing cooperation by groups and individuals. *Journal of Conflict Resolution, 22*, 679–690.

Lindskold, S., & Finch, M. L. (1981). Styles of announcing conciliation. *Journal of Conflict Resolution, 25*, 145–155.

Lindskold, S., & Han, G. (1988). GRIT as a foundation for integrative bargaining. *Personality and Social Psychology Bulletin, 14*, 335–345.

Lindskold, S., Han, G., & Betz, B. (1986a). Repeated persuasion in interpersonal conflict. *Journal of Personality and Social Psychology, 51*, 1183–1188.

Lindskold, S., Han, G., & Betz, B. (1986b). The essential elements of communication in the GRIT strategy. *Personality and Social Psychology Bulletin, 12*, 179–186.

Lindskold, S., Walters, P. S., Koutsourais, H., & Shayo, R. (1981). Cooperators, competitors, and response to GRIT. Unpublished manuscript, Ohio University.

Linssen, H., & Hagendoorn, L. (1994). Social and geographical factors in the explanation of the content of European nationality stereotypes. *British Journal of Social Psychology, 33*, 165–182.

Linville, P. W., Fischer, G. W., & Fischhoff, B. (1992). AIDS risk perceptions and decision biases. In J. B. Pryor & G. D. Reeder (Eds.), *The social psychology of HIV infection*. Hillsdale, NJ: Erlbaum.

Linville, P. W., Fischer, G. W., & Salovey, P. (1989). Perceived distributions of the characteristics of in-group and out-group members:

Empirical evidence and a computer simulation. *Journal of Personality and Social Psychology, 57*, 165–188.

Lippa, R. A. (2007). The preferred traits of mates in a cross-national study of heterosexual and homosexual men and women: An examination of biological and cultural influences. *Archives of Sexual Behavior, 36*, 193–208.

Lippa, R. A. (2008a). Sex differences and sexual orientation differences in personality: Findings from the BBC Internet survey. *Archives of Sexual Behavior, 37*, 173–187.

Lippa, R. A. (2008b). Sex differences in sex drive, sociosexuality, and height across 53 nations: Testing evolutionary and social structural theories. *Archives of Sexual Behavior* (www.springerlink.com/content/x754q0433g18hg81/).

Lipsitz, A., Kallmeyer, K., Ferguson, M., & Abas, A.(1989). Counting on blood donors: Increasing the impact of reminder calls. *Journal of Applied Social Psychology, 19*, 1057–1067.

Little, A., & Perrett, D. (2002). Putting beauty back in the eye of the beholder. *The Psychologist, 15*, 28–32.

Livingston, R. W. (2001). What you see is what you get: Systematic variability in perceptual-based social judgment. *Personality and Social Psychology Bulletin, 27*, 1086–1096.

Livingston, R. W., & Drwecki, B. B. (2007). Why are some individuals not racially biased? Susceptibility to affective conditioning predicts nonprejudice toward Blacks. *Psychological Science, 18*, 816–823.

Locke, E. A., & Latham, G. P. (1990). Work motivation and satisfaction: Light at the end of the tunnel. *Psychological Science, 1*, 240–246.

Locke, K. D., & Horowitz, L. M. (1990). Satisfaction in interpersonal interactions as a function of similarity in level of dysphoria. *Journal of Personality and Social Psychology, 58*, 823–831.

Locksley, A., Borgida, E., Brekke, N., & Hepburn, C. (1980). Sex stereotypes and social judgment. *Journal of Personality and Social Psychology, 39*, 821–831.

Locksley, A., Hepburn, C., & Ortiz, V. (1982). Social stereotypes and judgments of individuals: An instance of the base-rate fallacy. *Journal of Experimental Social Psychology, 18*, 23–42.

Locksley, A., Ortiz, V., & Hepburn, C. (1980). Social categorization and discriminatory behavior: Extinguishing the minimal intergroup discrimination effect. *Journal of Personality and Social Psychology, 39*, 773–783.

Lockwood, P. (2002). Could it happen to you? Predicting the impact of downward comparisons on the self. *Journal of Personality and Social Psychology, 87*, 343–358.

Lockwood, P., Dolderman, D., Sadler, P., & Gerchak, E. (2004). Feeling better about doing worse: Social comparisons within romantic relationships. *Journal of Personality and Social Psychology, 87*, 80–95.

Loewenstein, G., & Schkade, D. (1999). Wouldn't it be nice? Predicting future feelings. In D. Kahneman, E. Diener, & N. Schwarz (Eds.), *Understanding well-being: Scientific perspectives on enjoyment and suffering* (pp. 85–105). New York: Russell Sage Foundation.

Loewenstein, G., & Small, D. A. (2007). The Scarecrow and the Tin Man: The vicissitudes of human sympathy and caring. *Journal of General Psychology, 11*, 112–126.

Lofland, J., & Stark, R. (1965). Becoming a worldsaver: A theory of conversion to a deviant perspective. *American Sociological Review, 30*, 862–864.

Loftin, C., McDowall, D., Wiersema, B., & Cottey, T. J. (1991). Effects of restrictive licensing of handguns on homicide and suicide in the District of Columbia. *New England Journal of Medicine, 325*, 1615–1620.

Loftus, E. F. (1979a). *Eyewitness testimony*. Cambridge, MA: Harvard University Press.

Loftus, E. F. (1979b). The malleability of human memory. *American Scientist, 67*, 312–320.

Loftus, E. F. (2001, November). Imagining the past. *The Psychologist, 14*, 584–587.

Loftus, E. F. (2003). Make-believe memories. *American Psychologist, 58*, 867–873.

Loftus, E. F. (2007). Memory distortions: Problems solved and unresolved. In M. Garry & H. Hayne (Eds.), *Do justice and let the sky fall: Elizabeth Loftus and her contributions to science, law, and academic freedom*. Mahway, NJ: Erlbaum.

Loftus, E. F., & Bernstein, D. M. (2005). Rich false memories: The royal road to success. In A. F. Healy (Ed.), *Experimental cognitive psychology and its applications*. Washington, DC: American Psychological Association.

Loftus, E. F., & Klinger, M. R. (1992). Is the unconscious smart or dumb? *American Psychologist, 47*, 761–765.

Loftus, E. F., Miller, D. G., & Burns, H. J. (1978). Semantic integration of verbal information into a visual memory. *Journal of Experimental Social Psychology: Human Learning and Memory, 4*, 19–31.

Loftus, E. F., & Zanni, G. (1975). Eyewitness testimony: The influence of the wording in a question. *Bulletin of the Psychonomic Society, 5*, 86–88.

Lombardo, J. P., Weiss, R. F., & Buchanan, W. (1972). Reinforcing and attracting functions of yielding. *Journal of Personality and Social Psychology, 21*, 359–368.

London, K., & Nunez, N. (2000). The effect of jury deliberations on jurors' propensity to disregard inadmissable evidence. *Journal of Applied Psychology, 85,* 932–939.

London, P. (1970). The rescuers: Motivational hypotheses about Christians who saved Jews from the Nazis. In J. Macaulay & L. Berkowitz (Eds.), *Altruism and helping behavior.* New York: Academic Press.

Lonner, W. J. (1980). The search for psychological universals. In H. C. Triandis & W. W. Lambert (Eds.), *Handbook of cross-cultural psychology* (Vol. 1). Boston: Allyn & Bacon.

Lonner, W. J. (1989). The introductory psychology text and cross-cultural psychology: Beyond Ekman, Whorf, and biased I.Q. tests. In D. Keats, D. R. Munro & L. Mann (Eds.), *Heterogeneity in cross-cultural psychology.*

Lord, C. G., Desforges, D. M., Ramsey, S. L., Trezza, G. R., & Lepper, M. R. (1991). Typicality effects in attitude-behavior consistency: Effects of category discrimination and category knowledge. *Journal of Experimental Social Psychology, 27,* 550–575.

Lord, C. G., Lepper, M. R., & Preston, E. (1984). Considering the opposite: A corrective strategy for social judgment. *Journal of Personality and Social Psychology, 47,* 1231–1243.

Lord, C. G., Ross, L., & Lepper, M. (1979). Biased assimilation and attitude polarization: The effects of prior theories on subsequently considered evidence. *Journal of Personality and Social Psychology, 37,* 2098–2109.

Losch, M. E., & Cacioppo, J. T. (1990). Cognitive dissonance may enhance sympathetic tonus, but attitudes are changed to reduce negative affect rather than arousal. *Journal of Experimental Social Psychology, 26,* 289–304.

Lott, A. J., & Lott, B. E. (1961). Group cohesiveness, communication level, and conformity. *Journal of Abnormal and Social Psychology, 62,* 408–412.

Lott, A. J., & Lott, B. E. (1974). The role of reward in the formation of positive interpersonal attitudes. In T. Huston (Ed.), *Foundations of interpersonal attraction.* New York: Academic Press.

Loughman, S., & Haslam, N. (2007). Animals and androids: Implicit associations between social categories and nonhumans. *Psychological Science, 18,* 116–121.

Lovett, F. (1997). Thinking about values (report of December 13, 1996 *Wall Street Journal* national survey). *The Responsive Community, 7*(2), 87.

Lowenstein, D. (2000, May 20). Interview. *The World* (www.cnn.com/TRANSCRIPTS/0005/20/stc.00.html).

Lowenthal, M. F., Thurnher, M., Chiriboga, D., Beefon, D., Gigy, L., Lurie, E., Pierce, R., Spence, D., & Weiss, L. (1975). *Four stages of life.* San Francisco: Jossey-Bass.

Loy, J. W., & Andrews, D. S. (1981). They also saw a game: A replication of a case study. *Replications in Social Psychology, 1*(2), 45–59.

Lücken, M., & Simon, B. (2005). Cognitive and affective experiences of minority and majority members: The role of group size, status, and power. *Journal of Experimental Social Psychology, 41,* 396–413.

Lueptow, L. B., Garovich, L., & Lueptow, M. B. (1995). The persistence of gender stereotypes in the face of changing sex roles: Evidence contrary to the sociocultural model. *Ethology and Sociobiology, 16,* 509–530.

Luginbuhl, J., & Middendorf, K. (1988). Death penalty beliefs and jurors' responses to aggravating and mitigating circumstances in capital trials. *Law and Human Behavior, 12,* 263–281.

Lumsdaine, A. A., & Janis, I. L. (1953). Resistance to "counter-propaganda" produced by one-sided and two-sided "propaganda" presentations. *Public Opinion Quarterly, 17,* 311–318.

Lumsden, A., Zanna, M. P., & Darley, J. M. (1980). When a newscaster presents counter-additional information: Education or propaganda? Paper presented to the Canadian Psychological Association annual convention.

Luntz, F. (2003, June 10). Quoted by T. Raum, "Bush insists banned weapons will be found." Associated Press (story.news.yahoo.com).

Luo, S., & Klohnen, E. C. (2005). Assortative mating and marital quality in newlyweds: A couple-centered approach. *Journal of Personality and Social Psychology, 88,* 304–326.

Lutsky, L. A., Risucci, D. A., & Tortolani, A. J. (1993). Reliability and accuracy of surgical resident peer ratings. *Evaluation Review, 17,* 444–456.

Lüüs, C. A. E., & Wells, G. L. (1994). Determinants of eyewitness confidence. In D. F. Ross, J. D. Read, & M. P. Toglia (Eds.), *Adult eyewitness testimony: Current trends and developments* (pp. 348–362). New York: Cambridge University Press.

Lydon, J., & Dunkel-Schetter, C. (1994). Seeing is committing: A longitudinal study of bolstering commitment in amniocentesis patients. *Personality and Social Psychology Bulletin, 20,* 218–227.

Lykken, D. T. (1997). The American crime factory. *Psychological Inquiry, 8,* 261–270.

Lykken, D. T. (2000, Spring). Psychology and the criminal justice system: A reply to Haney and Zimbardo. *The General Psychologist, 35,* 11–15.

Lykken, D. T., & Tellegen, A. (1993). Is human mating adventitious or the result of lawful choice? A twin study of mate selection. *Journal of Personality and Social Psychology, 65,* 56–68.

Lynch, J. W., Kaplan, G. A., Pamuk, E. R., Cohen, R. D., Heck, K. E., Balfour, J. L., & Yen, I. H. (1998). Income inequality and mortality in metropolitan areas of the United States. *American Journal of Public Health, 88,* 1074–1080.

Lynch, J. W., Smith, G. D., Kaplan, G. A., & House, J. S. (2000). Income inequality and health: A neo-material interpretation. *British Medical Journal, 320,* 1200–1204.

Lynn, M., & Oldenquist, A. (1986). Egoistic and nonegoistic motives in social dilemmas. *American Psychologist, 41,* 529–534.

Lyons, L. (2003, September 23). Oh, boy: Americans still prefer sons. *Gallup Poll Tuesday Briefing* (www.gallup.com).

Lyubomirsky, S. (2001). Why are some people happier than others? The role of cognitive and motivational processes in well-being. *American Psychologist, 56,* 239–249.

Lyubomirsky, S., Sousa, L., & Dickerhoof, R. (2006). The costs and benefits of writing, talking, and thinking about life's triumphs and defeats. *Journal of Personality and Social Psychology, 90,* 692–708.

Ma, V., & Schoeneman, T. J. (1997). Individualism versus collectivism: A comparison of Kenyan and American self-concepts. *Basic and Applied Social Psychology, 19,* 261–273.

Maass, A. (1998). Personal communication from Universita degli Studi di Padova.

Maass, A. (1999). Linguistic intergroup bias: Stereotype perpetuation through language. In M. P. Zanna (Ed.), *Advances in Experimental Social Psychology, 31,* 79–121.

Maass, A., & Clark, R. D., III. (1984). Hidden impact of minorities: Fifteen years of minority influence research. *Psychological Bulletin, 95,* 428–450.

Maass, A., & Clark, R. D., III. (1986). Conversion theory and simultaneous majority/minority influence: Can reactance offer an alternative explanation? *European Journal of Social Psychology, 16,* 305–309.

Maass, A., Milesi, A., Zabbini, S., & Stahlberg, D. (1995). Linguistic intergroup bias: Differential expectancies or in-group protection? *Journal of Personality and Social Psychology, 68,* 116–126.

Maass, A., Volparo, C., & Mucchi-Faina, A. (1996). Social influence and the verifiability of the issue under discussion: Attitudinal versus objective items. *British Journal of Social Psychology,* **35,** 15–26.

Maccoby, E. E. (2002). Gender and group process: A developmental perspective. *Current Directions in Psychological Science,* **11,** 54–58.

Maccoby, N. (1980). Promoting positive health behaviors in adults. In L. A. Bond & J. C. Rosen (Eds.), *Competence and coping during adulthood.* Hanover, NH: University Press of New England.

Maccoby, N., & Alexander, J. (1980). Use of media in lifestyle programs. In P. O. Davidson & S. M. Davidson (Eds.). *Behavioral medicine: Changing health lifestyles.* New York: Brunner/ Mazel.

MacCoun, R. J., & Kerr, N. L. (1988). Asymmetric influence in mock jury deliberation: Jurors' bias for leniency. *Journal of Personality and Social Psychology,* **54,** 21–33.

MacDonald, G., & Leary, M. R. (2005). Why does social exclusion hurt? The relationship between social and physical pain. *Psychological Bulletin,* **131,** 202–223.

MacDonald, G., Zanna, M. P., & Holmes, J. G. (2000). An experimental test of the role of alcohol in relationship conflict. *Journal of Experimental Social Psychology,* **36,** 182–193.

MacDonald, T. K., & Ross, M. (1997). Assessing the accuracy of predictions about dating relationships: How and why do lovers' predictions differ from those made by observers? Unpublished manuscript, University of Lethbridge.

Mack, D., & Rainey, D. (1990). Female applicants' grooming and personnel selection. *Journal of Social Behavior and Personality,* **5,** 399–407.

MacLeod, C., & Campbell, L. (1992). Memory accessibility and probability judgments: An experimental evaluation of the availability heuristic. *Journal of Personality and Social Psychology,* **63,** 890–902.

MacLin, O. H., Zimmerman, L. A., & Malpass, R. S. (2005). PC_Eyewitness and the sequential superiority effect: Computer based lineup administration. *Law and Human Behavior,* **29,** 303–321.

Macrae, C. N., & Bodenhausen, G. V. (2000). Social cognition: Thinking categorically about others. *Annual Review of Psychology,* **51,** 93–120.

Macrae, C. N., & Bodenhausen, G. V. (2001). Social cognition: Categorical person perception. *British Journal of Psychology,* **92,** 239–255.

Macrae, C. N., Alnwick, M. A., Milne, A. B., & Schloerscheidt, A. M. (2002). Person perception across the menstrual cycle: Hormonal influences on social-cognitive functioning. *Psychological Science,* **13,** 532–536.

Macrae, C. N., Bodenhausen, G. V., Milne, A. B., & Jetten, J. (1994). Out of mind but back in sight: Stereotypes on the rebound. *Journal of Personality and Social Psychology,* **67,** 808–817.

Macrae, C. N., & Johnston, L. (1998). Help, I need somebody: Automatic action and inaction. *Social Cognition,* **16,** 400–417.

Maddux, J. E. (1993). The mythology of psychopathology: A social cognitive view of deviance, difference, and disorder. *The General Psychologist,* **29**(2), 34–45.

Maddux, J. E. (2008). Positive psychology and the illness ideology: Toward a positive clinical psychology. *Applied Psychology: An International Review,* **57,** 54–70.

Maddux, J. E., & Gosselin, J. T. (2003). Self-efficacy. In M. R. Leary, & J. P. Tangney (Eds.), *Handbook of self and identity.* New York: Guilford.

Maddux, J. E., & Rogers, R. W. (1983). Protection motivation and self-efficacy: A revised theory of fear appeals and attitude change. *Journal of Experimental Social Psychology,* **19,** 469–479.

Maddux, W. W., Galinsky, A. D., Cuddy, A. J. C., & Polifroni, M. (2008). When being a model minority is good . . . and bad: Realistic threat explains negativity towards Asian Americans. *Personality and Social Psychology Bulletin,* **34,** 74–89.

Maddux, W. W., Mullen, E., & Galinsky, A. D. (2008). Chameleons bake bigger pies and take bigger pieces: Strategic behavioral mimicry facilitates negotiation outcomes. *Journal of Experimental Social Psychology,* **44,** 461–468.

Madon, S., Jussim, L., & Eccles, J. (1997). In search of the powerful self-fulfilling prophecy. *Journal of Personality and Social Psychology,* **72,** 791–809.

Madon, S., Jussim, L., Keiper, S., Eccles, J., Smith, A., & Palumbo, P. (1998). The accuracy and power of sex, social class, and ethnic stereotypes: A naturalistic study in person perception. *Personality and Social Psychology Bulletin,* **24,** 1304–1318.

Madrian, B. C., & Shea, D. F. (2001). The power of suggestion: Inertia in 401(k) participation and savings behavior. *Quarterly Journal of Economics,* **116,** 1149–1187.

Mae, L., Carlston, D. E., & Skowronski, J. (1999). Spontaneous trait transference to familiar communicators: Is a little knowledge a dangerous thing? *Journal of Personality and Social Psychology,* **77,** 233–246.

Major, B., Kaiser, C. R., & McCoy, S. K. (2003). It's not my fault: When and why attributions to prejudice protect self-esteem. *Personality and Social Psychology Bulletin,* **29,** 772–781.

Malamuth, N. M. (1996). The confluence model of sexual aggression. In D. M. Buss & N. M. Malamuth (Eds.), *Sex, power, conflict: Evolutionary and feminist perspectives.* New York: Oxford University Press.

Malamuth, N. M. (2003). Criminal and noncriminal sexual aggressors: Integrating psychopathy in a hierarchical-mediational confluence model. In R. A. Prentky, E. Janus, & M. Seto (Eds.), *Sexually coercive behavior: Understanding and management.* New York: Annals of the New York Academy of Sciences.

Malamuth, N. M., & Check, J. V. P. (1981). The effects of media exposure on acceptance of violence against women: A field experiment. *Journal of Research in Personality,* **15,** 436–446.

Malamuth, N. M., Haber, S., Feshbach, S., & others. (1980, March). *Journal of Research in Personality,* **14,** 121–137.

Malkiel, B. (2007). *A random walk down Wall Street,* 9th edition. New York: Norton.

Malle, B. F. (2006). The actor-observer asymmetry in attribution: A (surprising) meta-analysis. *Psychological Bulletin,* **132,** 895–919.

Maner, J. K., Gailliot, M. T., & Miller, S. L. (2009). The implicit cognition of relationship maintenance: Inattention to attractive alternatives. *Journal of Experimental Social Psychology,* **45,** 174–179.

Maner, J. K., Kenrick, D. T., Becker, V., Robertson, T. E., Hofer, B., Neuberg, S. L., Delton, A. W., Butner, J., & Schaller, M. (2005). Functional projection: How fundamental social motives can bias interpersonal perception. *Journal of Personality and Social Psychology,* **88,** 63–78.

Maner, J. K., Miller, S. L., Schmidt, N. B., & Eckel, L. A. (2008). Submitting to defeat: Social anxiety, dominance threat, and decrements in testosterone. *Psychological Science,* **19,** 764–768.

Manis, M., Cornell, S. D., & Moore, J. C. (1974). Transmission of attitude-relevant information through a communication chain. *Journal of Personality and Social Psychology,* **30,** 81–94.

Manis, M., Nelson, T. E., & Shedler, J. (1988). Stereotypes and social judgment: Extremity, assimilation, and contrast. *Journal of Personality and Social Psychology,* **55,** 28–36.

Mann, L. (1981). The baiting crowd in episodes of threatened suicide. *Journal of Personality and Social Psychology,* **41,** 703–709.

Manning, R., Levine, M., & Collins, A. (2007). The Kitty Genovese murder and the social psychology of helping: The parable of the 38 witnesses. *American Psychologist,* **62,** 555–562.

Mar, R. A., & Oatley, K. (2008). The function of fiction is the abstraction and simulation of social experience. *Perspectives on Psychological Science, 3,* 173–192.

Marcus, A. C., & Siegel, J. M. (1982). Sex differences in the use of physician services: A preliminary test of the fixed role hypothesis. *Journal of Health and Social Behavior, 23,* 186–197.

Marcus, S. (1974). Review of *Obedience to authority.* New York Times Book Review, January 13, pp. 1–2.

Marcus-Newhall, A., Pedersen, W. C., Carlson, M., & Miller, N. (2000). Displaced aggression is alive and well: A meta-analytic review. *Journal of Personality and Social Psychology, 78,* 670–689.

Markey, P. M., Wells, S. M., & Markey, C. N. (2002). In S. P. Shohov (Ed.), *Advances in Psychology Research, 9,* 94–113. Huntington, NY: Nova Science.

Markman, H. J., Floyd, F. J., Stanley, S. M., & Storaasli, R. D. (1988). Prevention of marital distress: A longitudinal investigation. *Journal of Consulting and Clinical Psychology, 56,* 210–217.

Markman, K. D., & McMullen, M. N. (2003). A reflection and evaluation model of comparative thinking. *Personality and Social Psychology Review, 7,* 244–267.

Marks, G., & Miller, N. (1987). Ten years of research on the false-consensus effect: An empirical and theoretical review. *Psychological Bulletin, 102,* 72–90.

Markus, H. (2001, October 7). Culture and the good life. Address to the Positive Psychology Summit conference, Washington, DC.

Markus, H. R. (2005). On telling less than we can know: The too tacit wisdom of social psychology. *Psychological Inquiry, 16,* 180–184.

Markus, H., & Kitayama, S. (1991). Culture and the self: Implications for cognition, emotion, and motivation. *Psychological Review, 98,* 224–253.

Markus, H. R., & Kitayama, S. (1994). A collective fear of the collective: Implications for selves and theories of selves. *Personality and Social Psychology Bulletin, 20,* 568–579.

Markus, H., & Nurius, P. (1986). Possible selves. *American Psychologist, 41,* 954–969.

Markus, H., & Wurf, E. (1987). The dynamic self-concept: A social psychological perspective. *Annual Review of Psychology, 38,* 299–337.

Marmot, M. G., & Wilkinson, R. G. (Eds.) (1999). *Social determinants of health.* Oxford: Oxford University Press.

Marsden, P., & Attia, S. (2005). A deadly contagion? *The Psychologist, 18,* 152–155.

Marsh, H. W., Kong, C-K., & Hau, K-T. (2000). Longitudinal multilevel models of the big-fish-little-pond effect on academic self-concept: Counterbalancing contrast and reflected-glory effects in Hong Kong schools. *Journal of Personality and Social Psychology, 78,* 337–349.

Marsh, H. W., & O'Mara, A. (2008). Reciprocal effects between academic self-concept, self-esteem, achievement, and attainment over seven adolescent years: Unidimensional and multidimensional perspectives of self-concept. *Personality and Social Psychology Bulletin, 34,* 542–552.

Marsh, H. W., & Young, A. S. (1997). Causal effects of academic self-concept on academic achievement: Structural equation models of longitudinal data. *Journal of Educational Psychology, 89,* 41–54.

Marshall, R. (1997). Variances in levels of individualism across two cultures and three social classes. *Journal of Cross-Cultural Psychology, 28,* 490–495.

Marshall, W. L. (1989). Pornography and sex offenders. In D. Zillmann & J. Bryant (Eds.), *Pornography: Research advances and policy considerations.* Hillsdale, NJ: Erlbaum.

Martens, A., Kosloff, S., Greenberg, J., Landau, M. J., & Schmader, R. (2007). Killing begets killing: Evidence from a bug-killing paradigm that initial killing fuels subsequent killing. *Personality and Social Psychology Bulletin, 33,* 1251–1264.

Martin, L. L., & Erber, R. (2005). The wisdom of social psychology: Five commonalities and one concern. *Psychological Inquiry, 16,* 194–202.

Martin, R., Hewstone, M., & Martin, P. Y. (2008). Majority versus minority influence: The role of message processing in determining resistance to counter-persuasion. *European Journal of Social Psychology, 38,* 16–34.

Martin, R., Martin, P. Y., Smith, J. R., & Hewstone, M. (2007). Majority versus minority influence and prediction of behavioural intentions and behaviour. *Journal of Experimental Social Psychology, 43,* 763–771.

Martino, S. C., Collins, R. L., Kanouse, D. E., Elliott, M., & Berry, S. H. (2005). Social cognitive processes mediating the relationship between exposure to television's sexual content and adolescents' sexual behavior. *Journal of Personality and Social Psychology, 89,* 914–924.

Marty, M. (1988, December 1). Graceful prose: Your good deed for the day. *Context,* p. 2.

Maruyama, G., Rubin, R. A., & Kingbury, G. (1981). Self-esteem and educational achievement: Independent

constructs with a common cause? *Journal of Personality and Social Psychology, 40,* 962–975.

Marvelle, K., & Green, S. (1980). Physical attractiveness and sex bias in hiring decisions for two types of jobs. *Journal of the National Association of Women Deans, Administrators, and Counselors, 44*(1), 3–6.

Maslow, A. H., & Mintz, N. L. (1956). Effects of esthetic surroundings: I. Initial effects of three esthetic conditions upon perceiving "energy" and "well-being" in faces. *Journal of Psychology, 41,* 247–254.

Masserman, J. H., Wechkin, S., & Terris, W. (1964). "Altruistic" behavior in rhesus monkeys. *American Journal of Psychiatry, 121,* 584–585.

Mast, M. S., & Hall, J. A. (2006). Women's advantage at remembering others' appearance: A systematic look at the why and when of a gender difference. *Personality and Social Psychology Bulletin, 32,* 353–364.

Mastekaasa, A. (1995). Age variations in the suicide rates and self-reported subjective well-being of married and never-married persons. *Journal of Community & Applied Social Psychology, 5,* 21–39.

Mastroianni, G. R. (2002). Milgram and the Holocaust: A reexamination. *Journal of Theoretical and Philosophical Psychology, 22,* 158–173.

Mastroianni, G. R., & Reed, G. (2006). Apples, barrels, and Abu Ghraib. *Sociological Focus, 39,* 239–250.

Masuda, T., Gonzalez, R., Kwan, L., & Nisbett, R. E. (2008). Culture and aesthetic preference: Comparing the attention to context of East Asians and Americans. *Personality and Social Psychology Bulletin, 34,* 1260–1275.

Masuda, T., & Kitayama, S. (2004). Perceiver-induced constraint and attitude attribution in Japan and the U.S.: A case for the cultural dependence of the correspondence bias. *Journal of Experimental Social Psychology, 40,* 409–416.

Matheson, K., Cole, B., & Majka, K. (2003). Dissidence from within: Examining the effects of intergroup context on group members' reactions to attitudinal opposition. *Journal of Experimental Social Psychology, 39,* 161–169.

Matthews, K. A. (2005). Psychological perspectives on the development of coronary heart disease. *American Psychologist, 60,* 783–796.

Maxwell, G. M. (1985). Behaviour of lovers: Measuring the closeness of relationships. *Journal of Personality and Social Psychology, 2,* 215–238.

Mayer, J. D., & Salovey, P. (1987). Personality moderates the interaction of mood and cognition. In K. Fiedler

& J. Forgas (Eds.), *Affect, cognition, and social behavior*. Toronto: Hogrefe.

Mazur, A., & Booth, A. (1998). Testosterone and dominance in men. *Behavioral and Brain Sciences, 21,* 353–363.

Mazzella, R., & Feingold, A. (1994). The effects of physical attractiveness, race, socioeconomic status, and gender of defendants and victims on judgments of mock jurors: A meta-analysis. *Journal of Applied Social Psychology, 24,* 1315–1344.

Mazzoni, G., & Memon, A. (2003). Imagination can create false autobiographical memories. *Psychological Science, 14,* 186–188.

Mazzuca, J. (2002, August 20). Teens shrug off movie sex and violence. *Gallup Tuesday Briefing* (www.gallup.com).

McAlister, A., Perry, C., Killen, J., Slinkard, L. A., & Maccoby, N. (1980). Pilot study of smoking, alcohol and drug abuse prevention. *American Journal of Public Health, 70,* 719–721.

McAndrew, F. T. (1981). Pattern of performance and attributions of ability and gender. *Journal of Personality and Social Psychology, 7,* 583–587.

McAndrew, F. T. (2002). New evolutionary perspectives on altruism: Multilevel-selection and costly-signaling theories. *Current Directions in Psychological Science, 11,* 79–82.

McCann, C. D., & Hancock, R. D. (1983). Self-monitoring in communicative interactions: Social cognitive consequences of goal-directed message modification. *Journal of Experimental Social Psychology, 19,* 109–121.

McCarthy, J. F., & Kelly, B. R. (1978a). Aggression, performance variables, and anger self-report in ice hockey players. *Journal of Psychology, 99,* 97–101.

McCarthy, J. F., & Kelly, B. R. (1978b). Aggressive behavior and its effect on performance over time in ice hockey athletes: An archival study. *International Journal of Sport Psychology, 9,* 90–96.

McCauley, C. (1989). The nature of social influence in groupthink: Compliance and internalization. *Journal of Personality and Social Psychology, 57,* 250–260.

McCauley, C. (1998). Group dynamics in Janis's theory of groupthink: Backward and forward. *Organizational Behavior and Human Decision Processes, 73,* 142–163.

McCauley, C. (2004). Psychological issues in understanding terrorism and the response to terrorism. In C. E. Stout (Ed.) *Psychology of terrorism: Coping with the continuing threat, condensed edition* (pp. 33–65). Westport, CT: Praeger/Greenwood.

McCauley, C. R. (2002). Psychological issues in understanding terrorism

and the response to terrorism. In C. E. Stout (Ed.), *The psychology of terrorism* (Vol. 3). Westport, CT: Praeger/Greenwood.

McCauley, C. R., & Segal, M. E. (1987). Social psychology of terrorist groups. In C. Hendrick (Ed.), *Group processes and intergroup relations: Review of personality and social psychology* (Vol. 9). Newbury Park, CA: Sage.

McClure, J. (1998). Discounting causes of behavior: Are two reasons better than one? *Journal of Personality and Social Psychology, 74,* 7–20.

McConahay, J. B. (1981). Reducing racial prejudice in desegregated schools. In W. D. Hawley (Ed.), *Effective school desegregation*. Beverly Hills, CA: Sage.

McCrae, R. R., & Costa, P. T., Jr. (1999). A five-factor theory of personality. In L. A. Pervin & O. P. John (Eds.), *Handbook of personality: Theory and research*. New York: Guilford.

McCullough, J. L., & Ostrom, T. M. (1974). Repetition of highly similar messages and attitude change. *Journal of Applied Psychology, 59,* 395–397.

McDermott, T. (2005). *Perfect soldiers: The hijackers: Who they were, why they did it*. New York: HarperCollins.

McFall, R. M. (1991). Manifesto for a science of clinical psychology. *The Clinical Psychologist, 44,* 75–88.

McFall, R. M. (2000). Elaborate reflections on a simple manifesto. *Applied and Preventive Psychology, 9,* 5–21.

McFarland, C., & Ross, M. (1985). The relation between current impressions and memories of self and dating partners. Unpublished manuscript, University of Waterloo.

McFarland, S. G. (2005). On the eve of war: Authoritarianism, social dominance, and American students' attitudes toward attacking Iraq. *Personality and Social Psychology Bulletin, 31,* 360–367.

McFarland, S. G., Ageyev, V. S., & Abalakina-Paap, M. A. (1992). Authoritarianism in the former Soviet Union. *Journal of Personality and Social Psychology, 63,* 1004–1010.

McFarland, S. G., Ageyev, V. S., & Djintcharadze, N. (1996). Russian authoritarianism two years after communism. *Personality and Social Psychology Bulletin, 22,* 210–217.

McFarland, S., & Carnahan, T. (2009). A situation's first powers are attracting volunteers and selecting participants: A reply to Haney and Zimbardo (2009). *Personality and Social Psychology Bulletin, 35,* 815–818.

McGillicuddy, N. B., Welton, G. L., & Pruitt, D. G. (1987). Third-party intervention: A field experiment comparing three different models. *Journal of Personality and Social Psychology, 53,* 104–112.

McGillis, D. (1979). Biases and jury decision making. In I. H. Frieze, D. Bar-Tal, & J. S. Carroll, *New approaches to social problems*. San Francisco: Jossey-Bass.

McGlone, M. S., & Tofighbakhsh, J. (2000). Birds of a feather flock conjointly (?): Rhyme as reason in aphorisms. *Psychological Science, 11,* 424–428.

McGlynn, R. P., Tubbs, D. D., & Holzhausen, K. G. (1995). Hypothesis generation in groups constrained by evidence. *Journal of Experimental Social Psychology, 31,* 64–81.

McGrath, J. E. (1984). *Groups: Interaction and performance*. Englewood Cliffs, NJ: Prentice-Hall.

McGraw, A. P., Mellers, B. A., & Tetlock, P. E. (2005). Expectations and emotions of Olympic atheletes. *Journal of Experimental Social Psychology, 41,* 438–446.

McGregor, I., Newby-Clark, I. R., & Zanna, M. P. (1998). Epistemic discomfort is moderated by simultaneous accessibility of inconsistent elements. In E. Harmon-Jones and J. Mills (Eds.), *Cognitive dissonance theory 40 years later: A revival with revisions and controversies*. Washington, DC: American Psychological Association.

McGregor, I., Zanna, M. P., Holmes, J. G., & Spencer, S. J. (2001). Conviction in the face of uncertainty: Going to extremes and being oneself. *Journal of Personality and Social Psychology, 80,* 472–478.

McGuire, A. (2002, August 19). Charity calls for debate on adverts aimed at children. *The Herald* (Scotland), p. 4.

McGuire, W. J. (1964). Inducing resistance to persuasion: Some contemporary approaches. In L. Berkowitz (Ed.), *Advances in experimental social psychology* (Vol. 1). New York: Academic Press.

McGuire, W. J., McGuire, C. V., Child, P., & Fujioka, T. (1978). Salience of ethnicity in the spontaneous self-concept as a function of one's ethnic distinctiveness in the social environment. *Journal of Personality and Social Psychology, 36,* 511–520.

McGuire, W. J., McGuire, C. V., & Winton, W. (1979). Effects of household sex composition on the salience of one's gender in the spontaneous self-concept. *Journal of Experimental Social Psychology, 15,* 77–90.

McGuire, W. J., & Padawer-Singer, A. (1978). Trait salience in the spontaneous self-concept. *Journal of Personality and Social Psychology, 33,* 743–754.

McKelvie, S. J. (1995). Bias in the estimated frequency of names. *Perceptual and Motor Skills, 81,* 1331–1338.

McKelvie, S. J. (1997). The availability heuristic: Effects of fame and gender on the estimated frequency of male and female names. *Journal of Social Psychology, 137,* 63–78.

McKenna, F. P., & Myers, L. B. (1997). Illusory self-assessments—Can they be reduced? *British Journal of Psychology, 88,* 39–51.

McKenna, K. Y. A., & Bargh, J. A. (1998). Coming out in the age of the Internet: Identity demarginalization through virtual group participation. *Journal of Personality and Social Psychology, 75,* 681–694.

McKenna, K. Y. A., & Bargh, J. A. (2000). Plan 9 from cyberspace: The implications of the Internet for personality and social psychology. *Personality and Social Psychology Review, 4,* 57–75.

McKenna, K. Y. A., Green, A. S., & Gleason, M. E. J. (2002). What's the big attraction? Relationship formation on the Internet. *Journal of Social Issues, 58,* 9–31.

McKenzie-Mohr, D., & Zanna, M. P. (1990). Treating women as sexual objects: Look to the (gender schematic) male who has viewed pornography. *Personality and Social Psychology Bulletin, 16,* 296–308.

McMillen, D. L., & Austin, J. B. (1971). Effect of positive feedback on compliance following transgression. *Psychonomic Science, 24,* 59–61.

McMillen, D. L., Sanders, D. Y., & Solomon, G. S. (1977). Self-esteem, attentiveness, and helping behavior. *Journal of Personality and Social Psychology, 3,* 257–261.

McNeill, B. W., & Stoltenberg, C. D. (1988). A test of the elaboration likelihood model for therapy. *Cognitive Therapy and Research, 12,* 69–79.

McNulty, J. K., O'Mara, E. M., & Karney, B. R. (2008). Benevolent cognitions as a strategy of relationship maintenance: "Don't sweat the small stuff" . . . But it is not all small stuff. *Journal of Personality and Social Psychology, 94,* 631–646.

McPherson, M., Smith-Lovin, L., & Cook, J. M. (2001). Birds of a feature: Homophily in social networks. *Annual Review of Sociology, 27,* 415–444.

Mead, G. H. (1934). *Mind, self, and society.* Chicago: University of Chicago Press.

Medalia, N. Z., & Larsen, O. N. (1958). Diffusion and belief in collective delusion: The Seattle windshield pitting epidemic. *American Sociological Review, 23,* 180–186.

Medvec, V. H., Madey, S. F., & Gilovich, T. (1995). When less is more: Counterfactual thinking and satisfaction among Olympic medalists. *Journal of Personality and Social Psychology, 69,* 603–610.

Medvec, V. H., & Savitsky, K. (1997). When doing better means feeling worse: The effects of categorical cutoff points on counterfactual thinking and satisfaction. *Journal of Personality and Social Psychology, 72,* 1284–1296.

Meehl, P. E. (1954). *Clinical vs. statistical prediction: A theoretical analysis and a review of evidence.* Minneapolis: University of Minnesota Press.

Meehl, P. E. (1986). Causes and effects of my disturbing little book. *Journal of Personality Assessment, 50,* 370–375.

Mehl, M. R., & Pennebaker, J. W. (2003). The sounds of social life: A psychometric analysis of students' daily social environments and natural conversations. *Journal of Personality and Social Psychology, 84,* 857–870.

Mehlman, P. T., & 7 others. (1994). Low CSF 5-HIAA concentrations and severe aggression and impaired impulse control in nonhuman primates. *American Journal of Psychiatry, 151,* 1485–1491.

Meier, B. P., & Hinsz, V. B. (2004). A comparison of human aggression committed by groups and individuals: An interindividual-intergroup discontinuity. *Journal of Experimental Social Psychology, 40,* 551–559.

Meissner, C. A., & Brigham, J. C. (2001). Thirty years of investigating the own-race bias in memory for faces: A meta-analytic review. *Psychology, Public Policy, & Law, 7,* 3–35.

Meissner, C. A., Brigham, J. C., & Butz, D. A. (2005). Memory for own- and other-race faces: A dual-process approach. *Applied Cognitive Psychology, 19,* 545–567.

Meissner, C. A., Brigham, J. C., & Kelley, C. M. (2001). The influence of retrieval processes in verbal overshadowing. *Memory and Cognition, 29,* 176–186.

Meissner, C. A., Tredoux, C. G., Parker, J. F., & MacLin, O. R. (2005). Eyewitness decisions in simultaneous and sequential lineups: A dual-process signal detection theory analysis. *Memory and Cognition, 33,* 783–792.

Meleshko, K. G. A., & Alden, L. E. (1993). Anxiety and self-disclosure: Toward a motivational model. *Journal of Personality and Social Psychology, 64,* 1000–1009.

Mellers, B., Hertwig, R., & Kahneman, D. (2001). Do frequency representations eliminate conjunction effects? An exercise in adversarial collaboration. *Psychological Science, 12,* 269–275.

Mendonca, P. J., & Brehm, S. S. (1983). Effects of choice on behavioral treatment of overweight children. *Journal of Social and Clinical Psychology, 1,* 343–358.

Merari, A. (2002). Explaining suicidal terrorism: Theories versus empirical evidence. Invited address to the American Psychological Association.

Merikle, P. M., Smilek, D., & Eastwood, J. D. (2001). Perception without awareness: Perspectives from cognitive psychology. *Cognition, 79,* 115–134.

Merton, R. K. (1938; reprinted 1970). *Science, technology and society in seventeenth-century England.* New York: Fertig.

Merton, R. K. (1948). The self-fulfilling prophecy. *Antioch Review, 8,* 193–210.

Merton, R. K., & Kitt, A. S. (1950). Contributions to the theory of reference group behavior. In R. K. Merton & P. F. Lazarsfeld (Eds.), *Continuities in social research: Studies in the scope and method of the American soldier.* Glencoe, IL: Free Press.

Merz, J. F. & Caulkins, J. P. (1995). Propensity to abuse—propensity to murder? *Chance, 8,* 14.

Mesmer-Magnus, J. R., & DeChurch, L. A. (2009). Information sharing and team performance: A meta-analysis. *Journal of Applied Psychology, 94,* 535–546.

Messé, L. A., & Sivacek, J. M. (1979). Predictions of others' responses in a mixed-motive game: Self-justification or false consensus? *Journal of Personality and Social Psychology, 37,* 602–607.

Messick, D. M., & Sentis, K. P. (1979). Fairness and preference. *Journal of Experimental Social Psychology, 15,* 418–434.

Metalsky, G. I., Joiner, T. E., Jr., Hardin, T. S., & Abramson, L. Y. (1993). Depressive reactions to failure in a naturalistic setting: A test of the hopelessness and self-esteem theories of depression. *Journal of Abnormal Psychology, 102,* 101–109.

Meyers, S. A., & Berscheid, E. (1997). The language of love: The difference a preposition makes. *Personality and Social Psychology Bulletin, 23,* 347–362.

Mezulis, A. H., Abramson, L. Y., Hyde, J. S., & Hankin, B. L. (2004). Is there a universal positivity bias in attributions? A meta-analytic review of individual, developmental, and cultural differences in the self-serving attributional bias. *Psychological Bulletin, 130,* 711–747.

Michaels, J. W., Blommel, J. M., Brocato, R. M., Linkous, R. A., & Rowe, J. S. (1982). Social facilitation and inhibition in a natural setting. *Replications in Social Psychology, 2,* 21–24.

Mickelson, K. D., Kessler, R. C., & Shaver, P. R. (1997). Adult attachment in a nationally representative sample. *Journal of Personality and Social Psychology, 73,* 1092–1106.

Mikula, G. (1984). Justice and fairness in interpersonal relations: Thoughts and suggestions. In H. Taijfel (Ed.), *The social dimension: European developments in social psychology* (Vol. 1). Cambridge: Cambridge University Press.

Mikulincer, M., Florian, V., & Hirschberger, G. (2003). The existential function of close relationships: Introducing death into the science of love. *Personality and Social Psychology Review, 7,* 20–40.

Mikulincer, M., & Shaver, P. R. (2001). Attachment theory and intergroup bias: Evidence that priming the secure base schema attenuates negative reactions to out-groups. *Journal of Personality and Social Psychology, 81,* 97–115.

Mikulincer, M., Shaver, P. R., Gillath, O., & Nitzberg, R. A. (2005). Attachment, caregiving, and altruism: Boosting attachment security increases compassion and helping. *Journal of Personality and Social Psychology, 89,* 817–839.

Milgram, A. (2000). My personal view of Stanley Milgram. In T. Blass (Ed.), *Obedience to authority: Current perspectives on the Milgram paradigm.* Mahwah, NJ: Erlbaum.

Milgram, S. (1961, December). Nationality and conformity. *Scientific American,* pp. 45–51.

Milgram, S. (1965). Some conditions of obedience and disobedience to authority. *Human Relations, 18,* 57–76.

Milgram, S. (1974). *Obedience to authority.* New York: Harper and Row.

Millar, M. G., & Millar, K. U. (1996). Effects of message anxiety on disease detection and health promotion behaviors. *Basic and Applied Social Psychology, 18,* 61–74.

Millar, M. G., & Tesser, A. (1992). The role of beliefs and feelings in guiding behavior: The mismatch model. In L. Martin & A. Tesser (Eds.), *The construction of social judgment.* Hillsdale NJ: Erlbaum.

Miller, A. G. (1986). *The obedience experiments: A case study of controversy in social science.* New York: Praeger.

Miller, A. G. (2004). What can the Milgram obedience experiments tell us about the Holocaust? Generalizing from the social psychological laboratory. In A. G. Miller (Ed.), *The social psychology of good and evil.* New York: Guilford.

Miller, A. G. (2006). Exonerating harm-doers: Some problematic implications of social-psychological explanations. Paper presented to the Society of Personality and Social Psychology convention.

Miller, A. G., Ashton, W., & Mishal, M. (1990). Beliefs concerning the features of constrained behavior: A basis for the fundamental attribution error. *Journal of Personality and Social Psychology, 59,* 635–650.

Miller, C. E., & Anderson, P. D. (1979). Group decision rules and the rejection of deviates. *Social Psychology Quarterly, 42,* 354–363.

Miller, C. T., & Felicio, D. M. (1990). Person-positivity bias: Are individuals liked better than groups? *Journal of Experimental Social Psychology, 26,* 408–420.

Miller, D. T., Downs, J. S., & Prentice, D. A. (1998). Minimal conditions for the creation of a unit relationship: The social bond between birthdaymates. *European Journal of Social Psychology, 28,* 475.

Miller, D. T., & McFarland, C. (1987). Pluralistic ignorance: When similarity is interpreted as dissimilarity. *Journal of Personality and Social Psychology, 53,* 298–305.

Miller, D. W. (2001, November 23). Jury consulting on trial. *Chronicle of Higher Education,* pp. A15, A16.

Miller, G. E., & Blackwell, E. (2006). Turning up the heat: Inflammation as a mechanism linking chronic stress, depression, and heart disease. *Current Directions in Psychological Science, 15,* 269–272.

Miller, G. R., & Fontes, N. E. (1979). *Videotape on trial: A view from the jury box.* Beverly Hills, CA: Sage.

Miller, G., Tybur, J. M., & Jordan, B. D. (2007). Ovulatory cycle effects on tip earnings by lap dancers: Economic evidence for human estrus? *Evolution and Human Behavior, 28,* 375–381.

Miller, J. G. (1984). Culture and the development of everyday social explanation. *Journal of Personality and Social Psychology, 46,* 961–978.

Miller, K. I., & Monge, P. R. (1986). Participation, satisfaction, and productivity: A meta-analytic review. *Academy of Management Journal, 29,* 727–753.

Miller, L. C. (1990). Intimacy and liking: Mutual influence and the role of unique relationships. *Journal of Personality and Social Psychology, 59,* 50–60.

Miller, L. C., Berg, J. H., & Archer, R. L. (1983). Openers: Individuals who elicit intimate self-disclosure. *Journal of Personality and Social Psychology, 44,* 1234–1244.

Miller, L. E., & Grush, J. E. (1986). Individual differences in attitudinal versus normative determination of behavior. *Journal of Experimental Social Psychology, 22,* 190–202.

Miller, N. (2002). Personalization and the promise of contact theory. *Journal of Social Issues, 58,* 387–410.

Miller, N., & Campbell, D. T. (1959). Recency and primacy in persuasion as a function of the timing of speeches and measurements. *Journal of Abnormal and Social Psychology, 59,* 1–9.

Miller, N., & Marks, G. (1982). Assumed similarity between self and other: Effect of expectation of future interaction with that other. *Social Psychology Quarterly, 45,* 100–105.

Miller, N., Maruyama, G., Beaber, R. J., & Valone, K. (1976). Speed of speech and persuasion. *Journal of Personality and Social Psychology, 34,* 615–624.

Miller, N., Pedersen, W. C., Earleywine, M., & Pollock, V. E. (2003). A theoretical model of triggered displaced aggression. *Personality and Social Psychology Review, 7,* 75–97.

Miller, N. E. (1941). The frustration-aggression hypothesis. *Psychological Review, 48,* 337–342.

Miller, P. A., & Eisenberg, N. (1988). The relation of empathy to aggressive and externalizing/antisocial behavior. *Psychological Bulletin, 103,* 324–344.

Miller, P. A., Kozu, J., & Davis, A. C. (2001). Social influence, empathy, and prosocial behavior in cross-cultural perspective. In W. Wosinska, R. B. Cialdini, D. W. Barrett, & J. Reykowski (Eds.), *The practice of social influence in multiple cultures.* Mahwah, NJ: Erlbaum.

Miller, P. C., Lefcourt, H. M., Holmes, J. G., Ware, E. E., & Saley, W. E. (1986). Marital locus of control and marital problem solving. *Journal of Personality and Social Psychology, 51,* 161–169.

Miller, P. J. E., Niehuis, S., & Huston, T. L. (2006). Positive illusions in marital relationships: A 13 year longitudinal study. *Personality and Social Psychology Bulletin, 32,* 1579–1594.

Miller, P. J. E., & Rempel, J. K. (2004). Trust and partner-enhancing attributions in close relationships. *Personality and Social Psychology Bulletin, 30,* 695–705.

Miller, R. L., Brickman, P., & Bolen, D. (1975). Attribution versus persuasion as a means for modifying behavior. *Journal of Personality and Social Psychology, 31,* 430–441.

Miller, R. S. (1997). Inattentive and contented: Relationship commitment and attention to alternatives. *Journal of Personality and Social Psychology, 73,* 758–766.

Miller, R. S., & Schlenker, B. R. (1985). Egotism in group members: Public and private attributions of responsibility for group performance. *Social Psychology Quarterly, 48,* 85–89.

Miller, R. S., & Simpson, J. A. (1990). Relationship satisfaction and attentiveness to alternatives. Paper presented at the American Psychological Association convention.

Millett, K. (1975, January). The shame is over. *Ms.,* pp. 26–29.

Mims, P. R., Hartnett, J. J., & Nay, W. R. (1975). Interpersonal attraction and help volunteering as a function of physical attractiveness. *Journal of Psychology, 89,* 125–131.

Minard, R. D. (1952). Race relationships in the Pocohontas coal field. *Journal of Social Issues, 8*(1), 29–44.

Mio, J. S., Thompson, S. C., & Givens, G. H. (1993). The commons dilemma as a metaphor: Memory, influence, and implications for environmental conservation. *Metaphor and Symbolic Activity, 8,* 23–42.

Mirels, H. L., & McPeek, R. W. (1977). Self-advocacy and self-esteem. *Journal of Consulting and Clinical Psychology, 45,* 1132–1138.

Mirsky, S. (2009, January). What's good for the group. *Scientific American,* p. 51.

Mischel, W. (1968). *Personality and assessment.* New York: Wiley.

Mita, T. H., Dermer, M., & Knight, J. (1977). Reversed facial images and the mere-exposure hypothesis. *Journal of Personality and Social Psychology, 35,* 597–601.

Mitchell, G., Tetlock, P. E., Mellers, B. A., & Ordonez, L. D. (1993). Judgments of social justice: Compromises between equality and efficiency. *Journal of Personality and Social Psychology, 65,* 629–639.

Mitchell, J., McCrae, C. N, & Banaji, M. R. (2006). Dissociable medial prefrontal contributions to judgments of similar and dissimilar others. *Neuron, 18,* 655–663.

Mitchell, T. L., Haw, R. M., Pfeifer, J. E., & Meissner, C. A. (2005). Racial bias in mock juror decision-making: A meta-analytic review of defendant treatment. *Law and Human Behavior, 29,* 621–637.

Mitchell, T. R., & Thompson, L. (1994). A theory of temporal adjustments of the evaluation of events: Rosy prospection and rosy retrospection. In C. Stubbart, J. Porac, & J. Meindl (Eds.), *Advances in managerial cognition and organizational information processing.* Greenwich, CT: JAI Press.

Mitchell, T. R., Thompson, L., Peterson, E., & Cronk, R. (1997). Temporal adjustments in the evaluation of events: The "rosy view." *Journal of Experimental Social Psychology, 33,* 421–448.

Moffitt, T., Caspi, A., Sugden, K., Taylor, A., Craig, I. W., Harrington, H., McClay, J., Mill, J., Martin, J., Braithwaite, A., & Poulton, R. (2003). Influence of life stress on depression: Moderation by a polymorphism in the 5-HTT gene. *Science, 301,* 386–389.

Moghaddam, F. M. (2005). The staircase to terrorism: A psychological exploration. *American Psychologist, 60,* 161–169.

Monin, B., & Norton, M. I. (2003). Perceptions of a fluid consensus: Uniqueness bias, false consensus, false polarization, and pluralistic ignorance in a water conservation crisis. *Personality and Social Psychology, 29,* 559–567.

Monson, T. C., Hesley, J. W., & Chernick, L. (1982). Specifying when personality traits can and cannot predict behavior: An alternative to abandoning the attempt to predict single-act criteria. *Journal of Personality and Social Psychology, 43,* 385–399.

Monteith, M. J. (1993). Self-regulation of prejudiced responses: Implications for progress in prejudice-reduction efforts. *Journal of Personality and Social Psychology, 65,* 469–485.

Montoya, R. M. (2008). I'm hot, so I'd say you're not: The influence of objective physical attractiveness on mate selection. *Personality and Social Psychology Bulletin, 34,* 1315–1331.

Montoya, R. M., & Horton, R. S. (2004). On the importance of cognitive evaluation as a determinant of interpersonal attraction. *Journal of Personality and Social Psychology, 86,* 696–712.

Montoya, R. M., & Insko, C. A. (2008). Toward a more complete understanding of the reciprocity of liking effect. *European Journal of Social Psychology, 38,* 477–498.

Moody, K. (1980). *Growing up on television: The TV effect.* New York: Times Books.

Moons, W. G., & Mackie, D. M. (2007). Thinking straight while seeing red: The influence of anger on information processing. *Personality and Social Psychology Bulletin, 33,* 706–720.

Moons, W. G., Mackie, D. M., & Garcia-Marques, T. (2009). The impact of repetition-induced familiarity on agreement with weak and strong arguments. *Journal of Personality and Social Psychology, 96,* 32–44.

Moore, D. A., & Small, D. A. (2007). Error and bias in comparative judgment: On being both better and worse than we think we are. *Journal of Personality and Social Psychology, 92,* 972–989.

Moore, D. L., & Baron, R. S. (1983). Social facilitation: A physiological analysis. In J. T. Cacioppo & R. Petty (Eds.), *Social psychophysiology.* New York: Guilford.

Moore, D. W. (2003, March 18). Public approves of Bush ultimatum by more than 2-to-1 margin. Gallup News Service (www.gallup.com).

Moore, D. W. (2004, March 23). The civil unions vs. gay marriage proposals. *Gallup Tuesday Briefing* (www.gallup .com).

Moore, D. W. (2004, April 20). Ballot order: Who benefits? *Gallup Poll Tuesday Briefing* (www.gallup.com).

Mor, N., & Winquist, J. (2002). Self-focused attention and negative affect: A meta-analysis. *Psychological Bulletin, 128,* 638–662.

Moran, G., & Comfort, J. C. (1982). Scientific juror selection: Sex as a moderator of demographic and personality predictors of impaneled felony juror behavior. *Journal of Personality and Social Psychology, 43,* 1052–1063.

Moran, G., & Comfort, J. C. (1986). Neither "tentative" nor "fragmentary": Verdict preference of impaneled felony jurors as a function of attitude toward capital punishment. *Journal of Applied Psychology, 71,* 146–155.

Moran, G., & Cutler, B. L. (1991). The prejudicial impact of pretrial publicity. *Journal of Applied Social Psychology, 21,* 345–367.

Moran, G., Cutler, B. L., & De Lisa, A. (1994). Attitudes toward tort reform, scientific jury selection, and juror bias: Verdict inclination in criminal and civil trials. *Law and Psychology Review, 18,* 309–328.

Moran, G., Cutler, B. L., & Loftus, E. F. (1990). Jury selection in major controlled substance trials: The need for extended voir dire. *Forensic Reports, 3,* 331–348.

Moreland, R. L., & Zajonc, R. B. (1977). Is stimulus recognition a necessary condition for the occurrence of exposure effects? *Journal of Personality and Social Psychology, 35,* 191–199.

Morgan, C. A., III, Hazlett, G., Doran, A., Garrett, S., Hoyt, G., Thomas, P., Baranoski, M., & Southwick, S. M. (2004). Accuracy of eyewitness memory for persons encountered during exposure to highly intense stress. *International Journal of Law and Psychiatry, 27,* 265–279.

Morling, B., & Lamoreaux, M. (2008). Measuring culture outside the head: A meta-analysis of individualism-collectivism in cultural products. *Personality and Social Psychology Bulletin, 12,* 199–221.

Morris, W. N., & Miller, R. S. (1975). The effects of consensus-breaking and consensus-preempting partners on reduction of conformity. *Journal of Experimental Social Psychology, 11,* 215–223.

Morrow, L. (1983, August 1). All the hazards and threats of success. *Time,* pp. 20–25.

Moscovici, S. (1985). Social influence and conformity. In G. Lindzey & E. Aronson (Eds.), *The handbook of social psychology,* 3rd edition. Hillsdale, NJ: Erlbaum.

Moscovici, S. (1988). Notes towards a description of social representations. *European Journal of Social Psychology, 18,* 211–250.

Moscovici, S. (2001). Why a theory of social representation? In K. Deaux & G. Philogène (Eds.), *Representations of the social: Bridging theoretical traditions.* Malden, MA: Blackwell.

Moscovici, S., Lage, S., & Naffrechoux, M. (1969). Influence of a consistent minority on the responses of a majority in a color perception task. *Sociometry, 32,* 365–380.

Moscovici, S., & Zavalloni, M. (1969). The group as a polarizer of attitudes. *Journal of Personality and Social Psychology, 12,* 124–135.

Motherhood Project. (2001, May 2). Watch out for children: A mothers' statement to advertisers. Institute for American Values (www.watchoutforchildren.org).

Moyer, K. E. (1976). *The psychobiology of aggression.* New York: Harper & Row.

Moyer, K. E. (1983). The physiology of motivation: Aggression as a model. In C. J. Scheier & A. M. Rogers (Eds.), *G. Stanley Hall Lecture Series* (Vol. 3). Washington, DC: American Psychological Association.

Moynihan, D. P. (1979). Social science and the courts. *Public Interest, 54,* 12–31.

Muehlenhard, C. L. (1988). Misinterpreted dating behaviors and the risk of date rape. *Journal of Social and Clinical Psychology, 6,* 20–37.

Mueller, C. M., & Dweck, C. S. (1998). Praise for intelligence can undermine children's motivation and performance. *Journal of Personality and Social Psychology, 75,* 33–52.

Mueller, C. W., Donnerstein, E., & Hallam, J. (1983). Violent films and prosocial behavior. *Personality and Social Psychology Bulletin, 9,* 83–89.

Mullen, B. (1986a). Atrocity as a function of lynch mob composition: A self-attention perspective. *Personality and Social Psychology Bulletin, 12,* 187–197.

Mullen, B. (1986b). Stuttering, audience size, and the other-total ratio: A self-attention perspective. *Journal of Applied Social Psychology, 16,* 139–149.

Mullen, B., Anthony, T., Salas, E., & Driskell, J. E. (1994). Group cohesiveness and quality of decision making: An integration of tests of the groupthink hypothesis. *Small Group Research, 25,* 189–204.

Mullen, B., & Baumeister, R. F. (1987). Group effects on self-attention and performance: Social loafing, social facilitation, and social impairment. In C. Hendrick (Ed.), *Group processes and intergroup relations: Review of personality and social psychology* (Vol. 9). Newbury Park, CA: Sage.

Mullen, B., Brown, R., & Smith, C. (1992). Ingroup bias as a function of salience, relevance, and status: An integration. *European Journal of Social Psychology, 22,* 103–122.

Mullen, B., Bryant, B., & Driskell, J. E. (1997). Presence of others and arousal: An integration. *Group Dynamics: Theory, Research, and Practice, 1,* 52–64.

Mullen, B., & Copper, C. (1994). The relation between group cohesiveness and performance: An integration. *Psychological Bulletin, 115,* 210–227.

Mullen, B., Copper, C., & Driskell, J. E. (1990). Jaywalking as a function of model behavior. *Personality and Social Psychology Bulletin, 16,* 320–330.

Mullen, B., & Goethals, G. R. (1990). Social projection, actual consensus and valence. *British Journal of Social Psychology, 29,* 279–282.

Mullen, B., & Hu, L. (1989). Perceptions of ingroup and outgroup variability: A meta-analytic integration. *Basic and Applied Social Psychology, 10,* 233–252.

Mullen, B., & Riordan, C. A. (1988). Self-serving attributions for performance in naturalistic settings: A meta-analytic review. *Journal of Applied Social Psychology, 18,* 3–22.

Muller, S., & Johnson, B. T. (1990). Fear and persuasion: A linear relationship? Paper presented to the Eastern Psychological Association convention.

Mullin, C. R., & Linz, D. (1995). Desensitization and resensitization to violence against women: Effects of exposure to sexually violent films on judgments of domestic violence victims. *Journal of Personality and Social Psychology, 69,* 449–459.

Munro, G. D., Ditto, P. H., Lockhart, L. K., Fagerlin, A., Gready, M., & Peterson, E. (1997). Biased assimilation of sociopolitical arguments: Evaluating the 1996 U.S. presidential debate. Unpublished manuscript, Hope College.

Muraven, M., Tice, D. M., & Baumeister, R. F. (1998). Self-control as a limited resource: Regulatory depletion patterns. *Journal of Personality and Social Psychology, 74,* 774–790.

Murphy, C. (1990, June). New findings: Hold on to your hat. *The Atlantic,* pp. 22–23.

Murphy, C. M., & O'Farrell, T. J. (1996). Marital violence among alcoholics. *Current Directions in Psychological Science, 5,* 183–187.

Murphy-Berman, V., Berman, J. J., Singh, P., Pachauri, A., & Kumar, P. (1984). Factors affecting allocation to needy and meritorious recipients: A cross-cultural comparison. *Journal of Personality and Social Psychology, 46,* 1267–1272.

Murray, J. P., & Kippax, S. (1979). From the early window to the late night show: International trends in the study of television's impact on children and adults. In L. Berkowitz (Ed.), *Advances in experimental social psychology* (Vol. 12). New York: Academic Press.

Murray, S. L., Gellavia, G. M., Rose, P., & Griffin, D. W. (2003). Once hurt, twice hurtful: How perceived regard regulates daily marital interactions. *Journal of Personality and Social Psychology, 84,* 126–147.

Murray, S. L., & Holmes, J. G. (1997). A leap of faith? Positive illusions in romantic relationships. *Personality and Social Psychology Bulletin, 23,* 586–604.

Murray, S. L., Holmes, J. G., Gellavia, G., Griffin, D. W., & Dolderman, D. (2002). Kindred spirits? The benefits of egocentrism in close relationships. *Journal of Personality and Social Psychology, 82,* 563–581.

Murray, S. L., Holmes, J. G., & Griffin, D. W. (1996a). The benefits of positive illusions: Idealization and the construction of satisfaction in close relationships. *Journal of Personality and Social Psychology, 70,* 79–98.

Murray, S. L., Holmes, J. G., & Griffin, D. W. (1996b). The self-fulfilling nature of positive illusions in romantic relationships: Love is not blind, but prescient. *Journal of Personality and Social Psychology, 71,* 1155–1180.

Murray, S. L., Holmes, J. G., & Griffin, D. W. (2000). Self-esteem and the quest for felt security: How perceived regard regulates attachment processes. *Journal of Personality and Social Psychology, 78,* 478–498.

Murray, S. L., Holmes, J. G., MacDonald, G., & Ellsworth, P. C. (1998). Through the looking glass darkly? When self-doubts turn into relationship insecurities. *Journal of Personality and Social Psychology, 75,* 1459–1480.

Murstein, B. L. (1986). *Paths to marriage.* Newbury Park, CA: Sage.

Muson, G. (1978, March). Teenage violence and the telly. *Psychology Today,* pp. 50–54.

Mussweiler, T. (2006). Doing is for thinking! Stereotype activation by stereotypic movements. *Psychological Science, 17,* 17–21.

Myers, D. G. (1978). Polarizing effects of social comparison. *Journal of Experimental Social Psychology, 14,* 554–563.

Myers, D. G. (1993). *The pursuit of happiness.* New York: Avon.

Myers, D. G. (2000a). *The American paradox: Spiritual hunger in an age of plenty.* New Haven, CT: Yale University Press.

Myers, D. G. (2000b). The funds, friends, and faith of happy people. *American Psychologist, 55,* 56–67.

Myers, D. G. (2001, December). Do we fear the right things? *American Psychological Society Observer,* p. 3.

Myers, D. G. (2010). *Psychology,* 9th edition. New York: Worth Publishers.

Myers, D. G., & Bishop, G. D. (1970). Discussion effects on racial attitudes. *Science, 169,* 778–789.

Myers, J. E., Madathil, J., & Tingle, L. R. (2005). Marriage satisfaction and wellness in India and the United States: A preliminary comparison of arranged marriages and marriages of choice. *Journal of Counseling and Development, 83,* 183–190.

Myers, J. N. (1997, December). Quoted by S. A. Boot, Where the weather reigns. *World Traveler*, pp. 86, 88, 91, 124.

Myers, N. (2000). Sustainable consumption: The meta-problem. In B. Heap & J. Kent (Eds.), *Towards sustainable consumption: A European perspective*. London: The Royal Society.

Nadler, A. (1991). Help-seeking behavior: Psychological costs and instrumental benefits. In M. S. Clark (Ed.), *Prosocial behavior*. Newbury Park, CA: Sage.

Nadler, A., & Fisher, J. D. (1986). The role of threat to self-esteem and perceived control in recipient reaction to help: Theory development and empirical validation. In L. Berkowitz (Ed.), *Advances in Experimental Social Psychology* (Vol. 19). Orlando, FL: Academic Press.

Nadler, A., Goldberg, M., & Jaffe, Y. (1982). Effect of self-differentiation and anonymity in group on deindividuation. *Journal of Personality and Social Psychology*, **42**, 1127–1136.

Nagar, D., & Pandey, J. (1987). Affect and performance on cognitive task as a function of crowding and noise. *Journal of Applied Social Psychology*, **17**, 147–157.

Nagourney, A. (2002, September 25). For remarks on Iraq, Gore gets praise and scorn. *New York Times* (www.nytimes.com).

Nail, P. R., MacDonald, G., & Levy, D. A. (2000). Proposal of a four-dimensional model of social response. *Psychological Bulletin*, **126**, 454–470.

Nair, H., Manchanda, P., & Bhatia, T. (2008, May). Asymmetric social interactions in physician prescription behavior: The role of opinion leaders. Stanford University Graduate School of Business Research Paper No. 1970 (ssrn.com/abstract=937021).

National Center for Health Statistics. (1991). Family structure and children's health: United States, 1988 (by Deborah A. Dawson). *Vital and Health Statistics*, Series 10, No. 178, CHHS Publication No. PHS 91–1506.

National Center for Health Statistics. (2004, December 15). Marital status and health: United States, 1999–2002 (by Charlotte A. Schoenborn). *Advance Data from Vital and Human Statistics*, No. 351. Centers for Disease Control and Prevention.

National Research Council. (1993). *Understanding and preventing violence*. Washington, DC: National Academy Press.

National Research Council. (2002). *Youth, pornography, and the Internet*. Washington, DC: National Academy Press.

National Safety Council. (2008). Transportation mode comparisons, from *Injury Facts* (via correspondence with Kevin T. Fearn, Research & Statistical Services Department).

National Television Violence Study. (1997). Thousand Oaks, CA: Sage.

Naylor, T. H. (1990). Redefining corporate motivation, Swedish style. *Christian Century*, **107**, 566–570.

NCHS. (2008, August 6). National ambulatory medical care survey: 2006 summary. *National Health Statistics Report*, No. 3 (by D. K. Cherry, E. Hing, D. A. Woodwell, & E. A. Rechtsteiner). Centers for Disease Control and Prevention: National Center for Health Statistics (www.cdc.gov/nchs/data/nhsr/nhsr003.pdf).

Needles, D. J., & Abramson, L. Y. (1990). Positive life events, attributional style, and hopefulness: Testing a model of recovery from depression. *Journal of Abnormal Psychology*, **99**, 156–165.

Neff, L. A., & Karney, B. R. (2005). To know you is to love you: The implications of global adoration and specific accuracy for marital relationships. *Journal of Personality and Social Psychology*, **88**, 480–497.

Neidorf, S., & Morin, R. (2007, May 23). Four in ten Americans have close friends or relatives who are gay. Pew Research Center Publications (pewresearch.org).

Neimeyer, G. J., MacNair, R., Metzler, A. E., & Courchaine, K. (1991). Changing personal beliefs: Effects of forewarning, argument quality, prior bias, and personal exploration. *Journal of Social and Clinical Psychology*, **10**, 1–20.

Nelson, L., & LeBoeuf, R. (2002). Why do men overperceive women's sexual intent? False consensus vs. evolutionary explanations. Paper presented to the annual meeting of the Society for Personality and Social Psychology.

Nelson, L. D., & Morrison, E. L. (2005). The symptoms of resource scarcity: Judgments of food and finances influence preferences for potential partners. *Psychological Science*, **16**, 167–173.

Nelson, L. J., & Miller, D. T. (1995). The distinctiveness effect in social categorization: You are what makes you unusual. *Psychological Science*, **6**, 246.

Nelson, T. E., Acker, M., & Manis, M. (1996). Everyday base rates (sex stereotypes): Potent and resilient. *Journal of Personality and Social Psychology*, **59**, 664–675.

Nelson, T. E., Biernat, M. R., & Manis, M. (1990). Everyday base rates (sex stereotypes): Potent and resilient. *Journal of Personality and Social Psychology*, **59**, 664–675.

Nemeth, C. (1979). The role of an active minority in intergroup relations. In W. G. Austin and S. Worchel (Eds.), *The social psychology of intergroup relations*. Monterey, CA: Brooks/Cole.

Nemeth, C., & Wachtler, J. (1974). Creating the perceptions of consistency and confidence: A necessary condition for minority influence. *Sociometry*, **37**, 529–540.

Nemeth, C., & Chiles, C. (1988). Modelling courage: The role of dissent in fostering independence. *European Journal of Social Psychology*, **18**, 275–280.

Nemeth, C. J. (1997). Managing innovation: When less is more. *California Management Review*, **40**, 59–74.

Nemeth, C. J. (1999). Behind the scenes. In D. G. Myers, *Social psychology*, 6th edition. New York: McGraw-Hill.

Nemeth, C. J., Brown, K., & Rogers, J. (2001a). Devil's advocate versus authentic dissent: Stimulating quantity and quality. *European Journal of Social Psychology*, **31**, 1–13.

Nemeth, C. J., Connell, J. B., Rogers, J. D., & Brown, K. S. (2001b). Improving decision making by means of dissent. *Journal of Applied Social Psychology*, **31**, 48–58.

Nemeth, C. J., & Ormiston, M. (2007). Creative idea generation: Harmony versus stimulation. *European Journal of Social Psychology*, **37**, 524–535.

Nemeth, C. J., Personnaz, B., Personnaz, M., & Goncalo, J. A. (2004). The liberating role of conflict in group creativity: A study in two countries. *European Journal of Social Psychology*, **34**, 365–374.

Neumann, R., & Strack, F. (2000). Approach and avoidance: The influence of proprioceptive and exteroceptive cues on encoding of affective information. *Journal of Personality and Social Psychology*, **79**, 39–48.

New York Times. (2002, May 26). Fighting to live as the towers died (www.nytimes.com).

Newcomb, T. M. (1961). *The acquaintance process*. New York: Holt, Rinehart & Winston.

Newell, B., & Lagnado, D. (2003). Think-tanks, or think *tanks*. *The Psychologist*, **16**, 176.

Newell, B. R., Wong, K. Y., Cheung, J. C. H., & Rakow, T. (2008, August 23). Think, blink, or sleep on it? The impact of modes of thought on complex decision making. *Quarterly Journal of Experimental Psychology* (DOI: 10.1080/17470210802215202).

Newman, H. M., & Langer, E. J. (1981). Post-divorce adaptation and the attribution of responsibility. *Sex Roles*, **7**, 223–231.

Newman, L. S. (1993). How individualists interpret behavior:

Idiocentrism and spontaneous trait inference. *Social Cognition,* **11,** 243–269.

Newman, L. S., Duff, K., Schnopp-Wyatt, N., Brock, B., & Hoffman, Y. (1997). Reactions to the O. J. Simpson verdict: "Mindless tribalism" or motivated inference processes? *Journal of Social Issues,* **53,** 547–562.

Newport, F. (2007a, May 11). The age factor: Older Americans most negative about Iraq war (www.galluppoll.com).

Newport, F. (2007b, June 11). Majority of Republicans doubt theory of evolution. *Gallup Poll* (www.galluppoll.com).

Newport, F., Moore, D. W., Jones, J. M., & Saad, L. (2003, March 21). Special release: American opinion on the war. *Gallup Poll Tuesday Briefing* (www.gallup.com/poll/tb/goverpubli/s0030325.asp).

Nias, D. K. B. (1979). Marital choice: Matching or complementation? In M. Cook and G. Wilson (Eds.), *Love and attraction.* Oxford: Pergamon.

Nichols, J. (2003, February 9). Man overdoses online as chatters watch him die. *Grand Rapids Press,* p. A20.

Nicholson, C. (2007, January). Framing science: Advances in theory and technology are fueling a new era in the science of persuasion. *APS Observer* (www.psychologicalscience.org).

Nicholson, N., Cole, S. G., & Rocklin, T. (1985). Conformity in the Asch situation: A comparison between contemporary British and U. S. university students. *British Journal of Social Psychology,* **24,** 59–63.

Nie, N. H., & Erbring, L. (2000, February 17). Internet and society: A preliminary report. Stanford, CA: Stanford Institute for the Quantitative Study of Society.

Niedermeier, K. E., Kerr, N. L., & Messe, L. A. (1999). Jurors' use of naked statistical evidence: Exploring bases and implications of the Wells effect. *Journal of Personality and Social Psychology,* **76,** 533–542.

Nielsen. (2008a, May). *Nielsen's three screen report.* The Nielsen Company (www.nielsen.com).

Nielsen. (2008b, February 14). Nielsen reports DVR playback is adding to TV viewing levels. The Nielsen Company (www.nielsen.com).

Nielsen, M. E. (1998). Social psychology and religion on a trip to Ukraine (psychwww.com/psyrelig/ukraine/index.htm).

Niemi, R. G., Mueller, J., & Smith, T. W. (1989). *Trends in public opinion: A compendium of survey data.* New York: Greenwood Press.

Nigro, G. N., Hill, D. E., Gelbein, M. E., & Clark, C. L. (1988). Changes in the facial prominence of women and men over the last decade. *Psychology of Women Quarterly,* **12,** 225–235.

Nijstad, B. A., & Stroebe, W. (2006). How the group affects the mind: A cognitive model of idea generation in groups. *Personality and Social Psychology Review,* **10,** 186–213.

Nijstad, B. A., Stroebe, W., & Lodewijkx, H. F. M. (2006). The illusion of group productivity. A reduction of failures explanation. *European Journal of Social Psychology,* **36,** 31–48.

Nisbett, R. (2003). *The geography of thought: How Asians and Westerners think differently . . . and why.* New York: Free Press.

Nisbett, R. E. (1990). Evolutionary psychology, biology, and cultural evolution. *Motivation and emotion,* **14,** 255–263.

Nisbett, R. E. (1993). Violence and U.S. regional culture. *American Psychologist,* **48,** 441–449.

Nisbett, R. E., Fong, G. T., Lehman, D. R., & Cheng, P. W. (1987). Teaching reasoning. *Science,* **238,** 625–631.

Nisbett, R. E., & Masuda, T. (2003). Culture and point of view. *Proceedings of the National Academy of Sciences,* **100,** 11163–11170.

Nisbett, R. E., & Ross, L. (1980). *Human inference: Strategies and shortcomings of social judgment.* Englewood Cliffs, NJ: Prentice-Hall.

Nix, G., Watson, C., Pyszczynski, T., & Greenberg, J. (1995). Reducing depressive affect through external focus of attention. *Journal of Social and Clinical Psychology,* **14,** 36–52.

Noel, J. G., Forsyth, D. R., & Kelley, K. N. (1987). Improving the performance of failing students by overcoming their self-serving attributional biases. *Basic and Applied Social Psychology,* **8,** 151–162.

Nolan, J. M., Schultz, P. W., Cialdini, R. B., Goldstein, N. J., & Griskevicius, V. (2008). Normative social influence is underdetected. *Personality and Social Psychology Bulletin,* **34,** 913–923.

Nolan, S. A., Flynn, C., & Garber, J. (2003). Prospective relations between rejection and depression in young adolescents. *Journal of Personality and Social Psychology,* **85,** 745–755.

Nolen-Hoeksema, S. (2003). *Women who think too much: How to break free of overthinking and reclaim your life.* New York: Holt.

Noller, P. (1996). What is this thing called love? Defining the love that supports marriage and family. *Personal Relationships,* **3,** 97–115.

Noller, P., & Fitzpatrick, M. A. (1990). Marital communication in the eighties. *Journal of Marriage and Family,* **52,** 832–843.

Noon, E., & Hollin, C. R. (1987). Lay knowledge of eyewitness behaviour: A British survey. *Applied Cognitive Psychology,* **1,** 143–153.

Noor, M., Brown, R., Gonzalez, R., Manzi, J., & Lewis, C. A. (2008). On positive psychological outcomes: What helps groups with a history of conflict to forgive and reconcile with each other? *Personality and Social Psychology Bulletin,* **34,** 819–832.

NORC. (National Opinion Research Center) (1996). General social survey. National Opinion Research Center, University of Chicago (courtesy Tom W. Smith).

NORC. (National Opinion Research Center) (2005). Marriage and happiness data from National Opinion Research Center General Social Surveys, 1972 to 2004 (www.csa.berkeley, edu:7502).

Norem, J. K. (2000). Defensive pessimism, optimism, and pessimism. In E. C. Chang (Ed.), *Optimism and pessimism.* Washington, DC: APA Books.

Norem, J. K., & Cantor, N. (1986). Defensive pessimism: Harnessing anxiety as motivation. *Journal of Personality and Social Psychology,* **51,** 1208–1217.

Norenzayan, A., & Heine, S. J. (2005). Psychological universals: What are they and how can we know? *Psychological Bulletin,* **131,** 763–784.

North, A. C., Hargreaves, D. J., & McKendrick, J. (1997). In-store music affects product choice. *Nature,* **390,** 132.

Norton, M. I., Frost, J. H., & Arlely, D. (2007). Less is more: The lure of ambiguity, or why familiarity breeds contempt. *Journal of Personality and Social Psychology,* **92,** 97–105.

Nosek, B. A. (2007). Implicit-explicit relations. *Current Directions in Psychological Science,* **16,** 65–69.

Nosek, B. A., Smyth, F. L., Hansen, J. J., Devos, T., Lindner, N. M., Ranganath, K. A., Smith, C. T., Olson, K. R., Chugh, D., Greenwald, A. G., & Banaji, M. R. (2007). Pervasiveness and correlates of implicit attitudes and stereotypes. *European Review of Social Psychology,* **18,** 36–88.

Notarius, C., & Markman, H. J. (1993). *We can work it out.* New York: Putnam.

Nunez, N., Poole, D. A., & Memon, A. (2003). Psychology's two cultures revisited: Implications for the integration of science with practice. *Scientific Review of Mental Health Practice,* **2**(1), 8–19.

Nurmi, J-E., & Salmela-Aro, K. (1997). Social strategies and loneliness: A prospective study. *Personality and Individual Differences,* **23,** 205–215.

Nurmi, J-E., Toivonen, S., Salmela-Aro, K., & Eronen, S. (1996). Optimistic, approach-oriented, and avoidance strategies in social situations: Three studies on loneliness and peer relationships. *European Journal of Personality,* **10,** 201–219.

Nuttin, J. M., Jr. (1987). Affective consequences of mere ownership: The name letter effect in twelve European languages. *European Journal of Social Psychology, 17*, 318–402.

Nyhan, B., & Reifler, J. (2008). When corrections fail: The persistence of political misperceptions. Unpublished manuscript, Duke University.

O'Connor, A. (2004, May 14). Pressure to go along with abuse is strong, but some soldiers find strength to refuse. *New York Times* (www.nytimes.com).

O'Dea, T. F. (1968). Sects and cults. In D. L. Sills (Ed.), *International encyclopedia of the social sciences* (Vol. 14). New York: Macmillan.

O'Hegarty, M., Pederson, L. L., Yenokyan, G., Nelson, D., & Wortley, P. (2007). Young adults' perceptions of cigarette warning labels in the United States and Canada. *Preventing Chronic Disease: Public Health Research, Practice, and Policy, 30*, 467–473.

O'Leary, K. D., Christian, J. L., & Mendell, N. R. (1994). A closer look at the link between marital discord and depressive symptomatology. *Journal of Social and Clinical Psychology, 13*, 33–41.

Oaten, M., & Cheng, K. (2006a). Improved self-control: The benefits of a regular program of academic study. *Basic and Applied Social Psychology, 28*, 1–16.

Oaten, M., & Cheng, K. (2006b). Longitudinal gains in self-regulation from regular physical exercise. *British Journal of Health Psychology, 11*, 717–733.

Oceja, L. (2008). Overcoming empathy-induced partiality: Two rules of thumb. *Basic and Applied Social Psychology, 30*, 176–182.

Oddone-Paolucci, E., Genuis, M., & Violato, C. (2000). A meta-analysis of the published research on the effects of pornography. In C. Violata (Ed.), *The changing family and child development*. Aldershot, England: Ashgate Publishing.

Ohbuchi, K., & Kambara, T. (1985). Attacker's intent and awareness of outcome, impression management, and retaliation. *Journal of Experimental Social Psychology, 21*, 321–330.

Ohtaki, P. (1999, March 24). Internment-camp reporter makes homecoming visit. Associated Press. Reprinted in P. T. Ohtaki (Ed.), *It was the right thing to do!* (Self-published collection of Walt and Mildred Woodward–related correspondence and articles).

Oishi, S., Lun, J., & Sherman, G. D. (2007). Residential mobility, self-concept, and positive affect in social interactions. *Journal of Personality and Social Psychology, 93*, 131–141.

Oishi, S., Rothman, A. J., Snyder, M., Su, J., Zehm, K., Hertel, A. W., Gonzales, M. H., & Sherman, G. D. (2007). The socioecological model of procommunity action: The benefits of residential stability. *Journal of Personality and Social Psychology, 93*, 831–844.

Olfson, M., & Pincus, H. A. (1994). Outpatient therapy in the United States: II. Patterns of utilization. *American Journal of Psychiatry, 151*, 1289–1294.

Oliner, S. P., & Oliner, P. M. (1988). *The altruistic personality: Rescuers of Jews in Nazi Europe*. New York: Free Press.

Olson, I. R., & Marshuetz, C. (2005). Facial attractiveness is appraised in a glance. *Emotion, 5*, 498–502.

Olson, J. M., & Cal, A. V. (1984). Source credibility, attitudes, and the recall of past behaviours. *European Journal of Social Psychology, 14*, 203–210.

Olson, J. M., Roese, N. J., & Zanna, M. P. (1996). Expectancies. In E. T. Higgins & A. W. Kruglanski (Eds.), *Social psychology: Handbook of basic principles* (pp. 211–238). New York: Guilford.

Olson, K. R., Dunham, Y., Dweck, C. S., Spelke, E. S., & Banaji, M. R. (2008). Judgments of the lucky across development and culture. *Journal of Personality and Social Psychology, 94*, 757–776.

Olweus, D. (1979). Stability of aggressive reaction patterns in males: A review. *Psychological Bulletin, 86*, 852–875.

Olweus, D., Mattsson, A., Schalling, D., & Low, H. (1988). Circulating testosterone levels and aggression in adolescent males: A causal analysis. *Psychosomatic Medicine, 50*, 261–272.

Omoto, A. M., & Snyder, M. (2002). Considerations of community: The context and process of volunteerism. *American Behavioral Scientist, 45*, 846–867.

Open Secrets. (2005). 2004 election overview: Winning vs. spending (www.opensecrets.org).

Opotow, S. (1990). Moral exclusion and injustice: An introduction. *Journal of Social Issues, 46*, 1–20.

Oppenheimer, D. M. (2004). Spontaneous discounting of availability in frequency judgment tasks. *Psychological Science, 15*, 100–105.

Orbell, J. M., van de Kragt, A. J. C., & Dawes, R. M. (1988). Explaining discussion-induced cooperation. *Journal of Personality and Social Psychology, 54*, 811–819.

Orenstein, P. (2003, July 6). Where have all the Lisas gone? *New York Times* (www.nytimes.com).

Orive, R. (1984). Group similarity, public self-awareness, and opinion extremity: A social projection explanation of deindividuation effects. *Journal of Personality and Social Psychology, 47*, 727–737.

Ornstein, R. (1991). *The evolution of consciousness: Of Darwin, Freud, and cranial fire: The origins of the way we think*. New York: Prentice-Hall.

Osborne, J. W. (1995). Academics, self-esteem, and race: A look at the underlying assumptions of the disidentification hypothesis. *Personality and Social Psychology Bulletin, 21*, 449–455.

Osgood, C. E. (1962). *An alternative to war or surrender*. Urbana, IL: University of Illinois Press.

Osgood, C. E. (1980). GRIT: A strategy for survival in mankind's nuclear age? Paper presented at the Pugwash Conference on New Directions in Disarmament, Racine, WI.

Oskamp, S. (1991). Curbside recycling: Knowledge, attitudes, and behavior. Paper presented at the Society for Experimental Social Psychology meeting, Columbus, OH.

Osofsky, M. J., Bandura, A., & Zimbardo, P. G. (2005). The role of moral disengagement in the execution process. *Law and Human Behavior, 29*, 371–393.

Osterhouse, R. A., & Brock, T. C. (1970). Distraction increases yielding to propaganda by inhibiting counterarguing. *Journal of Personality and Social Psychology, 15*, 344–358.

Ostrom, T. M., & Sedikides, C. (1992). Out-group homogeneity effects in natural and minimal groups. *Psychological Bulletin, 112*, 536–552.

Oswald, A. (2006, January 19). The hippies were right all along about happiness. *Financial Times*, p. 15.

Oswald, A. J. (2008). On the curvature of the reporting function from objective reality to subjective feelings. Unpublished manuscript at www.andrewoswald.com.

Ouellette, J. A., & Wood, W. (1998). Habit and intention in everyday life: The multiple processes by which past behavior predicts future behavior. *Psychological Bulletin, 124*, 54–74.

Oxfam. (2005, March 26). Three months on: New figures show Tsunami may have killed up to four times as many women as men. Oxfam Press release (www.oxfam.org.uk).

Oyserman, D., Coon, H. M., & Kemmelmeier, M. (2002a). Rethinking individualism and collectivism: Evaluation of theoretical assumptions and meta-analyses. *Psychological Bulletin, 128*, 3–72.

Oyserman, D., Kemmelmeier, M., & Coon, H. M. (2002b). Cultural psychology, a new look: Reply to Bond (2002), Fiske (2002), Kitayama (2002), and Miller (2002). *Psychological Bulletin, 128*, 110–117.

Ozer, E. M., & Bandura, A. (1990). Mechanisms governing empowerment effects: A self-efficacy analysis. *Journal of Personality and Social Psychology, 58,* 472–486.

Packer, D. J. (2008). Identifying systematic disobedience in Milgram's obedience experiments: A meta-analytic review. *Perspectives on Psychological Science, 3*(4), 301–304.

Packer, D. J. (2009). Avoiding groupthink: Whereas weakly identified members remain silent, strongly identified members dissent about collective problems. *Psychological Science, 20,* 546–548.

Padgett, V. R. (1989). Predicting organizational violence: An application of 11 powerful principles of obedience. Paper presented at the American Psychological Association convention.

Page, S. E. (2007). *The difference: How the power of diversity creates better groups, firms, schools, and societies.* Princeton, NJ: Princeton University Press.

Page-Gould, E., Mendoza-Denton, R., & Tropp, L. R. (2008). With a little help from my cross-group friend: Reducing anxiety in intergroup contexts through cross-group friendship. *Journal of Personality and Social Psychology, 95,* 1080–1094.

Pallak, M. S., Mueller, M., Dollar, K., & Pallak, J. (1972). Effect of commitment on responsiveness to an extreme consonant communication. *Journal of Personality and Social Psychology, 23,* 429–436.

Pallak, S. R., Murroni, E., & Koch, J. (1983). Communicator attractiveness and expertise, emotional versus rational appeals, and persuasion: A heuristic versus systematic processing interpretation. *Social Cognition, 2,* 122–141.

Palmer, D. L. (1996). Determinants of Canadian attitudes toward immigration: More than just racism? *Canadian Journal of Behavioural Science, 28,* 180–192.

Palmer, E. L., & Dorr, A. (Eds.) (1980). *Children and the faces of television: Teaching, violence, selling.* New York: Academic Press.

Paloutzian, R. (1979). Pro-ecology behavior: Three field experiments on litter pickup. Paper presented at the Western Psychological Association convention.

Pandey, J., Sinha, Y., Prakash, A., & Tripathi, R. C. (1982). Right-left political ideologies and attribution of the causes of poverty. *European Journal of Social Psychology, 12,* 327–331.

Paolini, S., Hewstone, M., Cairns, E., & Voci, A. (2004). Effects of direct and indirect cross-group friendships on judgments of Catholics and Protestants in Northern Ireland: The mediating role of an anxiety-reduction mechanism. *Personality and Social Psychology Bulletin, 30,* 770–786.

Papastamou, S., & Mugny, G. (1990). Synchronic consistency and psychologization in minority influence. *European Journal of Social Psychology, 20,* 85–98.

Pape, R. A. (2003, September 22). Dying to kill us. *New York Times* (www .nytimes.com).

Parachin, V. M. (1992, December). Four brave chaplains. *Retired Officer Magazine,* pp. 24–26.

Parashar, U. D., Gibson, C. J., Bresse, J. S., & Glass, R. I. (2006). Rotavirus and severe childhood diarrhea. *Emerging Infectious Diseases, 12,* 304–306.

Park, B., & Rothbart, M. (1982). Perception of out-group homogeneity and levels of social categorization: Memory for the subordinate attributes of in-group and out-group members. *Journal of Personality and Social Psychology, 42,* 1051–1068.

Parke, R. D., Berkowitz, L., Leyens, J. P., West, S. G., & Sebastian, J. (1977). Some effects of violent and nonviolent movies on the behavior of juvenile delinquents. In L. Berkowitz (Ed.), *Advances in experimental social psychology* (Vol. 10). New York: Academic Press.

Parker, K. D., Ortega, S. T., & VanLaningham, J. (1995). Life satisfaction, self-esteem, and personal happiness among Mexican and African Americans. *Sociological Spectrum, 15,* 131–145.

Pascarella, E. T., & Terenzini, P. T. (1991). *How college affects students: Findings and insights from twenty years of research.* San Francisco: Jossey-Bass.

Patrick, H., Knee, C. R., Canevello, A., Lonsbary, C. (2007). The role of need fulfillment in relationship functioning and well-being: A self-determination theory perspective. *Journal of Personality and Social Psychology, 92,* 434–457.

Patterson, D. (1996). *When learned men murder.* Bloomington, IN: Phi Delta Kappan.

Patterson, G. R., Chamberlain, P., & Reid, J. B. (1982). A comparative evaluation of parent training procedures. *Behavior Therapy, 13,* 638–650.

Patterson, G. R., Littman, R. A., & Bricker, W. (1967). Assertive behavior in children: A step toward a theory of aggression. *Monographs of the Society of Research in Child Development* (Serial No. 113), *32,* 5.

Patterson, M. L. (2008). Back to social behavior: Mining the mundane. *Basic and Applied Social Psychology, 30,* 93–101.

Patterson, M. L., Iizuka, Y., Tubbs, M. E., Ansel, J., & Anson, J. (2006). Passing encounters East and West: Comparing Japanese and American pedestrian interactions. Paper presented to the Society of Personality and Social Psychology convention.

Patterson, M. L., Iizuka, Y., Tubbs, M. E., Ansel, J., Tsutsumi, M., & Anson, J. (2007). Passing encounters east and west: Comparing Japanese and American pedestrian interactions. *Journal of Nonverbal Behavior, 31,* 155–166.

Patterson, T. E. (1980). The role of the mass media in presidential campaigns: The lessons of the 1976 election. *Items, 34,* 25–30. Social Science Research Council, 605 Third Avenue, New York, NY 10016.

Paulhus, D. (1982). Individual differences, self-presentation, and cognitive dissonance: Their concurrent operation in forced compliance. *Journal of Personality and Social Psychology, 43,* 838–852.

Paulhus, D. L., & Lim, D. T. K. (1994). Arousal and evaluative extremity in social judgments: A dynamic complexity model. *European Journal of Social Psychology, 24,* 89–99.

Paulhus, D. L., & Morgan, K. L. (1997). Perceptions of intelligence in leaderless groups: The dynamic effects of shyness and acquaintance. *Journal of Personality and Social Psychology, 72,* 581–591.

Paulhus, D. L., & Williams, K. M. (2002). The Dark Triad of personality: Narcissism, Machiavellianism and psychopathy. *Journal of Research in Personality, 36,* 556–563.

Paulus, P. B. (1998). Developing consensus about groupthink after all these years. *Organizational Behavior and Human Decision Processes, 73,* 362–375.

Paulus, P. B., Brown, V., & Ortega, A. H. (1997). Group creativity. In R. E. Purser and A. Montuori (Eds.), *Social creativity* (Vol. 2). Cresskill, NJ: Hampton Press.

Paulus, P. B., Larey, T. S., & Dzindolet, M. T. (1998). Creativity in groups and teams. In M. Turner (Ed.), *Groups at work: Advances in theory and research.* Hillsdale, NJ: Erlbaum.

Paulus, P. B., Larey, T. S., & Ortega, A. H. (1995). Performance and perceptions of brainstormers in an organizational setting. *Basic and Applied Social Psychology, 17,* 249–265.

Payne, B. K. (2001). Prejudice and perception: The role of automatic and controlled processes in misperceiving a weapon. *Journal of Personality and Social Psychology, 81,* 181–192.

Payne, B. K. (2006). Weapon bias: Split-second decisions and unintended stereotyping. *Current Directions in Psychological Science, 15,* 287–291.

Pedersen, A., & Walker, I. (1997). Prejudice against Australian Aborigines: Old-fashioned and modern forms. *European Journal of Social Psychology, 27*, 561–587.

Pedersen, W. C., Gonzales, C., & Miller, N. (2000). The moderating effect of trivial triggering provocation on displaced aggression. *Journal of Personality and Social Psychology, 78*, 913–927.

Pegalis, L. J., Shaffer, D. R., Bazzini, D. G., & Greenier, K. (1994). On the ability to elicit self-disclosure: Are there gender-based and contextual limitations on the opener effect? *Personality and Social Psychology Bulletin, 20*, 412–420.

Pelham, B., & Crabtree, S. (2008, October 8). Worldwide, highly religious more likely to help others: Pattern holds throughout the world and across major religions. Gallup Poll (www.gallup.com).

Pennebaker, J. (1990). *Opening up: The healing power of confiding in others.* New York: William Morrow.

Pennebaker, J. W. (1982). *The psychology of physical symptoms.* New York: Springer-Verlag.

Pennebaker, J. W., & Lay, T. C. (2002). Language use and personality during crises: Analyses of Mayor Rudolph Giuliani's press conferences. *Journal of Research in Personality, 36*, 271–282.

Pennebaker, J. W., & O'Heeron, R. C. (1984). Confiding in others and illness rate among spouses of suicide and accidental death victims. *Journal of Abnormal Psychology, 93*, 473–476.

Pennebaker, J. W., Rimé, B., & Sproul, G. (1996). Stereotypes of emotional expressiveness of northerners and southerners: A cross-cultural test of Montesquieu's hypotheses. *Journal of Personality and Social Psychology, 70*, 372–380.

Penner, L. A. (2002). Dispositional and organizational influences on sustained volunteerism: An interactionist perspective. *Journal of Social Issues, 58*, 447–467.

Penner, L. A., Dertke, M. C., & Achenbach, C. J. (1973). The "flash" system: A field study of altruism. *Journal of Applied Social Psychology, 3*, 362–370.

Pennington, N., & Hastie, R. (1993). The story model for juror decision making. In R. Hastie (Ed.), *Inside the juror: The psychology of juror decision making.* New York: Cambridge University Press.

Penrod, S., & Cutler, B. L. (1987). Assessing the competence of juries. In I. B. Weiner & A. K. Hess (Eds.), *Handbook of forensic psychology.* New York: Wiley.

Penton-Voak, I. S., Jones, B. C., Little, A. C., Baker, S., Tiddeman, B., Burt, D. M., & Perrett, D. I. (2001). Symmetry, sexual dimorphism in facial proportions and male facial attractiveness. *Proceedings of the Royal Society of London, 268*, 1–7.

People. (2003, September 1). Nipped, tucked, talking, *People*, pp. 102–111.

Peplau, L. A., & Fingerhut, A. W. (2007). The close relationships of lesbians and gay men. *Annual Review of Psychology, 58*, 405–424.

Peplau, L. A., & Gordon, S. L. (1985). Women and men in love: Gender differences in close heterosexual relationships. In V. E. O'Leary, R. K. Unger, & B. S. Wallston (Eds.), *Women, gender, and social psychology.* Hillsdale, NJ: Erlbaum.

Pereira, J. (2003, January 10). Just how far does First Amendment protection go? *Wall Street Journal*, pp. B1, B3.

Perkins, H. W. (1991). Religious commitment, Yuppie values, and well-being in post-collegiate life. *Review of Religious Research, 32*, 244–251.

Perlman, D., & Rook, K. S. (1987). Social support, social deficits, and the family: Toward the enhancement of well-being. In S. Oskamp (Ed.), *Family processes and problems: Social psychological aspects.* Newbury Park, CA: Sage.

Perls, F. S. (1972). Gestalt therapy [interview]. In A. Bry (Ed.), *Inside psychotherapy.* New York: Basic Books.

Perls, F. S. (1973, July). *Ego, hunger and aggression: The beginning of Gestalt therapy.* Random House, 1969. Cited by Berkowitz in The case for bottling up rage. *Psychology Today*, pp. 24–30.

Perrin, S., & Spencer, C. (1981). Independence or conformity in the Asch experiment as a reflection of cultural or situational factors. *British Journal of Social Psychology, 20*, 205–209.

Persico, N., Postlewaite, A., & Silverman, D. (2004). The effect of adolescent experience on labor market outcomes: The case of height. *Journal of Political Economy, 112*, 1019–1053.

Persky, S., & Blascovich, J. (2005). Consequences of playing violent video games in immersive virtual environments, In A. Axelsson & Ralph Schroeder (Eds.), *Work and Play in Shared Virtual Environments.* New York: Springer.

Pessin, J. (1933). The comparative effects of social and mechanical stimulation on memorizing. *American Journal of Psychology, 45*, 263–270.

Pessin, J., & Husband, R. W. (1933). Effects of social stimulation on human maze learning. *Journal of Abnormal and Social Psychology, 28*, 148–154.

Peters, E., Romer, D., Slovic, P., Jamieson, K. H., Whasfield, L., Mertz, C. K., & Carpenter, S. M. (2007). The impact and acceptability of Canadian-style cigarette warning labels among U.S. smokers and nonsmokers. *Nicotine and Tobacco Research, 9*, 473–481.

Peterson, C., & Barrett, L. C. (1987). Explanatory style and academic performance among university freshmen. *Journal of Personality and Social Psychology, 53*, 603–607.

Peterson, C., & Bossio, L. M. (2000). Optimism and physical well-being. In E. C. Chang (Ed.), *Optimism and pessimism.* Washington, DC: APA Books.

Peterson, C., Schwartz, S. M., & Seligman, M. E. P. (1981). Self-blame and depression symptoms. *Journal of Personality and Social Psychology, 41*, 253–259.

Peterson, C., & Seligman, M. E. P. (1987). Explanatory style and illness. *Journal of Personality, 55*, 237–265.

Peterson, C., Seligman, M. E. P., & Vaillant, G. E. (1988). Pessimistic explanatory style is a risk factor for physical illness: A thirty-five-year longitudinal study. *Journal of Personality and Social Psychology, 55*, 23–27.

Peterson, C., & Steen, T. A. (2002). Optimistic explanatory style. In C. R. Snyder & S. J. Lopez (Ed.), *Handbook of positive psychology.* London: Oxford University Press.

Peterson, E. (1992). *Under the unpredictable plant.* Grand Rapids, MI: Eerdmans.

Peterson, J. L., & Zill, N. (1981). Television viewing in the United States and children's intellectual, social, and emotional development. *Television and Children, 2*(2), 21–28.

Pettigrew, T. F. (1958). Personality and socio-cultural factors in intergroup attitudes: A cross-national comparison. *Journal of Conflict Resolution, 2*, 29–42.

Pettigrew, T. F. (1969). Racially separate or together? *Journal of Social Issues, 2*, 43–69.

Pettigrew, T. F. (1978). Three issues in ethnicity: Boundaries, deprivations, and perceptions. In J. M. Yinger & S. J. Cutler (Eds.), *Major social issues: A multidisciplinary view.* New York: Free Press.

Pettigrew, T. F. (1979). The ultimate attribution error: Extending Allport's cognitive analysis of prejudice. *Personality and Social Psychology Bulletin, 55*, 461–476.

Pettigrew, T. F. (1980). Prejudice. In S. Thernstrom et al. (Eds.), *Harvard encyclopedia of American ethnic groups.* Cambridge, MA: Harvard University Press.

Pettigrew, T. F. (1986). The intergroup contact hypothesis reconsidered. In M. Hewstone & R. Brown (Eds.), *Contact and conflict in intergroup encounters.* Oxford: Blackwell.

Pettigrew, T. F. (1988). Advancing racial justice: Past lessons for future use.

Paper for the University of Alabama conference "Opening Doors: An appraisal of Race Relations in America."

Pettigrew, T. F. (1997). Generalized intergroup contact effects on prejudice. *Personality and Social Psychology Bulletin,* **23,** 173–185.

Pettigrew, T. F. (2003). Peoples under threat: Americans, Arabs, and Israelis. *Peace and Conflict,* **9,** 69–90.

Pettigrew, T. F. (2004). Intergroup contact: Theory, research, and new perspectives. In J. A. Banks & C. A. McGee Banks (Eds.), *Handbook of research on multicultural education.* San Francisco: Jossey-Bass.

Pettigrew, T. F. (2006). A two-level approach to anti-immigrant prejudice and discrimination. In R. Mahalingam (Ed.), *Cultural psychology of immigrants.* Mahwah, NJ: Erlbaum.

Pettigrew, T. F. (2008). Future directions for intergroup contact theory and research. *Intercultural Relations,* **32,** 187–199.

Pettigrew, T. F., Christ, O., Wagner, U., Meertens, R. W., van Dick, R., & Zick, A. (2008). Relative deprivation and intergroup prejudice. *Journal of Social Issues,* **64,** 385–401.

Pettigrew, T. F., Christ, O., Wagner, U., & Stellmacher, J. (2007). Direct and indirect intergroup contact effects on prejudice: A normative interpretation. *International Journal of Intercultural Relations,* **31,** 411–425.

Pettigrew, T. F., Jackson, J. S., Brika, J. B., Lemaine, G., Meertens, R. W., Wagner, U., & Zick, A. (1998). Outgroup prejudice in western Europe. *European Review of Social Psychology,* **8,** 241–273.

Pettigrew, T. F., & Meertens, R. W. (1995). Subtle and blatant prejudice in western Europe. *European Journal of Social Psychology,* **25,** 57–76.

Pettigrew, T. F., & Tropp, L. R. (2000). Does intergroup contact reduce prejudice: Recent meta-analytic findings. In Oskamp, S. (Ed.), *Reducing prejudice and discrimination* (pp. 93–114). Mahwah, NJ: Erlbaum.

Pettigrew, T. F., & Tropp, L. R. (2006). A meta-analytic test of intergroup contact theory. *Journal of Personality and Social Psychology,* **90,** 751–783.

Pettigrew, T. F., & Tropp, L. R. (2008). How does intergroup contact reduce prejudice? Meta-analytic tests of three mediators. *European Journal of Social Psychology,* **38,** 922–934.

Pettigrew, T. F., Wagner, U., & Christ, O. (2008). Who opposes immigration? Comparing German with North American findings. *DuBois Review,* **4,** 19–40.

Petty, R. E., & Briñol, P. (2008). Persuasion: From single to multiple to metacognitive processes. *Perspectives on Psychological Science,* **3,** 137–147.

Petty, R. E., & Cacioppo, J. T. (1979). Effects of forewarning of persuasive intent and involvement on cognitive response and persuasion. *Personality and Social Psychology Bulletin,* **5,** 173–176.

Petty, R. E., & Cacioppo, J. T. (1986). *Communication and persuasion: Central and peripheral routes to attitude change.* New York: Springer-Verlag.

Petty, R. E., Cacioppo, J. T., & Goldman, R. (1981). Personal involvement as a determinant of argument-based persuasion. *Journal of Personality and Social Psychology,* **41,** 847–855.

Petty, R. E., Haugtvedt, C. P., & Smith, S. M. (1995). Elaboration as a determinant of attitude strength: Creating attitudes that are persistent, resistant, and predictive of behavior. In R. E. Petty & J. A. Krosnick (Eds.), *Attitude strength: Antecedents and consequences.* Hillsdale, NJ: Erlbaum.

Petty, R. E., Schumann, D. W., Richman, S. A., & Strathman, A. J. (1993). Positive mood and persuasion: Different roles for affect under high and low elaboration conditions. *Journal of Personality and Social Psychology,* **64,** 5–20.

Petty, R. E., & Wegener, D. T. (1998). Attitude change: Multiple roles for persuasion variables. In D. Gilbert, S. Fiske, & G. Lindzey (Eds), *Handbook of Social Psychology,* 4th edition. New York: McGraw-Hill.

Pew Research Center. (2000, May 10). Tracking online life: How women use the Internet to cultivate relationships with family and friends. Washington, DC: Pew Internet and American Life Project.

Pew Research Center. (2003). Views of a changing world 2003. The Pew Global Attitudes Project. Washington, DC: Pew Research Center for the People and the Press (people-press.org/reports/pdf/185.pdf).

Pew Research Center. (2006, February 13). Not looking for love: Romance in America. Pew Internet and American Life Project (pewresearch.org).

Pew Research Center. (2006, March 14). Guess who's coming to dinner. Pew Research Center (pewresearch.org).

Pew Research Center. (2006, March 30). America's immigration quandary. Pew Research Center (www.people-press.org).

Pew Research Center. (2006, July 12). Little consensus on global warming: Partisanship drives opinion. Pew Research Center (people-press.org).

Pew Research Center. (2006, September 21). Publics of Asian powers hold negative views of one another. Pew Global Attitudes Project Report, Pew Research Center (pewresearch.org).

Pew Research Center (2007, May 22). *Muslim Americans: Middle class and mostly mainstream* (www.pewresearch.org).

Pew Research Center. (2007, July 18). Modern marriage: "I like hugs. I like kisses. But what I really love is help with the dishes." Pew Research Center (pewresearch.org).

Pew Research Center. (2008, September 17). Unfavorable views of both Jews and Muslims increase in Europe. Pew Research Center (www.pewresearch.org).

Phillips, D. L. (2003, September 20). Listening to the wrong Iraqi. *New York Times* (www.nytimes.com).

Phillips, D. P. (1982). The impact of fictional television stories on U.S. adult fatalities: New evidence on the effect of the mass media on violence. *American Journal of Sociology,* **87,** 1340–1359.

Phillips, D. P. (1985). Natural experiments on the effects of mass media violence on fatal aggression: Strengths and weaknesses of a new approach. In L. Berkowitz (Ed.), *Advances in experimental social psychology* (Vol. 19). Orlando, Fla.: Academic Press.

Phillips, D. P., Carstensen, L. L., & Paight, D. J. (1989). Effects of mass media news stories on suicide, with new evidence on the role of story content. In D. R. Pfeffer (Ed.), *Suicide among youth: Perspectives on risk and prevention.* Washington, DC: American Psychiatric Press.

Phillips, T (2004, April 3). Quoted by T. Baldwin & D. Rozenberg, "Britain 'must scrap multiculturalism.'" *The Times,* p. A1.

Phinney, J. S. (1990). Ethnic identity in adolescents and adults: Review of research. *Psychological Bulletin,* **108,** 499–514.

Pichon, I., Boccato, G., & Saroglou, V. (2007). Nonconscious influences of religion on prosociality: A priming study. *European Journal of Social Psychology,* **37,** 1032–1045.

Pierce, J. P., & Gilpin, E. A. (1995). A historical analysis of tobacco marketing and the uptake of smoking by youth in the United States: 1890–1977. *Health Psychology,* **14,** 500–508.

Pierce, J. P., Lee, L., & Gilpin, E. A. (1994). Smoking initiation by adolescent girls, 1944 through 1988. *Journal of the American Medical Association,* **27,** 608–611.

Piliavin, J. A. (2003). Doing well by doing good: Benefits for the benefactor. In C. L. M. Keyes & J. Haidt (Eds.), *Flourishing: Positive psychology and the life well-lived.* Washington, DC: American Psychological Association.

Piliavin, J. A., Evans, D. E., & Callero, P. (1982). Learning to "Give to unnamed strangers": The process of commitment to regular blood donation. In E. Staub, D. Bar-Tal, J. Karylowski, & J. Reykawski (Eds.), *The development and maintenance of prosocial behavior: International perspectives.* New York: Plenum.

Piliavin, J. A., & Piliavin, I. M. (1973). The Good Samaritan: Why *does* he help? Unpublished manuscript, University of Wisconsin.

Pincus, J. H. (2001). *Base instincts: What makes killers kill?* New York: Norton.

Pinel, E. C. (1999). Stigma consciousness: The psychological legacy of social stereotypes. *Journal of Personality and Social Psychology, 76,* 114–128.

Pinel, E. C. (2002). Stigma consciousness in intergroup contexts: The power of conviction. *Journal of Experimental Social Psychology, 38,* 178–185.

Pinel, E. C. (2004). You're just saying that because I'm a woman: Stigma consciousness and attributions to discrimination. *Self and Identity, 3,* 39–51.

Pingitore, R., Dugoni, B. L., Tindale, R. S., & Spring, B. (1994). Bias against overweight job applicants in a simulated employment interview. *Journal of Applied Psychology, 79,* 909–917.

Pinker, S. (1997). *How the mind works.* New York: Norton.

Pinker, S. (2002). *The blank slate.* New York: Viking.

Pinker, S. (2008). *The sexual paradox: Men, women, and the real gender gap.* New York: Scribner.

Pipher, M. (2002). *The middle of everywhere: The world's refugees come to our town.* Harcourt.

Plaks, J. E., & Higgins, E. T. (2000). Pragmatic use of stereotyping in teamwork: Social loafing and compensation as a function of inferred partner-situation fit. *Journal of Personality and Social Psychology, 79,* 962–974.

Platow, M. J., Haslam, S. A., Both, A., Chew, I., Cuddon, M., Goharpey, N., Mårerer, J., Rosini, S., Tsekouras, A., & Grace, D. M. (2004). "It's not funny if *they're* laughing": Self-categorization, social influence, and responses to canned laughter. *Journal of Experimental Social Psychology, 41,* 542–550.

Platz, S. J., & Hosch, H. M. (1988). Cross-racial/ethnic eyewitness identification: A field study. *Journal of Applied Social Psychology, 18,* 972–984.

Pliner, P., Hart, H., Kohl, J., & Saari, D. (1974). Compliance without pressure: Some further data on the foot-in-the-door technique. *Journal of Experimental Social Psychology, 10,* 17–22.

Plomin, R., & Daniels, D. (1987). Why are children in the same family so different from one another? *Behavioral and Brain Sciences, 10,* 1–60.

Polk, M., & Schuster, A. M. H. (2005). *The looting of the Iraq museum, Baghdad: The lost legacy of ancient Mesopotamia.* New York: Harry N. Abrams.

Pomazal, R. J., & Clore, G. L. (1973). Helping on the highway: The effects of dependency and sex. *Journal of Applied Social Psychology, 3,* 150–164.

Poniewozik, J. (2003, November 24). All the news that fits your reality. *Time,* p. 90.

Pooley, E. (2007, May 28). The last temptation of Al Gore. *Time,* pp. 31–37.

Popenoe, D. (2002). The top ten myths of divorce. Unpublished manuscript, National Marriage Project, Rutgers University.

Pornpitakpan, C. (2004). The persuasiveness of source credibility: A critical review of five decades' evidence, *Journal of Applied Social Psychology, 34,* 243–281.

Post, J. M. (2005). The new face of terrorism: Socio-cultural foundations of contemporary terrorism. *Behavioral Sciences and the Law, 23,* 451–465.

Postmes, T., & Spears, R. (1998). Deindividuation and antinormative behavior: A meta-analysis. *Psychological Bulletin, 123,* 238–259.

Postmes, T., Spears, R., & Cihangir, S. (2001). Quality of decision making and group norms. *Journal of Personality and Social Psychology, 80,* 918–930.

Potter, T., Corneille, O., Ruys, K. I., & Rhodes, G. (2006). S/he's just another pretty face: A multidimensional scaling approach to face attractiveness and variability. *Psychonomic Bulletin & Review, 14,* 368–372.

Pratkanis, A. R., Greenwald, A. G., Leippe, M. R., & Baumgardner, M. H. (1988). In search of reliable persuasion effects: III. The sleeper effect is dead. Long live the sleeper effect. *Journal of Personality and Social Psychology, 54,* 203–218.

Pratkanis, A. R., & Turner, M. E. (1996). The proactive removal of discriminatory barriers: Affirmative action as effective help. *Journal of Social Issues, 52,* 111–132.

Pratt, M. W., Pancer, M., Hunsberger, B., & Manchester, J. (1990). Reasoning about the self and relationships in maturity: An integrative complexity analysis of individual differences. *Journal of Personality and Social Psychology, 59,* 575–581.

Pratto, F. (1996). Sexual politics: The gender gap in the bedroom, the cupboard, and the cabinet. In D. M. Buss & N. M. Malamuth (Eds.), *Sex, power, conflict: Evolutionary and feminist perspectives.* New York: Oxford University Press.

Pratto, F., Sidanius, J., Stallworth, L. M., & Malle, B. F. (1994). Social dominance orientation: A personality variable predicting social and political attitudes. *Journal of Personality and Social Psychology, 67,* 741–763.

Pratto, F., Stallworth, L. M., & Sidanius, J. (1997). The gender gap: Differences in political attitudes and social dominance orientation. *British Journal of Social Psychology, 36,* 49–68.

Prentice, D. A., & Carranza, E. (2002). What women and men should be, shouldn't be, are allowed to be, and don't have to be: The contents of prescriptive gender stereotypes. *Psychology of Women Quarterly, 26,* 269–281.

Prentice-Dunn, S., & Rogers, R. W. (1980). Effects of deindividuating situational cues and aggressive models on subjective deindividuation and aggression. *Journal of Personality and Social Psychology, 39,* 104–113.

Prentice-Dunn, S., & Rogers, R. W. (1989). Deindividuation and the self-regulation of behavior. In P. B. Paulus (Ed.), *Psychology of group influence,* 2nd edition. Hillsdale, NJ: Erlbaum.

Presson, P. K., & Benassi, V. A. (1996). Illusion of control: A meta-analytic review. *Journal of Social Behavior and Personality, 11,* 493–510.

Price, G. H., Dabbs, J. M., Jr., Clower, B. J., & Resin, R. P. (1974). At first glance—Or, is physical attractiveness more than skin deep? Paper presented at the Eastern Psychological Association convention. Cited by K. L. Dion & K. K. Dion (1979). Personality and behavioral correlates of romantic love. In M. Cook & G. Wilson (Eds.), *Love and attraction.* Oxford: Pergamon.

Pritchard, I. L. (1998). The effects of rap music on aggressive attitudes toward women. Master's thesis, Humboldt State University.

Prohaska, V. (1994). "I know I'll get an A": Confident overestimation of final course grades. *Teaching of Psychology, 21,* 141–143.

Pronin, E. (2008). How we see ourselves and how we see others. *Science, 320,* 1177–1180.

Pronin, E., Berger, J., & Molouki, S. (2007). Alone in a crowd of sheep: Asymmetric perceptions of conformity and their roots in an introspection illusion. *Journal of Personality and Social Psychology, 92,* 585–595.

Pronin, E., Kruger, J., Savitsky, K., & Ross, L. (2001). You don't know me, but I know you: The illusion of asymmetric insight. *Journal of Personality and Social Psychology, 81,* 639–656.

Pronin, E., Lin, D. Y., & Ross, L. (2002). The bias blind spot: Perceptions of bias in self versus others. *Personality and Social Psychology Bulletin, 28,* 369–381.

Pronin, E., & Ross, L. (2006). Temporal differences in trait self-ascription: When the self is seen as an other. *Journal of Personality and Social Psychology, 90*, 197–209.

Prothrow-Stith, D. (with M. Wiessman) (1991). *Deadly consequences.* New York: HarperCollins.

Provine, R. R. (2005). Yawning. *American Scientist, 93*, 532–539.

Pruitt, D. G. (1986). Achieving integrative agreements in negotiation. In R. K. White (Ed.), *Psychology and the prevention of nuclear war.* New York: New York University Press.

Pruitt, D. G. (1998). Social conflict. In D. Gilbert, S. T. Fiske, & G. Lindzey (Eds.), *Handbook of social psychology,* 4th edition. New York: McGraw-Hill.

Pruitt, D. G., & Kimmel, M. J. (1977). Twenty years of experimental gaming: Critique, synthesis, and suggestions for the future. *Annual Review of Psychology, 28*, 363–392.

Pruitt, D. G., & Lewis, S. A. (1975). Development of integrative solutions in bilateral negotiation. *Journal of Personality and Social Psychology, 31*, 621–633.

Pruitt, D. G., & Lewis, S. A. (1977). The psychology of integrative bargaining. In D. Druckman (Ed.), *Negotiations: A social-psychological analysis.* New York: Halsted.

Pruitt, D. G., & Rubin, J. Z. (1986). *Social conflict.* San Francisco: Random House.

Pryke, S., Lindsay, R. C. L., Dysart, J. E., & Dupuis, P. (2004). Multiple independent identification decisions: A method of calibrating eyewitness identifications. *Journal of Applied Psychology, 89*, 73–84.

Pryor, J. B., DeSouza, E. R., Fitness, J., Hutz, C., Kumpf, M., Lubbert, K., Pesonen, O., & Erber, M. W. (1997). Gender differences in the interpretation of social-sexual behavior: A cross-cultural perspective on sexual harassment. *Journal of Cross-Cultural Psychology, 28*, 509–534.

Pryor, J. H., Hurtado, S., Saenz, V. B., Lindholm, J. A., Korn, W. S., & Mahoney, K. M. (2005). *The American freshman: National norms for Fall 2005.* Los Angeles: Higher Education Research Institute, UCLA.

Pryor, J. H., Hurtado, S., Sharkness, J., & Korn, W. S. (2007). *The American freshman: National norms for Fall 2007.* Los Angeles: Higher Education Research Institute, UCLA.

PTC. (2007, January 10). *Dying to entertain: Violence on prime time broadcast TV, 1998 to 2006.* Parents Television Council (www.parentstv .org).

Public Opinion. (1984, August/September). *Vanity Fair,* p. 22.

Purvis, J. A., Dabbs, J. M., Jr., & Hopper, C. H. (1984). The "opener": Skilled user of facial expression and speech pattern. *Personality and Social Psychology Bulletin, 10*, 61–66.

Putnam, R. (2000). *Bowling alone.* New York: Simon & Schuster.

Putnam, R. (2006, July 3). You gotta have friends: A study finds that Americans are getting lonelier. *Time,* p. 36.

Pyszczynski, T., Abdollahi, A., Solomon, S., Greenberg, J., Cohen, F., & Weise, D. (2006). Mortality salience, martyrdom, and military might: The great Satan versus the axis of evil. *Personality and Social Psychology Bulletin, 32*, 525–537.

Pyszczynski, T., & Greenberg, J. (1987). Self-regulatory perseveration and the depressive self-focusing style: A self-awareness theory of reactive depression. *Psychological Bulletin, 102*, 122–138.

Pyszczynski, T., Hamilton, J. C., Greenberg, J., & Becker, S. E. (1991). Self-awareness and psychological dysfunction. In C. R. Snyder & D. O. Forsyth (Eds.), *Handbook of social and clinical psychology: The health perspective.* New York: Pergamon.

Qirko, H. N. (2004). "Fictive kin" and suicide terrorism. *Science, 304*, 49–50.

Quartz, S. R., & Sejnowski, T. J. (2002). *Liars, lovers, and heroes: What the new brain science reveals about how we become who we are.* New York: Morrow.

Raine, A. (1993). *The psychopathology of crime: Criminal behavior as a clinical disorder.* San Diego, CA: Academic Press.

Raine, A. (2005). The interaction of biological and social measures in the explanation of antisocial and violent behavior. In D. M. Stoff & E. J. Susman (Eds.), *Developmental psychobiology of aggression.* New York: Cambridge University Press.

Raine, A. (2008). From genes to brain to antisocial behavior. *Current Directions in Psychological Science, 17*, 323–328.

Raine, A., Lencz, T., Bihrle, S., LaCasse, L., & Colletti, P. (2000). Reduced prefrontal gray matter volume and reduced autonomic activity in antisocial personality disorder. *Archives of General Psychiatry, 57*, 119–127.

Raine, A., Stoddard, J., Bihrle, S., & Buchsbaum, M. (1998). Prefrontal glucose deficits in murderers lacking psychosocial deprivation. *Neuropsychiatry, Neuropsychology, & Behavioral Neurology, 11*, 1–7.

Rajagopal, P., Raju, S., & Unnava, H. R. (2006). Differences in the cognitive accessibility of action and inaction regrets. *Journal of Experimental Social Psychology, 42*, 302–313.

Rajecki, D. W., Bledsoe, S. B., & Rasmussen, J. L. (1991). Successful personal ads: Gender differences and similarities in offers, stipulations, and outcomes. *Basic and Applied Social Psychology, 12*, 457–469.

Ramirez, J. M., Bonniot-Cabanac, M-C., & Cabanac, M. (2005). Can aggression provide pleasure? *European Psychologist, 10*, 136–145.

Rank, S. G., & Jacobson, C. K. (1977). Hospital nurses' compliance with medication overdose orders: A failure to replicate. *Journal of Health and Social Behavior, 18*, 188–193.

Rapoport, A. (1960). *Fights, games, and debates.* Ann Arbor: University of Michigan Press.

Rappoport, L., & Kren, G. (1993). Amoral rescuers: The ambiguities of altruism. *Creativity Research Journal, 6*, 129–136.

Rawls, J. (1971). *A theory of justice.* Cambridge, MA: Belknap Press of Harvard University Press.

Ray, D. G., Mackie, D. M., Rydell, R. J., & Smith, E. R. (2008). Changing categorization of self can change emotions about outgroups. *Journal of Experimental Social Psychology, 44*, 1210–1213.

Reed, D. (1989, November 25). Video collection documents Christian resistance to Hitler. Associated Press release in *Grand Rapids Press,* pp. B4, B5.

Regan, D. T., & Cheng, J. B. (1973). Distraction and attitude change: A resolution. *Journal of Experimental Social Psychology, 9*, 138–147.

Regan, D. T., & Fazio, R. (1977). On the consistency between attitudes and behavior: Look to the method of attitude formation. *Journal of Experimental Social Psychology, 13*, 28–45.

Regan, P. C. (1998). What if you can't get what you want? Willingness to compromise ideal mate selection standards as a function of sex, mate value, and relationship context. *Personality and Social Psychology Bulletin, 24*, 1294–1303.

Reicher, S., Spears, R., & Postmes, T. (1995). A social identity model of deindividuation phenomena. In W. Storebe & M. Hewstone (Eds.), *European review of social psychology* (Vol. 6). Chichester, England: Wiley.

Reid, P., & Finchilescu, G. (1995). The disempowering effects of media violence against women on college women. *Psychology of Women Quarterly, 19*, 397–411.

Reifman, A. S., Larrick, R. P., & Fein, S. (1991). Temper and temperature on the diamond: The heat-aggression relationship in major league baseball. *Personality and Social Psychology Bulletin, 17*, 580–585.

Reiner, W. G., & Gearhart, J. P. (2004). Discordant sexual identity in some genetic males with cloacal exstrophy assigned to female sex at birth. *New England Journal of Medicine,* **350,** 333–341.

Reis, H. T., & Aron, A. (2008). Love: Why is it, why does it matter, and how does it operate? *Perspectives on Psychological Science,* **3,** 80–86.

Reis, H. T., Nezlek, J., & Wheeler, L. (1980). Physical attractiveness in social interaction. *Journal of Personality and Social Psychology,* **38,** 604–617.

Reis, H. T., & Shaver, P. (1988). Intimacy as an interpersonal process. In S. Duck (Ed.), *Handbook of personal relationships: Theory, relationships and interventions.* Chichester, England: Wiley.

Reis, H. T., Wheeler, L., Spiegel, N., Kernis, M. H., Nezlek, J., & Perri, M. (1982). Physical attractiveness in social interaction: II. Why does appearance affect social experience? *Journal of Personality and Social Psychology,* **43,** 979–996.

Reisenzein, R. (1983). The Schachter theory of emotion: Two decades later. *Psychological Bulletin,* **94,** 239–264.

Reitzes, D. C. (1953). The role of organizational structures: Union versus neighborhood in a tension situation. *Journal of Social Issues,* **9**(1), 37–44.

Remley, A. (1988, October). From obedience to independence. *Psychology Today,* pp. 56–59.

Renaud, H., & Estess, F. (1961). Life history interviews with one hundred normal American males: "Pathogenecity" of childhood. *American Journal of Orthopsychiatry,* **31,** 786–802.

Renner, M. (1999). *Ending violent conflict.* Worldwatch Paper 146, Worldwatch Institute.

Ressler, R. K., Burgess, A. W., & Douglas, J. E. (1988). *Sexual homicide patterns.* Boston: Lexington Books.

Revkin, A. C. (2008, December 16). A cooler year on a warming planet. *New York Times* blog (www.nytimes.com).

Reynolds, J., Stewart, M., MacDonald, R., & Sischo, L. (2006). Have adolescents become too ambitious? High school seniors' educational and occupational plans, 1976 to 2000. *Social Problems,* **53,** 186–206.

Rhine, R. J., & Severance, L. J. (1970). Ego-involvement, discrepancy, source credibility, and attitude change. *Journal of Personality and Social Psychology,* **16,** 175–190.

Rhodes, G. (2006). The evolutionary psychology of facial beauty. *Annual Review of Psychology,* **57,** 199–226.

Rhodes, G., Sumich, A., & Byatt, G. (1999). Are average facial configurations attractive only because of their symmetry? *Psychological Science,* **10,** 52–58.

Rhodes, N., & Wood, W. (1992). Self-esteem and intelligence affect influenceability: The mediating role of message reception. *Psychological Bulletin,* **111,** 156–171.

Rhodewalt, F. (1987). Is self-handicapping an effective self-protective attributional strategy? Paper presented at the American Psychological Association convention.

Rhodewalt, F., & Agustsdottir, S. (1986). Effects of self-presentation on the phenomenal self. *Journal of Personality and Social Psychology,* **50,** 47–55.

Rhodewalt, F., Saltzman, A. T., & Wittmer J. (1984). Self-handicapping among competitive athletes: The role of practice in self-esteem protection. *Basic and Applied Social Psychology,* **5,** 197–209.

Rholes, W. S., Newman, L. S., & Ruble, D. N. (1990). Understanding self and other: Developmental and motivational aspects of perceiving persons in terms of invariant dispositions. In E. T. Higgins & R. M. Sorrentino (Eds.), *Handbook of motivation and cognition: Foundations of social behavior* (Vol. 2). New York: Guilford.

Rice, B. (1985, September). Performance review: The job nobody likes. *Psychology Today,* pp. 30–36.

Rice, M. E., & Grusec, J. E. (1975). Saying and doing: Effects on observer performance. *Journal of Personality and Social Psychology,* **32,** 584–593.

Richard, F. D., Bond, C. F., Jr., & Stokes-Zoota, J. J. (2003). One hundred years of social psychology quantitatively described. *Review of General Psychology,* **7,** 331–363.

Richards, Z., & Hewstone, M. (2001). Subtyping and subgrouping: Processes for the prevention and promotion of stereotype change. *Personality and Social Psychology Review,* **5,** 52–73.

Richardson, B. B. (2005, Spring–Summer). A conversation with Judith Lichtman, a.k.a. "the 101st Senator." ABA/YLD Women in the Profession Committee newsletter.

Richardson, D. S. (2005). The myth of female passivity: Thirty years of revelations about female aggression. *Psychology of Women Quarterly,* **29,** 238–247.

Richardson, J. D., Huddy, W. P., & Morgan, S. M. (2008). The hostile media effect, biased assimilation, and perceptions of a presidential debate. *Journal of Applied Social Psychology,* **38,** 1255–1270.

Richardson, L. F. (1960). Generalized foreign policy. *British Journal of Psychology Monographs Supplements,* **23.** Cited by A. Rapoport in *Fights, games, and debates* (p. 15). Ann Arbor: University of Michigan Press.

Richeson, J. A., & Trawalter, S. (2008). The threat of appearing prejudiced, and race-based attentional biases. *Psychological Science,* **19,** 98–102.

Richtel, M. (2007, June 2). For pornographers, Internet's virtues turn to vices. *New York Times* (www.nytimes.com).

Ridge, R. D., & Reber, J. S. (2002). "I think she's attracted to me": The effect of men's beliefs on women's behavior in a job interview scenario. *Basic and Applied Social Psychology,* **24,** 1–14.

Riek, B. M., Mania, E. W., & Gaertner, S. L. (2006). Intergroup threat and outgroup attitudes: A meta-analytic review. *Personality and Social Psychology Review,* **10,** 336–353.

Riess, M., Rosenfeld, P., Melburg, V., & Tedeschi, J. T. (1981). Self-serving attributions: Biased private perceptions and distorted public descriptions. *Journal of Personality and Social Psychology,* **41,** 224–231.

Rietzschel, E. F., Nijstad, B. A., & Stroebe, W. (2006). Productivity is not enough: A comparison of interactive and nominal brainstorming groups on idea generation and selection. *Journal of Experimental Social Psychology,* **42,** 244–251.

Riggs, J. M. (1992). Self-handicapping and achievement. In A. K. Boggiano & T. S. Pittman (Eds.), *Achievement and motivation: A social-developmental perspective.* New York: Cambridge University Press.

Riordan, C. A. (1980). Effects of admission of influence on attributions and attraction. Paper presented at the American Psychological Association convention.

Risen, J. L., Gilovich, T., & Dunning, D. (2007). One-shot illusory correlations and stereotype formation. *Personality and Social Psychology Bulletin,* **33,** 1492–1502.

Roach, M. (1998, December). Why men kill. *Discover,* pp. 100–108.

Robberson, M. R., & Rogers, R. W. (1988). Beyond fear appeals: Negative and positive persuasive appeals to health and self-esteem. *Journal of Applied Social Psychology,* **18,** 277–287.

Robertson, I. (1987). *Sociology.* New York: Worth Publishers.

Robins, L., & Regier, D. (Eds.). (1991). *Psychiatric disorders in America.* New York: Free Press.

Robins, R. W., & Beer, J. S. (2001). Positive illusions about the self: Short-term benefits and long-term costs. *Journal of Personality and Social Psychology,* **80,** 340–352.

Robins, R. W., Mendelsohn, G. A., Connell, J. B., & Kwan, V. S. Y. (2004). Do people agree about the causes of behavior? A social relations analysis of behavior ratings and causal attributions. *Journal of Personality and Social Psychology, 86,* 334–344.

Robinson, J. (2002, October 8). What percentage of the population is gay? *Gallup Tuesday Briefing* (www.gallup.com).

Robinson, M. D., & Ryff, C. D. (1999). The role of self-deception in perceptions of past, present, and future happiness. *Personality and Social Psychology Bulletin, 25,* 595–606.

Robinson, M. S., & Alloy, L. B. (2003). Negative cognitive styles and stress-reactive rumination interact to predict depression: A prospective study. *Cognitive Therapy and Research, 27,* 275–291.

Robinson, T. N., Wilde, M. L., Navracruz, L. C., Haydel, F., & Varady, A. (2001). Effects of reducing children's television and video game use on aggressive behavior. *Archives of Pediatric and Adolescent Medicine, 155,* 17–23.

Rochat, F. (1993). How did they resist authority? Protecting refugees in Le Chambon during World War II. Paper presented at the American Psychological Association convention.

Rochat, F., & Modigliani, A. (1995). The ordinary quality of resistance: From Milgram's laboratory to the village of Le Chambon. *Journal of Social Issues, 51,* 195–210.

Roehling, M. V., Roehling, P. V., & Odland, I. M. (2008). Investigating the validity of stereotypes about overweight employees. *Group and Organization Management, 23,* 392–424.

Roehling, M. V., Roehling, P. V., & Pichler, S. (2007). The relationship between body weight and perceived weight-related employment discrimination: The role of sex and race. *Journal of Vocational Behavior, 71,* 300–318.

Roehling, P. V., Roehling, M. V., Vandlen, J. D., Blazek, J., & Guy, W. C. (2009). Weight discrimination and the glass ceiling effect among top U.S. male and female CEOs. *Equal Opportunities International, 28,* 179–196.

Roese, N. J., & Hur, T. (1997). Affective determinants of counterfactual thinking. *Social Cognition, 15,* 274–290.

Roese, N. L., & Olson, J. M. (1994). Attitude importance as a function of repeated attitude expression. *Journal of Experimental Social Psychology, 66,* 805–818.

Roger, L. H., Cortes, D. E., & Malgady, R. B. (1991). Acculturation and mental health status among Hispanics: Convergence and new directions for research. *American Psychologist, 46,* 585–597.

Rogers, C. R. (1980). *A way of being.* Boston: Houghton Mifflin.

Rogers, C. R. (1985, February). Quoted by Michael A. Wallach and Lise Wallach in "How psychology sanctions the cult of the self." *Washington Monthly,* pp. 46–56.

Rogers, R. W., & Mewborn, C. R. (1976). Fear appeals and attitude change: Effects of a threat's noxiousness, probability of occurrence, and the efficacy of coping responses. *Journal of Personality and Social Psychology, 34,* 54–61.

Rogers, R. W., & Prentice-Dunn, S. (1981). Deindividuation and anger-mediated interracial aggression: Unmasking regressive racism. *Journal of Personality and Social Psychology, 41,* 63–73.

Rohrer, J. H., Baron, S. H., Hoffman, E. L., & Swander, D. V. (1954). The stability of autokinetic judgments. *Journal of Abnormal and Social Psychology, 49,* 595–597.

Rohter, L. (2004, December 19). U.S. waters down global commitment to curb greenhouse gases. *New York Times* (www.nytimes.com).

Rokeach, M. (1968). *Beliefs, attitudes, and values.* San Francisco: Jossey-Bass.

Rokeach, M., & Mezei, L. (1966). Race and shared beliefs as factors in social choice. *Science, 151,* 167–172.

Romer, D., Gruder, D. L., & Lizzadro, T. (1986). A person-situation approach to altruistic behavior. *Journal of Personality and Social Psychology, 51,* 1001–1012.

Roney, J. R. (2003). Effects of visual exposure to the opposite sex: Cognitive aspects of mate attraction in human males. *Personality and Social Psychology Bulletin, 29,* 393–404.

Rook, K. S. (1984). Promoting social bonding: Strategies for helping the lonely and socially isolated. *American Psychologist, 39,* 1389–1407.

Rook, K. S. (1987). Social support versus companionship: Effects on life stress, loneliness, and evaluations by others. *Journal of Personality and Social Psychology, 52,* 1132–1147.

Rooth, D-O. (2007). Implicit discrimination in hiring: Real-world evidence. IZA Discussion Paper No. 2764, University of Kalmar, Institute for the Study of Labor (IZA).

Rose, A. J., & Rudolph, K. D. (2006). A review of sex differences in peer relationship processes: Potential trade-offs for the emotional and behavioral development of girls and boys. *Psychological Bulletin, 132,* 98–131.

Rosenbaum, M. E. (1986). The repulsion hypothesis: On the nondevelopment of relationships. *Journal of Personality and Social Psychology, 51,* 1156–1166.

Rosenbaum, M. E., & Holtz, R. (1985). The minimal intergroup discrimination effect: Out-group derogation, not in-group favorability.

Paper presented at the American Psychological Association convention.

Rosenberg, L. A. (1961). Group size, prior experience and conformity. *Journal of Abnormal and Social Psychology, 63,* 436–437.

Rosenblatt, A., & Greenberg, J. (1988). Depression and interpersonal attraction: The role of perceived similarity. *Journal of Personality and Social Psychology, 55,* 112–119.

Rosenblatt, A., & Greenberg, J. (1991). Examining the world of the depressed: Do depressed people prefer others who are depressed? *Journal of Personality and Social Psychology, 60,* 620–629.

Rosenbloom, S. (2008, January 3). Putting your best cyberface forward. *New York Times,* Style section.

Rosenfeld, D., Folger, R., & Adelman, H. F. (1980). When rewards reflect competence: A qualification of the overjustification effect. *Journal of Personality and Social Psychology, 39,* 368–376.

Rosenhan, D. L. (1970). The natural socialization of altruistic autonomy. In J. Macaulay & L. Berkowitz (Eds.), *Altruism and helping behavior.* New York: Academic Press.

Rosenhan, D. L. (1973). On being sane in insane places. *Science, 179,* 250–258.

Rosenthal, D. A., & Feldman, S. S. (1992). The nature and stability of ethnic identity in Chinese youth: Effects of length of residence in two cultural contexts. *Journal of Cross-Cultural Psychology, 23,* 214–227.

Rosenthal, R. (1985). From unconscious experimenter bias to teacher expectancy effects. In J. B. Dusek, V. C. Hall, & W. J. Meyer (Eds.), *Teacher expectancies.* Hillsdale, NJ: Erlbaum.

Rosenthal, R. (1991). Teacher expectancy effects: A brief update 25 years after the Pygmalion experiment. *Journal of Research in Education, 1,* 3–12.

Rosenthal, R. (2002). Covert communication in classrooms, clinics, courtrooms, and cubicles. *American Psychologist, 57,* 839–849.

Rosenthal, R. (2003). Covert communication in laboratories, classrooms, and the truly real world. *Current Directions in Psychological Science, 12,* 151–154.

Rosenthal, R. (2006). Applying psychological research on interpersonal expectations and covert communication in classrooms, clinics, corporations, and courtrooms. In S. I. Donaldson, D. E. Berger, & K. Pezdek (Eds.), *Applied psychology: New frontiers and rewarding careers.* Mahwah, NJ: Erlbaum.

Rosenthal, R. (2008). Introduction, methods, results, discussion: The story of a career. In R. Levin, A. Rodriques, & L. Zelezny (Eds.), *Journeys in social psychology: Looking back to inspire the future.* New York: Psychology Press.

Rosenthal, R., & Jacobson, L. (1968). *Pygmalion in the classroom: Teacher expectation and pupils' intellectual development.* New York: Holt, Rinehart & Winston.

Rosenzweig, M. R. (1972). Cognitive dissonance. *American Psychologist, 27,* 769.

Roseth, C. J., Johnson, D. W., & Johnson, R. T. (2008). Promoting early adolescents' achievement and peer relationships: The effects of cooperative, competitive, and individualistic goal structures. *Psychological Bulletin, 134,* 223–246.

Ross, L. (1977). The intuitive psychologist and his shortcomings: Distortions in the attribution process. In L. Berkowitz (Ed.), *Advances in experimental social psychology* (Vol. 10). New York: Academic Press.

Ross, L. (1981). The "intuitive scientist" formulation and its developmental implications. In J. H. Havell & L. Ross (Eds.), *Social cognitive development: Frontiers and possible futures.* Cambridge, England: Cambridge University Press.

Ross, L. (1988). Situationist perspectives on the obedience experiments. Review of A. G. Miller's *The obedience experiments. Contemporary Psychology, 33,* 101–104.

Ross, L., Amabile, T. M., & Steinmetz, J. L. (1977). Social roles, social control, and biases in social-perception processes. *Journal of Personality and Social Psychology, 35,* 485–494.

Ross, L., & Anderson, C. A. (1982). Shortcomings in the attribution process: On the origins and maintenance of erroneous social assessments. In D. Kahneman, P. Slovic, & A. Tversky (Eds.), *Judgment under uncertainty: Heuristics and biases.* New York: Cambridge University Press.

Ross, L., & Lepper, M. R. (1980). The perseverance of beliefs: Empirical and normative considerations. In R. A. Shweder (Ed.), *New directions for methodology of behavioral science: Fallible judgment in behavioral research.* San Francisco: Jossey-Bass.

Ross, L., & Ward, A. (1995). Psychological barriers to dispute resolution. In M. P. Zanna (Ed.), *Advances in experimental social psychology* (Vol. 27). San Diego: Academic Press.

Ross, L., & Ward, A. (1996). Naive realism in everyday life: Implications for social conflict and misunderstanding. In T. Brown, E. Reed, & E. Turiel (Eds.), *Values and knowledge.* Hillsdale, NJ: Erlbaum.

Ross, M., & Fletcher, G. J. O. (1985). Attribution and social perception. In G. Lindzey & E. Aronson (Eds.), *The Handbook of Social Psychology,* 3rd edition. New York: Random House.

Ross, M., McFarland, C., & Fletcher, G. J. O. (1981). The effect of attitude on the recall of personal histories. *Journal of Personality and Social Psychology, 40,* 627–634.

Ross, M., & Newby-Clark, I. R. (1998). Construing the past and future. *Social Cognition, 16,* 133–150.

Ross, M., & Sicoly, F. (1979). Egocentric biases in availability and attribution. *Journal of Personality and Social Psychology, 37,* 322–336.

Rossi, A. S., & Rossi, P. H. (1990). *Of human bonding: Parent-child relations across the life course.* Hawthorne, NY: Aldine de Gruyter.

Roszell, P., Kennedy, D., & Grabb, E. (1990). Physical attractiveness and income attainment among Canadians. *Journal of Psychology, 123,* 547–559.

Rotenberg, K. J., Gruman, J. A., & Ariganello, M. (2002). Behavioral confirmation of the loneliness stereotype. *Basic and Applied Social Psychology, 24,* 81–89.

Rothbart, M., & Birrell, P. (1977). Attitude and perception of faces. *Journal of Research Personality, 11,* 209–215.

Rothbart, M., Fulero, S., Jensen, C., Howard, J., & Birrell, P. (1978). From individual to group impressions: Availability heuristics in stereotype formation. *Journal of Experimental Social Psychology, 14,* 237–255.

Rothbart, M., & Taylor, M. (1992). Social categories and social reality. In G. R. Semin & K. Fielder (Eds.), *Language, interaction and social cognition.* London: Sage.

Rothblum, E. D. (2007). Same-sex couples in legalized relationships: I do, or do I? Unpublished manuscript, Women's Studies Department, San Diego State University.

Rothman, A. J., & Salovey, P. (1997). Shaping perceptions to motivate healthy behavior: The role of message framing. *Psychological Bulletin, 121,* 3–19.

Rotter, J. (1973). Internal-external locus of control scale. In J. P. Robinson & R. P. Shaver (Eds.), *Measures of social psychological attitudes.* Ann Arbor: Institute for Social Research.

Rotton, J., & Frey, J. (1985). Air pollution, weather, and violent crimes: Concomitant time-series analysis of archival data. *Journal of Personality and Social Psychology, 49,* 1207–1220.

Rotundo, M., Nguyen, D-H., & Sackett, P. R. (2001). A meta-analytic review of gender differences in perceptions of sexual harrassment. *Journal of Applied Psychology, 86,* 914–922.

Rowe, D. C., Almeida, D. M., & Jacobson, K. C. (1999). School context and genetic influences on aggression in adolescence. *Psychological Science, 10,* 277–280.

Rowe, D. C., Vazsonyi, A. T., & Flannery, D. J. (1994). No more than skin deep: Ethnic and racial similarity in developmental process. *Psychological Review, 101,* 396–413.

Roy, M. M., Christenfeld, N. J. S., & McKenzie, C. R. M. (2005). Underestimating the duration of future events: Memory incorrectly used or memory bias? *Psychological Bulletin, 131,* 738–756.

Ruback, R. B., Carr, T. S., & Hoper, C. H. (1986). Perceived control in prison: Its relation to reported crowding, stress, and symptoms. *Journal of Applied Social Psychology, 16,* 375–386.

Rubin, A. (2003, April 16). War fans young Arabs' anger. *Los Angeles Times* (www.latimes.com).

Rubin, J. Z. (1986). Can we negotiate with terrorists: Some answers from psychology. Paper presented at the American Psychological Association convention.

Rubin, L. B. (1985). *Just friends: The role of friendship in our lives.* New York: Harper & Row.

Rubin, R. B. (1981). Ideal traits and terms of address for male and female college professors. *Journal of Personality and Social Psychology, 41,* 966–974.

Rubin, Z. (1973). *Liking and loving: An invitation to social psychology.* New York: Holt, Rinehart & Winston.

Ruby, R. (2007, June 26). Capital punishment's constant constituency: An American majority. Pew Research Center (pewresearch.org).

Rudolph, U., Roesch, S. C., Greitenmeyer, T., & Weiner, B. (2004). A meta-analytic review of help-giving and aggression from an attributional perspective: Contributions to a general theory of motivation. *Cognition and Emotion, 18,* 815–848.

Ruiter, R. A. C., Abraham, C., & Kok, G. (2001). Scary warnings and rational precautions: A review of the psychology of fear appeals. *Psychology and Health, 16,* 613–630.

Ruiter, S., & De Graaf, N. D. (2006). National context, religiosity, and volunteering: Results from 53 countries. *American Sociological Review, 71,* 191–210.

Rule, B. G., Taylor, B. R., & Dobbs, A. R. (1987). Priming effects of heat on aggressive thoughts. *Social Cognition, 5,* 131–143.

Rusbult, C. E. (1980). Commitment and satisfaction in romantic associations: A test of the investment model. *Journal of Experimental Social Psychology, 16,* 172–186.

Rusbult, C. E., Johnson, D. J., & Morrow, G. D. (1986). Impact of couple patterns of problem solving on distress and nondistress in dating relationships. *Journal of Personality and Social Psychology, 50,* 744–753.

Rusbult, C. E., Martz, J. M., & Agnew, C. R. (1998). The investment model scale: Measuring commitment level, satisfaction level, quality of alternatives, and investment size. *Personal Relationships, 5,* 357–391.

Rusbult, C. E., Morrow, G. D., & Johnson, D. J. (1987). Self-esteem and problem-solving behaviour in close relationships. *British Journal of Social Psychology, 26,* 293–303.

Rusbult, C. E., Olsen, N., Davis, J. L., & Hannon, P. A. (2001). Commitment and relationship maintenance mechanisms. In J. Harvey & A. Wenzel (Eds.), *Close romantic relationships: Maintenance and enhancement.* Mahwah, NJ: Erlbaum.

Rushton, J. P. (1975). Generosity in children: Immediate and long-term effects of modeling, preaching, and moral judgment. *Journal of Personality and Social Psychology, 31,* 459–466.

Rushton, J. P. (1991). Is altruism innate? *Psychological Inquiry, 2,* 141–143.

Rushton, J. P., & Bons, T. A. (2005). Mate choice and friendship in twins. *Psychological Science, 16,* 555–559.

Rushton, J. P., Brainerd, C. J., & Pressley, M. (1983). Behavioral development and construct validity: The principle of aggregation. *Psychological Bulletin, 94,* 18–38.

Rushton, J. P., & Campbell, A. C. (1977). Modeling, vicarious reinforcement and extraversion on blood donating in adults: Immediate and long-term effects. *European Journal of Social Psychology, 7,* 297–306.

Rushton, J. P., Chrisjohn, R. D., & Fekken, G. C. (1981). The altruistic personality and the self-report altruism scale. *Personality and Individual Differences, 2,* 293–302.

Rushton, J. P., Fulker, D. W., Neale, M. C., Nias, D. K. B., & Eysenck, H. J. (1986). Altruism and aggression: The heritability of individual differences. *Journal of Personality and Social Psychology, 50,* 1192–1198.

Russell, B. (1930/1980). *The conquest of happiness.* London: Unwin Paperbacks.

Russell, G. W. (1983). Psychological issues in sports aggression. In J. H. Goldstein (Ed.), *Sports violence.* New York: Springer-Verlag.

Russell, N. J. C., & Gregory, R. J. (2005). Making the undoable doable: Milgram, the Holocaust, and modern government. *American Review of Public Administration, 35,* 327–349.

Ruvolo, A., & Markus, H. (1992). Possible selves and performance: The power of self-relevant imagery. *Social Cognition, 9,* 95–124.

Ryan, R. (1999, February 2). Quoted by A. Kohn, In pursuit of affluence, at a high price. *New York Times* (www .nytimes.com).

Ryckman, R. M., Robbins, M. A., Kaczor, L. M., & Gold, J. A. (1989). Male and female raters' stereotyping of male and female physiques. *Personality and Social Psychology Bulletin, 15,* 244–251.

Rydell, R. J., McConnell, A. R., & Beilock, S. L. (2009). Multiple social identities and stereotype threat: Imbalance, accessibility, and working memory. *Journal of Personality and Social Psychology, 96,* 949–966.

Ryff, C. D., & Singer, B. (2000). Interpersonal flourishing: A positive health agenda for the new millennium. *Personality and Social Psychology Review, 4,* 30–44.

Saad, L. (2002, November 21). Most smokers wish they could quit. Gallup News Service (www.gallup.com/poll/ releases/pr021121.asp).

Saad, L. (2003, April 22). Giving global warming the cold shoulder. The Gallup Organization (www.gallup .com).

Saad, L. (2006, August 10). Anti-Muslim sentiments fairly commonplace. Gallup News Service (poll.gallup .com).

Saad, L. (2007, March 12). To Americans, the risks of global warming are not imminent: A majority worries about climate changes, but thinks problems are a decade or more away. Gallup Poll (www.galluppoll.com).

Sabini, J., & Silver, M. (1982). *Moralities of everyday life.* New York: Oxford University Press.

Sacerdote, B., & Marmaros, D. (2005). How do friendships form? NBER Working Paper No. 11530 (www.nber .org/papers/W11530).

Sachs, J. D. (2006, July). Ecology and political upheaval. *Scientific American, 291,* 37.

Sack, K., & Elder, J. (2000, July 11). Poll finds optimistic outlook but enduring racial division. *New York Times* (www .nytimes.com).

Sacks, C. H., & Bugental, D. P. (1987). Attributions as moderators of affective and behavioral responses to social failure. *Journal of Personality and Social Psychology, 53,* 939–947.

Safer, M. A., Bonanno, G. A., & Field, N. P. (2001). It was never that bad: Biased recall of grief and long-term adjustment to the death of a spouse. *Memory, 9,* 195–204.

Sagarin, B. J., Cialdini, R. B., Rice, W. E., & Serna, S. B. (2002). Dispelling the illusion of invulnerability: The motivations and mechanisms of resistance to persuasion. *Journal of Personality and Social Psychology, 83,* 526–541.

Sagarin, B. J., Rhoads, K. v. L., & Cialdini, R. B. (1998). Deceiver's distrust: Denigration as a consequence of undiscovered deception. *Personality and Social Psychology Bulletin, 24,* 1167–1176.

Sageman, M. (2004). *Understanding terror networks.* Philadelphia: University of Pennsylvania Press.

Saks, M. J. (1974). Ignorance of science is no excuse. *Trial, 10*(6), 18–20.

Saks, M. J. (1996). The smaller the jury, the greater the unpredictability. *Judicature, 79,* 263–265.

Saks, M. J. (1998). What do jury experiments tell us about how juries (should) make decisions? *Southern California Interdisciplinary Law Journal, 6,* 1–53.

Saks, M. J., & Hastie, R. (1978). *Social psychology in court.* New York: Van Nostrand Reinhold.

Saks, M. J., & Marti, M. W. (1997). A meta-analysis of the effects of jury size. *Law and Human Behavior, 21,* 451–467.

Sakurai, M. M. (1975). Small group cohesiveness and detrimental conformity. *Sociometry, 38,* 340–357.

Sales, S. M. (1972). Economic threat as a determinant of conversion rates in authoritarian and nonauthoritarian churches. *Journal of Personality and Social Psychology, 23,* 420–428.

Sales, S. M. (1973). Threat as a factor in authoritarianism: An analysis of archival data. *Journal of Personality & Social Psychology, 28,* 44–57.

Salganik, M. J., Dodds, P. S., & Watts, D. J. (2006). Experimental study of inequality and unpredictability in an artificial cultural market. *Science, 311,* 854–856.

Salmela-Aro, K., & Nurmi, J-E. (2007). Self-esteem during university studies predicts career characteristics 10 years later. *Journal of Vocational Behavior, 70,* 463–477.

Salovey, P., Mayer, J. D., & Rosenhan, D. L. (1991). Mood and healing: Mood as a motivator of helping and helping as a regulator of mood. In M. S. Clark (Ed.), *Prosocial behavior.* Newbury Park, CA: Sage.

Salovey, P., Schneider, T. R., & Apanovitch, A. M. (2002). Message framing in the prevention and early detection of illness. In J. P. Dillard & M. Pfau (Eds.), *The persuasion handbook: Theory and practice.* Thousand Oaks, CA: Sage.

Saltzstein, H. D., & Sandberg, L. (1979). Indirect social influence: Change in judgmental processor anticipatory conformity. *Journal of Experimental Social Psychology, 15,* 209–216.

Sampson, E. E. (1975). On justice as equality. *Journal of Social Issues, 31*(3), 45–64.

Sanbonmatsu, D. M., Akimoto, S. A., & Gibson, B. D. (1994). Stereotype-based blocking in social explanation. *Personality and Social Psychology Bulletin, 20,* 71–81.

Sancton, T. 1997, October 13). The dossier on Diana's crash. *Time*, pp. 50–56.

Sande, G. N., Goethals, G. R., & Radloff, C. E. (1988). Perceiving one's own traits and others': The multifaceted self. *Journal of Personality and Social Psychology, 54*, 13–20.

Sanders, G. S. (1981a). Driven by distraction: An integrative review of social facilitation and theory and research. *Journal of Experimental Social Psychology, 17*, 227–251.

Sanders, G. S. (1981b). Toward a comprehensive account of social facilitation: Distraction/conflict does not mean theoretical conflict. *Journal of Experimental Social Psychology, 17*, 262–265.

Sanders, G. S., Baron, R. S., & Moore, D. L. (1978). Distraction and social comparison as mediators of social facilitation effects. *Journal of Experimental Social Psychology, 14*, 291–303.

Sanderson, C. A., & Cantor, N. (2001). The association of intimacy goals and marital satisfaction: A test of four mediational hypotheses. *Personality and Social Psychology Bulletin, 27*, 1567–1577.

Sanislow, C. A., III, Perkins, D. V., & Balogh, D. W. (1989). Mood induction, interpersonal perceptions, and rejection in the roommates of depressed, nondepressed-disturbed, and normal college students. *Journal of Social and Clinical Psychology, 8*, 345–358.

Sanitioso, R., Kunda, Z., & Fong, G. T. (1990). Motivated recruitment of autobiographical memories. *Journal of Personality and Social Psychology, 59*, 229–241.

Sanna, L. J., Parks, C. D., Meier, S., Chang, E. C., Kassin, B. R., Lechter, J. L., Turley-Ames, K. J., & Miyake, T. M. (2003). A game of inches: Spontaneous use of counterfactuals by broadcasters during major league baseball playoffs. *Journal of Applied Social Psychology, 33*, 455–475.

Sansone, C. (1986). A question of competence: The effects of competence and task feedback on intrinsic interest. *Journal of Personality and Social Psychology, 51*, 918–931.

Sapadin, L. A. (1988). Friendship and gender: Perspectives of professional men and women. *Journal of Social and Personal Relationships, 5*, 387–403.

Sapolsky, R. (2005, December). Sick of poverty. *Scientific American*, pp. 93–99.

Sargent, J. D., Heatherton, T. F., & Ahrens, M. B. (2002). Adolescent exposure to extremely violent movies. *Journal of Adolescent Health, 31*, 449–454.

Sarnoff, I., & Sarnoff, S. (1989). *Love-centered marriage in a self-centered world*. New York: Schocken Books.

Sartre, J-P. (1946/1948). *Anti-Semite and Jew*. New York: Schocken Books.

Sassenberg, K., Moskowitz, G. B., Jacoby, J., & Hansen, N. (2007). The carry-over effect of competition: The impact of competition on prejudice towards uninvolved outgroups. *Journal of Experimental Social Psychology, 43*, 529–538.

Sato, K. (1987). Distribution of the cost of maintaining common resources. *Journal of Experimental Social Psychology, 23*, 19–31.

Saucier, D. A., & Miller, C. T. (2003). The persuasiveness of racial arguments as a subtle measure of racism. *Personality and Social Psychology Bulletin, 29*, 1303–1315.

Saucier, D. A., Miller, C. T., & Doucet, N. (2005). Differences in helping Whites and Blacks: A meta-analysis. *Personality and Social Psychology Review, 9*, 2–16.

Savitsky, K., Epley, N., & Gilovich, T. (2001). Do others judge us as harshly as we think? Overestimating the impact of our failures, shortcomings, and mishaps. *Journal of Personality and Social Psychology, 81*, 44–56.

Savitsky, K., & Gilovich, T. (2003). The illusion of transparency and the alleviation of speech anxiety. *Journal of Experimental Social Psychology, 39*, 618–625.

Savitsky, K., Van Voven, L., Epley, N., & Wright, W. M. (2005). The unpacking effect in allocations of responsibility for group tasks. *Journal of Experimental Social Psychology, 41*, 447–457.

Sax, L. J., Lindholm, J. A., Astin, A. W., Korn, W. S., & Mahoney, K. M. (2002). *The American freshman: National norms for Fall, 2002*. Los Angeles: Cooperative Institutional Research Program, UCLA.

Scarr, S. (1988). Race and gender as psychological variables: Social and ethical issues. *American Psychologist, 43*, 56–59.

Schachter, S. (1951). Deviation, rejection and communication. *Journal of Abnormal and Social Psychology, 46*, 190–207.

Schachter, S., & Singer, J. E. (1962). Cognitive, social and physiological determinants of emotional state. *Psychological Review, 69*, 379–399.

Schacter, D., Kaszniak, A., & Kihlstrom, J. (1991). Models of memory and the understanding of memory disorders. In T. Yanagihara & R. Petersen (Eds.), *Memory disorders: Research and clinical practice*. New York: Marcel Dekker.

Schafer, R. B., & Keith, P. M. (1980). Equity and depression among married couples. *Social Psychology Quarterly, 43*, 430–435.

Schaffner, P. E. (1985). Specious learning about reward and punishment. *Journal of Personality and Social Psychology, 48*, 1377–1386.

Schaffner, P. E., Wandersman, A., & Stang, D. (1981). Candidate name exposure and voting: Two field studies. *Basic and Applied Social Psychology, 2*, 195–203.

Schaller, M., & Cialdini, R. B. (1988). The economics of empathic helping: Support for a mood management motive. *Journal of Experimental Social Psychology, 24*, 163–181.

Schein, E. H. (1956). The Chinese indoctrination program for prisoners of war: A study of attempted brainwashing. *Psychiatry, 19*, 149–172.

Schiffenbauer, A., & Schiavo, R. S. (1976). Physical distance and attraction: An intensification effect. *Journal of Experimental Social Psychology, 12*, 274–282.

Schiffmann, W. (1999, February 4). An heiress abducted: Patty Hearst, 25 years after her kidnapping. Associated Press (www.abcnews.com).

Schimel, J., Arndt, J., Pyszczynski, T., & Greenberg, J. (2001). Being accepted for who we are: Evidence that social validation of the intrinsic self reduces general defensiveness. *Journal of Personality and Social Psychology, 80*, 35–52.

Schimel, J., Pyszczynski, T., Greenberg, J., O'Mahen, H., & Arndt, J. (2000). Running from the shadow: Psychological distancing from others to deny characteristics people fear in themselves. *Journal of Personality & Social Psychology, 78*, 446–462.

Schimel, J., Simon, L., Greenberg, J., Pyszczynski, T., Solomon, S., & Waxmonsky, J. (1999). Stereotypes and terror management: Evidence that mortality salience enhances stereotypic thinking and preferences. *Journal of Personality and Social Psychology, 77*, 905–926.

Schimmack, U., Oishi, S., & Diener, E. (2005). Individualism: A valid and important dimension of cultural differences between nations. *Personality and Social Psychology Review, 9*, 17–31.

Schkade, D. A., & Kahneman, D. (1998). Does living in California make people happy? A focusing illusion in judgments of life satisfaction. *Psychological Science, 9*, 340–346.

Schkade, D. A., & Sunstein, C. R. (2003, June 11). Judging by where you sit. *New York Times* (www.nytimes.com).

Schkade, D., Sunstein, C. R., & Hastie, R. (2007). What happened on deliberation day? *California Law Review, 95*, 915–940.

Schlenker, B. R. (1976). Egocentric perceptions in cooperative groups: A conceptualization and research review. Final Report, Office of Naval Research Grant NR 170–797.

Schlenker, B. R., & Leary, M. R. (1982). Social anxiety and self-presentation: A conceptualization and model. *Psychological Bulletin, 92,* 641–669.

Schlenker, B. R., & Leary, M. R. (1985). Social anxiety and communication about the self. *Journal of Language and Social Psychology, 4,* 171–192.

Schlenker, B. R., & Miller, R. S. (1977a). Group cohesiveness as a determinant of egocentric perceptions in cooperative groups. *Human Relations, 30,* 1039–1055.

Schlenker, B. R., & Miller, R. S. (1977b). Egocentrism in groups: Self-serving biases or logical information processing? *Journal of Personality and Social Psychology, 35,* 755–764.

Schlenker, B. R., & Weigold, M. F. (1992). Interpersonal processes involving impression regulation and management. *Annual Review of Psychology, 43,* 133–168.

Schlesinger, A. M., Jr. (1965). *A thousand days.* Boston: Houghton Mifflin. Cited by I. L. Janis (1972) in *Victims of groupthink.* Boston: Houghton Mifflin.

Schlesinger, A., Jr. (1949). The statistical soldier. *Partisan Review, 16,* 852–856.

Schlesinger, A., Jr. (1991, July 8). The cult of ethnicity, good and bad. *Time,* p. 21.

Schlosser, E. (2003, March 10). Empire of the obscene. *New Yorker,* pp. 61–71.

Schmader, T., Johns, M., & Forbes, C. (2008). An integrated process model of stereotype threat effects on performance. *Psychological Review, 115,* 336–356.

Schmid, R. E. (2008, July 8). Pet owners prefer McCain over Obama. Associated Press (news.yahoo.com).

Schmitt, D. P. & 128 others. (2004). Patterns and universals of adult romantic attachment across 62 cultural regions: Are models of self and of other pancultural constructs? *Journal of Cross-Cultural Psychology, 35,* 367–402.

Schmitt, D. P. (2003). Universal sex differences in the desire for sexual variety; tests from 52 nations, 6 continents, and 13 islands. *Journal of Personality and Social Psychology, 85,* 85–104.

Schmitt, D. P. (2005). Sociosexuality from Argentina to Zimbabwe: A 48-nation study of sex, culture, and strategies of human mating. *Behavioral and Brain Sciences, 28,* 247–311.

Schmitt, D. P. (2006). Evolutionary and cross-cultural perspectives on love: The influence of gender, personality, and local ecology on emotional investment in romantic relationships. In R. J. Sternberg (Ed.), *The psychology of love* (2nd ed.). New Haven, CT: Yale University Press.

Schmitt, D. P. (2007). Sexual strategies across sexual orientations: How personality traits and culture relate to sociosexuality among gays, lesbians,

bisexuals, and heterosexuals. *Journal of Psychology and Human Sexuality, 18,* 183–214.

Schmitt, D. P., & Allik, J. (2005). Simultaneous administration of the Rosenberg Self-Esteem Scale in 53 nations: Exploring the universal and culture-specific features of global self-esteem. *Journal of Personality and Social Psychology, 89,* 623–642.

Schmitt, D. P., Realo, A., Voracek, M., & Allik, J. (2008). Why can't a man be more like a woman? Sex differences in Big Five personality traits across 55 cultures. *Journal of Personality and Social Psychology, 94,* 168–182.

Schnall, S., & Laird, J. D. (2003). Keep smiling: Enduring effects of facial expressions and postures on emotional experience and memory. *Cognition and Emotion, 17,* 787–797.

Schneider, M. E., Major, B., Luhtanen, R., & Crocker, J. (1996). Social stigma and the potential costs of assumptive help. *Personality and Social Psychology Bulletin, 22,* 201–209.

Schneider, P. (2000, February 13). Saving Konrad Latte. *New York Times Magazine* (www.nytimes.com).

Schneider, T. R., Salovey, P., Pallonen, U., Mundorf, N., Smith, N. F., & Steward, W. T. (2000). Visual and auditory message framing effects on tobacco smoking. *Journal of Applied Social Psychology, 31*(4), 667–682.

Schoeneman, T. J. (1994). Individualism. In V. S. Ramachandran (Ed.), *Encyclopedia of Human Behavior.* San Diego: Academic Press.

Schofield, J. (1982). *Black and white in school: Trust, tension, or tolerance?* New York: Praeger.

Schofield, J. W. (1986). Causes and consequences of the colorblind perspective. In J. F. Dovidio & S. L. Gaertner (Eds.), *Prejudice, discrimination, and racism.* Orlando, FL: Academic Press.

Schooler, J. W. (2002). Verbalization produces a transfer inappropriate processing shift. *Applied Cognitive Psychology, 16,* 989–997.

Schor, J. B. (1998). *The overworked American.* New York: Basic Books.

Schroeder, D. A., Dovidio, J. F., Sibicky, M. E., Matthews, L. L., & Allen, J. L. (1988). Empathic concern and helping behavior: Egoism or altruism? *Journal of Experimental Social Psychology, 24,* 333–353.

Schulz, J. W., & Pruitt, D. G. (1978). The effects of mutual concern on joint welfare. *Journal of Experimental Social Psychology, 14,* 480–492.

Schulz-Hardt, S., Frey, D., Luthgens, C., & Moscovici, S. (2000). Biased information search in group decision making. *Journal of Personality and Social Psychology, 78,* 655–669.

Schuman, H., & Kalton, G. (1985). Survey methods. In G. Lindzey & E. Aronson (Eds.), *Handbook of Social Psychology* (Vol. 1). Hillsdale, NJ: Erlbaum.

Schuman, H., & Scott, J. (1989). Generations and collective memories. *American Sociological Review, 54,* 359–381.

Schutte, J. W., & Hosch, H. M. (1997). Gender differences in sexual assault verdicts. *Journal of Social Behavior and Personality, 12,* 759–772.

Schwartz, B. (2000). Self-determination: The tyranny of freedom. *American Psychologist, 55,* 79–88.

Schwartz, B. (2004). *The tyranny of choice.* New York: Ecco/HarperCollins.

Schwartz, S. H. (1975). The justice of need and the activation of humanitarian norms. *Journal of Social Issues, 31*(3), 111–136.

Schwartz, S. H., & Gottlieb, A. (1981). Participants' post-experimental reactions and the ethics of bystander research. *Journal of Experimental Social Psychology, 17,* 396–407.

Schwartz, S. H., & Rubel, T. (2005). Sex differences in value priorities: Cross-cultural and multimethod studies. *Journal of Personality and Social Psychology, 89,* 1010–1028.

Schwarz, N., & Clore, G. L. (1983). Mood, misattribution, and judgments of well-being: Informative and directive functions of affective states. *Journal of Personality and Social Psychology, 45,* 513–523.

Schwarz, N., & Kurz, E. (1989). What's in a picture? The impact of face-ism on trait attribution. *European Journal of Social Psychology, 19,* 311–316.

Schwarz, N., Strack, F., Kommer, D., & Wagner, D. (1987). Soccer, rooms, and the quality of your life: Mood effects on judgments of satisfaction with life in general and with specific domains. *Journal of Applied Social Psychology, 17,* 69–79.

Schweitzer, K., Zillmann, D., Weaver, J. B., & Luttrell, E. S. (1992, Spring). Perception of threatening events in the emotional aftermath of a televised college football game. *Journal of Broadcasting and Electronic Media,* pp. 75–82.

Sciolino, E. (2005, December 12). Immigrants' dreams mix with fury in a gray place near Paris. *New York Times* (www.nytimes.com).

Scott, J. P., & Marston, M. V. (1953). Nonadaptive behavior resulting from a series of defeats in fighting mice. *Journal of Abnormal and Social Psychology, 48,* 417–428.

Scottish Life (2001, Winter). Isle of Muck without a crime for decades. *Scottish Life,* p. 11.

Sears, D. O. (1979). Life stage effects upon attitude change, especially among the elderly. Manuscript prepared for Workshop on the Elderly of the Future, Committee on Aging, National Research Council, Annapolis, MD, May 3–5.

Sears, D. O. (1986). College sophomores in the laboratory: Influences of a narrow data base on social psychology's view of human nature. *Journal of Personality and Social Psychology, 51,* 515–530.

Sedikides, C. (1993). Assessment, enhancement, and verification determinants of the self-evaluation process. *Journal of Personality and Social Psychology, 65,* 317–338.

Sedikides, C., Gaertner, L., & Vevea, J. L. (2005). Pancultural self-enhancement reloaded: A meta-analytic reply to Heine (2005). *Journal of Personality and Social Psychology, 89,* 539–551.

Segal, H. A. (1954). Initial psychiatric findings of recently repatriated prisoners of war. *American Journal of Psychiatry, 61,* 358–363.

Segal, N. L. (1984). Cooperation, competition, and altruism within twin sets: A reappraisal. *Ethology and Sociobiology, 5,* 163–177.

Segal, N. L., & Hershberger, S. L. (1999). Cooperation and competition between twins: Findings from a Prisoner's Dilemma game. *Evolution and Human Behavior, 20,* 29–51.

Segall, M. H., Dasen, P. R., Berry, J. W., & Poortinga, Y. H. (1990). *Human behavior in global perspective: An introduction to cross-cultural psychology.* New York: Pergamon.

Segerstrom, S. C. (2001). Optimism and attentional bias for negative and positive stimuli. *Personality and Social Psychology Bulletin, 27,* 1334–1343.

Segerstrom, S. C., McCarthy, W. J., Caskey, N. H., Gross, T. M., & Jarvik, M. E. (1993). Optimistic bias among cigarette smokers. *Journal of Applied Social Psychology, 23,* 1606–1618.

Segerstrom, S., & Miller, G. E. (2004). Psychological stress and the human immune system: A meta-analytic study of 30 years of inquiry. *Psychological Bulletin, 130,* 601–630.

Seibt, B., & Forster, J. (2004). Stereotype threat and performance: How self-stereotypes influence processing by inducing regulatory foci. *Journal of Personality and Social Psychology, 87*(1), 38–56.

Selby, J. W., Calhoun, L. G., & Brock, T. A. (1977). Sex differences in the social perception of rape victims. *Personality and Social Psychology Bulletin, 3,* 412–415.

Seligman, M. (1994). *What you can change and what you can't.* New York: Knopf.

Seligman, M. E. P. (1975). *Helplessness: On depression, development and death.* San Francisco: W. H. Freeman.

Seligman, M. E. P. (1991). *Learned optimism.* New York: Knopf.

Seligman, M. E. P. (1992). Power and powerlessness: Comments on "Cognates of personal control." *Applied & Preventive Psychology, 1,* 119–120.

Seligman, M. E. P. (1998). The prediction and prevention of depression. In D. K. Routh & R. J. DeRubeis (Eds.), *The science of clinical psychology: Accomplishments and future directions.* Washington, DC: American Psychological Association.

Seligman, M. E. P. (2002). *Authentic happiness: Using the new positive psychology to realize your potential for lasting fulfillment.* New York: Free Press.

Seligman, M. E. P., Nolen-Hoeksema, S., Thornton, N., & Thornton, K. M. (1990). Explanatory style as a mechanism of disappointing athletic performance. *Psychological Science, 1,* 143–146.

Seligman, M. E. P., & Schulman, P. (1986). Explanatory style as a predictor of productivity and quitting among life insurance sales agents. *Journal of Personality and Social Psychology, 50,* 832–838.

Sengupta, S. (2001, October 10). Sept. 11 attack narrows the racial divide. *New York Times* (www.nytimes.com).

Sengupta, S. (2003, May 27). Congo war toll soars as U.N. pleads for aid. *New York Times* (www.nytimes.com).

Sentyrz, S. M., & Bushman, B. J. (1998). Mirror, mirror, on the wall, who's the thinnest one of all? Effects of self-awareness on consumption of fatty, reduced-fat, and fat-free products. *Journal of Applied Psychology, 83,* 944–949.

Seta, C. E., & Seta, J. J. (1992). Increments and decrements in mean arterial pressure levels as a function of audience composition: An averaging and summation analysis. *Personality and Social Psychology Bulletin, 18,* 173–181.

Seta, J. J. (1982). The impact of comparison processes on coactors' task performance. *Journal of Personality and Social Psychology, 42,* 281–291.

Shaffer, D. R., Pegalis, L. J., & Bazzini, D. G. (1996). When boy meets girls (revisited): Gender, gender-role orientation, and prospect of future interaction as determinants of self-disclosure among same- and opposite-sex acquaintants. *Personality and Social Psychology Bulletin, 22,* 495–506.

Shah, A. (2005, June 11). Poverty facts and stats (www.globalissues.org/TradeRelated/Facts.asp#fact1).

Shah, A. K., & Oppenheimer, D. M. (2008). Heuristics made easy: An effort-reduction framework. *Psychological Bulletin, 134,* 207–222.

Sharan, S., & Sharan, Y. (1976). *Small group teaching.* Englewood Cliffs, NJ: Educational Technology.

Sharan, Y., & Sharan, S. (1994). Group investigation in the cooperative classroom. In S. Sharan (Ed.), *Handbook of cooperative learning methods.* Westport, CT: Greenwood.

Shariff, A. F., & Norenzayan, A. (2007). God is watching you: Priming God concepts increases prosocial behavior in an anonymous economic game. *Psychological Science, 18,* 803–809.

Shaver, P. R., & Hazan, C. (1993). Adult romantic attachment: Theory and evidence. In D. Perlman & W. Jones (Eds.), *Advances in personal relationships* (Vol. 4). Greenwich, CT: JAI.

Shaver, P. R., & Hazan, C. (1994). Attachment. In A. L. Weber & J. H. Harvey (Eds.), *Perspectives on close relationships.* Boston: Allyn & Bacon.

Shaver, P., Hazan, C., & Bradshaw, D. (1988). Love as attachment: The integration of three behavioral systems. In R. J. Sternberg & M. L. Barnes (Eds.), *The psychology of love.* New Haven, CT: Yale University Press.

Shaw, J. S., III. (1996). Increases in eyewitness confidence resulting from postevent questioning. *Journal of Experimental Psychology: Applied, 2,* 126–146.

Shaw, M. E. (1981). *Group dynamics: The psychology of small group behavior.* New York: McGraw-Hill.

Sheese, B. E., & Graziano, W. G. (2005). Deciding to defect: The effects of video-game violence on cooperative behavior. *Psychological Science, 16,* 354–357.

Sheldon, K. M., Elliot, A. J., Youngmee, K., & Kasser, T. (2001). What is satisfying about satisfying events? Testing 10 candidate psychological needs. *Journal of Personality and Social Psychology, 80,* 325–339.

Sheldon, K. M., Ryan, R. M., Deci, E. L., & Kasser, T. (2004). The independent effects of goal contents and motives on well-being: It's both what you pursue and why you pursue it. *Personality and Social Psychology Bulletin, 30,* 475–486.

Sheldon, K. M., & Niemiec, C. P. (2006). It's not just the amount that counts: Balanced need satisfaction also affects well-being. *Journal of Personality and Social Psychology, 91,* 331–341.

Shell, R. M., & Eisenberg, N. (1992). A developmental model of recipients' reactions to aid. *Psychological Bulletin, 111,* 413–433.

Shelton, J. N., & Richeson, J. A. (2005). Intergroup contact and pluralistic ignorance. *Journal of Personality and Social Psychology, 88,* 91–107.

Sheppard, B. H., & Vidmar, N. (1980). Adversary pretrial procedures and testimonial evidence: Effects of lawyer's role and machiavelianism.

Journal of Personality and Social Psychology, 39, 320–322.

Shepperd, J. A. (2003). Interpreting comparative risk judgments: Are people personally optimistic or interpersonally pessimistic? Unpublished manuscript, University of Florida.

Shepperd, J. A., & Arkin, R. M. (1991). Behavioral other-enhancement: Strategically obscuring the link between performance and evaluation. *Journal of Personality and Social Psychology, 60,* 79–88.

Shepperd, J. A., Arkin, R. M., & Slaughter, J. (1995). Constraints on excuse making: The deterring effects of shyness and anticipated retest. *Personality and Social Psychology Bulletin, 21,* 1061–1072.

Shepperd, J. A., Grace, J., Cole, L. J., & Klein, C. (2005). Anxiety and outcome predictions. *Personality and Social Psychology Bulletin, 31,* 267–275.

Shepperd, J. A., & Taylor, K. M. (1999). Ascribing advantages to social comparison targets. *Basic and Applied Social Psychology, 21,* 103–117.

Shepperd, J. A., & Wright, R. A. (1989). Individual contributions to a collective effort: An incentive analysis. *Personality and Social Psychology Bulletin, 15,* 141–149.

Shergill, S. S., Bays, P. M., Frith, C. D., & Wolpert, D. M. (2003). Two eyes for an eye: The neuroscience of force escalation. *Science, 301,* 187.

Sherif, M. (1935). A study of some social factors in perception. *Archives of Psychology,* No. 187.

Sherif, M. (1937). An experimental approach to the study of attitudes. *Sociometry, 1,* 90–98.

Sherif, M. (1966). *In common predicament: Social psychology of intergroup conflict and cooperation.* Boston: Houghton Mifflin.

Sherman, D. K., Nelson, L. D., & Ross, L. D. (2003). Naive realism and affirmative action: Adversaries are more similar than they think. *Basic and Applied Social Psychology, 25,* 275–289.

Sherman, J. W. (1996). Development and mental representation of stereotypes. *Journal of Personality and Social Psychology, 70,* 1126–1141.

Sherman, J. W., Kruschke, J. K., Sherman, S. J., Percy, E. J., Petrocelli, J. V., & Conrey, F. R. (2009). Attentional processes in stereotype formation: A common model for category accentuation and illusory correlation. *Journal of Personality and Social Psychology, 96,* 305–323.

Sherman, J. W., Lee, A. Y., Bessenoff, G. R., & Frost, L. A. (1998). Stereotype efficiency reconsidered: Encoding flexibility under cognitive load. *Journal of Personality and Social Psychology, 75,* 589–606.

Sherman, S. J., Cialdini, R. B., Schwartzman, D. F., & Reynolds, K. D. (1985). Imagining can heighten or lower the perceived likelihood of contracting a disease: The mediating effect of ease of imagery. *Personality and Social Psychology Bulletin, 11,* 118–127.

Shermer, M. (2006). Answer on World Question Center 2006. The Edge (www.edge.org).

Shih, M., Pittinsky, T. L., & Ambady, N. (1999). Stereotype susceptibility: Identity salience and shifts in quantitative performance. *Psychological Science, 10,* 80–83.

Shiller, R. (2000). *Irrational exuberance.* Princeton: Princeton University Press.

Shipman, P. (2003). We are all Africans. *American Scientist, 91,* 496–499.

Shook, N. J., & Fazio, R. H. (2008). Interracial roommate relationships: An experimental field test of the contact hypothesis. *Psychological Science, 19,* 717–723.

Short, J. F., Jr. (Ed.) (1969). *Gang delinquency and delinquent subcultures.* New York: Harper & Row.

Shostak, M. (1981). *Nisa: The life and words of a !Kung woman.* Cambridge, MA: Harvard University Press.

Shotland, R. L. (1989). A model of the causes of date rape in developing and close relationships. In C. Hendrick (Ed.), *Review of Personality and Social Psychology* (Vol. 10). Beverly Hills, CA: Sage.

Shotland, R. L., & Stebbins, C. A. (1983). Emergency and cost as determinants of helping behavior and the slow accumulation of social psychological knowledge. *Social Psychology Quarterly, 46,* 36–46.

Shotland, R. L., & Straw, M. K. (1976). Bystander response to an assault: When a man attacks a woman. *Journal of Personality and Social Psychology, 34,* 990–999.

Showers, C., & Ruben, C. (1987). Distinguishing pessimism from depression: Negative expectations and positive coping mechanisms. Paper presented at the American Psychological Association convention.

Shrauger, J. S. (1975). Responses to evaluation as a function of initial self-perceptions. *Psychological Bulletin, 82,* 581–596.

Shrauger, J. S., & Schoeneman, T. J. (1979, May). Symbolic interactionist view of self-concept: Through the looking glass darkly. *Psychological Bulletin, 86,* 549–573.

Shriver, E. R., Young, S. G., Hugenberg, K., Bernstein, M. J., & Lanter, J. R. (2008, February). Class, race, and the face: Social context modulates the cross-race effect in face recognition. *Personality and Social Psychology Bulletin, 34,* 260–274.

Sidanius, J., & Pratto, F. (1999). *Social dominance: An intergroup theory of social hierarchy and oppression.* New York: Cambridge University Press.

Sidanius, J., Pratto, F., & Bobo, L. (1994). Social dominance orientation and the political psychology of gender: A case of invariance? *Journal of Personality and Social Psychology, 67,* 998–1011.

Sidanius, J., Van Laar, C., Levin, S., & Sinclair, S. (2004). Ethnic enclaves and the dynamics of social identity on the college campus: The good, the bad, and the ugly. *Journal of Personality and Social Psychology, 87,* 96–110.

Sigall, H. (1970). Effects of competence and consensual validation on a communicator's liking for the audience. *Journal of Personality and Social Psychology, 16,* 252–258.

Silk, J. B., Alberts, S. C., & Altmann, J. (2003). Social bonds of female baboons enhance infant survival. *Science, 302,* 1231–1234.

Silke, A. (2003). Deindividuation, anonymity, and violence: Findings from Northern Ireland. *Journal of Social Psychology, 143,* 493–499.

Silver, M., & Geller, D. (1978). On the irrelevance of evil: The organization and individual action. *Journal of Social Issues, 34,* 125–136.

Silver, N. (2009, May 9). Bush may haunt Republicans for generations (www.fivethirtyeight.com).

Silvia, P. J. (2005). Deflecting reactance: The role of similarity in increasing compliance and reducing resistance. *Basic and Applied Social Psychology, 27,* 277–284.

Silvia, P. J., & Duval, T. S. (2001). Objective self-awareness theory: Recent progress and enduring problems. *Personality and Social Psychology Review, 5,* 230–241.

Simmons, W. W. (2000, December). When it comes to having children, Americans still prefer boys. *The Gallup Poll Monthly,* pp. 63–64.

Simon, H. A. (1957). *Models of man: Social and rational.* New York: Wiley.

Simon, P. (1996, April 17). American provincials. *Christian Century,* pp. 421–422.

Simonton, D. K. (1994). *Greatness: Who makes history and why.* New York: Guilford.

Simpson, J. A. (1987). The dissolution of romantic relationships: Factors involved in relationship stability and emotional distress. *Journal of Personality and Social Psychology, 53,* 683–692.

Simpson, J. A., Campbell, B., & Berscheid, E. (1986). The association between romantic love and marriage: Kephart (1967) twice revisited *Personality and Social Psychology Bulletin, 12,* 363–372.

Simpson, J. A., Gangestad, S. W., & Lerma, M. (1990). Perception of physical attractiveness: Mechanisms involved in the maintenance of romantic relationships. *Journal of Personality and Social Psychology, 59,* 1192–1201.

Simpson, J. A., Rholes, W. S., & Nelligan, J. S. (1992). Support seeking and support giving within couples in an anxiety-provoking situation: The role of attachment styles. *Journal of Personality and Social Psychology, 62,* 434–446.

Simpson, J. A., Rholes, W. S., & Phillips, D. (1996). Conflict in close relationships: An attachment perspective. *Journal of Personality and Social Psychology, 71,* 899–914.

Sinclair, S., Dunn, E., & Lowery, B. S. (2004). The relationship between parental racial attitudes and children's implicit prejudice. *Journal of Experimental Social Psychology, 41,* 283–289.

Singer, M. (1979). Cults and cult members. Address to the American Psychological Association convention.

Singer, T., Seymour, B., O'Doherty, J. P., Stephan, K. E., Dolan, R. J., & Frith, C. D. (2006). Empathic neural responses are modulated by the perceived fairness of others. *Nature, 439,* 466–469.

Singh, D. (1993). Adaptive significance of female physical attractiveness: Role of waist-to-hip ratio. *Journal of Personality and Social Psychology, 65,* 293–307.

Singh, D. (1995). Female judgment of male attractiveness and desirability for relationships: Role of waist-to-hip ratio and financial status. *Journal of Personality and Social Psychology, 69,* 1089–1101.

Singh, D., & Randall, P. K. (2007). Beauty is in the eye of the plastic surgeon: Waist-hip ratio (WHR) and women's attractiveness. *Personality and Individual Differences, 43,* 329–340.

Singh, R., & Ho, S. J. (2000). Attitudes and attraction: A new test of the attraction, repulsion and similarity-dissimilarity asymmetry hypotheses. *British Journal of Social Psychology, 39,* 197–211.

Singh, R., & Teoh, J. B. P. (1999). Attitudes and attraction: A test of two hypotheses for the similarity-dissimilarity asymmetry. *British Journal of Social Psychology, 38,* 427–443.

Sissons, M. (1981). Race, sex, and helping behavior. *British Journal of Social Psychology, 20,* 285–292.

Sittser, G. L. (1994, April). Long night's journey into light. *Second Opinion,* pp. 10–15.

Sivarajasingam, V., Moore, S., & Shepherd, J. P. (2005). Winning, losing, and violence. *Injury Prevention, 11,* 69–70.

Six, B., & Eckes, T. (1996). Metaanalysen in der Einstellungs-Verhaltens-Forschung. *Zeitschrift fur Sozialpsychologie,* pp. 7–17.

Skaalvik, E. M., & Hagtvet, K. A. (1990). Academic achievement and self-concept: An analysis of causal predominance in a developmental perpsective. *Journal of Personality and Social Psychology, 58,* 292–307.

Skinner, B. F. (1971). *Beyond freedom and dignity.* New York: Knopf.

Skitka, L. J. (1999). Ideological and attributional boundaries on public compassion: Reactions to individuals and communities affected by a natural disaster. *Personality and Social Psychology Bulletin, 25,* 793–808.

Skitka, L. J., Bauman, C. W., & Mullen, E. (2004). Political tolerance and coming to psychological closure following the September 11, 2001, terrorist attacks: An integrative approach. *Personality and Social Psychology Bulletin, 30,* 743–756.

Skitka, L. J., & Tetlock, P. E. (1993). Providing public assistance: Cognitive and motivational processes underlying liberal and conservative policy preferences. *Journal of Personality and Social Psychology, 65,* 1205–1223.

Skurnik, I., Yoon, C., Park, D. C., & Schwarz, N. (2005). How warnings about false claims become recommendations. *Journal of Consumer Research, 31,* 713–724.

Slatcher, R. B., & Pennebaker, J. W. (2006). How do I love thee? Let me count the words: The social effects of expressive writing. *Psychological Science, 17,* 660–664.

Slater, M., Antley, A., Davison, A., Swapp, D., Guger, C., Barker, C., Pistrang, N., & Sanchez-Vives, M. V. (2006). A virtual reprise of the Stanley Milgram obedience experiments. *PloS One,* 1(1): e39 (DOI:10.1371/journal. pone.0000039).

Slavin, R. E. (1985). Cooperative learning: Applying contact theory in desegregated schools. *Journal of Social Issues,* 41(3), 45–62.

Slavin, R. E. (1990, December/ January). Research on cooperative learning: Consensus and controversy. *Educational Leadership,* pp. 52–54.

Slavin, R. E., & Cooper, R. (1999). Improving intergroup relations: Lessons learned from cooperative learning programs. *Journal of Social Issues, 55,* 647–663.

Slavin, R. E., Hurley, E. A., & Chamberlain, A. (2003). Cooperative learning and achievement: Theory and research. In W. M. Reynolds & G. E. Miller (Eds.), *Handbook of psychology: Educational psychology* (Vol. 7). New York: Wiley.

Slavin, R. E., & Madden, N. A. (1979). School practices that improve race relations. *Journal of Social Issues, 16,* 169–180.

Slotow, R., Van Dyke, G., Poole, J., Page, B., & Klocke, A. (2000). Older bull elephants control young males. *Nature, 408,* 425–426.

Slotter, E. B., & Gardner, W. L. (2009). Where do you end and I begin? Evidence for anticipatory, motivated self-other integration between relationship partners. *Journal of Personality and Social Psychology, 96,* 1137–1151.

Slovic, P. (1972). From Shakespeare to Simon: Speculations—and some evidence—about man's ability to process information. *Oregon Research Institute Research Bulletin,* 12(2).

Slovic, P. (2007). "If I look at the mass I will never act": Psychic numbing and genocide. *Judgment and Decision Making, 2,* 79–95.

Slovic, P., & Fischhoff, B. (1977). On the psychology of experimental surprises. *Journal of Experimental Psychology: Human Perception and Performance, 3,* 455–551.

Small, M. F. (1999, March 30). Are we losers? Putting a mating theory to the test. *New York Times* (www.nytimes. com).

Smedley, J. W., & Bayton, J. A. (1978). Evaluative race-class stereotypes by race and perceived class of subjects. *Journal of Personality and Social Psychology, 3,* 530–535.

Smelser, N. J., & Mitchell, F. (Eds.) (2002). *Terrorism: Perspectives from the behavioral and social sciences.* Washington, DC: National Research Council, National Academies Press.

Smith, A. (1976). *The wealth of nations.* Book 1. Chicago: University of Chicago Press. (Originally published, 1776.)

Smith, D. E., Gier, J. A., & Willis, F. N. (1982). Interpersonal touch and compliance with a marketing request. *Basic and Applied Social Psychology, 3,* 35–38.

Smith, H. (1976) *The Russians.* New York: Balantine Books. Cited by B. Latané, K. Williams, and S. Harkins in "Many hands make light the work." *Journal of Personality and Social Psychology,* 1979, *37,* 822–832.

Smith, H. J., & Tyler, T. R. (1997). Choosing the right pond: The impact of group membership on self-esteem and group-oriented behavior. *Journal of Experimental Social Psychology, 33,* 146–170.

Smith, H. W. (1981). Territorial spacing on a beach revisited: A cross-national exploration. *Social Psychology Quarterly, 44,* 132–137.

Smith, M. B. (1978). Psychology and values. *Journal of Social Issues, 34,* 181–199.

Smith, P. B. (2005). Is there an indigenous European social psychology? *International Journal of Psychology*, **40**, 254–262.

Smith, P. B., & Tayeb, M. (1989). Organizational structure and processes. In M. Bond (Ed.), *The cross-cultural challenge to social psychology.* Newbury Park, CA: Sage.

Smith, R. H., Turner, T. J., Garonzik, R., Leach, C. W., Urch-Druskat, V., & Weston, C. M. (1996). Envy and Schadenfreude. *Personality and Social Psychology Bulletin*, **22**, 158–168.

Smith, T. W. (1998, December). *American sexual behavior: Trends, sociodemographic differences, and risk behavior.* National Opinion Research Center GSS Topical Report No. 25.

Smith, V. L. (1991). Prototypes in the courtroom: Lay representations of legal concepts. *Journal of Personality and Social Psychology*, **61**, 857–872.

Smith, V. L., & Ellsworth, P. C. (1987). The social psychology of eyewitness accuracy: Misleading questions and communicator expertise. *Journal of Applied Psychology*, **72**, 294–300.

Smolowe, J. (1994, August 1). Race and the O. J. case. *Time*, pp. 24–25.

Smoreda, Z., & Licoppe, C. (2000). Gender-specific use of the domestic telephone. *Social Psychology Quarterly*, **63**, 238–252.

Snodgrass, M. A. (1987). The relationships of differential loneliness, intimacy, and characterological attributional style to duration of loneliness. *Journal of Social Behavior and Personality*, **2**, 173–186.

Snopes. (2008, accessed July 30). The naked truth (www.snopes.com/humor/iftrue/pollster.asp).

Snyder, C. R. (1978). The "illusion" of uniqueness. *Journal of Humanistic Psychology*, **18**, 33–41.

Snyder, C. R. (1980). The uniqueness mystique. *Psychology Today*, March, pp. 86–90.

Snyder, C. R., & Fromkin, H. L. (1980). *Uniqueness: The human pursuit of difference.* New York: Plenum.

Snyder, C. R., & Higgins, R. L. (1988). Excuses: Their effective role in the negotiation of reality. *Psychological Bulletin*, **104**, 23–35.

Snyder, C. R., & Smith, T. W. (1986). On being "shy like a fox": A self-handicapping analysis. In W. H. Jones et al. (Eds.), *Shyness: Perspectives on research and treatment.* New York: Plenum.

Snyder, M. (1981). Seek, and ye shall find: Testing hypotheses about other people. In E. T. Higgins, C. P. Herman, & M. P. Zanna (Eds.), *Social cognition: The Ontario symposium on personality and social psychology.* Hillsdale, NJ: Erlbaum.

Snyder, M. (1984). When belief creates reality. In L. Berkowitz (Ed.), *Advances in Experimental Social Psychology* (Vol. 18). New York: Academic Press.

Snyder, M. (1987). *Public appearances/private realities: The psychology of self-monitoring.* New York: Freeman.

Snyder, M. (1988). Experiencing prejudice firsthand: The "discrimination day" experiments. *Contemporary Psychology*, **33**, 664–665.

Snyder, M., Campbell, B., & Preston, E. (1982). Testing hypotheses about human nature: Assessing the accuracy of social stereotypes. *Social Cognition*, **1**, 256–272.

Snyder, M., Grether, J., & Keller, K. (1974). Staring and compliance: A field experiment on hitch-hiking. *Journal of Applied Social Psychology*, **4**, 165–170.

Snyder, M., & Haugen, J. A. (1994). Why does behavioral confirmation occur? A functional perspective on the role of the perceiver. *Journal of Experimental Social Psychology*, **30**, 218–246.

Snyder, M., & Haugen, J. A. (1995). Why does behavioral confirmation occur? A functional perspective on the role of the target. *Personality and Social Psychology Bulletin*, **21**, 963–974.

Snyder, M., & Ickes, W. (1985). Personality and social behavior. In G. Lindzey & E. Aronson (Eds.), *Handbook of social psychology*, 3rd edition. New York: Random House.

Snyder, M., & Swann, W. B., Jr. (1976). When actions reflect attitudes: The politics of impression management. *Journal of Personality and Social Psychology*, **34**, 1034–1042.

Snyder, M., Tanke, E. D., & Berscheid, E. (1977). Social perception and interpersonal behavior: On the self-fulfilling nature of social stereotypes. *Journal of Personality and Social Psychology*, **35**, 656–666.

Solano, C. H., Batten, P. G., & Parish, E. A. (1982). Loneliness and patterns of self-disclosure. *Journal of Personality and Social Psychology*, **43**, 524–531.

Solberg, E. C., Diener, E., & Robinson, M. D. (2003). Why are materialists less satisfied? In T. Kasser & A. D. Kanner (Eds.), *Psychology and consumer culture: The struggle for a good life in a materialistic world.* Washington, DC: APA Books.

Solberg, E. C., Diener, E., Wirtz, D., Lucas, R. E., & Oishi, S. (2002). Wanting, having, and satisfaction: Examining the role of desire discrepancies in satisfaction with income. *Journal of Personality and Social Psychology*, **83**, 725–734.

Solomon, H., & Solomon, L. Z. (1978). Effects of anonymity on helping in emergency situations. Paper presented at the Eastern Psychological Association convention.

Solomon, H., Solomon, L. Z., Arnone, M. M., Maur, B. J., Reda, R. M., & Rother, E. O. (1981). Anonymity and helping. *Journal of Social Psychology*, **113**, 37–43.

Solomon, S., Greenberg, J., & Pyszczynski, T. (2000). Pride and prejudice: Fear of death and social behavior. *Current Directions in Psychological Science*, **9**, 200–203.

Sommer, R. (1969). *Personal space.* Englewood Cliffs, NJ: Prentice-Hall.

Sommers, S. R., & Ellsworth, P. C. (2000). Race in the courtroom: Perceptions of guilt and dispositional attributions. *Personality and Social Psychology Bulletin*, **26**, 1367–1379.

Sommers, S. R., & Ellsworth, P. C. (2001). White juror bias: An investigation of prejudice against Black defendants in the American courtroom. *Psychology, Public Policy, and Law*, **7**, 201–229.

Sonne, J., & Janoff, D. (1979). The effect of treatment attributions on the maintenance of weight reduction: A replication and extension. *Cognitive Therapy and Research*, **3**, 389–397.

Sparrell, J. A., & Shrauger, J. S. (1984). Self-confidence and optimism in self-prediction. Paper presented at the American Psychological Association convention.

Spector, P. E. (1986). Perceived control by employees: A meta-analysis of studies concerning autonomy and participation at work. *Human Relations*, **39**, 1005–1016.

Speer, A. (1971). *Inside the Third Reich: Memoirs.* (P. Winston & C. Winston, trans.). New York: Avon Books.

Spence, A., & Townsend, E. (2007). Predicting behaviour towards genetically modified food using implicit and explicit attitudes. *British Journal of Social Psychology*, **46**, 437–457.

Spence, C. (2006). Mismatching money and need. *Stanford Social Innovation Review*, **4**, 49.

Spencer, S. J., Fein, S., Wolfe, C. T., Fong, C., & Dunn, M. A. (1998). Automatic activation of stereotypes: The role of self-image threat. *Personality and Social Psychology Bulletin*, **24**, 1139–1152.

Spencer, S. J., Steele, C. M., & Quinn, D. M. (1999). Stereotype threat and women's math performance. *Journal of Experimental Social Psychology*, **3**, 4–28.

Speth, J. G. (2008). Foreword. In A. A. Leiserowitz & L. O. Fernandez, *Toward a new consciousness: Values to sustain human and natural communities.* New Haven: Yale School of Forestry & Environmental Studies.

Spiegel, H. W. (1971). *The growth of economic thought.* Durham, NC: Duke University Press.

Spitz, H. H. (1999). Beleaguered *Pygmalion:* A history of the controversy over claims that teacher expectancy raises intelligence. *Intelligence, 27,* 199–234.

Spitzberg, B. H., & Hurt, H. T. (1987). The relationship of interpersonal competence and skills to reported loneliness across time. *Journal of Social Behavior and Personality, 2,* 157–172.

Spivak, J. (1979, June 6). *Wall Street Journal.*

Sporer, S. L. (2008). Lessons from the origins of eyewitness testimony research in Europe. *Applied Cognitive Psychology, 22,* 737–757.

Sporer, S. L., Trinkl, B., & Guberova, E. (2007). Matching faces. Differences in processing speed of out-group faces by different ethnic groups. *Journal of Cross-Cultural Psychology, 38,* 398–412.

Sprecher, S. (1987). The effects of self-disclosure given and received on affection for an intimate partner and stability of the relationship. *Journal of Personality and Social Psychology, 4,* 115–127.

Sprecher, S., Aron, A., Hatfield, E., Cortese, A., Potapova, E., & Levitskaya, A. (1994). Love: American style, Russian style, and Japanese style. *Personal Relationships, 1,* 349–369.

Sprecher, S., Sullivan, Q., & Hatfield, E. (1994). Mate selection preferences: Gender differences examined in a national sample. *Journal of Personality and Social Psychology, 66,* 1074–1080.

Sprecher, S., & Toro-Morn, M. (2002). A study of men and women from different sides of Earth to determine if men are from Mars and women are from Venus in their beliefs about love and romantic relationships. *Sex Roles, 46,* 131–147.

Srivastava, S., McGonigal, K. M., Richards, J. M., Butler, E. A., & Gross, J. J. (2006). Optimism in close relationships: How seeing things in a positive light makes them so. *Journal of Personality and Social Psychology, 91,* 143–153.

Stajkovic, A., & Luthans, F. (1998). Self-efficacy and work-related performance: A meta-analysis. *Psychological Bulletin, 124,* 240–261.

Stalder, D. R. (2008). Revisiting the issue of safety in numbers: The likelihood of receiving help from a group. *Social Influence, 3,* 24–33.

Stambor, Z. (2006, April). How reliable is eyewitness testimony? *APA Monitor,* pp. 26–27.

Stangor, C., Jonas, K., Stroebe, W., & Hewstone, M. (1996). Influence of student exchange on national stereotypes, attitudes and perceived group variability. *European Journal of Social Psychology, 26,* 663–675.

Stangor, C., Lynch, L., Duan, C., & Glass, B. (1992). Categorization of individuals on the basis of multiple social features. *Journal of Personality and Social Psychology, 62,* 207–218.

Stangor, C., & McMillan, D. (1992). Memory for expectancy-congruent and expectancy-incongruent information: A review of the social and social developmental literatures. *Psychological Bulletin, 111,* 42–61.

Stanley, D., Phelps, E., & Banaji, M. (2008). The neural basis of implicit attitudes. *Current Directions in Psychological Science, 17,* 164–170.

Stanovich, K. E., & West, R. F. (2008). On the relative independence of thinking biases and cognitive ability. *Journal of Personality and Social Psychology, 94,* 672–695.

Stapel, D. A., & Suls, J. (2004). Method matters: Effects of explicit versus implicit social comparisons on activation, behavior, and self-views. *Journal of Personality and Social Psychology, 87,* 860–875.

Staples, B. (1999a, May 2). When the "paranoids" turn out to be right. *New York Times* (www.nytimes.com).

Staples, B. (1999b, May 24). Why "racial profiling" will be tough to fight. *New York Times* (www.nytimes.com).

Staples, B. (2000, June 26). Playing "catch and grope" in the schoolyard. *New York Times* (www.nytimes.com).

Stark, E., Kim, A., Miller, C., & Borgida, E. (2008). Effects of including a graphic warning label in advertisements for reduced-exposure products: Implications for persuasion and policy. *Journal of Applied Social Psychology, 38,* 281–293.

Stark, R., & Bainbridge, W. S. (1980). Networks of faith: Interpersonal bonds and recruitment of cults and sects. *American Journal of Sociology, 85,* 1376–1395.

Stasser, G. (1991). Pooling of unshared information during group discussion. In S. Worchel, W. Wood, & J. Simpson (Eds.), *Group process and productivity.* Beverly Hills, CA: Sage.

Stasser, G., Kerr, N. L., & Bray, R. M. (1981). The social psychology of jury deliberations: Structure, process, and product. In N. L. Kerr & R. M. Bray (Eds.), *The psychology of the courtroom.* New York: Academic Press.

Statistics Canada. (2008). *Victims and persons accused of homicide, by age and sex.* (Table 253-003).

Staub, E. (1978). *Positive social behavior and morality: Social and personal influences* (Vol. 1). Hillsdale, NJ: Erlbaum.

Staub, E. (1989). *The roots of evil: The origins of genocide and other group violence.* Cambridge: Cambridge University Press.

Staub, E. (1991). Altruistic and moral motivations for helping and their translation into action. *Psychological Inquiry, 2,* 150–153.

Staub, E. (1992). The origins of caring, helping and nonaggression: Parental socialization, the family system, schools, and cultural influence. In S. Oliner & P. Oliner (Eds.), *Embracing the other: Philosophical, psychological, and theological perspectives on altruism.* New York: New York University Press.

Staub, E. (1996). Altruism and aggression in children and youth: Origins and cures. In R. Feldman (Ed.), *The psychology of adversity.* Amherst, MA: University of Massachusetts Press.

Staub, E. (1997a). Blind versus constructive patriotism: Moving from embeddedness in the group to critical loyalty and action. In D. Bar-Tal and E. Staub (Eds.), *Patriotism in the lives of individuals and nations.* Chicago: Nelson-Hall.

Staub, E. (1997b). *Halting and preventing collective violence: The role of bystanders.* Background paper for symposium organized by the Friends of Raoul Wallenberg, Stockholm, June 13–16.

Staub, E. (1999a). Behind the scenes. In D. G. Myers, *Social psychology,* 6th edition. New York: McGraw-Hill.

Staub, E. (1999b). The origins and prevention of genocide, mass killing, and other collective violence. *Peace and Conflict, 5,* 303–336.

Staub, E. (2003). *The psychology of good and evil: Why children, adults, and groups help and harm others.* New York: Cambridge University Press.

Staub, E. (2005a). The origins and evolution of hate, with notes on prevention. In R. J. Sternberg (Ed.), *The psychology of hate.* Washington, DC: American Psychological Association.

Staub, E. (2005b). The roots of goodness: The fulfillment of basic human needs and the development of caring, helping and nonaggression, inclusive caring, moral courage, active bystandership, and altruism born of suffering. In G. Carlo & C. P. Edwards (Eds.), *Moral motivation through the life span: Theory, research, applications. Nebraska Symposium on Motivation* (Vol. 51). Lincoln, NE: University of Nebraska Press.

Staub, E., & Bar-Tal, D. (2003). Genocide, mass killing, and intractable conflict. In D. Sears, L. Huddy, & R. Jervis (Eds.), *Handbook of political psychology.* New York: Oxford University Press.

Staub, E., & Pearlman, L. A. (2005a). Advancing healing and reconciliation. In L. Barbanel & R. Sternberg (Eds), *Psychological interventions in times of crisis* (pp. 213–243). New York: Springer.

Staub, E., & Pearlman, L. A. (2005b). Psychological recovery and reconciliation after the genocide in Rwanda and in other post-conflict settings. In R. Sternberg & L. Barbanel (Eds.), *Psychological interventions in times of crisis*. New York: Springer.

Staub, E., & Pearlman, L. A. (2009). Reducing intergroup prejudice and conflict: A commentary. *Journal of Personality and Social Psychology, 96,* 588–593.

Staub, E., Pearlman, L. A., Gubin, A., & Hagengimana, A. (2005). Healing, reconciliation, forgiving and the prevention of violence after genocide or mass killing: An intervention and its experimental evaluation in Rwanda. *Journal of Social and Clinical Psychology, 24,* 297–334.

Steblay, N. M. (1987). Helping behavior in rural and urban environments: A meta-analysis. *Psychological Bulletin, 102,* 346–356.

Steblay, N. M., Besirevic, J., Fulero, S. M., & Jimenez-Lorente, B. (1999). The effects of pretrial publicity on juror verdicts: A meta-analytic review. *Law and Human Behavior, 23,* 219–235.

Steblay, N., Dysart, J. E., Fulero, S., & Lindsay, R. C. L. (2001). Eyewitness accuracy rates in sequential and simultaneous lineup presentations: A meta-analytic comparison. *Law and Human Behavior, 25,* 459–473.

Steele, C. M. (1988). The psychology of self-affirmation: Sustaining the integrity of the self. In L. Berkowitz (Ed.), *Advances in experimental social psychology* (Vol. 21). Orlando, FL: Academic Press.

Steele, C. M. (1997). A threat in the air: How stereotypes shape intellectual identity and performance. *American Psychologist, 52,* 613–629.

Steele, C. M., & Aronson, J. (1995). Stereotype threat and the intellectual test performance of African Americans. *Journal of Personality and Social Psychology, 69,* 797–811.

Steele, C. M., Southwick, L. L., & Critchlow, B. (1981). Dissonance and alcohol: Drinking your troubles away. *Journal of Personality and Social Psychology, 41,* 831–846.

Steele, C. M., Spencer, S. J., & Aronson, J. (2002). Contending with group image: The psychology of stereotype and social identity threat. In Zanna, M. P. (Ed.), *Advances in experimental social psychology, 34,* 379–440. San Diego: Academic Press.

Steele, C. M., Spencer, S. J., & Lynch, M. (1993). Self-image resilience and dissonance: The role of affirmational resources. *Journal of Personality and Social Psychology, 64,* 885–896.

Steffen, P. R., & Masters, K. S. (2005). Does compassion mediate the intrinsic religion-health relationship? *Annals of Behavioral Medicine, 30,* 217–224.

Stein, A. H., & Friedrich, L. K. (1972). Television content and young children's behavior. In J. P. Murray, E. A. Rubinstein, & G. A. Comstock (Eds.), *Television and social learning.* Washington, DC: Government Printing Office.

Stein, D. D., Hardyck, J. A., & Smith, M. B. (1965). Race and belief: An open and shut case. *Journal of Personality and Social Psychology, 1,* 281–289.

Steinem, G. (1988). Six great ideas that television is missing. In S. Oskamp. (Ed.), *Television as a social issue: Applied Social Psychology Annual* (Vol. 8). Newbury Park, CA: Sage.

Steinhauer, J., & Holson, L. M. (2008, September 20). Text messages fly, danger lurks. *New York Times* (www.nytimes.com).

Stelter, B. (2008, November 25). Web suicide viewed live and reaction spur a debate. *New York Times* (www.nytimes.com).

Stelzl, M., Janes, L., & Seligman, C. (2008). Champ or chump: Strategic utilization of dual social identities of others. *European Journal of Social Psychology, 38,* 128–138.

Stelzl, M., & Seligman, C. (2004). The social identity strategy of MOATING: Further evidence. Paper presented at the Society of Personality and Social Psychology convention.

Stephan, C. W., & Stephan, W. G. (1986). Habla Ingles? The effects of language translation on simulated juror decisions. *Journal of Applied Social Psychology, 16,* 577–589.

Stephan, W. G. (1986). The effects of school desegregation: An evaluation 30 years after *Brown.* In R. Kidd, L. Saxe, & M. Saks (Eds.), *Advances in applied social psychology.* New York: Erlbaum.

Stephan, W. G. (1987). The contact hypothesis in intergroup relations. In C. Hendrick (Ed.), *Group processes and intergroup relations.* Newbury Park, CA: Sage.

Stephan, W. G. (1988). School desegregation: Short-term and long-term effects. Paper presented at the national conference "Opening Doors: An Appraisal of Race Relations in America," University of Alabama.

Stephan, W. G., Berscheid, E., & Walster, E. (1971). Sexual arousal and heterosexual perception. *Journal of Personality and Social Psychology, 20,* 93–101.

Stephens, N. M., Markus, H. R., & Townsend, S. S. M. (2007). Choice as an act of meaning: The case of social class. *Journal of Personality and Social Psychology, 93,* 814–830.

Sternberg, R. J. (1988). Triangulating love. In R. J. Sternberg & M. L. Barnes (Eds.), *The psychology of love.* New Haven, CT: Yale University Press.

Sternberg, R. J. (1998). *Cupid's arrow: The course of love through time.* New York: Cambridge University Press.

Sternberg, R. J. (2003). A duplex theory of hate and its development and its application to terrorism, massacres, and genocide. *Review of General Psychology, 7,* 299–328.

Sternberg, R. J., & Grajek, S. (1984). The nature of love. *Journal of Personality and Social Psychology, 47,* 312–329.

Stewart-Williams, S. (2007). Altruism among kin vs. nonkin: Effects of cost of help and reciprocal exchange. *Evolution and Human Behavior, 28,* 193–198.

Stillinger, C., Epelbaum, M., Keltner, D., & Ross, L. (1991). The "reactive devaluation" barrier to conflict resolution. Unpublished manuscript, Stanford University.

Stinson, V., Devenport, J. L., Cutler, B. L., & Kravitz, D. A. (1996). How effective is the presence-of-counsel safeguard? Attorney perceptions of suggestiveness, fairness, and correctability of biased lineup procedures. *Journal of Applied Psychology, 81,* 64–75.

Stinson, V., Devenport, J. L., Cutler, B. L., & Kravitz, D. A. (1997). How effective is the motion-to-suppress safeguard? Judges' perceptions of the suggestiveness and fairness of biased lineup procedures. *Journal of Personality and Social Psychology, 82,* 211–220.

Stix, G. (2008, March). When markets beat the polls. *Scientific American Mind,* pp. 38–45.

Stockdale, J. E. (1978). Crowding: Determinants and effects. In L. Berkowitz (Ed.), *Advances in experimental social psychology* (Vol. 11). New York: Academic Press.

Stokes, J., & Levin, I. (1986). Gender differences in predicting loneliness from social network characteristics. *Journal of Personality and Social Psychology, 51,* 1069–1074.

Stone, A. A., Hedges, S. M., Neale, J. M., & Satin, M. S. (1985). Prospective and cross-sectional mood reports offer no evidence of a "blue Monday" phenomenon. *Journal of Personality and Social Psychology, 49,* 129–134.

Stone, A. L., & Glass, C. R. (1986). Cognitive distortion of social feedback in depression. *Journal of Social and Clinical Psychology, 4,* 179–188.

Stone, J. (2000, November 6). Quoted by Sharon Begley, The stereotype trap. *Newsweek.*

Stone, J., Lynch, C. I., Sjomeling, M., & Darley, J. M. (1999). Stereotype threat effects on Black and White athletic performance. *Journal of Personality and Social Psychology, 77,* 1213–1227.

Stone, L. (1977). *The family, sex and marriage in England, 1500–1800.* New York: Harper & Row.

Stoner, J. A. F. (1961). A comparison of individual and group decisions involving risk. Unpublished master's thesis, Massachusetts Institute of Technology, 1961. Cited by D. G. Marquis in Individual responsibility and group decisions involving risk, *Industrial Management Review, 3,* 8–23.

Storms, M. D. (1973). Videotape and the attribution process: Reversing actors' and observers' points of view. *Journal of Personality and Social Psychology, 27,* 165–175.

Storms, M. D., & Thomas, G. C. (1977). Reactions to physical closeness. *Journal of Personality and Social Psychology, 35,* 412–418.

Stouffer, S. A., Suchman, E. A., DeVinney, L. C., Star, S. A., & Williams, R. M., Jr. (1949). *The American soldier: Adjustment during army life* (Vol. 1.). Princeton, NJ: Princeton University Press.

Strack, F., & Deutsch, R. (2004). Reflective and impulsive determinants of social behavior. *Personality and Social Psychology Review, 8*(3), 220–247.

Strack, F., Martin, L. & Stepper, S. (1988). Inhibiting and facilitating conditions of the human smile: A nonobtrusive test of the facial feedback hypothesis. *Journal of Personality and Social Psychology, 54,* 768–777.

Strack, S., & Coyne, J. C. (1983). Social confirmation of dysphoria: Shared and private reactions to depression. *Journal of Personality and Social Psychology, 44,* 798–806.

Straus, M. A., & Gelles, R. J. (1980). *Behind closed doors: Violence in the American family.* New York: Anchor/Doubleday.

Streeter, S. A., & McBurney, D. H. (2003). Waist–hip ratio and attractiveness: New evidence and a critique of "a critical test." *Evolution and Human Behavior, 24,* 88–98.

Stroebe, W., & Diehl, M. (1994). Productivity loss in idea-generating groups. In W. Stroebe & M. Hewstone (Eds.), *European review of social psychology* (Vol. 5). Chichester: Wiley.

Stroebe, W., Insko, C. A., Thompson, V. D., & Layton, B. D. (1971). Effects of physical attractiveness, attitude similarity, and sex on various aspects of interpersonal attraction. *Journal of Personality and Social Psychology, 18,* 79–91.

Stroebe, W., Lenkert, A., & Jonas, K. (1988). Familiarity may breed contempt: The impact of student exchange on national stereotypes and attitudes. In W. Stroebe & A. W. Kruglanski (Eds.), *The social psychology of intergroup conflict.* New York: Springer.

Stroebe, W., Stroebe, M., Abakoumkin, G., & Schut, H. (1996). The role of loneliness and social support in adjustment to loss: A test of attachment versus stress theory.

Journal of Personality and Social Psychology, 70, 1241–1249.

Stroessner, S. J., Hamilton, D. L., & Lepore, L. (1990). Intergroup categorization and intragroup differentiation: Ingroup-outgroup differences. Paper presented at the American Psychological Association convention.

Stroessner, S. J., & Mackie, D. M. (1993). Affect and perceived group variability: Implications for stereotyping and prejudice. In D. M. Mackie & D. L. Hamilton (Eds.), *Affect, cognition, and stereotyping: Interactive processes in group perception.* San Diego: Academic Press.

Strong, S. R. (1968). Counseling: An interpersonal influence process. *Journal of Counseling Psychology, 17,* 81–87.

Strong, S. R. (1978). Social psychological approach to psychotherapy research. In S. L. Garfield & A. E. Bergin (Eds.), *Handbook of psychotherapy and behavior change,* 2nd edition. New York: Wiley.

Strong, S. R. (1991). Social influence and change in therapeutic relationships. In C. R. Snyder & D. R. Forsyth (Eds.), *Handbook of social and clinical psychology.* New York: Pergamon.

Strong, S. R., Welsh, J. A., Corcoran, J. L., & Hoyt, W. T. (1992). Social psychology and counseling psychology: The history, products, and promise of an interface. *Journal of Personality and Social Psychology, 39,* 139–157.

Stroufe, B., Chaikin, A., Cook, R., & Freeman, V. (1977). The effects of physical attractiveness on honesty: A socially desirable response. *Personality and Social Psychology, 3,* 59–62.

Stukas, A. A., Snyder, M., & Clary, E. G. (1999). The effects of "mandatory volunteerism" on intentions to volunteer. *Psychological Science, 10,* 59–64.

Sue, S., Smith, R. E., & Caldwell, C. (1973). Effects of inadmissible evidence on the decisions of simulated jurors: A moral dilemma. *Journal of Applied Social Psychology, 3,* 345–353.

Suedfeld, P. (2000). Reverberations of the Holocaust fifty years later: Psychology's contributions to understanding persecution and genocide. *Canadian Psychology, 41,* 1–9.

Sullivan, A. (1999, September 26). What's so bad about hate? *New York Times Magazine* (www.nytimes.com).

Suls, J., & Tesch, F. (1978). Students' preferences for information about their test performance: A social comparison study, *Journal of Applied Social Psychology, 8,* 189–197.

Suls, J., Wan, C. K., & Sanders, G. S. (1988). False consensus and false uniqueness in estimating the prevalence of health-protective

behaviors. *Journal of Applied Social Psychology, 18,* 66–79.

Summers, G., & Feldman, N. S. (1984). Blaming the victim versus blaming the perpetrator: An attributional analysis of spouse abuse. *Journal of Social and Clinical Psychology, 2,* 339–347.

Sun, C., Bridges, A., Wosnitzer, R., Scharrer, E., & Liberman, R. (2008). A comparison of male and female directors in popular pornography: What happens when women are at the helm? *Psychology of Women Quarterly, 32,* 312–325.

Sundstrom, E., De Meuse, K. P., & Futrell, D. (1990). Work teams: Applications and effectiveness. *American Psychologist, 45,* 120–133.

Sunstein, C. R. (2001). *Republic.com.* Princeton: Princeton University Press.

Sunstein, C. R. (2007a). Group polarization and 12 angry men. *Negotiation Journal, 23,* 443–447.

Sunstein, C. R. (2007b). On the divergent American reactions to terrorism and climate change. *Columbia Law Review, 107,* 503–557.

Sunstein, C. R., & Hastie, R. (2008). *Four failures of deliberating groups.* Economics Working Paper Series, University of Chicago Law School (www.law.uchicago.edu).

Sunstein, C. R., Schkade, D., & Ellman, L. M. (2004). Ideological voting on federal courts of appeals: A preliminary investigation. *Virginia Law Review, 90,* 301–354.

Surgery.org. (2008). Cosmetic procedures in 2007. American Society for Aesthetic Plastic Surgery (www.surgery.org).

Surowiecki, J. (2004). *The wisdom of crowds.* New York: Doubleday.

Sussman, N. M. (2000). The dynamic nature of cultural identity throughout cultural transitions: Why home is not so sweet. *Personality and Social Psychology Review, 4,* 355–373.

Svenson, O. (1981). Are we all less risky and more skillful than our fellow drivers? *Acta Psychologica, 47,* 143–148.

Swami, V., Chan, F., Wong, V., Furnham, A., & Tovée, M. J. (2008). Weight-based discrimination in occupational hiring and helping behavior. *Journal of Applied Social Psychology, 38,* 968–981.

Swann, W. B., Jr. (1984). Quest for accuracy in person perception: A matter of pragmatics. *Psychological Review, 91,* 457–475.

Swann, W. B., Jr. (1996). *Self-traps: The elusive quest for higher self-esteem.* New York: Freeman.

Swann, W. B., Jr. (1997). The trouble with change: Self-verification and allegiance to the self. *Psychological Science, 8,* 177–180.

Swann, W. B., Jr., Chang-Schneider, C., & Angulo, S. (2007). Self-verification in relationships as an adaptive process. In J. Wood, A. Tesser, & J. Holmes (Eds.) *Self and relationships.* New York: Psychology Press.

Swann, W. B., Jr., & Gill, M. J. (1997). Confidence and accuracy in person perception: Do we know what we think we know about our relationship partners? *Journal of Personality and Social Psychology, 73,* 747–757.

Swann, W. B., Jr., Gómez, Á., Seyle, D. C., Morales, J. F., & Huici, C. (2009). Identity fusion: The interplay of personal and social identities in extreme group behavior. *Journal of Personality and Social Psychology, 96,* 995–1011.

Swann, W. B., Jr., & Pelham, B. (2002, July–September). Who wants out when the going gets good? Psychological investment and preference for self-verifying college roommates. *Self and Identity, 1,* 219–233.

Swann, W. B., Jr., & Predmore, S. C. (1985). Intimates as agents of social support: Sources of consolation or despair? *Journal of Personality and Social Psychology, 49,* 1609–1617.

Swann, W. B., Jr., & Read, S. J. (1981). Acquiring self-knowledge: The search for feedback that fits. *Journal of Personality and Social Psychology, 41,* 1119–1128.

Swann, W. B., Jr., Rentfrow, P. J., & Gosling, S. D. (2003). The precarious couple effect: Verbally inhibited men + critical, disinhibited women = bad chemistry. *Journal of Personality and Social Psychology, 85,* 1095–1106.

Swann, W. B., Jr., Sellers, J. G., & McClarty, K. L. (2006). Tempting today, troubling tomorrow: The roots of the precarious couple effect. *Personality and Social Psychology Bulletin, 32,* 93–103.

Swann, W. B., Jr., Stein-Seroussi, A., & Giesler, R. B. (1992a). Why people self-verify. *Journal of Personality and Social Psychology, 62,* 392–401.

Swann, W. B., Jr., Stein-Seroussi, A., & McNulty, S. E. (1992b). Outcasts in a white lie society. The enigmatic worlds of people with negative self-conceptions. *Journal of Personality and Social Psychology, 62,* 618–624.

Swann, W. B., Jr., Wenzlaff, R. M., Krull, D. S., & Pelham, B. W. (1991). Seeking truth, reaping despair: Depression, self-verification and selection of relationship partners. *Journal of Abnormal Psychology, 101,* 293–306.

Swap, W. C. (1977). Interpersonal attraction and repeated exposure to rewarders and punishers. *Personality and Social Psychology Bulletin, 3,* 248–251.

Sweeney, J. (1973). An experimental investigation of the free rider problem. *Social Science Research, 2,* 277–292.

Sweeney, P. D., Anderson, K., & Bailey, S. (1986). Attributional style in depression: A meta-analytic review. *Journal of Personality and Social Psychology, 50,* 947–991.

Swets, J. A., Dawes, R. M., & Monahan, J. (2000). Psychological science can improve diagnostic decisions. *Psychological Science in the Public Interest, 1,* 1–26.

Swim, J. K. (1994). Perceived versus meta-analytic effect sizes: An assessment of the accuracy of gender stereotypes. *Journal of Personality and Social Psychology, 66,* 21–36.

Swim, J. K., Aikin, K. J., Hall, W. S., & Hunter, B. A. (1995). Sexism and racism: Old-fashioned and modern prejudices. *Journal of Personality and Social Psychology, 68,* 199–214.

Swim, J., Borgida, E., Maruyama, G., & Myers, D. G. (1989). Joan McKay vs. John McKay: Do gender stereotypes bias evaluations? *Psychological Bulletin, 105,* 409–429.

Swim, J. K., & Cohen, L. L. (1997). Overt, covert, and subtle sexism. *Psychology of Women Quarterly, 21,* 103–118.

Swim, J. K., Cohen, L. L., & Hyers, L. L. (1998). Experiencing everyday prejudice and discrimination. In J. K. Swim & C. Stangor (Eds.), *Prejudice: The target's perspective.* San Diego: Academic Press.

Swim, J. K., & Hyers, L. L. (1999). Excuse me—What did you just say?!: Women's public and private reactions to sexist remarks. *Journal of Experimental Social Psychology, 35,* 68–88.

Swindle, R., Jr., Heller, K., Bescosolido, B., & Kikuzawa, S. (2000). Responses to nervous breakdowns in America over a 40-year period: Mental health policy implications. *American Psychologist, 55,* 740–749.

Symons, D. (1979). *The evolution of human sexuality.* New York: Oxford University Press.

t'Hart, P. (1998). Preventing groupthink revisited: Evaluating and reforming groups in government. *Organizational Behavior and Human Decision Processes, 73,* 306–326.

Tafarodi, R. W., Lo, C., Yamaguchi, S., Lee, W. W-S., & Katsura, H. (2004). The inner self in three countries. *Journal of Cross-Cultural Psychology, 35,* 97–117.

Tafarodi, R. W., & Vu, C. (1997). Two-dimensional self-esteem and reactions to success and failure. *Personality and Social Psychology Bulletin, 23,* 626–635.

Tajfel, H. (1970, November). Experiments in intergroup discrimination. *Scientific American,* pp. 96–102.

Tajfel, H. (1981). *Human groups and social categories: Studies in social psychology.* London: Cambridge University Press.

Tajfel, H. (1982). Social psychology of intergroup relations. *Annual Review of Psychology, 33,* 1–39.

Tajfel, H., & Billig, M. (1974). Familiarity and categorization in intergroup behavior. *Journal of Experimental Social Psychology, 10,* 159–170.

Talbert, B. (1997, February 2). Bob Talbert's quote bag. *Detroit Free Press,* p. 5E, quoting *Allure* magazine.

Tamres, L. K., Janicki, D., & Helgeson, V. S. (2002). Sex differences in coping behavior: A meta-analytic review and an examination of relative coping. *Personality and Social Psychology Review, 6,* 2–30.

Tang, S-H., & Hall, V. C. (1995). The overjustification effect: A meta-analysis. *Applied Cognitive Psychology, 9,* 365–404.

Tangney, J. P., Baumeister, R. F., & Boone, A. L. (2004). High self-control predicts good adjustment, less pathology, better grades, and interpersonal success. *Journal of Personality, 72,* 271–324.

Tanke, E. D., & Tanke, T. J. (1979). Getting off a slippery slope: Social science in the judicial processes. *American Psychologist, 34,* 1130–1138.

Tannen, D. (1990). *You just don't understand: Women and men in conversation.* New York: Morrow.

Tanner, R. J., Ferraro, R., Chartrand, T. L., Bettman, J. R., & Van Barren, R. (2008). Of chameleons and consumption: The impact of mimicry on choice and preferences. *Journal of Consumer Research, 34,* 754–766.

Tapp, J. L. (1980). Psychological and policy perspectives on the law: Reflections on a decade. *Journal of Social Issues, 36*(2), 165–192.

Tarmann, A. (2002, May/June). Out of the closet and onto the Census long form. *Population Today, 30,* 1, 6.

Taubes, G. (1992). Violence epidemiologists tests of hazards of gun ownership. *Science, 258,* 213–215.

Tavris, C., & Aronson, E. (2007). *Mistakes were made (but not by me): Why we justify foolish beliefs, bad decisions, and hurtful acts.* New York: Harcourt.

Taylor, D. A., Gould, R. J., & Brounstein, P. J. (1981). Effects of personalistic self-disclosure. *Personality and Social Psychology Bulletin, 7,* 487–492.

Taylor, D. M., & Doria, J. R. (1981). Self-serving and group-serving bias in attribution. *Journal of Social Psychology, 113,* 201–211.

Taylor, S. E. (1981). A categorization approach to stereotyping. In D. L. Hamilton (Ed.), *Cognitive processes in stereotyping and intergroup behavior.* Hillsdale, NJ: Erlbaum.

Taylor, S. E. (1989). *Positive illusions: Creative self-deception and the healthy mind.* New York: Basic Books.

Taylor, S. E. (2002). The tending instinct: How nurturing is essential to who we are and how we live. New York: Times Books.

Taylor, S. E., Crocker, J., Fiske, S. T., Sprinzen, M., & Winkler, J. D. (1979). The generalizability of salience effects. *Journal of Personality and Social Psychology, 37,* 357–368.

Taylor, S. E., & Fiske, S. T. (1978). Salience, attention, and attribution: Top of the head phenomena. In L. Berkowitz (Ed.), *Advances in experimental social psychology* (Vol. 11). New York: Academic Press.

Taylor, S. E., Fiske, S. T., Etcoff, N. L., & Ruderman, A. J. (1978). Categorical and contextual bases of person memory and stereotyping. *Journal of Personality and Social Psychology, 36,* 778–793.

Taylor, S. E., Lerner, J. S., Sherman, D. K., Sage, R. M., & McDowell, N. K. (2003a). Are self-enhancing cognitions associated with healthy or unhealthy biological profiles? *Journal of Personality and Social Psychology 85,* 605–615.

Taylor, S. E., Lerner, J. S., Sherman, D. K., Sage, R. M., & McDowell, N. K. (2003b). Portrait of the self-enhancer: Well adjusted and well liked or maladjusted and friendless? *Journal of Personality and Social Psychology, 84,* 165–176.

Taylor, S. E., Repetti, R. L., & Seeman, T. (1997). Health psychology: What is an unhealthy environment and how does it get under the skin? *Annual Review of Psychology, 48,* 411–447.

Taylor, S. P., & Chermack, S. T. (1993). Alcohol, drugs and human physical aggression. *Journal of Studies on Alcohol,* Supplement No. 11, 78–88.

Technical Working Group for Eyewitness Evidence. (1999). Eyewitness Evidence: A Guide for Law Enforcement. A research report of the U.S. Department of Justice, Office of Justice Programs, National Institute of Justice.

Tedeschi, J. T., Nesler, M., & Taylor, E. (1987). Misattribution and the bogus pipeline: A test of dissonance and impression management theories. Paper presented at the American Psychological Association convention.

Teger, A. I. (1980). *Too much invested to quit.* New York: Pergamon.

Teigen, K. H. (1986). Old truths or fresh insights? A study of students' evaluations of proverbs. *British Journal of Social Psychology, 25,* 43–50.

Teigen, K. H., Evensen, P. C., Samoilow, D. K., & Vatne, K. B. (1999). Good luck and bad luck: How

to tell the difference. *European Journal of Social Psychology, 29,* 981–1010.

Telch, M. J., Killen, J. D., McAlister, A. L., Perry, C. L., & Maccoby, N. (1981). Long-term follow-up of a pilot project on smoking prevention with adolescents. Paper presented at the American Psychological Association convention.

Tennen, H., & Affleck, G. (1987). The costs and benefits of optimistic explanations and dispositional optimism. *Journal of Personality, 55,* 377–393.

Tenney, E. R., MacCoun, R. J., Spellman, B. A., & Hastie, R. (2007). Calibration trumps confidence as a basis for witness credibility. *Psychological Science, 18,* 46–50.

Tennov, D. (1979). *Love and limerence: The experience of being in love.* New York: Stein and Day.

Terracciano, A., & 86 others. (2005). National character does not reflect mean personality trait levels in 49 cultures. *Science, 310,* 96–100.

Tesser, A. (1988). Toward a self-evaluation maintenance model of social behavior. In L. Berkowitz (Ed.), *Advances in experimental social psychology* (Vol. 21). San Diego, CA: Academic Press.

Tesser, A., Martin, L., & Mendolia, M. (1995). The impact of thought on attitude extremity and attitude-behavior consistency. In R. E. Petty and J. A Krosnick (Eds.), *Attitude strength: Antecedents and consequences.* Hillsdale, NJ: Erlbaum.

Tesser, A., Millar, M., & Moore, J. (1988). Some affective consequences of social comparison and reflection processes: The pain and pleasure of being close. *Journal of Personality and Social Psychology, 54,* 49–61.

Tesser, A., Rosen, S., & Conlee, M. C. (1972). News valence and available recipient as determinants of news transmission. *Sociometry, 35,* 619–628.

Testa, M. (2002). The impact of men's alcohol consumption on perpetration of sexual aggression. *Clinical Psychology Review, 22,* 1239–1263.

Tetlock, P. E. (1985). Integrative complexity of American and Soviet foreign policy rhetoric: A time-series analysis. *Journal of Personality and Social Psychology, 49,* 1565–1585.

Tetlock, P. E. (1998a). Close-call counterfactuals and belief-system defenses: I was not almost wrong but I was almost right. *Journal of Personality and Social Psychology, 75,* 639–652.

Tetlock, P. E. (1988b). Monitoring the integrative complexity of American and Soviet policy rhetoric: What can be learned? *Journal of Social Issues, 44,* 101–131.

Tetlock, P. E. (1999). Theory-driven reasoning about plausible pasts and probable futures in world politics: Are we prisoners of our preconceptions? *American Journal of Political Science, 43,* 335–366.

Tetlock, P. E. (2005). *Expert political judgment: How good is it? How can we know?* Princeton, NJ: Princeton University Press.

Tetlock, P. E., Peterson, R. S., McGuire, C., Chang, S., & Feld, P. (1992). Assessing political group dynamics: A test of the groupthink model. *Journal of Personality and Social Psychology, 63,* 403–425.

Thibodeau, R. (1989). From racism to tokenism: The changing face of blacks in *New Yorker* cartoons. *Public Opinion Quarterly, 53,* 482–494.

Thomas, G. C., & Batson, C. D. (1981). Effect of helping under normative pressure on self-perceived altruism. *Social Psychology Quarterly, 44,* 127–131.

Thomas, G. C., Batson, C. D., & Coke, J. S. (1981). Do Good Samaritans discourage helpfulness? Self-perceived altruism after exposure to highly helpful others. *Journal of Personality and Social Psychology, 40,* 194–200.

Thomas, K. W., & Pondy, L. R. (1977). Toward an "intent" model of conflict management among principal parties. *Human Relations, 30,* 1089–1102.

Thomas, L. (1971). Notes of a biology watcher: A fear of pheromones. *New England Journal of Medicine, 285,* 292–293.

Thompson, L. (1990a). An examination of naive and experienced negotiators. *Journal of Personality and Social Psychology, 59,* 82–90.

Thompson, L. (1990b). The influence of experience on negotiation performance. *Journal of Experimental Social Psychology, 26,* 528–544.

Thompson, L. (1998). *The mind and heart of the negotiator.* Upper Saddle River, NJ: Prentice-Hall.

Thompson, L., & Hrebec, D. (1996). Lose-lose agreements in interdependent decision making. *Psychological Bulletin, 120,* 396–409.

Thompson, L., Valley, K. L., & Kramer, R. M. (1995). The bittersweet feeling of success: An examination of social perception in negotiation. *Journal of Experimental Social Psychology, 31,* 467–492.

Thompson, L. L., & Crocker, J. (1985). Prejudice following threat to the self-concept. Effects of performance expectations and attributions. Unpublished manuscript, Northwestern University.

Thompson, S. C., Armstrong, W., & Thomas, C. (1998). Illusions of control, underestimations, and accuracy: A control heuristic explanation. *Psychological Bulletin, 123,* 143–161.

Thompson, W. C., Cowan, C. L., & Rosenhan, D. L. (1980). Focus of attention mediates the impact of negative affect on altruism. *Journal of Personality and Social Psychology, 38,* 291–300.

Thompson, W. C., Fong, G. T., & Rosenhan, D. L. (1981). Inadmissible evidence and juror verdicts. *Journal of Personality and Social Psychology, 40,* 453–463.

Thompson, W. C., & Schumann, E. L. (1987). Interpretation of statistical evidence in criminal trials. *Law and Human Behavior, 11,* 167–187.

Thomson, R., & Murachver, T. (2001). Predicting gender from electronic discourse. *British Journal of Social Psychology, 40,* 193–208 (and personal correspondence from T. Murachver, May 23, 2002).

Thornton, B., & Maurice, J. (1997). Physique contrast effect: Adverse impact of idealized body images for women. *Sex Roles, 37,* 433–439.

Tice, D. M., & Baumeister, R. F. (1997). Longitudinal study of procrastination, performance, stress, and health: The costs and benefits of dawdling. *Psychological Science, 8,* 454–458.

Tice, D. M., Butler, J. L., Muraven, M. B., & Stillwell, A. M. (1995). When modesty prevails: Differential favorability of self-presentation to friends and strangers. *Journal of Personality and Social Psychology, 69,* 1120–1138.

Tideman, S. (2003, undated). Announcement of Operationalizing Gross National Happiness conference, February 18–20, 2004. Distributed via the Internet.

Tierney, J. (2008, January 29). Hitting it off, thanks to algorithms of love. *New York Times* (www.nytimes.com).

Time. (1992, March 30). The not so merry wife of Windsor, pp. 38–39.

Time. (1994, November 7). Vox pop (poll by Yankelovich Partners Inc.), p. 21.

Timko, C., & Moos, R. H. (1989). Choice, control, and adaptation among elderly residents of sheltered care settings. *Journal of Applied Social Psychology, 19,* 636–655.

Timmerman, T. A. (2007). "It was a thought pitch": Personal, situational, and target influences on hit-by-pitch events across time. *Journal of Applied Psychology, 92,* 876–884.

Tindale, R. S., Davis, J. H., Vollrath, D. A., Nagao, D. H., & Hinsz, V. B. (1990). Asymmetrical social infuence in freely interacting groups: A test of three models. *Journal of Personality and Social Psychology, 58,* 438–449.

Tobin, R. J., & Eagles, M. (1992). U.S. and Canadian attitudes toward international interactions: A cross-national test of the double-standard hypothesis. *Basic and Applied Social Psychology, 13,* 447–459.

Todorov, A., Mandisodza, A. N., Goren, A., & Hall, C. C. (2005). Inferences of competence from faces predict election outcomes. *Science, 308,* 1623–1626.

Tomorrow, T. (2003, April 30). Passive tense verbs deployed before large audience; stories remain unclear (www240.pair.com/tomtom/pages/ja/ja_fr.html).

Tong, E. M. W., Tan, C. R. M., Latheef, N. A., Selamat, M. F. B., & Tan, D. K. B. (2008). Conformity: Moods matter. *European Journal of Social Psychology, 38,* 601–611.

Tormala, Z. L., Brinol, P., & Petty, R. E. (2006). When credibility attacks: The reverse impact of source credibility on persuasion. *Journal of Experimental Social Psychology, 42,* 684–691.

Tormala, Z. L., Clarkson, J. J., & Petty, R. E. (2006). Resisting persuasion by the skin of one's teeth: The hidden success of resisted persuasive messages. *Journal of Personality and Social Psychology, 91,* 423–435.

Toronto News. (1977, July 26).

Totterdell, P., Kellett, S., Briner, R. B., & Teuchmann, K. (1998). Evidence of mood linkage in work groups. *Journal of Personality and Social Psychology, 74,* 1504–1515.

Towles-Schwen, T., & Fazio, R. H. (2006). Automatically activated racial attitudes as predictors of the success of interracial roommate relationships. *Journal of Experimental Social Psychology, 42,* 698–705.

Towson, S. M. J., & Zanna, M. P. (1983). Retaliation against sexual assault: Self-defense or public duty? *Psychology of Women Quarterly, 8,* 89–99.

Trail, T. E., Shelton, J. N., & West, T. V. (2009). Interracial roommate relationships: Negotiating daily interactions. *Personality and Social Psychology Bulletin, 35,* 671–684.

Trampe, D., Stapel, D. A., & Siero, F. W. (2007). On models and vases: Body dissatisfaction and proneness to social comparison effects. *Journal of Personality and Social Psychology, 92,* 106–118.

Traut-Mattausch, E., Schulz-Hardt, S., Greitemeyer, T., & Frey, D. (2004). Expectancy confirmation in spite of disconfirming evidence: The case of price increases due to the introduction of the Euro. *European Journal of Social Psychology, 34,* 739–760.

Trautwein, Ul, & Lüdtke, O. (2006). Self-esteem, academic self-concept, and achievement: How the learning environment moderates the dynamics of self-concept. *Journal of Personality and Social Psychology, 90,* 334–349.

Travis, L. E. (1925). The effect of a small audience upon eye-hand coordination. *Journal of Abnormal and Social Psychology, 20,* 142–146.

Trawalter, S., Todd, A. R., Baird, A. A., & Richeson, J. A. (2008). Attending to threat: Race-based patterns of selective attention. *Journal of Experimental Social Psychology, 44,* 1322–1327.

Trewin, D. (2001). *Australian social trends 2001.* Canberra: Australian Bureau of Statistics.

Triandis, H. C. (1981). Some dimensions of intercultural variation and their implications for interpersonal behavior. Paper presented at the American Psychological Association convention.

Triandis, H. C. (1982). Incongruence between intentions and behavior: A review. Paper presented at the American Psychological Association convention.

Triandis, H. C. (1994). *Culture and social behavior.* New York: McGraw-Hill.

Triandis, H. C. (2000). Culture and conflict. *International Journal of Psychology, 55,* 145–152.

Triandis, H. C., Bontempo, R., Villareal, M. J., Asai, M., & Lucca, N. (1988). Individualism and collectivism: Cross-cultural perspectives on self-ingroup relationships. *Journal of Personality and Social Psychology, 54,* 323–338.

Trimble, D. E. (1993). Meta-analysis of altruism and intrinsic and extrinsic religiousness. Paper presented at the Eastern Psychological Association convention.

Triplett, N. (1898). The dynamogenic factors in pacemaking and competition. *American Journal of Psychology, 9,* 507–533.

Trolier, T. K., & Hamilton, D. L. (1986). Variables influencing judgments of correlational relations. *Journal of Personality and Social Psychology, 50,* 879–888.

Tropp, L. R., & Pettigrew, T. F. (2005a). Differential relationships between intergroup contact and affective and cognitive dimensions of prejudice. *Personality and Social Psychology Bulletin, 31,* 1145–1158.

Tropp, L. R., & Pettigrew, T. F. (2005b). Relationships between intergroup contact and prejudice among minority and majority status groups. *Psychological Science, 16,* 951–957.

Trost, M. R., Maass, A., & Kenrick, D. T. (1992). Minority influence: Personal relevance biases cognitive processes and reverses private acceptance. *Journal of Experimental Social Psychology, 28,* 234–254.

Trzesniewski, K. H., Donnellan, M. B., Moffitt, T. E., Robins, R. W., Poulton, R., & Caspi, A. (2006). Low self-esteem during adolescence predicts poor health, criminal behavior, and limited economic prospects during adulthood. *Developmental Psychology, 42,* 381–390.

Trzesniewski, K. H., Donnellan, M. B., & Robins, R. W. (2008). Do today's young people really think they are so extraordinary? An examination of secular changes in narcissism and self-enhancement. *Psychological Science, 19,* 181–188.

Tsang, J-A. (2002). Moral rationalization and the integration of situational factors and psychological processes in immoral behavior. *Review of General Psychology, 6,* 25–50.

Tumin, M. M. (1958). Readiness and resistance to desegregation: A social portrait of the hard core. *Social Forces, 36,* 256–273.

Turner, C. W., Hesse, B. W., & Peterson-Lewis, S. (1986). Naturalistic studies of the long-term effects of television violence. *Journal of Social Issues, 42*(3), 51–74.

Turner, J. C. (1981). The experimental social psychology of intergroup behaviour. In J. Turner & H. Giles (Eds.), *Intergroup behavior.* Oxford, England: Blackwell.

Turner, J. C. (1984). Social identification and psychological group formation. In H. Tajfel (Ed.), *The social dimensions: European developments in social psychology* (Vol. 2). London: Cambridge University Press.

Turner, J. C. (1987). *Rediscovering the social group: A self-categorization theory.* New York: Blackwell.

Turner, J. C., & Haslam, S. A. (2001). Social identity, organizations, and leadership. In M. E. Turner (Ed.), *Groups at work: Theory and research.* Mahwah, NJ: Erlbaum.

Turner, J. C., & Reynolds, K. J. (2004). The social identity perspective in intergroup relations: Theories, themes, and controversies. In M. B. Brewer & M. Hewstone (Eds.), *Self and social identity.* Malden, MA: Blackwell.

Turner, M. E., & Pratkanis, A. R. (1993). Effects of preferential and meritorious selection on performance: An examination of intuitive and self-handicapping perspectives. *Personality and Social Psychology Bulletin, 19,* 47–58.

Turner, M. E., & Pratkanis, A. R. (1994). Social identity maintenance prescriptions for preventing groupthink: Reducing identity protection and enhancing intellectual conflict. *International Journal of Conflict Management, 5,* 254–270.

Turner, M. E., & Pratkanis, A. R. (1997). Mitigating groupthink by stimulating constructive conflict. In C. K. W. De Dreu & E. Van de Vliert (Eds.), *Using conflict in organizations.* London: Sage.

Turner, M. E., Pratkanis, A. R., Probasco, P., & Leve, C. (1992). Threat cohesion and group effectiveness: Testing a social identity maintenance perspective on groupthink. *Journal of Personality and Social Psychology, 63,* 781–796.

Turner, N., Barling, J., & Zacharatos, A. (2002). Positive psychology at work. In C. R. Snyder & S. J. Lopez (Eds.), *The handbook of positive psychology.* New York: Oxford University Press.

Turner, R. N., Hewstone, M., & Voci, A. (2007a). Reducing explicit and implicit outgroup prejudice via direct and extended contact: The mediating role of self-disclosure and intergroup anxiety. *Journal of Personality and Social Psychology, 93,* 369–388.

Turner, R. N., Hewstone, M., Voci, A., Paolini, S., & Christ, O. (2007b). Reducing prejudice via direct and extended cross-group friendship. *European Review of Social Psychology, 18,* 212–255.

Turner, R. N., Hewstone, M., Voci, A., & Vonofakou, C. (2008). A test of the extended intergroup contact hypothesis: The mediating role of intergroup anxiety, perceived ingroup and outgroup norms, and inclusion of the outgroup in the self. *Journal of Personality and Social Psychology, 95,* 843–860.

Tutu, D. (1999). *No future without forgiveness.* New York: Doubleday.

Tversky, A. (1985, June). Quoted by Kevin McKean in Decisions, decisions, *Discover,* pp. 22–31.

Tversky, A., & Kahneman, D. (1973). Availability: A neuristic for judging frequency and probability. *Cognitive Psychology, 5,* 207–302.

Tverksy, A., & Kahneman, D. (1974). Judgment under uncertainty: Heuristics and biases. *Science, 185,* 1123–1131.

Tversky, A., & Kahneman, D. (1983). Extensional versus intuitive reasoning: The conjunction fallacy in probability judgment. *Psychological Review, 90,* 293–315.

Twenge, J. M. (1997). Changes in masculine and feminine traits over time: A meta-analysis. *Sex Roles, 36,* 305–325.

Twenge, J. M. (2006). *Generation me: Why today's young Americans are more confident, assertive, entitled—and more miserable than ever before.* New York: Free Press.

Twenge, J. M., Abebe, E., & Campbell, W. K. (2009). Fitting in or standing out: Trends in American parents' choices for children's names, 1880–2007. Unpublished manuscript.

Twenge, J. M., Baumeister, R. F., Tice, D. M., & Stucke, T. S. (2001). If you can't join them, beat them: Effects of social exclusion on aggressive behavior. *Journal of Personality and Social Psychology, 81,* 1058–1069.

Twenge, J. M., & Campbell, W. K. (2001). Age and birth cohort differences in self-esteem: A cross-temporal meta-analysis. *Personality and Social Psychology Review, 5,* 321–344.

Twenge, J. M., & Campbell, W. K. (2008). Increases in positive self-views among high school students: Birth cohort changes in anticipated performance, self-satisfaction, self-liking, and self-competence. *Psychological Science, 19,* 1082–1086.

Twenge, J. M., Catanese, K. R., & Baumeister, R. F. (2002). Social exclusion causes self-defeating behavior. *Journal of Personality and Social Psychology, 83,* 606–615.

Twenge, J. M., Catanese, K. R., & Baumeister, R. F. (2003). Social exclusion and the deconstructed state: Time perception, meaninglessness, lethargy, lack of emotion, and self-awareness. *Journal of Personality and Social Psychology, 85,* 409–423.

Twenge, J. M., & Foster, J. D. (2008). Mapping the scale of the narcissism epidemic: Increases in narcissism 2002–2007 within ethnic groups. *Journal of Research in Personality, 42,* 1619–1622.

Twenge, J. M., Konrath, S., Foster, J. D., Campbell, W. K., & Bushman, B. J. (2008). Egos inflating over time: A cross-temporal meta-analysis of the Narcissistic Personality Inventory. *Journal of Personality, 76,* 875–901.

Twenge, J. M., Zhang, L., Catanese, K. R., Dolan-Pascoe, B., Lyche, L. F., & Baumeister, R. F. (2007). Replenishing connectedness: Reminders of social activity reduce aggression after social exclusion. *British Journal of Social Psychology, 46,* 205–224.

Tyler, T. R., & Lind, E. A. (1990). Intrinsic versus community-based justice models: When does group membership matter? *Journal of Social Issues, 46,* 83–94.

Tzeng, M. (1992). The effects of socioeconomic heterogamy and changes on marital dissolution for first marriages. *Journal of Marriage and the Family, 54,* 609–619.

U. S. Supreme Court, Plessy v. Ferguson. (1986). Quoted by L. J. Severy, J. C. Brigham, & B. R. Schlenker, *A contemporary introduction to social psychology* (p. 126). New York: McGraw-Hill.

Uchino, B. N., Cacioppo, J. T., & Kiecolt-Glaser, J. K. (1996). The relationship between social support and physiological processes: A review with emphasis on underlying mechanisms and implications for health. *Psychological Bulletin, 119,* 488–531.

Ugwuegbu, C. E. (1979). Racial and evidential factors in juror attribution of legal responsibility. *Journal of Experimental Social Psychology, 15,* 133–146.

Uleman, J. S. (1989). A framework for thinking intentionally about unintended thoughts. In J. S. Uleman & J. A. Bargh (Eds.), *Unintended thought: The limits of awareness, intention, and control.* New York: Guilford.

Uleman, J. S., Saribay, S. A., & Gonzalez, C. M. (2008). Spontaneous inferences, implicit impressions, and implicit theories. *Annual Review of Psychology,* **59,** 329–360.

Unger, R. K. (1979). Whom does helping help? Paper presented at the Eastern Psychological Association convention, April.

Unger, R. K. (1985). Epistomological consistency and its scientific implications. *American Psychologist,* **40,** 1413–1414.

United Nations (UN). (1991). *The world's women, 1970–1990: Trends and statistics.* New York: United Nations.

United Nations (UN). (2006). *Ending violence against women: From words to action.* Study of the Secretary-General. New York: United Nations (www.un.org).

Unkelbach, C., Forgas, J. P., & Denson, T. F. (2008). The turban effect: The influence of Muslim headgear and induced affect on aggressive responses in the shooter bias paradigm. *Journal of Experimental Social Psychology,* **44,** 1409–1413.

USGS. (2006). United States energy and world energy production and consumption statistics. U.S. Geological Survey (energy.cr.usgs.gov/energy/stats_ctry/Stat1.html#ConsumptionUvsW).

Väänänen, A., Buunk, B. P., Kivimäke, M., Pentti, J., & Vahtera, J. (2005). When it is better to give than to receive: Long-term health effects of perceived reciprocity in support exchange. *Journal of Personality and Social Psychology,* **89,** 176–193.

Vaillant, G. E. (1977). *Adaptation to life.* Boston: Little, Brown.

Vaillant, G. E. (1997). Report on distress and longevity. Paper presented to the American Psychiatric Association convention.

Valcour, M. (2007). Work-based resources as moderators of the relationship between work hours and satisfaction with work-family balance. *Journal of Applied Psychology,* **92,** 1512–1523.

Valdesolo, P., & DeSteno, D. (2007). Moral hypocrisy: Social groups and the flexibility of virtue. *Psychological Science,* **18,** 689–690.

Valdesolo, P., & DeSteno, D. (2008). The duality of virtue: Deconstructing the moral hypocrite. *Journal of Experimental Social Psychology,* **44,** 1334–1338.

Valentine, T., & Mesout, J. (2009). Eyewitness identification under stress in the London Dungeon. *Applied Cognitive Psychology,* **23,** 151–161.

Valentine, T., Pickering, A., & Darling, S. (2003). Characteristics of eyewitness identification that predict the outcome of real lineups. *Applied Cognitive Psychology,* **17,** 969–993.

Vallone, R. P., Griffin, D. W., Lin, S., & Ross, L. (1990). Overconfident prediction of future actions and outcomes by self and others. *Journal of Personality and Social Psychology,* **58,** 582–592.

Vallone, R. P., Ross, L., & Lepper, M. R. (1985). The hostile media phenomenon: Biased perception and perceptions of media bias in coverage of the "Beirut Massacre." *Journal of Personality and Social Psychology,* **49,** 577–585.

van Baaren, R. B., Holland, R. W., Karremans, R. W., & van Knippenberg, A. (2003). Mimicry and interpersonal closeness. Unpublished manuscript, University of Nijmegen.

van Baaren, R. B., Holland, R. W., Kawakami, K., & van Knippenberg, A. (2004). Mimicry and prosocial behavior. *Psychological Science,* **15,** 71–74.

van Baaren, R. B., Holland, R. W., Steenaert, B., & van Knippenberg, A. (2003). Mimicry for money: Behavioral consequences of imitation. *Journal of Experimental Social Psychology,* **39,** 393–398.

Van Boven, L., & Gilovich, T. (2003). To do or to have? That is the question. *Journal of Personality and Social Psychology,* **85,** 1193–1202.

Van Boven, L., & Loewenstein, G. (2003). Social projection of transient drive states. *Personality and Social Psychology Bulletin,* **29,** 1159–1168.

van den Bos, K., & Spruijt, N. (2002). Appropriateness of decisions as a moderator of the psychology of voice. *European Journal of Social Psychology,* **32,** 57–72.

van Dijk, W. W., Finkenauer, C., & Pollmann, M. (2008). The misprediction of emotions in track athletics: Is experience the teacher of all things? *Basic and Applied Social Psychology,* **30,** 369–376.

van Honk, J., & Schutter, D. J. L. G. (2007). Testosterone reduces conscious detection of signals serving social correction. *Psychological Science,* **18,** 663–667.

Van Knippenberg, D., & Wilke, H. (1992). Prototypicality of arguments and conformity to ingroup norms. *European Journal of Social Psychology,* **22,** 141–155.

Van Laar, C., Levin, S., Sinclair, S., & Sidanius, J. (2005). The effect of university roommate contact on ethnic attitudes and behavior. *Journal of Experimental Social Psychology,* **41,** 329–345.

Van Vugt, M., De Cremer, D., & Janssen, D. P. (2007). Gender differences in cooperation and competition. *Psychological Science,* **18,** 19–23.

Van Vugt, M., & Spisak, B. R. (2008). Sex differences in the emergence of leadership during competitions within and between groups. *Psychological Science,* **19,** 854–858.

Van Vugt, M., Van Lange, P. A. M., & Meertens, R. M. (1996). Commuting by car or public transportation? A social dilemma analysis of travel mode judgements. *European Journal of Social Psychology,* **26,** 373–395.

Van Yperen, N. W., & Buunk, B. P. (1990). A longitudinal study of equity and satisfaction in intimate relationships. *European Journal of Social Psychology,* **20,** 287–309.

Vandello, J. A., & Cohen, D. (1999). Patterns of individualism and collectivism across the United States. *Journal of Personality and Social Psychology,* **77,** 279–292.

Vandello, J. A., Cohen, D., & Ransom, S. (2008). U.S. southern and northern differences in perceptions of norms about aggression: Mechanisms for the perpetuation of a culture of honor. *Journal of Cross-Cultural Psychology,* **39,** 162–177.

Vanderslice, V. J., Rice, R. W., & Julian, J. W. (1987). The effects of participation in decision-making on worker satisfaction and productivity: An organizational simulation. *Journal of Applied Social Psychology,* **17,** 158–170.

Vanman, E. J., Paul, B. Y., Kaplan, D. L., & Miller, N. (1990). Facial electromyography differentiates racial bias in imagined cooperative settings. *Psychophysiology,* **27,** 563.

Vargas, R. A. (2009, July 6). "City of Heroes" character "Twixt" becomes game's most hated outcast courtesy of Loyola professor. *The Times-Picayune* (www.nola.com).

Vasquez, E. A., Denson, T. F., Pedersen, W. C., Stenstrom, D. M., & Miller, N. (2005). The moderating effect of trigger intensity on triggered displaced aggression. *Journal of Experimental Social Psychology,* **41,** 61–67.

Vaughan, K. B., & Lanzetta, J. T. (1981). The effect of modification of expressive displays on vicarious emotional arousal. *Journal of Experimental Social Psychology,* **17,** 16–30.

Vazire, S., & Mehl, M. R. (2008). Knowing me, knowing you: The accuracy and unique predictive validity of self-ratings and other-ratings of daily behavior. *Journal of Personality and Social Psychology,* **95,** 1202–1216.

Vega, V., & Malamuth, N. M. (2007). Predicting sexual aggression: The role of pornography in the context of general and specific risk factors. *Aggressive Behavior, 33*, 104–117.

Verkuyten, M., & Yildiz, A. A. (2007). National (dis)identification and ethnic and religious identity: A study among Turkish-Dutch Muslims. *Personality and Social Psychology, 33*, 1448–1462.

Verplanken, B. (1991). Persuasive communication of risk information: A test of cue versus message processing effects in a field experiment. *Personality and Social Psychology Bulletin, 17*, 188–193.

Vescio, T. K., Gervais, S. J., Snyder, M., & Hoover, A. (2005). Power and the creation of patronizing environments: The stereotype-based behaviors of the powerful and their effects on female performance in masculine domains. *Journal of Personality and Social Psychology, 88*, 658–672.

Veysey, B. M., & Messner, S. F. (1999). Further testing of social disorganization theory: An elaboration of Sampson and Groves's "Community structure and crime." *Journal of Research in Crime and Delinquency, 36*, 156–174.

Vidmar, N. (1979). The other issues in jury simulation research. *Law and Human Behavior, 3*, 95–106.

Vidmar, N., & Laird, N. M. (1983). Adversary social roles: Their effects on witnesses' communication of evidence and the assessments of adjudicators. *Journal of Personality and Social Psychology, 44*, 888–898.

Vignoles, V. L., Chryssochoou, X., & Breakwell, G. M. (2000). The distinctiveness principle: Identity, meaning, and the bounds of cultural relativity. *Personality and Social Psychology Review, 4*, 337–354.

Viken, R. J., Treat, T. A., Bloom, S. L., & McFall, R. M. (2005). Illusory correlation for body type and happiness: Covariation bias and its relationship to eating disorder symptoms. *International Journal of Eating Disorders, 38*, 65–72.

Visher, C. A. (1987). Juror decision making: The importance of evidence. *Law and Human Behavior, 11*, 1–17.

Visintainer, M. A., & Seligman, M. E. (1983, July/August). The hope factor. *American Health*, pp. 59–61.

Visintainer, M. A., & Seligman, M. E. P. (1985). Tumor rejection and early experience of uncontrollable shock in the rat. Unpublished manuscript, University of Pennsylvania. See also M. A. Visintainer et al. (1982), Tumor rejection in rats after inescapable versus escapable shock. *Science, 216*, 437–439.

Visser, P. S., & Mirabile, R. R. (2004). Attitudes in the social context: The impact of social network composition on individual-level attitude strength. *Journal of Personality and Social Psychology, 87*, 779–795.

Vitelli, R. (1988). The crisis issue assessed: An empirical analysis. *Basic and Applied Social Psychology, 9*, 301–309.

Vivian, J. E., & Berkowitz, N. H. (1993). Anticipated outgroup evaluations and intergroup bias. *European Journal of Social Psychology, 23*, 513–524.

Vohs, K. D., Baumeister, R. F., & Ciarocco, N. J. (2005). Self-regulation and self-presentation: Regulatory resource depletion impairs impression management and effortful self-presentation depletes regulatory resources. *Journal of Personality and Social Psychology, 88*, 632–657.

Vohs, K. D., Baumeister, R. F., Schmeichel, B. J., Twenge, J. M., Nelson, N. M., & Tice, D. M. (2008). Making choices impairs subsequent self-control: A limited-resource account of decision making, self-regulation, and active initiative. *Journal of Personality and Social Psychology, 94*, 883–898.

Vohs, K. D., Mead, N. L., & Goode, M. R. (2006). The psychological consequences of money. *Science, 314*, 1154–1156.

Vohs, K. D., Mead, N. L., & Goode, M. R. (2008). Merely activating the concept of money changes personal and interpersonal behavior. *Current Directions in Psychological Science, 17*, 208–212.

Vohs, K. D., & Schooler, J. W. (2008). The value of believing in free will: Encouraging a belief in determinism increases cheating. *Psychological Science, 19*, 49–54.

Vollrath, D. A., Sheppard, B. H., Hinsz, V. B., & Davis, J. H. (1989). Memory performance by decision-making groups and individuals. *Organizational Behavior and Human Decision Processes, 43*, 289–300.

Von Hippel, W., Brener, L., & von Hippel, C. (2008). Implicit prejudice toward injecting drug users predicts intentions to change jobs among drug and alcohol nurses. *Psychological Science, 19*, 7–12.

von Hippel, W., Silver, L. A., & Lynch, M. B. (2000). Stereotyping against your will: The role of inhibitory ability in stereotyping and prejudice among the elderly. *Personality and Social Psychology Bulletin, 26*, 523–532.

Vonofakou, C., Hewstone, M., & Voci, A. (2007). Contact with out-group friends as a predictor of meta-attitudinal strength and accessibility of attitudes toward gay men. *Journal of Personality and Social Psychology, 92*, 804–820.

Vorauer, J. D. (2001). The other side of the story: Transparency estimation in social interaction. In G. Moskowitz (Ed.), *Cognitive social psychology: The Princeton symposium on the legacy and future of social cognition*. Mahwah, NJ: Erlbaum.

Vorauer, J. D. (2005). Miscommunications surrounding efforts to reach out across group boundaries. *Personality and Social Psychology Bulletin, 31*, 1653–1664.

Vorauer, J. D., Main, K. J., & O'Connell, G. B. (1998). How do individuals expect to be viewed by members of lower status groups? Content and implications of meta-stereotypes. *Journal of Personality and Social Psychology, 75*, 917–937.

Vorauer, J. D., & Ratner, R. K. (1996). Who's going to make the first move? Pluralistic ignorance as an impediment to relationship formation. *Journal of Social and Personal Relationships, 13*, 483–506.

Vorauer, J. D., & Sakamoto, Y. (2006). I thought we could be friends, but . . . Systematic miscommunication and defensive distancing as obstacles to cross-group friendship formation. *Psychological Science 17*, 326–331.

Vukovic, J., Jones, B. C., DeBruine, L. M., Little, A. C., Feinberg, D. R., & Welling, L. L. M. (2008). Circum-menopausal changes in women's face preferences. *Biology Letters* (DOI: 10.1098/rsbl.2008.0478).

Vul, E., & Pashler, H. (2008). Measuring the crowd within: Probabilistic representations within individuals. *Psychological Science, 19*, 646–647.

Wagner, R. V. (2006). Terrorism: A peace psychological analysis. *Journal of Social Issues, 62*, 155–171.

Wagner, U., Christ, O., & Pettigrew, T. F. (2008). Prejudice and group-related behavior in Germany. *Journal of Social Issues, 64*, 403–416.

Wagstaff, G. F. (1983). Attitudes to poverty, the Protestant ethic, and political affiliation: A preliminary investigation. *Social Behavior and Personality, 11*, 45–47.

Wald, M. L. (2008, July 27). Flight's first fatal trip. *New York Times* (www.nytimes.com).

Walinsky, A. (1995, July). The crisis of public order. *The Atlantic Monthly*, pp. 39–54.

Walker, L. J., & Frimer, J. A. (2007). Moral personality of brave and caring exemplars. *Journal of Personality and Social Psychology, 93*, 845–860.

Walker, M., Harriman, S., & Costello, S. (1980). The influence of appearance on compliance with a request. *Journal of Social Psychology, 112*, 159–160.

Walker, P. M., & Hewstone, M. (2008). The influence of social factors and implicit racial bias on a generalized own-race effect. *Applied Cognitive Psychology, 22*, 441–453.

Walker, R. (2004, December 5). The hidden (in plain sight) persuaders. *New York Times Magazine* (www.nytimes.com).

Wall, B. (2002, August 24–25). Profit matures along with baby boomers. *International Herald Tribune*, p. 13.

Wallace, C. P. (2000, May 8). Germany's glass ceiling. *Time*, p. B8.

Wallace, D. S., Paulson, R. M., Lord, C. G., & Bond, C. F., Jr. (2005). Which behaviors do attitudes predict? Meta-analyzing the effects of social pressure and perceived difficulty. *Review of General Psychology*, **9**, 214-227.

Wallace, M. *New York Times*, November 25, 1969.

Waller, J. (2002). *Becoming evil: How ordinary people commit genocide and mass killing.* New York: Oxford University press.

Walster (Hatfield), E. (1965). The effect of self-esteem on romantic liking. *Journal of Experimental Social Psychology*, **1**, 184–197.

Walster (Hatfield), E., Aronson, V., Abrahams, D., & Rottman, L. (1966). Importance of physical attractiveness in dating behavior. *Journal of Personality and Social Psychology*, **4**, 508–516.

Walster (Hatfield), E., & Festinger, L. (1962). The effectiveness of "overheard" persuasive communications. *Journal of Abnormal and Social Psychology*, **65**, 395–402.

Walster (Hatfield), E., Walster, G. W., & Berscheid, E. (1978). *Equity: Theory and research.* Boston: Allyn & Bacon.

Walther, J. B., Van Der Heide, B., Kim, S-Y., Westerman, D., & Tong, S. T. (2008). The role of friends' appearance and behavior on evaluations of individuals on Facebook: Are we known by the company we keep? *Human Communication Research*, **34**, 28–49.

Walum, H., Westberg, L., Heinningsson, S., Neiderhiser, J. M., Reiss, D., Igl, W., Ganiban, J. M., Spotts, E. L., Pedersen, N. L., Eriksson, E., & Lichtenstein, P. (2008). Genetic variation in the vasopressin receptor 1a gene (*AVPR1A*) associates with pair-bonding behavior in humans. *Proceedings of the National Academy of Sciences*, **105**, 14153–14156.

Ward, W. C., & Jenkins, H. M. (1965). The display of information and the judgment of contingency. *Canadian Journal of Psychology*, **19**, 231–241.

Warneken, F., & Tomasello, M. (2006). Altruistic helping in human infants and young chimpanzees. *Science*, **311**, 1301–1303.

Warnick, D. H., & Sanders, G. S. (1980). The effects of group discussion on eyewitness accuracy. *Journal of Applied Social Psychology*, **10**, 249–259.

Warr, P., & Payne, R. (1982). Experiences of strain and pleasure among British adults. *Social Science and Medicine*, **16**, 1691–1697.

Warren, N. C. (2005, March 4). Personal correspondence from founder of eHarmony.com.

Wason, P. C. (1960). On the failure to eliminate hypotheses in a conceptual task. *Quarterly Journal of Experimental Psychology*, **12**, 129–140.

Watkins, D., Akande, A., & Fleming, J. (1998). Cultural dimensions, gender, and the nature of self-concept: A fourteen-country study. *International Journal of Psychology*, **33**, 17–31.

Watkins, D., Cheng, C., Mpofu, E., Olowu, S., Singh-Sengupta, S., & Regmi, M. (2003). Gender differences in self-construal: How generalizable are Western findings? *Journal of Social Psychology*, **143**, 501–519.

Watkins, E. R. (2008). Constructive and unconstructive repetitive thought. *Psychological Bulletin*, **134**, 163–206.

Watson, D. (1982, November). The actor and the observer: How are their perceptions of causality divergent? *Psychological Bulletin*, **92**, 682–700.

Watson, R. I., Jr. (1973). Investigation into deindividuation using a cross-cultural survey technique. *Journal of Personality and Social Psychology*, **25**, 342–345.

Watt, S. E., & Badger, A. J. (2009). Effects of social belonging on homesickness: An application of the belongingness hypothesis. *Personality and Social Psychology Bulletin*, **35**, 516–530.

Weary, G., & Edwards, J. A. (1994). Social cognition and clinical psychology: Anxiety, depression, and the processing of social information. In R. Wyer & T. Srull (Eds.), *Handbook of social cognition* (Vol. 2). Hillsdale, NJ: Erlbaum.

Weary, G., Harvey, J. H., Schwieger, P., Olson, C. T., Perloff, R., & Pritchard, S. (1982). Self-presentation and the moderation of self-serving biases. *Social Cognition*, **1**, 140–159.

Webb, T. L., & Sheeran, P. (2006). Does changing behavioral intentions engender behavior change? A meta-analysis of the experimental evidence. *Psychological Bulletin*, **132**, 249-268.

Weber, B., & Hertel, G. (2007). Motivation gains of inferior group members: A meta-analytical review. *Journal of Personality and Social Psychology*, **93**, 973–993.

Weber, N., Wells, G. L., & Semmler, C. (2004). Eyewitness identification accuracy and response latency: The unruly 10–12-second rule. *Journal of Experimental Psychology: Applied*, **10**, 139–147.

Wegner, D. M., & Erber, R. (1992). The hyperaccessibility of suppressed thoughts. *Journal of Personality and Social Psychology*, **63**, 903–912.

Wehr, P. (1979). *Conflict regulation.* Boulder, CO: Westview.

Weiner, B. (1980). A cognitive (attribution)-emotion-action model of motivated behavior: An analysis of judgments of help-giving. *Journal of Personality and Social Psychology*, **39**, 186–200.

Weiner, B. (1981). The emotional consequences of causal ascriptions. Unpublished manuscript, UCLA.

Weiner, B. (1985). "Spontaneous" causal thinking. *Psychological Bulletin*, **97**, 74–84.

Weiner, B. (1995). Judgments of responsibility: A foundation for a theory of social conduct. New York: Guilford.

Weinstein, N. D. (1980). Unrealistic optimism about future life events. *Journal of Personality and Social Psychology*, **39**, 806–820.

Weinstein, N. D. (1982). Unrealistic optimism about susceptibility to health problems. *Journal of Behavioral Medicine*, **5**, 441–460.

Weiss, J., & Brown, P. (1976). Self-insight error in the explanation of mood. Unpublished manuscript, Harvard University.

Wells, G. L. (1984). The psychology of lineup identifications. *Journal of Applied Social Psychology*, **14**, 89–103.

Wells, G. L. (1986). Expert psychological testimony. *Law and Human Behavior*, **10**, 83–95.

Wells, G. L. (1992). Naked statistical evidence of liability: Is subjective probability enough? *Journal of Personality and Social Psychology*, **62**, 739–752.

Wells, G. L. (1993). What do we know about eyewitness identification? *American Psychologist*, **48**, 553–571.

Wells, G. L. (2005). Helping experimental psychology affect legal policy. In N. Brewer & K. D. Williams (Eds.), *Psychology and law: An empirical perspective.* New York: Guilford.

Wells, G. L. (2008). Field experiments on eyewitness identification: Towards a better understanding of pitfalls and prospects. *Law and Human Behavior*, **32**, 6–10.

Wells, G. L., & Bradfield, A. L. (1998). "Good, you identified the suspect": Feedback to eyewitnesses distorts their reports of the witnessing experience. *Journal of Applied Psychology*, **83**, 360–376.

Wells, G. L., & Bradfield, A. L. (1999). Distortions in eyewitnesses' recollections: Can the postidentification-feedback effect be moderated? *Psychological Science*, **10**, 138–144.

Wells, G. L., Charman, S. D., & Olson, E. A. (2005). Building face composites can harm lineup identification performance. *Journal of Experimental Psychology: Applied*, **11**, 147–156.

Wells, G. L., Ferguson, T. J., & Lindsay, R. C. L. (1981). The tractability of eyewitness confidence and its implications for triers of fact. *Journal of Applied Psychology, 66,* 688–696.

Wells, G. L., & Leippe, M. R. (1981). How do triers of fact enter the accuracy of eyewitness identification? Memory for peripheral detail can be misleading. *Journal of Applied Psychology, 66,* 682–687.

Wells, G. L., Lindsay, R. C. L., & Ferguson, T. (1979). Accuracy, confidence, and juror perceptions in eyewitness identification. *Journal of Applied Psychology, 64,* 440–448.

Wells, G. L., Lindsay, R. C. L., & Tousignant, J. P. (1980). Effects of expert psychological advice on human performance in judging the validity of eyewitness testimony. *Law and Human Behavior, 4,* 275–285.

Wells, G. L., Malpass, R. S., Lindsay, R. C. L., Fisher, R. P., Turtle, J. W., & Fulero, S. M. (2000). Mistakes in eyewitness identification are caused by known factors. Collaboration between criminal justice experts and research psychologists may lower the number of errors. *American Psychologist, 55,* 581–598.

Wells, G. L., Memon, A., & Penrod, S. D. (2006). Eyewitness evidence: Improving its probative value. *Psychological Science in the Public Interest, 7,* 45–75.

Wells, G. L., & Murray, D. M. (1983). What can psychology say about the *Neil v. Biggers* criteria for judging eyewitness accuracy? *Journal of Applied Psychology, 68,* 347–362.

Wells, G. L., & Olson, E. A. (2001). The other-race effect in eyewitness identification: What do we do about it? *Psychology, Public Policy and the Law, 7,* 230–246.

Wells, G. L., & Olson, E. A. (2003). Eyewitness testimony. *Annual Review of Psychology, 54,* 277–295.

Wells, G. L., Olson, E. A., & Charman, S. D. (2002). The confidence of eyewitnesses in their identifications from lineups. *Current Directions in Psychological Science, 11,* 151–154.

Wells, G. L., & Petty, R. E. (1980). The effects of overt head movements on persuasion: Compatibility and incompatibility of responses. *Basic and Applied Social Psychology, 1,* 219–230.

Wells, G. L., & Turtle, J. W. (1987). Eyewitness testimony research: Current knowledge and emergent controversies. *Canadian Journal of Behavioral Science, 19,* 363–388.

Wener, R., Frazier, W., & Farbstein, J. (1987, June). Building better jails. *Psychology Today,* pp. 40–49.

Wenzlaff, R. M., & Prohaska, M. L. (1989). When misery prefers company: Depression, attributions, and responses to others' moods. *Journal of Experimental Social Psychology, 25,* 220–233.

Werner, C. M., Kagehiro, D. K., & Strube, M. J. (1982). Conviction proneness and the authoritarian juror: Inability to disregard information or attitudinal bias? *Journal of Applied Psychology, 67,* 629–636.

Werner, C. M., Stoll, R., Birch, P., & White, P. H. (2002). Clinical validation and cognitive elaboration: Signs that encourage sustained recycling. *Basic and Applied Social Psychology, 24,* 185–203.

West, S. G., & Brown, T. J. (1975). Physical attractiveness, the severity of the emergency and helping: A field experiment and interpersonal simulation. *Journal of Experimental Social Psychology, 11,* 531–538.

West, S. G., Whitney, G., & Schnedler, R. (1975). Helping a motorist in distress: The effects of sex, race, and neighborhood. *Journal of Personality and Social Psychology, 31,* 691–698.

Weyant, J. M. (1984). Applying social psychology to induce charitable donations. *Journal of Applied Social Psychology, 14,* 441–447.

Weyant, J. M., & Smith, S. L. (1987). Getting more by asking for less: The effects of request size on donations of charity. *Journal of Applied Social Psychology, 17,* 392–400.

Whatley, M. A., Webster, J. M., Smith, R. H., & others. (1999). The effect of a favor on public and private compliance: How internalized is the norm of reciprocity? *Basic and Applied Social Psychology, 21,* 251–261.

Wheeler, L., Koestner, R., & Driver, R. E. (1982). Related attributes in the choice of comparison others: It's there, but it isn't all there is. *Journal of Experimental Social Psychology, 18,* 489–500.

White, G. L. (1980). Physical attractiveness and courtship progress. *Journal of Personality and Social Psychology, 39,* 660–668.

White, G. L., & Kight, T. D. (1984). Misattribution of arousal and attraction: Effects of salience of explanations for arousal. *Journal of Experimental Social Psychology, 20,* 55–64.

White, J. W., & Kowalski, R. M. (1994). Deconstructing the myth of the nonaggressive woman. *Psychology of Women Quarterly, 18,* 487–508.

White, K., & Lehman, D. R. (2005). Culture and social comparison seeking: The role of self-motives. *Personality and Social Psychology Bulletin, 31,* 232–242.

White, L., & Edwards, J. (1990). Emptying the nest and parental well-being: An analysis of national panel data. *American Sociological Review, 55,* 235–242.

White, M. (2000). *Historical atlas of the twentieth century* (users.erols.com/ mwhite28/warstat8.htm).

White, M. J., & Gerstein, L. H. (1987). Helping: The influence of anticipated social sanctions and self-monitoring. *Journal of Personality, 55,* 41–54.

White, R. (1984). *Fearful warriors: A psychological profile of U.S.-Soviet relations.* New York: Free Press.

White, R. K. (1968). *Nobody wanted war: Misperception in Vietnam and other wars.* New York: Doubleday.

White, R. K. (1986). *Psychology and the prevention of nuclear war.* New York: New York University Press.

White, R. K. (1996). Why the Serbs fought: Motives and misperceptions. *Peace and Conflict: Journal of Peace Psychology, 2,* 109–128.

White, R. K. (1998). American acts of force: Results and misperceptions. *Peace and Conflict, 4,* 93–128.

White, R. K. (2004). Misperception and war. *Peace and Conflict, 10,* 399–409.

Whitley, B. E., Jr. (1987). The effects of discredited eyewitness testimony: A meta-analysis. *Journal of Social Psychology, 127,* 209–214.

Whitman, D. (1996, December 16). I'm OK, you're not. *U.S. News and World Report,* p. 24.

Whitman, D. (1998). *The optimism gap: The I'm OK—They're not syndrome and the myth of American decline.* New York: Walker.

Whitman, R. M., Kramer, M., & Baldridge, B. (1963). Which dream does the patient tell? *Archives of General Psychology, 8,* 277–282.

Whittaker, J. O., & Meade, R. D. (1967). Social pressure in the modification and distortion of judgment: A cross-cultural study. *International Journal of Psychology, 2,* 109–113.

Whooley, M. A., de Jonge, P., Vittinghoff, E., Otte, C., Moos, R., Carney, R. M., Ali, S., Dowray, S., Na, B., Feldman, M. C., Schiller, N. B., & Browner, W. S. (2008). Depressive symptoms, health behaviors, and risk of cardiovascular events in patients with coronary heart disease. *Journal of the American Medical Association, 300,* 2379–2388.

Wicker, A. W. (1969). Attitudes versus actions: The relationship of verbal and overt behavioral responses to attitude objects. *Journal of Social Issues, 25,* 41–78.

Wicker, A. W. (1971). An examination of the "other variables" explanation of attitude-behavior inconsistency. *Journal of Personality and Social Psychology, 19,* 18–30.

Widom, C. S. (1989). Does violence beget violence? A critical examination of the literature. *Psychological Bulletin, 106,* 3–28.

Wiebe, D. J. (2003). Homicide and suicide risks associated with firearms in the home: A national case-control study. *Annals of Emergency Medicine*, **41**, 771–782.

Wiegman, O. (1985). Two politicians in a realistic experiment: Attraction, discrepancy, intensity of delivery, and attitude change. *Journal of Applied Social Psychology*, **15**, 673–686.

Wiesel, E. (1985, April 6). The brave Christians who saved Jews from the Nazis. *TV Guide*, pp. 4–6.

Wieselquist, J., Rusbult, C. E., Foster, C. A., & Agnew, C. R. (1999). Commitment, pro-relationship behavior, and trust in close relationships. *Journal of Personality and Social Psychology*, **77**, 942–966.

Wike, R., & Grim, B. J. (2007, October 30). Widespread negativity: Muslims distrust Westerners more than vice versa. Pew Research Center (pewresearch.org).

Wikipedia. (2008, accessed July 30). Strip search prank call scam (en. wikipedia.org).

Wilder, D. A. (1977). Perception of groups, size of opposition, and social influence. *Journal of Experimental Social Psychology*, **13**, 253–268.

Wilder, D. A. (1978). Perceiving persons as a group: Effect on attributions of causality and beliefs. *Social Psychology*, **41**, 13–23.

Wilder, D. A. (1981). Perceiving persons as a group: Categorization and intergroup relations. In D. L. Hamilton (Ed.). *Cognitive processes in stereotyping and intergroup behavior*. Hillsdale, NJ: Erlbaum.

Wilder, D. A. (1990). Some determinants of the persuasive power of in-groups and out-groups: Organization of information and attribution of independence. *Journal of Personality and Social Psychology*, **59**, 1202–1213.

Wilder, D. A., & Shapiro, P. N. (1984). Role of out-group cues in determining social identity. *Journal of Personality and Social Psychology*, **47**, 342–348.

Wilder, D. A., & Shapiro, P. N. (1989). Role of competition-induced anxiety in limiting the beneficial impact of positive behavior by out-group members. *Journal of Personality and Social Psychology*, **56**, 60–69.

Wilder, D. A., & Shapiro, P. (1991). Facilitation of outgroup stereotypes by enhanced ingroup identity. *Journal of Experimental Social Psychology*, **27**, 431–452.

Wildschut, T., Insko, C. A., & Pinter, B. (2007). Interindividual-intergroup discontinuity as a joint function of acting as a group and interacting with a group. *European Journal of Social Psychology*, **37**, 390–399.

Wildschut, T., Pinter, B., Vevea, J. L., Insko, C. A., & Schopler, J. (2003). Beyond the group mind: A quantitative review of the interindividual-intergroup discontinuity effect. *Psychological Bulletin*, **129**, 698–722.

Wilford, J. N. (1999, February 9). New findings help balance the cosmological books. *New York Times* (www.nytimes .com).

Wilkes, J. (1987, June). Murder in mind. *Psychology Today*, pp. 27–32.

Wilkinson, G. S. (1990, February). Food sharing in vampire bats. *Scientific American*, **262**, 76–82.

Wilkowski, B. M., & Robinson, M. D. (2008). The cognitive basis of trait anger and reactive aggression: An integrative analysis. *Personality and Social Psychology Bulletin*, **12**, 3–21.

Willard, G., & Gramzow, R. H. (2009). Beyond oversights, lies, and pies in the sky: Exaggeration as goal projection. *Personality and Social Psychology Bulletin*, **35**, 477–492.

Williams, D. K., Bourgeois, M. J., & Croyle, R. T. (1993). The effects of stealing thunder in criminal and civil trials. *Law and Human Behavior*, **17**, 597–609.

Williams, E. F., & Gilovich, T. (2008). Do people really believe they are above average? *Journal of Experimental Social Psychology*, **44**, 1121–1128.

Williams, J. E. (1993). Young adults' views of aging: A nineteen-nation study. In M. I. Winkler (Ed.), *Documentos: Conferencia del XXIV Congreso Interamericano de Psicologia* (pp. 101–123). Santiago, Chile: Sociedad Interamericana de Psicologia.

Williams, J. E., & Best, D. L. (1990). *Measuring sex stereotypes: A multination study*. Newbury Park, CA: Sage.

Williams, J. E., Satterwhite, R. C., & Best, D. L. (1999). Pancultural gender stereotypes revisited: The Five Factor model. *Sex Roles*, **40**, 513–525.

Williams, J. E., Satterwhite, R. C., & Best, D. L. (2000). Five-factor gender stereotypes in 27 countries. Paper presented at the XV Congress of the International Association for Cross-Cultural Psychology, Pultusk, Poland.

Williams, K. D. (2002). *Ostracism: The power of silence*. New York: Guilford.

Williams, K. D. (2007). Ostracism. *Annual Review of Psychology*, **58**, 425–452.

Williams, K. D., Cheung, C. K. T., & Choi, W. (2000). Cyberostracism: Effects of being ignored over the Internet. *Journal of Personality and Social Psychology*, **79**, 748–762.

Williams, K. D., Harkins, S., & Latané, B. (1981). Identifiability as a deterrent to social loafing: Two cheering experiments. *Journal of Personality and Social Psychology*, **40**, 303–311.

Williams, K. D., & Karau, S. J. (1991). Social loafing and social compensation: The effects of expectations of coworker performance. *Journal of Personality and Social Psychology*, **61**, 570–581.

Williams, K. D., Nida, S. A., Baca, L. D., & Latané, B. (1989). Social loafing and swimming: Effects of identifiability on individual and relay performance of intercollegiate swimmers. *Basic and Applied Social Psychology*, **10**, 73–81.

Williams, M. J., & Eberhardt, J. L. (2008). Biological conceptions of race and the motivation to cross racial boundaries. *Journal of Personality and Social Psychology*, **94**, 1033–1047.

Williams, T. M. (Ed.) (1986). *The impact of television: A natural experiment in three communities*. Orlando, FL: Academic Press.

Williamson, G. M., & Clark, M. S. (1989). Providing help and desired relationship type as determinants of changes in moods and self-evaluations. *Journal of Personality and Social Psychology*, **56**, 722–734.

Willis, F. N., & Hamm, H. K. (1980). The use of interpersonal touch in securing compliance. *Journal of Nonverbal Behavior*, **5**, 49–55.

Willis, J., & Todorov, A. (2006). First impressions: Making up your mind after a 100-ms exposure to a face. *Psychological Science*, **17**, 592–598.

Wilson, A. E., & Ross, M. (2001). From chump to champ: People's appraisals of their earlier and present selves. *Journal of Personality and Social Psychology*, **80**, 572–584.

Wilson, D. K., Kaplan, R. M., & Schneiderman, L. J. (1987). Framing of decisions and selections of alternatives in health care. *Social Behaviour*, **2**, 51–59.

Wilson, D. S., & Wilson, E. O. (2008). Evolution for "the good of the group." *American Scientist*, **96**, 380–389.

Wilson, D. W., & Donnerstein, E. (1979). Anonymity and interracial helping. Paper presented at the Southwestern Psychological Association convention.

Wilson, E. O. (1978). *On human nature*. Cambridge, MA: Harvard University Press.

Wilson, E. O. (2002, February). The bottleneck. *Scientific American*, **286**, 83–91.

Wilson, G. (1994, March 25). Equal, but different. *The Times Higher Education Supplement*, Times of London.

Wilson, J. P., & Petruska, R. (1984). Motivation, model attributes, and prosocial behavior. *Journal of Personality and Social Psychology*, **46**, 458–468.

Wilson, R. S., & Matheny, A. P., Jr. (1986). Behavior-genetics research in infant temperament: The Louisville twin study. In R. Plomin & J. Dunn (Eds.), *The study of temperament: Changes, continuities, and challenges.* Hillsdale, NJ: Erlbaum.

Wilson, S. J., & Lipsey, M. W. (2005). The effectiveness of school-based violence prevention programs for reducing disruptive and aggressive behavior. Revised Report for the National Institute of Justice School Violence Prevention Research Planning Meeting, May 2005.

Wilson, T. D. (1985). Strangers to ourselves: The origins and accuracy of beliefs about one's own mental states. In J. H. Harvey & G. Weary (Eds.), *Attribution in contemporary psychology.* New York: Academic Press.

Wilson, T. D. (2002). *Strangers to ourselves: Discovering the adaptive unconscious.* Cambridge: Harvard University Press.

Wilson, T. D., & Bar-Anan, Y. (2008). The unseen mind. *Science,* **321,** 1046–1047.

Wilson, T. D., Dunn, D. S., Kraft, D., & Lisle, D. J. (1989). Introspection, attitude change, and attitude-behavior consistency: The disruptive effects of explaining why we feel the way we do. In L. Berkowitz (Ed.), *Advances in experimental social psychology* (Vol. 22). San Diego: Academic Press.

Wilson, T. D., & Gilbert, D. T. (2003). Affective forecasting. *Advances in Experimental Social Psychology,* **35,** 346–413.

Wilson, T. D., & Gilbert, D. T. (2005). Affective forecasting: Knowing what to want. *Current Directions in Psychological Science,* **14,** 131–134.

Wilson, T. D., Laser, P. S., & Stone, J. I. (1982). Judging the predictors of one's mood: Accuracy and the use of shared theories. *Journal of Experimental Social Psychology,* **18,** 537–556.

Wilson, T. D., Lindsey, S., & Schooler, T. Y. (2000). A model of dual attitudes. *Psychological Review,* **107,** 101–126.

Wilson, W. R. (1979). Feeling more than we can know: Exposure effects without learning. *Journal of Personality and Social Psychology,* **37,** 811–821.

Winch, R. F. (1958). *Mate selection: A study of complementary needs.* New York: Harper & Row.

Windschitl, P. D., Kruger, J., & Simms, E. N. (2003). The influence of egocentrism and focalism on people's optimism in competitions: When what affects us equally affects me more. *Journal of Personality and Social Psychology,* **85,** 389–408.

Wines, M. (2005, September 23). Crime in South Africa grows more vicious. *New York Times* (www.nytimes.com).

Winquist, J. R., & Larson, J. R., Jr. (2004). Sources of the discontinuity effect: Playing against a group versus being in a group. *Journal of Experimental Social Psychology,* **40,** 675–682.

Winseman, A. L. (2005, March 8). Invitations, donations up among engaged congregation members. Gallup Poll (www.gallup.com).

Winter, F. W. (1973). A laboratory experiment of individual attitude response to advertising exposure. *Journal of Marketing Research,* **10,** 130–140.

Winter, R. J., & York, R. M. (2007, June). The "CSI effect": Now playing in a courtroom near you? *Monitor on Psychology,* p. 54.

Wiseman, R. (1998, Fall). Participatory science and the mass media. *Free Inquiry,* pp. 56–57.

Wisman, A., & Koole, S. L. (2003). Hiding in the crowd: Can mortality salience promote affiliation with others who oppose one's worldviews? *Journal of Personality and Social Psychology,* **84,** 511–526.

Wispe, L. G., & Freshley, H. B. (1971). Race, sex, and sympathetic helping behavior: The broken bag caper. *Journal of Personality and Social Psychology,* **17,** 59–65.

Wittenberg, M. T., & Reis, H. T. (1986). Loneliness, social skills, and social perception. *Personality and Social Psychology Bulletin,* **12,** 121–130.

Wittenbrink, B. (2007). Measuring attitudes through priming. In B. Wittenbrink & N. Schwarz (Eds.), *Implicit measures of attitudes.* New York: Guilford.

Wittenbrink, B., Judd, C. M., & Park, B. (1997). Evidence for racial prejudice at the implicit level and its relationship with questionnaire measures. *Journal of Personality and Social Psychology,* **72,** 262–274.

Wixon, D. R., & Laird, J. D. (1976). Awareness and attitude change in the forced-compliance paradigm: The importance of when. *Journal of Personality and Social Psychology,* **34,** 376–384.

Wohl, M. J. A., & Enzle, M. E. (2002). The deployment of personal luck: Sympathetic magic and illusory control in games of pure chance. *Personality and Social Psychology Bulletin,* **28,** 1388–1397.

Wojciszke, B., Bazinska, R., & Jaworski, M. (1998). On the dominance of moral categories in impression formation. *Personality and Social Psychology Bulletin,* **24,** 1251–1263.

Wolak, J., Mitchell, K., & Finkelhor, D. (2007). Unwanted and wanted exposure to online pornography in a national sample of youth Internet users. *Pediatrics,* **119,** 247–257.

Wolf, S. (1987). Majority and minority influence: A social impact analysis. In M. P. Zanna, J. M. Olson, & C. P. Herman (Eds.), *Social influence: The Ontario symposium on personality and social psychology,* Vol. 5. Hillsdale, NJ: Erlbaum.

Wolf, S., & Latané, B. (1985). Conformity, innovation and the psycho-social law. In S. Moscovici, G. Mugny, & E. Van Avermaet (Eds.), *Perspectives on minority influence.* Cambridge: Cambridge University Press.

Wolf, S., & Montgomery, D. A. (1977). Effects of inadmissible evidence and level of judicial admonishment to disregard on the judgments of mock jurors. *Journal of Applied Social Psychology,* **7,** 205–219.

Women on Words and Images. (1972). *Dick and Jane as victims: Sex stereotyping in children's readers.* Princeton: Women on Words and Images. Cited by C. Tavris & C. Offir (1977) in *The longest war: Sex differences in perspective* (p. 177). New York: Harcourt Brace Jovanovich.

Wood, J. V., Heimpel, S. A., & Michela, J. L. (2003). Savoring versus dampening: Self-esteem differences in regulating positive affect. *Journal of Personality and Social Psychology,* **85,** 566–580.

Wood, W., & Eagly, A. H. (2002). A cross-cultural analysis of the behavior of women and men: Implications for the origins of sex differences. *Psychological Bulletin,* **128,** 699–727.

Wood, W., & Eagly, A. H. (2007). Social structural origins of sex differences in human mating. In S. W. Gangestad & J. A. Simpson (Eds.), *The evolution of mind: Fundamental questions and controversies.* New York: Guilford.

Wood, W., Rhodes, N., & Whelan, M. (1989). Sex differences in positive well-being: A consideration of emotional style and marital status. *Psychological Bulletin,* **106,** 249–264.

Woodberry, R. D., & Smith, C. S. (1998). Fundamentalism et al: Conservative Protestants in America. *Annual Review of Sociology,* **24,** 25–56.

Woodward, W., & Woodward, M. (1942, March 26). Not time enough, "Not Time Enough." Editorial, *Bainbridge Review,* p. 1.

Woodzicka, J. A., & LaFrance, M. (2001). Real versus imagined gender harassment. *Journal of Social Issues,* **57**(1), 15–30.

Worchel, S., Andreoli, V. A., & Folger, R. (1977). Intergroup cooperation and intergroup attraction: The effect of previous interaction and outcome of combined effort. *Journal of Experimental Social Psychology,* **13,** 131–140.

Worchel, S., Axsom, D., Ferris, F., Samah, G., & Schweitzer, S. (1978). Deterrents of the effect of intergroup cooperation on intergroup attraction. *Journal of Conflict Resolution*, **22**, 429–439.

Worchel, S., & Brown, E. H. (1984). The role of plausibility in influencing environmental attributions. *Journal of Experimental Social Psychology*, **20**, 86–96.

Worchel, S., & Norvell, N. (1980). Effect of perceived environmental conditions during cooperation on intergroup attraction. *Journal of Personality and Social Psychology*, **38**, 764–772.

Worchel, S., Rothgerber, H., Day, E. A., Hart, D., & Butemeyer, J. (1998). Social identity and individual productivity within groups. *British Journal of Social Psychology*, **37**, 389–413.

Word, C. O., Zanna, M. P., & Cooper, J. (1974). The nonverbal mediation of self-fulfilling prophecies in interracial interaction. *Journal of Experimental Social Psychology*, **10**, 109–120.

Workman, E. A., & Williams, R. L. (1980). Effects of extrinsic rewards on intrinsic motivation in the classroom. *Journal of School Psychology*, **18**, 141–147.

World Bank (2003, April 4). *Gender equality and the millennium development goals.* Washington, DC: Gender and Development Group, World Bank (www.worldbank.org/gender).

Worringham, C. J., & Messick, D. M. (1983). Social facilitation of running: An unobtrusive study. *Journal of Social Psychology*, **121**, 23–29.

Wraga, M., Helt, M., Jacobs, E., & Sullivan, K. (2007). Neural basis of stereotype-induced shifts in women's mental rotation performance. *Social Cognitive and Affective Neuroscience*, **2**, 12–19.

Wright, D. B., & Hall, M. (2007). How a "reasonable doubt" instruction affects decisions of guilt. *Basic and Applied Social Psychology*, **29**, 91–98.

Wright, D. B., & Skagerberg, E. M. (2007). Postidentification feedback affects real eyewitnesses. *Psychological Science*, **18**, 172–178.

Wright, D. B., & Stroud, J. N. (2002). Age differences in lineup identification accuracy: People are better with their own age. *Law and Human Behavior*, **26**, 641–654.

Wright, D. B., Boyd, C. E., & Tredoux, C. G. (2001). A field study of own-race bias in South Africa and England. *Psychology, Public Policy, & Law*, **7**, 119–133.

Wright, E. F., Lüüs, C. A., & Christie, S. D. (1990). Does group discussion facilitate the use of consensus information in making causal attributions? *Journal of Personality and Social Psychology*, **59**, 261–269.

Wright, R. (1995, March 13). The biology of violence. *New Yorker*, pp. 69–77.

Wright, R. (1998, February 2). Politics made me do it. *Time*, p. 34.

Wright, R. (2003, June 29). Quoted by Thomas L. Friedman, "Is Google God?" *New York Times* (www.nytime.com).

Wright, R. (2003, September 11). Two years later, a thousand years ago. *New York Times* (www.nytimes.com).

Wright, S. C., Aron, A., McLaughlin-Volpe, T., & Ropp, S. A. (1997). The extended contact effect: Knowledge of cross-group friendships and prejudice. *Journal of Personality and Social Psychology*, **73**, 73–90.

Wrightsman, L. (1978). The American trial jury on trial: Empirical evidence and procedural modifications. *Journal of Social Issues*, **34**, 137–164.

Wrosch, C., & Miller, G. E. (2009). Depressive symptoms can be useful: Self-regulatory and emotional benefits of dysphoric mood in adolescence. Unpublished manuscript.

Wuthnow, R. (1994). *God and mammon in America.* New York: Free Press.

Wylie, R. C. (1979). *The self-concept (Vol. 2): Theory and research on selected topics.* Lincoln, NE: University of Nebraska Press.

Yamaguchi, S., Greenwald, A. G., Banaji, M. R., Murakami, F., Chen, D., Shiomura, K., Kobayashi, C., Cai, H., & Krendl, A. (2007). Apparent universality of positive implicit self-esteem. *Psychological Science*, **18**, 498–500.

Yang, S., Markoczy, L., & Qi, M. (2007). Unrealistic optimism in consumer credit card adoption. *Journal of Economic Psychology*, **28**, 170–185.

Yarmey, A. D. (2003a). Eyewitness identification: Guidelines and recommendations for identification procedures in the United States and in Canada. *Canadian Psychology*, **44**, 181–189.

Yarmey, A. D. (2003b). Eyewitnesses. In D. Carson and R. Bull, *Handbook of psychology in legal contexts*, 2nd edition. Chichester: Wiley.

Ybarra, O. (1999). Misanthropic person memory when the need to self-enhance is absent. *Personality and Social Psychology Bulletin*, **25**, 261–269.

Yelsma, P., & Athappilly, K. (1988). Marriage satisfaction and communication practices: Comparisons among Indian and American couples. *Journal of Comparative Family Studies*, **19**, 37–54.

Young, L. (2009). Love: Neuroscience reveals all. *Nature*, **457**, 148.

Yousif, Y., & Korte, C. (1995). Urbanization, culture, and helpfulness. *Journal of Cross-Cultural Psychology*, **26**, 474–489.

Yovetich, N. A., & Rusbult, C. E. (1994). Accommodative behavior

in close relationships: Exploring transformation of motivation. *Journal of Experimental Social Psychology*, **30**, 138–164.

Yuchtman (Yaar), E. (1976). Effects of social-psychological factors on subjective economic welfare. In B. Strumpel (Ed.), *Economic means for human needs.* Ann Arbor: Institute for Social Research, University of Michigan.

Yuille, J. C., & Cutshall, J. L. (1986). A case study of eyewitness memory of a crime. *Journal of Applied Psychology*, **71**, 291–301.

Yukl, G. (1974). Effects of the opponent's initial offer, concession magnitude, and concession frequency on bargaining behavior. *Journal of Personality and Social Psychology*, **30**, 323–335.

Yzerbyt, V. Y., & Leyens, J-P. (1991). Requesting information to form an impression: The influence of valence and confirmatory status. *Journal of Experimental Social Psychology*, **27**, 337–356.

Zadro, L., Boland, C., & Richardson, R. (2006). How long does it last? The persistence of the effects of ostracism in the socially anxious. *Journal of Experimental Social Psychology*, **42**, 692–697.

Zagefka, H., & Brown, R. (2005). Comparisons and perceived deprivation in ethnic minority settings. *Personality and Social Psychology Bulletin*, **31**, 467–482.

Zajonc, R. B. (1965). Social facilitation. *Science*, **149**, 269–274.

Zajonc, R. B. (1968). Attitudinal effects of mere exposure. *Journal of Personality and Social Psychology*, **9**, Monograph Suppl. No. 2, part 2.

Zajonc, R. B. (1970, February). Brainwash: Familiarity breeds comfort. *Psychology Today*, pp. 32–35, 60–62.

Zajonc, R. B. (1980). Feeling and thinking: Preferences need no inferences. *American Psychologist*, **35**, 151–175.

Zajonc, R. B. (1998). Emotions. In D. Gilbert, S. T. Fiske, & G. Lindzey (Eds.), *Handbook of social psychology*, 4th edition. New York: McGraw-Hill.

Zajonc, R. B. (2000). Massacres: Mass murders in the name of moral imperatives. Unpublished manuscript, Stanford University.

Zakaria, F. (2008). We need a wartime president. *Newsweek* (www.newsweek.com).

Zanna, M. P. (1993). Message receptivity: A new look at the old problem of open- vs. closed-mindedness. In A. Mitchell (Ed.), *Advertising: Exposure, memory and choice.* Hillsdale, NJ: Erlbaum.

Zanna, M. P., & Olson, J. M. (1982). Individual differences in attitudinal relations. In M. P. Zanna, E. T. Higgins, & C. P. Herman, *Consistency in social behavior: The Ontario symposium* (Vol. 2). Hillsdale, NJ: Erlbaum.

Zaragoza, M. S., & Mitchell, K. J. (1996). Repeated exposure to suggestion and the creation of false memories. *Psychological Science, 7,* 294–300.

Zauberman, G., & Lynch, J. G., Jr. (2005). Resource slack and propensity to discount delayed investments of time versus money. *Journal of Experimental Psychology: General, 134,* 23–37.

Zebrowitz, L. A., Collins, M. A., & Dutta, R. (1998). The relationship between appearance and personality across the life span. *Personality and Social Psychology Bulletin, 24,* 736–749.

Zebrowitz, L. A., Olson, K., & Hoffman, K. (1993). Stability of babyfaceness and attractiveness across the life span. *Journal of Personality and Social Psychology, 64,* 453–466.

Zebrowitz-McArthur, L. (1988). Person perception in cross-cultural perspective. In M. H. Bond (Ed.), *The cross-cultural challenge to social psychology.* Newbury Park, CA: Sage.

Zeelenberg, M., van der Pligt, J., & Manstead, A. S. R. (1998). Undoing regret on Dutch television: Apologizing for interpersonal regrets involving actions or inactions. *Personality and Social Psychology Bulletin, 24,* 1113–1119.

Zeisel, H., & Diamond, S. S. (1976). The jury selection in the Mitchell-Stans conspiracy trial. *American Bar Foundation Research Journal, 1,* 151–174 (see p. 167). Cited by L. Wrightsman, The American trial jury on trial: Empirical evidence and procedural modifications. *Journal of Social Issues,* 1978, *34,* 137–164.

Zhang, Y. F., Wyon, D. P., Fang, L., & Melikov, A. K. (2007). The influence of heated or cooled seats on the acceptable ambient temperature range. *Ergonomics, 50,* 586–600.

Zhong, C-B., Galinsky, A D., & Unzueta, M. M. (2008). Negational racial identity and presidential voting preferences. *Journal of Experimental Social Psychology, 44,* 1563–1566.

Zhong, C-B, & Leonardelli, G. F. (2008). Cold and lonely: Does social exclusion literally feel cold? *Psychological Science, 19,* 838–842.

Zhong, C-B., & Liljenquist, K. (2006). Washing away your sins: Threatened morality and physical cleansing. *Science, 313,* 1451–1452.

Zhou, X., Sedikides, C., Wildschut, T., & Gao, D-G. (2008). Counteracting loneliness: On the restorative function of nostalgia. *Psychological Science, 19,* 1023–1029.

Zick, A., Pettigrew, T. F., & Wagner, U. (2008). Ethnic prejudice and discrimination in Europe. *Journal of Social Issues, 64,* 233–251.

Zick, A., Wolf, C., Küpper, B., Davidov, E., Schmidt, P., & Heitmeyer, W. (2008). The syndrome of group-focused enmity: The interrelation of prejudices tested with multiple cross-sectional and panel data. *Journal of Social Issues, 64,* 363–383.

Zill, N. (1988). Behavior, achievement, and health problems among children in stepfamilies: Findings from a national survey of child health. In E. Mavis Hetherington and Josephine D. Arasteh (Eds.), *Impact of divorce, single parenting, and stepparenting on children.* Hillsdale, NJ: Erlbaum.

Zillmann, D. (1988). Cognition-excitation interdependencies in aggressive behavior. *Aggressive Behavior, 14,* 51–64.

Zillmann, D. (1989a). Aggression and sex: Independent and joint operations. In H. L. Wagner & A. S. R. Manstead (Eds.), *Handbook of psychophysiology: Emotion and social behavior.* Chichester: Wiley.

Zillmann, D. (1989b). Effects of prolonged consumption of pornography. In D. Zillmann & J. Bryant (Eds.), *Pornography: Research advances and policy considerations.* Hillsdale, NJ: Erlbaum.

Zillmann, D., & Paulus, P. B. (1993). Spectators: Reactions to sports events and effects on athletic performance. In R. N. Singer, N. Murphey, & L. K. Tennant (Eds.), *Handbook of research on sport psychology.* New York: Macmillan.

Zillmann, D., & Weaver, J. B., III. (1999). Effects of prolonged exposure to gratuitous media violence on provoked and unprovoked hostile behavior. *Journal of Applied Social Psychology, 29,* 145–165.

Zillmann, D., & Weaver, J. B. (2007). Aggressive personality traits in the effects of violence imagery on unprovoked impulsive aggression. *Journal of Research in Personality, 41,* 753–771.

Zillmer, E. A., Harrower, M., Ritzler, B. A., & Archer, R. P. (1995). *The quest for the Nazi personality: A psychological investigation of Nazi war criminals.* Hillsdale, NJ: Erlbaum.

Zimbardo, P. G. (1970). The human choice: Individuation, reason, and order versus deindividuation, impulse, and chaos. In W. J. Arnold & D. Levine (Eds.), *Nebraska symposium on motivation, 1969.* Lincoln: University of Nebraska Press.

Zimbardo, P. G. (1971). *The psychological power and pathology of imprisonment.* A statement prepared for the U.S. House of Representatives Committee on the Judiciary, Subcommittee No. 3: Hearings on Prison Reform, San Francisco, October 25.

Zimbardo, P. G. (1972). The Stanford prison experiment. A slide/tape presentation produced by Philip G. Zimbardo, Inc., P. O. Box 4395, Stanford, CA 94305.

Zimbardo, P. G. (2002, April). Nurturing psychological synergies. *APA Monitor,* pp. 5, 38.

Zimbardo, P. G. (2004a). A situationist perspective on the psychology of evil: Understanding how good people are transformed into perpetrators. In A. G. Miller (Ed.), *The social psychology of good and evil.* New York: Guilford.

Zimbardo, P. G. (2004b, May 3). Awful parallels: Abuse of Iraqi inmates and SPE. Comments to Social Psychology of Personality and Social Psychology listserv.

Zimbardo, P. G. (2007, September). Person x situation x system dynamics. *The Observer* (Association for Psychological Science), p. 43.

Zimbardo, P. G., Ebbesen, E. B., & Maslach, C. (1977). *Influencing attitudes and changing behavior.* Reading, MA: Addison-Wesley.

Zimmer, C. (2005, November). The neurobiology of the self. *Scientific American,* pp. 93–101.

Zitek, E. M., & Hebl, M. R. (2007). The role of social norm clarity in the influenced expression of prejudice over time. *Journal of Experimental Social Psychology, 43,* 867–876.

Zola-Morgan, S., Squire, L. R., Alvarez-Royo, P., & Clower, R. P. (1991). Independence of memory functions and emotional behavior. *Hippocampus, 1,* 207–220.

Zucker, G. S., & Weiner, B. (1993). Conservatism and perceptions of poverty: An attributional analysis. *Journal of Applied Social Psychology, 23,* 925–943.

Zuckerman, E. W., & Jost, J. T. (2001). What makes you think you're so popular? Self-evaluation maintenance and the subjective side of the "friendship paradox." *Social Psychology Quarterly, 64,* 207–223.

Zuwerink, J. R., Monteith, M. J., Devine, P. G., & Cook, D. A. (1996). Prejudice toward blacks: With and without compunction? *Basic and Applied Social Psychology, 18,* 131–150.

Credits

TEXT AND ILLUSTRATIONS

Chapter 2

Figure 2.5: Adapted from Figure 2, p. 435, in Bushman et al, 2009, "Looking again, and harder, for a link between low self-esteem and aggression," *Journal of Personality*, 77:2(April). © 2009, Copyright the Authors. Journal compilation © 2009, Wiley Periodicals, Inc.

Figure 2.8: From R. Inglehart & C. Welzel, 2005, *Modernization, Cultural Change, and Democracy*. © Ronald Inglehart and Christian Welzel 2005. Reprinted with permission of Cambridge University Press and the author.

Chapter 3

Figure 3.3: From J. P. Forgas, G. H. Bower, & S. E. Kranz, 1984, "The influence of mood on perceptions of social interactions," *Journal of Experimental Social Psychology*, 20. Reprinted with permission from Elsevier

Chapter 4

Figures 4.3, 4.4: Reprinted from B. J. Bushman & A. M. Bonacci, 2004, "You've got mail: Using e-mail to examine the effect of prejudiced attitudes on discrimination against Arabs,"*Journal of Experimental Social Psychology*, 40, pp. 753–759. Copyright 2004, with permission from Elsevier and Brad J. Bushman, Ph.D., University of Michigan.

Chapter 5

Figures 5.2 and 5.3: M. L. Patterson, Y. Iizuka, M. Tubbs, J. Ansel, M. Tsutsumi, & J. Anson, 2007, "Passing encounters East and West: Comparing Japanese and American pedestrian interactions," *Journal of Nonverbal Behavior*, 31, pp. 155–166. With kind permission of Miles Patterson and Springer Science and Business Media

Figure 5.5: From D. M. Buss, "The strategies of human mating," 1994, *American Scientist*, 82 (May-June), pp. 238–249, Figure 3. Reprinted with permission of Sigma Xi.

Figure 5.6: From D. M. Buss, 1995, "Evolutionary psychology: A new paradigm," *Psychological Inquiry*, 6:1, Fig 1, p. 3. Reprinted by permission of Taylor & Francis Group, http://www .informaworld.com.

Figure 5.7: Reprinted with permission of the Pew Global Attitudes Project, http://pewglobal.org

Figure 5.8: Adapted from A. H. Eagly & W. Wood, 1991, "Explaining sex differences in social behavior: A meta-analytic perspective," *Personality and Social Psychology Bulletin*, 17, pp. 306–315. Copyright © 1991. Reprinted by permission of Sage Publications, Inc.

Chapter 6

Figure 6.4: From Stanley Milgram, 1974, Figure 13, "Learner demands to be shocked," p. 91, and "The learner's schedule of protests in Milgram's 'Heart Disturbance' experiments: 75–300 volts," pp. 56–57. From *Obedience to Authority: An Experimental View*, by Stanley Milgram. Copyright © 1974 by Stanley Milgram. Reprinted by permission of HarperCollins Publishers and by Pinter & Martin, Ltd.

p. 203: From Roger Fisher in "Preventing Nuclear War," *Bulletin of the Atomic Scientists*, March 1981, pp. 11 17. Copyright © 2006 by Bulletin of the Atomic Scientists, Chicago, IL, 60602. Reproduced by permission of Bulletin of the Atomic Scientists, www.thebulletin.org.

Figure 6.5: From S. Milgram, 1965, "Some conditions of obedience and disobedience to authority," *Human Relations*, 18, pp. 57–76. Reprinted by permission of Sage Publications.

Chapter 9

Figure 9.1: "Changing racial attitudes of White Americans from 1958 to 2007." Data from Gallup polls (brain.gallup .com).

Figure 9.3: "Changing gender attitudes from 1958 to 2007." Data from Gallup polls (brain.gallup.com).

Figure 9.6: From P. G. Devine & R. S. Malpass, 1985, "Orienting strategies in differential face recognition," *Personality and Social Psychology Bulletin*, 11, pp. 33–40. Copyright © 1985. Reprinted by permission of Sage Publications, Inc.

Figure 9.8: "Overestimating Minority Populations." Source: 1990 Gallup Poll (Gates 1993). Data from Gallup Polls (brain.gallup.com)

Chapter 10

Figure 10.10: Adapted from Craig A. Anderson & Brad J. Bushman, 2001, "Effects of violent video games on

aggressive behavior, aggressive cognition, aggressive effect, psychological arousal and prosocial behavior: A meta-analytic review of the scientific literature," *Psychological Science*, 12, no. 5, pp. 353–359. Reprinted by permission of Blackwell Publishing.

Chapter 11

Figure 11.5: Reprinted by permission of Kristina M. Durante.

Figure 11.12: Used by permission of the National Opinion Research Center

Chapter 12

Figure 12.2: From M. A. Whatley, J. M. Webster, R. H. Smith, & A. Rhodes, 1999, "The effect of a favor on public and private compliance: How internalized is the norm of reciprocity?" *Basic and Applied Social Psychology*, 21, pp. 251–259. Reprinted by permission of Lawrence Erlbaum Associates

Figure 12.7: "Mismatched needs and donations" from C. Spence, 2006, "Mismatching money and need." In *Stanford Social Innovation Review*, 4, p. 49. Reprinted by permission.

Figure 12.11: "Have you done any of the following in the last month: Donate to charity." From *Gallup World Survey*, 2008. Data from Gallup Polls (brain .gallup.com)

Chapter 13

Figure 13.4: From P. E. Tetlock, 1988, "Monitoring the integrative complexity of American and Soviet policy rhetoric: What can be learned?" *Journal of Social Issues*, 454, no. 2, pp. 101–131. Reprinted by permission of Blackwell Publishing.

Figure 13.6: "George W. Bush's Job Approval Ratings Trend (2001–present). http://www.gallup.com/poll/116500/Presidential-Approval-Ratings-George-Bush.aspx. Reprinted by permission of Gallup Poll.

Chapter 14

Figure 14.1: From N. Nunez, D. Poole, & A. Memon, 2003, "Psychology's two cultures revisited: Implications for the integration of science and practice," *Scientific Review of Mental Health Practice*. Reprinted by permission.

Figure 14.4: From J. Dill & C. Anderson, 1998, "Loneliness, shyness and depression: The etiology and interpersonal relationships of everyday problems in living," in *Recent Advances in Interpersonal Approaches to Depression*, T. Joiner & J. Coyne, eds., 1998. Copyright © 1998 American Psychological Association. Reprinted by permission.

Chapter 15

Figure 15.2: From G. H. Fisher, 1968, "Ambiguity of form: Old and new," *Perception and Psychophysics*, 4, pp. 189–192. Reprinted with permission of Psychonomic Society, Inc.

Chapter 16

Figure 16.4: Adapted from Life Goals of First-year College Students in the U.S., 1966–2005. From UCLA Higher Education Research Institute, 2005. *The American Freshman: National Norms for Fall 2005*. Reprinted by permission.
Figure 16.5: From R. F. Inglehart, 2006, "Cultural change and democracy in Latin America," in Frances Hagopian, ed., *Contemporary Catholicism, Religious Pluralism and Democracy in Latin America*, Notre Dame University Press, 2006.
Figure 16.8: "Structure of the example national accounts framework," box 2, p. 21 from *The National Accounts of Well-Being Report*. © 2009 NEF. Used with permission.

PHOTOS
Front matter

p. v(top): Blend Images/Getty Images; p. v(middle): © Corbis; p. v(bottom): Terry Vine/Getty Images; p. vi: Jerry Marks Productions/Getty Images; p. vii: GoGo Images/Masterfile; p. viii: Getty Images/Digital Vision; p. ix: Nick White/Getty Images; p. x: Blend Images/Alamy; p. xi: Corbis/Age Fotostock; p. xii(bottom): © Fancy Photography/Veer; p. xiii(top): © IT Stock/PunchStock; p. xiii(bottom): Tony Anderson/Getty Images; p. xiv: © PhotoAlto/PunchStock; p. xv: Via Productions/Brand X Pictures/Jupiterimages; p. xviii: Getty Images/Photodisc

Part Openers

p. 33: © Gala/Superstock; p. 155: © Ace Stock Limited/Alamy; p. 305: © Larry Dale Gordon/Getty Images; p. 523: © Jeremy Sutton-Hibbert/Alamy

Chapter 1

p. 2: © Holger Hill/Getty Images; p. 11: R. C. James; p. 12: © David Young-Wolff/PhotoEdit; p. 20: © Corrance/Still Digital; p. 22: © Michael Newman/PhotoEdit; p. 23: Courtesy of the Survey Research Center at The University of Michigan; p. 26: © Mary Kate Denny/PhotoEdit

Chapter 2

p. 34: © HBSS/Age Fotostock; p. 39: © AP Images/Dima Gavrysh; p. 46(left): Courtesy Hazel Rose Markus; p. 46(right): Courtesy Shinobu Kitayama; p. 47: © AP Images/Peter Dejong; p. 49: © AP Images/Gene Blythe; p. 53: © Michael Newman/PhotoEdit; p. 60: © Marc Deville/Gamma/Eyedea Presse; p. 62: © Arlo Gilbert; p. 68: © Larry Dale Gordon/Getty Images; p. 75: © Tibor Bognar/Corbis

Chapter 3

p. 78: © Shawn Thew/epa/Corbis; p. 83: © Bettmann/Corbis; p. 84: © Shawn Thew/epa/Corbis; p. 93: © AP Images/J. Scott Applewhite; p. 98: © Trae Patton/NBCU Photo Bank via AP Images; p. 100: © Rob Melnychuk/Getty Images; p. 103: © Image Source Black/Alamy; p. 104: © Ellen Senisi/Image Works; p. 107: © AP Images/Michael Stephens; p. 108: Everett Collection; p. 109: Courtesy Kathryn Brownson, Hope College; p. 110: © Guy Cali/Stock Connection/PictureQuest; p. 111: © Esbin-Anderson/Image Works; p. 116: © AP Images/Michael Probst

Chapter 4

p. 122: © Ted Levine/Corbis; p. 126: Courtesy Mahzarin Banaji; p. 128: © Kevin P. Casey/Corbis; p. 132: © Phillip Zimbardo; p. 133: Photo courtesy of Washington Post via Getty Images; p. 136: © AP Images/Sayyid Azim; p. 137: Courtesy of Andy Martens, University of Canterbury; p. 139: © AP Images/Gary Kazanjian; p. 143: © Michael Newman/PhotoEdit; p. 144(top): Courtesy Leon Festinger; p. 144(bottom): © Ariel Skelley/Getty Images; p. 146(all): © Colin Young-Wolff/PhotoEdit; p. 147(top): Courtesy Fritz Strack; p. 147(bottom): © Kyodo News International, Inc.

Chapter 5

p. 156: © Larry Kolvoord/Image Works; p. 162: © Dorothy Littell/Stock Boston; p. 163(both): © Kees Keizer; p. 165: © AP Images/J. Scott Applewhite; p. 167: © Fujifotos/Image Works; p. 170(left): © Audrey Gottlieb; p. 170(right): © Bob Daemmrich/Image Works; p. 178: © Frederick M. Brown/Getty Images; p. 182(top): © AP Images/Suzanne Plunkett; p. 182(bottom left): © Spencer Grant/PhotoEdit; p. 182(bottom right): © Capital Features/Image Works; p. 185: © Will Hart/PhotoEdit; p. 187: Courtesy Alice Eagly

Chapter 6

p. 190: © MedioImages/Corbis; p. 195: From Provine, Robert, "Yawning," *American Scientist*, Volume 93, Fig. 6, page 536. Images courtesy Dr. Robert R. Provine, Department of Psychology, University of Maryland; p. 198: © William Vandivert; p. 202: Stanley Milgram, 1965, from the film *Obedience*, distributed by the Pennsylvania State University, PCR; p. 204: © AP Images; p. 205: Courtesy Alexandra Milgram; p. 206: © Benny Gool/Capetown Independent Newspaper; p. 207: © Empics; p. 209: © AP Images/APTN; p. 211: © James A. Sugar/Corbis; p. 212: © PhotoFest; p. 214: © AP Images; p. 217: Courtesy CNN; p. 218: © Anup Shah/Nature Picture Library; p. 219: © Zia Soleil/Getty Images; p. 221(left): © Bettmann/Corbis; p. 221(right): © Peter Kramer/Getty Images; p. 223: © AP Images/Joe Hermosa; p. 224: © Michael Newman/Photo Edit

Chapter 7

p. 228: © Photos 12/Alamy; p. 230: © Bob Daemmrich/Image Works; p. 238: Figures courtesy of Jeremy Bailenson, Nick Yee, and Stanford's Virtual Human Interaction Lab, http://vhil.stanford.edu; p. 239: © AP Images/Uwe Lein; p. 241(all): © Health Canada; p. 246(left): © AP Images/Jeff Chiu; p. 246(right): © Win McNamee/Getty Images; p. 247: © Time Life Pictures/Getty Images; p. 253: © Hulton Archive/Getty Images; p. 255: © AP Images/HO; p. 258: © AP Images/Richard Vogel; p. 261(top): Courtesy William McGuire, Yale University; p. 261(bottom): © Rachel Epstein/Image Works; p. 263: © Michelle D. Bridwell/PhotoEdit

Chapter 8

p. 266: © Sheng Li/Reuters/Corbis; p. 269: © Bob Winsett/Corbis; p. 271: © Mike Okoniewski; p. 273: Courtesy Herman Miller, Inc.; p. 274: Courtesy Alan G. Ingham; p. 276(top): © Royalty-Free/Corbis; p. 276(bottom): © David Young-Wolff/PhotoEdit; p. 277: © Joel W. Rogers/Corbis; p. 278: © AP Images/Laurent Rebours; p. 279: © Phillip Zimbardo; p. 282: © AP Images/Massimo Sambucetti; p. 286: © Tom Brakefield/Stock Connection/PictureQuest; p. 291: Courtesy Irving Janis; p. 293: © Kobal Collection; p. 297: Courtesy Daniel Kahneman; p. 302: © Mark Richards/PhotoEdit; p. 303: © Corbis

Chapter 9

p. 306: © Bob Daemmrich; p. 311: Andrew Redington/Getty Images; p. 312(top): © AP Images/Charles Dharapak; p. 312(bottom): © Jim Craigmyle/Getty Images; p. 314(both): J. Correll, B. Park, C. M. Judd, & B. Wittenbrink, 2002, "The police officer's dilemma: Using ethnicity to disambiguate potentially threatening individuals," *Journal of Personality and Social Psychology*, 83, p. 1316, Fig. 1. Images courtesy Josh Correll; p. 323: © Chris Leslie Smith/PhotoEdit; p. 324(left): © AP Images; p. 324(right): © Bonnie Kamin/PhotoEdit; p. 327(top): © Brand X Photos/PhotoDisc; p. 327(bottom): © Digital Vision/PhotoDisc; p. 328: © AP Images; p. 329: © 1999 Allan Tannenbaum; p. 333: James Blascovich; p. 335: © AP Images/Eugene Hoshiko; p. 340: © AP Images/Lynne Sladk; p. 343: © Bob Daemmrich/Stock Boston; p. 347: Courtesy Dr. Claude Steele; p. 348: © Paul Drinkwater/NBCU Photo Bank via AP Images; p. 344–345: From Johanne, Huart, Olivier Corneille, & Emilie Becquart, 2005, "Face-based categorization, context-based categorization, and distortions in the recollection of gender ambiguous faces," *Journal of Experimental Social Psychology*, 41, pp. 598–608, Fig. 1

Chapter 10

p. 352: © AP Images/Thibault Camus; p. 357: © Jeff Share/Black Star; p. 358: © Jose Mercado/Corbis Images; p. 360: © O. Burriel/Photo Researchers; p. 363(both): © Albert Bandura; p. 364: © Stephen Whitehorn/AA World Travel/Topfoto/Image Works; p. 366: © AP Images/Jack Smith; p. 367: © John Barr/Getty Images; p. 371: © Bettmann/Corbis Images; p. 382: Courtesy Craig A. Anderson; p. 383: © Gus van Dyk, Pilanesberg

Chapter 11

p. 392: © Alaska Stock/Alamy; p. 395: © Getty Images; p. 396: N. I. Eisenberger, M. D. Lieberman, & K. D. Williams, 2003, "Does rejection hurt? An fMRI study of social exclusion," *Science*, 302, pp. 290–292. © 2003 American Association for the Advancement of Science; p. 397: © Tony Freeman/PhotoEdit; p. 398: © PhotoDisc; p. 402(top left, top right): © AP Images/Michael Sohn; p. 402(bottom): © Peter Scholey/Getty Images; p. 405: © AP Images; p. 407: Courtesy Ellen Berscheid, University of Minnesota; p. 408(left): © Rick Smolan/Stock Boston; p. 408(center left): © John

Lund/Getty Images; p. 408(center right): © Catherine Karnow/Woodfin Camp; p. 408(right): © Marc Romanelli/Getty Images; p. 409(left): © Oliver Bodmer/Zuma Press; p. 409(right): From C. Braun, M. Gruendl, C. Marberger, & C. Scherber, 2001, "Beautycheck—Causes and consequences of human facial attractiveness," as presented at The German Students Award 2000/2001; p. 410(top): K. M. Durante, N. P. Li, & M. G. Haselton, 2008, "Changes in women's choice of dress across the ovulatory cycle: Naturalistic and laboratory task-based evidence," *Personality and Social Psychology Bulletin*, 34, pp. 1451–1460. Fig. 1, page 5. Images courtesy of Dr. Kristina Durante; p. 410(bottom left): © Terry Lilly/Zuma Press; p. 410(bottom right): © Mark Mainz/Getty Images; p. 412: © Granger Collection; p. 414: Courtesy James M. Jones; p. 419(all): Dr. Pawel Lewicki, University of Tulsa, Oklahoma; p. 422: © Joe Polillio; p. 423: From A. Aron, H. Fisher, D. J. Mashek, G. Strong, H. Li, & L. L. Brown, 2005, "Reward, motivation, and emotion systems associated with early-stage intense romantic love," *Journal of Neurophysiology*, 94, pp. 327–337. Image courtesy of Lucy L. Brown; p. 424: © AP Images/Jae C. Hong; p. 427: © Elizabeth Crews/Image Works

Chapter 12

p. 440: © Jim West/Alamy; p. 442(top): Courtesy Yad Vashem, The Holocaust Martyrs' and Heroes' Remembrance Authority; p. 442(bottom): © National Gallery Collection; By kind permission of the Trustees of the National Gallery, London; p. 445: Courtesy Dennis Krebs; p. 447: © Ellis Herwig/Stock Boston; p. 450: © AP Images/Pier Paolo Cito; p. 451: © Twentieth Century Fox/Shooting Star; p. 457: Courtesy Laura Myers; p. 460: © Ed Kashi/Corbis Images; p. 462: Courtesy John M. Darley, Princeton University; p. 463(top): © Peter Dazeley/Getty Images; p. 463(bottom): © Corbis Sygma; p. 468(both): Courtesy Lisa DeBruine; p. 471: © Lynn Burkholder/First Impressions; p. 478: © Leopold Page Photographic Collection, courtesy of USHMM Photo Archives (Photo #03411)

Chapter 13

p. 482: © Jeff Greenberg/Alamy; p. 484: © AP Images; p. 489: © Catherine Karnow/Corbis Images; p. 490: © Joseph Sohm, ChromoSohm/Corbis Images; p. 492: © Muzafer Sherif; p. 495: © Chris Morris/Black Star; p. 496: © Robert King/Getty Images; p. 501: Courtesy John Dixon, Lancaster University; p. 503(left): Courtesy Nicole Shelton; p. 503(right): Courtesy Jennifer Richeson. Photo by Stephen Anzaldi; p. 505: © AP Images; p. 507: © AP Images/Martin Meissner; p. 509: © Ian Shaw/Getty Images; p. 510: © AP Images; p. 511: © Bettmann/Corbis Images; p. 512: © AP Images; p. 514: © Mike Blake/Corbis; p. 517: © Mark Antman/Image Works

Chapter 14

p. 524: © Véronique Burger/Photo Researchers; p. 528: © AP Images/Robert Sorbo; p. 531: © Robin Nelson/PhotoEdit; p. 534: Courtesy Shelley Taylor; p. 535: © Punchstock UpperCut Images; p. 538: © Comstock/PictureQuest; p. 539: © Bob Daemmrich/Image Works; p. 543: © Jacques Chenet; p. 546: © Ellis Herwig/Stock Boston; p. 551: From *The Scotsman*, "If you are born and raised in Calton you can expect to die at 54," August 29, 2008, p. 22–23. Photo by Mike Gibbons/Spindrift Photo Agency

Chapter 15

p. 558: © AP Images/Vince Bucci, Pool; p. 562(both): Courtesy Chicago Tribune; p. 565: © AP Images/Chuck Burton; p. 566(both): Courtesy Elizabeth Loftus; p. 577: © Christopher Gardner/New Times/Corbis Images; p. 579: © John Giordano/Corbis; p. 581: © AP/Pool/Star Ledger; p. 588: © Alexander Jason/Getty Images

Chapter 16

p. 590: © Jewel Samad/Getty Images; p. 593(both): © NASA Goddard Space Flight Center; p. 595: © Ilene MacDonald/Alamy; p. 601: © AP Images/Ng Han Guan; p. 605: © Kayte M. Deioma/PhotoEdit

Name Index

No

Subject Index/Glossary

A

Abu Ghraib. *See* Iraq war
accentuation effect, 285
acceptance: Conformity that involves both acting and believing in accord with social pressure, 192. *See also* **conformity**
actor-observer difference: We observe others from a different perspective than we observe ourselves; in some experiments this has led to differing explanations for behavior, 108
adaptation-level phenomenon: The tendency to adapt to a given level of stimulation and thus to notice and react to changes from that level, 602–603
addiction, 424
advertising. *See* **persuasion**
affective forecasts, 48–50
age differences, 251–252, 308
aggression: Physical or verbal behavior intended to hurt someone. In laboratory experiments, this might mean delivering electric shocks or saying something likely to hurt another's feelings, 353–390
  and arousal, 368, 377, 380
  and aversive incidents, 365–368
  biological theories, 356–359
  cues for, 368–370, 388
  definitions, 355
  extent of, 353–354
  frustration-aggression theory, 359–362
  and gender, 173, 180
  and group influence, 382–385
  and pornography, 370–374
  reducing, 385–390
  social learning theory, 362–365, 387–388
  and television violence, 25–26, 374–379, 388
  and video games, 379–382
alcohol use, 223, 358
altruism: A motive to increase another's welfare without conscious regard for one's self-interests, 443, 454–459, 490–491. *See also* helping
American Society of Trial Consultants, 581
androgynous: From *andro* (man) + *gyn* (woman)—thus mixing both masculine and feminine characteristics, 181
anger, 361. *See also* **aggression**; emotions
anonymity, 279–281
anticipation, 398–399
anxiety, 71, 538–540
anxious-ambivalent attachment, 428
arbitration: Resolution of a conflict by a neutral third party who studies both sides and imposes a settlement, 514, 518–519
arousal
  and aggression, 368, 377, 380
  and cognitive dissonance, 150–151
  and group influence, 269–273, 278
  and love, 422–423
assertiveness training, 544

attachment, 426–428
attention, and persuasion, 258
attitude: A favorable or unfavorable evaluative reaction toward something or someone (often rooted in one's beliefs, and exhibited in one's feelings and intended behavior), 8, 123–152
  and change, 152
  and cognitive dissonance, 141–145, 150–151
  and conformity, 192, 206–207, 256
  dual attitudes, 51, 125–126, 310
  and moral hypocrisy, 124–125
  and persuasion, 233
  potency, 128–129
  and self-perception, 145–150, 151
  and self-presentation, 140–141
  and social influence, 125–127
  and theory of planned behavior, 127–128
  See also attitudes-follow-behavior principle; **prejudice**
attitude alignment, 414
attitude inoculation: Exposing people to weak attacks upon their attitudes so that when stronger attacks come they will have refutations available, 260–264
attitudes-follow-behavior principle, 8, 131–140
  and cognitive dissonance, 151
  and conformity, 192, 256
  and foot-in-the-door phenomenon, 134–136, 256
  and happiness, 555
  and helping, 478
  and morality, 136–138
  and peacemaking, 499
  and persuasion, 256
  and roles, 132–133
  and social movements, 138–139
  and spoken support, 133–134
  and treatment, 544–545
attraction, 396–420, 415–418
  and implicit egotism, 400
  mutual, 415–418, 420
  and proximity, 397–402, 420
  reward theory, 418–420
  and similarity, 412–415, 420
  See also physical attractiveness
attractiveness: Having qualities that appeal to an audience. An appealing communicator (often someone similar to the audience) is most persuasive on matters of subjective preference, 236–238, 239. *See also* physical attractiveness
attribution theory: The theory of how people explain others' behavior—for example, by attributing it either to internal dispositions (enduring traits, motives, and attitudes) or to external situations, 102–112
  and attraction, 417
  commonsense attributions, 104–105
  and conflict, 496
  and depression, 533

fundamental attribution error, 105–112, 487, 494
  and helping, 450–451, 478–479
  misattribution, 102–103
  and prejudice, 339–342
  and social dilemmas, 487
  spontaneous trait transference, 84, 104, 108
  and therapy, 546–547
audience, 250–253, 257
authoritarian personality: A personality that is disposed to favor obedience to authority and intolerance of outgroups and those lower in status, 320–321
autokinetic phenomenon: Self (*auto*) motion (*kinetic*). The apparent movement of a stationary point of light in the dark, 193
automatic processing: "Implicit" thinking that is effortless, habitual, and without awareness, roughly corresponding to "intuition." 89, 127
availability heuristic: A cognitive rule that judges the likelihood of things in terms of their availability in memory. If instances of something come readily to mind, we presume it to be commonplace, 95–97
aversive incidents, 365–368

B

bad vs. good events, 416
bandwagon effect, 289
bargaining: Seeking an agreement to a conflict through direct negotiation between parties, 514–515
Bay of Pigs invasion, 291
behavioral confirmation: A type of self-fulfilling prophecy whereby people's social expectations lead them to behave in ways that cause others to confirm their expectations, 116–117
behavioral medicine: An interdisciplinary field that integrates and applies behavioral and medical knowledge about health and disease, 540. *See also* **health psychology**
behavior problems, 532–544
  depression, 70, 532–536, 541–542
  loneliness, 430, 536–538
  shyness, 538–540
  treatment for, 544–548
behavior therapy, 544–545
belief perseverance: Persistence of one's initial conceptions, as when the basis for one's belief is discredited but an explanation of why the belief might be true survives, 84–85
benevolent sexism: A seemingly favorable attitude that puts women on a pedestal but sometimes conveys an assumption that women need men's protection, 316
Benzien, Jeffrey, 206